American Land
Planning Law

American Land Planning Law:

Cases and Materials

Norman Williams, Jr.

Professor of Law,
Vermont Law School

Visiting Professor of Law,
College of Law,
University of Arizona

Volume 2.

The Center for Urban Policy Research
Rutgers University
Building 4051 – Kilmer Campus
New Brunswick, New Jersey 08903

Second Printing—January, 1980

Published in the United States by The Center for Urban Policy Research
Rutgers University, New Brunswick, New Jersey 08903

Manufactured in the United States of America

Type set by New Jersey Appellate Printing Company, Inc.
Printed and manufactured by LithoCrafters, Inc.

Volume 1 of two volumes

Library of Congress Cataloging in Publication Data

Main entry under title:

American Land Planning Law

  Bibliography: P.
      1.   Regional Planning—Law
              and Legislation—United
States—Cases.   2.   City Planning
      and Redevelopment Law—United
States—Cases.   3.   Zoning Law—United
States—Cases.   I.   Williams, Norman

K.F.5692.   A4A47   346'.73'045

      77-17009

ISBN: 0-88285-041-5

Contents

M. ZONING FOR OPEN SPACE

SECTION 8   RESIDENTIAL v. NON-RESIDENTIAL ZONING

SECTION 9   COMMERCIAL ZONING

SECTION 10   INDUSTRIAL ZONING

SECTION 11   OTHER ZONING CONTROLS

A.   OFF STRIPT PARKING

PART C HOUSING AND URBAN DEVELOPMENT/RENEWAL

SECTION 12 THE BACKGROUND IN THE WEST

SECTION 13 EXCESS CONDEMNATION

SECTION 14 PUBLIC PURPOSE

SECTION 15 HOUSING AS A NUISANCE

SECTION 16 RESTRICTIVE HOUSING LEGISLATION

CONTENTS

SECTION 17   PUBLIC HOUSING

SECTION 18   URBAN REDEVELOPMENT/RENEWAL

J. Recent Developments in Exclusionary Zoning

VICKERS

v.

GLOUCESTER TOWNSHIP

37 N.J. 232, 181 A.2d 129(1962), appeal dismissed, 371 U.S. 233 (1963).

Supreme Court of New Jersey.

Argued Dec. 5, 1961.

Decided May 7, 1962.

Proceeding in lieu of prerogative writ to challenge the validity of a township zoning ordinance amendment precluding trailer camps and trailer parks in an industrial district. The Superior Court, Law Division, sustained the validity of the amendment. The Superior Court, Appellate Division, 68 N.J.Super. 263, 172 A.2d 218, reversed and the township appealed. The Supreme Court, Proctor, J., held that the township had the authority to enact the provision and that it was valid.

The opinion of the court was delivered by

PROCTOR, J.

In this proceeding plaintiff Harold E. Vickers challenges the validity of an amendment to the zoning ordinance of the defendant Gloucester Township. This amendment prohibits "Keeping, locating, establishing, maintaining or operating a trailer camp, trailer park * * *" in its industrial district.[1] After hearings, the Superior Court, Law Division, sustained the validity of the amendment. On plaintiff's appeal the Appellate Division reversed. 68 N.J.Super. 263, 172 A.2d 218 (1961). The township appeals to this court under R.R. 1:22–1(a).

---

1. The Definitions section of the amendment to the ordinance provides:
"442: TRAILER, TRAILER-COACH or CAMP-CAR: Any unit which is, or may be, used for living, sleeping, or business purposes by one or more persons and that is equipped with wheels or similar devices used for the purpose of transporting said unit from place to place, whether it be self-propelled or otherwise, and whenever the word 'trailer' is used herein it shall mean and include 'trailer coach' and 'camp car' * * *

443: TRAILER CAMP or TRAILER PARK: Any place, area, lot or track of land which is so designed or intended for placing or locating thereon a trailer, trailer-coach or camp-car, one or more, as above defined, other than a garage or other similarly enclosed type of building in which such vehicles may be placed."

On July 1, 1957, the township adopted a comprehensive zoning ordinance establishing Residence Districts "A," "B," "C," "D," a Business District, an Agricultural District and an Industrial District. The ordinance enumerated the uses permitted within all residence, business and agricultural districts, not mentioning trailer camps. The section regulating uses within the industrial district was drafted in different form; it permitted lands to be used and buildings to be erected for any lawful purpose with the exception of 41 specified uses. Trailer camps were not among the barred uses. By the terms of the ordinance dwellings which conformed to the requirements of the "A" residence district were permitted in the industrial district, provided prior approval of the Board of Adjustment was obtained. "A" residence district houses were required to be "One-family detached dwellings" located on a lot not less than 75 by 125 feet with at least 800 square feet of usable first floor area.

On September 3, 1957, the township adopted an ordinance entitled "An Ordinance to Regulate and Control Trailers, Trailer Coaches, Camp Cars and Trailer Camps in the Township of Gloucester." (Trailer Ordinance.) The effect of this ordinance and the zoning ordinance was to repeal a 1947 trailer ordinance barring trailer camps in the entire township and to ban such camps in the residence, business and agricultural districts, but permit them in the industrial district. At present there are no trailer camps in the township.

In April 1959 this court decided Napierkowski v. Township of Gloucester, 29 N.J. 481, 150 A.2d 481, which concerned the validity of the zoning ordinance as it applied to trailers in residential districts. We held "the provisions of the zoning ordinance prohibiting the location of trailers in residence districts ° ° ° bears a reasonable relationship to the purpose of zoning as outlined in R.S. 40:55–32, N.J.S.A., and should be upheld." Id., at p. 496, 150 A.2d at p. 488. We expressly left open the question of whether such uses could be completely excluded from the township. Id., at p. 497, 150 A.2d 481, 488.

On August 26, 1959, Vickers applied to the township for a permit to operate a trailer camp upon his ten acres of industrially zoned land which he had purchased in November 1957. While this application was pending, he acquired ten additional acres of land across the road from his prior holdings but still within the industrial district. The Township Committee denied his application in a letter dated December 8, 1959. As a result, Vickers instituted an action in lieu of prerogative writ on December 30, 1959, wherein he alleged he had complied with the Trailer Ordinance requirements and sought a judgment compelling the township to grant him permission to operate his proposed trailer camp. In their answer, the defendants stated that plaintiff's application was denied because his plans did not meet the requisite health standards and that the granting of the permit would be in violation of the zoning ordinance, subdivision ordinance and building code.

Much of the testimony introduced by the plaintiff at the trial on March 17, 1960, concerned his compliance with the requirements of the State Department of Health. Plaintiff also introduced evidence as to the characteristics of the township, particularly the area surrounding his property. This area is almost entirely in the industrial district (an "A" residential district is not far from Vickers' lands) and is for the most part undeveloped. Several buildings ranging from dilapidated shacks to modest homes are situated in the immediate vicinity of plaintiff's property. There are no residential developments or industrial plants in this area, nor are there any between plaintiff's land and the Freeway which runs through the township and is about two miles west of the property. An expert called by plaintiff testified that plaintiff's land could be appropriately used as a trailer camp site and that such use would not have an adverse economic effect upon the neighborhood.

Apparently realizing during the course of the trial that his application and plans did not meet the required standards of the State Department of Health, plaintiff moved for an opportunity to amend his application and plans as submitted. The court granted plaintiff's motion and further allowed the township to "take such administrative action and review what action they may be desirous of taking in the interim time, which means that the Court will hold this issue in abeyance until such time as those amendatory actions are taken on the part of both parties." The trial was adjourned for an unspecified period.

The plaintiff's amended plans were submitted to the Township Committee at a meeting held on April 1, 1960. At that meeting the Mayor announced that a "proposed amendment to the Zoning Ordinance to exclude trailer camps is being submitted to the Planning Board for its consideration and comment at its next meeting, to be held April 5, 1960." After this announcement the Committee meeting was adjourned until April 5, 1960, "to take up any action regarding such proposed zoning ordinance amendment, and any other things that may be considered at the adjourned meeting." At the Township Committee meeting held April 5, 1960, the amending ordinance barring trailer camps from the industrial district and an ordinance repealing the Trailer Ordinance were read for the first time. The Township Planning Board met and approved the amending ordinance on the same night. In a letter formally notifying the Township Committee of this action, the Planning Board stated:

> "The Board believes that trailer camps do not contribute anything to the general appearance of the local scenery and do not enhance the use or value of the local real estate and, in fact, do have a directly opposite effect, that the areas where they may exist are prejudiced thereby, that real estate values instead of being preserved or enhanced, would be de-

preciated, that the establishment of such camps would retard and, perhaps, choke the development of real estate for the area. To permit trailer camps and camp sites would not be in the interest of the general welfare of the community. The Board, therefore, registers its approval of the amendment ° ° ° "

This letter was read to the Township Committee at its next meeting which was held on April 22, 1960. At that meeting the zoning ordinance and the ordinance repealing the Trailer Ordinance were read for the second time and adopted by the Township Committee. The minutes disclose the following:

"Mayor Yost, Mr. Harrison and Mr. McCann in reply to statements and questions raised by the members of the public, stated, in substance, that the Township Committee in presenting the ordinance to amend the zoning ordinance was taking into consideration the over all planning for the township, present and future, and that the purpose of the amendment was to protect property values, both present and future, which might be adversely affected by a trailer camp, because a trailer camp is not attractive in appearance and that consideration must be given to the effect that such appearance would have on the development of the area in particular and the township in general.

Mayor Yost further pointed out that the township was in the heart of the Delaware Valley expansion that is taking place and that the township is growing fast and planning is necessary to cope with such growth."

Since the result of the ordinances was to prohibit trailer camps throughout the township, plaintiff on May 5, 1960, filed a second complaint in lieu of prerogative writ demanding a judgment declaring the ordinances invalid and inapplicable to the use of his property as a trailer camp. In its answer the township contended it had the power to enact the ordinances under its zoning powers and general police powers.

The second action came to trial on June 20, 1960, before the same judge who heard the first case, and the actions were consolidated. The parties stipulated that plaintiff's amended plans satisfied the prerequisite health standards applicable to trailer camps, thus leaving as the primary question whether the township had the power to adopt the amendment prohibiting trailer camps from its industrial district, which in effect barred them from the entire township. Also in issue was the legal propriety of the procedure followed in adopting the amendment, the plaintiff contending the Planning Board did not have the opportunity to properly consider the amendment as required by N.J.S.A. 40:55–35.

The testimony, zoning map and photographs submitted at the trial showed that the township is in the main a rural community of about 23 square miles in Camden County. However, the nature of the township is rapidly changing, it being in the throes of expansion. The population has grown from 7,950 in 1950 to about 17,500 in 1960, and the number of houses has increased from 2,594 in 1955 to 4,113 as of September 1959. The bulk of this expansion is concentrated in the northern and western sections. The southern section, where plaintiff's lands are situated, includes several residential districts and a business district, but is for the most part relatively undeveloped. The township's sanitary land-fill area, where non-garbage refuse is disposed and promptly covered by earth, is located about 100 yards from plaintiff's land. Although most of the southern section is in the industrial district, one-family houses can be constructed in that district if the Board of Adjustment gives permission. In fact, home developers have purchased 500 acres within the industrial district and adjacent to plaintiff's property. Mayor Yost and Mr. Moffa, Chairman of the Planning Board, stated the township was continually considering changes in the existing zones in order to benefit the township. The record and zoning map indicate that certain areas which had been previously zoned residential, have recently been reclassified industrial. There was also testimony that the township, in an effort to eliminate blighted structures, had on February 8, 1960, appointed a Public Officer who is actively engaged in a program to rid the township of properties which are in "bad condition," including those located in the vicinity of plaintiff's land.

Mayor Yost testified that many factors motivated the township to prohibit trailers. He said:

> "The Committee took many things into consideration; future over all planning of our Township; the acquisition of 500 acres of development ground bought by developers, adjacent to Mr. Vickers' property; also taking in connection with the Freeway, the other sections of our Township are farily well built up and the development is working further south.
>
>   ✽   ✽   ✽
>
> We feel that the trailers, as a general run, are unsightly, and couldn't see with the present growth, also with the view in mind of future growth of planning where trailers would add to it."

The trial court, after noting the expanding nature of the community, held that the challenged ordinances were valid because "this is a municipality where prohibition of trailer camps can be legislated," and it further held the adoption of the amendment accorded with the statutory procedure. The Appellate Division reversed, holding "the amendment of the zoning ordinance of April 22, 1960, must be set aside as an unreasonable and arbitrary exercise of the zoning power." It said at p. 270 of 68 N.J. Super. at p. 221 of 172 A.2d:

> "The entire picture presented very definitely gives the impression that the planned future of the township, as reflected by the high proportion industrial districts bear to the whole, does not contemplate that the township will become what is commonly called a 'residential town.' On the contrary it appears that the zoning power has been used in the hope of attracting industry.
>
>   ✽   ✽   ✽

Surely, in this vast rural area, there must be some portion in which the operation of trailer parks would be compatible with the scheme of zoning the township has seen fit to select, and yet would not adversely affect existing or future uses of property located anywhere in the township, and however zoned."

The Appellate Division further held the township was free to repeal its Trailer Ordinance and "its action in that regard will not be disturbed." In view of its disposition of the case, the Appellate Division found it unnecessary to pass upon the alleged procedural irregularity.

The parties agree the only issues on this appeal are: (1) In the circumstances, could the township through its zoning power totally exclude trailer camps from the municipality? and, (2) Were the procedural requirements of N.J.S.A. 40:55-35 met in the adoption of the zoning ordinance amendment?

As to the first issue, the township contends the zoning ordinance as amended represents a valid exercise of the municipality's power to "develop itself as an orderly and well integrated community," and that trailer camps with their accompanying disadvantages can only interfere with its planned growth. The plaintiff argues the township, although it can regulate the operation of trailer camps, cannot absolutely prohibit them, that such an attempt is invalid since it "goes beyond the essential objects of zoning." He asserts "there is everything to indicate that Gloucester Township is not the type of community where the absolute prohibition of mobile home parks is warranted."

Our Constitution empowers the Legislature to enact general laws under which municipalities may adopt zoning ordinances "limiting and restricting to specified districts and regulating therein, buildings and structures, according to their construction, and the nature and extent of their use, and the nature and extent of the uses of land, and the exercise of such authority shall be deemed to be within the police power of the State." N.J.Const. Art. IV, Sec. VI, par. 2. And our Constitution commands that all laws concerning local government, and zoning laws are in that class, be construed liberally in favor of municipal power. N.J. Const. Art. IV, Sec. VII, par. 11.

In N.J.S.A. 40:55-30 and N.J.S.A. 40:55-31 the Legislature has given municipalities extensive power to create districts and regulate structures and the use of land therein through zoning ordinances. The guiding purpose in exercising this power is set forth in R.S. 40:55-32, N.J.S.A. as:

"Such regulations shall be in accordance with a comprehensive plan and designed for one or more of the following purposes: to lessen congestion in the streets; secure safety from fire, panic and other dangers; promote health, morals or the general welfare; provide adequate light and air; prevent the overcrowding of land or buildings; avoid undue concentration of population. Such regulations shall be made with reasonable consideration, among other things, to the character of the district and its peculiar suitability for particular uses, and with a view of conserving the value of property and encouraging the most appropriate use of land throughout such municipality."

[1, 2] The role of the judiciary in reviewing zoning ordinances adopted pursuant to the statutory grant of power is narrow. The court cannot pass upon the wisdom or unwisdom of an ordinance, but may act only on the presumption in favor of the validity of the ordinance if overcome by an affirmative showing that it is unreasonable or arbitrary. Kozesnik v. Township of Montgomery, 24 N.J. 154, 167, 131 A.2d 1 (1957); see Cunningham, "Control of Land Use in New Jersey," 14 Rutgers L.Rev. 37, 48 (1959). By these standards which control judicial review, the plaintiff to prevail must show beyond debate that the Township in adopting the challenged amendment transgressed the standards of R.S. 40:55-32, N.J.S.A. In other words, if the amendment presented a debatable issue we cannot nullify the township's decision that its welfare would be advanced by the action it took.

[3] "It cannot be said that every municipality must provide for every use somewhere within its borders." Fanale v. Borough of Hasbrouck Heights, 26 N.J. 320, 325, 139 A.2d 749, 752 (1958). The fact that a municipality is largely undeveloped does not impose a contrary obligation. Sound planning and zoning look beyond the present into what lies ahead in the hopes of the planners. "It requires as much official watchfulness to anticipate and prevent suburban blight as it does to eradicate city slums." Lionshead Lake, Inc. v. Township of Wayne, 10 N.J. 165, 173, 89 A.2d 693, 697 (1952), appeal dismissed, 344 U.S. 919, 73 S.Ct. 386, 97 L.Ed. 708 (1953).

This court has considered several cases in which a municipality's zoning ordinance was attacked as unreasonable because it prohibited certain structures or uses.

In Duffcon Concrete Products, Inc. v. Borough of Cresskill, 1 N.J. 509, 64 A.2d 347, 9 A.L.R.2d 678 (1949) this court held a municipality could through its zoning ordinance permit light industry and totally exclude heavy industry.

In Lionshead Lake, Inc. v. Township of Wayne, supra, this court sustained a zoning ordinance provision barring the construction anywhere in the township (which included residential, business and industrial districts) of dwellings containing less than 768 square feet of living area. After alluding to health factors, the court said at p. 174 of 10 N.J., at p. 697 of 89 A.2d:

> "But quite apart from these considerations of public health which cannot be overlooked, minimum floor-area standards are justified on the ground that they promote the general welfare of the community and, as we have seen in Schmidt v. Board of Adjustment of the City of Newark, 9 N.J. 405, 88 A.2d 607 (1952), supra, the courts in conformance with the constitutional provisions and the statutes hereinbefore cited take a broad view of what constitutes general welfare. The size of the dwellings in any community inevitably affects the character of the community and does much to determine whether or not it is a desirable place in which to live."

In Fischer v. Township of Bedminster, 11 N.J. 194, 93 A.2d 378 (1952), this court upheld a zoning ordinance which placed most of the township in a residence zone with a minimum lot size of five acres for each residence. The court said, at p. 204, 93 A.2d at p. 383: "As much foresight is now required to preserve the countryside for its best use as has been needed to save what could be salvaged of our cities."

In Pierro v. Baxendale, 20 N.J. 17, 118 A.2d 401 (1955), this court sustained a zoning ordinance barring motels from a municipality which included residential, business and industrial districts. In so doing, we reiterated the proposition that "general welfare" is a broad concept and noted that it includes "public convenience" and "general prosperity."

In Fanale v. Borough of Hasbrouck Heights, supra, the validity of the zoning ordinance prohibiting the construction of apartment house anywhere in the borough was under attack. The borough was zoned for residence, business and industry. The plaintiff sought to construct an apartment house in the business district on a lot which contained a dilapidated residence. The plaintiff contended *inter alia* the ordinance was invalid because one and two-family houses were permitted in the industrial zone, while apartment houses were excluded. In sustaining the ordinance, we said at p. 328 of 26 N.J., at p. 753 of 139 A.2d:

> "True, as the ordinance now stands, one and two-family homes may be erected in those districts. Nonetheless, and apart from the unlikelihood of that development, a multi-family structure in an industrial setting would grossly accentuate the resulting problems. The matter is one of classification, and we cannot say a distinction between one and two-family houses as against multi-family ones even in industrial districts is devoid of reasonable factual support."

In Napierkowski v. Township of Gloucester, supra, the provisions of this township's zoning ordinance which prohibited trailers and trailer parks from the residential, business and agricultural districts were under attack. The plaintiff wanted to place a trailer on her four-acre tract for use as her permanent residence. Although the land was situated in a residential zone, the area about her plot was mainly rural and was likely to remain so for the reasonably foreseeable future. After noting that: (1) some states have upheld regulations limiting the time during which a trailer could remain in a municipality to short intervals thus making them strictly temporary abodes and effectively eliminating trailer parks which cater to trailers used as permanent residences; (2) other states have permitted municipalities to apply their house building codes to trailers, thus effectively barring all trailers since none could possibly comply; and (3) some states have permitted the uneqivocal prohibition of trailers throughout the municipality, we said at p. 493 of 29 N.J., at p. 487 of 150 A.2d:

> "The decisions elsewhere highlight the fact that the use of trailers as permanent residences present problems which are oft times inimical to the general welfare. * * * And from the point of view of aesthetic con-

siderations (which are inextricably intertwined with conservation of the value of property) trailers may mar the local landscape."

We conclude that the Township of Gloucester had the power to prohibit trailers from all residential districts, even though those districts include rural areas which will remain undeveloped for the reasonably foreseeable future. We said at p. 494 of 29 N.J., at p. 488 of 150 A.2d: "Zoning must subserve the long-range needs of the future as well as the immediate needs of the present and the reasonably foreseeable future. It is, in short, an implementing tool of sound planning."

[4] It is necessary to look at the total picture to determine whether the township's ordinance violated the statutory zoning standards in the light of the above decisions. As in all zoning cases, the question is whether the requirements of the ordinance are reasonable under the circumstances. Fanale v. Borough of Hasbrouck Heights, supra, at p. 325 of 26 N.J., at p. 749 of 139 A.2d.

It is clear the tide of suburban development has begun to engulf the rustic character of the township. Its population has more than doubled in the past ten years with a corresponding increase in the number of homes. There is every indication this markedly accelerated growth will continue; housing developers have acquired large tracts of land in the sparsely settled areas. While the record does not show any significant industrial development, the new Freeway and the Walt Whitman Bridge have recently opened up this particular section of south Jersey to the business and shipping centers of Philadelphia and Camden, and to the industrial and commercial areas along the Delaware River. See Napierkowski v. Township of Gloucester, supra, 29 N.J. at p. 494, 150 A.2d at p. 481. It is not unreasonable to anticipate that industry, creating new ratables which will help allay local tax problems, may be encouraged by sound planning and zoning to look favorably to this area for plant sites. Indeed, unless there is such planning and zoning, the municipality may suffer from the adverse effects of helter-skelter and deleterious property uses, thus discouraging industry from settling in the Township. Industry may shun the disharmony resulting from discordant uses side by side.

Choosing to take advantage of the community benefits which can flow from thoughtful planning, the township in 1957 adopted its first comprehensive zoning ordinance and recognized the difference between modern industrial development and unrestricted factory constructions. The ordinance excludes from the industrial district 41 nuisance type industries which were determined to be unsuitable to the kind of community planned. As to the permitted structures, there are restrictions as to lot size, percentage of area occupied by buildings, height of buildings and set-backs, and requirements for off-street parking and loading facilities. These provisions are in harmony with modern concepts of industrial planning which aim to promote an attractive industrial area, compatible in appearance with nearby residences. Much of the current industrial development in this State is in fact taking place in areas resembling parks where nuisance type plants are excluded and attractive architecture prevails. Such types of industry often lend to the prosperity of the entire municipality.

Trailer camps, because of their particular nature and relation to the public health, safety, morals and general welfare, present a municipality with a host of problems, and these problems persist wherever such camps are located. See Zullo v. Board of Health, Woodbridge Tp., 9 N.J. 431, 88 A.2d 625 (1952); "Regulation and Taxation of House Trailers," 22 U.Chi.L. Rev. 738, 739 (1955); "Trailer Parks vs. The Municipal Police Power," 34 Conn.B.J. 285 (1960); "Regulation of Mobile Homes," 13 Syracuse L.Rev. 125 (1961). In Fanale v. Borough of Hasbrouck Heights, supra, we said 26 N.J. at p. 325 of 26 N.J., at p. 752 of 139 A.2d: "Apartment houses are not inherently benign. On the contrary, they present problems of congestion and may have a deleterious impact upon other uses." This description is equally applicable to trailer camps. Clearly trailer camps bring problems of congestion with all their attendant difficulties. In the present case the plaintiff proposes to place each trailer on a 40 by 60 foot lot. The smallest lot upon which a one-family dwelling (the only type permitted in the zone) can be erected in the same zone is 75 by 125 feet. Therefore, in the same square area the township would have to cope with nearly four times as many trailer families and motor vehicles as would be present if the tract were devoted to one-family houses. As we recognized in Fanale, at p. 328, 139 A.2d 749, a town may properly conclude that, because of the gross difference in the resulting problems, it will permit in its industrial zone the types of residences which do not foster congestion while excluding those which bring with them heavy concentration of population.

And if the township is to avoid the "deleterious impact" which one use may have upon other uses and encourage "the most appropriate use of land throughout such municipality," it must be concerned with the future as well as the present values of property. Our recent decisions have uniformly held, in conformance with the constitutional provisions and the zoning statutes hereinbefore cited, that "general welfare" should be given a broad interpretation. Pierro v. Baxendale, supra; Fischer v. The Township of Bedminster, supra; Lionshead Lake, Inc. v. Township of Wayne, supra. If the zoning ordinance is reasonably calculated to advance the community as a social, economic and political unit, it furthers the general welfare and therefore is a proper exercise of the zoning power. Schmidt v. Board of Adjustment of the City of Newark, 9 N.J. 405, 88 A.2d 607 (1952).

[5] In the present case the township is seeking to create an attractive industrial zone. The purpose of the zoning ordinance is to guide the township in its transition from a *laissez faire* growth to a well-ordered community. The zoning ordinance does not presently envision exclusively indus-

trial districts since it permits dwellings to be erected in those areas. However, these houses can only be one-family detached dwellings on a lot not less than 75 by 125 feet. The governing body determined that such houses would be compatible with industrial uses. It thought that trailer camps would strike a discordant note and be detrimental to property values, present and prospective, and retard the progress of the township. The governing body stated "a trailer camp is not attractive in appearance" and considered this factor in reaching their conclusion. Aesthetics may properly be considered in establishing a zoning scheme "with a view of conserving the value of property and encouraging the most appropriate use of land." See Napierkowski v. Township of Gloucester, supra, 29 N.J. at p. 494, 150 A.2d at p. 150; Pierro v. Baxendale, supra, 20 N.J. at p. 28, 118 A.2d 401; Point Pleasant Beach v. Point Pleasant Pavilion, 3 N.J.Super. 222, 225, 66 A.2d 40 (App.Div.1949).

[6, 7] The township has begun to feel the effects of its potential for extensive and rapid development, and has concluded that the presence of trailer camps would hamper this potential. It believes that the prohibition of trailer camps is in keeping with the orderly growth of the township and best serves the interests of the entire municipality in its development as a desirable place in which to work and live. Since, as this court has held, municipalities can properly determine that the construction of small houses, Lionshead Lake, apartment houses, Fanale, and motels, Pierro, may have an adverse effect upon other properties throughout those municipalities (including industrial districts), and that living units which produce congestion can be excluded, we would be flying in the face of the broad powers granted to municipalities by the Constitution and zoning statutes as interpreted by our decisions if we held that the township in the present case must, against the will of its governing body, allow the construction and operation of trailer camps in its industrial district. Accordingly, we hold the plaintiff has failed to show the township acted unreasonably in amending its zoning ordinance to exclude trailer camps from its industrial district.

Since trailer camps are not permitted in the other districts, the effect of the amending ordinance prohibiting them in the industrial district is to bar them from the entire municipality. There are no trailer camps in the township at present. Plaintiff contends that total prohibition is illegal. However, we have held that a municipality need not provide a place for every use. Fanale v. Borough of Hasbrouck Heights, supra. We do not think that a municipality must open its borders to a use which it reasonably believes should be excluded as repugnant to its planning scheme. It must be remembered that once a use is legally established, even though conditions impel a revision of the zoning ordinance and the use strikes a jarring note, it cannot be eliminated by such a revision under existing law. See R.S. 40:55-48, N.J.S.A. If through foresight a municipality is able to anticipate the adverse effects of particular uses and its resulting actions are reasonable, it should be permitted to develop without the burdens of such uses. In his inaugural address on January 16, 1962, Governor Hughes recognized the need for a "planned development" of communities. He said:

> "[A] balanced distribution of people, jobs and industries between our urban and suburban communities is essential for the revitalization of urban life *and the orderly growth of suburban* areas. We cannot stand by while the bright face of New Jersey is disfigured by decay of its cities *and a haphazard growth of its suburbs.*" (Italics supplied)

Our conclusion that the township had the authority to adopt the amendment is based upon the facts presented, the circumstances of the township today and its projected development. We have noted that the township is in a state of flux. Its ultimate character remains indeterminate. In fact, there have been several amendments to the zoning ordinance since its enactment in 1957 and the testimony indicates more are contemplated. We are not unmindful of the reported improvements in design and rising popularity of trailers and the accompanying increased need for trailer camps. Mays, "Zoning for Mobile Homes," Journal of American Institute of Planners, 204 (1961). McKeever, "The Motionless Mobile Home," 19 Urban Land 1 (April 1960); Bartley, Mobile Home Parks and Comprehensive Community Planning, p. 3 (1960); Hodes and Roberson, The Law of Mobile Homes, p. 3 (1957); Note, "Toward an Equitable and Workable Program of Mobile Home Taxation," 71 Yale L.J. 702 (1962). It may be that circumstances will change and trailer camps will be an appropriate use in some areas of the township. If at that time the provisions of the ordinance become unreasonable they may be set aside. As we said in Pierro v. Baxendale, supra, 20 N.J. at p. 29, 118 A.2d 401, 408, "If and when conditions change, alterations in zoning restrictions and pertinent legislative and judicial attitudes need not be long delayed."

[8] It is of no significance that plaintiff's proposed trailer camp would not be detrimental to his immediate neighborhood as it now exists. The validity of a zoning ordinance is not to be determined by reference to an individual parcel of land. Fischer v. Township of Bedminster, supra, 11 N.J. at p. 205, 93 A.2d 378. Moreover, the township has embarked upon an active program designed to eliminate the blighted structures which are near plaintiff's property. We repeat what we said in Napierkowski v. Township of Gloucester, supra, 29 N.J. at 494, 150 A.2d at p. 488: "Zoning must subserve the long-range needs of the present and the reasonably foreseeable future." The township officials have a basis to expect plaintiff's neighborhood will not remain in its present run-down condition and they are justified in considering the envisioned betterment.

The only decision of an appellate court cited by the plaintiff to sustain his contention that total prohibition of trailer camps in a municipality is beyond the zoning power is Gust v. Township of Canton, 342 Mich. 436, 70 N.W.2d 772 (Sup.Ct.1955). There the court said, "The test of validity is not whether the prohibition may *at some time in the future* bear a real and substantial relationship to the public health, safety, morals or general welfare, but whether it does so *now*." (Italics supplied.) 70 N.W.2d 774, 775. This view is contrary to our concept of zoning which requires a looking beyond an immediate "now." Napierkowski v. Township of Gloucester, supra, 29 N.J. at p. 494, 150 A.2d 481. Therefore, we are not persuaded by a result based on the philosophy of the court in Gust.

Plaintiff further contends that even if the township could exclude trailer camps, the adopted amendment is void because the Planning Board did not have the opportunity to give proper consideration to the matter as required by N.J.S.A. 40:55-35.

The amendment was introduced by a first reading at the Township Committee meeting on April 5, 1960. Shortly thereafter, a recess was called to enable the Committeemen who were also members of the Planning Board to attend the Board meeting being held in the same building. After a 45-minute recess the Committee meeting reconvened and it was orally reported that the Planning Board had approved the amendment during that period. This approval was formally communicated to the Committee in a letter dated April 5, 1960, and read at its April 22, 1960, meeting before final adoption of the amendment.

The Chairman of the Planning Board had received a copy of the proposed amendment on April 3, 1960. He discussed the matter informally with several members prior to the meeting of April 5, 1960. The exclusion of trailers and trailer camps had been a subject of frequent discussion prior to the Napierkowski decision in 1959, and even more so since then, but this specific amendment was considered formally by the Planning Board for only 45 minutes.

The plaintiff asserts the action of the Planning Board violated the essential principle of N.J.S.A. 40:55-35 because the Board did not take a reasonable time to consider the specific amendment, and that it was in effect "a mere rubber stamp."

N.J.S.A. 40:55-35 prescribes the procedure for amending a zoning ordinance. It provides in pertinent part:

> "[N]o amendment or change shall become effective unless the ordinance proposing such amendment or change shall first have been submitted to the planning board, when such board exists, for approval, disapproval or suggestions, and the planning board shall have a reasonable time, not less than thirty days, for consideration and report ° ° °."

[9] The policy of the above provision is to afford the Planning Board a reasonable time, not less than 30 days, to perform its statutory function. However, it may act in less time and, if it does, the statutory prerequisite

is met. Wollen v. Fort Lee, 27 N.J. 408, 417, 142 A.2d 881 (1958). The statute does not specify a minimum period of time during which the Board must consider the amendment. The reasonableness of the time allowed depends on the facts in each case. The amendment in the present case was not a long and complicated document couched in ambiguous language. On the contrary, it was short and easily understood. The subject matter was discussed by the Board "from time to time" prior to the approval of the specific amendment. In view of the circumstances here, we cannot say the action of the Board did not represent its considered judgment arrived at independently. It could have reasonably concluded it was as prepared to pass upon the amendment on April 5 as it would be at some later time.

In light of the above, we hold that the township zoning ordinance amendment barring trailer camps from its industrial district was a valid exercise of its zoning power and was adopted in conformity with the statutory requirements.

The judgment of the Appellate Division is reversed and the judgment of the Law Division is reinstated.

For reversal: Chief Justice WEINTRAUB, and Justices JACOBS, FRANCIS, PROCTOR, and HANEMAN—5.

For affirmance: Justices HALL and SCHETTINO—2.

HALL, J. (dissenting).

The majority decides that this particular municipality may constitutionally say, through the exercise of the zoning power, that its residents may not live in trailers—or in mobile homes, to use a more descriptive term. I am convinced such a conclusion in this case is manifestly wrong. Of even greater concern is the judicial process by which it is reached and the breadth of the rationale. The import of the holding gives almost boundless freedom to developing municipalities to erect exclusionary walls on their boundaries according to local whim or selfish desire, and to use the zoning power for aims beyond its legitimate purposes. Prohibition of mobile home parks, although an important issue in itself, becomes, in this larger aspect, somewhat a symbol.

The instant case, both in its physical setting and in the issues raised, is typical of land use controversies now current in many New Jersey municipalities on the outer ring of the built up urban and suburban areas. These are municipalities with relatively few people and a lot of open space, but in the throes, or soon to be reached by the inevitable tide, of industrial and commercial decentralization and mass population migration from the already densely settled central cores. They are not small, homogeneous communities with permanent character already established, like the settled suburbs surrounding the cities in which planning and zoning may properly be geared around things as they are and as they will pretty much continue to be. On the contrary these areas are sprawling, heterogeneous governmental units, mostly townships, each really amounting to a region of considerable size in itself. Their present rural, semi-rural or mixed nature is about to change substantially and they are soon to become melded into the whole metropolitan area. Their political boundaries are artificial and hence of relatively little significance beyond defining one unit of local government. Their existing conglomeration of land uses is sectionally distributed—large or small scale agriculture, residences in separated communities and on good sized plots or acreage in the open country, business establishments in the populated sectors and along through highways, and perhaps a spot or two of industry much sought after to aid municipal tax revenues. Many differing land uses, both present and future, are and can be made comfortably compatible by reason of the distances involved and the varying characteristics of geographical sections. Present municipal services are not more extensive than necessary to serve a population scattered over a large territory. Increased facilities, especially schools, required to accommodate a sudden population growth of large proportions must be provided almost solely at local expense, which in New Jersey means from additional taxation on real estate within the municipal boundaries And it is elementary knowledge that small homes with children to be educated in local schools cannot pay their own way tax-wise.

Such municipalities, above all others, vitally need and may legally exercise comprehensive planning and implementing zoning techniques to avoid present haphazard development which can only bring future grief. They are entitled to aim thereby for a sound and balanced area, with varying uses confined to specified districts and appropriately regulated. They may even limit the pace of growth to coincide with the availability of the necessary additional facilities and services so as to minimize growing pains. See Fagin, "Regulating the Timing of Urban Development," 20 Law and Contemporary Problems 298 (1955). They do not have to permit an Oklahoma land rush or a western boom town. They need not allow every land use wherever someone wants to put it or the property is suitable and, in accordance with a comprehensive plan, may reasonably restrict districts to a particular future use even though another use would be equally suitable. They would be well advised to plan with adjoining communities, especially for joint public services and facilities. Intercommunity planning is also best able to accommodate those categories of uses that ought not be excluded everywhere, but which may be more desirably located in one municipality rather than another. Unfortunately, our statutory provisions for voluntary regional planning boards, R.S. 40:27-9 to 11, N.J.S.A., have been little used, if at all.

And this gets to the nub of what this, and similar cases, are really all about, i.e., the outer limit of the zoning power to be enjoyed by these municipalities most in need of comprehensive authority. What action is not legitimately encompassed by that power and what is the proper role of courts in reviewing its exercise?

The inquiry involves important fundamentals. In the broad sense the considerations are well posed in Williams, "Planning Law and Democratic Living," 20 Law and Contemporary Problems 317 (1955):

> "The main premises of American constitutional law represent a codification and institutionalization of the primary values of a democratic society —equality of opportunity and equality of treatment, freedom of thought and considerable freedom of action, and fairness. Under the American system, a more or less independent mechanism of judicial review is established to provide an independent check on whether specific governmental decisions conform to these standards. *While controversy has often raged about judicial action in other areas, it has always been recognized that it is an essential part of the judicial function to watch over the parochial and exclusionist attitudes and policies of local governments, and to see to it that these do not run counter to national policy and the general welfare.*
>
> Constitutional law should serve to shed light upon thinking about local planning, by requiring those concerned to do what they should be doing anyway—to work out the relationship between planning the future environment and the great issues connected with human freedom and opportunity.
>
>   o   o   o
>
> An intelligent application of constitutional law to the measures used in planning the environment will therefore force a searching inquiry into basic problems—and thus become in fact an excellent vehicle for getting at what is really involved in planning decisions. If such searching inquiries are to be undertaken, this means that no major problem in planning law can really be understood except by an analysis thereof in relation to the whole background of the changing physical, economic and social environment. In short, what is needed in planning law is a super-Brandeis-brief approach.
>
>   o   o   o
>
> The leaders of liberal-democratic thought are all too often so confused with abstractions ('health, safety, morals and welfare,' 'character of the neighborhood,' etc.), so full of respect for local autonomy, and so fearful of judicial review generally, as to be unable to understand the implications of what is going on. It has not been generally realized that in many instances the problems arising in this field of constitutional law are closely akin to those invilved in civil liberties law, and call for similar attitudes toward the exercise of governmental power." (Emphasis supplied) (at pp. 318, 319, 349-350).

Looking first at the judicial role in such matters, it may well be suggested there is nothing revolutionary or even novel in the majority's approach, the formulation of the decision or even in what is said. True it is that the opinion flows smoothly, beginning with common principles and presumptions of constitutional and statutory validity, continuing through recital of a succession of prior decisions in this court, to the seemingly irresistible conclusion that the local action is beyond successful attack. But as I see it, the result of this judicial process goes so far off the mark here as to point up in bold relief the necessity to pause for reappraisal of some of what has gone before and at least to halt what I think has developed into a most improper trend.

The decision formula runs as follows: The 1947 Constitution requires that zoning enabling laws be construed liberally in favor of municipal power. Any local exercise of that power is presumed valid until overcome by an affirmative showing of unreasonableness. Judicial review is so narrow that this showing can never be made if even a "debatable issue" exists. Such an issue exists in this case. Therefore the local prohibition stands.

The majority's spelling out of the "debatable issue" falls into this syllogistic pattern: Developing municipalities need not provide for every use. Cited precedent supports the local right to exclude uses on broad grounds. Planning and zoning in growing municipalities must look ahead to anticipate and prevent blight and to provide for "the hopes of the planners." Any zoning ordinance provision by such a municipality is proper if only it furthers the "general welfare" of the particular municipality in isolation. It does so if, in the single view of a majority of the local governing body, it "is reasonably calculated to advance the community as a social, economic and political unit" or aids in making the community a desirable place in which to work and live. Trailer camps present problems, are unattractive in appearance ("aesthetics may properly be considered in establishing a zoning scheme"), and may be detrimental to present and prospective property values, thereby retarding the "progress" of a municipality. Moreover, once allowed to exist, they become irremovable nonconforming uses with a permanent jarring note if future conditions impel zoning revision. Factually, since validity must be considered in the light of the particular circumstances, this township is in the path of growth potential and is presently in a state of flux. It is seeking the orderly development of a well integrated community. Its officials do not like the looks of trailer camps in industrial districts or anywhere else—they "are unsightly" and "do not contribute anything to the general appearance of the local scenery and do not enhance the use or value of the local real estate." Therefore their complete prohibition furthers the "general welfare" in the eyes of the local authorities. The court cannot go against their view.

As the first stone in building its thesis, the majority relies on the 1947 constitutional mandate, Art. IV, Sec. VII, par. 11, enjoining liberal construction of provisions in that document and of laws concerning local government. Analysis demonstrates that the mandate has no true application in this situation. It was intended to reverse the former rule of construction of municipal power which had required, as stated for example in N.J. Good Humor, Inc. v. Bradley Beach, 124 N.J.L. 162, 164-165 11 A.2d 113, 115 (E. & A. 1939), that

> "[a]ny reasonable or fair doubt of the existence of the asserted power, or any ambiguity in the statute whence it springs, or those in *pari materia,* is to be resolved against the municipality, and the power is denied. Mu-

nicipalities are to be confined within the limits that a strict construction of the grants of powers will assign to them."

See 1 Proceedings of the New Jersey Constitutional Convention of 1947 401. But municipalities are still governmental units carrying out only those state functions and duties delegated to them by the Legislature either expressly, by necessary or fair implication, or as incidental or essential to powers expressly conferred. The new constitutional provision did not create a new concept of limitless home rule or give omnipotence to a local government to do anything it desires without regard to the limits of the delegated power supposedly exercised. Magnolia Development Co., Inc. v. Coles, 10 N.J. 223, 89 A.2d 664 (1952); Fred v. Mayor and Council, Old Tappan Borough, 10 N.J. 515, 518, 92 A.2d 473 (1952); Grogan v. DeSapio, 11 N.J. 308, 316-317, 94 A.2d 316 (1953); Wagner v. Newark, 24 N.J. 467, 476-478, 132 A.2d 794 (1957).

In land use regulation, the Legislature has specifically defined and delineated the objects and methods of municipal action in accordance with expressed standards. Liberal construction cannot be applied in such matters so as to "constitute an authorization for a municipality to exercise the powers therein conferred without compliance with the provisions and procedures therein described," many of which are for the protection of property owners. Magnolia Development Co., Inc. v. Coles, supra (10 N.J., at p. 227, 89 A.2d 664), nor does it, speaking more generally, "connote an extension of the boundaries delineated by the statutory phraseology as commonly used," Grogan v. DeSapio, supra (11 N.J., at p. 316, 94 A.2d 316, 320). We are not here concerned with the physical scope of the zoning power, cf. United Advertising Corp. v. Borough of Raritan, 11 N.J. 144, 150, 93 A.2d 362 (1952), but rather with the propriety of its exercise in the light of the prescribed statutory scheme and standards and other inherent limitations. It is a misapplication of the constitutional mandate to utilize it, as the majority seems to do, for the purpose of glossing over or watering down the requisite inquiry as to reasonableness with reference to the particular action under review.

The other foundation stones of the majority's approach are the twin shibboleths of presumption of validity of municipal action and restraint on judicial review if the proofs do not overcome it "beyond debate." The trouble is not with the principles—if we did not have them, governments could not well operate at all—but rather with the perfunctory manner in which they have come to be applied. Undoubtedly influenced at the same time by loose application of the constitutional provision for liberal construction, Lionshead Lake, Inc. v. Township of Wayne, 10 N.J. 165, 172, 89 A.2d 693 (1952), appeal dismissed, 344 U.S. 919, 73 S. Ct. 386, 97 L.Ed. 708 (1953), our courts have in recent years made it virtually impossible for municipal zoning regulations to be successfully attacked. Judicial scrutiny has become too superficial and one-sided.[1] The state of the trend is exemplified in the language of the majority that "if the amendment presented a debatable issue we cannot nullify the Township's decision that its welfare would be advanced by the action it took."

In passing, a further principle may be noticed which seems to have been lost sight of in recent zoning decisions: "the presumption of validity ° ° ° is only a presumption and may be overcome or rebutted not only by clear evidence *aliunde*, but also by a showing on its face or in the light of facts of which judicial notice can be taken, of transgression of constitutional limitation or the bounds of reason." Moyant v. Paramus, 30 N.J. 528, 535, 154 A.2d 9, 12 (1959). Accordingly, it seems only fair to private citizens seeking judicial determination of their rights to require the municipality, with all its resources, to assume the burden of going forward to justify its action when the challenged measure gives good possibility on the surface of going to a doubtful extreme.[2]

While it has long been conventional for courts to test the validity of local legislation by the criterion of whether a fairly debatable issue is presented, and if so to sustain it, it makes all the difference in the world how a court deals with that criterion. Proper judicial review to me can be nothing less than an objective, realistic consideration of the setting—the evils or conditions sought to be remedied, a full and comparative appraisal of the public interest involved and the private rights affected, both from the local and broader aspects, and a thorough weighing of all factors, with government entitled to win if the scales are at least balanced or even a little less so. Of course, such a process involves judgment and the measurement can never be mathematically exact. But that is what judges are for—to evaluate and protect all interests, including those of individuals and minorities, regardless of personal likes or views of wisdom, and not merely to rubber-stamp governmental action in a kind of judicial *laissez-faire*. The majority approach attaches exclusive significance to the view of the governing body that, in its summary opinion, the "welfare" of the municipality would be

---

1. One student of the subject, writing in the fall of 1959, finds that since liberality of application of the principles was stated so strongly in Kozesnik v. Montgomery Township, 24 N.J. 154, 167, 131 A.2d 1 (1957), this court has sustained the challenged ordinance in every case but one. Cunningham, "Control of Land Use in New Jersey by Means of Zoning," 14 Rutgers L.Rev. 37, 48. And the record has not changed substantially since.

2. The instant case is a good example. At the inception, plaintiff, a single, small property owner, was seeking authority, on any possible basis, to use his particular land for a mobile home park, a then permissible use. The prohibitory ordinance amendment adopted in the middle of the litigation shifted the issue to the comprehensive one with which this dissent is concerned. His proofs—and the townships' too, for that matter—are sparse on the meaningful aspects of the ultimate controversy. Undoubtedly he was without the facilities or financial means to marshal and present the many-sided evidence needed to make a telling attack and even come close to meeting the heavy burden the majority imposes upon him and others similarly situated.

advanced. On this criterion it is hard to conceive of any local action which would not come within the "debatable" class.

The majority falls in line with a plainer expression of the same thought in two earlier cases upon which it relies—Lionshead Lake, Inc. v. Township of Wayne, supra (10 N.J. 165, 89 A.2d 693, concurring opinion) and Pierro v. Baxendale, 20 N.J. 17, 118 A.2d 401 (1955). In the latter the court said: "We are satisfied that at long last conscientious municipal officials have been sufficiently empowered to adopt reasonable zoning measures designed towards preserving the wholesome and attractive characteristics of their communities and the values of taxpayers' properties." (20 N.J., at p. 29, 118 A.2d at p. 408). In the former: "[The attacked provision] constituted important legislative action representing the governing body's best judgment as to what zoning restrictions were required to promote the health, morals and general welfare of the community as a whole. Decent respect for its problems and sincerity required that its action remain unimpaired in the absence of clear showing that it was arbitrary, unreasonable, or beyond the authority of the general Zoning Act." (10 N.J., at p. 179, 89 A.2d 693, 700). I think it is basically wrong for a court to take this point of view. Municipal legislative action is always assumed to have been taken conscientiously, sincerely and honestly. The test of validity is certainly something much more than bad faith or corruption. Local officials, no matter how conscientious and sincere in their own minds, may be legally wrong in formulating into legislation what they think is best for their community. The only place that question can be tested and individual rights and privileges safeguarded is in the courts. The judicial branch does not meet its full responsibility when, as here, its concept of review gives unquestioning deference to the views of local officials.

Turning to the way the majority looks at local zoning regulations from the substantive standpoint, it is asserted to be enough, as has been indicated, that the "general welfare" of the community is advanced. And the definition of the term, taken from prior cases, is so broad—anything "reasonably calculated to advance the community as a social, economic and political unit," including "public convenience" and "general prosperity"—one could hardly conceive of any land use regulation which would not fulfill it, especially when the governing body's determination is so controlling. All the other purposes and criteria of valid zoning set forth in the enabling act, R.S. 40:55-32, N.J.S.A., seem to be written out as unnecessary and of no bearing. The result is an extension of local control in directions and for purposes, under the guise of zoning, which go beyond the legitimate aims of the power. We should not forget some fundamentals. Zoning is land use control by *physical* planning to bring about physical results for public, not private, welfare. It is not a device to be used to accomplish any and all purportedly desirable *social* results unrelated to the statutorily stated purposes. The basic definition by the first authority in the field still holds good: "Zoning is the regulation by districts under the police power of the height, bulk and use of buildings, the use of land and the density of population." Bassett, Zoning 45 (1940). The purpose "to promote ° ° ° the general welfare" does not stand alone in the statute. Its meaning and scope must have some relation to the other specified standards and the whole authorized scheme. Certainly "general welfare" does not automatically mean whatever the municipality says it does, regardless of who is hurt and how much.

And no matter how broadly the concept is viewed, it cannot authorize a municipality to erect a completely isolationist wall on its boundaries. This was early recognized in the foundation case of Euclid v. Ambler Realty Co., 272 U.S. 365, 47 S. Ct. 114, 71 L.Ed. 303 (1926), where the court was careful to say: "It is not meant by this, however, to exclude the possibility of cases where the general public interest would so far outweigh the interest of the municipality that the municipality would not be allowed to stand in the way." 47 S. Ct. at 119, 71 L.Ed., at p. 311. Two of our own landmark decisions (one wonders what has lately happened to them) made it very plain, even though our zoning scheme is legislatively keyed to municipal lines, that validity of local use prohibitions is to be judged by, among other things, availability of other appropriate locations, Duffcon Concrete Products, Inc. v. Borough of Cresskill, 1 N.J. 509, 64 A.2d 347, 9 A.L.R.2d 678 (1949), and that one town's zoning should give due recognition to conditions across its boundaries, Borough of Cresskill v. Borough of Dumont, 15 N.J. 238, 104 A.2d 441 (1954). See Haar, "Regionalism and Realism in Land-Use Planning," 105 U.Pa.L.Rev. 515 (1957); Note, "Zoning Against the Public Welfare: Judicial Limitations on Municipal Parochialism," 71 Yale L.J. 720 (1962). Though the Cresskill cases dealt with built-up suburbs their underlying philosophy is equally applicable to developing municipalities in a vast metropolitan complex. They stand for the proposition that "general welfare" transcends the artificial limits of political subdivisions and cannot embrace merely narrow local desires.

I have at least equal difficulty with the breadth of another major aspect of the majority's thesis—that the local power to zone is especially *carte blanche* when the municipality is a relatively virgin one, and in the path of metropolitan expansion. The specter of future blight and a present inward vision of what the municipality hopes or dreams of someday becoming or remaining seem enough to sanction most any restriction, however drastic or provincial. This is, of course, partly true, since such municipalities may validly exercise comprehensive planning and zoning powers in many ways to meet their peculiar problems, present and prospective. Reasonableness depends on particular circumstances and some of the techniques legitimately available to them might be invalid if applied to relatively small built-up municipalities with settled character. But the reverse is also true. Euclid long ago noted: "A regulatory zoning ordinance, which would be clearly valid as applied to the great cities, might be clearly invalid as applied to rural communities." 47 S.Ct. at p. 118, 71 L.Ed., at p. 310. Some of the cases relied on by the majority—Duffcon Concrete Products, Inc. v. Borough of Cresskill, supra (1 N.J. 509, 64 A.2d 347, 9 A.L.R.2d 678) (a densely settled suburb may properly exclude industry, if it has some other place to go in the general area); Fanale v. Borough of Hasbrouck Heights, 26 N.J. 320, 139 A.2d 749 (1958) (such a community may say it has had enough of some problem-creating method of living); Pierro v. Baxendale, supra (20 N.J. at p. 17, 118 A.2d 401). (It may keep transient motels at least out of its residential districts even though it allows dwellings to be used for boarding and rooming houses)—have little substantive pertinency in passing on the propriety of regulations in virgin territories.

Townships like Gloucester, with their vast areas of vacant land, have plenty of room in which to accommodate the variety of land uses people of all income levels and individual desires may want to enjoy. Sound planning and zoning regulations by appropriate districts can easily make such uses compatible while avoiding detrimental impact on each other. The technique is to allow for differing uses by putting them in the right places and with accompanying restrictions. I am unconvinced that "adequate light and air," lessening "congestion in the streets," avoidance of "undue concentration of population," "safety from fire, panic and other dangers" and prevention of suburban blight reasonably require a minimum five-acre dwelling lot in 90% of a 24-square-mile township with a population of 1600, if that municipality is a growing one or about to be reached by the tide.[3]

In my opinion legitimate use of the zoning power by such municipalities does not encompass the right to erect barricades on their boundaries through exclusion or too tight restriction of uses where the real purpose is to prevent feared disruption with a so-called chosen way of life. Nor does it encompass provisions designed to let in as new residents only certain kinds of

---

3. The reference is to Fischer v. Township of Bedminster, 11 N.J. 194, 93 A.2d 378 (1952), also relied on by the majority. While the court used broad language, to be mentioned again shortly, the result of the case is supportable on the proofs set forth in the opinion. They showed a completely rural municipality, with land uses and population little changed from what they had been 122 years before. More important, it was said to be in the center of a group of municipalities having substantially the same characteristics and there is no indication given of the probability of a population invasion in the near future. All the expert evidence found the restriction reasonable under the circumstances. The court did say that changed conditions might make the approved restriction unreasonable at a later time. (11 N.J., at p. 205, 93 A.2d 378).

I do not mean to urge by what I have said or am about to say that every sparsely populated township cannot zone to maintain, reasonably, present basic rural land uses, at least until growth reaches it. Many such areas are so far away from the metropolitan center and suburbs that any substantial change will not come or be threatened for many years. I speak only of those municipalities where substantial growth has begun or is so practically imminent that it cannot validly be held off by local legislative walls denominated as zoning.

people,[4] or those who can afford to live in favored kinds of housing, or to keep down tax bills of present property owners. When one of the above is the true situation deeper considerations intrinsic in a free society gain the ascendency and courts must not be hesitant to strike down purely selfish and undemocratic enactments. I am not suggesting that every such municipality must endure a plague of locusts or suffer transition to a metropolis over night. I suggest only that regulation rather than prohibition is the appropriate technique for attaining a balanced and attractive community. The opportunity to live in the open spaces in decent housing one can afford and in the manner one desires is a vital one in a democracy. It seems contradictory to sustain so readily legislative policy at the state level forbidding various kinds of discrimination in housing, e.g., Levitt & Sons, Inc. v. Division Against Discrimination, 31 N.J. 514, 158 A.2d 177 (1960), appeal dismissed, 363 U.S. 418, 80 S.Ct. 1257, 4 L.Ed.2d 1515 (1960), and permitting the use of eminent domain and public funds to remove slums and provide decent living accommodations, e.g., Ryan v. Housing Authority of Newark, 125 N.J.L. 336, 15 A.2d 647 (Sup.Ct.1940); Wilson v. Long Branch, 27 N.J. 360, 142 A.2d 837 (1958), cert. den. 358 U.S. 873, 79 S.Ct 113, 3 L.Ed.2d 104 (1958), and at the same time bless selfish zoning regulations which tend to have the effect of precluding people who now live in congested and undesirable city areas from obtaining housing within their means in open, attractive and healthy communities.

Lionshead (10 N.J., at pp. 173-175, 89 A.2d 693), and Fischer in the breadth of some of its language (11 N.J., at pp. 204, 205, 93 A.2d 378), rationalize such exclusionary results, as does the majority here, by reference to the statutory zoning purposes, R.S. 40:55-32, N.J.S.A., of "conserving the value of property" and "encouraging the most appropriate use of land" and in the name of preservation of the character of the community or neighborhood. I submit these factors are perverted from their intended application when used to justify Chinese walls on the borders of roomy and developing municipalities for the actual purpose of keeping out all but the "right kind" of people or those who will live in a certain kind and cost of dwelling. What restrictions like minimum house size requirements, overly large lot area regulations and complete limitation of dwellings to single family units really do is bring about community-wide economic segregation. It is a proper thing to exclude factories from residential zones to conserve property

---

4. That this kind of motivation was not entirely absent in the barring of mobile homes from Gloucester Township is indicated by the statement at oral argument of the township's counsel, during the course of discussion of the local reasons for the action, that people who lived in trailers were a shifting population without roots and did not make good citizens. Aside from the fact that such characterizations are today without true foundation, the statement is an example of frequently found resentment and distrust by present residents of newcomers, including renters, who vote on school budgets and the election of local officials with the power over municipal appropriations, but who do not pay real estate taxes directly or in sufficient amount to cover the cost of local services rendered to them.

values and to encourage the most appropriate use of land throughout the municipality. It is quite another and improper thing to use zoning to control who the residents of your township will be. To reiterate, all the legitimate aspects of a desirable and balanced community can be realized by proper placing and regulation of uses, as the zoning statute contemplates, without destroying the higher value of the privilege of democratic living. For a fuller discussion see Williams, "Planning Law and Democratic Living," 20 Law and Contemporary Problems 317 (1955); Haar, "Zoning for Minimum Standards: The Wayne Township Case," 66 Harv.L.Rev. 1051 (1953); Haar, "Wayne Township: Zoning for Whom—In Brief Reply," 67 Harv.L. Rev. 986 (1954).

We should not perpetuate or augment this fundamental error of Lionshead. Prohibition of mobile home parks is of a piece with absolute minimum house sizes there approved and the same reasoning is utilized here to support it. Trailer living is a perfectly respectable, healthy and useful kind of housing, adopted by choice by several million people in this country today. Municipalities and courts can no longer refuse to recognize its proper and significant place in today's society and should stop acting on the basis of old wives' tales. A fair, modern appraisal is found in Note, "Toward an Equitable and Workable Program of Mobile Home Taxation," 71 Yale L.J. 702 (1962):

> "Between 1951 and 1956 the mobile home population doubled; it currently totals over 3,000,000 persons. The number of mobile homes in use grew from 550,000 in 1953 to 1,200,000 in 1959. This figure has been augmented by mobile homes recently produced—produced at a rate which exceeds 10 per cent of the private single family housing starts in this country.
>
> For many years communities viewed the house trailer as the source of at least three major problems: its presence was expected to blight surrounding areas, causing property values to fall; its occupants were often viewed as personally undesirable; and the municipal expense attributable to trailerites was expected to exceed the revenue which could be raised from them.
>
> Community fear of blight can be traced to the low quality of both the early trailers and their parking facilities. Economic conditions of the 'thirties, followed by wartime housing shortages and rapid relocations of the labor force, pressed many thousands of unattractive trailers into permanent use. Often these units were without running water or sanitary facilities. There were no construction standards to insure even minimum protection against fire or collapse. They were parked in areas which were usually crowded, poorly equipped, and generally unsuited to residential use. As a result, conditions in these parks seldom exceeded minimum health and sanitation standards. The specter of such parks teeming with tiny trailers made community apprehension understandable. But substantial improvements in the quality of both mobile homes and park facilities may have undermined the bases for this antipathy today. The mobile home currently produced is an atttractive, completely furnished, efficiently spacious dwelling for which national construction standards have been adopted and enforced by the manufacturers' associations. Some of today's parks are

landscaped, and feature ample lots imaginatively arranged around paved streets. Recreation facilities—such as swimming pools, boat docks and playgrounds—found in high quality parks could be the envy of conventional housing developments. *Although many parks have yet to match such progress, communities have ample power to require improvement of existing facilities and to set high standards for future park construction. They need only exercise it.*

Community distaste for trailer dwellers personally developed at a time when the trailerites were often considered footloose, nomadic people unlikely to make any positive contribution to community life. The early trailer was used primarily 'by tourists and transient workers; the permanent residents who did use trailers were likely to be low income workers with temporary positions. Mobile homes, however, can no longer be said to be inhabited primarily by migratory paupers; according to recent surveys, the present occupations and incomes of their occupants vary widely. Skilled workers, many of whom are engaged in construction or mineral development, now seem to form the largest single group of mobile home owners. Many mobile homes are also used by military personnel, young couples, and retired persons. Even professional people, perhaps attracted by the comfort available in a high quality mobile home and park, perhaps by tax economies, currently represent a large segment of the mobile home population. With the increasing variety of occupational groups living in mobile homes has come a substantial upgrading in income level. In 1958, the median income of mobile home dwellers ($5,250) was approximately the same as the national average ($5,300). There seems little justification, therefore, for any continuing personal antipathy toward mobile home dwellers as a group." (Emphasis supplied) (at pp. 702-704).

In the face of these facts, it is arbitrary to permit the prohibition of mobile home parks completely in a municipality where they can be placed in appropriate districts and in which there is a need or demand for them. To hold otherwise would be to allow any method of housing to be outlawed by local whim. I cannot understand how, in a large and roomy township, a properly situated and regulated mobile home park can have a detrimental effect on the value of all the property in the township or on its overall attractiveness any more than industrial and commercial districts or even small lot housing developments.[5]

---

5. It should be noted that, as we were advised at oral argument, the mobile home industry in this state now accepts the proposition that trailers properly belong in parks and may legitimately be barred by zoning as single dwellings on individual lots in residential zones. Napierkowski v. Township of Gloucester, 29 N.J. 481, 150 A.2d 481 (1959). The best modern planning thought seems to be that, since mobile home living is truly residential, parks should be situated in a residential type of environment and not in commercial and industrial districts. They are, in effect, a horizontal multi-residential use.—no more of a commercial venture than a rented garden apartment. The suggestion seems sound that they should be located in districts akin to multi-family residential zones away from busy highways, but with particular requirements of ground area, arrangement, buffers and the like to immunize any adverse impact on other uses in the vicinity. Bartley and Bair, Mobile Home Parks and Comprehensive Community Planning 77-79 (1960). The special exception technique, N.J.S.A. 40:55-39(b) would appear to be an especially appropriate method of handling both specific location and desirable physical regulations of each individual case.

Moreover, the aesthetic warrant for the prohibition, additionally relied upon by the majority, is not a reasonable basis for the exercise of zoning power in this situation. Without getting into all the ramifications surrounding the difficult question of how and to what extent aesthetics may validly be considered in zoning regulations, it certainly is not enough to sanction exclusion of a particular kind of use on the sole ground that its appearance offends the subjective sensibilities of the local governing body. Objective standards in this field are hard enough to fashion and work with, for even expert to fashion and work with, for even expert tastes vary so greatly. Bassett, Zoning 97-98 (1940). Letting a use be controlled by individual preferences and prejudice, devoid of standards entirely, is the antithesis of proper judicial review. The majority's view could as well support exclusion of modernistic dwelling architecture, split level homes, or even whole developments of identical houses if a bare majority of the township committee does not like their looks.

Nor is a use validly prohibited because it might later develop that the zone for it was improvidently chosen necessitating a change in classification, resulting in a nonconforming use. If this were to be a sound criterion, we could never have any planning or zoning of virgin areas, for the best theoretical views of planners may often not work out in practice and amendment is frequently found necessary.

I have no doubt that, if the issue in this case is approached in the way I have indicated it should be, the particular circumstances in Gloucester Township shown by the record are such that prohibition of mobile home parks throughout the municipality should be held unlawful. It is clearly a heterogeneous, growing municipality, very close by the Philadelphia metropolitan area, in the path of further expansion of varied kinds. The northern half of its 23 square miles is already quite densely settled, mostly with small home development and neighborhood business areas along and adjacent to old and new highways. The southern half is very largely undeveloped, with no established character as yet. Most of the vacant land throughout the township is zoned for industrial use, although there is none now. This classification seems more a device to block further home construction on any large scale (as witness the provision permitting dwellings therein only with approval of the Board of Adjustment) than evidence of any real hope of filling with industry the areas so zoned. Planning and zoning to date have been pretty much catch-as-catch-can and piecemeal. But practically all conceivable uses except nuisance industries and mobile home parks are permitted. There is plenty of room in the vast undeveloped areas for all manner of classification districts, which, by appropriate regulations, can compatibly exist without deleterious impact on each other and at the same time lead to the creation of a balanced and attractive community. There is nothing to indicate that a mobile home park is not a legally and factually appropriate use somewhere in such a scene. To hold that it is not exceeds the bounds of reason.

I would affirm the judgment of the Appellate Division. Justice SCHET-TINO joins in this opinion.

Questions and Notes

1. Justice Hall's dissent is probably the most famous zoning opinion between *Euclid* and *Mount Laurel,* and deservedly so. It was this opinion which first spelled out the problems of exclusionary zoning to the judiciary; and thirteen years later the New Jersey court came around with the *Mount Laurel* case (see below).

2. The majority opinion represents the ultimate development of the third-period attitude in New Jersey zoning. The dissent announces the advent of the fourth period.

3. Note that Hall's dissent focused immediately on the really basic issue, which is nothing less than the nature of judicial review, and calls for a more creative judicial review, going far beyond the "fairly debatable" test.

4. Equally important is the realistic description of the workings of exclusionary zoning, which broke almost wholly new ground. In this section, Hall's argument is essentially that, at least in a township where substantial areas are zoned to permit expansion of employment on presently-vacant land, there must be some place where inexpensive housing (like mobile homes) can be permitted.

CLARY

v.

EATONTOWN

41 N.J. Super. 47, 124 A.2d 54(1956).

Superior Court of New Jersey.
Appellate Division.

Argued June 4, 1956.
Decided July 10, 1956.

Action attacking the validity of zoning ordinances establishing minimum lot areas of 11,000 and 20,000 square feet respectively on the ground that the effect of the ordinances upon the property of the plaintiff was confiscatory. From a judgment of the Superior Court, Law Division, sustaining the validity of the ordinance the plaintiff appealed. The Superior Court, Appellate Division, Conford, J. A. D., held that the ordinances were valid.

Judgment affirmed

CONFORD, J. A. D.

This is an appeal from a judgment of the Superior Court, Law Division, sustaining the validity, as against the plaintiff, of a zoning ordinance adopted by the defendant borough November 10, 1954. The ordinance effects widespread revision of residential zoning throughout the municipality, principally by creating a scale of zones based upon minimum lot area and frontage. Some 58 acres of undeveloped land owned by plaintiff were placed in an R-3 residential zone, which requires a minimum lot area of 20,000 square feet and a 100-foot minimum frontage. The gravamen of the action is plaintiff's assertion that such a restriction on his property is unreasonable; that the character of most existing homes in the neighborhood and the size of the lots on which they are situated are such that it would be economically unfeasible to develop his property for residences on lots as large as 20,000 square feet and that the effect of the ordinance upon his property is consequently confiscatory.

Plaintiff also complains of the effect of the ordinance in restricting the utility of ten small building lots which he owns in what is known as the Chestnut Grove development, northwest of the 58-acre tract. These lots were placed by the ordinance in an R–4 residence zone calling for a minimum lot area of 11,000 square feet and a minimum frontage of 75 feet. The complaint is that the ordinance is unreasonable as to these properties because none of them can conform with all the requirements as to frontage, land area and side yard area.

Eatontown is a municipality of some six square miles in area, having a 1955 population of approximately 5,000. It is situated in Monmouth County, a part of the State which is experiencing rapid population growth, much of it through mass small-home residential developments. In 1940 its population was only 1,700, and in 1950 approximately 3,000. About one third of its land area is vacant and unused, except for occasional farming operations. The community may be described as primarily made up of middle class residents, homes having a value of over $20,000 being exceptional. Much, if not most, of the working population is employed either at nearby Fort Monmouth, the Eisner uniform plant at Red Bank, or at the Bendix plant on State Highway No. 35, which was erected within the last five years. The municipality is bisected in a north-south direction by State Highway No. 35 and east-west by State Highway No. 36. These highways, an approach spur to the Garden State Parkway, and two other thoroughfares have their confluence at what is generally known as the Eatontown Traffic Circle, situated at the geographical center of the municipality. * * *

In addition to the argument based upon the smallness of the homes and lots in surrounding developments plaintiff contends that a factor further militating against the utility of the Clary tract for better-type homes is the unattractiveness of each of the road approaches to the property. He stresses that the highways which lead to the Wyckoff Road approach on the south have the usual highway appurtenances of gasoline stations, trailer camps, diners, and miscellaneous business establishments; that an approach from the north, via Broad Street, involves traversing the unattractive commercial center of the town on Broad Street. Finally, his argument dwells upon the consideration that Eatontown is predominantly composed of working-class people living in small dwellings and that they characterize the kind of prospect interested in an Eatontown home. The central theme of plaintiff's case is that it is not economically feasible to develop the Clary tract for residence purposes on lots of 20,000 square feet because a lot of that area would require a home of such value that the parcel would sell for from $20,000 to $25,000, a product assertedly not marketable in Eatontown under the surrounding developmental circumstances. It is contended, in effect, that the reasonable residential zoning of Eatontown must be approached from the standpoint of its modest status in the surrounding geographical region—that the requirements of the region for better homes are adequately met by such nearby communities as Rumson, Fair Haven, Little Silver, and the Shrewsburys, which are characterized by higher-cost residential areas.

One realty expert for plaintiff, McGregor, who had sold most of the Elkwood homes, testified that land in the neighborhood was worth $1,000 a quarter-acre and that a house which "would be put on a 20,000 square foot lot" on the Clary tract, "where the land would sell for $1,000 a quarter of an acre," would be "at least $20,000, maybe $25,000." He did not believe any developer would undertake the development of the Clary tract on that basis and testified he knew of builders who had lost interest in the property after it was rezoned. He conceded, on cross-examination, however, that the fact that he might not be able to sell the property for that type of development "doesn't mean a thing," that "somebody might do it," and that the plaintiff had never authorized him to sell the land to any one for any given price. He also conceded that he knew of instances in Monmouth County where homes in residential developments on lots of 100 x 200 feet had been sold for $16,000.

Another realty expert for plaintiff, Morris, testified that in his opinion, "on a lot 20,000 square feet there should be a house from $22,000 to $25,000," in order "to make it economically feasible." He did not think that it would be practicable to sell homes of that value on the Clary tract because of the proximity of the smaller homes in the Elkwood development. He acknowledged, however, that directly across Wyckoff Road from the Clary tract there were homes on plots in excess of 20,000 square feet which he would value at about $20,000.

Theodore McGinness, a member of the Eatontown Planning Board, clerk of the tax board, and engaged in the real estate business in Eatontown, was called as a witness by plaintiff, primarily to testify concerning assessment records. He testified that homes on 20,000 square foot plots in the Clary tract would not "readily sell" for from $20,000 to $25,000. Later, however, as a witness for the defendant, he stated it to be his opinion that the Clary tract could be developed on plots of 20,000 square feet for homes which would sell for from $16,000 to $18,000. He referred to two other residential developments on Wyckoff Road south of State Highway No. 36, on plots of 20,000 square feet, which were in process of development and selling at prices from $14,000 to $21,000. He also testified to a projected "Wynnewood Homes Development," for which a plot plan had been officially approved, to be erected on the easterly side of Wyckoff Road southeast of the Clary tract and within the triangular portion of the R–3 zone district here in question. We gather from the transcript that the lots are about 20,000 square feet, but the plot plan, though admitted in evidence, has not been incorporated in the appendix.

Plaintiff produced as a witness Russell V. N. Black, a well-known zoning and planning expert, who gave it as his opinion that the zoning of the Clary property for minimum 20,000 square foot lots was "much too severe an upgrading" as against the surrounding homes on 7,500 square foot plots. His conclusion was that the zoning of the Clary tract in the respect mentioned was unreasonable. He said, however, that the "cost range of the houses" in the neighborhood is "really more determinative of the Clary tract than the actual size of the lots" of such houses. We judge this to mean that in his opinion the degree of "up-grading" of the subject tract should be measured in terms of comparison of the value of the homes in the surrounding area with that of such homes as might feasibly be projected for the Clary tract on lots of 20,000 square feet rather than in terms of comparison of the respective lot areas.

The plaintiff testified as a witness in his own behalf. He is a New York lawyer and has been beneficially interested in the Clary tract for some 20 years. It appears that the property was originally a hunting preserve on a large estate. It is on high ground, attractively landscaped with trees and shrubs and several brooks course through it. The plaintiff testified that he spends much of his time in keeping the property attractive. He said that he has had several inquiries concerning purchase of the property but that the prospects lost interest when told of the present zoning. He conceded, however, that he has never listed the property for sale nor communicated a sale price to any one. There is no evidence that he has ever attempted to market the property.

The principal witness for the defendant was Leo J. Carling, president of the Eatontown Planning Board. The board was created by the municipality in the spring of 1950 and undertook at once a comprehensive study of the borough for purposes of revision of the existing zoning of the municipality, then based upon an ordinance of 1940 which fixed no minimum lot areas for the residential zones. Carling himself became very active in planning activities statewide and later became a director of the New Jersey Federation of Official Planning Boards and of the Central Jersey Federation of Planning Boards. He has made an extensive study of the current literature in the field and has attended various lectures and conferences on planning and zoning held in New Jersey and also conferences in New York under the auspices of the New York Regional Planning Association. He testified that he has spent a great many hours riding and walking about all areas in the borough, "alone and in company of other members of the planning board." Early in the history of the board, a committee was designated to study and map existing land uses throughout the borough. A rough land-use map was prepared but was not kept as a permanent record.

The planning board eventually completed a draft of a revised zoning ordinance and submitted it to the mayor and council in August 1953. From that date until the adoption of the ordinance presently in question there were numerous meetings and conferences, formal and informal, between the planning board and the mayor and council respecting the subject matter thereof, and there were several public hearings on the proposed ordinance in various stages of its revision. As originally prepared by the board, the present R-3 zone district in which the Clary property is situated was set up as an R-2 zone district, calling for a minimum lot area of 32,000 square feet. After a public hearing, at which the Clary and Maida interests protested, the district was reduced to an R-3 residence zone (20,000 square feet). Over objection on the part of the plaintiff, Carling answered a question as to "what considerations the planning board took in determining to classify the Clary property in the R-3 zone," as follows:

"A. We considered the fact that this land and that adjacent to it, particularly the Maida properties, represented a sizable area, I think in the order of 90 acres of undeveloped land. It is known to be good residential land, or prime for residential development purposes. I believe Mr. Clary's land is the highest land on the east side of the borough, and as such would command a certain amount of careful consideration to preserve its value as a residential section of the borough.

"We took into account the fact that in the general area there are lands used for other purposes and residential purposes, and beyond that there are lands used and intended for use in business and industrial zones.

"*   *   *

"* * * To protect the value, then, of this land and the adjacent lands to it, we established a pattern of gradation, considering, let us say, the highway, Route 35, running more or less north and south throughout the center of the borough and used for business and industrial purposes, an area adjacent to it occupied by the Norwood Homes tract as a residential usage, not of the quality that we would expect to find on the Maida and Clary properties, but to serve as a buffer zone between the influences of business and industry on Mr. Clary's land. Similarly, a continuation of that same R-4 zone in the area which has been referred to in this case as the Cleveland Farm serves as a buffer from the general southwesterly section where the drive-in theatre is located. That same general pattern of thinking then followed all the way around the territory, and as a matter of fact, served for the basis of thinking in the entire zoning program and planning program.

"We did take into account as well the fact that modern homes require larger lot sizes because of their architecture, ranch type houses producing a greater building frontage than the older two-story or bungalow type of house. That called, then, for a greater frontage. To provide latitude in placing a house within the lot confines, the side yard and rear yard requirements have been established so that not all houses need be exactly the same or placed in the same precise position on the lot, thus again enhancing the value of the area as a community with a certain amount of distinctiveness about it, rather than the mass-produced effect of small lots and small houses precisely located in the only way that they can be located on a small lot. ° ° °"

The witness also testified that the planning board took into account the fact that since there was no public sewerage system in the municipality, larger lot areas would be desirable from a health standpoint, better to permit soil absorption of sewage. He mentioned the objective of preventing the "whole eastern section of the municipality" from being characterized as small-lot, low-cost housing and indicated that the area in question was the only high quality residential land available in that part of the borough for half-acre lots. They also gave consideration to the desirability of reduction of population density and such concomitant benefits as limitation of traffic.

Herbert H. Smith, a professional planning and zoning consultant whose qualifications have been noted by our courts, was engaged by the borough as a consultant in the drafting of the ordinance. He worked on the project some two weeks in manhours over a period of several months in the spring of 1954. While he did not prepare the zoning ordinance itself but only made technical suggestions, his work required him to become familiar with the municipality as a whole and the neighborhood of the subject property in particular. He was asked at the trial whether he had an opinion as to the reasonableness of the classification of the Clary tract under the zoning ordinance as enacted. He explained his affirmative answer as follows:

"Q. And what is that opinion?

A. Taking into account the studies that the community has made in conjunction with this zoning, the various ideas that they have for future development, the characteristics of the surrounding area and the potentialities of the entire community, I believe that the present zoning of this area is reasonable."

He was asked on cross-examination whether he would recommend that a tract of ground "surrounded" as is the Clary tract should "be up-graded so that the lots in that tract of land would have to be 170% larger" than lots on which homes had been erected nearby. He answered:

"A. Speaking strictly from a hypothetical standpoint in the proposition that you have presented, I would say that there would certainly be occasions that such an upping would be justified; that the factors that I have mentioned as having been taken into consideration in reaching an opinion on the Eatontown zoning ordinance would be among those factors."

The trial judge filed findings of fact and conclusions of law which, summarized, recite the "phenomenal population growth in recent years" in the Borough of Eatontown, "like many municipalities in Monmouth County," the character of the municipality as densely built up in the "old section" in the northerly part of the borough, with a diminishing density south, east and west; that the borough has no public sewer system and each dwelling requires individual septic tanks, and the Clary tract is "suitably and attractively located for the purpose of subdivision for residential development"; that the property could be profitably developed for sale to home owners on plots having a minimum area of 20,000 square feet, minimum lot frontage of 100 feet, improved by houses so that the parcel could be advantageously and profitably sold for from $15,000 to $17,000; and that the present trend in real estate development is toward larger plots to accommodate one-story or ranch-type houses. The court concluded its findings with a determination that the ordinance was "an exceptionally good one," adopted with the general view of benefiting the entire borough; that due consideration was given to various of the statutory objectives for zoning set forth in R.S. 40:55–32, N.J.S.A.; that careful consideration was given "to the character of the district in which plaintiff's property is located as well as to the character of the neighboring districts and to the remainder of the borough," and also to the peculiar suitability of plaintiff's property for its present use as well as its most appropriate and advantageous use to plaintiff. The conclusion of law was that the plaintiff had failed to sustain the burden of showing that the zoning ordinance was unreasonable, either generally or in its application to the plaintiff's properties, both the 58-acre tract and the small parcels in the Chestnut Grove area. Judgment was consequently entered for the defendant.

[1] Aside from all other considerations, we should, of course, give due weight to the opportunity of the trial judge to see and hear the witnesses and form a conclusion as to the reliability and weight of their testimony. This is particularly important in the present case, in view of the close factual issue at the trial as to the economical feasibility of development of the Clary tract for residential purposes under the limitations of the ordinance, since residential development is clearly the only practicable use of the property from an economic viewpoint. There were two real estate experts who purported to support the thesis that the property was not susceptible of economic development on a 20,000 square-foot minimum lot basis. There was one real estate expert in controversion. Two planning experts were divided on the issue of reasonableness. In such a sharp clash of opposing experts the factor of personal appraisal by the hearer of the demeanor of the witnesses and of the reliability and probative weight of their testimony becomes particularly weighty.

[2] Our first review problem is the sufficiency of the evidence to support the trial finding that the ordinance was not confiscatory as to plaintiff. We are unable, on the proofs adduced, to conclude that the finding is so far

unsupported by the evidence as to call for reversal. The conclusion of the trial court and of the defendant's experts on this score accords with the presumption that a municipal zoning ordinance is valid and reasonable in its impact upon property owners. Pierro v. Baxendale, 20 N.J. 17, 26, 118 A.2d 401 (1955); Cobble Close Farm v. Board of Adjustment, Middletown Township, 10 N.J. 442, 451, 92 A.2d 4 (1952). There was substantial evidence on the side of the defendant and our close study of the record does not satisfy us that the evidence *contra* on the issue of confiscation was such as to compel a conclusion in favor of plaintiff. We agree with and concur in the trial finding on that issue.

[3] There are other issues in the case as we view it which require more extended discussion. One of them may be stated as whether there is sound legal justification for the assumption underlying the premise implied by the allegation in the complaint herein that the ordinance in question has placed the Clary tract "within a zone in which the best use for which the property is adapted is prohibited" (paragraph 6). It might be difficult to refute the factual thesis that the Clary tract would be more readily marketable, and perhaps at a higher price, if it were in a zone permitting the construction of residences on plots of 11,000 square feet (as permitted in R–4 zones) or less. The plain implication of plaintiff's emphasis in argument has been that surrounding developments already constructed and completed, wholly or partially, so stamp the character of the Clary property as to fix a natural *optimum* market for residential development of the property on building tracts of the same size as those predominately found in Elkwood, Monmouth Park, Chestnut Grove and the Norwood homes. There is some factual basis for disputing this contention in view of the physical superiority of the Clary tract for attractive residences and the scattering of relatively large homes both north and east of the tract. But conceding agreement with the thesis made by plaintiff, it has no legal materiality in the light of the scope of the zoning power vested by the Legislature, with constitutional authorization, in the municipal governing body. As was stated for a unanimous Supreme Court in Cobble Close Farm v. Board of Adjustment, Middletown Township, supra (10 N.J. at page 452, 92 A.2d at page 9):

> "° ° ° Zoning regulations are not to be formulated or applied (as plaintiff argues is required by R.S. 40:55-32, N.J.S.A.) with a design to encourage the most appropriate use of *plaintiff's property* but rather 'with reasonable consideration, among other things, to the character of the district and its peculiar suitability for particular uses, and with a view of conserving the value of property and encouraging the most appropriate use of land *throughout such municipality.*' (Emphasis supplied.) Collins v. Board of Adjustment of Margate City, 3 N.J. 200, 69 A.2d 708 (1949); Duffcon Concrete Products, Inc. v. Borough of Cresskill, 1 N.J. 509, 64 A.2d 347, 9 A.L.R. 2d 678 (1949); Guaclides v. Englewood Cliffs, 11 N.J.Super. 405, 78 A.2d 435 (App.Div.1951)." (Emphasis by the court.)

[4] Put in another way, "The standard is not the 'advantage or detriment' to particular neighboring landowners," or, indeed, to the owner of the prop-

erty in question, "but rather the effect on the entire community as a social, economic and political unit." Raskin v. Morristown, 21 N.J. 180, 196, 121 A.2d 378, 386 (1956). It is not sufficient for the plaintiff to show that it would be more profitable for him to use his property in a manner prohibited by the ordinance; he must show an abuse of discretion resulting in an unreasonable exercise of the zoning power. Fischer v. Township of Bedminster, 11 N.J. 194, 206, 93 A.2d 378 (1952); Cobble Close Farm v. Board of Adjustment, Middletown Township, supra (10 N.J. at page 452, 92 A.2d 4); Berdan v. Paterson, 1 N.J. 199, 205, 62 A.2d 680 (1948). The essential question is whether it is clearly demonstrated that the ordinance classification has no "real and substantial relation" to one or more of the zoning considerations specified by the statute, R.S. 40:55–32, N.J.S.A. Roselle v. Wright, 21 N.J. 400, 408, 122 A.2d 506, 510 (1956). As was said by this court as to the similar restriction involved in the ordinance litigated in Rockaway Estates, Inc., v. Rockaway Township, 38 N.J.Super. 468, 478, 119 A.2d 461, 466 (App.Div.1955),

> "The core of plaintiff's opposition is really that the lot size requirement prevents the most profitable use of his land. But the welfare of the community for all time cannot be subordinated to the profit motive of an individual landowner."

[5, 6] Plaintiff indicates that his 58-acre tract might properly be zoned differently from the small plot developments which he cites if the prescribed minimum lot area were not so much greater than the average lot dimensions in those developments. He stresses the 167% "up-grading" represented by a 20,000 square-foot minimum as against the 7,500 square-foot lots on which nearby homes have actually been erected. But the same legal principles nevertheless continue to be applicable. Conceding, *arguendo,* that plaintiff would do better profitwise in developing his tract on lots intermediate in size between 7,500 square feet and 20,000 square feet (but note that the surrounding areas are all zoned 11,000 square-foot minimum), it remains true that the profitable criterion is not the test of validity and that the arbiter of lot sizes, as of all other specifications of the ordinance, within reason, is the governing body of the municipality, not the property owner's sense of what is appropriate. Moreover, in this regard, plaintiff's planning expert, Mr. Black, deflates the emphasis ascribed by plaintitff to the percentage comparison of zones by size of plot. He holds, as indicated above, that the relevant factor is comparison of improved parcel valuations rather than plot sizes. (Compare the ordinance involved in Fischer v. Township of Bedminster, supra, in which neighboring residential zones varied in prescribed minimum lot areas from one acre to five acres.) Taking a figure of $19,000 as the approximate median value for a prospective home on the Clary tract (as between the estimates of defendant's witness, McGinness, and plaintiff's real estate witnesses as to the type of home which would be expected to be erected on this tract, using 20,000 square foot plots), it is found that the gradation thereof above the valuation of the average home

in the surrounding developments is considerably more moderate and that in the instances of a number of homes near the Clary tract the values are closely comparable.

[7, 8] The evidence indicates strong concern by Eatontown over prospective over-population. It is by now, of course, well settled that control of density of population is a proper zoning objective and a commonly approved technique for that purpose is minimum building lot areas. Fischer v. Township of Bedminster, supra (five acres and one acre); Rockaway Estates Inc. v. Township of Rockaway, supra (40,250 square feet, 20,000 square feet, 6,000 square feet); 58 Am.Jur., Zoning, § 52, p. 974; 1 Yokley, Zoning Law and Practice (2d ed. 1953), § 170, p. 421; Annotation 141 A.L.R. 693; Dilliard v. Village of North Hills, 276 App.Div. 969, 94 N.Y.S.2d 715, 716 (App.Div.1950); Simon v. Town of Needham, 311 Mass. 560, 42 N.E.2d 516, 518, 141 A.L.R. 688 (Sup.Jud.Ct.1942); Franmor Realty Corp. v. Village of Old Westbury, 280 App.Div. 945, 116 N.Y.S.2d 68 (App.Div. 1952), motion for leave to appeal dismissed 304 N.Y. 843, 109 N.E.2d 714 (Ct.App. 1952); Flora Realty & Investment Co. v. City of Ladue, 362 Mo. 1025, 246 S.W.2d 771, 774, 777 (Sup.Ct.1952); Clemons v. City of Los Angeles, 36 Cal.2d 95, 222 P.2d 439, 443, 445 (Sup.Ct.1950); DeMars v. Zoning Commission of Town of Bolton, 142 Conn. 580, 115 A.2d 653, 654 (Sup.Ct.Err. 1955); Gignoux v. Village of Kings Point, 199 Misc. 485, 99 N.Y.S.2d 280, 284, 285 (Sup.Ct.1950). It will be noted that in the case last cited the court makes the point that the less restricted nature of contiguous property across a municipal boundary line does not make a residential zoning restriction unreasonable (99 N.Y.S.2d at page 285). The municipal authorities of Eatontown have evinced an appreciation not only of such mundane benefits from setting aside suitable areas for residences on larger plots, for example, as increased capacity of soil for sewage absorption and curtailment of traffic, but also the more intangible but no less respectable objective of community attractiveness. It is no longer to be doubted that this is an appropriate consideration within the statutory criterion of the "general welfare" R.S. 40:55–32, N.J.S.A. Pierro v. Baxendale, supra (20 N.J. at page 28, 118 A.2d 401); Lionshead Lake, Inc., v. Township of Wayne, 10 N.J. 165, 89 A.2d 693 (1952). In the Lionshead Lake case, supra, it was said (10 N.J. at page 174, 89 A.2d at page 697), "The size of the dwellings in any community inevitably affects the character of the community and does much to determine whether or not it is a desirable place in which to live." Mr. Justice Jacobs, concurring in the decision in that case, restated a previously expressed view (10 N.J. at page 177, 89 A.2d at page 699) " 'that it is in the public interest that our communities, so far as feasible, should be made pleasant and inviting so that primary considerations of attractiveness and beauty might well be frankly acknowledged as appropriate, under certain circumstances, in the promotion of the general welfare of our people.' "

[9] The testimony shows that the municipal fathers apprehended that the population rush into Monmouth and other shore counties in recent years

might, under a local *laissez-faire* zoning policy, blanket Eatontown with
small-lot, low-cost homes and, for the foreseeable future, prevent the community, particularly its northeast section, from having any better-type home
areas.   They were justified in attempting to prevent this by appropriate
zoning of yet undeveloped land.   Cf. Monmouth Lumber Co. v. Ocean
Township, 9 N.J. 64, 74, 87 A.2d 9 (1952); Collins v. Board of Adjustment of
Margate City, 3 N.J. 200, 209, 69 A.2d 708 (1949); Rockaway Estates Inc.
v. Rockaway Township, supra (38 N.J.Super, at page 473, 119 A.2d 461).

[10–12] We do not believe that the argument purportedly based upon
the rule requiring weight to be given to regional characteristics in planning
and zoning, Borough of Cresskill v. Borough of Dumont, 15 N.J. 238, 104
A.2d 441 (1954); Duffcon Concrete Products v. Borough of Cresskill, 1 N.J.
509, 513, 64 A.2d 347, 9 A.L.2d 678 (1949); Hochberg v. Borough of Freehold, 40 N.J.Super. 276, 288, 123 A.2d 46 (App.Div.1956); is soundly made
in relation to the fact situation before us.   While Eatontown debatably
might have been justified, on strictly regional considerations, in limiting its
residential development to small homes of the 7,500-11,000 square foot plot
site type, had it chosen to do so on the theory that regional requirements
for larger homes could more appropriately be met by such neighboring
residential communities as have already been mentioned, we cannot hold
that it was under any legislative zoning mandate to follow that course.
In our judgment, the local officials were entitled to plan and project higher
grade residential districts within their own community, without regard to
the presence of such developments in nearby municipalities, provided, always, this could be done without arbitrary or capricious treatment of land
in the light of existing conditions.   "A high class residence district is as
essential to the local economy as multi-family and apartment house areas.
Each has its place in a well rounded municipal development; each has its
part in a comprehensive plan for the utilization of local facilities for the
common welfare."   Cf. Collins v. Board of Adjustment of Margate City,
supra (3 N.J. at page 209, 69 A.2d at page 712).   Moreover, it seems to
us that in a society of constantly progressing concepts as to healthful and
wholesome living there should not be postulated any fixed limitations as
to the capacity of given localities to absorb and adjust to better homes, or
of higher-type housing to flourish in communities not previously experiencing it.   "The police function cannot be expressed in terms of a definitive
formula that will automatically resolve every case."   Katobimar Realty Co.
v. Webster, 20 N.J. 114, 122, 118 A.2d 824, 828 (1955).   It has also been
suggested on behalf of the municipality that residents in existing small
homes in Eatontown might well aspire, as their economic conditions improve, to the ownership of larger homes within the same community, and
we agree that this is a legitimate consideration for zone planning.   Furtherance of the social as well as the economic and political advantages of a
community are reasonable zoning objectives.   Fischer v. Township of Bedminster, supra (11 N.J. at page 203, 93 A.2d 378).

[13] The presently controlling concept of reasonableness in zoning stems from the federal cases construing the due process and equal protection clauses of the Fourteenth Amendment to the United States Constitution, and the New Jersey decisions have accepted interpretative rulings of the United States Supreme Court, beginning with Village of Euclid v. Ambler Realty Co., 272 U.S. 365, 47 S.Ct. 114, 71 L.Ed. 303 (1926), as authoritative. See Fischer v. Township of Bedminster, supra (11 N.J. at page 203, 93 A.2d 378); Pierro v. Baxendale, supra (20 N.J. at page 21, 118 A.2d 401); Raskin v. Morristown, supra (21 N.J. at page 196, 121 A.2d 378). The canon of construction enunciated by the Euclid case is: "If the validity of the legislative classification for zoning purposes be fairly debatable, the legislative judgment must be allowed to control." (272 U.S. at page 388, 57 S.Ct. at page 118.) The rule has been applied in cases where our Supreme Court has concluded that a zoning classification was unreasonable, Katobimar Realty Co. v. Webster, supra (20 N.J. at page 124, 118 A.2d 824), as well as in many where ordinances have withstood attack. In the recent Pierro case, supra, the court emphasized the tendency toward judicial abstention from interference with municipal zoning policy and judgment in upholding the ordinance there involved as not "wholly without reasonable basis" (20 N.J. at page 26, 118 A.2d at page 406). The court went on to say:

> "° ° ° It must always be remembered that the duty of selecting particular uses which are congruous in residential zones was vested by the Legislature in the municipal officials rather than in the courts. Once the selections were made and duly embodied in the comprehensive zoning ordinance of 1939 they became presumptively valid and they are not to be nullified except upon an affirmative showing that the action taken by the municipal officials was unreasonable, arbitrary or capricious. ° ° °" *(Ibid.)*

Courts should be at pains to give more than lip service to that rule and ought, in punctilious observance of the proper limitations of the judicial function, allow fullest flexibility to the range of well-informed local judgment as to the precise way in which local zoning can best serve the welfare of the particular community.

[14] In summary, we conclude that the municipal officials of Eatontown, after long study, aided by the labors of an industrious and conscientious planning board, arrived at a conception of graduated residential zoning conceived to be for the best interests of the entire community, now and prospectively; that all of the objectives which the evidence indicates motivated the planning board and the governing body are material and pertinent under the statute; that in setting up the 130-acre R-3 residence zone district, inclusive of the Clary tract, the municipality did give consideration to the actual development on the ground of neighboring residential area, as well as to the existing and potential character and development of the subject property and of the community as a whole; that its decision in the ordinance under attack to restrict building sites in that district to plots of 20,000

minimum square feet, while perhaps disputable as a matter of judgment, cannot be said to be so far removed from the category of fair debate as to warrant judicial nullification of such action as a classification without real or substantial relation to proper zoning standards and therefore clearly arbitrary and capricious. Insofar as the 58-acre Clary tract is concerned, therefore, we concur in the conclusion of the trial court that the ordinance is reasonable and valid.

[15, 16] By way of footnote, we turn to the attack made in the brief of plaintiff upon the admission, over objection, of the testimony of the president of the planning board concerning the considerations taken into account by that body in formulating the revised ordinance submitted to the mayor and council. That testimony has been discussed hereinabove. The justification for its admission on an issue of reasonableness would seem to be evident where the municipal action is shown to have been as closely associated with the work and recommendations of its planning board as here. Plaintiff cites cases which stand for the proposition that the intent of the lawgiver is to be found in the language used. See, for example, Burnson v. Evans, 137 N.J.L. 511, 514, 60 A.2d 891 (Sup.Ct.1948). The authority is not apposite. No issue is here drawn as to the meaning of the ordinance. The question is one as to its effect and reasonableness. Reasonableness is a two-sided coin. On one side is the adverse impact of the restriction upon him who asserts its unreasonableness. On the other are the social and policy considerations which led to the adoption of the regulation. The final assessment of reasonableness involves a balancing of the considerations on one side of the coin as against those on the other. The more cogent the social pressures impelling the adoption of the restriction the greater the permissible abrasion of the interests of the individual affected. The testimony in question went to the manifold considerations authorized by the zoning statute which inspired the particular restriction here attacked. While it has been held that an inquiry into legislative motivation will not be permitted in order to impugn the reasonableness of legislation valid on its face, 5 McQuillin, Municipal Corporations (3rd ed. 1949), § 16.90, p. 323, Sunny Slope Water Co. v. City of Pasadena, 1 Cal.2d 87, 33 P.2d 672, 677 (Sup.Ct.1934), yet courts will consider evidence with respect to the purpose, object, reason, necessity and effect of an ordinance where the factors bearing upon its reasonableness are not manifest on its face. 5 McQuillin, op. cit., supra, § 18.24, p. 460. As was said in People v. Leighton, 44 N.Y.S.2d 779, 781 (Cty.Ct.1943):

> "While the Court may determine the reasonableness or unreasonableness of a municipal ordinance by an inspection of it on its face, it sometimes becomes a question of fact whether under a given situation or circumstance the regulation or its administration is reasonable [and] evidence *aliunde* is admissible to determine that question."

There are many examples in the New Jersey decisions of the consideration of comparable testimony in zoning cases with no question raised as to admissibility. Mansfield & Swett, Inc., v. West Orange, 120 N.J.L. 145, 159, 198 A. 225 (Sup.Ct.1938); Brookdale Homes, Inc. v. Johnson, 123 N.J.L. 602, 605, 10 A.2d 477 (Sup.Ct.1940), affirmed 126 N.J.L. 516, 19 A.2d 868 (E. & A.1941); Scarborough Apartments, Inc., v. City of Englewood, 9 N.J. 182, 192, 193, 87 A.2d 537 (1952); Rockaway Estates, Inc., v. Rockaway Township, supra (38 N.J.Super. at pages 476, 477, 119 A.2d 461); Cf. State v. Mundet Cork Corp., 8 N.J. 359, 369, 86 A.2d 1 (1952); Prinz v. Paramus, 120 N.J.L. 72, 74, 198 A. 284 (Sup.Ct.1938), affirmed 121 N.J.L. 585, 3 A.2d 584 (E. & A.1939). The reliance by the court in the Rockaway Estates case, supra, on such testimony is evidenced by its comment (38 N.J.Super. at page 475, 119 A.2d at page 465) that "* * * the plan is comprehensive not only because the physical partition into zones appears to be reasonable but also because that partition in its broadest aspects portrays reasonable planning for the orderly development of the community in the future." Liberality in the reception of evidence for such purposes is found elsewhere, Ex Parte Bock, 125 Cal.App. 375, 13 P.2d 836 (D.Ct.App.1932); Bellerive Inv. Co. v. Kansas City, 321 Mo. 969, 13 S.W.2d 628, 641 (Sup.Ct.1929); Evison v. Chicago, St. P., M. & O. Ry. Co., 45 Minn. 370, 48 N.W. 6, 7, 11 L.R.A. 434 (Sup.Ct.1891).

We hold that the testimony of a member of a municipal planning board which submitted to and consulted with the members of the governing body concerning a proposed zoning ordinance, regarding the purposes and objects sought to be served and accomplished by the ordinance, is admissible, although, of course, in no wise controlling, when the issue is the reasonableness of the ordinance. * * *

[19] Plaintiff has argued the additional point that the trial judge was without jurisdiction to hear and decide the cause because his lawful term of office had previously expired. This precise question has been disposed of adversely to plaintiff's contention in Switz v. Middletown Township, 40 N.J.Super. 217, 122 A.2d 649 (App.Div.1956).

Judgment affirmed.

KIT-MAR BUILDERS, INC.

v.

TOWNSHIP OF CONCORD

439 Pa. 466, 268 A.2d 765(1970).

Supreme Court of Pennsylvania.

Feb. 24, 1970.

Rehearing Denied Sept. 14, 1970

The township zoning board of adjustment upheld decision denying contractor's request for rezoning and application for building permit. The contractor took its case to the Court of Common Pleas, Delaware County, at No. 8961 of 1967, Francis J. Catania, J., which made new findings of fact without taking additional testimony, and reversed the board. On township's appeal, the Supreme Court, at No. 218 January Term, 1969, Roberts J., held that zoning ordinance requiring lots no less than two acres along existing roads and no less than three acres in the interior was unconstitutional.

Affirmed.

Bell, C. J., concurred and filed opinion.

Jones, J., dissented and filed opinion in which Cohen, J., joined.

Pomeroy, J., dissented and filed opinion in which Jones, J., joined.

John W. Wellman, Solicitor, Chester, for appellant.

Harry F. Dunn, Jr., Media, for appellee.

Before BELL, C. J., and JONES, COHEN, EAGEN, O'BRIEN, ROBERTS and POMEROY, JJ.

ROBERTS, Justice.

Appellee Kit-Mar Builders, Inc., entered into an agreement to purchase a 140-acre tract of land in Concord Township, Delaware County. The agreement was contingent on the tract's being rezoned to permit the construction of single-family homes on lots of one acre, since the tract was then zoned to require lots of no less than two acres along the existing roads and no less than three acres in the interior. Appellee's request for rezoning and application for a building permit were denied; it then appealed to the zoning board of adjustment and announced that it would not seek to prove the hardship necessary to secure a variance but would instead attack the constitutionality of the zoning ordinance as applied to the property in question. The zoning board upheld the minimum lot requirements and appellee took its case to the court of common pleas. That court took no additional testimony but made new findings of fact and reversed the board. Concord Township then filed a petition for allowance of an appeal to this Court which we granted.

[1, 2] Initially we must note that the trial court erred in making new findings of fact without taking additional testimony. Without an indepen-

dent taking of evidence the trial court could not properly make its own findings of fact, but could only review the decision of the board to determine if an abuse of discretion or an error of law had been committed. See, e. g., National Land and Investment Company v. Easttown Township Board of Adjustment, 419 Pa. 504, 215 A.2d 597 (1965); Cleaver v. Board of Adjustment, 414 Pa. 367, 200 A.2d 408 (1964); Tidewater Oil Company v. Poore, 395 Pa. 89, 149 A.2d 636 (1959). However, it remains within the province of this Court to affirm the action of the trial court, even if that action was based on an erroneous procedure, if there are independent grounds for affirmance. See Sherwood v. Elgart, 383 Pa. 110, 117 A.2d 899, 63 A.L.R.2d 490 (1956). We conclude that, even accepting the findings of the zoning board, the ordinance here in question is unconstitutional under the test set forth in our decision in National Land and Investment Company v. Easttown Township Board of Adjustment, 419 Pa. 504, 215 A.2d 597 (1965).

[3-6] We decided in *National Land* that a scheme of zoning that has an exclusionary purpose or result is not acceptable in Pennsylvania. We do not intend to say, of course, that minimum lot size requirements are inherently unreasonable. Planning considerations and other interests can justify reasonably varying minimum lot sizes in given areas of a community.[1] "At some point along the spectrum, however, the size of lots ceases to be a concern requiring public regulation and becomes simply a matter of private preference." 419 Pa. at 524, 215 A.2d at 608.[2] The two and three acre minimums imposed in this case are no more reasonable than the four acre requirements struck down in *National Land*. As we pointed out in *National Land*, there are obvious advantages to the residents of a community in having houses built on four—or three—acre lots. However, minimum lot sizes of the magnitude required by this ordinance are a great deal larger

---

1. The fundamental proposition in cases involving property rights is that an individual generally should be able to utilize his own land as he sees fit. U.S. Const. Amends. V, XIV. Although zoning is, in general, a proper exercise of police power which can permissibly limit an individual's property rights, Village of Euclid v. Ambler Realty Co., 272 U.S. 365, 47 S.Ct. 114, 71 L.Ed. 303 (1926), it goes without saying that this restriction on the individual's right to use his own property cannot be unreasonable. E. g., Eller v. Board of Adjustment, 414 Pa. 1, 198 A.2d 863 (1964).

2. Cf. Sager, Tight Little Islands: Exclusionary Zoning, Equal Protection, and the Indigent, 21 Stand.L.Rev. 767, 791 (1969): "The policy issue thus becomes one of the quantum of acknowledged social injustice involved in a formal governmental unit excluding or segregating people on the basis of their means. If the question is one of the constitutionality of individuals acting in a fashion that excludes the poor from neighborhoods—through covenants of home value or size of land and structure or whatever—the balance struck may be different because of the values assigned to the individual's freedom to dispose of property. It would seem that the serious harm done to accepted egalitarian ends would at least preclude direct governmental promulgation of exclusionary land devices, unless those devices find their justification in the effectuation of governmental ends of overriding importance." Compare Shelley v. Kraemer, 334 U.S. 1, 68 S.Ct. 836, 92 L.Ed. 1161 (1948).

than what should be considered as a *necessary* size for the building of a house,[3] and are therefore not the proper subjects of public regulation. As a matter of fact, a house can fit quite comfortably on a one acre lot without being the least bit cramped.[4] Absent some extraordinary justification, a zoning ordinance with minimum lot sizes such as those in this case is completely unreasonable.

[7] As the primary justification for the zoning ordinance now before us the township contends that lots of a smaller size will create a potential sewerage problem.[5] It was on this question that the zoning board and the trial court made conflicting findings of fact. Whether a potential sewerage problem exists or not is irrelevant, however, since we *explicitly rejected* the argument that sewerage problems could excuse exclusionary zoning in *National Land:*

"We can not help but note also that the Second Class Township Code provides for establishing sanitary regulations which can be enforced by a

---

3. A three-acre lot, for instance, is an enormous tract on which to build a single house. This is best illustrated by pointing to some familiar landmarks and areas that encompass approximately three acres. For example, in the City of Pittsburgh, the area bounded by Smithfield Street and William Penn Place and Cherry Way, stretching from Forbes Avenue through Fifth Avenue and Oliver Avenue to approximately the half-way point in Mellon Square is about three acres in size. In Harrisburg, the Highway and Safety Building and its adjoining plaza is built on a lot of approximately three acres. In Philadelphia, the Lit Brothers Store lot, which takes up an entire square block bounded by 8th Street, Market Street, 7th Street, and Filbert Street, is only slightly more than three acres in size; the Wanamaker's store occupies somewhat less than three acres; and Rittenhouse Square, divided down the middle, would create two lots of about three acres each.

These figures are supported by letters from: Harrisburg—Ronald S. Pontins, Space and Facilities Planning Unit. Pennsylvania Department of Property and Supplies: Pittsburgh—Samuel Marsh, Pittsburgh Department of Public Works: Philadelphia—Paul F. Croley, Executive Vice President, Philadelphia Industrial Development Corporation. These letters are on file with the Prothonotary's office.

4. The Kaufmann's Department Store in Pittsburgh is built on approximately a one-acre lot, and clearly a house built on the same area would hardly want for elbow room. See note 2, supra.

5. Appellant also offers some other arguments which are so clearly makeweights as to barely require comment. For example, appellant notes that there is but one bus in the township. The rationale of *National Land* hardly allows a municipality to continue indefinitely an exclusionary zoning scheme because it refuses to purchase and operate a second bus. Likewise, it is claimed that the current road network is suitable only for the present population, which hardly explains why new roads should not be built to accommodate new people. As we said in dealing with the same argument in *National Land,* zoning may not be used "to avoid the increased responsibilities and economic burdens which time and natural growth invariably bring." 419 Pa. at 528, 215 A.2d at 610. Delaware County Community College Appeal, 435 Pa. 264, 256 A.2d 641 (1969); Lower Merion Twp. v. Enokay, Inc., 427 Pa. 128, 233 A.2d 883 (1967); Archbishop O'Hara Appeal, 389 Pa. 35, 131 A.2d 587 (1957). Finally, almost unbelievably, appellant maintains that two and three acre zoning would be more in conformity with the rural and historical surrounding of the neighborhood. These are exactly the kinds of aesthetic considerations which we explicitly rejected in *National Land.*

'sanitary board' regardless of the zoning for the area. The Code also provides for the installation and maintenance of sewer systems but the township has made no plans in this regard. In addition, under the township subdivision regulations, the zoning officer may require lots larger than the minimum permitted by the zoning ordinance if the result of percolation tests upon the land show that a larger land area is needed for proper drainage and disposal of sewage. These legislatively sanctioned methods for dealing with the sewage problem compel the conclusion that a four acre minimum is neither a necessary nor a reasonable method by which Easttown can protect itself from the menace of pollution." 419 Pa. at 526, 215 A.2d at 609.

Everything said in the quoted paragraph is equally applicable to the case now before us. We in effect held in *National Land* that because there were alternative methods for dealing with nearly all the problems that attend a growth in population, including sewage problems, zoning which had an exclusive purpose or effect could not be allowed. See Westwood Forest Estates, Inc. v. Village of South Nyack, 23 N.Y.2d 424, 428-429, 297 N.Y.S.2d 129, 133-134, 244 N.E.2d 700, 702-703 (1969): "This is not to say that the village may not, pursuant to its other and general police powers [i.e. not zoning power], impose other restrictions or conditions on the granting of a building permit to plaintiff, such as a general assessment for reconstruction of the sewage system, granting of building permits * * * in stages, or perhaps even a moratorium on the issuance of any building permits, reasonably limited as to time. But, whatever the right of a municipality to impose ' "a * * * temporary restraint of beneficial enjoyment * * * where the interference is necessary to promote the ultimate good either of the municipality as a whole or of the immediate neighborhood," ' such restraint must be kept ' "within the limits of necessity" ' and may not prevent permanently the reasonable use of private property for the only purposes to which it is practically adapted [citations omitted]."

We recently reaffirmed exactly this position in Delaware County Community College Appeal, 435 Pa. 264, 270, 254 A.2d 641, 645 (1969), where this Court, citing *National Land*, explicitly rejected a zoning exclusion as a proper method for dealing with sewerage problems:

> "The court below pointed out that once the special exception is granted, the college will still be required to make 'appropriate arrangements [for sewerage] * * * consistent with local ordinances and regulations and state statutes and regulations pertaining to sewerage disposal. * * * *If expansion is required, then it should be accomplished.*' We are in accordance with this view; *the Board could not properly make a broad scale zoning decision simply because of a potential sewerage problem in the future.*" (Emphasis added.)

We once again reaffirm our past authority and refuse to allow the township to do precisely what we have never permitted—keep out people, rather than make community improvements.

[8] The implication of our decision in *National Land* is that communities must deal with the problems of population growth. They may not refuse to confront the future by adopting zoning regulations that effectively restrict population to near present levels.[6] It is not for any given township to say who may or may not live within its confines, while disregarding the interests of the entire area. If Concord Township is successful in unnaturally limiting its population growth through the use of exclusive zoning regulations, the people who would normally live there will inevitably have to live in another community, and the requirement that they do so is not a decision that Concord Township should alone be able to make.

While our decision in *National Land* requires municipalities to meet the challenge of population growth without closing their doors to it, we have indicated our willingness to give communities the ability to respond with great flexibility to the problems caused by suburban expansion. Most notable in this regard is our decision in Village 2 at New Hope, Inc. Appeals, 429 Pa. 626, 241 A.2d 81 (1968), in which we approved planned unit development. "It would seem that this decision is a forerunner of a necessary change in the law of planned development. Caught between increasing population pressure and urban sprawl and the reluctance of the rural communities to absorb their fair share of the load, planners have been faced with an unpleasant choice. They are now equipped with a proper instrument to meet the challenge. The scope of this decision is by no means limited to residential and ancillary usage. It can just as effectively be applied to commercial and industrial development as well as to new combinations of land use which are only limited by the ingenuity of the planner and developer. Effective interrelations between the various component needs of the community can now be more easily realized. For instance, various types of housing, schools, and recreational facilities can be planned not only for the immediate needs of the community, but also to effectuate broad social purposes. The adverse economic impact of large-scale development can be mitigated if not entirely eliminated by the judicious juxtapositioning of revenue-producing development with residential and public uses. In this manner, achievement of good traffic separation, public transportation, visual enjoyment, and a host of other desiderata can be real-

---

6. "The question posed is whether the township can stand in the way of the natural forces which send our growing population into hitherto undeveloped areas in search of a comfortable place to live. We have concluded not. A zoning ordinance whose primary purpose is to prevent the entrance of newcomers in order to avoid future burdens, economic and otherwise, upon the administration of public services and facilities cannot be held valid." 419 Pa. at 532, 215 A.2d at 612.

Although *National Land,* and this problem in general, is postured as involving the constitutional due process rights of the land-owner whose property has been zoned adversely to his best interest, it cannot realistically be detached from the rights of other people desirous of moving into the area "in search of a comfortable place to live." See generally Sager, Tight Little Islands: Exclusionary Zoning, Equal Protection, and the Indigent, 21 Stan.L.Rev. 767 (1969).

ized as [sic] much reduced economic cost." Zucker and Wolffe, Supreme Court Legalizes PUD: New Hope from New Hope, 2 Land Use Controls 32, 33-34 (1968).

We will not turn our back on the approach to these problems which we adopted in *National Land* and *Village 2 at New Hope.* New and exciting techniques are available to the local governing bodies of this Commonwealth for dealing with the problems of population growth. Neither Concord Township nor Easttown Township nor any other local governing unit may retreat behind a cover of exclusive zoning. We fully realize that the overall solution to these problems lies with greater regional planning; but until the time comes that we have such a system we must confront the situation as it is. The power currently resides in the hands of each local governing unit, and we will not tolerate their abusing that power in attempting to zone out growth at the expense of neighboring communities.

Finally, we cannot ignore the fact that in the narrow confines of the case before us, Concord Township's argument that three-acre minimum zoning is necessary for adequate on-site sewerage is patently ridiculous. The township does not argue that on-site sewerage is impossible for the lots in question; instead it maintains that if houses are built on lots of one acre, as envisioned by appellee, not on lots of three acres, on-site sewerage will become unfeasible. This argument assumes that all of the lot where the house is not is necessary for waste effluence, which simply is not what happens. The difference in size between a three-acre lot and a one-acre lot is irrelevant to the problem of sewage disposal, absent the construction of a house of an unimaginably enormous magnitude.

This proposition is fully borne out by the Pennsylvania Department of Health Regulations for the Administration of the Pennsylvania Sewage Facilities Act, Act of January 24, 1966, P.L. (1965) 1535, 35 P.S. § 750.1 et seq., Regulation Chapter 4, Article 423, Standards for Individual Sewage Disposal Systems § 7.1-1. This regulation tells us that if the soil percolation rate on a given lot exceeds 60 minutes per inch no on-site sewage disposal will be permitted. Let us assume that the lots in question have the bare minimum percolation rates necessary to support on-site sewerage. Section 7.3 indicates that on a lot with the minimum acceptable percolation rate the required absorption area is only 330 square feet per bedroom. See § 7.3, Table IV.[7] Adding in the maximum isolation distances provided for in § 2, Tables I and II,[8] the required absorption area for a three bedroom house on a lot with the minimum acceptable percolation rate would be only a little more than 1,000 square feet. We can conclude from these Depart-

---

7. "7.3 Absorption Area Requirements for Private Residential (Provides for Garbage Grinder and Automatic-Sequence Washington Machines)
8. "2. *Isolation Distances*
The minimum isolation distances shown in Tables I and II shall be maintained between the sewage disposal system and the respective features itemized in the tables. Where conditions warrant, greater isolation distances may be required.

ment of Health regulations that a three bedroom house cannot be built with on-site sewerage if such a disposal system would require more than approximately a 1,000 square foot absorption area. One acre contains 43,560 square feet and three acres contain 130,680 square feet. It is obviously sheer fantasy for the township to claim that, because of an on-site sewerage problem, houses cannot be built on a one-acre lot, but can be built on a three-acre lot.

Thinly veiled justifications for exclusionary zoning will not be countenanced by this Court. We rejected them in *National Land* and in our very recent decision in *Delaware County Community College Appeal*, supra, and we reject them here.

Decree affirmed.

BELL, C. J., filed a concurring opinion.

JONES, J., filed a dissenting opinion, in which COHEN, J., joins.

POMEROY, J., filed a dissenting opinion, in which JONES, J., joins.

BELL, Chief Justice (concurring).

The basic question is whether an Ordinance which imposes a minimum lot requirement of not less than two acres along the existing roads, and no less than three acres in the interior of the township, is Constitutional.

TABLE IV

Percolation Rate (time for water to fall 1 in. in min.)	Septic Tank Effluent Required Absorption Area Sq. ft./bedroom	Aerobic Tank Effluent Required Absorption Area (Standard trenches, seepage beds, seepage pits)
15 or less	175	*120
16-30	250	*210
31-45	300	300
46-60	330	330

* indicates reduced absorption area other than required for conventional septic tank effluent. Aerobic sewage treatment systems utilizing reduced absorption areas for effluent disposal are experimental and shall be so indicated on the permit."

TABLE I

Septic Tank-Minimum Isolation Distances

Property Line	10 feet
Occupied Buildings	10 feet
Individual Water Supply	50 feet

TABLE II

Leaching System-Minimum Isolation Distances

Individual Water Supply	100 feet
Streams, Lakes or Other Surface Water	50 feet
Occupied Building	10 feet
Property Lines	10 feet"

The Constitution of Pennsylvania, in Article I, Section 1, and the Constitution of the United States, in the Fifth Amendment and in the Fourteenth Amendment, ordain and guarantee the right of private property. They further protect its "taking," except by due process of law, or, if taken for public use, without payment of just compensation.

Article I, Section 1, of the Constitution of Pennsylvania, P.S., assures these basic fundamental property rights by providing: "All men * * * have certain inherent and indefeasible rights, among which are those of enjoying and defending life and liberty, of *acquiring, possessing and protecting property* * * * "* See, Parker v. Hough, 420 Pa. 7, 10-11, 215 A.2d 667; Cleaver v. Board of Adjustment, 414 Pa. 367, 371-372, 200 A.2d 408; Andress v. Zoning Board of Adjustment, 410 Pa. 77, 87, 188 A.2d 709; Village of Euclid v. Ambler Realty Co., 272 U.S. 365, 47 S.Ct. 114, 71 L.Ed. 303 (1926).

In Parker v. Hough, 420 Pa. page 10-11, 215 A.2d page 669, supra, the Court accurately and succinctly said:

"An owner of property in this Commonwealth has a tremendously prized and fundamental Constitutional right to use his property as he pleases, subject to certain exceptions hereinafter set forth. Cleaver v. Board of Adjustment, 414 Pa. 367, 371-372, 200 A.2d 408; Andress v. Zoning Board of Adjustment, 410 Pa. 77, 87, 188 A.2d 709; Key Realty Co. Zoning Case, 408 Pa. 98, 104, 182 A.2d 187; Siciliano v. Misler, 399 Pa. 406, 409, 160 A.2d 422, 80 A.L.R.2d 1253; Sandyford Park Civic Assn. v. Lunnemann, 396 Pa. 537, 539, 152 A.2d 898; Lened Homes, Inc. v. Department of Licenses, 386 Pa. 50, 54, 123 A.2d 406; Lord Appeal, 368 Pa. 121, 125, 81 A.2d 533.

"As the Court aptly said in Cleaver v. Board of Adjustment, 414 Pa., supra, pages 371-372, 200 A.2d, page 411: ' " * * * ' "An owner of property is still entitled in Pennsylvania to certain unalienable constitutional rights of liberty and property. These include a right to use his own home [or property] in any way he desires, *provided he does not** (1) violate any provision of the Federal or State Constitutions; or (2) create a nuisance; or (3) *violate any covenant, restriction* or easement; or (4) violate any laws or zoning or police regulations *which are constitutional.*'** * * *" ' "

Many zoning cases, including the present one, fall into a twilight zone. For over a century it was the law of this Commonwealth that every person in the United States of America had a Constitutionally ordained right to own, possess, protect and use his property in any way he desired, so long as it did not injure or adversely affect the health or morals or safety of others. This was one of the two basic differences between America and Communism. Then along came "zoning" with its desirable and worthwhile objectives. The result was that all the aforesaid basic fundamental rights of an owner of property were restricted by a Judicially created higher right, namely, the general welfare of the people of that community. No one

---

* Italics, ours.
* Italics in Cleaver v. Board of Adjustment Opinion.
** Italics, ours.

knows, and the Courts have been unable to define what is meant by "general welfare." To some, it means the absolute, unqualified Constitutional right to liberty and property, subject to the above-mentioned restrictions. To some, it means what the Zoning Board or a Court believes is best for the community or township or county involved. To others, it means the right of our expanding population to live in any county or place in our Country they may desire. To still others, it means the right to have the Government purchase and set aside millions of acres of open land for the benefit of our Country. These rights are sometimes indefinite, sometimes overlapping, and sometimes conflicting.

This is one of those debatable cases which leave me in "no man's land."

Although zoning almost always has a worthwhile objective, since it is a restriction on and a deprivation of a property owner's Constitutionally ordained rights of property, it can be sustained only if it is clearly necessary to protect the health or safety or morals or general welfare of the people. Cleaver v. Board of Adjustment, 414 Pa. 367, 200 A.2d 408, supra; Parker v. Hough, 420 Pa. 7, 215 A.2d 667, supra; Eller v. Board of Adjustment, 414 Pa. 1, 198 A.2d 863. I believe that this zoning ordinance, which has no substantial relationship to health or safety or morals, is an Unconstitutional restriction upon an owner's basic right of the ownership and use of his property, and it can not be sustained under the theory or principle of "general welfare."

JONES, Justice (dissenting).

I agree with the writer of the majority opinion that the rural and suburban communities of our Commonwealth may not ignore the problems we all share with respect to population growth, and that any unjustified attempt by these communities to avoid these problems by exclusionary zoning should be resisted by our courts. However, we must bear in mind that zoning does, most often, have a legitimate and even laudable purpose, and we should not, therefore, hold a zoning ordinance to be invalid if it *does* have a legitimate, nonexclusionary purpose, *particularly where the ordinance is part of an overall plan which is specifically designed to face the problem of population growth.*

William K. Davis, who served on the Delaware County Planning Commission from 1960 to 1966 and was its Executive Director for the last four years, gave his assessment of the new Concord Township zoning plan as follows: "It was adopted by the township to recognize the need for change and departure from the zoning pattern that preceded this one. The township itself is in a transitory stage of development. There are growth trends, there is new housing in and around the township. *This to me represents an effort to move directly into future growth patterns,* to provide relief and land areas for growth to take place where the township officials think it most appropriate." (Emphasis supplied)

I begin my consideration of this appeal by reiterating the salutary principle of judicial self-restraint in this area of the law set forth in National

Land and Investment Co. v. Easttown Twp. Board of Adjustment, 419 Pa. 504, 521-522, 215 A.2d 597, 606-607 (1965) (hereinafter cited as *National Land*):

> "The days are fast disappearing when the judiciary can look at a zoning ordinance and, with nearly as much confidence as a professional zoning expert, decide upon the merits of a zoning plan and its contribution to the health, safety, morals or general welfare of the community. This Court has become increasingly aware that it is neither a super board of adjustment nor a planning commission of last resort. [Citing authorities]. Instead, the Court acts as a judicial overseer, drawing the limits beyond which local regulation may not go, but loathing to interfere, within those limits, with the discretion of local governing bodies. [Citing authority]. The zoning power is one of the tools of government which, in order to be effective, must not be subjected to judicial interference unless clearly necessary. For this reason, *a presumption of validity attaches to a zoning ordinance which imposes the burden to prove its invalidity upon the one who challenges it.* [Citing authorities]." (Emphasis supplied)

See also: Bilbar Const. Co. v. Easttown Twp. Bd. of Adjustment, 393 Pa. 62, 72, 141 A.2d 851, 855 (1958).

By reason of the technical and factual nature of the issues involved in a zoning appeal, the scope of review of a reviewing court is limited to determining whether the zoning board of adjustment abused its discretion or committed an error of law. See, *e.g.*, *National Land*, 419 Pa. 504, 523, 215 A.2d 597, 607 (1965); Cleaver v. Board of Adjustment, 414 Pa. 367, 380, 200 A.2d 408, 416 (1964); Tidewater Oil Co. v. Poore, 395 Pa. 89, 93, 149 A.2d 636, 638 (1959). I conclude from my examination of this record that the evidence before the board amply supported its decision to uphold the minimum lot requirements, and, accordingly, I would reverse the order of the court below.

The majority has stated that a zoning ordinance may not be upheld solely because of a sewage disposal problem, that the zoning ordinance presently in question was enacted exclusively to solve such a sewerage problem and, therefore, this ordinance is invalid. If either of the majority's first two points is incorrect, then its conclusion must also fall.

Two Pennsylvania cases have been cited as support for the proposition that sewerage problems cannot, per se, excuse minimum-acreage zoning requirements. In *National Land*, the first of these two cases, the township subdivision regulations authorized the township zoning officer to require lots larger than the minimum as stated in the zoning ordinance if the disposal of sewage so required. This Court held, therefore, that since other means were available to solve any sewerage problem, the township's use of a minimum-lot zoning ordinance was unnecessary and improper. There is no evidence in the instant case which might indicate that Concord Township's authorities have such power, and, accordingly, *National Land* is distinguishable on its facts.

Moreover, the position now taken by the majority, even if it were the same as in *National Land*, *totally* ignores intervening legislation which appears to specifically reject the broad proposition as now stated. *National Land* was handed down in 1965, when the applicable state zoning act was the Act of May 1, 1933, P.L. 103, art. XX, § 2001, added by Act of July 10, 1947, P.L. 1481, § 47, as amended, 53 P.S. §§ 67001-10. However, this Act was repealed in 1968 and replaced by the Act of July 31, 1968, P.L., 53 P.S. §§ 10601-20.

The former statute listed several objectives which, collectively, delineated the proper purpose for zoning regulations under that statute. 53 P.S. § 67003. The comparable section of the 1968 Act reads as follows: "The provisions of zoning ordinances shall be designed: (1) To promote, protect and facilitate *one or more* of the following: * * * sewerage * * *." 53 P.S. § 10604 (Pocket Parts) (Emphasis supplied). The new legislation differs from the 1947 Act in that it specifically states that any *one* of the listed problems may be the basis for a township's zoning ordinance. In contradistinction to the 1968 Act, the majority opinion states that a zoning ordinance may *not* be upheld solely because of a sewerage problem.

The second case cited by the majority as support for the first proposition, as stated above, is Delaware County Community College Appeal, 435 Pa. 264, 254 A.2d 641 (1969). That case, however, dealt with a situation in which the existing sewer facilities could amply handle the proposed facilities. The zoning board there merely anticipated a possible problem at some *future* time, as the result of other expansion which had not yet, in fact, been proposed. In the case at bar, however, the sewerage problem will be caused by *this* application; we do not have a "potential sewerage problem in the future." It should also be noted, parenthetically, that in the *Community College* case the Executive Director of the Delaware County Planning Commission testified that the proposed use (the college) *would* be consistent with the applicable comprehensive plan, supporting the position of the applicant in that case.[1]

The first proposition suggested by the majority is that the alleviation of a sewage disposal problem cannot, per se, justify a minimum-acreage zoning ordinance. As I have indicated above, this suggestion is not only directly contrary to the most recent state legislation, but it is also without support (as applied to the instant case) in either of the only two cases relied upon as authority in the majority opinion.

The second premise of the syllogism suggested by the majority is to the effect that the Concord Township zoning ordinance was enacted solely to solve a problem of sewage disposal. This point finds no more support in the record than does the first premise in the law. Several other factors were considered by the zoning board and were fully testified to at the hearing. One of these is that the local road network surrounding the tract

---

1. Compare that situation with the testimony of William K. Davis in the instant case, wherein he *opposes* the position of the applicant. *Supra* at page 772.

in question is already taxed to its capacity at certain times of the day. There is but one bus route in the township and no train service, and, therefore, we must assume that any additional residents of the community will use their automobiles for transportation. Moreover, most of the residences surrounding the tract are built on five-acre lots. Two- and three-acre zoning would be more in conformity with the rural and historical surroundings of the neighborhood. Finally, there is no guarantee as to source of a water supply for the new development. There is a municipal water main 1000 feet from the property but there is no evidence in the record that this source of water will be available for the new development.[2]

We note in passing that a new zoning map was adopted by the Township while the board was conducting its hearings. Land which had been zoned three acre under the old map, and which constituted 80% of the Township, was reduced in area to 10% of the Township, and the new map also substantially enlarged the one-acre and light industry areas.[3] While this information is not necessarily germane to the instant litigation, it does reveal that the Township is aware of its responsibility to readjust its zoning classifications to meet the needs of an increasing population. Evidence in the record indicates that under the present zoning classification the Township can absorb adequately all population increases until the year 1980. This evidence suggests that the officials of the Township are making a conscientious effort to develop the Township according to a systematic plan, and we should be loathe to upset that plan by striking down a zoning classification unless absolutely required to do so.

The real crux of the controversy in this case is indicated by the following statement in the majority opinion: "Finally, we cannot ignore the fact that in the narrow confines of the case before us, Concord Township's argument that three-acre minimum zoning is necessary for adequate on-site sewerage is *patently ridiculous.*" (Emphasis supplied) If, in fact, there is no support for the Township's contentions on this issue, *then* it might be argued that the situation does not justify this type of zoning, and we must, therefore, consider the evidence which was offered by the Township and how that evidence is to be judged.

The general rule for determining the constitutionality of a zoning act or ordinance was set forth by this Court in Colligan Zoning Case, 401 Pa. 125, 131, 162 A.2d 652, 654 (1960): "It is now well settled that zoning acts and ordinances passed under them are valid and constitutional as structural or general legislation whenever they are necessary for the preservation of

---

2. As previously noted, the 1968 Act lists several factors which, individually or collectively, may support a zoning ordinance. In addition to sewage disposal, the Act refers to "co-ordinated and practical community development, proper density of population. * * * disaster evacuation, * * * transportation, water, * * *." 53 P.S. § 10604(1) (Pocket Parts).

3. By way of contrast, the zoning ordinance involved in *National Land* upzoned the property in question from one to four acres.

public health, safety, morals or general welfare, and not unjustly discriminatory, or arbitrary, or unreasonable, or confiscatory in their application to a particular or specific piece of property." [4] The burden of proof is upon the applicant attacking the constitutionality of the zoning act to prove that it does not meet these standards.[5] As the majority has noted, the proper question for a reviewing court is whether the zoning board abused its discretion or committed an error of law in deciding that the ordinance in question is constitutionally sound.

In its determination that the instant petition involves no sewerage problem, the majority opinion totally and unjustifiably ignores *all* the evidence presented on this question by the Township and by the applicant. Whenever we are called upon to decide a complex scientific question, we must rely upon the testimony of experts and give great weight to the scientific conclusions which they reach. Where there is a conflict between the testimony offered by one side and that offered by the opposing side, the zoning board must consider *both* positions carefully to arrive at its conclusion as to which is correct. However, once the board has made its findings of fact and reached a conclusion, the function of a reviewing court is to examine the evidence before the board to determine whether the board's results are reasonably supported by the facts and by the law. The question is not whether we—at the appellate level—would have reached the same result, but rather whether the zoning board's determination was arbitrary and contrary to the weight of the evidence. Gilden Appeal, 406 Pa. 484, 487, 178 A.2d 562, 564 (1962).

At this point, it is necessary to briefly delineate the means by which the majority has concluded that the possibility of a sewerage problem is "patently ridiculous." I first note that there had been no reference whatsoever in the record, at any stage of these proceedings, to the Pennsylvania Department of Health Regulations until the promulgation of the majority opinion. The majority refers to the scientific opinions contained in these Regulations *as determinative* on the question of whether a sewerage problem exists, although the Regulations were never offered in evidence by either Concord Township or the petitioner. The patent impropriety of basing a decision on these Regulations which are beyond the scope of the record in this case is too clear to require elucidation. It should suffice to merely point out that scientists are continually questioning the opinions and conclusions of other scientists, even those opinions and conclusions which have been legislatively accepted. Therefore, it is extremely important that such

---

4. *See also* Exton Quarries, Inc. v. Zoning Bd. of Adjustment, 425 Pa. 43, 58-59, 228 A.2d 169 (1967); National Land, 419 Pa. 504, 511-512, 522, 215 A.2d 597 (1965); Bilbar Const. Co. v. Easttown Twp. Bd. of Adjustment, 393 Pa. 62, 72, 141 A.2d 851 (1958).

5. *See, e.g.,* Cleaver v. Board of Adjustment, 414 Pa. 367, 373, 200 A.2d 408 (1964); Bilbar Const. Co. v. Easttown Twp. Bd. of Adjustment, 393 Pa. 62, 70, 141 A.2d 851 (1958).

evidence be subjected to cross-examination, and that the opposing party (*i.e.*, the Township) be given the opportunity to present rebuttal evidence. These Regulations must certainly carry great weight in our consideration. Nevertheless, I believe it is improper to base a scientific conclusion solely upon Regulations which have not been referred to by the parties, the zoning board, or the lower court, and where a substantial amount of other evidence *has* been offered with all the safeguards of open-court examination.

Moreover, the Regulations themselves point out the issue which was actually disputed by the parties. According to § 7.1-1 thereof, an on-site sewerage system is impermissible *if* the percolation rate in the immediate area is over sixty minutes per inch.[6] The controversy at the hearing in the instant case, and the point on which the parties differ, is whether and to what extent the 140-acre tract in question is comprised of land with a percolation rate of over sixty minutes per inch. It is clear to me that if, as claimed by the Township, a substantial portion of the land cannot support on-site sewerage systems, then we would be dangerously derelict in our duty to protect the citizens of this Commonwealth if we permit this tract of 115 one-acre lots to be built, each lot with its own system.[7] Accordingly, we reach what should be the decisive question on this appeal: Can the evidence on the record support the conclusion of the Zoning Board that a substantial portion of this 140-acre tract cannot support on-site sewerage systems?

The only evidence offered by the applicant, Kit-Mar Builders, Inc., on the question of whether this land would be suitable for on-site sewerage systems if divided into one-acre lots, was given by David Clark. Mr. Clark is a professional engineer as well as the president of Kit-Mar Builders, Inc., the applicant. He testified as to the results of thirteen percolation tests which he personally conducted, and these tests indicated that the entire property would be satisfactory for on-site sewage disposal,[8] although Mr. Clark admitted, on cross-examination, that at least seven acres of the tract would not even be suitable for building because the ground was low and wet.

---

6. By way of clarification, the percolation test is the most commonly-used means of deciding whether an on-site sewerage system may be safely installed. It tests the length of time required for the soil to absorb water. Generally speaking, if it requires more than sixty minutes for one inch of water to be absorbed, then it is likely that the system will back up and not operate—i.e., the sewage might come to the surface of the land and collect there instead of dissipating.

7. The majority opinion states that it is "sheer fantasy" to claim, as does the Township, that although a one-acre lot would not support on-site sewage disposal, a three-acre lot would. The witnesses for the Township have simply reasoned that because substantial portions of this 140-acre tract have high percolation rates, it would be possible to lay out three-acre lots, each lot including an area with an acceptable percolation rate, although this could not be done with one-acre lots. I find nothing fantastic about this and, in any case, would be extremely, hesitant to adopt my *personal* assessment over the unrebutted testimony of expert witnesses.

8. The percolation rates obtained by Mr. Clark ranged from 2.8 minutes per inch up to 26.0 minutes per inch.

On the question of percolation rates, the Township offered the testimony of Harry H. Curtin, who has been conducting these tests for twenty years and is now the vice president of Roy F. Weston Company, an independent firm of consulting engineers. Mr. Curtin's firm conducted fifteen percolation tests, under his personal supervision. He testified that five of the tests gave completely unsatisfactory results,[9] that seven of the tests indicated the possibility of disposal problems,[10] and that three of the tests "would indicate that on-site systems might work in that particular area." [11] By way of summarizing Mr. Curtin's lengthy testimony, I refer to the following exchange on direct examination:

> "Q.   If in fact it was developed into one-acre lots with on-site sewerage systems, what in your opinion would be the results from a sanitary standpoint?
> A.   I would predict that there would be a high percentage of failures within five to ten years after these systems were put into use.
> Q.   And a failure consists of what?
> A.   Failure in a clay soil of this type would probably first mean back-up of sewage into the house or the overflow of these systems into yards and streets."

The evidence, therefore, which was offered as to percolation rates was contradictory, although both parties agreed that this was the standard method of measuring the feasibility of installing on-site sewerage systems.

On the question of whether a potential sewerage problem may exist, the Township also offered the testimony of Walter Satterthwaite, a consulting geologist for Roy F. Weston Company. Mr. Satterthwaite utilized a "base map" of the area in question, which map had been prepared by the United States Department of Agriculture. On the basis of criteria established by the Department of Agriculture as guide lines to determine soil acceptability for on-site waste disposal, Mr. Satterthwaite testified as to the extent to which the tract could support on-site sewerage systems. His findings were as follows: 40% of the area would not be acceptable for on-site sewerage; 52½% of the area would normally be all right, but might cause problems at some time; and on 7½% of the area the normal oxidation process would be effective. Mr. Satterthwaite summarized his testimony as follows, on cross-examination:

> "Q.   Now, you aren't saying by your testimony here that any dire consequences would happen to anyone who would possibly end up living on a one-acre lot on this property, are you?
> A.   It very likely could become quite a health hazard.
> Q.   Would you tell me how, sir?

---

9. The percolation rates ranged from 80 minutes per inch up to 160 minutes per inch.

10. The percolation rates ranged from 30 minutes per inch up to 50 minutes per inch.

11. The percolation rates ranged from 12 minutes per inch up to 24 minutes per inch.

A. By the inability of the soil to accept the effluent or by the altogether too rapid passage of sewage wastes through the soil into the surface of the ground or to the surface of streams and springs that are in the area."

The *potential* sanitation threat is compounded by a drainage problem attributable to the steep terrain in the interior of the tract where the land descends to a creek bed.

The Township also offered the testimony of Oliver Armitage, a licensed real estate broker and appraiser for fourteen years. Mr. Armitage stated his professional opinion, based upon the nature of the surrounding area and the market for houses, that "a residential subdivision of two or three acres is the most desirable method of developing this property." In fact, he pointed out that although in a more urbanized area there would tend to be a much greater demand for one-acre lots, in an area such as this 140-acre tract, the market would be stronger for two- or three-acre lots. His testimony agreed with that of William Davis, referred to above, who also pointed out that the present zoning plan would adequately absorb *all* population increases through 1980. No population estimates had been made beyond 1980.

Considering all the evidence before the zoning board, I find it impossible to say that the board was guilty of either an abuse of discretion or of committing an error of law when it upheld this zoning ordinance. The fact that the majority opinion takes no notice of the evidence offered by the Township is particularly distressing because of the "presumption of validity [which] attaches to a zoning ordinance [and] which imposes the burden to prove its invalidity *upon the one who challenges it*." *National Land*, 419 Pa. 504, 522, 215 A.2d 597, 607 (1965).

I am well aware that at times minimum-acreage requirements might be a crude way of dealing with a sewerage problem. Nevertheless, I feel that a potential sewerage problem may be a very important factor to be considered in evaluating a zoning ordinance, particularly in the light of the 1968 Zoning Act. Of course, if we hold that a potential sewerage problem is one factor to be considered, we might well be encouraging certain municipalities which desire to maintain high-acreage requirements to drag their feet as far as constructing municipal sewerage systems is concerned. If this appears to be the case, then in evaluating such a zoning ordinance we would be forced to discount the potential sewerage problem. On the other hand, we should not say that the sewerage problem must be overlooked entirely. Concord Township has no municipal sewerage system. If we strike down this zoning ordinance and if the sewerage problem is such that on-site systems would not be feasible, then the Township will be forced to incur the expense of installing a municipal system. Rural and suburban townships have relatively limited tax resources for the obvious reason that they are composed primarily of single-family residences, properties which do not yield high real estate tax revenues. To require these municipalities to incur the great expense of installing sewerage systems and to augment their limited municipal services to meet a population which is increasing more rapidly than anticipated, does not appear to me to be a sound way to face what is admittedly a serious problem of providing residential communities for a rapidly-growing population.

I dissent.

COHEN, J., joins in this dissenting opinion.

POMEROY, Justice (dissenting).

While agreeing in the main with the dissenting opinion of Mr. Justice Jones, I deem it desirable to make a brief separate explanation of the reasons I am unable to concur in the majority opinion.

Bilbar Const. Co. v. Easttown Twp. Bd. of Adj., 393 Pa. 62, 141 A.2d 851 (1958) was a decision upholding the validity of a one-acre minimum size lot in an opinion written by Chief Justice Charles Alvin Jones. (Mr. Justice, now Chief Justice, Bell dissented at length, and was joined by Justice Musmanno and Justice Benjamin R. Jones.) *Bilbar* seems to me to have been a wise opinion in the delicate area of judicial versus legislative prerogatives. Said the Court:

> "While the promotion of the public health, safety, morals or general welfare is the test for checking subjectively whether a municipality's exertion of its constitutional power to zone has been exceeded, courts do not apply the criteria in a vacuum. Someone must be injured by the ordinance's restrictions in order to raise the constitutional question, and the applicable objective test is whether the ordinance operates in an arbitrary, capricious, discriminatory or confiscatory manner as to the property of the complainant. The latter inquiry calls for judicial determination. But, as to the former, what serves the public interest is primarily a question for the appropriate legislative body in a given situation to ponder and decide. And, so long as it acts within its constitutional power to legislate in the premises, courts do well not to intrude their independent ideas as to the wisdom of the particular legislation. *Specifically, with respect to zoning enactments, judges should not substitute their individual views for those of the legislators as to whether the means employed are likely to serve the public health, safety, morals or general welfare.*" (Italics supplied.)

The Court in *Bilbar* reiterated the presumption of constitutional validity that attends legislative enactments, including those of municipal bodies in the form of ordinances, and the rule that "the burden of proof, when legislation is under attack on constitutional grounds, is on the one so asserting and never shifts." The Court went on to observe:

> "Even where there is room for difference of opinion as to whether an ordinance is designed to serve a proper public purpose, or if the question is fairly debatable, the courts cannot substitute their judgment for that of the authorities who enacted the legislation." (Citing cases.) pp. 71-72, 141 A.2d p. 856.

National Land and Investment Company v. Easttown Township Board of Adjustment, 419 Pa. 504, 215 A.2d 597 (1965), a decision with which I agree, struck down as unconstitutional, under the facts there prevailing, a four-acre minimum lot size. In so doing, the Court cited *Bilbar* approvingly several times, and acknowledged that "The zoning power is one of the tools of government which, in order to be effective, must not be subjected to judicial interference unless clearly necessary. For this reason, a presumption of validity attaches to a zoning ordinance which imposes the burden to prove its invalidity upon the one who challenges it." (p. 522, 215 A.2d p. 607) Addressing itself to the requirement of a minimum area for residential building, the Court said:

> "There is no doubt that in Pennsylvania, zoning for density is a legitimate exercise of the police power. [Citing *Bilbar* and *Volpe Appeal*, 384 Pa. 374, 121 A.2d 97.] Every zoning case involves a different set of facts and circumstances in light of which the constitutionality of a zoning ordinance must be tested. Therefore, it is impossible for us to say that any minimum acreage requirement is unconstitutional per se." (p. 523, 215 A.2d pp. 607-608)

Yet it is difficult to see, in light of the majority opinion in the case at bar, how any minimum acreage requirement for suburban residential use in excess of one acre can henceforth be sustained. Any minimum lot requirement is, almost by its name, exclusive in some degree in purpose and effect. Indeed, if the minimum lot size in the present case had been one acre, and the appellee had planned to develop the tract in question in ¾ acre lots, or ½ acre lots, the reasoning of the majority opinion would appear to be equally applicable to permitting such use. Perhaps it is significant that the majority opinion in the case at bar does not cite *Bilbar* a single time.

In all previous zoning cases, the Court has put the burden of proof on the challenger of the legislation involved. By the present decision the Court appears to reverse the burden, and says that "Absent some extraordinary justification, a zoning ordinance with minimum lot sizes such as those in this case is *completely unreasonable.*" The majority then holds that the Township has not shown such extraordinary justification for its 2 and 3 acre minimum lot size requirements, and that such requirements are accordingly unconstitutional. The rationale of this holding appears to be that Concord Township is "unnaturally limiting its population growth through the use of exclusive zoning regulations," with the result that "the people who would normally live there will inevitably have to live in another community."

The record, as I read it, does not indicate that the appellee sustained its burden, assuming it still had one, of showing unconstitutionality. If the burden has now shifted to the municipality to justify its minimum requirement, I think it was sufficiently met, though probably not by showing any justification which the majority would say was "extraordinary."

The record shows, to my satisfaction at least, that Concord Township, heretofore an essentially rural area, has been aware of a responsibility to

deal with the problem of population growth, and has responded constructively. Rather than executing a "retreat behind a cover of exclusive zoning," it has liberalized its ordinance to make it less exclusive, changing
the three acre minimum from 80% to 10% of the total land area and substantially increasing the area zoned for one acre or less; rather than "attempting
to zone out growth at the expense of neighboring communities," it has
projected its growth pattern for the next decade, and charted its zoning
pattern to accommodate it;[1] rather than using a waste disposal problem
as "a thinly veiled justification for exclusionary zoning," it has presented,
as but one relevant factor, competent testimony to indicate that 40% of the
tract in question is, because of topography and soil composition, in an area
of "severe limitation" for on-lot sewage disposal.

It is true that Concord Township has not utilized the Planned Unit Development technique approved by the Court in Village 2 at New Hope,
Inc. Appeals, 429 Pa. 626, 241 A.2d 81 (1968), but it is also true that it
has appointed a Township Planning Commission which since 1966 has been
engaged, with the help of a community planning consultant, and in conjunction with the Delaware County Planning Commission, in planning
for land use development, including feasibility studies relative to water
supply and sewage disposal. This process is not complete. Indeed, the
Township properly recognizes that planning is a continuous process. In
the words of the Township's consultant, William K. Davis, "The Township is endeavoring to embark on a full, new, comprehensive planning
program which I am—confident will lead to new proposals in land use,
new development areas perhaps, variety of other things. Because the
Township is in this period of transition, I think the town must be guarded
against the development of parcels at random * * *"[2]

Our function on this appeal, where no additional testimony was taken by
the lower court, is to look at the decision of the Board of Adjustment to
determine if in upholding the constitutionality of the two acre and three
acre minimum zoning, the Board committed an abuse of discretion or an
error of law. My reading of the record satisfies me that it did not.
National Land's substantive holding, as now stated by the majority, is that
the existence of alternative methods for dealing with problems attendant
upon population growth forbids zoning which has "an exclusive purpose
or effect." It appears that in the case at bar the Township has been ex-

---

1. The Township's 1966 population was 4,081 persons. It is anticipating a growth
by 1980 of more than double, to 8 to 10 thousand.

2. Professor Sager, in his interesting article cited several times by the majority
opinion (Sager, "Tight Little Islands: Exclusionary Zoning, Equal Protection, and
the Indigent," 21 Stanford L. Rev. 767, 797 (1969) acknowledges that "The restraint
on the number of households effectuated by large-lot-size restrictions is a restraint on
the total demand for [public] services and may permit the more rational and systematic
absorption of new residents." He goes on to state his conviction that "this argument
implies a planned and controlled change of the affected area, not a firm posture of opposition to change."

ploring the alternative methods, and has made its zoning less exclusive as part of a conscious effort to absorb the population thrust which it anticipates. That the particular tract here involved is zoned two and three acre minimum lot size does not demonstrate the contrary, or even that the appellee developer would have to go to another community, since one acre, or less, zoning is available in the Township.

I would reverse the decree of the Court below and reinstate the decision of the Board of Adjustment.

JONES, J., joins in the dissenting opinion.

APPEAL OF GIRSH

437 Pa. 237, 263 A. 2d 395(1970).

Supreme Court of Pennsylvania.

Feb. 13, 1970.
Rehearing Denied April 13, 1970.

Actions challenging constitutionality of zoning ordinance. The Court of Common Pleas, Delaware County, Edwin E. Lippincott, II, J., order dated 9/4/68 at No. 8517 of 1967, affirmed zoning board's sustaining of ordinance and appeal was taken. The Supreme Court, Roberts, J., No. 164 January Term, 1969, held that failure of zoning scheme of township, which had area of 4.64 square miles and population of almost thirteen thousand, to provide for apartments was unconstitutional though apartments were not explicitly prohibited by zoning ordinance.

Decree reversed.

Jones, Cohen and Pomeroy, JJ., dissented.

Louis F. Floge, Philadelphia, for appellant.

John W. Wellman, Chester, John R. McConnell, Philadelphia, for Township of Nether Providence.

E. Barclay Cale, Jr., John R. McConnell, Philadelphia, for the General Council of Civic Ass'ns of Nether Providence Twp. et al.

Before BELL, C. J., and JONES, COHEN, EAGEN, O'BRIEN, ROBERTS and POMEROY, JJ.

OPINION OF THE COURT

ROBERTS, Justice.

By agreement dated July 13, 1964, appellant contracted to purchase a 17½ acre tract of land, presently zoned R-1 Residential,[1] in Nether Provi-

---

1. R-1 Residential zones require minimum lot sizes of 20,000 square feet. The most common of the permissible land uses under the R-1 Residential classification is a single-family detached dwelling.

dence Township, Delaware County. Appellant agreed to pay a minimum of $110,000 (later changed by agreement to $120,000) for the property. He further agreed to request the Township Board of Commissioners to change the R-1 Residential zoning classification so that a high-rise apartment could be built on the property and to pay $140,000 if this request were granted.

Nether Providence is a first-class township with a population of almost 13,000 persons and an area of 4.64 square miles. Approximately 75% of the Township is zoned either R-1 or R-2 Residential, which permit the construction of single-family dwelling units on areas not less than 20,000 and 14,000 square feet, respectively. Multi-unit apartment buildings, although not *explicitly* prohibited, are not provided for in the ordinance. The Township contains the customary commercial and industrial districts, as well as two areas where apartments have been permitted and constructed only after variances were secured.

[1]   After the Board refused to amend the zoning ordinance, appellant sought a building permit to construct two nine-story luxury apartments, each containing 280 units.[2] The permit was refused since the R-1 Residential classification does not permit multiple dwellings. Appellant appealed to the Zoning Board of Adjustment and announced that he would attack the constitutionality of the zoning ordinance in lieu of seeking a variance. The Zoning Board sustained the ordinance and denied relief. The Court of Common Pleas of Delaware County affirmed, and appellant took this appeal. We hold that the failure of appellee township's zoning scheme to provide for apartments is unconstitutional and reverse the decree of the court below.

Initially, it is plain that appellee's zoning ordinance indeed makes no provision for apartment uses. Appellee argues that nonetheless apartments are not explicitly *prohibited* by the zoning ordinance. Appellee reasons that although only single-family residential uses are provided for, nowhere does the ordinance say that there shall be no apartments. In theory, an apartment use by variance is available, and appellee urges that this case thus is different from prior cases in which we severely questioned zoning schemes that did not allow given uses in an *entire* municipality. See Exton Quarries, Inc. v. Zoning Board of Adjustment, 425 Pa. 43, 228 A.2d 169 (1967); Ammon R. Smith Auto Co. Appeal, 423 Pa. 493, 223 A.2d 683 (1966); Norate Corp. v. Zoning Board of Adjustment, 417 Pa. 397, 207 A.2d 890 (1965).

[2-5]   Appellee's argument, although perhaps initially appealing, cannot withstand analysis. It is settled law that a variance is available *only* on narrow grounds, i.e., "where the property is subjected to an unnecessary hardship, unique or peculiar to itself, and where the grant thereof will not be contrary to the public interest. The reasons to justify the

---

2. Appellant stated in court that he would reduce the number of units per building to 216.

granting of a variance must be 'substantial, serious and compelling.' " Poster Advertising Company, Inc. v. Zoning Board of Adjustment, 408 Pa. 248, 251, 182 A.2d 521, 523 (1962). In light of this standard, appellee's land-use restriction in the case before us cannot be upheld against constitutional attack because of the *possibility* that an *occasional* property owner may carry the heavy burden of proving sufficient hardship to receive a variance. To be constitutionally sustained, appellee's land-use restriction must be reasonable. If the failure to make allowance in the Township's zoning plan for apartment uses is unreasonable, that restriction does not become any the more reasonable because once in a while, a developer may be able to show the hardship necessary to sustain a petition for a variance.[3] At least for the purposes of this case, the failure to provide for apartments anywhere within the Township must be viewed as the legal equivalent of an explicit total prohibition of apartment houses in the zoning ordinance.

Were we to accept appellee's argument we would encourage the Township in effect to spot-zone a given use on variance-hardship grounds. This approach distorts the question before us, which is whether appellee must provide for apartment living as part of its *plan* of development. Cf. Eves v. Zoning Board of Adjustment, 401 Pa. 244, 164 A.2d 7 (1960).

[6] By emphasizing the possibility that a given land owner *could* obtain a variance, the Township overlooks the broader question that is presented by this case. In refusing to allow apartment development as part of its zoning scheme, appellee has in effect decided to zone *out* the people who would be able to live in the Township if apartments were available. Cf. National Land and Investment Co. v. Easttown Twp. Board of Adjustment, 419 Pa. 504, 532, 215 A.2d 597, 612 (1965): "The question posed is whether the township can stand in the way of the natural forces which send our growing population into hitherto undeveloped areas in search of a comfortable place to live. We have concluded not. A zoning ordinance whose primary purpose is to prevent the entrance of newcomers in order to avoid future burdens, economic and otherwise, upon the administration of public services and facilities can not be held valid."

We emphasize that we are not here faced with the question whether we can compel appellee to zone *all* of its land to permit apartment develop-

---

3. We must start with the basic proposition that absent more, an individual should be able to utilize his own land as he sees fit. U.S.Const. Amends. V, XIV. Although zoning is, in general, a proper exercise of police power which can permissibly limit an individual's property rights, Village of Euclid, Ohio v. Ambler Realty Co., 272 U.S. 365, 47 S.Ct. 114, 71 L.Ed. 303 (1926), it goes without saying that the use of the police power cannot be unreasonable. E.g., Eller v. Board of Adjustment, 414 Pa. 1, 198 A.2d 863 (1964). If the zoning ordinance is unreasonable, it is no saving that some people may show the requisite degree of hardship to obtain a variance. The hardship necessary to sustain an application for a variance borders on economic disaster, but this provides no protection for the individual who is disadvantaged to a substantial, but lesser, extent. This infringement on this latter individual's right to use his own property cannot be allowed unless it is reasonable.

ment, since this is a case where *nowhere* in the Township are apartments permitted. Instead, we are guided by the reasoning that controlled in *Exton Quarries*, supra. We there stated that "The constitutionality of zoning ordinances which totally prohibit legitimate businesses * * * from an entire community should be regarded with particular circumspection; for unlike the constitutionality of most restrictions on property rights imposed by other ordinances, the constitutionality of total prohibitions of legitimate businesses cannot be premised on the fundamental reasonableness of allocating to each type of activity a particular location in the community." 425 Pa. at 58, 228 A.2d at 179. In *Exton Quarries* we struck down an ordinance which did not allow quarrying anywhere in the municipality, just as in Ammon R. Smith Auto Co. Appeal, supra, we did not tolerate a total ban on flashing signs and in *Norate Corp.*, supra, we struck down a prohibition on billboards everywhere in the municipality. Here we are faced with a similar case, but its implications are even more critical, for we are here dealing with the crucial problem of population, not with billboards or quarries. Just as we held in *Exton Quarries, Ammon R. Smith,* and *Norate* that the governing bodies must make some provision for the use in question, we today follow those cases and hold that appellee cannot have a zoning scheme that makes no reasonable provision for apartment uses.

[7] Appellee argues that apartment uses would cause a significant population increase with a resulting strain on available municipal services and roads, and would clash with the existing residential neighborhood. But we *explicitly* rejected both these claims in *National Land*, supra: "Zoning is a tool in the hands of governmental bodies which enables them to more effectively meet the demands of evolving and growing communities. It must not and can not be used by those officials as an instrument by which they may shirk their responsibilities. Zoning is a means by which a governmental body can plan for the future—it may not be used as a means to deny the future. * * * Zoning provisions may not be used * * * to avoid the increased responsibilities and economic burdens which time and natural growth invariably bring." 419 Pa. at 527-528, 215 A.2d at 610. Cf. Delaware County Community College Appeal, 435 Pa. 264, 254 A.2d 641 (1969); O'Hara's Appeal, 389 Pa. 35, 131 A.2d 587 (1957). That reasoning applies equally here. Likewise we reaffirm our holding in *National Land* that protecting the character—really the aesthetic nature—of the municipality is not sufficient justification for an exclusionary zoning technique. 419 Pa. at 528-529, 215 A.2d at 610-611.

This case presents a situation where, no less than in *National Land*, the Township is trying to "stand in the way of the natural forces which send our growing population into hitherto undeveloped areas in search of a comfortable place to live." Appellee here has simply made a decision that it is content with things as they are, and that the expense or change in character that would result from people moving in to find "a comfortable place to live" are for someone else to worry about. That decision is unacceptable. Statistics indicate that people are attempting to move away from the urban core areas, relieving the grossly over-crowded conditions that exist in most of our major cities. Figures show that most jobs that are being created in urban areas, including the one here in question, are in the suburbs. New York Times, June 29, 1969, p. 39 (City Edition). Thus the suburbs, which at one time were merely "bedrooms" for those who worked in the urban core, are now becoming active business areas in their own right. It follows then that formerly "outlying," somewhat rural communities, are becoming logical areas for development and population growth—in a sense, suburbs to the suburbs. With improvements in regional transportation systems, these areas also are now more accessible to the central city.

In light of this, Nether Providence Township may not permissibly choose to only take as many people as can live in single-family housing, in effect freezing the population at near present levels. Obviously if every municipality took that view, population spread would be completely frustrated. Municipal services must be provided *somewhere,* and if Nether Providence is a logical place for development to take place, it should not be heard to say that it will not bear its rightful part of the burden.[4] Certainly it can protect its attractive character by requiring apartments to be built in accordance with (reasonable) set-back, open space, height, and other light-and-air requirements,[5] but it cannot refuse to make any provision for apartment living. The simple fact that someone is anxious to build apartments is strong indication that the location of this township is such that people are desirous of moving in, and we do not believe Nether Providence can close its doors to those people.

It is not true that the logical result of our holding today is that a municipality must provide for all types of land use. This case deals with the right of people to *live on land,* a very different problem than whether

---

4. Perhaps in an ideal world, planning and zoning would be done on a *regional* basis, so that a given community would have apartments, while an adjoining community would not. But as long as we allow zoning to be done community by community, it is intolerable to allow one municipality (or many municipalities) to close its doors at the expense of surrounding communities and the central city.

5. As appellants indicate, the apartments here in question would cover only 2.7 acres of a 17.7 acre tract, would be located far back from the road and adjacent properties, and would be screened by existing high trees. Over half of the trees now on the tract would be saved.

It should be pointed out that much of the opposition to apartment uses in suburban communites is based on fictitious emotional appeals which insist on categorizing all apartments as being equivalent to the worst big-city tenements. See Babcock and Bosselman, Suburban Zoning and the Apartment Boom, 111 U.Pa. L.Rev. 1040, 1051–1072 (1963), wherein the authors also convincingly refute the arguments that apartments necessarily will: not "pay their own way"; cut off light and air; become slums; reduce property values; be destructive to the "character of the community"; and bring in "low-class" people.

appellee must allow certain industrial uses within its borders.[6]   Apartment living is a fact of life that communities like Nether Providence must learn to accept.   If Nether Providence is located so that it is a place where apartment living is in demand, it must provide for apartments in its plan for future growth; it cannot be allowed to close its doors to others seeking a "comfortable place to live."

The order of the Court of Common Pleas of Delaware County is reversed.

BELL, C. J., files a concurring opinion.

JONES, J., files a dissenting opinion in which COHEN and POMEROY, JJ., join.

BELL, Chief Justice (concurring).

This case poses for me a very difficult problem.   One of the most important rights, privileges and powers which (at least until recently) has differentiated our Country from Communist and Socialist Countries, is the right of ownership and the concomitant use of property.   The only limitation or restriction therof was "sic utere tuo ut alienum non laedas"—a right to use one's property in any way and manner and for any purpose the owner desires, except and unless it injures the property of another, or endangers or seriously affects the health or morals or safety of others.

Then along came zoning with its desirable objectives.   However, desirable or worthwhile objectives have too often been carried to an unfair or unwise or unjustifiable extreme, or an extreme which makes the Act or Ordinance illegal or unconstitutional.

This Ordinance cannot be sustained under the theory or unwitting pretense that it is necessary for, or has a substantial relationship to the protection of the health or morals or safety of the people of that Township, and, as Justice Roberts points out, it cannot and should not be legalized or Constitutionalized under the theory of "general welfare" * or "public interest or worthy objectives."   Furthermore, Courts, Legislators, zoning bodies and most of the public have forgotten or rendered meaningless Article I, Section 1, of the Constitution of Pennsylvania, which provides: "All men are born equally free and independent, and have certain inherent and indefeasible rights, among which are those of * * * acquiring, possessing and protecting property * * *."

---

6. Even in the latter case, if the Township instituted a total ban on a given use, that decision would be open to at least considerable question under our decision in *Exton Quarries,* supra.

In addition, at least hypothetically, appellee could show that apartments are not appropriate on the site where appellant wishes to build, but that question is not before us as long as the zoning ordinance in question is fatally defective on its face.   Appellee could properly decide that apartments are more appropriate in one part of the Township than in another, but it cannot decide that apartments can fit in *no* part of the Township.

* Aesthetics have no place or part in zoning, either as support or justification for, or rejection of any plan.   Moreover, it is sometimes forgotten that very few can ever agree on what is or is not "aesthetic."

I believe that a County or Township can "reasonably" regulate the location, size, height, setbacks, light and air requirements, etc. of apartment houses or buildings, but that neither a County nor a Township can *totally prohibit* all apartment houses or buildings. Cf. Exton Quarries Inc. v. Zoning Board of Adjustment, 425 Pa. 43, 228 A.2d 169. Whether an ordinance which makes no provision for, or authorization of, apartment houses is equivalent to a total prohibition thereof raises (at least, for me) a difficult question. However, I have come to the conclusion that the present zoning ordinance (1) *in practical effect* amounts to a prohibition of apartment houses, and (2) cannot be saved or legalized by a right to a variance which is grantable only upon proof of (a) unnecessary hardship upon and which is unique or peculiar to the property involved, as distinguished from the hardship arising from the impact of the zoning ordinance upon the entire district, and (b) where the proposed variance will not be contrary to the public safety, health, morals or general welfare: DiSanto v. Zoning Board of Adjustment, 410 Pa. 331, 189 A.2d 135; Sheedy v. Zoning Board of Adjustment, 409 Pa. 655, 187 A.2d 907; Brennen v. Zoning Board of Adjustment, 409 Pa. 376, 187 A.2d 180; Joseph B. Simon & Co. v. Zoning Board of Adjustment, 403 Pa. 176, 168 A.2d 317.

For these reasons, I concur in the Opinion of the Court.

JONES, Justice (dissenting).

Appellant attacks the constitutionality of the zoning ordinance in question on two levels. First, he maintains that it is unconstitutional for the Township to prohibit the construction of apartment buildings throughout the entire township. Second, he argues that the ordinance as applied to the Duer Tract in particular is unconstitutional because the property cannot reasonably be graded and developed for single-family residences.

The principles governing the disposition of cases involving a constitutional attack on a zoning ordinance have been oft-repeated in our case law. "The test of constitutionality of a zoning ordinance is whether it bears a substantial relation to the health, safety, morals or general welfare of the public: [Citing authority]. One who challenges the constitutionality of a zoning ordinance has no light burden and it is settled that before a zoning ordinance can be declared unconstitutional it must be shown that its provisions are clearly arbitrary and unreasonable, having no substantial relation to the public health, safety, morals or general welfare. If the validity of the legislative judgment is fairly debatable, the legislative judgment must be allowed to control: [Citing authorities]." Glorioso Appeal, 413 Pa. 194, 198, 196 A.2d 668, 671 (1964).[1]

Appellant's first argument is that the zoning ordinance is unconstitutional in that it makes no provision for apartment buildings anywhere in the

---

1. See also: National Land and Investment Co. v. Easttown Twp. Bd. of Adjustment, 419 Pa. 504, 511, 512, 215 A.2d 597 (1965); Colligan Zoning Case, 401 Pa. 125, 131, 162 A.2d 652 (1960); Billbar Constr. Co. v. Easttown Twp. Bd. of Adjustment, 398 Pa. 62, 72, 141 A.2d 851 (1958).

township. Appellant maintains that this Court looks askance at zoning ordinances which totally prohibit a legitimate use anywhere within the municipality, citing Exton Quarries, Inc. v. Zoning Board of Adjustment, 425 Pa. 43, 228 A.2d 169 (1967); Ammon R. Smith Auto Co. Appeal, 423 Pa. 493, 223 A.2d 683 (1966); Norate Corp. v. Zoning Board of Adjustment, 417 Pa. 397, 207 A.2d 890 (1965); Eller v. Board of Adjustment, 414 Pa. 1, 198 A.2d 863 (1964). Of these four cases, the authority most in point is *Exton*.[2]

In *Exton* we struck down a zoning ordinance as unconstitutional which prohibited any and all quarrying within the township. We noted that the township was sparsely settled and that the proposed quarry would be located some distance from the nearest residential neighborhood. We held that "a zoning ordinance which totally excludes a particular business from an entire municipality must bear a more substantial relationship to the public health, safety, morals and general welfare than an ordinance which merely confines that business to a certain area in the municipality." (425 Pa. at 60, 228 A.2d at 179.)

The Township, in support of its position that the zoning ordinance in question is constitutional, cites two decisions of our Court. In Dunlap Appeal, 370 Pa. 31, 87 A.2d 299 (1952), we upheld an ordinance which forbid the construction of row houses, and in Mutual Supply Co. Appeal, 366 Pa. 424, 77 A.2d 612 (1951), we upheld an ordinance which permitted only single-family dwellings in the face of a challenge from a coal mining company which wanted to build coal mining structures on the surface of the land which were necessary for the mining operations below the surface.[3]

My research indicates that the exact question presented on this appeal has never been decided at the appellate level in this Commonwealth. The one decision I have found most directly on point is Lofmer, Inc. v. Board of Adjustment of Easttown Twp., 11 Chester Cty. R. 66 (1963), in which the Court of Common Pleas of Chester County upheld the constitutionality of a zoning ordinance which changed the applicable zoning classification to prohibit apartment buildings. The court held that the fact that

---

2. In *Norate* we struck down an ordinance which prohibited all "off-site" advertising signs anywhere within the township. In *Ammon Smith* we struck down a similar ordinance banning all flashing signs. In *Eller* we voided an ordinance requiring minimum set-offs for mushroom houses on the grounds that the set-offs would require a person to own approximately 69 acres before he could grow mushrooms. I conclude that none of these three cases is cogent authority for the position advanced by the appellant.

3. In *Mutual Supply,* we stated in pertinent part: "The exclusion of industrial use involves an exercise of legislative discretion under the existing facts and circumstances. In the present instance, there was evidence that 'the highest and best use of the area is residential.' Within a half-mile radius of Mutual's surface plot there are not less than forty residences of an average value of $30,000 each. Of course, if the ordinance's exclusion of industrial use would conclusively prevent the appellants from mining and removing their coal for which they have full mining rights without liability for surface support, then a different question would be presented." (366 Pa. at 430, 431, 77 A.2d at 615.)

a zoning ordinance makes no provision for a particular use of property in the township does not, ipso facto, make the ordinance unconstitutional. I am in agreement with this conclusion.

Exton, upon which the majority opinion places the most reliance, can be distinguished on two grounds. First, *Exton* involved the total prohibition of a valid use. The ordinance now before us does not involve a total prohibition; the ordinance simply does not make provision for apartment buildings. While at first blush this might appear to be a distinction without a difference, there is, in reality, an important difference. Apartment buildings are permissible—and, in fact, have been constructed—if a variance is granted. Therefore, it is not correct to say that the Township totally prohibits the construction of apartment buildings.[4]

Second, the natural expansion of the majority's conclusion is that Nether Providence must provide for all types of high-density, residential land use. This is an unsound result. It makes no more sense to require a rural township to provide for high-rise apartments than to provide for industrial zones; likewise, it would not make sense to require an industrial municipality to provide for agricultural uses. By concluding that the township must provide for high-rise apartments, the majority also impliedly holds that every possible use, having no greater detrimental effect, must also be allowed. In my opinion, this decision places us in the position of a "super board of adjustment" or "planning commission of last resort," a position which we have heretofore specifically rejected. National Land and Investment Co. v. Easttown Twp. Bd. of Adjustment, 419 Pa. 504, 521-22, 215 A.2d 597, 606-607 (1965).

Even if I were to accept appellant's logic, it must still be affirmatively demonstrated that high-rise apartment buildings are a *suitable* land use within the township. The court below held that appellant had failed to carry his burden of proof, and I find no fault in this decision. The evidence indicates that 90% of the township is presently already developed. A land planner and municipal consultant testified that he had studied the remaining undeveloped properties within the township and concluded that none of them was suitable for high-rise apartments. Furthermore, the township is residential in nature with a relatively sparse population. A high-rise apartment project would produce a significant increase in population which would tax the limited municipal services available in the township.[5] Accordingly, I find it impossible to say on the face of this record that a township such as Nether Providence is constitutionally required to make provision for high-rise apartments in its zoning ordinances.[6]

4. *Cf.* Honey Brook Twp. v. Alenovitz, 430 Pa. 614, 243 A.2d 330 (1968).

5. Since I would hold that appellant failed to prove that high rise apartments would be a suitable land use in the township, *Exton* is inapposite, for there was no question in *Exton* that quarrying was a suitable land use.

6. Decisions in other jurisdictions support this conclusion. *See, e. g.,* Valley View Village, Inc. v. Proffett, 221 F.2d 412, 418 (6th Cir. 1955), (per Potter Stewart, J.);

I turn now to appellant's second contention, *viz.*, that the zoning ordinance permitting only single-family dwellings is unconstitutional as applied to the Duer Tract in particular. Appellant's first argument under this heading is that the ordinance has no relation to the public health, safety and welfare. I cannot agree. The proposed apartment complex would be the largest of its kind in Delaware County, housing an estimated 1,600 persons, and would increase the population of the township by 13%. We cannot refute the conclusion that such a large and rapid increase in population would place a strain on the township's limited municipal services and rural roads. Furthermore, except for the railroad tracks, the area surrounding the Duer Tract is composed exclusively of single-family dwellings. The proposed apartment towers would be incompatible with the existing residential neighborhood and would introduce a structure completely out of proportion to any other building in the township. Furthermore, the complex would present a density problem in this area of the township. The First Class Township Code specifically empowers local municipalities to zone for density;[7] I conclude that the ordinance in question is a proper application of that power.

Appellant's second argument is that the ordinance is unreasonable, arbitrary and discriminatory as applied to the Duer Tract because of the prohibitive expense involved in grading and preparing the land for single-family residences. There is no question that the property contains some topographical features which are less than desirable for the construction of single-family homes. The record is replete with conflicting testimony, however, as to how much expense would be required to grade the tract and divert the creek which runs through the property. There is evidence in the record to support the court's conclusion that these preparatory expenses would not make the cost of the homes prohibitively expensive. The court pointed out that a development of single-family houses is now being constructed on a neighboring tract which is very similar topographically to the Duer Tract. Furthermore, appellant made a firm commitment to buy the property regardless of whether he was successful in having the zoning classification changed. Apparently when he purchased the property, therefore, appellant concluded that he could successfully build and sell single-family homes on the tract.

Fanale v. Borough of Hasbrouck Heights, 26 N.J. 320, 129 A.2d 749, 752 (1958) (per Weintraub, C. J.); Connor v. Township of Chanhassen, 249 Minn. 205, 81 N.W.2d 789, 794–795 (1957); Fox Meadow Estates, Inc. v. Culley, 233 App.Div. 250, 252 N.Y.S. 178 (1931), *aff'd per curiam,* 261 N.Y. 506, 185 N.E. 714 (1933); Guaclides v. Borough of Englewood Cliffs, 11 N.J. Super. 405, 78 A.2d 435 (1951) (per William Brennan, J.).

7. Act of June 24, 1931, P.L. 1206, art. XXXI, § 3101, as amended, 53 P.S. § 58101. This section has been repealed by the recently enacted Pennsylvania Municipalities Planning Code. The new Code also empowers municipalities to zone for density. Act of July 31, 1968, P.L. —, N. 247, 603(4), 53 P.S. § 10603(4) (pp).

Therefore, I would hold that the Township is *not* constitutionally required to provide for multiple-unit apartment buildings in its zoning ordinance and that the ordinance in question is not unconstitutional as applied to the Duer Tract.

I dissent.

COHEN and POMEROY, JJ., join in this dissenting opinion.

Questions and Notes

1. In all these Pennsylvania cases, is the Court's concern with the rights of property owners as developers, or with the rights of third party non-beneficiaries, or both?

2. Is there a presumption of the validity of zoning restrictions in Pennsylvania?

3. Does the Court define the word exclusionary? What does the Court mean by this word? Do you conclude that there is, or is not, a rule of law in Pennsylvania that acreage requirements larger than a certain size are unconstitutional *per se*? What size? Why that size?

Those who take these cases seriously should take a look at more recent developments—for example, DeCaro v. Washington Township, 344 A.2d 725 (Pa., Comw. Ct., 1975).

4. What does the Pennsylvania court think about the preservation of rural character as a basis for zoning?

5. Who were the dissenting judges in each case?

On Kit-Mar

1. How many judges agreed with the prevailing opinion and endorsed it? Is there an opinion of the Court?

On Girsh

1. Were there any apartment buildings already in Nether Providence?

2. How did they get there?

3. How did the Court take into account the existence of such buildings?

4. What kind of an apartment building was proposed in this instance?

5. Would it be fair to say that, if each suburban township arranged its zoning to permit one or more luxury multiple dwellings, this would satisfy the Pennsylvania court's concern about exclusionary zoning? If so, is this the course which many townships are likely to take?

6. Is the implication in the opinion that, as soon as the site zoned for multiple dwellings is built upon, another site must be provided— and so on, ad infinitum?

ROCKLEIGH

v.

ASTRAL INDUSTRIES

29 N.J. Super. 154, 102 A.2d 84(1953).
Superior Court of New Jersey
Appellate Division.
Argued Dec. 7, 1953.
Decided Dec. 24, 1953.

Suit by municipality and another to restrain alleged unlawful extension of nonconforming use and for declaratory judgment delineating extent of operations which would be permitted under the nonconforming use. The Superior Court, Chancery Division, 23 N.J.Super. 255, 92 A.2d 851, entered judgment denying the relief sought, and plaintiffs appealed. The Superior Court, Appellate Division, Francis, J. A. D., held, inter alia, that construction of large water tank which was separated from main building being used for light industrial work pursuant to nonconforming use antedating ordinance zoning area for residential purposes and which was constructed solely to protect plant in event of fire by providing necessary water for new sprinkler system was an unlawful enlargement of the nonconforming use.

Reversed and remanded with directions.

FRANCIS, J. A. D.

This is a zoning case instituted in the Chancery Division of this court in which the interested municipality and a proximate property owner sought an injunction against alleged violation of the zoning ordinance and a declaratory judgment as to the permissible scope of the alleged violator's manufacturing operations. The trial court denied the relief sought and a review of the denial is now sought. 23 N.J. Super. 255, 92 A.2d 851 (Ch.1952).

The Borough of Rockleigh is a small community of 25 homes and 105 inhabitants in northern Bergen County. It is one mile square in area. The business activities are all located in one part of the borough and consist of a riding stable, a combination garage and welding shop, and the manufacturing plant of the respondent corporation, Astral Industries, Inc.

Appellant Pfeil Realty Co., consisting of Ward Greene, his wife Edith Greene, and one other person, is the owner of a 7½ acre parcel of land on the northeast corner of County Road and Willow Avenue in the borough. The Greenes reside in a substantial home thereon.

The plant of Astral Industries, Inc. is located on the southeast corner of the same intersection across the street from the Greene premises. The building stands on a plot 554 x 314 x 622 x 308 feet. Originally it was built for and used as an indoor polo field.

During World War II the building was purchased by the Aero Metalcraft Corporation and used for the manufacture of mufflers for planes, chairs, cabinets and parts for military tanks.

At this time the borough had a zoning ordinance, adopted in 1924, under which the premises were located in a residential zone. However, in 1944 the ordinance was amended to legalize the business activity of Aero Metalcraft by changing the zone and designating it as zone "D", light industrial.

In 1948 Aero Metalcraft became bankrupt and thereafter, in latter March or early April 1949, under an agreement with the trustee in bankruptcy, respondent Astral Industries, Inc. took possession and began manufacturing small refrigerators. On April 8, 1949 a contract of purchase was made with the trustee but it was not consummated until July 26, 1950, when the deed was delivered.

On April 5, 1949, while the manufacturing was still in progress, the zoning ordinance was again amended and the premises placed back in the residential zone. However, in this proceeding the municipality recognizes that Astral's pre-existing nonconforming use is not affected thereby so long as its operations are within those permitted in the light industrial zone.

This zone is described as follows:

"Section 4, District D Zone. (A) 2. Light manufacturing which is herein defined as the converting of raw, finished or unfinished material into an article or articles of a similar or different character, purpose or use, printing, publishing, engraving, woodworking, carpentering, cabinet making, of any nature which does not require power of any kind more than the equivalent of five (5) H.P. of electrical energy per machine and which does not involve or require hammering or striking together or beating of metal or hard substance."

When Astral assumed possession of the premises it recognized that the municipal fire-fighting facilities were extremely limited. Wells were and are the sole source of water. No water mains have ever been laid in the borough as the governing body is opposed to them. The reason assigned was that such mains probably would attract substantial numbers of home builders to the community, which in turn would require the establishment of schools, public buildings, a police department and other services normally supplied by government. The desire was to keep the community small and residential and to keep the tax burden down.

A study of the fire-fighting problem was made by respondent as a result of which a plan was proposed whereby the Hackensack Water Company would extend its mains into the borough and thus provide water for a tank of undisclosed size to be built on respondent's premises. Around August 1950 the plan was discussed with the mayor and then with the council, and the borough's opposition to extension of the mains along the public streets from Northvale, an adjoining municipality, to the plant was announced to respondent and a representative of the water company.

However, Astral proceeded with arrangements to accomplish its objective and assumed financial obligations to a total of $85,318.58 therefor. The total was made up of these items:

Water tank	$11,370.00
Tank foundation	2,000.00
Sprinkler pipe installation in factory	30,469.58
Excavation	800.00
Pump	3,779.00
Water mains	30,000.00
Boiler house operations	1,000.00
Oil tank for boiler	1,000.00
Boilers	4,500.00
Miscellaneous and labor	400.00

Substantial progress toward completion of the project was made by April 1951. The sprinkler system, for which the contract had been made in December 1950, was fully installed and some noticeable outside work had been completed, including a water hydrant near the public street.

On April 5, 1951 Astral applied for and was granted by the building inspector a permit for the construction on its property of a 250,000-gallon water tank. About the last week in March the mayor had heard talk about the tank and the matter was the subject of some discussion at the council meeting of April 3. However, no official action was taken at that time. Around April 7 or 8 the mayor saw visible signs of its construction and he said that it was fully erected, so far as outward appearance went, in a little over a week.

The tank is a mammoth structure; it is separated from the plant itself by 65 feet. The dimensions do not appear, but a sizeable picture hereof is included in appellant's appendix. In this picture, and making allowance for perspective, the tank seems to dwarf everything in sight, including trees, an electric light pole and the home of the Greenes, which can be seen to the right of and diagonally across the street, and it towers above the roof of the plant. The uncontradicted evidence is to the effect that its use will be limited to fire protection and particularly to feed the sprinkler system.

One month after the issuance of the building permit, appellants brought this action for injunction and declaratory judgment.

It is urged now, as it was in the trial court, that the tank constitutes an unlawful extension of a nonconforming use.

[1]   A prime purpose of a zoning ordinance is to provide for the orderly physical development of the community by confining particular uses of property to specified locations. Nonconforming uses, which must be recognized because they preceded the ordinance, are inconsistent with that spirit and purpose and they represent conditions which should be reduced to conformity as speedily as is compatible with justice. Gunther v. Board of Zoning Appeals, 136 Conn. 303, 71 A.2d 91 (Sup.Ct.Err.1949).

[2]   It is the policy of the law to restrict closely uses which do not accord with the zoning ordinance; although they may be continued, they may not be enlarged or extended. Adler v. Department of Parks, Irvington, 20 N.J.Super. 240, 89 A.2d 704 (App.Div.1952); Home Fuel Oil Co. v. Board

of Adjustment of Glen Rock, 5 N.J. Super. 63, 68 A.2d 412 (App.Div.1949);
Home Fuel Oil Co. v. Glen Rock, 118 N.J.L. 340, 192 A. 516 (Sup.Ct.1937);
DeVito v. Pearsall, 115 N.J.L. 323, 180 A. 202 (Sup.Ct.1935).

[3] The term "nonconforming use" comprehends both the physical structure on the land in question and the functional use of the land or structure.
And the restriction of extension or enlargement referred to in the cases relates to structure as well as use thereof. In fact, the Legislature, in sanctioning repair or restoration in the event of partial destruction of a nonconforming building, seems plainly to have had the original structure in mind. In
N.J.S.A. 40:55-48, it said:

> "Any nonconforming use or structure existing at the time of the passage
> of an ordinance may be continued upon the lot or in the building so oc-
> cupied and any *such* structure may be restored or repaired in the event of
> partial destruction thereof." (Italics ours.)

Respondent places great reliance upon the fact that the tank does not
represent any departure whatever from the present nature and extent of its
manufacturing operations or from the size or use of the existing physical
plant. The assertion is that the tank as a separate structure is simply and
wholly to protect the plant in the event of fire, by providing the necessary
water for the new sprinkler system.

[4] Such argument is not tenable as a justification for the construction
of the gargantuan tank as a new structure separated by 65 feet from the
main building. In our judgment this addition to the plant facilities is an
unlawful enlargement of the antecedent nonconforming use.

Additions to or enlargements of nonconforming structures have been condemned. For example, the construction of a fuel oil tank to hold 360,000
gallons of fuel oil, in addition to the existing six smaller tanks with a total
gallonage of 100,000 gallons (Home Fuel Oil Co. v. Glen Rock, 118 N.J.L.
340, 192 A. 516 (Sup.Ct.1937); a similar situation with the same company
12 years later (5 N.J.Super. 63, 68 A.2d 412 (App.Div.1949); a proposed
cinder block addition of sizeable proportions designed to enclose the rear
portion of a soda bottling plant (Pieretti v. Johnson, 132 N.J.L. 576, 41 A.2d
896 (Sup.Ct.1945)); the addition of a single-story frame structure, 16 by 24
feet, to a boardwalk shop in order to increase the storage space and to
provide a bedroom (Burmore Co. v. Smith, 124 N.J.L. 541, 12 A.2d 353
(E. & A. 1940)); the addition of three 10,000-gallon tanks for fuel oil,
located above ground, to augment a coal business being conducted on the
premises (Brandt v. Zoning Board of Adjustment, 16 N.J.Super. 113, 84 A.2d
18 (App.Div.1951)); the tearing down of a greenhouse and the erection of
another much larger one (DeVito v. Pearsall, 115 N.J.L. 323, 180 A. 202
(Sup.Ct.1935)).

In the last-mentioned case, the landowner argued that the entire lot had
been used for business and so he should be protected in that use. But
Justice Case, for the Supreme Court, said:

"Carried to its logical result, the argument made for the prosecutor is that if a nonconforming use is once established on a property, that use may be extended and enlarged to the length and breadth of the entire plot without restraint as to height and depth. We do not understand that to be the law." 115 N.J.L. at page 325, 180 A. at page 203.

Respondent criticizes the borough council for its wilful refusal to allow the water mains to be extended into the borough for the protection of its property in the event of fire. The record discloses that the public fire-fighting facilities consist of a volunteer fire department which operates a gasoline-driven portable fire pump with a capacity of 500 gallons of water a minute. The sprinkler system installed consists of 400 heads, and if the entire plant were involved in a fire at one time, "possibly" 4,000 gallons a minute would be needed.

[5] In this connection, it cannot go unnoticed that respondent was aware of the limited fire-fighting equipment of the municipality when it went into occupancy of the premises. This fact detracts substantially from the force of any claim of right to enlarge or add to the nonconforming structure.

[6] Stress is laid upon the circumstance that a permit was issued by the building inspector to build the tank, and that it and the entire system is substantially complete with the attendant large expense. Therefore, it is suggested, an estoppel exists against the municipality, which bars any injunctive remedy. However, such an argument loses sight of the company's deliberate action in the face of known opposition by the borough to the extension of the water mains. It overlooks also that the permit was unlawful because the building inspector had no authority to sanction the enlargement of a nonconforming use. Consequently no right can derive from the permit and under the circumstances presented no estoppel can arise from it. Adler v. Department of Parks, Irvington, supra, 20 N.J.Super. at page 243, 89 A.2d 704.

Appellant claims, also, that the business operations themselves have been extended beyond the nonconforming use which was authorized for the light industrial zone.

As already set forth, the ordinance permits such manufacturing as does not require power more than the equivalent of five horsepower of electrical energy per machine. The evidence discloses that when borough officials visited the plant shortly before the trial, they found 25-horsepower motors attached to three air compressors. The compressors were not in operation and respondent insists that there is no proof that the compressors either require or use more than five horsepower.

[7] We find no evidence that each compressor requires a 25-horsepower motor for purposes of operation. There is no proof, for example, that once such a motor is put in operation, its full horsepower is used, although the compressor may need only five horsepower. And judicial notice cannot be taken of any such fact. Cf. National Lumber Products Co. v. Ponzio, 133 N.J.L. 95, 42 A.2d 753 (Sup.Ct.1945).

The trial court agreed with respondent that an enlargement of a non-conforming use had not been shown and that in any event the circumstances established an estoppel against the borough. For the reasons already stated, we have concluded that both of these determinations were erroneous.

[8, 9] Respondent protests that the borough failed to prove that the zoning ordinance and the amendments thereto were adopted legally. In accordance with N.J.S. 2A:82-14, N.J.S.A., R.R. 4:45-1, a copy of the ordinance certified by the clerk was received in evidence. Cf. Ackerman v. Nutley, 70 N.J.L. 438, 441, 57 A. 150 (Sup.Ct.1904). The duty of establishing the invalidity of the presumptively valid ordinance then rested with respondent. The trial court was satisfied after a consideration of the evidence that the burden had not been met and we see no reason to disturb his finding.

[10] One further problem remains. Appellant insists that it is entitled to a declaratory judgment "delineating the extent of operation which would be permitted on the part of Astral Industries in the future * * *." The Declaratory Judgments Act (R.S. 2:26-66 et seq.) does not justify any such excursion into the future New Jersey Turnpike Authority v. Parsons, 3 N.J. 235, 69 A.2d 875 (1949).

Under all the circumstances, the judgment is reversed and the matter remanded for the issuance of a mandatory injunction directing dismantling of the water tank.

Questions and Notes

1. Note that this is a case of a community which simply does not want any development at all.

KENNEDY PARK HOMES ASSOCIATION

v.

LACKAWANNA

318 F. Supp. 669 (WDNY. 1970), affd., 436 F.2d 108 (CA 2nd, 1970), cert. den., 401 U.S. 1010(1971).
United States District Court,
W. D. New York
Aug. 13, 1970.

The Diocese of Buffalo, New York, committed itself to sell 30 acres of land in city of Lackawanna, New York, to nonprofit organization for low-income housing subdivision for minorities. The Diocese, such organization, a colored people's civic and political organization, and two individuals who intended to purchase homes in the subdivision brought suit against the city and its mayor and its councilmen charging violations of the equal protection and due process clauses of Fourteenth Amendment, the Civil Rights Act, and the Fair Housing Act of 1968. The United States intervened as plaintiff. The District Court, Curtin, J., held that the city council's resolutions amending zoning ordinance to restrict all land referred to therein to exclusive use as a park and recreation area and declaring moratorium prohibiting approval of all future subdivisions and mayor's refusal to sign "Sanitary 5" form denied equal protection of law to plaintiffs. The Court further held that sewer needs and park and recreation needs and flooding problems did not justify such action.

Relief granted to plaintiffs.

Judgment affirmed.

Will Gibson, Buffalo, N. Y., and Michael Davidson, New York City, for Kennedy Park Homes Association, Inc., Colored People's Civil and Political Organization, James M. Thomas and Samuel Martin.

Kevin Kennedy, Buffalo, N. Y. (Charles S. Desmond, Buffalo, N. Y., of counsel), for the Diocese of Buffalo.

Gerald W. Jones and Stephen P. Passek, Attys., Dept. of Justice, Washington, D. C. (Jerris Leonard, Asst. Atty. Gen. of United States, and H. Kenneth Schroeder, Jr., U. S. Atty., Western District of New York, on the brief), for United States.

Condon, Klocke, Ange & Gervase, Buffalo, N. Y. (John W. Condon, Jr., and Grace Marie Ange, of counsel), Buffalo, N. Y., for defendants.

DECISION AND ORDER

CURTIN, District Judge.

COMPLAINTS

On December 2, 1968, Kennedy Park Homes Association, Inc. (hereinafter referred to as K.P.H.A.), Colored People's Civic and Political Organization (hereinafter referred to as C.P.C.P.O.), James M. Thomas and Samuel Martin filed a complaint against the City of Lackawanna, Mayor Mark L. Balen, Director of Development Frank Cipriani, Chief Engineer Edward Kuwik and the then members of the Lackawanna City Council charging violations of the Equal Protection and Due Process Clauses of the Fourteenth Amendment, the Civil Rights Act (42 U.S.C. § 1983), and the Fair Housing Act of 1968 (42 U.S.C. § 3601 et seq.).

The complaint alleges that the Diocese committed itself to sell to K.P.H.A., a non-profit organization formed by the C.P.C.P.O., 30 acres of its approximately 80 acres of vacant land located in Lackawanna's third ward for development of a low income housing subdivision. The two individual plaintiffs allege that they intend to purchase homes in the proposed subdivision.

Plaintiffs contend that certain resolutions amending the City's zoning ordinances to restrict all land referred to therein to the exclusive use as a park and recreation area and declaring a moratorium prohibiting the approval of all future subdivisions were passed in October, 1968 by the City

Council for the purpose of denying low income families—whether they are elderly, Negro or Puerto Rican—the equal protection of the laws in obtaining decent housing. The Diocese contends the purpose of these resolutions was to deny it the right to use and dispose of its property.

Among other things, the plaintiffs seek a judgment declaring the defendants' use of the City's zoning and appropriation powers an unconstitutional deprivation of plaintiffs' rights and mandatory relief requiring the defendants to take steps toward the approval of the subdivision. Plaintiffs also seek to enjoin defendants from enforcing the October, 1968 zoning and moratorium ordinances.

On February 5, 1969, this court—the defendants offering no opposition—granted the United States of America leave to file a complaint in intervention pursuant to Section 902 of the Civil Rights Act (42 U.S.C. § 2000h-2). Plaintiff-Intervenor invokes this court's jurisdiction under Section 813 of the Civil Rights Act of 1968 (42 U.S.C. § 3613).

The allegations in the complaint in intervention are substantially the same as those in the plaintiffs' complaint. In its prayer for relief, the Plaintiff-Intervenor asks the court to enjoin the defendants from engaging in any other acts or practices which have the effect of depriving Negroes of their right to purchase or rent dwellings in Lackawanna without regard to their race or color.

ANSWERS

The original answer filed January 29, 1969, an amended answer filed February 17, 1969, and the answer to the complaint in intervention filed February 17, 1969 generally deny the allegations of the complaints. The answers also assert five "defenses": (1) Defendants allege that the City desires, and very much needs, a park and that construction of the proposed subdivision in the Martin Road area (the only large and centrally located vacant area left in Lackawanna) would forever foreclose the City's opportunity to have such a park; (2) Defendants allege that the sewers in the Martin Road area are so overloaded that they could not tolerate the additional sewerage of a new subdivision; (3) The Diocese of Buffalo has no standing to sue in this action; (4) The complaint fails to state a cause of action; and (5) The plaintiffs have failed to exhaust all administrative procedures to obtain the relief sought herein.

On June 19, 1969, the court granted the defendants leave to file a supplemental answer alleging the rescission of the October, 1968 ordinances on February 26, 1969. The thrust and purpose of the supplemental answer was to show that no legal impediment stood in the way of plaintiffs' proposed subdivision.

HISTORY OF LAWSUIT TO DATE

In addition to the complaints and answers discussed above, certain other pretrial proceedings bear noting to understand this lawsuit.

When the lawsuit was commenced, the plaintiffs applied for a temporary restraining order and a preliminary injunction restraining the defendants from rezoning the Martin Road area for parks and recreation and from enforcing the October, 1968 ordinances. No order was signed because the defendants consented to hold their park rezoning plans pending a final decision in this case.

After the defendants filed their supplemental answer setting forth the rescission of the October, 1968 ordinances, the plaintiffs submitted a "Sanitary 5" form to Mayor Balen for approval. The "Sanitary 5" form, with the mayor's approving signature, is in the nature of an application by the City on behalf of a subdivider to the Erie County Health Department for approval of a sewer extension.

On November 14, 1969, this court gave the defendants two weeks to report on their disposition on the "Sanitary 5" form. On November 28, 1969, the plaintiffs and the court were advised that the mayor refused to sign the "Sanitary 5" form. This refusal effectively stalled any further progress in plaintiffs' attempt to obtain approval for their subdivision plans.

Afterwards, the defendants moved for a judgment on the pleadings pursuant to Rule 12(c) of the Federal Rules of Civil Procedure. The defendants argued that their affirmative defenses and the subsequent rescission of the October, 1968, ordinances established a "complete defense" to the plaintiffs' actions. Pointing to the specific allegations of the complaints, the defendants contended that the only act of any of the defendants complained of in the complaints was the passage of the October, 1968 ordinances. Since the specific acts complained of were rescinded, the defendants argued, plaintiffs' actions were moot. This argument was directed against all plaintiffs, but especially against the Diocese whose right to dispose of its property, the defendants urged, was no longer impaired.

In light of the mayor's refusal to sign the "Sanitary 5" form, and noting that the complaint in intervention prayed for an injunction restraining *all acts* denying Negroes the equal protection of the law in obtaining decent housing, the court denied the defendants' motion in all respects.

Immediately prior to trial, extensive pre-trial statements of fact and memoranda of law were submitted by the parties. The trial began on April 9, 1970 and concluded on May 21, 1970, after 22 trial days. The parties then submitted post-trial briefs of facts and law. Oral argument was heard by the court on July 10, 1970. On all of the evidence introduced at the trial and arguments made by the parties, the court makes the following findings of fact and conclusions of law pursuant to Rule 52 of the Federal Rules of Civil Procedure.

COLORED PEOPLE'S CIVIC AND POLITICAL ORGANIZATION

The C.P.C.P.O. filed its original certificate of incorporation on August 9, 1929. This membership corporation was formed "to promote good fellowship and to extend the acquaintance of its members and for social and political gatherings and lectures, and other amusements for the general welfare and benefit of its members."

The organization apparently went through a period of inactivity until a reactivation in February, 1962. Richard Easley has been president of this organization from its reactivation to date.

Shortly after reactivation, the organization showed interest in housing. Most of the members were (and are) residents of Lackawanna's first ward and many of them are employed at the Bethlehem Steel plant.

The minutes of the C.P.C.P.O. are replete with references to housing discussions among the membership, to nonmember speakers concerning the housing situation, and to reports of C.P.C.P.O. representatives meeting with private and governmental officials about the housing problem. In January, 1968, for example, the C.P.C.P.O. made inquiries of Director of Development Frank Cipriani concerning available vacant land in Lackawanna. They made a written offer to purchase certain vacant land owned by the City in the second ward.

In March, 1968, the C.P.C.P.O. had obtained a "commitment" from the Diocese for approximately 30 acres of vacant land south of Martin Road. On March 15, 1968, the C.P.C.P.O. created K.P.H.A., a non-profit membership corporation for the development of low income housing. Two officers of C.P.C.P.O. became officers of K.P.H.A.

K.P.H.A. plans to act as its own general contractor in building the subdivision. However, to aid in this endeavor, it will call upon specialists in various fields. One step was taken early in 1969, when K.P.H.A. retained Cleon Cervas, a Buffalo real estate broker, to conduct a survey of potential home buyers in order to determine their eligibility for financing. After interviewing 23 individuals, Mr. Cervas tentatively determined that about 20 would be eligible for some kind of mortgage. Because of the uncertainty of when final applications would be made, these pre-qualifying interviews were terminated after the lawsuit was filed.

DIOCESE OF BUFFALO

The Catholic Diocese of Buffalo encompasses within its territorial jurisdiction the entire City of Lackawanna with its predominantly Catholic population.

The Diocese is one of the largest landowners in the City. In addition to several small parish churches and schools which occupy small parcels of land, the Diocese "owns" a large complex located near South Park Avenue and Ridge Road in the third ward known locally as "Father Baker's," which includes Our Lady of Victory Basilica, Our Lady of Victory Hospital, Father Baker's Orphanage, and a large high school facility. The Diocese also owns Holy Cross Cemetery and approximately 80 acres of vacant land, most of it situated in the area north and south of Martin Road.

The Diocese is represented by Attorney Kevin Kennedy, who participated in many of the negotiations for the purchase of vacant land not only with C.P.C.P.O..but also with the City officials.

LACKAWANNA

The City of Lackawanna is a municipal corporation established under the laws of the State of New York. A special census taken of Erie County in 1966 showed a total population of 28,717 in Lackawanna, of which 2,693 (9.4%) were nonwhite.

The City is divided into three wards, the boundaries of which are defined in the City Charter. The first ward is the westernmost ward in the City, completely bounded on the west by the Bethlehem Steel plant situated on Lake Erie. A series of railroad tracks runs along the entire eastern boundary of the first ward with a bridge serving as the only connection within the City between the first ward and the second and third wards. The second ward comprises the middle sector of the City, bounded entirely on the west by the railroad tracks and on the east by South Park Avenue. The third ward is the eastern sector of the City, bounded on the east by the Lackawanna city line.

The City is bounded on the north by the City of Buffalo, on the east by West Seneca and Orchard Park, on the south by the Town of Hamburg, and on the west by Lake Erie.

The 1966 census figures show that 98.9% of 2,693 nonwhites living in Lackawanna live in the first ward, and these nonwhites comprise 35.4% of the total first ward population. Comparison of census figures in 1950, 1960 and 1966 shows that the percentage of nonwhites in the first ward has increased from 25% in 1950 to 35.4% in 1966. There is sharp contrast between the first ward and the other two. The 1966 census figures show 29 (0.2%) nonwhites out of a total third ward population of 12,229. Comparison of census figures in 1950, 1960 and 1966 shows a doubling in the white population of the third ward from 6,324 in 1950 to 12,200 in 1966.

The population of the second ward has changed little through the years, but it must be noted that, out of a 1966 population of 8,974, there was only one non-white.

The most pervasive influence on all Lackawanna life is the Lackawanna plant of the Bethlehem Steel Corporation, located on the shores of Lake Erie in the westerly part of the first ward. This plant, established there in 1901 and operated by the Bethlehem Steel Corporation since the early 20's, has grown to a massive industrial operation employing over 20,000 men. At present, it takes up at least half of the entire land area of the first ward. Recently, increasing industrial needs have led to an encroachment by the corporation on former residential land. For example, New Village, Bethlehem constructed housing located in the northern part of the first ward, is gradually being demolished for conversion from residential to Bethlehem use.

Unloading docks for ore boats, rail facilities, blast furnaces, coke ovens, open hearths, and mills for the manufacture of rails, beams, sheet steel, and many other steel products are located at Lackawanna. The blast furnaces and open hearths, which are the major sources of air pollution, are located in the northern part of the plant. To the south are situated shipping areas and other mills which do not contribute as heavily to air pollution. Across Route 5 in the southern portion and immediately south of Bethlehem Park, a residential area, is the strip mill which manufactures sheet steel. The plant continues to the south on both sides of the highway into the Town of Hamburg. Included in the facilities in that area is the main office. Bethlehem Steel Corporation is the largest single taxpayer in the City and employs a full-time community relations man to work on City-plant problems.

At certain times in the steel making process, huge billowing clouds of dust, smoke, and other particles are spewed into the atmosphere, especially into the northern part of the first ward. However, the entire City of Lackawanna suffers from severe air pollution due primarily to the location of the Bethlehem Steel plant.

Nevertheless, there is a sharp contrast between the first ward and the other two wards in the amount of pollution, housing problems, congestion, and other environmental factors. The series of railroad tracks running along the eastern boundary of the first ward practically separate the first ward from the remainder of the City. The only connection between the first ward and the rest of the City is the single, long Ridge Road bridge. The east-west thoroughfares, located in Buffalo to the north and Hamburg to the south, are some distance removed and do not provide an effective means of travel from the first ward to other areas of Lackawanna.

The first ward is described in the Model City application which was prepared and submitted by the City of Lackawanna to the Department of Housing and Urban Development in 1967 in the following way:

> "* * * This area is in very poor structural condition because of the age of dwellings and the poor environmental characteristics fostered by the Bethlehem Steel Company.
>
>   *   *   *   *   *   *
>
> Visual evidence substantiates the belief that housing deterioration and overcrowding within the M.N.A. (Model Neighborhood Area—first ward) are more than twice those of the city as a whole.
>
>   *   *   *   *   *   *
>
> Another major contribution to the physical blighting of the area (M.N.A.) is the smoke which blows from the stacks of Bethlehem Steel, spreading dirt, dust and pollution throughout the area."

The first ward has the oldest, most dilapidated housing, the highest residential density with the most housing units per acre, and it has the largest number of persons per housing unit. The Erie County Department of

Health has classified the first ward as a "high risk area." There is a high infant mortality rate and tuberculosis is twice as prevalent as in the city as a whole. The juvenile crime rate is almost three times, and the adult crime rate is more than double, the city average.

The worst section of the first ward for housing and air pollution is in the area north of Ridge Road. Recently, of 126 housing units in that area, 74% of them was inhabited by blacks. The best housing in the first ward is in Bethlehem Park in the southern part. This housing was established by the Bethlehem Steel Company as an all-white residential area for employees of the Lackawanna plant. Until very recently, no blacks were allowed to live there.

In considering the issues in this case, the structure of city government and the duties of various city officials should be noted. A new Charter in 1964 considerably altered the makeup of city government. Under the old system, the mayor, elected for a two-year term, had a limited appointive power, no veto and, in the City Council, only voted to break legislative ties. At that time, there were four wards, each ward having one councilman. Because this system emphasized the role of the ward councilman, decision making reflected ward needs rather than the good of the City as a whole.

Under the new Charter, each ward has a councilman elected for a two-year term. In addition, there are two councilmen-at-large, elected for four years, making up a legislative body of five. The mayor, elected for a four-year term, now has a greatly increased and more effective role in city government. He is empowered to appoint the Directors of Public Safety, Public Works, Development, and Parks and Recreation. Important to this case, he also appoints the members of the Planning and Development Board. As chief executive officer of the city, each department head reports to the mayor.

Mayor Mark Balen became mayor on January 1, 1968. Since the early 60's, he was a councilman. He testified that the transition from the old system to the new required considerable adjustment because it was difficult for the citizens and the ward councilmen to become accustomed to the diminished role of the councilmen in city government. Before enactment of the Charter, it was not unusual for the councilmen to usurp normally executive or administrative roles of the officers of city government. The mayor felt that it would take citizens and city officials some time to become used to the new Charter.

A particular question created by the change in the Charter was the power to approve new subdivisions. Under the old system, a subdivision was approved by a three-fourths vote of the Council. No standards for approval other than those exercised by the vote of the Council were set. What is now required for approval of subdivisions under the new Charter is confusing. The opinion of Frank Cipriani, Director of Development, is that the Planning Board has this authority, but such authority is not clearly set forth in the Charter or the Administrative Code. Furthermore, it was not clear from the evidence what standards govern the issuance of building permits.

When Mark Balen assumed the office of mayor on January 1, 1968, he appointed Frank Cipriani Director of Development. The Director of Development is the Executive Director of the Planning and Development Board and also of the Zoning Board of Appeals. The composition of the Planning and Development Board is set forth in City Charter Chapter 8, Section 8.3. The board consists of seven members—one councilman appointed by the City Council, one City official, and five citizen members to be appointed by the mayor to serve three-year terms. After Mayor Balen had completed his appointments to the board, four members of the board resided in the third ward, three in the second, and none in the first. There were no black members on the board.

There are three low income housing projects in the City of Lackawanna, all located in the first ward. Baker Homes and the Gates Avenue Project are operated by the Lackawanna Municipal Housing Authority, and Albright Court is privately owned.

The amount of vacant land left in Lackawanna is limited. Most of it is located in the third ward, and much of this is owned by the Catholic Diocese of Buffalo. The City owns 74 vacant lots in the second ward.

PLANNING

Various planning studies and reports were admitted into evidence for the light they shed upon the City's problems—past, present, and future. Among the most important of these are: (1) The Model City application submitted by the City of Lackawanna to HUD on April 29, 1967; (2) The Master or Comprehensive Plan and supporting reports prepared by Patrick Kane of KRS Associates, Inc.; and (3) A Study of Parks and Recreation for Lackawanna, prepared by the National Recreation and Parks Association and finally submitted by a report dated June, 1968.

The Model City application described all aspects of City life in detail. Housing supply and condition, public facilities. health services, educational services, the crime problem, social services, employment, and many other details of life in the City of Lackawanna were enumerated. The Model Neighborhood Area to which particular attention is paid in the application is the first ward. Some quotations from the application accent some of Lackawanna's problems:

> "Lackawanna poses a unique problem in housing in as much as there is a physical boundary between the 'haves' and 'have-nots' in the city."

The first ward area is described in this way:

> "° ° ° There is a high percentage of Negro and other minority groups in this area. This adds to the difficulty of relocation since Lackawanna is in fact a segregated community."

The Model City application was the source of much of the statistical information set forth in other parts of this decision.

The Comprehensive Plan or Master Plan was prepared by Patrick Kane of KRS Associates, Inc., a planning consultant firm. The State of New York and Mr. Kane entered into a contract to provide professional assistance in the development of the Plan. His work on the Plan is carried out with the cooperation of HUD, State of New York, and City of Lackawanna officials.

A Comprehensive or Master Plan, according to Mr. Kane, is a long-range statement of development goals for a municipality that uses an analysis of present conditions, determines the trends in the community, and forecasts its needs in relation to land use, community facilities, transportation networks, zoning ordinances, and capital improvement programs that relate to the goals of the community. However, the Plan is not fixed. The purpose of the Plan is to provide a general framework so that the City can make an intelligent and responsible decision relative to its development.

Mr. Kane began his work early in 1966. He prepared a number of detailed studies and plans in conjunction with the development of the Lackawanna Comprehensive Plan. These documents covered such fields as land use, population trends, economic analysis, transportation and zoning. He met monthly with the Planning and Development Board and the Director. During 1966 and '67, the Director was Nicholas Colello. He was replaced on January 1, 1968 by Frank Cipriani. At each monthly meeting, Mr. Kane and members of the board discussed in detail the studies and reports as they were being prepared.

Mr. Kane presented three alternative land use plans to the board. Each plan designated the area south of Martin Road and east of the proposed McKinley extension as "residential—low density" and some or all of the area south of Martin Road and west of the proposed McKinley extension as recreation space.

Because of the poor environmental conditions, Kane wanted to restrict the residential use of the first ward as much as possible. However, because the board insisted upon keeping low densities in other parts of the City, he recognized that some residential use must be made of the first ward. The elimination of all residences in the first ward would create a difficult rehousing problem in Lackawanna because of lack of space in other parts of the City to provide housing at the densities required, and because of "the social problems which would result from the massive relocation of low income and minority groups into basically white and higher income areas of the City."

However, Planner Kane repeatedly urged the board not to use the area north of Ridge Road for residential purposes. He pointed out that this area suffered from the worst air pollution, had the most run-down housing, that private developers probably would not build there, that it would be difficult to obtain financing, and that Ridge Road separated this small area from the rest of the community so that the residents there would not receive proper services. Further, he urged elimination of Bethlehem Park because it is surrounded by industrial, railroad, and commercial enterprise, it is separated from the rest of the City, and it is too small to support schools, stores, and other community facilities. The elimination of housing in these areas would mean that there would be increased densities in other parts of the City.

However, in spite of Kane's urging, the board approved the continuance of Bethlehem Park for residential use, mainly single-family homes, and also adopted a resolution, on August 20, 1968, setting aside part of the area north of Ridge Road in the first ward for residential use, preferably apartments.

Another basic difference between the board and Mr. Kane arose over the board's demand for encouragement of single-family dwellings and the limitation of apartments. Kane protested that this would deprive many members of the community—the elderly, the poor, the single person, some minority families and the newly-married—of housing opportunity.

From March to August, 1968, Mr. Kane met several times with the board, principally to discuss the use of the land north of Ridge Road. During the same period, without his advice or consultation, the board conducted joint meetings with the Zoning Board of Appeals about the "sewer crisis" and the use of the Martin Road land. Their alleged concern was never called to his attention, nor did they ever discuss with him or ask him to change the proposals for the Martin Road area.

After the board adopted its resolution concerning the use of the Ridge Road area on August 20, 1968, Mr. Kane then began his work to put the Plan in final form and have it printed. In the summer of 1969, Mr. Kane sent on to Mr. Cipriani the proposed Final Report and told him it was ready for final printing. He also sent to Mr. Cipriani a letter for the mayor's signature, giving his official endorsement to the Plan. The Final Plan was circularized to various City officials. Mayor Balen signed the letter and the Plan, in final form, was printed in October, 1969 and distributed. The Martin Road land use remained unchanged in the final Plan.

PARKS AND RECREATION

Several of the City's actions challenged by the plaintiffs in this lawsuit are based, the defendants claim, on the City's urgent need for more recreation and park space. In 1962, the City included in its capital appropriations budget the sum of $25,000 for a recreational study to be made in 1967 or 1968. In 1966, the Capital Expenditures Board of the City recommended to the City legislators that a community recreation center costing $250,000, and an all-weather swimming pool costing $150,000 be included in the capital budget. In 1967, $25,000 was appropriated for recreation studies. Finally, on June 29, 1967, the City engaged the National Recreation and Park Association (hereinafter referred to as N. R. & P. A.) to do a study of the park and recreation facilities of the City at a cost of $2,400. Robert D. Buechner was in charge and Arthur T. Noren was a consultant, concerned primarily with the recreation program and financial considerations. Buechner concerned himself with site location and facilities.

Mr. Buechner and Mr. Noren worked in cooperation with the Lackawanna Department of Parks and Recreation and Mr. Kane, in connection with his report.

The N. R. & P. A. submitted two reports. The first was a preliminary report sent to the City Department of Parks and Recreation in November, 1967. The final report, dated June, 1968, was probably printed in August, 1968 and delivered to the City of Lackawanna early in October, 1968. After the preliminary report was delivered to the City in November, 1967, Mr. Buechner discussed it with Mr. Galanti, at that time Director of Parks and Recreation.

During 1968, he consulted further with the Department of Parks and Recreation and Mr. Kane about the final report. Both reports made similar recommendations for a community park and recreation center in the Martin Road area. Mr. Buechner recommended that a 40 or 50-acre community or district park, containing a community center with ice skating and swimming facilities and play fields for sports, be developed south of Martin Road and west of the proposed McKinley extension. The planner considered this site the best for a district park since this centrally located area was one of the last large areas left in the City, and because the most southerly portion of it bounded the south branch of Smokes Creek in a flood plain area.

According to the minimum standards of the N. R. & P. A., a community park for a city of 30,000 usually requires 70 acres, but Mr. Buechner testified that, because Lackawanna High School in the third ward and Friendship House in the first ward supplied many of the facilities usually found in a community park, 40 to 50 acres was sufficient to satisfy the recreation needs of the City of Lackawanna. Mr. Kane concurred in the N. R. & P. A. proposal.

During the planning process, neither Mr. Buechner nor Mr. Kane ever advised acquiring land east of the McKinley extension (eventually the K.P.H.A. site) for park or recreation. Nor did any City official ask the planners to consider this area to the east for park and recreation.

On February 15, 1968, the Planning and Development Board approved Alternate "C" which designated the area south of Martin Road and west of the Thruway for park and open space, and the area to the east (K.P.H.A.) for residential use. Moreover, the board at that time commented that the western area was too large for a park purpose, but decided to keep it designated "park and open space" until a more definite plan could be made.

The N. R. & P. A. also recommended the acquisition of South Park, which is within the city limits of Buffalo and borders Lackawanna to the north. An attempt by Mayor Balen to negotiate with the City of Buffalo in behalf of

Lackawanna to purchase South Park was strongly and quickly rebuffed by City of Buffalo officials.

It should be also noted that the N. R. & P. A. report recommended that the City acquire a 200-foot right-of-way along both branches of Smokes Creek for park and hiking trails. Since this land was in the flood plain, the use for recreation was strongly urged. The City has not taken any steps to implement this proposal.

In early 1968, an attempt was made by the City to acquire vacant land for recreation purposes when several meetings were held by City officials with Kevin Kennedy, attorney for the Diocese of Buffalo. Mr. Kennedy informed the Lackawanna officials that, although no land was available for sale at that time, the Diocese was willing to lease land to the City north of Martin Road for a playground area. The mayor declined this offer since he felt that the City had enough playgrounds; that it needed a large area for a park, and that a lease would not fit in well with long-range planning for Lackawanna.

The City claims that it is difficult to plan in the Martin Road area because the location of the proposed McKinley Parkway Extension is in doubt. For many years, the Department of Transportation of the State of New York and Lackawanna officials have discussed the construction of a north-south highway connecting McKinley Parkway at the Buffalo City Line to the north with McKinley Parkway Extension in the Town of Hamburg to the south. The corridor for this proposed highway parallels Abbott Road and borders the westerly bounds of the proposed K. P. H. A. site. Although the exact bounds of this highway have not been fixed, nevertheless, because another subdivision is built up on the other side of Martin Road to the north of K. P. H. A., the ultimate course of this highway will not prevent the planning and construction of homes in the K.P.H.A. area.

SEWERS

As noted elsewhere in this opinion, the City urges that many of its actions were taken because of a serious sewer situation in the City as a whole, and especially in the Martin-Abbott Road area. On some residential streets in that section, occasionally sewage has backed into cellars during heavy rainfalls.

The Lackawanna sewers are deficient in many other ways. For this reason, the City must spend a large sum of money to improve the system and upgrade it to state standards. For example, the sanitary and storm sewer lines are combined in many areas. Furthermore, on older residential streets the roof leaders and footing drains run to the sanitary sewer lines. Therefore, in periods of heavy rain, the storm water rushes into the sanitary line causing overflows and cellar backups. Thaddeus J. Pieczonka, Superintendent of the Lackawanna Sewage Treatment Plant since the early 1940's, explained the impact of this combination of systems:

"300 homes of four people each could be serviced by an 8-inch (sanitary sewer) pipe. Yet the same pipe would be full if all the footing drains and roofing drains were connected from 10 homes."

The Wilmuth Street Pumping Station located in the first ward is the main collection point for sanitary sewage in Lackawanna. From it, sewage is pumped to the primary treatment plant which is designed for a population of about 80,000 people. Adjacent to the Wilmuth Pumping Station is the Well Street Pumping Station, recently remodeled at a cost of about $500,000. The Well Street Station pumps storm water flow from the first ward into Smokes Creek and, if there are overflows from the Wilmuth Station, pumps that material, after chlorination, into the creek.

Another crucial part of the Lackawanna system is the Seal Street Pumping Station, located in the second ward near the railroad tracks and next to the south branch of Smokes Creek. The Pumping Station intercepts the overflow from sanitary sewers and discharges it directly into the creek, after chlorination, in order to prevent sewage backing up into cellars. The overflow usually occurs during rainy weather but, because of line blockages, spillages can happen when it is dry.

The pumping of sewage into the creek is a hazard to health and must be corrected. As Mr. Katra, former Lackawanna Chief Engineer, bluntly put it, "Dilution is no longer a solution to pollution."

The best way to describe one of the problems in the third ward is in Mr. Pieczonka's language:

"Just beyond St. Anthony Drive three 10-inch sewers funnel into one 15-inch sewer. This 15-inch sewer in turn empties into an 18-inch sewer on Martin Road. However, this 18-inch sewer on Martin Road has another 15-inch sewer coming in from upper Martin Road and another 10-inch sewer from Ludel Terrace. Eventually, this 18-inch Martin Road trunk, with all the above mentioned connections, enters a 15-inch sewer on South Park Avenue. This sewer on South Park cannot handle the load which then spills into the adjacent 30-inch interceptor leading to the Seal Street Pumping Station.

The Martin Road sewer becomes overloaded in the area near Maryknoll Drive even during light rains. Yet building another sewer on Martin Road will only aggravate the water pollution problem of Smokes Creek at Seal Place, because more raw sewage will be bypassed."

There are other citywide problems to solve. By order of New York State, Lackawanna must install a secondary treatment facility not later than 1972. In addition, Lackawanna must incorporate the sewers north of Ridge Road in the third ward into the Lackawanna system. For many years, the Buffalo Sewer Authority serviced this area at a rental of $250,000 a year. Because Buffalo insists that Lackawanna sever this connection, Lackawanna must spend a considerable sum to bring these sewers into the Lackawanna system.

The City of Lackawanna points to its Council minutes over the past ten years, noting the repeated reference to sewer problems and proposed sewer studies to indicate its continuing concern for a solution of this problem. However, many of the studies proposed have never been undertaken; many of the complaints received were filed without action; and many of the practical suggestions made for resolution of the problems have not been acted upon. From 1963 to 1967, when there were many complaints about sewer problems, the City of Lackawanna approved seven subdivision Sanitary 5 forms in the third ward area and issued many building permits after the subdivisions were approved. On two occasions after the FHA had rejected subdivision applications because of sewer and flooding problems, the City nevertheless issued building permits for construction in these subdivisions. However, it should be noted that one subdivision application, that for Sharon Park subdivision, was disapproved because of lack of sewer facilities and also because the State Department of Transportation requested that this area be reserved for a highway.

At least since 1964, and on several occasions after that, Mr. Pieczonka made recommendations to alleviate the third ward sewer problem. He suggested that Lackawanna (1) Build a new 24-inch sanitary sewer from Abbott Road directly to the Wilmuth Street Pumping Station; (2) Hire a consulting engineering firm to make a detail study of the Lackawanna sewer system; (3) Install the necessary pump and lines to force sewage from Seal Street to the treatment plant rather than have it discharge sewage into Smokes Creek; (4) Televise the Martin Road sewer from Abbott Road to South Park to determine if any obstruction exists in the sewer; and lastly, (5) Eliminate the roofing and footing drains from the older buildings. These last two suggestions could be undertaken quickly without large expense to the City.

A recent independent study made of all Erie County sewer systems strongly recommended that the roof leader connections be separated from the sanitary sewers in Lackawanna. A few years ago, the City passed an ordinance requiring this separation but an enforcement process was not begun until June, 1969 when the state directed that the connections had to be eliminated or the City would lose state aid.

The 1963 budget included an authorization for a comprehensive sewer study and a Council resolution of October, 1968 requested a similar study but, in spite of the claimed "sewer crisis," these studies have not been undertaken.

Furthermore, the City has taken no action either to examine or put into effect the other suggestions made by Mr. Pieczonka.

FLOOD PROBLEM

On about six occasions since 1942, Smokes Creek flooding has substantially damaged certain areas in Lackawanna. To prevent this, the Corps of Engineers undertook—and has almost completed—a flood control project. The Corps issued in 1965 a flood plain information report for the Smokes Creek basin.

The flood plain report provided contours for statistical prediction of floods. The levels used were: One flood in a period of 250 years; one in a period of 100 years; one in 50 years, and one in 10 years. As an example, the contour line shown at the 50-year level means that, based upon past history, the statistical prediction is that once every 50 years the water level will come to the level of the contour line shown on the map.

The report contained a number of recommendations. It urged that, by the use of zoning, restrictions be placed upon land most frequently flooded. Lackawanna is authorized to enact these ordinances, but has not done so as yet. The report strongly urged that flood plain areas be used for park or recreation, without the construction of expensive buildings. Some of the older residences in Lackawanna were constructed below the 50-year level and a few as low as the 10-year level.

During the testimony, there was reference to the Martin Road area flood problem. Martin Road itself is at a higher level than the Creek and well removed from any flooding area. Since the K.P.H.A. subdivision abuts Martin Road to the south, the north branch is not of particular concern to us. The land of the proposed subdivision drains from Martin Road in a southwesterly direction and eventually to the south branch. There is a ditch located in the southwesterly portion of the subdivision recently deepened and widened by the Corps of Engineers. This ditch facilitates the drainage of this subdivision and also provides drainage for the Ludel subdivision, which is generally to the east and on the other side of the Baltimore and Ohio tracks which run along the easterly side of the K.P.H.A. subdivision. The lands lying to the south and west of the subdivision are open fields dropping off gently to the south branch.

Some sublots, generally in the Southwestern part of the K.P.H.A. subdivision, lie within the contour of the 100-year projected flood area. There were five sublots also within the 50-year area. The site engineer for the Federal Housing Administration, in determining whether or not this area was suitable for a subdivision, considered the flood plain report and the improvements made and proposed by the Corps of Engineers. He determined that, if fill was provided in certain other areas and required standards met, the land was feasible for the construction of the proposed subdivision. Based upon the F.H.A. investigation, the plaintiffs received a letter of feasibility from the F.H.A. on March 18, 1969. By this letter, the F.H.A. states that financing assistance will be available for residential construction on this site if K.P.H.A. meets F.H.A. standards.

EVENTS LEADING UP TO THE PASSAGE OF THE OCTOBER, 1968 ORDINANCES

Other Recently Approved Subdivisions

As population statistics in 1966 indicate, there exists in the City of Lackawanna a *de facto* separation of the races. Almost all of the Negro population of the City lives within the first ward, while the population of the second and third wards is almost completely white. The population of the third ward has increased in recent years while the population of the first ward has decreased. One reason for this increased white population in the third ward is the number of subdivisions approved in Lackawanna's third ward from 1963 to 1967. A catalog of recently approved third ward subdivisions, derived from the official records of the Erie County Health Department, appears below:

1. *Willett Park Subdivision:* Sanitary 5 form signed by mayor; approved by Erie County Health Department July 16, 1963—68 lots.

2. *Pacific Subdivision:* Sanitary 5 form signed by mayor; approved by Erie County Health Department July 16, 1964—18 lots.

3. *Autumn Acres Subdivision:* Sanitary 5 form signed by the mayor; approved by Erie County Health Department July 23, 1965—138 lots.

4. *Burke Subdivision:* Sanitary 5 form signed by mayor; approved by the the Erie County Health Department September 9, 1965—7 lots.

5. *Meadowbrook Subdivision, Part 3:* Sanitary 5 form signed by mayor; approved by the Erie County Health Department April 20, 1965—11 lots.

6. *Smith Subdivision:* Sanitary 5 form signed by mayor; approved by the Erie County Health Department on February 2, 1965—52 lots.

7. *Majestic Acres Subdivision:* Sanitary 5 form signed by mayor; approved by the Erie County Health Department February 3, 1967—27 lots.

The records of the Buffalo Office of the Federal Housing Administration indicate the existence of the following additional subdivisions in Lackawanna's third ward, even though there is no reference to such subdivisions in the Lackawanna records or Erie County Health Department records:

1. *Abbott Heights Subdivision* (Edison Street). Subdivision deemed not feasible on April 7, 1964—32 lots.

2. *Ludel Subdivision* (Ludel Terrace and Sander Drive). Subdivision deemed not feasible January 8, 1964 but houses are in fact being constructed in the subdivision—83 lots.

It is also important to note the number of construction permits for residential units issued by the City in the third ward from 1964 to 1968. There were 129 permits issued in 1964, 163 in 1965, 108 in 1966, 84 in 1967, and 61 in 1968.

First Moratorium Resolution passed by the City Council on May 15, 1967

At a meeting of the City Council on May 15, 1967, Resolution 98 was moved by then Councilman (now Mayor) Balen and carried unanimously. It directed the Department of Development and Engineering to refuse to issue building permits in new subdivisions already approved and to refuse to approve any new subdivision applications. Four reasons were given by the Council for the passage of this resolution: (1) The existence of many newly approved subdivisions and streets in the third ward; (2) The constant flooding and sewer backups; (3) The present inadequacy of the sewer system; and (4) Certain new third ward subdivisions which were planned. (This ordinance was enacted long before discussions began about the proposed K.P.H.A. subdivision.)

On the same day, May 15, 1967, in addition to moving Resolution 98, Mr. Balen also requested the City Attorney to draw up an ordinance waiving the zoning ordinance to permit Frank Cipriani to build a multiple dwelling at Abbott and Pacific. This intersection is in the third ward, not far from the Martin Road area. The ordinance was adopted by the Council in August, 1967, vetoed by the mayor, and later, on motion of Mr. Balen, the mayor's vote was overridden. Because of difficulty of financing, Mr. Cipriani was not able to build the multiple dwelling desired.

At a City Council meeting on August 21, 1967, Resolution No. 112 was passed unanimously rescinding the May 15, 1967 moratorium resolution. The premises of this resolution were an improved sewer situation and a directive by the Council to the Engineering Department to make a sewer study. In rescinding the prior moratorium resolutions, the Council went on record admonishing against the approval of new subdivisions in the flood areas. At that meeting, even though the resolution rescinding the moratorium was passed unanimously. Councilman Balen asked for a legal opinion on the moratorium concept.

Entered in the minutes of the City Council meeting of September 18, 1967 was the opinion of the City Attorney, Nicholas Haragos, concerning the moratorium resolution passed on May 15, 1967. His opinion was that the May 15, 1967 moratorium was an illlegal "taking" of property because it inhibited the issuance of building permits in already approved subdivisions. The treatment was unequal because it disadvantaged owners of property in subdivisions by barring them from receiving permits, while allowing adjacent property owners to obtain them.

Other Events Occurring in 1967 Which Are Part of the Background of the Passage of the October, 1968 Ordinances

The October 19, 1967 minutes of the C.P.C.P.O. reflect the concern of the members about the demolition of housing in the first ward and the need for relocation plans. Mr. Colello, then Director of Development, attended that meeting and told the members that, in his opinion, no builders would build homes for them in the third ward.

At the October 23, 1967 meeting of the Planning and Development Board, Patrick Kane discussed the housing problem. He explained that, in order to provide proper housing for all of the residence of Lackawanna, it was necessary to use a variety of structures—single-family dwellings, town houses, garden apartments, and apartment dwellings. He pointed out that it was not possible to have only single-family dwellings because of the cost of land, the need to have certain densities of population so that the services of schools, parks, and stores could be properly provided, and the necessity to provide for residents of all ages and economic backgrounds. He told them that housing should be discouraged in areas of the City where the adverse effects of smoke, noise, or congestion could not be abated.

Because of these factors, special attention was required for the planning of housing in the first ward. He discussed the first ward situation in the following way:

> "Now why do we even want to put houses in the first ward again. They are not going to be as good there as they are going to be somewhere else. One reason is because it's a transitional neighborhood, a starter neighborhood. There [sic] people that live there can't afford to live somewhere else until they can get enough money to move. Or maybe because of the race issue. Again you can't live in the past on that issue because we have laws that are doing something about that every day. So if we think there is going to be a barrier against race across that railroad track, we may as well forget planning altogether."

He explained to them that, with the use of federal funds, old patterns of living had to change. He said:

> "An implied subject in all of this discussion we have had here, if we talk about changing the second ward, do you know how we are going to do it. We are going to do it with some kind of federal aid I'll guarantee you that and you know what that's going to mean. It's going to mean that that bridge has been broken and it's not going to be any one man holding any other man back from buying a home. We will never advertise this at a meeting because that's a dangerous approach to the general population just as saying that we are only going to build public housing. You don't say things like that publicly."

Emmett Wright, Chairman of the C.P.C.P.O. Housing Committee, spoke at the meeting. He told the board that the first ward Negro desired to move out of the first ward and acquire a single-family residence.

As early as December, 1967, the minutes of the C.P.C.P.O. reflect that Harold Thornton, a professional housing consultant, had been contacted by the organization to assist it in its efforts to obtain housing in the third ward. At the November 2, 1967 meeting of the C.P.C.P.O., a survey was taken to determine how many people would be interested in purchasing homes in a third ward subdivision development.

Early 1968 Events

In early January, 1968, representatives of the C.P.C.P.O. visited Frank Cipriani to inquire about city-owned land which may be available for sub-division development. Cipriani, who had been in office but a few days, replied that he knew of no city-owned land available at that time, but that he would investigate to see if such land eixsted. In a letter dated January 23, 1968, and before Cipriani responded to the inquiries of the C.P.C.P.O.

representatives, that organization offered to purchase 74 contiguous lots in the second ward near Electric and Van Wick Streets. The C.P.C.P.O. was later informed that their offer had been tabled by the City Council for study.

During this period, a group of ministers visited Mayor Balen to discuss with him the offer to purchase. The mayor told them that he thought that such purchases could only be completed after a public bid, but told them he would look into it. They heard nothing further from him.

During the same time period, newly-installed officers of the City of Lackawanna approached Attorney Kevin Kennedy about the City's possible acquisition of diocesan land in the Martin Road area. The first meeting occurred on January 8, 1968, with Frank Cipriani and other City officials present. Kennedy at that time informed them that there was presently no land for sale. He explained that the land around Martin Road was reserved for church use. Later in January, 1968, a second meeting in Kevin Kennedy's office was held concerning the City's proposed purchase of Martin Road land. Present at that meeting were Cipriani and Mayor Balen. Kennedy repeated his "no sale" position, but said he would let the City know if the Diocese should change its mind and decide to offer any of the Martin Road land for sale. At the previous meeting, Kennedy had suggested a short term lease of land north of Martin Road for the purpose of erecting a playground, but this suggestion was unacceptable to Mayor Balen.

In the early part of 1968, the Planning and Development Board was told that it would have to finally approve the comprehensive plan as soon as possible. At a meeting of the board on January 23, 1968, Mr. Kane explained to the new board members the nature of a comprehensive plan and summarized what had been accomplished to date on the Lackawanna plan. In January and February of 1968, five new members were appointed by Mayor Balen to the Planning and Development Board. After these appointments, there were four members of the board from the third ward, three from the second ward, none from the first ward, and no black members.

Another meeting of the Planning and Development Board was held on February 1, 1968. Mr. Kane made a further explanation of the past work of the board and explained to them the three alternative land use plans which the prior board had considered. In speaking to them about the first ward, he said:

> "The Negro has indicated tremendous concern about his suspected confinement to the first ward. At almost every one of the Planning Board meetings, collectively they have stated they do not feel that any residential use should be allowed to remain in the first ward. In piercing through what they say, what they really mean is don't keep us in the first ward, let us live where our income or our desires allow us. You have a tremendous pressure building up in your community on the part of the non-whites to go across the bridge."

On February 15, 1968, the new Planning Board took under consideration the three alternative land use plans submitted by Kane for approval as the final plan. These were the same alternatives considered by the former board. Each of these alternative plans designated the area south of Martin Road and east of the proposed McKinley extension as "residential-low density." Each designated some or all of the area south of Martin Road and west of the proposed McKinley extension as recreation space.

The basic difference in the various alternatives was the use of areas in the first ward. Alternative "A" preserves residential use in the area south of Ridge Road in the first ward, including Bethlehem Park. It eliminates, however, any residential use of the area north of Ridge Road in the first ward. Alternative "B" completely eliminates the first ward as an area for residential use. Alternative "C" provides for the continued residential use of the area in the first ward south of Ridge Road, but not including Bethlehem Park.

At the meeting of February 15, 1968, the Planning and Development Board generally approved Alternative "C" with certain modifications. The prior Planning and Development Board had approved Alternative "C" without modification. The modifications to Alternative "C" devised by the new board are: (1) First Ward: The retention of Bethlehem Park as a residential area and a stated preference for as many single-family dwellings as possible in areas previously designated medium density residential use; (2) Second Ward: High density residential area eliminated around commercial and governmental complex and, again, as many single-family homes as possible; and (3) Third Ward: The board expressed some doubt about consultant's intention with respect to the Ridgewood Village area, presently designated medium density area. Whatever his plans were, however, they went on record as preferring single-family dwellings. In addition, the board thought that the area in the Martin Road area designated in Alternative "C" for a possible school site and open space is "too large for open space or park area." They decided to leave this question open for future discussion.

At the March 12, 1968 meeting of the Planning and Development Board, the results of the February 15 meeting were reviewed and Mr. Kane presented Alternative "D" which, he represented, was a reflection of Alternative "C" with the modifications approved by the board of February 15. Mr. Kane noted that he had originally proposed increasing the City's population from 28,000 to 36,000. Alternative "D", by reducing densities, anticipated a population of 31,000 or 32,000. He again told them that their emphasis upon single-family homes for most of Lackawanna residents was not practical or desirable, since this would eventually cause a decline in population, a lower tax base, and a housing shortage for residents who do not need, or cannot afford, a single-family home.

The minutes of the March 28, 1968 meeting of the Planning and Development Board reflect that the board did not want Alternative "D" suggested by Mr. Kane. Alternative "D" did not propose the area north of Ridge Road in the first ward for a residential purpose. The board adopted a

946 RECENT DEVELOPMENTS IN EXCLUSIONARY ZONING

resolution approving Alternative "C" with the following modifications. In the first ward, it desired the continued residential use of Bethlehem Park and the use of the area north of Ridge Road for commercial purpose with some residential use, preferably apartments. In the second and third wards, it wanted the high residential density to be eliminated. In these wards, the board wanted single and two-family homes, with three and four-family apartments only when necessary to obtain a population of about 31,000.

At the same meeting, the board discussed rumors about the Martin Road property owned by the Diocese of Buffalo. Several members heard that the Diocese planned to sell this property to an organization for low income housing. The board directed Cipriani to conduct an inquiry regarding these rumors. Following the board's direction, Cipriani sent a letter to Kevin Kennedy about this matter.

In mid-March, 1968, the C.P.C.P.O. met with Attorney Kevin Kennedy concerning the sale of Martin Road property for the proposed subdivision. Shortly thereafter, on March 23, 1968, members of the C.P.C.P.O. incorporated K.P.H.A. as a housing or mortgagor company. In April, 1968, Buffalo and Lackawanna newspapers reported the proposed sale of Martin Road property by the Diocese to K.P.H.A.

In April, 1968, a petition was circulated in the third ward opposing the sale of land by the Diocese on the basis that the proposed housing would be "low income" housing. Another petition with 3,000 signatures was sent to Bishop McNulty of the Diocese, opposing the sale of the land "due to lack of schools and inadequate sewers." That petition carried the names of the incumbent mayor, the then president of the City Council, and the incumbent president of the City Council. Mayor Balen explained at trial that he did not sign the petition but that, in all likelihood, his wife did.

A meeting was held in Ridgewood Village in the third ward for the purpose of protecting the proposed subdivision. As the opposition mounted to the proposed subdivision, the newspapers covered the events in detail. One group particularly opposed to it was the third ward group known as "Taxpayers Interested in Civil Affairs" (known as TICA). A leader in the TICA organization was Henry Starzynski, who sent a strident letter to the Lackawanna Leader adamantly opposing the proposed sale to K.P.H.A.[1]

---

1. "Frank E. Hollins, Publisher
Lackawanna Leader
Dear Mr. Hollins:
    I wish to alert the citizenry of all the suburban areas within the geographical tangents of the 'Roman Catholic Diocese of Buffalo' to a problem so grave, with ultimate ramifications so serious as to directly jeopardize the very existence of our finest suburban communities. Residents of West Seneca, Cheektowaga, Lancaster, Amherst, Orchard Park and Hamburg should take particular note.
    As a 'Roman Catholic' I am appalled, shocked and ashamed of the arrogant, ruthless, viciously totalitarian powers assumed and exerted by Bishop McNulty and the Hierarchy of the Roman Catholic Diocese of Buffalo.

Human Rights Commission Activity in Face of Growing Concern about Proposed Subdivision

Because of the mounting opposition to the Kennedy subdivision in the third ward, and because of the possible racial overtones that lie behind this opposition, Emil Cohen, a Commissioner of the New York State Human Rights Division, requested Stanley Gworek, the Chairman of the Lackawanna Human Rights Commission, to hold special meetings to discuss the problems generated by the proposed construction of the third ward subdivision by the C.P.C.P.O. As a result of the State Commissioner's request to the Lackawanna Human Rights Commission, Chairman Gworek arranged to meet with TICA and other concerned white citizens and also to meet with the C.P.C.P.O. to discuss the problems facing the community as a result of the rumored subdivision.

On April 10, 1968, Gworek, together with Cohen, met with the TICA group and, during the course of this meeting, heard the people voice their concern over the sewer situation, the need for new schools, and their interest in protecting their property values which they thought would diminish if low income housing was constructed in the third ward. Cohen pointed out that there were practical and legal methods of insuring that

---

It has now become apparent that the Bishop and the Catholic Hierarchy have embarked on a calculated scheme to physically alter our choice suburban communities and thereby promote their religiously oriented philosophies while the unsuspecting property owners of these areas will be compelled to suffer the inherent agonizing consequences.

The first phase of an apparent Diocesan master plan is to be instituted on a Catholic Diocese tract of land on Martin Road in Lackawanna, where an integrated, low-cost housing development is to be injected. This low-cost housing development would be immediately adjacent to a developed area with homes and property presently valued at from $20,000 to $60,000.

The already overburdened taxpayers throughout our far-flung suburbs may well be faced with additional skyrocketed taxes inherent with these concentrated developments.

Zoning laws may well become flexible when strained by the 'men of the cloth.'

The Diocesan attorney, Mr. Kevin Kennedy has made various vain attempts to white-wash the dark consequences of this critical problem.

I urge all property owners throughout the Western New York suburban areas to evaluate their own position in relation to this potential danger.

It appears apparent that the Catholic Hierarchy of the Buffalo Diocese has joined the ranks of the many irresponsible politicians in this "give-away" ideology who are attempting to placate the shamelessly immoral, savagely violent groups who are rioting, burning and killing their way into a hideously shameful page of our nation's history.

These 'give-away' programs are tearing at the very fabric of our Nation's economy and our country's very existence, while the decent, toiling, tax-paying white and colored Americans alike are forced to pay the expenses of certain unscrupulous politicians and certain clergy as well.

HENRY PAUL STARZYNSKI
Lackawanna"

the high quality environment in the third ward neighborhoods would be maintained even if the first ward group constructed homes in the third ward. He suggested that restrictive covenants could be attached to the land, requiring certain minimum values on all houses to be constructed in a particular neighborhood. He ventured the opinion that the first ward people who wished to move to the third ward would be equally as concerned with schools and sewers as the people in the third ward present at the meeting. One man at the meeting interjected that "the Negro in the third ward have been accepted [sic] without incident and a grand scale integration now instead of the gradual way now being down [sic] will only cause more unrest and misunderstanding." At the end of this meeting, it was agreed that another meeting would be scheduled later in conjuction with the first ward group, at which representatives of both sides would meet and exchange their views.

The meeting with the first ward group was held on April 24, 1968 and again Gworek and Cohen conducted the meeting. Cohen briefly summarized the attitudes of the third ward group expressed at the first meeting. He stated that they were concerned with sewers, schools, and housing values. He noted that, "if these are the only objections to the sale of the land, we now have a common ground to begin." Harold Thornton, the K.P.H.A. consultant, acted as spokesman for the first ward group expressing their attitudes toward moving to the third ward and the recently evidenced opposition to this move. He referred to rumored threats of violent action if first ward families attempted to move to the third ward, but assured that arrangements had already been made through the Justice Department and the Attorney General's office if these threats had any basis in fact. He suggested a series of meetings be set up to orient both groups on the common problems of living together in the same community. As to the sewer problem, Thornton noted that the mayor's budget had some provisions for sewers in this area, but that further improvement had been hindered because of a personality conflict between the present administration and the City Council. As in the first meeting, it was agreed that another meeting would be held where representatives of this group would meet with representatives of the third ward group to discuss their problems.

On April 29, 1968, Emil Cohen wrote Stanley Gworek inquiring about the present prospects for the third meeting between the two groups. Apparently this meeting was never held.

On June 25 and 26, 1968, Gworek, with other members of the Lackawanna Human Rights Commission, traveled to New York City to discuss the K.P.H.A. plans with officials of the Department of Housing and Urban Development. This New York City meeting was arranged at least partially by Harold Thornton, acting for the K.P.H.A. At the New York City meeting, the anticipated Fair Housing Act of 1968 was discussed. He testified that he intended to return to Lackawanna and "prepare the parties involved for the inevitability of the action which seemed to * * * confront (Lackawanna) city officials with the things which were going to happen based on the new federal law * * *" He reported the results of the meeting to Councilmen DePasquale and Wodzinski.

However, Richard Easley, the president of C.P.C.P.O., and other members of that organization apparently misunderstood the reason why the Lackawanna Human Rights Commission had traveled to New York to meet with the HUD officials. Robert Pino, the Negro member of the Lackawanna Human Rights Commission, was chastised by Easley and others for meddling in C.P.C.P.O. affairs. The fact is, however, that the K.P.H.A. consultant, Harold Thornton, arranged the meeting and asked the members of the Lackawanna Human Rights Commission to attend.

April and May Meetings of the Planning and Development Board

On April 25, 1968, the Planning and Development Board met again. In speaking about the area north of Ridge Road in the first ward Mr. Kane informed the board that it would be "very hard to develop any kind of rational [sic] to support * * * (their) recommendation of residential use in this area." He pointed out to them that the part of that area which was available for residential use was too small and, furthermore, since Ridge Road was heavily traveled, it separated the north side from the rest of the area. After discussion, the board refused to follow Kane's advice and adhered to their former decision.

On May 1, 1968, Mr. Kane met again with the board. He attempted once more to persuade them not to use the area north of Ridge Road for residential purposes. The board was warned that private developers would refuse to build there, that housing would deteriorate, and that the land available was too small to provide the citizens there with necessary services needed for a residential neighborhood. In spite of that, the board again insisted that residential use, preferably apartments, be made of this area.

Meetings of the Zoning Board of Appeals and the Planning and Development Board

On January 17, 1968, the District Director of the Corps of Engineers wrote a letter to municipal officers in Erie County, including Lackawanna, explaining that the Corps had completed a flood plain information report for the area and offering assistance to communities in developing flood plain regulations.

Later, when the rumors started to circulate about the sale of the Diocesan land to K.P.H.A., Mr. Cipriani called a joint meeting of the Zoning Board of Appeals and the Planning and Development Board on April 20, 1968.

At a meeting of the Lackawanna Zoning Board of Appeals held on May 7, 1968, Mr. Cipriani discussed the Smokes Creek flood plain study and gave a copy of it to each member of the board. Mr. Cipriani pointed out to the board that "this report makes definite reference to the land on Martin Road and at the present time we are having quite a problem with this area. * * * They (Corps of Engineers) would prefer to see the flood plain areas developed for recreation * * *" He asked the members to read the report so that it could be discussed at a later meeting. It should be noted that Martin Road itself is well out of the flood plain area, and only the southwest part of the K.P.H.A. subdivision is within any part of the flooding zone.

On June 11, 1968, another joint meeting of the two boards was held. A Corps of Engineers representative explained the flood plain report in detail to the members.

Actions of the Planning and Development Board Immediately Prior to the City Council's Passage of the October, 1968 Ordinances.

As a result of the joint meeting held on June 11, 1968, Mr. Cipriani was instructed to request Edward Kuwik, the Chief Engineer of Lackawanna, to prepare a sewer study for the Martin Road area. At an August 1, 1968 meeting of the Planning and Development Board, Kuwik's response was to make available the March, April, and May, 1968 report prepared by Thaddeus Pieczonka, the Chief Chemist, which was distributed for consideration by members of the board.

Two meetings were held on August 20, 1968. The first was a special meeting of the Planning and Development Board called to consider the map prepared by Mr. Kane, which showed the land use proposal for the north of Ridge Road area. The sketch proposed that 15.9 acres be set aside for residential use. The board gave its final approval to that proposal.

This meeting was followed by a joint meeting of the Zoning Board of Appeals and the Planning and Development Board. Also present at that meeting were the City Clerk, Gerald DePasquale, and the Chief Chemist, Thaddeus Pieczonka. Cipriani stated that the meeting was called for the special purpose of discussing the acute sewer conditions existing in the southeast portion of the second and third wards of the City of Lackawanna. Noting that the board members had been given a copy of the March, April, and May, 1968 report of Mr. Pieczonka, Mr. Pieczonka was requested to interpret it. Mr. Pieczonka explained in detail how the sewer lines in this area became overloaded, causing either cellar backups or overflows of sewage into Smokes Creek. He informed them that, if the creek pollution was not corrected, the City would lose $55,000 a year in state financial aid. He recommended to the board a comprehensive sewer study, the separation of storm and sanitary sewers, the elimination of roof leaders from the sanitary system, televising of certain sewers to find obstructions, and the construction of a 24-inch sewer line from Abbott Road directly to the Wilmuth Pumping Station. He told the board that, in his opinion, it was most doubtful that the Erie County Department of Health would approve a subdivision application in an area where the City was bypassing raw sewage into a stream.

The first motion made at this meeting was to direct a communication to the City Council recommending that the Council hire a consulting engineer to make a study of the sewer problems in the entire southern part of the second and third wards of the City. This motion was passed unanimously.

No action was taken on Mr. Pieczonka's other recommendations. Instead, Mr. Cipriani initiated discussion about discouraging development in this area until the sewer problem was resolved. Pieczonka responded that, if both boards were going to go on record discouraging development in this area, that area should be defined as the southeast part of the second and third wards to the City Line of Lackawanna. A motion was then made that the joint boards issue a moratorium on all new subdivisions until such time as the sewer problems abated. This motion was carried unanimously.

Cipriani then initiated further discussion concerning the possible rezoning of the southeast portion of the second and third wards for the purpose of park and recreation. He pointed out that this suggestion would fill a two-fold need: (1) It would provide for the much needed park space in one of the last vacant areas in Lackawanna; and (2) It would insure against the worsening of sewer problems and the Smokes Creek flooding problems. In addition, the members discussed the flood plain report prepared by the Corps of Engineers. A motion was then made to recommend that the City Council rezone a portion of the area described by Mr. Pieczonka for recreation. The motion reads as follows:

> "* * * [T]he Zoning Board of Appeals and the Planning and Development Board recommend to the City Council that any and all vacant open land situated within the following boundary—south of the north branch of Smokes Creek, bounded by the B & O tracks on the east, on the south by the city line at Willett Road and on the west by South Park Avenue approximately 1,000 feet east of South Park Avenue, be designated for open space or park area."

The motion was passed unanimously.

When he testified, Mr. Pieczonka described the problem area as all of the southern part of the second and third wards south of the north branch of Smokes Creek, extending from South Park Avenue on the west to the city line on the east. The area encompassed by the board's resolution is much smaller than that described by Mr. Pieczonka. The area in the resolution did not include any part of the second ward or any part of the third ward east of the Baltimore and Ohio tracks.

Meetings with HUD about Sewers

Harold Thornton arranged a meeting in New York for Lackawanna and HUD officials to discuss the availability of federal assistance for

Lackawanna sewers. Although a number of Lackawanna officeholders went to New York on September 11, 1968, the day of the meeting, many of them did not attend. Mr. Cipriani and some members of the Council went, but neither Mayor Balen nor John O'Connor, City Engineer of Lackawanna, did. Mr. O'Connor explained his absence by saying that the City did not want to appear "totally committed." Mr. O'Connor's supervisor, Edward Kuwik, Chief Engineer, went but left before the meeting was over. Pieczonka and an Assistant City Attorney were not informed of the correct meeting time and, when they arrived, the meeting was almost finished.

On September 18, 1968, HUD officials inspected the Lackawanna treatment plant in Mr. Pieczonka's company. However, the conversation centered upon moneys available for secondary treatment. Mr. Pieczonka could not recall any discussion about the Martin Road problem.

October 1968 Ordinances: Their Passage and Rescission

The City Council, on October 7, 1968, heard a first reading of the rezoning and moratorium resolutions. The zoning ordinance[2] designated

---

2.
ZONING ORDINANCE AMENDMENT
CITY OF LACKAWANNA
BE IT ENACTED by the City Council of the City of Lackawanna, New York, as follows:

The Zoning Ordinances of the City of Lackawanna adopted by the Common Council on September 7, 1937 and all ordinances amendatory thereto and the Building Zone Map of the City of Lackawanna are amended as follows:

The following described area is hereby designated as an area exclusively designated for parks and recreation:

BEING ALL OF LOTS 435, 434, 433 AND PARTS OF LOTS 352, 353, 354, 355, 432, 431, 40 and 429, ALL BEING IN T. 10, R. 7 OF THE BUFFALO CREEK RESERVATION.

BEGINNING AT A POINT IN THE CENTER LINE OF THE NORTH BRANCH OF SMOKES CREEK WHERE IT INTERSECTS WITH THE WEST LINE OF GREAT LOT 352, TOWNSHIP 10, RANGE 7, THENCE RUNNING SOUTHERLY ALONG THE WEST LINE OF GREAT LOTS 352 AND 435, TOWNSHIP 10, RANGE 7 TO THE CENTER LINE OF WILLET ROAD, THENCE EASTERLY ALONG THE CENTER LINE OF WILLET ROAD TO THE WEST LINE OF THE NEW YORK STATE THRUWAY, THENCE RUNNING NORTHERLY ALONG THE NEW YORK STATE THRUWAY TO THE WEST LINE OF THE B. & O. RAILROAD, THENCE RUNNING NORTHWESTERLY ALONG THE WEST LINE OF THE B & O RAILROAD TO THE CENTER LINE OF NORTH BRANCH OF SMOKES CREEK, THENCE RUNNING WEST ALONG THE CENTER LINE OF THE NORTH BRANCH OF SMOKES CREEK TO THE WEST LINE OF GREAT LOT 352, TOWNSHIP 10, RANGE 7, THE POINT OR PLACE OF BEGINNING.

If any section, subsection, sentence, clause or phrase of this ordinance amendment is, for any reason, held to be invalid, such decision shall not affect the validity of the remaining portions of this ordinance.

The City Council hereby declares that it would have passed this ordinance amendment and each section, subsection, clause and phrase thereof, irrespective of the fact

an area in the third ward exclusively for parks and recreation. This area, smaller than that proposed by the Planning and Development Board, was in the third ward south of the north branch of Smokes Creek. However, it included the area where the K.P.H.A. subdivision was located, but excluded the area covered by Majestic Acres subdivision which was approved in 1966, and where sublots were still available for construction.

The second ordinance [3] created an indefinite moratorium on the ap-

---

that any one or more sections, subsections, sentences, clauses or phrases be declared invalid.

THIS ORDINANCE SHALL TAKE EFFECT IMMEDIATELY.
Dated: Lackawanna, New York
October 7, 1968
APPROVED:
/s/ MARK L. BALEN
MARK L. BALEN, Mayor
3.

ZONING ORDINANCE AMENDMENT
CITY OF LACKAWANNA

WHEREAS, the present sewer facilities, including the treatment facilities of the City of Lackawanna have been and are overtaxed, and

WHEREAS, the said facilities are in need of improvement, repair and maintenance because of such use, mandated requirements recently enacted by the state authorities, and

WHEREAS, the said need has principally occurred because of the growth of the City of Lackawanna, demand by the Buffalo Sewer Authority to provide its own sewer facilities, besides compliance with additional state requirements, and

WHEREAS, because of such circumstances, raw sewage is being discharged instead of being properly treated, thereby creating further menace to the public health, safety and welfare, and

WHEREAS, it appears provident and imperative that new housing, particularly new subdivisions, be restrained until these sewer facilities of the said City of Lackawanna are improved so as to meet present and future needs safely, thereby maintaining the health, welfare and safety of the public, therefore,

BE IT ENACTED by the City Council of the City of Lackawanna, New York as follows:

SECTION 1. That a state of emergency exists in the City of Lackawanna with respect to this problem which makes it imperative that this ordinance shall become effective forthwith.

SECTION 2. No approval of new subdivisions will be granted until this state of emergency terminates in the best interest of the city.

SECTION 3. All existing ordinances, orders, rules and regulations of the City of Lackawanna are hereby repealed insofar as they may be inconsistent with the provisions of this Ordinance.

SECTION 4. It is the intention of the City Council that each separate provision of this Ordinance shall be deemed independently of all other provisions herein, and

SECTION 5. It is further the intention of the City Council that if any provisions of this Ordinance be declared invalid, all other provisions shall remain valid and enforceable.
Dated: Lackawanna, New York,
October 7, 1968.
APPROVED:
/s/ MARK L. BALEN
MARK L. BALEN, Mayor

proval of new subdivisions because of the sewer problem. On October 14, 1968, a public hearing was held on the two ordinances. On October 21, 1968, the City Council read and voted final passage of both ordinances and they were signed into law by defendant, Mayor Mark L. Balen. The subdivision moratorium ordinance imposed a ban only on the approval of new subdivisions and had no effect on Majestic Acres, which was only half complete at the time of the passage of the ordinance. In addition, this ordinance did not have any effect on single-family residential construction proceeding in the third ward outside of subdivisions.

At the City Council meeting of October 24, 1968, the Council passed an ordinance expressing its desire to hire a sewer consultant to make a comprehensive study of the City's sewer problems. The City has not undertaken a study as yet pursuant to this resolution calling for a comprehensive sewer study.

At the October 24 meeting, the Council approved a resolution setting forth findings of fact and reasons for the adoption of the ordinances in the Martin Road area. Some of the reasons given were: (1) The sewage problems in the entire City, and in particular the third ward area; (2) That a recreation study recommended this area for a park and recreation; (3) That the Army Corps of Engineers has declared the area just south of this area as a flood land area; and (4) Because the Master Plan has earmarked this area for a recreation purpose.

On February 25, 1969 (after this lawsuit was commenced), the Council passed a resolution rescinding both the rezoning and the moratorium ordinances dated October 7, 1968. This rescission was to take effect immediately.

MAYOR'S REFUSAL TO SIGN SANITARY 5 FORM

Almost one year after the commencement of this lawsuit and approximately eight months after the City Council rescinded the October, 1968 ordinances, Mr. Will Gibson, attorney for K.P.H.A., C.P.C.P.O., and the two individual plaintiffs, sent a letter to John W. Condon, attorney for the defendants, requesting that a Sanitary 5 form and certain plans to construct a waste disposal system for the proposed subdivision be submitted to Mayor Balen for approval. On November 13, 1969, the Sanitary 5 form was forwarded to the mayor. The next day, all of the parties appeared in this court, and the court directed the Corporation Counsel for the City and defendants' counsel to advise the court within two weeks of the action taken by the mayor in regard to the Sanitary 5 form.

When Mayor Balen received the Sanitary 5 form, he contacted Mr. Vito Caruso from the consulting engineering firm of Nussbaumer & Clark and requested an opinion regarding the advisability of signing this Sanitary 5 form. Nussbaumer & Clark is a consulting engineering firm which has supervised sewer work for the City of Lackawanna for many years, and Mr. Caruso has been active in recent years in the Dorrance Avenue sewer project where the Lackawanna sewers are being disconnected from the Buffalo Sewer Authority. Although his knowledge of other sewers in Lackawanna was limited, within a week Mr. Caruso conducted a visual inspection of the Martin Road sewer situation, reviewed the Sanitary 5 form and the supporting data, and finally concluded that the sewers were inadequate for a new subdivision. He was not asked, nor did he consider, whether or not there was an alternative to an outright refusal to sign the Sanitary 5 form. He reported to the mayor that the sewers were inadequate for a new subdivision. The mayor refused to sign the Sanitary 5 form and this fact was reported in open court on November 28, 1969.

During this period another incident occurred which highlighted the fact that a "sewer crisis" was not the real reason for opposition to the K.P.H.A. undertaking. For a number of reasons, the Buffalo Baseball team was forced to terminate use of its Buffalo stadium. Because of this, during the fall of 1969 the Baseball Club was seeking a stadium to use for about five years, at which time it expected to be able to play in a new stadium.

Mayor Balen proposed to the Baseball Club that the Lackawanna Stadium on South Park Avenue be expanded, at a cost of about $500,000, to provide a temporary baseball park. This stadium is located about five and a half blocks from the K.P.H.A. site in the third ward and is part of the Lackawanna sewer system. The revamped stadium would accommodate about 7,000 additional patrons, but no thought was given to sewer problems or was Mr. Caruso ever consulted about it.

Mayor Balen made a special trip to New York to consult a bonding attorney. However, nothing came of these efforts since the proposal was defeated at a public referendum.

THE DISCRIMINATORY ACTIONS OF THE DEFENDANTS VIOLATED PLAINTIFFS' CONSTITUTIONAL AND STATUTORY RIGHTS

[1] The plaintiffs seek relief in this case by asserting causes of action under the Fourteenth Amendment (the Equal Protection Clause), the Civil Rights Act (42 U.S.C. § 1983), and the Fair Housing Act of 1968 (42 U.S.C. § 3601 et seq.). The cause of action created under each of these statutes or the amendment proscribes discriminatory conduct because of race or color.

[2,3] The Fair Housing Act of 1968 covers discriminatory conduct in fair housing situations by both public and private alleged wrongdoers. However, the nature of the discrimination proscribed under the Fair Housing Act is limited in that it does not include discrimination based on poverty. Under Section 1983 and the Fourteenth Amendment, the full range of discriminatory conduct is proscribed if, and only if, that action is taken by a party acting under color of state law. In other words, private discrimination is not actionable under Section 1983 and the Fourteenth Amendment.

Because this lawsuit deals specifically with an allegation of discrimination in housing based on race or color by wrongdoers acting under color of state law, the differences between the various sections and amendment are unimportant.

[4-6]   As long ago as Buchanan v. Warley, 245 U.S. 60, 38 S.Ct. 16, 62 L.Ed. 149 (1917), the Supreme Court pointed out that the Fourteenth Amendment does not allow conduct which results in racially discriminatory treatment, even though the purpose of the municipal action was to preserve the public peace and public welfare, a goal which represented a valid exercise of the police power.   Furthermore, a long line of cases in the Supreme Court dealing with equal protection of the laws has held that racial discrimination may be established either by proof of purpose or effect.   See Yick Wo v. Hopkins, 118 U.S. 356, 6 S.Ct. 1064, 30 L.Ed. 220 (1886) and, more recently, Reitman v. Mulkey, 387 U.S. 369, 87 S.Ct. 1627, 18 L.Ed.2d 830 (1967), and Hunter v. Erickson, 393 U.S. 385, 89 S.Ct. 557, 21 L.Ed.2d 616 (1969). "It is of no consolation to an individual denied the equal protection of the laws that it was done in good faith." Burton v. Wilmington Parking Authority, 365 U.S. 715, 725, 81 S.Ct. 856, 861, 6 L.Ed.2d 45 (1961).   Requirements which appear neutral on their face and theoretically apply to everyone, but have the inevitable effect of tying present rights to the discriminatory pattern of the past, are unlawful. United States v. Louisiana, 380 U.S. 145, 85 S.Ct. 817, 13 L.Ed.2d 709 (1965).   The official act may not place a special burden upon the minority.   Gaston County, N. C. v. United States, 395 U.S. 285, 89 S.Ct. 1720, 23 L.Ed.2d 309 (1969).

[7]   Judicial inquiry into the purpose or effect of governmental action is not limited to the moment that that action occurs.   Not only must the "immediate objective" of governmental action be considered, but the "historical context" and "ultimate effect" of such action must be considered as well.   Reitman v. Mulkey, *supra*.   The inquiry must further assess the "reality" of the "law's impact" and consider the "background" against which state action operates to determine that reality.   Hunter v. Erickson, *supra*.   Therefore, relevant to this inquiry are either past or prospective governmental actions which form a part of the background.

[8]   The history of Lackawanna is that of a racially separate community. Only a handful of blacks ever lived in the second or third ward.   The increased white population of the third ward is due substantially to the recently constructed subdivisions which were approved by the City over the last ten years.   These approvals were granted in spite of the City's awareness of the sewer problems and the desire of its citizens for increased park and recreation areas.   Private discriminatory conduct was well known to City officials.   The attempts by Negroes to move into the third ward are accompanied by instances of evasion and refusal by contractors, home owners, realtors, and subdividers.   In 1968, a more

dramatic example of the private sentiment against the proposed K.P.H.A. subdivision is the petition sent to Bishop McNulty.

The actions of the Planning and Development Board during 1968, taken independently and in conjunction with the Zoning Board of Appeals, and the consequent action of the City Council in October, 1968, indicate to the court that the Lackawanna City officials attempted to respond to the discriminatory sentiments of the community.

One example of this racially motivated response is the Planning and Development Board's demand that the area north of Ridge Road in the first ward be used partly for residential purposes. The prior Planning and Development Board followed the recommendation of the planner not to use this area for residences. However, in spite of the detailed warnings of Mr. Kane, the new board reversed the former position and determined that this area be used for residential purposes, preferably apartments. The result of this decision would be to accelerate the pattern of segregation. Of all of the alternatives presented to the Planning Board, the City chose the one which would minimize the first ward Negroes' opportunity to move to the better conditions of the third ward.

The evidence shows that the actions of the Planning and Development Board were taken specifically to block the K.P.H.A. subdivision. It was not until rumors began about the K.P.H.A. subdivision that the Planning and Development Board discussed the "sewer crisis" and the flood report, but their discussion and resolution of these problems show that they did not attempt to consider the facts developed in these reports in a rational manner but instead used both the "sewer crisis" and the flood report as clubs to defeat the K.P.H.A. proposal. At the same time, they were adopting the resolution which would keep population density levels low in the third ward—the best place to live—and high in the first—the worst place to live.

Discriminatory reasons guided the action of the City Council in its enactment of the October ordinances. It is true that the Council cited a number of reasons for their passage, but the main reasons given—sewer needs, park and recreation needs, and flooding problems—were clearly wrong on the facts and, under the circumstances, mere rationalization. For example, a finding that the park study specifically recommended this area rezoned as a park and recreation area is false. The fact is that the report of the N.R. & P.A. recommended only the area south of Martin Road and west of the proposed McKinley extension as a park area. The finding of fact that the original and the present Master Plan both earmarked the area known as "south of Martin Road" as a recreation area is false. The fact is that both plans and the supporting documents recommended the area south of Martin Road both for recreational and for residential purposes. The Master Plans and supporting reports recommended the area where K.P.H.A. wants to build a subdivision for a residential purpose.

Further, the mayor's action in refusing to sign the Sanitary 5 form, when considered in the "historical context," can only lead to the determination that his refusal was based upon discrimination. Admittedly, Mr. Caruso's knowledge of the sewers in this area was limited; his inspection was cursory, and no alternatives to refusal were requested or given.

Therefore, considering all of the evidence and especially the actions of the City in 1968 and 1969 in their historical context, the court concludes that the plaintiffs have met their burden of showing a denial of equal protection of the law. Affirmative acts were taken under color of law to inhibit the plaintiffs' constitutional and statutory rights.

Justification

[9] The defendants urge that the sewer crisis and the urgent need for park space justify the actions they took with respect to the proposed subdivision. However, the Supreme Court has held that, when the effect of a state action is to place upon a minority group a special burden or classification, the defendant has a heavy burden of justifying such action. It must show that it is necessary to serve a legitimate governmental interest. McLaughlin v. Florida, 379 U.S. 184, 196, 85 S.Ct. 283, 13 L.Ed.2d 222 (1964). It must also be shown that the governmental interest is compelling. Shapiro v. Thompson, 394 U.S. 618, 633-634, 89 S.Ct. 1322, 22 L.Ed.2d 600 (1969).

The defendants have failed to meet their burden of proof. First of all, they have never attempted to find out whether it was possible to deal with the sewer problems and park needs without infringing upon plaintiffs' rights. There were alternative courses of action which could have been taken in regard to both of these problems, which would have solved the City's needs and not impaired the rights of the plaintiffs.

There was no justification for rezoning this land for park purposes. The Planning and Development Board had designated it for residential use. No one recommended that it be used for park purposes either before or after the enactment of the ordinance.

In support of their position that the City Council was justified in rezoning the K.P.H.A. area for park and recreation space, the defendants called five recreation experts. The court affords little weight to their testimony. One of them, Mr. Noren, who participated with Mr. Buechner in the preparation of the N.R. & P.A. report and concurred in it, attempted to make a different site recommendation at trial. The other four were never consulted during 1968 before the enactment of the ordinance. Their sole function was to testify at trial. In each case, their recommendation was made considering only the park needs of the community without taking into account the other factors which Mr. Kane considered and discussed with Mr. Buechner.

[10]   The sewer problem did not justify the action taken by the Council in enacting the ordinance, or by the mayor in refusing to sign the Sanitary 5 form.   There is no question that preserving the environment and healthful living conditions in the community by providing adequate sewage collection is a legitimate governmental function, but the enactment of the subdivision moratorium was not necessary or compelling and, in fact, could not solve the sewer problem.

Neither the Planning and Development Board nor the Council discussed alternatives to the subdivision moratorium so that the sewer system could be improved and the subdivision completed.   For the most part, the board and Council ignored the recommendations made by the City's own expert, except for his suggestion to separate the roof leaders from the sanitary sewers, which work the City began only after the state threatened to cut off financial assistance.   They ignored other suggestions completely.

Many third ward and other residents of the City have complained about the sewers for at least the last ten years.   Nevertheless, during this period, the City continued to issue subdivision and building permits without facing up to a satisfactory solution to the sewer problem.   Defendants' lack of attention not only deprived the plaintiffs of an opportunity for housing, but all Lackawanna residents of an efficient sewer system.

Defendants Had a Duty to Consider and Affirmatively Plan for the Protection of Plaintiffs' Housing Rights

This court has already held that the facts warrant a finding that the acts of the defendants were a wilful contrivance to deprive plaintiffs of their housing rights.   That alone is sufficient to warrant relief to the plaintiffs, but it must be noted that some discrimination resulted from thoughtlessness or failure on the part of City officials to consider or plan for the housing needs of all Lackawanna residents.   The defendants may not escape responsibility by ignoring community needs or by failing to consider alternative solutions to city-wide problems.

If the plaintiffs are deprived of equal housing opportunity, the result is the same whether caused by open, purposeful conduct, by a subtle scheme, or by sheer neglect or thoughtlessness.   Adopting the language of Hobson v. Hansen, 269 F.Supp. 401, 497 (D.C., 1967), the Second Circuit, in Norwalk CORE v. Norwalk Redevelopment Agency, 395 F.2d 920, 931 (2d Cir.1968), held that

> " 'Equal protection of the laws' means more than merely the absence of governmental action designed to discriminate;* * * 'we now firmly recognize that the arbitrary quality of thoughtlessness can be as disastrous and unfair to private rights and the public interest as the perversity of a willful scheme.' "

In Southern Alameda Spanish Speaking Organization v. City of Union City, 424 F.2d 291, 295, 296 (9th Cir. 1970), the court held:

> " ° ° ° [I]t may well be, as matter of law, that it is the responsibility of a city and its planning officials to see that the city's plan as initiated or as it develops accommodates the needs of its low-income families, who usually—if not always—are members of minority groups."

The City officials in Lackawanna have the obligation to consider and plan for all of the citizens in the community. They have an obligation not only to plan for the sewer needs of the third ward citizens, but also the housing problem of the first. Industrial encroachment into former residential areas in the first ward which displaced people from their homes calls for as much attention as sewer backups in the third ward.

MISCELLANEOUS

[11] The court rejects the argument of the defendants that plaintiffs, C.P.C.P.O., K.P.H.A., the Diocese of Buffalo, and the individual plaintiffs, do not have standing to bring this suit. All plaintiffs have a personal stake in the outcome of this controversy. Baker v. Carr, 369 U.S. 186, 82 S.Ct. 691, 7 L.Ed.2d 663 (1962).

The court disregards as irrelevant the testimony of Peter Vinolus, attorney for the Lackawanna School Board, that the board is now considering acquiring the land to the west of the K.P.H.A. site for school purposes.

REMEDY

Because defendants' conduct has denied plaintiffs equal protection of the laws and the Constitution of the United States, and also the rights guaranteed by Title VIII of the Civil Rights Act of 1968, plaintiffs are entitled to relief. "We bear in mind that the court has not merely the power but the duty to render a decree which will so far as possible eliminate the discriminatory effects of the past as well as bar like discrimination in the future." United States v. Louisiana *supra*, 380 U.S. 154, 85 S.Ct. 822. Therefore, it is the order of this court:

1. That, within ten days after plaintiffs deliver the Sanitary 5 form with accompanying documents to the City of Lackawanna, it be executed by an appropriate official and forwarded to the Erie County Department of Health for future action.

2. That, if the Sanitary 5 form is disapproved by the Erie County Department of Health, defendants shall immediately take whatever action is necessary to provide adequate sewage service to the K.P.H.A. subdivision.

3. That defendants be enjoined from initiating steps to condemn, appropriate or otherwise acquire the Kennedy Park Subdivision site for use as park and recreation.

4. That defendants be enjoined from using any of the City's municipal powers regarding land use to prevent or interfere with the construction of Kennedy Park Subdivision.

5. That defendants affirmatively take whatever steps are necessary to allow the Kennedy Park Subdivision to begin construction.

6. That defendants be enjoined from issuing building permits for any construction in the second and third wards which will contribute additional sanitary sewage to the municipal system until Kennedy Park Subdivision has been granted permission to tap into the sewer system by the appropriate authority.

7. That defendants report to the court, the United States and the private plaintiffs what steps the City has taken to allow the connection of Kennedy Park Subdivision into the municipal sewer system; what problems they have encountered; and what they are doing about those problems. That, if appropriate and necessary, the court shall set a timetable for such reports.

8. That this court retain jurisdiction over this matter until Kennedy Park Homes Subdivision is completed.

9. That this court will defer consideration of the question of damage until a later date, to be fixed by order of the court.

The order of this court shall take effect immediately upon filing and service upon the attorney for the defendants. No stay of this judgment will be granted by this court pursuant to Rule 8(a) of the Federal Rules of Appellate Procedure.

So ordered.

SOUTHERN ALAMEDA
SPANISH SPEAKING ORGANIZATION

v.

UNION CITY

424 F.2d 291 (CA 9th, 1970), on remand, No. 51590, July 31, 1970

United States Court of Appeals,

Ninth Circuit.

March 16, 1970.

Action by Spanish-speaking organization for injunctive action directing city to implement zoning change permitting construction of federally financed housing project for low and moderate income families, notwithstanding city-wide referendum nullifying rezoning ordinance. The United States District Court for the Northern District of California, William T. Sweigert, J., denied motion for three-judge court and preliminary injunction and plaintiff appealed. The Court of Appeals, Merrill, Circuit Judge, held that contention that purpose and result of city-wide referendum was to discriminate racially and economically against Mexican-American residents and that result was to perpetuate discrimination within city against Mexican-American residents with low incomes did not require convening of three-judge court since validity of state law was not drawn in question and challenge was directed not against state's grant of power but against manner in which city had exercised power, notwithstanding that state statute provided for referendum.

Affirmed.

Richard F. Bellman and Lewis M. Steel (argued), New York City, Johnathan Rutledge, D'Army Bailey, Cruz Reynoso, San Francisco, Cal., Sol Rabken and Robert Carter, New York City, for appellants.

John V. Trump (argued), of Bell, Trump, Sheppard & Raymond, Fremont, Cal., for appellees.

Anthony J. Garcia, San Leandro, Cal. and Pete Tijerina, Mario Obledo, San Antonio, Tex., for Mexican-American Defense and Education Fund, Farber & McKelvey, Seymour Farber and Edwin Lukas, San Francisco, Cal., for American Jewish Congress and American Jewish Committee, amicus curiae.

Before MERRILL and KOELCSH, Circuit Judges, and TAYLOR, District Judge[*].

MERRILL, Circuit Judge:

The principal appellant, the Southern Alameda Spanish Speaking Organization (SASSO), was successful in obtaining the passage of a city ordinance rezoning a tract of land within Union City, California, to a multi-family residential category in order to permit the construction of a federally financed housing project for low and moderate income families. The ordinance was nullified almost immediately by a city-wide referendum. By this action appellants attack the referendum[1] and its results as infringing upon their constitutional rights under the due process and equal protection clauses of the Fourteenth Amendment, and seek injunctive action directing Union City to implement the zoning change notwithstanding the referendum.

In the District Court appellants sought, under 28 U.S.C. § 2281,[2] an order convening a three-judge court to entertain their constitutional claims. They also moved for a preliminary injunction directing Union City to put the

---

[*] Honorable Fred M. Taylor, United States District Judge for the District of Idaho, sitting by designation.

1. The original complaint was filed prior to the holding of the referendum and sought to enjoin the referendum itself. When appellants failed to secure that injunction, an amended and supplementary complaint was filed asserting the claim now presented.

2. 28 U.S.C. § 2281 provides:

"An interlocutory or permanent injunction restraining the enforcement, operation or execution of any State statute by restraining the action of any officer of such State in the enforcement or execution of such statute, or of an order made by an admin-

zoning changes into effect *pendente lite*. The District Court ruled against the appellants on both motions and that order is the subject of this appeal.

As incorporated in 1959 Union City combined two existing communities known as Decoto and Alvarado. The area was largely agricultural and the two communities were inhabited almost exclusively by Mexican-American residents.

Since incorporation Union City has absorbed residents both from Oakland to the north and San Jose to the south. The population has risen from about 6600 in 1960 to the current 14,000. During the same period the composition of the population has also changed; the Mexican-American percentage has declined from 55 per cent to about 35-40 per cent of the total.

A master plan for Union City was formally adopted in 1962, after public hearings. Under that plan, vacant land not then in use was generally zoned as agricultural, a "holding" classification subject to rezoning by city ordinance for urban use at the appropriate time. The plan did, however, anticipate future use and zoning. The land here in question (the "Baker Road Tract") was zoned agricultural under the plan but designated for purposes of rezoning as appropriate for single-family dwellings.

Since 1962, suburban pressures have created an increasing need for multi-family housing in Union City and several such units have already been accommodated through rezoning ordinances. These units have largely gone to meet the needs of new residents. The old residents of Decoto and Alvarado, due to limited incomes, have been unable to enjoy the housing so provided, and have had to remain in those districts, where a substantial portion of the housing is rated substandard. In 1967, city officials concerned with housing problems contracted with a consulting firm for a comprehensive study of local housing requirements. That study, still incomplete, has resulted in a number of recommendations and a draft master plan. The firm recommended that the city encourage housing projects for families with low and moderate incomes, sponsored by nonprofit corporations and financed through federal aid. The projected master plan designates the tract in question for multi-family dwellings. Although the 1962 plan has not been formally superseded, city officials have in large part accepted the firm's recommendations. They have informally abandoned the 1962 plan's designations of appropriate future use in favor of the updated designations regarded as more appropriate in light of the city's growth.

Appellant SASSO is qualified to sponsor federally assisted housing developments for low income persons and was organized for the purpose of improving housing and living conditions for the Spanish speaking people of Southern Alameda County. In December, 1968, it obtained an option to

---

istrative board or commission acting under State statute, shall not be granted by any district court or judge thereof, upon the ground of the unconstitutionality of such statute unless the application therefor is heard and determined by a district court of three judges under section 2284 of this title."

purchase the Baker Road tract, where it planned to construct a 280-unit medium density housing project. In accordance with this objective, SASSO applied to the City Planning Staff of Union City for rezoning. After appropriate studies, the Planning Staff recommended the application to the Planning Commission. Several months later the Planning Commission's recommendation for rezoning (medium density multi-family residential) was approved by the City Council after public hearings; an ordinance was passed on April 7, 1969.

The Baker Road tract is adjacent to several tracts of single-family homes. Opposition to the April 7 ordinance arose there and among other home owners; petitions seeking a referendum under § 4051, Cal. Elections Code,[3] were circulated and completed. Pursuant to § 4052, Cal.Elections Code,[4] the matter was submitted to the voters of Union City, who by a vote of 1149 to 845 rejected the ordinance. The referendum automatically restored the Baker Road tract to the agricultural holding category and the City Council was barred from rezoning the tract for medium density, multi-residential dwellings for a period of one year.

1. Police Power and Due Process

Appellants initially challenge the constitutionality of California's referendum procedures as applied to the zoning process. They contend that "referendum zoning" violates due process requirements.

The rights asserted are those of a landowner (SASSO) [5] to be free from arbitrary restrictions on land use. Appellants assert that regulation of land use by zoning is constitutionally permissible only where procedural safeguards assure that the resulting limitations have been determined, by legislatively promulgated standards, to be in the interest of public health, safety, morals, or the general welfare. They contend that the referendum process destroys the necessary procedural safeguards upon which a municipality's power to zone is based and subjects zoning decisions to the bias, caprice

---

3. § 4051, Cal. Elections Codes, provides:

"If a petition protesting against the adoption of an ordinance is ° ° ° submitted to the clerk of the legislative body of the city within 30 days of the adoption of the ordinance and is signed by not less than 10 percent of the voters of the city ° ° ° the effective date of the ordinance shall be suspended, and the legislative body shall reconsider the ordinance."

4. § 4052, Cal. Elections Code, provides:

"If the legislative body does not entirely repeal the ordinance against which the petition is filed, the legislative body shall submit the ordinance to the voters, either at a regular municipal election ° ° ° or at a special election ° ° °. The ordinance shall not become effective until a majority of the voters voting on the ordinance vote in favor of it. If the legislative body repeals the ordinance or submits the ordinance to the voters and a majority of the voters voting on the ordinance do not vote in favor of it, the ordinance shall not again be enacted by the legislative body for a period of one year after the date of its repeal by the legislative body or disapproval by the voters."

5. SASSO at the time held an option to purchase the Baker Road tract, for which it had paid $6,000, subject to forfeit.

and self-interest of the voter. They rely on Washington ex rel. Seattle Title Trust Co. v. Roberge, 278 U.S. 116, 49 S.Ct. 50, 73 L.Ed. 210 (1928), and Eubank v. City of Richmond, 226 U.S. 137, 33 S.Ct. 76, 57 L.Ed. 156 (1912).

Appellants' reliance on these cases is misplaced There, local ordinances permitted residents of a neighborhood, by majority vote (*Eubank*) or by withholding consent (*Washington*), to impose restrictions that otherwise had not legislatively been determined to be in the public interest. The resulting rule, as applied to appellants' contentions respecting procedural safeguards, would seem to be that an expression of neighborhood preference for restraints, uncontrolled by any legislative responsibility to apply acceptable public interest standards, is not such a determination of what is in the public interest as will justify an exercise of the police power to zone.

A referendum, however, is far more than an expression of ambiguously founded neighborhood preference. It is the city itself legislating through its voters—an exercise by the voters of their traditional right through direct legislation to override the views of their elected representatives as to what serves the public interest. See Spaulding v. Blair, 403 F.2d 862 (4th Cir. 1968). This question lay at the heart of the proposition put to the voters. That some voters individually may have failed to meet their responsibilities as legislators to vote wisely and unselfishly cannot alter the result.

Nor can it be said that the resulting legislation on its face was so unrelated to acceptable public interest standards as to constitute an arbitrary or unreasonable exercise of the police power. See Washington ex rel. Seattle Title Trust Co. v. Roberge, *supra;* Eubank v. City of Richmond, *supra;* Euclid, Ohio v. Ambler Realty Co., 272 U.S. 365, 395, 47 S.Ct. 114, 71 L.Ed. 303 (1926). Many environmental and social values are involved in a determination of how land would best be used in the public interest. The choice of the voters of Union City is not lacking in support in this regard.

[1] Thus in the present case neither the zoning process itself nor the result can be said to be such an arbitrary or unreasonable exercise of the zoning power as to be violative of appellants' right to due process of law. We agree with the District Court that no substantial constitutional question was presented by appellants' due process contentions, and that they warranted neither a three-judge court [6] nor a preliminary injunction.[7]

2. *Equal Protection*

Appellants contend that both the purpose and the result of the referendum were to discriminate racially and economically against the Mexican-American residents of Union City. They assert that the referendum was racially

6. In so ruling on the substantiality of the constitutional challenge to the California statute, we avoid considering whether the other prerequisites for three-judge court jurisdiction under 28 U.S.C. § 2281 are satisfied. See note 2, *supra.*

7. We note that on similar facts the 6th Circuit through somewhat different reasoning reached the same result. Ranjel v. City of Lansing, 417 F.2d 321, 324 (6th Cir. 1969), cert. denied, 397 U.S. 980, 90 S.Ct. 1105, 25 L.Ed.2d 390 (1970).

motivated and that its result was to perpetuate discrimination in Union City against Mexican-American residents with low incomes.

Under the facts of this case we do not believe that the question of motivation for the referendum (apart from a consideration of its effect) is an appropriate one for judicial inquiry. In this respect, Reitman v. Mulkey, 387 U.S. 369, 87 S.Ct. 1627, 18 L.Ed.2d 830 (1967), is distinguishable.

There a constitutional amendment, adopted by the people of California through a statewide ballot, resulted in the repeal of existing fair housing laws and prohibited all legislative action abridging the rights of persons to sell, lease or rent property to whomsoever they chose. In examining the constitutionality of the amendment, its purpose was treated as a relevant consideration.

Purpose was judged, however, in terms of ultimate effect and historical context. The only existing restrictions on dealings in land (and thus the obvious target of the amendment) were those prohibiting private discrimination. The only "conceivable" purpose, judged by wholly objective standards, was to restore the right to discriminate and protect it against future legislative limitation. The amendment was held to constitute impermissible state involvement (in the nature of authorization or encouragement) with private racial discrimination. 387 U.S. at 381, 87 S.Ct. 1627.

The case before us is quite different. As we have noted, many environmental and social values are involved in determinations of land use. As the District Court noted, " * * * [T]here is no more reason to find that [rejection of rezoning] was done on the ground of invidious racial discrimination any more than on perfectly legitimate environmental grounds which are always and necessarily involved in zoning issues."

If the voters' purpose is to be found here, then, it would seem to require far more than a simple application of objective standards. If the true motive is to be ascertained not through speculation but through a probing of the private attitude of the voters, the inquiry would entail an intolerable invasion of the privacy that must protect an exercise of the franchise. Spaulding v. Blair, *supra*.

Appellants' equal protection contentions, however, reach beyond purpose. They assert that the effect of the referendum is to deny decent housing and an integrated environment to low-income residents of Union City. If, apart from voter motive, the result of this zoning by referendum is discriminatory in this fashion, in our view a substantial constitutional question is presented.

Surely, if the environmental benefits of land use planning are to be enjoyed by a city and the quality of life of its residents is accordingly to be improved, the poor cannot be excluded from enjoyment of the benefits. Given the recognized importance of equal opportunities in housing,[8] it may

---

8. See Hunter v. Erickson, 393 U.S. 385, 89 S.Ct. 557, 21 L.Ed.2d 616 (1969); Jones v. Alfred H. Mayer Co., 392 U.S. 409, 88 S.Ct. 2186, 20 L.Ed.2d 1189 (1968); Reitman v. Mulkey, *supra;* Shelley v. Kraemer, 334 U.S. 1, 68 S.Ct. 836, 92 L.Ed. 1161 (1948); Block v. Hirsh, 256 U.S. 135, 41　S.Ct. 458, 65 L.Ed. 865 (1921).

well be, as matter of law, that it is the responsibility of a city and its planning officials to see that the city's plan as initiated or as it develops accommodates the needs of its low-income families, who usually—if not always—are members of minority groups.[9] It may be, as matter of fact, that Union City's plan, as it has emerged from the referendum, fails in this respect. These issues remain to be resolved.

[2] They do not, however, call for a three-judge court under 28 U.S.C. § 2281. It is not state law that has brought about the condition in Union City and the validity of state law is not drawn in question. State law has enabled Union City to act, but appellants' challenge is directed not against the state's grant of power but against the manner in which the city has exercised that power.[10]

[3] Nor do we feel that denial of preliminary injunction constituted abuse of discretion. An injunction here would not serve to freeze the status quo but would require that affirmative steps now be taken in the direction of the ultimate remedy sought by appellants. The fact that discrimination resulted from the referendum, and that Union City has failed to make satisfactory provision for low-income housing, is not so clear as to demand preliminary relief of this nature.

The order of the District Court is affirmed.

Questions and Notes

On Lackawanna

1. The statement of facts in this case gives a vivid picture of the resistance in an old manufacturing city to the expansion of the residential area available for the black population, and indeed of the town government's attitude towards the black population.

---

9. In Norwalk CORE v. Norwalk Redevelopment Agency, 395 F.2d 920 (2d Cir. 1968), the 2d Circuit has endorsed this broader view of equal protection within a housing context. That case held that plaintiffs had a cause of action even where there was no showing of discrimination in housing opportunities [failure to relocate persons displaced by urban renewal projects] brought about by public officials. *Id.* at 932. As the court there stated:

"The fact that the discrimination is not inherent in the administration of the the program * * * surely does not excuse the planners from making sure that there is available relocation housing for all displacees. 'Equal protection of the laws' means more than merely the absence of governmental action designed to discriminate; as Judge J. Skelley Wright has said, 'we now firmly recognize that the arbitrary quality of thoughtlessness can be as disastrous and unfair to private rights and public interest as the perversity of a wilfull scheme.' Hobson v. Hansen, 269 F. Supp. 401, 497 (D.D.C. 1967)." 395 F.2d at 931.

10. For the same reason, discriminatory purpose similar to that found in Reitman v. Mulkey, *supra,* would present no three-judge issue.

2. Describe the housing and environmental conditions in the First Ward, and contrast this with the residential character of the Third Ward.

3. What was the situation on sewer capacity, and what was the local policy on additional connections with the public sewer system?

4. In the answer to number 3, are you referring to proposed residential developments, or to any other large developments? Were there examples of the latter?

5. Note the passage about the city's obligation to plan for everybody's housing problems.

On Union City

1. Exactly what local government action was challenged in this suit?

2. Note the passage (similar to the one in *Lackawanna*) about the responsibility for planning for all groups.

3. Did the Court require that a permit be given for the precise site sought by Sasso?

4. For what happened after this opinion, see Williams, Sec. 66.16.

JAMES

v.

VALTIERRA

APPEAL FROM THE UNITED STATES DISTRICT COURT FOR THE
NORTHERN DISTRICT OF CALIFORNIA
402 U.S. 137 (1971)
Argued March 3-4, 1971—Decided April 26, 1971[*]

Appellees, who are eligible for low-cost public housing, challenged the requirement of Art. XXXIV of the California Constitution that no low-rent housing project be developed, constructed, or acquired by any state public body without the approval of a majority of those voting at a community election, as violative of the Supremacy, Privileges and Immunities, and Equal Protection Clauses of the United States Constitution. A three-judge District Court enjoined the enforcement of the referendum provision on the ground that it denied appellees equal protection of the laws, relying chiefly on *Hunter* v. *Erickson,* 393 U.S. 385.

---

[*] Together with No. 226, *Shaffer v. Valtierra et al.,* also on appeal from the same court, argued March 4, 1971.

Held: The California procedure for mandatory referendums, which is not limited to proposals involving low-cost public housing, ensures democratic decisionmaking, and does not violate the Equal Protection Clause. *Hunter v. Erickson, supra,* distinguished. Pp. 140-143.

313 F. Supp. 1, reversed and remanded.

BLACK, J., delivered the opinion of the Court, in which BURGER, C. J., and HARLAN, STEWART, and WHITE, JJ., joined. MARSHALL, J., filed a dissenting opinion, in which BRENNAN and BLACKMUN, JJ., joined, *post,* p. 143. DOUGLAS, J., took no part in the consideration or decision of the cases.

Donald C. Atkinson argued the cause and filed a brief for appellants in No. 154. *Moses Lasky* argued the cause for appellant in No. 226. With him on the briefs was *Malcolm T. Dungan.*

Archibald Cox argued the cause for appellees in both cases. On the brief were *Lois P. Sheinfeld* and *Anthony G. Amsterdam. Warren Christopher* and *Donald M. Wessling* filed a brief for appellee Housing Authority of the city of San Jose in both cases.

Briefs of *amici curiae* urging affirmance in both cases were filed by *Solicitor General Griswold, Assistant Attorney General Leonard,* and *Lawrence G. Wallace* for the United States, and by *Louis J. Lefkowitz,* Attorney General, *pro se, Samuel A. Hirshowitz,* First Assistant Attorney General, and *George D. Zuckerman, Dominick J. Tuminaro,* and *Lloyd G. Milliken,* Assistant Attorneys General, for the Attorney General of the State of New York.

MR. JUSTICE BLACK delivered the opinion of the Court.

These cases raise but a single issue. It grows out of the United States Housing Act of 1937, 50 Stat. 888, as amended, 42 U.S.C. §1401 *et seq.,* which established a federal housing agency authorized to make loans and grants to state agencies for slum clearance and low-rent housing projects. In response, the California Legislature created in each county and city a public housing authority to take advantage of the financing made available by the federal Housing Act. See Cal. Health & Safety Code §34240. At the time the federal legislation was passed the California Constitution had for many years reserved to the State's people the power to initiate legislation and to reject or approve by referendum any Act passed by the state legislature. Cal. Const., Art. IV, §1. The same section reserved to the electors of counties and cities the power of initiative and referendum over acts of local government bodies. In 1950, however, the State Supreme Court held that local authorities' decisions on seeking federal aid for public housing projects were "executive" and "administrative," not "legislative," and therefore the state constitution's referendum provisions did not apply to these actions.[1] Within six months of that decision the California voters adopted Article XXXIV of the state constitution to bring public housing decisions

---

1. *Housing Authority v. Superior Court,* 35 Cal. 2d 550, 557–558, 219 P.2d 457, 460–461 (1950).

under the State's referendum policy. The Article provided that no low-rent housing project should be developed, constructed, or acquired in any manner by a state public body until the project was approved by a majority of those voting at a community election.[2]

The present suits were brought by citizens of San Jose, California, and San Mateo County, localities where housing authorities could not apply for federal funds because low-cost housing proposals had been defeated in referendums. The plaintiffs, who are eligible for low-cost public housing, sought a declaration that Article XXXIV was unconstitutional because its referendum requirement violated: (1) the Supremacy Clause of the United States Constitution; (2) the Privileges and Immunities Clause; and (3) the Equal Protection Clause. A three-judge court held that Article XXXIV denied the plaintiffs equal protection of the laws and it enjoined its enforcement. 313 F. Supp. 1 (ND Cal. 1970). Two appeals were taken from the judgment, one by the San Jose City Council and the other by a single member of the council. We noted probable jurisdiction of both appeals. 398 U.S. 949 (1970); 399 U.S. 925 (1970). For the reasons that follow, we reverse.

The three-judge court found the Supremacy Clause argument unpersuasive, and we agree. By the Housing Act of 1937 the Federal Government has offered aid to state and local governments for the creation of low-rent public housing. However, the federal legislation does not purport to require that local governments accept this or to outlaw local referendums on whether the aid should be accepted. We also find the privileges and immunities argument without merit.

While the District Court cited several cases of this Court, its chief reliance plainly rested on *Hunter v. Erickson,* 393 U.S. 385 (1969). The first paragraph in the District Court's decision stated simply: "We hold Article XXXIV to be unconstitutional. *See* Hunter v. Erickson . . ." The court

---

2. "Section 1. No low rent housing project shall hereafter be developed, constructed, or acquired in any manner by any state public body until, a majority of the qualified electors of the city, town or county, as the case may be, in which it is proposed to develop, construct, or acquire the same, voting upon such issue, approve such project by voting in favor thereof at an election to be held for that purpose, or at any general or special election.

"For the purposes of this article the term 'low rent housing project' shall mean any development composed of urban or rural dwellings, apartments or other living accommodations for persons of low income, financed in whole or in part by the Federal Government or a state public body or to which the Federal Government or a state public body extends assistance by supplying all or part of the labor, by guaranteeing the payment of liens, or otherwise. . . .

"For the purposes of this article only 'persons of low income' shall mean persons or families who lack the amount of income which is necessary (as determined by the state public body developing, constructing, or acquiring the housing project) to enable them, without financial assistance, to live in decent, safe and sanitary dwellings, without overcrowding."

below erred in relying on *Hunter* to invalidate Article XXXIV. Unlike the case before us, *Hunter* rested on the conclusion that Akron's referendum law denied equal protection by placing "special burdens on racial minorities within the governmental process." *Id.*, at 391. In *Hunter* the citizens of Akron had amended the city charter to require that any ordinance regulating real estate on the basis of race, color, religion, or national origin could not take effect without approval by a majority of those voting in a city election. The Court held that the amendment created a classification based upon race because it required that laws dealing with racial housing matters could take effect only if they survived a mandatory referendum while other housing ordinances took effect without any such special election. The opinion noted:

> "Because the core of the Fourteenth Amendment is the prevention of meaningful and unjustified official distinctions based on race, [citing a group of racial discrimination cases] racial classifications are 'constitutionally suspect' . . . and subject to the 'most rigid scrutiny.' . . . They 'bear a far heavier burden of justification' than other classifications." *Id.*, at 391-392.

The Court concluded that Akron had advanced no sufficient reasons to justify this racial classification and hence that it was unconstitutional under the Fourteenth Amendment.

Unlike the Akron referendum provision, it cannot be said that California's Article XXXIV rests on "distinctions based on race." *Id.*, at 391. The Article requires referendum approval for any low-rent public housing project, not only for projects which will be occupied by a racial minority. And the record here would not support any claim that a law seemingly neutral on its face is in fact aimed at a racial minority. Cf. *Gomillion v. Lightfoot,* 364 U. S. 339 (1960). The present case could be affirmed only by extending *Hunter,* and this we decline to do.

California's entire history demonstrates the repeated use of referendums to give citizens a voice on questions of public policy. A referendum provision was included in the first state constitution, Cal. Const. of 1849, Art. VIII, and referendums have been a commonplace occurrence in the State's active political life.[3] Provisions for referendums demonstrate devotion to democracy, not to bias, discrimination, or prejudice. Nonetheless, appellees contend that Article XXXIV denies them equal protection because it demands a mandatory referendum while many other referendums only take place upon citizen initiative. They suggest that the mandatory nature of the Article XXXIV referendum constitutes unconstitutional discrimination because it hampers persons desiring public housing from achieving their objective when no such roadblock faces other groups seeking to influence other public decisions to their advantage. But of course a lawmaking pro-

---

3. See, *e.g.*, W. Crouch, The Initiative and Referendum in California (1950).

cedure that "disadvantages" a particular group does not always deny equal protection. Under any such holding, presumably a State would not be able to require referendums on any subject unless referendums were required on all, because they would always disadvantage some group. And this Court would be required to analyze governmental structures to determine whether a gubernatorial veto provision or a filibuster rule is likely to "disadvantage" any of the diverse and shifting groups that make up the American people.

Furthermore, an examination of California law reveals that persons advocating low-income housing have not been singled out for a mandatory referendums while no other group must face that obstacle. Mandatory referendums are required for approval of state constitutional amendments, for the issuance of general obligation long-term bonds by local governments, and for certain municipal territorial annexations. See Cal. Const., Art. XVIII; Art. XIII, § 40; Art. XI, § 2(b). California statute books contain much legislation first enacted by voter initiative, and no such law can be repealed or amended except by referendum. Cal. Const., Art. IV, § 24(c). Some California cities have wisely provided that their public parks may not be alienated without mandatory referendums, see, e. g., San Jose Charter § 1700.

The people of California have also decided by their own vote to require referendum approval of low-rent public housing projects. This procedure ensures that all the people of a community will have a voice in a decision which may lead to large expenditures of local governmental funds for increased public services and to lower tax revenues.[4] It gives them a voice in decisions that will affect the future development of their own community. This procedure for democratic decisionmaking does not violate the constitutional command that no State shall deny to any person "the equal protection of the laws."

The judgment of the three-judge court is reversed and the cases are remanded for dismissal of the complaint.

Reversed and remanded.

MR. JUSTICE DOUGLAS took no part in the consideration or decision of these cases.

MR. JUSTICE MARSHALL, whom MR. JUSTICE BRENNAN and MR. JUSTICE BLACKMUN join, dissenting.

---

4. Public low-rent housing projects are financed through bonds issued by the local housing authority. To be sure, the Federal Government contracts to make contributions sufficient to cover interest and principal, but the local government body must agree to provide all municipal services for the units and to waive all taxes on the property. The local services to be provided include schools, police, and fire protection, sewers, streets, drains, and lighting. Some of the cost is defrayed by the local governing body's receipt of 10% of the housing project rentals, but of course the rentals are set artificially low. Both appellants and appellees agree that the building of federally financed low-cost housing entails costs to the local community. Appellant Shaffer's Brief 34—35. Appellees' Brief 47. See also 42 U.S.C. §§ 1401–1430.

By its very terms, the mandatory prior referendum provision of Art. XXXIV applies solely to

"any development composed of urban or rural dwellings, apartments or other living accommodations for persons of low income, financed in whole or in part by the Federal Government or a state public body or to which the Federal Government or a state public body extends assistance by supplying all or part of the labor, by guaranteeing the payment of liens, or otherwise."

Persons of low income are defined as

"persons or families who lack the amount of income which is necessary . . . to enable them, without financial assistance, to live in decent, safe and sanitary dwellings, without overcrowding."

The article explicitly singles out low-income persons to bear its burden. Publicly assisted housing developments designed to accommodate the aged, veterans, state employees, persons of moderate income, or any class of citizens other than the poor, need not be approved by prior referenda.*

In my view, Art. XXXIV on its face constitutes invidious discrimination which the Equal Protection Clause of the Fourteenth Amendment plainly prohibits. "The States, of course, are prohibited by the Equal Protection Clause from discriminating between 'rich' and 'poor' *as such* in the formulation and application of their laws." *Douglas* v. *California,* 372 U. S. 353, 361 (1963) (HARLAN, J., dissenting). Article XXXIV is neither "a law of general applicability that may affect the poor more harshly than it does the rich," *ibid.,* nor an "effort to redress economic imbalances," *ibid.* It is rather an explicit classification on the basis of poverty—a suspect classification which demands exacting judicial scrutiny, see *McDonald* v. *Board of Election,* 394 U. S. 802, 807 (1969); *Harper* v. *Virginia Board of Elections,* 383 U. S. 663 (1966); *Douglas* v. *California, supra.*

The Court, however, chooses to subject the article to no scrutiny whatsoever and treats the provision as if it contained a totally benign, technical economic classification. Both the appellees and the Solicitor General of the United States as *amicus curiae* have strenuously argued, and the court below found, that Art. XXXIV, by imposing a substantial burden solely on the poor, violates the Fourteenth Amendment. Yet after observing that the article does not discriminate on the basis of race, the Court's only response to the real question in these cases is the unresponsive assertion that "referendums demonstrate devotion to democracy, not to bias, discrimination, or

---

* California law authorizes the formation of Renewal Area Agencies whose purposes include the construction of "low-income, middle-income and normal-market housing," Cal. Health & Safety Code § 33701 *et seq.* Only low-income housing programs are subject to the mandatory referendum provision of Art. XXXIV even though all of the agencies' programs may receive substantial governmental assistance.

prejudice." It is far too late in the day to contend that the Fourteenth Amendment prohibits only racial discrimination; and to me, singling out the poor to bear a burden not placed on any other class of citizens tramples the values that the Fourteenth Amendment was designed to protect.

I respectfully dissent.

Questions and Notes

1. Viewing the history of the Twentieth Century as a whole, would you say that a referendum is a democratic device?

VILLAGE OF BELLE TERRE

v.

BORAAS

416 U.S. 1

Argued Feb. 19, 20, 1974.

Decided April 1, 1974.

Civil rights action challenging constitutionality of village zoning ordinance limiting, with certain exceptions, the occupancy of one-family dwellings to traditional families or to groups of not more than two unrelated persons. The United States District Court for the Eastern District of New York, 367 F. Supp. 136, held the ordinance to be constitutional. The Court of Appeals, Second Circuit, 476 F. 2d 806, reversed, and an appeal was taken. The Supreme Court, Mr. Justice Douglas, held that the ordinance is not aimed at transients, involves no procedural disparity inflicted on some but not on others, involves no deprivation of any "fundamental" right, bears a rational relationship to a permissible state objective, and must be upheld as valid land-use legislation addressed to family needs, notwithstanding claims that the ordinance is unconstitutional as violative of equal protection and rights of association, travel and privacy.

Reversed.

Mr. Justice Brennan dissented with opinion.

Mr. Justice Marshall dissented with opinion.

✻   ✻   ✻

2 Cir., 476 F.2d 806, reversed.

Bernard E. Gegan, Brooklyn, N. Y., for appellants.

Lawrence G. Sager, New York City, for appellees.

Mr. Justice DOUGLAS delivered the opinion of the Court.

Belle Terre is a village on Long Island's north shore of about 220 homes inhabited by 700 people. Its total land area is less than one square mile.

It has restricted land use to one-family dwellings excluding lodging houses, boarding houses, fraternity houses, or multiple dwelling houses. The word "Family" as used in the ordinance means, "One or more persons related by blood, adoption, or marriage, living and cooking together as a single house-keeping unit, exclusive of household servants. A number of persons but not exceeding two (2) living and cooking together as a single housekeeping unit though not related by blood, adoption, or marriage shall be deemed to constitute a family."

Appellees (Dickmans) are owners of a house in the village and leased it in December, 1971 for a term of 18 months to Michael Truman. Later Bruce Boraas became a colessee. Then Anne Parish moved into the house along with three others. These six are students at nearby State University at Stony Brook and none is related to the other by blood, adoption, or marriage. When the village served the Dickmans with an "Order to Remedy Violations" of the ordinance,[1] the owners plus three tenants[2] thereupon brought this action under 42 U.S.C. § 1983 for an injunction declaring the ordinance unconstitutional. The District Court held the ordinance constitutional and the Court of Appeals reversed, one judge dissenting. 2 Cir., 476 F.2d 806. The case is here by appeal, 28 U.S.C. § 1254(2); and we noted probable jurisdiction, 414 U.S. 907, 94 S.Ct. 234, 38 L.Ed.2d 145.

This case brings to this Court a different phase of local zoning regulations than we have previously reviewed. Village of Euclid v. Ambler Realty Co., 272 U.S. 365, 47 S.Ct. 114, 71 L.Ed. 303, involved a zoning ordinance classifying land use in a given area into six categories. Appellee's tracts fell under three classifications: U-2 that included two-family dwellings; U-3 that included apartments, hotels, churches, schools, private clubs, hospitals, city hall and the like; and U-6 that included sewage disposal plants, incinerators, scrap storage, cemeteries, oil and gas storage and so on. Heights of buildings were prescribed for each zone; also the size of land areas required for each kind of use was specified. The land in litigation was vacant and being held for industrial development; and evidence was introduced showing that under the restricted use ordinance the land would be greatly reduced in value. The claim was that the land owner was being deprived of liberty and property without due process within the meaning of the Fourteenth Amendment.

The Court sustained the zoning ordinance under the police power of the State, saying that the line "which in this field separates the legitimate from the illegitimate assumption of power is not capable of precise delimitation.

---

1. Younger v. Harris, 401 U.S. 37, 91 S.Ct. 746, 27 L.Ed.2d 669 is not involved here as on Aug. 2, 1972, when this federal suit was initiated, no state case had been started. The effect of the "Order to Remedy Violations" was to subject the occupants to liability commencing August 3, 1972. During the litigation the lease expired and it was extended. Anne Parish moved out. Thereafter the other five students left and the owners now hold the home out for sale or rent, including to student groups.

2. Truman, Boraas, and Parish became appellees but not the other three.

It varies with circumstances and conditions." 272 U.S., at 387, 47 S.Ct., at 118. And the Court added "A nuisance may be merely a right thing in the wrong place, like a pig in the parlor instead of the barnyard. If the validity of the legislative classification for zoning purposes be fairly debatable, the legislative judgment must be allowed to control." *Id.*, at 388, 47 S.Ct., at 118. The Court listed as considerations bearing on the constitutionality of zoning ordinances the danger of fire or collapse of buildings, the evils of over-crowding people, and the possibility that "offensive trades, industries, and structures" might "create nuisance" to residential sections. *Ibid.* But even those historic police power problems need not loom large or actually be existent in a given case. For the exclusion of "all industrial establishments" does not mean that "only offensive or dangerous industries will be exluded." *Ibid.* That fact does not invalidate the ordinance; the Court held:

> "The inclusion of a reasonable margin to insure effective enforcement will not put upon a law, otherwise valid, the stamp of invalidity. Such laws may also find their justification in the fact that, in some fields, the bad fades into the good by such insensible degrees that the two are not capable of being readily distinguished and separated in terms of legislation." *Id.*, 388-389, 47 S.Ct., 118.

The main thrust of the case in the mind of the Court was in the exclusion of industries and apartments and as respects that it commented on the desire to keep residential areas free of "disturbing noises"; "increased traffic"; the hazard of "moving and parked automobiles"; thus "depriving children of the privilege of quiet and open spaces for play, enjoyed by those in more favored localities." *Id.*, at 394, 47 S.Ct., at 120. The ordinance was sanctioned because the validity of the legislative classification was "fairly debatable" and therefore could not be said to be wholly arbitrary. *Id.*, at 388, 47 S.Ct., at 118.

Our decision in Berman v. Parker, 348 U.S. 26, 75 S.Ct. 98, 99 L.Ed. 27, sustained a land use project in the District of Columbia against a land owner's claim that the taking violated the Due Process Clause and the Just Compensation Clause of the Fifth Amendment. The essence of the argument against the law was, while taking property for ridding an area of slums was permissible, taking it "merely to develop a better balanced, more attractive community" was not, 348 U.S., at 31, 75 S.Ct., at 102. We refused to limit the concept of public welfare that may be enhanced by zoning regulations.[3] We said:

---

3. Vermont has enacted comprehensive statewide land use controls which direct local boards to develop plans ordering the uses of local land *inter alia,* to "create conditions favorable to transportation, health, safety, civic activities and educational and cultural opportunities, [and] reduce the wastes of financial and human resources which result from either excessive congestion or excessive scattering of population. . . ." 10

"Miserable and disreputable housing conditions may do more than spread disease and crime and immorality. They may also suffocate the spirit by reducing the people who live there to the status of cattle. They may indeed make living an almost unsufferable burden. They may also be an ugly sore, a blight on the community which robs it of charm, which makes it a place from which men turn. The misery of housing may despoil a community as an open sewer may ruin a river.

"We do not sit to determine whether a particular housing project is or is not desirable. The concept of the public welfare is broad and inclusive. . . . The values it represents are spiritual as well as physical, aesthetic as well as monetary. It is within the power of the legislature to determine that the community should be beautiful as well as healthy, spacious as well as clean, well-balanced as well as carefully patrolled." *Id.*, 32-33, 75 S.Ct., 102.

If the ordinance segregated one area only for one race, it would immediately be suspect under the reasoning of Buchanan v. Warley, 245 U.S. 60, 38 S.Ct. 16, 62 L.Ed. 149 where the Court invalidated a city ordinance barring a Black from acquiring real property in a white residential area by reason of an 1866 Act of Congress, 14 Stat. 27, 42 U.S.C. § 1982 and an 1870 Act, 16 Stat. 144, both enforcing the Fourteenth Amendment. *Id.*, 78-82, 38 S.Ct. 19-21. See Jones v. Alfred H. Mayer Co., 392 U.S. 409, 88 S.Ct. 2186, 20 L.Ed.2d 1189.

In Seattle Title Trust Co. v. Roberge, 278 U.S. 116, 49 S.Ct. 50, 73 L.Ed. 210, Seattle had a zoning ordinance that permitted a "philanthropic home for children or for old people" in a particular district "when the written consent shall have been obtained of the owners of two thirds of the property within four hundred (400) feet of the proposed building." *Id.*, at 118, 49 S.Ct., at 50. The Court held that provision of the ordinance unconstitutional saying that the existing owners could "withhold consent for selfish reasons or arbitrarily and may subject the trustee [owner] to their will or caprice." *Id.*, at 122, 49 S.Ct., at 52. Unlike the billboard cases (Cusack Co. v. City of Chicago, 242 U.S. 526, 37 S.Ct. 190, 61 L.Ed. 472), the Court concluded that the Seattle ordinance was invalid since the proposed home for the aged poor was not shown by its maintenance and construction "to work any injury, inconvenience or annoyance to the community, the district or any person." *Id.*, 278 U.S., at 122, 49 S.Ct., at 52.

The present ordinance is challenged on several grounds: that it interferes with a person's right to travel; that it interferes with the right to migrate to and settle within a State; that it bars people who are uncongenial to the present residents; that the ordinance expresses the social preferences of the residents for groups that will be congenial to them;

Vermont Stat. Ann. § 6042 (1971 Supp.). Federal legislation has been proposed designed to assist States and localities in developing such broad objective land use guidelines. See S. Comm. on Interior and Insular Affairs, Land Use Policy and Planning Assistance Act, S. Rep. No. 93-197, 93d Cong., 1st Sess. (1973).

that social homogenity is not a legitimate interest of government; that the restriction of those whom the neighbors do not like trenches on the newcomers' rights of privacy; that it is of no rightful concern to villagers whether the residents are married or unmarried; that the ordinance is antithetical to the Nation's experience, ideology and self-perception as an open, egalitarian, and integrated society.[4]

[1, 2] We find none of these reasons in the record before us. It is not aimed at transients. Cf. Shapiro v. Thompson, 394 U.S. 618, 89 S.Ct. 1322, 22 L.Ed.2d 600. It involves no procedural disparity inflicted on some but not on others such as was presented by Griffin v. Illinois, 351 U.S. 12, 76 S.Ct. 585, 100 L.Ed. 891. It involves no "fundamental" right guaranteed by the Constitution, such as voting, Harper v. Virginia State Board, 383 U.S. 663, 86 S.Ct. 1079, 16 L.Ed.2d 169; the right of association, NAACP v. Alabama ex rel. Patterson, 357 U.S. 449, 78 S.Ct. 1163, 2 L.Ed.2d 1488; the right of access to the courts, NAACP v. Button, 371 U.S. 415, 83 S.Ct. 328, 9 L.Ed.2d 405; or any rights of privacy, cf. Griswold v. Connecticut, 381 U.S. 479, 85 S.Ct. 1678, 14 L.Ed.2d 510; Eisenstadt v. Baird, 405 U.S. 438, 453-454, 92 S.Ct. 1029, 1038-1039, 31 L.Ed.2d 349. We deal with economic and social legislation where legislatures have historically drawn lines which we respect against the charge of violation of the Equal Protection Clause if the law be "reasonable, not arbitrary" (quoting F. S. Royster Guano Co. v. Virginia, 253 U.S. 412, 415, 40 S.Ct. 560, 561, 64 L.Ed. 989) and bears "a rational relationship to a [permissible] state objective." Reed v. Reed, 404 U.S. 71, 76, 92 S.Ct. 251, 254, 30 L.Ed.2d 225.

[3] It is said, however, that if two unmarried people can constitute a "family," there is no reason why three or four may not. But every line drawn by a legislature leaves some out that might well have been included.[5] That exercise of discretion, however, is a legislative not a judicial function.

It is said that the Belle Terre ordinance reeks with an animosity to unmarried couples who live together.[6] There is no evidence to support it;

---

4. Many references in the development of this thesis are made to Turner, The Frontier in American History (1920), with emphasis on his theory that "democracy is born of free land." Id., 32.

5. Mr. Justice Holmes made the point a half century ago.

"When a legal distinction is determined, as no one doubts that it may be, between night and day, childhood and maturity, or any other extremes, a point has to be fixed or a line has to be drawn, or gradually picked out by successive decisions, to mark where the change takes place. Looked at by itself without regard to the necessity behind it the line or point seems arbitrary. It might as well or nearly as well be a little more to one side or the other. But when it is seen that a line or point there must be, and that there is no mathematical or logical way of fixing it precisely, the decision of the legislature must be accepted unless we can say that it is very wide of any reasonable mark." Louisville Gas & Electric Co. v. Coleman, 277 U.S. 32, 41, 48 S.Ct. 423, 426, 72 L.Ed. 770 (dissenting).

6. U.S. Dept. of Agriculture v. Moreno, 413 U.S. 528, 93 S.Ct. 2821, 37 L.Ed.2d 782 (1973), is therefore inapt as there a household containing anyone unrelated to the rest was denied food stamps.

and the provision of the ordinance bringing within the definition of a "family" two unmarried people belies the charge.

The ordinance places no ban on other forms of association, for a "family" may, so far as the ordinance is concerned, entertain whomever they like.

The regimes of boarding houses, fraternity houses, and the like present urban problems. More people occupy a given space; more cars rather continuously pass by; more cars are parked; noise travels with crowds.

[4, 5] A quiet place where yards are wide, people few, and motor vehicles restricted are legitimate guidelines in a land use project addressed to family needs. This goal is a permissible one within Berman v. Parker, *supra.*. The police power is not confined to elimination of filth, stench, and unhealthy places. It is ample to lay out zones where family values, youth values, and the blessings of quiet seclusion, and clean air make the area a sanctuary for people.

[6] The suggestion that the case may be moot need not detain us. A zoning ordinance usually has an impact on the value of the property which it regulates. But in spite of the fact that the precise impact of the ordinance sustained in *Euclid* on a given piece of property was not known, 272 U.S., at 397, 47 S.Ct., at 121, the Court, considering the matter a controversy in the realm of city planning, sustained the ordinance. Here we are a step closer to the impact of the ordinance on the value of the lessor's property. He has not only lost six tenants and acquired only two in their place; it is obvious that the scale of rental values rides on what we decide today. When *Berman* reached us it was not certain whether an entire tract would be taken or only the buildings on it and a scenic easement. 348 U.S., at 36, 75 S.Ct., at 104. But that did not make the case any the less a controversy in the constitutional sense. When Mr. Justice Holmes said for the Court in Block v. Hirsh, 256 U.S. 135, 155, 41 S.Ct. 458, 459, 65 L.Ed. 865, "property rights may be cut down, and to that extent taken, without pay," he stated the issue here. As is true in most zoning cases, the precise impact on value may, at the threshold of litigation over validity, not yet be known.

Reversed.

Mr. Justice BRENNAN, dissenting.

The constitutional challenge to the village ordinance is premised *solely* on alleged infringement of associational and other constitutional rights of *tenants*. But the named tenant appellees have quit the house, thus raising a serious question whether there now exists a cognizable "case or controversy" that satisfies that indispensable requisite of Art. III of the Constitution. Existence of a case or controversy must of course appear at every stage of review, see, *e. g.*, Roe v. Wade, 410 U.S. 113, 125, 93 S.Ct. 705, 712, 35 L.Ed.2d 147 (1973); Steffel v. Thompson, —— U.S. ——, —— n. 10, 94 S.Ct. 1209, ——, 39 L.Ed.2d —— (1974). In my view it does not appear at this stage of this case.

Plainly there is no case or controversy as to the named tenant appellees since, having moved out, they no longer have an interest, associational, economic or otherwise, to be vindicated by invalidation of the ordinance. Whether there is a cognizable case or controversy must therefore turn on whether the lessor appellees may attack the ordinance on the basis of the constitutional rights of their tenants.

The general "weighty" rule of practice is "that a litigant may only assert his own constitutional rights or immunities," United States v. Raines, 362 U.S. 17, 22, 80 S.Ct. 519, 523, 4 L.Ed.2d 524 (1960). A pertinent exception however ordinarily limits a litigant to the assertion of the alleged denial of another's constitutional rights to situations in which there is: (1) evidence that as a direct consequence of the denial of constitutional rights of the others, the litigant faces substantial economic injury, Pierce v. Society of Sisters, 268 U.S. 510, 535-536, 45 S.Ct. 571, 573-574, 69 L.Ed. 1070 (1925); Barrows v. Jackson, 346 U.S. 249, 255-256, 73 S.Ct. 1031, 1034-1035, 97 L.Ed. 1586 (1953), or criminal prosecution, Griswold v. Connecticut, 381 U.S. 479, 481, 85 S.Ct. 1678, 1679, 14 L.Ed.2d 510 (1965), Eisenstadt v. Baird, 405 U.S. 438, 92 S.Ct. 1029, 31 L.Ed.2d 349 (1972), and (2) a showing that the litigant's and the others' interests intertwine and unless the litigant may assert the constitutional rights of the others, those rights cannot effectively be vindicated. Griswold v. Connecticut, *supra*, Eisenstadt v. Baird, *supra;* see also NAACP v. Alabama ex rel. Patterson, 357 U.S. 449, 78 S.Ct. 1163, 2 L.Ed.2d 1488 (1958).

In my view, lessor appellees do not, on the present record, satisfy either requirement of the exception. Their own brief negates any claim that they face economic loss. The brief states that "there is nothing in the record to support the contention that in a middle class suburban residential community like Belle Terre, traditional families are willing to pay more or less than students with limited means like appellees." Brief of Appellees, pp. 54-55. And whether they face criminal prosecution for violations of the ordinance is at least unclear. The criminal summons served on them on July 19, 1972, was withdrawn because not preceded, as required by the Village's procedure, by an order requiring discontinuance of violations within 48 hours. An order to discontinue violation was served thereafter on July 31, but was not followed by service of a criminal summons when the violation was not discontinued within 48 hours.*

The Court argues that, because a zoning ordinance "has an impact on the value of the property which it regulates," there is a cognizable case or controversy. But even if lessor appellees for that reason have a personal stake, and we were to concede that landlord and tenant interests inter-

---

* In these circumstances, I agree with the Court that no criminal action was "pending" when this suit was brought and that therefore the District Court correctly declined to apply the principles of Younger v. Harris, 401 U.S. 37, 91 S.Ct. 746, 27 L.Ed.2d 669 (1971).

twine in respect of the ordinance, I cannot see, on the present record, how it can be concluded that "it would be difficult if not impossible," Barrows v. Jackson, *supra,* 346 U.S., at 257, 73 S.Ct., at 1035, for present or prospective unrelated tenant groups of more than two to assert their own rights before the courts, since the departed tenant appellees had no difficulty in doing so. Thus, the second requirement of the exception would not presently appear to be satisfied. Accordingly it is irrelevant that the house was let, as we are now informed, to other unrelated tenants on a month-to-month basis after the tenant appellees moved out. None of the new tenants has sought to intervene in this suit. Indeed, for all that appears, they too may have moved out and the house may be vacated.

I dissent and would vacate the judgment of the Court of Appeals and remand to the District Court for further proceedings. If the District Court determines that a cognizable case or controversy no longer exists, the complaint should be dismissed. Golden v. Zwickler, 394 U.S. 103, 89 S.Ct. 956, 22 L.Ed.2d 113 (1969).

Mr. Justice MARSHALL, dissenting.

This case draws into question the constitutionality of a zoning ordinance of the incorporated village of Belle Terre, New York, which prohibits groups of more than two unrelated persons, as distinguished from groups consisting of any number of persons related by blood, adoption or marriage, from occupying a residence within the confines of the township.[1] Appellees, the two owners of a Belle Terre residence, and three unrelated student tenants challenged the ordinance on the grounds that it establishes a classification between households of related and unrelated individuals, which deprives them of equal protection of the laws. In my view, the disputed classification burdens the students' fundamental rights of association and privacy guaranteed by the First and Fourteenth Amendments. Because the application of strict equal protection scrutiny is therefore required, I am at odds with my brethren's conclusion that the ordinance may be sustained on a showing that it bears a rational relationship to the accomplishment of legitimate governmental objectives.

I am in full agreement with the majority that zoning is a complex and important function of the State. It may indeed be the most essential function performed by local government, for it is one of the primary means by which we protect that sometimes difficult to define concept of quality of life. I therefore continue to adhere to the principle of Village of Euclid v. Ambler Realty Co., 272 U.S. 365, 47 S.Ct. 114, 71 L.Ed. 303 (1926), that deference should be given to governmental judgments concerning proper land use allocation. That deference is a principle which has served this Court well and which is necessary for the continued development of effective zoning and land use control mechanisms. Had the owners alone brought this suit alleging that the restrictive ordinance deprived them of

---

1. The text of the ordinance is reprinted at 1537, *ante.*

their property or was an irrational legislative classification, I would agree that the ordinance would have to be sustained. Our role is not and should not be to sit as a zoning board of appeals.

I would also agree with the majority that local zoning authorities may properly act in furtherance of the objectives asserted to be served by the ordinance at issue here: restricting uncontrolled growth, solving traffic problems, keeping rental costs at a reasonable level, and making the community attractive to families. The police power which provides the justification for zoning is not narrowly confined. See Berman v. Parker, 348 U.S. 26, 75 S.Ct. 98, 99 L.Ed. 27 (1954). And, it is appropriate that we afford zoning authorities considerable latitude in choosing the means by which to implement such purposes. But deference does not mean abdication. This Court has an obligation to ensure that zoning ordinances, even when adopted in furtherance of such legitimate aims, do not infringe fundamental constitutional rights.

When separate but equal was still accepted constitutional dogma, this Court struck down a racially restrictive zoning ordinance. Buchanan v. Warley, 245 U.S. 60, 38 S.Ct. 16, 62 L.Ed. 149 (1917). I am sure the Court would not be hesitant to invalidate that ordinance today. The lower federal courts have considered procedural aspects of zoning,[2] and acted to insure that land use controls are not used as means of confining minorities and the poor to the ghettos of our central cities.[3] These are limited but necessary intrusions on the discretion of zoning authorities. By the same token, I think it clear that the First Amendment provides some limitation on zoning laws. It is inconceivable to me that we would allow the exercise of the zoning power to burden First Amendment freedoms, as by ordinances that restrict occupancy to individuals adhering to particular religious, political or scientific beliefs. Zoning officials properly concern themselves with the uses of land—with, for example, the number and kind of dwellings to be constructed in a certain neighborhood or the number of persons who can reside in those dwellings. But zoning authorities cannot validly consider who those persons are, what they believe, or how they choose to live, whether they are Negro or white, Catholic or Jew, Republican or Democrat, married or unmarried.

---

2. See Citizens Ass'n of Georgetown v. Zoning Commission, 155 U.S. App. D.C. 233, 477 F.2d 402 (1973).

3. See Kennedy Park Homes Ass'n v. City of Lackawanna, 436 F.2d 108 (CA2 1970); Dailey v. City of Lawton, 425 F.2d 1037 (CA10 1970); cf. Gautreaux v. City of Chicago, 480 F.2d 210 (CA7 1973); Crow v. Brown, 457 F.2d 788 (CA5 1972); Southern Alameda Spanish Speaking Organization v. Union City, 424 F.2d 291 (CA9 1970). See generally, Sager, Tight Little Islands: Exclusionary Zoning, Equal Protection and the Indigent, 21 Stan. L. Rev. 767 (1969); Note, Exclusionary Zoning and Equal Protection, 84 Harv. L. Rev. 1645 (1971); Note, The Responsibility of Local Zoning Authorities to Nonresident Indigents, 23 Stan. L. Rev. 774 (1971).

My disagreement with the Court today is based upon my view that the ordinance in this case unnecessarily burdens appellees' First Amendment freedom of association and their constitutionally guaranteed right to privacy. Our decisions establish that the First and Fourteenth Amendments protect the freedom to choose one's associates. NAACP v. Button, 371 U.S. 415, 430, 83 S.Ct. 328, 336, 9 L.Ed.2d 405 (1963). Constitutional protection is extended not only to modes of association that are political in the usual sense, but also to those that pertain to the social and economic benefit of the members. *Id.*, at 430-431, 83 S.Ct., at 336-337; Brotherhood of R.R. Trainmen v. Virginia ex rel. Virginia State Bar, 377 U.S. 1, 84 S.Ct. 1113, 12 L.Ed.2d 89 (1964). See United Transportation Union v. State Bar of Michigan, 401 U.S. 576, 91 S.Ct. 1076, 28 L.Ed.2d 339 (1971); U. M. W. v. Illinois State Bar Ass'n, 389 U.S. 217, 88 S.Ct. 353, 19 L.Ed.2d 426 (1967). The selection of one's living companions involves similar choices as to the emotional, social, or economic benefits to be derived from alternative living arrangements.

The freedom of association is often inextricably entwined with the constitutionally guaranteed right of privacy. The right to "establish a home" is an essential part of the liberty guaranteed by the Fourteenth Amendment. Meyer v. Nebraska, 262 U.S. 390, 399, 43 S.Ct. 625, 626, 67 L.Ed. 1042 (1972); Griswold v. Connecticut, 381 U.S. 479, 495, 85 S.Ct. 1678, 1687, 14 L.Ed.2d 510 (1965). And the Constitution secures to an individual a freedom "to satisfy his intellectual and emotional needs within the privacy of his own home." Stanley v. Georgia, 394 U.S. 557, 564-565, 89 S.Ct. 1243, 1248, 22 L.Ed.2d 542 (1969); see Paris Adult Theatre I v. Slaton, 413 U.S. 49, 66-67, 93 S.Ct. 2628, 2640-2641, 37 L.Ed.2d 446 (1973). Constitutionally protected privacy is, in Mr. Justice Brandeis' words, "as against the government, the right to be let alone . . . the right most valued by civilized man." Olmstead v. United States, 277 U.S. 438, 478, 48 S.Ct. 564, 572, 72 L.Ed. 944 (1928) (dissenting opinion). The choice of household companions—of whether a person's "intellectual and emotional needs" are best met by living with family, friends, professional associates or others —involves deeply personal considerations as to the kind and quality of intimate relationships within the home. That decision surely falls within the ambit of the right to privacy protected by the Constitution. See Roe v. Wade, 410 U.S. 113, 153, 93 S.Ct. 705, 727, 35 L.Ed.2d 147 (1973); Eisenstadt v. Baird, 405 U.S. 438, 453, 92 S.Ct. 1029, 1038, 31 L.Ed.2d 349 (1972); Stanley v. Georgia, 394 U.S., at 564-565, 89 S.Ct., at 1247-1248; Griswold v. Connecticut, 381 U.S., at 483, 486, 85 S.Ct., at 1682; Olmstead v. United States, 277 U.S. 438, 478, 48 S.Ct. 564, 572, 72 L.Ed. 944 (1928) (Brandeis, J., dissenting); Moreno v. Department of Agriculture, 345 F. Supp. 310, 315 (D.C.D.C. 1972), aff'd, 413 U.S. 528, 93 S.Ct. 2821, 31 L.Ed.2d 782 (1973).

The instant ordinance discriminates on the basis of just such a personal lifestyle choice as to household companions. It permits any number of persons related by blood or marriage, be it two or twenty, to live in a single household, but it limits to two the number of unrelated persons bound by profession, love, friendship, religious or political affiliation or mere economics who can occupy a single home. Belle Terre imposes upon those who deviate from the community norm in their choice of living companions significantly greater restrictions than are applied to residential groups who are related by blood or marriage, and comprise the established order with the community.[4] The town has, in effect, acted to fence out those individuals whose choice of lifestyle differs from that of its current residents.[5]

This is not a case where the Court is being asked to nullify a township's sincere efforts to maintain its residential character by preventing the operation of rooming houses, fraternity houses or other commercial or high-density residential uses. Unquestionably, a town is free to restrict such uses. Moreover, as a general proposition, I see no constitutional infirmity in a town limiting the density of use in residential areas by zoning regulations which do not discriminate on the basis of constitutionally suspect criteria.[6] This ordinance, however, limits the density of occupancy of only those homes occupied by unrelated persons. It thus reaches beyond control of the use of land or the density of population, and undertakes to regulate the way people choose to associate with each other within the privacy of their own homes.

It is no answer to say, as does the majority that associational interests are not infringed because Belle Terre residents may entertain whomever they choose. Only last Term Mr. Justice Douglas indicated in concurrence that he saw the right of association protected by the First Amendment as involving far more than the right to entertain visitors. He found that right infringed by a restriction on food stamp assistance, penalizing households of "unrelated persons." As Mr. Justice Douglas there said, freedom of association encompasses the "right to invite a stranger into one's home" not only for "entertainment" but to join the household as well. Moreno v. Department of Agriculture, 413 U.S. 528, 538-545, 93 S.Ct. 2821, 2828-2831 (1973) (Douglas, J., concurring). I am still persuaded that the choice of those who will form one's household implicates constitutionally protected rights.

Because I believe that this zoning ordinance creates a classification which impinges upon fundamental personal rights, it can withstand constitutional

4. "Perhaps in an ideal world, planning and zoning would be done on a regional basis, so that a given community would have apartments, while an adjoining community would not. But as long as we allow zoning to be done community by community, it is intolerable to allow one municipality (or many municipalities) to close its doors at the expense of surrounding communities and the central city." Appeal of Girsh, 437 Pa. 237, 245 n.4, 263 A.2d 395, 399 n.4 (1970).
5. See generally, Note, On Privacy, Constitutional Protection for Personal Liberty, 48 N.Y.U. L. Rev. 670, 740-750 (1973).
6. See Palo Alto Tenants' Union v. Morgan, 487 F.2d 883 (CA.9 1973).

scrutiny only upon a clear showing that the burden imposed is necessary to protect a compelling and substantial governmental interest, Shapiro v. Thompson, 394 U.S. 618, 634, 89 S.Ct. 1322, 1331, 22 L.Ed.2d 600 (1969). And, once it be determined that a burden has been placed upon a constitutional right, the onus of demonstrating that no less intrusive means will adequately protect the compelling state interest and that the challenged statute is sufficiently narrowly drawn, is upon the party seeking to justify the burden. See Memorial Hospital v. Maricopa County, —— U.S. ——, 94 S.Ct. 1076, 39 L.Ed.2d (1973); Speiser v. Randall, 357 U.S. 513, 525-526, 78 S.Ct. 1332, 1341-1342, 2 L.Ed.2d 1460 (1958).

A variety of justifications have been proffered in support of the village's ordinance. It is claimed that the ordinance controls population density, prevents noise, traffic and parking problems, and preserves the rent structure of the community and its attractiveness to families. As I noted earlier, these are all legitimate and substantial interests of government. But I think it clear that the means chosen to accomplish these purposes are both over-and under-inclusive, and that the asserted goals could be as effectively achieved by means of an ordinance that did not discriminate on the basis of constitutionally protected choices of life style. The ordinance imposes no restriction whatsoever on the number of persons who may live in a house, as long as they are related by marital or sanguinary bonds—presumably no matter how distant their relationship. Nor does the ordinance restrict the number of income earners who may contribute to rent in such a household, or the number of automobiles that may be maintained by its occupants. In that sense the ordinance is under-inclusive. On the other hand, the statute restricts the number of unrelated persons who may live in a home to no more than two. It would therefore prevent three unrelated people from occupying a dwelling even if among them they had but one income and no vehicles. While an extended family of a dozen or more might live in a small bungalow, three elderly and retired persons could not occupy the large manor house next door. Thus the statute is also grossly over-inclusive to accomplish its intended purposes.

There are some 220 residences in Belle Terre occupied by about 700 persons. The density is therefore just above three per household. The village is justifiably concerned with density of population and the number of dependent children.[7] The burden of such an ordinance would fall equally upon all segments of the community. It would surely be better tailored to the goals asserted by the township than the ordinance before us today, for it would more realistically restrict population density and growth and

---

7. By providing an exception for dependent children, the township would avoid any doubts that might otherwise be posed by the constitutional protection afforded the choice of whether to bear a child. See Molino v. Mayor & Council of Glassborough, 116 N.J. Super. 195, 281 A.2d 401 (1971); cf. Cleveland Board of Education v. LaFleur, — U.S. —, 94 S.Ct. 791, 39 L.Ed.2d 52 (1974).

their attendant environmental costs. Various other statutory mechanisms also suggest themselves as solutions to Belle Terre's problems—rent control, limits on the number of vehicles per household, and so forth, but, of course, such schemes are matters of legislative judgment and not for this Court. Appellants also refer to the necessity of maintaining the family character of the village. There is not a shred of evidence in the record indicating that if Belle Terre permitted a limited number of unrelated persons to live together, the residential, familial character of the community would be fundamentally affected.

By limiting unrelated households to two persons while placing no limitation on households of related individuals, the village has embarked upon its commendable course in a constitutionally faulty vessel. Cf. United States v. Marshall, —— U.S. ——, 94 S.Ct. 700, 38 L.Ed.2d 618 (1973) (dissenting opinion). I would find the challenged ordinance unconstitutional. But I would not ask the village to abandon its goal of providing quiet streets, little traffic, and a pleasant and reasonably priced environment in which families might raise their children. Rather, I would commend the town to continue to pursue those purposes but by means of more carefully drawn and even-handed legislation.

I respectfully dissent.

Questions and Notes

1. What was the precise issue in this case?

2. Why did Mr. Justice Brennan feel that the case was moot? What plaintiffs were left by the time it reached the Supreme Court?

3. On what ground did Mr. Justice Marshall place his dissent? For further elaboration of this point, see the opinion in the Second Circuit Court of Appeals, 476 F.2d 806.

4. Why do you suppose Mr. Justice Douglas upheld the ordinance, and why did he talk so much about the advantages of quiet areas with big lawns?

5. In the Douglas opinion, how many zoning cases are cited (a) from the Supreme Court and (b) from the state courts? What are the dates of such cases?

6. What view did Mr. Justice Marshall take about regulation of density?

SOUTHERN BURLINGTON COUNTY N.A.A.C.P.

v.

TOWNSHIP OF MOUNT LAUREL

67 N.J. 151, 336 A.2d 713 (1975),
appeal dismissed and cert. denied, U.S. (   ).

Superior Court of New Jersey,
Law Division.

May 1, 1972.

Action seeking declaratory and injunctive relief against municipality's zoning ordinance. The Superior Court, Law Division, Martino, A. J. S. C., held that zoning ordinance permitting multifamily dwellings on a farm for a farmer, a member of the farmer's family or persons employed by the farmer, provided that such dwelling was no closer than 200 feet from the property boundary line, was required to be declared invalid where patterns and practices established that the municipality, through its zoning ordinances, had exhibited economic discrimination in that the poor had been deprived of adequate housing and the opportunity to secure construction of subsidized housing and the municipality had used federal, state, county and local finances and resources solely for the betterment of middle and upper income persons.

Order accordingly.

Carl S. Bisgaier, Camden, for plaintiffs (David H. Dugan, III, Camden, Director, Camden Regional Legal Services, Inc., attorney).

John F. Gerry, Camden, for defendants (Wallace, Douglas, Gerry & Mariano, Camden, attorneys).

MARTINO, A. J. S. C.

Plaintiffs herein consist of corporate entities and certain individuals, resident and nonresident, who seek declaratory and injunctive relief against a municipality's zoning ordinance. The right of the corporate entities to bring the action raises a question of qualification to do so, but since certain individual plaintiffs are township residents their right to sue will permit the court to dispose of the issue raised without a determination of the right to sue raised against the other plaintiffs.

The factual situation as it appears as to the resident plaintiffs clearly indicates one of them has moved into a house which was originally used as a summer quarters for a summer camp. The electrical wiring is in an exposed condition and she often gets shocks from the outlets; one space heater by the front door provides inadequate intermittent heat and she must use the gas stove to provide sufficient heat; cold air comes through the windows; drains do not work on occasion and the cesspool backs up into the toilet. She was told that the county board of health and the local building inspector want to be advised when she leaves so that they can "post" the house as unfit for human habitation. She has two children, ages four and two, and receives $282 a month from the Welfare Department. In 1969 the planning board of defendant township recommended blighted area treatment for the area in which she lives.

Another resident with two children and two grandchildren, a widow, lives in an area also recommended for blighted area treatment by the planning board. The dwelling in which she lives was the subject of the first receivership action brought in this State under the new Receivership Law— N.J.S.A. 2A:42-85 et seq. For five years she and her family had been living in the house without any indoor plumbing or hot or cold running water. As a result of the court proceedings the house was put in receivership and repairs ordered. As a result, her toilet is now functional and she has hot and cold running water. However, insufficient funds are available to repair a leaking roof, plaster continues to fall, the stove is broken, pipes leak in bathroom, the house is infected with vermin. She has attempted to find other quarters in Mount Laurel, but is unable to do so because of her present income. Her total annual income is $6,000.

Another plaintiff has lived with her husband and seven children in defendant township for 20 years. The house is old and crowded and the area is surrounded by industrial uses. She was unable to give the age of the building, although she has lived in it 20 years.

Defendant township stipulated that three other persons who are party plaintiffs were former residents of Mount Laurel but were forced to move to adjoining municipalities. One couple had been living in a converted chicken coop; the cesspool kept backing up and the quarters were infected with vermin. This couple was forced to move in 1970. Another plaintiff was born in defendant township but was forced to move to Camden. The family had lived in a structure in Mount Laurel called "Diamond Apts." Their quarters were heated by a single kerosene heater; there was little or no hot water; the cesspool backed up and the place was infected with vermin. The family consisted of a husband and wife and four children. Another plaintiff, separated from her husband, was forced to move to Camden because the house she and her four children lived in while a resident of Mount Laurel had ceilings that were cracked and opened. A coal furnace with air vents on the first floor heated the entire house. Water lines continually became frozen; the cesspool kept filling up and backing up.

Testimony has indicated that in defendant municipality the minimum building costs of a single-family home is approximately $23,000. This would be the cost of the home completely bare, built on nonunion wages. Testimony further revealed that such a home built at union wage and including minimal amenities would cost 10% to 20% more. This would result in an expense for a single-family home that would not qualify for federal subsidized programs within the reach of the resident plaintiffs herein neglected. Over the years defendant municipality has acted affirmatively to control development and to attract a selective type of growth. These plans were financed with state and federal funds. The township has consistently excluded trailers or mobile homes from its confines. Multi-family uses were generally prohibited as early as 1954 in the local ordinances and the amendments which followed.

While plaintiffs' testimony referred to clearly indicates the neglect of defendant municipality as to them, the suit by these individuals who appear of record is proposed as a class action for the benefit of many others who, it is alleged and not disputed, suffer from the same substandard type of housing accommodations and reside in defendant municipality.

Under certain factual circumstances our Supreme Court has upheld zoning ordinances which require minimum interior floor space, Lionshead Lake Inc. v. Wayne Tp., 10 N.J. 165, 89 A.2d 693 (1952), app. dism. 344 U.S. 919, 73 S.Ct. 386, 97 L.Ed. 708 (1953); which limit lot sizes for a single-family unit to five acres, Fischer v. Bedminster Tp., 11 N.J. 194, 93 A.2d 378 (1952); which absolutely prohibit the construction of any additional multi-family units, Fanale v. Hasbrouck Heights, 26 N.J. 320, 139 A.2d 749 (1958); which prohibit the use of mobile homes on an individual lot, Napierkowski v. Gloucester Tp., 29 N.J. 481, 150 A.2d 481 (1959), and which absolutely prohibit all mobile-home parks from a township, Vickers v. Gloucester Tp. Committee, 37 N.J. 232, 181 A.2d 129 (1962), cert. den. 371 U.S. 233, 83 S.Ct. 326, 9 L.Ed.2d 495 (1963).

Plaintiffs do not quarrel with the above-mentioned cases and, for the purpose of argument herein, are not suggesting that they be overruled. They maintain that, if anything, these cases clearly enumerate judicial standards which mandate that they prevail in the instant case. Following the *Lionshead* case, which will be discussed *infra,* our court in Pierro v. Baxendale, 20 N.J. 17, 118 A.2d 401 (1955), aptly noted:

> We are aware of the extensive academic discussion following the decisions in the *Lionshead* and *Bedminster* cases, *supra,* and the suggestion that the very broad principles which they embody may intensify dangers of economic segregation ° ° °. In the light of existing population and land conditions within our State these powers may *fairly* be exercised without in anywise endangering the *needs* or *reasonable expectations* of any segments of our people. If and when conditions change, alterations in zoning restrictions and pertinent legislative and *judicial* attitudes need not be long delayed. [at 29, 118 A.2d at 407, 408; emphasis added]

In defendant township multi-family dwellings are only permitted on a farm for a farmer, a member of the farmer's family, or persons employed by the farmer, provided the multiple-family dwelling is not closer than 200 feet from the property boundary line.

Minutes of various township committee meetings expressing the attitudes of the members of the governing body were introduced into evidence. Early in 1968 the mayor, when a discussion arose as to low-income housing, stated it was the intention of the township committee to take care of the people of Mount Laurel Township but not make any area of Mount Laurel a home for the county. A committeeman added that it was the intent of the township to clear out substandard housing in the area and thereby get better citizens. At a later meeting of the township committee in 1969 a variance to permit multi-family dwelling units was rejected because the committee did not see a need for such construction. At a meeting in 1970 a committeeman, during a discussion of homes being run down and worthless, indicated that the policy was to wait until these homes were vacant before the township took action, "because if these people are put out on the streets they do not have another place to go." At another meeting in September 1970 a township committeeman, when referring to pressure from the Federal and State Governments to encourage low-cost housing retorted that their most useful function was to evaluate and screen away all but the most beneficial plans. He added, "We must be selective as possible—approving only those applications which are sound in all respects—We can approve only those development plans which will provide direct and substantial benefits to our *taxpayers.*" (Emphasis added). All through the various admissions permitted to be introduced into evidence, the evidence clearly indicates the attitude of developers who proposed various developments which were not concerned with people of low incomes. Every proposal made leaned in the direction of homes for only those of high income.

A research specialist and planning attorney, who was a consultant to the Division of State and Regional Planning, Department of Community Affairs, and a reporter to the State Land Use Revision Commission charged with revising the State's enabling legislation regarding planning and zoning in New Jersey, as well as counsel to Governor Cahill's Housing Task Force Committee, called by defendant municipality as one of its experts, categorically stated that the lack of permissible multi-family provisions in the zoning ordinance was a very good indication that low-income families were not being provided for. While he indicated that Burlington County, as a part of the Camden region, had a possibility of 45,000 multiple-family units under existing ordinances, it must be conceded that under our present enabling statute each municipality now controls its own zoning destiny.

Another expert witness employed by defendant municipality indicated that 66% of the township is vacant land. In the R-1 zone, which is the district having the lowest zoning category, viz., 9,375 square feet, there is currently 928 acres of vacant land available for development. This witness, a planner for defendant township for the past 2½ years, conceded that nothing to his knowledge has been done to re-house the residents living in substandard dwellings in that community. He also conceded that he knew of no standard housing in defendant township available for residents on welfare; that people are living in substandard housing because the municipality will not condemn, in as much as our Relocation Law, N.J.S.A. 20:4-1 to 22, would require that these residents be otherwise located.

The effect of this practice would account for the photographic exhibits, which indicate the deplorable facilities now tenanted by residents of the township.

In James v. Valtierra, 402 U.S. 137, 91 S.Ct. 1331, 28 L.Ed.2d 678 (1971), involving a California constitutional provision which required that all public housing proposals be submitted to a referendum, the court upheld the right to referendum. However, the reason was that the referendum itself did not on its face socially discriminate. In Hunter v. Erickson, 393 U.S. 385, 89 S.Ct. 557, 21 L.Ed.2d 616 (1969), the same court invalidated a city charter which required all fair housing ordinances to be submitted to a referendum.

"The States, of course, are prohibited by the Equal Protection Clause from discriminating between 'rich' and 'poor' *as such* in the formulation and application of their laws." Douglas v. California, 372 U.S. 353, 361, 83 S.Ct. 814, 818, 819, 9 L.Ed.2d 811 (1963), cited by Justice Marshall, with Justice Brennan and Justice Blackmun concurring, in the dissent in James v. Valtierra, *supra.* Significantly, the dissent added that "It is far too late in the day to contend that the Fourteenth Amendment prohibits only racial discrimination; and to me, singling out the poor to bear a burden not placed on any other class of citizens tramples the values that the Fourteenth Amendment was designed to protect."

Very little weight should be placed on the majority opinion in James v. Valtierra, *supra,* as an argument on behalf of defendant municipality, because the court there said, "Furthermore, an examination of California law reveals that persons advocating low-income housing have not been singled out for mandatory referendums while no other group must face that obstacle."

In Southern Alameda Spanish Speaking Organization v. City of Union, 424 F.2d 291 (9 Cir. 1970), the court, while only passing on the right to referendum as in James v. Valtierra, *supra,* significantly stated:

> Surely, if the environmental benefits of land use planning are to be enjoyed by a city and the quality of life of its residents is accordingly to be improved, the poor cannot be excluded from enjoyment of the benefits. Given the recognized importance of equal opportunities in housing, it may well be, as a matter of law, that it is the responsibility of a city and its planning officials to see that the city's plan as initiated or as it develops accommodates the needs of its low-income families, who usually—if not always—are members of minority groups. [at 295-296]

In Hobson v. Hansen, 269 F.Supp. 401 (D.C.1967) aff'd *sub nom.* Smuck v. Hobson, 132 U.S.App.D.C. 372, 408 F.2d 175 (1969) (*en banc*), the trial court stated:

> The complaint that analytically no violation of equal protection vests unless the inequalities stem from a deliberately discriminatory plan is simply false. Whatever the law was once, it is a testament to our maturing concept of equality that, with the help of Supreme Court decisions in the last

decade, we now firmly recognize that the arbitrary quality of thoughtlessness can be as disastrous to private rights and the public interests as the perversity of a willful scheme. [at 497]

One of the earlier cases which appeared to follow the philosophy propounded by these plaintiffs was Brookdale Homes, Inc. v. Johnson, 123 N.J.L. 602, 10 A.2d 477 (Sup.Ct.1940), aff'd 126 N.J.L. 516, 19 A.2d 868 (E & A 1941). In that case an ordinance required a dwelling to be not less than 26 feet above the building foundation. The court held:

> ° ° ° [A]n ordinance under the zoning act must bear a reasonable relation to the powers conferred by that act. ° ° ° Restrictions imposed pursuant to the zoning act must tend at least in some degree to promote the public good; they must bear a "substantial relation to the public health, the public morals, the public safety or the public welfare in its proper sense."

It appears that plaintiff there sought the right to build a dwelling which would be only 21 feet high from its foundation. The Court of Errors and Appeals filed a dissenting opinion joined in by six jurists.

Twelve years later Lionshead Lake, Inc. v. Wayne Tp., *supra*, was decided. That case has been the subject of much academic discussion. "Wayne Township: Zoning for Whom—In Brief Reply," 67 Harv.L.Rev. 986 (1954); Haar, "Zoning for Minimum Standards, The Wayne Township Case," 66 Harv.L.Rev. 1051 (1953). Chief Justice Vanderbilt concluded that constitutional and statutory changes in the meantime had in effect adopted the reasoning of the dissenters in *Brookdale, supra,* and rendered inapplicable the majority decision of the Court of Errors and Appeals which had held invalid an ordinance imposing minimum restrictions on the size of dwellings to protect the character of a community and property values therein. However, the opinion did include the statement:

> We must bear in mind, finally, that a zoning ordinance is not like the law of the Medes and Persians; variances may be permitted, the zoning ordinance may be amended, and *if the ordinance proves unreasonable in operation it may be set aside at any time.* [10 N.J. at 172, 173, 89 A.2d at 697; emphasis added]

A dissenting opinion by the late Justice Oliphant, who was joined by the late Justice Wachenfeld, commented upon the very points raised by plaintiffs in the instant case, *i. e.,*

Certain well-behaved families will be barred from these communities, not because of any acts they do or conditions they create, but simply because the income of the family will not permit them to build a house at the cost testified to in this case. They will be relegated to living in the large cities or in multiple-family dwellings even though it be against what they consider the welfare of their immediate families. [at 182, 89 A.2d at 701.]

Nineteen years later University of Toledo Law Review, vol. I, No. 1 (Winter 1969), at 76, had occasion to state, "Justice Oliphant's dissent in *Lionshead* is eloquent testimony to his farsightedness."

Today there remains only one jurist on our Supreme Court who concurred with the majority in *Lionshead, supra.*

[I]n zoning there must be a rational relation between the regulation and the promotion of the general welfare within the reach of the statutorily prescribed areas of action, and that the means invoked be in keeping with the public need. Arbitrary deviation from the general rule is forbidden; and, by the same token, undue discrimination in treatment and classification vitiates the regulation. [Roselle v. Wright, 21 N.J. 400, 410, 122 A.2d 506 (1956)]

The thin dividing line between economic segregation and racial or ethnic segregation can be seen in two New Jersey cases. It is generally assumed that it would be unconstitutional for the government by enactment and administration of local zoning ordinances to segregate residential areas by income levels, for example, by restricting an area to those families with incomes over $10,000, or to homes costing $20,000. In Stein v. Long Branch (2 N.J.Misc. 121 (Sup.Ct.1924)) and Brookdale Homes, Inc. v. Johnson, (*supra*), (overruled in *Lionshead, supra*), the zoning ordinances provided that no residences should cost less than a certain amount. The provisions of these ordinances clearly intended to exclude those unable to afford the houses in question. [University of Toledo Law Review, *supra,* at 75]

Ten years ago Justice Hall, in his dissent in Vickers v. Gloucester Tp. Committee, *supra,* in a lengthy dissent which deserves close study, summed up the true function of zoning when he said:

In my opinion legitimate use of the zoning power by such municipalities does not encompass the right to erect barricades on their boundaries through exclusion or too tight restriction of uses where the real purpose is to prevent feared disruption with a so-called chosen way of life. Nor does it encompass provisions designed to let in as new residents only certain kinds of people, or those who can afford to live in favored kinds of housing, or to keep down tax bills of present property owners. When one of the above is the true situation deeper considerations intrinsic in a free society gain the ascendancy and *courts must not be hesitant to strike down purely selfish and undemocratic enactments.* [37 N.J. at 264, 265, 181 A.2d at 147; emphasis added.]

While a municipality can be said to permit a use not specifically permitted in a zone area by way of a variance, the Governor's message delivered March 27, 1972 clearly enunciated the long and tortuous delays in accomplishing any variant to the provisions of our present zoning ordinances, much to the frustration of and damage to the builder and ultimate owner. See "New Horizons in Housing," A Special Message by William T. Cahill, Governor of New Jersey. The message, ever mindful of the rights of the individual to live and let live, calls for a rejuvenation of the general welfare concept originally contemplated in zoning and planning. The message and the proposals it suggests may put to rest the problem that exists as to the poor and needy in the sphere of housing. The courts, however, must be ever watchful of any discriminatory acts of local units of government against the rights and privileges of the poor and underprivileged.

[1]   It must be conceded that there is a general principle against judicial inquiry into the exercise by a legislative body of its police powers. Courts have always had the power to scrutinize the issue of discrimination. The pleadings, the evidence and the issues framed in this action evoke judicial review beyond that posed by a generalized exercise of police power. The inquiry here was not limited to the terms of the ordinance; the court received evidence of the ordinance's purpose, its ultimate objective and all the circumstances attending its adoption and enforcement.

The problems which zoning has raised were nurtured by the decision of our United States Supreme Court in Village of Euclid v. Ambler Realty Co., 272 U.S. 365, 47 S.Ct. 114, 71 L.Ed. 305 (1926). Those who oppose multi-family dwelling units find solace in the words of the late Justice Sutherland, who described multiple-family dwellings as very often a mere parasite whose presence utterly destroys the residential character of the neighborhood and its desirability as a place of residence. While the *Euclid* decision may have in effect condoned legislative zoning discretion, it did warn that:

> It is not meant by this, however, to exclude the possibility of cases where the general public interest would so far outweigh the interest of the municipality that the municipality would not be allowed to stand in the way. [272 U.S. at 390, 47 S.Ct. at 119, 71 L.Ed. at 311]

The *Euclid* case in the lower court plainly indicated the exclusionary use of zoning that was being perpetuated. That court said:

> The plain truth is that the true object of the ordinance in question is to place all the property ° ° ° in a strait-jacket. The purpose to be accomplished is really to regulate the mode of living of persons who may hereafter inhabit it. In the last analysis, the result to be accomplished is to classify the population and segregate them according to their income or situation in life. [297 F. 307, 316 (N.D.Ohio 1924), rev'd 272 U.S. 365, 47 S.Ct. 114, 71 L.Ed. 303 (1926)]

[2]   Today, when municipalities give reasons for the exclusion of certain uses, although they gloss them with high-meaning phrases, they lack sincerity. It is not low-cost housing which ferments crime; it is the lower economic strata of society which moves in, yet no ordinance would dare to raise that objection to prohibit them and expect to succeed. Local legislative bodies know better than to state that more low-income producing structures will mean a higher tax rate. This is what the courts have abhorred as fiscal zoning. What local governing body would raise an objection to bringing a factory into a neighborhood because it would increase the

population of the economically poor? While it may be an argument that it would affect property values, and while it is proper to zone in certain instances against factories, it is improper to build a wall against the poor-income people. In Gomillion v. Lightfoot, 364 U.S. 339, 81 S.Ct. 125, 5 L.Ed.2d 110 (1960), the court made it clear that the Constitution nullifies sophisticated as well as simple-minded modes of discrimination.

In Duffcon Concrete Products v. Cresskill, 1 N.J. 509, 64 A.2d 347 (1949), the court gave some promise when it said:

> What may be the most appropriate use of any particular property depends not only on all the conditions, physical, economic and social, prevailing within the municipality and its needs, present and reasonably prospective, but also on the nature of the entire region in which the municipality is located and the use to which the land in that region has been or may be put most advantageously. The effective development of a region should not and cannot be made to depend upon the adventitious location of municipal boundaries, often prescribed decades or even centuries ago, and based in many instances on considerations of geography, of commerce, or of politics that are no longer significant with respect to zoning. [at 513, 64 A.2d at 349-350]

The judiciary cannot be expected to alleviate a condition that definitely calls for legislative action from either the national or state governments. The courts can only meet each specific situation as it is presented, and while one community may have facts which justify court intervention, the relief will not necessarily be the same in all areas unless the factual content justifies intervention, as this court believes in the case at hand. The Federal Government has left zoning problems to the states, and the states have largely, but not entirely, left them to the local governments. Housing, to be adequate for the poor, must be left primarily in the hands of a governmental body other than a local unit. The judiciary can only expect to give relief on a piecemeal basis, and "legislation" by the courts is often less than satisfactory.

Ever mindful of the admonitions set forth in the Constitutional mandate of the New Jersey Constitution, Art. IV, § VII, par. 11, enjoining liberal construction of provisions in that document and of laws concerning local government, I would parrot the words of Justice Hall in his dissent in *Vickers, supra,* 37 N.J. at 257, 181 A.2d at 143, when he said, "Analysis demonstrates that the mandate has no true application in this situation."

There has been too much conservatism in the definition of the words which refer to one of the purposes of zoning, *i. e.,* "to promote the general welfare." Some definitions would better apply to private welfare.

Our present State Supreme Court, in a different setting, said:

> We specifically hold, as matter of law in the light of public policy and the law of the land, that public or, as here, semi-public housing accommodations to provide safe, sanitary and decent housing, to relieve and replace substandard living conditions or to furnish housing for minority

or underprivileged segments of the population outside of ghetto areas is a special reason adequate to meet that requirement of N.J.S.A. 40:55-39 (d) and to ground a use variance. [DeSimone v. Greater Englewood Housing Corp. No. 1, 56 N.J. 428, 442, 267 A.2d 31, 38-39 (1970)]

[3] The patterns and practice clearly indicate that defendant municipality through its zoning ordinances has exhibited economic discrimination in that the poor have been deprived of adequate housing and the opportunity to secure the construction of subsidized housing, and has used federal, state, county and local finances and resources solely for the betterment of middle and upper-income persons. The zoning ordinance is, therefore, declared invalid.

Plaintiffs, in seeking declaratory and injunctive relief, argue that even if the zoning ordinance were declared invalid, the injury they suffer will not afford a remedy. They argue there is a desperate need for affirmative municipal action within parameters established by the court.

In Hawkins v. Shaw, 437 F.2d 1286, 1293 (5 Cir. 1971), the court declared that a municipality cannot discriminate in the use of municipal services and said that a town could be required to submit a plan for the equitable distribution of such services. See also, Crow v. Brown, 332 F. Supp. 382 (N.D.Ga.1971), aff'd 457 F.2d 788 (5 Cir. 1972).

[4] This court agrees with plaintiffs and, therefore, orders that defendant municipality shall, upon the entry of a judgment to conform with these findings and conclusions of law, immediately undertake a study to identify:

a. The existing sub-standard dwelling units in the township and the number of individuals and families, by income and size, who would be displaced by an effective code-enforcement program;

b. The housing needs for persons of low and moderate income:

1. Residing in the township;

2. Presently employed by the municipality or in commercial and industrial uses in the township;

3. Expected or projected to be employed by the municipality or in commercial and industrial uses, the development of which can reasonably be anticipated in the township.

Defendant shall, upon completion of the investigation referred to in the preceding paragraph, establish, to the extent possible, an estimated number of both low and moderate income units which should be constructed in the township each year to provide for the needs as identified in the preceding paragraph.

Defendant shall, upon completion of the analysis set forth in the preceding paragraphs, develop a plan of implementation, that is, an affirmative program, to enable and encourage the satisfaction of the needs as previously set forth. That plan shall include an analysis of the ways in which the township can act affirmatively to enable and encourage the satisfaction of the indicated needs and shall include a plan of action which the township has chosen for the purposes of implementing this program. The adopted plan shall encompass the most effective and thorough means by which municipal action can be utilized to accomplish the goals set forth above.

If for any reason the township shall find that circumstances exist which in any way interfere with or bar the implementation of the plan chosen, it shall set forth in explicit detail:

a. Each and every factor;

b. The way in which each factor interferes with or bars implementation of the plan;

c. Possible alternative plans or municipal action which temporarily or permanently, wholly or in part, eliminate the indicated factor or factors, and

d. The reason why the alternative plans have not been adopted.

To the extent possible, the aforementioned analysis, studies and plans shall be undertaken with the cooperation and participation of plaintiffs and their representatives.

The aforementioned analyses, studies, development of plans and other action shall be completed within 90 days from the date of judgment. The township shall serve copies of the analyses, studies and plans on plaintiffs' attorney and this court within 90 days. The parties shall appear before this court no later than ten days, or on a date set by this court, after service of said papers for a determination of whether defendants have complied with the order of this court and whether further action is necessary.

The judgment entered in this matter as to the invalidity of the zoning ordinance shall not become effective until this court shall decide that sufficient time has elapsed to enable the municipality to enact new and proper regulations for the municipality. Morris County Land, etc. v. Parsippany-Troy Hills, 40 N.J. 539, 193 A.2d 232 (1963).

This court retains jurisdiction until a final order issues requiring implementation of the plan as agreed upon.

SOUTHERN BURLINGTON COUNTY N. A. A. C. P.

v.

TOWNSHIP OF MOUNT LAUREL

67 N.J. 151, 336 A2d. 713 (1975),
appeal dismissed and cert. denied, 423 U.S. 808 (1976).

Supreme Court of New Jersey.

Argued Jan. 8, 1974.

Decided March 24, 1975.

Action was brought attacking system of land use regulation by township on ground that low and moderate income families are thereby unlawfully excluded from the municipality. The Superior Court, Law Division, 119 N.J.Super. 164, 290 A.2d 465, declared the township zoning ordinance totally invalid and appeal was taken. The Supreme Court, Hall, J., held that a developing municipality may not, by a system of land use regulation, make it physically and economically impossible to provide low and moderate income housing in the municipality for various categories of persons who need and want it; that ordinance permitting only single-family detached dwellings and which was so restrictive in its minimum lot area, lot frontage and building size requirements as to preclude single-family housing for even moderate income families was contrary to the general welfare; that release from consequences of tax system by limiting permissible types of housing to those having the fewest school children or those providing sufficient value to pay their own way could not be accomplished by restricting types of housing through the zoning process; and that ecological or environmental reasons was not a sufficient excuse for limiting housing to single-family dwellings on large lots.

Judgment modified.

Mountain and Pashman, JJ., filed concurring opinions.

John W. Trimble, Turnersville, for defendant-appellant and cross-respondent (Higgins, Trimble & Master, Turnersville, attorneys; Peter R. Thorndike, Camden, on the brief).

Carl S. Bisgaier of Camden Regional Legal Services, Inc., Camden, for plaintiffs-respondents and cross-appellants (Kenneth E. Meiser and Peter J. O'Connor, Camden, on the brief).

Norman Williams, Jr., Newark, for amicus curiae The Public Interest Research Group of N. J.

Melville D. Miller, Jr., Trenton, for amicus curiae Legal Services Housing Task Force, N. J. State Office of Legal Services.

The opinion of the Court was delivered by

HALL, J.

This case attacks the system of land use regulation by defendant Township of Mount Laurel on the ground that low and moderate income families are thereby unlawfully excluded from the municipality. The trial court so found, 119 N.J.Super. 164, 290 A.2d 465 (Law Div.1972), and declared the township zoning ordinance totally invalid. Its judgment went on, in line with the requests for affirmative relief, to order the municipality to make studies of the housing needs of low and moderate income persons presently or formerly residing in the community in substandard housing, as well as those in such income classifications presently employed in the township and living elsewhere or reasonably expected to be employed therein in the future, and to present a plan of affirmative public action designed "to enable and encourage the satisfaction of the indicated needs." Jurisdiction was retained for judicial consideration and approval of such a plan and for the entry of a final order requiring its implementation.

The township appealed to the Appellate Division and those plaintiffs, not present or former residents, cross-appealed on the basis that the judgment should have directed that the prescribed plan take into account as well a fair share of the regional housing needs of low and moderate income families without limitation to those having past, present or prospective connection with the township. The appeals were certified on our own motion before argument in the Division. R.2:12-1.[1]

The implications of the issue presented are indeed broad and far-reaching, extending much beyond these particular plaintiffs and the boundaries of this particular municipality.

There is not the slightest doubt that New Jersey has been, and continues to be, faced with a desperate need for housing, especially of decent living accommodations economically suitable for low and moderate income families.[2] The situation was characterized as a "crisis" and fully explored and documented by Governor Cahill in two special messages to the Legislature—*A Blueprint for Housing in New Jersey* (1970) and *New Horizons in Housing* (1972).

---

1. The judgment stayed the declaration of invalidity of the zoning ordinance until the court should decide "that sufficient time has elapsed to enable the municipality to enact new and proper regulations." The other provisions of the judgment were stayed pending appeal by subsequent order of the trial court.

2. "Low income" was used in this case to refer to those persons or families eligible, by virtue of limited income, for occupancy in public housing units or units receiving rent supplement subsidies according to formulas therefor in effect in the area. "Moderate income" was similarly used to refer to those eligible for occupancy in housing units receiving so-called Section 235 or 236 or like subsidies. In another case, Oakwood at Madison v. Township of Madison, 128 N.J. Super. 438, 445, 320 A.2d 223 (Law Div. 1974), the figures of income up to $7,000 a year for the first category and up to $10,000-$12,000 for the second were projected. While the formula figures vary depending on family size, the dollar amounts mentioned are close enough to represent the top income in each classification for present purposes. "Middle income" and "upper income" are the designations of higher income categories.

[1]   Plaintiffs represent the minority group poor (black and Hispanic)[3] seeking such quarters. But they are not the only category of persons barred from so many municipalities by reason of restrictive land use regulations. We have reference to young and elderly couples, single persons and large, growing families not in the poverty class, but who still cannot afford the only kinds of housing realistically permitted in most places—relatively high-priced, single-family detached dwellings on sizeable lots and, in some municipalities, expensive apartments. We will, therefore, consider the case from the wider viewpoint that the effect of Mount Laurel's land use regulation has been to prevent various categories of persons from living in the township because of the limited extent of their income and resources. In this connection, we accept the representation of the municipality's counsel at oral argument that the regulatory scheme was not adopted with any desire or intent to exclude prospective residents on the obviously illegal bases of race, origin or believed social incompatibility.

As already intimated, the issue here is not confined to Mount Laurel. The same question arises with respect to any number of other municipalities of sizeable land area outside the central cities and older built-up suburbs of our North and South Jersey metropolitan areas (and surrounding some of the smaller cities outside those areas as well) which, like Mount Laurel, have substantially shed rural characteristics and have undergone great population increase since World War II, or are now in the process of doing so, but still are not completely developed and remain in the path of inevitable future residential, commercial and industrial demand and growth. Most such municipalities, with but relatively insignificant variation in details, present generally comparable physical situations, courses of municipal policies, practices, enactments and results and human, governmental and legal problems arising therefrom. It is in the context of communities now of this type or which become so in the future, rather than with central cities or older built-up suburbs or areas still rural and likely to continue to be for some time yet, that we deal with the question raised.

Extensive oral and documentary evidence was introduced at the trial, largely informational, dealing with the development of Mount Laurel, in-

---

3. Plaintiffs fall into four categories: (1) present residents of the township residing in dilapidated or substandard housing; (2) former residents who were forced to move elsewhere because of the absence of suitable housing; (3) nonresidents living in central city substandard housing in the region who desire to secure decent housing and accompanying advantages within their means elsewhere; (4) three organizations representing the housing and other interests of racial minorities. The township originally challenged plaintiffs' standing to bring this action. The trial court properly held (119 N.J. Super. at 166, 200 A.2d 465) that the resident plaintiffs had adequate standing to ground the entire action and found it unnecessary to pass on that of the other plaintiffs. The issue has not been raised on appeal. We merely add that both categories of nonresident individuals likewise have standing. N.J.S.A. 40:55-47.1; *cf.* Walker v. Borough of Stanhope, 23 N.J. 657, 130 A.2d 372 (1957). No opinion is expressed as to the standing of the organizations.

cluding the nature and effect of municipal regulation, the details of the region of which it is a part and the recent history thereof, and some of the basics of housing, special reference being directed to that for low and moderate income families. The record has been supplemented by figures, maps, studies and literature furnished or referred to by counsel and the *amici*, so that the court has a clear picture of land use regulation and its effects in the developing municipalities of the state.

This evidence was not contradicted by the township, except in a few unimportant details. Its candid position is that, conceding its land use regulation was intended to result and has resulted in economic discrimination and exclusion of substantial segments of the area population, its policies and practices are in the best present and future fiscal interest of the municipality and its inhabitants and are legally permissible and justified. It further asserts that the trial court was without power to direct the affirmative relief it did.

I

The Facts

Mount Laurel is a flat, sprawling township, 22 square miles, or about 14,000 acres, in area, on the west central edge of Burlington County. It is roughly triangular in shape, with its base, approximately eight miles long, extending in a northeasterly-southwesterly direction roughly parallel with and a few miles east of the Delaware River. Part of its southerly side abuts Cherry Hill in Camden County. That section of the township is about seven miles from the boundary line of the city of Camden and not more than 10 miles from the Benjamin Franklin Bridge crossing the river to Philadelphia.

In 1950, the township had a population of 2817, only about 600 more people than it had in 1940. It was then, as it had been for decades, primarily a rural agricultural area with no sizeable settlements or commercial or industrial enterprises. The populace generally lived in individual houses scattered along country roads. There were several pockets of poverty, with deteriorating or dilapidated housing (apparently 300 or so units of which remain today in equally poor condition). After 1950, as in so many other municipalities similarly situated, residential development and some commerce and industry began to come in. By 1960 the population had almost doubled to 5249 and by 1970 had more than doubled again to 11,221. These new residents were, of course, "outsiders" from the nearby central cities and older suburbs or from more distant places drawn here by reason of employment in the region. The township is now definitely a part of the outer ring of the South Jersey metropolitan area, which area we define as those portions of Camden, Burlington and Gloucester Counties within a semicircle having a radius of 20 miles or so from the heart of Camden city. And 65% of the township is still vacant land or in agricultural use.

The growth of the township has been spurred by the construction or improvement of main highways through or near it. The New Jersey Turnpike, and now route I-295, a freeway paralleling the turnpike, traverse the municipality near its base, with the main Camden-Philadelphia turnpike interchange at the corner nearest Camden. State route 73 runs at right angles to the turnpike at the interchange and route 38 slices through the northeasterly section. Routes 70 and U.S. 130 are not far away. This highway network gives the township a most strategic location from the standpoint of transport of goods and people by truck and private car. There is no other means of transportation.

The location and nature of development has been, as usual, controlled by the local zoning enactments. The general ordinance presently in force, which was declared invalid by the trial court, was adopted in 1964. We understand that earlier enactments provided, however, basically the same scheme but were less restrictive as to residential development. The growth pattern dictated by the ordinance is typical.

Under the present ordinance, 29.2% of all the land in the township, or 4,121 acres, is zoned for industry. This amounts to 2,800 more acres than were so zoned by the 1954 ordinance. The industrial districts comprise most of the land on both sides of the turnpike and routes I-295, 73 and 38. Only industry meeting specified performance standards is permitted. The effect is to limit the use substantially to light manufacturing, research, distribution of goods, offices and the like. Some nonindustrial uses, such as agriculture, farm dwellings, motels, a harness racetrack, and certain retail sales and service establishments, are permitted in this zone. At the time of trial no more than 100 acres, mostly in the southwesterly corner along route 73 adjacent to the turnpike and I-295 interchanges, were actually occupied by industrial uses. They had been constructed in recent years, mostly in several industrial parks, and involved tax ratables of about 16 million dollars. The rest of the land so zoned has remained undeveloped. If it were fully utilized, the testimony was that about 43,500 industrial jobs would be created, but it appeared clear that, as happens in the case of so many municipalities, much more land has been so zoned than the reasonable potential for industrial movement or expansion warrants. At the same time, however, the land cannot be used for residential development under the general ordinance.

The amount of land zoned for retail business use under the general ordinance is relatively small—169 acres, or 1.2% of the total. Some of it is near the turnpike interchange; most of the rest is allocated to a handful of neighborhood commercial districts. While the greater part of the land so zoned appears to be in use, there is no major shopping center or concentrated retail commercial area—"downtown"—in the township.

The balance of the land area, almost 10,000 acres, has been developed until recently in the conventional form of major subdivisions. The general ordinance provides for four residential zones, designated R-1, R-1D, R-2 and R-3. All permit only single-family, detached dwellings, one house per lot—the usual form of grid development. Attached townhouses, apartments (except on farms for agricultural workers) and mobile homes are not allowed anywhere in the township under the general ordinance. This dwelling development, resulting in the previously mentioned quadrupling of the population, has been largely confined to the R-1 and R-2 districts in two sections—the northeasterly and southwesterly corners adjacent to the turnpike and other major highways. The result has been quite intensive development of these sections, but at a low density. The dwellings are substantial; the average value in 1971 was $32,500 and is undoubtedly much higher today.

The general ordinance requirements, while not as restrictive as those in many similar municipalities, nontheless realistically allow only homes within the financial reach of persons of at least middle income. The R-1 zone requires a minimum lot area of 9,375 square feet, a minimum lot width of 75 feet at the building line, and a minimum dwelling floor area of 1,100 square feet if a one-story building and 1,300 square feet if one and one-half stories or higher. Originally this zone comprised about 2,500 acres. Most of the subdivisions have been constructed within it so that only a few hundred acres remain (the testimony was at variance as to the exact amount). The R-2 zone, comprising a single district of 141 acres in the northeasterly corner, has been completely developed. While it only required a minimum floor area of 900 square feet for a one-story dwelling, the minimum lot size was 11,000 square feet; otherwise the requisites were the same as in the R-1 zone.

The general ordinance places the remainder of the township, outside of the industrial and commercial zones and the R-1D district (to be mentioned shortly), in the R-3 zone. This zone comprises over 7,000 acres—slightly more than half of the total municipal area—practically all of which is located in the central part of the township extending southeasterly to the apex of the triangle. The testimony was that about 4,600 acres of it then remained available for housing development. Ordinance requirements are substantially higher, however, in that the minimum lot size is increased to about one-half acre (20,000 square feet). (We understand that sewer and water utilities have not generally been installed, but, of course, they can be.) Lot width at the building line must be 100 feet. Minimum dwelling floor area is as in the R-1 zone. Presently this section is primarily in agricultural use; it contains as well most of the municipality's substandard housing.

The R-1D district was created by ordinance amendment in 1968. The area is composed of a piece of what was formerly R-3 land in the western part of that zone. The district is a so-called "cluster" zone. See generally 2 Williams, American Planning Law: Land Use and the Police Power, §§ 47.01-47.05 (1974). That writer defines the concept as follows:

    * * * Under the usual cluster-zoning provisions, both the size and the width of individual residential lots in a large (or medium-sized) development may be reduced, provided (usually) that the overall density of the entire tract remains constant—provided, that is, that an area equivalent to the total of the areas thus "saved" from each individual lot is pooled and retained as common open space.   The most obvious advantages include a better use of many sites, and relief from the monotony of continuous development.   § 47.01, pp. 212-213.

Here this concept is implemented by reduction of the minimum lot area from 20,000 square feet required in the R-3 zone to 10,000 square feet (12,000 square feet for corner lots) but with the proviso that one-family houses—the single permitted dwelling use—"shall not be erected in excess of an allowable development density of 2.25 dwelling units per gross acre." The minimum lot width at the building line must be 80 feet and the minimum dwelling floor area is the same as in the R-3 zone.   The amendment further provides that the developer must set aside and dedicate to the municipality a minimum of 15% and a maximum of 25% of the total acreage for such public uses as may be required by the Planning Board, including "but not limited to school sites, parks, playgrounds, recreation areas, public buildings, public utilities."   Some dwelling development has taken place in this district, the exact extent of which is not disclosed by the record.   It is apparent that the dwellings are comparable in character and value to those in the other residential zones.   The testimony was that 486 acres remained available in the district.[4]

A variation from conventional development has recently occurred in some parts of Mount Laurel, as in a number of other similar municipalities, by use of the land use regulation device known as "planned unit development" (PUD).   This scheme differs from the traditional in that the type, density and placement of land uses and buildings, instead of being detailed and confined to specified districts by local legislation in advance, is determined by contract, or "deal," as to each development between the developer and the municipal administrative authority, under broad guidelines laid down by state enabling legislation and an implementing local ordinance. The stress is on regulation of density and permitted mixture of uses within the same area, including various kinds of living accommodations with or without commercial and industrial enterprises.   The idea may be basically thought of as the creation of "new towns" in virgin territory, full-blown or in miniature, although most frequently the concept has been limited in practice, as in Mount Laurel, to residential developments of various sizes having some variety of housing and perhaps some retail establishments to serve the inhabitants.   See generally, 2 Williams, *supra*, §§ 48.01 to 48.12; *cf.* Cheney v. Village 2 at New Hope, Inc., 429 Pa. 626, 241 A.2d 81, 82-83 (1968).

---

4. The validity of cluster zoning and of particular ordinance provisions, including, as here, those requiring the dedication of open space for public uses, has never been passed upon by this court. See generally 2. Williams, *supra*, §§ 47.02, 47.03, 47.05.

New Jersey passed such enabling legislation in 1967 (L.1967, c. 61, amended c. 286, N.J.S.A. 40:55-54 et seq.), which closely follows a model act found in 114 U.Pa.L.Rev. 140 (1965), and Mount Laurel adopted the implementing enactment as a supplement to its general zoning ordinance in December of that year. While the ordinance was repealed early in 1971, the township governing body in the interim had approved four PUD projects, which were specifically saved from extinction by the repealer.[5]

These projects, three in the southwesterly sector and one in the northeasterly sector, are very substantial and involve at least 10,000 sale and rental housing units of various types to be erected over a period of years. Their bounds were created by agreement rather than legislative specification on the zoning map, invading industrial, R-1, R-1D, R-3 and even flood plain zones. If completed as planned, they will in themselves ultimately quadruple the 1970 township population, but still leave a good part of the township undeveloped. (The record does not indicate how far development in each of the projects has progressed.) While multi-family housing in the form of rental garden, medium rise and high rise apartments and attached townhouses is for the first time provided for, as well as single-family detached dwellings for sale, it is not designed to accommodate and is beyond the financial reach of low and moderate income families, especially those with young children. The aim is quite the contrary; as with the single-family homes in the older conventional subdivisions, only persons of medium and upper income are sought as residents.

A few details will furnish sufficient documentation. Each of the resolutions of tentative approval of the projects contains a similar fact finding to the effect that the development will attract a highly educated and trained population base to support the nearby industrial parks in the township as well as the business and commercial facilities. The approvals also sharply limit the number of apartments having more than one bed-

---

5. The ordinance was held, in a taxpayer's suit, to be unconstitutional under the zoning section of the state constitution (Art. IV, sec. VI, par. 2) and violative of the general zoning enabling act (N.J.S.A. 40:55-30 et seq.). Rudderow v. Township Committee of Mount Laurel Township, 114 N.J. Super. 104, 274 A.2d 854, decided in March 1971 by the same judge who determined the instant case. His judgment was reversed by the Appellate Division in December 1972, 121 N.J. Super. 409, 297 A.2d 583, after the ordinance has been repealed and the instant case heard and decided at the trial level. This court has never passed upon the PUD enabling legislation, any local implementing ordinances or any municipal approval of a PUD project. The basic legal questions involved in *Rudderow*, which include among others the matter of what requirements a municipal authority may, in effect, impose upon a developer as a condition of approval, are serious and not all easy of solution. We refer to the Mount Laurel PUD projects as part of the picture of land use regulation in the township and its effect. It may be noted that, at a hearing on the PUD ordinance, the then township attorney stated that "° ° ° providing for apartments in a PUD ordinance in effect would seem to overcome any court objection that the Township was not properly zoning in denying apartments."

room. Further, they require that the developer must provide in its leases that no school-age children shall be permitted to occupy any one-bedroom apartment and that no more than two such children shall reside in any two-bedroom unit. The developer is also required, prior to the issuance of the first building permit, to record a covenant, running with all land on which multi-family housing is to be constructed, providing that in the event more than .3 school children per multi-family unit shall attend the township school system in any one year, the developer will pay the cost of tuition and other school expenses of all such excess numbers of children. In addition, low density, required amenities, such as central air conditioning, and specified developer contributions help to push rents and sales prices to high levels. These contributions include fire apparatus, ambulances, fire houses, and very large sums of money for educational facilities, a cultural center and the township library.[6]

Still another restrictive land use regulation was adopted by the township through a supplement to the general zoning ordinance enacted in September 1972 creating a new zone, R-4, Planned Adult Retirement Community (PARC). The supplementary enactment designated a sizeable area as the zone—perhaps 200 acres—carved out of the R-1D and R-3 districts in the southwesterly sector. The enactment recited a critical shortage of adequate housing in the township suitable "for the needs and desires of senior citizens and certain other adults over the age of 52." The permission was essentially for single ownership development of the zone for multi-family housing (townhouses and apartments), thereafter to be either rented or sold as cooperatives or condominiums. The extensive development requirements detailed in the ordinance make it apparent that the scheme was not designed for, and would be beyond the means of, low and moderate income retirees. The highly restricted nature of the zone is found in the requirement that all permanent residents must be at least 52 years of age (except a spouse, immediate family member other than a child, live-in domestic, companion or nurse). Children are limited to a maximum of one, over age 18 residing with a parent and there may be no more than three permanent residents in any one dwelling unit.[7]

All this affirmative action for the benefit of certain segments of the population is in sharp contrast to the lack of action, and indeed hostility, with respect to affording any opportunity for decent housing for the township's own poor living in substandard accommodations, found largely in the section known as Springville (R-3 zone). The 1969 Master Plan Report recognized it and recommended positive action. The continuous official

---

6. The current township attorney, at oral argument, conceded without specification, that many of these various conditions which had been required of developers were illegal.

7. This court has not yet passed on the validity of any land use regulation which restricts residence on the basis of occupant age.

reaction has been rather a negative policy of waiting for dilapidated premises to be vacated and then forbidding further occupancy. An earlier non-governmental effort to improve conditions had been effectively thwarted. In 1968 a private non-profit association sought to build subsidized, multi-family housing in the Springville section with funds to be granted by a higher level governmental agency. Advance municipal approval of the project was required. The Township Committee responded with a purportedly approving resolution, which found a need for "moderate" income housing in the area, but went on to specify that such housing must be constructed subject to all zoning, planning, building and other applicable ordinances and codes. This meant single-family detached dwellings on 20,000 square foot lots. (Fear was also expressed that such housing would attract low income families from outside the township.) Needless to say, such requirements killed realistic housing for this group of low and moderate income families.[8]

The record thoroughly substantiates the findings of the trial court that over the years Mount Laurel "has acted affirmatively to control development and to attract a selective type of growth" (119 N.J.Super. at 168, 290 A.2d at 467) and that "through its zoning ordinances has exhibited economic discrimination in that the poor have been deprived of adequate housing and the opportunity to secure the construction of subsidized housing, and has used federal, state, county and local finances and resources[9] solely for the betterment of middle and upper-income persons." (119 N.J. Super. at 178, 290 A.2d at 473).

There cannot be the slightest doubt that the reason for this course of conduct has been to keep down local taxes on *property* (Mount Laurel is not a high tax municipality) and that the policy was carried out without regard for non-fiscal considerations with respect to *people,* either within or without its boundaries. This conclusion is demonstrated not only by what was done and what happened, as we have related, but also by innumerable direct statements of municipal officials at public meetings over the years which are found in the exhibits. The trial court referred to a number of them. 119 N.J.Super. at 169-170, 290 A.2d 465. No official testified to the contrary.

---

8. The record is replete with uncontradicted evidence that, factually, low and moderate income housing cannot be built without some form of contribution, concession or incentive by some level of government. Such, under various state and federal methods, may take the form of public construction or some sort of governmental assistance or encouragement to private building. Multi-family rental units at a high density, or, at most, low cost single-family units on very small lots, are economically necessary and in turn require appropriate local land use regulations.

9. Such "finances and resources" has reference to monies spent by various agencies on highways within the municipality, loans and grants for water and sewer systems and for planning, federal guarantees of mortgages on new home construction, and the like.

This policy of land use regulation for a fiscal end derives from New Jersey's tax structure, which has imposed on local real estate most of the cost of municipal and county government and of the primary and secondary education of the municipality's children. The latter expense is much the largest, so, basically, the fewer the school children, the lower the tax rate. Sizeable industrial and commercial ratables are eagerly sought and homes and the lots on which they are situate are required to be large enough, through minimum lot sizes and minimum floor areas, to have substantial value in order to produce greater tax revenues to meet school costs. Large families who cannot afford to buy large houses and must live in cheaper rental accommodations are definitely not wanted, so we find drastic bedroom restrictions for, or complete prohibition of, multi-family or other feasible housing for those of lesser income.

This pattern of land use regulation has been adopted for the same purpose in developing municipality after developing municipality. Almost every one acts solely in its own selfish and parochial interest and in effect builds a wall around itself to keep out those people or entities not adding favorably to the tax base, despite the location of the municipality or the demand for varied kinds of housing. There has been no effective inter-municipal or area planning or land use regulation. All of this is amply demonstrated by the evidence in this case as to Camden, Burlington and Gloucester counties. As to the similar situation generally in the state, see New Jersey Department of Community Affairs, Division of State and Regional Planning, Land Use Regulation, The Residential Land Supply (April 1972) (a study assembling and examining the nature and extent of municipal zoning practices in 16 counties as affecting residential land available for low and moderate income housing) and Williams and Norman, Exclusionary Land Use Controls: The Case of North-Eastern New Jersey, 22 Syracuse L.Rev. 475, 486-487 (1971). One incongruous result is the picture of developing municipalities rendering it impossible for lower paid employees of industries they have eagerly sought and welcomed with open arms (and, in Mount Laurel's case, even some of its own lower paid municipal employees) to live in the community where they work.

The other end of the spectrum should also be mentioned because it shows the source of some of the demand for cheaper housing than the developing municipalities have permitted. Core cities were originally the location of most commerce and industry. Many of those facilities furnished employment for the unskilled and semi-skilled. These employees lived relatively near their work, so sections of cities always have housed the majority of people of low and moderate income, generally in old and deteriorating housing. Despite the municipally confined tax structure, commercial and industrial ratables generally used to supply enough revenue to provide and maintain municipal services equal or superior to those furnished in most suburban and rural areas.

The situation has become exactly the opposite since the end of World War II. Much industry and retail business, and even the professions, have left the cities. Camden is a typical example. The testimonial and documentary evidence in this case as to what has happened to that city is depressing indeed. For various reasons, it lost thousands of jobs between 1950 and 1970, including more than half of its manufacturing jobs (a reduction from 43,267 to 20,671, while all jobs in the entire area labor market increased from 94,507 to 197,037). A large segment of retail business faded away with the erection of large suburban shopping centers. The economically better situated city residents helped fill up the miles of sprawling new housing developments, not fully served by public transit. In a society which came to depend more and more on expensive individual motor vehicle transportation for all purposes, low income employees very frequently could not afford to reach outlying places of suitable employment and they certainly could not afford the permissible housing near such locations. These people have great difficulty in obtaining work and have been forced to remain in housing which is overcrowded, and has become more and more substandard and less and less tax productive. There has been a consequent critical erosion of the city tax base and inability to provide the amount and quality of those governmental services—education, health, police, fire, housing and the like—so necessary to the very existence of safe and decent city life. This category of city dwellers desperately needs much better housing and living conditions than is available to them now, both in a rehabilitated city and in outlying municipalities. They make up, along with the other classes of persons earlier mentioned who also cannot afford the only generally permitted housing in the developing municipalities, the acknowledged great demand for low and moderate income housing.

II

The Legal Issue

The legal question before us, as earlier indicated, is whether a developing municipality like Mount Laurel may validly, by a system of land use regulation, make it physically and economically impossible to provide low and moderate income housing in the municipality for the various categories of persons who need and want it and thereby, as Mount Laurel has, exclude such people from living within its confines because of the limited extent of their income and resources. Necessarily implicated are the broader questions of the right of such municipalities to limit the kinds of available housing and of any obligation to make possible a variety and choice of types of living accommodations.

[2, 3] We conclude that every such municipality must, by its land use regulations, presumptively make realistically possible an appropriate variety and choice of housing. More specifically, presumptively it cannot foreclose the opportunity of the classes of people mentioned for low and moderate income housing and in its regulations must affirmatively afford that opportunity, at least to the extent of the municipality's fair share of the present and prospective regional need therefor. These obligations must be met unless the particular municipality can sustain the heavy burden of demonstrating peculiar circumstances which dictate that it should not be required so to do.[10]

We reach this conclusion under state law and so do not find it necessary to consider federal constitutional grounds urged by plaintiffs. We begin with some fundamental principles as applied to the scene before us.

[4] Land use regulation is encompassed within the state's police power. Our constitutions have expressly so provided since an amendment in 1927. That amendment, now Art. IV, sec. VI, par. 2 of the 1947 Constitution, authorized legislative delegation of the power to municipalities (other than counties), but reserved the legislative right to repeal or alter the delegation (which we take it means repeal or alteration in whole or in part). The legislative delegation of the zoning power followed in 1928, by adoption of the standard zoning enabling act, now found, with subsequent amendments, in N.J.S.A. 40:55-30 to 51.

[5-9] It is elementary theory that all police power enactments, no matter at what level of government, must conform to the basic state constitutional requirements of substantive due process and equal protection of the laws. These are inherent in Art. I, par. 1 of our Constitution,[11] the requirements of which may be more demanding than those of the federal Constitution, Robinson v. Cahill, 62 N.J. 473, 482, 490-492, 303 A.2d 273 (1973); Washington National Insurance Co. v. Board of Review, 1 N.J. 545, 553-554, 64 A.2d 443 (1949). It is required that, affirmatively, a zoning regulation, like any police power enactment, must promote public health, safety, morals or the general welfare. (The last term seems broad enough to encompass the others.) Conversely, a zoning enactment which is contrary to the general welfare is invalid. See generally, e. g., Roselle v. Wright, 21 N.J. 400, 409-410, 122 A.2d 506 (1956); Katobimar Realty Co. v. Webster, 20 N.J. 114, 122-123, 118 A.2d 824 (1955); Schmidt v. Board of Adjustment of Newark, 9 N.J. 405, 413-419, 88 A.2d 607 (1952); Collins v. Board of Ad-

---

10. While, as the trial court found, Mount Laurel's actions were deliberate, we are of the view that the identical conclusion follows even when municipal conduct is not shown to be intentional, but the effect is substantially the same as if it were.

11. The paragraph reads:
> All persons are by nature free and independent, and have certain natural and unalienable rights, among which are those of enjoying and defending life and liberty, of acquiring, possessing, and protecting property, and of pursuing and obtaining safety and happiness.

justment of Margate City, 3 N.J. 200, 206, 69 A.2d 708 (1949). Indeed these considerations are specifically set forth in the zoning enabling act as among the various purposes of zoning for which regulations must be designed. N.J.S.A. 40:55-32. Their inclusion therein really adds little; the same requirement would exist even if they were omitted. If a zoning regulation violates the enabling act in this respect, it is also theoretically invalid under the state constitution. We say "theoretically" because, as a matter of policy, we do not treat the validity of most land use ordinance provisions as involving matters of constitutional dimension: that classification is confined to major questions of fundamental import. *Cf.* Tidewater Oil Co. v. Mayor and Council of the Borough of Carteret, 44 N.J. 338, 343, 209 A.2d 105 (1965). We consider the basic importance of housing and local regulations restricting its availability to substantial segments of the population to fall within the latter category.

The demarcation between the valid and the invalid in the field of land use regulation is difficult to determine, not always clear and subject to change. This was recognized almost fifty years ago in the basic case of Village of Euclid v. Ambler Realty Co., 272 U.S. 365, 47 S.Ct. 114, 71 L.Ed. 303 (1926):

> The ordinance now under review, and all similar laws and regulations, must find their justification in some aspect of the police power, asserted for the public welfare. The line which in this field separates the legitimate from the illegitimate assumption of power is not capable of precise delimitation. It varies with circumstances and conditions. (272 U.S. at 387, 47 S.Ct. at 118, 71 L.Ed. at 310).

This court has also said as much and has plainly warned, even in cases decided some years ago sanctioning a broad measure of restrictive municipal decisions, of the inevitability of change in judicial approach and view as mandated by change in the world around us. Lionshead Lake, Inc. v. Township of Wayne, 10 N.J. 165, 172-173, 89 A.2d 693 (1952), appeal dismissed 344 U.S. 919, 73 S.Ct. 386, 97 L.Ed. 708 (1953) (approving requirement of minimum floor area for dwellings, the same in all residential districts); Fischer v. Township of Bedminster, 11 N.J. 194, 205, 93 A.2d 378 (1952) (sanctioning minimum lot area of five acres in a then rural municipality); Pierro v. Baxendale, 20 N.J. 17, 29, 118 A.2d 401 (1955) (holding valid an ordinance permitting boarding and rooming houses, but not hotels and motels, in residential districts); Vickers v. Township Committee of Gloucester Township, 37 N.J. 232, 250, 181 A.2d 129 (1962), cert. den. 371 U.S. 233, 83 S.Ct. 326, 9 L.Ed.2d 495 (1963) (sustaining ordinance provisions prohibiting mobile home parks throughout the township). The warning is perhaps best put in *Pierro*:

> We are aware of the extensive academic discussion following the decisions in the *Lionshead* and *Bedminster* cases, *supra,* and the suggestion that the very broad principles which they embody may intensify dangers of economic segregation which even the more traditional modes of zoning

> entail ° ° °. In the light of existing population and land conditions within
> our State these [municipal zoning] powers may fairly be exercised without
> in anywise endangering the needs or reasonable expectations of any seg-
> ments of our people. If and when conditions change, alterations in zoning
> restrictions and pertinent legislative and judicial attitudes need not be long
> delayed. (20 N.J. at 29, 118 A.2d at 407).

The warning implicates the matter of *whose* general welfare must be
served or not violated in the field of land use regulation. Frequently the
decisions in this state, including those just cited have spoken only in terms
of the interest of the enacting municipality, so that it has been thought, at
least in some quarters, that such was the only welfare requiring consideration. It is, of course, true that many cases have dealt only with regulations
having little, if any, outside impact where the local decision is ordinarily
entitled to prevail. However, it is fundamental and not to be forgotten
that the zoning power is a police power of the state and the local authority
is acting only as a delegate of that power and is restricted in the same manner as is the state. So, when regulation does have a substantial external
impact, the welfare of the state's citizens beyond the borders of the particular
municipality cannot be disregarded and must be recognized and served.

This essential was distinctly pointed out in *Euclid,* where Mr. Justice
Sutherland specifically referred to "° ° ° the possibility of cases where
the general public interest would so far outweigh the interest of the municipality that the municipality would not be allowed to stand in the way."
(272 U.S. at 390, 47 S.Ct. at 119, 71 L.Ed. at 311). Chief Justice Vanderbilt said essentially the same thing, in a different factual context, in the
early leading case of Duffcon Concrete Products, Inc. v. Borough of Cresskill, 1 N.J. 509, 64 A.2d 347 (1949), when he spoke of the necessity of
regional considerations in zoning and added this:

> ° ° ° The effective development of a region should not and cannot be
> made to depend upon the adventitious location of municipal boundaries,
> often prescribed decades or even centuries ago, and based in many instances
> on considerations of geography, of commerce, or of politics that are no
> longer significant with respect to zoning. The direction of growth of resi-
> dential areas on the one hand and of industrial concentration on the other
> refuses to be governed by such artificial lines. Changes in methods of
> transportation as well as living conditions have served only to accentuate
> the unreality in dealing with zoning problems on the basis of the territorial
> limits of a municipality. (1 N.J. at 513, 64 A.2d at 350).

See, to the same general effect, Borough of Cresskill v. Borough of Dumont,
15 N.J. 238, 247-249, 104 A.2d 441 (1954).

In recent years this court has once again stressed this non-local approach
to the meaning of "general welfare" in cases involving zoning as to facilities
of broad public benefit as distinct from purely parochial interest. See
Roman Catholic Diocese of Newark v. Ho-Ho-Kus Borough, 42 N.J. 556,
566, 202 A.2d 161 (1964), Id., 47 N.J. 211, 220 A.2d 97 (1966). In this

case we pointed out local action with respect to private educational projects largely benefitting those residing outside the borough must be exercised "with due concern for values which transcend municipal lines." (47 N.J. at 218, 220 A.2d at 101). Likewise in Kunzler v. Hoffman, 48 N.J. 277, 225 A.2d 321 (1966), a case unsuccessfully attacking a use variance granted a private hospital to serve the emotionally disturbed in a wide area of the state, we rejected the contention that local zoning authorities are limited to a consideration of only those benefits to the general welfare which would be received by residents of the municipality, pointing out that "general welfare" in the context there involved "comprehends the benefits not merely within municipal boundaries but also those to the regions of the State relevant to the public interest to be served." 48 N.J. at 288, 225 A.2d at 327.

This brings us to the relation of housing to the concept of general welfare just discussed and the result in terms of land use regulation which that relationship mandates. There cannot be the slightest doubt that shelter, along with food, are the most basic human needs. See Robinson v. Cahill, *supra* (62 N.J., at 483, 303 A.2d 273). "The question of whether a citizenry has adequate and sufficient housing is certainly one of the prime considerations in assessing the general health and welfare of that body." New Jersey Mortgage Finance Agency v. McCrane, 56 N.J. 414, 420, 267 A.2d 24, 27 (1970). Cf. DeSimone v. Greater Englewood Housing Corp. No. 1, 56 N.J. 428, 442, 267 A.2d 31 (1970). The same thought is implicit in the legislative findings of an extreme, long-time need in this state for decent low and moderate income housing, set forth in the numerous statutes providing for various agencies and methods at both state and local levels designed to aid in alleviation of the need. See, *e. g.*, Mortgage Finance Agency Law, N.J.S.A. 17:1B-5 (L.1970, c. 38); Department of Community Affairs Demonstration Grant Law, N.J.S.A. 52:27D-61 (L.1967, c. 82); Local Housing Authorities Law, N.J.S.A. 55:14A-2 (L.1938, c. 19); Housing Co-operation Law, N.J.S.A. 55:14B-2 (L.1938, c. 20); Redevelopment Companies Law, N.J.S.A. 55:14D-2 (L.1944, c. 169); State Housing Law, N.J.S.A. 55:14H-2 (L.1949, c. 303); Senior Citizens Nonprofit Rental Housing Tax Law, N.J.S.A 55:141-2 (L.1965, c. 92); Housing Finance Agency Law, N.J.S.A. 55:14J-2 (L.1967, c. 81); Limited-Dividend Nonprofit Housing Corporations or Associations Law, N.J.S.A. 55:16-2 (as amended L.1967, c. 112).

[10-12] It is plain beyond dispute that proper provision for adequate housing of all categories of people is certainly an absolute essential in promotion of the general welfare required in all local land use regulation. Further the universal and constant need for such housing is so important and of such broad public interest that the general welfare which developing municipalities like Mount Laurel must consider extends beyond their boundaries and cannot be parochially confined to the claimed good of the particular municipality. It has to follow that, broadly speaking, the presumptive obligation arises for each such municipality affirmatively to plan and provide, by its land use regulations, the reasonable opportunity for an appropri-

ate variety and choice of housing, including, of course, low and moderate cost housing, to meet the needs, desires and resources of all categories of people who may desire to live within its boundaries. Negatively, it may not adopt regulations or policies which thwart or preclude that opportunity.

It is also entirely clear, as we pointed out earlier, that most developing municipalities, including Mount Laurel, have not met their affirmative or negative obligations, primarily for local fiscal reasons. Governor Cahill summed it up in his 1970 special legislative message, A Blueprint for Housing in New Jersey, supra, at 10-11:

> We have reached a point in the State where the zoning criteria in many municipalities is two-fold; dwelling units of all kinds must be curtailed; industrial development must be encouraged. This is a far cry from the original concept of municipal zoning and planning ° ° °.
>
> The fundamental objective of (the) constitutional amendment and the implementing Municipal Zoning Enabling Act was local control of zoning and planning for the purpose of effecting the public good ° ° °. The original concept of local planning and zoning never contemplated prohibition in lieu of regulation nor the welfare of the few in place of the general welfare.

The exclusionary details are fully set forth in Land Use Regulation, The Residential Land Supply, previously referred to.

In sum, we are satisfied beyond any doubt that, by reason of the basic importance of appropriate housing and the long-standing pressing need for it, especially in the low and moderate cost category, and of the exclusionary zoning practices of so many municipalities, conditions have changed, and consistent with the warning in Pierro, supra, judicial attitudes must be altered from that espoused in that and other cases cited earlier, to require, as we have just said, a broader view of the general welfare and the presumptive obligation on the part of developing municipalities at least to afford the opportunity by land use regulations for appropriate housing for all.

[13] We have spoken of this obligation of such municipalities as "presumptive." The term has two aspects, procedural and substantive. Procedurally, we think the basic importance of appropriate housing for all dictates that, when it is shown that a developing municipality in its land use regulations has not made realistically possible a variety and choice of housing, including adequate provision to afford the opportunity for low and moderate income housing or has expressly prescribed requirements or restrictions which preclude or substantially hinder it, a facial showing of violation of substantive due process or equal protection under the state constitution has been made out and the burden, and it is a heavy one, shifts to the municipality to establish a valid basis for its action or non-action. Robinson v. Cahill, supra, 62 N.J. at 491-492 303 A.2d 273, and cases cited therein. The substantive aspect of "presumptive" relates to the specifics, on the one hand, of what municipal land use regulation provisions, or the absence thereof, will evidence invalidity and shift the burden of

proof and, on the other hand, of what bases and considerations will carry the municipality's burden and sustain what it has done or failed to do. Both kinds of specifics may well vary between municipalities according to peculiar circumstances.

We turn to application of these principles in appraisal of Mount Laurel's zoning ordinance, useful as well, we think, as guidelines for future application in other municipalities.

The township's general zoning ordinance (including the cluster zone provision) permits, as we have said, only one type of housing—single-family detached dwellings. This means that all other types—multi-family including garden apartments and other kinds housing more than one family, town (row) houses, mobile home parks—are prohibited.[12] Concededly, low and moderate income housing has been intentionally excluded. While a large percentage of the population living outside of cities prefers a one-family house on its own sizeable lot, a substantial proportion do not for various reasons. Moreover, single-family dwellings are the most expensive type of quarters and a great number of families cannot afford them.[13] Certainly they are not pecuniarily feasible for low and moderate income families, most young people and many elderly and retired persons, except for some of moderate income by the use of low cost construction on small lots.

[14, 15] As previously indicated, Mount Laurel has allowed some multi-family housing by agreement in planned unit developments, but only for the relatively affluent and of no benefit to low and moderate income families. And even here, the contractual agreements between municipality and developer sharply limit the number of apartments having more than one bedroom.[14] While the township's PUD ordinance has been repealed, we men-

---

12. Zoning ordinance restriction of housing to single-family dwellings is very common in New Jersey. Excluding six large, clearly rural townships, the percentage of remaining land zoned for multi-family use is only just over 1% of the net residential land supply in 16 of New Jersey's 21 counties (not included are Atlantic, Cumberland, Cape May, Salem and Hudson counties). See *Land Use Regulation, The Residential Land Supply, supra,* pp. 10-13. (It is well known that considerable numbers of privately built apartments have been constructed in recent years in municipalities throughout the state, not allowed by ordinance, by the use variance procedure. N.J.S.A. 40:55-39(d). While the special exception method, N.J.S.A. 40:55-39(b), is frequently appropriate for the handling of such uses, it would indeed be the rare case where proper "special reasons" could be found to validly support a subsection (d) variance for such privately built housing.) Pennsylvania has held it unconstitutional for a developing municipality to fail to provide for apartments anywhere within it. Appeal of Girsh, 437 Pa. 237, 263 A.2d 395 (1970).

13. Some authorities suggest that such dwellings are rapidly becoming financially possible only for those of relatively high income. See *New Jersey Trends,* ch. 24. Sternlieb, *Introduction: Is This The End of the American Dream House,* p. 302 (Institute for Environmental Studies, Rutgers University, 1974).

14. Apartment bedroom restrictions are also common in municipalities of the state which do allow multi-family housing. About 60% of the area zoned to permit multi-family dwellings is restricted to efficiency or one-bedroom apartments; another 20% permits two-bedroom units and only the remaining 20% allows units of three bedrooms or larger. See *Land Use Regulation, The Residential Land Supply, supra,* pp. 11-12.

tion the subject of bedroom restriction because, assuming the overall validity of the PUD technique (see footnote (5), *supra*), the measure could be re-enacted and the subject is of importance generally. The design of such limitations is obviously to restrict the number of families in the municipality having school age children and thereby keep down local education costs.[15] Such restrictions are so clearly contrary to the general welfare as not to require further discussion. *Cf.* Molino v. Mayor and Council of Borough of Glassboro, 116 N.J. Super. 195, 281 A.2d 401 (Law Div.1971).

Mount Laurel's zoning ordinance is also so restrictive in its minimum lot area, lot frontage and building size requirements, earlier detailed, as to pre-clude single-family housing for even moderate income families. Required lot area of at least 9,375 square feet in one remaining regular residential zone and 20,000 square feet (almost half an acre) in the other, with required frontage of 75 and 100 feet, respectively, cannot be called small lots and amounts to low density zoning, very definitely increasing the cost of pur-chasing and improving land and so affecting the cost of housing.[16] As to building size, the township's general requirements of a minimum dwelling floor area of 1,100 square feet for all one-story houses and 1,300 square feet for all of one and one-half stories or higher is without regard to required minimum lot size or frontage or the number of occupants (see Sente v. Mayor and Municipal Council of City of Clifton, 66 N.J. 204, 208-209, 330 A.2d 321 (1974)). In most aspects these requirements are greater even than those approved in Lionshead Lake, Inc. v. Township of Wayne, *supra*, 10 N.J. 165, 89 A.2d 693, almost 24 years ago and before population decen-tralization, outer suburban development and exclusionary zoning had at-tained today's condition. See also Williams and Wacks, Segregation of Residential Areas Along Economic Lines; Lionshead Lake Revisited, 1969 Wis.L.Rev. 827.[17] Again it is evident these requirements increase the size and so the cost of housing. The conclusion is irresistible that Mount Laurel permits only such middle and upper income housing as it believes will have sufficient taxable value to come close to paying its own governmental way.

---

15. For a full report on the fiscal aspects of multi-family housing, see New Jersey County & Municipal Government Study Commission, *Housing & Suburbs: Fiscal & Social Impact of Multifamily Development* (1974).

16. These restrictions are typical throughout the state. As shown in *Land Use Regulation, The Residential Land Supply, supra*, pp. 14-16, in the 16 counties covered by that study, only 14.1% of the available single-family land is allowed to be in lots of less than one-half acre, only 5.1% (and that mostly in urban counties) in those of less than 10,000 square feet, and 54.7% of it requires lots of from one to three acres.

The same study, pp. 17-18, demonstrates that only as to 13.5% of the available single-family land is a frontage of less than 100 feet required, 32.2% requires 100-149 feet, 23.3%, 150-199 feet and 31%, 200 feet or more.

17. Minimum floor area requirements exist as to all but 8% of the available resi-dential land supply in the 16 counties studies in *Land Use Regulation, The Residential Land Supply, supra*, pp. 18-20; the Mount Laurel dimensions are representative of those most commonly imposed.

Akin to large lot, single-family zoning restricting the population is the zoning of very large amounts of and for industrial and related uses. Mount Laurel has set aside almost 30% of its area, over 4,100 acres, for that purpose; the only residential use allowed is for farm dwellings. In almost a decade only about 100 acres have been developed industrially. Despite the township's strategic location for motor transportation purposes, as intimated earlier, it seems plain that the likelihood of anywhere near the whole of the zoned area being used for the intended purpose in the foreseeable future is remote indeed and that an unreasonable amount of land has thereby been removed from possible residential development, again seemingly for local fiscal reasons.[18]

[16] Without further elaboration at this point, our opinion is that Mount Laurel's zoning ordinance is presumptively contrary to the general welfare and outside the intended scope of the zoning power in the particulars mentioned. A facial showing of invalidity is thus established, shifting to the municipality the burden of establishing valid superseding reasons for its action and non-action.[19] We now examine the reasons it advances.

The township's principal reason in support of its zoning plan and ordinance housing provisions, advanced especially strongly at oral argument, is the fiscal one previously adverted to, *i.e.*, that by reason of New Jersey's tax structure which substantially finances municipal governmental and educational costs from taxes on local real property, every municipality may, by the exercise of the zoning power, allow only such uses and to such extent as will be beneficial to the local tax rate. In other words, the position is that any municipality may zone extensively to seek and encourage the "good" tax ratables of industry and commerce and limit the permissible types of housing to those having the fewest school children or to those providing sufficient value to attain or approach paying their own way taxwise.

[17, 18] We have previously held that a developing municipality may properly zone for and seek industrial ratables to create a better economic balance for the community *vis-a-vis* educational and governmental costs engendered by residential development, provide. that such was " * * * done reasonably as part of and in furtherance of a legitimate comprehensive plan for the zoning of the entire municipality." Gruber v. Mayor and Township Committee of Raritan Township, 39 N.J. 1, 9-11, 186 A.2d 489, 493 (1962). We adhere to that view today. But we were not there concerned with, and did not pass upon, the validity of municipal exclusion by zoning of types of housing and kinds of people for the same local financial end. We have

---

18. *Land Use Regulation, The Residential Land Supply, supra,* pp. 6-8, shows that in the 16 county area only 14.7% of the net land supply is zoned for industrial uses (including offices and research laboratories). 3.6% is zoned for commercial uses and the remainder (81.7%) for residential uses of all types.

19. The township has not been deprived of the opportunity to present its defense on this thesis, since the case was very thoroughly tried out with voluminous evidence on all aspects on both sides.

no hesitancy in now saying, and do so emphatically, that, considering the basic importance of the opportunity for appropriate housing for all classes of our citizenry, no municipality may exclude or limit categories of housing for that reason or purpose. While we fully recognize the increasingly heavy burden of local taxes for municipal governmental and school costs on home-owners, relief from the consequences of this tax system will have to be furnished by other branches of government. It cannot legitimately be ac-complished by restricting types of housing through the zoning process in developing municipalities.

[19] The propriety of zoning ordinance limitations on housing for ecol-ogical or environmental reasons seems also to be suggested by Mount Laurel in support of the one-half acre minimum lot size in that very considerable portion of the township still available for residential development. It is said that the area is without sewer or water utilities and that the soil is such that this plot size is required for safe individual lot sewage disposal and water supply. The short answer is that, this being flat land and readily amenable to such utility installations, the township could require them as improvements by developers or install them under the special assessment or other appropriate statutory procedure. The present environmental sit-uation of the area is, therefore, no sufficient excuse in itself for limiting housing therein to single-family dwelling on large lots. Cf. National Land and Investment Co. v. Kohn, 419 Pa. 504, 215 A.2d 597 (1965). This is not to say that land use regulations should not take due account of ecol-ogical or environmental factors or problems. Quite the contrary. Their importance, at last being recognized, should always be considered. Gen-erally only a relatively small portion of a developing municipality will be involved, for, to have a valid effect, the danger and impact must be sub-stantial and very real (the construction of every building or the improve-ment of every plot has some environmental impact)—not simply a make-weight to support exclusionary housing measures or preclude growth—and the regulation adopted must be only that reasonably necessary for public protection of a vital interest. Otherwise difficult additional problems relat-ing to a "taking" of a property owner's land may arise. See AMG Associates v. Township of Springfield, 65 N.J. 101, 112, n.(4), 319 A.2d 705 (1974).

[20-23] By way of summary, what we have said comes down to this. As a developing municipality, Mount Laurel must, by its land use regulations, make realistically possible the opportunity for an appropriate variety and choice of housing for all categories of people who may desire to live there, of course including those of low and moderate income. It must permit multi-family housing, without bedroom or similar restrictions, as well as small dwellings on very small lots, low cost housing of other types and, in general, high density zoning, without artificial and unjustifiable minimum requirements as to lot size, building size and the like, to meet the full panoply of these needs. Certainly when a municipality zones for industry and commerce for local tax benefit purposes, it without question must zone

to permit adequate housing within the means of the employees involved in such uses. (If planned unit developments are authorized, one would assume that each must include a reasonable amount of low and moderate income housing in its residential "mix," unless opportunity for such housing has already been realistically provided for elsewhere in the municipality.) The amount of land removed from residential use by allocation to industrial and commercial purposes must be reasonably related to the present and future potential for such purposes. In other words, such municipalities must zone primarily for the living welfare of people and not for the benefit of the local tax rate.[20]

[24] We have earlier stated that a developing municipality's obligation to afford the opportunity for decent and adequate low and moderate income housing extends at least to " * * * that municipality's fair share of the present and prospective regional need therefore." [21] Some comment on that conclusion is in order at this point. Frequently it might be sounder to have more of such housing, like some specialized land uses, in one municipality in a region than in another, because of greater availability of suitable land, location of employment, accessibility of public transportation or some other significant reason. But, under present New Jersey legislation,

---

20. This case does not properly present the question of whether a developing municipality may time its growth and, if so, how. See, e.g., Golden v. Planning Board of Town of Ramapo, 30 N.Y.2d 359, 334 N.Y.S.2d 138, 285 N.E.2d 291 (1972), appeal dismissed 409 U.S. 1003, 93 S.Ct. 436, 440, 34 L.Ed.2d 294 (1972); Construction Industry Association of Sonoma County v. City of Petaluma, 375 F. Supp. 574 (N.D.Cal.1974), appeal pending (citation of these cases is not intended to indicate either agreement or disagreement with their conclusions). We now say only that, assuming some type of timed growth is permissible, it cannot be utilized as an exclusionary device or to stop all further development and must include early provision for low and moderate income housing.

21. This was said with the realization that most of such housing will require some form of governmental subsidy or assistance at some level to construct and, if the present tax structure remains unchanged, perhaps also some assistance to the municipality itself in connection with the furnishing of the additional local services required. See recommendations, *Housing & Suburbs, Fiscal & Social Impact of Multi-family Development, supra,* p. 123 et seq.

We further agree with the statement in the separate summary of the cited study, p. 2: "We recognize that new development, whatever the pace of construction, will never be the source of housing for more than a small part of the State's population. The greater part of New Jersey's housing stock is found and will continue to be found in the central cities and older suburbs of the State * * *" (Substantial housing rehabilitation, as well as general overall revitalization of the cities, is, of course, indicated.) So, while what we decide today will produce no mass or sudden emigration of those of low and moderate income from the central cities and older suburbs to the developing municipalities, our conception of state law as applied to land use regulation affecting housing requires that the fair opportunity therefor be afforded at once, with the expectation and purpose that the opportunity will come to fruition in the near future through private or public enterprises, or both, and result in available housing in the developing municipalities for a goodly number of the various categories of people of low and moderate income who desire to live therein and now cannot.

zoning must be on an individual municipal basis, rather than regionally.[22] So long as that situation persists under the present tax structure, or in the absence of some kind of binding agreement among all the municipalities of a region, we feel that every municipality therein must bear its fair share of the regional burden. (In this respect our holding is broader than that of the trial court, which was limited to Mount Laurel-related low and moderate income housing needs.)

The composition of the applicable "region" will necessarily vary from situation to situation and probably no hard and fast rule will serve to furnish the answer in every case. Confinement to or within a certain county appears not to be realistic, but restriction within the boundaries of the state seem practical and advisable. (This is not to say that a developing municipality can ignore a demand for housing within its boundaries on the part of people who commute to work in another state.) Here we have already defined the region at present as "those portions of Camden, Burlington and Gloucester Counties within a semicircle having a radius of 20 miles or so from the heart of Camden City." The concept of "fair share" is coming into more general use and, through the expertise of the municipal planning adviser, the county planning boards and the state planning agency, a reasonable figure for Mount Laurel can be determined, which can then be translated to the allocation of sufficient land therefor on the zoning map. See generally, New Jersey Trends, ch. 27, Listokin, Fair Share Housing Distribution: An Idea Whose Time Has Come ?, p. 353.[23] We may add that we think that, in arriving at such a determination, the type of information and estimates, which the trial judge (119 N.J.Super. at 178, 290 A.2d 465) directed the township to compile and furnish to him, concerning the hous-

---

22. This court long ago pointed out "* * * the unreality in dealing with zoning problems on the basis of the territorial limits of a municipality." Duffcon Concrete Products, Inc. v. Borough of Cresskill, supra (1 N.J. at 513, 64 A.2d at 350). It is now clear that the Legislature accepts the fact that at least land use planning, to be of any value, must be done on a much broader basis than each municipality separately. Note the statutes establishing county planning boards, with the duty to prepare a county master plan and requiring that board's review and approval of certain subdivisions, N.J.S.A. 40:27-1 to 8; authorizing voluntary regional planning boards, N.J.S.A. 40:37-6 to 11; creating state planning and coordinating functions in the Department of Community Affairs and its Division of State and Regional Planning, N.J.S.A. 52: 27D-6 and 9 and 13:1B-5.1 and 15.52; and providing for New Jersey to join with New York and Connecticut in the establishment of the Tri-State Regional Planning Commission with extensive area planning functions, N.J.S.A. 32:22B-1 et seq. (Federal statutes and regulations require many federal grants for local public or regional planning agencies, consistent with works and installations to have approved comprehensive area plans.) Authorization for regional zoning—the implementation of planning—or at least regulation of land uses having a substantial external impact by some agency beyond the local municipality, would seem to be logical and desirable as the next legislative step.

23. The questions mentioned in this paragraph are more fully involved in Oakwood at Madison v. Township of Madison, supra, 128 N.J. Super. 438, 320 A.2d 223, appeal pending unheard in this court.

ing needs of persons of low and moderate income now or formerly residing in the township in substandard dwellings and those presently employed or reasonably expected to be employed therein, will be pertinent.

There is no reason why developing municipalities like Mount Laurel, required by this opinion to afford the opportunity for all types of housing to meet the needs of various categories of people, may not become and remain attractive, viable communities providing good living and adequate services for all their residents in the kind of atmosphere which a democracy and free institutions demand. They can have industrial sections, commercial sections and sections for every kind of housing from low cost and multi-family to lots of more than an acre with very expensive homes. Proper planning and governmental cooperation can prevent over-intensive and too sudden development, insure against future suburban sprawl and slums and assure the preservation of open space and local beauty. We do not intend that developing municipalities shall be overwhelmed by voracious land speculators and developers if they use the powers which they have intelligently and in the broad public interest. Under our holdings today, they can be better communities for all than they previously have been.

III

The Remedy

As outlined at the outset of this opinion, the trial court invalidated the zoning ordinance *in toto* and ordered the township to make certain studies and investigations and to present to the court a plan of affirmative public action designed "to enable and encourage the satisfaction of the indicated needs" for township related low and moderate income housing. Jurisdiction was retained for judicial consideration and approval of such a plan and for the entry of a final order requiring its implementation.

We are of the view that the trial court's judgment should be modified in certain respects. We see no reason why the entire zoning ordinance should be nullified. Therefore we declare it to be invalid only to the extent and in the particulars set forth in this opinion. The township is granted 90 days from the date hereof, or such additional time as the trial court may find it reasonable and necessary to allow, to adopt amendments to correct the deficiencies herein specified. It is the local function and responsibility, in the first instance at least, rather than the court's, to decide on the details of the same within the guidelines we have laid down. If plaintiffs desire to attack such amendments, they may do so by supplemental complaint filed in this cause within 30 days of the final adoption of the amendments.

[25] We are not at all sure what the trial judge had in mind as ultimate action with reference to the approval of a plan for affirmative public action concerning the satisfaction of indicated housing needs and the entry of a final order requiring implementation thereof. Courts do not build housing

nor do municipalities. That function is performed by private builders, various kinds of associations, or, for public housing, by special agencies created for that purpose at various levels of government. The municipal function is initially to provide the opportunity through appropriate land use regulations and we have spelled out what Mount Laurel must do in that regard. It is not appropriate at this time, particularly in view of the advanced view of zoning law as applied to housing laid down by this opinion, to deal with the matter of the further extent of judicial power in the field or to exercise any such power. See, however, Pascack Association v. Mayor and Council of Township of Washington, 131 N.J.Super. 195, 329 A.2d 89 (Law Div.1974), and cases therein cited, for a discussion of this question. The municipality should first have full opportunity to itself act without judicial supervision. We trust it will do so in the spirit we have suggested, both by appropriate zoning ordinance amendments and whatever additional action encouraging the fulfillment of its fair share of the regional need for low and moderate income housing may be indicated as necessary and advisable. (We have in mind that there is at least a moral obligation in a municipality to establish a local housing agency pursuant to state law to provide housing for its resident poor now living in dilapidated, unhealthy quarters.) The portion of the trial court's judgment ordering the preparation and submission of the aforesaid study, report and plan to it for further action is therefore vacated as at least premature. Should Mount Laurel not perform as we expect, further judicial action may be sought by supplemental pleading in this cause.

The judgment of the Law Division is modified as set forth herein. No costs.

MOUNTAIN and PASHMAN, JJ., concurring in the result.

For modification: Chief Justice HUGHES and Justices JACOBS, HALL, MOUNTAIN, SULLIVAN, PASHMAN and CLIFFORD—7.

Opposed: None.

MOUNTAIN, J. (concurring).

I agree with the conclusions reached in the Court's opinion and essentially with the opinion itself. In one important respect, however, I disagree. The Court rests its decision upon a ground of State constitutional law. I reach the same result by concluding that the term, "general welfare," appearing in N.J.S.A. 40:55-32, can and should properly be interpreted with the same amplitude attributed to that phrase in the opinion of the Court, as well as otherwise in the manner there set forth. I therefore would rest the conclusions we here announce upon an interpretation of the statute, and not upon the State constitution.

Accordingly, since I read the statute—without resort to the Constitution—to justify, if not compel, our decision, I find it unnecessary to express any view as to the merits of the constitutional argument set forth in the Court's opinion.

PASHMAN, J. (concurring).

With this decision, the Court begins to cope with the dark side of municipal land use regulation—the use of the zoning power to advance the parochial interests of the municipality at the expense of the surrounding region and to establish and perpetuate social and economic segregation.

The problem is not a new one. Early opponents of zoning advanced the possibility of such abuse as an argument against allowing municipalities the power to zone. *See, e. g.,* Ambler Realty Co. v. Euclid, 297 F. 307, 316 (N.D.Ohio 1924), rev'd 272 U.S. 365, 47 S.Ct. 114, 71 L.Ed. 303 (1926). Later, even those sympathetic to the goals and methods of zoning began to express concern. *See, e. g.,* Haar, "Zoning for Minimum Standards: The Wayne Township Case," 66 Harv.L.Rev. 1051 (1953). In that spirit, Justice Jacobs wrote for this Court in Pierro v. Baxendale, 20 N.J. 17, 29, 118 A.2d 401, 407 (1955):

> We are aware of the extensive academic discussion following the decisions in the *Lionshead* and *Bedminster* cases, *supra,* and the suggestion that the very broad principles which they embody may intensify dangers of economic segregation which even the more traditional modes of zoning entail. * * * In the light of existing population and land conditions within our State these powers may fairly be exercised without in anywise endangering the needs or reasonable expectations of any segments of our people. If and when conditions change, alterations in zoning restrictions and pertinent legislative and judicial attitudes need not be long delayed.

The growth of the new suburbs, first as affluent residential communities and, more recently, as sites for commercial and industrial development, leaving persons with low or even moderate incomes housed inadequately in the cities and the older, inner suburbs, far from new sources of employment, magnified the importance of the problem, moving it from the realm of speculation to that of physical and social reality. Justice Hall was among the first to recognize the new significance of the problem in his now classic dissent to Vickers v. Gloucester Tp., 37 N.J. 232, 252, 181 A.2d 129 (1962), appeal dismissed 371 U.S. 233, 83 S.Ct. 326, 9 L.Ed.2d 495 (1963). The facts of this case, as well as the information compiled by various governmental agencies, of which the Court may take notice, *e. g., Nat'l Comm'n on Urban Problems, Building the American City,* H.R. Doc.No.34, 91st Cong. 1st Sess. 211 (1968); *N.J. Dept. of Community Affairs, Land Use Regulation: The Residential Land Supply* (1972),[1] demonstrate that judicial action in this area is long overdue.

Therefore, I join in the thoughtful and eloquent majority opinion of Justice Hall. I differ from the majority only in that I would have the Court go farther and faster in its implementation of the principles announced today. The fact that abuses of the municipal zoning power are now widespread and derive from attitudes and premises deeply ingrained in the

---

1. Hereinafter cited as *Building the American City* and *The Residential Land Supply,* respectively.

suburban planning and zoning processes requires that the Court not restrict itself to the facts of this particular case but, rather, lay down broad guidelines for judicial review of municipal zoning decisions which implicate these abuses. *Cf.* Busik v. Levine, 63 N.J. 351, 363-64, 307 A.2d 571 (1973), appeal dismissed 414 U.S. 1106, 94 S.Ct. 831, 38 L.Ed2d 733 (1973).

I

The misuse of the municipal zoning power at issue in this case, generically described as "exclusionary zoning," *see, e. g.,* Brooks, *Exclusionary Zoning* 3 (Am. Soc'y. of Planning Officials 1970), involves two distinct but interrelated practices: (1) the use of the zoning power by municipalities to take advantage of the benefits of regional development without having to bear the burdens of such development; and (2) the use of the zoning power by municipalities to maintain themselves as enclaves of affluence or of social homogeneity.

Both of these practices are improper and to be strongly condemned. They are violative of the requirement, found both in the Constitution of 1947, Art. I, § 1 and the zoning enabling statute itself, N.J.S.A. 40:55-32, that municipal zoning ordinances further the general welfare. *Cf.* Cresskill v. Dumont, 15 N.J. 238, 247-49, 104 A.2d 441 (1954); Duffcon Concrete Products, Inc. v. Cresskill, 1 N.J. 509, 64 A.2d 347 (1949). They are inconsistent with the fundamental premise of the New Jersey zoning legislation that zoning is concerned with the physical condition of the municipality not its social condition. In a deeper sense, they are repugnant to the ideals of the pluralistic democracy which America has become.

The motivations for exclusionary zoning practices are deeply embedded in the nature of suburban development. In part, these practices are motivated by fear of the fiscal consequences of opening the community to all social and economic classes. Residents of the municipality anticipate that higher density development will require the construction of additional roads, sewers, and water systems, the provision of additional municipal services, and the increase of school expenditures, all of which must be financed through local property taxes. Often, although not universally, this is a reasonable concern, *see generally,* Sternlieb, *Residential Development, Urban Growth and Municipal Costs* (1973); N.J. Cty. & Mun. Gov. Study Comm'n. *Housing & Suburbs: Fiscal & Social Impact of Multifamily Development* (1974), and, as long as these costs are primarily financed through local property taxes, will continue to impel suburban communities to use the zoning laws to encourage commercial development and discourage settlement of less affluent families. *But cf.* Robinson v. Cahill, 62 N.J. 473, 303 A.2d 273 (1973), cert. denied 414 U.S. 976, 94 S.Ct. 292, 38 L.Ed.2d 219 (1973). Insofar as this fiscal situation prevails, suburban communities will find the temptation of exclusionary zoning alluring.

In addition, exclusionary zoning practices are also often motivated by fear of and prejudices against other social, economic, and racial groups.[2] *Nat'l Comm. Against Discrimination in Housing, Jobs and Housing: Final Summary Report on the Housing Component*, 25-29 (1972). Thus, in a recent survey of suburban municipal leaders, 42.6% identified social and racial conflict as being the chief impact of low and moderate cost subsidized housing on the municipality, while only 21.3% identified fiscal problems as the chief impact. *Cty. & Mun. Gov. Study Comm'n, Housing & Suburbs: Fiscal & Social Impact of Multifamily Development, supra* at 86. A large portion felt that even State assumption of the additional municipal costs of a balanced housing policy would not make a great impact on the genreal unacceptability of low or moderate income housing. *Id.* at 89. Nor are these attitudes, however disappointing we may find them at this late date, wholly surprising. Many people who settle in suburban areas do so with the specific intention of living in affluent, socially homogeneous communities and of escaping what they perceive to be the problems of the cities. *See generally, Clawson, Suburban Land Conversion in the United States*, 45 (1971). They do not wish their insular communities to be disturbed by the introduction of diverse social, racial, and economic groups. The experience of the nation over the past 20 years must serve as a caution that, however much we might wish it, we cannot expect rapid, voluntary reversal of such attitudes.

Exclusionary zoning may assume a wide variety of forms. Ultimately, the existence of such practices must be measured by exclusionary intent and actual or potential exclusionary effect. *Cf.* Hawkins v. Shaw, 437 F.2d 1286 (5 Cir. 1971); Hobson v. Hansen, 269 F.Supp. 401 (D.D.C.1967), aff'd sub nom. Smuck v. Hobson, 132 U.S.App.D.C. 372, 408 F.2d 175 (D.C.Cir. 1969). Some zoning devices, however, which are inherently exclusionary in effect or which lend themselves especially readily to abuse have come into widespread use and are a revealing gauge of the extent of exclusionary zoning in New Jersey:

1) *Minimum house size requirements*

As of 1970, 92% of the land in the Department of Community Affairs study area [3] zoned for single family housing was covered by some minimum house

---

2. Defendant contends that no such motivation is at work in this case. I, like my brethren, accept that claim.

3. The Department of Community Affairs surveyed the use of exclusionary devices in municipal zoning laws as of 1970. The study area included all developable land in New Jersey except that in Atlantic, Cape May, Cumberland, Hudson, and Salem Counties and in the Hackensack Meadowlands District. *The Residential Land Supply, supra.* All figures in this opinion as to the extent of use of various zoning provisions are based on that study. For other analyses of Department of Community Affairs data, see Special Message to the Legislature by Governor Cahill, *A Blueprint*

size requirement. More than 65% was zoned for houses with 1,000 square feet or more of floor space, and 38.9% for houses of 1,200 square feet or more. By contrast, the controversial case of Lionshead Lake v. Wayne Tp., 10 N.J. 165, 89 A.2d 693 (1953), appeal dismissed 344 U.S. 919, 73 S.Ct. 386, 97 L.Ed. 708 (1953, upheld a minimum of 768 square feet in all districts. There is wide variation from county to county and within the various counties.[4] In the so-called "outer-ring" counties in northern New Jersey—Morris, Somerset, Middlesex, and Monmouth[5]—houses of less than 1,000 square feet may be built on only about 10% of the land zoned for single family dwellings. On 77% of the land zoned for single family dwellings, houses must have 1,200 square feet or more of floor space. In the South Jersey outer-ring counties, Burlington, Camden, and Gloucester, the figures are 31.9% and 43.5% respectively.

The effect on the cost of housing of such requirements is obvious. If one assumes construction costs of $20 per square foot of floor space,[6] a 1,000 square foot minimum imposes a corresponding minimum figure of $20,000 upon the portion of the cost of a new house attributable to construction. A recent study of housing costs indicates that floor space is the single most important factor contributing to differences in prices for new housing, even more important than the socio-economic status of the municipality. *Sagalyn & Sternlieb, supra* at 48.

2) *Minimum lot size and minimum frontage requirements*

On two-thirds of the land in the Department of Community Affairs study area zoned in 1970 for single family dwellings, houses could not be built

---

for *Housing in New Jersey*, Dec. 7, 1970; Williams & Norman, "Exclusionary Land Use Controls: the Case of Northeastern New Jersey, 22 Syracuse L.Rev. 476 (1971); *Sagalyn & Sternlieb, Zoning and Housing Costs*, 93-115 (1972); *Nat'l Comm. Against Discrimination in Housing, Jobs and Housing; Final Summary Report on the Housing Component, supra* at 25-37.

4. The extreme case is Morris County, where 87% of the land zoned for single family housing had a 1,200 square foot minimum floor space requirement and 66.3% had a 1,600 square foot or more minimum. In Burlington, only 54.7% was zoned for 1,000 square feet or more and 24% had no minimum house size requirement at all.

5. The term "outer-ring" is used here in the same sense as it is used in the majority opinion, ante at 718. *See Williams & Norman, supra* at 479. It should be noted that this term is not used consistently by professional planners. The Regional Plan Association, the principal New York planning group, describes the counties referred to here as "outer-ring" counties as the "intermediate ring," reserving the former term for more outlying areas, Sussex, Warren, Hunterdon, and Ocean. *Clawson, supra* at 368. The Delaware Valley Regional Planning Commission, the principal Philadelphia planning group, does not describe suburban development in the Philadelphia region in terms of concentric "rings" at all, perhaps because development in that region has been more blotchy. *Id.* at 291.

6. This concededly is an oversimplified measure, *see Williams & Norman, supra* at 481 n.13, but one widely used by persons in the housing construction industry. *The Residential Land Supply*, at 18. The $20 figure was considered conservative at the time of publication of the Department of Community Affairs in 1972. *Id.*

on lots of less than an acre.   Upon only 5.1% could houses be built on 10,000 square feet or less.   Approximately 10% of such land in the outer-ring counties in South Jersey was zoned for 10,000 square foot lots or less; 45.9% was zoned for an acre or more.   In the North Jersey outer-ring counties only 1.2% of the land zoned for single family dwellings was available for use as lots of 10,000 square feet or less; 77% was zoned for one acre or larger lots.   Here, too, there are wide variations among counties.   In Camden, 24.5% of the land was zoned for lots of 10,000 square feet or less, and less than 34% for lots of an acre or more.   In Somerset County, only .2% of the land was zoned for lots of 10,000 square feet or less; 85.3% was zoned for lots of an acre or more, and 24.6% was zoned for three acres or more. By way of comparison, the American Public Health Association, a vigorous advocate of high minimum standards, recommends 6,000 square feet as a suitable minimum lot size based upon health considerations.   Am. *Public Health Ass'n Planning the Neighborhood*, 37 (1948).

Minimum frontage requirements frequently, although not invariably, are found together with minimum lot size requirements.   *The Residential Land Supply* at 21-24.   Only 13.5% of the land zoned in 1970 for single family housing in the Department of Community Affairs study area was zoned for 100 foot minimum frontage or less.   In that area, 54.3% was zoned for 150 feet or more.   This device was widely used in the northern outer-ring counties, where only 5% of the land is zoned for less than 100 foot frontage and 68.4% is zoned for more than 150 feet, but somewhat less widely used in the southern outer-ring counties, where 22.7% of the land was zoned for less than 100 foot frontage and 42.5% was zoned for more than 150 feet.

Analysis of the exclusionary impact of the widespread use of minimum lot size and minimum frontage requirements is a more complex task than that of analyzing minimum building requirements.   *See generally, Building the American City, supra* at 213-15; *Williams & Norman, supra* at 493-97; *Sagalyn & Sternlieb, supra* at 6-16, 66-67.   There is a significant correlation between lot size and price of housing in areas without sewage service and between frontage and price in areas with sewage service.   *Sagalyn & Sternlieb, supra* at 54-56.   At the very least, it can be said with certainty that extensive mapping for large lots or large lot widths drives up the costs of smaller lots and thereby significantly raises the overall price of housing. *Williams & Norman, supra* at 496-97.

3) *Prohibition of multifamily housing*

Realistically, much of the housing needs of persons with low or moderate incomes will have to be met through various forms of multifamily housing. *Williams & Norman, supra* at 481.   Hence, restrictions upon the construction of such housing have a highly exclusionary effect.   In the Department of Community Affairs study area, construction of multifamily housing was permitted on only 6.2% of the land zoned for residential uses.   If six aberrant rural municipalities are disregarded, the percentage falls to 1.1%.[7]   In the South Jersey outer-ring counties, only ½ of 1% is so zoned.   There is no land zoned for multifamily housing in Somerset County and only .006% is so zoned in Monmouth County.[8]

The effect of zoning against multifamily dwellings is magnified by restrictions upon the number of bedrooms which may be included in each dwelling unit.   In the Department of Community Affairs study area [9] 59% of the already limited area of land zoned for multifamily dwellings is restricted to one-bedroom or efficiency apartments.   On only 20.4% of this land is construction of apartments of three or more bedrooms permitted.   In addition, in many areas where some construction of larger apartments is permitted, they are limited to a small percentage of any individual development. *The Residential Land Supply, supra at* 11.   In the North Jersey outer-ring counties, 78% of the land zoned for multifamily housing is burdened with bedroom restrictions.   In the South Jersey outer-ring counties, 83% of the land zoned for multi-family housing is so restricted.   The situation is particularly acute in Burlington County, where 95.8% of the land zoned for multifamily housing has bedroom restrictions.

The Department of Community Affairs concluded from these figures that:

> ° ° ° [I]n general, the multi-family zoned land is geared to accommodate the housing needs of single people, married couples without children, and retired people, and not geared to the housing needs of the large part of the population living as families with children. [*The Residential Land Supply, supra* at 12; footnote omitted].

5) *Prohibition of mobile homes*

Mobile homes offer an alternate, less expensive form of housing.   They have long since ceased to be mere "house trailers" but have become an important form of mass produced semi-permanent housing.   Indeed, for many persons they may be the only form of new housing available.   However,

---

7. The communities are Lamberton Township (Burlington); Winslow Township (Camden); Franklin Township (Gloucester); Plumstead Township (Ocean); Montague Township (Sussex); Allamuchy Township (Warren).   All are distant from the path of development and rural in character.

8. It should be noted that despite these restrictions a significant amount of multi-family housing has been built in the suburbs in recent years.   Thus, even in Somerset County, which had no vacant land zoned for multifamily dwellings during the period between 1960 and 1970, 7,635 multifamily units were built in those 10 years.   This seems to have been achieved through variances and specially procured zoning ordinance amendments.   Such individually negotiated variances and amendments, however, have usually been accompanied by formal or informal restrictions limiting development to small high-rent units, which are wholly unsuited to the needs of families with low or moderate incomes. *Nat'l Comm. Against Discrimination in Housing, Jobs and Housing: Final Summary Report on the Housing Component, supra* at 35-37.

9. Here, too, Winslow, Franklin, Plumstead, and Montague Townships are aberrant and not included.

only .1% of the land zoned for residential use in the Department of Community Affairs study area was zoned for use by mobile homes. In the South Jersey outer-ring counties, .3% of the residential land was so zoned, the bulk of it being in Gloucester County, which had twice as much land zoned for mobile homes as the rest of the study area combined. None was zoned for this purpose in Camden County. No land was zoned for mobile homes in the northern outer-ring counties.[10]

6) *Overzoning for nonresidential uses*

Zoning a great proportion of the developable land in a municipality noncumulatively for nonresidential uses may have the effect of forcing the price of land zoned for residential purposes up beyond the reach of persons with low or moderate incomes. Neither statewide nor county wide figures provide unambiguous evidence of the use of such practice at present in New Jersey. *Land Use Regulation, supra* at 6-8; *Sagalyn & Sternlieb, supra* at 96. At the municipal level, the use of such practices is more evident in some areas. Thus, in Mt. Laurel itself, 29.2% of the land in the township, totaling 4,121 acres, is zoned for industrial uses, although only 100 acres within the township has actually been developed for such use in the past 10 years, and there is no reasonable prospect of industrial uses expanding to such proportions.

If anything, these figures underestimate the extent of exclusionary zoning in this State. A wide variety of other techniques may be used to achieve an exclusionary effect. In addition, a municipality need not use all of these techniques to achieve exclusionary ends. Municipalities which have large lot-size and frontage requirements may not have high building-size requirements and vice versa. Thus, only 18% of the land in the Department of Community Affairs study area zoned for single family residences permitted houses with less than 1,200 square feet of floor space to be constructed on a ¼ acre or less site with 100 foot or less frontage.

Forceful judicial intervention is necessitated not only by the already widespread use of exclusionary zoning practices and by the fact that the motivations for such are deeply ingrained in the suburban zoning and planning process, but also by certain extrinsic factors of which the Court may take notice.

First, the United States suffers from an acute national housing shortage. It has been estimated that over 10 million dwelling units would be needed to provide each family in the country with adequate housing. *Building the American City, supra* at 75. In New Jersey, it has been estimated that there is an immediate need for over 400,000 dwelling units. *Dep't of Community*

---

10. In a few municipalities in Gloucester and Burlington Counties mobile homes are permitted in some nonresidential use areas. In a few localities scattered through the State, mobile homes are permitted as conditional uses. *The Residential Land Supply, supra* at 13; *Williams & Norman, supra* at 488-89.

Affairs, The Housing Crisis in New Jersey, 1970 (1970).[11]   New Jersey, already the second most densely populated state in the country, is experiencing continuing population growth—it is estimated that by 1985 the total population will have increased from its 1970 figure of 7,200,000 to about 10,000,000.   Special Message to the Legislature by Governor Cahill, *A Blueprint for Housing in New Jersey,* Dec. 7, 1970, at 1.   Housing, particularly in urban areas is deteriorating.   The percentage of substandard units throughout the State increased from 14.8% in 1960 to 17.4% in 1969.   In Hudson County, the increase as from 22.3% to 31.3% .   *Housing Crisis in New Jersey, supra* at 14.   Some of these units dropped out of the housing market altogether.   It has been estimated that simply to keep up with population growth and to replace units which drop out of the housing market, 100,000 new units would have to be constructed in the State each year.   Special Message to the Legislature by Governor Cahill, *A Blueprint for Housing in New Jersey,* Dec. 7, 1970, at 1.   In fact, the construction of new housing in the State peaked in 1964, when permits were issued for the construction of 68,078 units, and has declined steadily since then.   In 1970, permits were issued for construction of only 39,897 units.   *Sagalyn & Sternlieb, Zoning & Housing Costs,* 98 (1972).

The brunt of this shortage is, of course, borne by persons with low or moderate incomes.   As of 1970, it was estimated that not only were half of all low income families in the State obliged to live in inadequate housing, but so were approximately 125,000 families with moderate incomes.   *Housing Crisis in New Jersey, supra* at iv.   The median cost of a new single family detached house was $30,000 in the northeastern region of the country in 1969.   *Sagalyn & Sternlieb, supra* at 20.   Prices since then have risen precipitously.   A study made in 1971 found median new house costs in suburban counties to range from $33,263 in Burlington to $62,500 in Somerset and $67,000 in Bergen.   *Id.* at 22.   Such housing was effectively beyond the reach of families with incomes of less than $15,000 per year.   *Housing Crisis in New Jersey, supra* at 42.   As of the time of that study, the median family income in New Jersey was $11,407 per year.   Analyses by both the federal and state governments, *Building the American City, supra* at 93; *Housing Crisis in New Jersey, supra* at 40-43, indicate that the majority of families can afford to neither rent nor buy new housing at current prices. Other authorities estimate that such housing may be beyond the financial capacity of as much as ¾ of all the families in the State, *Sagalyn & Sternlieb, supra* at 64, and as much as 90% of those families in which the head of the household is below the age of 35.   *Nat'l Comm. Against Discrimination in Housing, Housing and Jobs: Final Summary Report on the Housing Component, supra* at 22.   In theory, low and moderate income families should benefit even from construction of new housing which they themselves cannot afford because such housing creates vacancies which "filter down."   In

---

11. Hereinafter cited as *Housing Crisis in New Jersey.*

reality, however, most of these vacancies are absorbed by the enormous lag between population growth and new housing construction. *Sagalyn & Sternlieb, supra* at 42. The housing which does "filter down" to persons with low or moderate incomes is often badly dilapidated and in deteriorating neighborhoods. *Building the American City, supra* at 11; *Clawson, Suburban Land Conversion in the United States,* 330 (1970).

The existence of this housing shortage has been amply recognized by all branches of government in this State. *See, e. g.* Inganamort v. Borough of Fort Lee, 62 N.J. 521, 303 A.2d 298 (1973); N.J. Mortgage Finance Agency v. McCrane, 56 N.J. 414, 267 A.2d 24 (1970); Marini v. Ireland, 56 N.J. 130, 265 A.2d 526 (1970); Mortgage Finance Agency Law, N.J.S.A. 17:1B-5 (L.1970, c. 38); Department of Community Affairs Demonstration Grant Law, N.J. S.A. 52:27D-61 (L.1967, c. 82); Special Message to the Legislature by Governor Cahill, *A Blueprint for Housing in New Jersey,* Dec. 7, 1970; Special Message to the Legislature by Governor Cahill, *New Horizons in Housing,* Mar. 27, 1972.

Second, the growing movement of commerce and industry to the suburbs is imposing a heavy burden upon employees who are unable to obtain housing in these suburban areas. The trend, which began after World War II and has continued unabated, arises from a variety of causes—need for additional land for expansion, automated methods of handling goods which make single-floor layout of manufacturing plants economically desirable, increased access provided, by superhighways, desire for aesthetic surroundings, lower suburban property taxes, etc. *See generally,* Clawson, Suburban Land Conversion in the United States, 40 (1971). Retail establishments have also relocated in the suburbs, taking advantage of the shift in the affluent population, the access provided by suburban highways, and the more attractive surroundings. *Id.* at 40-41. The result has been a shift of blue-collar jobs from the cities to the suburbs. *Id.* at 40. Thus in the New York metropolitan region,[12] 75% of the 990,000 new jobs created between 1959 and 1967 were located outside of New York City. Jobs at manufacturing production sites outside New York City increased during that period by 138,440, while such jobs within New York City diminished by 47,110. Of the 100,600 new jobs created in retailing between 1959 and 1965, 95% were located outside of New York City. The new jobs created within New York City in recent years have been confined almost exclusively to services, finance, insurance, communications, utilities, government and manufacturing headquarters offices, all of which are fields with high percentages of white-collar employment. It appears that these trends will continue into the foreseeable future. It has been estimated that between 1970 and 1985 New York City will lose another 137,700 factory jobs, and the suburbs gain 122,700. *Nat'l Comm. Against Discrimination in Housing, Jobs and Housing,* 6-9 (1970). Job

---

12. As the term is used by the Regional Planning Association, which includes much of northern New Jersey.

movement in the Philadelphia metropolitan region displays an essentially identical pattern. *Nat'l Comm. Against Discrimination in Housing, Impact of Housing Patterns on Job Opportunities*, 21-26 (1968). This is, of course, the natural and foreseeable consequence of "fiscal zoning" that encourages the development within a municipality of commercial establishments, which are net tax-providers, and discourages the development of housing for persons who would work in such establishments, on the grounds that they are net revenue-absorbers.

This trend is one that imposes unfair burdens on the worker who is locked out of suburban residential areas. For blue-collar workers, commutation from the cities to suburban job locations is both time-consuming and prohibitively expensive. There is often no access at all by public mass transit and even when such transportation is available in theory it is frequently impractical in fact. *Nat'l Comm. Against Discrimination in Housing, The Impact of Housing Patterns on Job Opportunities, supra* at 27-30; *Nat'l Comm. Against Discrimination in Housing, Jobs and Housing, supra* at 23-26. *See generally, Babcock and Bosselman, Exclusionary Zoning: Land Use Regulation in the 1970s*, 114-15 (1973).

Third, even as we write, development proceeds apace. Once an area is developed, it becomes much more difficult to alter its social and economic character. There is a hazard that prolonged judicial inaction will permit exclusionary practices to continue to operate and will allow presently developing communities to acquire permanent exclusionary characteristics. The concern is not that New Jersey will soon be without developable land, but that large areas now in the process of development will have already acquired irrevocably exclusionary characteristics before the courts effectively intervene. Thus, the Delaware Valley Regional Planning Commission has estimated that the amount of developed land in the Philadelphia metropolitan area (including Burlington, Camden, Gloucester, and Mercer Counties) will increase by 38% between 1960 and 1985, *Clawson, supra* at 294, and the Regional Plan Association has estimated that intensive land use in the New York metropolitan area (which includes most of northern New Jersey) will double in the same period, *Clawson, supra* at 279.

Finally, we must take notice of the fact that the cost of building new housing has increased steadily over the past 10 years and shows all signs of continuing to increase in the future. Between 1963 and 1969, the median sales price of new single-family housing in the northeastern part of the United States rose from $20,000 to $30,500. *Sagalyn & Sternlieb, supra,* at 20. The costs of building rental housing had increased comparably. *See generally, Clawson, supra* at 82-83. As the costs of housing slip farther beyond the reach of persons of low and moderate incomes, the practical value of zoning reform diminishes and becomes increasingly contingent on the establishment of new State and federal housing subsidy programs.

Today's decision by its terms expressly concerns exclusionary zoning practices in municipalities which are developing but which "still are not completely developed and remain in the path of inevitable future residential, commercial and industrial demand and growth." *Ante* at 717. As to these communities, the Court holds:

> ° ° ° [E]very such municipality must, by its land use regulations, presumptively make realistically possible an appropriate variety and choice of housing. More specifically, presumptively it cannot foreclose the opportunity of the classes of people mentioned for low and moderate income housing and in its regulations must affirmatively afford that opportunity, at least to the extent of the municipality's fair share of the present and prospective regional need therefor. These obligations must be met unless the particular municipality can sustain the heavy burden of demonstrating peculiar circumstances which dictate that it should not be required so to do. [*Ante* at 724-725. footnote omitted].

The majority has chosen not to explore in this case either the extent of the affirmative obligations upon developing municipalities or the role of the courts in enforcing those obligations. It has also chosen not to consider the degree to which the principles applicable to developing municipalities are also applicable to rural ones and to largely developed ones. The facts set out above seem to me to demonstrate that exclusionary zoning is a problem of such magnitude and depth as to require that the Court extend these principles to all municipalities in the State, recognizing, of course, that they may have different implications for municipal conduct when applied in different areas, and that the Court establish a policy of active judicial enforcement, not only of the negative obligations imposed upon municipalities by this decision but also of the affirmative obligations.

II

I consider first the extent of the affirmative obligation to plan and provide for housing opportunities for persons with low and moderate incomes that municipalities assume when they choose to avail themselves of land use controls permitted by statute. Although this discussion will concern itself initially with developing municipalities, many of the same considerations also apply *mutatis mutandi* to developed municipalities and rural areas, as will subsequently become clear.

A municipality need not exercise at all the powers permitted it by the zoning and planning statutes, N.J.S.A. 40:55-30 et seq. and N.J.S.A. 40:55-1.1 et seq.[13] Once, however, it chooses to enter the field of land use regulation it assumes a duty—one of constitutional dimensions, deriving from N.J.Const. (1947), Art. I, § 1—to act affirmatively to provide its fair

---

13. As of 1971, 96% of all municipalities in New Jersey had zoning ordinances and 85% had subdivision controls. *Sagalyn & Sternlieb, Zoning and Housing Costs* 102 (1972). We need not consider here the affirmative duties of a municipality which once had but has now abandoned zoning or subdivision regulations.

share of the low and moderate income housing necessary to meet the regional housing needs. *Cf.* Southern Alameda Spanish Speaking Organization v. Union City, 424 F.2d 291, 295-6 (9 Cir. 1970); Williams, American Planning Law: Land Use and the Police Power §§ 66.15, 66.16 (1974).

The substantive content of this affirmative obligation will necessarily vary from municipality to municipality, depending upon, among other things, the intensity of the regional housing needs, the extent of previous exclusionary practices by the municipality, and the degree to which the municipality is benefiting, directly or indirectly, from regional economic development. A factor of special importance is the sufficiency of local housing opportunities for persons who might fill jobs created by new commercial and industrial development in the locality. *Cf. Building the American City, supra* at 243; ALI, *Model Land Development Code,* § 7-405 (Ten. Draft No. 3, 1971); *Babcock & Bosselman, Exclusionary Zoning: Land Use Regulation and Housing in the 1970s,* 114-15 (1973).

Every developing municipality has at least a duty to consider regional housing needs in all its planning activities, both formal and informal, including its formulation of the comprehensive plan underlying its zoning ordinance, N.J.S.A. 40:55-21, its adoption of a master plan, N.J.S.A. 40:55-1.10 and its consideration of applications for zoning variances, N.J.S.A. 40:55-39, and for approval of subdivision plats, N.J.S.A. 40:55-1.14.[14] In addition, since effective planning for regional needs is virtually impossible without some degree of intergovernmental cooperation, all developing municipalities also have an affirmative obligation to cooperate, where appropriate, in regional planning efforts, to cooperate, for example, with regional planning boards established pursuant to N.J.S.A. 40:27-9 and in area review procedures established under the Intergovernmental Cooperation Act, 42 U.S.C. § 4231 and implemented by U.S. Office of Management and Budget Circular A-95 (July 24, 1969) and N.J.A.C. 5:42-1.1 et seq. *See generally Babcock & Bosselman, Exclusionary Zoning: Land Use Regulation and Housing in the 1970s,* 135-47 (1973).

There is little hope that the private housing construction industry will be able to satisfy the State's housing needs in the foreseeable future, even if all exclusionary barriers are removed. *Building the American City, supra* at 93. To meet these needs, State or federal assistance will be required. This fact has been recognized by both the State Legislature and Congress in a lengthy series of statutes providing governmental subsidies for private construction and ownership of low and moderate income housing. *See. e. g.,* Housing and Community Development Act of 1974, 88 Stat. 633 (codified at various places in 12, 42 U.S.C.): National Housing Act of 1959, § 202, as amended, 12 U.S.C. § 1701q; National Housing Act,

---

14. While this opinion is principally directed towards municipalities, the same considerations also apply to planning at the county level when the county has chosen to exercise power to regulate land use permitted it by N.J.S.A. 40:27-1 et seq.

§§ 235, 236, as amended, 12 U.S.C. §§ 1715z, 1715z-1 et seq.;   Mortgage Finance Agency Law, N.J.S.A. 17:1B-4 et seq.;   Housing Finance Agency Law, N.J.S.A. 55:14J-1 et seq.;   Department of Community Affairs Demonstration Grant Act, N.J.S.A. 52:27D-59 et seq.   To a greater or lesser degree, all of the programs require active municipal cooperation.   Failure to actively cooperate in the implementation of such programs as effectively thwarts the meeting of regional needs for low and moderate income housing as does outright exclusion.   *See, e. g.,* Farmworkers of Florida Housing Projects, Inc. v. Delray Beach, 493 F.2d 799 (5 Cir. 1974);   Kennedy Park Home Ass'n v. Lackawanna, 318 F.Supp. 669 (W.D.N.Y. 1970), aff'd 436 F.2d 108 (2 Cir. 1970), cert. den. 401 U.S. 1010, 91 S.Ct. 1256, 28 L.Ed.2d 546 (1971).   Developing municipalities have a duty to make all reasonable efforts to encourage and facilitate private efforts to take advantage of these programs.

Finally, there may be circumstances in which the municipality has an affirmative duty to provide housing for persons with low and moderate incomes through public construction, ownership, or management.   *See, e. g.,* Community Development and Housing Act of 1974, Title II, 42 U.S.C. § 1401 et seq.;   Local Housing Authority Law, N.J.S.A. 55:14A-1;   *cf.* Mahaley v. Cuyahoga Metropolitan Housing Authority, 355 F.Supp. 1257 (N.D. Ohio 1973) rev'd 500 F.2d 1087 (6 Cir. 1974), cert. den. —— U.S. ——, 95 S.Ct. 781, 42 L.Ed.2d 805 (1975).

There are certain important limitations on the scope of these affirmative obligations.   While municipalities must plan and provide for regional housing needs, no municipality need assume responsibility for more than its fair share of these needs.   The purpose of land use regulation is to create pleasant, well-balanced communities, not to recreate slums in new locations. It is beyond dispute that when the racial and socioeconomic composition of the population of a community shifts beyond a certain point, the white and affluent begin to abandon the community.   While the attitudes underlying this "tipping" effect must not be catered to, the phenomenon must be recognized as a reality.   *See, e. g.,* Graves v. Romney, 502 F.2d 1062 (8 Cir. 1974), cert. den. —— U.S. ——, 95 S.Ct. 1354, 43 L.Ed.2d 440 (1975);   Otero v. New York City Housing Authority, 484 F.2d 1122 (2 Cir. 1973).   Municipalities have a legitimate interest in placing an upper limit on the extent of uses which, if permitted to expand without limit, might reasonably be feared to operate to the general detriment.   Tidewater Oil Co. v. Carteret, 84 N.J.Super. 525, 202 A.2d 865 (App.Div.1965), aff'd 44 N.J. 338, 209 A.2d 105 (1965).   The limitation of the municipality's affirmative duty to one of providing for its fair share of reasonable needs responds to this interest.   *Cf.* Mass.Gen.Laws Ann., c. 40B, §§ 20-23 (a statute authorizing the state to override local zoning restrictions for low and moderate income housing projects, but limiting the municipality's obligations to fixed annual and total maxima).   A number of regions have, in response to the problem of exclusionary zoning, voluntarily sought to put such fair share housing plans into effect. *See Babcock & Bosselman, supra* at 109-13.

Nor need a municipality altogether give up control of the pace and sequence of development. A municipality has a legitimate interest in insuring that residential development proceeds in an orderly and planned fashion, that the burdens upon municipal services do not increase faster than the practical ability of the municipality to expand the capacity of those services, and that exceptional environmental and historical features are not simply concreted over. *See e.g.,* Golden v. Ramapo Planning Board, 30 N.Y.2d 359, 334 N.Y.S.2d 138, 285 N.E.2d 291 (1972), appeal dismissed 409 U.S. 1003, 93 S.Ct. 436, 34 L.Ed.2d 294 (1972); Construction Industry Ass'n of Sonoma County v. Petaluma, 375 F.Supp. 574 (N.D.Cal. 1974); Mass.Gen.Laws Ann., c. 40B, §§ 20, 23.[15] On the other hand, such regulations must be reasonable, substantially related to the purpose which they seek to achieve, and must adopt the least exclusionary means practical. "Zoning is a means by which a governmental body can plan for the future—it may not be used as a means to deny the future." National Land and Investment Co. v. Kohn, 419 Pa. 504, 528, 215 A.2d 597, 610 (Pa.Sup.Ct.1965). By way of illustration, large lot zoning is commonly rationalized as a device for preventing premature development. Such zoning, it is claimed, merely creates holding zones. In practice, however, it appears that land zoned for large lots, even where intended as an interim holding zone, tends to become frozen in a pattern of low density development. *Williams & Norman, supra at* 495. Such zoning is not a reasonable device for regulating the pace and sequence of development. Its effects on development, if any, are merely exclusionary.

Finally, the affirmative duty to plan and provide for regional needs does not require the municipality to make any specific piece of property available for low or moderate income housing, absent a showing that there are inadequate alternative sites realistically available for that type of development. A municipality must zone in accordance with a comprehensive plan. N.J.S.A. 40:55-32. Once it has adopted a comprehensive plan which properly provides for the community's fair share of the regional housing needs, it is entitled to be able to enforce that plan through its zoning ordinances. To permit a developer to come in at a later date and demand, as a matter of right, that a piece of property not presently zoned to permit development of low or moderate cost housing be so zoned, is to undermine the entire premise of land use regulations. *Williams, supra* at § 66.15; *see* Confederacion de la Raza Unida v. Morgan Hill, 324 F.Supp. 895 (N.D. Cal.1971). The one exception to this principle is the situation in which the developer can show that, as a matter of practical fact, sufficient land is not available for development in the areas zoned for low or moderate

---

15. It should be emphasized that citation of these cases and statutes is not intended to indicate approval of the specific zoning provisions approved therein.

income housing. *See, e. g.*, Kennedy Park Homes Association v. Lackawanna, 318 F.Supp. 669 (W.D.N.Y.1970), aff'd 436 F.2d 108 (2 Cir. 1970), cert. den. 401 U.S. 1010, 91 S.Ct. 1256, 28 L.Ed.2d 546 (1971) (construction of multi-family housing in area zoned for it would perpetuate a segregated housing pattern and add to existing problem of overcrowding); Pascack Ass'n v. Washington Tp., 131 N.J. Super. 195, 329 A.2d 89 (Law Div.1974) (area zoned for multi-family housing was already largely occupied by other, non-residential uses, and was burdened with other zoning requirements that made construction of low or moderate income housing impractical).

The affirmative obligations of developing municipalities so far discussed are legally binding and judicially enforceable. It is a truism that courts have no inherent expertise in matters of land use planning. They are not equipped to sit as higher planning boards and substitute their judgment for municipal bodies lawfully established for the purpose of making planning and zoning decisions. Bow & Arrow Manor v. West Orange, 63 N.J. 335, 343, 307 A.2d 563 (1973); Kozesnik v. Montgomery Tp., 24 N.J. 154, 167, 131 A.2d 1 (1957). The decision as to how the municipality should go about performing the affirmative duties set out above is one initially to be made by the officials of the municipality itself. Nevertheless, if the municipality has failed to take affirmative steps to make realistically possible a variety and choice of housing so as to meet its fair share of the regional housing needs, its actions are presumptively illegal and the burden shifts to the municipality to justify them. The mere fact that local land use control issues are involved does not preclude the court from making such determinations, nor, if a court finds that the municipality has failed to meet its obligation, from exercising the full panoply of equitable powers to remedy the situation. Norwalk CORE v. Norwalk Redevelopment Agency, 395 F.2d 920 (2 Cir. 1968); Hawkins v. Shaw, 437 F.2d 1286 (5 Cir. 1971); Pascack Ass'n v. Washington Tp., 131 N.J.Super. 195, 329 A.2d 89 (LawDiv.1974).

Judicial enforcement of municipal obligations, both negative and affirmative, to plan and provide for a fair share of regional housing needs, even if only directed to one municipality, necessarily has grave implications for the entire region. In dealing with such cases courts must act both deliberately and imaginatively. In administering such relief the trial court ought to proceed in four steps:

   (1) identify the relevant region; [16]
   (2) determine the present and future housing needs of the region;

---

16. Relevant considerations might include: the area included in the interdependent residential housing market; the area encompassed by significant patterns of commutation; the area served by major public services and facilities, *e. g.*, parks, hospitals, cultural facilities, etc.; the area in which the housing problem can be solved. All of these considerations must be evaluated in terms of both present facts and projections of future development.

(3) allocate these needs among the various municipalities in the region; [17] and

(4) shape a suitable remedial order.

Cf. Williams, American Planning Law: Land Use and the Police Power § 66.38 (1974). Needless to say, all of these steps involve difficult factual determinations based upon expert testimony and statistical evidence. It may be well appropriate for the court to appoint independent experts or consultants for its assistance, *see* Pascack Ass'n v. Washington Tp., 131 N.J.Super. 195, 329 A.2d 89 (Law Div.1974); *cf.* Handleman v. Marwen Stores Corp., 53 N.J. 404, 251 A.2d 122 (1969); Polulich v. J. G. Schmidt Tool Die & Stamping Co., 46 N.J.Super. 135, 134 A.2d 29 (Cty.Ct. 1957); Manual for Complex Litigation, Pt. 1 §§ 1.42, 1.46 2.60, 3.40 (1973), or to invite participation by the Department of Community Affairs as *amicus curiae.*

Since conflicting decisions within a given region would be highly undesirable, all municipalities in the region should be joined as parties at the earliest practical point in the proceedings, if not at the instance of one of the parties, then on the motion of the court. R. 4:28-1, 4:30.

The trial court must be flexible and imaginative in molding remedies to fit the facts of each case, balancing the need to vindicate the rights of persons who have been or will be deprived of the opportunity for decent housing if no relief is granted against the principle of local decision-making in land use planning matters. Pascack Ass'n v. Washington Tp., *supra; see e. g.,* Kennedy Park Homes Ass'n v. Lackawanna, 318 F.Supp. 669 (W.D. N.Y.1970) aff'd 436 F.2d 108 (2 Cir. 1970) cert. den. 401 U.S. 1010, 91 S.Ct. 1256, 28 L.Ed.2d 546 (1971); Mahaley v. Cuyahoga Metropolitan

---

17. The following factors were considered in developing a fair share plan for the Dayton, Ohio area:

> [T]he needed low and moderate income dwelling units were assigned to the planning units using a composite of numbers resulting from six calculation methods: (1) equal share; (2) proportionate share of the county's households; (3) proportionate share of the county's households making less than $10,000 annually (or less than $7,000 in the three more rural counties); (4) the inverse of #3; (5) a share based on the assessed valuation per pupil of the school districts covering the planning units; and (6) a share based on the relative over-crowding of the school districts involved.

o   o   o

> The six factors used in the calculations, however, seemed to reflect some very basic determinations; the possibility of each sub-area being treated equally, the existing distribution of each county's households and lower income households, and two indicators of the receiving school districts' ability to accept new students. The latter two were used because the school question emerged as a critical concern whenever low and moderate income housing was mentioned for placement in a given area.

[Bertsch & Shafer "A Regional Housing Plan: The Miami Valley Regional Planning Commission Experience," I Planners Notebook No. 1 (1971) quoted in *Williams, supra* § 66.36.]

Housing Authority, 355 F.Supp. 1257 (N.D.Ohio 1973) rev'd on other grounds, 500 F.2d 1087 (6 Cir. 1974), cert. denied —— U.S. ——, 95 S.Ct. 781, 42 L.Ed.2d 805 (1975); United Farmworkers of Florida Housing Projects, Inc. v. Delray Beach, 493 F.2d 799 (5 Cir. 1974); Lakewood Homes, Inc. v. Lima Bd. of Adjustment, 23 Ohio Misc. 211, 52 Ohio Op.2d 213, 258 N.E.2d 470 (Ohio Ct.C.P. 1970); mod. 25 Ohio App.2d 125, 267 N.E.2d 595 (Ohio Ct.App.1971).

III

It can hardly be denied that there are some suburban municipalities which have already developed in an exclusionary mold. These communities, which have benefited from regional development, have, by their land use controls, contributed to the regional housing shortages. *Cf.* United States v. Black Jack, 372 F.Supp. 319 (E.D.Mo.1974). It would be both highly inequitable to absolve them of any responsibility for solving those problems and inconsistent with the legal analysis developed by the Court today. Although the majority does not reach this issue in the present case, I would hold that developed suburban municipalities which have availed themselves of the land use controls permitted by statute and which have not provided sufficient opportunities for development of low and moderate income housing to meet their fair share of regional needs, have both a negative obligation not to use zoning and subdivision controls to obstruct the construction of such housing and an affirmative duty to plan and provide for such housing, insofar as these obligations can be carried out without grossly disturbing existing neighborhoods. It is, of course, neither practical nor wise to demand that such communities rezone established neighborhoods; to do so would in all likelihood contribute to neighborhood instability and permit certain property owners and developers to obtain windfalls rather than actually effecting construction of low or moderate income housing.

Occasions, however, arise in every community when land becomes available for development or redevelopment. It is on these occasions that these obligations come into play most strongly. Thus the existence of an unmet regional need for low and moderate income housing in appropriate cases must be given great weight in considering applications for variances under N.J.S.A. 40:55-39(d) to permit the construction of such housing. De Simone v. Greater Englewood Housing Corp. No. 1, 56 N.J. 428, 267 A.2d 31 (1970); Brunetti v. Madison Tp., 130 N.J.Super. 164, 325 A.2d 851 (Law Div. 1974).

The discussion above of judicial enforcement applies equally to developed suburban communities, save only that in formulating relief the trial judge must be alert to take into consideration the delicacy and difficulty of altering the character of already developed areas.

IV

Substantial portions of New Jersey are neither experiencing a surge of development nor situated in the imminently foreseeable path of development. These include much of Cape May, Cumberland, and Salem Counties, portions of Atlantic, Ocean, Sussex and Warren Counties, and some rural areas in other parts of the State. In these municipalities, it is not meaningful to speak of failure to meet regional housing needs, not because there are no persons who are inadequately housed,[18] but because it is not yet meaningful to speak of "regional" needs nor is it clear that land use controls play a significant role in the housing shortage at the present time. Nevertheless, the time may well come when the frontiers of suburbia will reach these areas. Municipalities may not act to deter the future development of a diversified housing stock by establishing land use controls which are inherently exclusionary and which bear no substantial relationship to any legitimate zoning purpose.

Without purporting to exhaust the list of zoning devices which are presumptively objectionable, I would note that minimum house size requirements which bear no substantial relationship to health needs[19] and requirements as to the minimum or maximum number of bedrooms which a dwelling unit may contain, cf. Molino v. Glassboro, 116 N.J.Super. 195, 281 A.2d 401 (Law Div. 1971), are presumptively invalid. Zoning for excessively large lots and large frontages presents more difficult analytic problems, cf. Steel Hill Development, Inc. v. Sanbornton, 469 F.2d 956 (1 Cir. 1972), but excessive mapping for such lots is, absent extraordinary environmental factors, also presumptively invalid. Cf. Williams & Norman, supra at 496-97.

These obligations, too, are judicially enforceable, albeit without need for the more elaborate procedures appropriate for litigation concerning developing and developed areas which are discussed above.

V

The problems we begin to face today are of awesome magnitude and importance, both for New Jersey and for the nation as a whole. It will not do to approach them gingerly; they call out for forceful and decisive judicial action.

---

18. In 1970 the Department of Community Affairs, in its study, *Housing Crisis in New Jersey 1970,* reported that 13.9% of the dwelling units in Cape May County were substandard, 32.8% in Cumberland, 34.7% in Salem, 16.9% in Atlantic, 19.5% in Sussex, and 23.2% in Warren. All of the counties have significant populations near or below poverty level. *Id.*

19. Unjustifiable minimum house size requirements should, of course, be distinguished from housing code minimum space requirements which bear a real and substantial relationship to health needs. Sente v. Clifton, 66 N.J. 204, 200, 330 A.2d 321 (1974) (Pashman J. dissenting); *Building the American City, supra* at 215 n.19.

The flow of low and moderate income persons is toward urban areas, but the cities have neither the space nor the resources to house these people. The question is whether the suburbs will act to accommodate this growth in an orderly way or will simply and blindly resist. Two well-entrenched zoning objectives, low density land use and favorable fiscal balance, though sometimes at odds with each other, have on the whole cooperated to create a milieu of discriminatory zoning which threatens to make the next 30 years of suburban growth a disaster.

The shape of the possible disaster can now be foreseen. The inevitable alternative to assumption by suburban communities of an obligation to provide for their fair share of regional housing needs is an increase in the size of slums with all their attendant miseries. The consequences of such economic, social, and racial segregation are too familiar to need recital here. *See Nat'l Advisory Comm'n on Civil Disorders, Report* (1968). Justice must be blind to both race and income.

It is not the business of this Court or any member of it to instruct the municipalities of the State of New Jersey on the good life. Nevertheless, I cannot help but note that many suburban communities have accepted at face value the traditional canard whispered by the "blockbuster": "When low income families move into your neighborhood, it will cease being a decent place to live." But as there is no difference between the love of low income mothers and fathers and those of high income for their children, so there is no difference between the desire for a decent community felt by one group and that felt by the other. Many low income families have learned from necessity the desirability of community involvement and improvement. At least as well as persons with higher incomes, they have learned that one cannot simply leave the fate of the community in the hands of the government, that things do not run themselves, but simply run down.

Equally important, many suburban communities have failed to learn the lesson of cultural pluralism. A homogeneous community, one exhibiting almost total similarities of taste, habit, custom and behavior is culturally dead, aside from being downright boring. New and different life styles, habits and customs are the lifeblood of America. They are its strength, its growth force. Just as diversity strengthens and enriches the country as a whole, so will it strengthen and enrich a suburban community. Like animal species that over-specialize and breed out diversity and so perish in the course of evolution, communities, too, need racial, cultural, social and economic diversity to cope with our rapidly changing times.

Finally, many suburban communities have failed to recognize to whom the environment actually belongs. By environment, I mean not just land or housing, but air and water, flowers and green trees. There is a real sense in which clean air belongs to everyone, a sense in which green trees and flowers are everyone's right to see and smell. The right to enjoy these is connected to a citizen's right to life, to pursue his own happiness as he sees fit provided his pursuit does not infringe another's rights.

The people of New Jersey should welcome the result reached by the Court in this case, not merely because it is required by our laws, but, more fundamentally, because the result is right and true to the highest American ideals.

Questions and Notes

1. *Mt. Laurel* is, of course, the famous decision which has turned zoning around, at least with respect to one of its most basic attitudes. In effect, *Mt. Laurel* has overruled *Euclid* on one of its major holdings—the question of exclusion of multiple dwellings.

2. On whose behalf was this suit brought?

3. What evidence was there in the opinions as to the existence of such plaintiffs?

4. Was Mt. Laurel beginning to have some indications of rapid suburban development?

5. What kind of housing had been admitted to Mt. Laurel? Had the local authorities taken some pains to see to it that only certain types of families were accommodated?

6. What was the New Jersey Court's opinion on fiscal zoning (a) to improve the local tax base, and (b) to exclude "bad ratables"?

7. Is the Supreme Court's opinion based on state constitutional law, or federal constitutional law? Why?

8. What is the obligation of a developing municipality under the *Mt. Laurel* case? Why do you suppose this was limited to developing municipalities?

9. What remedy was provided (a) in the lower court opinion and (b) in the Supreme Court opinion?

CROSS-REFERENCES

In Hagman, see § 97.

In Rathkopf, see Index under "Area Restrictions" and "Exclusionary Zoning".

In Williams, see Index under "Acreage Zoning" and "Exclusionary Zoning".

In Yokley, see §§ 17-1 to 17-12.

SUPREME COURT OF NEW JERSEY

OAKWOOD AT MADISON INC.

v.

TOWNSHIP OF MADISON

A-80/81-75 (A-52/53-74). Questions by the Court.

117 N.J. Super. 11, 283 A.2d 353(1971)
and 128 N.J. Super. 438, 320 A.2d 223(1974),
72 N.J. 481, 371 A.2d 1192 (1977).

Gentlemen:

The Supreme Court has ordered reargument in the above case and has tentatively scheduled it for October 20 or 21, 1975. You are each requested to file supplementary briefs (simultaneously) on or before October 7 as to the following points:

1. Is it necessary, for fair share purposes, for the Court to fix a specific "region," or may the municipality zone on the basis of any area which it reasonably may regard as an appropriate region?

2. Is it sufficient that the ordinance permits satisfaction of the housing needs of low and moderate income people as a single category, or is it necessary that separate estimates of the housing needs for low income, as distinguished from moderate income, people, be formulated and the number of necessary housing units in each category be determined?

3. What are to be the determinants of the income qualifications for low income and moderate income categories, respectively, as of any given date?

4. In framing zoning regulations to achieve the opportunity for adequate low and moderate income housing, how does a municipality accommodate the lag in the rate of rise of median income behind the rate of rise in construction and land costs? During such a period, must the municipality continually revise the zoning ordinance to reduce the size and increase the density of permissible housing in order to accommodate such lag? Are the 1970-1975 figures in the record suitable for 1975 and beyond?

5. Can a developing municipality, in the light of the evidence in this case, "affirmatively afford the opportunity" for adequate low and moderate income housing (*Mt. Laurel*, 67 *N.J.* at 174) short of eliminating all minimum bulk, size or density requirements, not mandated by health statutes or regulations, in sufficiently large areas zoned residential?

6. In view of the absence of assurance of any degree of public subsidization of privately built housing, must the zoning regulations be such as to permit a developer, operating privately, to build housing of a character which will both meet normal profit incentives and be affordable by low and moderate income renters and purchasers? Or is a municipality entitled to assume that a given degree of subsidization will be forthcoming?

7. Are "density bonus" provisions in zoning ordinances valid as against existing zoning law or the general police power authority of municipalities (*i.e.* relaxation of requirements as to maximum units per acre or percentage of lot for building, in return for agreement by builder to rent some units at low rental rates)?

8. What other valid zoning devices are available to encourage construction of low and moderate income housing?

9. In order to affirmatively provide low and moderate income housing, may the zoning ordinance set aside residential zones in which, for purposes of single-family unattached houses, *maximum* lot widths, are fixed (*e.g.* 25 feet, 30 feet, 40 feet); or in which *minimum* density units per acre may be fixed for multi-unit housing? (*e.g.* 15 or 20).

10. In seeking to encourage lower housing costs to accommodate low income purchasers and renters, how does the municipality resolve the dilemma that low income families generally require more bedrooms than upper income families, which in turn increases the cost of construction of housing units?

11. If the Court affirms the determination of the trial court that the ordinance, as amended, still does not affirmatively provide adequately for low and moderate income housing, how specific should the Court be as to the terms of an ordinance which will satisfy *Mt. Laurel?* Do the interests of bringing this litigation to a final determination dictate some degree of specificity in the determination of the Court?

12. In connection with the latter question, would it be serviceable for the Court to appoint a Special Master to consult with the municipality and frame specific zoning guidelines to assist the municipality in meeting the Court's judgment?

13. Referring to the trial court's opinion, 128 *N.J. Super.* at 443, invalidating the AF multi-family zone because "construction of efficiency and one-bedroom units will dominate," how would plaintiff and *amici* modify the ordinance as to the AF zone to render it valid?

14. In considering what is Madison's fair share of low and moderate income housing for an appropriate region, is it not necessary to determine whether the areas which the municipality seeks to exempt from fair share requirements on ecological grounds, are factually entitled to such exemption (a question the trial court found unnecessary to decide)? Should there be a remand for that purpose?

15. Independently of the general question as to the validity or invalidity of the ordinance on the fair share issue, has the corporate plaintiff factually established its entitlement to be relieved of the restrictions of the ordinance as to its own property on grounds of unreasonableness to the point of confiscation? See *Schere v. Township of Freehold*, 119 *N.J. Super.* 433, certif. den. 62 *N.J.* 69.

16. Plaintiff and *amici* are invited to submit an outline of the basic contents of a zoning ordinance, including specific provisions governing residential zones, which in their opinion would satisfy that *Mt. Laurel* case.

17. Discuss the relevance of *Construction Industry Association of Sonoma County v. City of Petaluma* decided August 13, 1975, 9th Circuit Court of Appeals, which has been summarized at 44 Law Week 2093.

18. What effect, if any, should be given to the financial ability of the municipality to meet the fiscal requirements of additional schools, police, firemen, utilities, etc. in determining its fair share of moderate and low income housing?

URBAN LEAGUE OF GREATER NEW BRUNSWICK

v.

CARTERET

142 N.J. Super. 11, 359 A.2d 526(1976).
Decided: May 4, 1976

    ✿   ✿   ✿

FURMAN, J.S.C.

Plaintiffs attack the zoning ordinance of 23 of the 25 municipalities of Middlesex County as unconstitutionally exclusionary and discriminatory. Third party complaints against the cities of New Brunswick and Perth Amboy were dismissed after trial. The remedy sought by plaintiffs is an allocation to each municipality of its fair share of low and moderate income housing to meet the countywide need. Plaintiffs rely on *So. Burl. Cty. N.A.A.C.P. v. Tp. of Mt. Laurel*, 67 N.J. 151, *cert.* den. — U.S. — (1975), which imposes on a developing municipality the obligation to provide by land use regulations for its fair share of the present and prospective regional need for low and moderate income housing.

Plaintiffs comprise an organization and five persons who sue individually and as representatives of others similarly situated. The standing of all plaintiffs is challenged. Under *Warth v. Seldin*, 422 U.S. 490 (1975) the individual plaintiffs as nonresidents lack standing to urge federal constitutional and statutory infirmities in municipal zoning. But their standing as nonresidents to pursue state constitutional objections is sustained in *Mt. Laurel* at 159. The standing of the three organizations which were plaintiffs in *Mt. Laurel* was not at issue and not passed on in Justice Hall's opinion.

Plaintiff Urban League of Greater New Brunswick seeks housing for its members and others, mostly blacks and Hispanics, throughout the county and elsewhere nearby, encountering rebuffs and delays. Under the liberal criteria for standing which prevail in this state standing must be accorded to plaintiff Urban League. *Crescent Pk. Tenants Assoc. v. Realty Eq. Corp. of N.Y.*, 58 *N.J.* 98 (1971).

No monetary or other specific recovery and no counsel fee for maintaining class actions are sought. Unquestionably some others are similarly situated to plaintiff Champion, a white, who cannot find adequate low income housing in the county for her family of three, plaintiff Benson, a black, who cannot find adequate moderate income housing in the county for his family of eleven, plaintiff Tippett, a black, whose family of five is adequately housed in New Brunswick but who cannot find equivalent housing in an unsegregated neighborhood and plaintiff Tuskey, a white, who objects to the racial and economic imbalance in South Brunswick, the predominately white municipality in which he resides with his family, including two children attending public school. The class actions are maintainable under R. 4:32-1(a) and (b)(3).

At the close of plaintiffs' proofs the court dismissed the cause of action for wilful racial discrimination. The impact of low density zoning is most adverse to blacks and Hispanics, who are disproportionately of low and moderate income. But no credible evidence of deliberate or systematic exclusion of minorities was before the court. That dismissal must result in the dismissal also of the specific count for violation of Federal Civil Rights Acts, 42 *U.S.C.A* §§ 1981, 1982 and 3601 *et seq.*

The challenge to the exclusionary aspects of defendants' zoning ordinances remains. All three branches of government have recognized overwhelming needs for low and moderate income housing in the State as a whole.

In Executive Order No. 35, dated April 2, 1976, Governor Byrne set forth: ". . . there exists a serious shortage of adequate, safe and sanitary housing accommodations for many households at rents and prices they can reasonably afford, especially for low and moderate income households, newly formed households, senior citizens, and households with children."

The Legislature in the preamble to the New Jersey Housing Assistance Bond Act of 1975, L.1975, c.207, §2(a), made a finding: "Despite the existence of numerous Federal programs designed to provide housing for senior citizens and families of low and moderate income, construction and rehabilitation of such housing units has not proceeded at a pace sufficient to provide for the housing need of the State."

In *Mt. Laurel* Justice Hall concluded at 158: "There is not the slightest doubt that New Jersey has been, and continues to be, faced with a desperate need for housing, especially of decent living accommodations economically suitable for low and moderate income families." Other recent legislation dealing with the housing shortage is set out in *Mt. Laurel* at 179.

In Middlesex County the shortage of low and moderate income housing is critical. From 1960 to 1970 the number of new jobs in the county increased by 2.2 times the number of new housing units, and the number of new housing units, and the number of employees in the county residing outside the county increased by 291%. In 1960 the total vacant land in the county was zoned 24.9% for industry, 22.7% for one acre or larger single-family housing, 21.5% for less than one quarter acre single-family housing and 2.1% for multi-family housing. Ten years later the zoning countywide was markedly more exclusionary: 41.7% for industry, 38.7% for one acre or larger single-family housing, 4.9% for less than one quarter acre single-family housing and .5% for multi-family housing.

The pattern of dwindling low and moderate housing opportunities has continued in the county since 1970. Minimal modest lot single family housing has been built. Housing congestion is worsening in the urban ghettoes. New mobile homes are prohibited in all municipalities. Thirteen municipalities have enacted rent control ordinances in response to the multi-family housing shortage.[1] Vacancy rates are low. Despite overzoning for industry, new industry is reluctant to settle in the County because of the shortage of housing for its workers. Experts for various defendants acknowledged a substantial market and a pressing need for new low and moderate housing.

The issue whether Middlesex County is a housing region is of significance because of the adoption of the term "region" in *Mt. Laurel*. Housing which must be afforded by a developing municipality is defined as its fair share of the present and prospective regional need. In *Oakwood at Madison, Inc. v. Madison Tp.*, 117 *N.J. Super.* 11 (Law Div. 1971), certif. granted 62 *N.J.* 185 (1972), on remand 128 *N.J. Super.* 438 (Law Div. 1974), this court struck down a zoning ordinance which failed to provide for a fair proportion of the housing needs of the municipality's own population and of the region, holding that it was in derogation of the general welfare encompassing housing needs and therefore unconstitutional. Justice Hall noted in *Mt. Laurel* at 189: "The composition of the applicable 'region' will necessarily vary from situation to situation and probably no hard and fast rule will serve to furnish the answer in every case."

Middlesex County is part of the New York metropolitan region. Plainsboro and Cranbury and portions of South Brunswick and Monroe to the southwest of the county are in some measure also part of the Philadelphia metropolitan region. Those areas look predominately towards Trenton, Princeton and Hightstown in Mercer County for local shopping and services. In the north of the county South Plainfield, Dunellen and Middlesex and portions of Piscataway and Edison look predominately towards Plainfield in Union County for local shopping and services. The balance of the county is oriented within the county, towards New Brunswick, Perth Amboy or elsewhere, for local shopping and services.

---

1. East Brunswick, Edison, Highland Park, Metuchen, Middlesex, New Brunswick, North Brunswick, Old Bridge, Perth Amboy, Piscataway, Sayreville, South Brunswick, Woodbridge. Municipal police power to enact rent control ordinances was upheld in *Inganamort v. Bor. of Fort Lee*, 62 N.J. 521 (1973) because of the critical housing need.

Regions are fuzzy at the borders. Middlesex County is a Standard Metropolitan Statistical Area as fixed by the United States Office of Management and Budget. Such an area is specified as an integrated economic and social unit with a large population nucleus. Twenty of the 25 municipalities joined in a Community Development Block Grant application as an "urban county" under the regulations of the Housing and Community Development Act of 1974, 42 U.S.C.A. §5301 *et seq.*[2] A county master plan and a wealth of applicable statistics are available through the County Planning Board. Someone employed in any municipality of the county may seek housing in any other municipality, and someone residing in any municipality may seek employment in any other municipality. Residence within walking distance of the place of employment, or within the same municipality, is no longer a desideratum. Nor is the availability of public transportation a major factor. The county is crisscrossed by arterial highways, including the New Jersey Turnpike and the Garden State Parkway. Mobility by automobile is the rule. A large proportion even of low income wage earners within the county own automobiles and many of those travel regularly 20 miles or more to their places of employment. The entire county is within the sweep of suburbia. Its designation as a region for the purpose of this litigation, within larger metropolitan regions, is sustained.

In compliance with *Mt. Laurel* plaintiffs undertook to establish by a prima facie showing that each of the 23 defendant municipalities' zoning ordinances was constitutionally invalid because of failure to provide for a fair share of the low and moderate income housing needs of the region. That burden was met as to 11 municipalities, as will be analyzed *infra*. Dunellen was granted an outright dismissal. With a population of over 7,000 in a square mile area and about 42% low and moderate income households, Dunellen has less than 20 acres of vacant land, mostly unsuitable for housing, and no patently exclusionary provisions in its zoning ordinance.

In addition 11 municipalities, Carteret, Helmetta, Highland Park, Jamesburg, Metuchen, Middlesex, Milltown, South Amboy, South River, Spotswood and Woodbridge were granted dismissals conditional upon adoption of amendments to their zoning ordinances which are agreed to by their respective attorneys, accepted by plaintiffs and approved by the court. These amendments include the following: Deletion of limitations on the number of bedrooms or of rooms in multi-family housing;[3] deletion of special exception procedures for multi-family housing and provision for it as an allowable use;[4] reduction of excessive parking space requirements in multi-family housing;[5] reduction of excessive minimum floor area require-

---

2. Edison, New Brunswick, Perth Amboy, Sayreville and Woodbridge submitted their separate applications as "entitlement municipalities."
3. Carteret, Highland Park, Middlesex, South Amboy, Spotswood, Woodbridge. *Mt. Laurel* at 182-183.
4. Jamesburg, Middlesex, Milltown South Amboy, South River, Woodbridge.
5. Jamesburg, Milltown. Reductions to 1.5 parking spaces minimum per unit were agreed to.

ments in multi-family or single-family housing or both;[6] reduction of excessive minimum lot sizes for multi-family or single-family housing or both,[7] increase of maximum density of multi-family housing to 15 units per acre,[8] increase of maximum height of multi-family housing to 2½ stories or higher;[9] deletion of a multi-family housing ceiling of 15% of total housing units within a municipality;[10] rezoning from industry to multi-family residential [11] and from single-family to multi-family residential.[12] A number of these agreed revisions have been enacted.

The 11 municipalities which were dismissed conditionally from the litigation are substantially built up without significant vacant acreage suitable for housing, except Woodbridge with some 800 acres, Spotswood with about 200 acres and Jamesburg, South Amboy and South River with about 100 acres each. In view of the consent dismissals no issue is before the court whether these 11 municipalities are "developing municipalities" in the sense of that term in *Mt. Laurel*. Incontrovertibly a fair share allocation of a substantial number of new housing units to meet regional needs would be nugatory in a municipality with minimal vacant acreage. But a municipality is not exempt from the constitutional standards of reasonableness in its zoning because it is not "developing" within *Mt. Laurel*.

Exemption from *Mt. Laurel* was pressed by Cranbury and Plainsboro on another ground. *Mt. Laurel* at 160 cites as one of the characteristics of a developing municipality that it has undergone a great population increase since World War II. These two townships have not, in contrast to the explosive growth countywide. But their relatively static population is attributable in large measure to restrictive zoning. Past exclusionary practices cannot shield them from an obligation to meet their fair share of regional housing needs.

Eleven municipalities were not dismissed outright or conditionally and, as prescribed in *Mt. Laurel,* assumed the "heavy burden" of establishing peculiar circumstances justifying their failure to afford the opportunity for low and moderate income housing to the extent of their respective fair shares. These 11 municipalities comprise seven townships south of the Raritan River, Cranbury, East Brunswick, Old Bridge (formerly Madison), Monroe, North Brunswick, Plainsboro and South Brunswick, two townships

---

6. Jamesburg, Metuchen, Milltown, South Amboy, Spotswood, Woodbridge. Reductions to less than 1,000 square feet minimum per single-family unit, to less than 700 square feet minimum per one bedroom multi-family unit and to less than 550 square feet minimum per efficiency unit were agreed to.

7. Carteret, Highland Park, Middlesex, South River, Spotswood, Woodbridge. Reductions to less than 10,000 square feet minimum single-family lot and to less than 3 acre minimum multi-family lots were agreed to.

8. South Amboy.

9. South Amboy, South River.

10. South River.

11. South Amboy, Spotswood.

12. Helmetta, Milltown, South Amboy, South River, Spotswood, Woodbridge.

north of the Raritan River, Edison and Piscataway, and two boroughs, Sayreville south and South Plainfield north of the Raritan River.

The exclusionary zoning practices in some or all of these 11 municipalities, compounded in effect because of the proximity of several to each other, embrace overzoning for industry and low density residential housing, underzoning for high density single-family and multi-family residential housing, prohibition of multi-family housing and mobile homes, bedroom and density restrictions on multi-family housing excluding couples with two or more children, and floor area and other restrictions on multi-family housing forcing up construction costs.

Prior to a discussion seriatim of the 11 zoning ordinances, population, income, employment and vacant acreage tables are appropriate.

East Brunswick, Edison, Monroe, North Brunswick, Old Bridge, Piscataway, Sayreville, South Brunswick and South Plainfield underwent a population upsurge since 1950 even beyond the 120% gain in the county. Only Cranbury and Plainsboro trailed perceptibly behind.

	1950	Population 1960	1970	Increase 1950-1970
Cranbury	1,797	2,001	2,253	25%
East Brunswick	5,699	19,965	34,166	500%
Edison	16,348	44,799	67,120	310%
Monroe	4,082	5,831	9,138	124%
North Brunswick	6,450	10,099	16,691	159%
Old Bridge	7,366	22,772	48,715	561%
Piscataway	10,180	19,890	36,418	258%
Plainsboro	1,112	1,171	1,648	48%
Sayreville	10,338	22,553	32,508	214%
South Brunswick	4,001	10,278	14,058	251%
South Plainfield	8,008	17,879	21,142	164%
Middlesex County	264,872	433,856	583,813	120%

Based on the 1970 census, low income in the following table is figured as up to $7,000 per year and moderate income up to $10,000. Those limits approximate the bottom 20% and the next 20% in the State as a whole and compare closely in Middlesex County with the Federal Department of Housing and Urban Development standards of low income as up to 50% of median income and moderate income as 50% to 80% of median income. Among the 11 municipalities only Piscataway with Rutgers University married student housing and Plainsboro with farm labor housing exceed the county percentage of low and moderate income families. Most are within 15% of the county percentage. Edison and South Plainfield are within 25%. Only East Brunswick may be characterized as an elite community. In contrast New Brunswick and Perth Amboy both had 54% low and moderate income population, Jamesburg 49% and Helmetta 48%.

INCOME BY FAMILIES IN 1970

	% Low Income	% Moderate Income
Cranbury	20	11
East Brunswick	7	11
Edison	11	15
Monroe	12	21
North Brunswick	12	18
Old Bridge	12	19.5
Piscataway	14	21.5
Plainsboro	23	20.5
Sayreville	10	20
South Brunswick	12.5	17
South Plainfield	11	15
Middlesex County	15	19

Industrial employees in the following table are defined as employees in manufacturing, wholesale, transportation, utilities and construction. The projections for the year 2000 are based upon County Planning Board estimates, as modified upward in Edison, Monroe and Old Bridge according to fact findings by the court. In eight of the 11 municipalities there are glaring deficiencies in low and moderate income housing, as measured by low and moderate income population, for the industrial employees within that municipality. In East Brunswick the deficiency is less but over 40%. Only Monroe and Old Bridge apparently offer adequate housing opportunities for their blue collar workers. By the year 2000 the deficiencies in low and moderate income housing for industrial employees within each municipality would be of disastrous proportions under present zoning. See Justice Hall's statement in *Mt. Laurel* at 187: "Certainly when a municipality zones for industry and commerce for local tax purposes, it without question must zone to permit adequate housing within the means of the employees involved in such uses." It is pertinent to note that at present an estimated 75,000 resi-

INDUSTRIAL ACREAGE AND EMPLOYEES

	1967		2000 projected	
	acres in use	employees	acres in use	employees
Cranbury	185	1,362	678	7,876
East Brunswick	378	2,176	1,377	11,877
Edison	1,789	15,823	3,950	39,589
Monroe	266	460	1,860	15,033
North Brunswick	1,231	11,739	2,347	23,204
Old Bridge	1,685	494	2,685	9,824
Piscataway	346	6,898	1,388	16,746
Plainsboro	229	438	557	4,253
Sayreville	967	8,786	2,091	20,670
South Brunswick	718	3,586	1,872	18,695
South Plainfield	509	3,767	1,187	11,259

dents of the county are employed outside the county, as compared to an estimated 55,000 residents elsewhere who are employed within the county.

The vacant acreage statistics in the following table are compiled from answers to interrogatories by the respective municipalities, data of the State Department of Community Affairs and relevant testimony. Gross vacant acreage suitable for housing excludes identified environmentally critical land, that is, short term flood plains, aquifer outcrops and swamps essential to water resources, also grades of 12% or steeper and proposed park land. Net vacant acreage also excludes vacant land reasonably zoned for industry and commerce and all farmland in present use. Manifestly there is ample vacant land in all 11 municipalities suitable for 2,000 or more units of low and moderate income housing at densities of five to ten units per acre. The major land resources of the county in the more distant future must rest in Monroe, Old Bridge and South Brunswick. With such significant open acreages all 11 municipalities fit within the *Mt. Laurel* criterion of "developing municipalities."

	TOTAL ACREAGE	VACANT ACREAGE SUITABLE FOR HOUSING	
		Gross	Net
Cranbury	8,614	6,891	1,700
East Brunswick	14,342	3,521	1,600
Edison	27,289	5,756	2,200
Monroe	26,041	21,819	11,500
North Brunswick	7,628	2,717	1,600
Old Bridge	25,126	15,000	13,500
Piscataway	12,288	2,637	1,315
Plainsboro	7,680	5,437	1,130
Sayreville	10,560	4,083	1,800
South Brunswick	28,788	23,470	17,000
South Plainfield	5,344	1,542	740

Cranbury is an historic village in the midst of farmland. In active farm use are 4,468 acres or 52% of its total area. An aquifer underlies much of it. The Upper Millstone River on its southerly and westerly borders is dangerously polluted. Meadowland along the river is designated as regional open space in the county master plan of 1970. Two major highways bisect Cranbury. Its residents who are employed outside Cranbury travel about half to the north and east and half to the south and west. It has 44 substandard housing units [13] and 90 occupied by households requiring a governmental housing subsidy.

Cranbury's zoning ordinance permits no new multi-family housing, except conversions to two family. Minimum lot sizes of 15,000 square feet

---

13. Defined as deteriorated, dilapidated, overcrowded, without plumbing or without kitchen facilities.

are permitted only in the substantially built up village. Elsewhere the minimum lot size is 40,000 square feet. The township is overzoned for industry by over 2,000 acres and over 500% of projected demand. A zoning amendment is under study to permit multi-family housing, with some low and moderate income units, to the east of the village along Brainerd Lake. A sewer system would tie in to the Middlesex County Sewerage Authority.

Cranbury's present zoning ordinance falls short of the *Mt. Laurel* standard and must be struck down in view of available suitable acreage adjoining the village on which low and moderate income housing may be built without impairing the established residential character of the village or interfering with present farm uses.

East Brunswick is a relatively low density residential municipality centrally located and bisected by major highways. It has established middle and high income neighborhoods. Less than 1,000 acres is farmland in use. Much of its undeveloped land is environmentally sensitive: aquifer outcrops, tidal marshes along the Raritan and South Rivers, other flood plains along several brooks, and steep hilly terrain. Sewage disposal and drainage are problems because of the high water table and clay soil in many areas. The northernmost fringes of the pine barrens are in the township. It has 244 substandard housing units and 348 occupied by households requiring a governmental housing subsidy.

Its zoning ordinance provides preponderately for one acre and half acre single-family housing with cluster options. Minimum floor acres of 1,500 square feet and minimum frontages exceeding 100 feet in most zones substantially exclude low and moderate income housing. Virtually no vacant land is available for single-family housing on 10,000 square foot lots or for multi-family housing. Maximum densities of 12 units per acre and other restrictions on multi-family housing drive up construction costs. The township is overzoned for industry by over 1,100 acres and over 250% of projected demand. A master plan revision is being worked on.

East Brunswick's zoning ordinance must be held invalid under *Mt. Laurel*. Absence of sewer utilities is not *per se* an exemption from *Mt. Laurel*. As stated by Justice Hall at 186 even in soil with a permeability problem ". . . the township could require [sewer and water utilities] as improvements by developers or install them under the special assessment or other appropriate statutory procedure."

Edison is a hub of highway, rail and deep water transportation. It has 520 substandard housing units and 1,879 occupied by households requiring a governmental housing subsidy. As noted *supra* its low and moderate income population is about 25% below that of the county, and it falls markedly short of providing low and moderate income housing opportunities for its more than 15,000 industrial workers.

Its zoning ordinance authorizes diversity of housing but only 5% of its vacant land is zoned for multi-family housing, including 10 acres for high rise apartments, and only 5% for single-family housing on 7,500 square foot lots. No other residential zone offers a realistic possibility, even with cluster options, for low and moderate income housing because of lot size, floor area and frontage restrictions. The township is overzoned for industry by about 500 acres. Several housing projects are under way with governmental subsidies. The township is the subject of a consent judgment of the United States District Court to participate in various programs administered by the Department of Housing and Urban Development for new housing and rehabilitation of substandard housing and for sewage and other improvements.

Edison's zoning ordinance likewise must be struck down under *Mt. Laurel*, chiefly because of maldistribution of vacant land into low density rather than high density residential uses, to a lesser extent because of maldistribution of vacant land into industrial use. * * *

Old Bridge's zoning ordinance was struck down by this court in *Oakwood at Madison, supra*. The two previous trial records were stipulated. Identical conclusions are reached, with the additional factual determinations that Old Bridge is overzoned for industry beyond reasonable projections by over 3,000 acres and over 400% and that it has 489 substandard housing units and 1,271 occupied by households requiring a governmental housing subsidy. * * *

South Brunswick is a sprawling township in the path of development both from New York and Philadelphia. Major highways and public transportation by railroad and bus are available. Several thousand acres of vacant land zoned for single-family housing on one, three and five acre minimum lots are abandoned farmland. Aquifers underlie much of the township. Swamps, flood plains and aquifer outcrops rule out housing over extensive sections. Protection of aquifer recharge areas may be accomplished by retention ponds in medium and high density residential zones, as well as in industrial zones. An expert for the township conceded a population capacity of at least 100,000 without endangering environmentally sensitive land. Water and sewer utilities are lacking in much of the township. Such infrastructure is feasible. Development may fan out from the four scattered villages. The township has 149 substandard housing units and 284 occupied by households requiring a governmental housing subsidy.

Amendments to South Brunswick's zoning ordinance in recent years have lessened its exclusionary impact. Mandatory minimums of 5% low income and 5% moderate income units have been set in Planned Residential Developments, nevertheless less than the country's and the township's own proportions of low and moderate income households. The township is overzoned for single-family housing on lots of one acre or more with frontages of 120 feet or more, and for industry by over 7,000 acres and over 700%. No multi-family housing is permitted outside Planned Residential Developments. One such development under construction near Dayton and others proposed or under review would augment low and moderate income housing stock.

South Brunswick's zoning ordinance remains invalidly exclusionary under *Mt. Laurel* and must be struck down. * * *

The final issue is the remedy. The zoning ordinances of 11 defendant municipalities have been held unconstitutional. The 11 municipalities have been determined to be part of a region comprising Middlesex County for the purpose of this litigation. The remaining determination is the fair share allocation of low and moderate income housing to each of the 11 municipalities.

A factual finding must therefore be made as to the countywide low and moderate income housing need projected to 1985. New units will be required to replace present substandard housing, for most of those filling new jobs in the county, for increasing numbers of retired persons and for other increments to population. Against this total must be deducted rehabilitated units through governmental subsidies and otherwise, units "filtering through" as occupants move up to higher income housing and units projected to be built under present or revised zoning in New Brunswick, Perth Amboy and the 12 municipalities which were dismissed outright or conditionally from this litigation, in particular Woodbridge, Spotswood, Jamesburg, South Amboy and South River which have significant vacant acreages. Taking into account County Planning Board population and job growth projections to 1985, estimating one third of new jobs as low and moderate income and a ratio, as at present, of 73% of low and moderate income employees also residing within the county, the total additional low and moderate income housing need in the county to 1985 is fixed at 18,697 units.

The initial fair share allocation must be to correct the present imbalance, that is, to bring each defendant municipality up to the county proportion of 15% low and 19% moderate income population. The county proportion rather than the state proportion of 20% low and 20% moderate income is determined upon. The historic trend of urban dispersal from New York and Philadelphia is that per capita incomes in counties are higher in inverse ratio to distance from the central city. The allocation to correct imbalance results in the following additional low and moderate income housing units.

Subtracting 4,030 from the 18,697 low and moderate income housing units needed in the county to 1985, the balance is 14,667 or approximately 1,333 per municipality. There is no basis not to apportion these units equally. Each municipality has vacant suitable land far in excess of its fair share requirement without impairing the established residential character of neighborhoods. Land to be protected for environmental considerations has been subtracted from vacant acreage totals. No special factor, such as relative access to employment, justifies a deviation from an alloca-

Cranbury	18
East Brunswick	1,316
Edison	1,292
Monroe	23
North Brunswick	180
Old Bridge	301
Piscataway	0
Plainsboro	0
Sayreville	328
South Brunswick	156
South Plainfield	416
	4,030

tion of 1,333 low and moderate housing units, plus the allocation to correct imbalance, to each of the 11 municipalities.

Low and moderate income housing units should be divided 45% low and 55% moderate. Low income is defined as up to 50% of median income in the county and moderate income as 50 to 80% of median income, according to current data of the County Planning Board. Within each municipality there may be flexibility, for example, multi-family housing at densities of 10 or more units per acre, multi-family housing encompassing a diversity of housing but with mandatory minimums of low and moderate income units, mobile homes at densities of five to eight units per acre [14] and single-family housing at densities of four or more units per acre. A combination of these alternatives may be arrived at. Each municipality would receive credit for pending low and moderate income construction for which certificates of occupancy have not been granted as of the date of this judgment.

After the allocation to correct imbalance, Cranbury, East Brunswick, Edison, North Brunswick, Piscataway, Plainsboro, Sayreville and South Plainfield are ordered to rezone their respective net vacant acreage suitable for housing, as shown in the fourth table *supra*, 15% for low income and 19% for moderate income on the basis of 100% zoning for housing (which this judgment does not require). The housing units thus afforded should approximate the allocation of 1,333 units each. As to any municipality, if it appears that such rezoning would fall significantly short of the allocation of 1,333 units, plus the allocation to correct imbalance, application to modify this judgment may be brought.

Monroe, Old Bridge and South Brunswick, all with net vacant land suitable for housing exceeding 10,000 acres, are ordered to rezone to provide their respective allocations of 1,333 units, plus their respective alloca-

---

14. *Vickers v. Tp. Com. of Gloucester Tp.*, 37 N.J. 232 (1962), cert. den. 371 U.S. 233 (1963), upheld the constitutionality of a zoning ordinance which prohibits mobile homes anywhere in a sprawling, largely undeveloped municipality. But *Vickers* is not a bar to zoning, otherwise reasonable, to allow mobile homes.

tions to correct imbalance, by any combination of multi-family, mobile home or single-family housing.

As stated by Justice Hall in *Mt. Laurel* at 192: "Courts do not build housing . . . ." In implementing this judgment the 11 municipalities charged with fair share allocations must do more than rezone not to exclude the possibility of low and moderate income housing in the allocated amounts. Approvals of multi-family projects, including Planned Unit Developments, should impose mandatory minimums of low and moderate income units. Density incentives may be set. Mobile homes offer a realistic alternative within the reach of moderate and even low income households. Whether single-family housing is attainable for moderate income households may hinge upon land and construction costs. The 11 municipalities should pursue and cooperate in available Federal and State subsidy programs for new housing and rehabilitation of substandard housing, although it is beyond the issues in this litigation to order the expenditure of municipal funds or the allowance of tax abatements. See *Hills v. Gautreaux*, — U.S. — (1976) holding that a federal district court has the authority to order the Department of Housing and Urban Development to undertake a regional plan for low income and integrated housing to remedy housing discrimination fostered by H.U.D. practices in a central city, with the consent of suburban municipalities.

Judgement in accordance herewith to be effective after 90 days. Jurisdiction is retained.

K. *Accessory Uses*

BEVERLY HILLS
v.
BRADY

34 Cal. 2d 854, 215 P.2d 460(1950).
Supreme Court of California, in Bank.
March 10, 1950.

The City of Beverly Hills, a municipal corporation, sued William Brady to enjoin defendant from using premises in a residential zone for purposes allegedly in violation of city ordinance zoning the premises as residential. The Superior Court, Los Angeles County, Stanley Mosk, J., rendered a judgment adverse to plaintiff and plaintiff appealed. The Supreme Court, Shenk, J., held that defendant's activities were not violative of the zoning ordinance.

Judgment affirmed:

For prior opinion see 205 P.2d 1088.

SHENK, Presiding Justice.

Appeal by the plaintiff from an adverse judgment in an action to enjoin the defendant's alleged violation of zoning restrictions. The appeal is on the judgment roll.

Ordinance No. 443 of the city of Beverly Hills, adopted December 8, 1936, prohibits the establishment or conduct of any business in Zone R-1.5, classified as residential. The establishment or conduct of any business therein is declared unlawful. The word "business," in so far as material here, is defined as the purchase, sale or other transaction involving the handling or disposition of any article, substance or commodity for profit or livelihood, or the ownership or management of office buildings or offices. Under the heading "Use Restrictions" it is provided that no property may be used for any purpose other than that permitted for the zone in which it is located except that the City Council may after notice and public hearing allow such variance as is deemed in harmony with the general purpose of the ordinance, the protection of the property, and the character of the district upon conditions consistent therewith. In the consideration of the grounds of appeal it will be assumed that the foregoing provisions of the ordinance or their equivalent were in force prior to and during the period of the defendant's ownership and occupancy of his home which is located in Zone R-1.5.

The defendant is a licensed physician and acquired his present home in 1932. During all of the times here involved he was the author of a syndicated column devoted to discussion of health problems which is published in 130 newspapers in the United States and Canada. In the syndicated article he offers free, or for the ten or twenty-five cent cost of printing and mailing, various pamphlets containing further information on subjects discussed. Each day he receives one bag of mailed requests for pamphlets and sends out daily one mail bag of pamphlets which aggregate about 150,-000 pamphlets annually. The dictation and writing of his syndicated article, and the receipt and mailing of pamphlets are conducted with the help of secretaries in a room over the garage which is fitted with shelves, filing cabinets, desks and typewriters. The total annual receipts for the requested pamphlets amounts to approximately $16,400, and the total annual printing, mailing and salary cost exceeds that sum by about $300. These activities, as conducted by the defendant, do not interfere with the use or appearance of his home or premises as a residence, nor do they affect the residential or aesthetic character of the district.

The trial court assumed constitutional validity of the ordinance and concluded that the defendant was not engaged in a business within the meaning thereof. Denial of the prayer for injunctive relief followed.

The plaintiff concedes that the defendant's writing of his syndicated column is not prohibited by the use restrictions of the ordinance; but contends that the additional activities amount to the conduct of a publishing business and the sale or other transaction involving the handling or disposition of a commodity which is in violation of the ordinance; that such is the case although no profit is derived or expected therefrom; and that therefore the court's conclusion and judgment are not supported by the admitted facts.

Where the questioned activities amount to the conduct of a business depends upon the adopted definition of that word and the primary intent of the zoning restrictions. Obviously the conduct of industry pursued for profit was prohibited because of the general tendency to interfere with the residential character assigned to the district. The zoning restrictions are intended to retain the highest residential and aesthetic value to the property owners and the district. They are general protective measures for the benefit of the residents of the district and of the community as a whole. However, a protective measure for the individual owner was also included to insure that a home-maker would not be deprived of the reasonable use of his premises.

The mere statement of the facts as they relate to the general purpose of the restrictions would appear to be a sufficient answer to the plaintiff's contentions. Unquestionably an author may answer his mail and include requested literature. Here the mailing of pamphlets is merely incidental to the writing and publication of the syndicated article, which is conceded to be a permissive use. The pamphlets are not independently advertised, nor is the defendant in the business of publishing or selling the pamphlets at a profit. His livelihood is derived from the authoring of the syndicated articles. It is not contended that the activities interfere with the general character and aesthetic harmonies of the district. It must follow that there is support for the trial court's conclusion that the defendant is not conducting a business within the meaning of the ordinance.

Furthermore, assuming that there is involved the sale or handling of a commodity although no profit is derived or expected, or that such activities constitute a non-residential and prohibited use, the question then is whether the defendant could be deprived of the right, pursuant to the protective provision of the ordinance or otherwise, to pursue on his premises activities incidental to an unrestricted use when such activities do not interfere with the primarily residential character of the district or affect the aesthetic values sought to be preserved. The question may be largely one of degree. On the record the ordinance may not operate so as to deprive the defendant of the normal activities incidental to a use not prohibited by the ordinance. The correct answer is indicated by the present factual situation. Whether that condition may conceivably be affected by extensive future increase in the volume of activity in connection with the defendant's proper use of his residence premises is not now a matter for consideration. Application of zoning restrictions to particular facts is subject to investigation by the courts and each case is determinable on its individual merits. People v. Hawley,

207 Cal. 395, 411, 279 P. 136; McKay Jewelers, Inc., v. Bowron, 19 Cal. 2d 595, 603, 122 P.2d 543, 139 A.L.R. 1188. The conclusion of the trial court is warranted by a consideration of the particular factual situation and requires no further citation of authority to justify it.

The judgment is affirmed.

EDMONDS, CARTER, SCHAUER and SPENCE, JJ., concur.

CROSS-REFERENCES

In Anderson, see Index, this topic.

In Hagman, see § 54.

In Rathkopf, see ch. 23 and see Index, this topic.

In Williams, see ch. 74.

In Yokley, see Index, this topic.

L. *Community Facilities*

ATHERTON

v.

SUPERIOR COURT

159 Cal. App. 2d 417, 324 P.2d 328 (1958).
District Court of Appeal. First District,
Division 1, California.
April 17, 1958.
Rehearing Denied May 16, 1958.

Proceeding for a writ of prohibition to restrain the Superior Court from proceeding in an action of eminent domain pending in that court brought by school district in which the district seeks to condemn certain lands in the town for school purposes. The District Court of Appeal, Bray, J., held that zoning ordinances of the municipality did not control the right of the school district in which the municipality was included to designate the location of its schools and that the school district is a state agency and that the state had occupied the field of location of schools.

Alternative writ discharged and petition for peremptory writ denied.

Winston Churchill Black, San Francisco, for petitioner.

Keith C. Sorenson, Dist. Atty., Howard E. Gawthrop, Deputy Asst. Atty., Redwood City, for respondents.

Edmund G. Brown, Atty. Gen., Richard H. Perry, Deputy Atty. Gen., amici curiae in support of contentions of respondents.

BRAY, Justice.

Petitioner seeks a writ of prohibition to restrain the Superior Court of San Mateo County from proceeding in an action in eminent domain now pending in that court, numbered 76501, brought by respondent Menlo Park School District[1] against certain parties, in which said respondent seeks to condemn certain lands in said Town of Atherton for school purposes.[2]

Questions presented:

Do the zoning ordinances of a municipality control the right of a school district in which the municipality is included, to designate the location of its schools? Corollary to this are the questions (a) Is a school district a state agency? (b) If so, has the state occupied the field of location of schools?

There is no conflict as to the facts. Included in Menlo Park School District are the incorporated cities of Atherton and Menlo Park as well as unincorporated territory. The district desires to acquire land in Atherton for public school purposes. Petitioner is a municipal corporation of the sixth class. June 24, 1957, the city council adopted ordinance No. 225, entitled "An Interim Zoning Ordinance Relating to Public Buildings and the Location Thereof Declaring its Urgency and Providing that it Shall Take Effect Immediately." In substance it prevents any property in the Town of Atherton which is zoned for residential purposes from being used for any other purposes, specifically providing that no lands presently zoned residential may be used for the purpose of public buildings, including but not limited to schools. The ordinance was adopted pursuant to section 65806, Government Code, which provides that if the planning commission in good faith is conducting studies or holding hearings for the purpose of the adoption of any zoning ordinance or amendment thereto, the legislative body may adopt a temporary interim ordinance prohibiting any purposes which might conflict with such ordinance.

The same day the city council adopted a resolution proposing amendments to the town's zoning ordinance No. 146 as amended for the zoning of public buildings, including schools, and directing the planning commission to hold public hearings on the proposed amendments to determine whether or not zoning districts should be established in which public buildings, including schools, may be located. The planning commission has employed a planning consultant for expert advice on land uses in the town, is now making pertinent studies, and has held public hearings. If valid, the ordinances would prohibit the school district from locating its school as proposed.

July 3, 1957, respondent commenced its eminent domain action, in which it seeks to condemn approximately nine acres within respondent's corporate

1. Hereinafter referred to as respondent.
2. Argued and submitted with this proceeding is Landi v. Superior Court. See Cal. App., 324 P.2d 326.

limits for school purposes, which property is zoned for residential uses only under petitioner's comprehensive zoning plan (ordinance No. 146 as amended). The condemnation is in direct violation of ordinance No. 225. The superior court in said action refused to grant petitioner's request for an order staying proceedings in said action. The petition alleges that the planning commission is proceeding "in good faith" as required by section 65806, Government Code; that Atherton was incorporated in 1923 for the express purpose of assuring a continuance of its area as, and its area still is, a low density, estate type, residential community consisting of 3035 acres. It has no industrial or manufacturing plants or districts and no business district or business enterprises excepting two real estate offices and one gasoline service station existing as non-conforming uses. Atherton is primarily dependent for revenue to operate the municipality on real property taxes. Three different elementary school districts including respondent extend into the boundaries of Atherton and the portion of each in Atherton is much smaller than the outside portions. Approximately 7000 persons live in Atherton. Registered as in attendance in schools within the town limits are 6046 persons of whom 2696 are in elementary grades. Only 1640 of these persons reside in Atherton; 1206 of these are in the elementary grades. Approximately 33 elementary students resident in Atherton cannot attend any public school in the town and are attending one in unincorporated territory. 74.61 per cent of the land in Atherton is used for one family residences, 15 per cent for streets, 5.86 per cent for schools, 3.61 per cent for public utilities, fire protection and city hall, police and other municipal uses; .92 per cent for other uses. The major portion of respondent district lies within the city of Menlo Park. Menlo Park uses for school purposes only 1.5 per cent of its land as compared to the 5.86 per cent used in Atherton. A study by the American Institute for Planners, published jointly with the Federal Reserve Bank of Boston, for a city of the same size, type and kind as Atherton, shows that reasonable and proper zoning would require for school purposes only 1.31 per cent of the total town area, or 39.76 acres as compared to Atherton's present 5.86 per cent or 177.77 acres. In addition to the nine acres sought to be condemned, petitioner is informed that respondent intends to acquire additional acreage in Atherton. Listing the present public and private schools, petitioner contends that Atherton has more schools per capita and more students in proportion to residents, than any other city in the United States. In the past five years there have been attempts to build four additional schools in Atherton. One elementary district whose boundary does not include any of the territory of Atherton, attempted to acquire property in Atherton for a school which no Atherton resident would have been permitted to attend. Attending school in Atherton with its population of only 7000 are approximately 6000 students while no community on either side of Atherton has students therein exceeding one for every five residents. Because of needed traffic control, public safety and police protection every school in Atherton has to receive the special attention of a police officer and because of the unreasonable number of schools there is an unreasonable burden on the police department and an unreasonable expenditure for the benefit of a majority of students who contribute nothing thereto.

In its answer in the eminent domain action, petitioner has set forth that plaintiff has not acquired the conditional use permit required by ordinance No. 146. The superior court denied petitioner's motion for a judgment on the pleadings based upon the ground that respondent's complaint was barred by the provisions of said two ordinances.

Does Petitioner's Zoning Ordinance Control?

Petitioner contends that the issue in this case is whether a municipality under section 65806, Government Code, has the power by an interim ordinance to prohibit any other than specific uses pending studies by the planning commission. It attempted to do this in ordinance No. 225. We are only concerned with the power of the municipality by such an ordinance to prohibit a school district from acquiring public school sites, and not to the application of the ordinance in general.

Petitioner concedes that the power of eminent domain is inherent in the State of California and may be exercised by the state, or any of its agencies to which the power is delegated, but contends that the delegation of the power to schools is limited by the powers which it contends the municipalities have by virtue of section 11, article XI, Constitution, and section 65800, Government Code.

In order to determine these questions we must consider the question of whether a municipality has the power to zone school sites, whether by an interim ordinance or otherwise. Therefore, we must determine if a school district is a state agency, and if so, whether the state has occupied the field in the matter of location of school sites.

(a) *Is a School District a State Agency?*

[1] This question has been flatly answered in the affirmative in Hall v. City of Taft, 47 Cal.2d 177, 302 P.2d 574 : "The public schools of this state are a matter of statewide rather than local or municipal concern; their establishment, regulation and operation are covered by the Constitution and the state Legislature is given comprehensive powers in relation thereto. * * * School districts are agencies of the state for the local operation of the state school system. [Citations.] The beneficial ownership of property of the public schools is in the state." 47 Cal.2d at pages 179, 181, 302 P.2d at page 576.

(b) *State has Occupied the Field.*

[2] "The public school system is of statewide supervision and concern and legislative enactments thereon control over attempted regulation by local government units. [Citations.]" Hall v. City of Taft, supra, 47 Cal.2d at page 181, 302 P.2d at page 577.

Has the state occupied the field of school site location or has it expressly granted the power of school zoning to the municipalities? The answer is that the state has occupied the field. Evidence of this is the following statutes:

Section 18402, Education Code: "The State Department of Education shall establish standards for school sites." How can this be accomplished if a municipality may by zoning determine the location of such sites?

Section 18403, Education Code, provides that the governing board of a school district before acquiring property for a new school site or addition to a present school site shall "give the planning commission having jurisdiction notice in writing of the proposed acquisition." The planning commission in 30 days is required to submit to the school board "a written report of the investigation and its recommendations concerning acquisition of the site." "The governing board shall not acquire title to the property until the report of the planning commission has been received. *If the report does not favor the acquisition of the property for a school site, or for an addition to a present school site, the governing board of the school district shall not acquire title to the property until 30 days after the commission's report is received.*" (Emphasis added.) This shows that while the local planning commission may recommend concerning the location of a school site the ultimate determination of the site is in the school board.

Section 18404 provides that a school district board and a city school board, if the latter desires to locate a school within two miles of an airport, must notify the State Department of Education of the proposed acquisition of a school site, and if the state department does not report favorably, the school board must wait 30 days before acquiring title to the property. This power of recommendation in the state department is inconsistent with the right of a local planning commission to designate by zoning the area where a public school may be located.

Sections 65090 et seq., Government Code, deal with the appointment and powers of a city planning commission. In chapter 3, article 9, dealing with "Administration of Master or General Plan" appears section 65551, which provides that after the legislative body has adopted a master or general plan for the city no "public ground or open space" shall be acquired and "no public building or structure shall be constructed or authorized in the area" until its location, purpose and extent have been submitted to and reported upon by the planning commission. Section 65552 provides that if the power to acquire such "public ground or open space" public building or structure is vested in "some governmental body, commission, or board" other than the city council, then such body, commission or board shall submit to the planning commission its location, purpose and extent.

Section 65553 provides that the planning commission shall report its findings as to whether the proposed public improvement conforms to the adopted master or general plan.

Section 65554 provides: "If the planning commission disapproves the proposed public improvement, *its disapproval may be overruled by such other governmental body, board, or agency.*" (Emphasis added.) Such a power in the other government body is completely incompatible with a power in the municipality of zoning public schools.

[3] Petitioner points out that a planning commission has no legislative function, but may only study, administer and recommend, whereas the city council has the sole power to zone. Therefore, says petitioner, section 65554 deals only with the planning commission and is not binding on the city council. This contention overlooks the fact that the section is dealing with a master plan which has already been adopted by the city council and in which the council has zoned an area for a public ground or building. While the council may zone it, these sections provide that if the power to acquire such ground or building is in some other governmental body that body after reporting to the planning commission may entirely disregard the disapproval of the commission. There is no requirement that it then must go to the city council before it may acquire the property. "[P]ublic ground or open space," and "public building or structure," necessarily include public school grounds and buildings. Assuming that the city council under the statutes relied upon by petitioner, and hereafter discussed, in the instance has the power to zone schools, it is clear that such zoning is merely advisory or recommendatory and that under section 65554 such zoning is not binding on the school district.

[4] Petitioner contends that Atherton's power to zone comes from section 11, article XI, Constitution (the police power section): "Any county, city, town, or township may make and enforce within its limits all such local, police, sanitary and other regulations as are not in conflict with general laws." "A zoning ordinance falls within the classification of police measures." Hurst v. City of Burlingame, 207 Cal. 134, 138, 277 P. 308, 310. Petitioner concedes that under the qualification in the section, the Legislature has the power to grant to the school districts if they are state agencies the exclusive power of zoning school sites. Petitioner contends that the Legislature has not done so but on the other hand has done just the contrary and designated the municipalities as the body having the power to effect such zoning. Supporting its contention it cites the hereafter mentioned statutes which it contends control those above mentioned. Section 65800, Government Code: "Pursuant to the provisions of this chapter, the legislative body of any county or city by ordinance may: (a) Regulate the use of buildings, structures, and land as between agriculture, industry, business, residence *and other purposes.* * * * (d) Create civic districts around civic centers, public parks, and public buildings and grounds for the purpose of enabling a planning commission to review all plans for buildings or structures within the district prior to the issuance of a building permit in order to assure an orderly development in the vicinity of such public sites and buildings." (Emphasis added.) Section 65801: "For such purposes

the legislative body may divide a city, a county, or portions thereof into zones of the number, shape, and area it deems best suited to carry out the purpose of this chapter." Section 65806 gives the city council authority to adopt as an emergency measure a temporary interim zoning ordinance to protect the public safety, health and welfare, which ordinance may prohibit "*such and any other uses* which may be in conflict with such zoning ordinance." (Emphasis added.) Section 65462 provides of what the master or general plan shall consist, including "(a) A *land use* element which designates the proposed general distribution and general location and *extent of the uses* of the land for housing, business, industry, recreation, *education*, public buildings and grounds, and other categories of public and private uses of land." (Emphasis added.) Section 65470: "A master or general plan may include a public buildings element of the plan, showing *locations* and arrangements of civic and community centers, *public schools*, libraries, police and fire stations, and all other public buildings, including their architecture and the landscape treatment of their grounds." (Emphasis added.)

[5] We see nothing in any of the above statutes which in any way conflicts with the statutes hereinbefore mentioned which we hold evidence the occupancy of the field by the state. The sections referred to by petitioner necessarily include broad general language in order to cover all the situations, purposes and property with which zoning must be concerned. The word "education" in section 65462 does not conflict with the power of a school district to locate its schools. It must be construed with statutes dealing with zoning and the rights of the state. It must be remembered that in all municipalities there are private schools, the location of which is purely a municipal matter. Hence the reason for the words "education" and the words "other uses" and "other purposes" appearing in the above statutes. As to the word "public schools" in section 65470, no master plan would be complete without showing on it the location of public schools already in existence. It may also show areas which the city recommends for future schools. The quoted words in nowise show that the Legislature intended by the use of these words to repeal the evident power given school districts expressly as state agencies to locate their schools. The statutes relied upon by petitioner include "public buildings." Petitioner concedes that the inclusion of those words in the statutes does not in any manner interfere with the right of the state to locate a state building, or of a county to locate a county building, in any portion of a municipality it desires, regardless of any attempt of the municipality to zone the location of such buildings. Yet if its contention is correct that by the inclusion of the words "education" and "public schools" in the above statutes the Legislature was relinquishing the field of school site location to the municipalities, it necessarily would be equally true that by the inclusion of "public buildings" the Legislature was also relinquishing the field of state and county building site locations.

Zahn v. Board of Public Works, 195 Cal. 497, 234 P. 388, deals with the power of the city of Los Angeles to zone to exclude stores from certain

was "whether a municipal corporation's building regulations are applicable to the construction of a public school building by a school district in the municipality." 47 Cal.2d at page 179, 302 P.2d at page 576.   Taft, like areas.   Petitioner contends that the language (195 Cal. at pages 502-503, 234 P. at page 391) to the effect that a municipal zoning ordinance which regulates, restricts and segregates the location of "industries, the several classes of business ° ° ° and the several classes of public and semipublic buildings is a valid exercise of the police power, is a holding that Atherton has the power it claims here.   Obviously, the court did not have in mind nor was it passing upon the question involved in our case.   It was dealing solely with the power to zone business areas.

In Hall v. City of Taft, supra, 47 Cal.2d 177, 302 P.2d 574, the question Atherton, is a city of the sixth class.   Taft, as does petitioner here, relied on article XI, section 11 of the Constitution and contended that under the police power therein granted, it was given the power to adopt building regulations which would apply to school buildings within its boundaries, as the state had not occupied the field.   After holding, as we have hereinbefore shown, that a school district is a state agency, the court went on to hold that the state had completely occupied the field and that the city's regulations concerning "the activity involved" (47 Cal.2d at page 184, 302 P.2d at page 579) conflicted with general laws.   "A city may not enact ordinances which conflict with general laws on statewide matters [citations]."

[6] The Education Code sets out a complete system for providing necessary and adequate schools.   In addition to the statutes hereinbefore discussed there are the following: Section 5021:   "The Legislature hereby declares that it is in the interest of the State and of the people thereof, for the State to aid school districts of the State in providing necessary and adequate school buildings for the pupils of the Public School System, such system being a matter of general concern inasmuch as the education of the children of the State is an obligation and function of the State."   This language obviously includes the location of schools.   Section 5041:   "The Legislature hereby declares that it is in the interest of the State and of the people thereof for the State to aid school districts of the State in providing necessary and adequate school sites and buildings for the pupils of the Public School System, such system being a matter of general concern inasmuch as the education of the children of the State is an obligation and function of the State ° ° °"   Section 5022 appropriates a sum of $30,000,000 to be apportioned to school districts for "(1) The purchase and improvement of school building sites."   Section 18102(a) requires the board of education to "Advise with the governing board of each school district on the acquisition of new school sites, and after a review of available plots give the governing board of the district in writing a list of the approved locations in the order of their merit considering especially the matters of educational merit, reduction of traffic hazards, and conformity to the organized regional plans as presented in the master plan of the planning com-

mission having jurisdiction." While the department of education is thereby required to consider the master plan of a city, in approving a school site, the school district is not required to conform to the department's recommendations. Section 18404 hereinbefore discussed gives the local school board the power to disregard the department's recommendations as it only requires the board to delay for 30 days the acquiring of title to the property the board desires, if the department's recommendation is unfavorable. These sections, as was said in Hall v. City of Taft, supra, 47 Cal.2d 177, 188, 302 P.2d 574, 582, concerning the building construction sections, "tend more to indicate that the school districts could follow such regulations [of the municipalities] as well as those of the state but are not bound to do so."

"The governing board of any school district may, and when directed by a vote of the district shall, build and maintain a schoolhouse." Ed.Code, § 18151. Section 18153 gives the school board the power to establish additional schools in the district. Section 18152 gives the school board, where any school is overcrowded, the power to locate the school in temporary quarters, without restriction as to its location.

The comprehensive system of school control and operation by the school districts as shown in the statutes herein discussed is completely inconsistent with any power of a municipality to control the location of school sites.

Hall v. City of Taft, supra, 47 Cal.2d 177, 302 P.2d 574, placed its decision that the construction of school buildings by school districts is not subject to building regulations of a municipality upon another ground than that the state has completely occupied the field by general laws and that such regulations interfere with those laws.[3] " * * * When it engages in such sovereign activities as the construction and maintenance of its buildings, as differentiated from enacting laws for the conduct of the public at large, it is not subject to local regulations unless the Constitution says it is or the Legislature has consented to such regulation. Section 11 of the article XI of the state Constitution, supra, should not be considered as conferring such powers on local government agencies. Nor should the Government Code sections which confer on a city the power to regulate the construction of buildings within its limits, see Government Code, §§ 38601, 38660, be so considered. * * *" 47 Cal.2d at page 183, 302 P.2d at page 578. As stated in the Hall case (47 Cal.2d at page 181, 302 P.2d at page 577): "The beneficial ownership of property of the public schools is in the state."

[7] If, as the Hall case holds, the construction and maintenance of a school building is a sovereign activity of the state, it is obvious that the location and acquisition of a school site is necessarily and equally such an activity. Obviously, too, neither the Constitution nor the Legislature has

---

3. The brief of the Attorney General on behalf of Honorable Roy E. Simpson, Superintendent of Public Instruction and ex-officio Director of Education, as amicus curiae, stresses this ground.

consented to a municipal regulation of school sites. As said in Kentucky Institution for Education of Blind v. City of Louisville, 123 Ky. 767, 97 S.W. 402, 8 L.R.A., N.S., 553, as quoted in the Hall case (47 Cal.2d at page 183, 302 P.2d at page 579): "'"The principle is that the state, when creating municipal governments, does not cede to them any control of the state's property situated within them, nor over any property which the state has authorized another body or power to control. ° ° ° How can the city ever have a superior authority to the state over the latter's own property or in its control and management? From the nature of things it cannot have."'"

[8] As said in C. J. Kubach Co. v. McGuire, 199 Cal. 215, 217, 248 P. 676, 677: "In the interpretation of a legislative enactment it is the general rule that the state and its agencies are not bound by general words limiting the rights and interests of its citizens unless such public authorities be included within the limitation expressly or by necessary implication."

Under the statutes, the state has in nowise ceded to the municipalities its sovereign right to locate school sites. On the contrary, the state has expressly granted the power of location to its agencies, the school districts.

[9] Article IX, section 5, and article IV, section 25, subdivision 27, of the Constitution vest the Legislature with the absolute power to establish the state school system. "It is well settled that the school system of the state is a matter of general concern and not a municipal affair ° ° ° " Becker v. Council of City of Albany, 47 Cal.App.2d 702, 705, 118 P.2d 924, 926.

[10, 11] The fact that ordinance No. 225 is an interim ordinance intended to hold property in status quo under the period of study necessary to an ultimate determination of the city's master plan, does not give the city the power to prevent the district from exercising its right of eminent domain in acquiring a school site. As we have shown, the city has no right to zone against the district's right of location whether such zoning be intended to be temporary or permanent.

[12] Petitioner contends that the action of the school board in bringing the eminent domain action and particularly in choosing the school site thereby sought to be acquired is arbitrary and constitutes an abuse of the discretion vested in the board. This question cannot be determined in prohibition. It is possibly a matter of defense to be determined in the condemnation action.

The alternative writ is discharged and the petition for a peremptory writ is denied.

PETERS, P. J., and FRED B. WOOD, J., concur.

ROMAN CATHOLIC DIOCESE OF NEWARK

v.

HO-HO-KUS

42 N.J. 556, 202 A.2d 161(1964), and

47 N.J. 211, 220 A.2d 97(1966).

Supreme Court of New Jersey.

Argued Feb. 3, 1964 and April 20, 1964.

Decided June 24, 1964.

Action attacking validity of zoning ordinance amendment prohibiting schools in residence area. The Superior Court, Law Division, held the statute invalid, and defendants appealed. The case was certified before argument in Appellate Division. The Supreme Court, Weintraub, C. J., held that municipality may not zone against private school, or place it in one district rather than another, or refuse it variance, on ground that it is exempt from taxation.

Reversed and remanded.

Francis, J., dissented.

Samuel M. Lyon, Jr., Ridgewood, for defendant-appellant; Merritt Lane, Jr., Newark, for defendants-intervenors-appellants (Ross B. Abrash, Newark, on the brief; McCarter & English, Newark, attorneys, for defendants-intervenors-appellants).

Frederick J. Gassert, Newark, for plaintiffs-respondents (Thomas H. Gassert, Newark, of counsel; Gassert, Murphy & Gassert, Newark, attorneys).

Joseph A. Hoffman, Deputy Atty. Gen. (Arthur J. Sills, Atty. Gen., attorney).

The opinion of the court was delivered by

WEINTRAUB, C. J.

This is a zoning case. In October 1960 plaintiff, Roman Catholic Diocese of Newark, purchased a parcel of some 20 acres in the most highly restricted residence district (R-1) of the Borough of Ho-Ho-Kus upon which it intended to erect a regional high school for some 1,500 boys. At the time of the purchase, the zoning ordinance permitted the contemplated use, but plaintiff's plans led to a reconsideration of the ordinance and finally to an amendment which barred all schools from the R-1 district but continued to permit public and parochial schools through the high-school level in the other three residential districts.

The amendment was assailed upon sundry grounds, including the charge of arbitrariness and denial of due process of law. Much testimony was taken. No findings were made however, the trial court deeming the case to be controlled by chapter 138, L.1961, which was adopted during the pendency of the case. That statute, which appears in the annotated statutes as N.J.S.A. 40:55-33.1, reads:

"No planning or zoning ordinance heretofore or hereafter enacted by any municipality governing the use of land by, or for, schools shall, by any of its terms or provisions or by any rule or regulation adopted in accordance therewith, discriminate between public and private day schools, not operated for profit, of elementary or high school grade."

On its face, the ordinance in question applies equally to public and private schools, but the trial court held that a municipality cannot zone with respect to public schools and hence a zoning restraint upon a private school is necessarily discriminatory. We certified the ensuing appeal before argument in the Appellate Division.

We are unable to accept the trial court's view of the statute. The statute obviously was drawn on the thesis that a municipality may zone as to public schools and upon that premise sought to insure equality of zoning treatment for private schools. A legislator voting for that law could hardly have understood it to mean that thenceforth a private school shall be immune from zoning. That, of course, is the effect of the trial court's treatment of the statute. If the Legislature so intended, it would have said so in such simple terms. It would not ordain that private schools shall be subject to nondiscriminatory zoning in order to say they shall not be subject to any zoning at all.

If public schools are beyond the local zoning power, then the statute in question is meaningless and a nullity. We cannot, however, say the Legislature erred in assuming the zoning power does apply. No statute expressly exempts public schools from zoning and no judicial decision has found the exemption. Indeed, we heretofore assumed that public schools are subject to zoning. See Yanow v. Seven Oaks Park, Inc., 11 N.J. 341, 94 A.2d 482, 36 A.L.R.2d 369 (1953); Andrews v. Ocean Twp. Board of Adjustment, 30 N.J. 245, 152 A.2d 580 (1959); St. Cassian's Catholic Church v. Allen, 40 N.J. 46, 190 A.2d 667 (1963); but cf. Trinity, &c., Church v. Morris Plains Bd. of Adjustment, 72 N.J. Super. 425, 431-432, 179 A.2d 45 (App.Div.1962).

Plaintiff cites Bloomfield v. New Jersey Highway Authority, 18 N.J. 237, 244, 113 A.2d 658 (1955); Aviation Services, Inc. v. Morristown, 20 N.J. 275, 119 A.2d 761 (1956); and Washington Twp. v. Ridgewood, 26 N.J. 578, 141 A.2d 308 (1958), in which it was held that the particular public projects involved were not subject to the zoning ordinance of the municipality in which they were situate. In each of those cases there was the likelihood of a conflict in interest which could defeat or hamper the project if the zoning power were applicable. In Bloomfield the project was restaurant and service station facilities on a toll highway. In Aviation Services the project was a municipal airport authorized by statute to be developed within the borders of another municipality. And in Washington Township the statute authorized a municipality to condemn lands in another municipality in connection with its water needs. We concluded in each case that the Legislature intended the municipality in which the improvement was to be located should not be able to block it by zoning.

[1] Here the prospect of discord is quite remote, for the school districts, whether regional or not, share a common interest with the municipalities themselves. Ordinarily there is no reason for a school board and the local governing body to quarrel about zoning matters. Hence, although unquestionably the school board as the State's agent to discharge the State's constitutional duty to provide for a system of free public schools, Art. VIII, § IV, par. 1, is a distinct entity essentially independent of the local governing body, Gualano v. Board of School Estimate, 39 N.J. 300, 303, 188 A.2d 569 (1963); Botkin v. Westwood, 52 N.J.Super. 416, 425 et seq., 145 A.2d 618 (App.Div.), appeal dismissed, 28 N.J. 218, 146 A.2d 121 (1958), there is a community of interest which augurs for good relations between them. Of course the Legislature could place the public school beyond the zoning power as it is in some jurisdictions, see Town of Atherton v. Superior Court, 159 Cal.App.2d 417, 324 P.2d 328 (D.Ct.App.1958); Congregation Temple Israel v. City of Creve Coeur, 320 S.W.2d 451, 454 (Mo.Sup.Ct.1959), but we see no constitutional command that it do so.

[2] Plaintiff cites N.J.S.A. 18:11-11 which provides that the plans and specifications for a school building are not subject to municipal approval and a building permit shall not be required. Kaveny v. Montclair, 71 N.J.Super. 244, 176 A.2d 802 (App. Div.), certif. denied, 36 N.J. 597, 178 A.2d 388 (1962). That statute must be considered with R.S. 18:11-8, N.J.S.A. which requires approval of such plans and specifications by the State Board of Education. Indeed N.J.S.A. 18:11-11 comes from L. 1928, c. 186, where it appeared as a proviso to what is now R.S. 18:11-8, N.J.S.A. The reason for the 1928 statute is given in its sponsoring statement:

> "All work in connection with the erection or alteration of school buildings is under the supervision of the State Board of Education. The Attorney General has ruled that a local building permit is not necessary in connection with school work. Some still feel that a local permit is necessary. The purpose of this act is to definitely settle the question."

In short, the subject having been committed to a state agency, the municipal role was eliminated to avoid a division of responsibility.

Thus with respect to the sufficiency of the school plant itself the Legislature has both vested responsibility in a state agency and expressly barred the municipality. No such legislation exists as to zoning. In this connection we are referred to N.J.S.A. 18:2-4, subd. h under which the State Board of Education "may" withhold approval of a "secondary school" if its "location" shall not warrant its establishment or continuance. That statute quite plainly does not charge the State Board with responsibility for the total zoning interests of the community but rather enables the State Board permissively to disapprove a specific site because it is unsuitable in the limited context of the need for and utility of a secondary school.

And so also N.J.S.A. 40:55-1.13 does not bespeak a purpose to place schools beyond the zoning power. That statute, which applies only if a planning board has adopted a master plan or a portion of a master plan, provides that the governing body or other public agency "before taking action necessitating the expenditure of any public funds, incidental to the location, character or extent" of a project, shall refer the proposal to the planning board for review and recommendation. A "school board" is specifically listed among the agencies subject to this requirement. The statute provides that the recommendation of the planning board may be overridden, and for present purposes we may accept the Attorney General's opinion that a school board may override the recommendation without the concurrence of the municipal governing body. Op.A.G.1954, No. 8. The statute, however, does not relate to compliance with zoning restrictions. Rather it deals with the suitability of a specific site or location for a public improvement, see Saddle River Country Day School v. Saddle River, 51 N.J. Super. 589, 602, 144 A.2d 425 (App.Div.1958), affirmed o. b. 29 N.J. 468, 150 A.2d 34 (1959), and hence, although a school board has the final say with respect to the precise location, it does not follow that it may ignore the zoning ordinance.

[3] In summary, then, there is no statute under which zoning responsibility with respect to public schools has been vested in another agency or expressly denied to the municipality. We see no reason, therefore, to dispute the assumption in N.J.S.A. 40:55-33.1 that public schools are subject to local zoning.

We of course do not mean that the Legislature intended that the governing body may block public education by barring schools throughout the municipality or by relegating schools to areas that are obviously unsuitable. Rather the Legislature found it appropriate to permit the municipality to consider the total needs of the community in all of its zoning aspects to the end that schools will be in appropriate districts and upon plots of ample size and with suitable buffers to contain within the perimeter of the property those influences which could be unduly hurtful to others.

This discourse upon the amenability of public schools to zoning should not obscure the question before us. That question is whether the Legislature intended private schools to be beyond zoning control. While undoubtedly the public interest could be left with the school board, it would be poor policy to permit private schools to locate anywhere at all and to be unrestrained as to size of plot, sideyards, etc. The private organization is not accountable to the electorate directly or indirectly, and even if it wanted to keep in mind the total zoning interests of the community, still it could not draw up a power to condemn or to tax in its quest for the optimum location. We should hesitate to impute so questionable a purpose to the Legislature.

Plaintiff alternatively suggests the statute be read to permit zoning regulation as to lot size, setback, buffers, etc., but not as to land use. Thus a private school could locate its facilities in any district but would have to obey local regulations reasonably designed to insulate the neighborhood from the noise and activity which schools, especially secondary schools with their athletic facilities, can readily generate. This approach would be more palatable as a policy matter than the approach we rejected above, but the answer is that the Legislature has not adopted it.

The statute is plain enough if it is read without stress and strain. There is disagreement upon whether public schools may constitutionally be treated differently in zoning matters from private schools furnishing equivalent education. See Tustin Heights Ass'n v. Board of Supervisors, 170 Cal.App. 2d 619, 339 P.2d 914, 922-23 (D.Ct.App.1959); St. John's Roman Catholic Church v. Darien, 149 Conn. 712, 184 A.2d 42 (Sup.Ct.Err.1962); City of Miami Beach v. State, 128 Fla. 750, 175 So. 537 (Sup.Ct.1937); Catholic Bishop of Chicago v. Kingery, 371 Ill. 257, 20 N.E.2d 583 (Sup.Ct.1939); Diocese of Rochester v. Planning Board, 1 N.Y.2d 508, 154 N.Y.S.2d 849, 136 N.E.2d 827, 834 (Ct.App.1956); State v. Sinar, 267 Wis. 91, 65 N.W.2d 43 (Sup.Ct.1954). We adverted to the question without deciding it in Andrews, supra (30 N.J., at p. 252, 152 A.2d 580). The statute before us resolved that issue by requiring equality of treatment. We so read the statute in St. Cassian's Catholic Church, supra (40 N.J. 46, 190 A.2d 667). That case involved a variance for a parochial school granted before the statute was enacted, and the question was whether one of the conditions of the variance discriminated against the school in violation of the statute. We did not say the statute placed private schools beyond zoning control and hence the variance was no longer needed. Rather we accepted the continued vitality of the variance, and upheld the condition upon a finding that other public schools met the requirements of that condition and hence there was no discrimination in fact.

Here the ordinance applies equally to public and private schools. The borough is small, with an area of but 1.76 square miles and 3,988 residents as of the 1960 census. It is almost wholly residential. About half its area is in the R-1 district. The R-1 district has the highest requirements of the four residential districts, is countrified in atmosphere and facilities, and the homes are in the $60,000 class on lots of one-acre minimum. A public elementary school situate in the R-3 district is centrally located and there was testimony that it will meet the total need even when the municipality is fully developed. As to secondary education, the borough has provided for instruction by contract with the Village of Ridgewood at its high school. There was testimony that the borough would never need a secondary school of its own. Also in the R-3 district is St. Luke's Regional Parochial School, which is both an elementary and a secondary school, with a student population of 1,512, of whom 164 reside in the borough. In this setting the municipality barred both public and private schools from the R-1 district.

[4, 5] The ordinance is nondiscriminatory as between public and private schools. If there is a grievance, it is of another kind. The municipality has zoned in terms of its own local need, whereas plaintiff wishes to meet

a regional need through a facility of relatively little utility to the residents of the borough. Not every municipality will welcome a tax-exempt enterprise whose contribution is essentially extraterritorial. Hence motivations are suspect when at a late hour an ordinance is adopted to bar the improvement on a site already in hand. Perhaps the problem should be given to a state agency removed from the pull of local interests. Indeed, we directed reargument to explore the question whether the State Board of Education has jurisdiction of it. We are satisfied it does not and hence the case must be adjudged under a statutory scheme which leaves the zoning decision in municipal hands.

The substantial issue upon which the trial court made no finding is whether it is arbitrary to bar the use of plaintiff's property for a secondary school. The issue is constitutional insofar as it is claimed that the ban offends due process of law. The issue is also statutory insofar as it involves the question whether the municipality exceeded the statutory authority or departed from state policy. In this connection it is appropriate to comment upon so much of the testimony and argument as stresses the tax implications of the proposed use.

We have held that a municipality may consider revenues in its plan for a well balanced community. Gruber v. Raritan Twp., 39 N.J. 1, 9-11, 186 A.2d 489 (1962). Thus it may provide for industrial or commercial uses which are less demanding in public services than residential uses. It is, however, another matter to bar tax-exempt facilities on the ground that they are financially burdensome by reason of that exemption. The exemption is granted by the State because of the contribution of the exempt facility to the public good. It may be that an exemption will mean a net burden for the taxpayers of a particular municipality, but the municipality must nonetheless abide by state policy. Indeed, our Constitution of 1947 expressly preserved the then existing exemptions of real and personal property used exclusively for religious, educational, charitable or cemetery purposes and owned by a non-profit corporation or association. Art. VIII, § I, par. 2. And N.J.S.A. 40:55-33.1, while not bearing the interpretation given it in the trial court, does serve to evidence the Legislature's concern for nonprofit private schools which furnish elementary and high school education.

[6] No municipality may quarrel with this policy. Hence it may not zone against a private school, place it in one district rather than another, or refuse it a variance on the ground that it is exempt from taxation. See Diocese of Rochester v. Planning Board, supra (1 N.Y.2d 508, 154 N.Y.S.2d 849, 136 N.E.2d, at p. 836).

[7, 8] The matter is remanded for trial of the issue of arbitrariness in the light of the views we have expressed. We should add that if it is held to be unreasonable to bar the proposed use upon a finding that the zoning objective may be readily achieved by appropriate regulation as to plot size,

setback, buffers, etc., the municipality should be given an opportunity to legislate to that end.

[9-11] As to the other issues presented to us, we think it enough to state our conclusions. We see no merit in plaintiff's attack upon the procedure used in adopting the amendatory ordinance nor in the charge that a councilman had a disqualifying interest. Nor do we find substance in defendant's sundry constitutional attacks upon N.J.S.A. 40:55-33.1, and we add that as to the charge that the statute invidiously discriminates between profit and nonprofit private schools, the statute would not fall in its entirety if the challenge were good for the reason that the offending words would be severable, and hence the issue is not involved in this case.

[12] If it wishes plaintiff may seek a variance at this juncture, and if the variance should be denied, litigate the validity of that action along with the attack upon the ordinance itself.

The judgment is reversed and the matter remanded for further proceedings not inconsistent herewith.

For reversal: Chief Justice WEINTRAUB and Justices JACOBS, PROCTOR, HALL, SCHETTINO and HANEMAN—6.

For affirmance: Justice FRANCIS—1.

FRANCIS, J. (dissenting).

The courts of New Jersey have never been called upon to decide the specific question whether a municipality has authority to control the location of a public school by means of a zoning ordinance. In my judgment no such authority exists and therefore the provision of the Ho-Ho-Kus ordinance barring such schools from the R-1 residence zone is *ultra vires* and invalid. Thus, it cannot operate as a preventative measure against the Ho-Ho-Kus Board of Education. Consequently, the provision, if effective at all, undertakes to exclude only private schools from the zone. Such exclusion of private nonprofit high schools constitutes discrimination contrary to the intent and spirit of N.J.S.A. 40:55-33.1, L.1961, c. 138, and is therefore void.

But even if the statute were not in existence, so far as the plaintiff is concerned, the result should be the same. If public schools are not or cannot be banned from a residence district under a municipal ordinance, I do not believe a nonprofit private school can be excluded. See Brandeis School v. Village of Lawrence, 18 Misc.2d 550, 184 N.Y.S.2d 687 (Sup.Ct. 1959); In re O'Hara, 389 Pa. 35, 131 A.2d 587 (Sup.Ct.1957); Diocese of Rochester v. Planning Board, 1 N.Y.2d 508, 154 N.Y.S.2d 849, 136 N.E.2d 827 (Ct.App.1956); Catholic Bishop of Chicago v. Kingery, 371 Ill. 257, 20 N.E.2d 583 (Sup.Ct.1939); City of Miami Beach v. State ex rel. Lear, 128 Fla. 750, 175 So. 537 (Sup.Ct.1937). And an attempt to ban the latter would be arbitrary and discriminatory.

Education of our children has a place at the summit of community activities. Article VIII, § IV, paragraph 1 of the New Jersey Constitution imposes a mandate on the Legislature to provide for the maintenance and support of a thorough and efficient system of free public schools. Obedient to the directive, the lawmakers have legislated extensively in the field of both publicly and privately furnished education. A state board of education has been created and invested with broad supervisory power over all aspects of education. N.J.S.A. 18:2-1, 18:2-4. Likewise school districts were established throughout the State (see, e. g., N.J.S.A. 18:5-1.1), and provision made for appointment or election of boards of education to control and regulate the manner and means of furnishing of education therein subject to the over-all supervisory authority of the state board. R.S. 18:6-1 et seq., 18:7-1 et seq., N.J.S.A.

A local board of education is an independent, autonomous corporate instrumentality of government within its territorial limits. As such, within its sphere of operation, it is not subject to the will or direction of the governing body of the municipality in which it functions, except to the extent that interdependence or connection has been imposed by the Legislature, either expressly or by inescapable implication. Gualano v. Bd. of Estimate of Elizabeth School Dist., 39 N.J. 300, 303, 188 A.2d 569 (1963).

Local boards of education have power to do all things necessary for the lawful and proper conduct, equipment and maintenance of the public schools of the district. See, e. g., R.S. 18:6-17, N.J.S.A. And they are empowered to acquire land by purchase or condemnation for the purpose of building schools. N.J.S.A. 18:6-24, 18:7-74, 18:7-110. The power to purchase or condemn is nowhere made subject to zoning ordinances, nor can there be found any restriction on the location of property within the municipal boundaries which may be acquired for the purpose. In fact, in some situations the board may purchase or condemn up to 25 acres for such purpose "in any municipality or municipalities adjoining the [school] district." N.J.S.A. 18:7-74. Absent some limitation, it must follow that land in any residential area of the particular municipality is subject to condemnation. In State v. Ferriss, 304 S.W.2d 896 (Mo.Sup.Ct.1957), the school district sought to condemn a 32.26-acre tract in the City of Ladue as the site for a new school. The land was in a district zoned exclusively for residence. The school district had been given power by the legislature to condemn property for schools in much the same language as the New Jersey statute. The Supreme Court of Missouri held the zoning ordinance inapplicable. It said that clearly the school district was vested by express grant from the legislature with the absolute power to select, locate and procure the site in question by condemnation. And the court declared the authority of a municipality to abrogate state law is never implied or inferred. "It is only derived from express grant, never from a general grant of power. A state policy may not be ignored by a municipality unless it is specifically empowered so to do in terms clear and explicit." Since no such specific grant of power was shown, the city could not by its "zoning regulation prevent the location of a school within its borders and thereby prohibit

the performance by the school district of the duty imposed upon it by law."
304 S.W.2d, at p. 902.

Here it may be noted that in our State (subject to R.S. 18:14-5, N.J.S.A.,
not here pertinent), school districts are under a mandate also to provide
suitable public school facilities and buildings. R.S. 18:11-1, N.J. S.A. They
are subject to sanctions if they fail to do so. N.J.S.A. 18:11-2; and, see
Durgin v. Brown, 37 N.J. 189, 180 A.2d 136 (1962); Board of Educ. v.
Atwood, 73 N.J.L. 315, 62 A. 1130 (Sup.Ct.1906), affirmed 74 N.J.L. 638,
65 A. 999 (E. & A. 1907).

Further legislative indications that boards of education are not bound
by zoning ordinances are to be found. Such boards are not required to
obtain municipal approval of their plans and specifications for construction
of a school; nor do they have to seek a building permit from municipal
authorities. N.J.S.A. 18:11-11; Kaveny v. Board of Comm'rs., 69 N.J.Super.
94, 173 A.2d 536 (App.Div.1961), certif. denied 36 N.J. 597, 178 A.2d 388
(1962). Standard plans and specifications for school buildings are drawn
at the state level. R.S. 18:11-6, N.J.S.A. Plans and specifications for a
new public school must be approved by the state board of education and,
once approved, cannot be changed without state board permission. N.J.S.A.
18:11-8. Local plumbing codes do not apply to public schools. Kaveny
v. Board of Comm'rs., supra. Moreover, the State Commissioner of Education is authorized to order the making of physical changes in school buildings at any time. R.S. 18:11-12, N.J.S.A. The statute contains no language
suggesting that limitations of a zoning ordinance could stand in the way
of such changes. And, finally, the board of education may overrule any
action of a municipal planning board with respect to the location of a
public school. N.J.S.A. 40:55-1.13; and cf. Opinion, Attorney General, 1954,
No. 8. Such action at best would be advisory and not binding on the
board. Town of Atherton v. Superior Court, 115 Cal.App.2d 417, 324 P.2d
328 (D.Ct.App.1958).

In passing it may be noted as of particular pertinence here (since we are
concerned with the proposed establishment of a high school) that as far
back as 1911 the Legislature gave the State Board of Education authority
to withhold approval of the location of any "secondary school." L.1911, c.
231. Such a school is an intermediate one between the elementary grades
and the college or university. Webster's New International Dictionary (2d
ed. 1949), p. 2260; N.Y. Education Law, § 2. That statute has been continued in force unaffected throughout the years of the developing zoning
concept and was retained in the most recent revision. L.1954, c. 81; N.J.
S.A. 18:2-4(h). Thus, at least the state board would seem to have the
power to veto a site selected by the local board of education for a secondary school. Suppose the vetoed site were the only one available in the
only zone where schools were permitted under a municipal ordinance, and
a school was needed in the community. Is it conceivable that a prohibition
against schools even in the most highly restricted residential zone could

stand in the way of a school there? Incidentally, the veto power appears to be a broad one and undoubtedly should be considered adequate to permit the state board to deal reasonably with matters such as area of plot in relation to size of school, play yards, sidelines and front and rear setback lines.

The foregoing demonstrates convincingly that the Legislature has not empowered a municipality to bar a public high school from its most highly restricted residential zone. Or, to put it another way, the lawmakers have not withdrawn or withheld from local boards of education the authority to exercise their own independent judgment as to where their schools shall be located. Certainly the authority has not been withheld or withdrawn expressly so as to permit local zoning power to interfere. I believe Judge Conford was on sound ground when he said in Trinity Evangelical Lutheran Church v. Board of Adjustment, 72 N.J. Super. 425, 431, 179 A.2d 45, 49 (App.Div.1962):

> "Certainly a board of education could not have been denied leave to establish a public school at this location on either the theory that it was detrimental to the public health, safety and general welfare, or not reasonably necessary for the convenience of the community."

(The extent to which the local board of education may be subordinate to the state board as to the location of secondary schools, by virtue of N.J.S.A. 18:2-4(h), or as to the location of elementary schools under the broad statutory grants of power to the state board, need not be decided.) New Jersey is therefore in tune with the weight of authority throughout the country. See 1 Rathkopf, Law of Zoning and Planning (3d ed. 1964), p. 18-1 et seq.; Basset, Zoning, pp. 31, 196 (1940); 2 Metzenbaum, Law of Zoning (2d ed. 1955), p. 1455; 2 Yokley, Zoning Law and Practice (2d ed. 1953), § 247, p. 141; Note, "The Immunity of Schools from Zoning," 14 Syracuse L.Rev. 644 (1963).

The majority opinion says in effect that chapter 138 of the Laws of 1961 is inconsistent with the idea that the authority of local boards of education to locate their schools is paramount to the zoning power of the municipality. I agree that the statute may be somewhat ambiguous. Its meaning is not uncertain, however. One light which floods all of its recesses and illuminates the legislative intention beyond doubt is that the lawmakers wanted no discrimination between public and nonprofit private schools in the matter of their location in a municipality.

Moreover, I cannot agree that the statute obviously was drawn on the thesis that a municipality may zone as to public schools. Its text seems just as consistent with the thesis that since public schools are not subject to zoning restrictions, a municipality should not discriminate against nonprofit private schools by means of planning or zoning restrictions affecting them alone. Note, also, that the statute invalidates discriminatory ordinances "heretofore" adopted, as well as forbidding all new ones of like tenor.   Undoubtedly the Legislature was aware that some municipalities, unsure of their zoning power, *vis-à-vis* the school board in the absence of definitive judicial decision, had assumed to zone with respect to schools. And so it employed the terse language of the act to express its antidiscrimination idea.   That it did not use crystal clear expression ought not to stand in the way of the accomplishment of its intention.   Public policy favors nonprofit private schools.   That is the reason for their tax-exempt status.   With that policy in mind, doubts engendered by words or contextual arrangement ought to be resolved in favor of an interpretation preventing discrimination against such schools.

Since the Ho-Ho-Kus ordinance as a matter of law cannot apply to public schools, its effect is to prohibit nonprofit private schools in the R-1 residence district.   Discrimination is thus apparent and must be considered as within the condemnation of L.1961, c. 138.   More than this, the exclusion of schools from the district appears to have been aimed at plaintiff's high school.   The borough's brief says "there never will be sufficient children of high school age within the Borough so as to permit it to erect its own high school."   The amendment to the ordinance drawn with that knowledge in mind, and adopted by the governing body when plaintiff was actively seeking to build its school, rendered lip service to equality of treatment by ostensibly barring public as well as private schools from the zone.   But, in fact, it rendered actual service to the cause of discrimination.

But, even if the 1961 anti-discrimination act did not exist, the contested part of the ordinance would have to be invalidated as to plaintiff.   Accepting the premise which I consider unavoidable, that location of public schools is not subject to municipal zoning, the attempt to prohibit nonprofit private schools in the R-1 zone, where public schools may go in the discretion of the board of education, is discriminatory and arbitrary.   In order to subject private property to zoning, the restriction imposed must bear some substantial relation to the health, safety, morals or general welfare of the community.   In this connection it seems fair to say with respect to zoning that public schools and nonprofit private schools involve substantially the same considerations.   Private schools operated for profit may present a different question from a zoning standpoint.   Perhaps such institutions may be considered as establishing a business use in a residence zone.   That problem is not before us.   On the record of the present case, however, the various reasons advanced by the borough for excluding schools from the area would apply equally to a public high school.   Generally, speaking, they are: increased traffic, need for widening roads in the school area, interference with the tranquility of the residence area, alleged depreciation of other property in the zone, probable need for increased fire and police protection, loss of tax revenue, and other claims of possible increased municipal burden.   In view of the intense public interest in education, whether the schools furnishing it are publicly operated or privately run under a curriculum approved by state authority, the objections urged against the high school do not bear a sufficiently important relation to the public health, safety or welfare to justify the limitation sought to be imposed on the desired use of plaintiff's property.

In Diocese of Rochester v. Planning Board, supra, a zoning ordinance of the Town of Brighton barred a nonprofit private school from the Class A residential zone unless a permit was granted by the planning board. The Diocese sought and was denied permission to build a parochial school in the district. The Court of Appeals of New York reversed the denial, saying among other things:

> "The text writers agree that churches and schools should be allowed in Class A residential areas which are usually the quietest and least congested areas of a town. ° ° ° It is well established in this country that a zoning ordinance may not *wholly exclude* a church or synogogue from any residential district. Such a provision is stricken on the ground that it bears no substantial relation to the public health, safety, morals, peace or general welfare of the community. ° ° ° An ordinance will also be stricken if it attempts to exclude private or parochial schools from any residential area where public schools are permitted. ° ° °" 154 N.Y.S.2d at p. 858, 136 N.E.2d at p. 834.

After referring to a number of cases, the court held that objections to establishment of the school based upon alleged adverse effect on property values, decreased enjoyment of neighboring property, traffic hazards and loss of potential tax revenue as a matter of law were not sufficient to warrant the action of the planning board. Among other things, the opinion indicated also that it is not a proper function of government to interfere in the name of the public to exclude schools from residential districts for the purpose of securing to adjacent landowners the benefits of exclusive residential restrictions. With respect to loss of tax revenue, it pointed out that the Constitution had exempted such institutions as churches and nonprofit schools from taxation. And it said:

> "Thus the paramount authority of this State has declared a policy that churches and schools are more important than local taxes, and that it is in furtherance of the general welfare to exclude such institutions from taxation. This being the case, it cannot be seriously argued that the decision of respondents denying this permit because of a loss of tax revenue is in furtherance of the general welfare.
>
> ° ° ° °
>
> Thus church and school and accessory uses are, in themselves, clearly in furtherance of the public morals and general welfare. The church is the teacher and guardian of morals, ° ° ° and 'an educational institution, whose curriculum complies with the state law, is considered an aid to the general welfare.' ° ° ° These proposed structures will not interfere with the public health, nor can they be said to be a danger to the public peace or safety; ° ° °" Id., 154 N.Y.S.2d, at p. 861, 136 N.E.2d at pp. 836-837.

In conclusion, the action of the planning board was held to "bear no substantial relation to the promotion of the public health, safety, morals or general welfare of the community." Therefore, it was deemed arbitrary and unreasonable and was ordered annulled.

In Brandeis School v. Village of Lawrence, supra, the zoning ordinance was amended to exclude public and private schools from certain residential districts of the village. Plaintiff sought to establish its school in one of the residence districts in three buildings, two already in existence and a third to be constructed. It was to be a nonprofit school of elementary grades, with a secular curriculum approved by the state education authorities, and a religious curriculum as well. The students were to be drawn from five surrounding towns.

The proof showed, among other things, that the last public school built in the village was a high school in the same district as plaintiff's property. Plaintiff contended that when the high school was completed, the public school needs of the village were met and then the zoning ordinance was amended to keep out all private schools. It urged from the sequence of events that although ostensibly the amended ordinance treated public schools and private schools alike by banning both from the district, in reality it discriminated between public and private schools by excluding the latter when it was no longer necessary to make provision for public schools. (Mention is made of this factual situation because it is analogous to the course taken by Ho-Ho-Kus in adopting the amendment in dispute here.)

The trial court declared the amendment invalid saying that it bore no such substantial relation to the public welfare in the zoning sense as would justify its adoption. Possible disadvantages which might be visited on the neighborhood were treated as outweighed by the social value of the institution.

In addition, reference was made to the holding of the Court of Appeals in the Diocese of Rochester case, cited above, that an ordinance will be stricken if it attempts to exclude parochial schools from any residential area where public schools are permitted. And the court said:

> "While it may well be, as defendant's counsel has painstakingly shown, that public and private schools have many characteristics which distinguish them from one another organizationally, these differences are not of sufficient importance, in the light of our highest court's expressed views, to justify different treatment in a zoning ordinance. Therefore, the Court finds that the ordinance in question discriminates against private schools." 184 N.Y.S.2d, at p. 697.

In Board of Zoning Appeals v. Schulte, 241 Ind. 339, 172 N.E.2d 39 (Sup.Ct.1961), the zoning ordinance provided a church or school could not be built in the residence zone unless the Board of Zoning Appeals found it to be on a lot so located that the building would "substantially [serve] the public convenience and welfare and [would] not substantially or permanently injure the appropriate use of the neighboring property." The Archdiocese of Indianapolis desired to build a church and parochial school on property owned by it in the residence district of Meridian Hills. The Board of Zoning Appeals denied permission.

The denial was based upon evidence that property in the neighborhood would be depreciated if the church and school were permitted. The Supreme Court of Indiana, in reversing the board, said zoning ordinances must support their validity in the police power of the state, which can only be exercised in the general public interest of safety, health and morals, and that the right to use private property could not be restricted except upon that basis. And "[i]t was never intended that zoning laws should be used for the purpose of creating special privileges or private rights in property which result from creating an exclusive community." 172 N.E.2d, at p. 43.

Apparently the board's refusal gave some recognition also to the contention that the proposed facilities should be located on another street (where the court pointed out, the traffic was heavier) in order not to disturb the neighborhood where the traffic was admittedly lighter. The Supreme Court rejected that reason as invalid saying:

> "Traffic safety, particularly for children, is a matter of general public concern and far outweighs the private interest involved in a quiet neighborhood. It likewise occurs to us that the fact that the 75th Street area might be one in which families with few children or no children are to be found, could not be made the basis for excluding from such area projects of public welfare, such as the church and facilities, in which children are involved. To exclude children's activities by zoning restriction from [such] areas would appear to us to be the converse of what is normally considered general public welfare.
>
>   ❖   ❖   ❖
>
> ❖ ❖ ❖ We do not feel that any zoning board may zone on the basis that children are undesirable in certain areas and that families without children should be protected against such intrusions." 172 N.E.2d, at p. 42.

The court not only adjudged invalid the action of the Board of Zoning Appeals but indicated also that if the ordinance simply banned a church and school from the zone without providing for the review by the Board, denial of a variance would be invalid. 172 N.E.2d, at pp. 44-45.

The majority opinion here remands the case for a determination whether the amendment to the zoning ordinance constitutes arbitrary action. It seems to me that on the extensive factual record made below and the authorities I have cited, as well as Trinity Evangelical Lutheran Church v. Board of Adjustment, supra, the borough's action was clearly arbitrary. Under the circumstances, that decision should be made by us now.

For the reasons stated, I believe the ordinance is invalid as to the plaintiff, and that the judgment of the trial court should be affirmed.

The majority opinion indicates that, upon the remand ordered, plaintiff is not precluded from applying for a variance to the appropriate local authority and, if the result is adverse, join an attack thereon with the present proceeding. Although I have expressed the conviction that as a matter of law plaintiff is entitled to favorable judgment now, manifestly, in view of the majority holding on the issue before us, pursuit of a variance would be feasible. In that case, however, on the record before us, the right to a variance is obvious, subject only to the question whether in the discretion of the board of adjustment the grant should be made subject to any reasonable conditions relating to front and rear setback lines, side yards, play areas, etc. Andrews v. Ocean Twp. Board of Adjustment, 30 N.J. 245, 248, 152 A.2d 580 (1959).

N.J.S.A. 40:55-39(d) authorizes the granting of a variance for "special reasons." On the thesis that such reasons existed, this Court in Andrews approved allowance of a variance for establishment of a parochial school in a residential district zoned against it. We found "no infirmity" in the circumstance that the children to attend the school would be drawn from neighboring communities as well as from Ocean Township. Cf. Trinity Evangelical Lutheran Church v. Board of Adjustment, supra; Brandeis School v. Village of Lawrence, supra. We said also that the school not only involved no "detriment to the public good," but in fact served the public welfare. 30 N.J., at pp. 249, 251, 152 A.2d, at p. 582.

ROMAN CATHOLIC DIOCESE OF NEWARK

v.

HO-HO-KUS

47 N.J. 211, 220 A.2d 97 (1966).

Supreme Court of New Jersey.

Argued Feb. 7, 1966.

Decided May 23, 1966.

Action attacking validity of zoning ordinance amendment prohibiting schools in residence area. The Superior Court, Law Division, held statute invalid and defendants appealed. The case was certified before argument in the Appellate Division. The Supreme Court, 42 N.J. 556, 202 A.2d 161, reversed and remanded. The trial court found amendment invalid and appeal was taken and Supreme Court certified matter before argument in the Appellate Division. The Supreme Court held that religious corporation failed to sustain its burden of showing that municipality was arbitrary in barring use of society's property in residential zone for secondary school.

Judgment reversed and judgment entered in favor of defendants.

Francis, J., dissented.

Samuel M. Lyon, Jr., Ridgewood, for appellant Borough of Ho-Ho-Kus, Merritt Lane, Jr., Newark, for defendants-intervenors-appellants (Elliot A. Lawrence, Newark, on the brief, McCarter & English, Newark, attorneys for defendants-intervenors-appellants).

Thomas H. Gassert, Newark, for respondents (Frederick J. Gassert, Newark, of counsel, Joseph A. Clarken, Jr., Newark, on the brief, Gassert & Murphy, Newark, attorneys).

The opinion of the court was delivered.

PER CURIAM.

Plaintiff seeks to erect a regional high school on lands it acquired for that purpose. The lands are in the highest residential district called R-1. At the time of purchase the local zoning ordinance permitted the proposed use. The municipality thereafter amended the ordinance to bar all schools, public or private, from the R-1 district, permitting them however in its other three residential districts. This suit followed.

The trial court held the municipality lacked power to bar the proposed school, finding that L.1961, c. 138 (N.J.S.A. 40:55-33.1)[1] had that effect. So holding, the trial court did not reach the charge that the ordinance was otherwise arbitrary and a denial of due process. We however concluded the statute only forbade discrimination between public and private schools and that, subject to that restraint, municipalities could deal with schools under the zoning power. Roman Catholic Diocese of Newark v. Borough of Ho-Ho-Kus, 42 N.J. 556, 202 A.2d 161 (1964).

Accordingly we reversed the judgment. The matter was remanded for consideration of the issue of arbitrariness. In that connection we made particular reference to the municipality's argument before us that it could take into account the tax exemption such schools have. We said (42 N.J., at p. 565, 202 A.2d at p. 166):

> "The substantial issue upon which the trial court made no finding is whether it is arbitrary to bar the use of plaintiff's property for a secondary school. The issue is constitutional insofar as it is claimed that the ban offends due process of law. The issue is also statutory insofar as it involves the question whether the municipality exceeded the statutory authority or departed from state policy. In this connection it is appropriate to comment upon so much of the testimony and argument as stresses the tax implications of the proposed use.
>
> We have held that a municipality may consider revenues in its plan for a well balanced community. Gruber v. Mayor and Township Committee of

---

1. "No planning or zoning ordinance heretofore or hereafter enacted by any municipality governing the use of land by, or for, schools, shall, by any of its terms or provisions or by any rule or regulation adopted in accordance therewith, discriminate between public and private day schools, not operated for profit, of elementay or high school grade."

> Raritan Twp., 39 N.J. 1, 9-11, 186 A.2d 489 (1962). Thus it may provide for industrial or commercial uses which are less demanding in public services than residential uses. It is, however, another matter to bar tax-exempt facilities on the ground that they are financially burdensome by reason of that exemption. The exemption is granted by the State because of the contribution of the exempt facility to the public good. It may be that an exemption will mean a net burden for the taxpayers of a particular municipality, but the municipality, must nonetheless abide by state policy. Indeed, our Constitution of 1947 expressly preserved the then existing exemptions of real and personal property used exclusively for religious, educational, charitable or cemetery purposes and owned by a nonprofit corporation or association. Art. VIII, § I, par. 2. And N.J.S.A. 40:55-33.1, while not bearing the interpretation given it in the trial court, does serve to evidence the Legislature's concern for nonprofit private schools which furnish elementary and high school education.
>
> No municipality may quarrel with this policy. Hence it may not zone against a private school, place it in one district rather than another, or refuse it a variance on the ground that it is exempt from taxation."

After remand, the parties took additional testimony upon the question whether the amendment was prompted by the tax exemption. The trial court found it was not. The trial court concluded, however, that the amendment was arbitrary and hence invalid. Defendants again appealed, and we certified the matter before argument in the Appellate Division.

[1] We are satisfied plaintiff did not sustain its burden and hence that the judgment must be reversed.

In finding the ordinance invalid, the trial court, it seems to us, combined several approaches, each of which we are unable to accept. In part, the trial court seems to have been persuaded by decisions elsewhere which are not consistent with our basic conclusion that schools may be excluded from the highest residential district. In part, the trial court seems to have made a *de novo* evaluation of the legislative policy decision upon an inquiry into the zoning considerations. Finally the trial court appears to have tested the validity of the ordinance on the basis of the attributes of the particular parcel plaintiff owns. Basic to that test would be the belief that the Constitution or the zoning statute requires a zoning ordinance to authorize for each parcel every possible use to which it could be devoted.

[2-4] As to the last facet, we point out that although a zoning ordinance may be invalid in its impact upon a particular parcel, as where the parcel is zoned into idleness, no one suggests the lands here involved cannot be used for residential purposes. On the contrary, they are ideally suited for that use, and this being so, a constitutional issue does not arise merely because these lands, appropriately zoned for highest residential use, are so extensive or otherwise so featured that a forbidden use might be harbored safely within its perimeter upon some special plan or design. Zoning contemplates the delineation of appropriate districts and the equal treatment of all property within it. The Constitution does not require, nor does the statute require or even permit, a municipality to enact an ordinance which

deals separately with every owner's parcel and undertakes to prescribe the uses to which each parcel may be put by reason of its size or situation and the terms upon which each possible use may be made.

[5] Rather, the statutory vehicle for the accommodation of zoning with individual situations is either a special exception, where the ordinance appropriately so provides, or a variance, as authorized in N.J.S.A. 40:55-39. Here the relevant provision is subsection d which authorizes the board of adjustment to "Recommend in particular cases and for special reasons to the governing body of the municipality the granting of a variance to allow a structure or use in a district restricted against such structure or use," if "such relief can be granted without substantial detriment to the public good and will not substantially impair the intent and purpose of the zone plan and zoning ordinance." Indeed we said in our first opinion that plaintiff might wish to "seek a variance at this juncture, and if the variance should be denied, litigate the validity of that action along with the attack upon the ordinance itself." (42 N.J., at p. 567, 202 A.2d, at p. 166.)

[6-13] Plaintiff remains free to apply for a variance. In this connection some observations seem appropriate without in any way intimating an opinion as to the outcome of an application. The educational mission of a regional high school is clearly a "special reason" within the meaning of the statute just cited. Andrews v. Ocean Twp. Board of Adjustment, 30 N.J. 245, 152 A.2d 580 (1959). Hence the question will be whether a sound exercise of discretion requires that the school be permitted. In dealing with that question, the local authorities should consider the State policy favoring such exempt functions and the fact that regional needs must be met somewhere. Unfortunately under present law the tax burden falls upon the single municipality rather than the whole area which is benefited. Yet a variance may not be refused on that account. 42 N.J., at p. 566, 202 A.2d 161. Consideration should also be given to the limited number of sites available to a charity for the reason that it cannot invoke the power of eminent domain. It would not be amiss to weigh also the circumstance that here the proposed use was authorized by the ordinance at the time plaintiff purchased the property. Finally, and of special importance in deciding whether the property can be put to the proposed use without substantial detriment to the public good and without substantially impairing the intent and purpose of the zone plan and the zoning ordinance, is the question whether the parcel is of such size and situation that, with suitable conditions, the proposed use will not subject the area to the conditions and influences which were the basis of the original zoning decision to exclude schools from this district. The burden of supplying an adequate buffer would be upon plaintiff, and indeed it would be incumbent on plaintiff to propose specific measures and to demonstrate their sufficiency to that end.

We suggested in our first opinion that the problem might well be committed to a State agency. 42 N.J., at p. 565, 202 A.2d 161. Meanwhile the reconciliation between the local interests and the needs of private educational projects remains in local hands, there to be exercised, as the Legislature must have intended, with due concern for values which transcend municipal lines.

The judgment in favor of plaintiff is reversed and judgment entered in favor of defendants. No costs.

HALL and SCHETTINO, JJ., concur in result.

For reversal: Chief Justice WEINTRAUB and Justices JACOBS, PROCTOR, HALL, SCHETTINO and HANEMAN—6.

For affirmance: Justice FRANCIS—1.

HALL, J. (concurring).

This litigation actually involves the perplexing problem of the permissible extent of local land use control of regional, tax-exempt institutions—be they private schools of religious or secular sponsorship educating children from more than one municipality, or other beneficial non-governmental educational, religious, charitable, hospital and like institutions the services of which transcend local boundaries.

In treating this problem, the primary frame of reference is that under present law planning and zoning regulation in New Jersey must be confined within municipal lines and each municipality may legislate with substantially no regard for the over-all area of which it is a part. The second frame of reference, well illustrated in this case, is that such facilities necessarily increase in size and number with the density of population and require sizeable tracts of land. In such areas lands at all adequate for facilities of this kind are scarce and becoming more so. They generally do not belong in commercial or industrial areas and suitable sites are likely to be found only in sections already zoned for residential use. Moreover, the availability of appropriate land is even more restricted by the absence of the power of eminent domain. On the other hand, there can be no doubt that such institutions have a physical impact on a residential neighborhood which can be unduly dissonant unless buffers and other conditions are imposed. It is equally true that in almost every case they cost the municipal taxpayer some money because they usually create a need for additional governmental installations and services without any return in the form of taxes. Furthermore, local residents frequently share in the benefits of the institutions only to a limited extent and sometimes not at all.

I fear that so far we have come up with little of a constructive nature by way of an answer to this basic question and that, as far as the parties in interest in this case are concerned, after five years of litigation we have succeeded only in marching them up hills and down again, with more of the same in prospect. This unfortunate result may be due in part to legal and practical limitations on the judicial function in problems of this kind, the work-a-day solutions of which are better handled legislatively and administratively. Courts in deciding the constitutional and statutory issues presented in this class of cases cannot go much beyond establishing outer boundaries of the zoning power and setting forth guide lines to aid proper local implementation of the power so delineated. I suggest, however, that we have not gone as far as we can and should in these respects in this case.

Perhaps what I have to say here might well have been stated to some extent in connection with the opinion on the first appeal. 42 N.J. 556, 202 A.2d 161 (1964). However, the only issue then decided, by reason of the narrow basis on which the trial court disposed of this case, was that public schools, and thus private schools, are in this State within the zoning power, or at least certain aspects of it, as a matter of legislative contemplation. The majority felt that the unreached matter of the validity, in the Ho-Ho-Kus setting, of the ordinance amendment prohibiting all schools and other institutional uses except churches and public parks and playgrounds in the highest residential zone should first be determined by the trial court. I did not believe that we were intending to deal definitively with the *extent or implementation* of the power. Two references to that phase of the matter indicated to me that we were suggesting the trial court ought to consider it. The first was in this comment:

> "We of course do not mean that the Legislature intended that the governing body may block public education by barring schools throughout the municipality or by relegating schools to areas that are obviously unsuitable. Rather the Legislature found it appropriate to permit the municipality to consider the total needs of the community in all of its zoning aspects to the end that schools will be in appropriate districts and upon plots of ample size and with suitable buffers to contain within the perimeter of the property those influences which could be unduly hurtful to others." (42 N.J., at p. 563, 202 A.2d at p. 164).

The second was in the following suggestion:

> "The matter is remanded for trial of the issue of arbitrariness in the light of the views we have expressed. We should add that if it is held to be unreasonable to bar the proposed use upon a finding that the zoning objective may be readily achieved by appropriate regulation as to plot size, setback, buffers, etc., the municipality should be given an opportunity to legislate to that end." (42 N.J., at p. 566, 202 A.2d, at p. 166).

I did not understand, as the present majority states, that we had decided in the prior opinion the unqualified proposition "that schools may be excluded from the highest residential district."

The trial court on the remand simply found, however, the blanket prohibition of all schools in the R-1 zone to be unreasonable and arbitrary *in toto* on bases which I agree are legally untenable. The practical effect of the decision is to say that, at least in Ho-Ho-Kus, private schools must be permitted at any location in the highest residential district without any zoning conditions or safeguards. It seems little different in pragmatic result from that which would ensue if the view that the zoning power does not extend to any schools were to prevail.

While Ho-Ho-Kus could permit private schools and other tax-exempt institutions in residential districts without limitation, as many zoning ordinances do and as Ho-Ho-Kus did before the amendment in controversy, I do not think it can be compelled to. The amendment establishes, at the very least, that the municipality no longer wishes to go that far—a choice which I think a court must recognize as matter of law and fact. Not to do so is to follow the line of cases which say, in analogous situations, that such institutions are immune from any police power regulation in the land use control field on the ground that such regulation bears no substantial relation to the promotion of the public health, safety, morals or general welfare of the community because these uses are themselves in furtherance of the public morals and general welfare. See, e.g., Diocese of Rochester v. Planning Board, 1 N.Y.2d 508, 154 N.Y.S.2d 849, 136 N.E.2d 827 (Ct. App. 1956); Board of Zoning Appeals of Town of Meridian Hills v. Schulte, 241 Ind. 339, 172 N.E.2d 39 (Sup.Ct.1961); In re O'Hara's Appeal, 389 Pa. 35, 131 A.2d 587 (Sup.Ct.1957). Such reasoning confuses issues and disregards the long established basis for general police power regulation of all kinds of activities. Just because an institution is thought to be a good thing for the community is no reason to exempt it completely from restrictions designed to alleviate any baneful physical impact it may nonetheless exert in the interest of another aspect of the public good equally worthy of protection. Cf. Allendale Congregation of Jehovah's Witnesses v. Grosman, 30 N.J. 273, 152 A.2d 569 (1959), appeal dismissed 361 U.S. 536, 80 S.Ct. 587, 4 L.Ed.2d 538 (1960); School District of Philadelphia v. Zoning Board of Adjustment, 417 Pa. 277, 207 A.2d 864 (Sup.Ct.1965). Consequently I am in accord that the judgment of the trial court must be reversed.

What is most satisfactory to me, however, is that the plaintiff is now left with only the possibility of applying for a use variance for "special reasons" under N.J.S.A. 40:55-39d. That possibility may well be illusory indeed, under the current scope of judicial review of municipal administrative action, if the borough board of adjustment denies a recommendation or the governing body disapproves the recommendation in the event one is made. While I think it is safe to say that a court, on an administrative record akin to the present evidence, would sustain the grant of a variance, see Andrews v. Ocean Township Board of Adjustment, 30 N.J. 245, 152 A.2d 580 (1959); Black v. Town of Montclair, 34 N.J. 105, 167 A.2d 388 (1961); Burton v. Town of Montclair, 40 N.J. 1, 190 A.2d 377 (1963), it is not at all certain that the denial of a variance would be upset. See Mayer v. Montclair Board of Adjustment, 32 N.J. 130, 160 A.2d 30 (1960); cf. St. Cassian's Catholic Church v. Allen, 40 N.J. 46, 190 A.2d 667 (1963).

My conviction is that, while a municipality cannot be required to permit tax-exempt institutions at any location without conditions or restrictions, it also may not exclude them from any zone by unqualified prohibition.

Rather such institutions should have the right to locate on any appropriate site where the physical impact of their operations can be alleviated to a reasonable extent by the imposition of suitable conditions and restrictions. I have in mind, for example, a tract so situated and large enough to accommodate the projected functions and activities as well as motor vehicle traffic and parking in order that considerable insulation will thereby be created for the benefit of immediate neighbors, together with such additional buffers and restrictions as are needed. In addition, the exterior structural design should not be completely out of keeping with the district, as would be the case of a ten-story building in a high-class one-family area.

My reasons for this view are essentially found in the thesis I advanced in the dissenting opinion in Vickers v. Township Committee of Gloucester Township, 37 N.J. 232, 252, 181 A.2d 129 (1962), which need not be repeated at length. See also discussions in Haar, "Regionalism and Realism in Land-Use Planning," 105 U.Pa.L.Rev. 515 (1957); Note, "Churches and Zoning," 70 Harvard L.Rev. 1428 (1957); Note, "Zoning Against the Public Welfare: Judicial Limitations on Municipal Parochialism," 71 Yale L.J. 720 (1962). Regional or, for that matter, local institutions generally are too important to be prevented from locating on available, appropriate sites, subject to reasonable qualifications and safeguards, by the imposition of exclusionary or unnecessarily onerous municipal legislation enacted for the sake of preserving the established or proposed character of a community or some portion of it (which seems to be the principal reason for Ho-Ho-Kus' antipathy to plaintiff's school) or to further some other equally indefensible parochial interest. And, of course, if one municipality can so act, all can, with the result that needed and desirable institutions end up with no suitable place to locate. In my view, such action is not legitimately encompassed by the zoning power and the courts have the power to and should say so. The substantive question seems to me to fall clearly within the following language from the foundation case of Village of Euclid, Ohio v. Ambler Realty Co., 272 U.S. 365, 47 S.Ct. 114, 119, 71 L.Ed. 303, 311 (1926): "It is not meant by this, however, to exclude the possibility of cases where the general public interest would so far outweigh the interest of the municipality that the municipality would not be allowed to stand in the way."

Municipalities greatly prize the New Jersey system of substantial home rule. But it should encompass responsibilities as well as rights and they should not be heard to object that they must take some of the bitter with the sweet when the public good thereby advanced necessarily transcends municipal boundaries. That the particular institution which circumstance brings into the community may cost some additional tax moneys does not dictate a different approach. The next town may well have to undertake a similar burden next year. If none can exclude, all will be equally subject to the same possibility of bearing the burden.

Methods to deal with the right I would thus recognize can be provided for, it seems to me, in either of two ways. The first would be by advance provision in the zoning ordinance for such uses as special exceptions pursuant to N.J.S.A. 40:55-39b. The required ordinance standards therefor would have to be broad enough to give the board of adjustment the necessary flexibility in passing upon and imposing particular conditions in each case. If the ordinance does not so provide, as in the case of Ho-Ho-Kus, the "special reasons" variance under N.J.S.A. 40:55-39d ought to be available and adequate, provided the judiciary takes the view, stronger than that presently prevailing, as I think it can and should, that such a variance *must* be granted in appropriate fact situations subject to reasonable conditions prescribed by the local agency. See Cunningham, "Flexible Zoning and the New Jersey 'Special Reasons' Variance Procedure," 15 Zoning Digest 169 (1963). (This is in reality the judicial approach followed today with respect to hardship variances under N.J.S.A. 40:55-39c, even though the opinions state and purport to follow the same scope of review rule as in cases of use variances. See Ardolino v. Florham Park Board of Adjustment, 24 N.J. 94, 130 A.2d 847 (1957). Note my view as to the proper scope of judicial review of municipal legislative land use regulation action expressed in the Vickers dissent, 37 N.J., at pp. 258-261, 181 A.2d, at p. 140, the rationale of which I think is equally applicable to municipal administrative action. I have deep concern about according the same deference to the actions of such agencies as is done in the case of state administrative bodies.

As far as the present case is concerned, I would require that an application for a variance by the plaintiff be so considered both at the local level and on any judicial review.

SCHETTINO, J., joins in this opinion.

FRANCIS, J. (dissenting).

I cannot agree with the result reached by the majority for the reasons expressed in my dissent in the original case. 42 N.J. 556, 567, 202 A.2d 161 (1964).

In his concurring opinion Justice Hall has stated in crystal clear fashion an incidental but significant problem which inheres in controversies like the present one. In capsule form the issue may be expressed as regionalism vs. provincialism, with the latter now firmly ensconced in control as the result of recognition by the majority of my colleagues of the comprehensive zoning power of the local authorities with respect to public and private non-profit schools. And it follows, of course, that so long as such pervasive power continues to be paramount, the public welfare as represented by regional interests or needs will be subordinated to the parochial views of a single municipality. Thus it seemed to me originally, and the view is strengthened now by Justice Hall's observations, that problems arising out of the location of public or private non-profit secondary schools, particularly those designed to serve regional educational needs, should be resolved by the State Board of Education. In my judgment that board has plenary express or implied authority to deal with the subject to the exclusion of district lines established by a municipal zoning ordinance. 42 N.J., at p. 570, 202 A.2d 161.

Moreover, as the dissent indicated, the power of the State Board would not be exhausted by a simple approval or veto of a secondary school location selected by the school authorities, whether the particular school is to be regional or local in its service. And it is unlikely that local aesthetic considerations would be ignored or that community desires to have the physical impact of the school structure on the neighborhood lessened would be shunted aside. Regulation of such matters as "area of plot in relation to size of school, play yards, sidelines, front and rear setback lines," buffer areas, shrubbing, treeing and the like, is certainly within the implied power of the board, and undoubtedly would be engaged in with due regard for such neighborhood interests. 42 N.J., at p. 571, 202 A.2d 161.

Questions and Notes

On Atherton

1. What kind of a town is Atherton?
2. What percentage of the total area in Atherton was already used for schools?
3. Where (in what town) was the voting power in each of the school districts involved?
4. Why do you think these school districts chose to dump so many schools into Atherton?

On Hohokus

1. Note that, as usual, Justice Hall's opinion in the second Hohokus case spells out the essential issues much more clearly than any place else.

STATE

v.

NORTHWESTERN PREPARATORY SCHOOL

228 Minn. 363, 37 N.W. 2d 370(1949).
Supreme Court of Minnesota.
April 29, 1949.

Syllabus by the Court.

A zoning ordinance which permits in a residential area public schools and churches and schools accessory thereto and prohibits therein private schools is unconstitutional as applied to a private school owned and conducted by a nonstock and nonprofit corporation, the purpose of which is to train young men for competitive examinations for entrance into schools conducted by the armed services of the United States and for appointment to and service in certain of the armed services, as being in violation of the equal protection clause of U.S.Const. Amend. XIV.

Appeal from Municipal Court of Minneapolis; Theodore B. Knudson, Judge.

The Northwestern Preparatory School, Inc., and another were convicted of violating a zoning ordinance, and they appeal.

Judgment reversed with directions to enter judgment acquitting defendants.

Ben W. Palmer, of Minneapolis, for appellants.

John F. Bonner, City Atty. and Leo P. McHale, Asst. City Atty., both of Minneapolis, for respondent.

PETERSON, Justice.

Defendants appeal from the judgment convicting them of violating a zoning ordinance of Minneapolis.

The question for decision is whether a zoning ordinance [1] which permits in a residential area "Public Schools" and "Churches and Schools accessory thereto" and prohibits therein private schools, is unconstitutional as applied to a private school, owned and conducted by a corporation which has no capital stock and is not operated for profit, the purpose of which is to train young men for competitive examinations for entrance into schools conducted by the armed services of the United States and for appointment to and service in certain of the armed services, as being in violation of the due process and equal protection clauses of U.S.Const. Amend. XIV, and of Minn.Const. art. 1, §§ 2 and 7.

The facts have been stipulated. Section 3 of the zoning ordinance in question provides that in such an area there may be erected "Private" and

---

1. Minneapolis City Charter & Ordinances, 1872-1925, p. 527 (Zoning Ordinance of the City of Minneapolis, § 3).

"Two-family" dwellings, "Public Schools," "Churches and Schools accessory thereto," and certain other buildings not here material. The proper construction of the ordinance, as the parties assumed and the trial court held, is that it excludes private schools from such residential areas. Northwestern Preparatory School, Inc., is a nonstock and nonprofit corporation, the purpose of which is "the establishment and maintenance of a school for the thorough training of young men for the competitive and entrance examinations for the United States Military Academy at West Point, the United States Naval Academy at Annapolis, the United States Coast Guard Academy and for appointment to and service in the Army, Navy, Air Corps or other services for the United States of America." It owns and operates the Northwestern Preparatory School, which is located in an area zoned as a residential one. Defendant Gerald J. Roddy is president of the corporation and in charge of the school. Admittedly, the school is an institution of learning. It is a preparatory school of a special type. The offense charged is based not upon the type of building in which the school is operated, but solely upon the use of the building as a private school.

Defendants contend that the classification in question permitting in a residential area public schools and parochial schools accessory to churches and excluding therefrom private schools is arbitrary and that, because that is true, it violates the due process and equal protection clauses of U.S.Const. Amend. XIV, and of Minn. Const. art. 1, §§ 2 and 7. The city contends that the exclusion of private schools from areas zoned as residential is based upon a reasonable distinction between residences and schools and consequently that it constitutes a permitted exercise of the police power, and that to permit private schools of the kind here in question to locate in a residential area would permit also other privately owned colleges and schools, such as barber colleges, dancing academies, and the like, to locate there and thereby defeat the exercise of the city of the police power.

[1] It is recognized that zoning ordinances otherwise valid may be unconstitutional as applied to particular cases. Village of Euclid v. Ambler Realty Co., 272 U.S. 365, 47 S.Ct. 114, 71 L.Ed. 303, 54 A.L.R. 1016. We think this is such a case.

[2-4] The Fourteenth Amendment guarantees due process and equal protection as separate rights. Anderson v. City of St. Paul, 226 Minn. 186, 32 N.W.2d 538. The guarantee of equal protection of the laws requires equality of application of the laws—that all similarly circumstanced shall be treated alike. George Benz Sons, Inc., v. Ericson, 227 Minn. 1, 34 N.W.2d 725; Anderson v. City of St. Paul, supra. The provisions of the zoning ordinance here involved do not apply equally to public, parochial, and privately owned schools. So far as the purposes of the ordinance are concerned, there is no difference between public and parochial schools on the one hand and private schools on the other. While ownership, some of the subjects taught, and the discipline enforced may be different in each from what they are in the others, a private school has no effect upon a

residential area different from that of a public or parochial one. The distinction between the different kinds of schools, upon which the classification made in the ordinance rests, is not based upon alleged evils which it is claimed exist in the case of private schools and do not exist in the case of public or parochial schools. The distinction is based solely upon ownership. Such a distinction bears no relation to the purposes of the ordinance, and for that reason is arbitrary. The ordinance denies to private schools the rights which it accords to public and parochial schools under the same circumstances. Thereby the ordinance fails to accord to private schools the equal protection of the laws. In that particular it is unconstitutional denying to private schools the equal protection of the laws. See, Village of University Heights v. Cleveland Jewish Orphans' Home, 6 Cir., 20 F.2d 743, 54 A.L.R. 1008.

The city's arguments that other businesses which call themselves colleges and schools, but which really are not institutions of learning, also might locate in residential areas under such a rule have been answered in State v. Northwestern College of Speech Arts, Inc., 193 Minn. 123, 128, 258 N.W. 1, 3, where we held that barber colleges, dancing academies, riding schools, and the like are not institutions of learning.

Since we hold that the ordinance as applied to private schools is unconstitutional as violative of the equal protection clause of the Fourteenth Amendment, it is not necessary to decide whether it is also unconstitutional upon the other grounds urged. One ground for decision is enough.

Defendants are entitled as a matter of law to an acquittal.

Reversed with directions to enter judgment acquitting defendants.

STATE ex rel. WISCONSIN LUTHERAN HIGH SCHOOL CONFERENCE

v.

SINAR

267 Wis. 91, 65 N.W.2d 43 (1954),
appeal dismissed 349 U.S. 913 (1955).

Supreme Court of Wisconsin.
June 8, 1954.
Dissenting Opinion June 18, 1954.
Rehearing Denied Oct. 5, 1954.

Mandamus action by private, non-profit corporation to compel city building inspector to issue permit for construction of corporation's private high school, with appurtenant athletic grounds and facilities, upon corporation's land in class "A" residence zone. Property owner and taxpayer was interpleaded. The Circuit Court, Milwaukee County, William C. O'Connell, J., entered judgment adverse to defendants and denied motion to quash order sustaining demurrers, and defendants appealed. The Supreme Court, Brown, J., held that, under zoning ordinance provision forbidding erection of buildings within class "A" residence district other than single family dwellings or public schools and private high schools is not arbitrary or unreasonable and does not lack foundation in difference which bears fair, substantial, reasonable, and just relation to promotion of general welfare of community, and, therefore, refusal of building inspector to issue building permit for erection of private high school was proper.

Orders and judgment reversed, and cause remanded with directions to quash writ of mandamus.

Steinle and Broadfoot, JJ., dissented.

Action in mandamus brought by plaintiff-respondent which is a private, non-profit corporation and, for the purpose of this opinion, is an owner of land in a class "A" residence zone of the city of Wauwatosa. Its action sought to compel the defendant-appellant Sinar, as building inspector of the city, to issue a permit for the construction of plaintiff's private high school with appurtenant athletic grounds and facilities. The building inspector had previously denied an application for such permit on the ground that the proposed use of the premises is not allowed by the zoning law of the city of Wauwatosa which he has the duty to administer. He filed a motion to quash the alternative writ and, after hearing, the motion was denied by Otto H. Breidenbach, circuit judge, but with leave to file a return to the writ, which was done. In the meantime, E. L. Vanderjagt, a Wauwatosa resident, property owner and taxpayer, was interpleaded and filed an answer to plaintiff's petition. Plaintiff interposed a general demurrer to both the return and the answer.

After a hearing the demurrers were sustained and an order entered directing the entry of judgment and the issuance of a peremptory writ of mandamus. Judgment was entered and the writ issued but execution stayed pending appeal. Defendants appeal from the order denying the motion to quash, the order sustaining the demurrers, and from the judgment entered and docketed on the 10th day of December, 1953. At present there is no high school, public or private, in the class "A" residence zone.

Other material facts will be stated in the opinion. For convenience the arguments advanced by the defendants severally will be treated as though made jointly.

Herbert L. Mount, Milwaukee, for Sid H. Sinar.

Bender, Trump, McIntyre, Trimborn & Godfrey, Milwaukee, for Vanderjagt.

von Briesen & von Briesen, C. R. Dineen, and Richard J. McGinn, Milwaukee, for respondent.

BROWN, Justice.

Ch. 62, Stats., is the General Charter Law for the government of cities below the first class. The city of Wauwatosa is a city of the third class and is subject to ch. 62. Sec. 62.23(7), subsections (a), (b) and (c) grants to cities the power to zone their areas, as follows:

"(a) *Grant of power.* For the purpose of promoting health, safety, morals or the general welfare of the community, the council may by ordinance regulate and restrict the height, number of stories and size of buildings and other structures, the percentage of lot that may be occupied, the size of yards, courts and other open spaces, the density of population, and the location and use of buildings, structures and land for trade, industry, residence or other purposes provided that there shall be no discrimination against temporary structures. This subsection and any ordinance, resolution or regulation, heretofore or hereafter enacted or adopted pursuant thereto, shall be liberally construed in favor of the city and as minimum requirements adopted for the purposes stated. It shall not be deemed limitation of any power elsewhere granted.

"(b) *Districts.* For any and all of said purposes the council may divide the city into districts of such number, shape, and area as may be deemed best suited to carry out the purposes of this section; and within such districts it may regulate and restrict the erection, construction, reconstruction, alteration or use of buildings, structures or land. All such regulations shall be uniform for each class or kind of buildings and for the use of land throughout each district, but the regulations in one district may differ from those in other districts.

"(c) *Purposes in view.* Such regulations shall be made in accordance with a comprehensive plan and designed to lessen congestion in the streets; to secure safety from fire, panic and other dangers; to promote health and the general welfare; to provide adequate light and air; to prevent the overcrowding of land; to avoid undue concentration of population; to facilitate the adequate provision of transportation, water, sewerage, schools, parks and other public requirements. Such regulations shall be made with reasonable consideration, among other things, of the character of the district and its peculiar suitability for particular uses, and with a view to conserving the value of buildings and encouraging the most appropriate use of land throughout such city."

Pursuant to this authority the common council of Wauwatosa adopted a zoning ordinance whose provisions, material to this action, are as follows:

"5. That Section 14.03(1) of said Zoning Code defines 'A' Residence District Regulations as follows:

"(1) Use: No building or premises shall be used and no building shall be hereafter erected or altered within any 'A' Residence District, unless otherwise provided in this ordinance, except for the following uses:

"(a) Single Family Dwellings.

*   *   *

"(e) Public Schools and Private Elementary Schools."

[1, 2] The constitutionality of the general power of the state to zone property in the public interest is well established. It is a police power and

it may be delegated by the state to the cities. State ex rel. Tingley v. Gurda, 1932, 209 Wis. 63, 243 N.W. 317; State ex rel. Carter v. Harper, 1923, 182 Wis. 148, 196 N.W. 451, 33 A.L.R. 269. Like other examples of regulation under the police power, a specific zoning ordinance must meet the constitutional demands of due process and the equal protection of the law. It must "° ° ° provide those in similar circumstances, among whom no reasonable basis for distinction exists, with equal protection of the law, as is constitutionally required of all ordinances as well as statutes. ° ° ° " McQuillin, Municipal Corporations, 3d Ed., Sec. 25.61.

Reference to sec 14.03(1) (e) of the ordinance discloses that the erection of public high schools is permitted and the erection of private schools above the elementary rank is forbidden in the "A" residence district. The defendant inspector relied on this prohibition in refusing to issue a building permit to the plaintiff.

[3] The power to zone is granted to cities in order to promote the "health, safety, morals or the general welfare of the community." Sec. 62.23(7) (a), Stats., supra. We have recognized that the term "general welfare" includes considerations of public convenience, and general prosperity. State ex rel. Carter v. Harper, supra. The means adopted to promote these ends must, of course, bear a reasonable relation to the declared purpose. Id., 182 Wis. at page 152, 196 N.W. 451; Nectow v. City of Cambridge, 277 U.S. 183, 48 S.Ct. 447, 72 L.Ed. 842. Appellants have made it abundantly clear that respondent's projected school has many features which seriously impair the social and economic benefits to the entire community which the zoning law is designed to preserve and promote. It will add to the congestion of the surrounding streets. Athletic events will bring noisy crowds and if the contests are held at night, there will be bright lights to interfere with the peace and comfort of the neighborhood. The school property will be taken from the tax roll, thus increasing the financial burden of the city's taxpayers. The presence of the school will lessen the taxable value of nearby homes and will deter the building of new homes in the area. Other detriments are easily thought of. But, as respondent points out, each such discordant feature attends the presence of a public school to an equal degree. ° ° °

Respondent submits, therefore, that there is no difference in the effect on the community between the permitted public high school and the prohibited private one and hence the ordinance's discrimination between them is unreasonable, not founded on a difference in fact material to the object sought to be attained by building ordinances, and is a measure which denies to respondent the equal protection of the laws and deprives it of property without due process of law, contrary to the provisions of the Fourteenth Amendment of the United States Constitution. Therefore, it asserts, so far as this case is concerned, the ordinance is void.

[4] "° ° ° a classification to be valid must always rest on a difference which bears a fair, substantial, natural, reasonable, and just relation to the

object, act, or persons in respect to which it is proposed. * * * " 12 Am.Jur. p. 153, sec. 481, Const.Law.   Respondent cites Catholic Bishop of Chicago v. Kingery, 371 Ill. 257, 20 N.E.2d 583, and City of Miami Beach v. State ex rel. Lear, 128 Fla. 750, 175, So. 537.   These are cases whose facts are practically identical with the present one.   In them the respective courts held that there was no substantial difference between public and private schools in relation to the object sought to be accomplished by the zoning ordinance and therefore, in so far as it prohibited the presence of a private school while allowing a public one, it was void.   If these decisions were controlling authority upon us we would necessarily affirm the learned trial court for we can not distinguish them from ours in any material respect. But their authority is persuasive, only, and it fails to persuade.

[5, 6] The subject of public education and the establishment and operation of public schools is a governmental function of this state.   Art. X, Wis. Const. Chapters 36 to 42, Stats.   The City School Plan, secs. 40.50 to 40.60, Stats., has made the city the municipal entity for the administration of school affairs of those cities which have come under it, as the city of Wauwatosa has done.   State ex rel. Board of Education v. City of Racine, 1931, 205 Wis. 389, 236 N.W. 553.   In the performance of other governmental functions we do not restrict the behavior of persons or the use of property to the same extent that we do when only private interests are pursued and the fact that the standards are different commonly raises no suspicion that an illegal discrimination is thereby imposed or that the difference between municipality and citizen is insufficient to support separate classifications. For example, who considers he has a right to ignore speed laws because they need not be observed by the fire department responding to a call? Sec. 85.40(5), Stats.   Nor is the state controlled by a building requirement which an individual must observe.   City of Milwaukee v. McGregor, 1909, 140 Wis. 35, 121 N.W.642.   It may be that the essential differences between government and governed are so great that the two are in different classes *per se* at any time when governmental functions are involved and no ordinance is void by reason of discrimination, alone, merely because it gives a preference to the government, acting in its governmental capacity, which it withholds from private corporations or individuals.

[7] However, we decide the present appeal on the narrower ground that tangible differences material to the classification of the ordinance can be readily pointed out which sustain the distinction made by the ordinance between the schools.   To begin with, the term "public" is the antithesis of "private."   The public school is not a private one.   They serve different interests and are designed to do so.   The private school is founded and maintained because it *is* different.   Is that difference material to the purpose of zoning?   In many respects the two schools perform like functions and in probably all respects concerning noise, traffic difficulties and the other objectionable features already mentioned they stand on an equality, so that in several of the objects of zoning ordinances,—the promotion of

health, safety and morals, as laid down by sec. 62.23(7)(a), Stats., and developed by respondent's brief, we may not say that the two schools differ. But when we come to "the promotion of the general welfare of the community,"—"Ay, there's the rub." The public school has the same features objectionable to the surrounding area as a private one, but it has, also, a virtue which the other lacks, namely, that it is located to serve and does serve that area without discrimination. Whether the private school is sectarian or commercial, though it now complains of discrimination, in its services it discriminates and the public school does not. Anyone in the district of fit age and educational qualifications may attend the public high school. It is his right. He has no comparable right to attend a private school. To go there he must meet additional standards over which the public neither has nor should have control. The private school imposes on the community all the disadvantages of the public school but does not compensate the community in the same manner or to the same extent. If the private school does not make the same contribution to public welfare this difference may be taken into consideration by the legislative body in framing its ordinance. If education offered by a school to the residents of an area without discrimination is considered by the council to compensate for the admitted drawbacks to its presence there, that school may be permitted a location which is denied to another school which does not match the offer, and we can not say that such a distinction is arbitrary or unreasonable or that such discrimination between the two schools lacks foundation in a difference which bears a "fair, substantial, reasonable and just relation" to the promotion of the general welfare of the community, which is the statutory purpose of zoning laws in general and of the ordinance in question.

While we have not found any decisions sustaining the public v. private distinction between schools in zoning cases and respondent has found two to the contrary, *supra*, it has not been difficult to find supporting examples in other activities. Thus, an ordinance permitted only municipal parks in a residence district. A property owner set up a bathing beach ostensibly run as a private club but actually open to the public. He asserted that it was a park and that there was an illegal discrimination by the ordinance which permitted a municipal park but not a private one. The court said: " ° ° ° There is nothing unreasonable in the classification that makes a distinction between municipally owned and privately owned playgrounds and parks. ° ° ° " McCarter v. Beckwith, 1936, 247 App.Div. 289, 285 N.Y.S. 151, 154. The decision was affirmed without opinion, 272 N.Y. 488, 3 N.E.2d 882, and was denied certiorari 299 U.S. 601, 57 S.Ct. 194, 81 L.Ed. 443.

In Golf, Inc., v. District of Columbia, 1933, 62 App.D.C. 309, 67 F.2d 575, a corporation established a driving range in a residential area. The ordinance prohibited this activity although it would have been permitted if conducted under public auspices. The corporation contended that the zoning ordinance was void because it made an unreasonable classification. The decision rested on the distinction between public benefit and a more restricted advantage which we make in the instant case.

The headnote states:

> "Zoning regulations *held* not discriminatory because permitting use of lands in residential districts for public recreational purposes while denying to private individuals similar use, ° °."

In the opinion on page 577 of 67 F.2d 577, the court said:

> "It is also contended by the corporation that the regulations are discriminatory in that they permit the use of lands in residential zones in the District of Columbia for public recreational purposes, but deny a similar use to private individuals.
>
> "We cannot agree with this contention. A use of public parks or recreational grounds in a residential area for the common benefit of all the people of the District is not to be compared with the use of lands by a private corporation for its exclusive profit in a manner forbidden by the zoning regulations."

In City of Cincinnati v. Wegehoft, 1928, 119 Ohio 136, 162 N.W. 389, an effort was made to enjoin the city from building a fire house in an area zoned for residential purposes only, except that the ordinance provided that the city was exempt from such restriction as far as the erection of its own municipal buildings was concerned. The court held that this discrimination did not violate the state and federal constitutions.

Even more persuasive is our own leading case on zoning ordinances, State ex rel. Carter v. Harper, supra. The ordinance there under consideration contained a provision which allowed a public service corporation, upon a finding of public necessity and convenience, to erect buildings and put its property to use in its business in *any* zone. We said, 182 Wis. at page 162, 196 N.W. at page 456:

> "° ° ° It must be apparent that an ordinance enacted pursuant to state authority, which prevents the erection of buildings or the conduct of business deemed inimical to public interest, need not also prohibit the erection of buildings or the conduct of business which is essential to the comfort and convenience of the public, and which the duly constituted authority of the state determines to be necessary for the public service which a public utility is required to render. ° ° °"

The private corporation, because affected by the public interest, was enabled to conduct activities in zones where similar industries not so affected were forbidden to operate. If such preferential treatment of a mere private corporation did not invalidate the ordinance because of the public interest in the utility, how much stronger is the position of the appellants whose contention rests on an ordinance which gives the preference to the public,—the municipality,—itself! We consider the authority very strong in support of the conclusion which we have already reached independently, that no unconstitutional or otherwise illegal discrimination appears in the Wauwatosa zoning ordinance by reason of its exclusion of private high schools from "A" residence zones while accepting public schools of the same rank. Consequently, the refusal of appellant building inspector to issue a building permit for the erection of respondent's private high school was proper and must be sustained.

Orders and judgment reversed. Cause remanded with directions to quash the writ of mandamus.

STEINLE, Justice (dissenting).

The ordinance in question permits the establishment and operation of a public high school within the prescribed zone, but prohibits the erection and conducting of a private high school therein.

The majority say that since there is a substantial distinction between public and private schools in that particularly the public school must serve all, whereas the private school restricts admission, there is no illegal classification under the ordinance, and that the discrimination resulting therefrom is not unreasonable.

Zoning regulations are foundationed on police power. The ultimate purpose of zoning is associated with public health, safety, morals and general welfare.   *l*

In State v. Withrow, 1938, 228 Wis. 404, 280 N.W. 364, 116 A.L.R. 1310, this court held that the scope of the police power is confined to the enactment of regulations to promote the public health, safety and welfare.

In Geisenfeld v. Village of Shorewood, 1939, 232 Wis. 410, 287 N.W. 683, it was held that a zoning ordinance is unconstitutional and void if it is arbitrary and unreasonable and has no substantial relationship to the public health, safety, morals or general welfare of a municipality.

In State ex rel. Ford Hopkins Co. v. Mayor, 1937, 226 Wis. 215, 276 N.W.311, the court said that in the exercise of police power all classifications must be based upon substantial distinctions which makes one class really different from another.

The primary purpose of our high schools, private or public, is to educate pupils of a particular age. The state is interested to have all such children so educated in order that they may become good citizens. Private high schools as well as public high schools promote the general welfare and there is no substantial distinction in the purpose which they serve. If the private high schools did not exist, the public would be obliged to furnish facilities for those attending the private institutions.

In 47 Am.Jur., p. 459, sec. 220, the following observation is made:

> "* * * the only difference between a public and private school is that one is organized and maintained as one of the institutions of the state, whereas the other is maintained by private individuals or corporations."

The placement of a private high school in the area in question here would no more offend or interfere with the health, safety, morals and general welfare of the community than would the presence of a public high school which the city authorities under the ordinance are permitted to erect in the zoned section. As was well said in the case of Catholic Bishop of Chicago v. Kingery, 1939, 371 Ill. 257, 20 N.E.2d 583 at page 584:

> "We fail to perceive to what degree a catholic school of this type will be more detrimental or dangerous to the public health than a public school. It is not pointed out to us just how the pupils in attendance at the parochial school are any more likely to jeopardize the public safety than the public school pupils. Nor can we arbitrarily conclude that the prospective students of the new school will seriously undermine the general welfare. As a matter of fact such a school, conducted in accordance with the educational requirements established by State educational authorities, is promotive of the general welfare."

Other cases holding ordinances of this type invalid on the basis of improper classification are: City of Miami Beach v. State ex rel. Lear, 1937, 128 Fla. 750, 175 So. 537; Lumpkin v. Township Committee of Bernards, 1946, 134 N.J.L. 428, 48 A.2d 798; Roman Catholic Archbishop of Diocese of Oregon v. Baker, 1932, 140 Or. 600, 15 P.2d 391; State ex rel. Synod of Ohio of United Lutheran Church in America v. Joseph, 1942, 139 Ohio St. 229, 39 N.E.2d 515, 138 A.L.R. 1274; Women's Kansas City St. Andrew Society v. Kansas City, 8 Cir., 1932, 58 F.2d 593. State v. Northwestern Preparatory School, 228 Minn. 363, 37 N.W.2d 370; Phillips v. City of Homewood, 255 Ala. 180, 50 So.2d 267. Yanow v. Seven Oaks Park, Inc., 11 N.J. 341, 94 A.2d 482. See, also 8 McQuillin, Municipal Corporations (3rd ed.) p. 40, sec. 25.15.

It is a rule, as pointed out by the majority, that valid classification for zoning may be based on distinctions between municipal and private property and activities. However, it is significant that the courts of the country in zoning cases have treated private school situations differently than other endeavors of private enterprise. In the field of education the courts in zoning cases have made an exception to the rule and have not distinguished as between private and public schools. There is good reason for such exception.

Cases cited by the majority, to wit: McCarter v. Beckwith, 1936, 247 App.Div. 289, 285 N.Y.S. 151; Norway Pleasant Telephone Co. v. Tuntland, 68 S.D. 441, 3 N.W.2d 882 and Golf, Inc. v. District of Columbia, 1933, 62 App.D.C. 309, 67 F.2d 575 involve a privately owned park and a privately owned golf driving range, respectively. It seems, however, that there is a substantial distinction between schools and places of recreation. Private schools must comply with state standards in matters of education. Privately owned recreation places need not so comply. By law, schooling is required to a particular age. The state permits such schooling in either public or private establishment. It does not require recreation to be taken in either park or golf range. The private park or golf range is a profit-making venture. In the instant situation the owner of the land who petitions for the building permit is a nonprofit organization.

Since it appears that the private high school which respondent desires to erect on its land in the zoned area is in the same category as the public high schools of Wauwatosa, and of the type which that municipality is free to erect in the zoned section, and that such private high school would serve the same purpose of educating the children of the community and vicinity as do the public high schools of that city, I am forced to the conclusion that the barring of respondent's contemplated project by this zoning ordinance is discriminatory, arbitrary and unreasonable and clearly violative of sec. 1, art. 1, of the Wisconsin Constitution and contrary to section 1 of the Fourteenth Amendment of the Federal Constitution and therefore void. I would affirm the judgments of the circuit court.

I am authorized to say that Mr. Justice BROADFOOT joins in this dissent.

Questions and Notes

1. Is there any difference in the impact on a neighborhood, between public and private schools?

2. Is there any difference in the impact on a neighborhood, between private profit-making and private non-profit-making schools?

3. Why did the Wisconsin case uphold the distinction made between public and private schools?

CORPORATION OF PRESIDING BISHOP OF CHURCH OF JESUS CHRIST OF LATTER-DAY SAINTS

v.

PORTERVILLE

90 Cal. App. 2d 656, 203 P.2d 823(1949), appeal dismissed,
338 U.S. 805 (1949)

District Court of Appeal, Fourth District, California.

March 17, 1949.

Rehearing Denied April 13, 1949.
Hearing Denied May 12, 1949.

Appeal from Superior Court, Tulare County; Frank Lamberson, Judge. Proceeding by Corporation of the Presiding Bishop of the Church of

Jesus Christ of Latter-Day Saints, a Utah corporation sole, against the City of Porterville and others, for a writ of mandate to compel defendants to issue a permit for the construction of a church. From a judgment dismissing the petition, the plaintiff appeals.

Affirmed.

Johnson, Harmon, Stirrat & Henderson, of San Francisco, and Jamison & Jamison, of Porterville, for appellant.

Waldo E. Burford, City Atty., of Porterville, and William MacKenzie Brown and Leon Thomas David, both of Los Angeles, for respondents.

MUSSELL, Justice.

This appeal is from a judgment dismissing plaintiff's petition for writ of mandate. The judgment was based on an order sustaining the demurrer of defendants to the petition without leave to amend, dismissing the same and quashing the alternative writ of mandate theretofore issued.

The plaintiff, by its petition for a writ of mandate, sought to compel the defendants to issue a permit for the construction of a church on property owned by plaintiff in the City of Porterville. Plaintiff alleged that its application to erect a church upon its property was duly filed with the proper city officials and that defendant city building inspector refused to issue a permit for the erection of the church on the ground that the property involved was zoned by the city solely for the erection of single family dwellings.

A copy of the zoning ordinance of the City of Porterville was attached to the petition. By its provisions, as far as applicable here, the city was zoned as follows: R-1, wherein buildings are restricted to single family residences; R-2, to duplex or two-family residences; R-3, to multiple residences, and R-4, to permit unlimited residences. In R-1, only single family dwellings may be erected; in R-2, there are permitted all uses that are permitted under R-1, plus duplexes and two family residences; in R-3, all uses of R-1 and R-2 are permitted, plus apartment houses, multiple family dwellings, hotels, boarding and lodging houses, clubs, fraternities, sororities, hospitals, etc. In R-4, called "unlimited residence," all uses of the preceding zones are permitted, plus libraries, museums, schools, churches and religious institutions, etc.

At the time the property was acquired by plaintiff it was partly within the city and thereafter was taken within the city limits and included in an area limited in its use to single family dwelling units, being zone R-1. Plaintiff's application for a building permit stated that the use and occupancy to which the building was to be put was "to provide a chapel and classrooms for religious worship and study and accommodations for youth activities and other church activities."

[1, 2] Plaintiff's contention is that the zoning ordinance as applied to plaintiff to prevent its construction of a church for religious worship upon its property is invalid because, as so applied, it bears no substantial relation to the public health, safety, morals and general welfare and thus is beyond

the police power of the State to enact, and further, because the application of the ordinance to petitioner results in a restriction of religious worship in the absence of any grave or imminent danger justifying such a restriction. The precise question of whether or not there may be established, as a part of a comprehensive zoning plan, strictly private residential districts from which churches are excluded and in which they are prohibited, has apparently not been decided in this State, however, it has been held that general business enterprises, apartments, tenements and like structures may be excluded and prohibited in private residential districts. Miller v. Board of Public Works, 195 Cal. 477, 490, 234 P. 381, 38 A.L.R. 1479. As was said in Wilkins v. City of San Bernardino, 29 Cal.2d 332, 337, 175 P.2d 542, 547:

> "It is well settled that zoning ordinances, when reasonable in object and not arbitrary in operation, constitute a justifiable exercise of police power, and that the establishment, as part of a comprehensive and systematic plan, of districts devoted to strictly private residences or single family dwellings from which are excluded business or multiple dwelling structures, is a legitimate exercise of the police power. See Jones v. City of Los Angeles, 211 Cal. 304, 307, 295 P. 14; Miller v. Board of Public Works, 195 Cal. 477, 490, 234 P. 381, 38 A.L.R. 1479. ° ° ° Every intendment is in favor of the validity of the exercise of police power, and, even though a court might differ from the determination of the legislative body, if there is reasonable basis for the belief that the establishment of a strictly residential district has substantial relation to the public health, safety, morals or general welfare, the zoning measure will be deemed to be within the purview of the police power. (Citing cases.)"

In Miller v. Board of Public Works, supra, 195 Cal. at page 492, 234 P. at page 386, 38 A.L.R. 1479, it was said:

> "There are some decisions which do not uphold the validity of a zoning ordinance establishing strictly residential districts. We are of the opinion however, that the better reasoned cases are in favor of the validity of comprehensive zoning which establish strictly private home districts, and that the most which can be said of the cases to the contrary is that they merely show that this is a question upon which reasonable minds may differ."

[3, 4] We are in accord with this view and we conclude that since the city had power to zone the property herein affected, strictly for single family dwellings, there was no abuse of the power in prohibiting the erection and construction of church buildings therein. It is a matter of common knowledge that people in considerable numbers assemble in churches and that parking and traffic problems exist where crowds gather. This would be true particularly in areas limited to single family dwellings. There necessarily is an appreciable amount of noise connected with the conduct of church and "youth activities." These and many other factors may well enter into the determination of the legislative body in drawing

the lines between districts, a determination primarily the province of the city.

A single family residence may be much more desirable when not in an apartment house neighborhood or adjacent to a public building such as a church. The municipal legislative body may require that church buildings be erected to conform to health and safety regulations as provided in its building code and we see no reason to hold that churches may be erected in a single family residential area when a duplex, triplex, or other multiple dwelling can lawfully be excluded therefrom. The provision in the ordinance for a single family residential area affords an opportunity and inducement for the acquisition and occupation of private homes where the owners thereof may live in comparative peace, comfort and quiet. Such a zoning regulation bears a substantial relation to the public health, safety, morals and general welfare because it tends to promote and perpetuate the American home and protect its civic and social values.

[5] We find no merit in plaintiff's contention that the application of the ordinance to the plaintiff results in an unwarranted restriction of religious worship. The petitioner is not a congregation, but holds his property as a corporation sole, the existence of which depends upon the laws of the State. Having such right from the State, the enjoyment of the property is subject to reasonable regulations. The denial of a building permit did not prohibit any one from religious worship and there is nothing in the record before us to indicate that the church building could not be erected if located in the area zoned for that purpose.

[6] The petition fails to state a cause of action in that the facts alleged do not show that the ordinance in question is unreasonable and void as applied to plaintiff. The allegations are:

> "That said zoning ordinance as applied to your petitioner so as to prevent your petitioner from erecting a church on the above mentioned property, is unconstitutional and void, in that said ordinance is arbitrary and unreasonable and is without any substantial relation to the public health, safety, morals or general welfare; that said ordinance is not based upon a finding by the governing body of the city of Porterville that such zoning is necessary to the public health, safety, morals or general welfare of the community. That said ordinance ° ° ° is not based on the general welfare of the community and does not tend to preserve or promote the public health, safety, or morals, and constitutes an arbitrary exclusion of a church ° ° °. That said ordinance ° ° ° constitutes a deprivation of petitioner's property without due process of law ° ° ° "

Matters of fact necessary to support the legal conclusions alleged are not stated, and the petition therefore states no cause of action. Wilkins v. City of San Bernardino, supra, 29 Cal.2d 332, at page 344, 175 P.2d 542.

[7] The burden is upon the plaintiff to allege and prove physical facts from which the court could conclude as a matter of law that the ordinance

was unreasonable and invalid. Wilkins v. City of San Bernardino, supra, 29 Cal.2d 332, at page 338, 175 P.2d 542.

[8, 9] In enacting zoning ordinances, the municipality performs a legislative function and every intendment is in favor of the validity of such ordinances. Jardine v. City of Pasadena, 199 Cal.64, 72-73, 248 P. 225, 48 A.L.R. 509. It is presumed that the enactment as a whole is justified under the police power and adapted to promote the public health, safety, morals, and general welfare. Lockard v. City of Los Angeles, 33 Cal.2d—, 202 P.2d 38.

[10] There is reasonable justification for the action of the defendant city in prescribing the buildings which may be erected and constructed in the zone established for single family residences and in such cases the wisdom of the prohibitions and restrictions is a matter for legislative determination. Lockard v. City of Los Angeles, supra, 33 Cal.2d—, 202 P.2d 38.

[11] Plaintiff argues that the trial court should not have sustained the demurrer to the petition without leave to amend. The plaintiff, however, did not request leave to amend and the judgment contains a recital that petitioner "advised the Court that leave to amend would be futile." Plaintiff's contention in the trial court was as stated in his reply brief—"That the prohibition of churches in virtually all residential zones is on its face not a proper exercise of the police power, and that it violates the constitutional immunity of freedom of religious worship."

Where, as here, plaintiff elected to stand on the allegations of the petition, and declined to amend it, informing the court that amendment would be "futile," it cannot be held that there was an abuse of discretion in the ruling of the trial court.

Judgment affirmed.

BARNARD, P. J., and GRIFFIN, J., concur.

Hearing denied; SHENK and CARTER JJ., dissenting.

Questions and Notes

1. What type of housing did the court think had an impact on a single-family neighborhood similar to the impact of churches?
2. Note this is a California decision.

MOONEY

v.

ORCHARD LAKE

333 Mich. 389, 53 N.W. 2d 308(1952).

Supreme Court of Michigan.

May 16, 1952.

Suit by Edward Mooney, Roman Catholic Archbishop of the Archdiocese of Detroit, and another, against the Village of Orchard Lake, and others, to enjoin defendants from enforcing a zoning ordinance. The Circuit Court, Oakland County, in Chancery, George B. Hartrick, J., renderede a decree for plaintiffs, and defendants appealed. The Supreme Court, Dethmers, J., held that the ordinance which as a practical matter excluded churches and schools from the entire village, did not bear such a real and substantial relationship to public health, safety, morals or the general welfare as to constitute a reasonable and legitimate exercise of the police power.

Affirmed.

DETHMERS, Justice.

Defendants appeal from a decree enjoining them from enforcing a zoning ordinance so as to prevent plaintiffs' erection and maintenance of a church and school on premises owned by them before adoption of the ordinance and situated in a zone thereunder restricted to use for private dwellings only.

The trial court found as a fact, from the evidence in the case, which need not be recounted here, that although the ordinance appeared on its face to allow churches and schools, under special permit only, in three zones comprising about ten per cent of the village's area while prohibiting them in the fourth zone containing the balance of the village, nevertheless, when applied to existing facts and circumstances, it served, as a practical matter, to exclude churches and schools from the village. The finding is fairly supported by the record.

As authority for the proposition that churches and schools may not be excluded by ordinance from residential districts or zones plaintiffs rely on City of Sherman v. Simms, 143 Tex. 115, 183 S.W.2d 415; Ellsworth v. Gercke, 62 Ariz. 198, 156 P.2d 242; Roman Catholic Archbishop v. Baker, 140 Or. 600, 15 P.2d 391; State ex rel. Synod of Ohio of United Lutheran Church of America v. Joseph, 139 Ohio St. 229, 39 N.E.2d 515, 138 A.L.R. 1274; State ex rel. Roman Catholic Bishop v. Hill, 59 Nev. 231, 90 P.2d 217; North Shore Unitarian Society, Inc. v. Village of Plandome, Sup., 109 N.Y.S.2d 803; State ex rel. Tampa, Fla. Co. of Jehovah's Witnesses v. City of Tampa, Fla., 48 So.2d 78; Western Theological Seminary v. City of Evanston, 325 Ill. 511, 156 N.E. 778. Defendants undertake, with varying degrees of success, to demonstrate the inapplicability of those cases to the case at bar. In turn, their chief reliance is placed upon Corporation of Presiding Bishop v. City of Porterville, 90 Cal.App.2d 656, 203 P.2d 823, 825, appeal dismissed for want of federal question, 338 U.S. 805, 70 S.Ct. 78, 94 L.Ed. 487, rehearing denied 338 U.S. 939, 70 S.Ct. 342, 94 L.Ed. 579. There the ordinance divided the city of Porterville into four zones, in two of which residences only were permitted. The significant factor distinguishing that case from this is that the California court found that "there is nothing in the record before us to indicate that the church building could not be erected if located in the area zoned for that purpose." We are not insensitive to the persuasiveness of some of the reasoning in that case to the effect that churches may as lawfully be excluded as may multiple dwellings from single family residential areas. That, however, is not the question before us. On the basis of the record at bar the question to be determined is whether churches and schools may, in effect, be excluded by ordinance from the entire village.

[1-3] The right to full and free use and enjoyment of one's property in a manner and for such purpose as the owner may choose, so long as it be not for the maintenance of a nuisance injurious to others, is one of which he may not be deprived by government without due process of law nor may his property be taken by government without just compensation. U.S. Const. Amends. 5 and 14; Mich.Const 1908, art 2, § 16, and art. 13, § 1. The owner's right to use is, however, subject to reasonable regulation, restriction and control by the state in the legitimate exercise of its police powers. The test of legitimacy is the existence of a real and substantial relationship between the exercise of those powers in a particular manner in a given case and public health, safety, morals or the general welfare. Village of Euclid v. Ambler Realty Co., 272 U.S. 365, 47 S.Ct. 114 71 L.Ed. 303; Austin v. Older, 283 Mich. 667, 278 N.W. 727; Northwood Properties Co. v. Royal Oak City Inspector, 325 Mich. 419, 39 N.W.2d 25.

[4-6] The use of premises for church or school purposes does not amount to a nuisance. Smith v. First United Presbyterian Church, 333 Mich. 1, 52 N.W.2d 568. Does exclusion of church and school from the entire village bear a real and substantial relationship to public health, safety, morals or the general welfare and thus constitute a reasonable and legitimate exercise of the police power? Defendants say that a presumption prevails in favor of the reasonableness and validity of the ordinance unless the contrary is shown by competent evidence or appears on the face of the enactment and that the burden rests on plaintiffs to show that it has no real or substantial relationship to public health, safety, morals or the general welfare, citing Harrigan & Reid Co. v. Burton, 224 Mich. 564, 195 N.W. 60, 33 A.L.R. 142; Austin v. Older, supra; Portage Township v. Full Salvation Union, 318 Mich. 693, 29 N.W.2d 297, and Northwood Properties Co. v. Royal Oak City Inspector, supra; that plaintiffs offered no proofs in relation thereto; and that, if there are proofs both ways relating to the subject, it is not for

this court to weigh the same but only to see whether there is substantial testimony supporting the conclusion in that regard of the legislative authorities, in which case the latter is to be upheld, citing Detroit v. Michigan R. Commission, 209 Mich. 395 at 433, 177 N.W. 306; Washington Agency, Inc. v. Commissioner of Insurance, 309 Mich. 683 at 687, 16 N.W.2d 121. This is not a case such as those relied upon in this connection by defendants, as, for example, Northwood Co. v. R. O. City Inspector, supra, in which the proofs showed merely that the ordinance restricted a certain zone to use for single residences. There was no evidence in that case concerning the effects of the operation of the ordinance, the reasonableness thereof, nor the relationship between the objects sought to be accomplished and the public health, safety, morals or general welfare, for lack of which the presumption of validity was indulged. In the instant case, on the contrary, the ordinance, exhibits and testimony show that the ordinance operates to exclude churches and schools from the entire village. Consequently, we are confronted with an enactment showing on its face that which, combined with the competent evidence in the case, obviates the necessity for resort to the presumption of reasonableness and validity and raises a question for judicial determination.

The ordinance of 1787 for the governing of the great Northwest Territory, of which Michigan is a part, pronounced a conviction and purpose, reiterated in the Michigan Constitution of 1908, art. 11, § 1, which formed the cornerstone of the governmental structures of the territory and of the states subsequently carved therefrom, in these exalted terms:

"Religion, morality and knowledge being necessary to good government and the happiness of mankind, schools and the means of education shall forever be encouraged."

Hardly compatible is this with a presumption that exclusion of school and church from an entire municipality is conducive to public health, safety, morals or the general welfare, a presumption which we decline to indulge. A thesis so inconsistent with the spirit and genius of our free institutions and system of government and the traditions of the American people will not be accepted by way of presumption, nor at all in the absence of competent evidence establishing a real and substantial relationship between the attempted exclusion and public health, safety, morals or the general welfare and, hence, the reasonableness and validity of the restriction upon use of private property as a legitimate exercise of the state's police powers.

[7] Affirmed, without costs, a public question being involved.

NORTH, C. J., and REID, BOYLES, BUTZEL, CARR, BUSHNELL and SHARPE, JJ., concur.

DIOCESE OF ROCHESTER

v.

BRIGHTON

1 N.Y. 2d 508, 136 N.E. 2d 827 (1956).

Court of Appeals of New York.

July 11, 1956.

Proceeding to review decisions of planning board, zoning board of appeals, and town board. The Supreme Court, Special Term, Monroe County, Charles B. Brasser, J., 207 Misc. 1021, 141 N.Y.S.2d 487, entered an order dismissing the petition and plaintiffs appealed. The Supreme Court, Appellate Division, Fourth Judicial Department, Wheeler, J., 1 A.D.2d 86, 147 N.Y.S. 2d 392, affirmed with permission to appeal. The Court of Appeals, Froessel, J., held that where decisions of defendants in denying plaintiffs' application for a permit to erect a church and school with necessary accessory uses, were based on fact there was no school or church in the area, adverse effect upon property values in the area, loss of potential tax revenue, and decreased enjoyment of neighboring property, and bore no substantial relation to declared purpose of zoning ordinance to promote the public health, safety, morals or general welfare of the community, such decisions were arbitrary and unreasonable.

Orders below reversed with directions.

Van Voorhis, J., dissented.

Porter R. Chandler, New York City, and David H. Shearer, Rochester, for appellants.

Leo Peffer, Will Maslow and Shad Polier, New York City, for American Jewish Congress, amicus curiae, in support of appellants' position.

Charles J. Tobin, Jr., Albany, for New York State Catholic Welfare Committee, amicus curiae, in support of appellant's position.

Andrew L. Gilman and Harold S. Coyle, Rochester, for respondents.

William F. Strang, Rochester, for intervenors-respondents.

FROESSEL, Judge.

This is an appeal pursuant to leave of the Appellate Division, Fourth Department, from an order of that court which unanimously affirmed an order, entered in an article 78 proceeding, of Special Term, Monroe County. Special Term dismissed the petition on the merits on the ground that no triable issue of fact had been raised, and affirmed respondents' decisions denying petitioners' application for a permit to build a church and school with necessary accessory uses and for a variance.

Petitioners allege that the population of the Town of Brighton (a suburb of Rochester) has been rapidly increasing and is now about 23,000, of whom more than 6,000 are Catholic. At present there is in Brighton but one Catholic church, Our Lady of Lourdes. This church was erected in 1928, and is inconveniently located with respect to worshippers residing in the eastern part of the town and is inadequate to accommodate them. The only parochial school in the town is attached to Our Lady of Lourdes, and was erected in 1948. It is also inconvenient to and unable to accommodate Catholic pupils residing in eastern Brighton. In 1953 the Diocese of Rochester (hereinafter called the Diocese), recognizing the inadequacy of existing facilities for members of its faith, established a new parish in the eastern part of town.

After a diligent search, the only suitable property found to be centrally located and available (free from private restrictions) in the new parish was a tract of 14 acres owned by the estate of William A. E. Drescher, deceased, fronting on East Avenue in the town. On August 30, 1954 the Diocese agreed to purchase the Drescher property, and entered into a contract which conditioned the sale upon the Diocese's obtaining a permit from the planning board of the town to erect and use a church and school on the western portion of the property. The executor of the estate of William A. E. Drescher has joined in all the proceedings to date.

In 1933 the town board of Brighton adopted a zoning ordinance which, together with all amendments thereto and the zoning map of the town in effect at the time of the hearing, is incorporated by reference into the petition.

Section 2 of the ordinance states:

> "For the purpose of promoting the public health, safety, morals or the general welfare ° ° ° the Town of Brighton is hereby divided into four classes of districts, termed respectively:
>
> (1) Residential Districts
>
> (2) Commercial Districts
>
> (3) Industrial Districts
>
> (4) Agricultural Districts."

Section 18 further subdivides the residential districts into three classes known as "A", "B", and "C". Section 19 defines the uses permitted in a Class A area, with which we are concerned, and provides: "In Class A, no structure *or* the premises can be used and no structure shall be erected or altered which is arranged, intended or designed to be used in whole or in part for other than one of the following *uses and accessory uses:*

> (1) Single family one and two story or two and one-half story detached dwelling, with private garage.
>
> (2) *Educational or Religious Building*, Fire Station, Town Municipal Building, Police Station, Park and Park buildings, *if approved by the Planning Board.*" (Emphasis supplied.)

The Drescher property is located in a Class A residential district, and the Diocese accordingly made written application to the planning board and the board of appeals as follows: (1) to subdivide the property in order to set apart a large house located in the northwest corner as a life estate for the widow of William A. E. Drescher, deceased; (2) for "permission to construct on and use the remainder of the west parcel" for a Roman Catholic church and school; and (3) to subdivide the east and west parcels as shown by the accompanying map so as to provide two L-shaped lots on each of which there shall be one dwelling, each having a frontage on East Avenue of at least 100 feet or, in the alternative, for a variance from the provisions of the zoning ordinance permitting the continuance of said two dwellings as they now exist.

The application was accompanied by a map which showed the proposed location of the church; school; meeting room; kindergarten, small games, open field and hardtop play areas; and parking lot which would accommodate 144 cars. The application stated that approximately 4 acres on the eastern part of the property are covered by title restrictions confining their use to residences only.

This application came on for a public hearing before the planning board and the board of appeals on September 14, 1954, at which time all the interested parties were heard. The minutes of that hearing are incorporated by reference into the petition. At this hearing, Mr. Ely, chairman of the planning board, stated that the Diocese's application was "actually addressed to both the Planning Board and the Board of Appeals," the application for a permit being before the former. The attorney for the Diocese also stated that his application was being made under subdivision (2) of section 19 of the ordinance, and that the application for a variance "is only an incidental matter and hinges entirely on whether or not we are permitted to use the west parcel for the construction of the school and church." Evidence was then presented on behalf of the Diocese to the effect that Catholic parishes are territorial and that the church should be in the center of the parish; that there would be no traffic problem; that ample parking facilities are provided; that the proposed school is to be a grade school only, eventually accommodating 300 children; that there will be little change in appearance of the property on East Avenue; and that the new parish will serve about 380 families.

A number of residents of the area were heard in opposition, and they testified as to the inconvenience, annoyance and undesirability of having this church and school in the neighborhood. A real estate appraiser testified that in his opinion the proposed church and school would depreciate neighboring property from 5% to 10%.

Thereafter on November 15, 1954 the planning board filed its decision, dated October 14, denying the Diocese's application. This decision states that the exclusive question before the board is "whether there should be a church and school at the applied for location." In answering this question in the negative, the board based its decision on several explicitly stated grounds: (1) that the area in question has been completely built up, and that where such is the case and the locale is strictly residential in character, the imposition of a church and school would change the character of the residential use and enjoyment of the area and have an adverse effect on property values; (2) good planning, directed to enhancing property values, dictates that churches and schools should be built in areas where future residential development could accommodate itself to the church or school; and (3) good planning requires the maintenance of larger and more expensive homes which bear higher assessed values. The board stated that it was certain that the Drescher property would be subdivided and built upon, and therefore to allow a church and school at this location would result in a loss of potential tax revenue.

On the same day, a decision of the board of appeals (consisting of the same men as were on the planning board [Brighton Ordinance, § 50]) was filed, which denied the application for a variance. This decision states that since the application for a variance was made subsidiary to and hinged entirely upon the planning board's granting the application for a permit and since this permission was denied, "there is no purpose in granting or further considering the requested variance at this time." The board of appeals also stated that the application for a variance so as to allow a church and school on the property is also denied.

Section 53 of the ordinance provides that any determination of the planning board may be reviewed by the town board. Accordingly, on November 17, 1954 petitioners applied for a review of said decisions, and on November 26th argument was heard thereon. At this meeting, the attorney for the Diocese stated that he was not asking for a variance, but was seeking a permit pursuant to subdivision (2) of section 19 of the zoning ordinance. On *December 17, 1954* the town board filed a decision affirming the determinations of the planning board and board of appeals.

On *December 9, 1954* petitioners commenced a proceeding pursuant to subdivision 7 of section 267 of the Town Law, Consol.Laws, c. 62 and article 78 of the Civil Practice Act for an order annulling the determinations of these boards, and directing that a permit issue and a variance be granted. That petition is also incorporated by reference in a second proceeding.[1] This second petition, with which we are here concerned, was verified

---

1. Town Law, § 267, subd. 7, provides that any person aggrieved by the decision of any board of appeals or other board of the town may apply to the Supreme Court for relief by a proceeding under article 78 of the Civil Practice Act, and that such proceedings shall be governed by article 78 "except that (a) it must be instituted as therein provided *within thirty days after the filing of a decision* in the office of the town clerk." (Emphasis supplied.) Petitioners were fearful that if they failed to seek review by the town board they would be denied relief for failure to exhaust their administrative remedies. On the other hand, if the town board took more than 30 days to decide, as they actually did, petitioners would be precluded from reviewing the decisions of the planning board and board of appeals. They therefore pursued both remedies.

December 29, 1954 and seeks to review the determination "against" the Town of Brighton, the planning board, the board of appeals and the town board. It alleges that if the planning board and the board of appeals had discretion to grant or deny the applications, said discretion was exercised in an arbitrary and unreasonable manner, and that their decisions constituted an abuse of discretion. The petition further states that the ordinance and decisions thereunder are contrary to the Constitutions of the United States and the State of New York.

The prayer for relief requests an order (1) consolidating the two petitions pursuant to section 96 of the Civil Practice Act, since they arise out of the same transaction; (2) annulling the determinations and decisions of the named respondents which denied their application "and directing that a permit issue to petitioner ° ° ° to construct, maintain and operate a church and school with incidental" buildings, and further (3) "directing that a variance be granted so as to permit the erection, maintenance and operation of church and school buildings and to maintain incidental dwelling structures" on the property.

On February 11, 1955 the motion for consolidation was heard along with other motions, and it was ordered that the two proceedings be consolidated and that the later petition be deemed the petition in the consolidated proceeding. It was also ordered that the proceedings against the "Town of Brighton" be dismissed, and several property owners who had been permitted to intervene as respondents were authorized to answer.

Respondents' answer to the petition sets forth a number of denials and separate defenses. The first, second and third allege that the proposed playgrounds, parking lot and other combined uses are prohibited uses in a Class A district. The fourth defense alleges respondents' good faith, and a variety of elements taken into consideration, among them: that a serious loss of revenue would result if the permit were granted; that the use of property for the proposed objectives was not contemplated in a Class A zone and that under the ordinance such structures were to be limited to the Class C zone; that the proposed buildings and parking lot would cause serious traffic problems, would have an adverse effect on property values, and would affect the development of the area. The fifth defense alleges that the constitutionality of the ordinance is not in issue because petitioners applied for a permit and a variance and therefore "admitted the constitutionality and validity of the ordinance." The sixth and seventh defenses allege that the Diocese established the boundaries of its parish in its sole discretion, and by so doing it could not obtain the right to construct the proposed structures; and that the allegations of paragraph 9 of the petition, being conclusory, should be stricken. The eighth and final defense states that the petition "does not state facts to entitle petitioners to any relief" and asks that the petiion be dismissed or an order of affirmance entered.

Special Term and the Appellate Division both held that petitioners could not attack the constitutionality of the Brighton ordinance in this proceeding because their application to the planning board was an appeal to the discretion of that body and, for that purpose, assumed the validity of the ordinance. Inasmuch as no constitutional question was involved, both courts stated that they could not substitute their judgment for that of respondents so long as there was some basis in the record for the determination, and that respondents' decisions were not arbitrary or unreasonable. In addition, Special Term held that petitioners could not attack the ordinance as construed and applied, since no element of intentional discrimination was alleged in the petition.

[1] It is a general rule that a party cannot, in the same proceeding, rely upon a statute or retain benefits thereunder and attack its constitutionality. Fahey v. Mallonee, 332 U.S. 245, 67 S.Ct. 1552, 91 L.Ed. 2030; Buck v. Kuykendall, 267 U.S. 307, 45 S.Ct. 324, 69 L.Ed. 623; Shepherd v. Mount Vernon Trust Co., 269 N.Y. 234, 199 N.E. 201. The proper way to raise the constitutional question is by way of a separate action or proceeding, Baddour v. City of Long Beach, 279 N.Y. 167, 18 N.E.2d 18, 124 A.L.R. 1003, motion for reargument denied 279 N.Y. 794, 19 N.E.2d 90, appeal dismissed 308 U.S. 503, 60 S.Ct. 77, 84 L.Ed. 431; Romig v. Weld, 276 App.Div. 514, 517, 95 N.Y.S.2d 571, 573, and we are advised that such an independent action is now pending. Accordingly, many cases have stated that an application for a permit or variance under a zoning ordinance is primarily an appeal to the discretion of the board, which discretion is conferred upon it by the ordinance, and therefore by making the application the petitioner necessarily concedes, for the purpose of the application, the validity and constitutionality of the ordinance. Vernon Park Realty v. City of Mount Vernon, 307 N.Y. 493, 501, 121 N.E.2d 517, 521; Baddour v. City of Long Beach, 279 N.Y. 167, 177, 18 N.E.2d 18, 22, supra; Arverne Bay Constr. Co. v. Thatcher, 278 N.Y. 222, 226, 15 N.E.2d 587, 589, 117 A.L.R. 1110; Pforzheimer v. Seidman, 278 App.Div. 780, 103 N.Y.S.2d 886; Romig v. Weld, 276 App.Div. 514, 95 N.Y.S.2d 571, supra, motion for leave to appeal denied 277 App.Div. 833, 97 NY.S.2d 920; Holy Sepulchre Cemetery v. Board of Appeals of Town of Greece, 271 App.Div. 33, 39-40, 60 N.Y.S.2d 750, 754. This rule has also been adopted in other jurisdictions. Strain v. Zoning Board of Appeals, 137 Conn. 36, 74 A.2d 462; Heath v. Mayor & City Council of Baltimore, 187 Md. 296, 303, 49 A.2d 799; State ex rel. Synod of Ohio, etc. v. Joseph, 139 Ohio St. 229, 39 N.E.2d 515, 138 A.L.R. 1274; Allen v. Zoning Board of Review of City of Warwick, 75 R.I. 321, 323, 66 A.2d 369; see 8 McQuillin on Municipal Corporations [3d ed.], § 25.291, p. 553.

Petitioners argue, however, that since the enactment of chapter 771 of the Laws of 1952, repealing former subdivisions 7, 8 and 9 of section 267 of the Town Law, and adding new subdivision 7, under which this proceeding was specifically brought, they are entitled to raise the constitutional question here, and that the instant ordinance constitutes an unlawful delegation of legislative authority without any reasonable or ascertainable standards or guides for the exercise thereof. While there may be merit in this argument, we do not find it necessary to reach these questions, for, even if we deem the Brighton ordinance to be valid and constitutional for the purposes of this proceeding, the instant decision must nevertheless fall.

[2, 3] It is well settled that a court may not substitute its judgment for that of the board or body it reviews *unless* the decision under review is arbitrary and unreasonable and constitutes an abuse of discretion. People ex rel. Hudson-Harlem Valley Title & Mortgage Co. v. Walker, 282 N.Y. 400, 26 N.E.2d 952; Levy v. Board of Standards & Appeals, 267 N.Y. 347, 196 N.E. 284.

An ordinance, constitutional on its face (or deemed so) may be construed and applied in an unconstitutional manner. Snowden v. Hughes, 321 U.S. 1, 64 S.Ct. 397, 88 L.Ed. 497; Yick Wo v. Hopkins, 118 U.S. 356, 6 S.Ct. 1064, 30 L.Ed. 220; Zorach v. Clauson, 303 N.Y. 161, 100 N.E.2d 463. If the construction of an ordinance as applied to a particular piece of property and a particular set of facts is so arbitrary and unreasonable as to result in an invasion of property rights, the action of the zoning board thereunder will be invalidated. See Community Synagogue v. Bates, 1 N.Y.2d 445, 154 N.Y.S.2d 15, 136 N.E.2d 488; Vernon Park Realty v. City of Mount Vernon, 307 N.Y. 493, 498-499, 121 N.E.2d 517, 519, supra; City of Chicago v. Sachs, 1 Ill.2d 342, 115 N.E.2d 762; Board of Zoning Appeals of Decatur v. Decatur, Indiana Co. of Jehovah's Witnesses, 233 Ind. 83, 117 N.E.2d 115; State v. Northwestern Preparatory School, 228 Minn. 363, 37 N.W.2d 370; State ex rel. Roman Catholic Bishop of Reno v. Hill, 59 Nev. 231, 90 P.2d 217; Young Israel Organization of Cleveland v. Dworkin, Ohio App., 133 N.E.2d 174; State ex rel. Synod of Ohio, etc. v. Joseph, 139 Ohio St. 229, 39 N.E.2d 515, 138 A.L.R. 1274, supra.

[4, 5] Special Term recognized that petitioners could attack the constitutionality of the *decisions* herein, as distinguished from the constitutionality of the ordinance itself, but held that "in order to invoke this principle, it must appear that there is ' "an element of intentional or purposeful discrimination" by the enforcement authorities,' " 207 Misc. 1023, 141 N.Y.S.2d 489, quoting Zorach v. Clauson, 303 N.Y. 161, 174, 100 N.E.2d 463, 468, supra. In this respect Special Term was only partially correct. The language quoted from the Zorach case was uttered in answer to the constitutional objection that the New York "released time" program, as administered, denied petitioners the equal protection of the law. To sustain *such* a claim, there had to be some showing of discrimination against petitioners as a class apart from all other persons. The instant petition also alleges that petitioners were denied the equal protection of the law, and with regard to this particular objection Special Term was correct in rejecting the claim since no discriminaiton is alleged. However, the instant petition also alleges that petitioners have been deprived of their property without due process of law, and that they have deprived of their rights to the free exercise of religion and to impart and receive religious instruction and education. No discrimination need be alleged or proved to establish the claim that an

ordinance has been construed and applied so as to violate such constitutional rights.

[6. 7] The text writers agree that churches and schools should be allowed
in Class A residential areas which are usually the quietest and least congested areas of a town (Bassett on Zoning [1940 ed.], pp. 70-72, 200; 1
Rathkopf on Law of Zoning and Planning [3d ed., 1956], p. 259; Yokely on
Zoning Law and Practice [1st ed., 1948], § 183, p. 367). It is well established in this country that a zoning ordinance may not *wholly exclude* a
church or synagogue from any residential district. Such a provision is
stricken on the ground that it bears no substantial relation to the public
health, safety, morals, peace or general welfare of the community. North
Shore Unitarian Soc. v. Village of Plandome, 200 Misc. 524, 109 N.Y.S.2d
803; Ellsworth v. Gercke, 62 Ariz. 198, 156 P.2d 242; O'Brien v. City of
Chicago, 347 Ill.App. 45, 105 N.E.2d 917; Board of Zoning Appeals of Decatur v. Decatur, Indiana Co. of Jehovah's Witnesses, 233 Ind. 83, 117
N.E.2d 115, supra; State ex rel. Roman Catholic Bishop of Reno v. Hill, 59
Nev. 231, 90 P.2d 217, supra; Young Israel Organization of Cleveland v.
Dworkin, Ohio App., 133 N.E.2d 174, 179, supra; City of Sherman v. Simms,
143 Tex. 115, 183 S.W.2d 415. An ordinance will also be stricken if it
attempts to exclude private or parochial schools from any residential area
where public schools are permitted. Long Island University v. Tappan, 305
N.Y. 893, 114 N.E.2d 432, affirming 281 App.Div. 771, 118 N.Y.S.2d 767,
which unanimously affirmed 202 Misc. 956, 113 N.E.2d 795; Property Owners Ass'n of Garden City Estates v. Board of Zoning Appeals of Incorporated
Village of Garden City, 2 Misc.2d 309, 123 N.Y.S.2d 716; see Roman Catholic Welfare Corp. of San Francisco v. City of Piedmont, 45 Cal.2d 325, 289
P.2d 438; City of Miami Beach v. State ex rel. Lear, 128 Fla. 750, 175 So.
537; City of Chicago v. Sachs, 1 Ill.2d 342, 115 N.E.2d 762, supra; Catholic
Bishop of Chicago v. Kingery, 371 Ill. 257, 20 N.E.2d 583; Lumpkin v.
Township Committee of Bernards, 134 N.J.L. 428, 48 A.2d 798; State v.
Northwestern Preparatory School, 228 Minn. 363, 37 N.W.2d 370, supra.

[8] Section 2 of the ordinance states that it was enacted "For the purpose of promoting the public health, safety, morals or the general welfare."
If the planning board's refusal to grant a permit to petitioners in the instant
case results in the exclusion of this proposed church and school from the
Class A residential district of the Town of Brighton and, if such refusal bears
no substantial relation to the health, safety, morals or general welfare of
the community, such action is illegal. Board of Zoning Appeals of Decatur
v. Decatur, Indiana Co. of Jehovah's Witnesses, 233 Ind. 83, 91, 117 N.E.2d
115, supra.

Let us examine separately each of the reasons advanced by the planning
board to support its decision. In evaluating these reasons, it must be borne
in mind that churches and schools occupy a different status from mere
commercial enterprises and, when the church enters the picture, different
considerations apply. State ex rel. Tampa, Fla., Co. of Jehovah's Witnesses,

North Unit, Inc. v. City of Tampa, Fla., 48 So.2d 78; Board of Zoning Appeals of Decatur v. Decatur, Indiana Co. of Jehovah's Witnesses, supra.

1. *No church or school in a built-up area:* The planning board found that the area in question was almost completely built up, and that churches in the town had all previously been built in areas where future residential development could accommodate itself to a church and school. The board stated that to allow this proposed use in this built-up area, inhabited by people who have chosen to live there because it was strictly residential, would change the character of the residential use and enjoyment of the area.

[9] This in effect is a declaration by the board that a proposed church and school, such as we have here, could only be built in an outlying area. Since the board states that all of this Class A area except this tract is built up, this in effect precludes the Diocese, under this declaration of policy, from ever locating its church in a Class A district. In fact, in their answer, respondents expressly state that under their interpretation of the ordinances, the proposed church and school and accessory uses are limited to a location in a Class C zone. Thus the Diocese is forced to locate in an undeveloped section of the town without being able adequately to serve the territorial needs of its parishioners, in the hope that people of the Catholic faith will move near it. We know of no rule of law which requires that churches may only be established in sparsely settled areas. On the contrary, as was said in O'Brien v. City of Chicago, 347 Ill.App. 45, 51, 105 N.E.2d 917, 920, supra, "wherever the souls of men are found, there the house of God belongs."

In State ex rel. Synod of Ohio, etc. v. Joseph, 139 Ohio St. 229, 39 N.E.2d 515, 138 A.L.R. 1274, supra, a kindred situation was presented. In that case, the ordinance involved provided that only private homes could be erected in a Class I district " 'Provided that * * * churches, schools * * * may be erected and used within such district *by special permit* granted by the zoning commission,' " 139 Ohio St. at page 238, 39 N.E.2d at page 521, emphasis supplied. The permit was denied on the basis of a declared policy that no church was to be located in a Class I district while Class III (equivalent to Brighton Class C) or business property was available. The court found that the thrust of the ordinance was to allow churches and schools in a Class I district, but that the policy expressed amounted to a suspension of this express provision of the ordinance. The court held that such an exclusion was not in furtherance of the public health, safety, morals or general welfare; that there was no authority in the ordinance for such a policy; and that the denial of the permit to petitioner was therefore arbitrary and unreasonable and in violation of petitioner's rights. In reference to this policy the court found that the board was trying to create, by administrative act, an exclusive residential section and stated, 139 Ohio St. at page 249, 39 N.E.2d at page 524: "It is true that many people prefer not to reside next door to a church. But the way legally to effectuate this desire is by private mutual covenants between property owners imposing appropriate servitudes on the land. * * * We do not believe it is a proper function of government to interfere in the name of the public to exclude churches from residential districts for the purpose of securing to adjacent landowners the benefits of exclusive residential restrictions." (Accord, Bassett on Zoning [1940 ed.], p. 200.)

[10] The planning board of Brighton has attempted to impose the same type of policy in this case, notwithstanding an ordinance whose thrust also is to allow churches and schools in Class A areas. Such policy may not be upheld for the reasons hereinbefore stated.

[11] 2. *Adverse effect upon property values:* This ground will apply with equal force to any residential zone and, if such unauthorized standard is allowed to prevail, the planning board could keep churches and private schools from locating in any place in a Class A area. It has been held that this reason is insufficient to deny a permit for the building of a parochial school in a Class I residential area. Roman Catholic Archbishop of Diocese of Oregon v. Baker, 140 Or. 600, 15 P.2d 391. Moreover, in view of the high purposes, and the moral value, of these institutions, mere pecuniary loss to a few persons should not bar their erection and use.

[12, 13] 3. *Loss of potential tax revenue:* Section 1 of article XVI of the Constitution of this State provides that "real or personal property used exclusively for religious, educational or charitable purposes" shall always be exempt from taxation, and such institutions have been granted tax exemption, Tax Law, Consol. Laws, c. 60, § 4, subd. 6. Thus the paramount authority of this State has declared a policy that churches and schools are more important than local taxes, and that it is in furtherance of the general welfare to exclude such institutions from taxation. This being the case, it cannot be seriously argued that the decision of respondents denying this permit because of a loss of tax revenue is in furtherance of the general welfare. A higher authority than these boards has decreed otherwise, and it has been held that "No municipal corporation can justly refuse a permit to build a church only because the property will no longer be subject to taxation." State ex rel. Anshe Chesed Congregation v. Bruggemeier, 97 Ohio App. 67, 75, 115 N.E.2d 65, 69.

[14] 4. *Decreased enjoyment of neighboring property:* Noise and other inconveniences have been held to be insufficient grounds upon which to deny a permit to a church, State ex rel. Synod of Ohio, etc. v. Joseph, 139 Ohio St. 229, 39 N.E.2d 515, supra, or a parochial school, Roman Catholic Archbishop of Diocese of Oregon v. Baker, 140 Or. 600, 15 P.2d 391, supra.

5. *Traffic hazards:* Although nothing is mentioned in the planning board's decision about possible traffic hazards, evidence was presented on this question to that board, and much is made of it in respondents' answer and brief, apparently by way of afterthought. This was the very situation presented in Small v. Moss, 279 N.Y. 288, 18 N.E.2d 281, where the regulation was stricken as an improper delegation of legislative authority. There we

held that the commissioner of licenses had no power to deny a license to a theatre on the ground that traffic and parking problems would be created, since no such policy or standard was declared in the statute. Several jurisdictions have held that it is arbitrary and unreasonable to deny a permit to a church or parochial school because of possible traffic hazards that may be created. State ex rel. Tampa, Fla., Co. of Jehovah's Witnesses, North Unit v. City of Tampa, Fla., 48 So.2d 78, supra; Board of Zoning Appeals of Decatur v. Decatur, Indiana Co. of Jehovah's Witnesses, 233 Ind. 83, 117 N.E.2d 115, supra; Young Israel Organization of Cleveland v. Dworkin, Ohio App., 133 N.E.2d 174, supra; State ex rel. Synod of Ohio, etc. v. Joseph, 139 Ohio St., 229, 39 N.E.2d 515, supra; State ex rel. Anshe Chesed Congregation v. Bruggemeier, 97 Ohio App. 67, 115 N.E.2d 65, supra; Archbishop of Oregon v. Baker, 140 Or. 600, 15 P.2d 391, supra.

As to the right of the planning board to reject the so-called "'package deal'" offered in this case, it is clear today that the accessory uses proposed by the Diocese, which are allowed by the ordinance, are within the scope of a church's activities. "A church is more than merely an edifice affording people the opportunity to worship God. Strictly religious uses and activities are more than prayer and sacrifice." Community Synagogue v. Bates, supra, 1 N.Y.2d at page 453, 154 N.Y.S.2d at page 21, 136 N.E.2d at page 493. In a recent case, an Indiana court stated: "We are of the opinion that a convent or 'sisters' home' must be considered an integral part of any Roman Catholic church project, which is composed of four component parts, viz.: church, priests' mansion, a 'sisters' home', and school." Board of Zoning Appeals of City of Indianapolis v. Wheaton, 118 Ind. App. 38, 47, 76 N.E.2d 597, 601. An earlier case also included a parking lot and playgrounds as proper accessory uses to a church. Keeling v. Board of Zoning Appeals, 117 Ind.App. 314, 69 N.E.2d 613.

Thus church and school and accessory uses are, in themselves, clearly in furtherance of the public morals and general welfare. The church is the teacher and guardian of morals, State ex rel. Synod of Ohio, etc. v. Joseph, 139 Ohio St. 229, 39 N.E.2d 515, supra, and "an educational institution, whose curriculum complies with the state law, is considered an aid to the general welfare." Roman Catholic Archbishop of Diocese of Oregon v. Baker, 140 Or. 600, 613, 15 P.2d 391, 395, supra. These proposed structures will not interfere with the public health, nor can they be said to be a danger to the public peace or safety; if they were, the ordinance would not have permitted their location in the district (§ 19, subd. [2]). It could hardly be urged that such structures are more objectionable than those related to agriculture, which are expressly permitted in Class A districts without qualification (§ 19, subd. [5]).

[15] In the light of the foregoing cases, and under the facts presented by this record, *the decisions* of the planning board, the board of appeals and the town board of Brighton *bear no substantial relation to the promotion of the public health, safety, morals or general welfare of the community; they*

must therefore be deemed arbitrary and unreasonable and should be an-nulled. That is not to say that appropriate restrictions may never be im-posed with respect to a church and school and accessory uses, nor is it to say that under no circumstances may they ever be excluded from designated areas. In this case, however, and in reference to this property, the decisions of the town bodies are arbitrary and unreasonable.

Accordingly, the orders below should be reversed, the decisions of the town bodies annulled and the matter remitted to them for further proceed-ings, not inconsistent with this opinion. Inasmuch as the board of appeals has not passed upon the merits of the application for a variance, we do not pass upon this phase of the appeal.

[16] We are advised that Joseph F. Taylor, executor under the will of William A. E. Drescher, deceased, and one of petitioners-appellants herein, died on June 13, 1956. Our decision will therefore, be entered *nunc pro tunc* as of the date we last recessed, June 8, 1956.

VAN VOORHIS, Judge (dissenting).

The majority opinion states that it is a general rule that a party cannot, in the same proceeding, rely upon a statute or retain benefits thereunder and attack its constitutionality. It seems to me that petitioners are being upheld in doing that in this proceeding. The opinion says that the uncon-stitutionality of subdivision (2) of section 19 of the Brighton zoning ordi-nance is not being adjudged; in reality, as it seems to me, that is the basis for this decision. Subdivision (2) of section 19 of the ordinance, in form, permits the erection and use in Class A residential districts of "Educational or Religious Building, Fire Station, Town Municipal Building, Police Station, Park and Park Buildings, *if approved by the Planning Board.*" (Italics supplied.) The planning board has denied approval. The evidence is ample to sustain the view that the proposed use will depreciate the value of real property and change the nature of the neighborhood, and create a traffic hazard at that location. The decisive question is whether those are standards of judgment which can govern the decision of the planning board. The truth is that the zoning ordinance lays down no standards of judgment and supplies no guides to decision in accordance with which the planning board shall act. For that reason, the constitutionality of this part of the ordinance is doubtful. Zoning ordinances are required to regulate the use of districts according to a comprehensive plan. It is not zoning when the ordinance is subject to amendment at will by some board whose action is not regulated and controlled by any prescribed principles of decision. Con-cordia Collegiate Inst. v. Miller, 301 N.Y. 189, 93 N.E.2d 632, 21 A.L.R.2d 544; Little v. Young, 299 N.Y. 699, 87 N.E.2d 74. As is mentioned in the majority opinion, an action for declaratory judgment is now pending unde-termined in which the constitutionality of this provision in the Brighton zoning ordinance is at issue. But either this part of the ordinance is con-stitutional or it is not, and if we are to assume, as the majority opinion says that it does, that it is valid *for the purposes of the proceeding which is now before the court*, that means that in this particular lawsuit the power of the Brighton planning board to deny its approval in proper cases is conceded. We cannot affirm and deny its power to act at the same time. The point seems to me to be that this appeal is in a proceeding with a limited objective, which is to compel approval by the planning board of this project by virtue of the same provision in the ordinance whose validity is attacked. If this subdivision (2) of section 19 of the ordinance is void, as it may be held to be in the pending declaratory judgment action, then it cannot supply authority to the planning board to grant the approval which petitioners are seeking to get from it in this proceeding. In asking for its approval, petitioners have necessarily conceded, for the purposes of this proceeding, that the planning board has power to act. If it had power to exercise discretion, then it had discretion to deny their application.

The majority opinion states, I am aware, that the planning board had some power to act, but acted arbitrarily and capriciously in denying approval to petitioners: in other words, that it abused its discretion as a matter of law. It is to be decided in the declaratory judgment action whether the planning board had power to act at all. If subdivision (2) of section 19 be held to be unconstitutional, the ordinance is to be read as though that subdivision were not contained in it. In that event, there could have been no abuse of discretion by the planning board, since it would have had no discretion to abuse. An abuse of discretion should not be confused with lack of power. If the planning board had discretion to exercise, I am unable to perceive how its discretion could have been abused in this instance. Upon the other hand, there is a substantial question, not now before the court, concerning whether this clause permitting religious and educational buildings subject to the approval of the planning board has validity. It is premature to decide that question now, as I believe that the court is doing. Under the majority view, it would hardly be possible for the planning board to deny approval of a religious or educational use in a Class A residential district upon any basis or upon any ground. If the board can do nothing but approve, that signifies that it lacks discretion and that its power is nullified. That is equivalent to holding that the clause in the zoning ordinance purporting to empower it to act is void, which should await decision in the declaratory judgment action in which the constitutionality is being tested. That is the customary method of procedure. Dowsey v. Village of Kensington, 257 N.Y. 221, 177 N.E. 427, 86 A.L.R. 642; Baddour v. City of Long Beach, 279 N.Y. 167, 18 N.E.2d 18, 124 A.L.R. 1003; Holy Sepulchre Cemetery v. Board of Appeals of Town of Greece, 271 App.Div. 33, 60 N.Y.S.2d 750.

The object in following that orderly procedure is more than merely formal. If the clause empowering the planning board to approve is unconstitutional, the whole of subdivision (2) of section 19 disappears from the ordinance. It cannot be held that the Brighton Town Board would have enacted this subdivision permitting religious, educational and other specified buildings without insisting upon approval by the planning board in the individual case. The rule has been accurately stated regarding the partial unconstitutionality of statutes that "if the void portion was the inducement of the passage of the act or is so interwoven in the texture of the statute as to preclude the idea that the remainder of the statute can be of operative fitness to effectuate the will of the legislature, the whole statute is rendered of no effect." McKinney's Consol.Laws of N. Y., Book 2, pt. 1, Constitutional Interpretation, § 48, citing People v. Mancuso, 255 N.Y. 463, 472-473, 175 N.E. 177, 180, 76 A.L.R. 514; Hauser v. North British & Mercantile Ins. Co., 206 N.Y. 455, 100 N.E. 52, 42 L.R.A., N.S., 1139, and many other cases to the same effect. Concordia Collegiate Inst. v. Miller, 301 N.Y. 189, 93 N.E.2d 632, 21 A.L.R.2d 544, supra, and Little v. Young, 299 N.Y. 699, 87 N.E.2d 74, supra, are in point in this regard. Those cases dealt with amendments to zoning ordinances. Both held the amendments to be wholly void, and enforced the ordinances as they had been prior to the amendments by directing the issuance of building permits. No building permit is applied for here.

It does not appear from this record that the Town of Brighton had any prior zoning ordinance containing a different provision respecting churches or schools in Class A residential districts. If subdivision (2) of section 19 were to be adjudged unconstitutional, the existing ordinance would stand without containing any valid clause upon that subject. In that event, the questions would be confronted whether it would be unconstitutional to prohibit the erection or use of churches and schools in this zoning district, and what comprises a constitutionally mandated religious or educational use. The courts of other States have had occasion to consider various phases of that subject. State ex rel. Synod of Ohio, etc. v. Joseph, 139 Ohio St. 229, 39 N.E.2d 515; State ex rel. Hacharedi v. Baxter, 148 Ohio St. 221, 74 N.E.2d 242; Ellsworth v. Gercke, 62 Ariz. 198, 156 P.2d 242; City of Sherman v. Simms, 143 Tex. 115, 183 S.W.2d 514; cf. Annotation, 138 A.L.R. 1287; Corporation of Presiding Bishop of Church of Jesus Christ of Latter-Day Saints v. City of Porterville, 90 Cal.App.2d 656, 203 P.2d 823; City of Chico v. First Ave. Baptist Church of Chico, 108 Cal.App.2d 297, 238 P.2d 587. That important issue should not be decided inferentially and summarily in this article 78 proceeding.

The order appealed from should be affirmed, with costs.

CONWAY, C. J., and DESMOND, DYE, FULD and BURKE, JJ., concur with FROESSEL, J.

VAN VOORHIS, J., dissents and votes to affirm in an opinon.

Order of the Appellate Division and that of Special Term reversed, the determinations of the planning board, the board of appeals and the town board of Town of Brighton annulled, as of June 8, 1956, and the matter remitted to those bodies for further proceedings not inconsistent with the opinon herein.

Questions and Notes

On Orchard Lake

1. What is the original source of the authority cited here to support a special position for schools and churches?

2. Note the realistic approach to mapping—that is, if a type of land use is excluded from that district which is mapped on all (or almost all) the vacant land, this is equivalent to total exclusion.

On Brighton

1. What were the planning board's reasons for opposing the proposed church at this location?

2. What was the court's answer to each of those?

CONCORDIA COLLEGIATE INSTITUTE

v.

MILLER

301 N.Y. 189, 93 N.E. 2d 632 (1950).

Court of Appeals of New York,

July 11, 1950.

Proceedings in the matter of the application of the Concordia Collegiate Institute for a mandamus order directing Rudolph N. Miller, as Superintendent of Buildings of the Village of Bronxville, to disregard a building zone ordinance and issue a permit for erection of a library, science building and auditorium by petitioner. The Supreme Court, Special Term, Westchester County, Frederick G. Schmidt, J., 88 N.Y.S.2d 825, denied the application and dismissed the proceeding on the merits, and petitioner appealed. The Supreme Court, Appellate Division, Second Department, entered an order December 27, 1949, 276 App.Div. 872, 93 N.Y.S.2d 922, which unanimously affirmed the resettled order of the Supreme Court, Special Term, and the petitioner appealed on constitutional grounds. The Court of Appeals, Froessel, J., held that amended zoning ordinance which withdrew unrestricted permission granted under original ordinance to use property in a residence district for educational purposes but authorized board of appeals to grant such permission provided petitioner filed consents duly acknowledged of 80 per cent of the owners of property fronting on the streets enclosing the block within which the property intended for such use lay was invalid, and the provisions of the original ordinance were restored insofar as the user in question was concerned, and since no triable issue of fact was presented the application of the petitioner would be granted.

Orders reversed and application granted with costs in Court of Appeals and in the Appellate Division.

Raphael Link and Raphael Link, Jr., Bronxville, for appellant.

G. Burchard Smith, Mineola, and Arnold Frye and Barent L. Visscher, New York City, for respondent.

FROESSEL, Judge.

Petitioner-appellant is a nonprofit, domestic educational corporation under the supervision of the State Education Department. It has continuously owned and operated its property in the village of Bronxville, New York, as a school and campus site for about forty years. It purchased the property with the intent of using the whole of the site for a school program and of erecting thereon such buildings as from time to time it might deem necessary. As a duly chartered preparatory school and junior college, with nearly three hundred full-time students, its facilities have become inadequate and it is necessary that it expand. It has thus far invested upwards of a million and a half dollars in this property, and has provided additional funds for the erection of new school buildings on its present campus site in furtherance of the requirements and rules of the State Education Department. When it purchased the site in 1909, the land adjacent thereto consisted of farms and vacant acreage. The surrounding neighborhood is now built up with private residences.

In 1938 the Village of Bronxville enacted a zoning ordinance dividing the village into six residence districts and three business districts. Petitioner's property was placed in a residence "A" district. An "Educational or religious building" was expressly permitted by the ordinance (art. 3, § 1, subd. [b]) in residence districts. On February 10, 1941, an amendment to the zoning ordinance was adopted, repealing said subdivision (b), and in place thereof adding subdivision (f) to section 7 of article 12 of the ordinance providing for "Variances" which might be permitted by the board of appeals, as follows: "(f) Permit in any residence district the erection or alteration of a building for educational, religious or eleemosynary purposes and the use of premises for such purposes provided the petitioner files the consents duly acknowledged of 80% of the owners of property fronting on the streets enclosing the block within which lies the property intended for such use."

As a result of this amendment, assuming it to be valid, no educational building may be erected as a matter of right on petitioner's property, nor indeed in any of the residence districts which comprise 97% of the village territory. The remaining 3%—a very small area of about nineteen acres bordering on the tracks of the Harlem Division of the New York Central Railroad and situated at the other end of the village—is zoned for business, and no land is available in that area; but, even if available, it would be quite impracticable for petitioner to use any of such property. Thus petitioner is in effect precluded from erecting any school building in the entire village as a matter of right, and, while boardinghouses, multifamily houses, hospitals and hotels may be erected in residence districts, schools and churches may not.

On or about July 1, 1948, petitioner filed plans and specifications for the new school library, science building and auditorium on its campus site and applied for a permit. Respondent denied the application upon the ground that the uses of the proposed new buildings were not permitted.

In this article 78 proceeding, petitioner seeks a mandamus order directing respondent to issue a permit to erect the proposed buildings. On the pleadings and accompanying papers, Special Term, upon respondent's motion to dismiss grounded on legal insufficiency, held that no triable issue of fact was raised, denied the relief sought, and dismissed the proceeding on the merits; the Appellate Division unanimously affirmed.

Petitioner's proposed use is clearly not a permitted use under the amended ordinance, for, concededly, its property is within a residence "A" district. There is no issue between the parties as to the right of the village to regulate and restrict the location and use of buildings, structures and land for trade, industry, residence or other purposes for "the purpose of promoting the health, safety, morals, or the general welfare of the community." Village Law, Consol.Laws, c. 64, § 175. Petitioner, however, challenges the constitutionality of the zoning amendment adopted February 10, 1941, insofar as it affects petitioner, upon the ground that it is arbitrary, unreasonable and confiscatory and violates the Fourteenth Amendment of the Constitution of the United States and section 6 of article I of our State Constitution. It contends (1) that the provision requiring consents from 80% of the adjoining owners, before the board of appeals is even empowered to consider an application, imposes a restriction on an inoffensive and legitimate use of property, not by a legislative body but by other property owners, and that such delegation of power is repugnant to the due process clause; (2) that, even if such consents were obtain, the amendment would be bad, since the board of appeals is given no standards or guides to exercise its discretion as to what "educational, religious or eleemosynary purposes" may be permitted, and (3) that the ordinance as amended discriminates between public and private schools, and virtually bars schools as well as churches from the village.

[1] We are of the opinion that the 1941 amendment of the zoning ordinance is invalid. According to its provisions, it withdrew the unrestricted permission granted under the original ordinance to use property in a residence district for educational purposes, but authorized the board of appeals to grant such permission "provided the petitioner files the consents duly acknowledged of 80% of the owners of property fronting on the streets enclosing the block within which lies the property intended for such use." Without such consents, the board of appeals had absolutely no power under said subdivision (f). A fraction over 20% of the adjoining property owners could prevent any action by the board and they could thus finally determine, even by inaction, the kind of use that petitioner might make of its

property. Against that restriction not only petitioner but the board itself would be powerless. The action of such dissenting or indifferent owners is subject to no guides or standards and to no rule whatsoever.

In Eubank v. City of Richmond, 226 U.S. 137, 33 S.Ct. 76, 57 L.Ed. 156, Ann.Cas. 1914B, 192, where a statute required the "committee on streets" upon request of the owners of two thirds of the abutting property to establish a building line, the court said, 226 U.S. at pp. 143-144, 33 S.Ct. at page 77: "One set of owners determines not only the extent of use but the kind of use which another set of owners may make of their property. In what way is the public safety, convenience, or welfare served by conferring such power? The statute and ordinance, while conferring the power on some property holders to virtually control and dispose of the property rights of others, creates no standard by which the power thus given is to be exercised; in other words, the property holders who desire and have the authority to establish the line may do so solely for their own interest, or even capriciously." See, also, Carter v. Carter Coal Co., 298 U.S. 238, 311, 56 S.Ct. 855, 80 L.Ed. 1160.

A situation somewhat similar to the instant case was presented in Washington ex rel. Seattle Tit. Trust Co. v. Roberge, 278 U.S. 116, 49 S.Ct. 50, 73 L.Ed. 210, 86 A.L.R. 654. In that case, plaintiff trustee owned and maintained a philanthropic home for aged poor, and desired to erect a new building in place of a smaller old building at a cost of about one hundred thousand dollars. The local zoning ordinance did not permit a philanthropic home for aged poor in a "First Residence District," wherein the home was situated. The ordinance was amended in 1925 by permitting such a home "when the written consent shall have been obtained of the owners of two-thirds of the property within four hundred (400) feet of the proposed building." 278 U.S. at page 118, 49 S.Ct. at page 50. The trustee of the home sought unsuccessfully to procure a permit without having obtained the required consents. The State courts held the amendment valid, but they were reversed by the Supreme Court of the United States, which posed and answered the following question, 278 U.S. at page 120, 49 S.Ct. at page 51: "Is the delegation of power to owners of adjoining land to make inoperative the permission, given by § 3(c) as amended, repugnant to the due process clause?"

It held, 278 U.S. at pages 121-122, 49 S.Ct. at page 52: "Legislatures may not, under the guise of the police power impose restrictions that are unnecessary and unreasonable upon the use of private property or the pursuit of useful activities. * * * The facts disclosed by the record make it clear that the exclusion of the new home from the first district is not indispensable to the general zoning plan. And there is no legislative determination that the proposed building and use would be inconsistent with public health, safety, morals or general welfare. The enactment itself plainly implies the contrary. * * * The section purports to give the owners of less than one-half the land within 400 feet of the proposed building authority—uncontrolled by any standard or rule prescribed by legislative action—to prevent the trustee from using its land for the proposed home. The superintendent is bound by the decision or inaction of such owners. There is no provision for review under the ordinance; their failure to give consent is final. They are not bound by any official duty, but are free to withhold consent for selfish reasons or arbitrarily and may subject the trustee to their will or caprice. ° ° ° The delegation of power so attempted is repugnant to the due process clause of the Fourteenth Amendment."

The court distinguished the case of Cusack Co. v. City of Chicago, 242 U.S. 526, 37 S.Ct. 190, 61 L.Ed. 472, L.R.A. 1918A, 136, Ann.Cas.1917C, 594, involving billboards in residential districts, pointing out that billboards were liable to endanger the safety and decency of such districts, and that such billboards or other uses which by reason of their nature were liable to be offensive, were quite different from a home for the poor.

[2, 3] In the case now before us, we are not dealing with billboards or garages or other offensive uses in connection with which consent provisions may be proper, but with an educational use which is clearly in furtherance of the health, safety, morals and general welfare of the community, and is under the direct supervision, care and concern of the State itself. Zoning ordinances must find their justification in the police power exercised in the interest of the public. Village of Euclid v. Ambler Realty Co., 272 U.S. 365, 387, 47 S.Ct. 114, 71 L.Ed. 303, 54 A.L.R. 1016. "The governmental power to interfere by zoning regulations with the general rights of the land owner by restricting the character of his use, is not unlimited, and other questions aside, such restriction cannot be imposed if it does not bear a substantial relation to the public health, safety, morals, or general welfare." Nectow v. City of Cambridge, 277 U.S. 183, 188, 48 S.Ct. 447, 448, 72 L.Ed. 842.

Moreover, even though 80% of the adjoining property owners consented, the board of appeals in the instant case was given no standards or guides to exercise its discretion as to what "educational, religious or eleemosynary purposes" may be permitted. Respondent in his brief suggests numerous instances of educational institutions which he deems objectionable, yet the board is given no guide; to it is committed an unfettered and unrestricted discretion to approve or reject proposed educational uses. It has been repeatedly held that this may not be done. Matter of Little v. Young, 299 N.Y. 699, 87 N.E.2d 74; Packer Collegiate Inst. v. University of State of New York, 298 N.Y. 184, 81 N.E.2d 80; Matter of Small v. Moss, 279 N.Y. 288, 295, 18 N.E.2d 281, 283; Panama Refining Co. v. Ryan, 293 U.S. 388, 55 S.Ct. 241, 79 L.Ed. 446.

This disposes of respondent's claim that petitioner must seek relief under the 1941 amendment. His further contention that petitioner could obtain relief upon a proper showing of hardship, Village Law, § 179-b, is likewise without validity. Petitioner's property is in a residence zone, and it frankly concedes—what is in fact evident— that it cannot demonstrate that its land will not yield a reasonable return if used only for the purpose allowed in that zone, namely, for residences. Therefore, it asserts, it could not obtain a variance on the ground of hardship under our decisions, such as Matter of Otto v. Steinhilber, 282 N.Y. 71, 24 N.E.2d 851, and Matter of Hickox v. Griffin, 298 N.Y. 365, 83 N.E.2d 836, and even if the board of appeals should grant its application, the variance would be a nullity, and by no means immune from attack by owners of adjoining property.

In short, petitioner urges that it should not be compelled to seek as a matter of grace and special privilege what at best is an extremely unlikely result, in the face of an invalid statute that stands in the way of relief as a matter of right; the restriction itself constitutes an invasion of its property rights. Dowsey v. Village of Kensington, 257 N.Y. 221, 231, 177 N.E. 427, 430, 86 A.L.R. 642. Petitioner's contention in this respect is sound, and we are accordingly constrained to conclude that the amendment of February 10, 1941, violates the due process clause of the Fourteenth Amendment of the Federal Constitution and section 6 of article I of our State Constitution.

[4] The question still remains, however, whether, with the amendment eliminated, petitioner is entitled to issuance of the permit requested, since the 1941 amendment also repealed subdivision (b) of section 1 of article 3. The precise question was presented in Matter of Little v. Young, supra, where we affirmed the lower courts, which held that since the provision requiring approval was invalid, the accompanying repealing provisions also failed, and there remained no limitation in the ordinance upon an otherwise lawful use. In other words, since the 1941 amendment is invalid, the provisions of the 1938 ordinance are restored insofar as the user here in question is concerned. The local legislature in adding the 1941 amendment evinced no desire to bar permits for educational buildings. It recognized an educational use as harmonious with the public interest—and who indeed could consider it otherwise—but made it subject to the consent and approval hereinbefore outlined, which we find invalid. Hence, no limitation remains.

It is unnecessary to consider the remaining questions presented, such as the village's right to bar schools absolutely from residential districts and its right to discriminate between private and public schools. We do not reach these questions, and therefore need not decide them.

The orders of the Appellate Division and Special Terms should be reversed, and, since no triable issue of fact is presented, the application of petitioner should be granted, with costs in this court and in the Appellate Division.

The orders should be reversed and the application granted, with costs in this court and in the Appellate Division.

LOUGHRAN, C. J., and LEWIS, CONWAY, DESMOND, DYE and FULD, JJ., concur.

Orders reversed, etc.

Questions and Notes

1. What provision of the Bronxville zoning ordinance was involved here?

2. What kind of community facility was proposed here?

3. Under this ordinance, did the neighbors have an absolute veto, or was their opinion merely advisory?

4. This case is the origin of the New York doctrine that community facilities promote the general welfare, and therefore that their exclusion cannot be upheld on the ground that such exclusion would promote the general welfare. In this connection see also Rogers v. Association for the Help of Retarded Children, 308 N.Y. 126, 123 N.E.2d 806 (1954), involving a change of nonconforming use.

CROSS-REFERENCES

In Anderson, see §§ 9.02-9.07 and Index under "Public Uses."
In Hagman, see §§ 67-73.
In McQuillin, see Index under specific heading.
In Rathkopf, see ch. 18, 19, and see Index under "Hospital."
In Williams, see ch. 75-81.
In Yokley, see §§ 28-1 to 28-37.

M.   Zoning for Open Space

MORRIS COUNTY LAND IMPROVEMENT COMPANY

v.

PARSIPPANY-TROY HILLS

40 N.J. 539, 193 A.2d 232(1963).

Supreme Court of New Jersey.

Argued March 18 and 19, 1963.

Decided July 23, 1963.

Proceeding respecting constitutional validity of township zoning ordinance provisions restricting use of swampland. The Law Division sustained provisions and the appeal was certified before it was heard in the Appellate Division. The Supreme Court, Hall, J., held that township zoning ordinance which greatly restricted use of swampland and had for prime object retention of land substantially in its natural state, essentially for public purposes such as floodwater detention basin and preservation of wetland wildlife sanctuary, constituted a taking of land for public purpose without just compensation and was unconstitutional.

Reversed and remanded for entry of judgment consistent with opinion.

John T. Dolan, Newark, for plaintiff-appellant (Crummy, Gibbons & O'Neill, Newark, attorneys, John T. Dolan, Newark, of counsel).

Herbert S. Glickman, Morristown, for defendant-respondent (Scerbo, Hegarty, Mintz, Glickman, Kobin & Howe, Morristown, attorneys, Herbert S. Glickman, Morristown, on the brief).

The opinion of the court was delivered by

HALL, J.

The fundamental question in this case is the constitutional validity of provisions of defendant township's zoning ordinance which greatly restrict the use of swampland and have for their prime object the retention of the land substantially in its natural state, essentially for public purposes. The provisions not only control land uses in the district, but also strictly regulate any reclamation or improvement of land therein. The Law Division sustained the provisions in a prerogative writ action brought by the plaintiff, a land owner within the area. We certified its appeal on our own motion before it was heard in the Appellate Division.

Parsippany-Troy Hills is a large, sprawling township in Morris County, with a great quantity of vacant land, which has in late years undergone very considerable development activity, accompanied by concomitant increase in population, with the usually resultant problems of planning and zoning. A fuller description of the municipality and a chronology of land use regulation therein may be found in Newark Milk and Cream Co. v. Township of Parsippany-Troy Hills, 47 N.J.Super. 306, 321-327, 135 A.2d 682 (Law Div.1957).

The particular area here involved is a large swamp of 1500 or more acres known as Troy Meadows. It is located mostly in the southeasterly corner of the township extending to some extent easterly into East Hanover Township and to a slight degree southerly across the boundary of Hanover Township. It and other similar formations in nearby municipalities represent the remaining parts of what was once Lake Passaic, a huge body of water formed eons ago by action of the last glacier in blocking the original channel of the Passaic River. Now, Troy Meadows slowly drains, by means of small streams and man-made ditches running through it, into tributaries of the present Passaic River and forms a portion of that river's basin.

As might be expected, the elevation of the area is low in relation to the surrounding land and considerably below the grade of the roads encircling or running through it. The terrain is typical swampland, with a high water table and marsh grass and cattail vegetation. The surface soil is black or dark brown muck and peat, two to six feet deep, wet and very unstable. The second stratum, from two to four feet in thickness, consists of clay and silt materials which drain poorly and are highly compressible in nature. The bottom layer is composed of sand and gravel, found, on the average, seven or eight feet beneath the surface. The testimony in the case is uncontradicted that the two top layers will not bear structures, are unsuitable for fill and would have to be removed and the land filled with proper material before it could be used for any active purpose, except possibly the raising of fish or the growing of aquatic plants.

At the present time, there are practically no active land uses in the Parsippany-Troy Hills portion of the area. About 75% of it is owned by Wildlife Preserves, Inc. (Wildlife), a private noncommercial, but tax-paying corporation, interested in conservation and preservation of the natural state of the area as a public or *quasi*-public wildlife sanctuary and nature study refuge. This organization has been energetic and apparently quite influential in urging the local authorities to restrict use of all of the land accordingly. It has even opposed filling of any of the land on the basis that the effect of the fill on the water would be biologically adverse to the conservation of wildlife.

There is no doubt that the area in its present state, acting essentially as a sponge, constitutes a natural detention basin for flood waters in times of very heavy rainfall, which would otherwise run off more quickly and aggravate damaging flood conditions occurring with some frequency in municipalities farther down the Passaic River valley. During such periods, Troy Meadows itself is flooded to some extent, but apparently with little, if any, effect on surrounding higher land.

Plaintiff's property consists of 66 acres in the lower corner of the meadows, fronting several hundred feet on Perrine (or Troy) Road, a dirt highway which is the boundary line in this section with Hanover Township. This acreage is part of a large tract, the balance of which is located across the road in Hanover. The entire parcel was acquired in 1952. The Hanover portion consisted mostly of high land, with a small amount of swamp near the road. At the time of acquisition and since, it has been zoned for industrial use. Plaintiff operates a sand and gravel business at the location in Hanover and has filled in the swamp portion of its property in that township with overburden and other unusable material from the sand and gravel pit.

At the time of acquisition, plaintiff's 66 acres in Parsippany-Troy Hills, along with the rest of Troy Meadows, was zoned, like the high land to the west, in the most restrictive residential classification under the township's original zoning ordinance adopted in 1945. The validity of the inclusion of the swamp in such a zone is indeed most doubtful, but apparently it was never attacked and, since no one would build an expensive home in a marsh, it served the practical purpose of precluding all development.

In 1954 an amendment to the zoning ordinance established "The Indeterminate Zone Classification * * * to cover such parts of the Township as Troy Meadows, where the nature of the land is such that its most appropriate future use is dependent on decisions by others than the government of the Township, such as with respect to flood control, and any change of present use and condition should be subject to special and individual consideration." The amendment forbade any new use, or change in existing use except for agricultural purposes or the growing of fish, water fowl and water plants, and also forbade any dumping or other disposal of material or any change in the natural or existing grade of the land, without the obtaining of a special permit from the Township Committee. From the evidence in the instant case, it is apparent that these almost "freezing" regulations were enacted as a stopgap or interim measure with the expectation or hope that higher governmental authority might well acquire the area as part of a large and much discussed flood control project to benefit the entire Passaic Valley—a project which has not yet come to pass.

Plaintiff attempted no utilization whatever of its Parsippany-Troy Hills land from 1952 until June 1959 when it commenced to fill along the edge of the road with overburden and excess material from the gravel pit operation, without obtaining any permit. Wildlife made a complaint against it in the Municipal Court for violation of the indeterminate zone regulations. While the complaint was pending, plaintiff unsuccessfully applied to the governing body to rezone its property for industrial use. Thereafter, in January 1960, plaintiff was granted a limited permission by the Township Committee to place fill to a depth of 300 feet from Perrine Road at its own risk, since the matter of the revision of land uses in the area was then under study by the township. This permission was conditioned upon submission to, and approval by, the Township Engineer of a sketch showing grades. Plaintiff resumed filling, but did not submit the sketch.

In March 1960, after an extended consideration of the meadows area by planning consultants and township officials, the indeterminate zone provisions were repealed and a new zoning classification created for the area under the title "Meadows Development Zone." The first paragraph of the new regulations set forth the purpose:

> "The Meadows Development Zone classification is established to be applied to areas of the Township with a high water table. These areas can perform a function for the Township of Parsippany-Troy Hills, if they are properly regulated in their uses. Therefore, the following special regulations become necessary to provide for the most appropriate uses of land in the district which will permit development in harmony with its character and the regional requirements for the area."

The new regulations permitted the following uses as of right: agricultural uses; raising of woody or herbaceous plants; commercial greenhouses; raising of aquatic plants, fish and fish food (with a one-family dwelling as an adjunct to any of these uses, provided its lowest floor was a specified distance above flood level); outdoor recreational uses operated by a governmental division or agency; conservation uses "including drainage control, forestry, wildlife sanctuaries and facilities for making same available and useful to the public"; hunting and fishing preserves; public utility transmission lines and substations; radio or television transmitting stations and antenna towers; and township sewage treatment plants and water supply facilities.

The section went on to provide for what were designated as "uses which may be permitted as special exceptions by the Board of Adjustment under R.S. 40:55-39(b)," with the following preamble:

> "* * * In determining whether a special exception shall be granted, the Board shall apply the standards set forth for each particular use and, in addition, shall determine that in its development and operation the proposed use will conform to the general purposes for which the district is established, and will not impair present or potential use of adjacent properties, as may be permitted under the terms of this section."

These so-called permitted uses amounted, for the most part, to strict regulation of land reclamation in aid of uses allowed as of right.[1] Thus, a special exception, with particular conditions, was required for any permitted use which involved a change in any drainage ditch, for the removal of earth products, such as gravel, sand, fill-dirt and peat, and for the diking, damming or filling of any land within the zone with an existing elevation of less than 175 feet above sea level (apparently this limitation would encompass practically all the land in the zone). The standards and conditions for exceptions to permit removal of earth products and filling included intricate site plan approval by the Planning Board together with studies and reports by other township officials and agencies before favorable action could be taken by the Board of Adjustment. Moreover, no filling was allowed except by the use of material taken from land within

---

1. It may be, although we need not pass upon the question, that the restrictions on land reclamation, in some aspects at least, exceed the proper bounds of a zoning ordinance as being beyond the general purposes and powers of zoning, N.J.S.A. 40:55-30, 31 and 32, and are more appropriately the subject of a separate non-zoning ordinance. If this be the case, they would amount to exercise of other aspects of the police power, see e.g., R.S. 40:48-1(21) and 40:48-2 N.J.S.A. akin to soil removal and excavation ordinances. See Fred v. Mayor and Council of Borough of Old Tappan, 10 N.J. 515, 92 A.2d 473 (1952); L. P. Marron & Co. v. Township of Mahwah, 39 N.J. 74, 187 A.2d 593 (1963); Wulster v. Borough of Upper Saddle River, 41 N.J. Super. 199, 124 A.2d 323 (App. Div. 1956), certif. denied 22 N.J. 268, 125 A.2d 753 (1956). In this event, their validity would have to be tested accordingly, even though included in a zoning ordinance, and the provisions of the zoning enabling act authorizing the granting of variances, N.J.S.A. 40:55-39(c) and (d), and protecting nonconforming uses, R.S. 40:55-48, N.J.S.A., would have no application. As to the latter, cf. Welsh v. Town of Morristown, 98 N.J.L. 630, 633-635, 121 A. 697 (Sup. Ct. 1923), affirmed o.b., sub nom. Welsh v. Potts, 99 N.J.L. 528, 124 A. 926 (E. & A. 1924). For purposes of this case, it is sufficient that we assume all the Meadows Development Zone regulations to be properly included in the zoning ordinance.

the zone. In addition, approval was required of ponds and lakes which would inevitably be created by a filling operation (since the fill had to come from within the zone and the only suitable material was the sand and gravel found below the first two strata of soil).

The removal of earth products from the zone, as a use in itself, previously permitted, became prohibited by an amendment of these provisions in June 1960. This forbade such removal on a commercial or profit basis and completely banned taking earth products beyond the boundaries of the zone.[2]

Plaintiff continued to fill its lands after the adoption of the Meadows Development Zone provisions, without municipal authorization, until further complaints made by Wildlife put an end to the work. By that time the fill extended 1000 feet or more along the road to a depth of 150 feet or greater. It then applied to the Board of Adjustment in August 1960 for a special exception, allegedly in accordance with the ordinance, to fill its lands further as shown on a map submitted, to excavate for an 18-acre reservoir of unspecified depth, to use the material taken therefrom to supply the fill and to sell the excess to defray the cost of the operation. Since the application sought leave to do things forbidden by the ordinance, it amounted also to a request for variance. The application was ultimately denied in January 1961. This suit against the township and the Board of Adjustment followed.

The complaint asserted three causes of action, the first two against the township. The first count charged, in effect, that the Meadows Development Zone provisions of March 1960 and the June 1960 amendment thereto amounted to a taking of plaintiff's property without compensation and sought a declaration that they were unconstitutional and void. The second asked for an adjudication that plaintiff had acquired a nonconforming use of vacant land prior to the adoption of the meadowland zone provisions. The third count, directed against the Board of Adjustment, demanded that body's refusal to grant the special exception to fill and excavate be set aside as unreasonable and arbitrary.

---

2. The amendment also required adherence to the requirements of the township's soil removal ordinance. This ordinance, adopted in 1956, is not contained in the record, so the full extent of the intended interplay with the meadows zone provisions is not known to us. An amendment, passed in July 1960, was introduced in evidence, however. It absolutely prohibited the excavation or removal of earth, clay, rock, sand, gravel, top soil or soil for sale or for use other than on the premises from which taken, except in connection with the construction of buildings and in certain other instances not here pertinent. We presume the purpose of the amendment was to take out of the soil removal ordinance the usual provision found in such enactments allowing soil removal from premises upon the grant of a permit by municipal authorities, see L. P. Marron & Co. v. Township of Mahwah, 39 N.J. 74, 187 A.2d 593 (1963), and thus to coincide with the meadows ordinance provision prohibiting removal from the zone, as well as adding the further restriction against removal from the particular premises. Since no atack is made on the amendment to the soil removal ordinance, we need not specifically consider it further.

Taking the last count first, the trial judge held that the Board's action was not arbitrary or unreasonable and found a clear inference that the application to excavate for the 18-acre reservoir and to fill the land was in reality an attempt to extend plaintiff's sand and gravel business from across Perrine Road in Hanover Township to its land in the meadows by utilizing the unsalable material from the reservoir excavation to fill the remaining land and selling the marketable sand and gravel therefrom in its usual course of business. Plaintiff has not appealed from this portion of the judgment so this phase of the case need not be discussed further. We note in passing that the Board of Adjustment was very properly represented by separate counsel in the trial court.

[1] Plaintiff has raised a question not presented below which may well be disposed of at this juncture. It contends that a visit to the locale by the trial judge without notice to or the accompaniment of counsel constitutes reversible error as a matter of law. The testimony in the case had been concluded in the afternoon and court was adjourned until the next day when the judge was to render his oral decision. After adjournment the judge inspected the area in the company of a court officer, a native of the vicinity. The next morning he advised counsel of his visit, and put his observations on the record as a viewing judge is always under a duty to do, inquiring whether there were any corrections or comments. Plaintiff's counsel made no objection nor said anything.

[2] We see no merit whatever in the contention. It is obvious from the court's report of his view that the object of the visit was only to better understand the evidence. There is no question of the right of a trial judge sitting without a jury to inspect a site for this purpose. Peoples Trust Company v. Board of Adjustment of Borough of Hasbrouck Heights, 60 N.J.Super. 569, 576, 160 A.2d 63 (App.Div. 1959). Indeed, in many types of cases involving physical facts which may not be clearly portrayed by the spoken word, it is most desirable, if not almost imperative, that he do so, particularly where, as here, no photographs or meaningful maps were included in the proofs. The judge must not, however, under the present law in this State governed by the principle of the exclusiveness of the record, base his decision on facts ascertained from his personal inspection. Second Reformed Church v. Board of Adjustment of Borough of Freehold, 30 N.J.Super. 338, 104 A.2d 703 (App.Div. 1954).

[3] We find nothing in the trial court's report of his visit or in his oral opinion indicating in the slightest that he learned or relied upon facts *dehors* the proofs. Plaintiff does not point to anything contrariwise, but suggests there is no way of knowing for certain and that the possibility can only be avoided by a reversal. In effect, this position would practically preclude any view of a locale made by a trial court sitting without a jury. A judge must be relied upon to have made full disclosure as to the scope and results of his inspection. "* * * [W]e must assume that every judge * * * places truth above pride, and will shun the burden of conscious

wrong. The judicial process depends upon that faith." State v. LaPierre, 39 N.J. 156, 164, 188 A.2d 10, 14 (1963). While a judge should not make an inspection without giving all counsel notice of his intention and the opportunity to be present, there was no prejudicial error in this case.

Next to be considered is plaintiff's claim that it acquired a valid non-conforming use prior to the adoption of the Meadows Development Zone provisions in March 1960. This contention rests upon the filling of a small portion of its lands between June 1959 and March 1960 and the alleged in-validity of the 1954 indeterminate zone classification, which forbade even land reclamation without a special permit. (The permit for limited filling granted plaintiff in January 1960 under the indeterminate zone provisions is of no help to it since it admittedly did not comply with the prerequisite specified therein). The trial court found it unnecessary to pass upon the validity of the 1954 ordinance provisions, since it held that the land filling did not constitute a use within the contemplation of R.S. 40:55-48, N.J.S.A., permitting the continuance of nonconforming uses or structures existing at the time of passage of a zoning ordinance.

[4, 5] There are many reasons why plaintiff's claim cannot be sustained. We need only mention that given by the trial court, which is unquestionably sound. Filling land otherwise not usable is obviously not in and of itself an "existing use" cf it in the statutory sense; here it amounted, at most, only to preparation for some indefinite and conjectural future use. Plaintiff's evidence conceded as much, its vice-president testifying: "We hadn't made any use at the time. We were aiming to make a use of it." The aimed use was "[t]o improve the land for industrial purposes." This is clearly not enough to come under the statutory umbrella. "* * * [I]t is an existing *use occupying* the land, that the statute protects; the statute does not deal in mere intentions." Martin v. Cestone, 33 N.J.Super. 267, 269, 110 A.2d 54, 56 (App.Div.1954); Ardolino v. Florham Park Board of Adjustment, 24 N.J. 94, 104, 130 A.2d 847 (1957).

This brings us to the important and decisive question in the case—the matter of the validity of the 1960 Meadows Development Zone provisions. Plaintiff's attack is full-scale and is not confined to unconstitutional effect of the regulations as applied to its property. The trial court decided the issue this way:

> "There is no question at all but that the township governing council was conscious of the physical nature of this area and that it was concerned about the danger of flooding. There is a limit to fill without adequate safeguards. The ordinance here is predicated on the physical nature of the area to a substantial extent. The land at the present time is not suitable for any intensive use.

> *   *   *

> * * * I am mindful of the cases cited by the plaintiff which condemn action by a municipality through zoning to, in effect, acquire lands for public use. That is what the contention of the plaintiff here is, that this

ordinance, in effect, is designed to aid flood control in the area at the expense of the plaintiff ° ° °.

But I think that considering the entire problem presented, considering the nature of the immediate and the surrounding area, that the presumption of validity has not been overcome by the plaintiff and I will hold that the ordinance represents a reasonable exercise of the power to zone."

We find ourselves in fundamental disagreement with this conclusion.

There cannot be the slightest doubt from the evidence that the prime object of the zone regulations is to retain the land substantially in its natural state. As we have already said, the testimony is uncontradicted that the character of the surface soil is such that it is unsuited for any of the permitted uses, except possibly the raising of fish and aquatic plants. The first two layers would have to be removed and replaced with proper fill which would support structures where the use involved the construction of buildings, and with appropriate top soil where agriculture and similar soil uses were contemplated. And land reclamation along these lines is, for all practical purposes, rendered impossible. Apart from the matter of having to obtain permission subject to exceedingly difficult conditions, the regulations absolutely prohibit not only the removal of the unusable top two layers of earth from the zone (and, indeed, even from the particular premises within the zone under the amendment to the soil removal ordinance), but also forbid the importation from outside the zone of suitable fill material or soil. As a practical matter, the only available method seems to be to dredge fill material from the bottom stratum of sand and gravel in some other portion of the premises (which however, does not have the qualities of fertile top soil) and to fill the excavation as far as possible with the unusable upper layers from the area being excavated and filled. Even then it appears that a pond or a lake would probably result in the unfilled portion of the excavation because of the high water table. And the regulations also require approval of such a formation. Moreover, the regulations further provide that earth removal will be permitted only if it "will not impair the present and potential use of adjacent properties." This might well become another block to any land reclamation since, it will be recalled, Wildlife has objected to any filling on the ground of an adverse biological effect on the water and the swamp creatures in its sanctuary.

In addition, it will be noted that many of the previously listed permitted uses in the zone are public or *quasi*-public in nature, rather than of the type available to the ordinary private landowner as a reasonable means of obtaining a return from his property, i.e., outdoor recreational uses to be operated only by some governmental unit, conservation uses and activities, township sewage treatment plants and water facilities and public utility transmission lines, substations and radio and television transmitting stations and towers. All in all, about the only practical use which can be made of property in the zone is a hunting or fishing preserve or a wildlife sanctuary, none of which can be considered productive.

One has to conclude that the uses to which a private landowner may put h's property in the zone under the 1960 regulations are little more favorable to him than the almost "freezing" provisions which controlled the area when subject to the stop-gap Indeterminate Zone regulations. One also has the strong feeling that the ordinance changes made in 1960 were adopted essentially, not to benefit the landowner or to permit practical change in the natural state of the area, but rather because it was considered, and quite properly so, that the indeterminate zone provisions were or had become invalid for any number of reasons.

It is equally obvious from the proofs, and legally of the highest significance that the main purpose of enacting regulations with the practical effect of retaining the meadows in their natural state was for a public benefit. This benefit is twofold, with somewhat interrelated aspects: first, use of the area as a water detention basin in aid of flood control in the lower reaches of the Passaic Valley far beyond this municipality; and second, preservation of the land as open space for the benefits which would accrue to the local public from an undeveloped use such as that of a nature refuge by Wildlife (which paid taxes on it).

This prime public, rather than private, utilization can be clearly implied from the purpose sections of the zone regulations previously quoted. And it is established beyond any question by the testimony of the township's own witnesses. The Chief Engineer and Acting Director of the Division of Water Policy and Supply of the State Department of Conservation and Economic Development testified, in effect, that the ordinance provisions were soundly and reasonably conceived from the scientific standpoint to accomplish this flood alleviation purpose. He said that artificial filling of natural retention storage areas automatically increases the magnitude and volume of flood downstream and that limiting excavation to the area would result in retention of the capacity for natural storage. He was careful to point out, however, "that there is such a thing as an abuse of zoning police power. * * * [W]hen land is acquired for some specific purpose it is not proper necessarily to do it through the zoning police powers but should be done through purchase."

The township's expert planning consultant, who made the area studies and drafted and recommended to the municipal council the Meadows Development Zone ordinance provisions adopted in March 1960, testified that one of the main considerations was the vital function the area serves as a detention basin "in flood control in the overall Passaic Valley region"—and that another was to retain its natural state to "provide necessary open space, green space, in the developing of the suburban area." The Assistant Director of the Morris County Planning Board, who had also made studies of the area incorporated in a report and recommendations to the township, testified similarly and said, in effect, that this township was fortunate because Wildlife had acquired considerable amounts of property which were being utilized in a passive type of recreational use, whereas other municipalities "would have to go out and buy it." Both men spoke of consultation with Wildlife and virtual adoption of the views and area uses suggested by that organization in arriving at their recommendations. It is fair to conclude from the proofs that any other factors which were taken into consideration in arriving at the detailed regulations were clearly subordinate to these two public purposes.

[6, 7] Private property may not, of course, to be taken for public use without just compensation. N.J.Const., Art. I, par. 20. The measures here adopted to accomplish public benefits do not amount to a direct or outright taking, as were those struck down in Grosso v. Board of Adjustment of Millburn Township, 137 N.J.L. 630, 61 A.2d 167 (Sup.Ct.1948), where use of the plaintiff's property was precluded by placing the lot in the bed of a proposed street on the official map; in Hager v. Louisville & Jefferson County Planning & Zoning Commission, 261 S.W.2d 619 (Ky.Ct.App.1953), where the plaintiff's land was rendered useless by zoning it as ponding areas for temporary storage basins in accordance with a flood control plan; and in Miller v. City of Beaver Falls, 368 Pa. 189, 82 A.2d 34 (Sup.Ct.1951), where private utilization of the tract was inhibited for a period of years, pursuant to a statute, by its inclusion in a territory encompassed by an ordinance adopting a general plan for present and future parks.

But a taking may as well occur indirectly through excessive regulation under the police power. Thus, in Yara Engineering Corp. v. City of Newark, 132 N.J.L. 370, 40 A.2d 559 (Sup.Ct.1945), a so-called airport zoning ordinance, which restricted the height of structures within designated distances of an airport and otherwise regulated use of such property so as not to endanger or interfere with the landing or takeoff of aircraft, was held unconstitutional as amounting to an appropriation of rights in private property which could only be acquired by eminent domain. And in Joint Meeting of the City of Plainfield v. Borough of Middlesex, 69 N.J.Super. 136, 173 A.2d 785 (Law Div.1961), defendant zoned plaintiff's property exclusively for school, park and playground use as a method of depreciating its value for purposes of municipal purchase. The zoning was held invalid as unconstitutionally depriving the owner of the full value of its property. The universal truth of the pithy observation of Mr. Justice Holmes in Pennsylvania Coal Co. v. Mahon, 260 U.S. 393, 415, 43 S.Ct. 158, 160, 67 L.Ed. 322, 326 (1922), must not be disregarded:

> "The general rule at least is that while property may be regulated to a certain extent, if regulation goes too far it will be recognized as a taking. * * * We are in danger of forgetting that a strong public desire to improve the public condition is not enough to warrant achieving the desire by a shorter cut than the constitutional way of paying for the change."

While the issue of regulation as against taking is always a matter of degree, there can be no question but that the line has been crossed where the purpose and practical effect of the regulation is to appropriate private property for a flood water detention basin or open space. These are laudable public purposes and we do not doubt the high-mindedness of their motivation. But such factors cannot cure basic unconstitutionality. Nor is the situation saved because the owner of most of the land in the zone, justifiably desirous of preserving an appropriate area in its natural state as a wetland wildlife sanctuary, supports the regulations. Both public uses are necessarily so all-encompassing as practically to prevent the exercise by a private owner of any worthwhile rights or benefits in the land. So public acquistion rather than regulation is required. See Dunham, "Flood Control Via the Police Power", 107 U.Pa.L.Rev. 1098 (1959); Krasnowiecki and Paul, "The Preservation of Open Space in Metropolitan Areas", 110 U.Pa.L.Rev. 179, 184-189 (1961). Note, "Techniques for Preserving Open Spaces", 75 Harv.L. Rev. 1622 (1962); and, generally, Dunham, "A Legal and Economic Basis for City Planning", 58 Colum.L.Rev. 650, 658-670 (1958). Cf. Alford v. Finch, 155 So.2d 790 (Fla.Sup.Ct.1963).[3] Our statutes empower the State and its subdivisions to purchase or condemn property needed for flood control, see e. g, N.J.S.A. 58:16A-1 et seq., and N.J.S.A. 40:69-4.1 et seq., and that found desirable for open-space, park, playground, conservation and recreation purposes, see e. g., R.S. 40:61-1, N.J.S.A. and N.J.S.A. 13:8A-1, et seq. (New Jersey Green Acres Land Acquisition Act of 1961). And the federal government has provided for grants to states in aid of open space programs. 42 U.S.C.A. § 1500-1500e.

[8] We cannot agree with the trial court's thesis that, despite the prime public purpose of the zone regulations, they are valid because they represent a reasonable local exercise of the police power in view of the nature of the area and because the presumption of validity was not overcome. In our opinion the provisions are clearly far too restrictive and as such are constitutionally unreasonable and confiscatory. As was said in Kozesnik v. Montgomery Township, 24 N.J. 154, 182, 131 A.2d 1, 16 (1957): "That a restraint against all use [for the benefit of another private land owner] is confiscatory and beyond the police power and statutory authorization is too apparent

---

3. There is no substantial evidence in this case that the matter of intra-municipal flood control had any bearing on the adoption of the meadows zone regulations. It does not appear that the rise in the water level in the meadows in times of heavy rainfall affected any other area in the township. The emphasis was on permitting that rise within the area as a detention basin for the benefit of lower valley sections rather than on any effort to prevent or channel it. This case, therefore, does not involve the matter of police power regulation of the use of land in a flood plain on the lower reaches of a river by zoning, building restrictions, channel encroachment lines or otherwise and nothing said in this opinion is intended to pass upon the validity of any such regulations. See e.g., R.S. 58:1-26, N.J.S.A. and N.J.S.A. 40:56-1(o). See, generally, Dunham, "Flood Control Via the Police Power," 107 U. Pa. L. Rev. 1098 (1959); Water Resources Circular 3, Flood Damage Alleviation in New Jersey, Department of Conservation and Economic Development, Division of Water Policy and Supply (1961); Beuchert, "Zoning on the Flood Plain," 49 A.B.A.J. 258 (1963). Cf., Vartelas v. Water Resources Commission, 146 Conn. 650, 153 A.2d 822 (Sup. Ct. Err. 1959).

to require discussion." (insertion ours). The same result ordinarily follows where the ordinance so restricts the use that the land cannot practically be utilized for any reasonable purpose or when the only permitted uses are those to which the property is not adapted or which are economically infeasible. Gruber v. Mayor and Township Committee of Raritan Township, 39 N.J. 1, 12, 186 A.2d 489 (1962); Arverne Bay Construction Co. v. Thatcher, 278 N.Y. 222, 15 N.E.2d 587, 117 A.L.R. 1110 (Ct.App.1938). Judge Lehman's oft-quoted sentence in the latter case epitomizes the situation: "The only substantial difference, in such case, between restriction and actual taking, is that the restriction leaves the owner subject to the burden of payment of taxation, while outright confiscation would relieve him of that burden." (15 N.E.2d at p. 592). Of course, property need not be zoned to permit every use to which it is adapted nor must all property similarly situated be accorded identical treatment. To so require would frustrate the zoning objective of a well-balanced community according to a comprehensive plan. It is sufficient if the regulations permit some reasonable use of the property in the light of the statutory purposes. See Kozesnik v. Montgomery Township, supra (24 N.J., at p. 72, 131 A.2d, at p. 10).

We need not repeat the nullifying effect of the use and soil reclamation restrictions on any productive use of property in the zone, which is apparent on the face of the ordinance when viewed in the light of the explanatory testimony. Without reclamation, nothing but a passive use is possible. Land improvement is rendered practically impossible by the almost prohibitory filling and removal regulations, and, even if it could be attained, permitted private owner uses are most narrow indeed. The case is unique in that reclamation is necessary before any worthwhile use is possible, except the commercial removal of the sand and gravel natural resource. Certainly where land improvement can be accomplished under reasonable regulations and some productive uses, otherwise impossible, are thereby made feasible, a municipality is not justified in practically prohibiting all reclamation, thereby preventing a private owner from obtaining any return on his property. While the record here is sparse as to what reasonable productive uses could follow reclamation, we feel confident there must be some which could properly be allowed under appropriate regulation protecting other property in the meadow zone and land in adjoining zones from adverse impact. For example, as to plaintiff's land, there was no refutation of its contention that industrial use was feasible after filing, in view of the similar zoning across the boundary in Hanover and the means of access by roads from both that and East Hanover Townships. Land filling could very likely be accomplished under less stringent regulations which would still protect adjoining property and any properly recognizable broader local interest from harm. Natural resource removal under reasonable regulation might also be considered. See Kozesnik v. Montgomery Township, supra (24 N.J., at pp. 167-168, 131 A.2d, at p. 8). But these are matters for determination by the local legislative body rather than a court in the first instance. The point for present purposes is that the Meadow Development Zone provisions were enacted to prevent private productive use and to maintain the natural state of the land rather than to seek and adopt reasonable means and conditions under which the area could be safely and properly developed by those private owners desiring and entitled to do so.

It is certainly no answer at all to the basic deficiencies in the regulations to assert, as the township does, that they are sanctioned merely because they bear superficial relation to some of the essential considerations for valid zoning specified in R.S. 40:55-32, N.J.S.A.—viz. "consideration * * * [of] the character of the district and its peculiar suitability for particular uses"; prevention of the overcrowding of land; avoidance of undue concentration of population; and as a preventive measure against flooding—and because they represent a local legislative decision compatible with statutory purposes and applicable uniformly to all property similarly situated.

[9] The Meadow Development Zone provisions of March 1960 and the amendment thereto in June 1960 were enacted as a unified whole. It is quite impossible or at least impracticable, even if a proper function or responsibility of a court, to attempt to sift any wheat from the chaff and pick out certain uses or certain land reclamation provisions which might individually be valid. That which thereby could be saved would be so fractional and incomplete as not to amount to a comprehensive, reasonable regulation of the area. Therefore we must hold the provisions invalid in their entirety.

This result, in effect, leaves the area unzoned. The Indeterminate Zone provisions were intended only as a stopgap and were repealed. The original zoning classification in the most highly restricted residential zone amounted, for all practical purposes, to a prohibition of all uses and, if attacked, could hardly be expected to stand. The absence of all regulation would permit the establishment of any use by any means—a result which might well be damaging to the overall local public interest entitled to be served by appropriate exercise of the police power in the light of the special characteristics and particular problems of the district. Consequently we deem it proper for the judgment to be entered by the Law Division to direct that it not become effective for such period of time as the trial court shall find reasonably necessary to enable enactment of new and proper regulations for the area. See, Newark Milk and Cream Co. v. Township of Parsippany-Troy Hills, supra (47 N.J.Super., at p. 331, 135 A.2d, at p. 696).

The judgment of the Law Division is reversed and the cause remanded for the entry of a judgment consistent with this opinion.

For reversal and remandment: Chief Justice WEINTRAUB, and Justices JACOBS, FRANCIS, PROCTOR, HALL, SCHETTINO and HANEMAN —7

For affirmance: None.

Questions and Notes

1. Because of Justice Hall's great prestige, this opinion necessarily commands serious respect. However, just before his retirement from the bench, he in effect repudiated the holding (or at least raised serious questions about it) in another case on a totally different subject; see *A.M.G. Associates v. Township of Springfield*, 65 N.J. 101, 112 n.4, 319 A.2d 705, 711 n.4 (1974).

GREENHILLS HOME OWNERS CORPORATION

v.

GREENHILLS

202 N.E. 2d 192(1964), revd, 5 Ohio St. 2d 207, 215 N.E. 2d 403(1966).

Court of Appeals of Ohio, Hamilton County.

Sept. 14, 1964.

Three cases, consolidated on appeal, involving constitutionality of provision of the comprehensive zoning ordinance of a village. The Court of Common Pleas, Hamilton County, found the restrictions valid. An appeal was taken on questions of law. The Court of Appeals, Hildebrant, J., held that the fact that the federal government relied on use limitation in the village zoning ordinance when conveying property to a private owner did not add to or detract from the village's zoning powers.

Reversed and remanded.

Charles P. Taft, Thomas H. Mongan, Robert E. Dolle, Cincinnati; for plaintiff-appellant.

C. R. Beirne, Robert G. Woellner, Robert F. Dreidame, Cincinnati, for defendant-appellee.

HILDEBRANT, Judge.

Three cases consolidated on appeal on the same record and presented to this Court on questions of law.

The fundamental question in these cases is the constitutionality of Article VI of the comprehensive zoning ordinance of the City (formerly Village) of Greenhills adopted by the council of the Village on August 2, 1949. Article VI of the ordinance provides:

"ARTICLE VI. GREENBELT DISTRICT

"SECTION 1. *Use Regulations.* In a Greenbelt District no land shall be used and no building or structure shall be erected or altered to be used in whole or in part, unless otherwise provided for in this ordinance, except for the following purposes:

"a. Public park reservation, and playground.

"b. Public recreational buildings.

"c. Allotment gardens, farm, nursery, gardens.

"d. Public utilities.

"e. Bus passenger station.

"f. Signs erected by public authorities for an educational or directional nature for the welfare and convenience of the public.

"SECTION II. *Height Regulations.* In a Greenbelt District, no building shall be erected or altered to exceed in height 25 feet or one story. Unoccupied towers are excepted.

"SECTION III. *Prior Approval of Plans of Permitted Uses.* In a Greenbelt District, no land shall be used and no building or structure shall be erected or altered to be used in whole or in part for permitted uses, except after plans for the proposed use, building or structure, and the location thereof, shall have been submitted to the Village Planning Commission for their recommendation."

Subsection g. of SECTION I was added by amendment in 1959 to provide as follows:

"g. The erection of churches on lots or parcels not less than five acres within minimum lot width of 300 feet, a side yard width of not less than 30 feet and aggregating not less than 30 feet and aggregating a total of not less than 25% of the width of the lot, requiring setback line of not less than 125 feet from front or a side street with the further restriction that no building or group of buildings may be erected to occupy collectively more than 25% of the total lot area with no building or buildings exceeding height, exclusive of spiral or steeple."

The court held the restrictions of Article VI valid and denied the relief prayed for.

The plaintiff is a corporation for profit organized and existing under the laws of the state of Ohio.

The defendant is a municipal corporation organized and existing under the laws of the state of Ohio, with all the powers of local government extended by the constitution and laws of the state.

These cases arise by reason of the fact that the plaintiff seeks the necessary building permits to develop to its highest use the real estate it owns located in the "Greenbelt" area of the city, which is the subject of Article VI of the ordinance, and the city has refused to issue any of such permits, basing its refusal on the efficacy of Article VI of the ordinance.

The parties are in one hundred per cent disagreement on the issues presented to the court. Defendant states in its brief:

"The question presented to the Court is not whether a zoning ordinance may ordinarily be the means by which the use of property may be restricted to park purposes, but specifically whether in the light of all of the circumstances in this case, this ordinance was a valid means of controlling the use of the property for the benefit of the public and whether in the light of the circumstances in this case, this plaintiff is in any position to question the validity of the ordinance."

Plaintiff states in its reply brief:

> "This is a suit whereby the pleadings the Court is called upon to consider the constitutionality of an extremely restrictive zoning being maintained by a municipal corporation. That is the issue and the only issue."

The disagreement on the issues resulted in a six weeks' trial producing 1,574 pages of record and 156 exhibits, and a lengthy finding of fact detailing the history of a governmental experiment in public housing upon lands owned by the government at the time and later disposed of to facilitate veterans' housing.

The Greenhills project was one of three so-called "Greenbelt" towns, subsidized and developed on land owned by the United States, and developed ultimately by the Public Housing Administration. The village of Greenhills was incorporated as an Ohio municipality in 1939, situated on land owned by the government, which also included extensive surrounding territory. The original intention of the government was to insulate the towns with adequate open land providing a park and forest area devoted essentially to public purposes to be maintained during development of the area in such a manner as to preserve the essential character of the entire original development. So long as government ownership continued, it had absolute control of the land use of the entire area.

Congress determined to terminate the "Greenbelt" housing experiment and passed the necessary legislation, Public Law 65, Act May 19, 1949, 63 Stat. 68, requiring the sale of the "Greenbelt" towns, including the Greenhills area, by negotiated sale. The record shows that in effecting the sale, the government refused to dedicate the "Greenbelt" area by deed to the Village or any other public authority, but chose the method of fostering a zoning ordinance to be adopted by the Village of Greenhills as adequate to effectuate their original "Greenbelt" intentions. As a result, a comprehensive zoning ordinance was passed containing Article VI quoted above. The Commissioner of Public Housing testified:

> "We considered that the zoning ordinance adopted by the town of Greenhills was adopted before the sale of the property and was adequate protection for that land, that area, and for that reason we saw no necessity of deeding it to the town.
>
> "As a matter of fact, we didn't want to get into any arrangement where the government would have its long arm controlling a piece of property in Greenhills by a reverter clause or such that might be included in that kind of a deed or dedication."

Included in the government issued prospectus of sale was the following:

"*CONDITIONS OF SALE.*

"*Protective Covenants.*

"The deed will contain covenants embodying the following requirments of and limitations upon the successor owners of the properties:

"*Use Restrictions.*

"Any development program undertaken by the purchaser (or his successor) within the corporate area shall conform to use restrictions embodied in the zoning ordinance to be adopted by the Village of Greenhills."

Included in its offer of purchase (Def. Exhibit 81), was the following:

"*D. Park and Public Areas: Greenbelt.*

"The corporation will endeavor to convey all interior parks and playground areas as presently delineated on the Greenhills plan of development to the Village of Greenhills, and without charge. Similarly, the corporation will convey such portions of the Greenbelt area within the corporate limits as are not suited to development to the Village (or to other appropriate agencies of local government)."

The record shows plaintiff subsequently conveyed to the Village all interior parks and twenty-nine acres of "Greenbelt" to the Hamilton County Park Board.

The government and plaintiff entered into a contract of sale which included the following provisions:

"The Government shall convey the Project, including realty, personalty and mixed properties, 'WHERE IS AND AS IS' without warranty or guaranty as to quantity, quality, or location, by quitclaim instrument or instruments subject to all outstanding exceptions, reservations, restrictions, and contracts, affecting the Project on the date hereof, * * *." (Plaintiff's Exhibit 4, page 5.)

"Merger of Negotiations. All negotiations and agreements between the parties hereto and all persons who have acted on their behalf are merged into this Contract, and this Contract contains within its terms and provisions all of the terms and provisions, stipulations and conditions agreed to by the parties with reference to the sale and purchase of the Project." (Plaintiff's Exhibit 4, page 15).

Further, in Contract Exhibit 1 attached to Plaintiff's Exhibit 4 at page 14, paragraph (c), it is stated:

"That it shall not amend or revise its Articles of Incorporation, Code of Regulations, or plan of operation as constituted on the date hereof without the written consent of the Mortgagee, as long as this instrument, or any indebtedness secured hereby, remains outstanding and in effect."

Pursuant to contract, on January 16, 1950, the government executed and delivered its Quit Claim Deed to plaintiff, transferring the title thereto from government ownership to private ownership.

The Quit Claim Deed, at page 11, states:

"The above described properties are conveyed subject to:

"(a) All dedications, reservations, restrictions, exceptions, rights-of-way, easements, taxes, assessments and similar conditions and limitations outstanding and visible or of record."

The habendum clause of the Deed reads:

"TO HAVE AND TO HOLD the foregoing described premises, with all the privileges and appurtenances thereto belonging, to the said Grantee, its successors or assigns, so that neither the Grantor, nor its assigns, nor any other person claiming title through or under it, shall or will hereafter claim or demand any right or title to the premises, or any part thereof; but they and every one of them shall by these presents be excluded and forever barred."

On the same day, January 16, 1950, the government, by Deed of Dedication, transferred other property to the Village.

On October 10, 1951, the United States, for a consideration received to its full satisfaction, sold, transferred, assigned and set over to the Connecticut General Life Insurance Company, the purchase money mortgage given by plaintiffs herein. It, therefore, appears the United States, being fully paid, had no objection and could have no objection to the amendment of plaintiff's charter in 1953, some two years later, to its present corporate form.

In reaching its conclusion, the trial court apparently adopted defendant's statement as to the issues raised by the pleadings, and based its conclusion upon the voluminous record detailing the history of the "Greenbelt" housing experiment terminating in negotiated sale by order of Congress through Public Law 65 to private ownership.

The gist of the trial court's conclusion appears in its memorandum opinion filed herein at page 15 et seq. as follows:

"The essence of the Plaintiff's case is this: That it is the private owner of the Greenbelt and as such private owner its title thereto includes all the uses ordinarily inherent in private ownership, and that the restrictions unreasonably deprive the Plaintiff of these uses without compensation, even though it paid nothing for the property.

"But neither the Plaintiff nor any other private owner has ever had a title to the Greenbelt which includes these uses. The United States Government created the Village of Greenhills, including the Greenbelt, and was the public owner of it. Prior to the execution of the contract and the delivery of the deed, the United States Government, pursuant to, and in compliance with, the authority and purpose of Public Law 65, by means of the restrictions in Article VI of the Zoning Ordinance, transferred the control of the uses in question, for the benefit of the public, to the Village of Greenhills, another governmental agency. Thereafter, a specific amount determined as the value of the Greenbelt, upon the insistence of the Plaintiff, was deducted from the purchase price because the restrictions were intended to, and did, separate said uses from private ownership. Subsequently, the Quit Claim Deed conveyed the property subject to such restrictions, minus said uses as private property. Enforcement of the restrictions will not deprive the Plaintiff, without compensation, of any uses of the Greenbelt to which it is entitled as private proprety.

"Much of the voluminous evidence relates to defenses, such as dedication, estoppel, clean hands and laches. Although they present questions of a possible breach of the contract with the Federal Government and perhaps others, the primary purpose of these defenses is to bar the Plaintiff from raising the question of the validity of the restrictions. In view of the Court's conclusion that the restrictions are valid, it is unnecessary to determine the merit of any of such defenses for that purpose.

"The Court holds that the restrictions contained in Article VI of said Zoning Ordinance are valid but subject to modification at the option of the Village of Greenhills; * * *"

With the above conclusion this Court cannot agree.

[1] There is no dispute between the government and plaintiff as to ownership of the property, nor between the City and plaintiff as to ownership, yet the court, by its holding, assumed to decide a question of title, in effect saying that under the circumstances here a zoning ordinance of an Ohio municipality had the effect of limiting plaintiff's ownership and title to something less than full private ownership, contrary to the all important habendum clause in the deed.

A zoning ordinance is not a title instrument and not included in the chain of title to any of the real estate zoned thereby, and in construing the word "restrictions" as it appears in the contract and deed to refer to the zoning ordinance, the court confuses the function of zoning which is concerned solely with use of private property and not its title or ownership. Even if, under the claimed unusual circumstances here, the ordinance could affect the ownership and title, it must have been such an ordinance as was within the power of an Ohio municipal corporation to adopt, and in the first instance have been a valid constitutional enactment bearing some reasonable relationship to an exercise of the police power. There is no evidence in the record to that effect.

[2] Specifically, we think the statement that the United States, through Public Law 65, by means of Article VI of the zoning ordinance transferred control of the uses in question for public benefit to the Village, is untenable. As we see it, the government did not transfer any control but actually relinquished control as testified to by Housing Administrator, Egan (quoted supra).

The Village passed the ordinance—not the government—and even though requested by, sanctioned, approved and relied on by the seller, the validity of its action was at the time, and we think is now, limited by law to its constitutional powers as an Ohio municipal corporation. We fail to see how government approbation of its acts as an Ohio municipal corporation can either add or detract from its powers.

[3] This Court considers it is bound to decide the issues raised by the pleadings and that the sole issue in these cases is the constitutionality of highly restrictive zoning ordinance passed by an Ohio municipal corporation.

[4] It is further considered that the rights of the parties must be determined from the record as of now and are not dependent upon the means by which plaintiff acquired its title from the government, whether or not criticized by the defendant.

The government is not a party and possible defenses by it are not available to the defendant, and from an examination of plaintiff's Exhibit No. 1, it appears the City of Greenhills is completely encircled by the extensive "Greenbelt" of Winton Woods, owned and operated by the Hamilton County Park District, so that the original "Greenbelt" intent is a fait accompli and the essential character of the entire original project, with the cooperation of the plaintiff as shown by the record, has been maintained after disposal by the government in accord with the intent of Congress as shown by Senate Committee hearing and report (Defendant's Exhibit No. 79).

It further appears from plaintiff's Exhibit No. 1, that extensive areas of the original "Greenbelt" have been by the city rezoned for residential use, and substantial footage of the original Greenbelt, adjacent to the actual Winston Woods Greenbelt, is but of token width and proportions.

[5-7] Coming now to consider the provisions of the ordinance itself, from the evidence and a mere reading thereof, it is clear that the prime object of the zone regulations is to devote the land to public rather than private use. Its main purpose of providing a protective belt of park or forest land is for public benefit rather than a benefit to private use.

In the opinion of this Court, it is clearly an excessive regulation attempted under the police power, is confiscatory in fact and amounts to a taking of private property without just compensation. No citation is necessary to state this violates both the Constitution of the United States and the Constitution of the state of Ohio. The only substantial difference between these restrictions and an outright taking is that the owners are left with the burden of taxation which outright confiscation would avoid.

This Court approves the reasoning and conclusions and cites with approval the authorities relied upon in the very similar case of Morris County Land Improvement Company v. The Township of Parsippany-Troy Hills, 40 N.J. 539, 193 A.2d 232, wherein the court held:

> "Private property may not be taken for public use without just compensation."

"Township zoning ordinance which greatly restricted use of swampland and had for prime object retention of land substantially in its natural state, essentially for public purposes such as floodwater detention basin and preservation of wetland wildlife sanctuary constituted an unconstitutional taking of land for public purpose without just compensation."

"Zoning ordinance which so restricts use that land cannot practically be utilized for any reasonable purpose or where only permitted uses are those to which property is not adapted or which are economically infeasible is ordinarily confiscatory and beyond police power and statutory authorization."

We deem the principles decisive of the above case decisive here and, without unduly lengthening this opinion, find that Article VI of the Greenhills, Ohio zoning ordinance is unconstitutional and void and by excessive regulation amounts to a taking of private property without just compensation and is an unreasonable exercise of the police power having no reasonable relation to the public health, safety, morals or general welfare.

The judgments herein are accordingly reversed and the causes remanded for further proceedings according to law and this opinion.

HOVER, P. J., and LONG, J., concur.

GREENHILLS HOME OWNERS CORPORATION

v.

GREENHILLS

5 Ohio St. 2d 207, 215, N.E.2d 403 (1966).

Supreme Court of Ohio.

March 16, 1966.

Rehearing Denied April 13, 1966.

Three separate actions seeking mandamus, declaratory judgments and injunctions were consolidated for trial. The Court of Common Pleas, Hamilton County, found restrictions of comprehensive zoning ordinance valid. The Court of Appeals, Hildebrant, J., 202 N.E.2d 192, reversed, and appeals were taken on questions of law. The Supreme Court, Schneider, J., held, inter alia, that where Home Owners Corporation procured village adoption of comprehensive zoning ordinance part of which restricted use of portion of land to public park and recreational purposes only, corporation failed to disclose to village legal advice that restriction was unconstitutional, and thereafter the corporation purchased substantially all the land affected by the ordinance and received a reduction in purchase price to extent that portion of land restricted was transferred substantially without consideration, corporation was estopped from attacking such restriction on ground that it constituted a taking of private property without compensation or due process.

Judgments of Court of Appeals reversed and final judgments granted in favor of defendants.

*   *   *

Charles P. Taft, Thomas H. Mongan and Robert E. Dolle, Cincinnati, for appellee.

C. R. Beirne, Cincinnati, and Robert G. Woellner, City Solicitor, for appellants.

Lindhorst & Dreidame and Robert F. Dreidame, Cincinnati, for intervenor-appellants.

SCHNEIDER, Judge.

In the 1930's, the United States of America erected a model town, in the rural outskirts of Hamilton County, which it called "Greenhills." Surrounding a central commercial area, single-family and multi-family residences were constructed for rental to lower-income family units. Churches, schools and other public meeting houses were provided. The plan included public commons, parkways and playgrounds interspersed with curving streets and graceful walks. Circumscribing all was a corridor of varying width of grassland and woodland, as a rampart against the intrusion of further urbanization from within as well as from without.

The town was incorporated as an Ohio municipal corporation. After World War II, the government determined to sell the town as an entity to any person or group of persons which could reasonably be found capable of continuing to operate it in accordance with the original plan. Alarmed by this decision, a group of citizens and tenants associated themselves together as a corporate body, the Greenhills Home Owners Corporation (GHOC), for the purpose of qualifying as that purchaser. The purchase was finally accomplished but not without many long months of agonizing negotiations within the corporation and with the Federal Housing Administration as agent for the United States.

The circumferential strip of woodland, known as "Greenbelt," is the focal point of the controversy between GHOC, the plaintiff-appellee, and the village (now a city), a defendant-appellant. A large number of residents of the community whose interests parallel those of the municipal corporation itself joined the proceedings in the trial court as intervening defendants and appear here separately as appellants. The three separate actions seek mandamus, declaratory judgments and injunctions, and were consolidated for trial. The objective of GHOC was the invalidation of the zoning ordinance of Greenhills to the extent that it thwarts GHOC in developing Greenbelt for residential use. The Court of Common Pleas found for the village, holding that the ordinance's restriction of Greenbelt to no other use except public park reservation, playgrounds, public recreational buildings, allotment gardens, farms, nurseries, gardens, public utilities, churches and bus passenger stations, constituted, under all the circumstances, as revealed by an exceedingly complex record, a valid restriction engrafted upon the title of GHOC to Greenbelt. In appeals on questions of law, the Court of Appeals found the zoning ordinance to be unconstitutional so far as it limits the use of Greenbelt as indicated and reversed the judgments of the Court of Common Pleas.

Our view of the matter will not require a lengthy excursion among the myriad facets of a basically simple case, vastly overcomplicated, to paraphrase the trial judge.

Although its conception and birth were the subject of meticulous study and planning by government experts, Greenhills, for the decade and one-half during which it remained under the ownership of the government, was, unlike the usual community, unneedful of, and in fact without, a zoning ordinance to protect its existing arrangements and to control its future development according to its original plan. As overlord, the United States regulated the use of every inch of land and of every blade of grass. However, prior to its purchase of Greenhills, GHOC determined to see to it that zoning was adopted.

After the professional planner who had previously designed Greenhills for the United States was engaged to draft a zoning ordinance incorporating his original concepts of the model community, including the Greenbelt, and after that draft was presented to the proper village authorities for consideration, GHOC delegated its vice-president and a member of its board of directors, Charles Stamm, as its permanent emissary to the planning commission and council of the village in the matter of the adoption of that draft, notwithstanding that two other board members were also members of the planning commission and two other board members were village councilmen.

For over a year and a half prior to August 1949, the labors of the commission and the council extended throughout day and night, in informal meetings and formal hearings. On the second day of that month and year, without any objection whatsoever, so the written records indicate, a zoning ordinance identical to the original draft as to that part which is in controversy here was duly adopted by the council after favorable recommendation by the planning commission.

In addition to the Greenbelt district, the ordinance divided the entire village into four other districts, three involving residential uses and one for commercial purposes. It regulates the density of uses within the districts, the height of structures, lot usage, and so on. In short, it is a comprehensive zoning ordinance in that it provides for that variety of land uses deemed necessary to the preservation of that portion of the village plan already executed and to the orderly completion of that plan.

Always in attendance at each meeting considering the zoning ordinance, and always insistent that the ordinance be adopted, was GHOC's representative, Stamm, fortified by the official written position of GHOC's board of directors that the proposal ought to be adopted. From time to time, other officers and directors of GHOC appeared at those meetings to support the passage of the proposed ordinance.

After its adoption, the negotiations for the purchase of the town, which had been lopping along at a flaccid pace, swiftly reached the end of their course. But not before the United States was prevailed upon by GHOC to reduce the purchase price by $98,969, representing the appraised value of the 331 acres of Greenbelt at $299 an acre, because Greenbelt had been zoned as indicated and hence unavailable for the use now desired by GHOC.

The village and the intervenors contend that GHOC's promotion of the ordinance containing the Greenbelt restrictions was pursuant to the insistence of the United States that zoning appropriate to its original conception as a "Greenbelt" town be adopted prior to any sale. Thus, it is claimed that GHOC was, if not the agent of the United States, the principal actor in an endeavor which was a *sine qua non* to GHOC's qualification as the purchaser. Alternatively, appellants claim that the promotion of the ordinance was designed to strike $100,000 from the purchase price. GHOC, of course, emphatically denies both contentions and pleads that its participation in securing the ordinance was simply for the purpose of advancing the general welfare of the community. In our view, the truth of falsity of these claims, to which a major portion of the six-week trial was devoted, is immaterial. Equally immaterial is whether the United States even knew of GHOC's participation in seeking the zoning ordinance, although the trial court found that it did.

The critical facts were never in dispute. GHOC did actively promote, as hereinbefore indicated, a comprehensive zoning ordinance over the course of a year and a half. During all this time GHOC was the potential purchaser of substantially every square foot of land subject to that ordinance. GHOC did, in fact, purchase that land. And GHOC thereby became the beneficiary of every good (neither the greatest nor the least of which was a reduction in the purchase price) and the endurer of every evil, if any, flowing from that ordinance.

There is, however, testimony from Stamm alone that in the course of the struggle to secure adoption of the ordinance and, despite the absence of any written objections, he registered the protest that the Greenbelt restriction should not be enacted. However, the fact, that GHOC's legal counsel had advised its board that in his opinion those restrictions were unconstitutional, was never communicated to any of the village authorities either by Stamm or by anyone else. Without weighing the evidence, Stamm's account of his objections, although vague as to dates, times or specific language, but construed most liberally in favor of GHOC, amounts to this paraphrase: "We (GHOC) want this zoning ordinance but we object to the Greenbelt provisions. However, if the village will not adopt the ordinance without Greenbelt, then we urge its adoption as drafted and we can adjust our differences at a later time."

At best, this objection was qualified, and, lacking the disclosure that GHOC had convinced itself of the unconstitutionality of the objectionable feature, it was tantamount to inequitable conduct toward the village authorities and the citizens who expected the zoning ordinance, among other things, to preserve an important characteristic of the village.

[1] The first rule controlling these cases is that a court will not exercise its power to determine the constitutionality of a legislative enactment unless it is absolutely necessary to do so. State ex rel. Lieux v. Village of Westlake, 154 Ohio St. 412, 96 N.E.2d 414. And, such necessity is absent where other issues are apparent in the record which will dispose of the case on its merits. Crowell, Commr. v. Benson, 285 U.S. 22, 52 S.Ct. 285, 76 L.Ed. 598.

[2] These precepts were ignored by the Court of Appeals in declaring the ordinance unconstitutional solely on the basis of Morris County Land Improvement Co. v. Township of Parsippany-Troy Hills, 40 N.J. 539, 193 A.2d 232. The restriction declared invalid in that case was an amendment to an existing comprehensive zoning plan, which further limited a single area to water-life and flood control purposes without any participation in or consent to its enactment by the owner of the land affected. Furthermore, a comparison of that situation with the limitations of Greenbelt in this case, is as unrealistic as it is premature. Similar limitation is inherent in every ordinance or zoning regulation which requires "open space" on all building lots. Such required "open space" is perpetually "used" to preserve maximum density of the active uses of land to prevent overcrowding and to minimize health and safety hazards. In these cases, the "open space" is located in one area. Therefore, it is no more correct to hold that Greenbelt is not "in use" than to hold that "open space," in the form of "set-backs" and minimum yard requirements, is not "in use."

The ordinance here may well violate the constitutional rights of GHOC quite apart from the reasoning of the Court of Appeals. Conversely, it may well be constitutional in spite of the rule of Morris County Land Improvement Co.

But the enduring value of the rule restraining precipitous constitutional determinations is well illustrated by these cases. The decision of the Common Pleas Court would tend to overemphasize zoning as an element of the law of real property. On the other hand, the decisions of the Court of Appeals might well cast premature doubt on the validity of so-called "development plans" now prevalent in zoning practice.

[3] Therefore, the second rule of law which we adopt as applicable here and from whose strictures GHOC has clearly failed to remove itself is tautly drawn in Board of Levy Commissioners of Fulton County v. Johnson, 178 Ky. 287, 199 S.W. 8, L.R.A.1918E, 202, to the effect that where there is clear evidence that a party seeking to assail a regulation as unconstitutional

"aided in procuring the legislation and derived benefit therefrom and that to set it aside would work a hardship or injustice on others who were misled to their prejudice into believing that the legislation was valid," estoppel will deny any right to pursue the attack on validity.

The rule has been recognized in less stringent form by this court in Mott v.Hubbard, Treas., 59 Ohio St. 199, 53 N.E. 47, and City of Mount Vernon v. State ex rel. Berry, 71 Ohio St. 428, 73 N.E. 515. It has been applied in many other jurisdictions. See, for example, Great Falls Mfg. Co. v. Attorney General, 124 U.S. 581, 8 S.Ct. 631, 31 L.Ed. 527; Wall v. Parrot Silver & Copper Co., 244 U.S. 407, 37 S.Ct. 609, 61 L.Ed. 1229; St. Louis Malleable Casting Co. v. George C. Prendergast Constr. Co., 260 U.S. 469, 43 S.Ct. 178, 67 L.Ed. 351; Daniels v. Tearney, 102 U.S. 415, 26 L.Ed. 187; Vickery v. Board of Comrs. of Hendricks County, 134 Ind. 554, 32 N.E. 880; Foley v. State ex rel. King, Atty, Genl., 157 Okl. 202, 11 P.2d 928; Hoertz v. Jefferson Southern Pond Draining Co., 119 Ky. 824, 84 S.W. 1141; De Noma v. Murphy, 28 S.D. 372, 133 N.W. 703; Owens v. Corporation Comm. of Okla., D.C., 41 F.2d 799; and Convent of Sisters of St. Joseph of Chestnut Hill v. City of Winston-Salem, 243 N.C. 316, 90 S.E.2d 879. See, also, 16 American Jurisprudence 2d 328 et seq., Section 131 et seq.; 48 Harv.L.Rev. 988; 34 Col.L.Rev. 1498; and 34 N.C.L.Rev. 514.

[4] As already shown, procuration and benefit are manifest in this record. Only injustice to the appellants can flow from a judgment in favor of the appellee who is, therefore, estopped from having it. Accordingly, the judgments of the Court of Appeals are reversed and final judgments are granted in favor of the appellants.

Judgments reversed.

TAFT, C. J., and ZIMMERMAN, MATTHIAS, O'NEILL, HERBERT and PAUL W. BROWN, JJ., concur.

Questions and Notes

1. Greenhills was one of the garden cities/towns built by the Resettlement Administration near the end of the 1930's.

2. Why was the town sold off into private ownership after the war?

3. In fixing the price for the sale, what account was taken of the limited rights acquired by the purchaser in the green belt area?

4. Did the Homeowners Corporation support the passage of the ordinance?

5. In view of this, how did the Homeowners Corporation have the gall to attempt to break the ordinance?

McCARTHY

v.

CITY OF MANHATTAN BEACH

257 P.2d 679(1953), revd, 41 Cal. 2d 879, 264 P.2d 932(1953),
cert. denied, 348 U.S. 817(1954).

District Court of Appeal, Second District, Division 3, California.

May 27, 1953.

Rehearing Denied June 9, 1953.

Hearing Granted July 22, 1953.

In suit for judgment declaring void ordinance permitting only recreational activities on ocean beach land on which plaintiffs had intended to construct houses on pilings, the Superior Court, Los Angeles County, rendered judgment in favor of defendant, and plaintiffs appealed. The District Court of Appeal, Wood, J., held that the ordinance, as applied to plaintiffs' property, was confiscatory and constituted a taking of such property for public use without compensation and without due process of law.

Reversed.

Cosgrove, Cramer, Diether & Rindge, John N. Cramer, Leonard A. Diether, J. D. Barnum, Jr., Los Angeles, for appellants.

Clyde Woodworth, City Atty., Manhattan Beach, and Dunlap, Holmes, Ross & Woodson, Pasadena, for respondent.

WOOD, Justice.

Action for declaratory relief. Plaintiffs appeal from judgment in favor of defendant.

Plaintiffs are owners of approximately three-fifths of a mile of sandy beach frontage in the City of Manhattan Beach (hereinafter referred to as city). In 1941, the city adopted an ordinance (No. 502), section 10 of which is to the effect that said land could be used only for beach recreational activities and for the operation of beach facilities for such activities for an admission fee; that the only structures permitted thereon were lifeguard towers, open smooth wire fences and small signs. Plaintiffs have not used the property for such purposes and have not received any income therefrom, but they have paid taxes thereon ranging in amounts from approximately $4,200 in 1940 to approximately $9,000 in 1950. In 1950 plaintiffs made application to the city for a modification of the ordinance which would permit the construction of single residences on the property. The application was denied. In the first cause of action herein, the plaintiffs sought a declaration that section 10 of said ordinance,[1] as applied to appellants' property, was unconstitutional in that it deprives them of their property without due process of law in violation of section 1 of the 14th amendment to the Constitution of the United States; it denies them the equal protection of the laws in violation of section 1 of said amendment; and it takes their property for public use without compensation. They also alleged that said section is unreasonable, arbitrary and discriminatory, and is an abuse of legislative discretion: In the second cause of action, they sought a declaration that the ordinance was invalid because it was not passed in good faith, but was passed pursuant to a scheme, conceived by the mayor and councilmen, to keep plaintiffs' property unimproved so that it could be used by the public for park purposes, and to depreciate its value so that it might be acquired by eminent domain for park purposes at the lowest possible amount of money.

The said property of plaintiffs extends from 1st Street, which is the south boundary of the city (and is also the north boundary of the City of Hermosa Beach) to 13th Street. The width of the strip of land varies from 174 feet to 186 feet. Its west boundary is the line of mean high tide of the Pacific Ocean. Its east boundary is the west side of the former right of way of the Pacific Electric Railway Company, which right of way is now a state park. That right of way is 50 feet wide. East of, and adjacent to, the right of way is a cement walk, 15 feet wide, which is referred to as "The Strand." East of the strand there are residential and business houses. The land, from east to west—that is facing oceanward from the strand, has a slope varying from 1 to 2 feet vertical in 10 feet horizontal. At the south end of the land, the strand is approximately 2 feet above the Pacific Electric right of way; and at 12th Street (near the north end of the land), the strand rises to an elevation of not less than 15 feet above the right of way.

The accompanying photograph (Exhibit 2) shows plaintiffs' property and adjacent and other nearby property. North is at the top of the

---

1. "Section 10. B-1 Beach Recreation District.

"A. Land Uses Permitted

"1-The following beach recreation activities: swimming, surf-fishing and athletics including operation of beach facilities for the above activities for an admission fee;

"2-Rental of the following beach equipment: back-rests, chairs, benches, picnic tables and stoves, umbrellas, wind screens, surf-rafts, surf-boards, surfing bags, paddleboards, kayaks, canoes, and other small boats.

"B. Other Uses

"No use other than those specifically mentioned in this section as permitted uses or those determined by action of the Commission * * * to be not more obnoxious or detrimental to the welfare of the community, shall be permitted * * *

"C. Structures Permitted

"1-No buildings, structures, walls, or fences shall be erected in the B-1 District, except life guard towers and open smooth wire fences neither of which shall have a height greater than four (4) feet above the grade of the nearest portion of the strand.

"2-No sign shall be permitted or displayed in the B-1 District other than directional signs as specified below * * *."

photograph. The row of houses at the bottom of the photograph (extending north and south, nearest to the ocean) is in Hermosa and will be referred to as the Hermosa houses. The south boundary of plaintiffs' property (1st Street—the boundary between Manhattan and Hermosa) is at a point in the photograph about 4 houses north of the Hermosa houses. The north boundary of plaintiffs' property (13th Street) is at a point about 5 houses north of the pier (the south pier).

In 1923, the city council passed an ordinance (No. 249), dividing the city into an industrial district and a residential district. Under that ordinance plaintiffs' land was in the residential district.

In 1924, the city, claiming title to said land by reason of alleged dedication of the land for public use by the subdividers, commenced an action to quiet title. In 1935, the superior court rendered judgment therein against the city, quieting title in the predecessors in interest of the present plaintiffs. On February 15, 1938, the judgment was affirmed by the Supreme Court. City of Manhattan Beach v. Cortelyou, 10 Cal.2d 653, 76 P.2d 483.

In 1929, while the quiet title action was pending, the council passed an ordinance (No. 337—amending the 1923 ordinance) which provided that no building should be erected westerly of the right of way, except a one-story one-family dwelling house with garage.

On March 17, 1938, about one month after the decision of the Supreme Court, the city passed a resolution to the effect that the withdrawal of said property (plaintiff's) from use as a public beach would be a great hardship to the public generally; the property should be acquired by the public for continued use as a public beach and particularly at a time when no structures had been erected thereon; the city did not have sufficient funds with which to acquire the property; and the city recommended to the county and the state that steps be taken looking to the acquisition of the property at the earliest possible moment in order to minimize the cost of such acquisition and to continue the use of the property as a public beach.

Thereafter, over a period of several years, the plaintiffs and defendant cooperated in various unsuccessful efforts to cause the property to be acquired for public use by the city or county or state.

In July, 1938, the mayor and the city attorney told Mr. McCarthy that they did not want appellants to sell the property or improve it because that would increase its value and the city wanted to acquire it within its means.

On July 21, 1938, the city council passed a resolution which recited that: The city did not have adequate funds for the acquisition of said property; it is deemed essential that said property "should nevertheless be preserved for public use"; that the board of supervisors of the county give immediate consideration to the matter of leasing the property from appellants.

On July 20, 1939, the city council passed a resolution instructing the city attorney to attend a meeting of the state park commission and request it to make arrangements for the preservation of the property for public use.

On July 25, 1939, pursuant to instructions from the city council, the city attorney sent a letter to the governor requesting that in the event that he called a special session of the Legislature he include in the call the consideration of an act which would allocate money for the acquisition of the property. In that letter it was stated that unless something is done the appellants proposed to sell the property to various persons, and if that should be done the cost of acquisition would be materially increased since the property was not improved.

On February 1, 1940, the council instructed the city attorney to attend a session of the Legislature for the purpose of ascertaining the progress of legislation regarding the allocation of money for acquiring the property.

On June 24, 1940, Mr. McCarthy sent a letter to the mayor stating that, upon assurance from the city officials that arrangements were being made to acquire the property, he had delayed putting the property on the market; he was arranging to enclose the property and charge admission for the use of it; he had cooperated fully in an effort to make it possible for the city to acquire the property but since it apparently was unable to do so, he had no alternative except to secure as much revenue from the property as he could in order to pay the taxes.

On July 1, 1940, the city passed an ordinance which made it unlawful for anyone to construct a barbed wire fence in the city without first obtaining written permission from the council.

On August 12, 1940, Mr. McCarthy sent a letter to the council stating that he understood the property was zoned for residential purposes; that under existing conditions it could not be sold or subdivided for such purposes and consequently he was paying taxes on property limited to use, by the zoning ordinance, for which it could not be utilized profitably; and he requested that the city rezone the property for business purposes. On August 22, 1940, the council denied the request.

On June 26, 1941, as above stated, the council passed said zoning ordinance No. 502, which is the subject of this action.

On March 1, 1945, the council passed a resolution which stated that: The city is without adequate funds with which to acquire the property; at the present time no improvements exist upon the property, and good policy dictates "that now is the time during which the same should be acquired by and for the public"; the board of supervisors is requested to give its earliest consideration to the acquisition of the property to the end that it may be preserved for public use.

On September 8, 1948, the state commenced an action to condemn the property for park purposes. The action has been at issue since November, 1949, but it has not been set for trial.

On November 15, 1950, appellants made the application, above referred to, for a modification of ordinance No. 502, which would permit the construction of single residences on the property. The application was referred to the city planning commission and, after hearings, the application was denied by the commission on January 10, 1951. On March 6, 1951, the council denied said application.

The court found, in part, that: The property is subject, from time to time, to erosion and replacement by reason of storms and wave action of the ocean; any residences which could be constructed upon said property would necessarily be erected on pilings, and that reasonable minds might differ as to the safety of residence properties so constructed; the construction of residence properties on pilings and, subject to erosion and replacement by the waves of the ocean, might create problems by reason of possible uses of the areas underneath the residences for immoral purposes; one of the principal characteristics of the city is that it is a beach city bordering upon the Pacific Ocean; said property has been suitable, at all times since the adoption of said ordinance, for use and has been used by the residents of the city and the public generally for beach recreation purposes; it is not true that the city, through its mayor and its councilmen, or otherwise, conceived any scheme designed to accomplish the keeping of the property unimproved so that it could be used by the city and visitors to the city as a beach recreation area; it is not true that the city conceived any scheme to depreciate the value of the property so as to enable public authorities to acquire the property for the lowest possible amount of money. The court also found that reasonable minds might reasonably differ, and in 1941 might have reasonably differed as to the following matters: Whether the property is or was suitable for residential or commercial development; whether the city would be subjected to liability by reason of the necessity of employing lifeguards, wrecking crews and salvage employees to protect the property and installations thereon from the ravages of high tides and storms; the propriety of the enactment of said section 10; and the proper classification of the property as being within a beach recreation district.

Ordinance 502 purported to be a city-wide zoning plan. It provided for 10 zoning districts in the city. The 4 districts which are material here are: R-2, for two-family residences; R-3, for limited multiple family residences; B-1, a beach recreation district; and C-1, for retail commercial purposes. All the property east of and next to the strand, facing oceanward, was in zone R-2, R-3 or C-1. The property west of the strand was in zone B-1. That property consisted of appellants' property, the beach frontage in the city which is north of plaintiffs' property, and the Pacific Electric right of way. The beach frontage north of plaintiffs' property was acquired by the state as a state park prior to the passage of said ordinance 502. The Pacific Electric right of way also was acquired by the state as a state park (in 1948). At the time this action was commenced, the only privately owned property in zone B-1 (beach recreation district) was appellants' property.

Section 1 of said ordinance 502 provides: "In order to provide the economic and social advantages resulting from an orderly planned use of land resources and to conserve and promote the public health, safety and general welfare, there is hereby adopted and established an Official Land Use Plan for the City of Manhattan Beach. ° ° °"

Appellants contend in effect that the evidence does not support the material findings; that the evidence demonstrates that said section 10 has no substantial relation to public objects which government may legally accomplish; and said section is arbitrary and unreasonable, and was not designed to accomplish a legitimate public purpose.

It was stipulated that Col. Leeds, who was called as a witness by appellants, was eminently qualified as a civil and consulting engineer. He testified that he had made a study of appellants' property; that as a former United States district engineer in this area and a former State Sea Coast engineer he had a degree of familiarity with the Southern California coast, and with Coast and Geodetic Survey charts; he had examined profile maps made by the county surveyor of the area immediately landward and seaward from the shoreline—showing an elevation above and below the shoreline at intervals of 200 or 500 feet; he had examined the two aerial photographs of appellants' property; as Coast engineer he had observed property that had been damaged as a result of action of the sea; he had observed the conditions at Redondo Beach in recent years where structures on the shore had been damaged. He was asked the following question: "Assume ° ° ° that the easterly 35 feet of plaintiffs' property is to be devoted for a street ° ° ° and that plaintiffs' property is to be subdivided into lots approximately 30 feet in width, and each of the lots would face on the street ° ° ° just mentioned; in your opinion, can houses be constructed upon said lots which would comply with the provisions of the zoning ordinance ° ° ° 502 ° ° ° on said lots safely?" He replied, "Yes." He testified that his answer pertained to construction of such a house as of the date of adopting the ordinance in 1941, and at all times thereafter up to the present. He also testified that he would place the structure on concrete or steel piles, the top of which would be at an elevation of approximately 20 feet above mean lower low water, and in his opinion, the top of the foundation could be placed "somewhat lower as a matter of safety"; he prepared a diagram (Exhibit 62) which is entitled "Representative Profile Across McCarthy Property"— and also recites "Showing Possible Development"; the diagram sets off 35 feet (next to the Pacific Electric right of way) to be dedicated for public use as a road; then it sets off 75 feet (next to the road) as an assumed suitable space on which to construct a house—with a 1-foot setback from the road—which would leave (on the average at each lot) approximately a minimum of 60 feet between the house and mean high tide; on some of the wider lots there would be 6 or 7 feet more between the houses and mean high tide; the approximate elevation of the top of the piling above mean lower low water would be between 16 and 17 feet; that such elevation would be 12.4 feet above mean high tide; if the house extended 75 feet from the road, the top of the piling at that point (75 feet from the road) would be on the average about 12 feet above the sand; that, in his opinion, if a house were constructed as indicated on the diagram, it could be constructed without fear of damage from the ocean. On cross-examination, he testified that he did not know that on occasions the Pacific Electric right of way at Manhattan Beach had been under water; he did not know that water came up over the strand in 1938; he had not made any investigation as to whether the city would approve the 35-foot road; he had not seen a subdivision plan for the property; in forming his opinion regarding the safety of constructing houses on appellants' property, he considered the presence of houses at Hermosa Beach, just south of the southerly limits of Manhattan Beach (as shown on the aerial photographs, Exhibits 1 and 2); the front of the houses that he would build on appellants' property would be on a line, which if extended southerly into Hermosa Beach, would be westerly of the front of said houses in Hermosa Beach; the line of mean high tide is 4.6 feet above mean lower low tide; the highest estimated possible tide in Southern California is 8 feet above mean lower low tide; a tide is measured as a level surface,—not as wave or wind action might send the water farther up on the beach; the height to which water is projected shoreward depends upon wave and wind action—ground swells are a form of wave; damage to piers and structures on beaches is usually caused by ground swells, which are usually produced by distant storms or submarine earthquakes; he would construct the building on pilings driven about 10 feet below lower low water, so that if an unanticipated storm should occur, it could gouge out several feet of the beach and the house would still stand and be safe; succeeding lesser waves will soon restore the gouged out places; the profiles of the beach at Hermosa are somewhat different from those in Manhattan; the attack of waves, wind or ground swells upon the shoreline is seriously influenced by the underwater configuration of the earth; in front of the Manhattan-Hermosa area there is a ridge, and therefore the severest attacks do not occur there; there have been very destructive waves at Redondo; how far a wave would extend shoreward, above the 8-foot (possible) high tide, depends upon many things, including the contour of the beach; the contour is normally a good indication of how far the waves have gone; the crest of the beach is normally around 12 to 15 feet. He was asked the following question: "Would you feel, Colonel, that intelligent and reasonable minds might reasonably differ as to the possible danger of construction of residences in accordance with the scheme indicated on Exhibit 62?" He replied: "Yes, I think you would find difficulty in getting all engineers to agree on one solution as being the only solution. It would depend on the degree of safety that you wanted, and various other factors. Only a very, very foolish engineer claims to be infallible."

Mr. Flanagan, a building inspector and secretary of the planning commission of Manhattan Beach, testified that he had been an employee of that city since 1937; there have been some heavy storms at the beach; on one occasion a fishing barge drifted onto the beach; in a heavy storm he has seen the breakers come over the Pacific Electric right of way or splash over it.

Mr. Sights, who is and has been for 17 years chief of police at Manhattan Beach, testified that on two or three occasions he has seen water against the westerly edge of the Pacific Electric right of way—in the areas near 1st, 5th and 9th Streets; one of the occasions was about 17 years ago, when a barge was washed ashore on 1st Street.

[1] It was stipulated that the judge might view the property and that he might consider as evidence everything he saw in viewing the premises. The judge viewed the premises in the presence of an attorney for appellants, an attorney for respondent, and the clerk of the court. Thereafter, the judge made a statement in open court regarding the observations he had made. Among other things, he said that the westerly side of the proposed 35-foot road (north of the pier in the vicinity of a row of sand dunes) is at least 12 feet lower than the general level of the Pacific Electric right of way; the westerly side of the proposed road is obviously subject to flooding at extremely high tides or during storms; about 500 feet south of the pier, the distance from the westerly side of the proposed road to the line of kelp and debris is about 75 feet, and the area within that distance is sand and generally level with a gentle slope seaward; from 6th Street to the south boundary of appellants' property there is an outcropping of soil; on the seaward side of the houses in Hermosa Beach, shown in the foreground of the photographs in evidence, there is a 20-foot cement walk; adjoining the walk there is a concrete wall, the top of which is level with the walk; the top of the walk is about 2 feet above the sand to the west of it; the distance from the wall to the break of the beach is about 65 feet; the front line of the houses in Hermosa, if continued northward, would be about 12 feet west of the westerly side of the proposed 35-foot roadway; the houses that might be built on plaintiffs' property would extend seaward of that line to the extent that appellants' houses would exceed 12 feet; if the proposed houses were built on plaintiffs' property westerly of the proposed 35-foot road, they would be right on the beach and unless they were protected by an adequate seawall they would be subject to a constant hazard of destruction by the sea. It may be noted that the judge's statement with reference to the necessity for "an adequate sea wall" was not consistent with the finding that houses would be built on piling, as Colonel Leeds testified. Also, as respects the sand beaches of Southern California, it is a matter of common knowledge that piers and other structures built upon piling, in areas washed by the waves, do not have the effect of eroding or washing away the sand, and endure indefinitely.

[2-5] Principles of law applicable in cases involving questions as to validity of zoning ordinances are stated in Clemons v. City of Los Angeles, 36 Cal.2d 95, at pages 98 and 99, 222 P.2d 439. Generally stated some of those principles are (1) a zoning ordinance enacted pursuant to a comprehensive plan, when reasonable and not arbitrary, will be sustained as a

proper exercise of police power; (2) every intendment is in favor of its validity, and a court will not, except when the limitation is clearly arbitrary, interfere with the legislative discretion; (3) it is presumed that the ordinance is adapted to promote the public health, safety, morals, and the general welfare; and (4) a court may differ with the legislative body as to the propriety of enacting the ordinance, but if the question is one upon which reasonable minds might differ, the court will not interfere with the legislative body's determination of policy.

It appears that from 1923 to June 26, 1941 (when ordinance No. 502 was passed), the property was zoned as residential property; that on August 12, 1940 (while it was zoned as residential property), Mr. McCarthy requested that it be zoned for business purposes (the request was denied); and that on November 15, 1950 (while the property was zoned for beach recreation activities under ordinance 502), he requested that it be rezoned for residential purposes (the request was denied).

It also appears that the city, after it had failed in 14 years of litigation to quiet title in itself, and it being financially unable to buy the property, recommended that the county or state buy it so that it might continue to be used as a public beach; and that the city, after it had tried unsuccessfully for approximately three years (after the Supreme Court decision) to cause the county or state to buy the property, and it being unable to buy the property, passed ordinance 502 which in practical effect has caused the property to remain available for public use without requiring the city, county or state to expend any money therefor; and to remain without income to plaintiffs, but subject to heavy taxes—about $9,000 per year.

[6-9] The engineering expert, called by appellants, testified to the effect that houses built upon pilings in a specified manner on appellants' property would be safe. That testimony was not contradicted by an engineering or construction expert. Even though the trial judge viewed the property, pursuant to stipulation, his conclusions as to tide, wave or wind action, based upon his observations of the property during a time of calm as distinguished from a time of storm, would not be evidence. The trial judge, in stating his observations, said that the houses would be subject to a constant hazard of destruction by the sea. He also stated in effect that during storms the houses would be within the area affected by the storms. In Fendley v. City of Anaheim, 110 Cal.App. 731, 294 P. 769, it was claimed that a power plant of defendant jarred and shook plaintiffs' residence and thereby caused damage. The judge therein viewed the premises in the daytime. The reviewing court said, 110 Cal.App. at page 736, 294 P. at page 771, that no observation was made by the trial court "at nighttime when most of the discomforts complained of appeared. We are of the opinion that under such circumstances the inspection of the premises by the court cannot add sufficient weight to sustain the questioned finding [that the operation of the plant caused no discomfort to plaintiffs]." In Wall v. United States Mining Co., C.C. 232 F. 613, it was held that where

the factual issue is a matter for expert testimony, the impressions obtained by a trial judge as to that issue, in viewing the premises, should not be considered as against the opinion of an expert. The observations of the trial judge herein as to the location and surface conditions of appellants' property and nearby property in Manhattan and Hermosa could be considered as evidence to aid the judge in understanding the evidence presented in the courtroom. The conclusions of the trial judge, based upon his observations of the premises, regarding the safety of houses constructed upon pilings, would not be controlling as against the opinion of the expert. The trial judge, however, was not required to find in accordance with the opinion of the expert. The finding of the court was contrary to that opinion. As above stated, there was no other testimony of an engineering or construction expert. The question therefore arises as to what the basis was for the finding that reasonable minds might differ as to the safety of houses constructed upon pilings. A statement of the judge, made during the trial, indicates that he based the finding, in part at least, upon his observations of the premises. He said: "I have an unusually high regard for Colonel Leeds and I know him to be an extremely well-qualified engineer, but I also have viewed the property, and what I have observed is evidence, and I think that that is a question upon which reasonable minds might differ." As above stated, the judge's conclusions as to safety, based upon his observations, were not evidence; and his opinion as to safety, based upon his observations, was not controlling as against the opinion of the expert. It might be that the judge based the finding in part upon the answer of the expert to the question by defense counsel as to whether he felt that "reasonable minds might reasonably differ as to the possible danger of construction of residences *in accordance with the scheme indicated on Exhibit 62?*" That answer was, in part, "Yes, I think you would find difficulty in getting all engineers to agree on one solution as being the only solution. It would depend on the degree of safety that you wanted, and various other factors." That was not an answer that reasonable minds might reasonably differ as to the safety of houses *built on pilings*—it was an answer that such minds might reasonably differ as to the safety of houses built *in accordance with the scheme indicated on Exhibit 62.* As indicated by the answer, it might well be that engineers would not agree as to the safety of the one proposed solution,—and that a certain proposed solution might cause differences in opinion as to the degree of safety. The fact that engineers might not agree as to the safety of a proposed plan, such as the one indicated on Exhibit 62, would not signify that engineers would differ in opinion as to the safety of houses built in accordance with other plans, such as higher, stronger, or differently arranged pilings. The said answer of the expert was not a sufficient basis for the finding that reasonable minds might differ as to the safety of *houses built on pilings.* A question remains as to whether that finding was supported by the presumption that section 10 of the ordinance was adapted or suited to promoting public safety. Various circumstances here, when considered together, show that the presumption alone was not sufficient to support the finding. Some of those circumstances are: (1) The testimony of the expert was contrary to the presumption,— and the judge did not reject the expert's testimony on the ground that he considered the expert was not qualified, but he rejected it because he preferred to base his opinion, as to safety of houses built on pilings, upon his observations of the premises—which opinion, as above stated, was not evidence. (2) In 1923, the city zoned the property for residences and it remained zoned for that purpose for 18 years—until 1941 when the present ordinance was enacted. (3) There was no evidence that there was any change in the physical condition of the property or any disadvantageous change in the action of the ocean. (4) The pictures of the property, received in evidence as Exhibits 1 and 2, show that on an easement across appellants' property for roadway purposes (where the pier is) there are houses adjoining each side of the pier, which houses presumably were built by the city. (5) Along the ocean front in Hermosa Beach, a few feet from the south boundary of appellants' property, there is a row of dwelling houses which is approximately in the same position, with reference to distance from mean high tide, as the row of proposed houses on appellants' property would be from that tide—those houses in Hermosa are not built on pilings but, at a point 20 feet oceanward from the houses (as hereinabove described), there is a cement wall which is about 2 feet higher than the sand. (The pictures indicate that those houses have been there many years.) (6) After the city had failed to quiet title in itself, following 14 years of litigation, and after it had failed in 3 additional years of negotiating for condemnation of the property, it enacted section 10 (prohibiting residences thereon) allegedly on the basis of promoting public safety, although the property had been zoned for residences during all the period of the litigation and negotiations. In summary, it appears that the testimony of the expert that houses built upon pilings would be safe was uncontradicted, notwithstanding the observations of the property by the judge; that the expert did not say that reasonable minds might differ as to the safety of houses built upon pilings, irrespective of height or kind of pilings; and that the presumption that section 10 was adapted to promoting public safety should not prevail as against the various circumstances herein which indicate that the section was not so adapted. The finding that reasonable minds might differ as to the safety of residences constructed on pilings is not supported by the evidence.

[10] Appellants also contend that another finding was not supported by the evidence. That finding is that the construction of houses on pilings might create problems by the possible uses of the areas under the residences for immoral purposes. Counsel for respondent (city) asked the chief of police if, in his opinion, he would have encountered any police problems if the McCarthy property had been improved by constructing residences on pilings. Appellants' objection to that question, upon the ground that it

called for a conclusion, was overruled. The witness then said that he definitely believed that such improvement would cause a police problem because along other beach frontages where homes were built on pilings they "had trouble with juveniles, sex perverts; we have had that under our piers a number of times." On cross-examination, he testified to the effect that he was not familiar with any such police problem in other beach cities involving houses on pilings. Such opinion evidence as to public morals was not sufficient to warrant the enactment of section 10 as a measure that would promote public morals. The fact that it is easier to police the vacant property than it is to police the improved property is not a proper basis for restricting the appellants in the use of their property. The said finding to the effect that the construction of houses on pilings might create police problems is not supported by the evidence.

[11] As above stated, appellants' property could have been used for residential purposes prior to the enactment of said section 10. The city recognized that the property was of high value,—a value which the city, itself, was not able to pay in order to acquire the property for public use. Appellants were and are required to pay high taxes on the property. Said section 10 rendered the property of comparatively little value for the limited uses designated in the section. In practical effect, as above stated, the enactment of section 10 accomplished for the city and the public, without paying any compensation, substantially the same result that would have been accomplished by eminent domain. In Arverne Bay Const. Co. v. Thatcher, 278 N.Y. 222, 15 N.E.2d 587, 592, 117 A.L.R. 1110, the court said: "An ordinance which *permanently* so restricts the use of property that it cannot be used for any reasonable purpose goes, it is plain, beyond regulation, and must be recognized as a taking of the property. The only substantial difference, in such case, between restriction and actual taking, is that the restriction leaves the owner subject to the burden of payment of taxation, while outright confiscation would relieve him of that burden." In Pennsylvania Coal Co. v. Mahon, 260 U.S. 393, 413, 43 S.Ct. 158, 159, 67 L. Ed. 322, 325, Justice Holmes said: "Government hardly could go on if to some extent values incident to property could not be diminished without paying for every such change in the general law. As long recognized some values * * * must yield to the police power. But obviously the implied limitation must have its limits or the contract and due process clauses are gone. *One fact for consideration in determining such limits is the extent of the diminution. When it reaches a certain magnitude, in most if not in all cases, there must be an exercise of eminent domain and compensation to sustain the act.* So the question depends upon the particular facts." (Italics added.) In Householder v. Town of Grand Island, Sup., 114 N.Y.S.2d 852, an ordinance required a 90-foot setback from a street, and as the result thereof all the owner's land except a strip 1 foot wide, at one end of his property, and 8 feet wide at the other end, was taken. The court said, 114 N.Y.S.2d at page 855: "Such an ordinance is confiscatory and unenforcible. It is an attempt

to accomplish by so called 'set back ordinance' without any compensation what can legally be done, if at all, only by the exercise of the power of eminent domain." In Skalko v. City of Sunnyvale, 14 Cal.2d 213, at page 216, 93 P.2d 93, at page 94, it was said: "Legislatures may not, under the guise of the police power, impose restrictions that are unnecessary and unreasonable upon the use of private property or the pursuit of useful activities." In practical effect section 10 of the ordinance, as applied to appellants' property, is confiscatory and constitutes a taking of plaintiffs' property for public use without compensation and without due process of law. Under the evidence here, said section, as applied to plaintiffs' property, is unconstitutional and invalid.

In view of our conclusion that section 10 of the ordinance is invalid, as applied to appellants' property, it is not necessary to consider claimed errors in the rejection of evidence.

The judgment is reversed.

SHINN, P. J., and VALLEE, J., concur.

McCARTHY

v.

CITY OF MANHATTAN BEACH

41 Cal. 2d 869,

264 P.2d 932 (1953), cert. denied, 348 U.S. 817(1954).

Supreme Court of California.

In Bank.

Dec. 30, 1953.

Rehearing Denied Jan. 27, 1954.

In suit for judgment declaring void ordinance permitting only recreational activities on beach land on which plaintiffs had intended to construct houses on pilings, the Superior Court, Los Angeles County, Arnold Praeger, J., rendered judgment in favor of defendant, and plaintiffs appealed. The Supreme Court, Spence, J., held, inter alia, that it would be presumed that city could perform its duty in affording police protection to safeguard plaintiffs' property, and that hence public destruction of fence plaintiffs had placed around their property while it was still zoned for residential use would not be germane to issue of reasonable zoning under present ordinance.

Affirmed.

Schauer and Shenk, JJ., dissented.

Prior opinion, 257 P.2d 679.

Cosgrove, Cramer, Diether & Rindge, John N. Cramer, Leonard A. Diether and J. D. Barnum, Jr., Los Angeles, for appellants.

Clyde Woodworth, City Atty., Inglewood, Dunlap, Holmes, Ross & Woodson, Pasadena, for respondent.

SPENCE, Justice.

Plaintiffs sought a judgment declaring that a certain zoning ordinance restricting the use of their ocean-front property to beach recreational purposes is "null and void" as applied to them. In the first cause of action they challenged the constitutionality of the zoning restriction insofar as it affects their land, claiming that it violates the due process and equal protection clauses of both the federal and state constitutions and results in a taking of their property for public use without compensation. U.S.C.A. Const. Amend. XIV, §1: Cal.Const. Art.I, §13. They also alleged that the restrictive use is unreasonable, arbitrary, and discriminatory, and is an abuse of legislative discretion. In their second cause of action they challenged the validity of the zoning restriction on the ground that it was not passed in good faith but was adopted pursuant to a scheme, conceived by the mayor and members of the city council, to depress the value of plaintiffs' property so that it could be acquired for public park purposes at the lowest possible price. The trial court decided in favor of the city; and settled legal principles sustain the propriety of its judgment.

Plaintiffs are the owners of approximately three-fifths of a mile of sandy beach frontage in the city of Manhattan Beach. The property extends from 1st Street, which is the south boundary of the city adjoining Hermosa Beach, to 13th Street. It is a strip of land varying in width from 174 to 186 feet and having an average slope of 1 to 2 feet vertical in 10 feet horizontal. It is bounded on the west by the Pacific Ocean and on the east by a state park, which was formerly a 50-foot right of way belonging to the Pacific Electric Railway Company. To the east of this former right of way and extending along the city's entire ocean frontage is a cement walk, 15 feet wide, and called "The Strand." Back therefrom are residential and business houses. As it parallels plaintiffs' property running from south to north, the strand varies in elevation from 2 to 15 feet above the Pacific Electric's former right of way, which in time of storm and on other occasions has been covered with water.

In 1924 the city brought a quiet title action with respect to the property now owned by plaintiffs, upon the claim of the subdividers' dedication of the land for public use according to certain recorded maps. The action, tried in 1935, resulted in a judgment against the city and title was quieted in plaintiffs' predecessors in interest. The judgment was affirmed on February 15, 1938. City of Manhattan Beach v. Cortelyou, 10 Cal.2d 653, 76 P.2d 483. Since at least 1900 the property has been continuously used for public beach purposes. 10 Cal.2d at page 665, 76 P.2d 483. In 1929 it was classified under the city's ordinance (No. 337) into a single-family residence district. Following the final judgment in the quiet title action and over a period of several years, plaintiffs and the city cooperated in various unsuccessful efforts to cause the property to be acquired through sale or lease by the public authorities. Resolutions were passed by the city from time to time declaring its present lack of funds for acquisition of the property but recommending that the county or state allocate money so that continued "use of the property as a public beach" could be preserved. In discussion of the matter with plaintiff Neil S. McCarthy, both the mayor and city attorney expressed their hope that the property would not be sold or improved so as to increase the cost of its acquisition by the public authorities.

On June 24, 1940, Mr. McCarthy advised the mayor by letter that upon assurance from the city officials that arrangements were being made to acquire the property, he had delayed putting it on the market during the main selling season; and that in the hope then of deriving some revenue from the property, he was arranging to enclose it and charge admission for its use. An emergency ordinance passed by the city on July 1, 1940, prohibited the erection of any barbed wire fence in the city without first obtaining a written permit from the city council. McCarthy secured such a permit and immediately began construction of the desired fence. It was never fully completed, as parts of it were destroyed by the public at various times during its building and finally it became necessary to remove the fence entirely. On July 30, 1940, McCarthy by letter notified the city council of these difficulties, demanded police protection, and stated his intention of holding the city responsible for all damages suffered.

By letter of August 12, 1940, McCarthy advised the city council of his belief that the property could not be sold or subdivided for residential purposes and requested a rezoning of the property for business purposes. Pursuant to the recommendation of the city planning commission after a public hearing, the city council on August 22, 1940, denied the request. Then on June 26, 1941, the city council adopted the zoning ordinance in question (No. 502), whereby under section 10 plaintiffs' property could be used only for beach recreational activities and for the operation of beach facilities for such activities for an admission fee; and the only structures permitted thereon were lifeguard towers, open smooth wire fences and small signs. Meanwhile the city was still interested in plaintiffs' property for a public park and carried on negotiations with the state looking toward its acquisition. In 1948 the state commenced an action to condemn the property for park purposes but it has not yet been brought to trial.

Plaintiffs made no use of their property as permitted by the 1941 zoning ordinance nor did they receive any income therefrom. In 1950 they applied to the city for a modification of the ordinance so as to change the classification of their property from "Beach Recreational District" to "Single Family Residence District." Plaintiffs had paid taxes on their property ranging from approximately $4,200 in 1940 to approximately $9,000 in 1950. The rezoning application was referred to the city planning commission and, after public hearings, was denied on January 10, 1951. The city council denied the application on March 6, 1951. Plaintiffs thereupon brought this action for declaratory relief.

The trial court found, in part, that plaintiffs' property is, from time to time, subject to erosion and replacement by reason of storms and wave action of the Pacific Ocean; that any residences which could be constructed upon the property would necessarily be erected on pilings, and reasonable minds might differ as to the safety of residence properties so constructed; that such construction might also create police problems by reason of possible uses of the areas underneath the residences for immoral purposes; that one of the principal characteristics of the city is its beach advantage bordering upon the Pacific Ocean; that at all times since adoption of the 1941 ordinance, plaintiffs' property has been suitable for use and has been used by the city and visitors thereto for beach recreational purposes; that it is not true that the city, through its mayor and councilmen, or otherwise, conceived any scheme designed to accomplish the keeping of the property unimproved so it could be used as a public beach recreational area or to depreciate the value of the property so as to enable the public authorities to acquire it at the lowest possible price. The court also found that "reasonable minds might reasonably differ and might have in the year 1941 reasonably differed" as to the following matters: whether the property is or was suitable for residential or commercial development; whether the city would be subject to liability by reason of the necessity of employing lifeguards, wrecking crews and salvage employees to protect the property and installations thereon from the ravages of high tides and frequent storms; the propriety of the enactment of the zoning restriction declared in section 10 of the 1941 ordinance; and the proper classification of the property as being within a beach recreational district. Upon such findings the court concluded that the zoning restriction is a valid enactment within the city's police power; that it does not deprive plaintiffs of their property without due process of law or deny them the equal protection of the laws; that it has a foundation in reason and is not a mere arbitrary or irrational exercise of power; and that the scheme of classification and districting followed in the ordinance "has been applied fairly and impartially in the instance of plaintiffs' property." The appeal is from the judgment entered in substantially this same language.

[1-4] As stated in Clemons v. City of Los Angeles, 36 Cal.2d 95, 222 P.2d 439, 441, a zoning ordinance enacted pursuant to a comprehensive plan of community development, "when reasonable in object and not arbitrary in operation," will be sustained as a proper exercise of the police power; every intendment is in favor of its validity, and a court will not, "except in a clear case of oppressive and arbitrary limitation," interfere with the legislative discretion; it is presumed to be adapted to promotion of the public health, safety, morals and general welfare; and though the

court may differ with the zoning authorities as to the "necessity or propriety" of the regulation so long as it remains a "question upon which reasonable minds might differ," there will be no judicial interference with the municipality's determination of policy.

Ordinance 502 comprehends a city-wide zoning plan. It provides for 10 zoning districts in the city. Only four districts are material here: R-2 for two-family residences; R-3, for limited multiple-family residences; B-1, a beach recreational district; and C-1, for retail commercial purposes. The property west of the strand is in zone B-1. That property consists of plaintiffs' land, the beach frontage adjoining on the north thereof, and the Pacific Electric's former right of way. Prior to the passage of this ordinance, the beach frontage north of plaintiffs' land was acquired by the state for state park purposes, and some years thereafter (1948) the mentioned right of way was similarly acquired for park purposes. Accordingly, when plaintiffs commenced this action, theirs was the only privately owned property in zone B-1.

Section 1 of ordinance 502 declares: "In order to provide the economic and social advantages resulting from an orderly planned use of land resources and to conserve and promote the public health, safety and general welfare, there is hereby adopted and established an Official Land Use Plan for the City of Manhattan Beach * * *." A planning consultant who had assisted in drafting the zoning ordinance testified that the intent of the district classifications was to "produce a plan meeting all of the various zoning needs of the city * * * a balanced plan * * * including, among other things, one section * * * eminently suited * * * for beach recreation." He further stated that in his opinion the cost of home-building would be relatively high on the beach frontage and therefore inclusion of that beach area in zone R-1 might be deemed "unreasonable zoning"; that home-building in that area might also destroy certain values which residential sections developed just back of the strand had long enjoyed; and that he therefore had recommended to the city planning commission the creation of the "beach recreation zone which would give the owners of the property the right to derive an income from it." Another expert witness on zoning problems testified that the ordinance properly provided for a beach recreational area to "take advantage" of the city's natural resource or asset, its "ocean frontage," which accounted for its original development as a community.

The secretary of the planning commission, who had been an employee of the city since 1937 and its building inspector for the past nine years, testified that there had been some heavy storms at the beach; that barge boats and barge tenders had drifted onto the beach; that in a heavy storm he had seen the breakers come over the Pacific Electric's former right of way—splash over it. The city's chief of police for the past seventeen years testified that on two or three occasions he had seen water against the westerly edge of the right of way—in the areas near 1st, 5th and 9th

Streets; that one of the occasions was some seventeen years ago, when a barge was washed ashore on 1st Street.

In support of their claim that their property was suitable for residential development, plaintiffs called as a witness Colonel Leeds, a qualified civil and consulting engineer. He testified that any residence construction on plaintiffs' property would have to be on pilings; that he would place the structure on concrete or steel piles, the top of which would be at an elevation of approximately 20 feet above mean low water; that he had prepared a diagram, admitted in evidence as plaintiffs' Exhibit 62, showing residential development of plaintiffs' property, allowing 35 feet west of the Pacific Electric's former right of way (the state park strip) for a public roadway and the next 75 feet oceanward for the construction of houses on pilings; that in his opinion houses so erected would be safe from damage from the ocean. On cross-examination, he testified that he did not know that on occasion the Pacific Electric's former right of way at Manhattan Beach had been under water; that he did not know that heavy sea and storm water had come up over the strand in 1938 and caused severe damage; that he had not made any investigation as to whether the city would approve a 35-foot roadway; that he had seen no subdivision plan for this beach area; that in forming his opinion as to the safety of constructing houses on plaintiffs' property, he had considered the presence of houses at Hermosa Beach, adjoining plaintiffs' property on the south, and that the front of the houses built on plaintiffs' property would be westerly of the front of the houses on Hermosa Beach; that the height to which water is projected shoreward depends upon wave and wind action—ground swells are a form of wave; that damage to piers and structures on beaches is usually caused by ground swells, which are produced by distant storms or submarine earthquakes—in other words, there may be heavy ground swells along a beach on a perfectly calm day; that he would construct the houses on pilings driven about 10 feet below low water, so that if an unanticipated storm should occur, it could gouge out several feet of the beach and the house would still stand and be safe. He was then asked the following question: "Would you feel, Colonel, that intelligent and reasonable minds might reasonably differ as to the possible danger of construction of residences in accordance with the scheme indicated on Exhibit 62?" He replied: "Yes, I think you would find difficulty in getting all engineers to agree on one solution as being the only solution. It would depend on the degree of safety that you wanted, and various other factors. Only a very, very foolish engineer claims to be infallible." Plaintiffs argue that such admission was limited to the proposed residential plan of Colonel Leeds and did not signify that engineers would differ in opinion as to the safety of houses built in accordance with other plans, such as higher, stronger or differently arranged pilings. This may be true as an abstract proposition, but there was no testimony to that effect. Obviously, as the city concedes, many structures are apparently safely erected many miles out in the ocean, such as offshore oil drilling and pumping derricks, and undoubtedly it would be possible at considerable expense to have safe residential construction on plaintiffs' property if the pilings were driven deeply enough and the houses built high enough to eliminate threatening ocean tide and wave action. However, the question is not whether it may be humanly possible to build houses on plaintiffs' property which would be safe in times of storms, high tides and ground swells, but whether such beach property is suitable for residential development pursuant to some representative plan such as that proposed by Colonel Leeds and as to which he himself admitted there could be a difference of opinion in regard to the safety factor.

It was stipulated that the judge might view the property and that he might consider as evidence everything that he saw in making such inspection. The visit was made in the company of an attorney for plaintiffs, an attorney for the city, and the clerk of the court. Thereafter the judge made a statement in open court regarding his observations. Among other things, he noted that the westerly side of the proposed 35-foot roadway was at least 12 feet lower than the general level of the Pacific Electric's former right of way; that the westerly side of the proposed roadway was beach that was obviously subject to flooding at extremely high tides or during storms; that if the proposed houses were built on plaintiffs' property westerly of the proposed 35-foot roadway, they would be right on the beach and unless they were protected by an adequate sea wall, they would be subject to a constant hazard of destruction by the sea. After stating that counsel during the visit to the premises had expressed no difference of opinion with his observations, the judge made the further remark that his view of plaintiffs' property demonstrated to him that the safety of the proposed construction of houses thereon was "a question upon which reasonable minds might differ."

[5-7] The trial judge's view of plaintiffs' property with the consent of counsel is evidence in the case and "may be used alone or with other evidence to support the findings." Noble v. Kertz & Sons Feed etc. Co., 72 Cal.App.2d 153, 159, 164 P.2d 257, 260; see, also, Wilkins v. City of San Bernardino, 29 Cal.2d 332, 348, 175 P.2d 542; Safeway Stores v. City Council, San Mateo, 86 Cal.App.2d 277, 284, 194 P.2d 720; Wheeler v. Gregg, 90 Cal.App.2d 348, 366, 203 P.2d 37; Sindell v. Smutz, 100 Cal.App. 2d 10, 15-16, 222 P.2d 903.

Plaintiffs argue that the trial judge's observations are not evidence because he did not view the premises under storm conditions. They cite on this point Fendley v. City of Anaheim, 110 Cal.App. 731, 294 P. 769. The plaintiffs there claimed that defendant's operation of a power plant jarred their residence and caused damage. The evidence established that most of the discomforts occurred at nighttime. There was no evidence to the contrary and in such circumstances, the trial court's inspection of the premises in the daytime was an insufficient basis to sustain its finding that the operation of the plant caused no discomfort to plaintiffs. Here, however, neither the expert witness, Colonel Leeds, nor the trial judge purported to recite existing conditions and physical facts observed on a visit to plaintiffs' property during time of storm: There was, moreover, undisputed evidence that in stormy weather sea water had extended further landward than plaintiffs' property. The trial judge merely applied such uncontradicted evidence to his own observations of the physical topography of the premises in determining the safety of residential development on piling construction along the beach frontage. Expert testimony is to be given the weight to which it appears in each case to be justly entitled. In the event of conflict, the law ordinarily makes no distinction between expert testimony and evidence of other character; either may be accepted by the trier of fact as the basis for findings on disputed factual issues. Arais v. Kalensnikoff, 10 Cal.2d 428, 432, 74 P.2d 1043, 115 A.L.R. 163; Liberty Mut. Ins. Co. v. Industrial Acc. Comm., 33 Cal.2d 89, 94, 199 P.2d 302; see, also, Gibson Properties Co. v. City of Oakland, 12 Cal.2d 291, 297-298, 83 P.2d 942.

[8, 9] In addition, the court found, upon the testimony of the city's chief of police, that the construction of houses on pilings might create police problems by reason of the possible use of the areas under the residences for immoral purposes. Municipal ordinances tending to minimize opportunity for immoral practices in relation to other types of construction such as billboards have been held within the police power. Cusack Co. v. City of Chicago, 242 U.S. 526, 529, 37 S.Ct. 190, 61 L.Ed. 472. In the light of these considerations, the zoning restriction of plaintiffs' property for beach recreational purposes appears to be a legitimate exercise of the city's police power in the interests of public health, safety, morals and general welfare. Where substantial reason exists to support the determination of the city council in matters of opinion or policy affecting zoning plans and the propriety of the districting classification is "fairly debatable" in furtherance of the community development, courts will not substitute their judgment for that of the municipal authority. Lockard v. City of Los Angeles, 33 Cal.2d 453, 462, 202 P.2d 38, 7 A.L.R.2d 990.

[10, 11] The fact that plaintiffs, may suffer some financial detriment does not require invalidation of the zoning restriction, for "every exercise of the police power is apt to affect adversely the property interest of somebody." Zahn v. Board of Public Works, 195 Cal. 497, 512, 234 P. 388, 394. As was said in Wilkins v. City of San Bernardino, supra, 29 Cal.2d 332, at page 338, 175 P.2d 542, at page 547, "It is implicit in the theory of police power that an individual cannot complain of incidental injury, if the power is exercised for proper purposes of public health, safety, morals and general welfare, and if there is no arbitrary and unreasonable application in the particular case." While plaintiffs recognize that some values incident to property must yield to the police power, they argue that the zoning restriction as applied to their beach land goes beyond mere regulation and constitutes an unwarranted interference with the use of their property so as to exceed the scope of permissible zoning. They cite in particular the

case of Pennsylvania Coal Co. v. Mahon, 260 U.S. 393, 413, 43 S.Ct. 158, 159, 67 L.Ed. 322. But as there stated, "the question depends upon the particular facts." That was an action between two private parties, the statute involved admittedly destroyed previously existing rights of property and contract as reserved between the parties, and the propriety of the statute's prohibition upon the single valuable use of the property for coal-mining operations was considered in relation to special benefits to be gained by an individual rather than by the whole community. In those circumstances application of the statute to the property was held to effect such diminution in its value as to be unconstitutional and beyond the legitimate scope of the police power.

[12] Factually dissimilar cases cannot avail plaintiffs in their attack upon the zoning restriction upon due process grounds. Typical of such cited cases is Panhandle Eastern Pipe Line Co. v. State Highway Com., 294 U.S. 483, 55 S.Ct. 563, 79 L.Ed. 1090, where the state in the purported exercise of its police power attempted to have a private property owner make at its own expense changes in structural improvements for public safety in travel upon the highway. It was held that such changes could be required of the property owner only upon the payment of compensation —a principle of decision well recognized in relation to the exercise of the police power within constitutional limits. City of Oakland v. Schenck, 197 Cal. 456, 461, 241 P. 545.

Here plaintiffs produced no evidence of value relative to the use of their property either before or after passage of the 1941 ordinance. Admittedly they have been paying substantial taxes on their property. Prior to the 1941 ordinance and while the property was zoned for residential use, plaintiffs claimed that it could not be so utilized profitably and they then unsuccessfully sought a rezoning for business purposes. Since 1941, with the zoning limitation upon their property as a beach district and subject to commercial operation for beach recreational purposes, plaintiff have still made no use of their property as authorized but seek its return to residential classification, a districting which they had previously deemed undesirable. Now they maintain that the 1941 restriction effects a confiscatory taking of their property but they have made no showing that their beach frontage could not be put to beneficial use in conformity with the zoning limitation. The city's planning expert expressly testified that plaintiffs' property was zoned for beach instead of residential use so as to give "the owners * * * the right to derive an income" therefrom. So distinguishable are cases cited by plaintiffs where the relative values in respective uses of the zoned property were shown, e. g. Long v. City of Highland Park, 329 Mich. 146, 45 N.W.2d 10, 12; State ex. rel. Tingley v. Gurda, 209 Wis. 63, 243 N.W. 317, 320; where changed conditions rendered previous zoning limitations unsuitable, e. g. Arverne Bay Const. Co. v. Thatcher, 278 N.Y. 222, 15 N.E.2d 587, 591-592, 117 A.L.R. 1110; Skalko v. City of Sunnyvale, 14 Cal.2d 213, 216, 93 P.2d 93; where "spot" zoning created an "island" in the middle of a larger area devoted to other uses, e. g. Maxwell v. Incorporated Village of Rockville Centre, Sup., 84 N.Y.S.2d 544, 545-546; Reynolds v. Barrett, 12 Cal.2d 244, 251, 83 P.2d 29; where the zoning restriction deprived the property owner of all beneficial or profitable use of the property, e. g. Eaton v. Sweeney, 257 N.Y. 176, 177 N.E. 412, 414.

[13, 14] Plaintiffs refer to McCarthy's above-mentioned letter to the city council in the summer of 1940 advising of the public destruction of the fence they were attempting to build on their property. They contend that the city was thereby put on notice that plaintiffs could not successfully maintain any fence around their beach property and charge a fee for its use for recreational activities because of the threat of "mob violence." But that alleged destruction occurred when plaintiffs' property was zoned for residential use and more than a year prior to the enactment of the 1941 ordinance. The city's liability for such damage is fixed by statute, Government Code, § 50140, subject to the one-year period of limitations for commencement of the action, Ibid, § 50141. But in any event such act of mob violence, so remote in point of time, is not germane to the issue of reasonable zoning of plaintiffs' property under the 1941 ordinance, and it must be presumed that the city could perform its duty in affording police protection to safeguard plaintiffs' property. The physical facts and surrounding circumstances, not the possible action of unidentified third persons, provide the test for determining the validity of zoning regulations. Lockard v. City of Los Angeles, supra, 33 Cal.2d 453, 461, 202 P.2d 38; Clemons v. City of Los Angeles, supra, 36 Cal.2d 95, 100, 222 P.2d 439.

[15, 16] The trial court properly disregarded plaintiffs' contention that the 1941 zoning restriction of their property was not made in good faith but was a maladministration of the city's police power pursuant to a scheme or plan of action to depress the value of plaintiffs' beach property so that it could eventually be acquired by the public authorities at the lowest price possible, and meanwhile be used for public recreational purposes. The record simply shows that following the 1938 determination of the city's quiet title action in favor of plaintiffs' predecessors in interest in the beach property, City of Manhattan Beach v. Cortelyou, supra, 10 Cal.2d 653, 76 P.2d 483, plaintiffs and the city endeavored together—through extended informal negotiations evidenced by the city council's resolutions and the interchange of voluminous correspondence—to interest the public authorities in the purchase of plaintiffs' land for permanent beach recreational purposes; that in 1940 plaintiffs sought an amendment of the ordinance then zoning their property for residential purposes, so as to permit some business use thereon and said request, after public hearings, was denied; that in 1941 the zoning ordinance in question was passed, restricting plaintiffs' property to beach recreational purposes pursuant to an overall city-wide zoning plan, but permitting commercial use to be made of plaintiffs' property according to the zoning limitation; that thereafter, and for nine years, plaintiffs made no attempt to use their property so as to derive

any income pursuant to the purposes authorized by the 1941 ordinance but the city and plaintiffs still continued to negotiate and work together in an effort to further public acquisition of plaintiffs' property; that in November, 1950, plaintiffs made their first move in objection to the zoning restriction, when they sought its modification to permit residential construction thereon though they had previously been dissatisfied with such residential limitation and wanted the property available for business use; and then upon the denial of their request in early 1951, plaintiffs brought this declaratory relief action.   While plaintiffs charge that the "scheme" was initiated shortly after the city lost its quiet title action and included the state's condemnation suit brought ten years later in 1948 (and still pending), plaintiffs did not call one city official to the witness stand to testify on the matter.   See Safeway Stores v. City Council, San Mateo, supra, 86 Cal.App.2d 277, 287, 194 P.2d 720.   The only evidence, except physical facts, as to the purpose of the 1941 zoning restrictions, was the abovementioned testimony of the city's planning experts, attesting to the adoption of the city-wide zoning plan in the interest of the general welfare.   The trial court, in its comments upon the evidence and plaintiffs' specific charges, determined that the city council had not been actuated by any improper motive or intent in the matter.

Plaintiffs' claims are entirely immaterial in view of the settled rule that "the purpose or motive of the city officials in passing an ordinance is irrelevant to any inquiry concerning the reasonableness of the ordinance. * * * If the conditions justify the enactment of the ordinance, the motives prompting its enactment are of no consequence. If the conditions do not justify the enactment, the inquiry as to motive becomes useless. * * *" Sunny Slope Water Co. v. City of Pasadena, 1 Cal.2d 87, 99, 33 P.2d 672, 677.   The cases which plaintiffs cite as example of the maladministration of the police power involve factual dissimilarities, which render them inapplicable here: Grand River Dam Authority v. Grand-Hydro., 200 Okl. 157, 201 P.2d 225, at page 228, where the state passed an act removing the principal value of the property and then sought to "acquire the property by condemnation, basing the reimbursement to the owner on the reduced value," State ex rel. Tingley v. Gurda, supra, 209 Wis. 63, 243 N.W. 317; Grand Trunk Western R. Co. v. City of Detroit, 326 Mich. 387, 40 N.W.2d 195; and Long v. City of Highland Park, supra, 329 Mich. 146, 45 N.W.2d 10, where the ordinance effected "spot" zoning and there was evidence showing significant relative value differentials in use of the property; and Dobbins v. Los Angeles, 195 U.S. 223, 25 S.Ct. 18, 49 L.Ed. 169, where a private citizen was led in good faith to make large expenditures on certain property pursuant to the terms of an ordinance and thereafter, without change in existing conditions within the city, a second ordinance was passed prohibiting the previously authorized use, thereby destroying a considerable property investment.

Plaintiffs also argue the error of several rulings of the trial court in the rejection of evidence. The first concerns certain testimony of Mr. McCarthy relative to conversations had with city officials and offered in support of plaintiffs' claim of improper motive on the part of the city council in its adoption of the 1941 zoning restriction on plaintiffs' property. Objection to this testimony was properly sustained. The assigned motive or purpose of various city officials in passing a zoning ordinance was irrelevant to any inquiry concerning its reasonableness in municipal overall planning. Sunny Slope Water Co. v. City of Pasadena, supra, 1 Cal. 2d 87, 99, 33 P.2d 672.

[17] Plaintiffs next assert that the trial court committed prejudicial error in rejecting certain expert testimony relative to the suitability of plaintiffs' property for subdivision for residential purposes. But such testimony had only cumulative value in that its admission would have added nothing to what was already before the court through Colonel Leeds' statements as to the feasibility of the residential development of the beach property and his proposed plan. There was no dispute that plaintiffs property could be so subdivided and the court recognized that fact after viewing the premises. Under the circumstances plaintiffs suffered no prejudice from the ruling.

Plaintiffs finally argue the point of the trial court's disposition of McCarthy's above-mentioned letter of July, 1940, notifying the city of the public destruction of the fence which was being erected on the property. The record shows some confusion on this phase of the case. This letter, upon objection, was originally rejected by the trial court but marked for identification. Then later in the trial when McCarthy testified as to the particular acts of "mob violence" experienced more than a year before the 1941 zoning regulation was adopted, the trial court commented that his testimony was "related in the document that is in evidence (the letter)." As aforestated, possible damage to plaintiffs property through mob violence and the city's liability therefor are matters wholly covered by statute, Gov. Code, §§ 50140-50141, and not germane to the issue of reasonableness of the zoning process in city-wide planning. But regardless of this consideration, the trial court apparently treated the particular letter as in evidence, corroborating McCarthy's testimony, and plaintiffs now have no ground for complaint.

[18] As the record has been reviewed, the zoning restriction of the 1941 ordinance (§ 10) on the use of plaintiffs' property appears to be a fair, just and reasonable regulation for the general welfare of the city as a whole, and not so burdensome that it contravenes the constitutional guarantees in protection of property rights. See City of Miami Beach v. Hogan, Fla. 1953, 63 So.2d 493, 494-495.

The judgment is affirmed.

EDMONDS and TRAYNOR, JJ., concur.

CARTER, Justice (concurring).

I concur in the judgment of affirmance because I can see no escape from the proposition that the record in this case presents a factual situation as to the reasonableness of the ordinance here in question upon which reasonable minds might differ. Such being the case it cannot fairly or honestly be said as a matter of law that as applied to plaintiff's property the ordinance is so unreasonable as to constitute an arbitrary and unconstitutional exercise of the police power by the defendant.

I have heretofore given expression to my views with respect to the validity of zoning ordinances enacted by city councils and boards of supervisors which arbitrarily and unreasonably limit and restrict the use of private property under the guise that such limitation and restriction constitute a reasonable exercise of the police power. See, County of San Diego v. McClurken, 37 Cal.2d 683, 692, 234 P.2d 972; Clemons v. City of Los Angeles, 36 Cal.2d 95, 107, 222 P.2d 439; Ayres v. City Council of Los Angeles, 34 Cal.2d 31, 43, 207 P.2d 1, 11 A.L.R.2d 503; Lockard v. City of Los Angeles, 33 Cal.2d 453, 468, 202 P.2d 38, 7 A.L.R.2d 990; Wilkins v. City of San Bernardino, 29 Cal.2d 332, 345, 175 P.2d 542.

In the McClurken, Lockard and Wilkins cases, supra, the trial court had held the zoning ordinance in each of said cases unconstitutional as applied to the property there involved and this Court by a bare majority reversed the trial court notwithstanding the record contained overwhelming evidence that the ordinance in each of said cases was so arbitrary and unreasonable as to seriously impair the value of the property affected by the ordinance. In the Wilkins case the trial judge viewed the premises. This is likewise true in the case at bar. It has been repeatedly held that the observations of a trial judge in viewing the premises or scene of the controversy is evidence in the case upon which findings may be based. Neel v. Mannings, Inc., 19 Cal.2d 647, 122 P.2d 576; Gates v. McKinnon, 18 Cal.2d 179, 114 P.2d 576; Ethel D. Co. v. Industrial Acc. Comm., 219 Cal. 699, 28 P.2d 919; People v. Milner, 122 Cal. 171, 54 P. 833; Gastine v. Ewing, 65 Cal.App. 2d 131, 150 P.2d 266; MacPherson v. West Coast Transit Co., 94 Cal.App. 463, 271 P.509; Vaughan v. County of Tulare, 56 Cal.App. 621, 205 P. 21.

Notwithstanding this circumstance a bare majority of this Court held that the findings that the enforcement of the ordinance would be oppressive, confiscatory and an unreasonable restriction on plaintiff's property rights were not supported by the evidence.

At page 352 of 29 Cal.2d, at page 555 of 175 P.2d of my dissent in the Wilkins case, supra, I stated: "The effect of the majority opinion in this case is to commit to the legislative body the solution of all questions of both fact and law which arise when a zoning ordinance is attacked for unreasonableness in its application to certain property unjustly affected thereby. This is contrary to the rule which has been uniformly followed in the prior decisions of this court hereinabove cited and discussed. The decision of the trial court is in accord with these decisions and should therefore be affirmed." In the Lockard case, supra, the majority of this Court stated in 33 Cal.2d at page 462, 202 P.2d at page 43: "The findings and conclusions of the trial court as to the reasonableness of a zoning ordinance are not binding on an appellate court if the record shows that the question is debatable and that there may be a difference of opinion on the subject. The appellate courts look beyond such determinations and consider in some detail the basic physical facts appearing in the record, such as the character of the property of the objecting parties, the nature of the surrounding territory, the use to which each has been put, recent trends of development, etc., to ascertain whether the reasonableness of the ordinance is fairly debatable." In my dissent in that case I stated in 33 Cal.2d at page 473, 202 P.2d at page 49: "In essence, what the majority opinion holds is this: That the validity of such an ordinance depends upon whether four members of this Court think it is reasonable as applied to plaintiffs' property, they being the judges of both fact and law. Such being the case, the function of the trial court is that of a mere referee to hear the evidence and make his recommendation which has no binding effect as a factual determination. This is indeed a new and unique legal philosophy of law without constitutional or statutory postulate."

In every zoning case which has come before this Court since I have been a member of it, I have taken the position that the law should be that the determination of the reasonableness of zoning ordinances as applied to private property is a question of fact to be determined by the trial court and if its determination is supported by sufficient competent evidence, such determination is binding upon an appellate court the same as in other cases where factual situations are involved. It has been my position that under the Constitution and laws of this state, fact finding powers are reposed in juries and trial judges and that where factual determinations are made by juries and trial judges upon sufficient competent evidence and no error has been committed prejudicial to the party against whom such determination is made, the appellate courts of this state are bound by such determinations as such courts have no fact finding powers and their only function is to determine issues of law; that an issue of fact becomes an issue of law only where no fact is left in doubt, and no deduction or inference can be drawn in support of an issue that the court can say, as a matter of law, that the issue has not been established. And even where the facts are undisputed, if reasonable minds might draw different conclusions from the evidence the issue is one of fact to be determined by the trier of fact. This is the traditional rule which has been followed by this Court since its institution in 1850 with the exception of the past two or three years when this Court has assumed the role of a fact finding tribunal both in zoning ordinance cases and many other cases, see dissenting opinion in Gray v. Brinkerhoff, 41 Cal. 2d—, 258 P.2d 834.

As stated at the beginning of this opinion the record in this case presents a factual situation as to the reasonableness of the ordinance here involved, as applied to plaintiff's property, upon which reasonable minds might differ, the trial judge viewed the premises and made findings to the effect that the ordinance as applied to plaintiff's property was and is reasonable. In view of this state of the record and the law as it has been declared by this Court, I can see no escape from the affirmance of the judgment.

SCHAUER, Justice (dissenting).

I dissent. In my view the opinion of the District Court of Appeal, authored by Justice Parker Wood and concurred in by Presiding Justice Shinn and Justice Vallee (reported in 257 P.2d 679-690), adequately discusses and correctly resolves all issues of law presented on this appeal.

From 1923 to June 26, 1941 (when ordinance No. 502 was passed), plaintiffs' property was zoned as residential property. Not until after the city failed in an attempt to quiet title to the property, and in efforts to purchase it, extending over several years, did the city, in 1941, pass ordinance 502, thereby zoning the property so as to limit it to beach recreation activities and cause it to remain available for public use without requiring the public or any public body to expend any money therefor, and to remain without income to plaintiffs but subject to some $9,000 in annual taxes. At the time this action was commenced plaintiffs' was the only privately owned property falling within the beach recreation zone (B-1). Moreover, the city had failed to provide plaintiffs with police protection to avoid destruction of a fence designed to protect the property from the encroaching public. These circumstances appear to me to constitute a clear and deliberate taking of the property for public use without the payment of compensation therefor.

Such taking of private property without compensation, as effected in this case, appears to me to go beyond any reasonable application of the police power of a constitutional state which would maintain capitalism as the foundation of its institutions. Capitalism is not to be ashamed of or whittled away. It encompasses the economic system which has brought our country to world leadership. It denotes a way of living in society and of having dealings with others for reciprocal benefits and with mutual gain; it thrives on free enterprise and competition; and it furnishes incentive to be diligent, efficient and thrifty. It means that a man is free, not a slave; that he alone or collectively with others may bargain for his labor and receive and possess the price thereof; that he alone or collectively with others may invest his earnings in real or other property; and that in either event he shall be protected in his right to work and in the ownership and enjoyment of his wealth.

The fact that a particular property is desirable for the public use does not make its private ownership unlawful or warrant using the power of government to destroy its value. Our Constitution envisages a taking for public use in all proper cases but it no more permits to the state a taking without paying fair compensation than it does to an individual. As between the state and an individual our first concern always should be to guard the rights of the individual, not to build up the power of the state. Under my view of constitutional American procedures the state, when it takes private property for the public use, must, if purchase for a fair price cannot be negotiated, proceed under the power of eminent domain, condemn the property desired, and pay the reasonable value as fixed by a jury. Taking the property as is here done does not appear to me to be encompassed within a reasonable exercise of police power by a constitutional state; it smacks more of calculated and arbitrary confiscation by a police state. Besides all that, I should like to think that the scheme here resorted to was beneath the honor of a self-respecting American municipality.

For the reasons more fully developed in the able opinion of Mr. Justice Wood, above referred to, I would reverse the judgment.

SHENK, Justice (dissenting).

I dissent. I agree with the District Court of Appeal of the Second Appellate District, Division 3, and would reverse the judgment for the reasons stated by that court in its opinion reported in 257 P.2d 679-690, inclusive.

Rehearing denied; SHENK and SCHAUER, JJ., dissenting.

Questions and Notes

1. This is perhaps the ultimate example of the California case law, with rather rough treatment for developers.
2. Why did Manhattan Beach not pay for the land as a park?
3. What was the safety argument in this case?
4. What was the moral argument?

TURNPIKE REALTY COMPANY

v.

TOWN OF DEDHAM

284 N.E.2d 891 (Mass., 1972), cert. denied, 409 U.S. 1108(1973).

Supreme Judicial Court of Massachusetts, Norfolk.

Argued April 6, 1972.

Decided June 26, 1972.

Action by landowner to determine, inter alia, validity of an amendment to a zoning bylaw as applied to his land. The Land Court, Silverio, J., ruled that bylaw was valid, and landowner excepted. The Supreme Judicial

Court, Spiegel, J., held, inter alia, that authority to enact flood plain zoning bylaws was contained in general grant of power to zone for public health, safety, and welfare, and was not limited by section of enabling law which provided that a zoning bylaw could provide that lands deemed subject to seasonal or periodic flooding could not be used for residence or other purposes in such a manner as to endanger the health or safety of the occupants thereof.

Exceptions overruled.

Antonino F. Iovino, Boston, for petitioner.

Herbert P. Wilkins, Boston (Acheson H. Callaghan, Jr., and Jeffrey Swope, Boston, with him) for respondent.

John A. Perkins, Town Counsel, joined in a brief.

Before TAURO, C. J., and SPIEGEL, BRAUCHER, and HENNESSEY, JJ.

SPIEGEL, Justice.

The petitioner, the owner of 61.9 acres of land in Dedham, brought this petition in the Land Court under the provisions of G.L. c. 185, § 1 (j½), and c. 240, § 14A, to determine, inter alia, the validity of an amendment to a zoning by-law as applied to the land of the petitioner. The judge in his decision ruled that the by-law "was a valid exercise of the authority and powers conferred upon the respondent . . . by . . . [G.L. c.] 40A and is in full force and effect as to the petitioner's land." The case is here on the petitioner's exceptions to several of the judge's findings and to his denial of a number of the petitioner's requests for rulings.

The petitioner acquired the land in question in 1947. It is made up of uplands and lowlands and includes two knolls, one of 3.2 acres and the other of .2 acres, which rise above the elevation of the petitioner's lowland. The land is bounded by Route 1, the Boston-Dedham boundary line, the Charles River, and the Mother Brook. At the annual town meeting in 1963 the respondent amended its "zoning by-laws and [z]oning [m]ap" by adopting a zoning bylaw establishing a "Flood Plain District," which included "the land of the petitioner, except for a minor portion thereof." Prior to the amendment the entire area involved in this case was in a general residence zoning district. The judge found that the knolls were included in the flood plain district. The remaining land of the petitioner is "a low swampy area" bordering on the Charles River.

Pertinent portions of the by-law, with paragraph numbers added by us for clarity of reference, are as follows: "[1] The purpose of the Flood Plain District is to preserve and maintain the ground water table; to protect the public health and safety, persons and property against the hazards of flood water inundation; for the protection of the community against the costs which may be incurred when unsuitable development occurs in swamps, marshes, along water courses, or in areas subject to floods; and to conserve natural conditions, wild life, and open spaces for the education, recreation and general welfare of the public. [2] Within a Flood Plain District no structure or building shall be erected, altered or used, and no premises shall be used except for one or more of the following uses: Any woodland, grassland, wetland, agricultural, horticultural, or recreational use of land or water not requiring filling. Buildings and sheds accessory to any of the Flood Plain uses are permitted on approval of the Board of Appeals. Notice of each such Flood Plain building permit application shall be given to the Town Public Works Department, to the Town Board of Health, to the Town Planning Board, and to the Town Conservation Commission as well as all other parties required. [3] The Board of Appeals, in hearing such application, shall consider, in addition to any other factors said Board deems pertinent, the following aspects with respect to flooding and Flood Plain District zoning provisions: that any such building or structure shall be designed, placed, and constructed to offer a minimum obstruction to the flow of water; and that it shall be firmly anchored to prevent floating away. [4] If any land in the Flood Plain district is proven to the satisfaction of the Board of Appeals after the question has been referred to the Planning Board, the Board of Health, and the Board of Selectmen, and reported on by all three boards or the lapse of thirty days from the date of referral without a report, as being in fact not subject to flooding or not unsuitable because of drainage conditions for any use which would otherwise be permitted if such land were not, by operation of this section, in the Flood Plain district, and that the use of such land for any such use will not interfere with the general purposes for which Flood Plain districts have been established, and will not be detrimental to the public health, safety, or welfare, the Board of Appeals may, after a public hearing with due notice, issue a permit for any such use. [5] Except as provided above, there shall be in the Flood Plain District: No land fill or dumping in any part of the District. No drainage other than Flood Control works by an authorized public agency. No damming or relocation of any water course except as part of an over-all drainage basin plan. No building or structure. No permanent storage of materials or equipment. [6] In any Flood Plain District after the adoption of this provision, no land, building, or structure shall be used for sustained human occupancy except dwellings theretofore lawfully existing, or land, buildings or structures which comply with the provisions of this by-law."

The petitioner attacks the validity of the by-law on several grounds. Many of its arguments overlap. We treat with its central contentions as it has presented them in its brief.

1. A recurrent argument throughout the petitioner's brief is that the prime purpose of the by-law was to "retain . . . [its] land in its natural state and as a flood water detention basin." It appears to rely to a considerable extent on various statements made by members of the Dedham conservation commission which suggest that their primary interest in urging the adoption of the by-law was for the above reasons. This demonstrates, it argues, that the by-law was "not regulatory, but confiscatory."

[1] The validity of this by-law does not hinge upon the motives of its supporters. See Caires v. Building Commr. of Hingham, 323 Mass. 589, 596, 83 N.E.2d 550. The reasons for the creation of the flood plain district are clearly set forth in the by-law itself. There is no need to speculate about the "prime purpose" of the by-law. Whether the stated purposes are within the authority granted by the Zoning Enabling Act, G.L. c. 40A, is a question which we will consider in the course of this opinion.

2. The petitioner takes the position that lands which are not subject to flooding from "natural" causes cannot or should not be included in a flood plain district, and that the judge's rulings denying the petitioner's requests on this point were erroneous.[1] It admits that its land was on occasions "covered with water" because of the overflow from the Charles River but charges this to mismanagement of the Mother Brook bascule gate[2] by one Salvatore Trementozzi, an employee of the Metropolitan District Commission. The petitioner seeks to characterize this flooding as "artificial."

The Mother Brook bascule gate was completed in 1959 as part of flood control work on the Charles River to reduce the effect of flooding. Trementozzi testified that when the gate is lowered, water is diverted into Mother Brook; when it is raised, water remains in the Charles River. He also testified that he made the decision "on a regular basis" whether to raise or lower the gate. On certain dates when the petitioner's land was flooded, Trementozzi decided not to lower the gate. The petitioner argues that the flooding over its land could have been prevented by "proper" operation of the gate. The evidence, however, in no way suggests that Trementozzi's management of the gate was unreasonable, or that "the locus was . . . an area which was being utilized by Trementozzi, at the expense of the petitioner, for public purposes."

Although the judge did not make explicit findings of fact on this point, it is clear that he considered the petitioner's contention. In any event, we are of opinion that the judge was correct in denying the petitioner's requests for rulings on this issue.

3. The petitioner argues that "the enactment of the by-law was arbitrary, capricious and unreasonable and went beyond the authority granted in the last sentence of" c. 40A, § 2, which reads as follows: "A zoning . . . by-law may provide that lands deemed subject to seasonal or periodic flooding shall not be used for residence or other purposes in such a manner as to endanger the health or safety of the occupants thereof."

The preamble of the by-law sets out its purposes: (numbers added for clarity of reference "[1] to preserve and maintain the ground water table;

---

1. These requests were: "7. The word 'flooding' in the enabling statute . . . means flooding from natural causes. . . . 11. The enabling statute does not authorize the inclusion of lands in a Flood Plain district which are not subject to seasonal or periodic flooding from natural causes."

2. Webster's Third New Intl. Dictionary defines "bascule" as follows: "[A]n apparatus or structure in which one end is counterbalanced by the other on the principle of the seesaw or by weights."

[2] to protect the public health and safety, persons and property against the hazards of flood water inundation; [3] for the protection of the community against the costs which may be incurred when unsuitable development occurs in swamps, marshes, along water courses, or in areas subject to floods; [4] and to conserve natural conditions, wild life, and open spaces for the education, recreation and general welfare of the public."

[2, 3] We first state our view that the last sentence of G.L. c. 40A, § 2, does not in any way limit the authority of a municipality to enact a flood plain zoning by-law. Even before the last sentence became part of the enabling act,[3] we believe that a municipality could validly have enacted a flood plain zoning by-law under the general grant of authority in G.L. c. 40A, § 2 (to promote the "health, safety, convenience, morals or welfare"), and for the reasons set forth in G.L. c. 40A, § 3 ("to secure safety from fire, panic and other dangers"). See Dunham, Flood Control Via the Police Power, 107 U. of Pa.L. Rev. 1098, 1118-1121. Although it might be argued that such authority to enact flood plain zoning could not be implied before the insertion of the last sentence of G.L. c. 40A, § 2, and that we must therefore regard the objective of such flood plain zoning as limited to the protection of "occupants" of residences on land subject to flooding, we think it "just as logical to regard . . . [the last sentence of G.L. c. 40A, § 2] as a clarification of an ambiguity and a legislative interpretation of the original act." See Fitz-Inn Auto Parks, Inc. v. Commissioner of Labor & Indus. 350 Mass. 39, 42, 213 N.E.2d 245. We believe that the test governing the validity of a flood plain zoning by-law or ordinance is the same as that governing any other zoning by-law or ordinance. "The test is whether there has been shown any substantial relation between the amendment and the furtherance of any of the general objects of the enabling act. Caires v. Building Commr. of Hingham, 323 Mass. 589, 593, 83 N.E.2d 550. Lamarre v. Commissioner of Pub. Works of Fall River, 324 Mass. 542, 545, 87 N.E.2d 211. The promotion of the public welfare, as that term is fairly broadly construed, is chief among the purposes of the enabling statute." Lanner v. Board of Appeal of Tewksbury, 348 Mass. 220, 228, 202 N.E.2d 777, 784.

More specifically, three basic public policy objectives of restricting use of flood plains have been advanced: (1) the protection of individuals who might choose, despite the flood dangers, to develop or occupy land on a flood plain; (2) the protection of other landowners from damages resulting from the development of a flood plain and the consequent obstruction of the flood flow; (3) the protection of the entire community from individual choices of land use which require subsequent public expenditures for public works and disaster relief. See Dunham, Flood Control Via the Police Power, 107 U. of Pa.L.Rev. 1098, 1110-1117.

---

3. The sentence was added by Sr. 1954, c. 368, § 2, as part of a general revision of the Zoning Enabling Act.

[4] The first three stated purposes of the by-law are consistent with these objectives.[4] The fourth purpose would fall into the category of "[a]esthetic considerations." Barney & Carey Co. v. Milton, 324 Mass. 440, 448, 87 N.E.2d 9, 14. In the *Barney and Carey* case, we said: "Aesthetic considerations may not be disregarded in determining the validity of a zoning by-law, but they do not alone justify restrictions upon private property merely for the purpose of preserving the beauty of a neighborhood or town." Furthermore, we said: "Regard for the preservation of the natural beauty of a neighborhood makes the enactment of a zoning regulation desirable but does not itself give vitality to the regulation." Since the by-law is fully supported by other valid considerations of public welfare, the additional purpose of conserving "natural conditions, wild life, and open spaces" does not bring it into conflict with the enabling act.

[5] The petitioner asserts that several other portions of the by-law are unreasonable and unduly burdensome. We do not agree. Paragraph 2 limits the uses of land in a flood plain district: "Within a Flood Plain District no structure or building shall be erected, altered or used, and no premises shall be used except for one or more of the following uses: Any woodland, grassland, wetland, agricultural, horticultural, or recreational use of land or water not requiring filling. Buildings and sheds accessory to any of the Flood Plain uses are permitted on approval of the Board of Appeals." Paragraph 3 contains specific considerations for the board of appeals in entertaining applications for construction of "accessory" buildings: i. e., "that any such building or structure shall be designed, placed, and constructed to offer a minimum obstruction to the flow of water; and that it shall be firmly anchored to prevent floating away." Paragraph 4 contains a separate and much broader exception than the "accessory" building exception of paragraph 2: "If any land in the Flood Plain district is proven to the satisfaction of the Board of Appeals after the question has been referred to the Planning Board, the Board of Health, and the Board of Selectmen, and reported on by all three boards or the lapse of thirty days from the date of referral without a report, as being in fact not subject to flooding or not unsuitable because of drainage conditions for any use which would otherwise be permitted if such land were not, by operation of this section, in the Flood Plain district, and that the use of such land for any such use will not interfere with the general purposes for which Flood Plain districts have been established, and will not be detrimental to the public health, safety, or welfare, the Board of Appeals may, after a public hearing with due notice, issue a permit for any such use." The petitioner asserts that these three paragraphs are conflicting. It contends that the board of appeals would be without authority to grant a permit for an "accessory" building (paragraph 2) "for it must be proven, under paragraph 4, to its 'satisfaction' that the land is not subject to flooding; and, therefore, any provision that a

---

4. It appears that the first purpose, preserving and maintaining the ground water table, is related to preventing depletion of the water supply.

building provide a minimum obstruction to the flow of water or be anchored to prevent its floating away (as in paragraph 3) is in conflict with paragraph 4." Similarly, it claims, the board could not grant a permit under paragraph 4 for any "use which would otherwise be permitted if such land were not . . . in the Flood Plain district" if such use does not meet the requirements of paragraph 3, or is contrary to the uses permitted in paragraph 2.

The judge correctly reconciled paragraphs 2 through 4 by distinguishing between the special permit procedure applicable to "accessory" buildings, and the special permit procedure relating to land "not subject to flooding or not unsuitable because of drainage conditions." The two procedures are independent. Restrictions concerning the water flow and anchoring make sense only when related to "accessory" buildings. Paragraph 4, by contrast, was intended to prevent injustice resulting from the establishment of zoning districts based on "the physical characteristics of substantial areas." Leahy v. Inspector of Bldgs. of New Bedford, 308 Mass. 128, 132, 31 N.E.2d 436, 438. An example of the type of situation where a landowner might resort to the procedure under paragraph 4 would be the two "knolls" on the petitioner's land which rise above the general level of the swamp.

[6] 4. The petitioner contends that several aspects of the by-law are vague and ambiguous. It argues that the phrase "Except as provided above" in paragraph 5 (which, inter alia, denies the right to fill, build, or permanently store materials or equipment) could refer to any of the four previous paragraphs. We think it clearly refers to the two types of special permits set out in paragraphs 2, 3 and 4. For instance, if the petitioner were granted a special permit to build an "accessory" building, paragraph 5 would not prevent it from filling its land for this purpose.

[7, 8] The petitioner particularly objects to the phrase "to the satisfaction of the Board of Appeals" in paragraph 4. It argues that there is no standard to measure "satisfaction" and thus an owner is subject to the "caprice and whim of men." As we have recently stated in the case of MacGibbon v. Board of Appeals of Duxbury, 356 Mass. 635, 637-638, 255 N.E.2d 347, "The delegation of authority to the board of appeals to act on applications for special permits for exceptions to the zoning by-law cannot leave the decision subject to the 'untrammeled discretion' or 'unbridled fiat' of the board. . . . The Zoning Enabling Act and the by-law together must provide adequate standards for the guidance of the board in deciding whether to grant or to withhold special permits. . . The standards need not be of such a detailed nature that they eliminate entirely the element of discretion from the board's decision." In the *MacGibbon* case, we concluded that sufficient standards for the board of appeals were contained in G.L. c. 40A, § 4, and § 8(d) of the Duxbury by-law, which provided that: "[t]he Board of Appeals may, in appropriate cases and subject to appropriate conditions and safeguards, make special exceptions to the terms of the by-law in harmony with their general purpose and intent, and in accordance with the specified rules contained in this by-law." In the instant case, the standards

to be applied by the board are at least as precise. The board must find that the land is not subject to flooding or not unsuitable because of drainage conditions for a particular use; and that such use will not interfere with the general purposes of the flood plain district, and will not be detrimental to the "public health, safety, or welfare." Moreover, the decision of the board is subject to judicial review under G.L. c. 40A, § 21, and, as in the *MacGibbon* case, may be reversed if it is "based on a legally untenable ground, or is unreasonable, whimsical, capricious or arbitrary." P. 639, 255 N.E.2d p. 350.

5. The petitioner further maintains that the special permit procedure is valueless because no permit under paragraph 4 for any use permitted by the underlying general residence zone could validly be granted because it would not be "in harmony with the general purpose and intent of the . . . by-law." G.L. c. 40A, § 4. If such permit were granted, the petitioner states, it would be "subject to annulment by action taken under [G.L.] c. 40A, § 16, by persons aggrieved or by mandamus proceedings.'

[9] The possibility that a special permit granted to a landowner would be contested in court and annulled does not render the by-law invalid. Moreover, in order for a special permit to be granted under paragraph 4, land would first have to be proven "not subject to flooding or not unsuitable because of drainage conditions." If this were the case, a special permit could be granted since it would not be in conflict with the general purpose of the by-law, which is to protect several classes of people from over-development of land subject to flooding.

6. We next discuss the petitioner's contention that the by-law, both on its face and as applied to its particular land, is unconstitutional.

[10-12] We have previously reviewed the purposes of the by-law and have determined that they comply with the authority granted by the enabling statute, G.L. c. 40A. To hold the by-law unconstitutional, we would have to hold that its terms are "clearly arbitrary and unreasonable, having no substantial relation to the public health, safety, morals, or general welfare." Euclid v. Ambler Realty Co., 272 U.S. 365, 395, 47 S.Ct. 114, 121, 71 L.Ed. 303. Wilbur v. Newton, 302 Mass. 38, 39, 18 N.E.2d 365, and cases cited. "Every presumption is to be afforded in favor of the validity of . . . [a by-law] and if its reasonableness is fairly debatable the judgment of the local authorities who gave it its being will prevail." Schertzer v. Somerville, 345 Mass. 747, 751, 189 N.E.2d 555, 558, and cases cited. The petitioner must sustain a "heavy burden" of showing that the by-law is in conflict with (a) the enabling act, G.L. c. 40A, or (b) applicable constitutional provisions. Pierce v. Wellesley, 336 Mass. 517, 521, 146 N.E.2d 666.

The general necessity of flood plain zoning to reduce the damage to life and property caused by flooding is unquestionable. See Dunham, Flood Control Via the Police Power, 107 U. of Pa.L.Rev. 1098; Note, Flood Plain Zoning for Flood Loss Control, 50 Iowa L.Rev. 552; Comment, State Flood-

Plain Zoning, 12 De Paul L.Rev. 246; Comment, Zoning the Flood Plains of Ohio, 1969 U. Toledo L.Rev. 655. See also Task-Force on Federal Flood Control Policy, A Unified National Program for Managing Flood Losses, 1966 H.R.Doc.No.465, 89th Cong., 2d Sess., 3. The principal criterion as to the reasonableness of the inclusion of the petitioner's land in the flood plain district is the extent of the flood hazard to its land. The judge's decision on this point contains the following: "There was extensive evidence on elevation, topography, dams, flood control, flood gates all bearing on the issue whether or not the locus was subject to 'seasonal' or 'periodic' flooding; this included photographs, exhibits reflecting the elevation of the locus in relation to the Charles River . . . as well as evidence concerning the level of the Charles River from 1954 to 1967. . . . The evidence indicated that there was a reasonable basis for the judgment of the town meeting that the land to be included in the 'Flood Plain District' is, in fact, subject to seasonal or periodic flooding and that the determination of the Town Meeting that the locus was subject to flooding was not unreasonable or capricious. A view of the locus further supported this testimony and disclosed that most of the locus consisted of lowlands covered with marshgrass and scrub growth. The only apparent areas on 'high' ground within the locus consisted of the 3.2 acre and .2 acre knolls."

The evidence clearly supported the judge's conclusion. One Robert A. Barrows, an expert hydrologist, testified for the respondent that, in his opinion, the petitioner's land "will have water on it, ranging anywhere from practically nothing up to . . . three feet of water annually." He further testified that once the flow in the Charles River exceeds 1,280 cubic feet a second, which is equivalent to the approximate elevation of the petitioner's land (92.5 feet), the petitioner's land will be flooded. The flow of the Charles River, according to Barrows, exceeded that level in 1936, 1938, 1955 and 1968. Barrows stated that he personally went to the petitioner's land in March, 1968, and observed that it was covered with "approximately four to five feet of water."

As we have stated, the restrictions in the by-law serve to protect not only those who might choose to develop or occupy the land in spite of the dangers to themselves and their property (see Pinnick v. Clearly, Mass.[a], 271 N.E.2d 592 and cases cited), but also other people in the community from the harmful effects of flooding.[5] Similarly, there is a substantial public interest in avoiding the public works and disaster relief expenditures connected with flooding.

In Vartelas v. Water Resources Commn., 146 Conn. 650, 654, 153 A.2d 822, the court stated: "The police power regulates use of property because

---

a. Mass. Adv. Sh. (1971) 1129, 1150-1151.

5. Barrows testified that if the petitioner's land was filled, this "could cause the water to rise higher at other points."

uncontrolled use would be harmful to the public interest. Eminent domain, on the other hand, takes private property because it is useful to the public."

The petitioner, moreover, has not been deprived of all beneficial uses of its property. The by-law specifically permits "Any woodland, grassland, wetland, agricultural, horticultural or recreational use of land or water not requiring filling." Although it is clear that the petitioner is substantially restricted in its use of the land, such restrictions must be balanced against the potential harm to the community from overdevelopment of a flood plain area. In Morris County Land Improvement Co. v. Township of Parsippany-Troy Hills, 40 N.J. 539, 193 A.2d 232, 242, fn. 3, a case heavily relied upon by the petitioner, the court stated: "There is no substantial evidence in this case that the matter of intra-municipal flood control had any bearing on the adoption of the meadows zone regulations. . . . This case, therefore, does not involve the matter of police power regulation of the use of land in a flood plain on the lower reaches of a river by zoning, building restrictions, channel encroachment lines or otherwise and nothing said in this opinion is intended to pass upon the validity of any such regulations."

7. The petitioner introduced testimony of an expert witness that prior to the enactment of the by-law the best use of the petitioner's land was for apartment buildings, and after the enactment the best use was for agriculture. He further testified that the value of the lowlands was $431,000 prior to becoming subject to the by-law, and $53,000 after the by-law's enactment, a reduction in value of about eighty-eight per cent. The petitioner argues that the reduction was of such magnitude that the enactment of the by-law must be considered the equivalent of a taking without just compensation.

The judge after referring to the testimony of the petitioner's expert as set out above stated that "[t]he respondent's witness testified that the value of the lowlands was not affected by the Flood Plain District as the nature of the terrain was such as to make the construction of housing on the locus under the General Residence Zone not economically feasible."

The transcript shows there was evidence contrary to the figures stated by the petitioner's expert. Although the judge in his decision made references to the testimony of both the petitioner's and the respondent's witnesses regarding the value of the land before and after the enactment of the by-law, he did not set any value thereon. He stated: "Although there was a substantial diminution in value of the locus, the mere decrease in the value of a particular piece of land is not conclusive evidence of an unconstitutional deprivation of property."

[13] There is no set formula to determine where regulation ends and taking begins. Although a comparison of values before and after is relevant . . . it is by no means conclusive, see Hadacheck v. Sebastian . . . [239

U.S. 394, 36 S.Ct. 143, 60 L.Ed. 348], where a diminution in value from $800,000 to $60,000 was upheld." Goldblatt v. Hempstead, 369 U.S. 590, 594, 82 S.Ct. 987, 990, 8 L.Ed.2d 130. See Euclid v. Ambler Realty Co., 272 U.S. 365, 47 S.Ct. 114, 71 L.Ed. 303. See also Caires v. Building Commr. of Hingham, 323 Mass. 589, 594, 83 N.E.2d 550; Massachusetts Broken Stone Co. v. Weston, 346 Mass. 657, 661, 195 N.E.2d 522; Anderson v. Wilmington, 347 Mass. 302, 304, 197 N.E.2d 682. But see Dooley v. Town Plan & Zoning Commn. of Fairfield, 151 Conn. 304, 310, 197 A.2d 770.

[14] We realize that it is often extremely difficult to determine the precise line where regulation ends and confiscation begins. The result depends upon the "peculiar circumstances of the particular instance." Pittsfield v. Oleksak, 313 Mass. 553, 555, 47 N.E.2d 930, 932. In the case at bar we are unable to conclude, even though the judge found that there was a substantial diminution in the value of the petitioner's land, that the decrease was such as to render it an unconstitutional deprivation of its property.

[15] 8. The petitioner argues that the finding and ruling of the judge that the 3.2 acre and .2 acre knolls were included in the flood plain district and subject to the by-law was contrary to the evidence. However, the evidence on this point was conflicting. The town engineer, at the request of the town conservation commission, made a zoning map as it related to flood plain districts. He was instructed to put in the flood district "all the swamp areas" below ninety-eight feet, and to designate them by coloring them green. The elevations of the knolls were 121 feet and 111 feet. Both were colored in the flood plain district despite elevations in excess of ninety-eight feet. They were shown as colored on the map at the town meeting which adopted the by-law. The town clerk testified that the map he submitted to the Attorney General was a "true copy of the Flood Plain District as created by vote of the Town Meeting."

In finding and ruling that the knolls were included in the flood plain district, the judge appeared to reason that although their inclusion "may have been inadvertent," the petitioner "would not have been able to utilize these areas for the purposes authorized under the underlying zone (General Residence) without obtaining a special permit from the Board of Appeals for access to it over the surrounding flood plain district zone." See Parmenter v. Board of Appeals of Grafton, Mass.[b], 274 N.E.2d 351. As we have previously stated, this is a situation which the special permit procedure under paragraph 4 was intended to cover.

9. The petitioner argues that under G.L. c. 40A, § 2, the respondent was required to make a "reasonable determination" that land to be included in a flood plain district is in fact subject to seasonal or periodic flooding. It contends, in summary, that flood plain zoning is a radical departure from ordinary zoning concepts, and that the Legislature intended that a narrower standard of validity be used.

---

b. Mass. Adv. Sh. (1971) 1332.

[16, 17] We have previously stated our view that the authority to enact flood plain zoning by-laws is contained in the general grant of power to zone for the public health, safety, and welfare, and is not limited by the last sentence of G.L. c. 40A, § 2. There is nothing to indicate that our familiar rule should not apply: " '[a]ll rational presumptions are made in favor of the validity of every legislative enactment. Enforcement is to be refused only when it is in manifest excess of legislative power.' Commonwealth v. Finnigan, 326 Mass. 378, 379, 96 N.E.2d 715, 716; Massachusetts Commn. Against Discrimination v. Colangelo, 344 Mass. 387, 390, 182 N.E.2d 595; Coffee-Rich, Inc. v. Commissioner of Pub. Health, 348 Mass. 414, 422, 204 N.E.2d 281." Mobil Oil Corp. v. Attorney Gen. Mass.[c], 280 N.E.2d 406, 415. The same is true of a zoning by-law. Caires v. Building Commr. of Hingham, 323 Mass. 589, 594, 83 N.E.2d 550; Lanner v. Board of Appeal of Tewksbury, 348 Mass. 220, 228, 202 N.E.2d 777. We find nothing wrong with the judge's ruling that the respondent "acted reasonably when, in the words of the [e]nabling [a]ct, it impliedly 'deemed' the locus to be subject to 'seasonal' or 'periodic' flooding." No express findings by the town meeting were required.

10. All of the petitioner's contentions have been considered. There was no error.

Exceptions overruled.

TAURO, Chief Justice (concurring).

The judge below has raised the question of "substantial diminution" in value without indicating the extent of the diminution. The majority opinion takes the position that the court is unable to conclude that the "substantial diminution" in value caused by the by-law was such as to render the by-law unconstitutional. In my view, this statement in the majority opinion might be used (possibly without justification) as a reason for the administrative denial of future petitions for special building permits. For this reason, I would add the following statement to the opinion:

> "[W]e need not now decide whether the . . . [petitioner is] the 'uncompensated victim . . . of a taking invalid without compensation.' Commissioner of Natural Resources v. S. Volpe & Co. Inc., 349 Mass. 104, 111, 206 N.E.2d 666, 671. That decision may depend in part on the board's . . . action on the . . . [possible petitioner's] application for . . . [a] special permit." MacGibbon v. Board of Appeals of Duxbury, 356 Mass. 635, 641, 255 N.E.2d 347, 352.

---

c. Mass. Adv. Sh. (1972) 561, 571.

JUST

v.

MARINETTE COUNTY

56 Wis. 2d 7, 201 N.W. 2d 761(1972).

Supreme Court of Wisconsin.

Oct. 31, 1972.

Consolidated actions wherein landowners sought a declaratory judgment that shoreland zoning ordinance of county was unconstitutional and county sought a mandatory injunction to restrain landowners from placing fill material on their property without first obtaining a conditional use permit as required by ordinance. The Circuit Court, Marinette County, James E. Martineau, J., entered judgments that were in favor of county, and landowners appealed, and state intervened on appeal as a party respondent because of constitutional issue. The Supreme Court, Hallows, C. J., held that shoreland zoning ordinance of Marinette County which prevents with exception of special permit situations changing of natural character of land within 1,000 feet of a navigable lake and 300 feet of a navigable river because of land's interrelation to contiguous water is not unconstitutional as being confiscatory or unreasonable. It was further held that where trial court dismissed action commenced by landowners, though they sought a declaratory judgment and though their rights were declared, dismissal was in conflict with procedure which Supreme Court had made clear should be followed, namely, that a complaint should not be dismissed when contrary to plaintiffs' contention, but rather judgment should set forth declaratory adjudication.

Modified and, as modified, affirmed.

These two cases were consolidated for trial and argued together on appeal. In case number 106, Ronald Just and Kathryn L. Just, his wife (Justs), sought a declaratory judgment stating: (1) The shoreland zoning ordinance of the respondent Marinette County (Marinette) was unconstitutional, (2) their property was not "wetlands" as defined in the ordinance, and (3) the prohibition against the filling of wetlands was unconstitutional. In case number 107, Marinette county sought a mandatory injunction to restrain the Justs from placing fill material on their property without first obtaining a conditional-use permit as required by the ordinance and also a forfeiture for their violation of the ordinance in having placed fill on their lands without a permit. The trial court held the ordinance was valid, the Justs' property was "wetlands," the Justs had violated the ordinance and they were subject to a forfeiture of $100. From the judgments, the Justs appeal.

[1] On this appeal the state of Wisconsin has intervened as a party-respondent pursuant to sec. 274.12(6), Stats., because of the issue of con-

stitutionality. The state considers the appeal to be a challenge to the underlying secs. 59.971 and 144.26, Stats., and a challenge to the state's comprehensive program to protect navigable waters through shoreland regulation.

Evrard, Evrard, Duffy, Holman, Faulds & Peterson, Wayne R. Peterson, Green Bay, for appellants.

James E. Murphy, Corp. Counsel, Marinette, for Marinette County.

Robert W. Warren, Atty. Gen., Steven M. Schur, Asst. Atty. Gen., Madison, for impleaded respondent.

McBurney, Musolf & Whipple, Carlyle H. Whipple, Madison, amici curiae.

HALLOWS, Chief Justice.

Marinette county's Shoreland Zoning Ordinance Number 24 was adopted September 19, 1967, became effective October 9, 1967, and follows a model ordinance published by the Wisconsin Department of Resource Development in July of 1967. *See* Kusler, Water Quality Protection For Inland Lakes in Wisconsin: A Comprehensive Approach to Water Pollution, 1970 Wis.L.Rev. 35, 62-63. The ordinance was designed to meet standards and criteria for shoreland regulation which the legislature required to be promulgated by the department of natural resources under sec. 144.26, Stats. These standards are found in 6 Wis. Adm.Code, sec. NR 115.03, May, 1971, Register No. 185. The legislation, secs. 59.971 and 144.26, Stats., authorizing the ordinance was enacted as a part of the Water Quality Act of 1965 by ch. 614, Laws of 1965.

Shorelands for the purpose of ordinances are defined in sec. 59.971(1), Stats., as lands within 1,000 feet of the normal high-water elevation of navigable lakes, ponds, or flowages and 300 feet from a navigable river or stream or to the landward side of the flood plain, whichever distance is greater. The state shoreland program is unique. All county shoreland zoning ordinances must be approved by the department of natural resources prior to their becoming effective. 6 Wis.Adm.Code, sec. NR 115.04, May, 1971, Register No. 185. If a county does not enact a shoreland zoning ordinance which complies with the state's standards, the department of natural resources may enact such an ordinance for the county. Sec. 59.971 (6), Stats.

[2] There can be no disagreement over the public purpose sought to be obtained by the ordinance. Its basic purpose is to protect navigable waters and the public rights therein from the degradation and deterioration which results from uncontrolled use and development of shorelands. In the Navigable Waters Protection Act, sec. 144.-26, the purpose of the state's shoreland regulation program is stated as being to "aid in the fulfillment of the state's role as trustee of its navigable waters and to promote public health, safety, convenience and general welfare."[1] In sec. 59.971(1), which

---

1. "144.26 Navigable waters protection law (1) To aid in the fulfillment of the state's role as trustee of its navigable waters and to promote public health, safety, convenience and general welfare, it is declared to be in the public interest to make studies,

grants authority for shoreland zoning to counties, the same purposes are reaffirmed.[2] The Marinette county shoreland zoning ordinance in secs. 1.2 and 1.3 states the uncontrolled use of shorelands and pollution of navigable waters of Marinette county adversely affect public health, safety, convenience, and general welfare and impair the tax base.

The shoreland zoning ordinance divides the shorelands of Marinette county into general purpose districts, general recreation districts, and conservancy districts. A "conservancy" district is required by the statutory minimum standards and is defined in sec. 3.4 of the ordinance to include "all shorelands designated as swamps or marshes on the United States Geological Survey maps which have been designated as the Shoreland Zoning Map of Marinette County, Wisconsin or on the detailed Insert Shoreland Zoning Maps." The ordinance provides for permitted uses [3] and conditional uses.[4] One of the conditional uses requiring a permit under

---

establish policies, make plans and authorize municipal shoreland zoning regulations for the efficient use, conservation, development and protection of this state's water resources. The regulations shall relate to lands under, abutting or lying close to navigable waters. The purposes of the regulations shall be to further the maintenance of safe and healthful conditions; prevent and control water pollution; protect spawning grounds, fish and aquatic life; control building sites, placement of structure and land uses and reserve shore cover and natural beauty . . ."

2. "59.971 Zoning of shorelands on navigable waters (1) To effect the purposes of s. 144.26 and to promote the public health, safety and general welfare, counties may, by ordinance enacted separately from ordinances pursuant to s. 59.97, zone all lands (referred to herein as shorelands) in their unincorporated areas within the following distances from the normal highwater elevation of navigable waters as defined in s. 144.26(2)(d): 1,000 feet from a lake, pond or flowage; 300 feet from a river or stream or to the landward side of the flood plain, whichever distance is greater. If the navigable water is a glacial pothole lake, the distance shall be measured from the high watermark thereof."

3. "3.41 Permitted Uses.

(1) Harvesting of any wild crop such as marsh hay, ferns, moss, wild rice, berries, tree fruits and tree seeds.

(2) Sustained yield forestry subject to the provisions of Section 5.0 relating to removal of shore cover.

(3) Utilities such as, but not restricted to, telephone, telegraph and power transmission lines.

(4) Hunting, fishing, preservation of scenic, historic and scientific areas and wildlife preserves.

(5) Non-resident buildings used solely in conjunction with raising water fowl, minnows, and other similar lowland animals, fowl or fish.

(6) Hiking trails and bridle paths.

(7) Accessory uses.

(8) Signs, subject to the restriction of Section 2.0."

4. "3.42 Conditional Uses. The following uses are permitted upon issuance of a Conditional Use Permit as provided in Section 9.0 and issuance of a Department of Resource Development permit where required by   Section 30.11, 30.12, 30.19, 30.195 and 31.05 of the Wisconsin Statutes.

(1) General farming provided farm animals shall be kept one hundred feet from any non-farm residence.

sec. 3.42(4) is the filling, drainage or dredging of wetlands according to the provisions of sec. 5 of the ordinance. "Wetlands" are defined in sec. 2.29 as "(a)areas where ground water is at or near the surface much of the year or where any segment of plant cover is deemed an aquatic according to N. C. Fassett's "Manual of Aquatic Plants." Section 5.42(2) of the ordinance requires a conditional-use permit for any filling or grading "Of any area which is within three hundred feet horizontal distance of a navigable water and which has surface drainage toward the water and on which there is: (a) Filling of more than five hundred square feet of any wetland which is contiguous to the water . . . (d) Filling or grading of more than 2,000 square feet on slopes of twelve per cent or less."

In April of 1961, several years prior to the passage of this ordinance, the Justs purchased 36.4 acres of land in the town of Lake along the south shore of Lake Noquebay, a navigable lake in Marinette county. This land had a frontage of 1,266.7 feet on the lake and was purchased partially for personal use and partially for resale. During the years 1964, 1966, and 1967, the Justs made five sales of parcels having frontage and extending back from the lake some 600 feet, leaving the property involved in these suits. This property has a frontage of 366.7 feet and the south one half contains a stand of cedar, pine, various hard woods, birch and red maple. The north one half, closer to the lake, is barren of trees except immediately along the shore. The south three fourths of this north one half is populated with various plant grasses and vegetation including some plants which N. C. Fassett in his manual of aquatic plants has classified as "aquatic." There are also non-aquatic plants which grow upon the land. Along the shoreline there is a belt of trees. The shoreline is from one foot to 3.2 feet higher than the lake level and there is a narrow belt of higher land along the shore known as a "pressure ridge" or "ice heave," varying in width from one to three feet. South of this point, the natural level of the land ranges one to two feet above lake level. The land slopes generally toward the lake but has a slope less than twelve per cent. No water flows onto the land from the lake, but there is some surface water which collects on land and stands in pools.

The land owned by the Justs is designated as swamps or marshes on the United States Geological Survey Map and is located within 1,000 feet of the normal high-water elevation of the lake. Thus, the property is included in a conservancy district and, by sec. 2.29 of the ordinance, classified as "wetlands." Consequently, in order to place more than 500 square feet of fill on this property, the Justs were required to obtain a conditional-use

(2) Dams, power plants, flowages and ponds.
(3) Relocation of any water course.
(4) Filling, drainage or dredging of wetlands according to the provisions of Section 5.0 of this ordinance.
(5) Removal of top soil or peat.
(6) Cranberry bogs.
(7) Piers, Docks, boathouses."

permit from the zoning administrator of the county and pay a fee of $20 or incur a forfeiture of $10 to $200 or each day of violation.

In February and March of 1968, six months after the ordinance became effective, Ronald Just, without securing a conditional-use permit, hauled 1,040 square yards of sand onto this property and filled an area approximately 20-feet wide commencing at the southwest corner and extending almost 600 feet north to the northwest corner near the shoreline, then easterly along the shoreline almost to the lot line. He stayed back from the pressure ridge about 20 feet. More than 500 square feet of this fill was upon wetlands located contiguous to the water and which had surface drainage toward the lake. The fill within 300 feet of the lake also was more than 2,000 square feet on a slope less than 12 percent. It is not seriously contended that the Justs did not violate the ordinance and the trial court correctly found a violation.

The real issue is whether the conservancy district provisions and the wetlands-filling restrictions are unconstitutional because they amount to a constructive taking of the Justs' land without compensation. Marinette county and the state of Wisconsin argue the restrictions of the conservancy district and wetlands provisions constitute a proper exercise of the police power of the state and do not so severely limit the use or depreciate the value of the land as to constitute a taking without compensation.

[3-8] To state the issue in more meaningful terms, it is a conflict between the public interest in stopping the despoilation of natural resources, which our citizens until recently have taken as inevitable and for granted, and an owner's asserted right to use his property as he wishes. The protection of public rights may be accomplished by the exercise of the police power and condemnation has been said to be a matter of degree of damage to the property owner. In the valid exercise of the police power reasonably restricting the use of property, the damage suffered by the owner is said to be incidental. However, where the restriction is so great the landowner ought not to bear such a burden for the public good, the restriction has been held to be a constructive taking even though the actual use or forbidden use has not been transferred to the government so as to be a taking in the traditional sense. Stefan Auto Body v. State Highway Comm. (1963), 21 Wis.2d 363, 124 N.W.2d 319; Buhler v. Racine County (1966), 33 Wis.2d 137, 146 N.W.2d 403; Nick v. State Highway Comm. (1961), 13 Wis.2d 511, 109 N.W.2d 71, 111 N.W.2d 95; State v. Becker (1934), 215 Wis. 564, 255 N.W. 144. Whether a taking has occurred depends upon whether "the restriction practically or substantially renders the land useless for all reasonable purposes." Buhler v. Racine County, supra. The loss caused the individual must be weighed to determine if it is more than he should bear. As this court stated in *Stefan*, at pp. 369-370, 124 N.W.2d 319, p. 323, ". . . if the damage is such as to be suffered by many similarly situated and is in the nature of a restriction on the use to which land may be put and ought to be borne by the individual as a member of society for the

good of the public safety, health or general welfare, it is said to be a reasonable exercise of the police power, but if the damage is so great to the
individual that he ought not to bear it under contemporary standards, then
courts are inclined to treat it as a 'taking' of the property or an unreasonable
exercise of the police power."

[9]   Many years ago, Professor Freund stated in his work on The Police
Power, sec. 511, at 546-547, "It may be said that the state takes property
by eminent domain because it is useful to the public, and under the police
power because it is harmful . . . From this results the difference between
the power of eminent domain and the police power, that the former recog-
nises a right to compensation, while the latter on principle does not." Thus
the necessity for monetary compensation for loss suffered to an owner by
police power restriction arises when restrictions are placed on property in
order to create a public benefit rather than to prevent a public harm. Rathkopf, The Law of Zoning and Planning, Vol. 1, ch. 6, pp. 6-7.

[10]   This case causes us to reexamine the concepts of public benefit in
contrast to public harm and the scope of an owner's right to use of his
property. In the instant case we have a restriction on the use of a citizens'
property, not to secure a benefit for the public, but to prevent a harm from
the change in the natural character of the citizens' property. We start with
the premise that lakes and rivers in their natural state are unpolluted and
the pollution which now exists is man made. The state of Wisconsin under
the trust doctrine has a duty to eradicate the present pollution and to
prevent further pollution in its navigable waters. This is not, in a legal
sense, a gain or a securing of a benefit by the maintaining of the natural
status quo of the environment. What makes this case different from most
condemnation or police power zoning cases is the interrelationship of the
wetlands, the swamps and the natural environment of shorelands to the
purity of the water and to such natural resources as navigation, fishing, and
scenic beauty. Swamps and wetlands were once considered wasteland,
undesirable, and not picturesque. But as the people became more sophisticated, an appreciation was acquired that swamps and wetlands serve a
vital role in nature, are part of the balance of nature and are essential to
the purity of the water in our lakes and streams. Swamps and wetlands
are a necessary part of the ecological creation and now, even to the un-
initiated, possess their own beauty in nature.

[11, 12]   Is the ownership of a parcel of land so absolute that man can
change its nature to suit any of his purposes? The great forests of our
state were stripped on the theory man's ownership was unlimited. But in
forestry, the land at least was used naturally, only the natural fruit of the
land (the trees) were taken. The despoilage was in the failure to look
to the future and provide for the reforestation of the land. An owner
of land has no absolute and unlimited right to change the essential natural
character of his land so as to use it for a purpose for which it was unsuited
in its natural state and which injures the rights of others. The exercise of

the police power in zoning must be reasonable and we think it is not an unreasonable exercise of that power to prevent harm to public rights by limiting the use of private property to its natural uses.

[13] This is not a case where an owner is prevented from using his land for natural and indigenous uses. The uses consistent with the nature of the land are allowed and other uses recognized and still others permitted by special permit. The shoreland zoning ordinance prevents to some extent the changing of the natural character of the land within 1,000 feet of a navigable lake and 300 feet of a navigable river because of such land's interrelation to the contiguous water. The changing of wetlands and swamps to the damage of the general public by upsetting the natural environment and the natural relationship is not a reasonable use of that land which is protected from police power regulation. Changes and filling to some extent are permitted because the extent of such changes and fillings does not cause harm. We realize no case in Wisconsin has yet dealt with shoreland regulations and there are several cases in other states which seem to hold such regulations unconstitutional; but nothing this court has said or held in prior cases indicate that destroying the natural character of a swamp or a wetland so as to make that location available for human habitation is a reasonable use of that land when the new use, although of a more economical value to the owner, causes a harm to the general public.

[14, 15] Wisconsin has long held that laws and regulations to prevent pollution and to protect the waters of this state from degradation are valid police-power enactments. State ex rel. Martin v. Juneau (1941), 238 Wis. 564, 300 N.W. 187; State ex rel. LaFollette v. Reuter (1967), 33 Wis.2d 384, 147 N.W.2d 304; Reuter v. Department of Natural Resources (1969), 43 Wis.2d 272, 168 N.W.2d 860. The active public trust duty of the state of Wisconsin in respect to navigable waters requires the state not only to promote navigation but also to protect and preserve those waters for fishing, recreation, and scenic beauty. Muench v. Public Service Comm. (1952), 261 Wis. 492, 53 N.W.2d 514, 55 N.W.2d 40. To further this duty, the legislature may delegate authority to local units of the government, which the state did by requiring counties to pass shoreland zoning ordinances. Menzer v. Elkhart Lake (1971), 51 Wis.2d 70, 186 N.W.2d 290.

[16, 17] This is not a case of an isolated swamp unrelated to a navigable lake or stream, the change of which would cause no harm to public rights. Lands adjacent to or near navigable waters exist in a special relationship to the state. They have been held subject to special taxation, Soens v. City of Racine (1860), 10 Wis. 271, and are subject to the state public trust powers, Wisconsin P. & L. Co. v. Public Service Comm. (1958), 5 Wis.2d 167, 92 N.W.2d 241; and since the Laws of 1935, ch. 303, counties have been authorized to create special zoning districts along waterways and zone them for restrictive conservancy purposes.[5] The restrictions in the Marinette

---

5. In Jefferson County v. Timmel (1952), 261 Wis. 39, 51 N.W.2d 518, the constitutionality of a conservancy district use restriction was upheld as being based on

county ordinance upon wetlands within 1,000 feet of Lake Noquebay which prevent the placing of excess fill upon such land without a permit is not confiscatory or unreasonable.

Cases wherein a confiscation was found cannot be relied upon by the Justs. In State v. Herwig (1962), 17 Wis.2d 442, 117 N.W.2d 335, a "taking" was found where a regulation which prohibited hunting on farmland had the effect of establishing a game refuge and resulted in an unnatural, concentrated foraging of the owner's land by waterfowl. In State v. Becker, supra, the court held void a law which established a wildlife refuge (and prohibited hunting) on private property. In Benka v. Consolidated Water Power Co. (1929), 198 Wis. 472, 224 N.W. 718, the court held if damages to plaintiff's property were in fact caused by flooding from a dam constructed by a public utility, those damages constituted a "taking" within the meaning of the condemnation statutes. In Bino v. Hurley (1955), 273 Wis. 10, 76 N.W.2d 571, the court held unconstitutional as a "taking" without compensation an ordinance which, in attempting to prevent pollution, prohibited the owners of land surrounding a lake from bathing, boating, or swimming in the lake. In Piper v. Ekern (1923), 180 Wis. 586, 593, 194 N.W. 159, 162, the court held a statute which limited the height of buildings surrounding the state capitol to be unnecessary for the public health, safety, or welfare and, thus, to constitute an unreasonable exercise of the police power. In all these cases the unreasonableness of the exercise of the police power lay in excessive restriction of the natural use of the land or rights in relation thereto.

Cases holding the exercise of police power to be reasonable likewise provide no assistance to Marinette county in their argument. In More-Way North Corp. v. State Highway Comm. (1969), 44 Wis.2d 165, 175 N.W.2d 749, the court held that no "taking" occurred as a result of the state's lowering the grade of a highway, which necessitated plaintiff's reconstruction of its parking lot and loss of 42 parking spaces. In Wisconsin Power & Light Co. v. Columbia County (1958), 3 Wis.2d 1, 87 N.W.2d 279, no "taking" was found where the county, in relocating a highway, deposited gravel close to plaintiff's tower, causing it to tilt. In Nick v. State Highway Comm., supra, the court held where property itself is not physically taken by the state, a restriction of access to a highway, while it may decrease the value of the land, does not entitle the owner to compensation. In *Buhler* the court held the mere depreciation of value was not sufficient ground to enjoin the county from enforcing the ordinance. In Hasslinger v. Hartland (1940), 234 Wis. 201, 290 N.W. 647, the court noted that "(a)ssuming an actionable nuisance by the creation of odors which make occupation of plaintiffs' farm inconvenient . . . and impair its value, it cannot be said that defendant has dispossessed plaintiffs or taken their property."

---

a valid exercise of police power. The purpose for this conservancy district, however, was for highway safety and not for the prevention of pollution and the protection of the public trust in navigable waters.

The Justs rely on several cases from other jurisdictions which have held zoning regulations involving flood plain districts, flood basins and wetlands to be so confiscatory as to amount to a taking because the owners of the land were prevented from improving such property for residential or commercial purposes. While some of these cases may be distinguished on their facts, it is doubtful whether these differences go to the basic rationale which permeates the decision that an owner has a right to use his property in any way and for any purpose he sees fit. In Dooley v. Town Plan & Zon. Com. of Town of Fairfield (1964), 151 Conn. 304, 197 A.2d 770, the court held the restriction on land located in a flood plain district prevented its being used for residential or business purposes and thus the restriction destroyed the economic value to the owner. The court recognized the land was needed for a public purpose as it was part of the area in which the tidal stream overflowed when abnormally high tides existed, but the property was half a mile from the ocean and therefore could not be used for marina or boathouse purposes. In Morris County Land I. Co. v. Parsippany-Troy Hills Tp. (1963), 40 N.J. 539, 193 A.2d 232, a flood basin zoning ordinance was involved which required the controversial land to be retained in its natural state. The plaintiff owned 66 acres of a 1,500-acre swamp which was part of a river basin and acted as a natural detention basin for flood waters in times of very heavy rainfall. There was an extraneous issue that the freezing regulations were intended as a stop-gap until such time as the government would buy the property under a flood-control project. However, the court took the view the zoning had an effect of preserving the land as an open space as a water-detention basin and only the government or the public would be benefited, to the complete damage of the owner.

In State v. Johnson (1970), Me., 265 A.2d 711, the Wetlands Act restricted the alteration and use of certain wetlands without permission. The act was a conservation measure enacted under the police power to protect the ecology of areas bordering the coastal waters. The plaintiff owned a small tract of a salt-water marsh which was flooded at high tide. By filling, the land would be adapted for building purposes. The court held the restrictions against filling constituted a deprivation of a reasonable use of the owner's property and, thus, an unreasonable exercise of the police power. In MacGibbon v. Board of Appeals of Duxbury (1970), 356 Mass. 635, 255 N.E.2d 347, the plaintiff owned seven acres of land which were under water about twice a month in a shoreland area. He was denied a permit to excavate and fill part of his property. The purpose of the ordinance was to preserve from despoilage natural features and resources such as salt marshes, wetlands, and ponds. The court took the view the preservation of privately owned land in its natural, unspoiled state for the enjoyment and benefit of the public by preventing the owner from using it for any practical purpose was not within the limit and scope of the police power and the ordinance was not saved by the use of special permits.

[18] It seems to us that filling a swamp not otherwise commercially usable is not in and of itself an existing use, which is prevented, but rather is the preparation for some future use which is not indigenous to a swamp. Too much stress is laid on the right of an owner to change commercially value-less land when that change does damage to the rights of the public. It is observed that a use of special permits is a means of control and accomplish-ing the purpose of the zoning ordinance as distinguished from the old con-cept of providing for variances. The special permit technique is now com-mon practice and has met with judicial approval, and we think it is of some significance in considering whether or not a particular zoning ordinance is reasonable.

A recent case sustaining the validity of a zoning ordinance establishing a flood plain district is Turnpike Realty Company v. Town of Dedham (June, 1972), 72 Mass. 1303, 284 N.E.2d 891. The court held the validity of the ordinance was supported by valid considerations of public welfare, the con-servation of "natural conditions, wildlife and open spaces." The ordinance provided that lands which were subject to seasonal or periodic flooding could not be used for residences or other purposes in such a manner as to endanger the health, safety or occupancy thereof and prohibited the erection of structures or buildings which required land to be filled. This case is analogous to the instant facts. The ordinance had a public purpose to pre-serve the natural condition of the area. No change was allowed which would injure the purposes sought to be preserved and through the special-permit technique, particular land within the zoning district could be ex-cepted from the restrictions.

[19] The Justs argue their property has been severely depreciated in value. But this depreciation of value is not based on the use of the land in its natural state but on what the land would be worth if it could be filled and used for the location of a dwelling. While loss of value is to be con-sidered in determining whether a restriction is a constructive taking, value based upon changing the character of the land at the expense of harm to public rights is not an essential factor or controlling.

We are not unmindful of the warning in Pennsylvania Coal Co. v. Mahon (1922), 260 U.S. 393, 416, 43 S.Ct. 158, 160, 67 L.Ed. 322:

> "... We are in danger of forgetting that a strong public desire to improve the public condition is not enough to warrant achieving the desire by a shorter cut than the constitutional way of paying for the change."

This observation refers to the improvement of the public condition, the securing of a benefit not presently enjoyed and to which the public is not entitled. The shoreland zoning ordinance preserves nature, the environ-ment, and natural resources as they were created and to which the people have a present right.[6] The ordinance does not create or improve the public

---

6. On the letterhead of the Jackson County Zoning and Sanitation Department, the following appears: "The land belongs to the people . . . a little of it to those dead . . . some to those living . . . but most of it belongs to those yet to be born . . ."

condition but only preserves nature from the despoilage and harm resulting from the unrestricted activities of humans.

[20] We note the lower court dismissed the action commenced by the Justs, although it sought a declaratory judgment and the rights of the Justs were declared. This dismissal is in conflict with the procedure which this court has made clear should be followed, namely, that the complaint should not be dismissed when contrary to the plaintiffs' contention, but rather the judgment should set forth the declaratory adjudication. City of Milwaukee v. Milwaukee County (1965), 27 Wis.2d 53, 67, 133 N.W.2d 393; David A. Ulrich, Inc. v. Saukville (1959), 7 Wis.2d 173, 181, 96 N.W.2d 612; Denning v. Green Bay (1955), 271 Wis. 230, 72 N.W.2d 730.

In commenting on the propriety of its deciding the issue of constitutionality of the ordinance, the trial court quoted State v. Stehlek (1953), 262 Wis. 642, at 645, 56 N.W.2d 514, 516:

> "The exercise of the power to declare laws unconstitutional by inferior courts, should be carefully limited and avoided if possible. The authorities are to the effect that unless it appears clearly beyond a reasonable doubt that the statute is unconstitutional, it is considered better practice for the court to assume the statute is constitutional, until the contrary is decided by a court of appellate jurisdiction."

This view has consistently been followed. State ex rel. Fieldhack v. Gregorski (1956), 272 Wis. 570 at 574, 76 N.W.2d 382; White House Milk Co. v. Reynolds (1960), 12 Wis.2d 143, 106 N.W.2d 441; Associated Hospital Service, Inc. v. City of Milwaukee (1961), 13 Wis.2d 447, 474, 109 N.W.2d 271; City of Milwaukee v. Hoffmann (1965), 29 Wis.2d 193, 198, 138 N.W.2d 223. In *Gregorski* the district court of Milwaukee held a statute constitutional and we affirmed the holding of constitutionality by the circuit court when it denied a writ of prohibition. We pointed out the above language did not justify an inference the trial court could not pass upon the constitutionality of a statute. In *White House* we reversed the circuit court's holding of unconstitutionality and quoted the *Stehlek Case* without comment. In *Associated Hospital* the circuit court denied summary judgment on the ground the constitutionality question required hearing evidence. We recognized the circuit court's power to decide the issue and stated we were hesitant "to lay down any rule governing the exercise of discretion by trial courts, when confronted with an issue of constitutionality of a statute on demurrer or motion for summary judgment . . ." but stated "it is better practice for it to assume the statute is constitutional until the appellate court has passed upon it except where unconstitutionality is apparent beyond a reasonable doubt." In *Hoffmann* we affirmed the circuit court which reversed the county court in holding a city ordinance unconstitutional and pointed out the county court had decided a question of constitutionality when one party was not represented by counsel, the other side had stated it was not ready for trial, without the benefit of briefs and without giving a written reason for the holding.

Although the practice for trial courts not to hold laws unconstitutional has not been uniformly followed, nevertheless, it is our belief many lawyers have and are bringing to the federal courts cases involving questions of constitutionality of state laws because of the limitation placed on state courts in the exercise of the power to declare a law unconstitutional.

[21, 22] We think that when a constitutional issue is now presented to the trial courts of this state, it is the better practice for those courts to recognize its importance, have the issue thoroughly briefed, and fully presented. The issue should be decided as any other important issue with due consideration. The practice of assuming constitutionality, until the contrary is decided by an appellate court, is no longer necessary or workable. Of course, a presumption of constitutionality exists until declared otherwise by a competent court, which we think the trial courts of Wisconsin are, because a regularly enacted statute is presumed to be constitutional and the party attacking the statute must meet the burden of proof of showing unconstitutionality beyond a reasonable doubt.

The Judgment in case number 106, dismissing the Justs' action, is modified to set forth the declaratory adjudication that the shoreland zoning ordinance of respondent Marinette County is constitutional; that the Justs' property constitutes wetlands and that particularly the prohibition in the ordinance against the filling of wetlands is constitutional; and the judgment, as so modified, is affirmed. The judgment in case number 107, declaring a forfeiture, is affirmed.

Questions and Notes

1. The above two cases give some idea of the way the state courts may move to uphold strict restrictions against development on environmentally sensitive land. (If in fact they do move in that direction, at the present time there is a split of authority on the point.) In the Massachusetts case, the court characteristically accepted the restriction as rather natural, presenting no great problem. In the Wisconsin case, the court developed a completely different theory of the nature of property rights for environmentally sensitive land—essentially, that in such a situation there was no such thing as development rights, so that in effect this case did not involve any question of taking (or even restricting) existing rights.

CROSS-REFERENCES

In Anderson, see §§ 8.37, 8.41, and see Index under "Open Space."

In Hagman, see §§ 182, 192.

In Rathkopf, see ch. 34-22, 6A.

In Williams, see ch. 157-160, and see Index, this topic, and particularly 1977 supplement, § 158.24.

In Yokley, see §§ 4-25 and 1975 Cumulative Supplement §§ 2-4, 9-9.

Section 8

Residential v.

Non-Residential Zoning

HFH, LTD.

v.

SUPERIOR COURT OF LOS ANGELES COUNTY

125 Cal. Rptr. 365, 542 P.2d 237(1975).

Supreme Court of California

In Bank.

Nov. 12, 1975.

Landowners sought review of order by the Superior Court, Los Angeles County, sustaining municipality's demurrer to landowners' complaint alleging inverse condemnation of landowners' property and landowners sought writ of mandate directing such Court to overrule its demurrer. The Supreme Court, Tobriner, J., held that landowners' 5.87-acre plot, which had decreased in market value as a result of municipality's adoption of a general zoning plan, was not "taken or damaged" within meaning of constitutional provisions forbidding uncompensated taking or damaging of property; that general zoning plan adopted by municipality was an "enactment" within meaning of Tort Claims Act, which provided municipality immunity for injuries caused by its adoption of or failure to adopt an enactment, and thus landowners were not entitled to append damage claims to their pending mandate action; and that fundamental fairness did not require finding that municipality's zoning action constituted inverse condemnation of landowners' property.

Alternative writs discharged; peremptory writs denied.

Clark, J., dissented and filed opinion.

Opinion, 116 Cal.Rptr. 436, vacated.

William J. Birney, Oliver, Stoever & Laskin, Richard Laskin and C. Edward Dilkes, Los Angeles for petitioners.

No appearance for respondent.

J. Kenneth Brown, City Atty., Ebben & Brown and Thomas F. Winfield III, Los Angeles for real parties in interest.

Evelle J. Younger, Atty. Gen., Robert H. O'Brien, Asst. Atty. Gen., Nicholas C. Yost and E. Clement Shute, Jr., Deputy Attys. Gen., John H. Larson, County Counsel (Los Angeles), S. Robert Ambrose and William F. Stewart, Deputy County Counsel, Burt Pines, City Atty. (Los Angeles), Claude E. Hilker, Asst. City Atty., Sally Disco, Deputy City Atty., Fred Caploe, Atkinson, Farasyn & Smith, Mountain View, Rutan & Tucker, James E. Erickson, John J. Murphy, Roger A. Grable, Thomas P. Clark, Jr., Santa Ana, Richard R. Hanna, So. Lake Tahoe, Gary A. Owen, Riverside, Kenneth C. Rollston, Carlyle W. Hall, Jr., Timothy B. Flynn, Pacific Palisades, A. Thomas Hunt, John R. Phillips, Brent N. Rushforth and Frederic P. Sutherland, Los Angeles, as Amici Curiae on behalf of real parties in interest.

Gordon Pearce, Los Angeles, C. Edward Gibson, Luce, Forward, Hamilton & Scripps, C. Douglas Alford, Louis E. Goebel, Ronald W. Rouse, San Diego, P. M. Barceloux, Burton J. Goldstein, Albert E. Levy, Ralph Golub, San Francisco, Keith S. Humphreys, Ronald E. Stewart, Chico, Goldstein, Barceloux & Goldstein, San Francisco, Paul Hamilton, Virgil Roberts, Pacht, Ross, Warne, Bernhard & Sears, Los Angeles, M. Reed Hunter, Thomas Seaton, San Francisco, Fulop, Rolston, Burns & McKittrick, Irwin F. Fulop, Marvin G. Burns, Beverly Hills, John Petrasich, Hollywood, Kenneth B. Bley, Los Angeles, Edmund S. Schaffer, Beverly Hills, Gideon Kanner, Donald G. Hagman, Los Angeles, Michael Atherton, Malovos & Chasuk, Mountain View, Cox Cummins & Lamphere, Martinez, Desmond, Miller & Desmond, Sacramento, Fadem, Berger & Stocker, Beverly Hills, Feeney & Sparks, San Francisco, Bressani, Hansen & Blos, San Jose, Jacobs, Jacobs, Nelson & Witmer, Santa Ana, Nichols, Stead, Boileau & Lamb, Pomona, Loube, Lewis & Blum, Oakland, Thorpe, Sullivan, Workman, Thorpe & O'Sullivan, Ronald A. Zumbrun, Donald M. Pach, Sacramento, and Thomas E. Hookano, Davis, as Amici Curiae on behalf of petitioners.

TOBRINER, Justice.

We face in these mandate proceedings [1] the narrow issue of whether a complaint alleging that a zoning action taken by a city council reduced the market value of petitioners' (hereafter plaintiffs) land state a cause of action

---

1. The two cases before us originated in separate lawsuits concerning the same parcel of land. All parties agree that they present identical legal issues; they were consolidated in the Court of Appeal for this reason, and we shall hereafter refer to them as a single proceeding.

in inverse condemnation; we conclude that it does not. We also face numerous amici, some of whom urge on us significant changes in the law of liability and compensation in public land use regulation; we have concluded that neither the state and federal Constitutions nor public policy compel or counsel these changes.

[1] We take the facts in this case from the allegations of the complaints, assuming as we must the truth of any properly pleaded factual allegations. (E.g., *Serrano v. Priest* (1971) 5 Cal.3d 584, 591, 96 Cal.Rptr. 601, 487 P.2d 1241.) Plaintiffs, a limited partnership (HFH) and a Delaware corporation (Von's), contracted to purchase the parcel in question from a common grantor. At the time the plaintiffs entered this contract with their grantor, the land in question lay in an agricultural zone and possessed no improvements of any kind. Plaintiffs conditioned the sale upon the grantor's ability to procure commercial zoning for the 5.87-acre tract; the City of Cerritos (the real party in interest) "in the latter part of the year 1965 or the early part of 1966" did classify the property as commercial, and in 1966 the plaintiffs became the owners of the parcel, according to the allegations of the complaint.

Plaintiffs thereafter submitted, and the city approved, a parcel map on which the plaintiffs subdivided the property in a manner appropriate for commercial uses. Subsequently, however, a period of some five years elapsed; during that time plaintiffs do not claim any development or establishment of a more intensive use of the land. In July 1971, with the land still in this undeveloped state, according to the allegations before us, the city placed a moratorium upon more intensive uses of the property by temporarily zoning it as agricultural, the classification it had borne before plaintiffs acquired it. Plaintiffs do not allege that this moratorium interfered with any use of the land which they then planned nor do they allege that they then challenged this reclassification.

In October 1971, the city adopted a general plan indicating that some land in the area of plaintiffs' properties was appropriate for "neighborhood commercial uses," but did not alter the agricultural classification of plaintiffs' tracts. The 1971 general plan designated the bulk of the land in the area of plaintiffs' properties for "low density residential" uses. (City of Cerritos October 1971 General Plan Map; Evid. Code, § 452, subd. (b).)

Having apparently concluded that their interests would best be served by selling rather than developing the land, plaintiffs in early 1972 entered into a $400,000 contract of sale with Diversified Associates, Inc. (not party to this action) conditioned upon the reclassification of the tract as commercial. In an attempt to bring about the condition which would enable them profitably to sell their land, plaintiffs applied to the planning commission for commercial zoning of the tract. Both the Commission and the city council, to which plaintiffs took an appeal, rejected this application, and instead zoned the property as single family residential. Concurrently with taking this action, the city zoned as commercial other properties on different corners of an intersection on which plaintiffs' land abuts. Plaintiffs, of course, had hoped to secure for their land a commercial classification in order to effectuate the conveyance of the land under the conditions of the contract of sale with Diversified Associates, Inc.

[2]   Plaintiffs allege that the situation of their properties rendered them "useless" for single family residential purposes; they do not, however, allege that the properties are useless for *other* purposes consonant with the zoning category in which they now lie.[2]   As a consequence, according to plaintiffs, their land, which they purchased for some $388,000 and hoped to sell for $400,000, suffered a decline in market value to $75,000.

[3]   The trial court sustained a demurrer without leave to amend to plaintiffs' cause of action in inverse condemnation and plaintiffs sought review.[3]

1. *Inverse condemnation does not lie in zoning actions in which the complaint alleges mere reduction of market value.*

The courts of this state have recognized the constitutional values served by actions in inverse condemnation and have not hesitated to validate com-

---

2. Plaintiffs also complain of the deprivation "of any reasonably beneficial use of . . . said properties commensurate with its value." In the same section of their complaints, however, they allege a remaining fair market value of $75,000. The substantial value of their land rebuts the allegation that they cannot enjoy any reasonably beneficial use of it. As to use "commensurate with value," we note the tautological quality of this statement: "Value" is of course not an objective quality, but a social attribute of legal rights. Only if we concluded that plaintiffs enjoyed a vested right in a previous zoning classification would the city's action have deprived them of a use commensurate with value; our courts have, however, clearly and frequently rejected the position that landowners enjoyed a vested right in a zoning classification. (E.g., *Morse v. San Luis Obispo County* (1967) 247 Cal.App.2d 600, 55 Cal.Rptr. 710.)

3. The trial court also sustained demurrers to other counts, granting leave to amend for purposes of adding a cause of action in mandate. These counts are not before us, for plaintiffs seek review only of the order sustaining the demurrer to the inverse condemnation count and pray for a writ of mandate directing the trial court to overrule that demurrer.

At oral argument plaintiffs and their amici curiae stressed the trial court's failure to allow amendment of their pleading. We recognize, of course, the requirement of liberality in permitting amendment of pleadings "in furtherance of justice." (Code Civ.Proc., § 473; e. g., *Klopstock v. Superior Court* (1941) 17 Cal.2d 13, 19-20, 108 P.2d 906.) Nothing in this policy of liberal allowance, however, requires an appellate court to hold that the trial judge has abused his discretion if on appeal the plaintiffs can suggest no legal theory or state of facts which they wish to add by way of amendment. Speaking to circumstances like those of the instant case, we have said: "[T]he burden is on the plaintiff to demonstrate that the trial court abused its discretion. [Citations omitted.] Plaintiff must show in what manner he can amend his complaint and how that amendment will change the legal effect of his pleading." (*Cooper v. Leslie Salt Co.* (1969) 70 Cal.2d 627, 636, 75 Cal.Rptr. 766, 772, 451 P.2d 406, 412; *Filice v. Boccardo* (1962) 210 Cal.App.2d 843, 847, 26 Cal.Rptr. 789.) Thus plaintiffs, while implying that they might in an unspecified manner amend their complaint to state a cause of action, fail to suggest any relevant facts with which they could supplement their pleading. We shall therefore determine this question below without reference to other possible facts which might enable them successfully to state a cause of action in inverse condemnation. (Cf. fn. 14, *infra.*)

plaints appropriately employing this theory of recovery.[4] At the same time, we have recognized mandamus as the proper remedy for allegedly arbitrary or discriminatory zoning,[5] and have in appropriate cases struck down land use restrictions which suffered from procedural or substantive deficiencies.[6]

We have never, however, suggested that inverse condemnation lay to challenge a zoning action whose only alleged effect was a diminution in the market value of the property in question. (E.g., *Morse v. County of San Luis Obispo* (1967) 247 Cal.App.2d 600, 55 Cal.Rptr. 710.) While this state of the law is sufficiently clear to admit of little doubt, we shall briefly review its development and basis.

[4] Zoning developed slowly in the later part of the 19th century. In its early stages it was frequently indistinguishable from the power to abate public nuisances,[7] but the first decades of this century saw the enactment of more comprehensive zoning laws and the development of the concept of city planning.[8] Shortly after these changes began to take effect, challenges in both state and federal courts raised the question of the constitutionality of these restrictions of the individual's previous ability to do with his land what he chose, bounded only by the laws of public and private nuisance. While the legal context in which this question arose differed from case to case, the courts of this state and the United States Supreme Court firmly rejected the notion that the diminution of the value of previously unrestricted land by the imposition of zoning could constitute a taking impermissible in the absence of compensation.[9] We have long adhered to that position.[10]

---

4. *Albers v. County of Los Angeles* (1965) 62 Cal.2d 250, 42 Cal.Rptr. 89, 398 P.2d 129; *Holtz v. Superior Court* (1970) 3 Cal.3d 296, 90 Cal.Rptr. 345, 475 P.2d 441; *Aaron v. City of Los Angeles* (1974) 40 Cal.App.3d 471, 115 Cal.Rptr. 162; see generally 10 California Law Revision Commission Reports (1971) California Inverse Condemnation Law.

5. E. g., *Selby Realty Co. v. City of Buenaventura* (1973) 10 Cal.3d 110, 128, 109 Cal. Rptr. 799, 514 P.2d 111.

6. *Broadway, Laguna, etc., Assn. v. Board of Permit Appeals* (1967) 66 Cal.2d 767, 59 Cal. Rptr. 146, 427 P.2d 810; *Hamer v. Town of Ross* (1963) 59 Cal.2d 776, 31 Cal.Rptr. 335, 382 P.2d 375; *Johnston v. Board of Supervisors* (1947); 31 Cal.2d 66, 187 P.2d 686; *Skalko v. City of Sunnyvale* (1939) 14 Cal.2d 213, 93 P.2d 93; *Tustin Heights Assn. v. Board of Supervisors* (1959) 170 Cal.App.2d 619, 339 P.2d 914.

7. *In re Hang Kie* (1886) 69 Cal. 149, 10 P. 327; see *Mugler v. Kansas* (1887) 123 U.S. 623, 8 S.Ct. 273, 31 L.Ed. 205.

8. California enacted its first statewide zoning law in 1917. (Stats.1917, ch. 734, p. 1419).

9. E. g., *Welch v. Swasey* (1909) 214 U.S. 91, 29 S.Ct. 567, 53 L.Ed. 923; *Euclid v. Ambler Realty* (1926) 272 U.S. 365, 47 S.Ct. 114, 71 L.Ed. 303; *Miller v. Board of Public Works* (1925) 195 Cal. 477, 234 P. 381.

10. E. g., *McCarthy v. City of Manhattan Beach* (1953) 41 Cal.2d 879, 264 P.2d 932; *Consolidated Rock Products Co. v. City of Los Angeles* (1962) 57 Cal.2d 515, 20 Cal.Rptr. 638, 370 P.2d 342; see *Selby v. City of San Buenaventura* (1973) 10 Cal.3d 110, 109 Cal.Rptr. 799, 514 P.2d 111; *State of California v. Superior Court (Veta)* (1974) 12 Cal.3d 237, 115 Cal.Rptr. 497, 524 P.2d 1281.

To demonstrate the settled nature of the issue before us we point out that the United States Supreme Court faced the same question in the first major constitutional challenge to modern zoning to come before it. (*Euclid v. Ambler Realty Co.* (1926) 272 U.S. 365, 47 S.Ct. 114, 71 L.Ed. 303.) Tendering allegations almost identical to those urged here, the appellee in *Euclid* claimed that "the tract of land in question is vacant and has been held for years for the purpose of selling and developing it for industrial uses, for which it is especially adapted, being immediately in the path of progressive industrial development; that for such uses it has a market value of about $10,000 per acre, but if the use be limited to residential purposes the market value is not in excess of $2,500 per acre. . . ." (*Id.*, at p. 384, 47 S.Ct. at p. 117.) The court upheld the zoning against the claim that it constituted a taking of the property in question, settling some half century ago the question in the instant case.

The record of this court stands equally clear. In one of the seminal zoning cases coming before us, in considering and rejecting a contention that a zoning ordinance forbidding the establishment of a non-conforming use in a residential area unconstitutionally deprived the landowners of their property, we quoted with approval the following language of the Wisconsin Supreme Court: " 'It is thoroughly established in this country that the rights preserved to the individual by these constitutional provisions are held in subordination to the rights of society. Although one owns property, he may not do with it as he pleases any more than he may act in accordance with his personal desires. . . . [I]ncidental damages to property resulting from governmental activities, or laws passed in the promotion of the public welfare are not considered a taking of the property for which compensation must be made. (*Carter v. Harper* [1923] 182 Wis. 148 [, 153], 196 N.W. 451: . . .)" (*Miller v. Board of Public Works, supra*, 195 Cal., 477, 488, 234 P.381, 385.)

In an attempt to escape the clear import of such rulings plaintiffs emphasize that their complaint sounds in inverse condemnation, and that they therefore need only show some diminution in value rather than the arbitrary or confiscatory action imposed by the line of cases they seek to avoid. Several appellate courts in California have considered and rejected precisely this contention.[11]

[5, 6] The Court of Appeal in *Morse v. County of San Luis Obispo, supra*, 247 Cal.App.2d 600, 55 Cal. Rptr. 710, spoke as follows in affirming a judgment of dismissal following the sustaining of a demurrer to a complaint seeking damages in inverse condemnation for the down-zoning of

---

11. *State of California v. Superior Court (Veta)* (1974) 12 Cal.3d 237, 115 Cal.Rptr. 497, 524 P.2d 1281; *Selby Realty Co. v. City of Buenaventura* (1973) 10 Cal.3d 110, 109 Cal.Rptr. 799, 514 P.2d 111; *Gisler v. County of Madera* (1974) 38 Cal.App.3d 303, 112 Cal.Rptr. 919; *Morse v. County of San Luis Obispo* (1967) 247 Cal.App.2d 600, 55 Cal.Rptr. 710; *Smith v. County of Santa Barbara* (1966) 243 Cal.App.2d 126, 52 Cal.Rptr. 292.

property: "Plaintiffs are apparently attempting to recover profits they might have earned if they had been successful in getting their land rezoned to permit subdivision into small residential lots, but *landowners have no vested right in existing or anticipated zoning ordinances.* (*Anderson v. City Council* [1964] 229 Cal.App.2d 79, 88-90, 40 Cal.Rptr. 41). A purchaser of land merely acquires a right to continue a *use* instituted before the enactment of a more restrictive zoning.[12]   Public entities are not bound to reimburse individuals for losses due to changes in zoning, for within the limits of the police power 'some uncompensated hardships must be borne by individuals as the price of living in a modern enlightened and progressive community.' (*Metro Realty v. County of El Dorado* [1963] 222 Cal.App.2d 508, 518, 35 Cal. Rptr. 480, 486. . . .)" (247 Cal. App.2d at pp. 602-603, 55 Cal.Rptr. at p. 712; emphasis added.)

[7, 8]   We have only recently reaffirmed this principle in *Selby Realty Co. v. City of Buenaventura, supra,* 10 Cal.3d 110, 109 Cal.Rptr. 799, 514 P.2d 111;[13] we held in that case that a landowner could not employ inverse condemnation to challenge a zoning ordinance which required him to dedicate part of his land to the city as a condition of receiving a building permit: "The sixth cause of action sounds in inverse condemnation and alleges that the city has 'taken' plaintiff's property without compensation. Again, insofar as this cause of action is based upon the adoption of the general plan, there is no 'taking' of the property. . . . The appropri-

---

12. Plaintiffs have failed to allege any existing use that was in nonconformity with the residential zoning classification now in effect; as far as the allegations of their complaint disclose, the land remains in the same state as the day the plaintiffs acquired it. Thus we need not here consider the question of a nonconforming use which the zoning authority seeks to terminate or remove; for plaintiffs have alleged that they enjoy a vested right, not in an existing *use*, but in a mere zoning *classification* on vacant land. This case therefore raises no issue of the constitutionality of a zoning regulation which requires the termination of an existing use. (Cf. *Livingston Rock, etc., Co. v. County of Los Angeles* (1954) 43 Cal.2d 121, 127, 272 P.2d 4.)

13. Plaintiffs argue that *Selby* is distinguishable because that case involved a uniform zoning classification while in the instant case plaintiffs have tendered allegations of discriminatory zoning classification. The asserted distinction lacks substance. Plaintiffs have a remedy in a mandate action against discriminatory zoning. (Code Civ.Proc., § 1094.5.) Both their complaint and their briefs in this case, however, urge that the injury constituting the taking was the reduction in market value of the land. If such a reduction constituted an injury, it would occur regardless of the legality of the zoning action occasioning it; indeed we have held that the wrongfulness of the state's action is irrelevant in an inverse condemnation case. (E. g., *Holtz v. Superior Court* (1970) 3 Cal.3d 296, 302, 90 Cal.Rptr. 345, 475 P.2d 441.) Thus, *if* plaintiffs have suffered an injury cognizable under California Constitution, article I, section 19, they stand entitled to compensation regardless of the public agency's wrongfulness in causing the injury. If, on the other hand, the city has acted arbitrarily or discriminatorily in passing the zoning ordinance of which they complain, plaintiffs stand entitled to relief by administrative mandate. Since governmental fault is irrelevant in an inverse condemnation action, *Selby's* discussion of the impropriety of inverse condemnation as a remedy for allegedly improper zoning is apposite to the instant case.

ate method by which to consider such a claim is by a proceeding in mandamus under section 1094.5 of the Code of Civil Procedure." (10 Cal.3d at pp. 127-128, 109 Cal.Rptr. 799, at p. 810, 514 P.2d at p. 122.) [14]

Plaintiffs' amici curiae, however, strenuously argue that California Constitution, article I, section 19 [former article I, section 14], which provides that "[p]rivate property may be taken *or damaged* for public use only when just compensation . . . has first been paid . . . ." (emphasis added) requires a ruling in their favor. Emphasizing the italicized words, plaintiffs contend first, that the California Constitution provides wider protection than the federal, and second, that the city in enacting the challenged zoning ordinances "damaged" their property and must therefore pay compensation. Only the first of these contentions is accurate.

This court has recognized the broader protections granted landowners by the addition of "or damaged" to the language of our state's compensation clause. (*Albers v. County of Los Angeles* (1965) 62 Cal.2d 250,

---

14. Neither *Selby* nor this case presents the distinct problems arising from inequitable zoning actions undertaken by a public agency as a prelude to public *acquisition* (*Klopping v. City of Whittier* (1972) 8 Cal.3d 39, 104 Cal.Rptr. 1, 500 P.2d 1345; *Peacock v. County of Sacramento* (1969) 271 Cal.App.2d 845, 77 Cal.Rptr. 391); or from zoning classifications invoked in order to evade the requirement that land *used* by the public must be acquired in eminent domain proceedings (*Sneed v. County of Riverside* (1963) 218 Cal.App.2d 205, 32 Cal.Rptr. 318). Thus in *Klopping* the city in question made public announcements that it intended to acquire the plaintiff's land, then unreasonably delayed commencement of eminent domain proceedings, with the predictable result that the property became commercially useless and suffered a decline in market value. We held only that the plaintiff should be able to include in his eminent domain damages the decline in value attributable to this unreasonable precondemnation action by the city. The case thus in no way resembles the instant one, in which plaintiffs make no allegations that the city intends to condemn the tract in question.

Similarly in *Peacock* the county had refused to permit any development of the land in question (barring even the growth of most vegetation), while assuring the owner that the restrictions were of no consequence because the county intended to acquire the land for an airport. When, after denying the owner any use of his property for five years, the county renounced its intent to acquire the land, the Court of Appeal affirmed a trial court finding that " '[t]he exceptional and extraordinary circumstances heretofore enumerated constituted a take [*sic*] of the subject property by inverse condemnation.' " (271 Cal.App.2d at 854, 77 Cal.Rptr. at 398.) Again one sees that the down-zoning to a taking only in connection with inequitable precondemnation actions by the public agency.

Finally, the cases hold that a public agency may not use a zoning ordinance to evade the requirement that the state acquire property which it uses for public purposes. Thus in *Sneed*, the county, rather than acquiring land for an air navigation easement, simply enacted a zoning ordinance forbidding any structure or vegetation more than three inches high and proceeded to operate flights over the area thus restricted. The Court of Appeal held that the plaintiff had stated a cause of action in inverse condemnation. Unlike the instant case, *Sneed* involved a zoning ordinance creating an actual public use of the property.

42 Cal.Rptr. 89, 398 P.2d 129; *Reardon v. San Francisco* (1879) 66 Cal. 492, 6 P.317; cf. *County of San Diego v. Miller* (1975) 13 Cal.3d 684, 119 Cal.Rptr. 491, 532 P.2d 139.) Yet in arguing that the additional phrase covers this case, plaintiffs mistake its meaning. Intended to reach situations in which government activity damaged land without taking it, the provision in question does not apply to this case, in which undamaged land has allegedly suffered only a diminution of market value.[15]

Plaintiffs fail to distinguish between the "damaged" property which is a requisite for a finding of compensability and the "damages" by which courts measure the compensation due. Reasoning backwards, plaintiffs erroneously contend that since they can calculate damages (by measuring decline in market value), they must have been "damaged" within the meaning of the state Constitution.

[9] Because a zoning action which merely decreases the market value of property does not violate the constitutional provisions forbidding uncompensated taking or damaging, the trial court correctly sustained without leave to amend the demurrer to the cause of action in inverse condemnation.[16] (Cal.Const., art. I, § 19 [former art. I, § 14].) * * * *

3. *Although amici argue that "fairness" requires that inverse condemnation lie to challenge zoning actions, both considerations of policy and the limitations of judicial institutions lead to a contrary conclusion.*

Numerous amici who have entered this case on behalf of the plaintiffs urge that the constitutional values of "fairness" protected by the compensation clauses of the state and federal Constitutions require us to hold that inverse condemnation lies for any zoning action which reduces the market value of any tract of land.[17] Without attempting a detailed discussion of

---

15. As we explained in *Holtz v. Superior Court* (1970) 3 Cal.3d 296, 310, 90 Cal. Rptr. 345, 354, 475 P.2d 441, 450: "Our decision in the instant case, and the *Albers* decision more generally, in effect recognize that, under article I, section 14 [present article I, second 19] *physical damages* proximately resulting from a public improvement be considered as direct a 'cost' as the property actually condemned or the materials actually utilized in its construction." (Emphasis added.) Thus, while we have not hesitated to afford individuals the full measure of the protection indicated by the history of article I, section 19, no California case has ever interpreted the "or damaged" phrase of our state Constitution to cover mere diminution of market value of property.

16. This case does not present, and we therefore do not decide, the question of entitlement to compensation in the event a zoning regulation forbade substantially *all* use of the land in question. We leave the question for another day.

17. Citing *County of San Diego v. Miller* (1975) 13 Cal.3d 684, 119 Cal.Rptr. 491, 532 P.2d 139, plaintiffs and their amici argue that the only consideration in this case relates to the "fairness" of the principle for which they contend; to this somewhat broad argument two answers present themselves. First, plaintiffs ignore the context of *San Diego;* the issue in that case was the distribution of a condemnation award which all conceded to be appropriate, not whether otherwise lawful state action constituted a "taking." Second, on a more basic level, we are deeply mindful of the

the many points raised by amici or a review of the still more voluminous secondary literature on the taking issue,[18] we shall briefly indicate the grounds for our declining to do so.

In this case, as in most instances, zoning is not an arbitrary action depriving someone of property for the purpose of its use by the public or transfer to another; rather it involves reciprocal benefits and burdens which the circumstances of this case well illustrate. The shopping center which plaintiffs seem at various times to have contemplated erecting, would derive its value from the existence of residential housing in the surrounding area. That residential character of the neighborhood, we may assume, results in part from the residential zoning of the area around the tract in question.[19] Plaintiffs in this case therefore find themselves in a somewhat uncomfortable position: they wish to reap the benefit in the form of higher market values of their land, of the restrictive zoning on other properties, but do not wish to bear the reciprocal burden of such zoning when it applies to their property. They thus would avoid the enforcement of residential zoning on their property while benefiting from its enforceability as to other property.

The long settled state of zoning law renders the possibility of change in zoning clearly foreseeable to land speculators and other purchasers of property, who discount their estimate of its value by the probability of such change. The real possibility of zoning changes for the tract in question finds ample demonstration in plaintiffs' insistence that their grantor procure such a change before conveying the land to them. Having obtained the benefits of such rezoning, but having failed to take advantage of it by building, they now assert that the termination of such rezoning rendered the

---

"basic equitable principles of fairness." (*United States v. Fuller* (1973) 409 U.S. 488, 490, 93 S.Ct. 801, 35 L.Ed.2d 16) which shape this area of the law. We set forth below some of the considerations which cast doubt on plaintiffs' claim even under this broad and only tenuously legal rubric of constitutional "fairness."

18. E. g., Berger. *A Policy Analysis of the Taking Problem* (1974) 49 N.Y.U.L. Rev. 165; Bosselman et al., The Taking Issue (1974); Costonis, *Development Rights Transfer: An Exploratory Essay* (1973) 83 Yale L.J. 75;————, *The Chicago Plan: Incentive Zoning and the Preservation of Urban Landmarks* (1972) 85 Harv.L. Rev. 574; Hagman, A New Deal: *Trading Windfalls for Wipeouts* (1974) 40 Planning 9; Michelman, *Property, Utility, and Fairness: Comments on the Ethical Foundations of "Just Compensation" Law* (1967) 80 Harv.L.Rev. 1165; Rose, *A Proposal for the Separation and Marketability of Development Rights as a Technique to Preserve Open Space* (1974) 2 Real Est.L.J. 635; Van Alstyne, *Taking or Damaging by Police Power: The Search for Inverse Condemnation Criteria* (1970) 44 So.Cal.L.Rev. 1.

19. As one of plaintiffs' amici has written in another context, "[W]hile one can conceptually separate windfalls caused by government [e. g., by zoning actions] from those caused by the community, they are very hard to disentangle and measure." (Hagman, *A New Deal: Trading Windfalls for Wipeouts* (1974) 40 Planning 9; see also Costonis, *Development Rights Transfer: An Exploratory Essay, supra,* 83 Yale L.J. 75; Rose, *A Proposal for the Separation and Marketability of Development Rights as a Technique to Preserve Open Space, supra,* 2 Real Est.L.J. 635.)

city liable in damages. A distinguished commentator has thus described plaintiffs' situation: "[They] bought land which [they] knew might be subjected to restrictions; and the price [they] paid should have been discounted by the possibility that restrictions would be imposed. Since [they] got exactly what [they] meant to buy, it can perhaps be said that society has effected no redistribution so far as [they are] concerned, any more than it does when it refuses to refund the price of [their] losing sweepstakes ticket." (Michelman, *Property, Utility, and Fairness: Comments on the Ethical Foundations of "Just Compensation" Law* (1967) 80 Harv.L.Rev. 1165, 1238; see also Berger, *A Policy Analysis of the Taking Problem* (1974) 49 N.Y.U.L.Rev. 165, 195-196.)

We are urged in this case to redefine the state and federal constitutional requirements of just compensation and to require payment for any zoning action which results in the diminution of market value. That we do not do so reflects less our belief that no problems exist with the present law in this area than our conviction that legislative rather than judicial action holds the key to any useful reform. The welter of proposals for action to remedy the inequities in the scheme of land use regulation which fall short of invoking constitutional protection bear ample witness to the ferment in this area.[20] Without passing on the desirability or legality of any of the proposed plans, we note that almost without exception they require legislative action for their implementation.[21] The complexity of the schemes proposed and the administrative machinery required for their effectuation obviously exceed anything readily feasible as a judicial remedy. Thus even if we were wholeheartedly to concede the wisdom of these plans, they would lie beyond our remedial powers.[22]

Finally, we note that our conclusion in no sense turns on the verbal distinction between "taking" and "police power." While these terms have a venerable history in discussions of this question, at best they have served as a shorthand method of indicating the result; neither hard nor easy cases are decided by such merely verbal lines. Rather, the far more basic con-

---

20. See footnote 18, *supra.*

21. E. g., Costonis, *Development Rights Transfer: An Exploratory Essay* (1973) 83 Yale L.J. 75; Rose, *A Proposal for the Separation and Marketability of Development Rights as a Technique to Preserve Open Space, supra,* 2 Real Est.L.J. 635; Berger, *A Policy Analysis of the Taking Problem, supra,* 49 N.Y.U.L.Rev. 165; Michelman, *Property, Utility and Fairness: Comments on the Ethical Foundations of "Just Compensation" Law supra,* 80 Harv.L.Rev. 1165, 1252: "[T]he courts recognize that they cannot, through the enunciation of doctrine which decides cases, adequately stake out the limits of fair treatment; that if the quest for fairness is left to a series of occasional encounters between the courts and public administrators it can but partially be fulfilled; and that the political branches, accordingly, labor under their own obligations to avoid unfairness regardless of what the courts may require."

22. Moreover, we do not accept the suggestion of some of plaintiffs' amici that we recognize their cause of action as a way of goading the Legislature into actions felt to be desirable.

siderations of reciprocity discussed above have shaped the decisions in this area,[23] decisions which reconcile property rights and social needs.

[12]   Plaintiffs in this case desire a change in long standing principles of the law of just compensation; they ask that we hold municipal zoning bodies liable for full compensation for any fall in market price due to zoning actions. Yet plaintiffs can cite no case and little by way of other considerations to support their claim of entitlement to compensation by reason of a change in zoning. Hoping to build a shopping center, they purchased a tract previously zoned as agricultural land. For reasons which do not appear in the record, they did not build for five years, although no zoning impediments are alleged to have existed. Now they desire to sell that land at a profit to yet another developer and complain that the city has in the meantime concluded that its interests would best be served by residential rather than commercial development of the tract in question. Unable to make the desired profit from the sale of their land, they now seek to recoup it from the city; in so doing they mistake the law.

Zoning and other land use regulation, long an established feature of our lives, expresses both a concern for our present quality of life and our collective fiduciary responsibility to the future; that it bears this weight and expresses this concern does not mean that it may not fall short of constitutional standards. These considerations do, however, caution us not capriciously to discard established constitutional boundaries in this area.

The alternative writs are discharged, and the peremptory writs denied.

WRIGHT, C. J., and McCOMB, MOSK, SULLIVAN and RICHARDSON, JJ., concur.

CLARK, Justice (dissenting).

I dissent.

Article I, section 19 of the California Constitution provides: "Private property may be taken *or damaged* for public use only when just compensation . . . has first been paid to . . . the owner." (Italics added.) While this court has usually applied the "or damaged" language in the context of physical damage to property (*Albers v. County of Los Angeles* (1965) 62 Cal.2d 250, 42 Cal.Rptr. 89, 398 P.2d 129; *Bacich v. Board of Control* (1943)

---

23. Professor Michelman has written: "We have, in effect, been searching for a useful and satisfying way to identify the 'evil' supposedly combatted by the constitutional just compensation provisions, and have now suggested equating it with a capacity of some collective actions to imply that someone may be subjected to immediately disadvantageous or painful treatment for no other apparent reason . . . than that someone else's claim to satisfaction has been ranked as intrinsically superior to his own. . . . We should, then, consider carefully the extent to which the 'fairness' or utility rationale is already reflected, even if inexplicitly, in the judicial doctrines which presently compose the main corpus of our just compensation lore. My conclusion is that these doctrines do significantly reflect the line of thought which has been elaborated in these pages. . . . " Michelman, *Property, Utility, and Fairness: Comments on the Ethical Foundations of "Just Compensation" Law, supra,* 80 Harv.L.Rev. 1165, 1224-1226.

23 Cal.2d 343, 144 P.2d 818), we have never limited compensation to physical damage. In fact, in *Reardon v. San Francisco* (1885) 66 Cal. 492, 6 p. 317, this court rejected such an interpretation, noting that the word *damaged* "refers to something more than a direct or immediate damage to private property, such as its invasion or spoliation. There is no reason why this word should be construed in any other than its ordinary and popular sense. It embraces more than the taking." (*Id.* at p. 501, p. 6 at p. 322.) " 'The tendency under our system is too often to sacrifice the individual to the community; and it seems very difficult in reason to show why the [government] should not pay for property which it destroys or impairs the value, as well as for what it physically takes.' " (*Bacich v. Board of Control, supra,* 23 Cal.2d 343, 351, 144 P.2d 818, 823.)

The 80 percent decrease in fair market value of the subject property clearly constitutes damage to plaintiffs. The issue then is whether plaintiffs' damage is compensable under the California Constitution.

California has long recognized that while "the police power is very broad in concept, it is not without restriction in relation to the taking or damaging of property. When it passes beyond proper bounds in its invasion of property rights, it in effect comes within the purview of the law of eminent domain and its exercise requires compensation. [Citations.]" (*House v. L. A. County Flood Control Dist.* (1944) 25 Cal.2d 384, 388, 153 P.2d 950, 952; see *Berman v. Parker* (1954) 348 U.S. 26, 75 S.Ct. 98, 99 L.Ed. 27.)

The point at which an injury becomes compensable is determined by balancing two fundamental—yet inconsistent—policy considerations. (*Bacich v. Board of Control, supra,* 23 Cal.2d 343, 144 P.2d 818.) "[O]n the one hand the policy underlying the eminent domain provision in the Constitution is to distribute throughout the community the loss inflicted upon the individual by the making of public improvements. . . . On the other hand, fears have been expressed that compensation allowed too liberally will seriously impede, if not stop, beneficial public improvements because of the greatly increased cost." (*Id.* at p. 350, 144 P.2d at p. 823.)

This balancing of policies in determining the point at which compensation is constitutionally mandated also has long been recognized by the United States Supreme Court. In *Pennsylvania Coal Co. v. Mahon* (1922) 260 U.S. 393, 43 S.Ct. 158, 67 L.Ed. 322, the court noted that "Government hardly could go on if to some extent values incident to property could not be diminished without paying for every such change in the general law. As long recognized some values are enjoyed under an implied limitation and must yield to the police power. But obviously the implied limitation must have its limits. . . . One fact for consideration in determining such limits is the extent of the diminution. When it reaches a certain magnitude, in most if not in all cases there must be an exercise of eminent domain and compensation to sustain the act." (*Id.* at p. 413, 43 S.Ct. at p. 159.)

As this court has recently recognized in viewing these conflicting policies, the ultimate test whether compensation is constitutionally required, resolves itself into one of fairness. (*County of San Diego v. Miller* (1975) 13 Cal.3d 684, 689, 119 Cal.Rptr. 491, 532 P.2d 139, *Southern California Edison Company v. Bourgerie* (1973) 9 Cal.3d 169, 173-175, 107 Cal.Rptr. 76, 507 P.2d 964.)[1]

We should address any problem of loss suffered by governmental action as one demanding application of a rule cf fairness. (Cf. *Muskopf v. Corning Hospital Dist.* (1961) 55 Cal.2d 211, 11 Cal.Rptr. 89, 359 P.2d 457.) Although earlier cases have failed to apply the rule of fairness to losses occasioned by downzoning, there is no justification for treating such losses differently from those due to other governmental action.

As Justice Traynor in his concurring opinion in *House v. L. A. County Flood Control Dist., supra,* 25 Cal.2d 384, 396-397, 153 P.2d 950, 956, correctly pointed out, in determining fairness "[i]t is irrelevant whether or not the injury to the property is accompanied by a corresponding benefit to the public purpose to which the improvement is dedicated, since the measure of liability is not the benefit derived from the property, but the loss to the owner [citations]."

In conjunction with the statement of Justice Traynor, the cautionary note of the United States Supreme Court in *Pennsylvania Coal Co. v. Mahon, supra,* 260 U.S. 393, 416, 43 S.Ct. 158, 160, 67 L.Ed. 322, should not be overlooked. "We are in danger of forgetting that a strong public desire to improve the public condition is not enough to warrant achieving the desire by a shorter cut than the constitutional way of paying for the change."

The great harm which might result from downzoning was recognized in *Metro Realty v. County of El Dorado* (1963) 222 Cal.App.2d 508, 516, 35 Cal.Rptr. 480, 485, involving an ordinance of short duration. The court stated that although the temporary restriction was a mere inconvenience, "the same restriction indefinitely prolonged might possibly metamorphize into oppression."

Compensation in appropriate downzoning cases also meets the policy reflected by the eminent domain provision. As recently reaffirmed by this court in *Holtz v. Superior Court* (1970) 3 Cal.3d 296, 303, 90 Cal.Rptr. 345, 349, 475 P.2d 441, 435, quoting from *Clement v. State Reclamation Board* (1950) 35 Cal.2d 628, 220 P.2d 397, "[T]he underlying purpose of our constitutional provision in inverse—as well as ordinary—condemnation is 'to distribute throughout the community the loss inflicted upon the individual by the making of public improvements' (*Bacich v. Board of Control* (1943) 23 Cal.2d 343, 350, 144 P.2d 818, 823); 'to socialize the burden . . .—to afford relief to the landowner in cases in which it is unfair to ask him to bear a burden that should be assumed by society [citation].' "

---

1. "The constitutional requirement of just compensation derives as much content from the basic equitable principles of fairness . . . as it does from technical concepts of property law." (*United States v. Fuller* (1973) 409 U.S. 488, 490, 93 S.Ct. 801, 803, 35 L.Ed.2d 16; also quoted in *Southern California Edison Co. v. Bourgerie, supra,* 9 Cal.3d at p. 175, 107 Cal.Rptr. 76, 507 P.2d 964, see *Mid-Way Cabinet, etc., Mfg. v. County of San Joaquin* (1967) 257 Cal.App.2d 181, 192, 65 Cal.Rptr. 37.)

Zoning is enacted for the public benefit. The need for "resolute sophistication in the face of occasional insistence that compensation payments must be limited lest society find itself unable to afford beneficial plans and improvements," was aptly stated by Professor Michelman in his well-noted law review article: [2] "What society cannot, indeed, afford to impoverish itself. It cannot afford to instigate measures whose costs, including costs which remain 'unsocialized,' exceed their benefits. Thus, it would appear that any measure which society cannot afford or, putting it another way, is unwilling to finance under conditions of full compensation, society cannot afford at all."

Not all governmental downzoning must be compensated. However, the compensatory "or damaged" provision of the California Constitution should apply when by public action land has (1) suffered substantial decrease in value, (2) the decrease is of long or potentially infinite duration and (3) the owner would incur more than his fair share of the financial burden.

Applying this fairness test to the instant factual situation, plaintiffs have stated a valid cause of action in inverse condemnation. The 80 percent decrease in value of plaintiff's property—from a market value of $400,000 to $75,000—is obviously substantial. Because the action is taken pursuant to Government Code section 65300, this decrease clearly is of long duration.[3] Of the four quadrants of the subject intersection, three are zoned for commercial use and *only* plaintiffs' quadrant has been rezoned to "low-density single family residential." Plaintiffs therefore are being forced to shoulder a burden that surrounding landowners have not been made to share.[4]

Applying the tripartite test of fairness to downzoning should not impose an undue burden on governmental agencies. Once the landowner establishes his cause of action for damage, the condemnation agency has several alternatives including: (1) compensating the landowner for the decrease in value; (2) paying total value for the land and acquiring title; (3) rescinding the downzoning, in which case the agency would be abandoning a condemnation, becoming liable to the landowner for interim damage, costs and attorney's fees. Cf. Code Civ.Proc., § 1255a; *City of Los Angeles v. Ricards* (1973) 10 Cal.3d 385, 110 Cal.Rptr. 489, 515 P.2d 585.) The first two alternatives assume the validity of the zoning ordinance and therefore are inapplicable when the ordinance itself is invalid.[5] In the

---

2. Michelman, *Property, Utility and Fairness: Comments on the Ethical Foundations of "Just Compensation" Law* (1967) 80 Harv.L.Rev. 1165, 1181.

3. Section 65300 of the Government Code states: "Each planning agency shall prepare and the legislative body of each county and city shall adopt a comprehensive, *long-term general plan* for the physical development of the county or city, and of any land outside its boundaries which in the planning agency's judgment bears relation to its planning." (Italics added.)

4. The facts of this case do not present a situation where the property was upzoned and then subsequently downzoned while in the hands of the same owner.

5. Whether the present zoning classification of the property is valid has not yet been decided by the trial court or by this court, as that issue is not before us. However, previous California cases have held that land use regulation creating an island

case of an invalid ordinance, the court in issuing mandate should follow the third alternative, awarding interim damage, costs and attorney's fees.[6]

Plaintiffs have stated a cause of action in inverse condemnation. Therefore, it was error for the trial court to sustain the demurrer without leave to amend. Accordingly I would grant the writ directing the trial court to overrule the demurrer.

BRADEN

v.

MUCH

403 Ill. 507, 87 N.E.2d 620 (1949).

Supreme Court of Illinois.

May 19, 1949.

Rehearing Denied Sept. 19, 1949.

Appeal from Superior Court, Cook County; Donald S. McKinlay, Judge.

Suit for injunction by Zedrick T. Braden and others against Sam Much and others. From the decree complainants appeal directly to the Supreme Court after the trial court certified that the validity of an ordinance was involved.

Affirmed.

Braden, Hall, Barnes & Moss and C. Francis Stradford, Chicago, for appellants.

Rudnick & Wolfe and Benjamin S. Adamowski, Corp. Counsel, Chicago (L. Louis Karton, Maurice J. Nathanson, and Sydney R. Drebin, Chicago, of counsel).

DAILY, Justice.

Appellants filed a complaint in equity in the superior court of Cook County to restrain appellee the city of Chicago from proceeding under an amendatory ordinance enacted on March 14, 1946, rezoning certain property in the city of Chicago from an apartment house district to a specialty shop district, and to compel appellee Sam Much to remove from his premises a building erected thereon. The trial court sustained appellees' objections to the report of the master in chancery and dismissed the complaint for want

of residential use surrounded by less restrictively zoned property constituted an invalid exercise of the legislative power. (*Hamer v. Town of Ross* (1963) 59 Cal.2d 776, 31 Cal.Rptr. 335, 382, P.2d 375; *Reynolds v. Barrett* (1938) 12 Cal.2d 244, 83 P.2d 29.)

6. Government Code section 818.2 providing that a public entity is not liable for injury caused by the enactment of a law is inapplicable when the governmental action rises to the level of a taking or damaging within the eminent domain provisions of the Constitution.

of equity. As the trial court has certified that the validity of the ordinance is involved, this matter comes to us on a direct appeal.

Appellants allege in their amended complaint that they are property owners on East Forty-fifth Place in the City of Chicago, and that on April 5, 1923, the Chicago zoning ordinance made the entire district an apartment house district. On March 14, 1946, the city council passed an ordinance changing the area bounded by East Forty-fifth Street, the alley next east of South Parkway, East Forty-fifth Place, and South Parkway, from an apartment house district to a specialty shop district.

Appellants further allege that they are property owners in the district, and purchased their homes after the passage of the 1923 ordinance; that the said amendatory ordinance was not passed in conformity with the statute, in that no public hearing was held before the board of appeals pursuant to notice, and no report of the findings of fact by the board was made; that the ordinance as amended is unreasonable, arbitrary and unjust, and was not passed with a view to maintaining, improving or protecting the safety, health, morals or general welfare of the people; and that it contravenes section 2 of article II of the State constitution, Smith-Hurd Stats. Const., and the fourteenth amendment of the Federal constitution. They further allege that appellee Sam Much is constructing a building to be used for commercial purposes on the property owned by him. Appellees answered by way of denial and alleged that the property was not to be used for commercial purposes, but for shops and specialities, in accordance with the zoning ordinance.

The evidence discloses that the amendatory ordinance of March 14, 1946, was introduced on January 16, 1946, upon a petition signed by property owners, dated January 2, 1946, and referred to the committee on buildings and zoning; that the ordinance was set for public hearing to be held February 21, 1946, at 10:30 A.M., in room 203 of the city hall building in the city of Chicago; that notice by publication was made in the Chicago Journal of Commerce of said public hearing, and that a meeting was actually held by the committee pursuant to the notice, after which the committee, by its chairman, reported that the ordinance providing for the amendment be recommended for passage by the city council; that the ordinance was ordered deferred and published by the city council at a meeting held February 28, 1946; that the ordinance was passed on March 14, 1946, and published in the Chicago Journal of Commerce on April 10, 1946.

The evidence further indicates that, in addition to giving the notice required by statute, (Ill.Rev.Stat.1945, chap. 24, par. 73—8,) and by the Chicago zoning ordinance, it had been the custom in the city of Chicago for investigators to give actual notice to the property owners affected by amendments to the zoning ordinances by delivering them copies of the notice, or by putting them in the mailboxes on the property. The investigator in this case testified that he had followed the custom in this respect, but appellants testified that they had never received a copy of the notice.

The property of appellee Much is located on the northeast corner of the intersection of South Parkway and Forty-fifth Place. It has a frontage on South Parkway of 75 feet and on Forty-fifth Place of 150 feet. The building was so constructed that the front of the same appears clearly to be on South Parkway which is a main arterial thoroughfare leading into Washington Park from Thirty-second Street. The properties of the several appellants are located on both sides of Forty-fifth Place, east of South Parkway, and between it and Evans Avenue. None of the property owned by any of the appellants is within the area that is rezoned by the amendatory ordinance.

Immediately north of Much's property, on South Parkway, is a 3-flat building, in the basement of which is a beauty shop. On the southeast corner of Forty-fifth Street and South Parkway is a 6-flat building in which is located a drugstore, a flower store and a cleaning shop. On the northeast corner of South Parkway and Forty-fifth Street, one block north of his property, is the Metropolitan Funeral System Building which houses a chapel and funeral parlor and a ballroom. At the intersection of Forty-third Street and South Parkway, on both sides of the street, are many business places, drugstores and doctors' and lawyers' offices. Likewise, south of the property, between Forty-sixth Street and Forty-seventh Street, both sides of South Parkway is zoned for business and contains numerous apartment buildings, including those owned by the several appellants and is, generally speaking, a quiet residential neighborhood, although there is a grocery store located in that neighborhood directly across the street from the properties owned by appellants Braden and Trammel.

Expert witnesses called on behalf of appellants testified that the effect of the building constructed by appellee Much would depreciate the value of the properties in the area from 15 percent to 25 or 35 percent. However, upon cross-examination, one of them admitted that the value of his property zoned for specialty shops would be about $170 to $175 per front foot, whereas, if zoned exclusively for apartment uses it would have a value of but $100 per front foot. Another testified that the value of the Much property for apartments would be $200 per foot for the first 25 feet and $100 per foot for the balance, and that if zoned for specialty shops the value would not be more than $250 per front foot.

Witnesses for appellees testified that the highest and best use of Much's property was a specialty-shop use, and that there is no demand for vacant property on South Parkway between Forty-fourth Street and Forty-seventh Street, for apartment or residential purposes. The chief draftsman in the county assessor's office testified that for tax purposes the property on South Parkway is valued at $60 a front foot, while the property on Forty-fifth Place is valued at $25 a front foot. Appellee Sam Much testified that he secured a permit from the city of Chicago to erect a building, consisting of three stores, on the property, and that the cost of construction was $49,000.

The master found in his report that appellants were influenced in purchasing their property by the fact that the area was zoned for apartment or residential use; that there was no evidence that the change was made for the public good; that appellants did not know of the proposal to amend, or of the amendment to the zoning ordinance; that the only notice given was by publication in the Chicago Journal of Commerce; that there was no evidence of a public hearing before the passage of the ordinance, and that the equities of the case were with appellants and against appellees. He recommended that a decree should be entered in favor of appellants in accordance with his findings and conclusions granting the prayer of the complaint.

The chancellor, in sustaining the objections of appellees to the master's report, found that the action of the city council in passing the amendatory ordinance was not arbitrary and that they acted wholly and absolutely within their province under the law; that the requisite notice prescribed by section 73—8 of the Revised Cities and Villages Act (Ill.Rev.Stat.1945, chap. 24, par. 73—8,) for an amendatory ordinance was given, and that, in addition thereto, notice was given in accordance with the customs of the city of Chicago by placing a copy of the notice in the mailbox of each of the property owners in the area to be affected, and that a public hearing was held pursuant to the notice by the committee on buildings and zoning.

[1] We have previously held that a complaint in equity, praying for general equitable relief and an injunction, is a proper remedy to test the validity of a zoning ordinance. 2700 Irving Park Bldg. Corp. v. City of Chicago, 395 Ill. 138, 69 N.E.2d 827; Western Theological Seminary v. City of Evanston, 325 Ill. 511, 156 N.E. 778.

Section 73—8 of the Revised Cities and Villages Act (Ill.Rev.Stat.1945, chap. 24, par. 73—8,) provided as follows: "The regulations imposed and the districts created under the authority of this article may be amended from time to time by ordinance after the ordinance establishing them has gone into effect, but no such amendments shall be made without a hearing before some commission or committee designated by the corporate authorities. At least fifteen days' notice of the time and place of the hearing shall be published in the official paper of, or in a paper of general circulation in the municipality." * * *

[5-7] It has long been established that municipalities may adopt zoning ordinances as an exercise of their police power, and may thereby impose a reasonable restraint upon the use of private property. Anderman v. City of Chicago, 379 Ill. 236, 40 N.E.2d 51; Johnson v. Village of Villa Park, 370 Ill. 272, 18 N.E.2d 887. The ordinance must have a real substantial relation to the public health, safety, morals or general welfare. Western Theological Seminary v. City of Evanston, 325 Ill. 511, 156 N.E. 778. Whether the means employed bear any real substantial relation to the public health, comfort, safety or welfare, or are essentially arbitrary or unreasonable, is a

question subject to judicial review. Offner Electronics, Inc. v. Gerhardt, 398 Ill. 265, 76 N.E.2d 27.

[8, 9] In ascertaining whether a particular zoning ordinance is in the interest of the public welfare, each case must be determined upon its own peculiar facts. Johnson v. Village of Villa Park, 370 Ill. 272, 18 N.E.2d 887. The extent to which property values are diminished by the provisions of the zoning ordinance must be given consideration. Offner Electronics, Inc. v. Gerhardt, 398 Ill. 265, 76 N.E.2d 27. The character of the neighborhood and the use to which nearby property is put may also be taken into consideration. Forbes v. Hubbard, 348 Ill. 166, 180 N.E. 767. If the gain to the public by the ordinance is small when compared to the hardship upon the individual property owner by the restrictions of the zoning ordinance, no valid basis for the exercise of the police power exists. The element of value is not controlling, but is proper to be considered and may be persuasive in passing upon the validity of the ordinance. Quilici v. Village of Mt. Prospect, 399 Ill. 418, 78 N.E.2d 240; Metropolitan Life Ins. Co. v. City of Chicago, 402 Ill. 581, 84 N.E.2d 825.

When the foregoing well-known principles applicable to zoning ordinances are applied to the facts in the instant case, we find that the area in which appellee's property is located is one which is fast becoming a specialty-shop district. South Parkway, both to the north and to the south of the property, is an arterial thoroughfare, with business enterprises interspersed among apartment and residential properties fronting upon it. It is difficult to evaluate the ratio between the depreciation in value of appellant's property by the amendatory ordinance, as compared with the appreciation of appellee's property and other property located in the rezoned area. The record discloses that other property owners lying within the area joined with the appellee in seeking the amendment to the ordinance. There is apparently little demand for property for residential purposes along South Parkway. The highest and best use to which property located in that area can be put seems to be for specialty-shop purposes; and likewise, the evidence indicates that the value of the property in the area which has been rezoned is greater than the value of the property adjoining thereto.

[10, 11] We are therefore of the opinion that the city council did not act in an arbitrary or unreasonable manner in passing its amendatory ordinance. The judgment of a legislative authority will not be disturbed merely because the court, if it were establishing zoning districts or making variations therein, would not have done the same thing the legislative body did. The rule is that when the question of reasonableness is fairly debatable, courts will not interfere with the legislative judgment. Avery v. Village of La Grange, 381 Ill. 432, 45 N.E.2d 647; Burkholder v. City of Sterling, 381 Ill. 564, 46 N.E.2d 45; Zadworny v. City of Chicago, 380 Ill. 470, 44 N.E.2d 426.

[12] Nor can we concur with the position of appellants that the amendatory ordinance would make their property worthless, and is therefore confiscatory. Granting that their property may be depreciated to a certain extent by the introduction of specialty shops in that vicinity, it is not the amendatory ordinance of 1946, alone, that has brought that condition about. The fact is that the vicinity has, for some years, by normal expansion and otherwise, become more and more commercial. The zoning of streets lying along the edges of residential districts, for business and commercial purposes, is a recognized method of zoning. Officer Electronics, Inc., v. Gerhardt, 398 Ill. 265, 76 N.E.2d 27; People ex rel. Joseph Lumber Co. v. City of Chicago, 402 Ill. 321, 83 N.E.2d 592. The situation is somewhat analogous to that set forth in Offner Electronics, Inc., v. Gerhardt, 398 Ill. 265, 76 N.E.2d 27, 32, in which we said: "Plaintiff's property is not characterized by the residential area to the west of it on North Sawyer Avenue but, instead, by the business district on Kedzie Avenue of which it is a component part." The converse of the situation is true here. Appellee's property is not characterized by the residential area to the east of it, in which lies the property belonging to appellants, but rather, by the properties on both sides of it on South Parkway, of which it is a component part.

The position of appellants is, in at least one respect, similar to the position of appellee Much. At the time they purchased their property, it was zoned for residential and apartment purposes, and they had reason to rely upon the rule of law that it would not be changed, unless for the public good. On the other hand, at the time that Much applied for a building permit for the construction of his building, the area was zoned for specialty-shop purposes, and he had reason to rely upon the same rule of law. Since the city council, in passing the amendatory ordinance, found that it was for the public good, and since we have found nothing in the record which invalidates the ordinance, the position of appellee Much must prevail over that of appellants.

A careful review of the entire record discloses that the decree of the superior court of Cook County, dismissing appellants' complaint for want of equity, was correct and it is affirmed.

Decree affirmed.

Questions and Notes

1. The discussion in this opinion is the ultimate in the theory that the purpose of zoning is to protect property rights. How did the court attempt to apply this theory here?

2. Note that what was involved was the elimination of a break in strip commercial zoning along a major highway. For other Illinois cases on this point, see Zilien v. City of Chicago, 415 Ill. 488, 114 N.E.2d 717 (1953). The Illinois court's attitude on this is rather unique.

WILSON

v.

MOUNTAINSIDE

42 N.J. 426, 201 A.2d 540(1964).

Supreme Court of New Jersey.

Argued Dec. 3, 1963.

Decided June 22, 1964.

Action in lieu of prerogative writ to set aside denial of variance or to strike down residential classification as invalid. The Superior Court, Law Division, decided all issues against the property owners and their appeal was certified on application while pending in the Appellate Division. The Supreme Court, Hall, J., held that where the interior of the property owners' tract deeply penetrated a fully developed, high-caliber residential section which would unquestionably be harmed to a very considerable degree by commercial use of the whole parcel, and where plaintiffs sought relief on the ground of unreasonableness of residential classification only as to the tract in its entirety, their demand must be denied in toto.

Affirmed without prejudice to future application or action.

Melvin J. Koestler, Elizabeth, for plaintiffs-appellants (Koestler & Koestler, Elizabeth, attorneys).

Irvine B. Johnstone, Jr., Westfield, for defendants-respondents.

The opinion of the court was delivered by

HALL, J.

This case tests the validity of the use zoning of plaintiffs' 12-acre tract fronting on U.S. Highway Route 22 in the Borough of Mountainside, Union County. They were denied a recommendation for a variance by the board of adjustment, N.J.S.A. 40:55-39(d), to permit commercial utilization of the entire parcel instead of a limited business use in one corner allowed by an earlier variance and single-family residential use specified for the parcel by the current municipal zoning ordinance. This action in lieu of prerogative writ was then instituted in the Law Division to set aside the denial and, alternatively, to strike down the residential classification as invalid. In addition, the suit sought a declaration that particular provisions of the zoning ordinance imposing certain special regulations on the establishment of businesses and industrial uses, as well as comparable provisions of the planning board ordinance, constitute an improper method of land use control. The trial court decided all issues against plaintiffs. We certified their appeal on application while it was pending in the Appellate Division. R.R. 1:10-1A.

The thrust of the attack was a claim of unreasonable ordinance classification of plaintiffs' property for residential use and a contention that all highway frontage zoning in the borough was void by reason of an illegal method of control whereby such frontage had been limited by the ordinance to residential use over a long period of years and indiscriminate individual deviations therefrom for business and industrial uses had been regularly allowed through administrative action. The additional assault on the special regulatory provisions of the current ordinances is broadly a part of the latter aspect of the attack. It is most important to keep in mind that plaintiffs sought relief not just with respect to that portion of their property close to the highway but for its entire depth of nearly 900 feet.

The basis asserted for the variance was, save in one respect relating to alleged peculiar physical characteristics of the interior of the property, the same as that grounding the claim of invalidity of the zoning classification. Consequently, plaintiffs confined their proof before the trial judge on this issue to the evidence they offered in the board of adjustment to support the variance application together with their cross-examination of opposing witnesses. The defense evidence substantially consisted of a live repetition of the opposition testimony before the board. In view of the broad sweep of the contentions, the geographical and historical facts of the community as well as of the particular property are essential for consideration of the issues.

Mountainside is situated some 12 miles southwest of Newark in the midst of what has become in the last 10 to 15 years a heavily developed ring surrounding the North Jersey central urban core. The ring development, residential, commerical and industrial, extends a considerably further distance. If it is thought of as a half wheel, the spokes are made up of several through highways passing through the ring and on into further parts of the State and beyond. Route 22 is one of the most important of these spokes, running from U. S. Route 1 near Newark Airport generally westerly through the densely developed areas of Union and eastern Somerset counties into west central New Jersey, central Pennsylvania and further. At least three quarters of Mountainside's four-square-mile area lies on the southerly slope of the Watchung hills. Route 22, a divided highway with two or more traffic lanes in each direction, traverses the entire two and one-half mile width of the borough from east to west at foot of the slope. The balance of the community extends south of this highway to the boundary of the Town of Westfield. Beyond the sizeable amount of county parklands, located both on the top of the ridge and bordering Westfield, the business development along Route 22 to be described, and a few neighborhood stores located some little distance south of the highway near the Westfield line, the land use is entirely that of highclass, single-family residences. These dwellings, now housing a population of about 6500 which has increased more than five-fold since 1940, cover the hilly slope to a considerable extent and also occupy most of the limited amount of available land south of the highway. None front thereon except a small number which antedated the highway business development and still remain in residential use and two or three constructed since in connection with a business use on a particular property. The growth along the highway has not been residential but of a distinctly commercial character, for the most part unrelated to the single-family dwelling development of the remainder of the community, and in many respects typical of what has happened in numerous other New Jersey towns bisected by through highways where there has been no limitation of access thereto by abutting owners or from intersecting local streets.

The highway, first designated State Route 29, was constructed a little over 30 years ago. As distinct from a virgin right of way as in most of its other courses, through Mountainside it utilized the route of an existing county road known as Springfield Road, which ran from Scotch Plains on the west to the center of Springfield on the east. Mountainside was at that time really only a country village, off the beaten track, with a population of about 1000. The land uses on Springfield Road, though it was the main thoroughfare, were mixed, but by no means dense—a number of large and small houses on large and small lots, some properties even devoted to small scale agriculture with roadside stands, a few scattered local stores and service establishments, community service buildings and a very considerable amount of vacant frontage.

The tract now owned by plaintiffs lay on the north side of the county road about equidistant from the Scotch Plains and Springfield borders and 1500 feet or so east of the intersection of New Providence Road, which runs from Westfield over the hill to the Summit area. Its southwest corner was then, and now, occupied by an old mansion type structure, at that time used as an orphanage. The balance of the parcel was and still is vacant land. Slightly to the east of it on the county road was a church. Apparently to save the church from destruction in view of the need to widen the road for the new highway, the highway was divided near the orphanage structure for several hundred feet, the east bound lanes going south of the church on the right of way of the county road and the west bound lanes occupying a new road bed on a curve and rise between the church and the orphanage property. An island was thus created, known as Chapel Island, on which the church remained, and frontage of about 960 feet on the north side of the west bound lanes of the highway resulted for what is now plaintiffs' property. (Since the original construction, the State has acquired the easterly 600 feet of this frontage, to a depth of 100 feet, subject to a right of access to the interior across the same. This strip, like some others similarly acquired along other parts of the highway, has remained vacant and apparently it is intended that it always remain in that condition as some kind of a buffer.) The 12-acre tract thereby became trapezoidal in shape, with a depth of almost 900 feet and a rear line approximately 375 feet long.

The history of highway land use control in Mountainside is divided into two periods. The first commenced with the initial zoning ordinance adopted in 1933 and extended to late 1955, when the second and current period began upon the enactment of a new ordinance.

The pattern of purported regulation during the first period amounted, legislatively, to a classification of all highway frontage for single-family residential use only, save for a few ordinance amendments permitting commercial use on specifically described parcels and the creation in 1952 of a very small industrial zone at the extreme easterly end of the borough. The classification was completely without regard to existing nonresidential uses or any foresight or plan to deal with the pressures and changes which an interstate highway would inevitably bring. The ordinance limitations were coupled with an almost incredible, deliberate course of administrative action by the board of adjustment and governing body which can only be characterized as about as great a perversion of proper zoning as could be imagined. This was the indiscriminate granting of variances for nonresidential uses, with the result that the blanket residential classification meant practically nothing even if it could be conceived of as intrinsically valid *in toto*. The evidence shows that from 1945 until the passage of the 1955 ordinance 44 use variances for highway property were granted, and only six denied, for the whole gamut of uses which has become so distressingly familiar in almost solidly lining through highways in metropolitan and suburban areas—gasoline stations, garages, restaurants, motor courts, bowling alleys, driving ranges, real estate and other offices, stores, showrooms and warehouses, service establishments, light manufacturing businesses, and so on *ad infinitum*, involving new buildings, enlarged use of existing business structures, conversion of former residences and the like. The record further shows that, almost without exception, these variances were also illegal (had they been seasonably attacked) because recommended by the board of adjustment without any findings whatever of justifying reasons or satisfaction of statutory criteria. The conclusion is irresistible either that allowance was dictated by whim, caprice or even favoritism or, at the very best, that the board of adjustment and the governing body had no conception of, or were improperly advised as to, their legal duties, limitations and general responsibilities.

Among the variances so granted was one to McIntyre, plaintiffs' predecessor in title, in 1949 to use the former orphanage building on the southwest corner of the tract, including land on which it stands and surrounding it 362 feet front by 232 feet deep, for a retail furniture business. (This frontage roughtly covers that between the westerly end of the property and the westerly end of the previously described strip owned by the State). McIntyre conducted such a business until he sold the entire property to plaintiffs in 1955, who continued it thereafter. The business was, however, inactive at the time of trial, allegedly because of general modern inadequacy of the ancient structure.

It is apparent that by 1955 the municipality realized the tragic error of its ways and has since sought at least to bring those ways to a halt by the adoption of the new ordinance in that year and subsequent abandonment of land use control by administrative action. Between the end of World War II and 1955, the phenomenal increase in the use of motor transportation both for people and products, the population explosion with consequent vast development home building, and the movement of business and industry to sites out of the cities, had produced radical changes in the use of vast quantities of vacant land in the ring area. While established highways made most of this physically and economically possible, they had become badly overburdened and, especially by reason of the great number of business establishments constructed along them in suburban and even rural areas, they had to serve not only their primary function of moving traffic but also that of providing access to the abutting businesses, the customers and employees of which in turn added to the traffic volume. And most of these highway businesses, as in Mountainside, were intended to serve or employ not those living in the near neighborhood but rather people from beyond the community who found them conveniently accessible by motor. Route 22 had become, in its first 25 or 30 miles west of Newark, one of the most overcrowded of these highways both in volume of traffic and number of commercial and industrial establishments lining its sides. There were few substantial gaps between the latter. It was and is an important interstate truck and passenger car route, a "rubber railroad" for commuters and others who had acquired homes in the broad area which it serves and a "Main Street" for the patrons of its businesses. Its traffic density and hazards and general ugly appearance, due in large measure to lack of appropriate planning and zoning controls in so many municipalities, are notorious. In Mountainside itself, traffic, increasing year by year, had reached a flow of 40,000 to 50,000 vehicles per day at the time of trial.

Consistent with this over-all pattern, by 1955 the easterly mile of Mountainside's highway frontage running from a short distance east of plaintiffs' property to the Springfield line, in which most of the previously described variances had been granted, was an almost indescribable hodgepodge of business enterprises of the type described. Few people still lived there, and it had admittedly lost all value for residential purposes. The chairman of the planning board in his testimony called it "a commercial slum * * * a mess * *". The 1955 ordinance divided this one-mile frontage into two use classifications. The easterly part was placed in an industrial zone which included not only the highway frontage but a very considerable amount of land in the rear thereof on both sides of the road. The only uses permitted anywhere in this zone are non-nuisance manufacturing, processing, warehousing and allied activities. Retail and residential uses (except for a caretaker) are specifically prohibited. The westerly part of the mile which ran to the westerly end of this intensive commercial development, a point just short of Chapel Island and about 1000 feet east of plaintiffs' property, was strip zoned by the ordinance in a restricted commercial zone, defined as "intended for the conduct of low-traffic generating, light manufacturing business and professional purposes." Only manufacturing, processing, and warehousing, professional offices and laboratories and warehouses are permitted. Retail sales and services and all residential uses are expressly forbidden. All of the numerous retail establishments along this mile which had been previously established by variance or other means were thereby rendered nonconforming. The evidence shows that the municipal thesis behind the restrictive zoning of this mile of frontage was that, while limitation to residential use could no longer be justified, the permitted uses would generate less additional highway traffic than retail businesses. The development therein since the 1955 ordinance has been in conformity with its limitations and no variances have been granted.[1]

The remaining highway frontage from the restricted commercial zone west to the Scotch Plains line was retained in the single-family residential classification in 1955. The only additional permitted uses are public buildings, churches, general agricultural activities and professional offices and studios contained in a residence building.[2] This distance is rather naturally divided into easterly and westerly segments for our purposes.

The easterly segment, in which plaintiffs' property is located, runs for about 3000 feet from the end of the restricted commercial zone to just beyond the New Providence Road intersection. It is the present character of this segment, coupled with its proximity to the intensive commercial development to the east and the general detrimental effect of the highway itself, which grounds plaintiffs' contention of intrinsic ordinance unreasonableness in limiting their property to residential use (and the limited business use permitted by the 1949 variance).[3]

This frontage underwent much less change in the 1945-1955 decade in comparison with the business development to the east, perhaps due to the fact of public ownership of a good part of the land, much of which has remained vacant. But by 1955 the great majority of uses were

---

1. The reasonableness of the 1955 zoning of this portion of the highway frontage is not attacked and we express no opinion with respect thereto.

2. The only zone in the borough provided for retail business by the ordinance is the small pocket occupied by the neighborhood stores south of the highway at the Westfield border. Light manufacturing and processing are also allowed therein. Incidentally, this zone is also the only area where filling stations or public garages are permitted and the total number in the borough is limited to 18.

3. While the complainant naturally sought invalidation of the classification only as to plaintiffs' property, the theory and proofs might well be equally applicable to much of the other privately held highway frontage in the segment.

public or retail business, the latter antedating the construction of the highway or established by virtue of variances granted in the ten-year period. Only one private structure has been erected since, an office building replacing a deteriorated dwelling for which a variance was allowed in 1957. This has been the only private variance granted along the entire borough highway frontage since the 1955 ordinance. In 1945 there were perhaps a dozen dwellings in the stretch. Today only five remain which are used exclusively for residential purposes (out of a total of about 20 buildings). There has been no dwelling construction in the segment for many, many years.

At the time of the trial the south side of the highway showed the following land uses, running westerly from the end of the restricted commercial zone: opposite Chapel Island, a long strip of vacant county park lands, a retail liquor store with apartment above, the borough fire house, the borough hall, and two old dwellings used also as tourist homes; beyond Chapel Island, two homes, a dwelling property also used as a nursery, another home, a vacant state-owned tract, a long stretch of land occupied by a large public school and playground, and, at the southeast corner of New Providence Road, the rescue squad headquarters. At the southwest corner of the intersection, and for several hundred feet beyond, is a concentration of commercial activity—a gas station which antedated 1933, the new office building previously referred to, a large roadside restaurant business which was also started prior to the enactment of the first zoning ordinance, and a very substantial truck sales and service establishment which was the beneficiary of an admittedly ill-advised variance ten or more years ago. On the north side, again running westerly from the restricted commercial zone and opposite Chapel Island, we find a high bank of vacant land, 800 feet or so long and 100 feet deep, owned by the State (the rear of the houses in a development to the north is just beyond this strip), and the previously described 600-foot state-owned strip along a portion of plaintiffs' property; beyond Chapel Island, plaintiffs' furniture business in the old orphanage building, a house, a real estate office with living quarters above and a strip of vacant state and municipally owned land running to the northeast corner of New Providence Road. On the northwest corner is an old home.

The remaining segment of highway frontage, running west from the area just described to the Scotch Plains line, is one of the few unspoiled gaps in the first 30 miles of Route 22, with a notable absence of commercial activity and, indeed, of development or growth of any kind. In view of the municipality's course of zoning conduct between 1945 and 1955, this is probably more fortuitous than the result of good planning, but plaintiffs do not suggest that the present residential zoning is inappropriate. What active land uses there are remain residential (with the exception of a dog kennel operated in connection with a house), substantially as they were at the time of the building of the highway. Apparently there has been little pressure for change and there has been no construction of any kind fronting the highway for a very long period of time. While two variances for office buildings on the north side were granted during the 1945-1955 period, one of which was allowed to the chairman of the board of adjustment, both were fortunately abandoned before construction began. Speaking more particularly, the south side of the highway frontage is blocked from private growth by complete state ownership thereof to a depth of 100 or 200 feet, with apparently no access through it. The land behind, some in Mountainside and some in Westfield, has recently been developed with expensive homes which back upon the state-owned stretch. The mile of north side frontage consists of a relatively small number of parcels, a few vacant and the balance occupied by a dozen of so large, old homes, many almost in the estate class and most set well back from the road on large and beautiful tracts, whose owners are apparently content to continue their properties in exclusively residential usage.

Something should be said about the nature of housing development in Mountainside close to the highway, because of its bearing on the utility of the interior of plaintiffs' tract. In recent years a very large number of homes have been built on streets which parallel or intersect the highway, especially on the north side thereof and west of the restricted commercial zone. The rear or side of many of these homes is within 100 to 300 feet of the highway, generally separated therefrom by vacant highway frontage. As previously indicated, none have been built fronting the road. The evidence indicates that there has been a ready market for high class dwellings so situated, but apparently none for homes on the frontage. In other words, people are willing to live fairly close to the bustle, noise and dirt of the highway but not directly upon it. With more particular reference to plaintiffs' tract, the three non-highway sides are fully built up, commencing 100 to 200 feet north of the road, with substantial homes fronting on side streets and closely backing upon the boundaries of the tract. The approximate 900-foot depth of plaintiffs' parcel therefore results in a wide gore penetrating a fully settled residential area.

It should also be mentioned that the interior of plaintiffs' property originally sloped considerably upward from the grade of the highway comparable for the most part to the grade of the surrounding lands. Plaintiffs and their predecessor over the years removed the dirt making up the slope, so that now the entire tract is approximately at the highway level. The result is that the property is now substantially bowl-like with banks 10 to 20 feet high on the three interior sides on the land above which sit the surrounding homes previously mentioned. There is access to the interior, other than from the highway, by a paper thoroughfare running through the bank from one of the surrounding streets.

What plaintiffs seek to do with the property, as shown by the variance application (a previous request to rezone the tract for the same purposes was refused by the borough governing body), is to utilize the whole for construction of a small shopping center. They propose to demolish the old orphanage building at the southwest corner and erect a 30,000-square-foot home furnishing store on its site, to build a two-story department store with a ground area of 50,000 square feet near the southeast corner fronting the highway, and another 30,000-square-foot building set back somewhere in between to house a restaurant, offices, bank or like use. The rear of the parcel would be laid out for a parking area to accommodate 1000 cars of patrons and employees. A landscaped buffer strip along the interior lines at the foot of the bank is also included.

I.

As precise discussion of plaintiffs' contentions is reached, attention is first directed to a collateral claim of procedural error in the Law Division action which arose in this fashion. At the original board of adjustment hearing on the variance application, plaintiffs' proofs were aimed to establish the right to a variance on a claim of unreasonableness of the use classification of their property (which proofs also later served as the evidence in support of their Law Division count to avoid the zoning) as well as on the basis of economic hardship in residential development of the tract arising from alleged peculiar characteristics of the property. The variance was strenuously objected to by residential property owners whose homes were near plaintiffs' tract or close to the highway in other sections. They were represented by counsel but offered no opposing proofs. The board apparently did not have counsel to advise it. Some time after the Law Division action was commenced, in which, as we have said, a reversal of the variance denial was one aspect of the relief sought, the municipality moved to remand the matter to the board of adjustment for further proofs in opposition to the variance to be offered on behalf of the governing body. Apparently it was felt that some of the board's findings in denying the application might be considered improper ones (i. e., a statement that the board was familiar with the property and area without setting forth on the record the details of that knowledge and the setting forth of the irrelevant reason for denial that no showing had been made of local need for the commercial development proposed by plaintiffs) or that other findings might not be sufficiently supported by the record. The remand was allowed by the trial court over plaintiffs' objection of impropriety in allowing a case in opposition to the variance thus to be made after the administrative proceeding had been closed and determined. The remand resulted in extensive further hearings, at which the board was advised by its own counsel, with voluminous opposition testimony offered by the borough attorney. At the conclusion the variance was again denied with new findings which did not contain the deficiencies that might have been urged with respect to the first determination. Plaintiffs urge that this court disregard the opposition evidence introduced at the further hearings and review the denial of the variance only on the basis of the proofs presented to the board at the original hearing.

[1] The point is really an academic one because we are satisfied, as will later be mentioned more fully, that plaintiffs did not sufficiently establish a valid basis for a variance on their own proofs at the original hearing and so the opposition testimony at the further hearings was not harmful to them. Moreover, most of that testimony bore on the issue of the intrinsic reasonableness of the ordinance use classification of the property and undoubtedly would have been presented at the trial on that issue even if it had never been offered before the board. (In fact a large part of it was reintroduced by live repetition at the trial.) Consequently the effect of the remand was really only unfortunate further delay in an already protracted litigation.

[2] The discretionary power in a court to remand an administrative action under review for further proceedings by the agency in the interests of justice is unquestionable. New Jersey Turnpike Authority v. Jersey City, 36 N.J. 332, 340, 177 A.2d 539 (1962). Most of the remands which have been ordered in zoning variance cases have been in situations where the agency *granted* relief and the court desired further findings by the agency or further evidence to support the findings made. It is at least unusual to remand on application of an opponent of a variance to permit the presentation of a new case in opposition where the agency *denied* relief. Protection of the public interest may justify such a course in particular situations as an appropriate exercise of judicial discretion. As a matter of hindsight this remand was unnecessary and proved only dilatory. Perhaps even at the time it was unwise to grant it, but we cannot conceive that any actual prejudice on the merits resulted to plaintiffs and it is certainly no ground for reversal of the trial court's judgment.

II.

(A)

We turn to plaintiffs' contention that Mountainside's scheme of highway land use control prior to, and even under, the 1955 ordinance, is illegal as amounting to zoning by administrative control contrary to the requirements of the enabling act. N.J.S.A. 40:55-30 et seq. The result apparently suggested is *ipso facto* nullification of the highway use classifications, at least to the extent of the limitation to residential use still imposed by the 1955 ordinance on the segment in which plaintiffs' property is located running from the end of the restricted commercial zone to just beyond the New Providence Road intersection.

[3, 4] The point is, of course, based on the pre-1955 course of conduct involving blanket zoning of the town's entire highway frontage exclusively for residential use, which could not be sustained *in toto*, and indiscriminate granting of numerous variances for business and industrial uses. The posi-

tion is so obviously correct insofar as the situation up to 1955 is concerned that the municipality concedes as much and little time need be spent in discussion of it. The statute requires zoning by districts, in accordance with a comprehensive plan, under uniform regulations for each class or kind of use throughout the district, imposed with reasonable consideration to the character of the district and its peculiar suitability for particular uses. N.J.S.A. 40:55-30, 31 and 32. Rockhill v. Chesterfield Township, 23 N.J. 117, 128 A.2d 473 (1957). The legitimate function of the use variance authorized by N.J.S.A. 40:55-39(d) is that of sparing application only to relieve the occasional individual property from validly based general limitations of the ordinance for special reasons. Cf. Andrews v. Ocean Township Board of Adjustment, 30 N.J. 245, 152 A.2d 580 (1959). It is the antithesis of the statutory requirement to impose blanket use restrictions without regard to the character of the district and use suitability and then generally and indiscriminately permit innumerable contrary uses by administrative action. Such a course of administrative control implicitly recognizes that the blanket ordinance restrictions cannot be justified. The scheme here utilized up to 1955 was even worse than that struck down in Rockhill, supra (23 N.J. 117, 128 A.2d 473) where an analogous method was at least expressly articulated and provided for in the ordinance. If the 1955 ordinance had not been adopted, we would have no hesitancy in completely nullifying the prior provisions limiting highway frontage to residential use and requiring the borough to rezone the entire area in compliance with the statutory criteria.

[5] But the 1955 ordinance recognized, by its creation of the highway industrial and restricted commercial zones, that restriction to residential use in the sectors covered thereby was no longer proper. And we agree with the trial court that there is no sufficient evidence to support plaintiffs' claim of continuance since that time of the former practice of indiscriminate variance allowance in the sections of the highway where the residential classification was retained. Only three highway variances have been granted since 1955. One was to permit enlargement of the borough hall in violation of sideyard requirements, another to sanction construction of the rescue squad building because of doubt whether it was strictly a public structure allowed by the ordinance in a residential zone, and the third, in 1957, covered the office building just west of the New Providence Road intersection which was built between a filling station and a restaurant to replace a deteriorated dwelling. The first two would not merit condemnation under the pre-1955 practice; the third, perhaps appropriate because of its situs, on the thesis that retention of the residential classification in the segment is justified, does not, standing alone as it does, evidence continuance of the prior wrongful course of action. Plaintiffs' present contention is, therefore, factually unsupported and is without merit so long as the municipality refrains from reverting to its pre-1955 ways.

(B)

At this point we may well consider a further claim representing another aspect of the contention of land use regulation by administrative control in violation of enabling act requirements. This claim seeks a declaration that certain special regulatory provisions, found in section 9 of the 1955 zoning ordinance (which incidentally had their origin in the previous ordinance) and identically in Article IX of the planning board ordinance, applying to the establishment of any business, commercial or industrial use are invalid. The contention is an abstract one and we do not choose to pass upon it definitively here, since we are holding that plaintiffs are not entitled to use their premises for the proposed business enterprise and therefore the regulations objected to can have no present application to them. Nonetheless, the general importance of the matter and the fact that it was specifically ruled upon by the trial judge make it desirable for us to express some tentative and limited observations.

The provisions in question require that no person may commence or enlarge the operation of any business or industry in Mountainside or change the location of one previously established until permission has been issued by the secretary of the planning board. Such permission is to be obtained on written application to and favorable action by the planning board. The application must include building and plot plans and a detailed description of the operations to be performed, prospective number of employees, type and numbers of machines and equipment to be operated, products to be manufactured or sold, and estimated amounts of water to be consumed and the volume of sewage and incoming and outcoming vehicular traffic. (The applicant may appeal to the governing body in the event of unfavorable board action.)

The scope of and criteria governing board consideration are best described by verbatim recital of one paragraph of the section:

"No permit for the operation of such business or industry shall be issued until the Planning Board has approved such business or industry. Upon written request for a hearing made by the applicant to the Planning Board an opportunity to be heard shall be granted to the applicant within thirty (30) days thereafter. The Planning Board, in considering and reviewing the application, including all information submitted by the applicant, and in arriving at its decision, whether a hearing shall be requested or not, shall be guided by, and take into consideration, the public health, safety and general welfare, and shall give particular consideration to the following factors:

(a) Present and future anticipated consumption of water and volume of sewage.

(b) Concentration of traffic in vicinity of business or industry.

(c) Available facilities for parking.

(d) Present or potential fire hazard.

(e) Possibility of creation of a public nuisance due to odor, dust, smoke, noise or objectionable illumination.

RESIDENTIAL V. NON-RESIDENTIAL ZONING

(f) Possibility of unusual hazards.

(g) Land values and uses.

(h) Architectural style and design in relation to existing commercial and industrial buildings.

(i) Such other factors as may bear upon or relate to a coordinated, adjusted and harmonious physical development of the premises in question with surrounding lands and buildings and with the master map of the Borough of Mountainside.

If after examining the application and all information submitted by the applicant, and after hearing, if one be requested by the applicant, the Planning Board shall be of the opinion that the proposed location or relocation of said business or industry will not create conditions inimical to the public health, welfare and safety, nor obstruct the proper development of the premises in question in conjunction with the surrounding lands and buildings, according to the master map of the said Borough, will not result in present or future excessive consumption of water or excessive sewage, concentration of traffic in the vicinity of the business or industry, create present or potential fire hazard, create a public nuisance due to odor, dust, smoke, noise or objectional illumination, create unusual hazards, or be detrimental to or impair land values and uses, will provide satisfactory parking facilities and result in an architectural style and design in harmony with existing commercial and industrial buildings, permission to operate said new business or industry or to relocate said business or industry shall be granted to the applicant by the said Planning Board."

The regulations are obviously intended to impose additional restrictions where the general character of the proposed use is expressly permitted at the location by use classification provisions of the ordinance. Plaintiffs contend that the considerations specified are so broad, go so far and, in any event, do not set forth adequate standards, that administrative control of the establishment of a business or industry on a capricious and illegal basis must necessarily result and that the situation will be as legally bad as the pre-1955 course of action. The municipality urges—and the trial judge found them valid in entirety on this basis— that the regulations are intended to go no further than the device of site plan approval and the like by the planning board under N.J.S.A. 40:55-1.13 held proper in prior decisions. See Kozesnik v. Montgomery Township, 24 N.J. 154, 178, 184-186, 131 A.2d 1 (1957); Newark Milk and Cream Company v. Parsippany-Troy Hills Township, 47 N.J.Super. 306, 332-333, 135 A.2d 682 (Law Div. 1957); and compare Brundage v. Township of Randolph, 54 N.J.Super. 384, 395, 148 A.2d 841 (App.Div.1959), affirmed o. b. 30 N.J. 555, 154 A.2d 581 (1959). The municipality obviously refers particularly to the method therein approved of delegating to the planning board, rather than the building inspector or some other agency, the task of deciding whether legitimate land use control considerations are met on the basis of sufficient standards contained in the zoning ordinance. A pertinent example here is assurance that manufacturing operations will meet the ordinance standard of not producing "injurious or offensive noise, fumes, smoke, odor or vibrations," the detailed requirements of which as to every conceivable enterprise may well be thought incapable of exact advance specification in the ordinance.

If the provisions of this section are to be interpreted to mean that this, plus general site plan approval as defined in the cited cases and assurance of compliance with any other applicable detailed provisions contained in other sections of the ordinance, e. g., parking and loading facilities, were all it is to encompass, it seems valid enough. (There is nothing in the record to indicate how the provisions have been construed or applied in practice.) But the face of the quoted paragraph in the considerations and criteria there specified as governing board actions seems to go much beyond and we find this statement in defendants' brief: "The ordinance in question recognizes that the business use is allowed in the area in question but that it will be allowed only provided it does not interfere with the public health, welfare and safety of the community." Without now going into details, this appears to open Pandora's box and offers the possibility of inquiring into and denial of the right to establish an individual business, otherwise authorized by the ordinance, for reasons which may well have no valid connection with legitimate land use control under the present statutory scheme and, at the least, not protected by sufficient standards. While we have serious doubts in the abstract as to validity to the full extent of the considerations and criteria set forth in the section, we prefer to await a case directly involving the application of the regulations before expressing a definitive opinion.

III.

[6] This brings us to the pivotal question of the reasonableness, in the constitutional sense, of the continued zoning of plaintiffs' property against business use. It is crucial in our minds that the claim is made and relief desired only on the basis of the entire 12 acres. Plaintiffs' argument is presented on the thesis that unreasonableness as to the highway frontage infects the entire 900-foot depth. This is clearly not so under the proofs. We perceive a vast difference as to that large portion of the tract to the rear of the part covered by the variance and the 100-foot-deep state-owned strip, irrespective of the reasonableness of the use classification of the frontage. To put it shortly, there is just no evidence to support the proposition that the interior of plaintiffs' land is unsuitable, in the context of constitutional reasonableness, for the residential use prescribed by the ordinance. Indeed, plaintiffs' own proofs confirm this conclusion. Furthermore, the interior of the tract deeply penetrates a fully developed, high-caliber residential section which would unquestionably be harmed to a very considerable degree by commercial use of the whole parcel. Consequently, since plaintiffs seek relief on the ground of unreasonableness only as to the tract in its entirety, we conclude that their demand must be denied *in toto*.

We have intimated that a far different and much harder question would be presented if the reasonableness point were confined to the highway area encompassed by plaintiffs' current variance. We think that we should make some comment thereon because the municipality's theory of defense, substantially adopted by the trial judge in reaching the same result we do, proceeded on the basis of valid present limitation to residential use of all the highway frontage from the end of the restricted commercial zone to the Scotch Plains boundary, as if to secure a judicial holding to that effect. We have so much question of the soundness of the basis urged that we do not want this opinion to be construed as deciding the question one way or the other.

[7] Analysis of the municipality's thesis, built largely upon the expert testimony of a municipal planner, discloses several aspects, many of considerable importance on the very troublesome question of through highway zoning generally. The first aspect asserts that the extended frontage just referred to has a predominantly residential character and utilizes an arithmetical method of proof by totalling the front foot usages in various categories. The trouble here is that a distorted picture is painted and the character difference shown by the evidence between the segment running from the end of the restricted commercial zone through the several business enterprises just beyond the New Providence Road intersection and the segment west thereof is not recognized as it seems it should be. Areas as distinct as these two are today require at least separate consideration, if not separate treatment. As our earlier analysis of the facts demonstrates, the land uses in the segment in which plaintiffs' frontage is located are not predominantly residential any longer and the use pattern there does not follow that prescribed by the ordinance. Secondly, it is urged that the use classification in the vicinity of plaintiffs' property is rendered valid because it is in accordance with the municipality's comprehensive plan. That plan is said to envision a predominantly residential community, with business and industry confined to areas specified by the ordinance and highway development otherwise closely restricted in order to have as little detrimental effect as possible on the residential characteristics of the community. This is all very well, but it is elementary that every district use classification is not saved simply because it is part of a comprehensive community plan. The plan to be a valid and effective influence in support of zoning regulations must not be a capricious one and its existence will generally not *ipso facto* insulate from scrutiny or invalidity the use classification of a substantial area which is established to be realistically unreasonable. We suggest that, while there may be sound bases to sustain the use classification in the area in question, the two just discussed are not too convincing.

Implicit in the municipality's thesis seems to be the deeper thought that further business use along a through highway may be prohibited for the sake of seeking thereby to prevent a bad traffic situation or an ugly roadside from becoming worse, even if, as seems clear from the evidence here, the only permitted use (residential) is so practically unlikely to be utilized that the result will be the deterioration of existing dwellings and the zoning of vacant highway frontage into permanent idleness. To put the idea in another way, may a municipality which had no early valid plan of regulation and with the hodgepodge highway strip development and land use control history of Mountainside validly say that it has had enough, even though abutting highway owners, particularly holders of vacant land, may end up with only the expensive privilege of paying taxes? Cf. *Fanale v. Hasbrouck Heights*, 26 N.J. 320, 139 A.2d 749 (1958), where, however, it would appear that remaining permitted uses were feasible. Or when a situation has gone so far to the bad, is it legally impossible to halt its further development completely? The questions are intriguing and most difficult, involving many public and private interests of vast consequence. We do not attempt to answer them here, beyond the observation that it seems unlikely a court would allow a municipality to repent of its past sins completely at the expense of the abutting highway land owner. Perhaps the best answer to frontage use problems on unlimited access highways is governmental acquisition of adjacent vacant strips, as has occurred in several points in Mountainside (although the record is not clear that these acquisitions were made for this purpose).

IV.

[8] Finally we come to plaintiffs' claim that they were wrongly denied a variance for the entire tract. The answer is clear. The board of adjustment was eminently correct in refusing to recommend it and the Law Division equally so in upholding the board. The matter is so plain that a contrary result could not be sustained as a proper exercise of board authority.

Plaintiffs offered two alleged "special reasons," N.J.S.A. 40:55-39(d), to support their application. On their own proofs, neither reason alone, nor the two in combination, was established to be sufficient. The first was the claim of intrinsic use classification unreasonableness of the tract as a whole, which we have already rejected as factually without merit. The second projected certain peculiar physical characteristics of the tract which it was urged would make residential development more difficult. The reason is summarized in plaintiffs' reply brief:

"* * * the plaintiffs do not claim that there is any physical impossibility of constructing one family houses, but that it is economically unfeasible to develop the property for one family houses because the shape and location of the tract, the surrounding development of streets, the stream crossing the property, etc., would make development highly expensive whereas the proximity to the highway makes the property less desirable for one family residence and less salable and the combination of factors would price the developed property out of the market."

The claim is really one of inability to make as much money as if commercial development were permitted, for the proofs did not sufficiently show that development costs would be excessively high on a competitive basis or that houses which might be built on the tract could not be sold at some profit. It is fundamental that mere economic hardship of these limited dimensions is not a sufficient special reason to ground a variance. See e. g., Home Builders Association of Northern New Jersey v. Borough of Paramus, 7 N.J. 335, 343, 81 A.2d 753 (1951).

[9] Moreover, as the board of adjustment rightly found from the evidence, the additional negative criteria required by N.J.S.A. 40:55-39, i. e., that the relief could be granted without substantial detriment to the public good or substantial impairment of the zone plan and ordinance, were certainly not met. The proofs clearly established the contrary. Schoelpple v. Woodbridge Township, 60 N.J.Super. 146, 158 A.2d 338 (App.Div.1960).

[10] We feel we ought to speak additionally on the argument of defendants that a proper reason, sufficient in itself, to deny the variance in this case is that plaintiffs bought the property knowing it was zoned for residential purposes and therefore may not assert hardship as a variance reason. The suggested theory is that purchase with such knowledge amounts to a self-created hardship.

There is a good deal of general and loose language in our earlier cases which we believe has led to confusion and misconception with respect to the factual situation posed and which demands clarification. For example, the following is found in Ardolino v. Florham Park Board of Adjustment, 24 N.J. 94, 106, 130 A.2d 847 853 (1957):

> "In the evaluation of a claim of undue hardship, the purchase of land after the adoption of an ordinance prescribing a greater requirement than can be complied with is a circumstance to be considered, Beirn v. Morris, 14 N.J. 529, 535, 103 A.2d 361 (1954). It is not conclusive by any means, but it is unquestionably a material element bearing on the issue, Lumund v. Board of Adjustment of the Borough of Rutherford, 4 N.J. 577, 581, 73 A.2d 545 (1950) and weighs heavily against the plaintiffs' claim, Home Builders Ass'n of Northern New Jersey v. Paramus Borough, supra, 7 N.J. 335, 343, 81 A.2d 753 (1951)."

But as that case went on to point out, in considering the concept in relation to the particular facts, the quoted language is not to be applied automatically to deny relief on that ground alone where nothing had been done by the owner or his predecessors, after the adoption of the ordinance provision in question, to create the condition as to which variance relief is sought on the basis of hardship.

We wish to make it clear that if a prior owner would be entitled to such relief, that right is not lost to a purchaser simply because he bought with knowledge of the zoning regulation involved. This situation is not within the realm of the self-created hardship which will generally bar relief. As is said in 2 Rathkopf, Law of Zoning and Planning (3d ed. 1960) c. 48, p. 48-20:

"Despite the fact that some courts have used language which, taken upon its face, would indicate that even where a unique hardship existed with respect to land which would have warranted the person owning the property prior to the enactment of the ordinance to apply for and receive a variance, the mere act of purchase with knowledge of the ordinance bars the purchaser from the same relief, it is apparent that few higher court decisions have actually so decided. In each case in which the refusal of a variance was upheld and in which such language was used, the facts showed either that there was an affirmative act which created the hardship peculiar to the property involved or that there was not sufficient evidence that the property was not reasonably adapted for a conforming use."

Perhaps we ought also to say out of an abundance of caution, that the disposition of this case shall not prejudice, in either direction, any future application or action by plaintiffs seeking relief with respect to the highway frontage encompassed by the current variance, either by way of modification of the present limitations of that variance as to building and precise use or otherwise.

The judgment of the Law Division is affirmed.

For affirmance: Chief Justice WEINTRAUB and Justices JACOBS, FRANCIS, PROCTOR, HALL, SCHETTINO and HANEMAN—7.

For reversal: None.

BARONE

v.

BRIDGEWATER

45 N.J. 224, 212 A.2d 129(1965).

Supreme Court of New Jersey.

Argued March 15, 1965.

Decided July 6, 1965.

Highway zoning case. The trial court found the zoning unreasonable as applied to plaintiffs' lands. The Appellate Division reversed in an unreported opinion. The Supreme Court granted certification on the plaintiffs' application. The Supreme Court, Hall, J., held that the evidence supported the existing residential-agricultural use classification.

Judgment of Appellate Division affirmed.

Mark L. Stanton, Dunellen, for appellants (Doren & Stanton, Dunellen, attorneys; Mark L. Stanton, Dunellen, of counsel; Raymond P. DeMarco, Dunellen, on the brief).

Charles A. Reid, Jr., Plainfield, for respondent.

The opinion of the court was delivered by

HALL, J.

[1]　This is a highway zoning case. The locale fronts the same road—U.S. Highway Route 22—as that involved in Wilson v. Borough of Mountainside, 42 N.J. 426, 201 A.2d 540 (1964), but some 12 miles farther west in Bridgewater Township, Somerset County. The suit attacks the residential-agricultural use classification of the most easterly half mile of the highway frontage in the township running from the Green Brook Township boundary west to the Mountain Avenue overpass intersection. The classification was imposed by the township's original ordinance in 1937 and continued in essence by the comprehensive revision thereof adopted in 1962. Plaintiffs are some, but not all, of the abutting property owners in the strip on both sides of the highway. The trial court found the zoning unreasonable as applied to plaintiffs' lands. The Appellate Division reversed in an unreported opinion. We granted certification on the plaintiffs' application. 43 N.J. 357, 204 A.2d 591 (1964). The basic issue, as is usual in this type of case, is whether the challengers have sustained their rather heavy burden of demonstrating that the municipal ordinance classification is so far without reason and arbitrary as to require invalidation.

[2, 3]　Since the complaint is exceedingly sketchy and the pretrial order no more informative, plaintiffs' thesis has to be gathered from their proofs and argument. Although the testimony of some of the plaintiffs themselves is not entirely consistent with the theory advanced by their counsel and expert witnesses, it is plain enough that the case was presented below and is argued here primarily on the contention that the impact of this busy highway on abutting lands in the area in question, in and of itself and essentially without regard to other considerations, requires such lands, to a depth of at least 400 or 500 feet, to be zoned for commercial and industrial uses. Plaintiffs' counsel at the trial spoke of their aim as "to open it wide open for business." Indeed, if plaintiffs' theory were to be accepted, it is difficult to imagine lands anywhere fronting on such a road which would not have to be so zoned—a conclusion we are not prepared to accept as an abstract proposition. Rather the land use regulation of such properties should be determined by consideration of a congery of the particular historical, geographical and economic facts in each instance.

The trial judge professed not to rely on such a broad approach, mentioning some business uses present in the area and nearby, the general lack of development of the affected lands over the years and his opinion that "the possibility of sale to anyone desiring residential property" was "extremely remote," despite substantial municipal testimony tending oppositely. Nonetheless, the wider thesis is not entirely absent from his conclusions, as witness the emphasis placed on "the devotion of land to its most appropriate use and the general character of the district and its peculiar suitability for a particular use."

[4]　The Appellate Division, in reversing, dealt with the matter in a very general fashion, relying mainly on the presumption of validity. Despite

the involvements of the case, there was little discussion of the facts or the various considerations to be taken into account. The court simply concluded "* * * that there is at least a debatable question that the ordinance in dispute is in accord with the comprehensive plan for the orderly development of land uses within Bridgewater Township * * *" Although Wilson v. Borough of Mountainside, supra, 42 N.J. 426, 201 A.2d 540, was decided before this cause was argued in the Appellate Division, it is not cited nor is the opinion's conclusion considered in the light of our holding in Wilson concerning the relationship between a comprehensive municipal zoning plan and the ordinance use classification of a particular area. It was there said: "* * * it is elementary that every district use classification is not saved simply because it is part of a comprehensive community plan. The plan to be a valid and effective influence in support of zoning regulations must not be a capricious one and its existence will generally not *ipso facto* insulate from scrutiny or invalidity the use classification of a substantial area which is established to be realistically unreasonable." 42 N.J., at p. 449, 201 A.2d, at p. 552. In view of the Appellate Division's manner of treatment, we feel obligated to review the factual and other considerations more fully than generally is the case when we are passing upon a determination of that tribunal in a zoning controversy. Cf. Tidewater Oil Co. v. Mayor and Council of Carteret, 44 N.J. 338, 344-345, 209 A.2d 105 (1965).

In Wilson, we described in some detail Route 22, its traffic load, and the present state of the almost solid commercial and industrial development of every kind and description along its frontage west from the intersection with U.S. Route 1 near Newark Airport. 42 N.J., at pp. 434-435, 201 A.2d 540. That description need not be repeated here. The important thing is that the intense concentration of such roadside uses rather abruptly stops at the Green Brook Township-Bridgewater Township line, the easterly end of the area here in question. While the volume and nature of the traffic continues westward for several miles further, the break in abutting uses is obvious to the observer. From this point on for the eight or nine miles of the course of Route 22 through Bridgewater, highway development has not been extensive or cluttered except for a relatively short distance in the general area where the road adjoins the Borough of Somerville and other through highway routes intersect, in which section a regional business zone of considerable size was provided by the 1962 ordinance. The reason for the difference between Bridgewater and communities to the east is historical.

Route 22, originally known as State Highway 29, was built through the eastern half of Bridgewater Township about 1930. It ran a virgin course north of the settled sections, through vacant, essentially rural, land. Although there was no township zoning until 1937, only a few business structures were erected along it in the early years. The first zoning ordinance (1937), we are advised, placed the whole area through which the road passed in a residential-agricultural zone. Whether that classification was and remained justified for every foot of township highway frontage is beside the point. The fact would appear to be that the township authorities then, with some vision, decided to prevent the highway blight which, as related in Wilson, has since descended upon the municipalities to the east adopting the opposite policy of encouraging or tolerating beyond redemption highway commercial and industrial development by one means or another, and to seek to maintain the highway for its true function of transportation of people and goods rather than as a "Main Street" as well. To be particularly stressed is that Bridgewater's highway zoning was not appreciably broken down by the granting of indiscriminate variances or other devices. Few variances were allowed and, while until about the time of the 1962 revision there was no great amount of residential building along the highway, most nonresidential uses pre-existed the 1937 ordinance and were nonconforming. The appearance throughout was definitely one of open spaces and lack of development rather than the contrary.

This status has been especially true of that segment running westerly from the Green Brook line to the Thompson Avenue overpass intersection, which is a mile and a half or so west of Mountain Avenue. In describing the segment, note should be made of the topography. For several miles east of Mountain Avenue, the highway runs just south of the base of the first range of the Watchung Mountains. This is the situation in the area from the Green Brook boundary to Mountain Avenue specifically involved in this case. On the north side of the highway the land is generally quite level to a depth of 400 feet or so and then rises rather sharply up the mountain side. On the south side, the terrain is flat for an almost infinite distance. From Mountain Avenue to Thompson Avenue, the mountain juts out and the highway cuts through the lower slope. (West of Thompson Avenue, it continues straight while the mountain angles to the northwest some distance away from it, making for a wide expanse of level land for several miles.)

Looking first at the Mountain Avenue-Thompson Avenue portion of this segment, which adjoins the area in question directly on the west, the Borough of Bound Brook breaks into Bridgewater Township for a distance of about a half mile west from Mountain Avenue, extending beyond the north side of the highway about 600 feet. The borough zoning is residential on both sides of the highway. A number of expensive residences are located within the 600 foot strip on the north side, many of the rear yards of which are not far distant therefrom. As was disclosed at oral argument, a substantial housing development is now in process on the south side, with the rear of a number of houses within 100 feet or so of the right of way. Bridgewater Township then resumes on both sides of the highway. On the north side there are some older homes fronting thereon and on the south side two high grade housing developments have recently been constructed with the rear of many of the houses within a few feet of the highway. There are only four commercial uses in this one and one-half mile stretch, all nonconforming. Three are at the Thompson Avenue intersection and one (a tavern) at the road intersection next easterly, directly adjoining one of the housing developments mentioned. The township residential zoning, which, as has been indicated, starts at the Green Brook boundary, continues as far as the Thompson Avenue intersection.[1]

Turning specifically to the Green Brook-Mountain Avenue section with which we are directly concerned, on the north side there are 11 land owners, only five of whom are plaintiffs, holding plots of varying shapes and sizes ranging from a sliver to substantial acreage. There was obviously no planned plot layout when the various parcels were sold off after the highway was cut through. They vary in frontage from 100 feet to more than 500 feet and in depth from about 250 feet to 800 feet or more. There are five houses fronting on the highway (one unoccupied), four of the owners of which are not plaintiffs. The fifth is owned by a party who operates an adjoining florist shop and large greenhouses several hundred feet to the rear. Aside from this highway business use, there are a substantial nursery (a permitted use), the owner of which also owns a 100-foot lot on the south side where he maintains an office and sales building, a gasoline service station, and a hamburger and hot dog restaurant with which a gold fish and skating pond is also operated. The owner of this latter enterprise purchased the highway frontage on which the parcel is located only a few years ago and also, within the past couple of years, erected a substantial home on the rear portion of his property about 350 feet north of the highway. There is another good-sized home of fairly recent vintage on an adjoining rear plot whose owner is also not a plaintiff. The only parcel of vacant land on this side is that at the Mountain Avenue intersection, substantially reduced as to Route 22 frontage by recent state acquisition for the overpass and approaches. See condemnation litigation in connection therewith reported as State by State Highway Com'r v. Speare, 86 N.J. Super. 565, 207 A.2d 552 (App.Div.1965). The remaining land acreage now fronts principally and for more than 1000 feet on Mountain Avenue, an entirely high quality residential road slanting up the mountain. The business uses described all antedated the 1937 ordinance and the houses fronting the highway were certainly built not later than 1947. The service station and the hamburger restaurant have been beneficiaries of variances

---

1. The township highway area west of Thompson Avenue was rezoned by the 1962 revision. As previously noted, the topography is vastly different and there had been practically no residential development over the years. Interstate Route 287, very recently constructed, crosses and parallels Route 22 for some distance in this area. The revised zoning places it, as far as Somerville, in limited industrial, limited industrial and commercial, and a special quarrying classification, requiring, respectively, five-acre, ten-acre and 100-acre minimum lot sizes, with substantial additional restrictions to prevent intensive and cluttered development. This area is so different from that east of Thompson Avenue that it cannot be conceived to have any bearing on the appropriateness of the use classification of the section involved in this case. Indeed Bridgewater Township is so vast and sectionally heterogeneous in its characteristics and present and potential land uses that it is difficult to think of a single, over-all zoning or planning objective for the entire municipality.

to permit some modernization. Both of these owners testified that their interest in seeking to invalidate the present zoning is to permit enlargement of the service station and a change in the nature of the retail business conducted at the restaurant site (both of which could be appropriate subjects for further variance applications.)

In some contrast, the land in the area on the south side of the highway is level and substantially vacant. There are seven owners. Going east from Mountain Avenue, there is a vacant strip about 250 feet deep and perhaps 1000 feet long which adjoins the large Thomae Park residential development, the houses in which are built up quite close to the strip. The owner is not a plaintiff. Next comes a golf driving range, a nonconforming use, on a plot some 800 feet deep with over 500 feet of highway frontage. The owner, who has erected a large home on the rear of the property, is a plaintiff but did not testify. This parcel adjoins a vacant tract of 20 acres or more, the owner of which is not a party. Then there are two triangular tracts of a bit over an acre each. One contains the remains of a long abandoned diner, the owner of which is a plaintiff, placed there just before the 1937 ordinance was adopted. A prospective purchaser sought to invalidate the original residential zoning in 1938 in order to erect a service station and bunkhouse. The effort was unsuccessful. Vogel v. Board of Adjustment, 121 N.J.L. 236, 2 A.2d 189 (Sup.Ct.1938). There is an old house on the second of these parcels. The owner is a plaintiff but did not testify. The final piece on this side, except for the nurseryman's 100-foot lot, is another parcel of very considerable acreage, vacant except for the shell of a house commenced in 1950 but never completed. The owner is not a party and there was nothing but unreliable hearsay offered as to the reason for its present status.

To recapitulate, there are 17 parcels in separate ownership in the whole area in question. Only eight of the owners are plaintiffs, and of those, but four testified. There are six houses fronting the highway; just two of the owners are parties. There are but five commercial uses, including the nursery and driving range which are better characterized as land uses since they do not involve permanent structures of any size. Only three of these commercial occupants testified and two were concerned solely with enlargement or change of business use in their present enterprises. Only three of the landowners who may be said to own any substantial amount of vacant land joined the suit. Their holdings probably do not equal even half of the unimproved land available in the section. While this relative paucity of interest in the litigation without explanation is probably of no great legal moment, it is some indication, in view of the fact that the attack is on the basis that the whole area is malzoned, that the present zoning regulations are not thought to be onerous by many of the affected landowners.

Plaintiffs emphasize the relative lack of development in the area over the years as conclusively indicating the unreasonableness of the zoning limitation to residential and agricultural uses. Their lay and expert testimony was directed to a claim of confiscation because commercial use is prohibited and people will not build residences fronting on the highway nor will lending institutions place mortgages thereon. The evidence does not support the claimed conclusion. While the south side of the highway remains substantially vacant, there are only two vacant parcels of any size on the north side, even counting the nursery as one. While three of the four owners who testified stated that they had received no inquiries relating to acquisition of their properties for residential purposes but that some overtures over the years had been made to them by persons interested in possible retail business and motel ventures, there was no testimony that any owner had actually tried to sell his property and had been unable to find a buyer because of the zoning restrictions. The fourth lay witness, the gas station operator, appeared not interested in disposing of his property.

Why particular land in a certain municipality does not develop in accordance with a zoning plan may be due to any number of conceivable reasons, most of which have little or no bearing on the validity of the zoning classification. Contentment of the present ownership, holding of land for speculative advancement in value in hopes of a zone change, and abandance of other land similarly classified and presently more desirable are among such conceivable reasons. Plaintiffs' planning expert conceded that the mere fact residentially zoned land had not developed does not justify placing it in another use classification, absent other reasons. The language of Justice Case in Vogel, supra (121 N.J.L., at p. 238, 2 A.2d, at p. 190) in 1938, where invalidation of the residential classification on the south side diner property was refused and the denial of a variance for a further business affirmed, still has some pertinency despite the changing years:

> "Of necessity there are border areas where the reason[s] for restrictions are not so apparent because it is inevitable that zones of varying degrees of restriction must abut and that restricted lands in proximity to unrestricted lands will be in a somewhat prejudiced position. But that is a consequence upon the exercise of the constitutional authority. Also, it is clear that every foot of land in a zone restricted to residences may not be so located that an attractive residence can advantageously be erected thereon. But if the act of a municipality in zoning is to be anything more than a gesture, the determination of the zoning board thereon should, in the absence of palpable abuse of discretion, be honored."

[5, 6] A local realtor, the other of plaintiffs' opinion witnesses, with no qualifications as a zoning expert, stressed the highest and best use of the area property as commercial and industrial, but that is no weighty factor in zoning classification determination. If it were, the whole concept of uniform zoning by districts in implementation of the statutory purpose (N.J.S.A. 40:55-32) to encourage the most appropriate use of land *through-out the municipality* would have to fall. Both witnesses mentioned that

housing development of the area would require large tracts and stressed the difficulty of assembly of the present parcels into single ownership for such purposes. They agreed, however, that modern highway commercial or industrial uses also require similar large tracts for practical reasons and because of lot size and other regulations for such uses found in current municipal ordinances. It would seem indisputable that any commercial or industrial development with direct highway access would generate more highway traffic and additional hazards than residential development, especially if the latter backed upon rather than fronted the highway and access was from side roads only. Both experts agreed that structural and other uses in the area to date had not gone so far as to preclude either residential or business development. While the varying size and shape of present parcels would present some difficulties in any type of extensive development, it is well to keep in mind in this connection the testimony of plaintiffs' planner that "* * * zoning doesn't look to the nature of the ownership. It looks, among other things, to the ownership and available land." From the standpoint of the determination of appropriate zoning of a particular sector by the preponderance of actual uses therein, the physical facts support the township's testimony that the nature and extent of current uses does not in itself dictate either commercial or residential classification, rather than plaintiffs' asserted conclusion that business uses predominate and zoning of that character is therefore required.

[7]   Plaintiffs further urge that commercial use zoning of the strip in question is dictated by the intense concentration of highway business and industrial enterprises permitted and existing throughout the Green Brook Township frontage to the east. The argument is that Bridgewater must take into account and, indeed, be controlled by the character and volume of the uses in the adjoining municipality. See Borough of Cresskill v. Borough of Dumont, 15 N.J. 238, 104 A.2d 441 (1954). The point is not a sound one in the factual context at hand. The rationale of Cresskill is that a neighboring community must consider, in its own zoning, adverse effects thereof on its neighbor. It would certainly be a perversion to twist this salutary concept to require a municipality to zone its highway frontage so that all of the detrimental effects its neighbors have brought about will be duplicated within its borders in spite of its long continued effort to prevent that very consequence.

The township offered several bases in support of the reasonableness of its decision to retain this area, along with the section as far west as Thompson Avenue, in the residential-agricultural classification in the 1962 comprehensive ordinance revision. Its witness was the planning consultant who made the studies and recommendations to the township authorities which ultimately resulted in that enactment. While some of the reasons are of doubtful strength and need not be discussed, the principal consideration advanced—and the factor which we believe to be decisive—was that these lands are sufficiently adaptable for and physically capable of residential development as to warrant classification for that use. This conclusion is grounded, first, in the fact that in very recent years successful and attractive residential developments have grown up along Route 22 frontage. This has been accomplished by backing the closest houses to the highway side-line rather than fronting them on it and providing access by side roads rather than directly from the highway. The three projects of this character very close to these lands on the south side of the highway in Bound Brook and Bridgewater west of Mountain Avenue, as well as the large Thomae Park development within 300 feet of the highway and adjoining the golf driving range on the southwest, furnish ample proof. We noted the same type of development farther east in Wilson v. Borough of Mountainside, supra, 42 N.J. 426, 201 A.2d 540, and comment was made at oral argument of the very extensive garden apartment construction on the mountainside in North Plainfield. *Secondly,* the municipality demonstrated by actual plans presented at the trial that such development is physically feasible here. On the south side, the land can be laid out as an extension of the Thomae Park section, utilizing the full highway frontage. In fact, a road connection for this purpose is included in the Thomae Park layout. On the north side, the area to the rear of the approximate 300-foot depth of most of the present uses, may be similarly planned with access provided from Mountain Avenue.

While plaintiffs' experts disputed such a prospective utilization in a general fashion, we think it is evident that the township's proofs in this regard may not be cast aside and, when viewed with plaintiffs' evidence, are sufficient to require a court to say, in fulfillment of its appropraite role in reviewing a municipal zoning ordinance provision, that a debatable question, at least, of the reasonableness of the local legislative action thereby results. Under elementary principles therefore, the ultimate conclusion necessarily is that the attacking party has not sustained his burden and the ordinance provision must be sustained.

The judgment of the Appellate Division is affirmed.

For affirmance: Chief Justice WEINTRAUB and Justices JACOBS, FRANCIS, PROCTOR, HALL, SCHETTINO and HANEMAN—7.

For reversal: None.

Questions and Notes

On Mountainside

1. How deep was the tract involved here?

2. What was the court's attitude on residential zoning of (a) the highway frontage, plus normal depth for commercial development, and (b) the area further back?

3. Describe the Mountainside zoning system as it was applied along this highway from 1933 to 1955.

4. What foreign country has a somewhat similar system of decision-making on land use?

5. What was the court's attitude to this system?

6. What was Justice Hall's view on municipal repentance at the expense of adjacent property owners?

7. This is also a leading case on site plan review, which is not specifically authorized under the present enabling legislation. What is site plan review, and why is it used?

On Bridgewater

1. Describe the Bridgewater system of residential zoning along major highways. How does this differ from the usual layout, and what are its advantages?

2. Where in these materials have we run across the same system? Compare the Ayres case, p. 161 *supra*.

CRESSKILL

v.

DUMONT

15 N.J. 238, 104 A.2d 441 (1954).

Supreme Court of New Jersey

Argued March 22, 1954.

Decided April 5, 1954.

Suits challenging amendment to zoning ordinance of defendant borough, which amendment would change one block from residential zone to business district. The Superior Court, Law Division, 28 N.J. Super. 26, 100 A.2d 182, entered decision setting aside the amendment, and defendant borough appealed to the Superior Court, Appellate Division, and the appeal was certified to Supreme Court on its own motion. The Supreme Court, Vanderbilt, C. J., held, inter alia, that the proposed change did not promote any of the statutory purposes relating to zoning, and that the amendment, which in effect granted a zoning variance, was required to be set aside as constituting spot zoning.

Judgment affirmed.

Guy W. Calissi, Hackensack, argued the cause for the appellant.

Arthur J. O'Dea, Hackensack, Frank H. Hennessy, Englewood, William A. Fasolo, Hackensack, argued the cause for the respondents.

The opinion of the court was delivered by

VANDERBILT, C. J.

From a decision of the Law Division of the Superior Court setting aside an amendment to its zoning ordinance the defendant Borough of Dumont appealed. We certified the borough's appeal on our own motion while it was pending in the Appellate Division.

The focal point of the action is Block 197 on the tax map of Dumont, which as a result of the challenged amendment to the zoning ordinance would be changed from an A and B residential zone to a D business district. Two separate complaints were filed, the first by three neighboring boroughs of Cresskill, Demarest and Haworth and by several residents of these boroughs as well as by several residents of Dumont. The second complaint was filed by William A. Wendland and Marjorie Wendland, his wife, who are property owners on the block in question.

The first complaint in effect charges that the amendatory ordinance is not in accordance with the comprehensive zoning plans in effect in the boroughs of Cresskill, Demarest, Dumont and Haworth in that it fails to take into consideration the physical, economic, and social conditions prevailing throughout the entire area of those four municipalities and the use to which the land in that region can and may be put most advantageously, and that regard was given solely to the political boundaries of the Borough of Dumont in utter disregard of the contiguous residential areas of the plaintiff boroughs. Lastly, the complaint charges that the amendment is invalid in that it represents "spot zoning" for the benefit of an individual property owner and thus constitutes a variance from the previously existing ordinance obtained without recourse to the Board of Adjustment of the Borough of Dumont, as prescribed by statute. The complaint filed by the Wendlands asserts that the amendatory ordinance is not in accordance with the comprehensive plan for zoning in Dumont, that the amendment will destroy the present character of the plaintiffs' lands, that it constitutes "spot zoning" and is an invalid attempt to grant a variance.

The defendant filed a separate answer to each complaint, claiming in each instance that the ordinance was a valid exercise of the zoning power. As to the first complaint, filed by the three boroughs and the individual plaintiffs, it claimed that neither the boroughs nor such individuals as were not residents of Dumont were proper parties, and that those plaintiffs who were residents of Dumont had no standing because their property rights were not affected. As to the complaint of the Wendlands the defendant claimed that the action was not brought in good faith and that the complaint failed to state a claim on which relief could be granted. The cases were consolidated for trial.

According to the 1950 census the four boroughs had a combined population of approximately 20,000. Dumont, with a population of 13,013, was the largest, while Cresskill was second was 3,534. Demarest had a population of 1,786, while Haworth followed with 1,612. Block 197 is a rectangularly shaped area at the extreme northeast corner of Dumont and

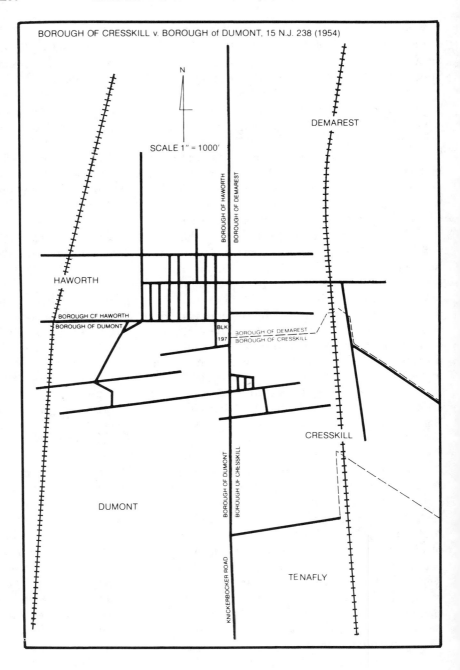

BOROUGH OF CRESSKILL v. BOROUGH of DUMONT, 15 N.J. 238 (1954)

extends north and south approximately 787 feet along Knickerbocker Road, a heavily travelled county highway, on the east and Franklin Street on the west. The block is approximately 195 feet wide, bordering on Massachusetts Avenue on the north and DeLong Avenue on the south. Massachusetts Avenue is the dividing line between the Boroughs of Dumont and Haworth, while Knickerbocker Road separates Dumont from the Boroughs of Cresskill and Demarest, with the result that across these two streets on the north and east sides of Block 197 are lands in adjoining municipalities. The properties adjoining Block 197 on the west and south are in Dumont.

The areas covered by the four municipalities are on the broad slope west of the Palisades. It is only in relatively recent years that the countryside has been converted from a rural to a highly developed suburban region. Due to their comparatively late change in character these boroughs have been able to avoid the misfortunes of other municipalities which developed before the recognition in this State of zoning. All four boroughs are to a high degree residential in character with a total of between 6,000 and 7,000 dwelling units in all. The character of the entire region can best be understood by noting that throughout the entire length of Knickerbocker Road, which is a main county highway extending north from Englewood to the New York State line, with the exception of one small business area, there are only three business establishments, two of which are nonconforming uses. With the exception of a small area zoned for business, Cresskill is exclusively residential with no industrial district, and the area along Knickerbocker Road opposite Block 197 is strictly zoned for single-family dwellings. Similarly Demarest is almost entirely residential and the area adjoining Knickerbocker Road facing the block in question is zoned exclusively for single-family dwellings. Haworth has a small business zone but the borough is almost entirely residential and the area across Massachusetts Avenue to the north facing Block 197 is zoned exclusively for residential purposes.

Although Dumont has a small industrial and business zone, it also is principally zoned for residences. In Dumont the area extending west and south from Block 197 for approximately one-half a mile in both directions is zoned for residential use only, except for one corner lot near the property in question which was rezoned from a residential to a business district by an amendment to the ordinance, an action which the trial court characterized as "obviously spot zoning and illegal." In the immediate vicinity of Block 197 and to the west of it are over 100 one-family houses in the $17,000-price class, which are in the process of construction, and the mayor of Dumont testified that 200 to 220 residences are to be constructed in that area.

In the adjoining area in Cresskill, Demarest and Haworth the properties are strictly residential with the exception of a gasoline service station, a tavern, and a construction storage yard, all of which are nonconforming uses in the residential zone and are about one-third of a mile from Block

197. There is an attractive and ample business center in Dumont approximately half a mile from Block 197. There are also business centers in Cresskill, Demarest and Haworth at distances varying from nine-tenths of a mile to a mile and a tenth from Block 197. The shopping needs of the community are adequately cared for by these business centers.

The amendment to the zoning ordinance to change Block 197 to a "D Business District" had been under consideration by the Borough Council and the Planning Board of Dumont for three or four years, according to the mayor. On November 26, 1952, it was submitted to the planning board, which unanimously approved it. On December 9, 1952, it was adopted by unanimous vote of the governing body of the borough at a meeting at which no objection was made by any residents of the borough, although representatives of the other three boroughs strenuously opposed it. Section 4 of the basic zoning ordinance of the borough adopted in 1942 provided that "D Business District is primarily intended for the conduct of commerce, general business and the sale of commodities and all such uses shall be permitted." The section then goes on to prohibit manufacturing, trucking, livery stables, slaughter houses and the like. It would appear, however, that such business activities as department and retail stores, theaters, motels, restaurants, garages and bowling alleys are permitted.

The only witnesses produced by the defendant borough were the mayor, a real estate appraiser, and a real estate broker. The mayor testified that Block 197 "was a logical place to put a business area, in keeping with the plan of the Borough. The best interests of the public would be served by placing a shopping center in an easily accessible area, that would have adequate off-street parking." He further stated that both the planning board and the council had considered traffic problems, parking facilities, the element of safety, the comprehensive zoning plan of the borough and other important factors before voting upon the ordinance, and that it was the opinion of both the planning board and the council that the most appropriate use of this area was as a shopping center. The real estate appraiser testified that "If this area was set aside for business, and proper planning by a modern developer, for a shopping center, it is my opinion that it would help not only Dumont, but it would help the neighborhood." The real estate broker testified that "The effect of the value, I think, won't be altered more than very, very slightly; and the benefits through having a better business section close by would more than offset what might be considered slight depreciation in value."

The plaintiffs, on the other hand, produced several witnesses who testified as to the undesirable aspects of the zoning amendment both from the standpoint of traffic conditions and as it related to the comprehensive zoning plan both of the Borough of Dumont and of the three adjoining boroughs. There was testimony that Knickerbocker Road is a heavily travelled two-lane county highway where the traffic congestion, lack of parking facilities, and the general safety problem have for some time been a matter of public concern, and that the rezoning of Block 197 as a business district would increase these problems to the detriment of public generally and especially of the residents of this area. There was also testimony that a new shopping center was unnecessary, since existing shopping facilities were adequate. Mr. Hugh R. Pomeroy, a zoning expert, testified that, "in [his] opinion the rezoning of Block 197 to a D district classification, under the Dumont zoning ordinance, is not in accordance with comprehensive zoning for the Borough of Dumont." He also stated that considering the surrounding area in all four boroughs as a whole the zoning of this property for business use was not in accordance with a comprehensive plan considered in an intercommunity sense. Another of plaintiffs' experts testified that the rezoning would have the effect of depreciating the value of residential property in Block 197 as well as all other residential properties in the immediate vicinity. There was substantial testimony of other witnesses to support these conclusions.

The trial judge held that the ordinance was invalid since it did not promote the public welfare, was not in accordance with any comprehensive plan, and did not promote any of the statutory purposes relating to zoning.

I.

[1] The appellant first argues that the plaintiffs were not proper parties to the action and that therefore its motion to dismiss the complaint should have been granted. In this regard the appellant directs its attack primarily toward the three municipal plaintiffs and the individual plaintiffs who reside in the other boroughs. It is unnecessary, however, for us to decide this issue, because the Wendlands own property on Block 197, the very area affected by the amendatory ordinance. Clearly they have sufficient interest to bring this action. Speakman v. Mayor and Council of Borough of North Plainfield, 8 N.J. 250, 258, 84 A.2d 715 (1951); Menges v. Township of Bernards, 4 N.J. 556, 559, 73 A.2d 540 (1950). The fact that they did not testify is not significant, since they were parties plaintiff and all evidence produced on the plaintiffs' case inured to their benefit. It is therefore immaterial whether the municipal and remaining individual plaintiffs have adequate status to challenge the ordinance and the question is therefore reserved.

II.

[2] The appellant also contends that the trial court erred in considering the property in adjoining municipalities, claiming that only property lying within the borough itself is to be taken into consideration by the borough authorities in their zoning. In this regard it cites Article IV, Sec. VI, par. 2 of the New Jersey Constitution:

> "The Legislature may enact general laws under which municipalities, other than counties, may adopt zoning ordinances limiting and restricting

RESIDENTIAL V. NON-RESIDENTIAL ZONING

to specified districts and regulating therein, buildings and structures, according to their construction, and the nature and extent of the uses of land, and the exercise of such authority shall be deemed to be within the police power of the State. Such laws shall be subject to repeal or alteration by the Legislature."

The pertinent statutory provisions (N.J.S.A. 40:55-30 et seq.) are as follows:

"Any municipality may by ordinance, limit and restrict to specified districts and may regulate therein, buildings and structures according to their construction, and the nature and extent of their use, and the nature and extent of the uses of land, and the exercise of such authority, subject to the provisions of this article, shall be deemed to be within the police power of the State. Such ordinance shall be adopted by the governing body of such municipality, as hereinafter provided, except in cities having a board of public works, and in such cities shall be adopted by said board.

"The authority conferred by this article shall include the right to regulate and restrict the height, number of stories, and sizes of buildings, and other structures, the percentage of lot that may be occupied, the sizes of yards, courts, and other open spaces, the density of population, and the location and use and extent of use of buildings and structures and land for trade, industry, residence, or other purposes." N.J.S.A. 40:55-30.

"For any or all of said purposes the governing body or board of public works may divide the municipality into districts of such number, shape, and area as may be deemed best suited to carry out the purposes of this article, and it may regulate and restrict the erection, construction, reconstruction, alteration, repair, or use of buildings or other structures, and the nature and extent of the uses of land, within such districts.

"All such regulations shall be uniform for each class or kind of buildings or other structures or uses of land throughout each district, but the regulations in one district may differ from those in other districts." N.J.S.A. 40:55-31.

"Such regulations shall be in accordance with a comprehensive plan and designed for one or more of the following purposes: to lessen congestion in the streets; secure safety from fire, panic and other dangers; promote health, morals or the general welfare; provide adequate light and air; prevent the overcrowding of land or buildings; avoid undue concentration of population. Such regulations shall be made with reasonable consideration, among other things, to the character of the district and its peculiar suitability for particular uses, and with a view of conserving the most appropriate use of land throughout such municipality." R.S. 40:55-32, N.J.S.A.

The appellant spells out from the language of these constitutional and statutory provisions that the responsibility of a municipality for zoning halts at the municipal boundary lines without regard to the effect of its zoning ordinances on adjoining and nearby land outside the municipality. Such a view might prevail where there are large undeveloped areas at the borders of two contiguous towns, but it cannot be tolerated where, as here, the area is built up and one cannot tell when one is passing from one borough to another. Knickerbocker Road and Massachusetts Avenue are not Chinese walls separating Dumont from the adjoining boroughs. At the very least Dumont owes a duty to hear any residents and taxpayers of adjoining municipalities who may be adversely affected by proposed zoning changes and to give as much consideration to their rights as they would to those of residents and taxpayers of Dumont. To do less would be to make a fetish out of invisible municipal boundary lines and a mockery of the principles of zoning. There is no merit to the defendant's contention. The views set forth in Duffcon Concrete Products, Inc. v. Borough of Cresskill, 1 N.J. 509, 513, 64 A.2d 347, 349, 9 A.L.R.2d 678 (1949) apply here with equal force:

> "What may be the most appropriate use of any particular property depends not only on all the conditions, physical, economic and social, prevailing within the municipality and its needs, present and reasonably prospective, but also on the nature of the entire region in which the municipality is located and the use to which the land in that region has been or may be put most advantageously. The effective development of a region should not and cannot be made to depend upon the adventitious location of municipal boundaries, often prescribed decades or even centuries ago, and based in many instances on considerations of geography, of commerce, or of politics that are no longer significant with respect to zoning. The direction of growth of residential areas on the one hand and of industrial concentration on the other refuses to be governed by such artificial lines. Changes in methods of transportation as well as in living conditions have served only to accentuate the unreality in dealing with zoning problems on the basis of the territorial limits of a municipality, improved highways and new transportation facilities have made possible the concentraton of industry at places best suited to its development to a degree not contemplated in the earlier stages of zoning. The same forces make practicable the presently existing and currently developing suburban and rural sections given over solely to residential purposes and local retail business services coextensive with the needs of the community. The resulting advantages enure alike to industry and residential properties and, at the same time, advance the general welfare of the entire region."

See also Monmouth Lumber Co. v. Ocean Township, 9 N.J. 64, 73-74, 87 A.2d 9 (1952), De Benedetti v. Township of River Vale, 21 N.J.Super. 430, 435, 91 A.2d 353 (App.Div.1952).

That comprehensive planning requires municipal officials to give consideration to adjoining and nearby properties in other municipalities is recognized not only by the decisions of our courts but also by various legislative enactments. As long ago as 1930, in defining the purposes of municipal planning the Legislature provided that municipal planning boards should give attention to "neighboring territory" and the "environs" of the municipality:

> "In the preparation of the plan and map the planning board shall cause to be made careful and comprehensive surveys and studies of present conditions and future growth of the municipality, *due regard being taken to its relation to neighboring territory*. The plan and map shall be made

with the general purpose of guiding and accomplishing a coordinated, adjusted and harmonious development of the municipality *and its environs* which will, in accordance with present and future needs, best promote health, safety, morals, order, convenience, prosperity and general welfare, as well as efficiency and economy in the process of development, including, among other things, adequate provision for traffic and recreation, the promotion of safety from fire and other dangers, adequate provision for light and air, the promotion of the healthful and convenient distribution of population, the promotion of good civic design and arrangement, wise and efficient expenditure of public funds, and the adequate provision of public utilities and other public requirements." R.S. 40:55-10, N.J.S.A. (all italics here and hereafter in this opinion supplied).

In the enactment of the new Municipal Planning Act, L.1953, c. 433, the foregoing section was repealed but its objectives as to the consideration of territory outside of the municipal boundaries was continued and enlarged:

"The master plan may include in its scope *areas outside the boundaries of the municipality* which the planning board deems to bear an essential relation to the planning of the municipality. The studies in connection with the master plan shall be conducted wherever possible *with the co-operation of adjacent planning agencies.*" N.J.S.A. 40:55-11.

"The master plan shall be made with the general purpose of guiding and accomplishing a coordinated, adjusted and harmonious development of the municipality *and its environs* which will, in accordance with present and future needs, best promote health, safety, morals, order, convenience, prosperity and general welfare, as well as efficiency and economy in the process of development and the maintenance of property values previously established." N.J.S.A. 40:55-1.12.

Although the exercise of zoning powers is a constitutional responsibility of the municipalities, Article IV, Sec. VI, par. 2, supra, it is to be noted that the Legislature has also provided for both county planning boards, R.S. 40:27-1, N.J.S.A., and regional planning boards, R.S. 40:27-9, N.J.S.A., thus indicating its intention to extend planning beyond municipal lines.

III.

[3] The vital problem here, and that upon which our decision necessarily rests, is whether, as charged by the respondents, the ordinance constitutes "spot zoning." R.S. 40:55-32, N.J.S.A. provides that zoning regulations "shall be in accordance with a comprehensive plan" to promote the specified statutory purposes. The test is whether the zoning change in question is made with the purpose or effect of establishing or furthering a comprehensive zoning scheme calculated to achieve the statutory objectives or whether it is "designed merely to relieve the lot of the burden of the restriction of the general regulation by reason of conditions alleged to cause such regulation to bear with particular harshness upon it." Conlon v. Board of Public Works of City of Paterson, 11 N.J. 363, 366, 94 A.2d 660, 662 (1953). If it is in the latter category, the ordinance is invalid since it is not " 'in ac-

cordance with a comprehensive plan' " and in effect is " 'a special exception or variance from the restrictive residential regulation, thereby circumventing the board of adjustment to which is committed by our Zoning Act * * * the *quasi*-judicial duty of passing upon such matters, at least initially, in accordance with prescribed standards. * * * ' " Speakman v. Mayor and Council of Borough of North Plainfield, supra, 8 N.J. 250, 257, 84 A.2d 715, 718. Our inquiry therefore has been directed to ascertaining whether in view of the purposes of the zoning act the action of the borough in rezoning Block 197 represents sound judgment based on the policy of the statute "to advance the common good and welfare" or whether it is arbitrary and unreasonable and furthers "purely private interests." Schmidt v. Board of Adjustment of City of Newark, 9 N.J. 405, 422, 88 A.2d 607, 615 (1952).

[4] The Borough of Dumont, as we have seen, is predominantly a residential community composed largely of one-family dwellings, as are the contiguous boroughs. The area surrounding Block 197 is, of course, residential and has been so zoned for years. The mayor testified that 200 to 220 one-family dwellings are to be constructed on the property adjoining Block 197 on the west. There is not the slightest indication that the character of the neighborhood is changing. The only exception to residential use in Dumont within one-half mile of the block in question is a small corner lot which the trial court properly characterized as a case of spot zoning at its worst. The business zone of Dumont, at which there is a fine shopping center, is one-half mile away. The comprehensive zoning plan of the borough reveals an intention to maintain this whole area as a residential one and the testimony clearly shows that the block is suitable for the construction of residences. There is no reason why it should not and cannot be used profitably for that purpose. On the other hand, the changing of Block 197 to a business use will not "lessen congestion in the streets; secure safety from fire, panic, and other dangers; * * * prevent the overcrowding of land or buildings; avoid undue concentration of population," as is required by R.S. 40:55-32, N.J.S.A., supra. On the contrary, the proposed use of the land cannot fail to achieve objectives that zoning was designed to prevent. One has but to remember that Knickerbocker Road, though an important artery of traffic from Englewood to the New York line, is merely a two-lane street to realize the consequences which would flow from the congestion of traffic at Block 197 in the event of the construction of a shopping center there. We fully concur in the finding of the trial court that the ordinance under review "does not promote any of the statutory purposes relating to zoning."

Here the very purpose of the ordinance was to permit the construction of a shopping center on this one block. The council has in effect granted the owner a zoning variance, clearly an action beyond its powers. It follows therefore that the ordinance must be set aside as "spot zoning" in violation of the comprehensive plan of the borough and contrary to the provisions of the zoning law.

The judgment below is affirmed.

OLIPHANT, J., concurring in result.

For affirmance: Chief Justice VANDERBILT and Justices HEHER, OLIPHANT, BURLING, JACOBS and BRENNAN—6.

For reversal: Justice Wachenfeld—1.

Questions and Notes

1. Describe the precise location of this tract in relation to municipal boundaries. (It has often been said that this is the sort of fact situation which could occur only on a law school exam.).

2. What was the holding on the standing of municipalities to sue in this situation?

3. What is the significance of municipal boundaries when they are located between potentially conflicting land uses?

4. For what happened after this decision, see Williams, sec. 85.01.

5. For the earlier Cresskill case (Cresskill I), see below, p. 1372.

ARVERNE BAY CONSTRUCTION CO.

v.

THATCHER

278 N.Y. 222, 15 N.E. 2d 587(1938).

Court of Appeals of New York.

May 24, 1938.

Appeal from Supreme Court, Appellate Division, Second Department.

Action by the Arverne Bay Construction Company against Edwin H. Thatcher as Commissioner of Buildings of the Borough of Brooklyn, City of New York, and another, to secure an adjudication that the restrictions placed on the usage of plaintiff's property by a zoning ordinance were unconstitutional. From a judgment of the Appellate Division, 253 App. Div. 285, 2 N.Y.S.2d 112, reversing a judgment of the Special Term, declaring the zoning resolution confiscatory, unconstitutional, and void, the plaintiff appeals.

Judgment of Appellate Division reversed and judgment of Special Term affirmed.

John P. McGrath, of Brooklyn, for appellant.

William C. Chanler, Corp. Counsel, of New York City (Paxton Blair and Francis J. Bloustein, both of New York City, of counsel), for respondents.

LEHMAN, Judge.

The plaintiff is the owner of a plot of vacant land on the northerly side of Linden boulevard in the borough of Brooklyn. Until 1928 the district in which the property is situated was classified as an "unrestricted" zone, under the Building Zone Resolution of the city of New York (New York Code of Ordinances, Appendix B). Then, by amendment of the ordinance and the "Use District Map," the district was placed in a residence zone. The plaintiff, claiming that its property could not be used properly or profitably for any purpose permitted in a residence zone and that, in consequence, the zoning ordinance imposed unnecessary hardship upon it, applied to the Board of Standards and Appeals, under section 21 of the Building Zone Resolution, for a variance which would permit the use of the premises for a gasoline service station. The application was denied, and, upon review in certiorari proceedings, the courts sustained the determination of the board. People ex rel. Arverne Bay Construction Co. v. Murdock, 247 App.Div. 889, 286 N.Y.S. 785; affirmed, 271 N.Y. 631, 3 N.E.2d 457.

[1-3] Defeated in its attempt to obtain permission to put its property to a profitable use, the plaintiff has brought this action to secure an adjudication that the restrictions placed upon the use of its property by the zoning ordinance result in deprivation of its property without due process of law and that, in so far as the ordinance affects its property, the ordinance violates the provisions of the Constitution of the United States and the Constitution of the State of New York. U.S.C.A. Const. Amend. 14; Const. N.Y. art. 1, § 6. In this action it demands as a right what has been refused to it as a favor. The defendant challenges the right of the plaintiff to urge the invalidity of the zoning ordinance after denial of an application for a variance made under its provisions. At the outset, and before considering the merits of the plaintiff's cause of action, we must dispose of this challenge to the plaintiff's right to maintain this action.

The application for the favor of a variance is an appeal primarily to the discretion of the board, conferred upon it by the ordinance. It necessarily assumes the validity of the ordinance. A successful attack upon the validity of the ordinance destroys the foundation of any discretion conferred by the statute. To invoke the discretion of the board, an owner of property must show "unnecessary hardship." When that has been shown the board may grant "a special privilege" denied to others differently situated. People ex rel. Fordham Manor Reformed Church v. Walsh, 244 N.Y. 280, 155 N.E. 575. Without such "special privilege," strict enforcement of a general rule restricting the use of all property within a district might work such hardship upon a particular owner that in effect it would deprive the owner of his property without compensation. The power to grant a variation might give such flexibility to the rule or its application that a property owner can, without violation of its terms, make reasonable use of his property. Dowsey v. Village of Kensington, 257 N.Y. 221, 177 N.E. 427, 86 A.L.R. 642.

[4-7] The rule established by that case is this: To sustain an attack upon the validity of the ordinance an aggrieved property owner must show that if the ordinance is enforced the consequent restrictions upon his property preclude its use for any purpose to which it is reasonably adapted. Thus it must appear either that the ordinance does not authorize a variation of the general rule which would admit of such use or that such variation has been refused by the administrative board in the exercise of a discretion which the ordinance confers upon it. Only two possible questions can be presented for decision upon an application for a variation: First, does the ordinance confer upon the administrative board power to grant the variation which is asked; second, if the board has power to grant it, does the exercise of a wise discretion call for the use of the power in the particular case? The issue whether without such variation the strict enforcement of the general rule would work such hardship as to constitute the taking of property without due process of law is not directly presented upon an application for a variation, and it follows that the denial of the application cannot be a binding adjudication that, without such variation, enforcement of the general rule will not deprive the applicant of his property without due process of law. True, where the board in the exercise of its discretion denies an application for a variation which it has *power* to grant, argument may be made that a refusal to exercise such discretion can, legally, be based only upon a finding that even without such variation there is no unnecessary hardship, and that the enforcement of the general rule would not deprive the owner of his property or preclude a reasonable use of the property. Then the same considerations which induced the board to deny the application might constrain the court to decide that the statute is valid. None the less, the questions presented would not be identical and the denial of the application for a variance would not be a conclusive adjudication of the validity of the statute; and that would be true even though the courts had, upon review by certiorari, sustained the determination of the board. We proceed, then, to a consideration of the merits of the plaintiff's claim, and in our discussion it will appear that in this case the denial of the application for a variation may have been based upon considerations which cannot affect the judgment of the court in passing upon the validity of the ordinance in so far as it applies to the plaintiff's property.

The amendment to the zoning ordinance, about which complaint is made, changed from an unrestricted zone to a residential district the property abutting on Linden boulevard for a distance of four miles, with the exception of a small section at a railroad crossing. The district is almost undeveloped. There had been no building construction in that area for many years prior to the amendment. The chairman of the building zone commission which drafted the zoning ordinance, testifying as an expert witness for the defendant, described the district as in a "transition state from the farms as I knew them thirty and forty years ago south of this location." There are some old buildings used for non-conforming purposes, left from the days when the district was used for farming. There are only three buildings in Linden boulevard in a distance of about a mile. One of these buildings is a cow stable and a second building is used as an office in connection with the dairy business conducted there. A gasoline station erected on that boulevard would, it is plain, not adversely affect the health, morals, safety or general welfare of the people who now live in that neighborhood. Justification, if any, for the ordinance restricting the use of the property on Linden boulevard to residential purposes must be found in the control over future development which will result from such restrictions.

Without zoning restrictions, the self-interest of the individual property owners will almost inevitably dictate the form of the development of the district. The plaintiff claims, and has conclusively shown at the trial, that at no time since the amendment of the zoning resolution could its property be profitably used for residential purposes. The expert witness for the city, to whose testimony we have already referred and whose qualifications are universally recognized, admits that such a residential improvement would, even now after the lapse of ten years, be "premature." The property, then, must for the present remain unimproved and unproductive, a source of expense to the owner, or must be put to some non-conforming use. In a district otherwise well adapted for residences a gasoline station or other non-conforming use of property may render neighboring property less desirable for use as a private residence. The development of a district for residential purposes might best serve the interests of the city as a whole and, in the end, might perhaps prove the most profitable use of the property within such district. A majority of the property owners might conceivably be content to bear the burden of taxes and other carrying charges upon unimproved land in order to reap profit in the future from the development of the land for residential purposes. They could not safely do so without reasonable assurance that the district will remain adapted for residence use and will not be spoilt for such purpose by the intrusion of structures used for less desirable purposes. The zoning ordinance is calculated to provide such assurance to property owners in the district and to constrain the property owners to develop their land in manner which in the future will prove of benefit to the city. Such considerations have induced the Appellate Division to hold that the ordinance is valid.

[8, 9] There is little room for disagreement with the general rules and tests set forth in the opinion of the Appellate Division. The difficulty arises in the application of such rules and tests to the particular facts in this case. We are not disposed to define the police power of the State so narrowly that it would exclude reasonable restrictions placed upon the use of property in order to aid the development of new districts in accordance with plans calculated to advance the public welfare of the city in the future. We have said that "the need for vision of the future in the governance of cities has not lessened with the years. The dweller within the gates, even more than the stranger from afar, will pay the price of blindness." Hesse

v. Rath, 249 N.Y. 436, 438, 164 N.E. 342. We have, indeed, recognized that long-time planning for zoning purposes may be a valid exercise of the police power, but at the same time we have pointed out that the power is not unlimited. "We are not required to say that a merely temporary restraint of beneficial enjoyment is unlawful where the interference is necessary to promote the ultimate good either of the municipality as a whole or of the immediate neighborhood. Such problems will have to be solved when they arise. If we assume that the restraint may be permitted, the interference must be not unreasonable, but on the contrary must be kept within the limits of necessity." People ex rel. St. Albans-Springfield Corporation v. Connell, 257 N.Y. 73, 83, 177 N.E. 313, 316. The problem presented upon this appeal is whether or not the zoning ordinance as applied to the plaintiff's property is unreasonable.

Findings of the trial judge, sustained by evidence presented by the plaintiff, establish that, in the vicinity of the plaintiff's premises, the city operates an incinerator which "gives off offensive fumes and odors which permeate plaintiff's premises." About 1,200 or 1,500 feet from the plaintiff's land, "a trunk sewer carrying both storm and sanitary sewage empties into an open creek * * *. The said creek runs to the south of plaintiff's premises and gives off nauseating odors which permeate the said property." The trial judge further found that other conditons exist which, it is plain, render the property entirely unfit, at present, for any conforming use. Though the defendant urges that the conditions are not as bad as the plaintiff's witnesses have pictured, yet as the Appellate Division has said: "It must be conceded, upon the undisputed facts in this case, that this property cannot, presently or in the immediate future, be profitably used for residential purposes." 253 App. Div. 285, 286, 2 N.Y.S.2d 112, 114.

[10-13] We may assume that the zoning ordinance is the product of far-sighted planning calculated to promote the general welfare of the city at some future time. If the State or the city, acting by delegation from the State, had plenary power to pass laws calculated to promote the general welfare, then the validity of the ordinance might be sustained; for we have nothing to do with the question of the wisdom or good policy of municipal ordinances. Village of Euclid, Ohio v. Ambler Realty Co., 272 U.S. 365, 393, 47 S.Ct. 114, 120, 71 L.Ed. 303, 54 A.L.R. 1016. The legislative power of the State is, however, not plenary, but is limited by the Constitution of the United States and by the Constitution of the State. It may not take private property without compensation even for a public purpose and to advance the general welfare. Eaton v. Sweeny, 257 N.Y. 176, 177 N.E. 412. "The protection of private property in the Fifth Amendment presupposes that it is wanted for public use. but provides that it shall not be taken for such use without compensation. A similar assumption is made in the decisions upon the Fourteenth Amendment. Hairston v. Danville & Western R. Co., 208 U.S. 598, 605, 28 S.Ct. 331, 52 L.Ed. 637, 13 Ann.Cas. 1008. When this seemingly absolute protection is found to be qualified by the

police power, the natural tendency of human nature is to extend the qualification more and more until at last private property disappears. But that
cannot be accomplished in this way under the Constitution of the United
States." Pennsylvania Coal Co. v. Mahon, 260 U.S. 393, 415, 43 S.Ct. 158,
160, 67 L.Ed. 322, 28 A.L.R. 1321.

In the prevailing opinion in that case, Mr. Justice Holmes pointed out
that "the general rule at least is that while property may be regulated to a
certain extent, if regulation goes too far it will be recognized as a taking"
(page 415, 43 S.Ct. page 160). Whether a regulation does go too far is "a
question of degree—and therefore cannot be disposed of by general propositions," and here Mr. Justice Holmes gave warning that "we are in danger
of forgetting that a strong public desire to improve the public condition is
not enough to warrant achieving the desire by a shorter cut than the constitutional way of paying for the change" (page 416, 43 S.Ct. page 160).
The dissent of Mr. Justice Brandeis in that case is not based upon difference of opinion in regard to general principles, but upon different evaluation of the degree of the restrictions there challenged.

[14-16] The warning of Mr. Justice Holmes should perhaps be directed
rather to Legislatures than to courts; for the courts have not hesitated to
declare statutes invalid wherever regulation has gone so far that it is clearly
unreasonable and must be "recognized as taking"; and unless regulation does
clearly go so far the courts may not deny force to the regulation. We
have already pointed out that in the case which we are reviewing, the
plaintiff's land cannot at present or in the immediate future be profitably
or reasonably used without violation of the restriction. An ordinance which
permanently so restricts the use of property that it cannot be used for any
reasonable purpose goes, it is plain, beyond regulation, and must be recognized as a taking of the property. The only substantial difference, in such
case, between restriction and actual taking, is that the restriction leaves the
owner subject to the burden of payment of taxation, while outright confiscation would relieve him of that burden.

The situation, of course, might be quite different where it appears that
within a reasonable time the property can be put to a profitable use. The
temporary inconvenience or even hardship of holding unproductive property
might then be compensated by ultimate benefit to the owner or, perhaps,
even without such compensation, the individual owners might be compelled
to bear a temporary burden in order to promote the public good. We do
not pass upon such problems now, for here no inference is permissible that
within a reasonable time the property can be put to a profitable use or that
the present inconvenience or hardship imposed upon the plaintiff is temporary. True, there is evidence that the neighborhood is improving and that
some or all of the conditions which now render the district entirely unsuitable for residence purposes will in time be removed. Even so, it is conceded that prognostication that the district will in time become suited for

residences rests upon hope and not upon certainty, and no estimate can be made of the time which must elapse before the hope becomes fact.

[17] During the nine years from 1928 to 1936, when concededly the property was unsuitable for any conforming use, the property was assessed at $18,000, and taxes amounting to $4,566 were levied upon it, in addition to assessments of several thousand dollars; yet, so far as appears, the district was no better suited for residence purposes at the time of the trial in 1936 than it was when the zoning ordinance was amended in 1928. In such case the ordinance is clearly more than a temporary and reasonable restriction placed upon the land to promote the general welfare. It is in substance a taking of the land prohibited by the Constitution of the United States and by the Constitution of the State.

[18-20] We repeat here what under similar circumstances the court said in People ex rel. St. Albans-Springfield Corporation v. Connell, supra, page 83, 177 N.E. page 316: "we are not required to say that a merely temporary restraint of beneficial enjoyment is unlawful where the interference is necessary to promote the ultimate good either of the municipality as a whole or of the immediate neighborhood." There the court held that the "ultimate good" could be attained and a "productive use" allowed by a variation of the zoning ordinance that "will be temporary and provisional and readily terminable." Here the application of the plaintiff for any variation was properly refused, for the conditions which render the plaintiff's property unsuitable for residential use are general and not confined to plaintiff's property. In such case, we have held that the general hardship should be remedied by revision of the general regulation, not by granting the special privilege of a variation to single owners. Levy v. Board of Standards and Appeals of City of New York, 267 N.Y. 347, 196 N.E. 284. Perhaps a new ordinance might be evolved by which the "ultimate good" may be attained without depriving owners of the productive use of their property. That is a problem for the legislative authority, not for the courts. Now we hold only that the present regulation as applied to plaintiff's property is not valid.

The judgment of the Appellate Division should be reversed and that of the Special Term affirmed, with costs in this court and in the Appellate Division.

CRANE, C. J., and O'BRIEN, HUBBS, LOUGHRAN, FINCH, and RIPPEY, JJ., concur.

Judgment accordingly.

WEST BROS. BRICK CO.

v.

ALEXANDRIA

169 Va. 271, 192 S.E. 881(1937),

appeal dismissed, 302 U.S. 658(1937).

Supreme Court of Appeals of Virginia.

Sept. 23, 1937.

Appeal from Circuit Court of City of Alexandria; Walter T. McCarthy, Judge.

Suit by the West Brothers Brick Company, Incorporated, against the City of Alexandria, Virginia. From an adverse judgment, the complainant appeals.

Affirmed.

Argued before CAMPBELL, C. J., and HOLT, HUDGINS, GREGORY, BROWNING, EGGLESTON, and SPRATLEY, JJ.

John S. Barbour, of Fairfax, for appellant.

Carl L. Budwesky, of Alexandria, and Thomas B. Gay, of Richmond, for appellee.

HOLT, Justice.

West Brothers Brick Company, Inc., appellant here and complainant below, contends that it has a right to mine and remove a bed of clay on a certain tract of land owned by it and lying within the corporate limits of the city of Alexandria. The city contends that this company has no such right and refuses to permit the prosecution of that proposed undertaking. An injunction was sought and refused; hence this appeal.

This lot is an eighteen-acre tract practically undeveloped, triangular in shape, bounded on the south by First street, on the west by Henry street, on the northwest at the apex of the triangle by the property of the Richmond, Fredericksburg & Potomac Railroad, and on the northeast and east by the Washington and Alexandria Road, sometimes known as the Old Georgetown Road.

To the east and one block from its eastern apex runs the Mount Vernon Memorial Boulevard. All of the land lying to the south between it and the center of the business section of the city, distant nine blocks away, has been set apart for residential purposes.

The West brothers were brickmakers and had for many years followed that vocation at their plant in what is now known as Arlington county, Va. That business was taken over by the plaintiff corporation on May 20, 1902, which since then has been making both brick and hollow tile. It is an undertaking of moment. In 1926 it was greatly enlarged and now represents an investment of about a half million dollars and has a pay roll on which are between two and three hundred men. The plant itself is about two miles from the city limits and about four miles from the lot in controversy. This company owned and owns about one hundred and thirty acres of clay land, but in 1927, anticipating that their supply of raw material might some day be exhausted, it commenced a quest which turned out to be successful and located this lot, on which there is a bed of clay from eight to fourteen feet deep, suitable for its purposes and well adapted to the making of high-class tile. It was carefully inspected and then purchased at the price of $47,000. At that time about 20 per cent. of that lot lay within the city limits, the balance being in the county. More than a year after this purchase these limits were extended. This extension went into effect on January 1, 1930, and includes all of this eighteen-acre lot.

It seemed desirable to the city that there be established within its limits certain zones or territorial sections to be set apart for certain designated uses. To that end it secured the services of Irving C. Root, city planner for the Maryland National Capitol Park & Planning Commission, and an expert with twenty years' experience in work of this kind. He was employed to prepare, and undertook to prepare a comprehensive zoning plan, showing property adapted to residential, commercial, and industrial uses, and in conjunction with a commission appointed for the purpose was engaged in this work for about a year. There were public hearings held by it and one at least by the mayor and city council, after which and on July 25, 1931, that council, acting under authority of chapter 122A of the Code, sometimes known as the Enabling Act (Acts 1926, c. 197, as amended by Acts 1930, c. 205), adopted a comprehensive ordinance, known as Zoning Ordinance 109; the plan adopted being substantially that recommended by its commission. This plan thus adopted classified all of appellant's eighteen-acre tract as residential except a 100-foot strip which bordered on Henry street and which was set apart for industrial uses.

This situation continued without protest until the latter part of 1934, when appellant petitioned the city council to rezone its land to the end that it might all be classed as industrial—this in order that it might obtain permission to begin excavation of its underlying clay bed. At that hearing counsel for the Brick Company appeared on its behalf. Relief was resisted by A. S. Doniphan, an adjoining property owner. Written protests were also received from the Alexandria Chamber of Commerce and the Sixth Ward Citizens Association. Petitioner's request was denied by a vote of six or three. Thereafter and on July 1, 1935, the bill in this cause was filed, its prayer being that a declaratory decree be entered quieting the right and title of said complainant to the use of its premises and enjoining the city and its officials from interferring therewith. It was heard on depositions, answer, and exhibits; the court, upon consideration thereof, being of the opinion that complainant was not entitled to the relief prayed for, did so decree.

Evidence for the complainant shows, or tends to show, the following facts:

This land, sometimes spoken of as the Taylor land or lot, was, to the extent that it was used at all, used as farm land when purchased by petitioner. On it were five or six residential buildings of little value; nor had there been any residential developments of moment in its neighborhood. Mr. West, president of the plaintiff company, tells us of conditions:

"To the west is a large ice manufacturing plant and to the south of that was a lumber yard and mill plant; to the east there were some small stores, as I remember, sort of a roadside stand selling groceries and eatables, such as motorists would stop and buy. To the south was a warehouse, I think known as Janney's Warehouse, and also there are other small industries in the immediate vicinity. I might state there was also a colored settlement immediately south of this property consisting largely of some very dilapidated types of colored dwellings. I might also state there is a railroad track along the Washington-Alexandria roadway between the highway and this property line, which railroad track, I think, connected with the Janney's Warehouse."

A number of other witnesses, among them Mr. Ezra, a member of the zoning commission, has testified. The substance of their evidence is that this land is better suited for industrial than for residential purposes and that there has never been any real residential development in its immediate vicinity. We have seen that four blocks along its western edge, fronting on Henry street and which lie between it and the Potomac yards, were set aside for industrial purposes and are not involved in this litigation.

Both brick and tile are made. For the latter a more plastic clay is necessary. This necessary characteristic appears in the underlying stratum on the Taylor lot and makes it valuable. Its gross value has been placed at $18 a cubic yard. From this, of course, must be deducted all costs incident to its use. If its use is forbidden, that part of plaintiff's plant devoted to that work must some time be abandoned, unless other available supplies can be uncovered; but it is also true that this deposit was neither relied upon nor known when the tile plant and kilns were built.

So far as this testimony deals with existing conditions as distinguished from opinions, it has not been seriously questioned.

For the city, Mr. Allwine, manager for the Portner properties, testified: That estate has large holdings in Alexandria, one of which is a lot east of this Taylor land and separated from it by the Washington and Alexandria Road. That lot, this witness thinks, is valuable for residential purposes, but that such value would be wholly destroyed if the Brick Company be permitted to develop its property in the manner desired. Negotiations for the sale of the Portner property to Mr. Hillegeist at the price of $42,000 are now under way. He represents a number of men who plan to build on it an apartment to consist of thirteen units, together with an underground garage which will accommodate 104 cars, all at a cost of something under $2,000,000. This proposed development would be seriously affected if the Brick Company's plans are carried out.

Mr. Root, another witness for the city, is a city planner with twenty years' experience. He was employed by Alexandria and worked with its zoning commission for about a year. Existing conditions were studied and future possibilities were considered, based upon the center of population, traffic lanes, transportation facilities, etc. Public hearings were had, and the conclusion was reached that a residential development here was most desirable; one of the features considered being the proximity of the Mount Vernon Memorial Boulevard. Speaking of that factor, he said:

> "It was one of the factors, because the agreement between the City and the Federal Government regarding the development of that Memorial Boulevard called for its residential use, and being protected for residential use and undoubtedly available for structures of a high character, it was assumed by myself that the influence of that high residential character would extend a considerable distance in that direction from the Memorial Boulevard."

He also tells us why those lots fronting on Henry street were classed as industrial:

> "The property, the portion of this West Brothers property facing the ice plant, which is zoned industrial, should also be zoned industrial because it would be obviously unfair to say that one side of the road should be zoned industrial and the other side should be denied a similar use, but that is only for the depth of the frontage actually facing on the ice company property; and the city plan contemplated the division of the rest of the West Brothers property into building lots, one tier of which would back on this industrial zoning on the west side of the property so that in that way there would be a screen created by the residence that would back on the industrial property, and so the industrial use would have less injurious effect on the balance of the West Brothers property."

Mr. Reardon, another witness, was a member of the zoning commission. Among the reasons which influenced him are these:

> "That property and all the property at the head of Washington Street there was considered an anticipated very high class development along the Boulevard, and due to the development, the Mall development in Washington, it was felt and believed and is still believed that that end of Washington Street would be a most desirable residential section."

Mr. Kane, another member of that commission, said that he realized that this property was not highly desirable for residential purposes but that it would in the future be well suited for homes of a less expensive type.

Other witnesses thought that this classification was fair, and they testify as to the undesirable conditions which would necessarily follow the excavations which the Brick Company proposes to make.

That territory south of the Potomac and contiguous to Washington has in recent years witnessed extraordinary developments. The time is not distant when Alexandria and Arlington county will constitute one urban community, and for this city planning is not only desirable but necessary. Zoning ordinances are devices of recent invention and are intended to conserve those elements which make life in cities livable. Necessarily private rights and public interests sometimes clash. Such conflict is as old as law itself. Sic utero tuo, etc., is an ancient maxim, whose applicability is constantly being extended at the expense of private interests. Plainly the owner of a lot on Franklin street in Richmond should not be permitted to operate a fertilizer factory there, nor is this invasion of private rights confined to matters so patent. Until recently in Virginia, a dairyman might sell his milk to all who wished to purchase. Now, before he can sell at all, he must secure the consent of a commission. Courts take cognizance of public and social developments and balance them as best they can against private rights.

[1] Conflicts between constitutional guaranties and the police power constantly arise, and indeed are inevitable. To them this is said to be a proper approach: "Where the police power conflicts with the Constitution, the latter is supreme, but the courts will not restrain the exercise of such power, except where the conflict is clear and plain." Buck v. Bell, 143 Va. 310, 130 S.E. 516, 519, 51 A.L.R. 855.

[2-8] Zoning ordinances have everywhere been adopted. Their validity was once challenged, but they are now generally recognized as a proper use of the police power. McQuillen's Municipal Corporations, vol. 2, p. 1051. And certainly they are valid in Virginia, Nusbaum v. Norfolk, 151 Va. 801, 145 S.E. 257; Gorieb v. Fox, 145 Va. 554, 134 S.E. 914, 916, Id., 274 U.S. 603, 47 S.Ct. 675, 71 L.Ed. 1228, 53 A.L.R. 1210; Eubank v. City of Richmond, 110 Va. 749, 67 S.E. 376, 19 Ann.Cas. 186; Id., 226 U.S. 137, 33 S.Ct. 76, 57 L.Ed. 156, 42 L.R.A. (N.S.) 1123, Ann.Cas. 1914B, 192, so long as they are not arbitrary and unreasonable. Under settled rules of construction, they must be sustained if their reasonableness is debatable. Martin v. Danville, 148 Va. 247, 138 S.E. 629, 630; Euclid, Ohio, v. Ambler Realty Co., 272 U.S. 365, 47 S.Ct. 114, 118, 71 L.Ed. 303, 54 A.L.R. 1016. The city council of Alexandria is better acquainted with the necessities of that city than we are. In Gorieb v. Fox, supra, this court said:

> "The Legislature may, in the exercise of the police power, restrict personal and property rights in the interest of public health, public safety, and for the promotion of the general welfare."

This power "embraces regulations designed to promote the public convenience or the general prosperity, as well as regulations designed to promote the public health, the public morals, or the public safety." Bacon v. Walker, 204 U.S. 311, 27 S.Ct. 289, 291, 51 L.Ed. 499.

"The power is not limited to regulations designed to promote public morals, or public safety, or to the suppression of what is offensive, disorderly, or unsanitary, but extends to so dealing with conditions which exist as to bring out of them the greatest welfare of the people by promoting public convenience or general prosperity." Wulfsohn v. Burden (1925) 241 N.Y. 288, 150 N.E. 120, 122, 43 A.L.R. 651.

Æsthetic considerations alone are not enough but they should be considered.

"It seems to us that æsthetic considerations are relative in their nature. With the passing of time, social standards conform to new ideals. As a race, our sensibilities are becoming more refined, and that which formerly did not offend cannot now be endured. That which the common law did not condemn as a nuisance is now frequently outlawed as such by the written law. This is not because the subject outlawed is of a different nature, but because our sensibilities have become more refined and our ideals more exacting. Nauseous smells have always come under the ban of the law, but ugly sights and discordant surroundings may be just as distressing to keener sensibilities. The rights of property should not be sacrificed to the pleasure of an ultra-æsthetic taste. But whether they should be permitted to plague the average or dominant human sensibilities well may be pondered." State ex rel. Carter v. Harper, 182 Wis. 148, 158, 196 N.W. 451, 455, 33 A.L.R. 269. It might be hard to prove that a city dump was hurtful to health, but plainly it should not be located in a residential district. The days of kitchen middenz are gone.

Indeed the inalienable rights of the individual are not what they used to be.

All of these considerations address themselves primarily to the Legislature (city council), and its judgment stands unless there has been plain abuse of its wide discretion.

In the instant case, these are those whose unanimity of conclusions is relied upon by the city: We have an expert city planner with twenty years' experience; we have the judgment of the zoning commission; we have the judgment of the mayor and city council when the ordinance framed by its commission was in substance adopted; and we have the judgment of that council at a later date, which, after a full hearing, declined to reclassify this land. It would be extraordinary, indeed, if their conclusions upon questions of fact were so utterly wrong as not to be debatable.

[9] Zoning ordinances, in the main, deal not with present conditions, but with conditions to come. They are not designed to Haussmannize a city, but to guide its future growth. Necessarily any plan of that nature must be in some degree arbitrary. It is seldom that there is any definite reason for holding that a lot on one side of a line should be devoted to one purpose and that just across it to another. The adaptability of certain territorial sections of cities to certain uses fade into each other. One end of a field may be, beyond peradventure, suited to industrial developments, the other to private homes. Intervening there must be a twilight zone. If the Legislature cannot be relied upon to say where lines must run, who can be vested with that discretion? Demonstrative accuracy is an impossibility.

"The boundary line of a zoning district must be fixed in some locality. In the very nature of things it must always be more or less arbitrary, because the property on one side of a line cannot, in the very nature of things, be very different from the property on the other side of the line." In re Dawson (1929) 136 Okl. 113, 277 P. 226, 228.

[10] This statute is not retroactive and was not intended to make unlawful any use of a building or premises lawful when it went into effect, and so under the doctrine of nonconforming uses complainant contends that it desires but to continue a use already in effect.

In support of this contention we are cited to Appeal of Haller Baking Company, 295 Pa. 257, 145 A. 77, 79. That was a case in which a major stable was forbidden within a certain district. A major stable was one which could accommodate four or more horses. When the Pennsylvania statute took effect, fewer than four horses were stabled there, although there were accommodations for twenty-five. The court held that there had been no abandonment and said:

> "This stable had been used continuously until 1924. Since then the quantity diminished very materially, but it was still used for its original purpose, and it is appellant's purpose and effort to continue the use. This does not show an intention to abandon, nor would the fact than on the day of the adoption of the ordinance, or a number of days before, no horses were in the building. A property right such as is involved in this case, having attached, cannot be lost by that circumstance."

In the instant case, this clay bed had never been used. It was bought, as we are told, for future use, and not having been used at all, the doctrine of nonconforming uses has no application.

[11-14] It is next said that the ordinance as construed and applied violates the statute under which it was passed.

"The Title of this Act (Acts 1926, c. 197, p. 345, Va.Code §§ 3091 (1) to 3091 (26) is as follows:

> " 'An Act to enable the council ° ° ° of cities ° ° ° to divide the municipal area into one or more districts and in such Districts to *regulate* the use of land and of buildings or other structures, and the height thereof, and also to establish building lines and to regulate and restrict the construction and location of buildings and other structures ° ° °.' "

And in support of this contention we are cited to Opinion of the Justices, 232 Mass. 605, 124 N.E. 319, 321, in which it was held that the power to regulate the uses of property did not confer the power to utterly prohibit its use and that the regulations themselves must be within reasonable limits.

These principles are well recognized in Virginia. Private property shall not be taken or damaged for public uses without just compensation. Constitution of Virginia, § 58. Likewise we are told that the exercise of the police power of the state shall never be abridged. Constitution of Virginia, § 159. We would be less than frank if we did not concede that these two great principles clash at times. Plainly the city of Richmond has a right to say that an abattoir shall not front on Monroe Park. Such a regulation would be in the interest of the public and possibly at the expense of some lot owner. The owner might still use his lot, but not for that purpose. This power of the state to regulate is incidental to every private title. Under the guise of regulation property cannot be taken, but no demand for compensation can be sustained because of some reasonable regulation which may affect its use or even its value. It is not true that a man may always do what he will with his own. Personal liberty itself is regulated. One cannot set his field afire and burn up his neighbor's fences. All of this rests upon established principles.

In Gorieb v. Fox, supra, it is said: "It is not contradicted that the legislature may confer the police power of the state upon cities and towns located therein. The extent of this power is difficult to define, but it is elastic, and expands automatically to protect the public against the improper use of private property to the injury of the public interest. It must never be exercised except in a reasonable manner and for the welfare of the public."

In that case there is cited with approval from Town of Windsor v. Whitney, 95 Conn. 357, 111 A. 354, 356, 12 A.L.R. 669, this statement:

> "The line between eminent domain and the police power is a hard one to hold with constancy and consistency, and it is not surprising that now and again these two great powers of government have been confused. A few years ago it was, so far as the rule had been announced, undoubted that restrictions could not be imposed upon a private property solely for aesthetic considerations. Later it has been said by high authority that aesthetic considerations may be regarded in connection with recognized police power consideration. And now Dillon in the latest edition of his Municipal Corporations, § 695, says:
>
> "'The law on this point is undergoing development, and perhaps cannot be said to be conclusively settled as to the extent of the police power.'"

In that same case it is said: "The State may regulate the use of property to the point of forbidding thereon certain businesses in themselves lawful."

These regulations, among their incidental effects, in terms of money may diminish the value of land so regulated. For such injuries the law affords no remedy. It is damnum absque injuria.

Evidence is not needed to tell us that an eighteen-acre clay pit within a city's limits and near a great national boulevard would be an eyesore and a nuisance.

[15-18] Next it is said that the act itself is invalid in that its title does not express its purpose, or at any rate does not express a purpose to prohibit the lawful use of land. Its title is:

> "An Act to authorize the councils ° ° ° of cities ° ° ° to divide the municipal area into one or more districts, and in such districts to regulate the use of land and of buildings or other structures."

This brings us back to matters heretofore considered. No general use of this land is prohibited; certain uses are, though they may be in themselves lawful. Ordinarily it is lawful for a man to cover his lot with a building, but under the power to regulate, this right may be overborne. The owner may be told to set it back, and the fact that he may suffer loss in this loss of space gives him no right to relief.

Moreover, this constitutional provision, "No law shall embrace more than one object which shall be expressed in its title" (section 52), is to be liberally construed. Bunkley v. Commonwealth, 130 Va. 55, 108 S.E. 1. If the title be not misleading and if those things are done which are germane to it, that is enough. This constitutional provision was intended to prevent the insertion of rights or reservations which cannot bear the light of public scrutiny and which, if uncovered, would not be tolerated. Where this is done that provision should be enforced to the letter.

[19, 20]   Next it is said that complainant's property has been both damaged and taken without just compensation, contrary to the provisions of sections 6, 11, and 58 of the Constitution of Virginia. Plainly this property has not been taken although it has undoubtedly been damaged, but, as we have seen, that damage which is incidental to a lawful exercise of police power is not the damage contemplated by these protective provisions invoked.

In Gorieb v. Fox, supra, this court said:

> "The Virginia Constitution declares that the exercise of the police power of the state shall never be abridged. Section 159.
>
> "The Legislature may, in the exercise of the police power, restrict personal and property rights in the interest of public health, public safety, and for the promotion of the general welfare. Eubank v. City of Richmond, 110 Va. [749], 751, 67 S.E. 376, 19 Ann. Cas. 186; Welch v. Swasey, 193 Mass. 364, 79 N.E. 745, 23 L.R.A.(N.S.) 1160, 118 Am. St. Rep. 523; Freund on Police Power, §§ 118, 128; Attorney General v. Williams, 174 Mass. [476], 477, 55 N.E. 77, 47 L.R.A. 314; People v. D'Oench, 111 N.Y. [359], 361, 18 N.E. 862; Barbier v. Connolly, 113 U.S. 27, 5 S.Ct. 357, 28 L.Ed. 923; Bacon v. Walker, 204 U.S. 311, 27 S.Ct. 289, 51 L.Ed. 499."

General welfare can no more be defined than can police power. These are terms which take on new definitions when we come to face new conditions. General welfare in Alexandria today may warrant regulations which would have been fantastic in Sherwood Forest.

Finally it is said that the statute and the ordinance as construed and applied in this case is violative of section 1 of the Fourteenth Amendment to the Constitution of the United States.

[21, 22]   The right of municipalities in Virginia under their police power to enact zoning ordinances can no longer be successfully challenged. Gorieb v. Fox, supra. In that case, confirmed on appeal to the Supreme Court, 274 U.S. 603, 47 S.Ct. 675, 71 L.Ed. 1228, 53 A.L.R. 1210, Mr. Justice Sutherland, commenting upon the ordinance under review, said that it must be sustained unless it is clearly arbitrary and unreasonable, having no substantial relation to the public health, safety, morals, or general welfare, citing Euclid, Ohio, v. Ambler Realty Co., supra.

This rule is restated in Martin v. Danville, supra, in this form:

> "It is a settled rule of the Supreme Court of the United States, if the question of reasonableness is fairly debatable, to hold that it will not substitute its judgment for that of the legislative body charged with the primary duty and responsibility of deciding the question."

See, also, Zahn v. Board of Public Works, 274 U.S. 325, 47 S.Ct. 594, 71 L.Ed. 1074; all of which goes back to this familiar principle: Courts uphold acts of the Legislature whenever their constitutionality is debatable: presumptions are in their favor.

Euclid, Ohio, v. Ambler Realty Co., supra, is an instructive case. It is there pointed out that regulations now uniformly sustained would, half a century ago, have been rejected as arbitrary and unreasonable, and that the exclusion of industrial enterprises from residential districts bears a rational relation to the health and safety of the community. Attention is called to the fact that the law of nuisances is to be remembered. "A nuisance may be merely a right thing in the wrong place."

Judge Way, in discussing this particular statute, though not the zone in judgment, said:

> "Taking the view most favorable to plaintiff's contention, this court cannot say as a matter of law that the question as to how plaintiff's property should be zoned is not debatable. It is fairly debatable, and the court may not arbitrarily substitute its judgment for that of the legislative body of the city on a question so vitally affecting the public safety and welfare." Downham v. City Council of Alexandria (D.C.) 58 F.(2d) 784, 787.

[23] The fact that the location of lines may be in some degree arbitrary will not defeat the statute.

It was in the power of Alexandria to mark out as suitable for industrial purposes all of the land which lay between its center and the Potomac yards. It might have set apart that territory for residential purposes only, and it might have divided it between these two uses. The conclusion which the city did reach was reached after mature consideration and after public hearings.

Had it all been set apart for residences, business might have complained; had it all been set apart for business, home owners might have objected, and it was in this light that this zoning commission, seeking to conserve the interests of the public generally, drew lines which are now charged to be utterly arbitrary and unreasonable, and its judgment after public hearing has been more than once confirmed.

As we understand complainant's contention, it does not attack the general power of cities to enact zoning ordinances, but it does contend that this under review, as applied to the facts in the instant case, is both arbitrary and unreasonable—that is to say, a statute valid as to one set of facts may be invalid as to another. Nashville, C. & St. L. Ry. v. Walters, 294 U.S. 405, 55 S.Ct. 486, 79 L.Ed. 949.

It was there also pointed out that the police power could be invoked to include regulations promoting public convenience and general welfare, as well as those which relate directly to public health, safety, and morals. How can it be said that this potential reservoir of stagnant water will not in days to come affect the welfare and comfort of this community? It would be a public and continuing nuisance. This pit, as has been suggested, might be used as a city dump; it is suited to no other purpose. Nor is it necessary that one be supersensitive in order to find it artistically objectionable.

Many cases are cited as showing, or tending to show, the unreasonableness of the ordinance in judgment. Among them are these:

Re Kelso, 147 Cal. 609, 82 P. 241, 2 L.R.A.(N.S.) 796, 109 Am.St.Rep. 178. That was decided more than thirty years ago. A San Francisco ordinance prohibited the operation of a quarry in a given district. The court said that there were many ways of operating a quarry, some of which could harm no one. It recognized the fact that one operated by blasts might be prohibited and that its operations might be hedged about by valid regulations which would make it unprofitable. If that case intended to hold that the city cannot forbid the operation of quarries, operated as quarries are ordinarily operated, where people live or are accustomed to move, then it is out of touch with latter day extensions of police power.

The Supreme Court dealt with this subject in Hadacheck v. Sebastian, Chief of Police of Los Angeles (1915) 239 U.S. 394, 36 S.Ct. 143, 60 L.Ed. 348, Ann.Cas. 1917B, 927. There an ordinance which prohibited the manufacture of brick in a designated district was upheld, but the right to dig clay there was in terms left open. It did hold that vested interest could not defeat the proper exercise of police power which is in substance what has been held in Virginia. One has a vested interest in all of his city lot, but we have held that he may not always cover it by a building.

Pennsylvania Coal Company v. Mahon, 260 U.S. 395, 43 S.Ct. 158, 67 L.Ed. 322, 28 A.L.R. 1321, deals with the right of a coal company to remove that commodity under conditions denied by statute. There the coal company gave to the complainant a deed in which it reserved the right to mine, and since this right had been reserved, the plaintiff had no right to forbid its use. It is true that that decision goes beyond an adjudication of private rights and holds the statute to be an unwarranted exercise of police power. An interesting discussion of it will be found in Marblehead Land Co. v. City of Los Angeles (C.C.A.) 47 F.(2d) 528, where the court points out that there is no distinction between diminution in the value of land by limitations upon its use and where the owner is prevented from developing underlying mineral resources, citing Zahn v. City of Los Angeles, supra.

In Nectow v. City of Cambridge, 277 U.S. 183, 48 S.Ct. 447, 448, 72 L.Ed. 842, a landowner in a district zoned as residential undertook successfully to have that classification set aside as arbitrary and unreasonable. The court, proceeding upon familiar principles, said:

> "The governmental power to interfere by zoning regulations with the general rights of the land owner by restricting the character of his use, is not unlimited, and, other questions aside, such restriction cannot be imposed if it does not bear a substantial relation to the public health, safety, morals, or general welfare. Euclid, Ohio, v. Ambler Realty Co., supra [272 U.S. 365, at] page 395, 47 S.Ct. 114 [71 L.Ed. 303, 54 A.L.R. 1016]. Here, the express finding of the master, already quoted, confirmed by the court below, is that the health, safety, convenience, and general welfare of the inhabitants of the part of the city affected will not be promoted by the disposition made by the ordinance of the loans in question. This finding of the master, after a hearing and an inspection of the entire area affected, supported, as we think it is, by other findings of fact, is determinative of the case. That the invasion of the property of plaintiff in error was serious and highly injurious is clearly established; and, since a necessary basis for the support of that invasion is wanting, the action of the zoning authorities comes within the ban of the Fourteenth Amendment and cannot be sustained."

No new principles of law were invoked; the court merely applied those which it had repeatedly approved to the facts found by the master. He held the classification to be unreasonable and his finding the court followed.

A leading case and one quite applicable to that in judgment is Marblehead Land Co. v. City of Los Angeles, supra, decided in 1931, certiorari denied on October 19th of that year. There in issue was the right to sink an oil well. The company owned 291 acres of land, seven miles distant from the heart of the city, and theretofore used as a farm. This land was well adapted to residential uses, but the nearest dwelling was eleven hundred feet away. Large sums of money had been invested and the possibilities of returns thereon were unlimited. The ordinance was sustained. See, also, Beveridge v. Harper & Turner Oil Trust, 168 Okl. 609, 35 P.(2d) 435, and Cromwell-Franklin Oil Co. v. Oklahoma City (D.C.) 14 F.Supp. 370.

In Leary v. Adams (1933) 226 Ala. 472, 147 So. 391, 395, money losses were considered. The court said:

> "Petitioner presents a strong appeal from the standpoint of financial loss occasioned by this restriction. But, as said by the North Carolina court in City of Elizabeth City v. Aydlett, 201 N.C. 602, 161 S.E. 78, 81: 'Financial loss is not the test; the question is whether the scheme is sound, and the classification fair. If the question is fairly debatable, the court will not substitute its judgment for that of the legislative body which creates the ordinance.'"

On this point, see Hadacheck v. Sebastian, 239 U.S. 394, 36 S.Ct. 143, 60 L.Ed. 348, Ann.Cas. 1917B, 927, and Chicago, B. & Q. Ry. Co. v. People of Illinois ex rel. Drainage Com'rs, 200 U.S. 561, 26 S.Ct. 341, 50 L.Ed. 596, 4 Ann.Cas. 1175.

[24-27] The enactment of zoning ordinances and cases which test them are all within the recollection of most of us. General rules applicable

thereto are now well settled. They must not be wholly unreasonable, but they are presumed to be valid and to have been promulgated by those familiar with local conditions. Vested interests will not defeat them, and of course constitutional rights are not to be measured in terms of money. That, however, is a consideration to be remembered. Great financial losses should not be inflicted where benefits to others are negligible, but public welfare and public convenience do control and are in themselves terms constantly adjusted to meet new conditions. Upon those who would set aside such ordinances rests a heavy burden of proof. They stand when their validity is debatable.

[28, 29] An eighteen-acre clay pit in a growing town, contiguous either to residences or business establishments, would doubtless be objectionable. Where it is forbidden by statute (a zoning ordinance), the burden of showing that it is necessary, or even desirable, as adding to the comfort and welfare of the city, does not rest upon it. Statutes are presumed to be valid expressions of legislative will and stand until this is disproven.

The decree appealed from should be affirmed, and it is so ordered.

Affirmed.

BROWNING, J., dissents.

Questions and Notes

1. Why did the courts, at least in earlier days, treat the mining of earth products as something essentially different from any other type of land use?

CHENEY

v.

VILLAGE 2 AT NEW HOPE, INC. APPEAL

429 Pa. 626, 241 A.2d 81 (1968).

Supreme Court of Pennsylvania

April 24, 1968.

Action challenging validity of ordinances creating planned unit development district and rezoning tract of land from low density residential to planned unit development. On appeal from decision of zoning board of adjustment upholding the ordinances, the Common Pleas Court, Bucks County, at No. 321 December Term 1965, Edwin H. Satterthwaite, P. J., reversed the board and certiorari was granted. The Supreme Court, Nos. 110, 111, 112, 113, 114 January 1968, Roberts, J., held that borough council by creating planned unit development district permitting as possible uses, inter alia, single-family attached or detached dwellings, apartments, public or private parks, ski slopes, hotels and restaurants did not vest in planning commission authority greater than that permitted under zoning enabling legislation and did not abrogate its legislative function by permitting mixture of uses.

Appeals from certain orders quashed, orders in other appeals vacated and records remanded, and order in other appeal reversed.

✻ ✻ ✻

Leonard L. Wolffe, Philadelphia, Edward I. Dobin, Curtin & Heefner, Morrisville, Carl K. Zucker, Philadelphia, for appellant.

William Eastburn, III, Doylestown, for appellees, Mayor and Borough Council of Borough of New Hope, and Watson G. Janney, Sec.

David H. Moskowitz, William Miller, Cornwells Heights of counsel, for appellees Sheldon Cheney et al.

Before MUSMANNO, JONES, COHEN, EAGEN, O'BRIEN and ROBERTS, JJ.

OPINION OF THE COURT

ROBERTS, Justice.

Under traditional concepts of zoning the task of determining the type, density and placement of buildings which should exist within any given zoning district devolves upon the local legislative body. In order that this body might have to speak only infrequently on the issue of municipal planning and zoning the local legislature usually enacts detailed requirements for the type, size and location of buildings within each given zoning district, and leaves the ministerial task of enforcing these regulations to an appointed zoning administrator, with another administrative body, the zoning board of adjustment, passing on individual deviations from the strict district requirements, deviations known commonly as variances and special exceptions. At the same time, the overall rules governing the dimensions, placement, etc. of primarily public additions to ground, e. g., streets, sewers, playgrounds, are formulated by the local legislature through the passage of subdivision regulations. These regulations are enforced and applied to individual lots by an administrative body usually known as the planning commission.

This general approach to zoning fares reasonably well so long as development takes place on a lot-by-lot basis, and so long as no one cares that the overall appearance of the municipality resembles the design achieved by using a cookie cutter on a sheet of dough. However, with the increasing popularity of large scale residential developments, particularly in suburban areas, it has become apparent to many local municipalities that land can be more efficiently used, and developments more aesthetically pleasing, if zoning regulations focus on density requirements rather than on specific rules for each individual lot. Under density zoning, the legislature determines what percentage of a particular district must be devoted to open space, for example, and what percentage used for dwelling units.

The task of filling in the particular district with real houses and real open space then falls upon the planning commission usually working in conjunction with an individual large scale developer. See Chrinko v. South Brunswick Twp., Planning Bd., 77 N.J.Super. 594, 187 A.2d 221 (1963). The ultimate goal of this so-called density or cluster concept of zoning is achieved when an entire self-contained little community is permitted to be built within a zoning district, with the rules of density controlling not only the relation of private dwellings to open space, but also the relation of homes to commercial establishments such as theaters, hotels, restaurants, and quasi-commercial uses such as schools and churches. The present controversy before this Court involves a frontal attack upon one of these zoning districts, known in the trade as a Planned Unit Development (hereinafter PUD).

Spurred by the desire of appellant developer to construct a Planned Unit Development in the Borough of New Hope, in December of 1964 Borough Council began considering the passage of a new zoning ordinance to establish a PUD district in New Hope. After extensive consultation with appellant, council referred the matter to the New Hope Planning Commission for further study. This body, approximately six months after the project idea was first proposed, formally recommended to council that a PUD district be created. Council consulted with members of the Bucks County Planning Commission on the text of the proposed ordinance, held public hear'ngs, and finally on June 14, 1965 enacted ordinance 160 which created the PUD district, and ordinance 161 which amended the Borough zoning map, rezoning a large tract of land known as the Rauch farm from low density residential to PUD. Pursuant to the procedural requirements of ordinance 160, appellant presented plans for a Planned Unit Development on the Rauch tract to the Borough Planning Commission. These plans were approved on November 8, 1965, and accordingly four days later two building permits, known as zon'ng permits 68 and 69, were issued to appellant. (Some question exists as to the current status of these permits, see text infra.) Subsequently, permit number 75 was issued. Appellees, all neighboring property owners opposing the issuance of these permits, appealed to the zoning board of adjustment. The board, after taking extensive testimony, upheld ordinances 160 and 161 and accord'ngly affirmed the issuance of the permits. Appellees then appealed to the Bucks County Court of Common Pleas. That tribunal took no additional testimony, but reversed the board, holding the ordinances invalid for failure to conform to a comprehensive plan and for vesting too much discretion in the New Hope Planning Commission. This Court granted certiorari under Supreme Court Rule 68½.

[1, 2] The procedural posture of this case is identical to that of National Land & Investment Co. v. Easttown Twp. Bd. of Adjustment, 419 Pa. 504, 523, 215 A.2d 597, 607 (1965). Our scope of review may thus be stated by reference to that decision: "The zoning enabling act being silent as to a

right of appeal, we consider this case on broad certiorari, reviewing the testimony, the evidence, and the entire record. Keystone Raceway Corp. v. State Harness Racing Comm'n, 405 Pa. 1, 173 A.2d 97 (1961); Schmidt v. Philadelphia Zoning Bd. of Adjustment, 382 Pa. 521, 114 A.2d 902 (1955). Because the court below took no additional testimony, we will look at the decision of the board of adjustment to determine if, in upholding * * * [ordinances 160 and 161], the board committed an abuse of discretion or an error of law. Upper Providence Twp. Appeal, 414 Pa. 46, 198 A.2d 522 (1964)." Applying this standard, we hold that no error of law or abuse of discretion was committed by the New Hope Board of Adjustment, and that therefore the Court of Common Pleas of Bucks County must be reversed.

I.

Approximately one year before the PUD seed was planted in New Hope, Borough Council had approved the New Hope Comprehensive Plan. This detailed land use projection clearly envisioned the Rauch tract as containing only single family dwellings of low density. The court below therefore concluded that the enactment of ordinance 160, and more specifically the placing of a PUD district on the Rauch tract by ordinance 161 was not "in accordance with a comprehensive plan," as required by the Act of February 1, 1966, P.L. (1965)— § 3203, 53 P.S. § 48203. See also Eves v. Zoning Bd. of Adjustment, 401 Pa. 211, 164 A.2d 7 (1960).

[3] The fallacy in the court's reasoning lies in its mistaken belief that a comprehensive plan, once established, is forever binding on the municipality and can never be amended. Cases subsequent to *Eves* have made it clear, however, that these plans may be changed by the passage of new zoning ordinances, provided the local legislature passes the new ordinance with some demonstration of sensitivity to the community as a whole, and the impact that the new ordinance will have on this community. As Mr. Chief Justice Bell so artfully stated in Furniss v. Lower Merion Twp., 412 Pa. 404, 406, 194 A.2d 926, 927 (1963): "It is a matter of common sense and reality that a comprehensive plan is not like the law of the Medes and the Persians; it must be subject to reasonable change from time to time as conditions in an area or a township or a large neighborhood change." This salutary rule that comprehensive plans may be later amended by the passage of new zoning ordinances has been approved not only in *Furniss*, but also in Donahue v. Zoning Bd. of Adjustment, 412 Pa. 332, 194 A.2d 610 (1963) and Key Realty Co. Zoning Case, 408 Pa. 98, 182 A.2d 187 (1962).

[4] Given this rule of law allowing post-plan zoning changes, and the presumption in favor of an ordinance's validity, see *National Land*, supra, 421 Pa. at 521-522, 215 A.2d at 607, we are not in a position, having reviewed the record in the present case, to say that the zoning board committed an abuse of discretion or an error of law when it concluded that ordinances 160 and 161 were properly passed. Presented as it was with evidence that the PUD district had been under consideration by council

for over six months and had been specifically recommended by the borough planning commission, a body specially equipped to view proposed ordinances as they relate to the rest of the community, we hold that the board, with its sound discretion, could have concluded that council passed the ordinances with the proper overall conditions in mind. The PUD district established by ordinance 160 is not the type of use which by its very nature could have no place in the middle of a predominantly residential borough. It is not a steel mill, a fat rendering plant, or a desiccated egg factory. It is, in fact, nothing more than a miniature residential community.

Closely tied to the comprehensive plan issue is the argument raised by appellees that ordinances 160 and 161 constitute spot zoning outlawed by *Eves*, supra. Given the fact situation in *Eves*, however, as well as the post-*Eves* cases, we do not believe that there is any spot zoning here. In *Eves*, the municipality created a limited industrial district, F-1, which, by explicit legislative pronouncement, was not to be applied to any particular tract until the individual land owner requested that his own tract be so re-zoned. The obvious evil in this procedure did *not* lie in the fact that a limited industrial district might be placed in an area previously zoned, for example, residential. The evil was the *pre-ordained* uncertainty as to where the F-1 districts would crop up. The ordinance all but invited spot zoning where the legislature could respond to private entreaties from land owners and re-zone tracts F-1 without regard to the surrounding community. In *Eves*, it was almost impossible for the F-1 districts to conform to a comprehensive plan since tracts would be re-zoned on a strictly ad hoc basis.

[5] Quite to the contrary, no such "floating zone" exists in the present case. On the very day that the PUD district was created by ordinance 160, it was brought to earth by ordinance 161; and, as discussed supra, this *was* done "in accordance with a comprehensive plan." Speaking of a similar procedure in Donahue v. Zoning Bd. of Adjustment, 412 Pa. 332, 194 A.2d 610 (1963), this Court faced squarely an attack based upon *Eves* and responded thusly:

> "It was this case by case review [in *Eves*] which demonstrated the absence of a comprehensive plan and which sought to enable the Board of Supervisors [the local legislative body] to exercise powers they did not statutorily possess.
>
> In the instant case, the new classification was established and the zoning map amended within a very short period of time [in the case at bar, on the same day]. Under the rules of statutory construction which are likewise applicable to ordinances, see Cloverleaf Trailer Sales Co. v. Pleasant Hills Borough, 366 Pa. 116, 76 A.2d 872 (1950); Philadelphia to Use of Polselli v. Phillips, 179 Pa.Super. 87, 116 A.2d 243 (1955); these ordinances should be read together as one enactment. See Statutory Construction Act, May 28, 1937, P.L. 1019, § 62, 46 P.S. § 562, 1952. So construed, Ordinances 151 [creating new zone] and 155 [amending zoning map] do not create the 'floating zone,' anchored only upon case by case application by landowners, which we struck down in *Eves*. While it is true that the

change here was made upon request of a particular landowner, this does not necessarily create the evils held invalid in *Eves* where the defects were specifically created by the very terms of the ordinances. It is not unusual for a zoning change to be made on request of a landowner, and such change is not invalid if made in accordance with a comprehensive plan." 412 Pa. at 334-335, 194 A.2d at 611.

We think *Donahue* is completely controlling on the issue of alleged spot zoning and compels the conclusion that ordinances 160 and 161 do not fall on that ground. See also the excellent discussion of *Eves* and its progeny in Krasnowiecki, Legal Aspects of Planned Unit Development, Technical Bull. 52, Urban Land Institute, pp. 20-22 (1965).

II.

The court below next concluded that even if the two ordinances were properly *passed*, they must fall as vesting authority in the planning commission greater than that permitted under Pennsylvania's zoning enabling legislation. More specifically, it is now contended by appellees that complete project approval by the planning commission under ordinance 160 requires that commission to encroach upon legislative territory whenever it decides where, within a particular PUD district, specific types of building should be placed.

In order to appreciate fully the arguments of counsel on both sides it is necessary to explain in some detail exactly what is permitted within a PUD district, and who decides whether a particular land owner has complied with these requirements. Admittedly the range of permissible uses within the PUD district is greater than that normally found in a traditional zoning district. Within a New Hope PUD district there may be: single family attached or detached dwellings; apartments; accessory private garages; public or private parks and recreation areas including golf courses, swimming pools, ski slopes, etc. (so long as these facilities do not produce noise, glare, odor, air pollution, etc., detrimental to existing or prospective adjacent structures); a municipal building; a school; churches; art galleries; professional offices; certain types of signs; a theatre (but not a drive-in); motels and hotels; and a restaurant. The ordinance then sets certain overall density requirements. The PUD district may have a maximum of 80% of the land devoted to residential uses, a maximum of 20% for the permitted commercial uses and enclosed recreational facilities, and must have a minimum of 20% for open spaces. The residential density shall not exceed 10 units per acre, nor shall any such unit contain more than two bedrooms. All structures within the district must not exceed maximum height standards set out in the ordinance. Finally, although there are no traditional "set back" and "side yard" requirements, ordinance 160 does require that there be 24 feet between structures, and that no townhouse structure contain more than 12 dwelling units.

The procedure to be followed by the aspiring developer reduces itself to presenting a detailed plan for his planned unit development to the planning commission obtaining that body's approval and then securing building permits. Of course, the planning commission may not approve any development that fails to meet the requirements set forth in the ordinance as outlined above.

[6] We begin with the observation that there is nothing in the borough zoning enabling act which would prohibit council from creating a zoning district with this many permissible uses. The applicable section of the borough code is the Act of February 1, 1966, P.L. (1965)—§ 3201, 53 P.S. § 48201. Under this section, council is given the power to regulate and restrict practically all aspects of buildings themselves, open spaces, population density, location of structures, etc., the only limitation on this power being that it be exercised so as to promote the "health, safety, morals or the general welfare" of the borough. Under the same act, section 1601, 53 P.S. § 46601, empowers council to adopt ordinances to govern the use of public areas, such as streets, parks, etc., again with the only limitation being that such ordinances create "conditions favorable to the health, safety, morals and general welfare of the citizens." Thus, if council reasonably believed that a given district could contain *all* types of structures, without *any* density requirements whatsoever, so long as this did not adversely affect health, safety and morals, such a district could be created. In fact, it is common knowledge that in many industrial and commercial districts just such a wide range of uses is permitted. Given such broad power to zone, we cannot say that New Hope Borough Council abrogated its legislative function by creating a PUD district permitting the mixture of uses outlined supra, especially given the density requirements.

We must next examine the statutory power of the borough planning commission to determine whether such an administrative body may regulate the internal development of a PUD district. The Act of February 1, 1966, P.L. (1965)—§ 1155, 53 P.S. § 46155 requires that all plans for land "laid out in building lots" be approved by the planning commission before they may be recorded. Thus, the traditional job of the commission has been to examine tract plans to determine whether they conform to the applicable borough ordinances. The ordinances most frequently interpreted and applied by the planning commission are those dealing with streets, sewers, water and gas mains, etc., i. e., the so-called public improvements. However, the statute contains no language which would prohibit the planning commission from approving plans with reference to ordinances dealing with permissible building uses as well. The primary reason that planning commissions have not traditionally interpreted this type of ordinance is that such regulations do not usually come into play until the landowner wishes to begin the actual construction of a particular building. By this time, the relevant subdivision plan has already been approved by the commission; thus the task of examining the plans for a particular structure to see whether it conforms to the regulations for the zoning district in which it will be erected devolves upon the local building inspector who issues the building permit.

However, in the case of PUD the entire development (including specific structures) is mapped out and submitted to the administrative agency at once. Accordingly, the requirements set forth in a PUD ordinance must relate not only to those areas traditionally administered by the planning commission, but also to areas traditionally administered by the building inspector. Therefore, quite logically, the job of approving a particular PUD should rest with a single municipal body. The question then is simply which one: Borough Council (a legislative body), the Planning Commission (an administrative body), or the Zoning Board of Adjustment (an administrative body)?

There is no doubt that it would be statutorily permissible for council itself to pass a PUD ordinance and simultaneous zoning map amendment so specific that no details would be left for any administrator. The ordinance could specify where each building should be placed, how large it should be, where the open spaces are located, etc. But what would be the practical effect of such an ordinance? One of the most attractive features of Planned Unit Development is its flexibility; the chance for the builder and the municipality to sit down together and tailor a development to meet the specific needs of the community and the requirements of the land on which it is to be built. But all this would be lost if the Legislature let the planning cement set before any developer could happen upon the scene to scratch his own initials in that cement. Professor Krasnowiecki has accurately summed up the effect on planned unit development of such legislative planning. The picture, to be sure, is not a happy one:

> "The traditional refuge of the courts, the requirement that all the standards be set forth in advance of application for development, does not offer a practical solution to the problem. The complexity of pre-established regulations that would automatically dispose of any proposal for planned unit development, when different housing types and perhaps accessory commercial areas are envisaged, would be quite considerable. Indeed as soon as various housing types are permitted, the regulations that would govern their design and distribution on every possible kind of site, their relationship to each other and their relationship to surrounding properties must be complex unless the developer's choice in terms of site, site plan, and design and distribution of housing is reduced close to zero. It is not likely * * * that local authorities would want to adopt such a set of regulations." Krasnowiecki, Planned Unit Development: A Challenge to Established Theory and Practice of Land Use Control, 114 U. Pa.L.Rev. 47, 72 (1965).

Left with Professor Krasnowiecki's "Hobson's choice" of no developer leeway at all, or a staggering set of legislative regulations sufficient to cover every idea the developer might have, it is not likely that Planned Unit

Development could thrive, or even maintain life, if the local legislature assumed totally the role of planner.

[7] The remaining two municipal bodies which could oversee the shaping of specific Planned Unit Developments are both administrative agencies, the Zoning Board of Adjustment and the Planning Commission. As this Court views both reality and zoning enabling act, the Zoning Board of Adjustment is not the proper body. The Act of February 1, 1966, P.L. (1965)—§ 3207, 53 P.S. § 48207(g) specifically sets forth the powers of a borough zoning board of adjustment. These powers are three in number, and only three. The board may (1) hear and decide appeals where there is an alleged error made by an administrator in the enforcement of the enabling act or any ordinance enacted pursuant thereto; (2) hear and decide special exceptions; and (3) authorize the grant of variance from the terms of existing ordinances. These powers in no way encompass the authority to review and approve the plan for an entire development when such plan is neither at variance with the existing ordinance nor is a special exception to it; nor does (1) above supply the necessary power since the board would not be reviewing an alleged administrative error.

[8] Moreover, from a practical standpoint, a zoning board of adjustment is, of the three bodies here under discussion, the one least equipped to handle the problem of PUD approval. Zoning boards are accustomed to focusing on one lot at a time. They traditionally examine hardship cases and unique uses proposed by landowners. As Professor Krasnowiescki has noted: "To suggest that the board is intended, or competent, to handle large scale planning and design decisions is, I think, far fetched." Technical Bulletin 52, Urban Land Institute, p. 38 (1965). We agree.

Thus, the borough planning commission remains the only other body both qualified and statutorily permitted to approve PUD. Of course, we realize that a planning commission is not authorized to engage in actual re-zoning of land. But merely because the commission here has the power to approve more than one type of building for a particular lot within the PUD district does not means that the commission is usurping the zoning function. Indeed, it is acting in strict *accordance* with the applicable zoning ordinance, for that ordinance, No. 160, *permits* more than one type of building for a particular lot. To be sure, if the commission approved a plan for a PUD district where 30% of the land were being used commercially, *then* we would have an example of illegal re-zoning by an administrator. But no one argues in the present case that appellant's plan does not conform to the requirements of ordinance 160.

[9] Nor is this Court sympathetic to appellees' argument that ordinance 160 permits the planning commission to grant variances and special exceptions. We fail to see how a development such as appellant's that meets every single requirement of the applicable zoning ordinance can be said to be the product of a variance or a special exception. The very essence of variances and special exceptions lies in their *departure* from ordinance

requirements, not in their compliance with them. We therefore conclude that the New Hope Planning Commission has the power to approve development plans submitted to it under ordinance 160.

*   *   *

BELL, C. J., took no part in the consideration or decision of this case.

CROSS-REFERENCES

In Anderson, see §§ 8.22-8.32, 26.60-26.61.

In Hagman, see Index under "Zones" and "Zoning," and ch. 17.

In McQuillin, see Index under "Residential Districts."

In Rathkopf, see ch. 14-6, ch. 71-43 and 71-45, and Index under "Residence District."

In Williams, see ch. 82-93, and ch. 48.

In Yokley, see § 28 and 1975 Cumulative Supplement, §§ 3-7 and 3-8.

Section 9

Commercial Zoning

MURPHY MOTOR SALES, INC.

v.

FIRST NATIONAL BANK OF ST. JOHNSBURY

122 Vt. 121, 165 A.2d 341 (1960).

Supreme Court of Vermont.

Nov. 1, 1960.

Suit in equity to restrain defendant from moving diner onto property located in residential zone. The Court of Chancery, Caledonia County, F. Ray Keyser, Sr., P. J., dismissed the complaint, and an appeal was taken. The Supreme Court, Shangraw, J., held that where prohibited uses of property in residential district were clearly set forth in St. Johnsbury zoning regulation which was specific as to prohibited uses, describing them, there was no room for construction, and in absence of any reference therein to diners, operation of diner on premises located in residential zone was not prohibited thereby.

Affirmed.

John A. Swainbank, St. Johnsbury, for plaintiff.

Arthur L. Graves, James B. Campbell, St. Johnsbury, for defendant.

Before HULBURD, C. J., and HOLDEN, SHANGRAW, BARNEY and SMITH, JJ.

SHANGRAW, Justice.

This is a suit in equity seeking to restrain the defendant from moving a diner which it owns onto the premises of Sherman R. Warren, and his wife Thea R. Warren, at 69 Portland Street in the Village of St. Johnsbury, Vermont. The bill of complaint alleges that the Warren property is located in a residential zone, and that the operation of the diner in such residential zone is contrary to the force, effect, intent and spirit of the zoning regulations of the Village. One phase of this case was before this court at the January Term, 1960 on another issue, and the appeal was dismissed for jurisdictional reasons. 121 Vt. 403, 159 A.2d 94.

The defendant filed its answer and demurrer. A temporary restraining order was issued and upon hearing was dissolved June 23, 1959. On March 18, 1960 the chancellor made a decree sustaining the demurrer and dismissing the complaint. While several grounds were set forth in the demurrer the principal issue presented is the question of whether the zoning regulations restrict the placing of a restaurant, diner or eating establishment in the area in question.

The plaintiff owns and operates a motel on the south side of Portland Street immediately west of the house lots of Sherman R. Warren and Thea R. Warren. The plaintiff's motel is not in a residential zone. Plaintiff makes no claim that the operation of the diner will be a nuisance per se, or that it will be operated contrary to the standards of the State Board of Health. Since the bringing of this bill of complaint the diner has been moved to the Warren premises.

The zoning ordinances under consideration were originally enacted by the village December 12, 1930, and subsequently amended and effective June 24, 1953. There are three residential zones and seven industrial zones set up by the regulations. All other sections of the village are trading zones. The Warren property is in an area designated as a residential zone.

Section 1 of the zoning regulations declares that the territory within the corporate limits "is divided into use districts or zones" and subsequent sections set forth the bounds of the residential and other zones. Section 13 is specific as to the prohibited uses, describing them, of property within a residential zone. It is a prohibitive form of a zoning regulation, and contains no prohibition or reference to a restaurant, diner, or quick-lunch room.

The plaintiff's contention is that section 13 excludes all business activity whatsoever from a residential zone, and that a diner or quick-lunch room is a non-residential or commercial enterprise.

Section 13 does not contain a general exclusion, or saving clause, such as stating at the outset that no business or manufacturing establishment, etc., or other appropriate words, shall be maintained or conducted within a residential area. The types of business prohibited are clear. The prohibited uses are set forth clearly, and there is no room for construction of this zoning regulation. Had the village intended to prohibit a diner in a residential zone it could have said so. There are many business activities that are not mentioned in section 13 some of which are equally as objectionable as those prohibited.

[1] Quoting from 58 Am.Jur. Zoning, § 73, page 988, "The rule has been laid down that where a zoning ordinance provides merely that certain specified trades, businesses, or uses shall not be permitted in a specified zone any business other than those expressly excluded may be conducted therein,

provided it is so carried on as not to be in and of itself a nuisance." Citing Kirk v. Mabis, 215 Iowa 769, 246 N.W. 759, 87 A.L.R. 1055. A court may not legislate in the guise of construction, and may not insert in a zoning regulation a provision not included by the legislative body. Glass v. Zoning Board of Appeals, City of Yonkers, 5 A.D.2d 991, 173 N.Y.S.2d 448, 450.

[2, 3] Zoning laws which curtail and limit uses of real property must be given a strict construction, since they are in derogation of common law rights, and provisions thereof may not be extended by implication. In re Willey, 120 Vt. 359, 365, 140 A.2d 11; 440 E. 102nd St. Corp. v. Murdock, 285 N.Y. 298, 34 N.E.2d 329; Toulouse v. Board of Zoning Adjustment, 147 Me. 387, 87 A.2d 670, 673; 8 McQuillin Municipal Corporations (3rd Ed.) 25, 72 p. 162. Any ambiguity or uncertainty must be decided in favor of the property owner. Kubby v. Hammond, 68 Ariz. 17, 22, 198 P.2d 134; City of Little Rock v. Williams, 206 Ark. 861, 177 S.W.2d 924.

[4-7] We have here a zoning regulation having the force and effect of a legislative enactment. Village of St. Johnsbury v. Aron, 103 Vt. 22, 151 A. 650. In construing such a regulation the general rule applicable to the construction of statutes applies. 101 C.J.S. Zoning § 128, p. 881. Where the meaning of a statute is plain, courts have the duty to enforce the statute according to its obvious terms, and there is no necessity for construction. Blanchard v. Blanchard's Est., 109 Vt. 454, 199 A. 233. Furthermore, great care should be exercised by the court not to expand proper construction of a statute into judicial legislation. State v. Reynolds, 109 Vt. 308, 310, 1 A.2d 730.

[8] The bill of complaint alleges that the Warrens intend to operate the diner when moved. Therefore, going to the heart of the controversy, we have considered the case in this light, rather than merely passing upon the limited question as to whether the mere moving of the diner by the defendant was prohibited by the zoning regulations. In view of the governing principles stated in this opinion, and applicable here, we hold that the operation of the diner in question on the Warren premises located in a residential zone is not prohibited by section 13 of the zoning regulations of the Village of St. Johnsbury. With this view of the case it is not necessary to pass upon the indispensability of Mr. and Mrs. Warren as parties in this proceeding.

The decretal order sustaining the demurrer and dismissing the bill of complaint is affirmed.

Questions and Notes

1. What provisions in the local zoning law led to this odd result?
2. Was the decision technically correct?

MARSHALL

v.

SALT LAKE CITY

105 Utah 111, 141 P.2d 704.

Supreme Court of Utah.

Sept. 25, 1943.

Appeal from District Court, Third District, Salt Lake County; B. P. Leverich, Judge.

Action by H. L. Marshall against Salt Lake City and the Mayor and Commissioners thereof to enjoin issuance of permits to erect business buildings on certain lands in a residential district of defendant city. From a judgment granting a permanent injunction, defendants appeal.

Reversed and remanded.

E. R. Christensen, Gerald Irvine, and A. Pratt Kesler, all of Salt Lake City for appellants.

Hurd & Hurd and E. A. Walton, all of Salt Lake City, for respondent.

LARSON, Justice.

Can a city, as a part of a general zoning plan, create small general utility zones throughout residential districts, for the purpose of placing within convenient distance of the inhabitants of the residential district certain small businesses, handling daily conveniences and necessities for the home?

That is the real question involved in this appeal. The questions presented on the record, and argued as grounds for reversal of the judgment, are more specific, and may be stated thus:

1. Was the court in error in hearing the matter under plaintiff's pleadings?

2. Is the citys' zoning plan, as evidenced by the zoning ordinance, invalid under the statutes?

3. Was the city's power to zone limited by the contractual business restrictions in the recorded deed to the property owned by Gibbs?

Plaintiff commenced this action at the instigation of a group of residents of the southeast bench section of Salt Lake City, for the purpose of obtaining an interpretation by the court, of certain provisions of the zoning ordinance of Salt Lake City. That ordinance had its historic origin prior to 1920, when the city commission, by ordinance, established a city planning commission and commenced the preparation of a comprehensive zoning plan.

Tentative plans were prepared by 1924, and a series of sectional and general public meetings held from May 1925 to September 1927, during which time the sectional plans were consolidated into one general zoning plan for the whole city. In 1925, the State Legislature enacted a law granting to Utah cities the power to zone the cities and make regulations governing the same. This was known as Chap. 119, Laws of Utah 1925;

became Art. 3, Chap. 15, R.S.U.1933; now U.C.A. 1943, Title 15, Chap. 8, Art. 3. In May 1927, pursuant to this statute, the city commission enacted an ordinance creating a city zoning commission. The zoning commission, after public hearing, submitted to the city commission a plan for the zoning of the city into Use Districts. In August 1927, the city commission adopted an ordinance embodying such zoning plan and regulations governing the same, dividing the city into seven Use Districts, designated as: 1. Residential "A". 2. Residential "B". 3. Residential "B2". 4. Residential "C". 5. Commercial. 6. Industrial. 7. Unrestricted. The only uses permitted in Residential "A" districts were one and two family private dwellings, schools, churches, libraries, parks, farming and truck gardening. Uses permitted in Residential "C" districts, in addition to all uses permitted in Residential "A", included retail shops, fire and police stations, banks, theatres, lunch rooms, drug stores, shoe repair shops, barber shops, garages and service stations. These are the only two district classifications with which we are concerned in this action. The southeast bench section of the city, being that part east of Thirteenth East Street, and south of Sunnyside Avenue, is generally, with the exceptions hereinafter noted, and which give rise to the action classified and designated as Residential "A". At that time it was sparsely settled, and within it were four places where there was small residential utility business operating. The main thoroughfares in the section, which are designated in the city's traffic regulations as "through streets", were 9th, 13th, and 17th South Streets, and 13th, 15th, 17th and 21st East Streets. The zoning ordinance designated as Residential "C" that land then being used for business uses permitted in Residential "C", and also designated as Residential "C" a small area on each corner of the intersections of the aforementioned main thoroughfares in the district.

The plaintiff is the owner of Lots 2, 3, and 4 (50 foot lots) facing west on 17th East Street; the north side of said lots being 51 feet south of the southeast corner of the intersection of 13th South Street and 17th East Street. Plaintiff owned these lots prior to the adoption of the zoning ordinance, at which time there was a dwelling house on the center lot (No. 3). In 1931, after the adoption of the zoning ordinance, the house was enlarged so part of it was placed upon No. 2, the north lot. Lot No. 1, the corner lot, north of plaintiff's property was owned by one Callister, and will hereafter be referred to as the Callister property, and with Lot 2, the north lot of plaintiff, and the property on the other corners of this street intersection, were zoned as Residential "C", and were later in 1936 rezoned as Residential "B3", a new classification more restricted than "C", in that it did not permit garages.

The classification of these last mentioned lots so as to permit uses other than family dwellings is the redoubt upon which plaintiff first concentrated his heavy artillery.

The other land involved in the action, and upon the classification of which plaintiff directed his second assault, involved thirteen lots at 19th

East Street and Hubbard Avenue, two blocks east and four blocks north of plaintiff's property, and will hereafter be referred to as the Gibbs property. This property, with other lands immediately abutting it, was at one time owned by the Douglas Heights Land and Improvement Company. By warranty deed, recorded in the office of the County Recorder of Salt Lake County, February 1, 1913, in Book "8G" of Deeds, it conveyed to the Hubbard Investment Company some of those lands, including the Gibbs property. The deed contained certain building restrictions, one reading "nor shall any building for business purposes be erected on any of said land." As far as the records show, the building restrictions have never been abrogated, modified or changed. This property, all vacant, was originally zoned as Residential "A". By amendment to the ordinances in 1936, the Gibbs property, along with the Callister property and plaintiff's north lot, was rezoned as Residential "B3". In 1939 Callister and Gibbs made applications to the city for permits to erect upon their respective tracts, types of buildings permitted in Residential "B3", but not permitted in Residential "A". This action, to enjoin such buildings, resulted.

The trial court found for plaintiff and issued a permanent injunction. Defendant appeals. Hereinafter, the parties will be referred to as "Plaintiff'" and "the City". From the factual background we consider in order the three propositions wherewith the city assails the judgment.

1. Plaintiff's first complaint in a single cause of action assailed and challenged the validity of the original zoning ordinance, and of each amending ordinance, on grounds specified in the complaint, directed at the passage of the ordinances, and also at their substance, as being ambiguous, unworkable, and not understandable. It asserted that said ordinances and each of them were wholly null and void; that the city was without any authority to grant the permits sought by Callister and Gibbs; and prayed for a permanent injunction. Defendants demurred to the complaint. Without a ruling on the demurrer, plaintiff filed an amended complaint, setting up two causes of action. The first cause of action pleads the zoning ordinances as generally valid, but assails that part of the ordinance which created within Residential "A" Districts small districts classed Residential "C" and Residential "B3", as beyond the power of the city, and a violation of the statute providing for zoning upon grounds specifically set out, which covers generally the grounds upon which the zoning ordinances in toto were assailed in the original complaint, with some further grounds added. This cause of action is confined and directed rather definitely to the classification of the Callister and other property at the intersection of 13th South and 17th East Streets, as Residential "C" or Residential "B3". The second cause of action in the amended complaint is directed at the action and ordinance reclassifying or redesignating the Gibbs property on Hubbard Avenue as Residential "B3".

*   *   *

2. Are those provisions of the city zoning ordinances which place the Callister property and the Gibbs property in class Residential "C" or Residential "B3" invalid? The trial court held them invalid as beyond the power granted the city by the statute, and as unreasonable, unlawful, discriminatory and void for five specified grounds set out in the findings. As to the Gibbs property, the court also found that the land was, by deed, under certain building restrictions which prohibited erection of any business building thereon. The city assails these findings as to every point in urging a reversal of the judgment.

Were the city zoning ordinances to the extent that they provided for small spot Residential "C" or Residential "B3" districts within Residential "A" districts a violation of the statute requiring a comprehensive zoning plan? The point argued here is whether the provisions of the ordinance creating these very small areas for limited business purposes detached from "C" or "B3" districts constitute "spot zoning", and not zoning by districts. The statute authorizing city zoning was first enacted in Chapter 119, Laws of Utah 1925. It has remained unchanged, and is now Article 3 of Chapter 8, Title 15, U.C.A.1943, being sections 15-8-89 to 15-8-107. It provides:

15-8-89. "* * * the legislative body of cities and towns is empowered to regulate * * * the location and use of buildings, structures, and land for trade, industry, residence or other purposes."

15-8-90. "* * * the legislative body may *divide the municipality into districts* of such number, shape and area as may be deemed best suited to carry out the purposes of this article, * * *"

15-8-91. "Regulations to Comprehensive Plan. Such regulations shall be made *in accordance with a comprehensive* plan, designed to lessen congestion in the streets, to secure safety from fire, panic and other dangers, to promote health and general welfare, to provide adequate light and air, to prevent the overcrowding of land, to avoid undue concentration of population, to facilitate adequate provision for transportation, water, sewage, schools, parks and other public requirements. Such regulations shall be made with reasonable consideration, among other things, to the character of the district and its peculiar suitability for particular uses, and with a view to conserving the value of buildings and encouraging the most appropriate use of land throughout the city."

15-8-92. "The legislative body municipality shall provide for the manner in which such regulations and restrictions and the boundaries of such districts shall be determined, established and enforced, and from time to time amended, supplemented or changed. * * *"

The trial court held and the city assails that holding, that the statutory requirement that the city be divided into *Use Districts* has implicit in it the idea that districts shall be of considerable size, and intersection corners do not constitute a district as used in the statute. It was also held that "a comprehensive plan" implied that districts must be comprehensive, that is, of considerable size. The trial Court took the position that small areas like those here involved constituted "spot zoning" or "lot zoning", and therefore permitted in restricted districts uses and conditions which the zoning statute sought to prevent. As shown by the above quotes from the statute, the city is authorized to regulate and restrict "the *location and use* of buildings, structures and land for trade, industry, residence and other purposes" and to accomplish this "may divide the municipality into *Districts* of such number, shape and area as may be deemed best suited to carry out the purposes of this Article." (Italics ours) This is done under the police power and by the statute must be done in accordance with a comprehensive plan, designed, inter alia, to lessen congestion in the street, promote the general welfare, facilitate transportation, and other public requirements. It shall be done with reasonable consideration of the character of the district, its suitability for particular uses "and with a view to conserving * * * and encouraging the most appropriate use of land." Sec. 15-8-91, supra. That the statute contemplates a division and regulation by *districts,* instead of regulation by single lots or small groups of lots, is evident. The regulation of the use of property by lots or by very small areas is not zoning and does violence to the purpose and provisions of the statute. It would not, and could not, accomplish the purpose of the law as set forth in the statute quoted supra. *Wippler v. Hohn,* 341 Mo. 780, 110 S.W.2d 409; *Mueller v. C. Hoffmeister Undertaking & Livery Co.,* 343 Mo. 430, 121 S.W.2d 775; *Guaranty Const. Co. v. Town of Bloomfield,* 168 A. 34, 11 N.J.Misc. 613; *Linden Methodist Episcopal Church v. City of Linden,* 113 N.J.L. 188, 173 A. 593; *Huebner v. Philadelphia Sav. Fund Soc.,* 127 Pa.Super. 28, 192 A. 139; *Wickham v. Becker,* 96 Cal.App. 443, 274 P. 397. But it does not necessarily follow that what was here done constitutes "spot zoning" or is violative of the statute. Historically speaking, the leading case on zoning is *Euclid, Ohio, v. Ambler Realty Co.,* 272 U.S. 365, 395, 47 S.Ct. 114, 121, 71 L.Ed. 303, 54 A.L.R. 1016, which established the constitutionality of comprehensive zoning plans. It is there said:

"It is enough for us to determine, as we do, that the ordinance in its general scope and dominant features, so far as it provisions are here involved, is a valid exercise of authority, leaving other provisions to be dealt with as cases arise directly involving them. * * *

"The exclusion of buildings devoted to business, trade, etc. from residential districts, bears a rational relation to the health and safety of the community. Some of the grounds for this conclusion are promotion of the health and security from injury of children and others by separating dwelling houses from territory devoted to trade and industry; suppression and prevention of disorder; facilitating the extinguishment of fires, and the enforcement of street traffic regulations and other general welfare ordinances; aiding the health and safety of the community, by excluding from residential areas the confusion and danger of fire, contagion, and disorder, which in greater or less degree attach to the location of stores, shops, and factories. Another ground is that the construction and repair of streets may be rendered easier and less expensive, by confining the greater part of the heavy traffic to the streets where business is carried on. * * *

"The segregation of industries, commercial pursuits, and dwellings to particular districts in a city, when exercised reasonably may bear a rational relation to the health, morals, safety, and general welfare of the community. The establishment of such districts or zones may, among other things, prevent congestion of population, secure quiet residence districts, expedite local transportation, and facilitate the suppression of disorder, the extinguishment of fires, and the enforcement of traffic and sanitary regulations. The danger of fire and the risk of contagion are often lessened by the exclusion of stores and factories from areas devoted to residences, and, in consequence, the safety and health of the community may be promoted. * * *

"* * * The exclusion of places of business from residential districts is not a declaration that such places are nuisances or that they are to be suppressed as such, but it is a part of the general plan by which the city's territory is allotted to different uses, in order to prevent, or at least to reduce, the congestion, disorder, and dangers which often inhere in unregulated municipal development."

To the same effect is *State v. City of New Orleans*, 154 La. 271, 97 So. 440, 33 A.L.R. 260. See also *Salt Lake City v. Western Foundry & Stove Repair Works*, 55 Utah 447, 187 P. 829; *Smith v. Barrett*, 81 Utah 522, 20 P.2d 864; *Feraut v. City of Sacramento*, 204 Cal. 687, 269 P. 537.

City zoning is authorized only as an exercise of the police power of the state. It must therefore have for its purposes and objectives matters which come within the province of the police power. When exercised by a city, it is of necessity confined by the limitations fixed in the grant by the state, and to accomplishment of the purposes for which the state authorized the city to zone. Those purposes, which control and must be subserved by any zoning, are set forth in Section 15-8-91, U.C.A. 1943, quoted *supra*. The elements required of a zoning plan are: It must be comprehensive; it must be designed to protect the health, safety, and morals of the inhabitants; to promote the general welfare; avoid overcrowding and congestion in traffic and population; facilitate transportation and other public service; and meet the ordinary or common requirements of happy convenient and comfortable living by the inhabitants of the districts, and the city as a whole. A zoning plan should not be jettisoned merely because it may be vulnerable to attack from one of these "pill boxes". It must be considered as a whole to see if it is designed to accomplish such purpose; if it could promote the general welfare; or even if it is reasonably debatable that it is in the interest of the general welfare, that act should be upheld. The wisdom of the plan, the necessity for zoning, the number and nature of the districts to be created, the boundaries thereof and the uses therein permitted, are matters which lie in the discretion of the governing body of the city. Unless the action of such body is arbitrary, discriminatory or unreasonable, or clearly offends some provision of the constitution or statute, the court must uphold it, if within the grant of power to the municipality. *Miller v. Board of Public Works,* 195 Cal. 477, 234 P. 381, 38 A.L.R. 1479; *Sundeen v. Rogers,* 83 N.H. 253, 141 A. 142, 57 A.L.R. 950; *Mehlos v. City of Milwaukee,* 156 Wis. 591, 146 N.W. 882, 51 L.R.A.,N.S., 1009, Ann.Cas.1915C, 1102; *Euclid, Ohio, v. Ambler Realty, supra.*

The basic purpose of zoning is to "bring about an orderly development of cities, to establish districts into which business, commerce, and industry shall not intrude, and to fix certain territory for different grades of industrial concerns. * * * The exercise [of this power] must have a substantial relation to the public good within the spheres held proper." *White's Appeal,* 287 Pa. 259, 134 A. 409, 412, 53 A.L.R. 1215. "It is a fundamental theory of the zoning scheme that it shall be for the general good, to secure reasonable neighborhood uniformity, and to exclude structures and occupations which clash therewith." *Guaranty Const. Co. v. Town of Bloomfield, supra.* See also in *Linden M. E. Church v. City of Linden, supra; Sugar v. North Baltimore Methodist Protestant Church,* 164 Md. 487, 165 A.703.

It is primarily the duty of the city to make the classifications. If a classification is reasonably doubtful, the judgment of the court will not be substituted for the judgment of the city. *Wippler v. Hohn,* 341 Mo. 780, 110 S.W.2d 409. But the principle is fundamental that the city, in zoning, must do so by districts and not by *indiscriminate* spot zoning. *Mueller v. C. Hoffmeister Undertaking & Livery Co., supra.* But the requirement that zoning be by districts does not require that districts be confined and rigidly limited to one particular type of use.

Zoning is done for the benefit of the city as a whole, and the limitations imposed on respective districts must be done with a view to the benefit of the district as a whole, and not from consideration of particular tracts. *Michigan-Lake Bldg. Corp. v. Hamilton,* 340 Ill. 284, 172 N.E. 710; *Wippler v. Hohn, supra; Mueller v. C. Hoffmeister Undertaking & Livery Co., supra.* Said the Massachusetts court in *Leahy v. Inspector of Buildings of City of New Bedford,* 308 Mass. 128, 31 N.E.2d 436, 438: "The establishment of zoning districts is based upon the physical characteristics of substantial areas and their suitability for use for certain purposes in view of the present and future requirements of the public health, morals, safety and general welfare."

Metzenbaum in his Law of Zoning, page 144, after discussing the need for zoning ordinances to eliminate the evils of "mixed" streets and intermingled classes of uses, prophetically views the future when he says:

"The benefits of preceding legislation would be defeated and would prove to be of comparatively little view in meeting the newest conditions of American life, unless the police power would prove elastic enough to meet these most recently created conditions.

"Today a much broader line of procedure is required, a wider course of action and a *more far reaching plan,* if the welfare of the people is to be safeguarded, and this broad, wide and embracing plan, finds not a panacea, but its best expression, and its wisest utilization in regulating the use for which territories may be employed."

And again, on page 129, the same author speaking of the creation of districts says: "In a comprehensive plan, the whole territory of the municipality is divided into districts some of which may be large, some small * * * each with its own standards of use, height and occupancy; each selected by the consideration of the community health and general welfare as applied to that particular district; the whole constituting a comprehensive plan for the best manner of conserving and assuring the greatest safety and welfare of the entire community."

In *Smith v. Collison,* 119 Cal.App. 180, 6 P.2d 277, 278, the California Court said: "Comprehensive zoning is regulation with forethought to a uniform plan or design to restrict construction and development reasonable and with fairness to each district."

Metzenbaum, on page 149, says it is "a use districting *reasonably applied* in order to protect the public welfare, safety and health." The California Court in *Miller v. Board of Public Works, supra* [195 Cal. 477, 234 P. 388, 38 A.L.R. 1479], said that the plan must tend to promote the health, safety, morals, and general welfare of the community, in such a way as "will redound to the welfare of the city as a whole". The preservation of the public health, morals, safety and welfare are not to be determined or gauged in dollars and cents alone, nor in protection from contagious diseases or moral charlatans. The public health involves the preservation of the mental, moral, and civic health of the inhabitants as well as physical health. A citizenry mentally alert and alive to the interests of the city and its inhabitants, filled with pride and confidence in the community and nation, awake to its weaknesses, needs and possibilities, is as much a matter of public concern and effort, as is the prevention of epidemics. Again, a mentally healthy and alert citizenship is one of the most effective ways of preserving the physical health. So, too, the moral health of the people is a matter of grave public concern. The higher the sense of public responsibility, of private citizens and public officers alike, the greater the assurance of safety in person, liberty, and property. The higher the moral tone, the morale of the people, the cleaner will be the city, the more beautiful the homes and parks; the more peace and quiet that abounds, the greater the joy of life and living in the community. The public health, safety, morals, and welfare, as those terms are used with reference to government and its exercise of police power are inseparably linked to, and founded upon, the peace of mind, happiness and contentment of its citizens. A government such as ours is merely a form for cooperative action, set up by free men, to enable them to live and operate as a unit, insuring the preservation to each life, liberty and the pursuit of happiness, and imposing only such restrictions upon the individual as shall be necessary to preserve and protect the welfare of society as a whole. A chain is no stronger than its weakest link, so society is no better or stronger than the units of, and upon, which it is builded. The unit upon, and out of which our present society is built is the family and the home. A basic and very important element in determining public welfare, especially as applied to regulations and restrictions governing residences and residential property, is its need or effect upon the homes and home life of the people. It is certainly the prerogative, and probably the duty of organized society, to take those measures and do those things which tend to preserve in their beauty, integrity and social force, the homes and homelife of its citizens. Those things, therefore, which contribute or reasonably may contribute to the convenience and enjoyment of the family home, and the homelife of the people generally, in such a way as may affect their health, safety, morals and general welfare are within the scope of the police power, and may properly form the basis for action by the city in zoning.

The creation of residential districts from which industry, commerce and business generally are excluded, is for the quiet and convenient enjoyment of homes and the safety and comfort of the people and especially of the children who make homes and homelife something to be preserved as the soul's anteroom to heaven. As to what restrictions and limitations should be imposed upon property, and what uses thereof should be permitted, has been by the legislature, committed to the judgment and discretion of the governing body of the city. As long as that body stays within the grant, and purposes fixed by the legislature, the courts will not gainsay (its) judgment. In *Walton v. Tracy Loan & Trust Co.*, 97 Utah 249, 92 P.2d 724, 726, we said: "No one would doubt that the exercise of the zoning power is definitely a legislative function and activity."

The test of the validity of a zoning ordinance was given by the California Court in Ex parte Ellis, 25 Cal.App.2d 99, 76 P.2d 516, at page 518, in this language. "The tests of validity in such cases are: Does the ordinance bear a reasonable relation to the public health, morals, safety or general welfare; have the districts been created according to a fair and rational plan?"

The same court, in *Zahn v. Board of Public Works*, 195 Cal. 497, 234 P. 388, at page 395, says: "It must be conceded that, where a given situation admittedly presents a proper field for the exercise of the police power, the extent of its invocation and application is a matter which lies very largely in legislative discretion ([State ex rel.] *Carter v. Harper*, 182 Wis. 148, 196 N.W. 451 [33 A.L.R. 269]), and we are well satisfied that the weight of authority dealing with the subject of zoning may now be regarded as establishing that 'every intendment is to be made in favor of zoning ordinances, and courts will not, except in clear cases, interfere with exercise of power' thus manifested."

And in *Euclid, Ohio, v. Ambler Realty, supra,* we read: "If the validity of the legislative classification * * * be fairly debatable, the legislative judgment must be allowed to control."

The governing body of the city has a large discretion in determining the plan of zoning. *Stone v. Cray,* 89 N.H. 483, 200 A. 517; *Acker v. Baldwin,* Cal.Sup., 108 P.2d 899; *Reschke v. Village of Winnetka,* 363 Ill. 478, 2 N.E.2d 718; *City of Aurora v. Burns,* 319 Ill. 84 149 N.E. 784. Only if its action is confiscatory, discriminatory, or arbitrary, will the court invoke the rule of the decalogue, "Thou shalt not." Here the general zoning plan of the city set within a reasonable walking distance of all homes in Residential "A" districts the possibilities of such homes securing daily family conveniences and necessities, such as groceries, drugs, and gasoline for the family car, with free air for the tires and water for the radiator, so the wife and mother can maintain in harmonious operation the family home, without calling Dad from his work to run errands. To effectuate this objective, there were created, on a definite, unified plan, at the intersections of definite fixed through streets, these small residential utility districts, limited and confined to such uses. Being set up on such a definite and comprehensive plan it cannot be said to be arbitrary or discriminatory. Neither does it come within the scope of the cases dealing with "spot zoning" which are based upon special privileges granted, or restrictions imposed, without regard to a unified plan. The cases relative to "spot zoning" are generally cases where a particular small tract, within a large district was specially zoned *so as to impose upon its restrictions* not imposed upon the surrounding lands, or grant to it special privileges not granted generally, not done in pursuance of any general or comprehensive plan. *Geisenfeld v. Village of Shorewood,* 232 Wis. 410, 287 N.W. 683; State ex rel. *Tingley v. Gurda,* 209 Wis. 63, 243 N.W. 317; *Rowland v. City of Racine,* 223 Wis. 488, 271 N.W. 36, 38; where it was also held that one who attacks a zoning ordinance "must show that it is unreasonable in respect to [his] property". *City of Little Rock v. Pfeifer,* 169 Ark. 1027, 277 S.W. 883. The city commission evidently decided that this method would promote the public welfare, by keeping the home as the sphere of the mother's influence, the father's haven of rest, and the children's paradise. It was not for the trial court to say it could not do so. In so acting it was in error.

* * *

McDONOUGH, Justice (concurring in the result).

I concur in the result. The designation of the described tracts at the intersecting through highways, as described in the opinion of Mr. Justice LARSON, as Zone "C" Districts, cannot be said as a matter of law not to have been made in accordance with a "comprehensive plan" designed "to promote the health and general welfare"; nor can it be said not to have been done with reasonable consideration for the character of the district in question and its peculiar suitability for the particular uses to which the ordinance permitted it to be devoted. This being so, it is not our province to interfere with the legislative discretion which placed such districts in that particular zone.

I concur in what is said in the opinion relative to the second cause of action.

MOFFAT, J., and FAUST, District Judge, concur in the result.

WOLFE, C. J., not participating.

PRATT, Justice, on leave of absence.

MAURER

v.

AUSTIN SQUARE

6 Ohio App.2d 41, 215 N.E. 2d 724(1966).

Court of Appeals of Ohio,

Summit County.

Feb. 15, 1966.

Action to restrain allegedly threatened violation of city building and zoning codes. The Court of Common Pleas issued a permanent injunction, and the defendant appealed on questions of law and fact. The Court of Appeals, Duffy, J., held that proposed shopping center, which was intended to provide business services to entire city of some 35,000 and to people in areas surrounding city up to radius of five miles from property involved, would constitute violation of zoning ordinance limiting retail stores and services to those devoted to supplying neighborhood needs, and construction thereof would be restrained.

Judgment accordingly.

Slabaugh, Walker, Pflueger, Roderick & Myers, Howard C. Walker, Sr., and Harold D. Parker, Akron, for appellees.

Roetzel, Hunsick, & Michaels and Bernard J. Roetzel, Akron, for appellants.

DUFFEY, Judge.

This is an appeal on questions of law and fact from the issuance of a permanent injunction. The action was brought under Section 713.13, Revised Code, to prevent an allegedly threatened violation of the Building and Zoning Codes of the city of Barberton.

Appellees are property owners in the vicinity of a proposed "shopping center." Appellant Austin Square, Inc., is the owner of a 26-acre tract in Barberton. The property is zoned as a "Planned Local Business District"

(PBL) pursuant to a comprehensive zoning code adopted in 1960 (ordinance No. 129-A-1960). Appellants intend to erect a one-story structure, with malls and a concourse, containing 4,850,730 cubic feet, 210,629 square feet, and costing approximately $2,250,000. It will house some 35 or more retail store units, the largest of which will be a "branch" of the M. O'Neil Company covering some 82,000 square feet. The parking capacity would have space for about 1,500 vehicles at one time.

The trial court found, and we agree, that the facility is designed and intended to provide business services to the entire city of Barberton and to people in areas surrounding the city up to a radius of five miles from the property.

[1] The question of special damage was not pressed before this court, but is a preliminary requirement. We find that appellees will suffer special damages and are entitled to sue under Section 713.13, Revised Code.

Appellants have questioned the application of provisions for Local Business Districts (BL) under Section 1163.05 to Planned Local Business Districts (PBL) under Section 1163.20 of the City Code. In our opinion, the provisions of Section 1163.20 are cumulative and in addition to those in Section 1163.05.

The principal issue is the validity of a provision of Section 1163.05, subparagraph 1b, which, as pertinent here, provides:

"Sec. 1163.05 PERMITTED USES; LOCAL BUSINESS DISTRICT

"1. *Main Uses:*

"* * *

"b. *Retail stores and services* conducted wholly within enclosed buildings and devoted to supplying *neighborhood needs* to the following limited extent: * * *." (Emphasis added.)

A detailed list of categories of permitted retail sales and services is provided, together with limits on open air or "yard" rules. Subparagraph 2 provides:

"2. *Similar Main Uses.* Any other *retail neighborhood* store, shop, or services not listed above or in any subsequent use classification, and determined as similar by the Commission according to standards set forth in Sec. 1181.11. Main uses enumerated in the General Business District may be permitted in a Local Business District if a Conditional Use Permit is granted." (Emphasis added.)

As a comparison, Section 1163.06, provides in part:

"Sec. 1163.06 PERMITTED USES; GENERAL BUSINESS DISTRICT

"1. *Main Buildings and Uses:*

"a. All stores, services, dwellings and other uses permitted in Local Business Districts; and "b. Additional retail business stores and services conducted wholly within enclosed buildings and devoted to supplying all community needs to the following extent: * * *."

Numerous categories are listed. They are substantially more extensive than those listed for the Local Business District.

Section 1163.01 is the "intent" statement for the Business District Chapter of the Code. The purposes of the local and general districts are stated as:

"* * *

"4. to provide Local Business Districts in close proximity and serving the ordinary shopping needs of the *immediate neighborhood,* and which do not attract large volumes of traffic; and

"5. to provide General Business Districts which require larger storage space, are open in evenings and generate large volumes of traffic, serving the extraordinary needs of the entire community; and * * *." (Emphasis added.)

Appellants contend that the provision of Section 1163.05 which limits a facility to supplying only "neighborhood needs" is too vague and indefinite and therefore invalid. In enacting its zoning code, the city of Barberton exercised a legislative power granted to it by Article XVIII of the Constitution of Ohio. The appellants' contention is, therefore, a claim that the limitation is unconstitutional on its face. In their brief, appellants argue that there is no definition of a neighborhood in the ordinance, that each succeeding planning commission could define it for themselves, and that the size of a facility would be related to "the current neighborhood population."

[2] A neighborhood is a concept rather than a thing. As with all concepts, it is necessarily relative. The meaning depends in large part upon the general context and the specific usage. Constitutional requirements do not demand impossible precision. It is only necessary that the legislative body provide a statement of its policy and set such guides as can be fairly understood. The elaboration by application to particular circumstances may be accomplished by administrative agencies and the courts. For example, who is an "owner" or what may be "fair competition" or "reasonable value" takes on meaning from the regulatory field involved and from the specific usage.

The pertinent definition of "neighborhood" found in Webster's New International Dictionary, Third Edition (1964), is:

"* * * 4a: a number of people forming a loosely cohesive community within a larger unit (as a city, town) and living close or fairly close together in more or less familiar association with each other within a relatively small section or district of usually somewhat indefinite boundaries and usually having some common or fairly common identifying feature (as approximate equality of economic condition, similar social status, similar national origins or religion, similar interests) and usually some degree of self-sufficiency as a group (as through local schools, churches, libraries, business establishments, cultural and recreational facilities) b: the particular section or district that is lived in by these people and that is marked by .individual features (as type of homes and public establishments) that together establish a distinctive appearance and atmosphere c: an area or region of usually vague limits that is usually marked by some fairly distinctive feature of the inhabitants or terrain ° ° °."

The Ohio Legislature has employed the neighborhood concept in establishing a standard for valuation under the special assessment statutes. See Section 727.02, Revised Code, and Early v. Leatherman, Treas. (1955), 100 Ohio App. 448, 137 N.E.2d 287, applying a requirement based upon "lots in the neighborhood." The "neighborhood" is also one of the basic concepts in legal doctrines pertaining to the enforcement or waiver of private restrictive covenants. See Restrictions—Change of Neighborhood —4 A.L.R.2d 1111, supplemented in 88 A.L.R. 405, and 54 A.L.R. 812; 15 Ohio Jurisprudence 2d 131, Covenants, Section 134.

[3] In the context of zoning, a "neighborhood" necessarily refers to an area having common geographical, physical and social characteristics which affect its physical development or maintenance. In the context of Section 1163.05, it also necessarily means that the geographical area is in the vicinity of the business district in question.

[4] In the large urban centers, the concept of a neighborhood, both as a social unit and as a geographical area, has undergone great changes. Burgeoning population and physical growth have obliterated some of the more obvious identifying characteristics which are still apparent in small community neighborhoods. However, for planning purposes, certain factors form the usual basis for establishing the approximate boundaries— and neighborhood boundaries are always only approximate. In imposing land-use controls, pertinent city planning factors to identify a neighborhood area are: physical characteristics or "barriers" such as railroads, streams, major traffic arteries; public facilities such as schools, parks and recreation centers; economic equivalence; traffic patterns; and cultural factors, not the least of which might well be the historical origin of the area.

[5, 6] While the regulatory purpose of land-use control and factors such as those just stated are the basis for defining a neighborhood, there is obviously room for reasonable differences as to the exact boundaries of any particular neighborhood. The purpose and effectiveness of the requirement of Section 1163.05 do not require identification of exact boundaries. Further, the determination of the neighborhood is in the first instance a matter for trained city planners and should be left to the appropriate agency and its staff. Compare Grant v. Washington Twp. (1963), 1 Ohio App.2d 84, at 89, 203 N.E.2d 859.

If appellants wish a determination of the neighborhood in relation to this particular PBL District, it can be made by the Planning Commission in the review of Development Plans submitted under Section 1163.20, subparagraph 3, and Section 1181.06. Obviously, such a determination must be reasonable and would be subject to judicial review.

[7] Appellants have pointed out that the ordinance does not contain any limitations on the size of the structure or number of outlets in a PBL District. However, we fail to see how the city's use of the "neighborhood" concept rather than imposing specific controls has any bearing on the validity of the former. Limits on the size of structures, the total outlets, etc., would have the advantage of greater ease in application and perhaps are the more traditional controls found in zoning codes. They have not always been too successful. Perhaps this is what induced the Barberton consultant to choose a broader approach. Whether this newer approach is administratively sound and capable of effective enforcement is for the city council to decide. As a court, we only determine that it is sufficiently definite to be constitutional.

[8] In determining whether an injunction should issue, it is not necessary in this case to know what the neighborhood is. If the area to be served is greater than anything that could reasonably be said to be the neighborhood for the proposed facilities, then a violation has been shown.

The southeast third of the city of Barberton is separated from the north and west portions of the city by a physical barrier consisting of the parallel lines of the Tuscarawas River, the Ohio Canal, the Pennsylvania Railroad, and the Akron and Barberton Belt Railroad. Appellants' property is almost in the middle of this southeast portion of the city. In the context of a regulation by the city of Barberton, it is difficult to conceive how the neighborhood of appellants' business district could extend northward or westward beyond the boundaries of this southeast portion. However, the evidence shows that the service area for which this development is designed includes the entire city of some 35,000 and all the people for several miles beyond the city in all directions. That might be a neighborhood in the context of the state of Ohio. It is not a neighborhood under any reasonable application of the Barberton ordinance.

[9] In holding that the contemplated development would constitute a violation of the ordinance, we do not in any way suggest that such a shopping area should not be developed. Perhaps it should, and probably it ultimately will be. However, this court is not the Planning Commission, nor the experts on its staff, nor members of the city council. If the present zoning is retained, a determination of the "neighborhood" to be served should be made, and upon that basis a decision given to the appellants as to permissible development plans for this district. At present, no such determinations have been requested or made.

The original building permit application and the permit itself did not comply with the requirements of Sections 105-2 and 106-3 of the Barberton Building Code. See Bloom v. Wides (1955), 164 Ohio St. 138, 128 N.E.2d 31. When subsequently "revised" permits were obtained in the name of the owner, Austin Square, Inc., there was no compliance with Zoning Code Section 1163.20, subparagraph 3, requiring submission of the development plans to the Planning Commission, nor with Section 1171.20 requiring sub-mission of drawings to the commission.

Appellants point out that a "site plan" was submitted to the commission by the Bernard Construction Company in connection with the first appli-cation and permit. Assuming that Bernard's submission can inure to the benefit of Austin Square, Inc., under its later application, the evidence shows that those plans were materially altered without submission to the Planning Commission. The orientation of the parking lanes, the number and location of traffic dividers and planting areas, the direction of traffic flow, even the quantity of square feet in the structure were changed. We are aware that the planning director testified that the plans were "essen-tially" the same. The plans themselves show substantial changes in the very matters upon which the commission should pass. The city attorney apparently felt that submission of these altered plans to the Planning Com-mission was not necessary. Perhaps he relied upon Section 105-5 of the Building Code. However, the later enacted provisions of the Zoning Code are quite explicit. See Sections 1181.-06 and 1187.01. Accordingly, the three permits in evidence are not valid.

[10] Appellants' brief contains some discussion of laches and equitable defenses. These equitable principles are available as defenses to equitable enforcement of private restrictive covenants. It seems very dubious that those doctrines have any place in a statutory injunction action to enforce regulatory laws, the violation of which affects the public interest, and which is made a crime. In any event, upon review of the record, we find that appellees asserted their rights by timely action and that appellants were not misled.

The journal entry of the Common Pleas Court based upon the excellent opinion of Judge Lamneck grants a permanent injunction in rather broad terms. If either party is dissatisfied with the wording of that entry, this court will consider any proposal that may be offered.

A judgment will be entered for the plaintiffs-appellees, not inconsistent with this opinion.

Judgment accordingly.

BRYANT, P. J., concurs.

DUFFY, Judge (concurring).

I concur on the basis of the last four paragraphs of the opinion.

BRYANT, P. J., and DUFFY and DUFFEY, JJ., of the Tenth Appellate District, sitting by designation in the Ninth Appellate District.

Questions and Notes

1. What was the service area of the proposed shopping center?

2. Describe the salient characteristics of the type of development envisaged by the existing zoning of this tract.

BOROUGH OF POINT PLEASANT BEACH

v.

POINT PLEASANT PAVILION

3 N.J. Super., 222, 66 A.2d 40(1949).

Superior Court of New Jersey

Appellate Division, Part A.

May 12, 1949.

Appeal from Recorder's Court.

Point Pleasant Pavilion, Inc., was convicted of violating a zoning ordinance of the Borough of Point Pleasant Beach, and it appeals.

Reversed.

Before JACOBS, Senior Judge, and EASTWOOD and BIGELOW, JJ.

William R. Blair, Jr. and Parsons, Labrecque, Canzona & Combs, all of Red Bank, for defendant-appellant.

W. Douglas Blair, of Point Pleasant, for plaintiff-respondent.

JACOBS, Senior Judge.

This is an appeal from a judgment of the Recorder's Court convicting the appellant of violation of Section 811 of the Zoning Ordinance of the Borough of Point Pleasant Beach. The appellant is the owner of property used for amusement purposes and located at the boardwalk near Arnold Avenue in the Borough of Point Pleasant Beach. From 1941 to 1945 a ferris wheel and "kiddie rides" were located at the premises. In 1945 the ferris wheel was discontinued and, thereafter, kiddie rides, including a "kiddie whip," were operated. On March 18, 1948, the appellant obtained a permit authorizing an extension of the platform on which the kiddie rides had been operated and, thereafter, began constructing an "adult whip" which was substantially completed by May 12, 1948. On May 13, 1948, the Borough adopted an amendatory ordinance which revised its zoning requirements and embodied a new paragraph designated as Section 811 and reading as follows: "Section 811: All businesses, except parking lots, tennis courts, miniature golf courses and miniature railways, shall be conducted under cover of permanent buildings constructed according to the requirements of this Ordinance and all other ordinances of the Borough of Point Pleasant Beach. No part of the business operation including the areas used by persons patronizing said business shall be in the open."

On July 9, 1948, a complaint was filed in the Recorder's Court charging the appellant with violating Section 811 by operating its adult whip "in the open and not under cover of a permanent building." The appellant did not dispute that it operated its adult whip in the open but contended before the Recorder that Section 811 was invalid. It introduced evidence that kiddie rides and adult whips were almost invariably operated in the open throughout the country; that to attempt to place them under cover of permanent buildings would result in increased concentration of noise, exclusion of sun and air and "wouldn't be healthy"; that its premises joined the boardwalk at Point Pleasant Beach in an area devoted primarily to "concessions and amusements"; and that a substantial number of the businesses adjoining the boardwalk were conducted, entirely or in part, without the cover of permanent buildings. No evidence to the contrary was presented by the Borough which asserts in its brief that Section 811 "is admittedly directed against the unsightliness of open air business operations, whether it be the sale of hot dogs from a wash tub on a vacant lot, the selling of merchandise from open air stands, or the operation of the appellant's amusement device in the open."

[1] The municipality's restriction on the use of appellant's property, whether it be grounded upon its zoning authority, R.S. 40:55-30 et seq., N.J.S.A., or other permissible exercise of the police power, R.S. 40:52-1, N.J.S.A., must have reasonable relation to the public health, safety, or general welfare. See Pfister v. Clifton, Sup.Ct.1945, 133 N.J.L. 148, 152, 43 A.2d 275. While the authority to regulate for the general welfare has been said to be broad enough to include regulations for the promotion of the public convenience and the general prosperity as well as those for the health, morals and safety of the public see Mansfield & Swett, Inc., v. West Orange, Sup.Ct.1938, 120 N.J.L. 145, 154, 198 A. 225, our courts have been reluctant to extend it to encompass instances where sightliness is the only justification advanced. See Passaic v. Paterson Bill Posting Co., Err. & App.1905, 72 N.J.L. 285, 62 A. 267, 111 Am.St. Rep. 676, 5 Ann.Cas. 995; Vassallo v. Orange, Err. & App.1940, 125 N.J.L. 419, 15 A.2d 603; Pfister v. Clifton, supra.

[2] In Murphy v. Town of Wesport, Sup.Ct. of Err.1944, 131 Conn. 292, 40 A.2d 177, 156 A.L.R. 568, Chief Justice Maltbie collected the pertinent cases and pointed out that although the earlier decisions nullified regulations designed predominately with regard to aesthetic considerations, there are some recent persuasive decisions to the contrary. Much can be said for the view implicit in his opinion that it is in the public interest that our communities, so far as feasible, should be made pleasant and inviting and that primary considerations of attractiveness and beauty might well be frankly acknowledged as appropriate, under certain circumstances, in the promotion of the general welfare of our people. Compare the dissenting opinion in Brookdale Homes, Inc. v. Johnson, Err. & App.1941, 126 N.J.L. 516, 521, 19 A.2d 868, 870, where Mr. Justice Heher stated that, "Police regulation on esthetic grounds is generally deemed to be an invasion of the right of private property, but it would seem that on principle such is within the police power if so far promotive of the interests of the public at large, through the resultant community development and profit, as to outweigh the incidental restraint upon private ownership." It seems to us that the recent decision by our Supreme Court, without dissent, in

Duffcon Concrete Products, Inc., v. Borough of Cresskill, Sup.Ct.1949, N.J., 64 A.2d 347, represents a wholesome and comparable departure in related direction.

We are not prepared to say that the Borough of Point Pleasant Beach would be wholly helpless in meeting the problem which might result from unrestricted operation of open amusements along its boardwalk. On the contrary, we are inclined to the belief that the problem may not be dominantly aesthetic but may directly involve considerations of health, safety, morals and public convenience well within the universally accepted concepts of the welfare clause. Cf. Piaget-Del Corp. v. Kulik, Sup.Ct.1945, 133 N.J.L. 485, 45 A.2d 125; Id., Sup.Ct.1946, 134 N.J.L. 147, 46 A.2d 379. However, the real difficulty in the present case is that no attempt has been made by the Borough to adopt a regulation reasonably calculated to meet the problem as thus stated. Instead, it adopted Section 811 which, in comprehensive fashion, seeks to wipe out all business anywhere in the Borough (apart from four very limited classes) which might require operation, in whole or in part, in the open. Thus, the ordinance, under its terms, is broad enough to exclude the customary gasoline station, cf. First Church of Christ v. Board of Adjustment, Sup.Ct.1941, 127 N.J.L. 325, 22 A.2d 569, affirmed Err. & App.1942, 128 N.J.L. 376, 26 A.2d 246, and the familiar "Good Humor man" see New Jersey Good Humor, Inc., v. Bradley Beach, Err. & App.1940, 124 N.J.L. 162, 11 A.2d 113. Similarly, it would exclude terrace service at hotels and restaurants and, indeed, numerous legitimate and acceptable business operations outside the confines of the "cover of permanent buildings". We believe the restriction, to the extent imposed, is unnecessary and has no reasonable relation to such public purposes as may properly be sought to be served. See Mr. Justice Heher's remarks in New Jersey Good Humor Inc. v. Bradley Beach, supra, 124 N.J.L. at page 168, 11 A.2d at page 117: "The restraints and regulations imposed for the general good and welfare must needs have the virtue of reasonableness. There cannot be, in the name of police regulation, an unreasonable and oppressive curtailment of personal or property rights. A measure that goes fairly beyond the public need designed to be served does not take the category of a valid police regulation. While the term 'need', as so used, is not strictly defined, the relief sought must come within the compass of a reasonable requirement for the common good and welfare. Hourigan v. Township of North Bergen, 113 N.J.L. 143, 172 A. 193, 785; Mansfield & Swett, Inc., v. West Orange, supra."

Cf. New York Used Car Trade Association v. Magee, Ch.Div.1948, N.J., 61 A.2d 751.

We have concluded that Section 811 is unreasonable on its face and that the appellant's conviction thereunder must be set aside. Accordingly, we find no occasion to consider other issues presented.

The judgment below is reversed.

PACKER

v.

NEW YORK

62 N.Y.S. 2d 54(1946), affd. mem., 271 App. Div. 874,
66 N.Y.S. 2d 634(1946), leave to appeal denied, 296 N.Y. 1060(1946),
71 N.E. 2d 778

Supreme Court, Special Term, Bronx County.

May 1, 1946.

Proceeding in the matter of the application of Rose Packer for an order of certiorari against the Board of Standards and Appeals of the City of New York and the members thereof, to review a determination of the respondent board denying petitioner's application for permission to use premises zoned for business purposes as a retail, rental, self-service laundry. On respondents' motion to vacate order of certiorari and affirm the determination of the board.

Motion to vacate order of certiorari denied and determination of Board of Standards and Appeals reversed and annulled.

Goldwater & Flynn, of New York City (Monroe Goldwater, Milton Small, and Leon Liner, all of New York City, of counsel), for petitioner.

John J. Bennett, Corp. Counsel, of New York City (Charles J. Weinstein and James Hurley, both of New York City, of counsel) for respondents.

SHIENTAG, Justice.

The petitioner is the owner of premises located at 1740 Bathgate Avenue, in the Borough of the Bronx, which are zoned for business purposes. On the premises there is a one-story building erected in 1925 and occupied by stores since then.

In 1945, the petitioner filed an application in the Department of Housing and Buildings in the Borough of the Bronx, for permission to use the first floor, north half of the building, as a retail, rental self-service laundry in which there was proposed to be installed coin-operated automatic washing machines. The Borough Superintendent of the Bronx denied the application on October 4, 1945, giving as his reason that the "Proposed use of store in a business district as a retail rental laundry, is contrary to Art. 2, Section 4(a) (51) of the Zoning Resolution." The Bronx Borough Superintendent considered the proposed business use to be a "wet wash" laundry and that such use was expressly prohibited in a business district. Section 4(a) (51) of the Zoning Resolution provides:

> "§ 4 Business Districts. (a) In a business district no building or premises shall be used, and no building shall be erected which is arranged, intended or designed to be used, for any of the following specified trades, industries or uses: * * *
>
> "(51) Steam or wet wash laundry."

The matter comes on before me on a motion to vacate the order of certiorari issued out of this court on December 5, 1945 and to affirm the decision of the Board of Standards and Appeals.

The machines proposed to be installed are the normal type of automatic home laundry machines which have been advertised for use in private homes. The model has a cylinder of twenty inches in diameter and a depth of twelve inches and accommodates ten pounds of clothing at one time. The only change from the model used in private homes is the addition of a coin-operated box. It is proposed, in the premises in question, to install a series of such machines which are to be used by the general public. The store is to be under the supervision of attendants.

A woman desiring to wash clothes brings to the store a package containing the clothes and places them in the cylinder or tub of the machine. The door is then closed and the coin inserted in the meter. Electric controls are set by the customer to regulate the washing, rinsing and drying as desired. The clothes are washed, rinsed three times and damp dried automatically without being removed. The only services rendered by the attendant are to weigh the clothes, make change and make minor repairs on the machines in the event of a break-down. The store premises contain no machinery other than the automatic laundries which have the appearance of medium-sized refrigerators. Hot water for the machines is supplied by the boiler in the basement, the boiler being no larger than that required for any apartment building or office building.

The operation does not require the use of any large machinery, evil-smelling chemicals, large vats, chimney or boiler flues, a large labor force, nor are there any wagons or trucks depositing or removing bundles of clothing. It is urged that this type of operation will permit those who are not fortunate enough to possess their own automatic washing machines, and those who do not live in modern apartment houses maintaining such machines for the use of the tenants, to wash their clothes without the labor usually incident to that operation when performed by housewives in their own homes.

[1] I am of the opinion that the laundry operation proposed does not involve the results normally associated with the carrying on of a public laundry business, commonly referred to as a "steam or wet wash laundry." See Laundry Machinery, New International Encyclopedia, Second Edition, Volume 13; Encyclopedia Britannica, 14th Ed. Vol. 3, p. 768; Williams v. Blue Bird Laundry Co., 85 Cal.App. 388, 259 P. 84. The record is devoid of any definition of the term "steam or wet wash laundry." That term which is used in subdivision 51, above referred to, is included in a long list of obnoxious trades, most of which constitute a nuisance per se. The term "wet wash" is merely descriptive of a type of product produced by any large commercial laundry as distinguished from any other products produced by it.

[2] The resolution must be read as a whole in construing the subdivision under review. So read it is clear that it was intended to eliminate the menace to health and property arising out of the use of buildings, in business districts, for trades that are obnoxious and offensive. Significantly enough the resolution does not prohibit the use of laundries generally in business districts. The prohibition is limited to a "steam or wet wash laundry." The use of the alternative form is loose and inaccurate, since there is no technical distinction in the operative procedure as between a steam laundry and a wet wash laundry, the difference being merely whether the product is returned to the customer in a damp or in a dry state.

[3-6] The respondents rest their position on the literal meaning of the words "wet wash laundry" rather than on the manifest spirit of the resolution. Giving a reasonable interpretation to the term; having in mind its context and the object sought to be accomplished, it seems clear that "wet wash" laundry refers to the wet or damp product of a large laundry factory. "In the interpretation of statutes, the spirit and purpose of the act and the objects to be accomplished must be considered. The legislative intent is the great and controlling principle. Literal meanings of words are not to be adhered to or suffered to 'defeat the general purpose and manifest policy intended to be promoted,' all parts of the act must be read and construed together for the purpose of determining the legislative intent, and if the statute is ambiguous and two constructions can be given, the one must be adopted which will not cause objectionable results or cause inconvenience, hardship, injustice, or mischief, or lead to absurdity." People v. Ryan, 274 N.Y. 149, 152, 8 N.E.2d 313, 315.

The legislative background of the resolution shows that it was not intended to cover the type of operation proposed. The amendment in controversy was apparently adopted on the basis of a letter from the City Planning Commission to the Secretary of the Board of Estimate (Report No. 1035 dated May 29, 1940), which letter in referring to the addition of subdivision 51 states:

> "Section 4(a) (50 and 51)—auto wrecking and steam laundries. Experience has indicated that both auto wrecking yards and steam laundries may be highly objectionable and should, therefore, be excluded, from business districts, a justifiable exception in the case of hotel and hospital laundries."

No mention is made of "wet wash" laundries in the letter from the City Planning Commission. This would seem to indicate that the term "wet wash laundry" was intended to be merely descriptive of the type of operation covered by the term "steam laundry." Furthermore, the lumping together of steam laundries and auto-wrecking yards emphasizes that the intention of the legislators was to restrict objectionable trades and that subdivision 51 was intended only to refer to those laundry operations which in essence amounted to nuisance per se. In the type of operation proposed the proprietor will not launder the clothing of customers but will merely supply the facilities by which each customer may launder her own clothing. The atmosphere of this so-called "launderette service" is far removed from the common conception of a steam or wet wash laundry. Labels applied to old processes should not be construed so as to retard the development of new techniques designed for the improvement of living conditions and for the convenience and the welfare of the general public.

Accordingly, the motion to vacate the order of certiorari is denied. The determination of the Board of Standards and Appeals is reversed and annulled.

Settle order.

<hr />

MacMILLAN

v.

McCAFFREY

201 N.Y. Misc. 574, 106 N.Y.S. 2d 673(1950).

Supreme Court, Special Term, New York County, Part III.

Nov. 30, 1950.

Action by Edward MacMillan against Edward T. McCaffrey, as Commissioner of Licenses of the City of New York, and another for a declaratory judgment and plaintiff moved for an injunction pendente lite, enjoining and restraining the defendants from suspending or revoking plaintiff's license for the operation of a launderette store because of installation of an extractor and a dryer, and from interfering with plaintiff's operation and conduct of the launderette store. The Special Term, Eder, J., held that the installation of the extractor and dryer in the launderette store did not transform it into a wet wash or steam laundry within the meaning of the zoning resolution.

Motion granted: judgment for plaintiff.
Goldwater & Flynn, New York City, for plaintiff.
John P. McGrath, Corp. Counsel, New York City, for defendants.
EDER, Justice.

This is an action for a declaratory judgment and plaintiff, in connection therewith, moves for an injunction pendente lite, enjoining and restraining the defendants from suspending or revoking plaintiff's license for the operation of a launderette store because of installation of an extractor and a dryer, and from interfering with plaintiff's operation and conduct of said launderette store. The cause was submitted upon an agreed statement of facts and the case is now ready for final determination of the sole issue of law involved, viz. the application of Article II, section 4(a) (51) of the New York City zoning resolution to plaintiff's launderette operation.

Plaintiff owns and operates a launderette store pursuant to a license duly issued to him by the commissioner of licenses of the City of New York, on July 10, 1950, bearing No. 412550. Such an establishment, it has been held, does not come within the purview of Article II, section 4(a) (51) of the New York City zoning resolution, as amended to January 23, 1950, which prohibits the conduct and operation in a business district of a steam or wet wash laundry; that such an enterprise is a retail self-service laundry, which may be availed of by the general public for use by depositing a coin,—the charge for the service,—in coin operated automatic washing machines. This status of such launderette business was determined in Packer v. Board of Standards and Appeals of City of New York, Sup., 62 N.Y.S.2d 54, opin. Shientag, J., affirmed 271 App.Div. 874, 66 N.Y.S.2d 634, leave to appeal denied, 296 N.Y. 1060, 71 N.E.2d 778.

Plaintiff, on or about April 3, 1950, duly filed an application with the Department of Housing and Buildings for permission to alter the store premises in question, proposing to install, among other equipment, twenty washing machines, one extractor and one dryer in connection with the establishment and operation of a launderette at said premises. The application was approved; such approval provided for installation of twenty Bendix automatic washing machines but did not include the extractor and dryer. This approval was transmitted to the Department of Licenses and the commissioner of licenses on or about July 10, 1950. The commissioner of licenses, after investigation by him, determined that the provisions of the several applicable laws and requirements were fully satisfied and approved plaintiff's application for a laundry license, as mentioned.

Shortly thereafter, on or about July 17, 1950, plaintiff caused to be installed in his said launderette store one Telecoin-Back extractor (also known as a spinner) and one Telecoin-Ace dryer for use with the said twenty Bendix automatic washing machines. This subsequent installation of said extractor and dryer in the operation of the laundry business by plaintiff was reported by an inspector of the Department of Licenses and thereafter plaintiff was cited to appear at a hearing on August 8, 1950, before the Department of Licenses and the license commissioner regarding the operation of the extractor and dryer in plaintiff's said launderette.

As a result of the hearing plaintiff was informed by said department and commissioner that the installation of said extractor and dryer was contrary to the architects plans which had previously been approved by the Department of Housing and Buildings and the borough superintendent of Queens in connection with plaintiff's application for a license to operate a laundry and that it was necessary for plaintiff to secure the approval of the Department of Housing and Buildings for the installation of said extractor and dryer, and plaintiff was informed that if he did not secure such approval his license would be revoked or suspended.

On August 29, 1950, the Department of Licenses and the license commissioner then wrote to the Department of Housing and Buildings, Borough of Queens, directing attention to the installation of the extractor and dryer and requesting information as to whether it met with said departments approval. On September 5, 1950 response was made to this letter that the installation of the said extractor and dryer had not been and would not be approved by said Housing and Buildings Department.

Thereafter and on or about September 15, 1950 an amended application was filed by plaintiff showing the existence of this additional machinery, viz. one extractor and one dryer, and the approval of the Department of Housing and Buildings was asked. This was refused in a decision rendered on September 29, 1950 upon the ground that the installation of the extractor and dryer in the existing launderette store created a steam laundry in a business use district contrary to Article II, section 4(a) (51) of said zoning resolution.

Article II, section 4(a) provides:

> "In a business district no building or premises shall be used, and no building shall be erected which is arranged, intended or designed to be used for any of the following specified trades, industries or uses:
>
> *   *   *
>
> "(51) Steam or wet wash laundry other than in a hotel or hospital."

The borough superintendent predicated his refusal to approve the installation of the extractor and dryer upon a departmental opinion or memorandum of the commissioner of housing and buildings to the effect that he was in accord with an opinion of the Board of Standards and Appeals that the use of additional machinery, such as extractors (spinner) and dryers in the operation of a launderette was not covered or contemplated in the decision in the Packer case, supra.

It appears that prior to this refusal the Board of Standards and Appeals, under calendar No. 606-49-A, passed upon an appeal from the refusal of the borough superintendent of Queens to rescind his approval of the installation of ten Norge washing machines, a Huebsch dryer and spinner (extractor), which it appears was predicated or at least influenced by a report made by a committee of the Board of Standards and Appeals, dated February 24, 1950 and which also guided and influenced the adoption ·of the departmental ruling issued by the commissioner of housing and buildings. So far as here pertinent this report reads: "It appears that supplementary machines, such as dryers and spinners, have customarily been permitted by the Department of Housing and Buildings subsequent to the Packer decision. In the opinion of the Board, however, there is no warrant for permitting such supplementary equipment under the Packer decision and this report does not contemplate permission to have them in addition to the self-service washing machines."

On October 3, 1950 the Department of Licenses informed plaintiff that a hearing would be held on October 10, 1950 by it in connection with the installation of said extractor and dryer. A hearing was held and the evidence disclosed that the extractor used in the operation of plaintiff's laundry for a nine pound package of wash consumed, in time, five minutes, and that the dryer used consumes in its operating time about fifteen minutes; that in the operation of these units they make no vibration and emit no noise, dirt or spray.

The evidence also established that the function of the extractor is to remove as much loose water from the wash as possible; that the function of the dryer is to actually dry the wash; all moisture and dampness are removed. The evidence also established that no steam, wet or live, is employed in any of the operations carried on in the premises and that the business is operated as a self-service automatic laundry whereby the general public has access to the machines and operates them by depositing a coin therein; that it is essentially retail in nature; that no laundry is picked up outside the premises and brought there by the operator or any one connected with its operation.

Testimony was also adduced by the plaintiff that he cannot successfully operate his launderette store without the additional equipment of the extractor and dryer for the reason that the public demand these services in a launderette store.

It appears at said hearing the license department and the license commissioner stated that the sole reason they had for revoking or suspending plaintiff's license to operate said launderette store was because plaintiff failed to secure the approval of the department of housing and buildings of his application and architect's plans as amended, which were filed with the department of housing and buildings. It also appears that at the conclusion of the hearing the commissioner of licenses announced that in view of the adverse report received from the department of housing and buildings, dated September 5, 1950, the department of licenses would require plaintiff to remove the extractor and dryer by November 1, 1950, and that if this was not done the laundry license would be revoked or suspended.

The parties have stipulated the above facts and by reason of the dispute with respect to the right of plaintiff to operate and conduct his launderette store, a judicial determination is sought concerning said restrictive provision of said zoning resolution and the nature and effect thereof on the licensing authority of the commissioner of licenses and the rules and regulations with reference to licensing laundries, promulgated thereunder.

In the light of the ruling in the Packer case, supra, the issue narrows itself down to whether the defendants were justified in acting as they did by virtue of the views expressed in the report of the committee of the Board of Standards and Appeals, above alluded to that in their opinion the decision in the Packer case, supra, did not include or contemplate the installation of an extractor or dryer in the operation of a launderette store and was not to be regarded as a decisive ruling in that regard and hence warranted holding that until the approval of the Department of Housing and Buildings was obtained the use of an extractor and dryer was improper and must be removed under penalty of suspension or loss of the license to operate a laundry.

[1, 2] It is quite apparent to this court that the use of an extractor and dryer is in reality, incidental, but yet needful to the proper and successful operation of a launderette, and, therefore, implicit in the ruling in the Packer case permitting a launderette store to be operated is the right to use in connection therewith an extractor and dryer requisite to the successful operation of such a business and establishment. To hold that a launderette store may be operated but not with essential additional and incidental equipment is to create not only chaos but absurdity. The canon of sensible construction should be and is invoked by the courts to prevent an absurd result. Of what value is a license to operate if the license is to be denied or may be refused the right to use essential equipment or needful additions?

[3] I am of opinion that in the light of the situation disclosed that the plaintiff, having been granted a license, it carried with it, the absolute right to install the additional and essential equipment like an extractor and dryer and did not require any additional license therefor.

[4] I am also of opinion that the view taken by the defendants that the installation of the extractor and dryer converted or transformed the launderette store into a steam or wet wash laundry was an erroneous determination and without support in logic and law. The fact is, as one of reality, that the use of these units did not in the slightest degree, change its basic character as a self-service retail laundry operation.

The objectionable features which characterize a steam or wet wash laundry, and alluded to in the Packer case, are not present in the operation of a launderette store and service as conducted by plaintiff. Indeed, this is substantially admitted in the said committee report of the Board of Standards and Appeals wherein it is stated that "supplementary machines, such as dryers and spinners (extractors) have customarily been permitted by the Department of Housing and Buildings subsequent to the Packer decision."

The legality of this permitted use of an extractor and dryer was never thought to be questioned by the defendants until the said committee of the Board of Standards and Appeals expressed an opinion that the Packer decision did not contemplate in its effect that an extractor and dryer constituted and were included as additional and essential units in the operation of a launderette establishment, viz., their use in addition to the self-service washing machines. It was not any conclusion of illegality that persuaded the defendants to take their stand as they have done, but, rather, to accomplish an agreement of views and department harmony that the commissioners and departments have acquiesced in the same opinion as expressed in said committee's report.

The court regards the action and threatened action of the defendants as erroneous and illegal, even though their stand is taken in good faith; it cannot serve to deprive the plaintiff of the right to operate his launderette store without fear and free from the threat of suspension or revocation of his license to operate his launderette store, and such threatened suspension or revocation of his laundry license is without legal right.

In the opinion of the court only sheer disregard of reality can induce a conclusion that the installation and use of the extractor and dryer has transformed the launderette into a steam or wet wash laundry and hence it has come within the restrictive provision of the zoning resolution.

The court accordingly declares that the Board of Standards and Appeals erred in its announcement and ruling under Calendar No. 606-49-A, and incorrectly construed the meaning of Article II, Section 4(a) (51) of the zoning resolution aforementioned, and that defendants' action based thereon threatening to suspend or revoke plaintiff's laundry license was and is illegal, and further declaration is made that it is lawful for plaintiff to install an extractor and dryer in his retail self-service.

Questions and Notes

1. Why are these cases included here?

2. There was even another decision following these, New York Ambassador, Inc. v. Board of Standards and Appeals of New York City, 281 App. Div. 342, 119 N.Y.S.2d 805 (1st Dep't. 1953), appl. rev., 305 N.Y. 791, 113 N.E. 2d 302 (1953).

3. What do you conclude with respect to use lists as a zoning technique in commercial districts? How much difference does it make if the regulations are phrased in the permissive, or alternatively in the prohibitory, form?

CROSS-REFERENCES

In Anderson, see §§ 8.02, 8.33, 11.01-11.86.
In Hagman, see § 57.
In McQuillin, see § 25.110.
In Rathkopf, see ch. 10-4, 14-1, 15-8.
In Williams, see ch. 94-100.
In Yokley, see §§ 4-2, 4-7.

FRED F. FRENCH INVESTING COMPANY

v.

CITY OF NEW YORK

39 N.Y. 2d 587, 385 N.Y.S.2d 5,

350 N.E. 2d 381, appeal dismissed, 97 Sup. Ct. 515 (1976).

Court of Appeals of New York.

May 4, 1976.

The purchase money mortgagee of a Manhattan residential complex brought an action to declare unconstitutional a 1972 amendment to the New York City zoning resolution and seeking compensation as for "inverse" taking by eminent domain. The amendment purported to create a "Special Park District," and rezoned two private parks in the complex exclusively as parks open to the public; it further provided for the granting to property owners of transferable development rights usable elsewhere. The Supreme Court, New York County, Wilfred A. Waltemade, J., declared the amendment void, and the Supreme Court, Appellate Division, First Department, 47 A.D.2d 715, 366 N.Y.S.2d 346, affirmed. On the parties' cross appeals, the Court of Appeals, Breitel, C. J., held, inter alia, that the state could not, under the guise of regulation by zoning, deprive a property owner of the reasonable income productive or other private use of his property and thus destroy all but a bare residue of its economic value.

Affirmed.

W. Bernard Richland, Corp. Counsel, New York City (Alfred Weinstein and L. Kevin Sheridan, New York City, of counsel), for appellant-respondent.

Bernard S. Meyer, Mineola, for respondent-appellant.

Lowell D. Willinger and Edward Brodsky, New York City, for respondents-appellants.

David W. Peck and Howard T. Milman, New York City, for the Tudor City Association, amicus curiae.

BREITEL, Chief Judge.

Plaintiff Fred F. French Investing Co., purchase money mortgagee of Tudor City, a Manhattan residential complex, brought this action to declare unconstitutional a 1972 amendment to the New York City Zoning Resolution and seeks compensation as for "inverse" taking by eminent domain. The amendment purported to create a "Special Park District", and rezoned two private parks in the Tudor City complex exclusively as parks open to the public. It further provided for the granting to the defendant property owners of transferable development (air) rights usable elsewhere. It created the transferable rights by severing the above-surface development rights from the surface development rights, a device of recent invention.

Special Term, in a studied and painstaking opinion, declared the amendment unconstitutional and restored the former zoning classification, R-10, permitting residential and office building development. The Appellate Division, 47 A.D.2d 715, 366 N.Y.S.2d 346 unanimously affirmed, without opinion. By its appeal, the city seeks review of the declaration of unconstitutionality and the denial of its summary judgment motion on the issue of damages. By their cross appeals, plaintiff mortgagee and defendants, owners and mortgage interest guarantor, seek review of the denial of their summary judgment motions for compensation based on an "inverse" taking.

The issue is whether the rezoning of buildable private parks exclusively as parks open to the public, thereby prohibiting all reasonable income productive or other private use of the property, constitutes a deprivation of property rights without due process of law in violation of constitutional limitations.

[1, 2] There should be an affirmance. While the police power of the State to regulate the use of private property by zoning is broad indeed, it is not unlimited. The State may not, under the guise of regulation by zoning, deprive the owner of the reasonable income productive or other private use of his property and thus destroy all but a bare residue of its economic value. Such an exercise of the police power would be void as violative of the due process clauses of the State and Federal Constitutions (N.Y.Const., art. I, § 6; U.S.Const., 14th Amdt., § 1). In the instant case, the city has, despite the severance of above-surface development rights, by rezoning private parks exclusively as parks open to the public, deprived the owners of the reasonable income productive or other private use of their property. The attempted severance of the development rights with uncertain and contingent market value did not adequately preserve those rights. Hence, the 1972 zoning amendment is violative of constitutional limitations.

Tudor City is a four-acre residential complex built on an elevated level above East 42nd Street, across First Avenue from the United Nations in mid-town Manhattan. Planned and developed as a residential community, Tudor City consists of 10 large apartment buildings housing approximately 8,000 people, a hotel, four brownstone buildings, and two 15,000 square-foot private parks. The parks, covering about 18½% of the area of the complex, are elevated from grade and located on the north and south sides of East 42nd Street, with a connecting viaduct.

On September 30, 1970, plaintiff sold the Tudor City complex to defendant Ramsgate Properties for $36,000,000. In addition to cash, plaintiff took back eight purchase money mortgages, two of which covered in part the two parks. Payment of the mortgage interest for three years was personally guaranteed by defendant Helmsley. Ramsgate thereafter conveyed, subject to plaintiff's mortgages, properties including the north and south parks to defendants, North Assemblage Co. and South Assemblage Co. Each of the mortgages secured in part by the parks has been in default since December 7, 1972.

Soon after acquiring the Tudor City property, the new owner announced plans to erect a building, said to be a 50-story tower, over East 42nd Street between First and Second Avenues. This plan would have required New York City Planning Commission approval of a shifting of development rights from the parks to the proposed adjoining site and a corresponding zoning change. Alternatively, the owner proposed to erect on each of the Tudor City park sites a building of maximum size permitted by the existing zoning regulations.

There was immediately an adverse public reaction to the owner's proposals, especially from Tudor City residents. After public hearings, the City Planning Commission recommended, over the dissent of one commissioner, and on December 7, 1972 the Board of Estimate approved, an amendment to the zoning resolution establishing Special Park District "P". By contemporaneous amendment to the zoning map, the two Tudor City parks were included within Special Park District "P".

Under the zoning amendment, "only passive recreational uses are permitted" in the Special Park District and improvements are limited to "structures incidental to passive recreational use". When the Special Park District would be mapped, the parks are required to be open daily to the public between 6:00 a.m. and 10:00 p.m.

The zoning amendment permits the transfer of development rights from a privately owned lot zoned as a Special Park District, denominated a "granting lot", to other areas in midtown Manhattan, bounded by 60th Street, Third Avenue, 38th Street and Eighth Avenue, denominated "receiving lots". Lots eligible to be receiving lots are those with a minimum lot size of 30,000 square feet and zoned to permit development at the maximum commercial density. The owner of a granting lot would be permitted to transfer part of his development rights to any eligible receiving lot, thereby increasing its maximum floor area up to 10%. Further increase in the receiving lot's floor area, limited to 20% of the maximum commercial density, is contingent upon a public hearing and approval by the City Planning Commission and the Board of Estimate. Development rights may be transferred by the owner directly to a receiving lot or to an individual or organization for later disposition to a receiving lot. Before development rights may be transferred, however, the Chairman of the City Planning Commission must certify the suitability of a plan for the continuing maintenance, at the owner's expense, of the granting lot as a park open to the public.

It is notable that the private parks become open to the public upon mapping of the Special Park District, and the opening does not depend upon the relocation and effective utilization of the transferrable development rights. Indeed, the mapping occurred on December 7, 1972, and the development rights have never been marketed or used.

Plaintiff contends that the rezoning of the parks constitutes a compensable "taking" within the meaning of constitutional limitations.

The power of the State over private property extends from the regulation of its use under the police power to the actual taking of an easement or all or part of the fee under the eminent domain power. The distinction, although definable, between a compensable taking and a noncompensable regulation is not always susceptible of precise demarcation. Generally, as the court stated in *Lutheran Church in Amer. v. City of New York*, 35 N.Y.2d 121, 128-129, 359 N.Y.S.2d 7, 14, 316 N.E.2d 305, 310: "[G]overnment interference [with the use of private property] is based on one of two concepts—either the government is acting in its enterprise capacity, where it takes unto itself private resources in use for the common good, or in its arbitral capacity, where it intervenes to straighten out situations in which the citizenry is in conflict over land use or where one person's use of his land is injurious to others. (Sax, Taking and the Police Power, 74 Yale L.J. 36, 62, 63.) Where government acts in its enterprise capacity, as where it takes land to widen a road, there is a compensable taking. Where government acts in its arbitral capacity, as where it legislates zoning or provides the machinery to enjoin noxious use, there is simply noncompensable regulation."

[3] As noted above, when the State "takes", that is appropriates, private property for public use, just compensation must be paid. In contrast, when there is only regulation of the uses of private property, no compensation need be paid. Of course, and this is often the beginning of confusion, a purported "regulation" may impose so onerous a burden on the property regulated that it has, in effect, deprived the owner of the reasonable income productive or other private use of his property and thus has destroyed its economic value. In all but exceptional cases, nevertheless a regulation does not constitute a "taking", and is therefore not compensable, but amounts to a deprivation or frustration of property rights without due process of law and therefore invalid.

True, many cases have equated an invalid exercise of the regulating zoning power, perhaps only metaphorically, with a "taking" or a "confiscation" of property, terminology appropriate to the eminent domain power and the concomitant right to compensation when it is exercised. Thus, for example, in *Arverne Bay Constr. Co. v. Thatcher*, 278 N.Y. 222, 232, 15 N.E.2d 587, 592, the court stated "An ordinance which *permanently* so restricts the use of property that it cannot be used for any reasonable purpose goes, it is plain, beyond regulation, and must be recognized as a taking of the property." Similarly, in *Pennsylvania Coal Co. v. Mahon*, 260 U.S. 393, 415, 43 S.Ct. 158, 160, 67 L.Ed. 322, a police power and not an eminent domain case, Mr. Justice Holmes stated: "while property may be regulated to a certain extent, if regulation goes too far it will be recognized as a taking" (see, also, e. g., *Lutheran Church in Amer. v. City of New York*, 35 N.Y.2d 121, 129, 132, 359 N.Y.S.2d 7, 14, 16, 316 N.E.2d 305, 310, 312 *supra* ["confiscatory"]; *Matter of Golden v. Planning Bd. of Town of Ramapo*, 30 N.Y.2d 359, 380, 334 N.Y.S.2d 138, 154, 285 N.E.2d 291, 303, app. dsmd. 409 U.S. 1003, 93 S.Ct. 436, 440, 34 L.Ed.2d 294 ["taking"]; *Salamar Bldrs. Corp. v. Tuttle*, 29 N.Y.2d 221, 225, 325 N.Y.S.2d 933, 937, 275 N.E.2d 585, 588 ["taking"]; *Vernon Park Realty v. City of Mount Vernon*, 307 N.Y. 493, 499, 121 N.E.2d 517, 519 ["confiscatory"]).

The metaphor should not be confused with the reality. Close examination of the cases reveals that in none of them, anymore than in the *Pennsylvania Coal* case *(supra)*, was there an actual "taking" under the eminent domain power, despite the use of the terms "taking" or "confiscatory". Instead, in each the gravamen of the constitutional challenge to the regulatory measure was that it was an invalid exercise of the police power under the due process clause, and the cases were decided under that rubric (see *Arverne Bay Constr. Co. v. Thatcher*, 278 N.Y. 222, 223, 225, 229, 231, 15 N.E.d 587, 588, 590, 591, *supra; Pennsylvania Coal Co. v. Mahon*, 260 U.S. 393, 395-396, 414, 43 S.Ct. 158 67 L.Ed. 322, *supra; Lutheran Church in Amer. v. City of. New York*, 35 N.Y.2d 121, 123, 125, 130-131, 359 N.Y.S.2d 7, 9, 11, 15—16, 316 N.E.2d 305, 307, 311-32, *supra; Matter of Golden v. Planning Bd. of Town of Ramapo*, 30 N.Y.2d 359, 363-364, 377, 334 N.Y.S.2d 138, 140-141, 151, 285 N.E.2d 291, 293-294, 301, *supra* [due process and equal protection clauses]; *Salamar Bldrs. Co. v. Tuttle*, 29 N.Y.2d 221, 223, 224-225, 226, 335 N.Y.S.d 933, 935, 936-937, 938, 275 N.E.2d 585, 586, 587-588, 589, *supra; Vernon Park Realty v. City of Mount Vernon*, 307 N.Y. 493, 498, 499, 121 N.E.2d 517, 519, *supra*). As has been cogently pointed out by Professor Costonis: "the goal of [challenges to regulatory measures] in conventional land use disputes is to preclude application of the measure to the restricted parcel on the basis of constitutional infirmity. What is achieved, in short, is declaratory relief. The sole exception to this mild outcome occurs where the challenged measure is either intended to eventuate in actual public ownership of the land or has already caused government to encroach on the land with trespassory consequences that are largely irreversible." (Costonis, "Fair" Compensation and the Accommodation Power: Antidotes for the Taking Impasse in Land Use Controversies, 1975 Col.L.Rev. 1021, 1035; for examples of the exceptions described see *Keystone Assoc. v. State of New York*, 33 N.Y.2d 848, 352 N.Y.S.2d 194, 307 N.E.2d 254, affg. on opn. at App.Div. 39 AD2d 176, 333 NYS.2d 27; *Matter of Keystone Assoc. v. Moerdler*, 19 N.Y.2d 78, 85-86, 278 N.Y.S.2d 185, 187-188, 224 N.E.2d 700, 701-702.)

[4] In the present case, while there was a significant diminution in the value of the property, there was no actual appropriation or taking of the parks by title or governmental occupation. The amendment was declared

void at Special Term a little over a year after its adoption. There was no physical invasion of the owner's property; nor was there an assumption by the city of the control or management of the parks. Indeed, the parks served the same function as before the amendment, except that they were now also open to the public. Absent factors of governmental displacement of private ownership, occupation or management, there was no "taking" within the meaning of constitutional limitations (see *City of Buffalo v. Clement Co.*, 28 N.Y.2d 241, 255-257, 321 N.Y.S.2d 345, 357-359, 269 N.E.2d 895, 903-905). There was, therefore, no right to compensation as for a taking in eminent domain.

Since there was no taking within the meaning of constitutional limitations, plaintiff's remedy, at this stage of the litigation, would be a declaration of the amendment's invalidity, if that be the case. Thus, it is necessary to determine whether the zoning amendment was a valid exercise of the police power under the due process clauses of the State and Federal Constitutions.

[5] The broad police power of the State to regulate the use of private property is not unlimited. Every enactment under the police power must be reasonable (see, e. g., *People v. Goodman*, 31 N.Y.2d 262, 265-266, 338 N.Y.S.2d 97, 100-101, 290 N.E.2d 139, 141-142; *Goldblatt v. Hempstead*, 369 U.S. 590, 594-595, 82 S.Ct. 987, 8 L.Ed.2d 130) An exercise of the police power to regulate private property by zoning which is unreasonable constitutes a deprivation of property without due process of law (N.Y. Const., art. I, § 6; U.S. Const.; 14th Amdt § 1; *Vernon Park Realty v. City of Mount Vernon*, 307 N.Y. 493, 499, 121 N.E.2d 517, 519, *supra; Nectow v. Cambridge*, 277 U.S. 183, 188-189, 48 S.Ct. 447, 72 L.Ed. 842; see 1 Rathkopf, Law of Zoning and Planning [4th ed.], § 4.02).

What is an "unreasonable" exercise of the police power depends upon the relevant converging factors. Hence, the facts of each case must be evaluated in order to determine the private and social balance of convenience before the exercise of the power may be condemned as unreasonable (see, e. g., *Village of Belle Terre v. Boraas*, 416 U.S. 1, 4, 94 S.Ct. 1536, 39 L.Ed.2d 797; *Euclid v. Ambler Co.*, 272 U.S. 365, 387, 47 S.Ct. 114, 71 L.Ed. 303; *Stevens v. Town of Huntington*, 20 NY.2d 352, 355-356, 283 N.Y.S.2d 16, 18-19, 229 N.E.2d 591, 593-594).

[6, 7] A zoning ordinance is unreasonable, under traditional police power and due process analysis, if it encroaches on the exercise of private property rights without substantial relation to a legitimate governmental purpose. A legitimate governmental purpose is, of course, one which furthers the public health, safety, morals or general welfare. (See, e. g., *Salamar Bldrs. Corp. v. Tuttle*, 29 N.Y.2d 221, 224-225, 325 N.Y.S.2d 933, 936-937, 275 N.E.2d 585, 587-588, *supra; People v. Scott*, 26 N.Y.2d 286, 291, 309 N.Y.S.2d 919, 925, 258 N.E.2d 206, 210; *Nectow v. Cambridge*, 277 U.S. 183, 187-188, 48 S.Ct. 447, 72 L.Ed 842, *supra; Euclid v. Ambler Co., supra*, 272 U.S. at p. 397, 47 S.Ct. 114; 1 Rathkopf, op. cit., at pp. 4-3,

4-26.) Moreover, a zoning ordinance, on similar police power analysis, is unreasonable if it is arbitrary, that is, if there is no reasonable relation between the end sought to be achieved by the regulation and the means used to achieve that end (see, e. g., *Salamar Bldrs. Corp. v. Tuttle, supra* 29 N.Y.2d at pp. 226-227, 325 N.Y.S.2d at pp. 938-939, 275 N.E.2d at pp. 588-589; *Matter of Board of Educ. v. City Council of City of Glen Cove*, 29 N.Y.2d 681, 682, 325 N.Y.S.2d 415, 416, 274 N.E.2d 749; 1 Rathkopf, *op. cit.*, at pp. 4-3, 4-26).

[8] Finally, and it is at this point that the confusion between the police power and the exercise of eminent domain most often occurs, a zoning ordinance is unreasonable if it frustrates the owner in the use of his property, that is, if it renders the property unsuitable for any reasonable income productive or other private use for which it is adapted and thus destroys its economic value, or all but a bare residue of its value (see, e. g., *Lutheran Church in Amer. v. City of New York*, 35 N.Y.2d 121, 130, 359 N.Y.S.2d 7, 15, 316 N.E.2d 305, 311, *supra; Vernon Park Realty v City of Mount Vernon*, 307 N.Y. 493, 499, 121 N.E.2d 517, 519, *supra; Shepard v. Village of Skaneateles*, 300 N.Y. 115, 118, 89 N.E.2d 619, 620; *Arverne Bay Constr. Co. v. Thatcher*, 278 N.Y. 222, 226, 232, 15 N.E.2d 587, 589, 592, *supra; Matter of Eaton v. Sweeney*, 257 N.Y. 176, 183, 177 N.E. 412, 414; 1 Rathkopf, *op. cit.*, § 6.02, at p. 6-2).

The ultimate evil of a deprivation of property, or better, a frustration of property rights, under the guise of an exercise of the police power is that it forces the owner to assume the cost of providing a benefit to the public without recoupment. There is no attempt to share the cost of the benefit among those benefited, that is, society at large. Instead, the accident of ownership determines who shall bear the cost initially. Of course, as further consequence, the ultimate economic cost of providing the benefit is hidden from those who in a democratic society are given the power of deciding whether or not they wish to obtain the benefit despite the ultimate economic cost, however initially distributed (Dunham, Legal and Economic Basis for Planning, 58 Col.L.Rev. 650, 665). In other words, the removal from productive use of private property has an ultimate social cost more easily concealed by imposing the cost on the owner alone. When successfully concealed, the public is not likely to have any objection to the "cost-free" benefit.

In this case, the zoning amendment is unreasonable and, therefore, unconstitutional because, without due process of law, it deprives the owner of all his property rights, except the bare title and a dubious future reversion of full use. The amendment renders the park property unsuitable for any reasonable income productive or other private use for which it is adapted and thus destroys its economic value and deprives plaintiff of its security for its mortgages. Indeed, as Rathkopf has characterized it, the case is an "extreme example" of a deprivation (1 Rathkopf, *op. cit.*, at p. 6-55; contra Marcus, Mandatory Development Rights Transfer and the Taking Clause: The Case of Manhattan's Tudor City Parks, 24 Buffalo L.Rev. 77, 93-94, 105).

[9] It is recognized that the "value" of property is not a concrete or tangible attribute but an abstraction derived from the economic uses to which the property may be put. Thus, the development rights are an essential component of the value of the underlying property because they constitute some of the economic uses to which the property may be put. As such, they are a potentially valuable and even a transferable commodity and may not be disregarded in determining whether the ordinance has destroyed the economic value of the underlying property (cf. *Newport Assoc. v. Solow,* 30 N.Y.2d 263, 268, 332 N.Y.S.2d 617, 621, 283 N.E.2d 600, 602 [concurring opn.], cert. den. 410 U.S. 931, 93 S.Ct. 1372, 35 L.Ed.2d 593).

Of course, the development rights of the parks were not nullified by the city's action. In an attempt to preserve the rights they were severed from the real property and made transferable to another section of mid-Manhattan in the city, but not to any particular parcel or place. There was thus created floating development rights, utterly unusable until they could be attached to some accommodating real property, available by happenstance of prior ownership, or by grant, purchase, or devise, and subject to the contingent approvals of administrative agencies. In such case, the development rights, disembodied abstractions of man's ingenuity, float in a limbo until restored to reality by reattachment to tangible real property. Put another way, it is a tolerable abstraction to consider development rights apart from the solid land from which as a matter of zoning law they derive. But severed, the development rights are a double abstraction until they are actually attached to a receiving parcel, yet to be identified, acquired, and subject to the contingent future approvals of administrative agencies, events which may never happen because of the exigencies of the market and the contingencies and exigencies of administrative action. The acceptance of this contingency-ridden arrangement, however, was mandatory under the amendment.

The problem with this arrangement, as Mr. Justice Waltemade so wisely observed at Special Term, is that it fails to assure preservation of the very real economic value of the development rights as they existed when still attached to the underlying property (77 Misc.2d 199, 201, 352 N.Y.S.2d 762, 764). By compelling the owner to enter an unpredictable real estate market to find a suitable receiving lot for the rights, or a purchaser who would then share the same interest in using additional development rights, the amendment renders uncertain and thus severely impairs the value of the development rights before they were severed (se Note, The Unconstitutionality of Transferable Development Rights, 84 Yale L.J. 1101; 1110-1111). Hence, when viewed in relation to both the value of the private parks after the amendment, and the value of the development rights detached from the private parks, the amendment destroyed the economic value of the property. It thus constituted a deprivation of property without due process of law.

None of this discussion of the effort to accomplish the highly beneficial purposes of creating additional park land in the teeming city bears any relation to other schemes, variously described as a "development bank" or the "Chicago Plan" (see Costonis, The Chicago Plan: Incentive Zoning and the Preservation of Urban Landmarks, 85 Harv.L.Rev. 574; Costonis, Development Rights Transfer: An Exploratory Essay, 83 Yale L.J. 75, 86-87). For under such schemes or variations of them, the owner of the granting parcel may be allowed just compensation for his development rights, instantly and in money, and the acquired development rights are then placed in a "bank" from which enterprises may for a price purchase development rights to use on land owned by them. Insofar as the owner of the granting parcel is concerned, his development rights are taken by the State, straightforwardly, and he is paid just compensation for them in eminent domain. The appropriating governmental entity recoups its disbursements, when, as, and if it obtains a purchaser for those rights. In contrast, the 1972 zoning amendment shortcircuits the double-tracked compensation scheme but to do this leaves the granting parcel's owner's development rights in limbo until the day of salvation, if ever it comes.

With respect to damages caused by the unlawful zoning amendment the issue is not properly before the court. The owner never made such an unequivocal claim and still does not. Instead, it claims compensation for value appropriated as for an "inverse" taking in eminent domain. The mortgagees and personal guarantor make parallel claims. That view of the invalid amendment is not adopted for the reasons discussed at length earlier. The city, on the other hand, seeks a declaration with respect to such damages, but in the absence of allegation or proof that such damages lie, are claimed, or how they have been incurred, there can be no abstract declaration, and therefore there is none.

It would be a misreading of the discussion above to conclude that the court is insensitive to the inescapable need for government to devise methods, other than by outright appropriation of the fee, to meet urgent environmental needs of a densely concentrated urban population. It would be equally simplistic to ignore modern recognition of the principle that no property has value except as the community contributes to that value. The obverse of this principle is, therefore, of first significance: no property is an economic island, free from contributing to the welfare of the whole of which it is but a dependent part. The limits are that unfair or disproportionate burdens may not, constitutionally, be placed on single properties or their owners. The possible solutions undoubtedly lie somewhere in the areas of general taxation, assessments for public benefit (but with an expansion of the traditional views with respect to what are assessable public benefits), horizontal eminent domain illustrated by a true "taking" of development rights with corresponding compensation, development banks, and other devices which will insure rudimentary fairness in the allocation of economic burdens.

Solutions must be reached for the problems of modern zoning, urban and rural conservation, and last but not least landmark preservations, whether by particular buildings or historical districts. Unfortunately, the land planners are now only at the beginning of the path to solution. In the process of traversing that path further, new ideas and new standards of constitutional tolerance must and will evolve. It is enough to say that the loose-ended transferable development rights in this case fall short of achieving a fair allocation of economic burden. Even though the development rights have not been nullified, their severance has rendered their value so uncertain and contingent, as to deprive the property owner of their practical usefulness, except under rare and perhaps coincidental circumstances.

The legislative and administrative efforts to solve the zoning and landmark problem in modern society demonstrate the presence of ingenuity (see, e. g., *Lutheran Church in Amer. v. City of New York,* 35 N.Y.2d 121, 359 N.Y.S.2d 7, 316 N.E.2d 305, *supra; Newport Assoc v. Solow,* 30 N.Y.2d 263, 332 N.Y.S.2d 617, 283 NE.2d 600, *supra; Matter of Golden v. Planning Bd. of Town of Ramapo,* 30 N.Y.2d 359, 334 N.Y.S.2d 138, 285 N.E.2d 291, *supra*). That ingenuity further pursued will in all likelihood achieve the goals without placing an impossible or unsuitable burden on the individual property owner, the public fisc, or the general taxpayer. These efforts are entitled to and will undoubtedly receive every encouragement. The task is difficult but not beyond management. The end is essential but the means must nevertheless conform to constitutional standards.

Accordingly, the order of the Appellate Division should be affirmed, without costs, and the certified question answered in the affirmative.

JASEN, GABRIELLI, JONES, WACHTLER, FUCHSBERG and COOKE, JJ., concur.

Order affirmed, etc.

Questions and Notes

In June 1977, the highest New York court strongly (and unanimously) upheld the validity of a landmark designation on Grand Central Station, with an accompanying denial of a permit for a proposed second office tower over the station. In a noteworthy opinion, Chief Judge Breitel also made two other holdings of the highest importance. First, that the constitutional requirement to permit some reasonable return on property ("the nation-wide rule") need not apply to that part of the value of property which has been created by public investment. Second, that it is appropriate, in calculating a "reasonable return," to take into consideration the value of reasonably transferable development rights—a decision which clearly recognizes the validity of the principle of transferability. See Penn Central Transportation Co. v. City of New York, New York Court of Appeals, June 23, 1977, aff'd. 50 App. Div. 2d 265, 377 N.Y.S. 2d 20 (1st Dep't. 1975).

Section 10

Industrial Zoning

THOMAS

v.

BEDFORD

11 N.Y. 2d 428, 230 N.Y.S.2d. 684, 184 N.E. 2d 285(1962).

Court of Appeals of New York.

July 6, 1962.

Action challenging constitutionality of rezoning ordinance. The Supreme Court, Westchester County, Special Term, James D. Hopkins, J., 29 Misc.2d 861, 214 N.Y.S.2d 145, dismissed the complaint on the merits, and plaintiff appealed. The Appellate Division of the Supreme Court in the Second Judicial Department, by judgment entered January 24, 1962, 15 A.D.2d 573, 222 N.Y.S.2d 1021, unanimously affirmed, and plaintiffs appealed on constitutional grounds. The Court of Appeals, Fuld, J., held that town board's action in rezoning 123 acre tract from residential to research office use was not arbitrary, where it was adopted after careful study and consultation with experts and extensive hearings, conformed with comprehensive plan, and imposed requirements even more stringent to those applying to residential area.

Judgment affirmed.

Harold Riegelman, H. H. Nordlinger and James D. Stillman, New York City, for appellants.

Ambrose Doskow, New York City, Edwin H. Uellendahl and Ernest A. Gleit, New York City, for respondents.

FULD, Judge.

In March of 1960, the Town of Bedford amended its 1946 zoning ordinance to rezone certain property from residence 2-A (two acres) and residence 4-A (four acres) use to an RO (research office) use. The plaintiffs, who live in 2-A and 4-A districts adjacent to or close by the rezoned area, brought the present action to declare the amendment unconstitutional and void and to enjoin the town officials from acting thereunder. The court at Special Term dismissed the complaint and the Appellate Division unanimously affirmed the judgment. The appeal is taken to this court as of right upon constitutional grounds.

The Town of Bedford is situated in northern Westchester County about 38 miles from New York City. Its population has nearly doubled since 1940. About 80 per cent of its land, much of it vacant, is zoned for two-acre or four-acre residential use; three per cent is devoted to industrial and commercial uses, the remainder to residential uses of less than two acres. The property here involved consists of 123 acres located in Bedford Village, which is in the Katonah section of the town. It has a frontage of about 3,000 feet on Route 22 or Jay Street, the village's main thoroughfare. Once a single estate, it is now divided into three parcels. One consists of 37 acres of vacant land bordering on Jay Street and belonging to Ruth Alice N. Halsband, the former owner of the entire tract. The second comprises 18 acres owned and operated under a special permit by Hickrill Chemical Research Foundation, an eleemosynary chemical research laboratory founded by Mrs. Halsband and her former husband, now deceased, and headed by her son, Frank Weil. The third contains 68 acres sold by Mrs. Halsband in 1957 to the Harvey School which has been in existence for some 37 years.

Before the town effected the rezoning now challenged, the portion of the property along Jay Street was in a 2-A district and the balance in a 4-A zone. The property surrounding it is for the most part similarly zoned, although there are located nearby the American Legion Club, with swimming pool and picnic tables, the John Jay home, an historical shrine, and, about a mile away, the Westfield State Farm, a prison for women. The subject property is about a half mile from the intersection of Route 22 and the Sawmill River Parkway, about a mile from the Katonah Railway Station and not far from the Cross River Reservoir, a part of the New York City watershed system.

The new RO classification reflects a type of land use which has become widespread since World War II in suburban sections surrounding New York City and other large metropolitan areas. The Town Planning Board of Bedford and its consultants had initiated plans for such zoning in 1956 and the present property figured in those plans. Partly because the ultimate location of Route 22 was then in doubt, however, no action was taken in the matter until 1959, when Frank Weil sought to sell the Hickrill property to Reichhold Chemicals, Inc., for a research and development laboratory.

This, to cull from the testimony of Mr. Weil, "triggered a refreshed interest in the whole idea of RO zoning". New studies and reports were made and hearings held and in October, 1959 the Town Board amended the 1946 zoning ordinance to establish an RO district, and the Planning Board recommended three areas, one of them being the subject property. Considerable opposition developed—part of it based on the incomplete status of a Town Development Plan which had been in progress for some years. However, the Town Board did no more than postpone decision on the matter in order to revise and make more strict the provisions relating to access and area requirements. Finally, on March 8, 1960, after a public hearing, the Town Board unanimously adopted a resolution rezoning the subject property for RO purposes, and 23 days later further limitations in connection with RO uses were approved; the Bedford RO classification became the most restricted in the entire county.

The minimum size for an RO development was 25 acres, the building area being limited to 10 per cent of the lot and the total floor area to 15 per cent. The maximum height was three stories. Setback regulations, including those for parking space, were strict, and parking areas were required to be screened from neighboring properties. Developments employing more than 50 people were compelled to provide direct access to a state or county highway. No uses were permitted which would result in the dissemination of dust or smoke, in vibration, excessive light, noise or traffic congestion. The Town Board was required to approve all proposed plans and could condition its approval upon adequate screening and shading to reduce the "emission of artificial light" at night. In short, many of the restrictions upon RO uses were more rigorous than those for 4-A districts.

[1] In any area of even moderate density, comprehensive and balanced zoning is essential to the health, safety and welfare of the community (Town Law, Consol. Laws, c. 62, § 261; Village Law, Consol. Laws, c. 64, § 175). The task of achieving this goal devolves upon the local legislative body, and its "judgment must be allowed to control" if the classification is "fairly debatable". (Rodgers v. Village of Tarrytown, 302 N.Y. 115, 121, 96 N.E.2d 731, 733, quoting from Euclid v. Ambler Co., 272 U.S. 365, 388, 47 S.Ct. 114, 71 L.Ed. 303; see, also, Shepard v. Village of Skaneateles, 300 N.Y. 115, 118, 89 N.E.2d 619, 620; Town of Islip v. Summers Coal & Lbr. Co., 257 N.Y. 167, 169, 170, 177 N.E. 409, 410.) In other words, the courts may not interfere unless the local body's determination is arbitrary, and "the burden of establishing such arbitrariness is imposed upon him who asserts it." (Rodgers v. Village of Tarrytown, 302 N.Y. 115, 121, 96 N.E.2d 731, 733, supra.)

[2, 3] These principles apply with equal force to rezoning, where there is presented the additional problem of adjusting a durable and uniform zoning pattern to altered conditions, whether local or county. As we wrote in the Rodgers case (302 N.Y. 115, 121, 96 N.E.2d 731, 733), "While stability and regularity are undoubtedly essential to the operation of zoning

plans, zoning is by no means static. Changed or changing conditions call for changed plans, and persons who own property in a particular zone or use district enjoy no eternally vested right to that classification if the public interest demands otherwise. Accordingly, the power of a village to amend its basic zoning ordinance in such a way as reasonably to promote the general welfare cannot be questioned."

[4] In the present case, the plaintiffs take the position that the town enacted a comprehensive zoning ordinance in 1946 which fully met, and still meets, the needs of the community and that it may not be amended without a showing of need, based on financial considerations or arising from changed conditions. At the same time, they declare that they have no general objection to an RO classification as such, but only to the fact that it has been placed in the portion of the town selected. What the plaintiffs are attempting to do, it seems clear, is to reverse the presumption that the ordinance is valid and place upon the town officials the burden of proving that they acted reasonably. The town, of course, is not required to establish a need for rezoning; the burden of proving arbitrariness rests upon the plaintiffs.

[5] The zoning under attack was reasonable and in accordance with a comprehensive plan. It was adopted after careful study and consultation with experts and after extensive hearings at which interested persons were given an opportunity to be heard; even the plaintiffs' own expert did not assert that the new zoning failed to follow a comprehensive plan. Furthermore, changing conditions completely justified the change which was effected. With the enormous and continuing population growth and the expansion of business into suburban communities in the metropolitan area, the town planners necessarily realized that increasing urbanization of the town was inevitable. Observing the trend in the suburbs toward the development of campus-type laboratory and research projects, they very properly decided that this type of zoning might preserve a fair measure of peace and serenity in their locality in the face of growing demands for business and commercial use of vacant land.

To state the matter briefly, by insisting upon a minimum of 25 acres for a research development and a building area limited to 10 percent of the land, with provision for setback and screening requirements far more stringent than those for 2-A and 4-A districts, the town has effected a balance between the pressure of changing conditions and the preservation of the rural atmosphere so much desired by residents of the area.

[6] The plaintiffs' charge of "spot zoning" has been adequately dealt with in Justice Hopkins' careful and thorough opinion at Special Term, and little need be added to what he wrote. Such spot zoning, we have said, is the "process of singling out a small parcel of land for a use classification totally different from that of the surrounding area, for the benefit of the owner of such property and to the detriment of other owners". (Rodgers v. Village of Tarrytown, 302 N.Y. 115, 123, 96 N.E.2d 731, 735,

supra.) Whether the size of the "parcel" here involved, comprising an area of 123 acres, is sufficient, without more, to exonerate the town officials from the charge leveled against them, we need not say. Since the Town Board acted in accordance with a comprehensive plan, even the singling out of one lot or the creation of a small area in the center of a large zone devoted to a different use will not be condemned as spot zoning. (See, e. g., Shepard v. Village of Skaneateles, 300 N.Y. 115, 89 N.E.2d 619, supra; Nappi v. LaGuardia, 295 N.Y. 652, 64 N.E.2d 716.) The vice of spot zoning is its inevitable effect of granting to a single owner a discriminatory benefit at the expense and to the detriment of his neighbors, without any public advantage or justification. That is not the situation here. As we have already noted, the introduction of RO zoning was contemplated as part of a comprehensive plan, albeit an alteration of the original 1946 plan, to preserve the quiet and spaciousness of a community increasingly subject to pressure from a rapidly growing population and from business expansion in the metropolitan area.

The judgment should be affirmed, with costs.

DESMOND, C. J., and DYE, FROESSEL, VAN VOORHIS, BURKE and FOSTER, JJ., concur.

Judgment affirmed.

Questions and Notes

1. What is an RO District? Why are such districts so popular with municipal officials?

2. Where else have we seen a similar district?

TIDEWATER OIL COMPANY

v.

CARTERET

80 N.J. Super. 283, 193 A.2d 412 (1963),

revd., 84 N.J. Super. 525, 202 A.2d 865(1964),

(appellate opinion) affd., 44 N.J. 338, 209 A.2d 105(1965)

Superior Court of New Jersey

Law Division.

July 23, 1963.

Action challenging zoning ordinance which called for exclusion of new petroleum industries, including manufacturing, processing and storage, from Heavy-Industrial Zone on waterfront land particularly suited for heavy industry operating by deep-water shipment. The Superior Court, Middlesex County, Law Division, Furman, J. S. C., held that the ordinance was invalid as not reasonably related to or in furtherance of statutory zoning purposes. Judgment accordingly.

Lewis S. Jacobson, Perth Amboy, for plaintiffs (Sam Weiss, Newark, on the brief; Jacobson & Winter, Perth Amboy, attorneys).

Emory C. Risley, Newark, for intervenor (Stryker, Tams & Dill, Newark, attorneys).

Benedict W. Harrington, Newark, for defendants (Kessler, Kessler & Harrington, Newark, attorneys).

FURMAN, J.S.C.

The zoning ordinance of the Borough of Carteret, enacted May 8, 1963, is under attack for constitutional and statutory flaws, The plaintiffs are the owner and the contract purchaser of premises fronting on the Arthur Kill in the Heavy Industrial B Zone and two individual citizens and taxpayers. The intervening plaintiff is the owner of premises adjoining the plaintiffs' in the B Zone, which it has listed with real estate brokers for sale as an industrial property. The present land and uses are a lumber business on the plaintiffs' property and a varied metallurgical and chemical industry on the intervenor's property, including detinning of tin scrap and manufacture of organic solvents. Plaintiff Tidewater Oil Company proposes to operate a petroleum storage tank terminal.

The Borough of Carteret is four square miles in area, with a population in excess of 20,000. Its easterly boundary is the Arthur Kill. Its northerly boundary is the Rahway River. The Arthur Kill, dividing New Jersey and Staten Island, has a dredged 35 foot channel at or near the pier line on the Carteret shore. The Rahway River has a mean depth of 25 feet for a short distance upstream from its junction with the Arthur Kill. Thereafter its channel adjoining Carteret is four to nine feet and not navigable by ocean-going tankers.

The borough enacted its first zoning ordinance in December 1958. The Heavy Industrial Zone comprised the entire waterfront along the Arthur Kill and the waterfront along the Rahway River from the Arthur Kill west to the New Jersey Turnpike. While the district varied in depth inland from the waterways, most of its southerly portion extended 1000 to 2000 feet from the Arthur Kill to Roosevelt Avenue and most of its northerly portion extended about 3000 feet from the Rahway River to Roosevelt Avenue, which makes a right-angle turn from a north-south to an east-west thoroughfare.

The designation as heavy industrial conformed to the character of the district for 60 years or longer. Much of the land is reclaimed by fill. Heavy industry, including petroleum storage facilities, chemical, fertilizer and other manufacturing industries are massed along the Arthur Kill. Some undeveloped land with pockets of marshland and tidal creeks is south of the Rahway River. Two large petroleum tank "farms" are north of Roosevelt Avenue. Storage tanks for naphtha and sulfur are south and east of Roosevelt Avenue. A major chemical industry located here after 1958 but most of the changes in the intervening period involved plant additions or improvements.

The adjoining residential and business zones likewise retained their essential character between 1958 and 1963, built-up and heavily populated. New home construction was minimal except in housing developments one-half mile or more from the Heavy Industrial Zone and a senior citizens housing project with nine buildings and 50 units completed in 1962 within a short distance of the plaintiffs' and intervenor's properties.

The zoning ordinance of 1958 was ruled invalid for procedural defects in a letter opinion by Judge Molineux in Cinege v. Borough of Carteret. No judgment was filed because of a stipulation of dismissal. Plaintiff Tidewater Oil Company broached its plan to construct a petroleum storage tank terminal in Carteret to borough officials, including the then mayor and members of the council, in the summer of 1962. A use permit was requisite under the 1958 ordinance, contingent upon proof to the board of adjustment that a proposed industry was not dangerous or objectionable to the public. Tidewater proceeded in conformity with the 1958 ordinance. The preliminary negotiations raised no serious objections. Tidewater agreed to build an off-street parking area and a Little League baseball field, to plant trees and shrubs along Roosevelt Avenue and to participate *pro rata* with other industries in the event the borough condemned land of the Central Railroad of New Jersey for a public road bisecting various industrial properties parallel to the Arthur Kill and Roosevelt Avenue.

A new mayor and two new members of the six-member council assumed office on January 1, 1963. The plaintiffs applied for a building permit and a use permit for the construction of a petroleum storage tank terminal on February 1, 1963. An unofficial meeting was held by the members of the governing body 11 days later. About 150 citizens attended. Opposition to Tidewater was vehement and overwhelming. Councilman Hutnick moved with a second that Tidewater be kept out of the Borough of Carteret. The board of adjustment held a public hearing on the use permit application on February 26 and March 5, 1963, but adjourned for 60 days without concluding the hearing and without a decision, upon advice from Mayor Banick and Councilman Boncelet that a new zoning ordinance affecting the plaintiffs' property was under consideration.

On February 28, 1963 the planning board discussed for an hour or more a proposal to divide the Heavy Industrial Zone into A and B zones, with restrictions against petroleum industries in the latter zone. An amendment to the zoning ordinance of December 1958 accomplishing this result was drafted with the participation of the planning board and recommended for adoption to the governing body, at a special meeting of the planning board on March 5, 1963. The governing body enacted this amendment on March 20, 1963. The area in the Heavy Industrial Zone south of Roosevelt Avenue, including the plaintiffs' and intervenor's properties, was established as the B zone.

This zoning amendment remained in force less than two months. The council members and the incoming mayor viewed with concern the continuing doubtful validity of the 1958 ordinance. The planning board considered a complete new ordinance at a regular meeting on March 28, 1963 and voted to recommend its enactment at a special meeting on April 1, 1963. The borough council adopted it on May 8, 1963. The Heavy Industrial A Zone, north of Roosevelt Avenue, and the Heavy Industrial B Zone, south of Roosevelt Avenue, are identical with the zones which were created by the amendment of March 20, 1963. As pertinent here, the zoning ordinance of May 8, 1963 permits heavy industrial uses in both A and B zones, except that the following uses are permitted in the A zone but prohibited in the B zone:

"The storage, manufacturing, refining or blending, of oil, oils, gas, gasoline, petroleum, crude oil, tars or any of the volatile, flammable, or explosive component parts of oil, gasoline, kerosene, petroleum, or crude oil or oils, or any of the inflammable, volatile or explosive liquids which are or can be derivative from gasoline, crude oil, tars or parts thereof, excepting however, storage of oil, fuel oil, gas or gasoline or petroleum for on-the-premises consumption of heat, fuel, power or other required consumption on the same premises in said zone where they are stored or maintained, and not for off-the-premises distribution or consumption.

No tanks or other containers or structures for storage or maintenance of such articles for off-the-premises distribution, use or consumption shall be erected, built, constructed, maintained, used or operated but only such as are essential for on-the-premises consumption in connection with a manufacturing or processing use or pursuit of another nature permitted in said zone. The lone exceptions will be those persons, companies, corporations, etc., who are and have been carrying on such functions or operations prior to the date of the adoption of the ordinance."

The plaintiffs assert the zoning ordinance should be set aside because of noncompliance with N.J.S.A. 40:55-35, which requires submission of proposed zoning enactments to the planning board, and with N.J.S.A. 10:4-1, the "Right to Know" Law. In addition, both the plaintiffs and the intervenor challenge the restriction against petroleum industries in the Heavy Industrial B Zone as arbitrary, without reasonable relation to the statutory zoning purposes (R.S. 40:55-32), N.J.S.A., and as discriminatory in its classification of permitted and prohibited uses. A further contention that the plaintiffs were entitled to building and use permits because of expenditures and commitments in reliance upon prior law must be stricken for lack of supporting proof. See Crecca v. Nucera, 52 N.J.Super. 279, 145 A.2d 477 (App.Div.1958).

[1] The court is satisfied that neither N.J.S.A. 40:55-35 nor N.J.S.A. 10:4-1 was violated in the planning board procedure. The planning board discussed the proposed division into Heavy Industrial A and B Zones at two regular and two special meetings. The regular meeting of March 28, 1963 was legally advertised as a public hearing on the ordinance ultimately adopted. No newspaper notice was published of the meeting of April 1, 1963 when the planning board voted to recommend adoption of the new zoning ordinance. An arrow sign directed members of the public to the meeting room, the public was not barred, the door of the meeting room was open throughout and a newspaper reporter was in attendance. Newspaper notice or advertisement is not a *sine qua non* for a public meeting. The meeting of April 1, 1963 was a public meeting, not a secret caucus or executive session. Cf. Wolf. v. Zoning Board of Adjustment of Park Ridge, 79 N.J.Super. 546, 192 A.2d 305 (App.Div.1963).

The planning board transmitted the new zoning ordinance with map and an accompanying letter stating its approval to the mayor and council, subsequent to the April 1, 1963 meeting. In addition to the specific documents, which are self-explanatory, the members of the governing body had available the planning board minutes setting forth details of its consideration of the zoning amendment which it participated in drafting prior to its adoption on March 20, 1963, and of the identical provisions of the new ordinance of May 8, 1963.

With the determination of the procedural issues against the plaintiffs, the court must test the constitutional and statutory sufficiency of the zoning ordinance of the Borough of Carteret, under substantive principles applied to the facts in proof. The municipal zoning power, specifically authorized by N.J.Const., Art. IV, § VI, par. 2, and subject to liberal construction by Art. IV, § VII, par. 11, may be exercised for the following purposes pursuant to R.S. 40:55-32, N.J.S.A.:

> "Such regulations shall be in accordance with a comprehensive plan and designed for one or more of the following purposes: to lessen congestion in the streets; secure safety from fire, panic and other dangers; promote health, morals or the general welfare; provide adequate light and air; prevent the overcrowding of land or buildings; avoid undue concentration of population. Such regulations shall be made with reasonable consideration, among other things, to the character of the district and its peculiar suitability for particular uses, and with a view of conserving the value of property and encouraging the most appropriate use of land throughout such municipality."

The decisive issue is whether the exclusion of new petroleum industries in the Heavy Industrial B Zone is in accordance with a classification of land uses reasonably related to and in furtherance of one or more of the statutory zoning purposes. The exclusion is broad. Storage, manufacturing, refining and blending of petroleum, gasoline, oils, tars, any of their volatile, inflammable or explosive components, or any of the volatile, inflammable or explosive liquids which are or can be derivative from gasoline, crude oil or tars are prohibited in the B zone, except for consumption on the premises for heat, fuel, power or in connection with a permitted manufacturing or processing use.

Without detailed expert testimony, the court cannot specify the exact number of nonconforming uses created in the B zone by the zoning amendment of March 20, 1963 and the comprehensive enactment of May 8, 1963. A majority of the organic chemicals in general industrial use are petroleum based. Substantially all of them may be derived from petroleum and thus meet the B zone restriction, although manufactured in practice from other hydrocarbons. Manufacture or storage of naphtha and benzene by other industries in the B zone and manufacture of various coatings by the intervenor would be barred as new uses.

[2] The Arthur Kill waterfront in the Borough of Carteret is prime land for heavy industry operating by deep-water shipment of raw materials and rail, highway or barge reshipment of products. It is in the category of a natural resource. Plaintiff Tidewater examined 40 sites in the New York metropolitan area and picked its proposed Carteret site as one of three most advantageous. The land elevations are higher on the average in the B zone than in the A zone, without marshland or tidal creeks. The available land for new industry in the A zone fronts on the Rahway River, which lacks a deep-water channel. A municipality may seek a balancing of heavy and light industry through planning and zoning. It may not exclude an extensive segment of heavy industry as a new use, in this case the petroleum, organic chemical and related manufacturing and processing industries, although permitted in another district, unless the prohibition is reasonably founded upon one or more of the legislative zoning objectives.

[3, 4] In determining the reasonableness of such an enactment, the court may consider the physical characteristics and suitability of the districts in which an industry is permitted and in which it is barred, and the extent of existing operations in the industry in both districts, elsewhere in the municipality and in nearby municipalities. The creation of nonconforming uses is evidential that a zoning ordinance does not reasonably fulfill the statutory purpose of encouraging the most appropriate use of land throughout the municipality. Zampieri v. River Vale Tp., 29 N.J. 599, 607, 152 A.2d 28 (1959).

The evidence before this court is that industries prohibited in the Heavy Industrial B Zone are operating on a widespread scale in both the A and B zones and in nearby municipalities along the Arthur Kill; that the B zone is suited to them because of its land elevations and access to deep water and reshipment facilities; that the undeveloped land in the A zone is less suited to them, and that both A and B zones abut upon residential and business concentrations.

[5] The plaintiffs contend that the officials of the Borough of Carteret had a predominant purpose to block Tidewater. Undoubtedly the Tidewater application alerted them to possible objections concerned with public health and safety, as well as to public opposition. A municipality need not anticipate all objectionable land uses. Upon learning that one is proposed, it may legislate to bar it through its zoning power. Unless in bad faith, an ordinance is not invalid *per se* because designed against one property owner, if reasonably related to the statutory zoning purposes. The court finds no bad faith in the zoning enactment of the Borough of Carteret.

[6] In determining the reasonableness of legislation, a court may search out the factors impelling it and its apparent objectives. Zampieri v. River Vale Tp., supra, and Glen Rock Realty Co. v. Board of Adjustment, etc., of Glen Rock, 80 N.J. Super. 79, 192 A.2d 865 (App.Div.1963). Because of the testimony of all but one member of the governing body and most members of the planning board, speculation is at a minimum. Their concern was with the threat of fires and explosions, both on the premises and in tank trucks passing through the public streets, with added traffic congestion and with the loss of employment opportunities.

[7] Legislation may attack an evil where it is worst. Two Guys From Harrison, Inc. v. Furman, 32 N.J. 199, 229, 160 A.2d 265 (1960). Two preliminary comments are appropriate. All factors bearing upon fire and traffic safety and traffic volume apply to new petroleum or related industries in the A zone as well as in the B zone. Existing petroleum storage tanks in the A zone are within 300 to 400 feet of dwelling houses. Tank trucks making deliveries and shipments from either zone would pass through residential and business areas, by schools and churches. One slight distinction is that the route is longer from most points in the B zone to the New Jersey Turnpike interchange at Roosevelt Avenue in Carteret.

Secondly, permitted industries in the B zone are serviced by trucks, in many cases heavy trucks. But the governing body may have considered that tank trucks up to 44 feet in length were a recognized problem and that it need not conjecture that other industries might generate as much or more traffic with trucks of comparable lengths.

The evidence on the threat of fires and explosions dealt exclusively with petroleum storage facilities and tank trucks. Expert witnesses developed to the satisfaction of the court that a petroleum storage terminal is a relatively safe installation, rated as a lower fire risk than, for example, a lumber business. Scientific advances have reduced the fire and explosion threat to negligibility. Floating roofs eliminate the vapor space. Venting techniques to eliminate pressure are improved. The conversions from rolled to extruded steel and from riveting to welding have virtually eliminated the possibility of tank rupture. Other safeguards are foam chambers and dikes. Similar advances in technique have substantially foreclosed the threat of fire, explosion or rupture in tank trucks even upon collision. The borough has experienced only two accidents involving tank trucks since 1950.

[8] A municipality acting under the zoning power to secure safety from fire or explosion must take into consideration prevailing industrial techniques based upon scientific advances. A municipality may deny a use permit to a property owner who fails to avail himself of established safeguards in his plans for the construction of industrial facilities. It has other statutory remedies and common law remedies to redress nuisances. But it cannot rule out an entire industry through apprehension of safety standards deviations.

The zoning restriction under attack applies to manufacturing and processing as well as storage operations involving petroleum products. Evidence is lacking as to their fire and explosion risks. By definition volatile, inflammable or explosive components or liquid derivatives of petroleum may not be manufactured or refined in the Heavy Industrial B Zone. The court must assume dangers to the public in such operations in the absence of specific countervailing testimony.

The effect of the zoning ordinance of May 8, 1963 is to permit manufacturing and processing industries labelled dangerous in Heavy Industrial A Zone and to prohibit them in Heavy Industrial B Zone. To be sustained as valid, such differing legislative treatment must be reasonably justified by distinctions between the two zones or their environs. With respect to the physical characteristics and suitability of the two zones, the evidence is plain that petroleum industries dependent upon deep-water transportation must look to industrial sites along the Arthur Kill waterfront, which is in the proscribed B zone or pre-empted by existing industries in the A zone.

Between the adjoining areas no substantial distinctions are found. Numerous dwellings, both one-family and multi-family, back upon both Heavy Industrial Zones. Churches, schools and other public places dot the right-angle course of Roosevelt Avenue, the western boundary of the B zone and the southern boundary of the A zone. The individual members of the public are entitled to an equal measure of legislative protection in matters of public safety. Assuming fire and explosion hazards in the petroleum industry, the residents south of the Heavy Industrial A Zone are exposed to it, the residents west of the Heavy Industrial B Zone are shielded from it by the ordinance under attack.

The threat of traffic congestion has two aspects. More vehicles, particularly bulky vehicles, may impair traffic flow. The accident rate may increase with an added volume of traffic. Roosevelt Avenue is the main artery into and out of the Borough of Carteret. With the opening of the New Jersey Turnpike interchange, heavy truck traffic has built up along Roosevelt Avenue within the borough and from urban and industrial centers south of the borough.

Roosevelt Avenue, opposite plaintiffs' property, is approximately 35 feet wide with an asphalt surface. The Columbus School is directly across from the private access road to the plaintiffs' property at the corner of Roosevelt and Carteret Avenues. By traffic counts the volume of traffic on Roosevelt Avenue is approximately one-half of capacity during most of the daylight and evening hours and close to two-thirds of capacity during peak hours. Capacity is figured as 900 vehicles, combining trucks and passenger cars, in each direction per hour. There is a school crossing on Carteret Avenue but not on Roosevelt Avenue, in view of the small number of residences east of Roosevelt Avenue.

Before the planning board and governing body plaintiff Tidewater projected truck traffic statistics for its proposed operation on the plaintiffs' property. The forecast was 95 round trips, or 190 trips in-and-out per day, with the heaviest volume about 12 trucks per hour at peak hours.

The court is satisfied that congestion from tank trucks servicing petroleum industries in the B Zone would be negligible. Through the use permit technique access roads of sufficient width to prevent tank trucks' blocking two-way traffic can be assured. Carteret Avenue may by ordinance be limited to light traffic. Accordingly, no reasonable relation is found between the exclusion of petroleum industries in the Heavy Industrial B Zone and the zoning objective of lessening congestion in the streets. Cf. Bogert v. Washington Twp., 25 N.J. 57, 65, 135 A.2d 1 (1957).

Some borough officials stressed as a factor in their legislative action the employment advantages of manufacturing and processing industries in contrast to storage operations. The zoning ordinance of May 8, 1963 is not so drawn. As discussed supra, manufacturing and processing as well as storage of petroleum, its components and derivatives are barred. A zoning ordinance cannot be defended constitutionally on a ground inapplicable to it, by conjecture that it might apply to and support another zoning ordinance.

A further objectionable aspect of the zoning ordinance under attack should be pointed out. By its specific terms nonconforming uses in the Heavy Industrial B Zone may be expanded. The statutory sanction of pre-existing nonconforming uses (R.S. 40:55-48, N.J.S.A.) is designed to guarantee constitutional rights. Authorization to increase or enlarge nonconforming uses is not constitutionally mandatory but derogates from and tends to nullify valid legislative objectives.

[9] The court therefore determines that the exclusion of new petroleum industries in the Heavy Industrial B Zone is not in accordance with a classification of land uses reasonably related to and in furtherance of the statutory zoning purposes.

TIDEWATER OIL COMPANY

v.

CARTERET

84 N.J.Super. 525, 202 A.2d 105(1965), aff'd. 44 N.J. 338,
20 A.2d 105 (1965).

Superior Court of New Jersey

Appellate Division.

Argued June 15, 1964.

Decided July 1, 1964.

A final judgment of the Superior Court, Law Division, declared invalid
certain portions of a zoning ordinance, 80 N.J.Super. 283, 193 A.2d 412.
The defendants appealed. The Superior Court, Appellate Division, Freund,
J. A. D., held that where action was in furtherance of a valid zoning purpose, a municipality could divide an area which had long been devoted
to heavy industrial uses into two zones and prohibit storage and refining
of petroleum in one zone where it did not exist and allow in the other
where it had long existed to a large extent.

Remanded with directions to enter judgment in favor of municipality.

Benedict W. Harrington, Newark, for appellants (Kessler, Kessler & Harrington, Newark, attorneys).

Emory C. Risley, Newark, for intervenor-respondent (Stryker, Tams &
Dill, Newark, attorneys).

Sam Weiss, Newark, for respondents (Jacobson & Winter, Perth Amboy,
attorneys; Sam Weiss, Newark, on the brief).

Before Judges CONFORD, FREUND and SULLIVAN.

The opinion of the court was delivered by

FREUND, J. A. D.

Defendants appeal from a final judgment of the Superior Court, Law
Division, declaring invalid those portions of the Borough of Carteret zoning
ordinance, as adopted May 8, 1963, which divided the then existing heavy
industrial zone into two parts, and placed use restrictions on one which
were not made applicable to the other.

The factual background is fully set forth in the trial court's opinion, see
Tidewater Oil Co. v. Mayor, etc. of Carteret, 80 N.J.Super. 283, 285-288,
193 A.2d 412 (LawDiv.1963), and we adopt the factual discussion therein
except where inconsistent with or amplified by what is stated in this opinion. We further adopt the trial court's findings of fact that the May 8
amendment was enacted in good faith, and did not violate vested rights
on the part of any of the plaintiffs. In this regard, it is clear that while it
was Tidewater's application to build a petroleum storage facility which

gave rise to the municipal concern with a spread of that kind of industry in the borough, see Roselle v. Mayor and Council of Borough of Moonachie, 49 N.J.Super. 35, 40, 139 A.2d 42 (App.Div.1958), and therefore some of the testimony deals with "keeping Tidewater out," the ultimate objective of the governing body was keeping the petroleum storage industry out of the entire section of the heavy industrial area where it had not yet penetrated, rather than merely excluding Tidewater.

For purposes of convenience we reiterate the facts crucial to an appellate determination of the present cause. Carteret's original heavy. industrial zone, as designated in its initial zoning ordinance of 1958, was, by amendment in March 1963, divided into two zones, the "Heavy Industrial A Zone" and the "Heavy Industrial B Zone." For technical reasons, the entire zoning ordinance, including this amendment, was reenacted on May 8, 1963. Although geographically and geophysically Zone B is as well (if not better) adapted for petroleum storage and refining as Zone A, the past industrial development of the Carteret waterfront (Arthur Kill on the eastern boundary and the Rahway River on the northern boundary) was such that the area now in Zone A is occupied to a great extent by large petroleum storage tanks, but that in Zone B is free of such "tank farms." Zone B does contain, however, several heavy industrial facilities which involve the manufacture and storage of petroleum derivatives. Under the May 8 ordinance the uses permitted in Zone A are exactly those which were permitted under the original single heavy industrial zone ordinance, but the following uses, permitted in Zone A, were prohibited in Zone B:

"1-1 The storage, manufacturing, refining or blending, of oil, oils, gas, gasoline, petroleum, crude oil, tars or any of the volatile, flammable, or explosive component parts of oil, gasoline, kerosene, petroleum, or crude oil or oils, or any of the inflammable, volatile or explosive liquids which are or can be derivative from gasoline, crude oil, tars or parts thereof, excepting however, storage of oil, fuel oil, gas or gasoline or petroleum for on-the-premises consumption for heat, fuel, power or other required consumption on the same premises in said zone where they are stored or maintained, and not for off-the-premises distribution or consumption.

1-2 No tanks or other containers or structures for storage or maintenance of such articles for off-the-premises distribution, use or consumption shall be erected, built, constructed, maintained, used or operated but only such as are essential for on-the-premises consumption in connection with a manufacturing or processing use or pursuit of another nature permitted in said zone. The lone exceptions will be those persons, companies, corporations, etc., who are and have been carrying on such functions or operations prior to the date of the adoption of the ordinance."

[1] The trial court found that the exclusion of new petroleum industries in Zone B was "not in accordance with a classification of land uses reasonably related to and in furtherance of the statutory zoning purposes." 80 N.J.Super., at p. 296, 193 A.2d, at p. 419. The appeal from that determina-

tion was argued before this court on June 15, 1964. That very night the borough council voted unanimously to adopt an amendment to section XII-1 of the zoning ordinance, which prescribed the permitted and prohibited uses for Zone B. It is well settled that, in respect of zoning uses, the law in effect at the time an appellate court decides a cause generally governs the disposition thereof, not the law prevailing when the case was decided in the trial court. Roselle v. Mayor and Council of Borough of Moonachie, 48 N.J.Super. 17, 21-22, 136 A.2d 773 (App.Div.1957). All the parties concede this case is to be decided on the basis of the ordinance as amended June 15, 1964. Supplemental briefs have been submitted in relation to the issues encompassed thereby. The broad question now before us is whether or not the ordinance of May 8, 1963, as altered by the June 15, 1964 amendment, is a valid exercise of the municipal police power as applied to this municipality.

The 1964 amendment, insofar as it parallels the former section XII-1, reads:

"1. In the Heavy Industrial 'B' (H.I.B.) Zone, a lot may be used and a structure erected, altered or occupied for any use permitted in the Heavy Industrial 'A' (H.I.A.) Zone, except for the following prohibited uses:

1-1. The storage or refining of oil, gas, gasoline, petroleum, crude oil or tars is not permitted excepting, however, storage of oil, fuel oil, gas, gasoline or petroleum for on-the-premises consumption for heat, fuel, power or other required consumption on the same premises in said zone where they are stored or maintained, and not for off-the-premises consumption or distribution is permitted.

1-2. No tanks or other structures for the storage or refining of oil, oils, gas, gasoline, petroleum, crude oil or tars for off-the-premises distribution or consumption shall be erected, built, constructed, maintained, used or operated."

Subparagraph 1-3 states that no industrial or manufacturing uses shall be permitted in Zone B except after the zoning board issues a permit. Conditions for the grant of such a permit are then described. There is no challenge here as to the validity of this procedure.

It is thus seen that, basically, the prohibition in Zone B under the 1963 ordinance was not only of petroleum storage and refining but also of all manufacturing and processing involving petroleum derivatives. The 1964 ordinance eliminated the prohibition of the latter. This serves, accordingly, to dispose of the basis for that portion of the trial court's invalidation of the zoning plan which rests on the creation thereby of a large number of nonconforming uses in Zone B. As the ordinance now stands, the prohibition in Zone B is confined to the storage or refining of petroleum and petroleum products. As to this, there is no resulting nonconformity since there are no existing petroleum storage or refining facilities in Zone B.

Since, however, much of both the trial court's opinion and the briefs of plaintiffs may be regarded as addressed to the supposed illegality of the present zone plan even as confined to a prohibition of petroleum storage and refining in Zone B (the uses Tidewater wants to make of the property it has selected), we will address ourselves to the arguments advanced in that regard. Basically, the contention is that the municipal split of the former Industrial Zone into A and B zones, barring petroleum storage, etc., from the latter, though purporting to rest on considerations of safety and traffic and similar factors, is actually so unjustified by the facts pertinent to those considerations, in the light of the evidence adduced at the trial, as to render the legislative action arbitrary and capricious. While the argument is not sound even as related to safety and traffic, as we shall demonstrate, it is necessary to point out that the municipal zoning viewpoint in adopting this zone scheme was somewhat more comprehensive than as assumed by plaintiffs.

Both judicial notice and the evidence in this case reveal that the northeast coastal section of New Jersey, particularly around New York Bay and its indentations, surrounding Carteret on all sides, is fertile territory for oil storage terminals. Moreover, such facilities tend, as a municipal representative in this case testified, to "mushroom" in an area where begun. Carteret's waterfront heavy industrial area had over the years developed massive petroleum storage facilities in its northern sector, now classified as Zone A. With the making known of Tidewater's intent to establish such a facility in the southern portion of the heavy industrial area it was feared according to one of the councilmen that the proposed and other oil plants would "push out" the more diversified kinds of industries, generally of a processing or manufacturing type, then in the area, which it was felt were better for the community in terms of tax ratables, job opportunities for residents of the town, and freedom from "inherent dangers," as well as avoiding traffic congestion. A member of the planning board testified to a fear of the town's becoming swamped with mammoth oil tank installations. He said: "We have tanks all around [us]. In fact we are surrounded by them."

In deciding where to draw the line for preventing expansion of "tank farms" in the heavy industrial area, the planning board and council made the entirely logical decision to restrict such operations to the portion of the area then already penetrated, and indeed long dominated, by such facilities. This was the northern segment lying on both the Rahway River and the Arthur Kill, generally north of Roosevelt Avenue. That area, moreover, was low and swampy, and thus less suitable for the diversified industries which would find better accommodation on the high, firm ground along the Kill in the southern portion of the industrial area, now classified as Zone B.

A great deal of emphasis was placed in the testimony for the municipality on the feared impact of a large number of added tank truck movements on the traffic situation in the borough. This municipality is unusually vulnerable to truck traffic congestion. It has only one or two streets capable of feeding heavy motorized traffic into and out of the municipality. These vary from 30 to 35 feet in width. According to the borough's proofs, two-way traffic of 44-foot tank trucks would present a real problem on such streets, especially at turns and where vehicles are parked at roadside. There is no road access out of the borough from the north except *via* the New Jersey Turnpike. Road access to the west and south is available, but is very limited in degree. The proofs are that the main artery, Roosevelt Avenue, is already heavily laden in the vicinity of the Carteret Zone B with oil truck and other industrial traffic from the Hess plant and other industries in Woodbridge, to the south. The added tank trucks, not alone from the proposed Tidewater plant, but from others which might establish petroleum depots in Zone B if the present ordinance were invalidated, could, it was feared, add greatly to traffic congestion throughout the entire municipality. The borough argues that there are no private roads on industrial lands in Zone B of any substantial length to help handle the industrial traffic problem there, as contrasted with the presence of such an auxiliary private road in Zone A.

The borough officials were also concerned with the safety problem involved in large aggregations of petroleum tanks concentrated within a few hundred feet of schools, churches and homes. They realize that, to a degree, this condition already exists in Zone A, but they argue that they have a right to prevent its spread to areas of the town not yet affected. Plaintiffs have, as noted in the opinion of the trial court, attempted to prove that the danger of fire or explosion from modern, properly erected oil storage tanks is inconsequential. However, our courts have referred to the fact that gasoline is a "highly inflammable and explosive substance." Reingold v. Harper, 6 N.J. 182, 191, 78 A.2d 54 (1951); Reinauer Realty Corp. v. Nucera, 59 N.J.Super. 189, 202, 157 A.2d 524 (App.Div.), certification denied 32 N.J. 347, 160 A.2d 845 (1960) (involving an application for a variance for construction of 600,000-gallon tanks for storage of gasoline and fuel oil). It does not seem to us that the officials of Carteret were capricious in giving weight to the dangers of fire or explosion (perhaps including the hazard from falling aircraft) from concentrations of large oil tanks close to population centers in classifying zones for appropriate land uses.

Plaintiffs, in addition to minimizing the factual pertinence of the zoning factors relied upon by the borough in creating Zone B, stress heavily that the area in question has prime economic utility for the petroleum business, particularly because of its location on deep water. It is not denied, however, that many other types of industry find it advantageous to be located on deep water in New York Bay.

With the foregoing expanded factual setting of this controversy in mind, we turn to the legal questions of municipal zoning power presented.

[2] There can be no doubt that a municipality has the power, through zoning, to determine the development of its municipal character by prohibiting, either partially or entirely, certain activities or uses, if within

reason. See, e.g., Morris v. Postma, 41 N.J. 354, 196 A.2d 792 (1964) (drive-in restaurants); Vickers v. Township Com. of Gloucester Tp., 37 N.J. 232, 181 A.2d 129 (1962), and Hohl v. Readington Tp., 37 N.J. 271, 181 A.2d 150 (1962) (trailer camps); Fanale v. Borough of Hasbrouck Heights, 26 N.J. 320, 139 A.2d 749 (1958) (apartment houses); Pierro v. Baxendale, 20 N.J. 17, 118 A.2d 401 (1955) (hotels and motels); Duffcon Concrete Products v. Borough of Cresskill, 1 N.J. 509, 64 A.2d 347, 9 A.L.R. 2d 678 (1949) (all heavy industry). The question is whether Carteret may, in furtherance of valid zoning purposes and without practicing invidious discrimination, divide an area which has long been devoted to heavy industrial uses into two zones which are in roughly equal proximity to other zones and of variable adaptability to the petroleum industry, and prohibit the storage (and refining) of petroleum in one of those zones, where it does not now exist, and allow it in the other, where it has long existed to a large extent. Noting that each case of this sort must be decided on its own facts, Fanale v. Borough of Hasbrouck Heights, supra, 26 N.J., at p. 326, 139 A.2d 749, we hold that the municipality may, under the evidence in this case, do so.

[3] Conceding, *arguendo*, that Zone A and Zone B are equally suited to the petroleum storage industry, the general proposition that all property in like circumstances should be treated alike, see, e.g., Roselle v. Wright, 21 N.J. 400, 409, 122 A.2d 506 (1956), Beirn v. Morris, 14 N.J. 529, 535, 103 A.2d 361 (1954), is one which in certain instances "must yield in realities." Kozesnik v. Montgomery Twp., 24 N.J. 154, 172, 131 A.2d 1, 11 (1957).

> "Dissimilar treatment does not inevitably bespeak capriciousness. If all property similarly situated had to be accorded identical treatment, the objective of a well-balanced community might be frustrated. If the public welfare is found to lie in the creation of a number of districts for various uses, lines must be drawn somewhere, and it may well happen, especially in rural areas, that little will distinguish properties on both sides of a given line. The final test must be whether the municipality is seeking to advance the community interest rather than some private or sectional advantage. Raskin v. Town of Morristown, supra (21 N.J. 180, 121 A.2d 378)." Id.

[4-6] While the entire waterfront area, originally included in the single heavy industrial zone, has long been open to the petroleum industry, the development of that area, as was noted above, has been such that the establishment of petroleum storage facilities has in fact been limited to that portion which is now designated Zone A. The establishment of zoning lines according to the uses to which the area being divided is presently subject, even though the land on each side of that line has identical physical characteristics, is as perfectly legitimate a differentiation as the drawing of zone lines according to geographical distinctions. Compare Bogert v. Washington Twp., 25 N.J. 57, 63, 135 A.2d 1 (1957). The principle is the same even if the area zoned against a given use, and where it has not yet taken hold,

has superior economic utility for the use than the zone where it has become established. The question is still the over-all reasonableness of the municipal zoning treatment. In our view, the fears of the community at large that Tidewater's proposed use of property in Zone B for purposes of a petroleum storage terminal would in the not distant future be followed by other similar activities in that area are not unjustified. Indeed, the very adaptability of the area for that use, plus the fact that much of the entire surrounding area in and out of Carteret has already been so appropriated, indicate the likelihood of such a development. The objective of keeping its heavy industrial area diversified, rather than having it contain nothing more than acre upon acre of "tank farms," is surely a legitimate one in the pursuit of the "objective of a well-balanced community."

[7, 8] Zoning ordinances are not of course, immutable; reasonable changes therein, based upon "changed viewpoints as to the needs and interests of the entire community," are valid exercises of the zoning power. Gruber v. Mayor and Tp. Com. of Raritan Tp., 39 N.J. 1, 11, 186 A.2d 489 (1962); see also Kozesnik v. Montgomery Twp., supra, 24 N.J., at p. 167, 131 A.2d 1. In the instant case, private economic interests should not be permitted to veto the wishes of the community at large when it discovers that its original plan for heavy industry threatens to take an undesired turn. The fact that the land in Zone B is well adapted for the purposes to which Tidewater would put it does not mean the borough is obligated to refrain from prohibiting the proposed use. Only where the zoning prohibitions are so restrictive as to allow nothing but economically unfeasible or otherwise inappropriate uses, while forbidding practical utilization of the land will they be stricken down as confiscatory. Morris County Land Improvement Co. v. Parsippany-Troy Hills Tp., 40 N.J. 539, 557, 193 A.2d 232 (1963); and see Finn v. Wayne Tp., 53 N.J. Super. 405 412-414, 147 A.2d 563 (App.Div.1959). This, of course, is not contended to be the case here. As was said in the Morris County Land case:

> "Of course, property need not be zoned to permit every use to which it is adapted nor must all property similarly situated be accorded identical treatment. To so require would frustrate the zoning objective of a well-balanced community according to a comprehensive plan. It is sufficient if the regulations permit some reasonable use of the property in the light of the statutory purposes. See Kozesnik v. Montgomery Township, supra (24 N.J., at p. 172, 131 A.2d, at p. 10)." 40 N.J., at p. 557, 193 A.2d, at p. 242 (Emphasis added).

[9] Indeed, uses which were at one time approved may by reason of their very number, and perhaps for that reason only, become undesirable. Under these circumstances a municipality has the power to prohibit the proliferation thereof. See Fanale v. Borough of Hasbrouck Heights, supra, 26 N.J., at p. 326, 139 A.2d 749; Kozesnik v. Montgomery Twp., supra, 24 N.J., at p. 173, 131 A.2d 1; compare Shipman v. Town of Montclair, 16 N.J.Super. 365, 370-371, 84 A.2d 652 (App.Div.1951).

[10] We conclude, therefore, that despite the economic suitability of Zone B for petroleum storage, Carteret has the right to "draw the line and shut the door" on further expansion of petroleum tank storage facilities, particularly where, as here, no such facilities presently exist in Zone B.

[11] It remains to consider whether such action is in furtherance of a valid zoning purpose, see R.S. 40:55-32, N.J.S.A. The present Zone B is occupied by various and diversified industrial enterprises. The continuance of at least a portion of a heavy industrial zone in such a diversified state is, in our view, a valid zoning purpose. It is in furtherance of "the general welfare" within the generally accepted broad interpretation of that phrase. See Vickers v. Township Com. of Gloucester Tp., supra, 37 N.J., at p. 247, 181 A.2d 129; Hochberg v. Board of Adjustment of the Borough of Freehold, 40 N.J.Super. 271, 276, 286, 123 A.2d 53 (App.Div.1956).

[12] We have already mentioned our opinion that Carteret's fears concerning the eventual complete domination of Zone B by tank farms is not unjustified. Whether such a state of affairs is desirable or not is for the community, not the courts, to determine, and absent a complete lack of reasonableness the judiciary will not interfere. See Kozesnik v. Montgomery Twp., supra, 24 N.J., at p. 168, 131 A.2d 1.

[13] It is inferable from the evidence here that the local officials could reasonably believe that more employment would result from diversified manufacturing and similar industrial activity than from the tank storage of petroleum. Further, there was a showing of reason in the municipal fear that domination of this area by tank farms would constitute a substantial aggravation of the local traffic problem. The trial court found that Tidewater's projected figures as to the traffic its storage facilities would involve was not an appreciable increase over the present traffic. But a determination as to the traffic implications of the zoning problems cannot be limited to a consideration of only the effect of Tidewater's proposed activity, for if the zoning ordinance is struck down the door would be open for the establishment of other petroleum storage facilities in Zone B. The fact that Tidewater may have shown that its traffic alone would not add appreciably to that which it would replace is not sufficient to overcome the presumption of reasonableness which attaches to the borough's determination that the traffic which would result from the operation of all expectable petroleum storage facilities in the general area, if open to all, would be burdensome. Cf. Cobble Close Farm v. Bd. of Adjustment Middletown Tp., 10 N.J. 442, 451-453, 92 A.2d 4 (1952).

In all the foregoing respects the judiciary is not to weigh the evidence as to the factors militating for one zoning course of action rather than another. If there is any reasonable basis at all grounded in the statutory zoning considerations, for the municipal decisions of policy and classification reflected in the ordinance, they are to be respected by the courts.

We thus conclude that the basic zoning decisions reflected by the May 1963 ordinance as to land uses in the heavy industrial zones of Carteret (with the June 1964 modification) represent a valid exercise of the zoning power of the municipality.

Plaintiffs argue by supplemental memorandum, however, that the June 1964 amendment of the zoning ordinance add still further illegalities to the ordinance. Specifically, they assert that the only difference in the amendments is that

> "industries *now* prohibited in the B Zone, viz., the storage and refining of the *basic* petroleum products, do not now operate in the *B* zone of Carteret.
> * * * But the exclusion of the *now* prohibited industries from the B Zone bears no substantial relation to the zoning purposes of [R.S. 40:55-32]. There is no reasonably conceivable basis of fact, under our zoning statute or under the general police power of municipalities, that can justify prohibiting such industries while at the same time permitting in the same zone the manufacturing and blending of the same basic petroleum products, *and* the storage, manufacturing, refining and blending of any of the volatile, flammable or inflammable and *explosive* components and derivatives of the basic petroleum products." (Emphasis theirs.)

Plaintiffs stress the fact that uses which are potentially more dangerous, such as the storage or manufacture of explosives, may be approved under the ordinance if the proponents thereof satisfy the zoning board that the particular operation can be conducted without danger to or adverse effect upon properties in any residential or commercial zone, but that under no circumstances could a proponent of petroleum tank storage facilities even have the opportunity of proffering proof as to those issues. "Here," they argue, "lies the discrimination."

[14, 15] There is no merit in the argument. It is elementary that in any police power measure the legislative body may strike at the evil where it deems it worst, and it need not root out all harms in order to validly proscribe some. Here, after reflection during the course of this litigation, the municipality has presumptively concluded that there is no substantial zoning harm in permitting relatively small, diversified industrial operations in Zone B, notwithstanding they involve handling petroleum derivatives of inflammable or explosive quality. The zoning dangers or public convenience of clusters of gigantic petroleum storage facilities may be attended to by the municipality without judicial interference based upon any notion that inadequate attention is being paid by the municipality to other alleged zoning evils. Cf. Morris v. Postma, supra, 41 N.J., at p. 361, 196 A.2d 792.

Finally, we point out that the June 1964 amendment also eliminated that feature of the 1963 ordinance which affirmatively authorized expansion of nonconforming uses in Zone B and was properly criticized in the opinion of the trial court.

Since we find that the ordinance as it now stands is entirely valid, we remand the cause to the trial court with directions to enter judgment in favor of the municipality. No costs.

TIDEWATER OIL COMPANY

v.

CARTERET

44 N.J. 338, 209 A.2d 105 (1965).

Supreme Court of New Jersey.

Argued Feb. 2, 1965.

Decided April 12, 1965.

Action to determine validity of borough zoning ordinance forbidding one plaintiff from erecting and operating in "Heavy Industrial B" zone a "tank farm" to store petroleum products for bulk sale, distribution, and ultimate off-sale consumption. The Superior Court, Law Division, 80 N.J. Super. 283, 193 A.2d 412, declared portions of ordinance invalid, and the defendants appealed. The Superior Court, Appellate Division, 84 N.J.Super. 525, 202 A.2d 865, reversed determination and found that ordinance was valid, and plaintiffs appealed without grant of certification. The Supreme Court held that the case was not appealable from the Appellate Division as of right, and that, in view of peculiar municipal geographical situation and long settled land use development, use classification which permitted such "tank farm" in "Heavy Industrial A" zone but not in "Heavy Industrial B" zone, despite alleged allowance of more objectionable uses, was adequately sustained on basis of traffic and safety problems.

Affirmed.

Sam Weiss, Newark, for plaintiffs-appellants (Jacobson & Winter, Perth Amboy, attorneys, Sam Weiss, Newark, of counsel).

Benedict W. Harrington, Newark, for defendants-respondents (Kessler, Kessler & Harrington, Newark, attorneys, Benedict W. Harrington, Newark, on the brief).

The opinion of the court was delivered

PER CURIAM.

This case challenges the validity of provisions of the zoning ordinance of the Borough of Carteret which forbid plaintiff Tidewater Oil Company (Tidewater) from erecting and operating in the "Heavy Industrial B" zone a "tank farm" to store petroleum products for bulk sale, distribution and ultimate off-premises consumption. The nub of the claim is that this use is permitted in the "Heavy Industrial A" zone, that uses more objectionable are allowed in the B zone and that the prohibition is therefore arbitrary and unlawfully discriminatory.

The trial court struck down the proscription as "not in accordance with a classification of land uses reasonably related to and in furtherance of the statutory zoning purposes." 80 N.J.Super. 283, 296, 193 A.2d 412, 419 (Law

Div.1963). The sections in question were amended during the pendency of the borough's appeal to the Appellate Division. That court, reversing the determination of the trial court, found the ordinance as it then stood to be entirely valid. 84 N.J.Super. 525, 202 A.2d 865 (1964).

I

Plaintiffs appealed the judgment to this court without the grant of certification, asserting it to be a cause "involving a question arising under the Constitution of the United States or this State" and so entitled to further review as of right. N.J.Const. Art. VI, sec. V, par. 1(a); R.R. 1:2-1(a). Defendants' motion to dismiss the appeal on the ground that the issue does not fall within the proper scope of the quoted phrase was reserved for determination until argument of the appeal on the merits. This requires first attention.

[1] The very limited provision for double appeals without leave arises as an aspect of the new judicial structure of this State created by the Constitution of 1947, which is based on the sound tenet of judicial administration that there should ordinarily be only one appeal as of right. Midler v. Heinowitz, 10 N.J. 123, 129, 89 A.2d 158 (1952). The exception of additional review in cases involving constitutional questions has to be based on the thinking that matters of interpretation or application of the organic documents of government and of fundamental rights and obligations warrant a second judicial look if the losing party wants it because they are intrinsically of basic importance. By the same token, the constitutional question should be a real and not merely a superficial one. Consequently this court determined in the early days of the new system that a constitutional question, in the sense intended by the appellate jurisdiction section of the 1947 instrument, must be "substantial," Starego v. Soboliski, 11 N.J. 29, 32, 93 A.2d 169 (1952), cert. denied 345 U.S. 925, 73 S.Ct. 784, 97 L.Ed. 1356 (1953), and not "merely colorable," State v. Pometti, 12 N.J. 446, 450, 97 A.2d 399 (1953).

[2, 3] It is clearly not enough if the asserted question is only remotely or speciously connected to the constitution by the loose or contrived use of broad constitutional terminology. Shibboleth mouthing of constitutional phrases like "due process of law" and "equal protection of the laws" does not *ipso facto* assure absolute appealability. Otherwise every cause in which nothing more is really at stake than a claim of mere trial error, for example, could be twisted to authorize a second appeal as of right. 536 Broad St. Corp. v. Valco Mortgage Co., Inc., 5 N.J. 393, 395, 75 A.2d 865 (1950); Starego v. Soboliski, supra; State v. Caprio, 14 N.J. 64, 101 A.2d 9 (1953), cert. denied 347 U.S. 952, 74 S.Ct. 677, 98 L.Ed. 1098 (1954); State v. Greenberg, 16 N.J. 568, 571-572, 109 A.2d 669 (1954); State v. De Meo, 20 N.J. 1, 5, 118 A.2d 1, 56 A.L.R.2d 905 (1955); Colacurcio Contracting Corp. v. Weiss, 20 N.J. 258, 119 A.2d 449 (1955); Klotz v. Lee, 21 N.J. 148, 121 A.2d 369 (1956); Essex County v. Hindenlang, 24 N.J. 517, 132 A.2d 807 (1957); State v. Schneider, 33 N.J. 451, 165 A.2d 299 (1960), cert. denied 365 U.S.

859, 81 S.Ct. 824, 5 L.Ed.2d 822 (1961); Amelchenko v. Freehold Borough, 42 N.J. 541, 545, 201 A.2d 726 (1964). In addition, there must appear indication of true merit from the constitutional point of view i.e., that the issue tendered is not frivolous and has not already been the subject of a conclusive judicial determination. State v. Pometti, supra, 12 N.J., at p. 450, 97 A.2d 399. See Camden County v. Pennsauken Sewerage Authority, 15 N.J. 456, 105 A.2d 505 (1954); Butler Oak Tavern v. Division of Alcoholic Beverage Control, 20 N.J. 373, 381, 120 A.2d 24 (1956); Fifth St. Pier Corp. v. City of Hoboken, 22 N.J. 326, 126 A.2d 6 (1956).

[4, 5] The plaintiffs' conclusional contention that the ordinance prohibition of the proposed use by Tidewater is unconstitutionally capricious and discriminatory is broadly cast in the familiar due process and equal protection concepts of the Fourteenth Amendment. But the supporting argument boils down, as in most cases of this kind, to a claim that, in this particular factual setting, the ordinance treatment is unreasonable because not within the purposes and essential considerations or the requirement of uniform regulations specified by the zoning enabling act as necessary to undergird valid local legislation. N.J.S.A. 40:55-31 and 32. While these statutory prerequisites have loose constitutional connotations, the fundamental question here resolves itself into a matter of application of statutory standards to a particular factual situation under long established principles. At this relatively advanced stage of the law of land use regulation, it will be the rare case concerned with the validity of use classification which will present an issue of sufficient constitutional involvement for purposes of the double appeal provision. See Vickers v. Township Committee of Gloucester Township, 37 N.J. 232, 234, 181 A.2d 129 (1962), cert. denied and appeal dismissed 371 U.S. 233, 83 S.Ct. 326, 9 L.Ed.2d 495 (1963), and Morris v. Postma, 41 N.J. 354, 196 A.2d 792 (1964), where fundamental questions of the right to exclude common uses from an entire municipality were at stake. We recognize, of course, that new constitutional questions of substance may arise in a generally settled field of law. Also it should be noted that constitutional issues sufficient in the early development of a new area for such appeal purposes may become so settled through the course of judicial decisions as one day to become no longer worthy of a second review without leave. We conclude that cases falling into the type of this one are not appealable from the Appellate Division as of right.

We appreciate that the approach to constitutional appealability which we have projected as the proper one in all cases does pose difficulties both for the unsuccessful party in the Appellate Division in deciding what means to employ to seek an additional review and for this court in attempting to pass fairly upon a motion to dismiss such an appeal taken under claim of right. The litigant's attorney may well not be certain whether his case qualifies without the necessity of certification. We have difficulty because the question presented by ordinarily brief motion papers may not be determinable without a full study of the briefs and the entire appendix, generally not then before us. Unless the situation is obvious on the face, the practice has been to reserve the motion until argument on the merits, which means the appeal is as fully heard as if there were no question of the right to bring it. If the alleged issue is then found to be insubstantial and a dismissal on that ground results, there has been a complete waste for everyone involved. See, e. g., Stiers v. City of Union City, 41 N.J. 243, 196 A.2d 5 (1963).

[6] We think therefore, that in any case where the right to appeal from the Appellate Division is not clear beyond doubt, the proposed appellant should petition for certification, outlining fully his claim for an appeal as of right, as well as any other appropriate reasons indicating why this court should allow further review even if it believes that the case does not present a sufficient constitutional question. The court will then have before it the complete appendix and the briefs below. If a proper constitutional question does appear, the rules provide that "certification shall be granted." R.R. 1:10-4(e). If it does not, an appeal may be allowed through certification for other reasons. In no case will a litigant suffer by falling between the millstones and this court will be better able to fulfill its proper function.

While there is no absolute right of appeal here, we feel we should determine the case on its merits since the dimensions of "causes ° ° ° involving a question arising under the Constitution," have previously not been fully clear.

II

[7] The validity of the ordinance provisions in question discriminating between the adjoining heavy industrial zones with respect to the storage of petroleum products for off-premises consumption, in the form they took at the time of the decision of the Appellate Division, revolves primarily around local geography and history. The prior opinions recite the entire factual complex at length and we need not repeat it. Suffice it to say that, in the light of the peculiar geographical situation of this municipality and its long settled land use development, the use classification between the two zones is adequately sustained on the basis of the traffic and safety problems as outlined in the opinion of the Appellate Division. 84 N.J.Super., at pp. 533-534, 202 A.2d 865. That tribunal's thesis, projected at 84 N.J.Super. 532-533, 536, 538, 202 A.2d 865 that the classification differences are also validly grounded upon the objective of "diversification of industry"—to prevent alleged possible "mushrooming" and concentration of a single industry to the ultimate exclusion of others thought locally more desirable from the standpoint of tax ratables or employment opportunities for community residents—was not necessary for the result reached and we express no opinion on it.

[8] There remains Tidewater's contention that it should be permitted to introduce evidence seeking to attack the validity of the amendment adopted while the case was pending in the Appellate Division. This amendment narrowed the zone B exclusion to petroleum refining and storage and thus made more pointed, says Tidewater, the matter of the claimed mushrooming

tendency of "tank farms." It urges that a zoning objective to avoid such a result had not previously been relied upon by the borough at trial or in argument and, as we understand it, the evidence sought to be presented would aim at establishing that petroleum storage terminals have no such tendency or effect. Since consideration of such an objective is not required in this case, further evidence relating to it would be of no moment.

The judgment of the Appellate Division is affirmed.

For affirmance: Chief Justice WEINTRAUB and Justices JACOBS, FRANCIS, PROCTOR, SCHETTINO and HANEMAN—6.

For affirmance, joining Part I of opinion and concurring in result only as to Part II of opinion: Justice HALL—1.

For reversal: None.

Questions and Notes

1. What kind of land use was prohibited here? Why is this so unpopular?

2. Was there any physical differentiation of the land between Industrial A and B Districts? What do you conclude about the validity of existing land use as a criterion for mapping (and differentiating) districts?

3. What other familiar grounds for zoning distinctions were involved here?

INTERNATIONAL HARVESTER COMPANY
v.
CHICAGO

43 Ill. App. 2d 440, 193 N.E. 2d 856(1963).

Appellate Court of Illinois

First District, Third Division.

Sept. 18, 1963.

Administrative review action to reverse a decision of city zoning board of appeals granting a special use permit to operate a metal salvage and material yard in a district zoned for general manufacturing. The decision was affirmed by the Superior Court, Cook County, D. S. McKinlay, J., and the findings of fact must be made by zoning board of appeals as a basis for objectors appealed. The Appellate Court, Dempsey, J., held, inter alia, that findings of fact must be made by zoning board of appeals as a basis for granting special use permit and that satisfactory showing by applicant that proposed use will conform with performance standards required by zoning ordinance for district in which the special use is to be located is a condition precedent to the granting of special use permit.

Reversed.

Stevenson, Conaghan, Hackbert, Rooks & Pitts, Chicago, for appellants.

John C. Melaniphy, Schuyler, Stough & Morris, Chicago, for appellees.

DEMPSEY, Justice.

One of the defendants, the Kedzie Iron & Metal Company, Inc., filed an application for a special use permit with the Zoning Board of Appeals of the City of Chicago. Its application was approved. Three objectors (the plaintiffs-appellants) brought an administrative review action seeking to reverse the decision of the zoning board. The Superior Court affirmed the decision and the objectors have appealed.

The property in question has been used as a coalyard since 1927. It is located on the west side of the street at 4844-56 South Kedzie Avenue, Chicago, in the midst of a district zoned for general manufacturing. It is irregular in shape and is bound by Kedzie Avenue on the east, by a bank of elevated railroad tracks on the south, by a spur railroad track on the west and by a building, in which food is processed, on the north. There is a brick fence on the Kedzie Avenue side which prevents a person on the sidewalk from seeing in. The testimony was that the applicant intended to build fences at least 8 feet high on the other sides and would remove from the premises six coal silos, each 55 feet high and 20 feet in diameter.

The application stated that the property was to be used.

> "° ° ° for the purposes of buying, selling at retail or wholesale and trading in, bartering, and exchanging new and used metals, scrap iron, scrap metals, wrecking and demolishing personal property for the purposes of salvaging all iron, metals and kindred articles therein contained, and to do any and all acts necessary and proper appertaining to the conduct of a metal salvage and material yard."

A special use of the type requested is permissible in a general manufacturing district (M2-3) if the Zoning Board of Appeals decides that the application meets the standards prescribed by the City's ordinance. Municipal Code of Chicago, ch. 194A, secs. 11.10-2, 11.10-4, 10.4, 10.4-2.

The pertinent portions of the zoning ordinance and the required standards are these:

> "Sec. 11.10-1 Purpose. The development and execution of a comprehensive zoning ordinance is based upon the division of the City into districts within which districts the use of land and buildings and the bulk and location of buildings and structures in relation to the land are substantially uniform. It is recognized, however, that there are variations in the nature of special uses which, because of their unique characteristics, cannot be properly classified in any particular district or districts, without consideration in each case, of the impact of those uses upon neighboring land and for the public need for the particular use at the particular location. Such variations in the nature of special uses fall into two categories:

> "(1) Uses either municipally operated, or operated by publicly regulated utilities or uses traditionally affected with a public interest; and

"(2) Uses entirely private in character but of such an unusual nature that their operations may give rise to unique problems with respect to their impact upon neighboring property or public facilities.

"Sec. 11.10-2 Authorization. Variations in the nature of special uses may be authorized by the Zoning Board of Appeals. ° ° °"

"Sec. 11.10-4 Standards. No special use shall be granted by the Zoning Board of Appeals unless the special use:

"(1) a. Is necessary for the public convenience at that location;

"b. Is so designed, located and proposed to be operated that the public health, safety and welfare will be protected; and

"(2) Will not cause substantial injury to the value of other property in the neighborhood in which it is to be located; and

"(3) It is within the provisions of 'Special Uses' as set forth in rectangular boxes appearing in Articles 7, 8, 9, and 10; and

"(4) Such special use shall conform to the applicable regulations of the district in which it is to be located."

The "applicable regulations of the district," [(4) above] refer in this instance to the performance standards established for an M2-3 general manufacturing district. These standards concern noise, vibration, smoke, glare, heat, fire hazards, explosive hazards and toxic, particulate and odorous matters. Chapter 194A, secs. 10.5 to 10.11-2, Municipal Code.

As to subsections (1), (2) and (3), it is the contention of the plaintiffs that the zoning board made insufficient findings of fact and that the evidence did not support the findings which were made; as to subsection (4), it is the contention that the applicant should have presented proof of intended compliance, but did not, and that the board should have made findings of fact, but did not.

[1] Although we are of the opinion that there is no evidence to support the finding of the Board of Appeals that the special use was "necessary for the public convenience at that location," as required in subsection (1) (a), and although we believe that the applicant's evidence was insufficient to justify the finding that the special use would not cause "substantial injury to the value of other property in the neighborhood," and the case must be reversed for these reasons alone, we will, nevertheless, consider the important underlying issues presented by this appeal: (1) whether in cases of special use the Zoning Board of Appeals must make findings of fact and (2) whether the applicant for a special use permit must show that the proposed special use will conform with the performance standards set forth in the ordinance for the district in which the special use is to be located. The first issue has been before this court in one other case (Rosenfeld v. Zoning Board of Appeals, 19 Ill.App.2d 447, 154 N.E.2d 323); the second has never been presented and is said by the plaintiffs to be a case of first impression not only in Illinois but in the United States.

The special use is a zoning device of comparatively recent origin which is being employed with increasing frequency. Where it is authorized by zoning ordinances, the device enables the zoning authorities to place into a zoned district, in addition to the uses permitted in that district, certain others designated as special uses. The device has been called "an effective method of dealing with a narrow but difficult problem of land use control." (Kotrich v. County of DuPage, 19 Ill.2d 181, 166 N.E.2d 601) and, on the other hand, it is said to afford—under certain conditions—an "obvious opportunity * * * for special privilege for the granting of favors to political friends or financial benefactors, for the witholding of permits from those not in the good graces of the authorities, and so on." (Special concurring opinion, Ward v. Village of Skokie, 26 Ill.2d 415, 186 N.E.2d 529.)

[2] No statute approving the special use procedure has been enacted by the Illinois legislature but its validity has been upheld as a means of implementing the zoning powers conferred by statute. Kotrich v. County of DuPage, supra. Since the legislature has not directly authorized the procedure, there is no statutory requirement that the granting of a permit for a special use "* * * shall be accompanied by findings of fact specifying the reason or reasons * * *" such as there is for zoning variations. (Ill.Rev.Stat., ch. 24, § 11-13-11 (1961).) The City ordinance which we are considering is also silent as to findings of fact for special use, but such findings must be made to support the granting of variations. Chapter 194A, sec. 11.7-1 provides:

> "11.7-1 Purpose. The Board of Appeals shall determine and vary the regulations of this comprehensive amendment in harmony with their general purpose and intent, only in the specific instances hereinafter set forth, where the Board *makes a finding of fact based upon the standards hereinafter prescribed,* that there are practical difficulties or particular hardships in the way of carrying out the strict letter of the regulations of this comprehensive amendment."

The same is true of section 11.7-3 which lays down the standards for variations. This section provides:

> "11.7-3. Standards for Variations. The Board of Appeals shall not vary the regulations of this comprehensive amendment, as authorized in Section 11.7-4 hereof *unless it shall make findings* based upon the evidence presented to it in each specific case that: * * *."

It is the plaintiffs' position that there is no essential difference between a variation and a special use, and, since the ordinance requires that findings must be made to support the grant of a variation, the same requirement should be engrafted on the grant of a special use.

[3]   There is a difference between a variation and a special use and the difference was noted in the Rosenfeld case, 19 Ill. App.2d 447, 154 N.E.2d 323:

> "It differs from a 'variance' in that a 'special use' is a permission by the Board to an owner to use his property in a manner contrary to the ordinance provided that the intended use is one of those specifically listed in the ordinance and provided that the public convenience will be served bv the use, while a variance is a grant of relief to an owner from the literal requirements of the ordinance where literal enforcement would cause him undue hardship.   Yokley, Zoning Law and Practice, sec. 134."

The same distinction was recognized in Kotrich v. County of DuPage, supra.   (See also, Yokley, Zoning Law and Practice, 2nd Ed., sec. 133, p. 324; and Metzenbaum, Law of Zoning, 2nd Ed., ch. IX-f-2(b), p. 813.)

Nevertheless, the ordinance (section 11.10-2) speaks of special uses as "Variations in the nature of special uses" and states (in section 11.10-3):

> "An application for a variation in the nature of a special use shall be filed and processed in the manner prescribed for applications for other variations and shall be in such form and accompanied bv such information as shall be established from time to time by the Zoning Board of Appeals."

This language may indicate a legislative intent to equate special uses with variations.

In addition to the language of the ordinance, we must take into consideration the factor that the Administrative Review Act, Ill.Rev.Stat., ch. 110, § 274 (1961), under which appeals are taken from the decisions of the Board of Zoning Appeals, provides: "The findings and conclusions of the administrative agency on questions of fact shall be held to be prima facie true and correct."

The Rosenfeld case, supra, was a case under the Administrative Review Act and the appeal was from a decision of the Chicago Zoning Board of Appeals which made no findings of fact.   This court stated:

> "We agree with plaintiffs that if the Board must make findings of fact specifying the reasons for granting a variation, Chap. 24, sec. 73—4(g) Ill. Rev. Stat. (1955), it ought to make findings of fact as a basis for granting a 'special use.'   It is true neither the statute nor the ordinance requires this, but fairness and orderly review procedure does."

The above statement from the Rosenfeld case was given sanction in Kotrich v. County of DuPage, supra.   The Kotrich case was a declaratory judgment proceeding which involved the validity of a special use permit granted by the defendant, the Board of Supervisors of DuPage County. After sustaining the statutory authority of the county to provide for special uses, the court proceeded to plaintiff's contention that since the impact of a special use is like that of a variation, the statutory requirement that written findings of fact must accompany a variation should be applied to special uses. The court rejected this contention. However, the court limited its holding by clearly pointing out that the special use permit before the court was granted by a legislative body, and that the judicial review was sought in an independent action on a new record made in court. The court did not extend its holding to a review brought under the Illinois Administrative Review Act. The court commented on the Rosenfeld case as follows:

> "It is true that in Rosenfeld v. Zoning Board of Appeals, 19 Ill.App.2d 447, 154 N.E.2d 323, the Appellate Court set aside a special use permit in part for lack of written findings of fact, although it recognized that findings were not required by the zoning ordinance or the enabling act. In that case, however, the special use was granted by the zoning board of appeals of Chicago and review was under the Illinois Administrative Review Act. Ill. Rev.Stat.1959, chap. 110, pars. 264-279. Review under that act is on the record made in the administrative agency and its findings of fact are to be held *prima facie* true and correct. Ill.Rev.Stat.1959, chap. 110, par. 274. Orderly and efficient review procedure under the act may, therefore, require that the administrative agency make written findings. The same reasoning does not apply in the present case where the special use permit was granted by a legislative body and judicial review is had in an independent action on a new record made in court."

In Maywood Park Trotting Ass'n v. Illinois Racing Comm., 15 Ill.2d 559, 155 N.E.2d 626, the court made this comment about findings under the Administrative Review Act:

> "Generally, the requirements with respect to administrative findings are more exacting than those relating to the findings of trial courts. Judicial recognition of the practical reasons for requiring administrative findings is almost universal. Davis, Administrative Law Treatise, vol. 2, sec. 16.01, p. 435."

The author cited by the court, in section 16.05 of his treatise, gives the reasons why courts judicially impose the requirement of findings of fact:

> "The practical reasons for requiring administrative findings are so powerful that the requirement has been imposed with remarkable uniformity by virtually all federal and state courts, irrespective of a statutory requirement. The reasons have to do with facilitating judicial review, avoiding judicial usurpation of administrative functions, assuring more careful administrative consideration, helping parties plan their cases for rehearings and judicial review, and keeping agencies within their jurisdiction." Davis, Administrative Law Treatise, vol. 2, chapter 16, sec. 16.05.

[4] Because of the language of the ordinance, because findings of fact are needed to enable a reviewing court to properly fulfill its function under the purpose and policy of the Administrative Review Act, and because of the

decision in the Rosenfeld case and the partial approval given that decision by the Supreme Court in the Kotrich case, we conclude, even though the ordinance does not directly require the Zoning Board of Appeals to make specific findings of fact, that these should be made when an application for a special use is granted.

We turn now to the issue of whether an application for a special use must show that the proposed use. will meet the performance standards required by the ordinance for the district in which the special use is to be located. When the present application was submitted to the Commissioner of City Planning (pursuant to sec. 11.10-2) the Commissioner recommended:

> "That the application to locate and establish a junk yard in an M2-3 General Manufacturing District, on premises at 4844-56 S. Kedzie Avenue, be granted provided all regulations of the zoning ordinance can be met, especially those pertaining to performance standards."

The zoning board, however, made no finding in reference to these standards —in fact its decision did not mention them at all and the comments of the chairman, during the course of the hearing, suggest that the board did not consider them as being conditions precedent to the granting of a special use permit.

[5] The performance standards are intricate and confusing and proof of intended compliance would obviously be difficult; nevertheless, a careful study of the ordinance leads to the ineluctable conclusion that these standards were meant to be conditions precedent as well as subsequent. They are conditions precedent in that there must be a satisfactory showing by the applicant that the proposed use will conform with these standards before the permit is granted. They are conditions subsequent in that the use, if granted, must continue to observe these standards and the applicant may be penalized if violations occur.

We are of the opinion that findings of fact must be made in cases of special use; that in the present case no findings were made in reference to the performance standards; that the findings which were made in reference to the other standards were too general and just repeated verbatim the language of section 11.10-4 of the ordinance, and in one or two instances the findings were not supported by substantial evidence.

The order of the Superior Court must, therefore, be reversed.

Reversed.

SCHWARTZ, P. J., and McCORMICK, J., concur.

Questions and Notes

1. Is this a developer's or a neighbor's case?

2. What type of zoning regulation is involved here? Is it easier, or more difficult, to defend than conventional use lists?

3. Why do courts like findings as a basis for judicial review? Compare the Topanga case, p. 83 *supra*.

DUFFCON CONCRETE PRODUCTS

v.

CRESSKILL

1 N.J. 509, 64 A.2d 347 (1949).

Supreme Court of New Jersey.

March 7, 1949.

Appeal from former Supreme Court.

Certiorari by Duffcon Concrete Products, Inc., against the Borough of Cresskill, to review the decision of the Mayor and Council rejecting the recommendation of the Board of Adjustment that an exception from zoning restrictions be granted to prosecutor. From judgment of former Supreme Court setting aside its zoning ordinance, 137 N.J.L. 81, 58 A.2d 104, the Borough of Cresskill appeals.

Reversed.

Walter H. Jones, of Hackensack, for appellant.

James A. Major and Breslin & Breslin, all of Hackensack, for appellee.

John A. Errico, of Bloomfield, for Joint Council of Municipal Planning Boards in Essex County, N.J., amicus curiae.

VANDERBILT, Chief Justice.

This is an appeal by the Borough of Cresskill from a judgment of the former Supreme Court setting aside its zoning ordinance.

The Borough is a small residential community in Bergen County, comprising about 1,300 acres and having a population of approximately 2,300 persons. In an effort to retain its residential character, the defendant in 1941 adopted a stringent zoning ordinance, establishing four zones, three of which are entirely residential and the fourth ("D" zone) is for "commercial districts for business centers." The pertinent portion of the ordinance dealing with the "D" zone reads (Article 4, § 4):

> "A. In any Commercial 'D' District, no building or premises shall be used and no building or part of a building shall be erected which is arranged, intended or designed to be used in whole or in part by any fabricating, manufacturing, converting, altering, finishing or assembling where mechanical power exceeding one horsepower electric motor is used, and where the major object of the establishment is to produce goods for sale other than at retail on the premises, or to furnish a service other than for residents of the locality, and where more than five mechanics or workers are habitually engaged on such work except that in the following listed industries the maximum number of workers engaged on such work shall be as specified below:
>
> "Carpet cleaning employing two workers.
>
> "Dry cleaning shop employing two workers.

"Dyeing where not more than one dyer is employed.

"Enameling, japanning or lacquering, only where the liquid is applied in tanks of not over five cubic feet capacity.

"Tinsmiths, plumbing, gas, steam or hot water fitting shop employing two workers on the premises.

"Milk bottling or distributing station employing three workers.

"No manufacturing except as above set forth shall be permitted in any Commercial 'D' District."

Early in 1946 the prosecutor purchased a tract of vacant land situated in a commercial zone but abutting on a residential district and distant only two blocks from the public school. Without making any inquiry of the borough officials, the prosecutor filled in the land at an estimated cost of $6,000.00 and in the middle of May, 1946, without obtaining a permit or applying for a variance, commenced the manufacture of concrete slabs in the open. The slabs were made for sale but not at retail on the premises. The manufacturing operations utilized the services of approximately forty employees and among other things, a large concrete mixer driven by a ten horsepower motor and a pneumatic drill. The attendant noise, vibration, dirt and dust was considerable and, in addition, trucks moving to and from the site caused traffic snarls during certain periods of the day on the county highway bordering the tract.

Not until the end of June, 1946, following almost two months of operation in entire disregard of the provisions of the zoning ordinance, did the prosecutor apply to the Borough authorities for permission to conduct its business. The application was in the form of plans for a proposed structure in which the manufacturing of the concrete slabs would be carried on. After a hearing a variance was denied by the local board of adjustment, the governing body concurring. New plans were submitted to the board of adjustment in September, 1946, and by a divided vote a variance was this time recommended. The recommendation, however, was rejected and the variance was denied by the governing body. Thereupon the prosecutor was granted a writ of certiorari to review the action of the municipality. On review the former Supreme Court held that the restriction in the ordinance against heavy industry was beyond the constitutional limits of municipal zoning power and that the discretion confided to the board of adjustment and the governing body bv the ordinance to grant a variance was subject to no adequate standard to guide them and it accordingly set aside the action of the municipal bodies.

The quoted portion of the ordinance constitutes an effective exclusion of all heavy industry from the Borough. The chief meritorious question thus hinges upon the power of the municipality so to legislate. There is no constitutional or statutory provision which would lead us to conclude that a municipality in the adoption of a comprehensive zoning scheme is compelled to set apart a portion of its territory for heavy industrial use without regard to its suitability therefor.

It has been argued that such is the intent of the concluding phrase of R.S. 40:55-30, N.J.S.A., where the legislative grant of authority to zone is stated to "include the right to regulate and restrict ° ° ° the location and use and extent cf use of buildings and structures and land for trade, industry, residence, or other purposes." But R.S. 40:55-32, N.J.S.A. which goes to the heart of the zoning legislation discloses very clearly the contrary intent of the Legislature.

> "Such regulations shall be in accordance with a comprehensive plan and designed for one or more of the following purposes: to lessen congestion in the streets; secure safety from fire, panic and other dangers; promote health, morals or the general welfare; provide adequate light and air; prevent the overcrowding of land or buildings; avoid undue concentration of population. Such regulations shall be made with reasonable consideration, among other things, to the character of the district and its peculiar suitability for particular uses, and with a view of conserving the value of property and encouraging the most appropriate use of land throughout such municipality."

What may be the most appropriate use of any particular property depends not only on all the conditions, physical, economic and social, prevailing within the municipality and its needs, present and reasonably prospective, but also on the nature of the entire region in which the municipality is located and the use to which the land in that region has been or may be put most advantageously. The effective development of a region should not and cannot be made to depend upon the adventitious location of municipal boundaries, often prescribed decades or even centuries ago, and based in many instances on considerations of geography, of commerce, or of politics that are no longer significant with respect to zoning. The direction of growth of residential areas on the one hand and of industrial concentration on the other refuses to be governed by such artificial lines. Changes in methods of transportation as well as in living conditions have served only to accentuate the unreality in dealing with zoning problems on the basis of the territorial limits of a municipality, improved highways and new transportation facilities have made possible the concentration of industry at places best suited to its development to a degree not contemplated in the earlier stages of zoning. The same forces make practicable the presently existing and currently developing suburban and rural sections given over solely to residential purposes and local retail business services coextensive with the needs of the community. The resulting advantages enure alike to industry and residential properties and, at the same time, advance the general welfare of the entire region.

[1] In the present cause the Court will take notice not only of the residential character of the Borough of Cresskill and the suitability of its location for such development, situated as it is on the western slope of the

Palisades, but also of the availability and use of the extensive bottom lands of the Hackensack River Valley within the region for industrial purposes. It cannot be doubted that in these circumstances the zoning scheme contemplated by the ordinance here under consideration comprehends, in the language and intent on the statute, "the most appropriate use of land throughout such municipality," R.S. 40:55-32, N.J.S.A.

Nor, when it is viewed in the light of these considerations, can the ordinance be said to be an arbitrary or unreasonable limitation upon the use of private property violative of either the Federal or state constitutions. The unhappy consequences which have invariably followed the establishment of heavy industry in residential areas are everywhere at hand—intense concentration of population, substandard housing and living conditions, increased fire and traffic hazards, disturbing noises, dirt and odors, with a consequent decline in the value of residential property. Numberless communities in this and other states present the sorry picture of what has been aptly characterized as urban blight. To hold that the state, through its municipal agencies, under conditions such as are here present may not thus afford protection to the health, safety, morals and general welfare of its inhabitants would be to deny one of the fundamental reasons for the existence of government. As Mr. Justice Sutherland stated in Village of Euclid v. Ambler Realty Co., 1926, 272 U.S. 365, 47 S.Ct. 114, 118, 71 L.Ed. 303, 310, 54 A.L.R. 1016, one of the leading cases dealing with the constitutional aspects of zoning;

> "Building zone laws are of modern origin. They began in this country about 25 years ago. Until recent years, urban life was comparatively simple; but, with the great increase and concentration of population, problems have developed, and constantly are developing which require, and will continue to require, additional restrictions in respect of the use and occupation of private lands in urban communities. Regulations, the wisdom, necessity, and validity of which, as applied to existing conditions are so apparent that they are now uniformly sustained, a century ago, or even half a century ago, probably would have been rejected as arbitrary and oppressive. Such regulations are sustained, under the complex conditions of our day, for reasons analogous to those which justify traffic regulations, which, before the advent of automobiles and rapid transit street railways would have been condemned as fatally arbitrary and unreasonable. And in this there is no inconsistency, for, while the meaning of constitutional guaranties never varies, the scope of their application must expand or contract to meet the new and different conditions which are constantly coming within the field of their operation. In a changing world it is impossible that it should be otherwise. * * *"

[2] Sound social, economic and governmental policy dictates a separation, where possible, of residential areas and industrial areas. In the case of our older and fully developed communities, it is now too late to do more than preserve such beneficial features as may have survived the period of spontaneous and uncontrolled growth and by such costly measures as slum clearance and low-cost housing to attempt to rectify the unwholesome con-

ditions caused by our earlier lack of foresight. Proper zoning today how-ever, can do much in our newly developing communities to provide and to maintain safer and more healthy living conditions. And where, as here, there exists a small residential municipality the physical location and cir-cumstances of which are such that it is best suited for continuing residen-tial development and, separated therefrom but in the same geographical region, there is present a concentration of industry in an area peculiarly adapted to industrial development and sufficiently large to accommodate such development for years to come, the power of the municipality to restrict its territory to residential purposes with ample provision for such small businesses, trades and light industries as are needed to serve the residents, is clear. Cf. Hamlett v. Snedeker, 1945, 246 App.Div. 758, 283 N.Y.S. 906.

[3, 4] The provisions in the ordinance creating a local board of adjust-ment with authority to make special exceptions and to recommend variances are in compliance with the legislative directions contained in R.S. 40:55-36, N.J.S.A. Without such provisions the ordinance would be void, Somers v. Borough of Bradley Beach, Err. & App.1935, 115 N.J.L. 135, 178 A. 755. The guiding standards which govern the exercise of the powers of the board of adjustment are carefully set forth in R.S. 40:55-39, N.J.S.A. Once the board of adjustment is provided for in the zoning ordinance, its powers stem directly from the statute, R.S. 40:55-39, N.J.S.A., and may not in any way be circumscribed, altered or extended by the municipal governing body. Under these circumstances, the inclusion in the zoning ordinance of a word for word recital of the statutory powers of the board of adjustment would be superfluous.

The judgment of the former Supreme Court is reversed.

For reversal: Chief Justice VANDERBILT, Justices HEHER, WACHEN-FELD and ACKERSON—4.

Concur in result: Justice OLIPHANT—1.

Questions and Notes

1. What type of land use was involved here? Does this fit well into a residential neighborhood?

2. The question of total exclusion from a town usually comes up in connection with industrial land use.

3. What is the significance of municipal boundaries in zoning?

CORTHOUTS

v.

NEWINGTON

140 Conn. 284, 99 A.2d 112 (1953).

Supreme Court of Errors of Connecticut.

Aug. 4, 1953.

Action for declaratory judgment by a landowner to determine the constitutionality of an amendment to a zoning ordinance prohibiting residential building in an area zoned for industry, but not presently used for industry, in the Town of Newington. The case was tried to the court. The Superior Court of Hartford County, Troland, J., declared amendment unconstitutional and void and the town appealed. The Supreme Court of Errors, Baldwin, J., held that ordinance was void insofar as it prohibited a landowner from making residential use of his property in an area zoned for industry but without industrial growth.

Error in part, judgment directed.

Inglis and O'Sullivan, JJ., dissented.

William W. Sprague, Hartford, for appellants (defendants).

Frank A. Francis, Hartford, with whom was John J. Devine, Jr., Hartford, for appellee (plaintiff).

Before BROWN, C. J., and BALDWIN, CORNELL, INGLIS and O'SULLIVAN, JJ.

BALDWIN, Associate Justice.

The plaintiff brought an action against the defendant town and its zoning commission to enjoin the enforcement of an amendment to the zoning ordinance of the town which prohibited, in an industrial zone, the use of land for residential purposes. The action has been treated by the parties as one for a declaratory judgment to determine whether the amendment is a lawful and constitutional exercise of the powers vested in the town and the commission. We will so consider it. The trial court rendered judgment in favor of the plaintiff and the defendants have appealed.

The material facts in the finding, with certain additions which are warranted, can be stated as follows: The town of Newington is neither a thickly settled nor an industrial community. Its population in 1930 was 4552; in 1940, 5449; in 1950, 9110. On August 26, 1930, a zoning ordinance was adopted which divided the town into districts designated as residence "A" and "B," business, industrial No. 1 and industrial No. 2. Newington Zoning Ordinance, Art. 1, § 2 (1949). The regulations for an industrial district No. 2 permit uses which are generally described as heavy industrial. Id., Art. 2, § 10. The total area of the town is 8382 acres. Out of this, approximately 6600 acres are confined to "A" residence districts, 95 acres to

"B" residence districts, 185 acres to business districts, 11 acres to industrial district No. 1 and 627 acres to industrial district No. 2. After more than twenty years of zoning, only 38.5 acres in industrial district No. 2 have been built upon or are occupied by industry. The right of way of the New York, New Haven and Hartford railroad crosses the westerly part of the town. When the zoning regulations were originally adopted, the land on both sides of the right of way to a depth of 600 feet was placed in an industrial district No. 2.

On December 14, 1951, the plaintiff purchased a tract of land for the purpose of erecting dwelling houses. His land, approximately 30 acres in extent, is situated in the westerly part of the town near the New Britain town line. It lies 150 feet west of the railroad right of way, which at this point is at a substantially lower level. There are several dwelling houses in the residence "B" zone west of and adjacent to the plaintiff's land. The more westerly portion of it, containing about 11.5 acres, is located in a "B" residence district. The remainder lies within the industrial district No. 2 hereinbefore referred to. There is a right of way appurtenant to it for a railway siding across land of the Hartford Electric Light Company which lies immediately adjacent to the railroad tracks. The city of New Britain has a right of way varying from twenty-five to fifty feet in width across the plaintiff's land for a trunk-line sewer. When the plaintiff made his purchase, the zoning ordinance permitted the use of land in an industrial district for residential purposes. Newington Zoning Ordinance, Art. 2 § 10 (1949). Effective February 1, 1952, the zoning commission amended the regulations pertaining to an industrial district No. 2 so as to prohibit within such a district, the erection of a dwelling of any kind except the residence of a janitor or a caretaker of premises or a plant of a permitted industry. Newington Zoning Ordinance, Art. 2, §10-33b. The plaintiff's land is adapted to development for residential use, for which there is a demand. Such use is the highest and best to which it can be put. Unless it can be devoted to residential purposes, in all probability it will remain unused for many years. It is not adapted to industrial use, for which there is not any present demand in Newington and none is expected. Although the amendment prohibits the use of land in an industrial district No. 2 for residential purposes, the ordinance allows such land to be used for community buildings, hotels, clubhouses, hospitals, churches, schools, playgrounds and businesses generally.

The Newington zoning ordinance follows the prescribed pattern in that it enumerates the uses which are permitted in residence districts, and lists only those which are prohibited in business and industrial districts. Generally, the districts of less restricted uses admit the uses of the more restricted ones. Baker, Legal Aspects of Zoning, p. 66; Yokley, Zoning Law & Practice, pp. 64, 66. Before the amendment under consideration was adopted, there was no prohibition against the use of land in an industrial district for residential purposes. The amendment proscribes what has usually been considered as the highest use to which land can be put, namely, residential use, in an industrial district where uses regarded as among the lowest and most burdensome are permitted. This is a marked departure from what has heretofore been accepted as standard practice. It is not altogether novel, however. Some communities already have ordinances which prohibit a residential use in an industrial district. Rathkopf, Law of Zoning & Planning (2d Ed.) (Sup. & Dig.1951, p. 58); Baker, op. cit., p. 66; Williams, Law of City Planning & Zoning, p. 277.

[1, 2] Zoning regulations constitute a valid exercise of the police power only when they have a "rational relation to the public health, safety, welfare, and prosperity of the community" and are "not such an unreasonable exercise of [the police] power as to become arbitrary, destructive or confiscatory. State v. Hillman, 110 Conn. 92, 100, 105, 147 A. 294, 297. Whether a zoning ordinance meets this test must be determined in the light of existing conditions, in order that the purpose for which the police power is invoked may be promoted. Euclid, Ohio v. Ambler Realty Co., 272 U.S. 365, 387, 47 S.Ct. 114, 71 L.Ed. 303. The ordinance must comply with the requirements of, and serve the purposes stated in, the statute. General Statutes § 837; Fairlawns Cemetery Ass'n, Inc. v. Zoning Commission, 138 Conn. 434, 440, 86 A.2d 74. We are not called upon to decide in this case whether, as a general proposition, a zoning ordinance which prohibits a residential use in an industrial district is valid. It is easy to conceive a situation where the erection and occupation of dwelling houses on land in an industrial area in close proximity to manufactories using highly inflammable or explosive materials or giving off noxious odors or pernicious gases would have a direct relation to the public health, safety and welfare and justify prohibitory legislation against the use of such land for residential purposes. But the combination of circumstances in the case at bar does not even simulate such a situation.

[3] The question presented to the trial court was whether, upon the facts, the amendment constituted a valid exercise of the police power with respect to the plaintiff's property. Euclid, Ohio v. Ambler Realty Co., supra. It is true that the amendment serves one of the purposes of zoning in that it stabilizes the property use in this industrial district. Kuehne v. Town Council, 136 Conn. 452, 461, 72 A.2d 474; Thayer v. Board of Appeals, 114 Conn. 15, 23, 157 A. 273. A completely arbitrary and unreasonable division and regulation could accomplish that. To be justifiable, an ordinance placing a drastic limitation upon the use of the plaintiff's land, on the one hand, must reasonably serve the public health, safety and welfare, on the other. 8 McQuillin, Municipal Corporations (3d Ed.) § 25.40. The facts disclose that the plaintiff's land is adaptable to, and in demand for, residential purposes. The amendment prevents such use and commits it to industrial purposes. The land is not needed now—nor will it be needed in the near future—for industrial development.

This is not a case where an owner of land is seeking to have the commission rezone the portion of it which is located within an industrial district. The plaintiff is simply insisting that he be permitted to devote his land to residential use until such time as need of it for industrial purposes arises. Since the amendment, in effect, prevents the plaintiff from using his land for any feasible purpose, it is unreasonable and confiscatory.

[4] The trial court has found no facts to indicate that the amendment would serve the public health, safety and welfare in any way, nor would the corrections to the finding claimed by the defendants, if made, show that it would have that effect. It is to be noted that the amendment prohibits dwellings in an industrial district No. 2, while under other provisions of the same ordinance hotels, hospitals, schools and public playgrounds are allowed therein. The amendment is thus inconsistent with these other provisions so far as serving the public health, safety and welfare is concerned. This is a very material consideration in this case, where the plaintiff is seeking relief from the effect which the amendment has upon the use of his land. The facts found fail to demonstrate that the drastic curtailment imposed by the amendment is warranted. Strain v. Mims, 123 Conn. 275, 288, 193 A. 754; 8 McQuillin, op. cit., § 25.42. We hold the amendment to be invalid in so far as it affects the plaintiff's property. Strain v. Mims, supra, 123 Conn. 290, 193 A. 754.

There is error in part, the judgment is set aside and the case is remanded with direction to render judgment that the amendment to the Newington zoning ordinance described as article 2, § 10-33b, is, as respects the plaintiff's property, unreasonable and confiscatory, and therefore void.

In this opinion BROWN, C. J., and CORNELL, J., concurred.

INGLIS and O'SULLIVAN, JJ., dissented.

PEOPLE ex rel. SKOKIE TOWN HOUSE BUILDERS

v.

MORTON GROVE

16 Ill.2d. 183, 157 N.E. 2d 33(1959)

Supreme Court of Illinois.

March 20, 1959.

Landowner brought mandamus proceeding against village and its building commission to compel issuance of necessary permits for construction of four townhouse buildings in commercial district. The Circuit Court, Cook County, Harry M. Fisher, J., entered judgment adverse to the village and its building commissioner, and they appealed. The Supreme Court, House,

J., held that where landowner, in reliance on village zoning ordinance before it was amended to prohibit future construction of any dwelling units in districts other than those designated as dwelling districts, paid for plans for construction of four townhouse buildings in commercial district and paid village $1,630 for permits and contractor's permits and $200 as a deposit for sidewalks, and there was no repayment or tender of the $1,830 by village, landowner would be deemed to have acquired a vested right under the zoning ordinance before its amendment, so as to entitle landowner to complete construction of town-houses.

Judgment affirmed.

John B. Moser and Thomas A. Matthews, Chicago, for appellant.

Richard Weinberger, Chicago, for appellee.

HOUSE, Justice.

The village of Morton Grove and Timothy Walsh, its building commissioner, appeal directly to this court from a summary judgment entered in the circuit court of Cook County upon the *mandamus* petition of Skokie Town House Builders, Inc., ordering the appellants to issue necessary permits for the construction of four townhouse buildings. A constitutional issue was presented to and decided by the trial court.

The case was tried upon the pleadings and stipulations of facts. Appellee is engaged in the business of construction and selling residential buildings. On June 20, 1957, it purchased certain lots in a class E commercial district which, under the ordinance then in force, were also available for group or row-dwelling usage. Immediately thereafter, it had plans and specifications prepared for the construction of four town houses upon the lots and had the property surveyed. On June 25 appellee applied for the necessary building permits which were issued the same day. A few days later the building commissioner revoked the permits. The village officials refused to reissue the permits and the appellee in March, 1958, filed its petition for a writ of *mandamus*. On April 22, 1958, the 1946 zoning ordinance was amended so as to prohibit the future construction of any dwelling units in districts other than those designed as dwelling districts.

The appellants in their answer to the petition contended that the deputy commissioner who issued the permits had no authority to do so and that they were properly revoked because the appellee's proposed buildings failed by some nine inches to meet the minimum rear-yard requirements. In addition, they pleaded the amended zoning ordinance as an affirmative defense.

In its reply, Skokie Town House Builders, Inc., argued that the rear-yard deficiency was not asserted by the village until after the *mandamus* action was instituted, and that upon being advised of this deficiency, it corrected its building plan to remove the objection, but the building commissioner refused to accept the revised plot plan. It also contended that the zoning amendment was void in that it violated the due process clauses of both the State and Federal constitutions, S.H.A.Const. art. 2, § 2; U.S. Const. Amend.

14, and was not, in any event, applicable to appellee's property because it had acquired a vested right in the 1946 ordinance by reason of its prior expenditures in reliance thereon.

Thereafter appellee filed its motion for summary judgment supported by the affidavit of its secretary which related in some detail the nature of the expenditures. The appellants filed motions to strike the reply and affidavit for alleged deficiencies and requested an extension of time to file counter-affidavits. Upon hearing, the court entered an order denying the motions of appellants and granting summary judgment to appellee.

Appellants' first contention is that the trial court erred in issuing the writ of *mandamus* because the appellee failed to exhaust its administrative remedies. At the time appellee applied for the permit, the zoning ordinance required a rear yard of 24.742 feet but the plans and specifications contained a plot plan showing a rear yard of only 24 feet. After appellee filed its petition for a writ of *mandamus*, it learned of appellants' objection and engaged an architect to prepare a revised plot plan showing a rear yard of a full 25 feet. It then tendered this amended plot plan to the building commissioner who refused to accept it for filing without even examining it. This fact was brought out in appellee's reply and it consented therein to the building permit being issued in accordance with the revised plot plan. The *mandamus* order of the trial court directs that the permits issue in accordance with the plans previously filed as amended by the revised plot plan. * * *

Appellants next contend that the trial court erroneously concluded that the amending ordinance was unconstitutional. Appellee argues that the trial court properly held this zoning ordinance excluding future residential development in commercial and industrial districts void *per se*. It asserts that such an ordinance conflicts sharply with the generally acknowledged principle that zoning is intended to preserve rather than to restrict dwellings.

Most of the earlier zoning ordinances were based upon this principle, and, generally, the districts of less restricted uses admitted the uses of the more restricted districts. (Babcock, Classification and Segregation Among Zoning Districts, 1954 Ill. Law Forum 186, 204; Baker, Legal Aspects of Zoning, p. 66; Yokley, Zoning Law & Practice, pp. 64, 66.) Recently, however, many municipalities have adopted noncumulative type zoning ordinances which exclude most, if not all, future residences from commercial and industrial districts. (Babcock, 1954 Ill.Law Forum 186; Kneier, The Future of Zoning, 1954 Ill.Law Forum 281; Rathkopf, The Law of Zoning and City Planning, 296 (3d ed. 1956).) This is the first case presented to us which involves such an ordinance. The primary question is whether such a limitation upon the scope of municipal powers is embodied as a limitation in law under the constitution and the zoning statutes.

[2-4] It has long been the rule that zoning is a proper exercise of the police power of the State and that the power to zone can be exercised by

the legislature or by the municipalities to which this power may be delegated. City of Aurora v. Burns, 319 Ill. 84, 149 N.E. 784. Governmental restrictions on the use of private property can be imposed, however, only if they bear a substantial relationship to the preservation of the public health, safety, morals or general welfare. Western Theological Seminary v. City of Evanston, 325 Ill. 511, 156 N.E. 778. Thus, the only constitutional limitation upon a municipality's power to exclude future residences from commercial and industrial districts is that the exclusion bear a substantial relationship to the preservation of the public health, safety, morals, or general welfare.

[5] There are many arguments in favor of this type of ordinance, although such an ordinance is a radical departure from our thinking and opinions in the past. We note a few. The dangers of heavy traffic are greater in mixed residential-industrial or residential-commercial districts than in districts devoted to just one purpose. Industrial and commercial districts are not good places to bring up families from a health standpoint; and the presence of children in and about industrial and commercial districts leads to a demand for school, park and play-ground facilities in an area where there is either no land available or the land available is ill-suited to such uses. In short, whether industry and commerce are excluded from the residential areas, or residences from industrial and commercial areas, it is not unreasonable for a legislative body to assume that separation of the areas would tend in the long run to insure a better and a more economical use of municipal services, such as schools, providing police protection, preventing and fighting fires, and better use of street facilities. The general welfare of the public may be enhanced if industry and commerce are provided with a favorable climate. The sale of a few lots at important points in a district may make industrial or commercial expansion impossible or prohibitively expensive. To protect the residents in the district, traffic may be slowed down unduly and thus detract from the efficiency of production and trade. In final analysis, it seems clear that industry and commerce are also necessary and desirable and that a proper environment for them will promote the general welfare of the public. We are of the opinion that the exclusion of residences from a commercial or industrial district is within the police power of the State.

[6, 7] It is elementary that a municipality possesses no inherent police power and can only legislate upon or with reference to that which is authorized by the General Assembly. Father Basil's Lodge, Inc. v. City of Chicago, 393 Ill. 246, 65 N.E.2d 805. Thus, a municipality's power to exclude future residences from commercial and industrial areas must be found in article 73 of the Revised Cities and Villages Act. Ill.Rev.Stat.1957, c. 24, pars. 72-1 to 73-12. Section 73-1 delegates to municipalities the power, "(4) to classify, regulate and restrict * * * the location of buildings designed for specified industrial, business, residential, and other uses;"

and the same section delegates the power "(7) to prohibit uses, buildings, or structures incompatible with the character of such districts." We are of the opinion that these delegations of power encompass the power to exclude future residences from industrial and commercial districts.

[8] Caution will have to be used in the application of noncumulative ordinances because of the existing admixture of residential, commercial and industrial uses. The present character of a district may make an ordinance unreasonable and discriminatory, or there may be no reasonably immediate use of the land for commercial purposes, thereby denying an owner his constitutional privileges with respect to his land, or an ordinance may not be part of a comprehensive and consistent plan. We are not beset by such questions in this case. There are no facts pleaded to indicate that the application of the amended ordinance to the lots in question would be discriminatory, and we have indicated that the ordinance is not discriminatory as a matter of law. The amended ordinance was enacted in the exercise of a power conferred upon the village of Morton Grove and is presumably valid. Kinney v. City of Joliet, 411 Ill. 289, 103 N.E.2d 473.

The trial court could properly order the writ of *mandamus* to issue only if the amended ordinance could not have been applied to the appellee. Appellants contend that the trial court erroneously concluded that appellee had acquired a vested right under the 1946 zoning ordinance which would entitle it to complete the construction of its town houses as originally authorized. Appellants' contention is based on two propositions. First, a property owner cannot, by making expenditures or incurring obligations in contemplation of putting his land to a certain use, prevent the municipality from rezoning his property and applying the amended zoning ordinance against his property to prevent that use. They state that the decision in Deer Park Civic Ass'n v. City of Chicago, 347 Ill.App. 346, 106 N.E.2d 823, to the extent that it is inconsistent with this proposition is incorrect. Second, they did not admit appellee had made the expenditures and incurred the obligations as alleged, and, therefore, a summary judgment holding that appellee had acquired a vested right by reason of prior expenditures and obligations was not warranted.

Appellants' first proposition has been eliminated by our holding in Fifteen Fifty North State Building Corp. v. City of Chicago, 15 Ill.2d 408, 155 N.E.2d 97 (filed subsequent to their brief), wherein we adopted the view expressed in the Deer Park Civic Ass'n case that where there has been a substantial change of position, expenditures or incurrence of obligations made in good faith by an innocent party under a building permit or in reliance upon the probability of its issuance, such party has a vested property right and he may complete the construction and use of the premises for the purposes originally authorized, irrespective of subsequent zoning or a change in zoning classification.

The appellee in support of its motion for summary judgment filed the affidavit of its secretary which related expenditures it made and obligations it incurred in reliance on the 1946 ordinance and the probability of a building permit being issued. The affiant stated that certain sums had been paid for plans, plot plans, and commitment for mortgage loan; together with $1,630 for permits and contractor's permits and $200 as a deposit for sidewalks to the appellant village. He also stated that an oral general construction contract had been entered into for $195,758.56.

It was stipulated by the parties that the petitioner caused to be prepared plans and specifications for the construction of four town houses of four units each and had caused the property to be surveyed. It was further stipulated that appellee had purchased the land upon which the town houses were to be built for $26,000. Appellee admitted in its second amended answer to the petition that $1,630 had been paid to it for the permits and $200 for a sidewalk deposit.

It will thus be noted that, while there is no admission of the exact amounts paid, it was stipulated that plans and specifications and plot plans had been procured. Furthermore, the expenditure of $1,830 was admitted and the record shows no repayment or tender. The conclusion that there were admitted substantial changes of position and expenditures within the meaning of the rule in the Fifteen Fifty North State Building Corp. case is, in our opinion, justified.

Appellants complaint that their written interrogatory was ignored and that their motion to strike the affidavit in support of the motion for summary judgment should have been granted. They also allege error in the Court's refusal to extend time for preparing counter-affidavits and taking depositions. None of these objections are well taken. They primarily deal with and were aimed at the alleged construction contract. As we have pointed out, there was a sufficient showing of expenditures so that it was unnecessary for the trial court to go into the question of the incurring of general contract obligations.

[9] On the basis of the record before us, we are of the opinion that the trial court did not err in holding that appellee had acquired a vested right under the 1946 zoning ordinance which would entitle it to complete the construction of the town houses and that it properly ordered a writ of *mandamus* to be issued. The judgment of the circuit court of Cook County is, therefore, affirmed.

Questions and Notes

On Newington

1. How was the land zoned? How much land?

2. What did the court think about the prospects for conforming development?

3. Was this a ruling on the general principle of excluding new residential construction from industrial districts?

4. Did the court think such a regulation was unusual? (It wasn't; see Williams, Sec. 104.02).

On Morton Grove

1. Did this case involve residences in manufacturing or in commercial districts?

2. What is the more recent attitude on residence above commercial?

3. What were the arguments about separation of residential and commercial? Do these apply equally well to manufacturing districts?

4. Is there a distinction between different kinds of residences in commercial districts?

CROSS-REFERENCES

In Anderson, see §§ 8.02, 8.34, 8.35, and see Index, this topic.
In Hagman, see § 57.
In McQuillin, see § 25.116, generally.
In Rathkopf, see Ch. 12-1, Ch. 14-4, and see Index, this topic.
In Williams, see Ch. 104-106.
In Yokley, see §§ 4-2, 4-8, 28-36 and see Index, this topic.

Section 11
Other Zoning Controls

A. Off-Street Parking

RONDA REALTY CORP.

v.

LAWTON

414 Ill. 313, 111 N.E. 2d 310(1953).

Supreme Court of Illinois.

March 23, 1953.

Action was brought to determine validity of city zoning ordinance providing that where there are more than two apartments in a building, a private garage or automobile compound for storage of one-passenger automobile for each of 33 percent of number of apartments shall be erected or established and maintained on lot used for the apartment house.   The Circuit Court of Cook County, Elmer J. Schnackenberg, J., entered judgment finding ordinance unconstitutional and void, and defendants appealed.   The Supreme Court, Daily, J., held that the ordinance is unconstitutional as a denial of equal process of law.

Judgment affirmed.

John J. Mortimer, Corporation Counsel, and Francis J. Mahon, both of Chicago (L. Louis Karton and Harry H. Pollack, Chicago, of counsel), for appellants.

Julius J. Schwartz, Leonard Gordon, and Richard F. Watt, all of Chicago, for appellee.

DAILY, Justice.

This is an appeal from a judgment of the circuit court of Cook County which found subparagraph (2) of section 8 of the Chicago zoning ordinance (Municipal Code of Chicago, sec. 194A-8(2), to be unconstitutional and void. The trial court has certified that the validity of a municipal ordinance is involved and, that in its opinion, the public interest requires a direct appeal to this court.

The leading facts show that appellee, which is the Ronda Realty Corporation, applied to the commissioner of buildings of the city of Chicago, for a permit to remodel appellee's apartment building at 4201-15 North Sheridan Road, from twenty-one to fifty-three apartments. Accompanying the application was a certificate, by the secretary of the appellee, to the effect that on the premises there would be off-street facilities for parking eighteen automobiles. The commissioner issued the permit, whereupon thirteen tenants of the building, who are some of the appellants here, appealed to the zoning board of appeals seeking to reverse the action of the commissioner. The ground of the appeal was that the remodeling would result in the creation of fifty-three apartments; that section 194A-8(2) of the Municipal Code of Chicago requires an apartment building to provide off-street automobile parking facilities on the lot where the apartment building is maintained at the ratio of one automobile for each three apartments; that there is only space on appellee's lot for parking eight automobiles; that fifty-three apartments would require eighteen parking spaces and therefore the commissioner should not have issued the permit.

A hearing was held before the zoning board of appeals, which body, after hearing evidence and viewing the premises, concluded that there were not enough off-street parking facilities on appellee's property to comply with the ordinance and entered an order reversing the action of the commissioner and revoking the permit. Appellee then filed a complaint in the circuit court for review under the provisions of the Administrative Review Act (Ill. Rev.Stat.1951, chap. 110, pars. 264-279) setting forth the facts and pleading the invalidity of the ordinance relied upon by the board. On the hearing for review, the court stated that it was deciding the case purely on a question of law and not on questions of fact, and entered its judgment that the section of the ordinance relied upon was unconstitutional and void in that it discriminated against appellee and deprived it of equal protection of the law. The order of the zoning board of appeals was reversed and the issuance of the building permit sustained. The tenants, the commissioner of buildings, the zoning board of appeals and the city of Chicago have perfected the appeal to this court.

The errors assigned in this court present but one decisive issue, namely, whether subparagraph (2) of section 8 of the zoning ordinance is invalid because it creates an unlawful classification, discriminatory in its nature. The complete provisions of section 8 of the ordinance are as follows:

"194A-8. (Section 8.) Apartment House Districts. Permitted uses in Apartment House districts are:

"(1) Any use permitted in a Family Residence district without restrictions except such as are applicable to auxiliary uses and any other use permitted in a Duplex Residence or Group House district;

"(2) Apartment house, provided that where there are more than two apartments in the building a private garage or automobile compound for the storage of one passenger automobile for each of 33 per cent of the number of apartments shall be erected or established and maintained on the lot used for the apartment house;

"(3) Boarding or lodging house, hotel, hospital, home for dependents or nursing home;

"(4) Boarding school, vocational school, college or university, when not operated for pecuniary profit;

"(5) Club, fraternity or sorority house, when not operated for pecuniary profit;

"(6) Public art gallery, library or museum;

"(7) Auxiliary uses, subject to the following limitations:
"A sign may be maintained on any lot area or building, if the sign is not more than 2 square feet in area and if it is located not nearer to the street line than the building line and if it does not advertise anything except the names and occupations of the occupants;

"A restaurant may be maintained in a hotel, if the public entrance to the restaurant is from the lobby of the hotel and no sign advertising the restaurant is visible to persons outside of the hotel.

[1-8] The right of cities to enact zoning ordinances thereby imposing a reasonable restraint upon the use of private property, and the rules of law governing the validity of such ordinances are reasonably well settled. The right which every property owner has to use his property in his own way and for his own purposes is subject always to the exercise of police power and it is in the exercise of this power that zoning ordinances are adopted. To be a valid exercise of the police power, however, the ordinance must bear a substantial relationship to the public health, safety, comfort or welfare. To those ends, legislative bodies may classify persons if the classification is based on some reasonable distinction having reference to the object of the legislation. Chicago Park Dist. v. Canfield, 382 Ill. 218, 47 N.E.2d 61; Josma v. Western Steel Car & Foundry Co., 249 Ill. 508, 94 N.E. 945. Laws will not be regarded as special or class legislation merely because they affect one class and not another, provided they affect all members of the same class alike. A classification which is not purely arbitrary and is reasonably adapted to secure the purpose for which it was intended will not be disturbed by the courts unless it can be clearly seen that there is no fair reason for the distinction made. Stearns v. City of Chicago, 368 Ill. 112, 13 N.E.2d 63, 114 A.L.R. 1507. Also, in this regard,

we have held that even though a zoning ordinance is based upon proper statutory authority and is reasonably designed to protect the public health or safety, it cannot, in such guise, under the rights guaranteed by the Illinois and Federal constitutions, effect an arbitrary discrimination against the class on which it operates by omitting from its coverage persons and objects similarly situated. Statutory classifications can only be sustained where there are real differences between the classes, and where the selection of the particular class, as distinguished from others, is reasonably related to the evils to be remedied by the statute or ordinance. Charles v. City of Chicago, 413 Ill. 428, 109 N.E.2d 790; Marallis v. City of Chicago, 349 Ill. 422, 182 N.E. 394, 83 A.L.R. 1222; Josma v. Western Steel Car & Foundry Co., 249 Ill. 508, 94 N.E. 945.

[9, 10] Tested in the light of these established rules of law, we believe it is manifest that subparagraph (2) of section B creates an unlawful classification, both arbitrary and discriminatory in its nature. Of all the different types of structures upon which the section is made to operate, it is only apartment buildings that are required to furnish off-street parking facilities. The evils to be remedied on crowded city streets are well known, but we do not see that the singling out of apartment buildings from the other types of buildings embraced by the ordinance is reasonably related to the elimination of those evils. Appellants urge that the classification is not discriminatory because it applies to all apartment buildings equally and because it is apartment buildings, more than any other type structure permitted, which contribute the most to street congestion caused by parked automobiles. We see neither a fair nor reasonable basis for such a classification nor its reasonable relation to the object and purpose of the ordinance. The street congestion problems created by boarding or rooming houses, hotels, and the like, are not essentially different from those caused by apartment buildings. All are similarly situated in their relation to the problems of congestion that are caused by parking cars in the street, and all contribute proportionately to the evil sought to be remedied. Indeed, we think it is not unreasonable to say that the scope and nature of the congestion may be greater in the case of large rooming houses and hotels than in the case of apartment houses. First, due to the comparative number of persons accommodated and, second, because the apartment dweller suggests a resident of some permanency who would seek to alleviate the problem of parking on the street, whereas the hotel or rooming house guest suggests a transient who makes no effort to solve his parking problem. It is our conclusion that the differences in kind between apartment buildings and numerous other structures upon which the section is made to operate are not such as to warrant the distinction made by subparagraph (2). Relieving congestion in the streets is no doubt a proper legislative purpose, but imposing the burden on one kind of property, while excepting other kinds not significantly different, is not a valid means for its accomplishment. A statute or ordinance cannot be sustained which applies to

some cases and does not apply to other cases not essentially different in kind. Josma v. Western Steel Car & Foundry Co., 249 Ill. 508, 94 N.E. 945.

It follows that the circuit court was correct in holding subparagraph (2) of section 8 of the ordinance invalid. The judgment of the circuit court is therefore affirmed.

Judgment affirmed.

RIDGEVIEW CO.

v.

FLORHAM PARK

57 N.J. Super. 142, 154 A.2d 23 (1959).

Superior Court of New Jersey

Law Division.

July 30, 1959.

Action in lieu of prerogative writ challenging validity of provisions of borough zoning ordinance. The Superior Court, Law Division, Stanton, J.S.C., held, inter alia, that where borough zoning ordinance established business zone broad enough to include shopping center, failed to exclude buildings containing more than one store and made no limitation on ground floor area of a building, providing it did not cover more than 20% of land, provisions in ordinance requiring that an individual store occupy no less than 1,500 square feet and no more than 5,000 square feet of ground were arbitrary and unreasonable and not designed to further proper objects of zoning.

Judgment rendered declaring certain provisions invalid.

Young & Sears, Boonton, for plaintiffs.

Salmon & Bennett, Chatham, for Borough of Florham Park.

Frank J. Valgenti, Jr., Madison, for defendant Sixth Nat. Corp.

STANTON, J. S. C.

This is an action in lieu of prerogative writ challenging the validity of certain provisions of the zoning ordinance of the Borough of Florham Park.

The action was brought also against the board of adjustment of the borough. The first count of the complaint filed on June 6, 1958 alleges that on January 30, 1958 the corporate plaintiff applied for a variance for the erection of a commercial retail structure, having a ground floor area in excess of 5,000 square feet. The borough enacted a general revision of its zoning ordinance on August 3, 1954. The following addition by way of amendment was made on February 5, 1957:

"Section 7.1 B(a)—The maximum ground floor area permitted for any individual store shall be 5000 square feet. The minimum floor area permitted for any individual store shall be 1500 square feet."

The application for a variance was denied by the board of adjustment on April 23, 1958. This count challenged that determination.

In the second count the corporate plaintiff alleged that on the same date it applied for a variance to erect two commercial retail structures on a parcel of land described in the complaint and said to be situate partly in the B-2 business zone and partly in the R-3 residential zone, one having a ground floor area in excess of 5,000 square feet, and the other less than 1,500 square feet. This application was also denied. In this count relief was sought solely against the board of adjustment.

In the third count the corporate plaintiff challenges the validity of section 7.1 B(a) of the zoning ordinance on the ground that its provisions are arbitrary, capricious, unlawful, discriminatory, and bear no relation to the purposes of zoning as set forth in R.S. 40:55-30 et seq., N.J.S.A. It questioned on like grounds the placing of lot 2 in Block 19, partly in a B-2 zone and partly in a R-3 zone.

To meet an objection that the corporate plaintiff was not the owner of the lands in question, the complaint was amended to add as plaintiffs certain individuals who held legal title to the property and who had entered into contractual relations with the corporate plaintiff for its sale.

By an amendment of the zoning ordinance adopted on October 21, 1958 all of the lands here involved were placed in the B-2 zone. It also added section 4.3, which created a 50-foot buffer area in a B-2 zone where it abuts a residential zone, and it amended section 9.5.1(g) so as to require six square feet of parking area for each square foot of gross floor area of business, commercial and personal service establishments and retail stores. It also revised the zoning map.

On November 24, 1958 the plaintiffs filed their second amendment to the complaint wherein they charged that the said provisions of the amendatory ordinance are invalid.

By a consent order Sixth National Corp., the owner of a shopping center in the vicinity, was permitted to intervene as a party defendant. Before trial there was a dismissal by stipulation of the first and second counts of the complaint. This eliminated the board of adjustment from the action.

The revised ordinance of 1954 fixed the maximum percentage of coverage of all buildings in a B-2 zone at 30%; by the February 5, 1957 amendment this was reduced to 20%. In the revised ordinance the parking space ratio was fixed at 2 to 1; the amendment of February 5, 1957 increased it to 4 to 1, and that of October 21, 1958, to 6 to 1.

The borough contends that the challenged provisions of the ordinance are in all respects valid. The defendant Sixth National Corp. asserted as a separate defense that it "has a vested right to the enjoyment of the ordinance, its privileges and burdens, as presently effective and regulatory." In its answer to the second amendment of the complaint, it stated that it had no interest in the allegation thereof "other than to assert and protect its rights under the provisions of Section 7.1B(a) of the zoning ordinance of the Borough * * *." This section fixes the minimum and maximum floor area for an individual store.

The testimony in the case came with one exception from experts. Robert F. Edwards, who has been engaged in the city and town planning field since 1941, and who is presently employed in that work by the Town of Montclair, testified he had never seen a maximum ground floor limitation in any ordinance except that of the City of Summit, where a maximum of 80,000 square feet is fixed for shopping centers. He said the effect of the instant provision is to eliminate supermarkets which he said have an average ground floor area in excess of 5,000 square feet; and he added such markets are in reality neighborhood stores. He said that it eliminates furniture stores which require display areas; and has the effect of eliminating variety stores, which ordinarily require space in excess of 5,000 square feet. He referred to the average ground floor area of stores in shopping centers as disclosed in professional reports, some of them being as follows:

Bakery	1200	—	1800	sq. ft.	
Bank	2000	—	3600	"	"
Barber shop	1000			"	"
Candy store	1000			"	"
Laundry pick-up store	750	—	2000	"	"
Furniture	900	—	12000	"	"
Grocery	5000	—	8000	"	"
Hardware	1500	—	4000	"	"
Jewelry stores	1200	—	2000	"	"
Women's wear	1200	—	4000	"	"
Variety stores	10000			"	"

With respect to the minimum floor area requirement, he said he was aware of no such provision in any zoning ordinance as regards business buildings, though such a provision is common in the case of dwellings.

He testified that the provision with respect to maximum floor area bears no relation to any of the purposes of zoning set forth in R.S. 40:55-32, N.J.S.A., except possibly to the overcrowding of land. However, that is eliminated here by reason of the restriction of land coverage to 20%. He expressed the opinion that the maximum floor area requirement was extremely unreasonable. As to the minimum requirement, he stated that there is no reasonable relationship between it and the statutory purpose of zoning, and that in his opinion it was entirely unreasonable.

He testified that the plaintiffs' property is situate within a triangle bounded by South Orange Avenue, Ridgedale Avenue, and Park Street. The apex of the triangle formed by South Orange Avenue and Park Street is zoned for residential use, the lower part of it having its base on Ridgedale Avenue is zoned for B-2 use. In this latter part there are both business and residential uses. The property of Sixth National Corp. is located on Ridgedale Avenue, opposite the plaintiffs' property. Several other stores are situate on that side of Ridgedale Avenue, and between these stores and South Orange Avenue is a large roller-skating rink. Across South Orange Avenue from the triangle there is a large area of land mostly vacant, but near Ridgedale Avenue there is a gasoline station, and opposite the apex of the triangle there is a large building containing bowling alleys open to the public. The lands opposite plaintiffs' property on Park Street are zoned for residential use, except for a parcel on the corner formed by it and Ridgedale Avenue upon which there is erected an old dwelling, which is now used for office purposes. The witness described the floor areas of the various stores in the vicinity which vary in size between 900 feet and 6,100 feet approximately.

The witness pointed out that Sixth National Corp. has eight stores in one building with the following floor areas:

1	—	936	sq. ft.
3	—	1224	" "
1	—	1368	" "
1	—	1584	" "
1	—	2520	" "
1	—	6120	" "
Total	—	16200	" "

He showed that because of the parking and buffer zone requirements, the plaintiffs can build on approximately only 12% of their land, although the ordinance permits a 20% land coverage.

Mr. Edwards testified that he did considerable research with respect to the parking ratio provision. He gave figures from various professional bulletins with respect to the parking needs of different types of business, and the average ratios in effect, and stated as his opinion that a ratio of 3 to 1 in the area in question would be reasonable and satisfactory. He said that a ratio of 6 to 1 was entirely too high for a supermarket use. He stated that some types of stores require much less than others, for instance, furniture stores, where the ratio would vary between 1 to 1, and 2 to 1.

He pointed out that the shopping center of the Sixth National Corp. has no buffer area but does have parking in the front and rear of the building. He estimated that the area available for parking is about 3 to 1. He gave it as his opinion that no lot in the B-2 area has a 6 to 1 parking ratio, with the result that all are nonconforming. He expressed the opinion that the parking provision is not at all realistic or practical but excessively high and unreasonable.

The plaintiff called as a witness Peter F. Pasbjerg, a mortgage banker and realtor of Newark, with considerable experience in leasing and managing shopping centers in New Jersey and Pennsylvania. He stated that the range of 1,500 feet minimum and 5,000 feet maximum for stores is neither practical nor economical. He stated that all supermarkets, even those under individual operation, are more than 5,000 square feet. He said that today the average floor area of supermarkets is about 20,000 square feet; that variety stores, including the five-and-ten-cent store type, require more than 5,000 square feet. He pointed out that in shopping centers having floor areas of 40,000 to 100,000 square feet, the majority of the individual stores are under 1,500 square feet. He mentioned that candy stores, barber shops, cleaning stores, shoe repairing shops, and the like, generally occupy less than 1,000 square feet.

It appeared from the testimony of an officer of the plaintiff corporation that it planned a group of stores, including one of 12,800 square feet for a variety store, and another of 15,000 square feet for a supermarket, with a number of smaller ones to be used in the cleaning, drug, bakery, shoe and apparel businesses. He stated that because of the parking and buffer provisions only 12% of the lands in question will be available for building, although the permissive land coverage is 20%.

Donald J. Irving, a planning consultant called by the defendants, testified that his firm worked on the borough's master plan and the 1954 revision of the zoning ordinance; that he personally had done no work for the borough since 1955; that the borough is generally residential, with some industry and business; that there are two swamp areas in the borough; that the water table is high, and there is a considerable area of land which is subject to flooding; that the population in 1950 was about 2,100, and is now between 5,000 and 6,000. He expressed the opinion that a buffer area between business parking areas and residential districts is reasonable. He stated that a 5,000 square foot maximum ground floor limitation for stores is proper zoning because larger stores might cause traffic congestion. He stated that the idea behind the B-2 zone in the borough was to provide services to meet community-wide needs. The desire was to eliminate traffic from outside the borough, although it was conceded that such traffic could not be excluded. He testified that he could not say whether his firm had recommended the ordinance changes involved here, but added that it did not recommend the 6 to 1 parking ratio.

On cross-examination he was asked his opinion as to the provision for a minimum limitation of 1,500 square feet for stores. This was objected to by the borough's attorney as not within the scope of the direct examination, and the question was thereupon withdrawn.

The witness, when asked about the difference between a supermarket operating in one 15,000 square foot store and in three stores each having 5,000 square feet, stated that he did not think the latter would be a practical operation. He said that one 20,000-foot store would generate more traffic than four 5,000-foot stores, but he could not substantiate his opinion.

Hugh R. Pomeroy, a planner of considerable experience, also testified for the defendants. He stated that the ordinance was designed for business to meet local needs, to maintain the residential character of the community, to minimize the impact of nonresidential use and to limit traffic from outside the borough, although conceding that people cannot be kept out; this despite the fact that South Orange Avenue, a heavy traffic artery, runs through the B-2 district. He expressed the opinion that a buffer zone of the type provided in this ordinance does not violate the principle of uniformity; that the limit on the maximum size stores was reasonable, but admitted that no other ordinance in this State has such a provision, but he referred to a few communities in the nation having neighborhood zoning where there are maximum limitations on store areas. No such ordinance was produced and no precise figures on limitation were given. With respect to the minimum limitation, he volunteered that it was not good zoning and did not conform with the borough's stated aims. He admitted that the parking ratio was high, but still within reasonable limits. He said that in the large Macy-Bamberger Shopping Center in Bergen County, the parking ratio is only 2 to 1. He conceded also that 3 to 1 is an acceptable ratio for neighborhood stores, but that 6 to 1 was not unreasonable because of what might evolve in the future. He expressed the opinion that one 15,000 square foot store would generate more traffic than three 5,000-foot units, because of sales attraction and the heavier turnover of a large store. No traffic studies were given to prove this statement, it was merely his estimate. The witness stated that in his opinion, the regional composite was adequate for the borough; that it needed only neighborhood stores and its requirements beyond that could be serviced by the adjoining communities, principally Chatham and Madison.

The trend in modern day zoning beyond the health, safety, and morals theory of earlier zoning is recognized in the following cases: Duffcon Concrete Products v. Borough of Cresskill, 1 N.J. 509, 64 A.2d 347, 9 A.L.R.2d 678 (1949); Schmidt v. Board of Adjustment of City of Newark, 9 N.J. 405, 88 A.2d 607 (1952); Lionshead Lake, Inc. v. Township of Wayne, 10 N.J. 165, 89 A.2d 693 (1952); Fischer v. Township of Bedminister, 11 N.J. 194, 93 A.2d 378 (1952); Pierro v. Baxendale, 20 N.J. 17, 118 A.2d 401 (1955). However, the comment of Chief Justice Weintraub in Kozesnik v. Montgomery Township, 24 N.J. 154, 169, 131 A.2d 1, 9 (1957), where he was discussing Pierro v. Baxendale, supra, and Katobimar Realty Co. v. Webster, 20 N.J. 114, 118 A.2d 824 (1955), which cases were said to be in conflict and to have created doubt as to what was the prevailing view of the Supreme Court, is apropos here: "In both cases this court divided 4 to 3, but the division did not reflect disagreement as to basic principle but rather as to the application of the principle to the facts of the case." The statement points up the situation in the instant case.

[1] It is recognized that certain uses may be excluded from a community by a zoning ordinance, as in Duffcon Concrete Products v. Borough of Cresskill, supra, where heavy industry was prohibited, and in Fanale v. Borough of Hasbrouck Heights, 26 N.J. 320, 139 A.2d 749 (1958), where apartment houses were banned.

It is important to note that the ordinance in this case provides for a business zone which is broad enough to include a shopping center; and a building containing a number of stores is not excluded. There is no limitation upon the ground floor area of a building, provided it does not cover more than 20% of the land. The plaintiffs have no desire to erect buildings beyond that limitation. What the plaintiffs challenge here are the minimum and maximum limitations put on the ground floor area of individual stores within a conforming building. This, in effect, is an attempt to control the location of partitions within such a building.

As regards the off-street parking requirement, the plaintiffs do not question the right of the ordinance *per se* to require off-street parking in connection with store operations, but they do contend that the ratio 6 to 1 is unreasonable and arbitrary.

As to the buffer zone, the challenge appears to be with respect to the depth of it, namely, 50 feet rather than to a buffer zone in general.

The defendants attempted no real defense of the minimum floor area provision of the ordinance, though they did not concede its invalidity. However, one of their own experts said it was unreasonable and poor zoning; they objected to an expression of opinion by their other expert with respect to it.

The parking provision is far out of line when compared with the average parking ratios as fixed by ordinance elsewhere, and as seen in practice in shopping centers elsewhere including that of the defendant Sixth National Corp. and it can hardly be said to have had the full support of the planning experts called by the defendants. And we have here the fact that the parking ratio set at 2 to 1 in the revised ordinance of 1954 was changed to 4 to 1 on February 5, 1957, and to 6 to 1 on October 21, 1958. This is very drastic change in regulation within a short period of time.

We cannot find any case in this State or elsewhere supporting minimum or maximum limitations on ground floor area of a store, nor were we cited to any ordinance within this State containing such a provision. As was stated above, there was some testimony of Mr. Pomeroy as to ordinance limitations elsewhere as to maximum area, but it was vague and general.

[2, 3] It is well recognized that zoning ordinances are not immutable, they may be amended from time to time, but there should be some change in circumstances justifying it or some showing that experience has proved that the earlier provision was made in error. A landowner has no vested right in district classifications, though one of the essential purposes of zoning regulations is the stabilization of property uses. Rockhill v. Chesterfield Twp., 23 N.J. 117, 129, 128 A.2d 473 (1957); Kozesnik v. Montgomery Twp., 24 N.J. 154, 167, 131 A.2d 1 (1957).

The law recognizes no vested right such as the defendant Sixth National Corp. claims in its answer. Its intervention in this case, the character of its defense, and the claims which it makes to vested rights, indicate rather strongly that it desires to keep out of the borough any type of business which might adversely affect it through competition offered to its tenants. There is no proof here of any improper motivation in the enactment of the amendments under discussion. However, there is clearly present in the atmosphere of the case the idea that Sixth National Corp. desires to limit such competition.

[4-6] There is a fairly debatable question with respect to the reasonableness of the buffer provision in the ordinance, and that being so, the presumption of its validity will stand. However the other challenged provisions are clearly unreasonable, arbitrary and not designed to further the objectives of zoning, as expressed in R.S. 40:55-32, N.J.S.A. There is in the ordinance as amended a lack of the uniformity within the same district which is required by R.S. 40:55-31, N.J.S.A.

Accordingly judgment may be entered declaring Sections 7.1 B(a) and 9.5.1(g) of the zoning ordinance invalid.

Questions and Notes

On Ronda

1. This is one of the few decisions in the field, apart from those on racial and economic segregation, which is based directly on considerations of equal protection.
2. Why could this argument not be met by the usual doctrine on equal protection, which is that in dealing with a problem it is proper to proceed one step at a time?
3. Note that this is a characteristic Illinois decision of the time.

On Florham Park

1. What parking ratios had Florham Park adopted for commercial development? Do you get the impression that the Florham Park authorities knew what they wanted?
2. What is the reason for the maximum size limit on individual stores?
3. Is there any point in a minimum size limit for stores?

DENVER

v.

DENVER BUICK, INC.

141 Col. 121, 347 P.2d 919 (1959 and 1960),

overruled, 522 P.2d 720 (Colo. 1975).

Supreme Court of Colorado.

En Banc.

As Modified on Denial of Rehearing and Dissenting Opinion Filed

Jan. 11, 1960.

Action by property owners to test validity of certain portions of municipal zoning ordinance, wherein other property owners were allowed to intervene as additional parties plaintiff. The District Court of the City and County of Denver, William A. Black, J., entered decree that District B-6, in which plaintiffs' land was located, was subject to same regulations as District B-5, which was not appreciably different in characteristics, and that the portions of the ordinance requiring off-street parking in District B-6 were unconstitutional, and municipal corporation brought error. The Supreme Court, Moore, J., held that provisions of the ordinance purporting to require installation of off-street parking facilities by owner of land as condition which must be fulfilled before such owner would be permitted to make use of land for business purposes authorized in district within which land was located were repugnant to due process and to provision of state Constitution that private property shall not be taken or damaged for public or private use without just compensation, but that it was beyond power of District Court to decree that District B-6 was subject to same regulations as District B-5.

Affirmed in part; reversed in part.

Sutton, J., dissented in part. Doyle and Day, JJ., dissented.

John C. Banks, Earl T. Thrasher, Hans W. Johnson, Denver, for plaintiff in error.

Theodore Epstein, Creamer & Creamer, Denver, for defendants in error Denver Buick, Salco Corp. and Gohan.

Dayton Denious, Omer L. Griffin, Denver, for defendants in error Weaver-Beatty Motor Co. and Roy J. Weaver.

Grant, Shafroth & Toll, Denver, for defendant in error Rainbo Bread Co.

MOORE, Justice.

This cause is here on writ of error to review a judgment of the district court of the City and County of Denver entered in an action there filed to test the validity of certain portions of the zoning ordinance of the city.

Plaintiffs in error were defendants, and the Denver Buick, Inc., Mollie Cohan, Lou Cohan, and Salco Corporation were plaintiffs, in the trial court. Rainbo Bread Company, Weaver-Beatty Motor Company and Roy J. Weaver were permitted to intervene as additional parties plaintiff. In this opinion we will refer to defendants in error as plaintiffs or interveners or by their individual names, and plaintiffs in error will be referred to as defendants or by name. All parties plaintiff attacked the validity of Ordinance No. 392, Series of 1956, adopted by the City and County of Denver. They prayed for a judgment, declaring their rights thereunder, and for a decree restraining defendants from enforcing the ordinance.

Defendants filed a motion to dismiss the action on the ground that the complaints of plaintiffs and interveners failed to state a claim upon which relief could be granted. This motion was overruled. Defendants thereupon filed an answer and the cause was tried to the court without the intervention of a jury.

Although the complaint of plaintiffs, which was adopted by interveners, contained seventeen different claims for relief, the trial court, with the consent of counsel for the parties, grouped all of said claims, except the fifteenth, under five main issues, as follows:

"(1) Is the ordinance unconstitutional because of its title under the Charter?

"(2) Was the ordinance passed in conformity with the Charter concerning notice to the property owners?

"(3) Was a public hearing held as contemplated under the Charter?

"(4) If the ordinance was passed as provided by the Charter, is that portion of the ordinance which restricts the owners of the district which is designated C on Defendants' Exhibit No. 6 unconstitutional for any of the reasons set forth in the plaintiffs' or interveners' complaint?

"(5) Is the answer of the defendant City and County pertaining to the affirmative defense of resorting to administrative remedies a good defense?"

The fifteenth claim of plaintiffs, relating to nonconforming uses, was considered apart from the issues above stated.

Under the questioned ordinance as originally adopted all the property involved herein was located in a district classified as B-4. This classification was changed to B-6 by an amendment as appears from the first affirmative defense contained in the answer of defendants, as follows:

"On December 29, 1956, pursuant to Ordinance No. 451, Series of 1956, that land and that property alleged by plaintiffs to be theirs was classified, among other lands, as a B-6 District under the Zoning Ordinance of the City and County of Denver and was made subject to the restrictions and regulations established for that district by Ordinance No. 450, Series of 1956, effective December 29, 1956 (a copy of which Ordinance No. 450, marked Exhibit 'A' is attached hereto and by such reference is made a part hereof.)"

Plaintiffs answered the above allegations in the following language:

"7. That the said B-6 Classification is meaningless, arbitrary, capricious, and void, and is an endeavor to circumvent the clearly discriminatory and abusive provisions of the B-4 District, while conferring none of the benefits of the B-5 District, all directly in violation of the rights of the Plaintiffs as set forth in their Ninth through Seventeenth Claims for Relief, each of which is incorporated herein and made specifically a part hereof, with specific reference to the said purported ordinances 450 and 451."

A second affirmative defense contained in the answer of defendants alleges in substance that all the ordinances under attack provide for administrative relief from the provisions thereof, and that plaintiffs have not availed themselves of these remedies. Plaintiffs allege that these allegations state no defense for the reason that the ordinance is unconstitutional and void.

April 4, 1958, the trial court entered its findings and judgment. That portion of the decree to which defendants object and which is now before us for review reads as follows:

"Wherefore, It Is Ordered, Adjudged And Decreed:

"1. That the B-6 District is a part in law and use of the B-5 District, and subject to the same regulations.

"2. That Article 614 of Ordinance 392 of the Series of 1956 as it relates to the so-called B-6 District requiring off-street parking violates the City Charter and particularly Chapter 219 B, in that the regulations are not uniform.

"3. That Article 614 of Ordinance 392, Series of 1956, is unconstitutional and violates Article II, Section 15, and Article II, Section 25 of the Colorado State Constitution.

"4. That Article 614 of Ordinance 392, Series of 1956, is unconstitutional in that it is oppressive, discriminatory and an invasion of the plaintiffs' and interveners' rights to use of their property.

"5. That off-street parking is a public and municipal function, and a property owner's property cannot be taken for a public use without just compensation.

"6. That the properties of the plaintiffs and interveners are subject to the regulations pertaining to the so-called B-5 District and none other.

"7. That Councilman's Bill 403, Ordinance 392, Series of 1956, repeals Ordinance 14, Series of 1925.

"8. That the operation of an apartment by the plaintiff Salco Corporation is a conforming use under the Ordinance."

Questions to be Determined

First. *Where a zoning ordinance of a municipality contains provisions which purport to require the installation of off-street parking* *facilities by the owner of land as a condition which must be fulfilled before such owner will be permitted to make use of his land for business purposes authorized in the district within which the land is located; are such provisions unconstitutional when tested by the due process clause of the state and federal constitutions and by Article II, Section 15, of the State Constitution which provides, inter alia, that "private property shall not be taken or damaged, for public or private use, without just compensation"?*

[1] We answer this question in the affirmative, and hold that such provisions are repugnant to each of said constitutional guarantees. We think it essential to again state some basic principles of constitutional law to which we are indebted as a nation of freedom loving people, and to which we must steadfastly adhere if individual freedoms and liberties are to survive.

[2-5] In City and County of Denver v. Thrailkill, 125 Colo. 488, 244 P.2d 1074, 1079, this court held that the restraint upon the freedom of one who provides transportation for hire to make use of public streets was "completely out of harmony with the American constitutional concept of fundamental freedoms and liberties, under which the individual has the right to engage in a lawful business which is harmless in itself and useful to the community, unhampered by unreasonable and arbitrary governmental interference or regulation." Without reservation we are firm in our adherence to the principle that "the privilege of a citizen to use his property according to his own will is not only a liberty but a property right, subject only to such restraints as the common welfare may require." People ex rel. Schimpff v. Norvell, 368 Ill. 325, 13 N.E.2d 960, 961. If a restriction upon the use of property is to be upheld as a valid exercise of the police power it must bear, "a fair relation to the public health, safety, morals or welfare," and have "a definite tendency to promote or protect the same." In determining the validity of restraints upon freedom imposed by statute or ordinance, "The determination we are called upon to make is whether the ordinance has a *real and substantial* relation to the accomplishment of those *objectives* which form the basis of police regulation." City and County of Denver v. Thrailkill, supra [244 P.2d 1079] (emphasis supplied). Bohn v. Board of Adjustment of City and County of Denver, 129 Colo. 539, 271 P.2d 1051.

In Buchanan v. Warley, 245 U.S. 60, 38 S.Ct. 16, 18, 62 L.Ed. 149, the Supreme Court of the United States asserted that:

> "Property is more than the mere thing which a person owns. It is elementary that it includes the right to acquire, *use,* and dispose of it. The Constitution protects *these essential attributes* of property." (Italics ours.)

[6]   As forcefully stated by the former Chief Justice of the Supreme Court of the United States, Charles Evans Hughes, at ceremonies commemorating the establishment of a government of *free* people:

> "We protect the fundamental right of minorities in order to save democratic government from destroying itself by the excesses of its own power. The firmest ground for confidence in the future is *that more than ever we realize* that, while democracy must have its orginization and controls, *its vital breath is individual liberty.*" (Emphasis supplied.)

It is the unquestioned duty and responsibility of the judicial branch of government, through the decision of controversies which come before it, to safeguard and maintain the constitutional provisions which guarantee the maximum free and unrestricted use of property by the citizen, and to strike down those enactments which unreasonably and unnecessarily fasten upon him new restraints upon freedom of action in the use and enjoyment thereof.

[7, 8]   Any legislative action which takes away any of the essential attributes of property, or imposes unreasonable restrictions thereon, violates the due process clause of the Constitutions of the United States and the State of Colorado.   In Bettey v. City of Sidney, 79 Mont. 314, 257 P. 1007, 1009, 56 A.L.R. 872, we find the following most significant language:

> "The constitutional guaranty that no person shall be deprived of his property without due process of law may be violated without the physical taking of property for public or private use.   Property may be destroyed, or its value may be annihilated; it is owned and kept for some useful purpose and it has no value unless it can be used. Its capability for enjoyment and adaptability to some use are essential characteristics and attributes without which property cannot be conceived; and hence any law which destroys it or its value, or takes away any of its essential attributes, deprives the owner of his property."

In Chicago, B. & Q. Ry. Co. v. State of Illinois, 200 U.S. 561, 26 S.Ct. 341, 350, 50 L.Ed. 596, we find the following:

> "The constitutional requirement of due process of law, which embraces compensation for private property taken for public use, applies in every case of the exertion of government power.   If, in the execution of any power, *no matter what it is,* the government, Federal or state, finds it necessary to take private property for public use, it must obey the constitutional injunction to make or secure just compensation to the owner." (Emphasis supplied.)

[9, 10]   At the common law the owner of property has a vested right to make the fullest legitimate use of such property.   It follows, therefore, that express legislative prohibition within the perimeter of constitutional permission is necessary in order to place restrictions upon the legitimate use of property.   The ordinance here in question, purporting to command

a specific use of property as a condition precedent to the right to do business, is in derogation of the common law and *must be strictly construed in favor of the person against whom its provisions are sought to be applied.* City and County of Denver v. Thrailkill, supra; Hart v. Board of Examiners, 129 Conn. 128, 26 A.2d 780; National Exhibition Co. v. City of St. Louis, 235 Mo.App. 485, 136 S.W.2d 396.

This court has been careful to protect constitutional rights in construing the zoning ordinance of 1925, the provisions of which were far less drastic than those now before us. With reference to the 1925 Act this court said:

> "In broad outline, but only so, we have held the zoning ordinance invoked by the building inspector to be constitutional." Hedgcock v. People ex rel. Arden Realty & Investment Co., 98 Colo. 522, 57 P.2d 891, 893.

In Colby v. Board of Adjustment of Denver, 81 Colo. 344, 255 P. 443, 446, "in broad outline" the old ordinance was held constitutional but this court there said:

> "This decision is not to be construed as passing upon or approving each and every provision of the Denver zoning ordinance, nor as fixing its application to every circumstance that may arise."

In numerous instances this court has held that even the old, less drastic zoning ordinance operated to deny constitutional rights to persons adversely affected by its terms. People ex rel. Friedman v. Webber, 110 Colo. 161, 132 P.2d 183, and cases there cited.

[11] Section 614 of the Zoning Ordinance here in question deals with the subject of off-street parking as related to the several district classifications. In so far as District B-5 (the main down town area) is concerned, it is provided that "Off Street Parking Requirements shall be of no force and effect in this district." But in District B-6 in which the property here involved is located, the ordinance classifies the off-street parking requirements into eight different trade categories, with different parking requirements for each. The utter unreasonableness of these off-street parking requirements is made crystal clear by a letter, introduced in evidence, which was written by defendant to the plaintiff Lou Cohan. The latter had applied for a building permit, which was denied. During the course of his frustrated effort to put his property to use in lawful business enterprises, he received the following letter in explanation of the denial of his application to build:

> "Plans submitted do not indicate the specific amount of floor area to be assigned to each of several classes of use. Nor is there indicated the precise area intended to be devoted to off-street parking. Our engineer, applying

various techniques for estimating, has estimated that automobile sales (Parking Class 6) would occupy 3,000 square feet and thus require 1500 square feet of off-street parking; that office uses (Parking Class 2) would occupy 106,000 square feet, requiring 53,000 square feet of off-street parking; and that a restaurant (Parking Class 4) would occupy 5000 square feet, requiring 15,000 square feet of off-street parking—for a total of 69,500 square feet of off-street parking. Attachment A of your application for construction permit indicates that 'a substantial portion' of approximately 37,000 square feet of basement and sub-basement area would be used for parking purposes. From this it is evident that the off-street parking proposed to be provided does not meet the requirements of Article 614. Again, additional information would be required to determine the exact amount of the proposed excess."

With reference to parking provisions of the ordinance the learned trial judge stated in his decree that:

" ° ° ° the off-street parking requirements in the B-6 District are confiscatory, oppressive, discriminatory, unreasonable and unconstitutional, and to enforce the provisions thereof would deprive the plaintiffs and intervenors of their property without due process of law."

With this statement we agree.

[12] In Bohn v. Board of Adjustment of City and County of Denver, 129 Colo. 539, 271 P.2d 1051, 1054, this court said:

"It is a fundamental principle recognized by all the authorities that any regulation or restriction upon the use of property which bears no relation to public safety, health, morals or general welfare, cannot be sustained as a proper exercise of the police power of the municipality."

The legal effect of the argument of the City is that it has a problem of concentration of traffic in the streets and that accordingly there is a right, under the zoning ordinance, to appropriate for off-street parking substantial portions of property of citizens desiring to use that property for a legitimate purpose, and to prohibit the use of that property for any purpose until its owners devote a substantial portion thereof to parking; and this despite the fact that in District B-5 which is in all respects similar to B-6 in general usage, no such requirement exists! No such power exists in the city thus to take private property for a public purpose without compensation to the owner for the taking. It would be quite as proper to argue that the city had the right, under the guise of "zoning" to require dedication of private property for the street itself, if it were considered that a given street was generally inadequate to carry the traffic; and to prohibit the use of property for any legitimate purpose until such dedication was made. If it be true that a traffic problem exists, it cannot be legally solved by confiscation of private property without compensation, under a pretense of "zoning."

The alert business man as a matter of voluntary action fully realizes the advantages which are to be gained by affording parking facilities to his customers. However, he cannot be compelled to do so under penalty of forfeiting the right to make a beneficial use of his property. The city has ample power to control the "congestion of traffic" by adoption of regulations adequate for the purpose, which are directly related to that problem. Compulsory, involuntary off-street parking maintained at the expense of a property owner as a price tag or tribute for the exercise of the constitutional right to do business, is "completely out of harmony with the American constitutional concept of fundamental freedoms and liberties." It has no definite or substantial tendency to promote or protect those objectives which form the basis of police power.

We direct attention to the opinion of this court in Willison v. Cooke, 54 Colo. 320, 130 P. 828, 832, 44 L.R.A.,N.S., 1030, from which we quote:

> "One of the essential elements of property is the right to its unrestricted use and enjoyment; and as we have seen, that use cannot be interfered with beyond what is necessary to provide for the welfare and general security of the public. Enforcing the provisions of the ordinances in question does not deprive the petitioner of title to his lots. He would not be ousted of possession. He would still have the power to dispose of them; but, although there would be no actual or physical invasion of his possession, he would be deprived of the right to put them to a legitimate use, which does not injure the public, and this, without compensation or any provision thereof. This would clearly deprive him of his property without compensation, and without due process of law, which your federal and state constitutions not only inhibit, but which would be repugnant to justice, independent of constitutional provisions on the subject."

[13] In Hedgcock v. People ex rel. Reed, 91 Colo. 155, 13 P.2d 264, 265, this court recognized that where "public health and safety will be best conserved" reasonable restrictions may be imposed upon the use of property. However in that case we find the following apt language, "* * but not less fundamental is the *inherent right of the owner [of property] to erect buildings covering such portions thereof as he may elect*, and put his property to any legitimate use." (Emphasis supplied.)

[14] And finally upon this question we direct attention to pertinent language of Mr. Justice Holmes in Pennsylvania Coal Co. v. Mahon, 260 U.S. 393, 43 S.Ct. 158, 160, 67 L.Ed. 322:

> "The protection of private property in the Fifth Amendment presupposes that it is wanted for public use, but provides that it shall not be taken for such use without compensation. * * * The general rule at least is that while property may be regulated to a certain extent, if regulation goes too far it will be recognized as a taking. * * * We are in danger of forgetting that a strong public desire to improve the public condition is not enough to warrant achieving the desire by a shorter cut than the con-

stitutional way of paying for the change." See also Arverne Bay Const. Co. v. Thatcher, 278 N.Y. 222, 15 N.E.2d 587, 117 A.L.R. 1110.

* * *

Third. *Are the various provisions and restrictions set forth in Ordinance No. 392 Series of 1956 unlawfully and unreasonably discriminatory in that they impose certain obligations and restrictions upon the property in the B-F District so as to work undue hardships within that District while favoring the B-5 District by not imposing those restrictions and obligations upon the property within the B-5 District, and thus creating a condition of sub-serviency by one district in favor of the other?*

[17] This question is answered in the affirmative. The trial court determined from knowledge common to any citizen, and from the language of the ordinance itself, that there is no applicable or apparent difference in the characteristics of District B-6 and B-5 except that in the latter the uses authorized include operation of a pawnshop or music studio, while these privileges are denied in the B-6 District. Indeed, a reading of Sections 612.9-1 and 612.10 respectively lead to no other conclusion. With reference to the B-6 District the ordinance reads:

"This district, at present, is a large area located immediately adjacent to the B-5 District, for which it acts as a service area * * *."

We know of nothing which justifies any such conclusion. The trial court took notice that within the District B-6 are a great many buildings and business enterprises which serve the entire city of Denver, the state, and large districts outside the state.

The regulations of the ordinance as to B-5 do not require off-street parking, but in the B-6 District the ordinance demands off-street parking facilities and sets up a maze of oppressive rules and regulations pertaining thereto. None of these requirments are made as to the B-5 District. Gross floor area provisions are set up in the B-6 District, none of which appears in the B-5 District. The city regulates private property in the B-6 District so as to require off-street parking based on nature and type of the trade or business, use of the building, size of the building to be erected, number of employees in excess of five, the religious belief of employees, the grade in school of children, furnishing services to the B-5 District, protecting an adjoining residential district, and serving as a shopping center for the adjoining residential districts; while no such regulations are required in the adjoining B-5 District although all types of business and buildings permitted are the same in both districts, with the two exceptions above noted.

[18] This is not to say, however, that the trial court was correct in that part of its decision wherein it finds that the property in the B-6 District is subject to the ordinance as set forth in the B-5 District. Such a result involves a legislative function beyond the power of the court, and we must

overrule the judgment of the trial court in so far as it purports to place property in the B-6 District into that classified B-5.

Fourth. *Where a zoning ordinance is adopted by a city council and becomes a law on a given date; will a provision thereof purporting to fix the effective date of the ordinance as of a time prior to its adoption be upheld?*

[19] The answer to this question is "No." In the instant case the ordinance in question was enacted and became law on November 7, 1956. A provision therein purported to relate back the effective date of the ordinance to February 11, 1955. It is sufficient to say that the Constitution of Colorado, art. 2, § 11, provides that no law "retrospective in its operation" shall be passed by the General Assembly. What the legislature cannot do at the state level in this connection, the city council cannot do in municipal affairs.

[20] It follows that any person who applied for a building permit prior to November 7, 1956, was entitled to have his application considered under the only zoning law in force at that time, and that law was the zoning ordinance of 1925, as amended.

Judgment of the trial court is affirmed in all respects except as to that part of the same which declares the property in the B-6 District to be subject to the ordinance as it pertains to the B-5 District.

FRANTZ, J., specially concurring.

SUTTON, J., concurs in part and dissents in part.

DAY and DOYLE, JJ., dissent.

FRANTZ, Justice (specially concurring).

I believe in the rightness of the opinion of Mr. Justice MOORE, and further believe that some aspects of his opinion can bear amplification.

Justification of this zoning ordinance in the name of progress, and on the theory that the Constitutions, Federal and state, are flexible enough to sustain it, is not in my opinion warranted. All too frequently acceptance of legislation is urged because it represents progress, and because the flexibility of both Constitutions allegedly has come to mean documents of boundless accommodation, Protean in their adjustments. Beguiling indeed are these notions, and hence their advancement as arguments for a proposition should be scrutinized and analyzed with care.

Let us examine and evaluate aspects of the ordinance in question. Is there sanction in the law for the provision regarding off-street parking?—for the provision placing technical demands upon one who desires to keep alive a nonconforming use?—for the provision giving the ordinance a retrospective operation?

Answers to these questions begin with certain fundamental, immemorial rules of property law. In ignoring or overlooking these basic tenets the law has been reduced to a state of contrarieties, where ownership envisions *rights* in the law of property, but only *privileges* in the law of zoning and city planning. It is imperative that we return to basic concepts, for then we can get direction and proceed correctly toward our goal—the amelioration of municipal ills.

What derives from the ownership of property? The ordinance under attack here is typical of one answer to the question. In so far as zoning applies, the owner has an inchoate, limited right to put his property to a use; he must go to an agency for a permit to develop his property in a certain way. The zoners and city planners have devised laws by which the owner must seek and obtain a license to do some particular thing with his property. Through these laws certain rights in property are placed under lock and key, and in their place arises a privilege to improve one's property, granted only after application and then only as the law permits.

Today a zoning board issues a permit to the owner to put his property to a certain use. This board exercises a legislatively imposed discretion in passing upon the application for the permit. And this permit bestows a privilege upon the owner. Such permit "partakes of a personal privilege and grant which attaches to the land. The right in so far as it is a personal privilege is not assignable, and it must be exercised * * * within a reasonable time after its issuance." Hanley v. Cook, 245 Mass. 563, 139 N.E. 654. See Rhyne, Municipal Law, page 893.

There is another answer to the question of what derives from ownership. It has been tested in the crucible of time, and by reason of its merit constitutional provisions were conceived and cast in its mold. By it an owner has more than a conferable privilege to use his property. He has a legal right, subject to certain restraints, to enjoy and use his property; his ownership, and his enjoyment and use springing therefrom, are not privileges, but are rights which this government was instituted to protect.

If this be not true, of what avail is it that "All persons have certain natural, essential and inalienable rights, among which may be reckoned the right * * * of acquiring, possessing and protecting property * * *," covenanted in Article II, Section 3, of our Constitution? Of what avail that "Private property shall not be taken or damaged, for public or private use, without just compensation," assured in Article II, Section 15? Of what avail that "No person shall be deprived of life, liberty or property, without due process of law," solemnly pledged in Article II, Section 25? Of what avail that a state may not "deprive any person of life, liberty, or property, without due process of law," guaranteed in Amendment XIV, Section 1, of the Federal Constitution?

Property had a well-defined meaning at the time these Constitutions were adopted. "The natural right one may have to use his own property as he wills is subject always to the limitation that in its use others shall not be injured. That which is hurtful to the comfort, safety, and welfare of society may always be prohibited under the inherent or plenary power of the state, notwithstanding the incidental inconvenience or loss individuals may suffer thereby. This power is the law of necessity, and is founded upon the maxim, 'Salus populi suprema lex.' The exercise of the power

is essential to the maintenance of society, and the establishment of government itself presupposes the surrender to it by the individual citizen of the
right to regulate, and even forbid, such use of his private property as would
prove injurious to the citizens generally. City of Chicago v. Rogers Park
Water Co., 214 Ill. [212], 73 N.E. 375; Mugler v. [State of] Kansas, 123
U.S. 623, 665, 8 S.Ct. 273, 31 L.Ed. 205. *It is equally true, however, that
the owner of property has the right to put it to any use he desires, provided in so doing he does not imperil or threaten harm to others. Legislative restrictions* of the use of property are imposed only upon the theory
of necessity; that is, they *are necessary for the safety, health, comfort, or
general welfare of the public."* Curran Bill Posting & Distributing Co. v.
City of Denver, 47 Colo. 221, 107 P. 261, 263, 27 L.R.A.,N.S., 544. (Emphasis supplied.) Cf. Mooney v. Village of Orchard Lake, 333 Mich. 389,
53 N.W.2d 308; O'Connor v. City of Moscow, 69 Idaho 37, 202 P.2d 401,
9 A.L.R.2d 1031 (both zoning cases). See Colby v. Board of Adjustment,
81 Colo. 344, 255 P. 443.

It has been said that "[i]f the right of use be denied, the value of the
property is annihilated and ownership is rendered a barren right." Spann v.
City of Dallas, 111 Tex. 350, 235 S.W. 513, 515, 19 A.L.R. 1387; O' Connor
v. City of Moscow, supra. Unless the contemplated use of property imperils
the safety, health, comfort or general welfare of the community, it appears
that a denial of such use would be invalid. And a zoning restriction must
have a reasonable and substantial relation to the safety, health, morals or
general welfare; the connection may not be tenuous, vague or remote. 101
C.J.S. Zoning § 7, p. 683 et seq. See Hedgcock v. People, 91 Colo. 155,
13 P.2d 264.

Is there such a relation to safety, health, morals or general welfare as
warrants the provision in the ordinance for off-street parking? As in
the numerous zoning ordinances of other cities requiring the installation of off-street parking facilities in order to make use of property,
justification for the provision in question is urged on the ground that Denver
has a traffic problem: certain streets in the industrial, commercial and business areas of the city are choked with moving and parked cars, and further
uses of property will magnify the condition. To the extent that contemplated uses magnify the condition, the ordinance is said to be proper and
effectual in that it will constitute a holding-of-the-line against intensifying
the problem.

Although courts generally cannot question the wisdom and policy of a
zoning law, they have the duty to determine "that the power must not be
exercised so arbitrarily or unreasonably as to make the [zoning] ordinance
unconstitutional in its operation and effect," Colby v. Board of Adjustment,
supra [81 Colo. 344, 255 P. 445]. If the effect of off-street parking facilities is to intensify the traffic condition, is ineffectual on examination, and
putting it into operation would destroy the thing it purports to protect,

clearly it would be unconstitutional. Property would then be taken in violation of cited constitutional provisions.

And that would be the very effect of the operation of the off-street parking provision. Parking space in these areas has reached flood-tide; moving and parked vehicles are jamming the streets; therefore, make possible more parking areas by requiring owners of buildings to provide off-street facilities, and thereby concentrate more moving traffic in the areas. Alleviate the lesser of two evils, the parked car, so that the greater, the moving vehicle, can be put in increased mass movement. A self-defeating condition inevitably follows such a development, for with more parking facilities available, more vehicles are attracted to the area, and traffic becomes denser.

If an owner builds a large structure on his land (and let us assume it is a useful building presenting no aspects of being a nuisance), does it imperil safety, health, morals or general welfare because no provision is made for parking facilities? It may be a building requiring, because of the nature of the business conducted therein, very few employees, and very few persons may be attracted to it for trade. On the other hand, it may house businesses having many employees and bringing to it many people. The building may be located on very busy streets, heavily burdened with moving and parked vehicles. In either case, automotive traffic attracted to the building may be a minute part of one per cent or it may be one per cent of the total traffic on the streets around the structure on any or every day.

Continuing with our illustration: the total traffic represents 100%, and the problem of how to handle this total traffic is one of municipal concern. It is primarily a street problem; it involves movement of vehicles with despatch, convenience and safety. Even the total parking may be an inconsequential percentage of the total traffic using the streets around the building. Other streets in the area may have substantially less traffic and less parking. In all these illustrations we are dealing with variants, all of which go to the question of the reasonableness of the provision requiring the installation of parking facilities.

Is there a reasonable connection between traffic congestion and a large building to which may be attracted considerably less than one per cent of the parked and moving cars on the street? In most instances the street, its width, its accessibility to other important streets, the directness with which persons using it can reach points of interest or of business, and probably other factors create the problem of traffic congestion. As can be seen, in essence the problem begins in the street and ends there.

In fact, there is authority for the proposition that mounting traffic burdens or hazards are matters which constitute police problems and are not within the province of the zoning authorities. Greenberg v. City of New Rochelle, 206 Misc. 28, 129 N.Y.S.2d 691, affirmed 284 App. Div. 891, 134 N.Y.S.2d 593, appeal dismissed 308 N.Y. 736, 124 N.E.2d 716; Property

Owners Ass'n, etc. v. Board of Zoning Appeals, 2 Misc.2d 309, 123 N.Y.S.2d 716, 718.

Adelphi College, located in the village of Garden City, N.Y., made application to the Zoning Board for permission to erect stands which would accommodate 3,958 persons, and the Board approved stands for only 2,000 persons, subject to certain conditions. As stated by the Supreme Court of New York in Property Owners Ass'n, etc. v. Board of Zoning Appeals, supra: "The principal question raised upon the hearing related to a possible increase in traffic and parking upon the village streets which allegedly would be detrimental to the residents but the evidence does not justify a conclusion that the presence or absence of permanent seats would have that effect." In the syllabus is a succinct statement of the holding of the court, viz.: "Great increase in traffic and parking on village streets, if a college were granted permission to erect seating stands adjacent to its athletic field in village were problems for police, not village zoning authorities."

This total traffic condition represents a municipal and public problem to be solved. Property dedicated to its solution is property devoted to a public use. Involuntary dedication of such property to such use is a taking of the property. Only a resort to sophistry may sustain the ordinance as not constituting the taking of property for a public use.

Indeed, there is argument that only persons going to a building will be permitted to use the parking facility provided for the building. It is argued that parking is furnished for their convenience, and therefore it is not requiring an owner to put his property to a public use. If that be true, then it is a taking for private use, a taking for more doubtful validity.

How far can a city go in requiring accessory uses? Could a city require an apartment house builder who intends to accept families with children to furnish classrooms for such children in order to ameliorate traffic congestion and related problems on the streets on which his building will be located? In order to keep children off the streets, whether such children are tenants or visitors of tenants, could the city require such builder to furnish playgrounds and a gymnasium—yes, and supervisors to maintain safety and order while these facilities are being used? Could the city require the builder of an office building to construct over-or underpasses for tenants and their patrons where the building would be located on heavily travelled streets? Instances could be multiplied, but these questions test the measure of the proposed power of a city.

As a matter of fact, the illustrations suggested by the foregoing questions have better basis for being held valid than the reality with which we are dealing, for in each of the illustrations the problem of safety has a closer relevance to the use of the property than the off-street parking provision has to the uses of property described in the instant ordinance.

❖   ❖   ❖

SUTTON, Justice (specially concurring in part and dissenting in part).

I

Although I am of the opinion that the particular zoning ordinance in question has in some particulars gone beyond the permissible limits of propriety and cannot meet certain constitutional requirements, I cannot agree with the majority opinion when it would deny to zoning authorities the right and power to adopt reasonable zoning laws which would properly regulate land and its use so that we city dwellers can live in a less frenetic and more orderly society.

It requires no citation of authority to establish that zoning is constitutionally possible only under the police powers of a state. In other words, all such ordinances or statutes must have a reasonable relation to the public health, safety or morals.

Let us examine the first question posed by the majority opinion and its answer relating to whether a municipality can require any type of off-street parking.

Admittedly off-street parking requirements for new construction or new uses of existing property dilute the bundle of an owner's rights, which in theory permits him to do whatever he chooses with his property. But such rights of ownership have never been absolute. Originally in England, from whence comes our common law, all property belonged to the Crown and ownership could revert to the King on failure of its possessor to perform certain conditions. Later the Crown lost these rights of reversion but the owner was required to pay taxes to the state for the privilege of ownership. Failure to pay resulted then as now in the loss of the property to the government.

In other words, though we recognize and firmly believe in the right to acquire and own private property, property rights are not absolute and property bears its share of responsibility for the orderly functioning of government by carrying part of the tax burden with the corollary restrictions that it cannot be used to the detriment of the public, and is always subject to the police power. Thus, for example, the law for centuries has prohibited a man from creating or permitting nuisances on his land which annoy or harm the public or a member thereof; and, in the event of public disaster the state under its police powers can even destroy private property without liability for compensation to its owners.

Zoning and planning laws have evolved in modern civilizations to permit huge masses of people to dwell together in restricted areas with the least possible friction commensurate with the widest and freest use of the land used in such areas.

The determination of municipal officials in zoning matters should not be approached by the courts with a general feeling of suspicion (Van Itallie v. Borough of Franklin Lakes, 1958, 28 N.J. 258, 146 A.2d 111). When zoning ordinances are reasonable and applied uniformly they do not violate due process of law (see McMahon v. City of Dubuque, Iowa, 8 Cir.,

1958, 255 F.2d 154). Under general rules of construction courts have an obligation in construing the validity of city ordinances to apply such construction, if possible, as will avoid an unconstitutional result. City of New Orleans v. Leeco, 1954, 226 La. 335, 76 So.2d 387 This is subject, however, to the exception that when the subject matter sought to be regulated is something which was permitted at common law, then the restriction is strictly construed in favor of the person against whom its provisions are sought to be applied. City and County of Denver v. Thrailkill, 1952, 125 Colo. 488, 500, 244 P.2d 1074. The latter does not mean, however, that the police powers can never be used to meet new situations which arise, for example, due to the growth of cities and vehicular traffic, and which need new but constitutional solutions. The exception is but one more test to properly protect freedoms against unwarranted governmental encroachment on private rights; it is not a bar to make government powerless to act for the general welfare under its police powers.

We live in a dynamic, growing society and what may have been unreasonable or arbitrary governmental interference or regulation in one period of our national history has often been recognized and accepted in later years as both necessary and constitutional when applied reasonably and equally to all people or property within a certain uniform class.

I firmly agree with the basic constitutional concepts set out by the majority opinion. It is in their application to some of the facts of this case that I respectfully dissent. In other words, the issue here is: what is a reasonable and necessary exercise of the police power? This degree of use "* * *" cannot be disposed of by general propositions * * *" as the majority opinion so succinctly quotes Mr. Justice Holmes as saying in Pennsylvania Coal Co. v. Mahon, 1922, 260 U.S. 393, 43 S.Ct. 158, 160, 67 L.Ed. 322.

This ordinance could not, contrary to the statement in the majority opinion, "* * * prohibit the use of that property for any purpose until its owners devote a substantial portion thereof to parking; * * *." In this regard I point out that the owners obviously can continue their present uses without interference and possibly change to others which do not require more parking area than may now exist.

It is not amiss to ask what is off-street parking attempting to do in this ordinance. Without determining whether this particular regulation is reasonable, it is obvious to all that traffic congestion and the need for adequate parking is a public problem of paramount importance in Denver. The public welfare, if nothing more, would require public officials to seek reasonable and legal solutions thereto. Such officials recognize a duty not to let the public stew in its own juice, so to speak, of traffic confusion and parking. This ordinance seeks to help correct the problem by requiring owners to provide certain off-street parking if and when they build new buildings or make structural alterations or change their uses in zoning districts where the problem exists. The majority opinion states this can only be done by condemnation and payment of compensation from public funds, whereas I believe it is properly the subject of reasonable zoning regulations. Apparently many others concur, for by 1953, according to Yokley on Zoning Law and Practice, Vol. 2, 2nd Ed. § 208, p. 76, "* * * 265 known localities in thirty-three states have enacted (zoning) ordinances or amendments thereto requiring off-street parking accommodations for designated property uses." We can presume that in the interval the list has grown considerably larger.

In McMahon, supra the federal circuit court not only upheld the constitutionality of an Iowa zoning ordinance but went on to point out that all regulations impose limitations upon the full use and enjoyment of property and in a sense take away property rights. McMahon, supra cites Anderson v. Jester, 1928, 206 Iowa 452, 221 N.W. 354, 357, which held: "That full use and enjoyment of a plot of ground is prohibited, that the excluded use is the most profitable to which the land can be put, or that the prohibition deprives the owner of profit that would otherwise be derived from such use, or that esthetic considerations incidentally enter into the determination does not invalidate the regulation."

The McMahon opinion further pointed out that though the zoning authorities had refused to rezone two corners of a wide intersection as commercial just because the other two were so zoned, it was not illegal or arbitrary saying it was a reasonable legislative determination that the district line should stop there; and it emphasized that lower market value and highest use of the land are not necessarily determinative factors to be considered in determining the validity of zoning regulations.

In Colby v. Board, 1927, 81 Colo. 344, 255 P. 443, 446, in discussing the constitutionality of a Denver zoning ordinance, this court pointed out that such laws are for the promotion of the public welfare and that "A full perspective, (of community growth and development) however, in a case like this, requires not merely that the present be depicted, but that the future be envisaged."

In addition to Yokley's comments supra it appears that many jurisdictions recently have either by implication or express holding upheld the principle of reasonable off-street parking. Among those so holding by implication are: Fleishon v. Philadelphia Zoning Board of Adjustment, 1956, 385 Pa. 295, 122 A.2d 673 (permits revoked as not being valid because no access provided to parking space; however, required off-street parking was not ruled upon); Hill v. Kesselring, 1949, 310 Ky. 483, 220 S.W.2d 858, 10 A.L.R.2d 1301 (remanded for further hearing on adequacy of off-street parking, traffic hazards on deadend street, etc. for a proposed church); Roselle v. Wright, 1955, 37 N.J. Super. 507, 117 A.2d 661 (ordinance required off-street public parking, petitioner desired permit for private storage of a few trucks and was denied it; reversed as to denial of off-street parking permit); Ronda Realty Corp. v. Lawton, 1953, 414 Ill. 313, 111 N.E.2d 310 (off-street parking re-

quirements only for apartment houses *and not for other multiple use buildings in same zone*, held discriminatory).

I find the following decisions upholding off-street parking in direct fashion:
Allendale Congregation of Jehovah's Witnesses v. Grosman, 1959, 30 N.J.
273, 152 A.2d 569; City of New Orleans v. Leeco, Inc., supra (where one
of several points decided was that defendant Leeco, Inc. had complied with
the off-street parking requirements for a theatre); State ex rel. Killeen
Realty Co. v. City of East Cleveland, 1958, 108 Ohio App. 99, 153 N.E.2d
177, 178 (owner sought permit to build supermarket; one question involved
was off-street parking. Headnote 7 summarizes this point by saying: "Zoning ordinance of city being within exercise of the police power, provisions
thereof regulating off-street parking are constitutional").

The true test as to whether off-street parking is constitutional seems to be
whether the requirement is applied uniformly in a district and whether the
amount of space required bears a reasonable relation to the use proposed.
See 58 Columbia Law Review 666-667 (1958) for a discussion of various
lines of demarcation laid down by the courts in various zoning controversies.

In Allendale, supra, a church had been denied a building permit because
it did not propose to provide the required off-street parking space required
by the zoning ordinance. The supreme court of New Jersey unanimously
upheld the denial saying that the requirement was not invalid on its face
and did not violate either the state or federal constitutions. I quote some
pertinent parts of the court's language [30 N.J. 273, 152 A.2d 571]:

> "The plaintiff's real contention is that off-street parking requirements of
> the amendatory ordinance are invalid on their face and as applied because
> they abridge 'freedom of assembly and worship contrary to the state and
> federal constitutions.' We consider this contention to be without merit.
> The off-street parking requirements are made indiscriminately applicable to
> all buildings where substantial numbers of people are likely to gather via
> private motor vehicles and are well designed to promote the public safety
> and general welfare by lessening 'congestion in the streets.' See R.S. 40:
> 55-32, N.J.S.A.; James v. Bd. of Adjustment of Town of Montclair, 40 N.J.
> Super. 206, 212, 122 A.2d 660 (Law Div. 1956); 2 Rathkopf, The Law
> of Zoning and Planning (3rd ed. 1956), 397. They do not restrict the
> plaintiff's freedom of worship and assembly at its present quarters or at
> any suitable quarters in the AA residential zone or in any of the other
> zones in the borough or even at the plaintiff's relatively small lot on Hill-
> side Avenue, if its plans are altered to reduce its proposed seating capacity
> and increase its proposed off-street parking facilities so as to comply with
> the terms of the amendatory ordinance. On the record before us we are
> not at all at liberty to say that the requirements have not been imposed
> in good faith and for the public interest or that they are unnecessary or
> excessive or that they are not substantially related to the promotion of the
> public safety and general welfare; they appear to come well within the
> principles expressed in cases which have here to fore held that property
> used for church purposes, along with property used for other purposes,
> may be lawfully subjected to reasonable zoning restrictions. (Citing num-
> erous authorities.)

"In Appeal of Trustees of Congregation of Jehovah's Witnesses, Bethel Unit, 183 Pa. Super. 219, 130 A.2d 240, 243 (Super. Ct. 1957), appeal dismissed for want of a substantial federal question [Swift v. Borough of Bethel, Pa.], 355 U.S. 40, 78 S.Ct. 120, 2 L.Ed.2d 71 (1957), the Borough of Bethel had adopted an ordinance which contained an off-street parking requirement applicable to churches, schools, auditoriums, stadiums and similar places of assembly; it also provided that no such places shall be permitted within 1/4 mile of each other. In a decision adverse to the appellant Jehovah's Witnesses, the board of adjustment found that its proposed church premises violated the off-street parking requirement and the 1/4 mile requirement. The Pennsylvania court, in sustaining the board's decision, first noted that each of the requirements bore a reasonable relation to the safety of the public and then made these comments which are:

" 'Certainly freedom of worship does not mean that churches are exempt from reasonable police power regulation. Our Supreme Court in Kurman v. Zoning Board of Adjustment of City of Philadelphia, 351 Pa. 247, 40 A.2d 381, determined that setback requirements are applicable to properties used for church purposes. The concepts of religious freedom, freedom of speech and the press which are embodied in the First Amendment have never been construed as absolute rights and beyond the power of reasonable regulation under the police power. Board of Zoning Appeals of Decatur v. Decatur, Indiana Co. of Jehovah's Witnesses, 233 Ind. 83, 117 N.E.2d 115, 123. The language used at page 123 of 117 N.E.2d [dissenting opinion] is applicable to the present case: 'It is quite evident that the members of the appellee could be killed just as dead going to and from church as going to and from a theater or a basketball game. It is a proper exercise of the police power to protect appellee's members from their own negligence as well as from the negligence of the traveling public. There would be just as much logic in holding that the members of appellee when going to church were not required to comply with the traffic regulations as in holding that the appellee is not required to make reasonable provisions for a lessening of the traffic hazards by off-street parking.

" ' "If it was a proper exercise of the police power for the city by its zoning ordinance to require the appellee to comply with the average setback line of the residences, which only has a very remote bearing on traffic hazards, a fortiori it was a reasonable exercise of the police power to require appellee to provide space for 25 cars to park off the streets. The right of appellee to exercise its religious freedom is not violated in either case." ' " (Citing numerous authorities.)

As I see it, times have changed, and the constitutional police power of the states is now being recognized in this country as the only reasonable and practical way to cope with this ever growing Frankenstein called "Traffic congestion". It is my firm belief that such regulations, when reasonable and applied equally, are not only constitutional but necessary to urban survival.

In Brodhead v. City and County of Denver, 1952, 126 Colo. 119, 247 P.2d 140, this court recognized the validity of Denver's attempt to solve this problem in some measure by creating publicly owned off-street parking facilities. But as in most communities where this has been done it has not been enough. Yokley in Vol. 2 at page 78 says about this problem:

"It must be beyond debate that the private parking lot and the private parking garage have failed to meet the crisis and solve the problem in most large cities. This failure has brought into being a two-fold municipal activity—the public parking of automobiles and the inclusion of off-street parking provisions in municipal zoning ordinances."

And on page 82 in Vol. 2 Yokley says:

"The question that has occurred to many thoughtful communities, as the passing of time has aggravated the problem of traffic congestion, is this: We have building codes and master plans and their policing partner, the zoning law; why then, can they not be put to good use by requiring, at least in the case of new construction, that reasonable off street parking facilities be furnished for the employees and patrons of the building so constructed and used?

"Thus, in the areas immediately outside the central business district, the theatre, the department store, the medical center, the commercial business, the industrial plant, the supermarkets, the streamlined drug store—all would be required to have some care and responsibility for the parking problems of their employees and patrons without requiring the public agency to step in and take a hand in clearing the streets of vehicular traffic.

"It is beyond debate that some businesses, by their very nature, attract vehicular traffic and create congestion in the public thoroughfares. What have the municipalities done to solve this problem from the standpoint of zoning?"

Another well-known authority ("Municipal Law" (1957) by Charles S. Rhyne, page 967) has commented on this as follows:

"Off-street parking requirements for dwellings, apartments, businesses, theatres, churches and other uses are common in zoning ordinances today. A recent decision by the Supreme Court of Illinois held that a Chicago zoning ordinance requiring apartment houses to provide private garages or automobile compounds for its tenants was invalid as discriminatory since boarding houses, rooming houses and similar uses which create traffic and other problems were not required to comply with this requirement. (Ronda Realty Corp. v. Lawton, 1953, 414 Ill. 313, 111 N.E.2d 310, 312-313). But similar provisions in other zoning ordinances have been sustained. Thus zoning ordinances have been held valid which required theatres to provide one parking space for each eight seats: ([City of] New Orleans v. Leeco, Inc., 1954, 226 La. 335, 76 So.2d 387, 390) and lunch counters, (Mirschel v. Weissenberger, 1950, 277 App.Div. 1039, 100 N.Y.S.2d 452, no confiscation or discrimination shown.) and churches (Hill v. Kesselring, 1949, 310 Ky. 483, 220 S.W.2d 858, 861-863 [10 A.L.R.2d 1301].) to furnish suitable parking facilities. However, the latter case was remanded to the lower court for additional evidence on the adequacy of the off-street parking facilities to be furnished by the church. But a zoning ordinance requiring 'all places of assembly' to provide 100 square feet of off-street parking space for every person in attendance was held not a valid reason for denial of a building permit for a church which had more off-street parking space than the seating capacity of the church. (State [ex rel Tampa, Fla., etc.] v. [City of] Tampa, Fla.1945, 48 So.2d 78, mandamus granted to compel issuance of building permit because there had been substantial compliance and because there was no showing of a connection between the ordinance and public health, safety, and morals.) Likewise, a zoning ordinance requiring one off-street parking space for every six seats in a church was held unconstitutional as a restraint upon the right of freedom of worship and assembly, and unreasonable in view of the fact that services would be held during minimum traffic hours and sufficient parking space for all vehicles was available for all ordinary services. (Board of Zoning Appeals [of Decatur] v. Decatur, Ind. Co. of Jehovah's Witnesses, 1954, 233 Ind. 83, 117 N.E.2d 115, 119-121.)" (Cases cited are inserted from footnotes.)

One of the public purposes of zoning and planning is "to lessen congestion in the streets" and the 1923 Denver Charter Amendment (Sec. 219A, § 3) expressly so provides. Heretofore some traffic congestion has been solved by public parking garages, by prohibiting all parking on certain thoroughfares and by restricting the period of time one may park in other areas. Some cities have even found it necessary to prohibit all stopping of vehicles on certain highways. All this is done in the exercise of the police powers of the state or city.

The reasoning of the majority opinion is that it is a taking of private property for a public use without condemnation and just compensation to require even reasonably computed off-street parking. I fail to see how that is so if an ordinance only requires an owner to provide parking on his own property for his own vehicles, or a reasonable amount of parking space for himself and those who use his property. In reality it is an application to zoning of the accepted but distinct nuisance principle that one shall not so use his property so as to interfere with either his neighbors or the public. When parking is an incident of a new land use, why should it not be required on the land itself just as the type of business or residential use can itself be lawfully regulated?

The specially concurring opinion of Mr. Justice Frantz goes further then the majority opinion and urges that if the off-street parking is only for persons going to the building in question "* * *" then it is a taking for private use, a taking of more doubtful validity." For the reasons herein set forth I cannot agree that this principle results in a taking of property or that it is of doubtful validity. It is primarily for the public welfare and to lessen congestion in the streets. The fact that incidentally it is also for the use and benefit of those who use the property in question does not suffice to void it.

Clearly the law could not require an owner to permit the general public to use his property for parking purposes, but that is not the case here. It is only the reasonableness of this requirement that we should concern ourselves with since I consider the principle itself to be a proper constitutional exercise of legislative power. And, if necessary I would remand this action to the trial court for the taking of testimony on the need and reasonableness of the regulation and for a determination thereof.

The majority opinion labels this requirement "° ° ° a price tag or tribute for the exercise of the constitutional right to do business ° ° °", which in my opinion ignores the widely recogn'zed right and power of governments, local, state and national, to not only tax businesses but also the right to regulate them when deemed reasonably necessary for police purposes or to prevent nuisances.

I need not describe here the various types of provisions which exist elsewhere in other zoning ordinances detailing how off-street parking should be computed. Suffice it to say that representative samples appear in Yokley supra and in Rathkopf, 3rd ed. on "The Law of Zoning and Planning".

Thus contrary to my learned colleagues, I conclude that reasonable off-street parking requirements, when equally applied, do not "unreasonably and unnecessarily fasten upon him (the citizen) new restraints upon freedom of action in the use and enjoyment" of his property as the majority opinion states. I urge that we declare this part of the ordinance invalid only if we are convinced after a thorough study that these particular provisions are unreasonable and, as pointed out above, before we can determine that question evidence should be taken upon a retrial of the action. This would allow the city to correct its error by amendment if it in fact has erred. I also concur with Mr. Justice Doyle in his dissenting opinion filed in this case as to the views he expresses and authorities he cites on the need for and validity of reasonable off-street parking requirements.

            ❄   ✿   ✿

III

The majority opinion, like the trial court, finds that this ordinance unlawfully and unconstitutionally places so-called down town Denver in one business zone and arb'trarily denies the same type of zoning to plaintiffs' lands which for many years have been used for similar business purposes. I believe this to be a matter of legislative discretion. Though the uses may be similar in great part in both zones, the types of structure obviously are not the same in many particulars, nor is the nature or character of the business carried on generally the same. I would also remand th's phase of the proceedings to the trial court to take and hear evidence thereon to determine the reasonableness thereof. And, if reasonable, as well it might be, for differences are apparent to all who view the Denver skyline, I would uphold such a classification.

IV

The majority opinion holds that all the permits sought herein should issue because this ord'nance cannot be held to be retroactive, Article II, Section 11, of the Colorado Constitution being cited in support thereof. I agree that any of these plaintiffs, and all others similarly situated, who had applied for permits under the prior ordinance and before the adoption of this one, must now, and from the beg'nning should have been given their building permits, subject to the terms of the former ordinance. I so concur, fully aware that in Colby, supra, 81 Colo. at page 352, 255 P. at page 446 this court had held that no one can secure vested rights against the operation of the police power.

Heretofore the attitude of this court, as well as those in many other jurisdictions, has been as expressed in Colby (see 8 McQuillin "Municipal Corporations", 3rd ed. 471, § 25.181, and Allendale, supra). However, Colby neglected to consider the Colorado const'tutional provision cited by the majority herein and we are of course bound by the latter and I would expressly overrule Colby on that point. Even if we were not so bound it seems to me that only in the rarest of instances could a zoning authority be justified under the police power in denying a permit under existing law while a new ordinance or an amendment to an existing ordinance is being drafted and adopted. Each of such cases would have to rest on its own facts and a real emergency be shown before I could support such reasoning. This is so because it is palpably unjust, for example, to say that an owner who has spent large sums on plans and specifications, in reliance on the law as it is, should forfeit his rights and what he has spent on architects' fees for the public good without just compensation. It seems to me that in all cases, except in case of an actual crisis in public health, morals or safety, builders should have the right to rely upon the law as it is, not what some public official thinks it should or will be at some time in the future.

To summarize, I would hold the concept of off-street park'ng valid; hold this particular non-conforming use section invalid; hold the zoning district classifications in question valid; and order certain permits issued as indicated. If we deem it necessary to have more evidence to reject or sustain this particular off-street parking section or the zoning classification in question, I would remand the case to the trial court to determine these matters after hearing further evidence thereon.

DOYLE, Justice (dissenting).

I respectfully dissent from the decision and reasoning expressed in the majority opinion. My objections fall into two classes and I shall preface my specific objections with some general observations.

First, the opinion seems unlimited in its sweeping terms. It expresses a philosophical aversion to all zoning efforts. The decision itself is limited to a holding that the off-street parking and non-conforming use provisions of the zoning ordinance are invalid. Its expressions of viewpoint are at variance with the basic premise that a city can be planned and that restrictions for the general good of the community can be imposed. While conceding that arbitrary regulation of property is invalid, I had thought that the power of the municipality to impose restrict'ons in the interests of the community so basic and fundamental that it cannot now be questioned. From earliest times restrictions on the use of property have been a necessary product of the development of the town or the urban community. Such restrictions are upheld unless shown to be arbitrary and capricious.

In the year 1923 the City of Denver enacted a Charter Amendment (Sec. 219A) which authorized in broad and general terms the enactment by council of zoning and planning legislation. Sections A, B and C emphasize the scope of this grant of power and read as follows:

"A—Grant of Power. For the purpose of promoting health, safety, morals or the general welfare of the community, the council of the city and county of Denver is hereby empowered to regulate and restrict the height, number of stories and size of buildings and other structures, the percentage of lots that may be occupied, the size of yards, courts and other open spaces, the density of population and the location and use of buildings, structures and land for trade, industry, residence or other purposes.

"B—Districts. For any or all of said purposes, the council may divide the city and county of Denver into districts of such manner, shape and area as may be deemed best suited to carry out the purposes of this amendment; and within such districts it may regulate and restrict the erection, construction, reconstruction, alteration, repair or use of buildings, structures or land. All such regulations shall be uniform for each class or kind of buildings throughout each district, but the regulations in one district may differ from those in other districts.

"C—Purposes in View. Such regulations shall be made in accordance with a comprehensive plan, and designed to lessen congestion in the streets; to secure safety from fire, panic and other dangers; to promote health and the general welfare; to provide adequate light and air; to prevent the overcrowding of land; to avoid undue concentration of population; to facilitate the adequate provisions of transportation, water, sewerage, schools, parks and other public requirements. Such regulations shall be made with reasonable consideration, among other things, to the character of the district and its peculiar suitability for particular uses, and with a view to conserving the value of buildings and encouraging the most appropriate use of land throughout the city and county of Denver."

Early decisions of this Court have also recognized the need for this type of regulation. See, for example, Colby v. Board of Adjustment of Denver, 1927, 81 Colo. 344, 255 P. 443, 446, which noted the passing of the horse and buggy era and wherein it was stated:

" ° ° ° The justice writing the opinion in Village of Euclid [Ohio] v. Ambler Realty Co. [272 U.S. 365, 47 S.Ct. 114, 71 L.Ed. 303], supra, remarks on the decided trend of opinion toward a broader view of zoning ordinances, and refers to state courts reversing themselves, citing instances. Even so, we do not apprehend that we are now offending the rule of stare decisis, as applied to any of our previous decisions. We are only applying old principles to new conditions, or to the changed facts of modern life. Thus, a horse and buggy day decision in the livery stable case, Phillips v. City of Denver, 19 Colo. 179, 34 P. 902, intimately allied with those times, would be incongruous now if not considered in the light of modern industrial and civic development. It would be applying the law to an obsolete situation. The same may be said of brickyards in a residence zone under the state of this record. ° ° ° "

In a more recent decision, Cross v. Bilett, 1950, 122 Colo. 278, 221 P.2d 923, 926, 928, the Court commented as follows:

" * * * With the growth of congested urban populations, containing areas of attractive residential development, with values greatly dependent on conformity, and with the increasing public concern for quiet, safety and beauty, there have been enacted zoning laws under appropriate legislative or constitutional authority in most municipalities in the United States and in many rural areas. The concept of public welfare thereunder has broadened. Under such ordinances uses permitted and legal in one district of the city are prohibited in another. Such prohibition is based not strictly upon the inherent danger to the public health, public morals, the public safety, or the public welfare of the prohibited use generally, but upon its interference with the appropriate use of property and the maintenance of its value in the zone in which such use is sought. We have repeatedly upheld such restrictions. So in Flinn v. Treadwell, 120 Colo. 117, 207 P.2d 967, we held valid a provision requiring in a 'B' residential district a front yard of not less than twenty-five feet in depth, directly contrary to the old ruling in Willison v. Cooke [54 Colo. 320, 130 P. 828, 44 L.R.A., N.S., 1030], supra. * * * "

An early definitive and recognized decision upholding zoning is that of the Supreme Court of the United States in Village of Euclid, Ohio v. Ambler Realty Co., 1925, 272 U.S. 365, 47 S.Ct. 114, 118, 71 L.Ed. 303. Mr. Justice Sutherland, who was not noted for his liberal economic philosophy nevertheless recognized that the community has the power to impose restrictions on the use and occupation of lands in urban communities. It was there stated:

" * * * Building zone laws are of modern origin. They began in this country about 25 years ago. Until recent years, urban life was comparatively simple; but, with the great increase and concentration of population, problems have developed, and constantly are developing, which require, and will continue to require, additional restrictions in respect of the use and occupation of private lands in urban communities. Regulations, the wisdom, necessity, and validity of which, as applied to existing conditions, are so apparent that they are now uniformly sustained, a century ago, or even half a century ago, probably would have been rejected as arbitrary and oppressive. Such regulations are sustained, under the complex conditions of our day, for reasons analogous to those which justify traffic regulations, which, before the advent of automobiles and rapid transit street railways, would have been condemned as fatally arbitrary and unreasonable. And in this there is no inconsistency, for, while the meaning of constitutional guaranties never varies, the scope of their application must expand or contract to meet the new and different conditions which are constantly coming within the field of their operation. In a changing world it is impossible that it should be otherwise. But although a degree of elasticity is thus imparted, not to the *meaning*, but to the *application* of constitutional principles, statutes and ordinances, which, after giving due weight to the new conditions, are found clearly not to conform to the Constitution, of course, must fall. * * * "

The majority opinion here quotes from Mr. Justice Holmes in an eminent domain opinion, which apparently dealt with what constitutes a taking. However, that distinguished jurist acknowledged that the state has the authority to impose restrictions for the general good and that it is not the function of a judge to substitute his own economic and political viewpoint for that of the legislature. In his now famous dissenting opinion in the case of Lochner v. State of New York, 1905, 198 U.S. 45, 25 S.Ct. 539, 546, 49 L.Ed. 937 he stated:

> " ° ° ° This case is decided upon an economic theory which a large part of the country does not entertain. If it were a question whether I agreed with that theory, I should desire to study it further and long before making up my mind. But I do not conceive that to be my duty, because I strongly believe that my agreement or disagreement has nothing to do with the right of a majority to embody their opinions in law. It is settled by various decisions of this court that state constitutions and state laws may regulate life in many ways which we as legislators might think as injudicious or if you like as tyrannical, as this, and which, equally with this, interfere with the liberty to contract. Sunday laws and usury laws are ancient examples. A more modern one is the prohibition of lotteries. The liberty of the citizen to do as he likes so long as he does not interfere with the liberty of others to do the same, which has been a shibboleth for some well-known writers, is interfered with by school laws, by the Post-office, by every state or municipal institution which takes his money for purposes thought desirable, whether he likes it or not. *The 14th Amendment does not enact Mr. Herbert Spencer's Social Statics.* The other day we sustained the Massachusetts vaccination law. ° ° ° " (Emphasis supplied.)

Another expression of the basic philosophy that community exis*ence requires curtailment of rights is found in the opinion of Chancellor Earl in Losee v. Buchanan, 1873, 51 N.Y. 476.

> "By becoming a member of civilized society, I am compelled to give up many of my natural rights, but I receive more than a compensation from the surrender by every other man of the same rights, and the security, advantages and protection which the law gives me. ° ° ° We must have factories, machinery, dams, canals, and railroads. They are demanded by the manifold wants of mankind, and lie at the basis of all our civilzations. ° ° ° Most of the rights of property, as well as of the person, in the social state, are not absolute but relative, and they must be so arranged and modified, not unnecessarily infringing upon natural rights, as upon the whole to promote the general welfare."

Second, the third part of the majority opinion wherein the classification of B 5 and B 6 is condemned as an unlawful discrimination is especially broad in its effect. It appears to kill all the regulations in the B 6 zone in one fell swoop without regard to whether they are reasonable or arbitrary, applicable or inapplicable. This ruling is certain to leave chaos and uncertainty in its wake. Does the 1925 ordinance with its onerous height and other restrictions now apply in this B 6 section or is this section now free altogether from any zoning regulation? These and other equally difficult questions will have to be faced as the aftermath of the "tornado" which is the majority decision.

Third, fundamental canons of procedure have been overlooked. This legislation cannot be judged by a mere reference to its terms. It is not invalid *per se.* If a judgment were to be made from examination of the legislation alone, it would be more logical to conclude that it is well founded factually and that it does bear a relationship to the public health and safety. The plaintiffs can succeed in this case, according to my view, only by proving the unconstitutionality of this legislation beyond a reasonable doubt. See Consumers' League of Colorado v. Colorado & Southern R. Co. 53 Colo. 54, 125 P. 577; People ex rel. Rogers v. Letford, 102 Colo. 284, 79 P.2d 274; Mosko v. Dunbar, 135 Colo. 172, 309 P.2d 581.

The instant legislation has been killed without even requiring proof of its invalidity. In fact, the Court refused to allow the plaintiff to introduce evidence to show the reasonable basis for its enactment. It strikes me that a question which has the scope and magnitude of that before us should not be decided in a vacuum; evidence should be received to the end that the court might be in a position to determine whether the enactment as applied to the facts is reasonable or arbitrary.

I also have *specific* objections to the rulings of the majority.

1. *Off-Street Parking*

If the court had determined that these particular off-street parking requirements were unnecessary, unreasonable and onerous as applied to these plaintiffs and the uses which they have proposed, I would be inclined to concur in the decision. I cannot, however, join in a condemnation of all off-street parking as an invalid exercise of the police power. It is not possible to conclude in the absence of evidence that the land use and the parking requirement ratios which are set up in the ordinance are unreasonable, and it is impossible to conclude that such requirements do not contribute to a solution of the tremendous urban problem of traffic congestion. On the other hand, no evidence is needed to establish that this is a problem of great magnitude and that it is not going to go away by the simple expedient of ignoring it. The number of automobiles and the extent and consequent traffic congestion will constitute a problem at all times in the future. Courts are not better qualified to solve these questions than legislators and enactments which are intended to look toward such solutions should not be voided merely because we might disagree with them.

The majority fail to cite any decisions which specifically support its conclusion. There are cases which hold particular off-street parking requirements invalid upon the basis of their special arbitrariness. All of these, however, proceed on the premise that off-street parking generally is valid. See Rhyne, Municipal Law, 967.

The relationship of off-street parking to the general welfare is ably outlined in 2 Yokley, Zoning Law and Practice (2d ed.),

"While traffic is not the moving factor in the drafting of zoning ordinances, most comprehensive zoning ordinances now make some provision for the proper programming of present and future traffic improvements. It has been found that this can best be done through the medium of off-street parking requirements for certain classes of buildings and structures.

"Amendments to zoning ordinances incorporating off-street parking requirements are now widespread in application, many cities having found that provisions in zoning ordinances which make imperative the provision for parking facilities constitute an excellent application of the zoning concept in alleviating traffic congestion.

"At this writing it appears, from information furnished by David R. Levin, Chief of the Land Studies Section of the Bureau of Roads, Department of Commerce, that 265 known localities in thirty-three different states have enacted ordinances or amendments thereto requiring off-street parking accommodations for designated property uses.

"The effects of zoning on transportation are immediately apparent when it is realized that the volume of the traffic which the urban street must accommodate is directly related to the height, bulk and function of the buildings comprising the community.

"As we have had occasion to state before,

" 'Among the many problem pressing for solution in the crowded metropolitan areas of America, traffic congestion still takes its rightful place near the top of the list.'

"For our cities to prosper, it is imperative that an adequate supply of off-street terminal spaces be provided, particularly in central business districts, in order to meet the ever expanding demand for the parking of automobiles. It is equally as essential to provide for off-street truck berths. The use of curb space for the parking of autos and loading and unloading of trucks blots out a final hope for vehicular capacities of city streets already bled white by the many encroachments thereon. Increasing proportions of the population prefer private autos to mass transportation for travel to central business districts and employment centers. Nothing could better illustrate this than the arguments of mass transporation utilities for higher fares in order to meet increased operating expenses in the face of revenue losses due to decreased patronage by former riders who prefer to use private transportation facilities. This argument highlights almost every rate hearing in which increased fares are sought.

"It must be beyond debate that the private parking lot and the private parking garage have failed to meet the crisis and solve the problem in most large cities. This failure has brought into being a two-fold municipal activity —the public parking of automobiles and the inclusion of off-street parking provisions in municipal zoning ordinances. ° ° ° "

The decisions which uphold off-street parking generally deal in each instance with the legality of the specific regulation as applied to particular fact. This is apparent from the discussion in Rhyne, supra. No case that we have been able to find invalidates the *principle* of off-street parking. For example, in City of New Orleans v. Leeco (In re Wimberly), 226 La. 335, 76 So.2d 387, the Court enforced an off-street parking require-

ment as applied to movie theaters.   In Roselle v. Wright, 37 N.J.Super.
507, 117 A.2d 661, 667, the Court held an off-street parking requirement
for a storage garage to be unreasonable in view of its particular terms,
but at the same time recognized the validity of such regulation where it
bears a substantial relationship to the public health, safety, morals or general welfare.   The Court said:

> " ° ° ° That provision as applied to stores, warehouses, office buildings, or
> other commercial structures, to which it may reasonably be anticipated large
> numbers of people would come by means of automobiles, thus giving rise to
> congestion in the public streets, appears to be entirely reasonable and
> logical. ° ° ° "

See also Allendale Congregation of Jehovah's Witnesses v. Grosman, 1950,
30 N.J. 273, 152 A.2d 569.   This holds a requirement of one parking space
for every three seats in a church to be reasonable.

State ex rel. Killeen Realty Co. v. City of East Cleveland, 1958, 108
Ohio App. 99, 153 N.E.2d 177, recognizes that such provisions are valid
and cites McSorley v. Fitzgerald, 359 Pa. 264, 59 A.2d 142 and many other
cases which deal with similar and related problems.   Mirschel v. Weissenberger, 277 App.Div. 1039, 100 N.Y.S.2d 452, recognizes the general validity of such requirements and also holds that the vesting of authority in
a board to make particular determinations does not constitute an unlawful delegation of legislative authority.   See also Fleishon v. Philadelphia
Zoning Board, 385 Pa. 295, 122 A.2d 673 and Hill v. Kesselring, 310 Ky.
438, 220 S.W.2d 858, 10 A.L.R.2d 1301 and see Fonoroff, The Relationship
of Zoning to Traffic Generators, 20 Law and Contemporary Problems 197
(1955).   Town of Islip v. F.E. Summers Coal & Lumber Co., 1931, 257
N.Y. 167, 177 N.E. 409 is analogous in that it upholds a zoning ordinance
requiring building setbacks.   The language of the Court per Pound, J.,
is here relevant:

> "The question is whether the zoning ordinance of the town of Islip is
> unconstitutional in so far as it requires a setback of ten feet from the street
> on that part of Montauk avenue which is zoned for business purposes.   The
> court below has held that such ordinance is detrimental and prejudicial to
> the use of the premises for building purposes, and unconstitutional as a
> taking of private property for public purposes without just compensation.

> "[1] Can it be said that the ordinance in this respect on its face 'passes
> the bounds of reason and assumes the character of a merely arbitrary fiat?'
> Village of Euclid, Ohio v. Ambler Realty Co., 272 U.S. 365, 389, 47 S.Ct.
> 114, 119, 71 L.Ed. 303, 54 A.L.R. 1016. 'If the validity of the legislative
> classification for zoning purposes be fairly debatable, the legislative judg-
> ment must be allowed to control.' Village of Euclid, Ohio v. Ambler Realty
> Co., supra, at page 388 of 272 U.S., 47 S.Ct. 114, 118; Wulfsohn v. Burden,
> 241 N.Y. 288, 296, 150 N.E. 120, 43 A.L.R. 651.

> "[2] In the light of these rulings, how can a court say upon mere inspec-
> tion of the zoning ordinance that the end in view is not reasonably pursued

by its adoption in order to lessen congestion in the streets and thereby to promote the public safety? Town Law, Consol.Law, c. 62, § 349-o. * * * "

In summary, I am of the opinion that the off-street parking regulations which the majority holds invalid are not *per se* unconstitutional. Moreover, the evidence at the trial fails to demonstrate specific invalidity as applied to plaintiffs and does not establish beyond reasonable doubt a lack of relationship between these regulations and the public health, safety and welfare. They should, therefore, be upheld.

* * *

3. *Authority of the City Council to Distinguish Between the B-5 and the B-6 Districts.*

The holding of the majority that there is no appreciable difference between the downtown property and that which is south of Colfax Avenue, the dividing line adopted by the City Council, ignores the facts. To be sure, there may be similarities between the two districts, but there are also substantial differences which justify the adoption of the dividing line. Certainly the legislature must be in a position to create districts and to determine differences and to declare land uses in accordance with its findings. The Charter provision itself which the majority considers narrow in scope and which I regard as broad and comprehensive certainly contemplates this type of legislative decision. We need only look out of the windows of our own offices to observe the very marked differences. The B-6 district by no stretch of the imagination can be classified as a conconcentrated commercial area such as B-5. The ground south of Colfax Avenue, which is here in question, is in the process of changing from residential to commercial. The Council has classified it as a secondary rather than a primary commercial district, and it is within its power, as I view it, to so determine. Adoption of ground rules to govern *development* is much easier than adoption of rules which seek to effect changes after the area has quickened and it cannot be said that the classification of this district as a secondary commercial area is unreasonable or unrealistic. On the contrary, the holding that there is no appreciable difference between this district and the traditional "downtown" district seems to me to be extremely unrealistic and arbitrary.

Finally, I fail to see that it is unreasonable discrimination to require this developing commercial area to provide off-street parking. The impossibility of requiring off-street parking in the so-called downtown district is at once apparent. It seems to me reasonable to distinguish between these two areas and to demand that new constructions in the developing commercial area comply with the off-street parking requirement.

4. *The Question Whether this Legislation is Invalid by Reason of its Being Retrospective.*

Merely because the plaintiffs applied for building permits prior to November 7, 1956, the effective date of this ordinance, does not mean that it may not be constitutionally applied to them. In order to hold that legislation is invalid because of its being retrospective, it must appear that the provision authorizing retrospective application is more than just form and operates so as to deprive them of a substantive right that had matured prior to the enactment of the ordinance. I cannot agree that the mere application for a building permit can result in one's having a vested right to build in accordance with the application, and that is the effect of the majority's alternative holding.

The holding that the mere filing of an application for a building permit creates a constitutionally protected property right is not supported in the majority opinion by citation to any authority. My research indicates that the authorities on the subject are to the contrary. The Court of Appeals of New York in 1930 affirmed a decision which restrained the defendant from erecting apartment houses by a zoning ordinance which became effective after the issuance of a permit for said construction but before any work had been commenced on the building. Rice v. Van Vranken, 225 N.Y. 541, 175 N.E. 304. It is interesting to note that the then chief justice of that court was Benjamin Cardozo. For a more recent decision adhering to the decision in Van Vranken see Application of Kunz, Sup.1954, 128 N.Y.S. 2d 680. The authorities there cited make clear that the underlying basis for extending the protections of substantive due process to this sort of situation depends on the extent to which the applicant has taken steps in justifiable reliance on the permit, such as performing substantial work and incurring significant expenses and obligations. Similarly, where attempt has been made to commence an undertaking prior to the date of an ordinance declaring it to be a nonconforming use, the courts have applied the principle of the Van Vranken case to prevent this race to the courthouse where there has been no substantial commitment of resources in reliance on the preexisting law. Smith v. Juillerat, 161 Ohio St. 424, 119 N.E.2d 611; Ohio State Students Trailer Park Coop. v. County of Franklin, Ohio App. 1953, 123 N.E.2d 542. Judged by these principles the plaintiffs have failed to show deprivation of any substantive rights. Article II, sec. 11 of the Constitution of Colorado prohibits only a law retrospective *in its operation*. As to these plaintiffs this ordinance is retrospective only in form. They have attempted to exploit the law rather than justifiably rely on it.

In conclusion, it is my opinion that the ordinance should be upheld and that we should determine that these plaintiffs have failed to establish that the ordinance, or any provision of it, operates to deprive them of any constitutional right. The mere fact that plaintiffs cannot, under the adopted plan, use the land so that they can make the maximum economic use of its does not justify the far-reaching and sweeping conclusion contained in the majority opinion. There cannot be a zoning plan applicable to all of the people of the city and having for its purpose the orderly development of the city which will at the same time permit every individual to use his property exactly as he sees fit. So long as the scheme itself is reasonable, it should be upheld. If particular individuals can show that a specific provision is unreasonably oppressive, it then becomes appropriate to strike down that particular provision. The present plaintiffs have failed to demonstrate the impossibility of their living and prospering under this ordinance. The judgment of the district court should be reversed and the denial of the building permit by the zoning administrator should be upheld.

DAY, J., concurs in this dissent.

DAY, Justice (dissenting).

Probably more has been written in this case than is necessary or desirable. Nevertheless it should be considered that in approaching this problem my brethren have given scant attention to the right of the people of Denver to govern themselves, the fundamental concept of our democracy. The people of Denver in their charter, which is their own home rule "constitution," by free ballot have expressed themselves as to how their own property should be used for the benefit of all of them. This they can do in local matters if the charter itself is not violative of the state constitution. This charter has been quoted but not upheld. Yet every power they have granted and the purposes and objectives they have enumerated do not violate the constitution. In it the people have given to their city council *authority* to enact ordinances to carry out the intent and purpose and objectives of the charter. The people have set forth the purposes, all of which fit very well within the powers reserved to them in governing themselves. While it is true that the people cannot by vote impose upon an electorate restrictions that are clearly unconstitutional, their vote is particularly helpful in this case because of the duty imposed upon the judiciary to give constitutionality to their enactments if at all possible. The public welfare, toward which end the people may enact laws under the police powers, is subject to a narrow construction as in the majority opinion or to a liberal construction as in the states which have upheld the constitutionality of off-street parking ordinances. So we do not have a situation here where the unconstitutionality of the ordinance is clear-cut, unequivocal, and beyond reasonable doubt. Such ordinances have been so universally adopted and accepted by other communities—265 of them— that we think the vote on the charter was meant to convey to a doubtful judiciary what was to be the public policy of Denver in regard to problems affecting its future growth. If a free people cannot go to the polls and by their vote regulate the orderly development of their own city, and their own neighborhoods, then we have taken away from them far more than is attempted to be given by the majority opinion. The people have set forth quite explicitly what they think is good for the whole. They are now told, not by a benevolent despot but by a solicitous judiciary, what is really good for them.

The English poet, William Cowper, wrote of Robinson Crusoe and his life alone for five years on a desert island,

> "I am monarch of all I survey
> My right there is none to dispute;
> From the centre all round to the sea,
> I am lord of the fowl and the brute."

This may have been all right for Robinson Crusoe but if there are great numbers of Robinson Crusoes in a home rule city, can each proclaim such right? I think not.

Writing of two shipwrecked passengers also cast on a desert isle, W. S. Gilbert, in his delightful ballad telling the story of the foundering of the Ballyshannon and the drowning of all the passengers except Gray and Somers, wrote,

> "There passengers, by reason of their clinging to a mast,
> Upon a desert island were eventually cast.
> They hunted for their meals, as Alexander Selkirk used,
> But they couldn't chat together—they had not been introduced.
>
> ❋   ❋   ❋
>
> And somehow thus they settled it without a word of mouth
> That Gray should take the northern half while Somers took the south."

It is the purpose of the poet to demonstrate that as soon as two people are thrown together and are likely to conflict, some regulation is in order. Though Gray and Somers may have been able to divide the island "without word of mouth," a growth in population would have required a clear understanding of the rights and duties of each. These rules, as now expressed in charters and ordinances, were necessary to protect the people and to promote their common good.

Some of the specific grants of power given by the people in their vote to their own elected city council, which appear now to be of no effect, are: To regulate and restrict the size of buildings and other structures, the percentage of lot that may be occupied, the size of yards, courts and other open spaces, the density of population, *the use of buildings, structures and land.* Among the expressed purposes specifically sought to be accomplished by zoning regulations and the charter—all, in my opinion, constitutional—were: To provide a comprehensive plan designed to lessen congestion in the streets, to secure safety from fire, panic and other dangers, to *prevent overcrowding of land* and to *avoid undue concentration of population,* to facilitate adequate provisions of transportation. The people and their comprehensive plan to prevent a duplication of or a compounding of the conditions prevalent in the downtown area (which developed unrestrained and which cannot be undone now) are to be held for naught.

The history of Denver, beginning with the years of no regulation in the use of property or in the size of the construction thereon, followed by the decades of inadequate ordinances and the deadly blows some of the decisions of this court struck at attempts to legislate in the field, has left the city with many scars. Judicial notice can be taken of what is plainly visible and of common knowledge. Our early fathers and the rugged individualists of pioneer days, most solicitous of the individual property rights, created a city which has been having a great struggle to meet the demands of growth. As a consequence of this individualism, there are encountered in every district dead-end streets, streets blocked by buildings and houses erected on the individual whim of the property owner without regard to contiguous plats, existing streets or adjacent property development. Opposition to or lack of uniform set-back requirements, all urged in the name of freedom of use, created conditions where streets cannot be widened, or, if they are, the movement of traffic splashes snow and water on the front stoop. Areas now designated as "blighted," heavily dotted with buildings standing vacant or, in many instances, commanding only nominal rents, attest not to the fact that the buildings are many years old, for many are well built and functional, but rather they stand as monuments to the lack of planning (such as was hoped to be achieved by the charter) which permitted buildings and houses to be jammed up one against the other. It was inevitable that under such circumstances the very owners themselves closed their property and in some instances sold for the best price obtainable. The colossal waste is apparent everywhere, and there is scant comfort in the present day that these "protected properties" now are looking to the federal government for a proposed program of urban renewal whereby their property will be purchased, torn down, and others will be given a chance to commence anew. But what value will be the new start if the area is developed under old concepts? If this potentially fine city in the next seventy-five years is to be allowed to develop with little more plan, legislation or restraint than were the downtown areas east and south from the river to Broadway, it doesn't tax the imagination to picture the catastrophic consequences.

Questions and Notes

1. Is the logic of the argument in the majority opinion directed against off-street parking requirements, or against zoning in general?

2. How and where did the majority judges think parking spaces should be provided? Is that an efficient use of land and public funds?

3. What was the reason for the exemption from parking requirements in the downtown area?

4. The ghost of *Denver Buick* long haunted Colorado land use law —until it was finally overruled.

RADCLIFFE COLLEGE

v.

CAMBRIDGE

350 Mass. 613, 215 N.E.2d 892(1966).

Supreme Judicial Court of Massachusetts.

Middlesex.

Argued Feb. 9, 1966.

Decided April 20, 1966.

Proceeding on petition in Land Court for declaration that zoning ordinance did not apply to proposed college library. The Land Court, McPartlin, J., granted relief, and the city appealed. The Supreme Judicial Court, Whittemore, J., held that statute prohibiting ordinances, limiting use of land for educational purposes did not operate to invalidate off-street parking requirement of zoning ordinance as applied to college's proposed library, since requirement that land be used for parking did not reduce its availability for educational purposes.

Reversed.

Andrew T. Trodden, City Solicitor, for respondent.

Philip M. Cronin, Boston (Robert I. Hunneman, Boston, with him), for petitioner.

Before SPALDING, WHITTEMORE, CUTTER, KIRK, SPIEGEL, and REARDON, JJ.

WHITTEMORE, Justice.

This is a petition in the Land Court pursuant to G.L. c. 185, § 1(j½), and c. 240, § 14A, inserted, respectively, by § 1 and § 2 of St.1934, c. 263. It describes land in Cambridge on a part of which the petitioner is building a library and seeks (1) a declaration that art. VII, § 2, of the Cambridge zoning ordinance, requiring provision for off street parking of automobiles, is inapplicable to the petitioner's land; and (2) an order that the superintendent of buildings of the city shall not withhold, in reliance on art. VII, § 2, a building permit or certificate of occupancy for the proposed library.

The petitioner is a public educational institution incorporated by St. 1894, c. 166. City of Worcester v. New England Inst. & New England Sch. of Accounting, Inc., 335 Mass. 486, 489, 140 N.E.2d 470. It is the owner of a quadrangular parcel of land (containing according to an exhibit, about 478,797 square feet[1]) bounded on the north by Linnaean Street, on the east by Walker Street, on the south by Shepard Street, and on the west by Garden Street. The library is in a rectangular area of over

---

1. The separate lot figures on another exhibit total 487,698 square feet.

80,000 square feet on the southwest corner at Garden and Shepard streets in a residence C-2 zone. The zoning ordinance, art. VII, § 2, requires for off street parking a one car space for each 1,000 feet of gross floor area. Relying thereon, the city superintendent of buildings refused to issue a permit for the library until the college provided off street parking spaces for ninety cars. The college under protest submitted a plan showing ninety spaces within the quadrangle. If not required to comply with art. VII, § 2, it intends to provide thirty-six parking spaces for library employees. At present there are twelve parking spaces in the quadrangle.

The college claims to be exempt from art. VII, § 2, by reason of G.L. c. 40A, § 2, as amended through St.1959, c. 607, § 1, which provides "that no ordinance or by-law which prohibits or limits the use of land for any church or other religious purpose or for any educational purpose which is religious, sectarian, denominational or public shall be valid ° ° ° "

The judge ruled that the college is a tax exempt public educational institution; that all its land in Cambridge is used for public educational purposes within the meaning of G.L. c. 40A; and that the library will be used for such purposes. He concluded by ruling that art. VII, § 2, of the ordinance limits the use of the land of the college for a public educational purpose, and is invalid as it applies to the college's land. A final decree was entered embodying the rulings in this last sentence. The city appealed. The evidence is not reported, but the judge's decision contains comprehensive findings of fact.

The judge granted the petitioner's fourth request reading: "The provisions of the Cambridge Zoning Ordinance, Article VII, Section 2 requiring designated amount of parking spaces per square foot of gross floor area, are inapplicable to ° ° ° [the petitioner's] property under General Laws, C. 40A, sec. 2." The respondent's request for a ruling to the contrary was denied. The college's request that it is "exempt from the provisions of the Cambridge Zoning Ordinance" under G.L. c. 40A, § 2, was denied. The judge granted the city's request, in substance to the contrary, which read: "The issue of total exemption of the petitioner from the provisions of the Cambridge Zoning Ordinance under General Laws, c. 40A, sec. 2, is not raised by the pleadings and the evidence and no ruling upon that issue is required."

The college argues that it is "exempt" from the ordinance (apparently all provisions) because of G.L. c. 40A, § 2. The rulings upon the requests show that the judge did not intend so to rule. The actual issue in the pleadings is whether art. VII, § 2, applies to the library site, but the wording of the decree, supported by findings, reaches at least the entire quadrangle. The only present controversy is as to the library site, but there is in G.L. c. 240, § 14A no requirement that a controversy be shown. Woods v. City of Newton, Mass.,[a] 208 N.E.2d 508.

---

a. Mass.Adv.Sh. (1965) 989, 991

Parking spaces required by art. VII, § 2, may, by art. VII, § 3, cl. 1, b, be "on lots not more than two thousand feet away from the building to be served," and, by art. VII, § 3, cl. 4, they "may be enclosed in a structure or be open." By art. VII, § 2, c,[2] dormitory parking spaces may be deducted from the number required for the library. There was testimony that "the college authorities were consulted in the development of the ordinance."[3]

The buildings in the quadrangle, totaling eleven in 1955, are all used for dormitories except for a small building used as an art studio. There were 1170 undergaduates in the college in 1964-1965 of whom 899 lived in the dormitories in the quadrangle. It was expected that 873 undergraduates would live in the dormitories in the year 1965-1966. Some of the dormitories contain dining and reception halls. Recently several buildings were removed to make space for the library. An open area in the center of the quadrangle is used by undergraduates as an athletic field. The college plans to erect in the quadrangle five new dormitories to house 350 undergradautes. "This development is contingent upon the effect of the Cambridge Zoning Ordinance in regard to providing parking spaces, and if spaces must be provided, the development will be adversely affected ° ° °   [C]ompliance with ° ° ° the Zoning Ordinance would cause the college to use in addition to the space needed for the future development of the college, many of those parts of the quadrangle area which are now landscaped by lawns, bushes, shrubs and trees, and are used for recreation ° ° °   These landscaped features contribute to the attractiveness of the area, and if eliminated would detract from the appearance of the quadrangle. The parking problems [in the streets] around the quadrangle area are caused partly by the residents in the area, and partly by the employees and undergraduates of the college." Students are required to register their automobiles at the college. In 1964-1965 there were fifty-three cars so registered.

[1] Adequate provision for parking or housing the automobiles of persons using dwellings and other buildings has become of general public concern. Public convenience and safety are adversely affected by crowded streets. Available street spaces are limited and unable to accommodate the increasing number of automobiles. Street parking regulations are ineffective. These, as general phenomena, are matters of common knowledge; the findings show that they exist in the area about the college quadrangle.[4] The

---

2. "Where an institution provides domitory residence accommodations, the number of parking spaces provided as a result thereof may be deducted from the requirements established to satisfy the needs of classrooms, libraries, lecture halls, laboratories, or similar educational areas normally used by such residential students."

3. There was also testimony that "they were represented on the advisory committee which worked on the preparation of the ordinance and that the ordinance shows an endeavor to correlate the problems of the different educational uses and needs of the colleges with the normal residential, commercial, and industrial community uses and needs which prevail in the City."

4. "The traffic problem of the City of Cambridge is one of its major municipal problems. One of the important purposes of the Zoning Ordinance was to supply the

reasonable premise of a requirement for off street parking spaces for new buildings is that parking automobiles nearby is an established function of the use of any building wherein people live, work, study or congregate for other purposes. Such a requirement is analogous to the statutory requirements of public corridors and exits of certain size and number and somewhat analogous to requirements of fire walls, fire escapes and fireproof construction.

The issue presented is whether the broad language of G.L. c. 40A, § 2, has barred the imposition in a zoning ordinance of any such requirement however appropriate and desirable. The statute has not been construed in this aspect. In Attorney Gen. v. Inhabitants of Town of Dover, 327 Mass. 601, 100 N.E.2d 1, we held that a by-law adopted in 1946 which, in effect, prohibited the use of land for sectarian educational purposes was invalid under the statute (G.L. c. 40, § 25, inserted by St.1933, c. 269 § 1, as amended by St.1950, c. 325, § 1) which, with amendments, is now G.L. c. 40A, § 2. We said (p. 604, 100 N.E.2d p. 3) that "[t]here can be no doubt that the statute was intended as an expression of a general policy to take away from all municipalities all power to limit the use of land for * * * [the specified] purpose[s]." In Sisters of the Holy Cross of Mass. v. Town of Brookline, 347 Mass. 486, 492-494, 495, 198 N.E.2d 624, we struck down dimensional requirements of a zoning by-law that affected the use of the land, pointing out that imposing the dimensional requirements for a single family house upon a proposed multipurpose college building of Holy Cross would virtually nullify the use exemption. The point was reserved (fn. p. 495, 198 N.E.2d 624) whether dimensional requirements not affecting the use of the land would validly apply to a religious or educational institution.

[2, 3] Providing for the parking or housing of the automobiles of students, instructors, and employees of an educational institution is within the broad scope of the educational powers of the institution just as is providing for the feeding and housing of such personnel. These are secondary functions incidental to the main educational purpose. Hence, a regulation that requires that some of the college land be used for parking does not lessen the availability of all or any of the institution's land for some appropriate educational purpose. We think the statute does not bar such regulation. Plainly the statute does not do so in express terms. At most the

---

best solutions possible for the control of this problem. * * * The traffic problems which predominate are caused by congestion as a result of on street parking, and bring secondary complications in the difficulty of keeping the streets clean and of keeping them properly plowed of snow. * * * Shepard Street is considered one of the most difficult streets to control for parking because of the intense residential development which already exists around it, much of which predates the use of the automobile. There are special traffic regulations in winter time that apply to both Garden Street and Shepard Street. Under the present conditions it is difficult for fire trucks to get into Shepard Street. It is planned to limit future parking to one side of Shepard Street. Walker Street is another narrow street with the same problems as Shepard Street. Garden Street and Linnaean Street which are greater in width do not create as intense a problem as that of the other two streets."

Cambridge ordinance requires choices among the proper educational purposes of the institution. In so doing it does not impede the reasonable use of the college's land for its educational purposes. We rule, therefore, that it does not limit "the use of [its] land for any * * * educational purpose" within the meaning of G.L. c. 40A, § 2.

[4, 5] The city's brief recognizes the possibility that the ordinance may call for more parking spaces than will be needed to accommodate cars that will be brought to the neighborhood by the new library. A variance would not, as the city suggests, be available to overcome such a hardship. Russell v. Zoning Bd. of Appeals of Brookline, Mass.,ᵇ 209 N.E.2d 337. But we discern no basis for concluding that the ordinance, as applied to the library, is so arbitrary as to be invalid. The findings show that there will not now be an unreasonable number of parking spaces for the quadrangle as it is now used.⁵ It is not clear, however, that in its further application to five new dormitories the ordinance would not require a greater number of spaces than could in reason be deemed necessary to take care of the cars brought to the quadrangle by the use made of it by the college. In these circumstances we think the decree should be of limited scope. Before a controversy arises as to additional parking spaces, amendment of the ordinance (by provision for exceptions under G.L. c. 40A, § 4, or by other amendment) or some other change in circumstances may avoid it.

The decree is reversed. A decree is to enter declaring that, applied to the library in the quadrangle as now used, the ordinance is valid.

So ordered.

Questions and Notes

1. This is a typical Massachusetts opinion, short and to the point.

2. Note the impact of the Massachusetts statute (upheld in Attorney General v. Dover, 327 Mass. 601, 100 N.E.2d (1951)), prohibiting zoning against churches.

---

b. Mass.Adv.Sh. (1965) 1179, 1181.

5. The ordinance (art. VII, § 1, cl. 2) provides that "[b]uildings and land uses in existence on the effective date of this ordinance are not subject to these parking requirements * * *."

VERNON PARK REALTY

v.

MOUNT VERNON

307 N.Y. 493, 121 N.E. 2d 517(1954).

Court of Appeals of New York.

July 14, 1954.

Action for judgment declaring a city zoning ordinance and amendments thereto limiting business use of plaintiff's realty to parking of automobiles and incidental services to be unconstitutional insofar as they affected plaintiff's property. The Appellate Division of the Supreme Court, in the Second Judicial Department entered a judgment on October 28, 1953, 125 N.Y.S.2d 112, 282 App.Div. 890, which unanimously affirmed the judgment of the Supreme Court in favor of plaintiff, 122 N.Y.S.2d 78, entered in Westchester County upon a decision of the court on a trial at special term, Coyne, J., declaring defendant's zoning ordinance of 1927, as amended in 1949, and 1952, unconstitutional as to plaintiff, and the city appealed as of right on constitutional grounds. The Court of Appeals, Dye, J., held that the ordinance as amended was unconstitutional.

Judgment affirmed.

Fuld, J., dissented.

Harry Zimmerman, Corporation Counsel, Mount Vernon (William Macy, New York City, of counsel), for appellant.

J. Robert Bleakley, White Plains, William F. Bleakley, New York City, John F. Minicus, Yonkers, for respondent.

DYE, Judge.

The City of Mount Vernon appeals as of right on constitutional grounds from a judgment declaring invalid and void insofar as they affected the plaintiff's property, the City Zoning Ordinance and Zoning Map of the City of Mount Vernon, enacted and adopted March 22, 1927, as amended March 9, 1949, and the amendment thereto, chapter 4A, enacted and adopted January 16, 1952.

The subject premises are known locally as the "Plaza", consisting of an open area containing approximately 86,000 square feet adjacent to the New York, New Haven & Hartford Railroad station. It is in the middle of a highly developed Business "B" district (Zoning Ordinance, 1927, ch. 12) and as such constitutes an island completely surrounded by business buildings. It has always been used by the patrons of the railroad and others for the parking of private automobiles. When the city first enacted a zoning ordinance, the Plaza was placed in a Business "B" district (Zoning Ordinance adopted 1922), later being changed without objection to a Residence "B" district (Zoning Ordinance adopted 1927), following which the parking of automobiles was continued as a valid nonconforming use. In 1932, upon the application of the railroad and its then tenant, the city granted a variance to permit the installation of a gasoline filling station. Later and in 1951 the railroad sold the premises to the plaintiff, the title being closed June 21, 1951. The purchaser applied without success for a variance to permit the erection of a retail shopping center, a prohibited use as the zoning ordinance then read (Zoning Ordinance adopted 1927, chs. 9-10).

[1, 2] The plaintiff then commenced this action for a judgment declaring the 1927 ordinance unconstitutional, unreasonable and void and not binding on the plaintiff insofar as the same pertains to the use of plaintiff's premises, and for injunctive relief. After joinder of issue and on January 16, 1952, the common council amended the zoning ordinance by adding thereto a new district to be known as "D. P. D." (Designed Parking District). In substance, the effect of this amendment was to prohibit the use of the property for any purpose except the parking and storage of automobiles, a service station within the parking area and the continuance of prior nonconforming uses (Zoning Ordinance as amended January 16, 1952, ch. 4A). Faced with this change in classification, the plaintiff amended its complaint so as to include an attack on both the zoning ordinance and the 1952 amendment. The amended complaint alleges that the ordinance and its 1952 amendment, as pertaining to the plaintiff's property, work an undue hardship as to use, destroy the greater part of its value, are discriminatory as a denial of the equal protection of the law, and amount to a taking of private property without just compensation contrary to due process and, as such, are constitutionally invalid and void. The city justifies the ordinance and its amendment by reason of the congested traffic and parking conditions now existing in Mount Vernon which, it says, have become so acute as to reach a strangulation point. However compelling and acute the community traffic problem may be, its solution does not lie in placing an undue and uncompensated burden on the individual owner of a single parcel of land in the guise of regulation, even for a public purpose. True it is that for a long time the land has been devoted to parking, a nonconforming use, but it does not follow that an ordinance prohibiting any other use is a reasonable exercise of the police power. While the common counsel has the unquestioned right to enact zoning laws respecting the use of property in accordance with a well-considered and comprehensive plan designed to promote public health, safety and general welfare, General City Law, Consol.Laws, c. 21, § 83, such power is subject to the constitutional limitation that it may not be exerted arbitrarily or unreasonably, Nashville, C. & St. L. Ry. v. Walters, 294 U.S. 405, 55 S.Ct. 486, 79 L.Ed. 949; Brous v. Smith, 304 N.Y. 164, 106 N.E.2d 503, and this is so whenever the zoning ordinance precludes the use of the property for any purpose for which it is reasonably adapted. Arverne Bay Construction Co. v. Thatcher, 278 N.Y. 222, 15 N.E.2d 587, 117 A.L.R. 1110. By the same token, an ordinance valid when adopted will nevertheless be stricken down as invalid when, at a later time, its operation under changed

conditions proves confiscatory, Abie State Bank v. Bryan, 282 U.S. 765, 51 S.Ct. 252, 75 L.Ed. 690, such, for instance, as when the greater part of its value is destroyed, Dowsey v. Village of Kensington, 257 N.Y. 221, 177 N.E. 427, 86 A.L.R. 642, for which the courts will afford relief in an appropriate case. Eaton v. Sweeny, 257 N.Y. 176, 177 N.E. 412.

[3] On this record, the plaintiff, having asserted an invasion of his property rights, cf. Rodgers v. Village of Tarrytown, 382 N.Y. 115, 96 N.E.2d 731, has met the burden of proof by establishing that the property is so situated that it has no possibilities for residential use and that the use added by the 1952 amendment does not improve the situation but, in fact, will operate to destroy the greater part of the value of the property since, in authorizing its use for parking and incidental services, it necessarily permanently precludes the use for which is most readily adapted, i. e., a business use such as permitted and actually carried on by the owners of all the surrounding property. Under such circumstances, the 1927 zoning ordinance and zoning map and the 1952 amendment, as they pertain to the plaintiff's property, are so unreasonable and arbitrary as to constitute an invasion of property rights, contrary to constitutional due process and, as such, are invalid, illegal and void enactments. U.S.Const. 5th and 14th Amends.; N.Y.Const. art. I, §§ 6, 7; Rockdale Construction Corporation v. Incorporated Village of Cedarhurst, Nassau County, 301 N.Y. 519, 93 N.E.2d 76; Arverne Bay Construction Co. v. Thatcher, supra; Dowsey v. Village of Kensington, supra; Eaton v. Sweeny, supra; Euclid, Ohio v. Ambler Co., 272 U.S. 365, 47 S.Ct. 114, 71 L.Ed. 303; Pennsylvania Coal Co. v. Mahon, 260 U.S. 393, 43 S.Ct. 158, 67 L.Ed. 322; Town of Islip v. F. E. Summers Coal & Lumber Co., 257 N.Y. 167, 177 N.E. 409.

[4] Mention should be made of appellant's contention that plaintiff has no right to bring this action because it has not shown good faith in that the contract of purchase provided for a reconveyance of the premises to the seller, at the option of the purchaser, in the event that, within one year from the date of closing title, the purchaser was unable to obtain from the city or through court action a change of zoning so as to permit use of the premises for a business purpose, and, in that it purchased the property with knowledge of the zoning restrictions. There is no merit to this claim of lack of good faith. The plaintiff took title to the property by deed prior to the enactment of the 1952 amendment and could not very well have known or anticipated that the city, under the guise of regulating traffic would permanently limit the use of the property to the parking of automobiles and incidental services, such as we have said constituted an illegal invasion of the plaintiff's property rights. Under such circumstances, the validity of the zoning ordinance and its zoning map may be attacked at any time and at any stage of the proceedings. The right to challenge the validity of an ordinance by action for a declaratory judgment is not to be confused with a proceeding under article 78 of the Civil Practice Act to review a discretionary determination of a zoning

board, as in Hickox v. Griffin, 298 N.Y. 365, 83 N.E.2d 836. There, the evidence was deemed insufficient to warrant granting a variance of the zoning ordinance under applicable principles of law. Otto v. Steinhilber, 282 N.Y. 71, 24 N.E.2d 851; Ernst v. Board of Appeals on Zoning of City of New Rochelle, 298 N.Y. 831, 84 N.E.2d 144. Nor should this right of action be confused with the question of who may bring an article 78 proceeding as a "person aggrieved." Hickox v. Griffin, supra; Taxpayers' Ass'n of South East Oceanside v. Board of Zoning Appeals of Town of Hempstead, 301 N.E. 215, 93 N.E.2d 645. Our recent case, Clark v. Board of Zoning Appeals of Town of Hempstead, 301 N.Y. 86, 92 N.E.2d 903, is not authority to the contrary. There, too, the issue was a reasonable exercise of administrative discretion. The ordinance as a valid enactment was not challenged.

[5-8] Purchase of property with knowledge of the restriction does not bar the purchaser from testing the validity of the zoning ordinance since the zoning ordinance in the very nature of things has reference to land rather than to owner (Bassett on Zoning, p. 177). Knowledge of the owned cannot validate an otherwise invalid ordinance. The owner's right to attack the validity of a zoning ordinance is not waived by the circumstance that he has on a previous occasion applied for a variance. Such an application is, primarily, an appeal to the discretion of the board and, for that purpose, the validity of the ordinance is assumed but that does not operate to confer validity if, in fact, as here, the zoning ordinance is clearly confiscatory. Cf. Arverne Bay Construction Co. v. Thatcher, supra. Conversely, an attack on the legality of a zoning ordinance prior to any request for a variance has long been accepted as proper procedure. Dowsey v. Village of Kensington, supra.

In view of all that has been said, we find it unnecessary to mention the appellant's other points beyond saying that we regard them as wholly lacking in merit.

The judgment appealed from should be affirmed, with costs.

FULD, Judge (dissenting).

I cannot agree that the zoning ordinance of the City of Mount Vernon here under attack is unconstitutional.

A zoning ordinance is confiscatory and, hence unconstitutional only when it "so restricts the use of property that it cannot be used for any reasonable purpose", Arverne Bay Construction Co. v. Thatcher, 278 N.Y. 222, 232, 15 N.E.2d 587, 592, 117 A.L.R. 1110, or when it restricts it "to a use for which the property is not adapted". Dowsey v. Village of Kensington, 257 N.Y. 221, 231, 177 N.E. 427, 430, 86 A.L.R. 642. But, if "the validity of the legislative classification for zoning purposes be fairly debatable, the legislative judgment must be allowed to control." Euclid, Ohio v. Ambler Co., 272 U.S. 365, 388, 47 S.Ct. 114, 118, 71 L.Ed. 303; see, also, Shepard v. Village of Skaneateles, 300 N.Y. 115, 118, 89 N.E.2d 619, 620. It seems to me that neither the 1927 ordinance nor its 1952 amendment is so unreasonable as to permit us to interfere with the judgment of Mount Vernon's Common Council.

In the present case, although the 1927 ordinance placed the property in a residential zone, all of the area was in fact employed for parking purposes since 1922. That being so we may not ignore realities and say that the ordinance was invalid because it singled out a small area in the midst of a large business zone for residential use. For all practical purposes, the district continued, as it had been, zoned for parking. Adjacent to the New York, New Haven & Hartford Railroad, the area served the community's obvious need for parking facilities. Accordingly, the continuance—indeed, even the creation—of a special parking zone was more than warranted. Serving, as it did, the parking needs of railroad passengers, permitting easier access to the trains and reducing congestion in the crowded business section, the ordinance not only afforded the owner an entirely reasonable use for his property, but advanced the public good and well-being.

Nor may the ordinance be condemned because it affected but a small area. It has long been recognized that, if it is done for the general welfare of the community as a whole, a municipality may, as part of a comprehensive zoning plan, set aside even a single plot in the center of a large zone devoted to a different use. See, e. g., Rodgers v. Village of Tarrytown, 302 N.Y. 115, 124, 96 N.E.2d 731, 734; Nappi v. LaGuardia, 295 N.Y. 652, 64 N.E.2d 716; Higbee v. Chicago, B. & Q. R. Co., 235 Wis. 91, 292 N.W. 320, 128 A.L.R. 734. And land adjacent to a railroad station has been regarded as a particularly appropriate subject for such treatment. See Higbee v. Chicago, B. & Q. R. Co., supra, 235 Wis. 91, 292 N.W. 320.

The ordinance being valid in 1927, it is valid today unless conditions have changed. Not even respondent claims that they have, and the fact is that, except for the erection of a gas station on part of the space involved,[1] neither the area nor the surrounding business district has undergone any alteration. There has, of course, been an increase in population and in the number of automobiles, but that—a general and widespread change affecting all of Mount Vernon—only serves to render the long-continued parking use still more suitable and necessary. It is, perhaps, true, that a parking lot may not afford a purchaser as great a return on his money as a shopping center, but that circumstance, standing alone, does not justify invalidation of the ordinance. See, e. g., Shepard v. Village of Skaneateles, supra, 300 N.Y. 115, 120, 89 N.E.2d 619, 621; Wulfsohn v. Burden, 241 N.Y. 288, 302, 150 N.E. 120, 124, 43 A.L.R. 651.

There is at least one other reason for upholding the 1927 ordinance. While mere acquiescence in an unconstitutional ordinance cannot serve to

---

1. In 1932, the Railroad Company which owned the property until 1951, and its then tenant applied for and obtained a variance, permitting the construction of a gasoline filling station.

validate it, see, e. g., Wuttke v. O'Connor, 306 N.Y. 677, 117 N.E.2d 128, the fact that for over twenty-five years the owner railroad actually occupied the property satisfactorily as a parking space—without objection or the slightest claim that it effected a confiscation—cannot be overlooked. Since an ordinance is unconstitutional only if it bars "any reasonable" use of property, it is difficult to see how it may be attacked successfully as confiscatory or invalid where it appears that the land was put to a "reasonable" use for a quarter of a century under conditions which have up to the present remained unchanged. And, that being so, a vendee, such as respondent, who buys with full knowledge of the applicable zoning regulations, certainly stands in no better or stronger position than his predecessor in title. Cf., e. g., Wuttke v. O'Connor, 306 N.Y. 677, 117 N.E.2d 128, supra; People ex rel. Arseekay Syndicate v. Murdock, 265 N.Y. 158, 191 N.E. 871.

The 1927 law, being, as I believe, constitutional, no fault may be found with the 1952 amendment. That merely brought about by enactment what had previously been accomplished by a nonconforming use and is no more subject to attack than the 1927 ordinance.

If I be right, if the ordinance and amendment are constitutional, it is unnecessary to decide whether the option—given to respondent, when it acquired the premises, to reconvey them back to the seller if unable to obtain a "change of zoning so as to permit buildings for offices or for stores on the premises"—prevents it from attacking the ordinance as invalid.

I would reverse the judgment rendered below.

LEWIS, Ch. J., and CONWAY, DESMOND, FROESSEL and VAN VOORHIS, JJ., concur with DYE, J.; FULD, J., dissents in opinion.

Judgment affirmed.

Questions and Notes

1. What was the long-time existing use of this tract?
2. Where was it located?
3. Why did Mt. Vernon not buy it?

Cross-References

In Anderson, see § 8.40.
In Hagman, see § 76.
In Rathkopf, see Index, this topic.
In Williams, see ch. 107-108.
In Yokley, see § 27.

B.   Non-Conforming Issues

JONES

v.

LOS ANGELES

211 Cal. 304, 295 P.14(1930).

Supreme Court of California.

Dec. 31, 1930.

Rehearing Denied Jan. 30, 1931.

LANGDON, J.

This is an action to enjoin the enforcement of a zoning ordinance of the city of Los Angeles. The said ordinance was enacted independently of the general zoning plan of the city, and its restrictive provisions are directed toward one type of business. It provides that outside of certain designated districts, it shall be unlawful for any person, firm or corporation "to erect, establish, operate, maintain or conduct any hospital, asylum, sanitarium, home, retreat or other place for the care or treatment of insane persons, persons of unsound mind, or persons affected by or suffering from mental or nervous diseases." Penalties of fine and imprisonment are specified for its violation.

In March, 1927, the city of Los Angeles annexed the territory known as the Mar Vista District. At that time, there were already in operation in this district four sanitariums for the treatment of nervous diseases: The Casa Del Mar Sanitarium, the Marshall Manor Sanitarium, the St. Erne Sanitarium, and the Wittman Home for Children. These institutions take as patients only persons suffering from the milder forms of mental disorder. No insane persons are admitted. Each institution has been established by a substantial investment in land, buildings, and equipment.

The above-mentioned zoning ordinance, adopted on August 11, 1927, some months after the annexation of the Mar Vista District, excluded that territory from the area in which the establishment and maintenance of such sanitariums was permitted. When the ordinance went into effect, plaintiffs, as the owners of the institutions, sought to enjoin its enforcement. The superior court of Los Angeles county, in each of the actions, denied the relief prayed for, and appeals were then taken. Because their grounds are practically identical, the four appeals were, by stipulation, consolidated, and will be considered together in this opinion.

[1, 2] A preliminary question which may readily be disposed of relates to the availability of the equitable remedy. It is settled that where a penal

statute causes irreparable damage to property rights, the injured party may attack its constitutionality by an action to enjoin its enforcement. San Diego Tuberculosis Ass'n v. East San Diego, 186 Cal. 252, 200 P. 393, 17 A. L. R. 513; Abbey Land Co. v. San Mateo County, 167 Cal. 440, 139 P. 1068, 52 L. R. A. (N. S.) 408, Ann. Cas. 1915C, 804. Hence, if the ordinance is unconstitutional in its application to these plaintiffs, they are entitled to the decree which they seek.

[3, 4] Viewing the ordinance as part of a general zoning plan, and disregarding for the moment the question of its applicability to plaintiffs, there can be no doubt of its validity. That zoning ordinances, when reasonable in object and not arbitrary in operation, constitute a justifiable exercise of police power, is now well established; and it is equally well established that the power extends to the regulation of uses of property which do not actually amount to nuisances. As Mr. Justice Lennon said in Miller v. Board of Public Works, 195 Cal. 477, 487, 234 P. 381, 384, 38 A. L. R. 1479: " ° ° ° The police power as evidenced in zoning ordinances, has a much wider scope than the mere suppression of the offensive uses of property ° ° ° it acts, not only negatively, but constructively and affirmatively, for the promotion of the public welfare." And in Village of Euclid v. Ambler Realty Company, 272 U.S. 365, 387, 47 S. Ct. 114, 118, 71 L. Ed. 303, 54 A. L. R. 1016, we find a similar statement: "Building zone laws are of modern origin. ° ° ° Regulations, the wisdom, necessity, and validity of which, as applied to existing conditions, are so apparent that they are now uniformly sustained, a century ago, or even half a century ago, probably would have been rejected as arbitrary and oppressive. ° ° ° And in this there is no inconsistency, for while the meaning of constitutional guaranties never varies, the scope of their application must expand or contract to meet the new and different conditions which are constantly coming within the field of their operation." See, also, Baker, Legal Aspects of Zoning, p. 113; Bettman, Constitutionality of Zoning, 37 Harv. L. Rev. 834, 837.

[5] The evidence shows and the lower court found that the restricted districts were mainly residential in character. This is sufficient to justify the exclusion of businesses such as that carried on by plaintiffs. The decisions uphold the validity of ordinances excluding from residential districts property uses much less incongruous than these, as, for example, flats, stores, and business buildings. See State v. Houghton, 164 Minn. 146, 204 N. W. 569, 54 A. L. R. 1012; Ware v. Wichita, 113 Kan. 153, 214 P. 99; State v. New Orleans, 154 La. 271, 97 So.440, 33 A. L. R. 260; Spector v. Building Inspector, 250 Mass. 63, 145 N. E. 265.

[6-8] The objection most vigorously urged by plaintiffs is that the ordinance violates the constitutional guarantee of equal protection of the laws in that the classification of permitted and prohibited districts is arbitrary and unreasonable. It is not contended, nor could the contention be made, that the permitted zones are too small or unsuited to plaintiffs' businesses.

The permitted districts cover considerably more than one-third of the area of the city and include the downtown business district, as well as various other built-up sections. Hence the instant case does not come within the principles of those decisions which hold an ordinance discriminatory where it makes the permitted area unreasonably small. See In re White, 195 Cal. 516, 234 P. 396. It appears, however, that in the permitted districts are certain densely populated areas, and in the prohibited districts there is some territory which is sparsely populated. This is attacked as discriminatory, chiefly on the authority of In re Throop, 169 Cal. 93, 145 P. 1029; Curtis v. Los Angeles, 172 Cal. 230, 156 P. 462; and In re Smith, 143 Cal. 368, 77 P. 180. The first of these cases was concerned with the use of a stone crusher, the second with stables, and the third with gas works. They are representative of the older group of decisions dealing with the power of a municipality to prohibit or regulate the conduct of businesses which are in the nature of public nuisances. To test the validity of zoning legislation by the strict language of some of the nuisance cases would be to ignore the change in both legislative and judicial views on this subject, a change which has been remarked upon by a number of authorities. See Miller v. Board of Public Works, supra; Village of Euclid v. Ambler Realty Company, supra; State v. Houghton, supra. It cannot be seriously contended that relative density of population in the permissive and restricted districts is a controlling test of the validity of a zoning plan, so far as the claim of discriminatory classification is concerned. The object of the present ordinance is to exclude hospitals for the treatment of insanity and nervous diseases from these districts which are devoted to residential purposes, because it is in such districts that they adversely affect the public welfare. This being so, it is immaterial whether the restricted district is densely or sparsely populated, if it is residential. The ordinance is concerned with the nature of the district. A growing residential area is as reasonable an object of protection as one which is fully built up. On the other hand, while the permitted districts include some territory which is densely populated, that territory is not residential in character. It is devoted to business purposes and hence requires none of the special regulation deemed desirable to foster and protect the development of homes and the maintenance of a proper environment for children. Moreover, the argument of plaintiffs, carried to its logical conclusion, would destroy the usefulness of zoning ordinances as an effective means of city planning, for it would require an examination of the regulation solely on the basis of present conditions. But zoning legislation looks to the future. It is a constructive movement in municipal legislation and, as such, it has received the approval of our courts. Miller v. Board of Public Works, supra; Zahn v. Board of Public Works, 195 Cal. 497, 234 P. 388.

[9] An appellate court should not permit itself to be drawn into a minute examination of alleged discriminatory operation of such ordinances if, broadly considered, a reasonable basis of classification exists. Zahn v.

Board of Public Works, supra; Bettman, Constitutionality of Zoning, 37 Harv. L. Rev. 834, 850. Bearing in mind the object of the ordinance and the findings of the court, we are satisfied that no unconstitutional discrimination has been made.

[10] We have thus arrived at this conclusion: The ordinance in question, in so far as it prohibits the establishment of hospitals for the treatment of nervous diseases in certain districts in the city of Los Angeles, and permits their establishment in other specified districts, is valid. The businesses so restricted are proper subjects of such regulation, and hence the ordinance does not result in a denial of due process. The classification of districts is reasonable and not arbitrary, and therefore there is no denial of equal protection of the laws. This much is clear, we feel, with respect to the *establishment of new businesses* of this character in the prohibited districts. But does the same result necessarily follow with regard to existing businesses in these districts? In other words, does the broad view of the police power which justifies the taking away of the *right to engage in such businesses* in certain territory, also justify the *destruction of existing businesses?* We do not think that it does.

We have already emphasized the fact that courts, in their consideration of zoning legislation, have not deemed themselves bound by their prior decisions on the legislative regulation or prohibition of nuisances. They have recognized that the right to use private property may be restricted by an ordinance which follows a reasonable plan, even though the use is neither a nuisance per se, nor a menace to health, safety, or morals in the particular district from which it is excluded. It would seem, therefore, at first glance, that the zoning decisions reach the conclusion that businesses may be prohibited in the sense of being excluded from specified districts, although they do not come within any reasonable view of what constitutes a nuisance. An examination of those decisions, however, reveals the fact that nearly all of them deal with the attempt to establish businesses in the prohibited areas. They decide nothing more than this: The right to engage in a lawful and not dangerous business in a certain area may be taken away in pursuance of a reasonable zoning scheme. They do not decide that an established and not dangerous business, operating in a lawful manner in a certain territory, may be eradicated in pursuance of a reasonable zoning scheme. That problem, which is the important problem of this case, has, so far as we are aware, only been squarely presented to appellate courts in a few instances. The reason for the paucity of decisions is illuminating: Zoning laws have almost invariably been prospective in nature. Indeed, in some states, including Kansas, Ohio, Wisconsin, Illinois, Massachusetts, Maine, and New Hampshire, the enabling statutes which give the zoning power to municipalities, expressly provide that no retroactive ordinances shall be passed. See Baker, Legal Aspects of Zoning, p. 158, note 220.

As a matter of practice, also, those who have drafted ordinances have usually proceeded with due regard for valuable, vested property interests, and have permitted existing, nonconforming uses to remain. They are very generally agreed that the destruction of an existing nonconforming use would be a dangerous innovation of doubtful constitutionality, and that a retroactive provision might jeopardize the entire ordinance. "Zoning * * * holds that an ounce of prevention if worth a pound of cure and that it is fairer to all concerned to prevent the establishment in residence districts of objectionable business than to drive them out once they were established. * * * Zoning looks to the future, not the past, and it is customary to allow buildings and businesses already in the district to remain, although of a class which cannot be established. If such a business constitutes a nuisance, it can still be removed under the police power, but the zoning acts in themselves do not customarily interfere with existing conditions." Chamberlain and Pierson, Zoning Laws and Ordinances, 10 Am. Bar Assn. J. 185. "Retroactive operation of the provisions of the ordinance is generally avoided. * * *" Bettman, Constitutionality of Zoning, 37 Harv. L. Rev. 834, 853. "Retroactive zoning is not to be recommended. * * *" Young, City Planning and Restrictions on the Use of Property, 9 Minn. L. Rev. 593, 628. "The purpose of zoning, which is said to be the crystallization of present conditions and the constructive control of future development, does not require that existing uses be changed. Hence it has been generally assumed that any attempt to make zoning ordinances retroactive would meet with the opposition of the courts and might result in their declaring the ordinance as a whole unconstitutional." Retroactive Zoning Ordinances, 39 Yale L. J. 735, 737. "Nonconforming uses may be required to be removed, but the majority of the cases seem to indicate that if this procedure is attempted the ordinance will be declared unconstitutional because unreasonable." Byrne, The Constitutionality of a General Zoning Ordinance, 11 Marquette L. Rev. 189, 214. See, also, Baker, supra, p. 145.

These same views have been expressed in a number of decisions. In Pelham View Apartments, Inc., v. Switzer, 130 Misc. Rep. 545, 224 N.Y.S. 56, 58, a building permit had been issued for the erection of an apartment house, and the petitioner had borrowed money, bought property, prepared plans, and begun construction, in reliance upon the permit. Thereafter, a new zoning law was enacted, under which such a permit could not be granted, and an attempt was made to revoke it. The court said: "While it is unfortunate that the erection of this apartment house may be distasteful to people living in the neighborhood, and while perhaps it is unfortunate that their property should be thus affected, yet the protection of such rights must be legally done, and the public officials representing the people cannot legally be permitted to change the zoning law, and cancel a permit previously issued under the original zoning act, where an innocent purchaser of real estate has in good faith acted upon such official action of the city, and has thereby acquired vested rights under his permit. * * * It would be nothing short of confiscation, and a complete disregard of constitutional rights, if a municipality could revoke a building permit issued under the conditions as presented in this case." See, also, People v. Stanton, 125 Misc. Rep. 215, 211 N. Y. S. 438.

In Atkinson v. Piper, 181 Wis. 519, 195 N.W. 544, retrocative legislation of this type was strongly disapproved, and the court construed the particular act as prospective in its operation, although the buildings in question were only in the process of construction. The Wisconsin court made a similar decision in the later case of Rosenberg v. Village of Whitefish Bay, 199 Wis. 214, 225 N. W. 838, where construction was not yet under way, but the owner of the land had incurred expenses in the preparation of plans for the structure.

In holding another statute not to be retroactive, the New Jersey court said in Frank J. Durkin Lumber Co. v. Fitzsimmons (Err. & App.) 147 A. 555, 558: " * * * May a municipality, without making compensation, estop an owner from continuing a use that is in actuality, that was begun and continued lawfully, and that becomes unlawful only because the municipality has so ordained? * * * Recognizing that the granting of a permit and the subsequent beginning of work thereunder do clothe the owner with certain rights against municipal interference, this court very recently, in two instances, refused a municipality the privilege of revoking a permit theretofore given. * * * It seems that a logical application of the same principle is to recognize *the right to continue, as against subsequent zoning interference, a use that was actually instituted*, that was lawful when instituted, and that has been actively and constantly maintained." (Italics ours.)

In Adams v. Kalamazoo Ice & Fuel Co., 245 Mich. 261, 222 N. W. 86, 87, the court said: "The ordinance excepts from its restrictive provisions, existing nonconforming uses, but even if it did not contain such an exception, we cannot hold its restrictions retroactive, though defendant, anticipating its enactment, purchased the property and placed its small distributing building thereon. Threatened invasion of a residence district by business may be an impelling reason for affording protection by way of a zoning ordinance, *but such an ordinance may not operate to remove business found there.*" (Italics ours.)

In response to the charge that exemption of existing nonconforming uses would be discriminatory, the courts have very generally held the exemption to be valid and necessary. Baker, supra, p. 144. As the court said in City of Aurora v. Burns, 319 Ill. 84, 149 N. E. 784, 788: "The building zone ordinance * * * permits lawful uses of building at the time of the passage of the ordinance although not in conformity with its provisions, to continue thereafter. This exception is made so that the ordinance shall not have a retroactive operation. It would be manifestly unjust to deprive the owner of property of the use to which it was lawfully devoted when the ordinance became effective." In Spector v. Building Inspector, 250 Mass. 63, 145 N. E. 265, 268, the same conclusion is reached: "To exempt buildings already devoted to a use from a prohibition of such use of other buildings or buildings thereafter erected in a specified area is not unequal but lawful." This court has also spoken to the same effect in Zahn v. Board of Public Works, 195 Cal. 497, where it is said on page 512, 234 P. 388, 394: "As to the objection that the ordinance was not retrospective, but permitted the continuance of existing uses, it will suffice to say that for the purpose of zoning it is not necessary that existing uses shall be removed. ° ° ° The ordinance was enacted with the purpose of directing the present and future development of the city and no attempt was made to remold its past development. To have required, preliminarily to an enactment for future development, that all past development, not in harmony therewith, should be removed, might be impractical. That the council did not attempt such a task has no tendency to show discrimination against property to be developed in the future." See, also, A. C. Blumenthal & Co., Inc., v. Cryer, 71 Cal. App. 668, 236 P. 216.

It therefore appears that the instant case involves a situation materially different from that presented in the usual zoning case. The exercise of power in this instance is, on the whole, far more drastic than in those in which a mere right to engage in a particular business is restricted. We are asked to uphold a municipal ordinance which destroys valuable businesses, built up over a period of years. If we do so on the ground that this is a proper exercise of the police power in the enactment of zoning legislation, then it follows that the same thing may be done to apartment houses, flats, or stores. The establishment of many lawful and not dangerous businesses in a city would then become an extremely hazardous undertaking. At any time, in pursuance of a reasonable plan for its future development, the city could prohibit the continuance of the businesses, and make property valueless which was previously constructed and devoted to a useful purpose. It may well be that in the course of years one of the outlying permitted districts in the present scheme will become residential in character, and will, by another ordinance, be placed in the prohibited area. If the plaintiffs, at great expense, re-establish themselves in that district, they might be pursued and again eradicated. All this is to be justified under the police power as a proper taking of private property for public use, without compensation. The approval of such a doctrine would be a blow to rights in private property such as this court has never before witnessed. Only a paramount and compelling public necessity could sanction so extraordinary an interference with useful business.

What is the public necessity here? We have considered the ordinance solely as modern zoning legislation, for such is undoubtedly its character. There is, it is true, testimony in the record to show that the district was in some respects a less agreeable residential section than it would be if the businesses of plaintiffs were removed. Neighbors complained that the presence of the sanitariums depreciated the value of their own property. There is similar testimony as to occasional noises made by unruly patients, and of several patients having escaped; although in this connection the trial court found that "none of the inmates of any of said four sanitariums ° ° ° has ever injured in any manner whatsoever any of the inhabitants of said Mar Vista District or elsewhere, nor has any of said inmates ever attacked or attempted to do bodily injury unto any of said inhabitants."

[11, 12] From the evidence the court found that the conduct and operation of plaintiffs' businesses will tend to and does "impair and endanger the health, safety, morals, convenience, comfort and welfare of the public, and will prevent the said district from obtaining its proper growth and from fully developing into the residential district to which it is devoted." Another finding is that "it is not true that said sanitarium ° ° ° will not create, and is not a nuisance." Assuming that the above statements are intended as a finding that the sanitariums of plaintiffs are nuisances as now conducted, it hardly seems supported by the record. For a discussion of similar evidence, see Jardine v. Pasadena, 199 Cal. 64, 75, 248 P. 225, 48 A. L. R. 509. But even such a finding does not go to the root of the matter, and is, so far as the validity of this ordinance is concerned, wholly immaterial. The individual, or the city, still has the right to enjoin acts which constitute a private or public nuisance and this right is given as a protection against the improper conduct of any lawful business. Jardine v. Pasadena, supra; Adams v. Kalamazoo Ice & Fuel Co., 245 Mich. 261, 222 N. W. 86. This ordinance expressly applies to any hospitals, asylums, and sanitariums for the care or treatment of persons suffering from "mental or nervous diseases." It affects all such places in the same manner, irrespective of whether they are conducted properly or improperly. The question of its constitutional validity must therefore be considered apart from the particular conditions alleged to exist in the establishment maintained by plaintiffs.

[13] As so considered, we are satisfied that it cannot find support in the legislative power to prohibit nuisances. A properly conducted sanitarium for the care and treatment of persons affected with "mental or nervous diseases" cannot, we feel, be held to constitute a nuisance. Mr. Justice Olney said in San Diego Tuberculosis Ass'n v. East San Diego, 186 Cal. 252, 254, 200 P. 393, 394, 17 A. L. R. 513: "That a well-conducted, modern hospital, even one for the treatment of contagious and infectious diseases, is not such a menace, but, on the contrary, one of the most beneficent of institutions needs no argument." This language was approved and a similar conclusion was reached in Jardine v. Pasadena, supra. In Mayor & Council of Wilmington v. Turk, 14 Del. Ch. 392, 129 A. 512, an ordinance which prohibited the maintenance of a private hospital in a residential district was held to be unreasonable in the particular case. These decisions are concerned with businesses closely analogous to those involved in the instant case. A case directly in point is Ex parte Whitwell, 98 Cal. 73, 32 P. 870, 19 L. R. A. 727, 35 Am. St. Rep. 152, which fully supports our conclusion that a properly conducted institution for the treatment of nervous diseases is not a nuisance.

[14] We repeat, therefore, that the ordinance involved herein is to be supported upon principles of zoning and not as a prohibition directed

against actual nuisances. With this conclusion as a basis, it becomes necessary to determine whether that part of the ordinance which prohibits the further operation or maintenance of plaintiffs' businesses is a reasonable means by which the zoning power may be exercised. And here the distinction between the power to prohibit nuisances and the power to zone is exceedingly important. The power over nuisances is more circumscribed in its objects; but once an undoubted menace to public health, safety, or morals is shown, the method of protection may be drastic. Private businesses may be wholly prohibited, where their danger is sufficiently great; and other businesses, no matter how well established and how great the resulting loss, may be excluded from certain districts where, by reason of the circumstances, their maintenance has become a public nuisance in those districts. In these cases, the public welfare demands even the destruction of existing property interests. Examples of decisions of this type are Ex parte Quong Wo, 161 Cal. 220, 118 P. 714, involving a laundry, and Hadacheck v. Sebastian, 239 U. S. 394, 36 S. Ct. 143, 60 L. Ed. 348, Ann. Cas 1917B, 927, involving a brick yard. While the latter case is an extreme illustration of the hardship which may result from an exercise of police power, it can be justified on the ground of nuisance regulation. It is not a zoning case at all. See 39 Yale L. J. 735, 738, note 19.

[15] Zoning is not so limited in its purposes. It may take into consideration factors which bear no relation to the public health, safety, or morals, but which come within the meaning of the broader term "general welfare." It deals with many uses of property which are in no way harmful. If its objects are so much broader than those of nuisance regulation, if its invasion of private property interests is more extensive, and if the public necessity to justify its exercise need not be so pressing, then does it not follow that its means of regulation must be more reasonable and less destructive of established interests? Must we say that the property of some of the residents of a district can be taken from them, without compensation, in order to make more attractive and pleasant the lives of other residents? "This background of nuisance law in the development of zoning occasionally leads to erroneous results. Property regulation by means of zoning is not restricted to what is disorderly or offensive * * * in attempting to apply to all types of zoning ordinances the summary methods of prevention and suppression which are employed in the case of nuisances, municipalities obviously fail to take into account the fact that zoning not only includes but also supplements nuisance regulation. A restriction imposed to prohibit an offensive use is not a taking of property for which compensation must be made and in the abatement of nuisances retroactive measures are valid. Granting that a zoning ordinance may operate retroactively where there is clearly an element of nuisance, it does not follow that a similar disposition may be made of every type of nonconforming use dealt with in zoning." 39 Yale L. J. 738. "No one gainsays that a municipal government within its police power has the right to prescribe rules regulating the character of buildings to be erected and the

material to be used within certain prescribed boundaries. ° ° ° But such ordinances must ° ° ° relate to the future. Of course, that does not prevent cities from moving to abate nuisances whenever occurring." Brown v. Grant (Tex. Civ. App.) 2 S.W.(2d) 285, 287.

Seemingly in opposition to these widely held views is the conclusion reached by the Supreme Court of Louisiana, with respect to an ordinance of the city of New Orleans which prohibited the establishment or maintenance of any business within a specified district, and provided that all businesses then in operation in the district should be liquidated in one year. In State v. McDonald, 168 La. 172, 121 So. 613, and in State v. Jacoby, 168 La. 752, 123 So. 314, the ordinance was held valid as applied to businesses in operation prior to its passage, which had failed to liquidate within the prescribed period. An examination of the language of the opinions indicates that the court did not consider the general question of the validity of retroactive zoning laws, but was concerned with the particular situation before it, and saw no material injury to the owner of the property. In the first case (State v. McDonald, supra, at page 616 of 121 So., the court said: "In the instant case there is nothing ° ° ° in the record on which the court would be authorized or justified in declaring the attacked provision of the ordinance harsh, arbitrary, or unreasonable. ° ° ° For all that appears, the business may be a small retail grocery business located in an outlying section far removed from the business center of the city. The defendants have not shown, and the court is unable to conjecture, any substantial reason why such a business could not be liquidated and closed out within a year." In the second case, State v. Jacoby, supra, at page 317 of 123 So., the objection of the owner was disposed of in the same manner: "Defendant's drug store is a small one, and it is obvious that one year affords ample time within which to liquidate the business and close it."

These decisions are, we think, distinguishable from the instant case; but even if they were not distinguishable, we should not be disposed to follow them, for they exhibit, in our opinion, a confusion between the objects of zoning and nuisance regulation. See 39 Yale L. J. 738.

A more drastic decision, perhaps, is Village of Euclid v. Ambler Realty Co., 272 U. S. 365, 47 S. Ct. 114, 71 L. Ed. 303, 54 A. L. R. 1016, already mentioned in this opinion. There the ordinance created a residential district which included a large tract of land owned by the Ambler Realty Company, which had been held vacant for industrial purposes. The effect of the restrictive provisions of the ordinance was materially to impair the market value of the land. Although the lower federal court was of the opinion that this was an unreasonable interference with private property, the Supreme Court of the United States finally upheld it, three justices dissenting. This is an extreme case, and has been recognized as such by zoning authorities. Thus, Baker says (page 144): "The ordinance involved in this case does not seem to be a reasonable application of the zoning principle, and the result is a distinct surprise." However harsh be the result of this decision, it is nevertheless in no sense decisive of the instant case, for it did not involve a retroactive ordinance. The Supreme Court recognized the difficulty that would be encountered in laying down a test of the validity of a restriction based solely upon the value of the property interest affected, yet in the subsequent case of Nectow v. Cambridge, 277 U. S. 183, 48 S. Ct. 447, 72 L. Ed. 842, it was held that a similar restriction involving a "serious and highly injurious" invasion of property was, under the particular circumstances, unreasonable. No general test can be derived from these or other cases, all of which reiterate the well-worn doctrine that each one must be decided on its particular facts. See Mayor of Wilmington v. Turk, 14 Del. Ch. 392, 129 A. 512. But we think that there is a decided difference between an ordinance which operates to limit the future use of property, no matter how great the impairment of its value, and one which requires the discontinuance of an existing use. In the first situation, we see merely the familiar example of an intangible and speculative future value being reduced as a result of the necessities of city planning; in the second we see the destruction of a going business. This latter action, if sanctioned by law, may have a serious and damaging effect on private enterprise generally, in addition to its manifest injury to the persons whose businesses are prohibited.

We do not mean to hold that those engaged in the zoning of cities must always be faced with the impossibility of eradicating the non-conforming uses. In some jurisdictions this problem has been dealt with by provisions against alteration or enlargement of existing structures, or rebuilding after their destruction. See State v. Hillman, 110 Conn. 92, 147 A. 294; Appeal of Ward, 289 Pa. 458, 137 A. 630; City of Earle v. Shackleford, 177 Ark. 291, 6 S.W.(2d) 294. But ordinarily the added benefit to the majority of the residents of the restricted district should not be received at the expense of others. If the city desires to abolish the nonconforming use, this may be a legitimate object of the police power, but the means of its exercise must not include the destruction of the property interest without compensation. The words of Mr. Justice Holmes in Pennsylvania Coal Co. v. Mahon, 260 U. S. 393, 413, 43 S. Ct. 158, 159, 67 L. Ed. 322, 28 A. L. R. 1321, are very much in point:

> "As applied to this case the statute is admitted to destroy previously existing rights of property and contract. The question is whether the police power can be stretched so far.

> "Government hardly could go on if to some extent values incident to property could not be diminished without paying for every such change in the general law. As long recognized some values are enjoyed under an implied limitation and must yield to the police power. But obviously the implied limitation must have its limits or the contract and due process clauses are gone. One fact for consideration in determining such limits is the extent of the diminution. When it reaches a certain magnitude, in most if not all cases there must be an exercise of eminent domain and compensation to sustain the act. So the question depends upon the particular facts. The greatest weight is given to the judgment of the legisla-

ture but it always is open to interested parties to contend that the legislature has gone beyond its constitutional power."

Further on, the learned justice remarks:

"The general rule at least is that while property may be regulated to a certain extent, if regulation goes too far it will be recognized as a taking. ° ° ° In general it is not plain that a man's misfortunes or necessities will justify his shifting the damages to his neighbor's shoulders. ° ° ° We are in danger of forgetting that a strong public desire to improve the public condition is not enought to warrant achieving the desire by a shorter cut than the constitutional way of paying for the change."

The principles set forth in the Pennsylvania Coal Company Case were approved in Piper v. Ekern, 180 Wis. 586, 194 N. W. 159, 162, 34 A. L. R. 32, where a statute limiting the height of buildings surrounding the state capitol was held unconstitutional. The court said: " ° ° ° In one sense such a restriction under the police power does not transfer property from the private owner to the public, as is the case where the power of eminent domain is exercised; nevertheless such restriction may be of such a nature as to practically accomplish the same result. ° ° ° It has also been held that any regulation which deprives any person of the profitable use of his property constitutes a taking of property and entitles him under the Constitution to compensation, unless the invasion of rights is so slight as to permit the regulation to be justified under the police power. ° ° ° " See, also, Isenbarth v. Bartnett, 206 App. Div. 546, 201 N. Y. S. 383.

Even where the destruction of private property is warranted by vital public necessity, it is sometimes the legislative practice to compensate the injured owner. Such, for example, was the case with our legislation directed toward the eradication of bovine tuberculosis by the destruction of diseased cattle. See Patrick v. Riley (Cal. Sup.) 287 P. 455.

[16, 17] Our conclusion is that where, as here, a retroactive ordinance causes substantial injury and the prohibited business is not a nuisance, the ordinance is to that extent an unreasonable and unjustifiable exercise of police power. Whether, under our present law, there exists the power to eliminate the nonconforming use by payment of compensation for the loss suffered, is a question not presented by this case, and one which we therefore do not attempt to determine.

It follows that the present ordinance is valid in so far as it prohibits the further establishment of businesses of this type in the restricted districts; and is invalid in its application to these plaintiffs.

The judgment is therefore reversed.

We concur: WASTE, C. J.; RICHARDS, J.; SEAWELL, J.; CURTIS, J.; PRESTON, J.

Questions and Notes

1. Which type of development arrived first, in this far Western part of Los Angeles? Which type came later, and filled up the neighborhood?

2. In this situation, how much of a blighting influence would you say the sanitarium was on single-family residences? (See the pictures in Williams, v.5, plate 18.)

3. If you were setting up a test case on the principle of amortizing out non-conforming uses, do you think it would be a good idea to select a case involving a somewhat similar use, permitted in the next zoning district?

STANDARD OIL CO.

v.

TALLAHASSEE

87 F. Supp. 145 (N.D. Fla., 1949), affd., 183 F.2d 410

(CA 5th, 1950), cert. den., 340 U.S. 892 (1950).

United States District Court

N. D. Florida, Tallahassee Division.

Nov. 30, 1949.

Action by Standard Oil Company against City of Tallahassee to enjoin the enforcement of a zoning ordinance.

The District Court, De Vane, J., held that the zoning ordinance requiring the discontinuance of filling station was valid and dissolved temporary injunction and dismissed the action.

Ausley, Collins & Truett, Tallahassee, Fla., for plaintiff.

James Messer, Jr., City Attorney, Tallahassee, Fla., for defendant.

DE VANE, District Judge.

This is a suit by plaintiff to enjoin the enforcement of a zoning ordinance (No. 542), adopted by the City of Tallahassee, Florida on April 27, 1948.

Plaintiff operates a gasoline service station at the dead-end intersection of Lafayette Street with Monroe Street in Tallahassee, across Monroe Street from the main entrance to the State Capitol. The property owned by plaintiff was purchased in 1938 for the purpose of erecting thereon a service station as an outlet for the sale of plaintiff's products. At the time of the purchase of said property there did not exist any restrictions by municipal ordinance or otherwise against the use of said property for such purpose. Plaintiff expended considerable money in the construction of the service station thereon, opening the same for business on or about November 1, 1938.

Under the zoning ordinance then in effect said property was located in what was designated as residence district "B", which permitted the construction and operation of service stations in such districts. Amendments were made, from time to time, to the zoning ordinance, which will be more fully referred to later. The latest amendment required plaintiff to discontinue the operation of its service station on or before May 1, 1949.

This suit was filed prior to May 1, 1949 and on April 30, 1949 a temporary restraining order was issued by this court enjoining the City from enforcing the ordinance against plaintiff until after final hearing in this case.

A review of the history of zoning laws passed by the State Legislature and of zoning ordinances adopted by defendant will aid in the determination of the issues before the court in this case. Chapter 15520, Sp.Laws of Florida, Acts of 1931, specifically authorized the City of Tallahassee to regulate the location and use of buildings and lands within the City, pursuant to a comprehensive zoning plan. Subsequently practically the same grant of authority was given all municipalities in the State through the enactment of Chapter 19539, Laws of Florida, Acts of 1939, Chapter 176, Fla.Stat.1941, F.S.A. The constitutionality of this legislation has been upheld by the Supreme Court of Florida in numerous decisions, some of which are cited below. State ex rel. Taylor v. City of Jacksonville, 101 Fla. 1241, 133 So. 114; State ex rel. Skillman v. City of Miami, 101 Fla. 585, 134 So. 541; City of Miami Beach v. Ocean & Inland Co., 147 Fla. 480, 3 So.2d 364; Miami Shores Village v. William N. Brockway Post No. 124, 156 Fla. 673, 24 So.2d 33.

Pursuant to authority granted to it by Chapter 15520, supra, the City of Tallahassee, by ordinance No. 263, adopted April 13, 1936, approved and put into effect a comprehensive zoning plan for the City. The area within which plaintiff's property is located was designated as a residence district "A" and under the terms of said ordinance service stations could not be operated within said area.

Ordinance No. 280, adopted December 22, 1936, changed the designation of the area to residence district "B" and permitted the operation of service stations within said area. It was during the period when this ordinance was in effect that plaintiff purchased the property involved in this suit and constructed its service station thereon.

Ordinance No. 334, adopted January 24, 1939, removed from residence district "B" the area within which plaintiff's property is located and added it to business district "A". This ordinance prohibited the construction of any more service stations within all said business distrct and there was also included in this ordinance the following provision: "No additional motor vehicle service station or stations shall be constructed or operated within the above described parts of this area of the City of Tallahassee, after the effective date of this ordinance; and further that all locations or cites within said parts or areas of the City now used for motor vehicle service stations shall be discontinued as such on and after January 1, 1949."

Ordinance No. 542, adopted April 27, 1948, again changed the area in which plaintiff's property is located from a business district to a residence district "A". It is this ordinance which plaintiff seeks to enjoin.

Business district "A", established by ordinance No. 334, adopted January 24, 1939, included not only the area in which plaintiff's property is located, but also included the main business district of the City lying adjacent to and immediately north of the area in which plaintiff's property is located. The provision with reference to the discontinuance of the operation of service stations in said business district "A" before January 1, 1949 was also applicable to this area and all service stations in what is now the main business district lying between Pensacola Street on the south and Park Avenue on the north have been forced to discontinue operation. Two other service stations formerly located in the same district as plaintiff was and is now located also ceased operation before the dead-line given them and plaintiff is the only one of the five stations affected by this ordinance No. 334 still in operation.

This resume of the zoning laws and ordinances applicable to the City of Tallahassee clearly shows that the City had been vested with authority to enact such ordinances and had exercised such authority prior to the acquisition by plaintiff of the property involved in this suit and plaintiff acquired the property with full knowledge of the right of the City to modify its zoning ordinances to meet the needs of this rapidly growing City.

The principle grounds upon which the validity of this ordinance is attacked may be summarized as follows:

1. The property of plaintiff is located one block south of the principal business district of the City. The trend in this area is towards business and not residential use and the business district should, therefore, be extended south to include plaintiff's property.

2. The classification of said area as residential is arbitrary and unreasonable and has no relation to the announced purposes of said ordinance.

3. The ordinance is unreasonable, arbitrary and confiscatory because it would greatly depreciate the value of plaintiff's property, its highest and best use being for a service station or other business purpose.

4. The ordinance permits non-conforming uses in other business and residential districts and to deny such right to plaintiff constitutes an arbitrary and unreasonable discrimination.

5. The exemption from the terms of said ordinance of all existing non-conforming uses within said residence district, except service stations, and the creation of an "island" business district "A" inside said residence district "A" in close proximity to plaintiff's property, is discriminatory and denies plaintiff the equal protection of the law, to which it is entitled.

6. The ordinance cannot be sustained on the ground that it will promote the health, safety, morals, convenience and general welfare of the inhabitants of the City and for this reason is an illegal exercise of the authority vested in the City under the laws of the State.

[1] The facts in the case are not in essential dispute—they were in large part stipulated. Considering first grounds 1 and 2, the evidence shows that the property of plaintiff is located one block south of the principal business district, although the evidence does not sustain the contention of plaintiff that the trend in the area in which plaintiff's property is located is towards business and not residential use. Ordinance No. 334, adopted January 24, 1939, changed the area within which plaintiff's property is located from residence district "B" to business district "A" and the area retained such designation until the adoption of ordinance No. 542 on April 27, 1948 when the area was changed from business district "A" to residence district "A". The evidence shows that during this period there was little business development in the area. As a matter of fact, businesses, other than service stations, were never prohibited in the area prior to the adoption of ordinance No. 542, on April 27, 1948, and there had been little businesses development of any kind in the area, despite rapid growth in other sections of the City. In view of this historical development of the area affected the court need not concern itself with the wisdom of the City in enacting the zoning ordinance questioned. Godson v. Town of Surfside, 150 Fla. 614, 8 So.2d 497; City of Miami Beach v. Ocean & Inland Co., 147 Fla. 480, 3 So.2d 364; State ex rel. Skillman v. City of Miami, 101 Fla. 585, 134 So. 541; State ex rel. Henry v. City of Miami, 117 Fla. 594, 158 So. 82.

[2] Passing next to ground 3, the evidence supports plaintiff's contention that the value of its property will be greatly depreciated if plaintiff is prohibited from the use of said property as a service station. The testimony is to the effect that the property, with improvements thereon, is worth approximately $55,000.00 as a service station; that the improvements are unfit for any other use and that the bare land is worth not to exceed $5,000.00 for residential purposes. However, it is well settled that a zoning ordinance is not invalid because it has the effect of depreciating the value of certain property affected by it. State ex rel. Townsend v. Farrey, 133 Fla. 15, 182 So. 448; City of Miami Beach v. Ocean & Inland Co., 147 Fla. 480, 3 So.2d 364; Marblehead Land Company v. City of Los Angeles, 9 Cir., 47 F.2d 528; Hadacheck v. Sebastian, 239 U.S. 394, 36 S: Ct. 143, 60 L.Ed. 348, Ann.Cas., 1917B, 927.

[3-5] Considering together grounds 4 and 5, the evidence supports the contention of plaintiff that the ordinance in question permits non-conforming uses in other residential districts and that it exempts from the terms of said ordinance all non-conforming uses within the district where plaintiff's property is located, except plaintiff's service station. The ordinance also permits the continued operation of a service station about five blocks east of plaintiff's property, which was in a residence districe "B" when it was constructed

but is now in the same residence district "A" in which plaintiff's property is located. The ordinance prohibits the continued operation of service stations only in that part of residence district "A" adjacent to the State Capitol and the other service station lies outside this area. The evidence also shows the creation of a small business district "A" in close proximity to plaintiff's property. These objections, however, are likewise not sufficient to strike down the ordinance. The power of the City to require discontinuance of existing uses is well established law in Florida. State ex rel. Henry v. City of Miami, 117 Fla. 594, 158 So. 82; Knowles v. Central Allapattae Properties, 145 Fla. 123, 198 So. 819. In State ex rel. Skillman v. City of Miami, 101 Fla. 585, 134 So. 541, the Supreme Court of Florida sustained an ordinance zoning a limited area on Biscayne Boulevard, Miami, Florida against the maintenance and operation of funeral homes. In State ex rel. Dallas Inv. Co. v. Peace, 139 Fla. 394, 190 So. 607 the Supreme Court of Florida held valid an ordinance in the City of Miami prohibiting the erection of a gasoline filling station within 350 yards of any church, hospital, school or other public institution or within 750 feet of another filling station. Plaintiff's service station is within close proximity to the State Capitol, several State office buildings and a public school, which constitutes sufficient ground for the City to require the discontinuance of plaintiff's service station. See also, State ex rel. Henry v. City of Miami, supra; Texas Co. v. City of Tampa, 5 Cir., 100 F.2d 347; Hadacheck v. Sebastian, supra and State ex rel. National Oil Works of Louisiana v. McShane, 159 La. 723, 106 So. 252.

Lastly, when evidence was proffered that the ordinance did not promote the health, safety, morals or general welfare of the inhabitants of the City, the court ruled out all such evidence except that bearing upon the general welfare. Defendant made no contention that the ordinance in any way promoted the health, morals or convenience of the inhabitants of the City, but did insist that both safety and general welfare were involved. The court refused to hear testimony on the issue of safety for the reason that the City was unable to produce any evidence satisfactorily showing that any hazards existing at the intersection of Lafayette and Monroe Streets were not equally present at other service stations located in the City. Evidence on this question, therefore, was confined to general welfare.

The character of the use of much of the property immediately adjacent or contiguous to and abutting the property of plaintiff has not changed essentially, except to the extent hereinafter specified, since the construction of the service station by plaintiff. In fact, it has not changed essentially in many years. Much of the development for several blocks east and south of plaintiff's property has been for years and still is an eyesore in the community. Despite the fact the area was zoned for business for many years, no businesses of any consequence were established in the area. The purpose of the zoning ordinance now under attack is to remove this eyesore. Some progress in this direction is being made in certain parts of the City adjacent to the district in which plaintiff's property is located, but the progress is slow and there remains much to be desired.

As heretofore pointed out, the service station of plaintiff is located at the dead-end intersection of Lafayette and Monroe Streets and just across Monroe Street from the main entrance to the State Capitol. Monroe Street is the principal thoroughfare in the City of Tallahassee. The residence district in which plaintiff's property is located contains several city blocks lying west, south and east of the State Capitol. Six large State office buildings adjacent to the Capitol are also located in the district. Most of the property acquired by the City and State, on which the State office buildings are located, were occupied by residences before acquisition and by far the greatest use made of the property in the district is for residential purposes. While it is true that most of the residences are far below standard and many of them shacks that fact contributes to rather than impedes the development of the property for high-class residential use. Apartment house development for use by State employees working in the Capitol Center office buildings is not only possible but very probable. It is at least an end worth striving to accomplish. It may safely be said that the area at least lends itself to a development of this character more readily than any other that would not constitute a nuisance to the State's property located in the area.

[6] The Supreme Court of Florida has held that in judging the merits of a controversy of this kind the facts peculiar to the particular case will govern and the court will not substitute its judgment for that of the legislative body of the City. City of Miami Beach v. Ocean & Inland Co., supra [147 Fla. 480, 3 So.2d 366]. In the case just cited the court also said: "We do not comprehend how it can be successfully urged that the maintenance of safety, health or morals are involved but only whether in the circumstances of this particular case the restrictions are so unnecessary to the general welfare of the inhabitants that the curtailment of the rights of the plaintiff are unreasonable and arbitrary."

And the court went on to say further: "We will determine the reasonableness of the regulations as applied to the factual situation meanwhile keeping before us the accepted rules that the court will not substitute its judgment for that of the city council; that the ordinance is presumed valid (State ex rel. Taylor v. City of Jacksonville, supra) and that the legislative intent will be sustained if 'fairly debatable'. Euclid Ohio v. Ambler Realty Co., 272 U.S. 365, 47 S.Ct. 114, 71 L.Ed. 303, 54 A.L.R. 1016.

Many cases have been before the Supreme Court of Florida involving the validity of zoning ordinances, some of which have been struck down and others sustained. The court has reviewed most of these cases and finds and holds that the legal principles announced by the court in City of Miami Beach v. Ocean & Inland Co., supra, are applicable to this case and upon the authority of that case and the other cases cited the relief sought here will be denied.

An Order will be entered in conformity with this Memorandum Decision dissolving the temporary restraining order and dismissing the suit.

STANDARD OIL CO.

v.

TALLAHASSEE

87 F. Supp. 145 (N. D. Fla. 1949), affd., 183 F.2d 410

(CA 5th, 1950), cert. den., 340 U.S. 892 (1950).

United States Court of Appeals

Fifth Circuit.

June 30, 1950.

Rehearing Denied July 28, 1950.

The Standard Oil Company sued the City of Tallahassee to enjoin enforcement of a city zoning ordinance which required discontinuance of use of a site owned by plaintiff for a gasoline filling station. The United States District Court for the Northern District of Florida, Dozier A. DeVane, J., 87 F. Supp. 145, rendered a judgment adverse to plaintiff, and plaintiff appealed. The Court of Appeals, McCord, Circuit Judge, held that ordinance was justified as a reasonable exercise of the police power of city and was not invalid as being arbitrary and unreasonable and as bearing no relation to the general welfare to the city.

Judgment affirmed.

Hutcheson, Chief Judge, dissenting.

McCORD, Circuit Judge.

This action was brought by Standard Oil Company, a corporation organized under the laws of Kentucky, against the City of Tallahassee, a municipal corporation of the state of Florida, to enjoin the enforcement of a city zoning ordinance adopted by that municipality on April 27, 1948.

On April 30, 1949, a temporary restraining order was granted by the district court enjoining the City of Tallahassee from enforcing said ordinance against plaintiff pending a final hearing and disposition of the cause. On November 30, 1949, after considering the pleadings, stipulation or counsel, and the testimony adduced upon a full hearing of the case, the district court held the ordinance valid and enforceable, whereupon the temporary restraining order was dissolved and the suit dismissed.

The main question presented is whether the zoning ordinance involved is justified as a reasonable exercise of the police power of the municipality to promote the general welfare of its inhabitants, or whether, as it affects plaintiff's property, it is so arbitrary and unreasonable as to constitute a confiscation of its property without due process of law, or so discriminatory as to deny appellant the equal protection of the law.

The material facts, as stipulated by the parties and found by the trial court, reveal that Standard Oil Company owns and operates a gasoline service station at the intersection of Lafayette and Monroe Streets in the City of Tallahassee, across from the main entrance to the State Capitol. The property on which the service station is located was purchased in 1938 for the purpose of constructing a station thereon, which was to be used as a retail outlet for the sale of plaintiff's gasoline and oil products. At the time of its purchase there were no restrictions by ordinance against the use of the property for such purpose.

Chapter 15,520, Special Laws of Florida, Acts of 1931, specifically authorized the City of Tallahassee to regulate the location and use of buildings and lands within that City, pursuant to a comprehensive zoning plan. Subsequently, practically the same grant of authority was given all municipalities in the State through the enactment of Chapter 19,539, Laws of Florida, Act of 1939, F.S.A. § 176.01 et seq.

On April 13, 1936, acting under authority granted to it by Chapter 15,520 of the Special Laws of Florida, the City of Tallahassee adopted a comprehensive zoning plan for the City. The area within which plaintiff's property is located was then designated as a residence district "A" and under the terms of the zoning ordinance service stations could not be operated within the area. However, a later zoning ordinance adopted that same year changed the designation of the area to residence district "B", and under this new classification service stations could be constructed and operated within the area. It was during the period when this latter ordinance was in effect that plaintiff purchased the property in dispute and constructed its service station thereon.

On January 24, 1939, the City adopted Ordinance No. 334, which removed from residence district "B" the area within which plaintiff's property is located, and added it to business district "A". This zoning ordinance also provided as follows: "No additional motor vehicle service station or stations shall be constructed or operated within the above described parts of this area of the City of Tallahassee, after the effective date of this ordinance; and further that all locations or cites within said parts or areas of the City now used for motor vehicle service stations shall be discontinued as such on and after January 1, 1949."

Finally, by zoning Ordinance No. 542, adopted April 27, 1948, the City again changed the area in which plaintiff's property is located from a business district to a residence district "A". The above provision of Ordinance

No. 334, requiring the discontinuance of the operation of service stations in said area by January 1, 1949, was also made applicable to the area in which plaintiff's service station is located. It is this ordinance which plaintiff here seeks to enjoin.

There is evidence to the effect that plaintiff has spent considerable money in the construction, operation, and maintenance of its service station since it was first opened for business on or about November 1, 1938, and that the value of its property will be greatly depreciated if it is prohibited under the ordinance from using it for such purpose. However, it is without dispute that the City of Tallahassee had authority to enact such zoning ordinances, and that it had exercised such authority prior to plaintiff's purchase of the property here involved. Plaintiff originally acquired the property with full knowledge of the right of the City to modify its zoning ordinances so as to conform to its requirements as a rapidly growing municipality. Moreover, the evidence further shows that other service stations formerly located in the same district where plaintiff's station is located have ceased operation before the deadline given them under the ordinance, and that plaintiff's station is the only one of five service stations affected by the zoning ordinance which is still in operation.

[1, 2] The courts have generally recognized that they should not inhibit a reasonable exercise of the zoning power of a municipality carried out pursuant to legislative grant by the state. Moreover, it has been held that a presumption of validity attends the enactment of such zoning ordinances. City of Miami Beach v. Ocean & Inland Co., 147 Fla. 480, 3 So.2d 364; Godson v. Town of Surfside, 150 Fla. 614, 8 So.2d 497.

[3] Legislation conferring the zoning power upon various Florida municipalities has been repeatedly sustained as constitutional by the Supreme Court of Florida. State ex rel. Taylor v. City of Jacksonville, 101 Fla. 1241, 133 So. 114; State ex rel. Skillman v. City of Miami, 101 Fla. 585, 134 So. 541; Miami Shores Village v. William N. Brockway Post, No. 124, 156 Fla. 673, 24 So.2d 33. And in such cases, we are not permitted to substitute our judgment for that of the city council, or to question the wisdom or policy of that body in adopting the ordinance under attack, so long as it does not infringe constitutional guaranties. City of Miami Beach v. Ocean & Inland Co., 147 Fla. 480, 3 So.2d 364; Godson v. Town of Surfside, 150 Fla. 614, 8 So.2d 497; State ex rel. Dallas Inv. Co. v. Peace, 139 Fla. 394, 190 So. 607.

[4, 5] The power of a municipality to require by ordinance the discontinuance of an existing property use also appears to be well established law in Florida. Knowles v. Central Allapattae Properties, 145 Fla. 123, 198 So. 819; State ex rel. Skillman v. City of Miami, 101 Fla. 585, 134 So. 541; State ex rel. Dallas Inv. Co. v. Peace, 139 Fla. 394, 190 So. 607. Here, plaintiff's service station is near the State Capitol and the State Supreme Court Building, as well as several other state office buildings and a public school. It therefore becomes manifest that its discontinuance under the ordinance

cannot be viewed as arbitrary and unreasonable, or as having no relation to the safety and general welfare of the community affected. Hadacheck v. Sebastian, 239 U.S. 394, 36 S.Ct. 143, 60 L.Ed. 348; Ann.Cas.1917B, 927; State ex rel. Henry v. City of Miami, 117 Fla. 594, 158 So. 82; See also, Texas Co. v. City of Tampa, 5 Cir., 100 F.2d 347; Marblehead Land Company v. City of Los Angeles, 9 Cir., 47 F.2d 528.

[6, 7] We find no merit in appellant's contention that enforcement of this ordinance would entail any unjust discrimination, or would be tantamount to depriving it of its property without due process merely because the site was acquired and improved at considerable expense before the zoning ordinance was enacted. The general rule here applicable is that considerations of financial loss or of so-called "vested rights" in private property are insufficient to outweigh the necessity for legitimate exercise of the police power of a municipality. Hadacheck v. Sebastian, 239 U.S. 394, 36 S.Ct. 143, 60 L.Ed. 348; Ann.Cas.1917B, 927; Reinman v. City of Little Rock, 237 U.S. 171, 35 S.Ct. 511, 59 L.Ed. 900; Village of Euclid v. Ambler Realty Co., 272 U.S. 365, 47 S.Ct. 114, 71 L.Ed. 303, 54 A.L.R. 1016; Knowles v. Central Allapattae Properties, 145 Fla. 123, 198 So. 819; See also, State ex rel. Oil Service Co. v. Stark, 96 W.Va. 176, 122 S.E. 533; Atlantic Coast Line R. R. Co. v. City of Goldsboro, 232 U.S. 548, 34 S.Ct. 364, 58 L.Ed. 721; Chicago & A. R. Co. v. Tranbarger, 238 U.S. 67, 35 S.Ct. 678, 59 L.Ed. 204; Cf. City of West Palm Beach v. Edward U. Roddy Corporation, Fla., 43 So.2d 709.

The judgment is

Affirmed.

HUTCHESON, Chief Judge (dissenting).

With the principles announced in the majority opinion I am in complete accord. Agreeing fully, though, with Captain Cuttle's famous *dictum*, "The bearings of that observation lies in the application of it," I must dissent from the application of the principles to the facts of this case as testified to and as found by the trial court.

Fully canvassing the evidence in the light of the contentions made and specifically rejecting those that the ordinance promoted health, safety, or morals, the court, though he agreed with the defendant that the value of his property would be ruined and that the zoned property was not adapted to the use for which it was zoned, to-wit, residence property, yet sustained the ordinance on two considerations, which were inadequate to sustain it. One of these, a consideration of fact, was that the property was within close proximity to the state capitol, several state office buildings and a public school. The other, a consideration of law, was that the court should not substitute its judgment for that of the legislative body of the city.

In view of the decision in Standard Oil Co. v. Bowling Green, 244 Ky. 362, 50 S.W.2d 960, 86 A.L.R. 648 and of the two decisions of the Supreme Court of Florida, relied on by appellant and decided since the decision of this case below,[1] in all of which the court, recognizing that even in this age of enlightenment the Constitution still protects the citizen against arbitrary and unreasonable action, I am in no doubt that in sustaining this admittedly confiscatory ordinance, a good general principle, the public interest in zoning, has been run into the ground, the tail of legislative confiscation by caprice has been permitted to wag the dog of judicial constitutional protection.

On Petition for Rehearing

PER CURIAM.

A majority of the Judges who originally heard and participated in the decision of the above styled and numbered cause are of opinion the decision was correct, and the petition for rehearing is therefore Denied.

Questions and Notes

1. Where was the land involved?
2. How long was the period for amortization?
3. How was the land zoned during this period?
4. Were other filling stations affected by the same regulations? How did they react?
5. Did the courts regard this case as presenting a serious and difficult question?
6. The Florida decisions cited have nothing whatever to do with the case.

---

1. City of West Palm Beach v. Edward U. Roddy Corp., 43 So.2d 709; City of Miami v. First Trust Co., 45 So.2d 681.

LOS ANGELES

v.

GAGE

127 Cal. App. 2d 442, 274 P.2d 34(1954).

District Court of Appeal, Second District,

Division 3, California.

Sept. 16, 1954.

Hearing Denied Nov. 10, 1954.

City brought action against owners of realty to enjoin use of realty in violation of zoning ordinance of city. The Superior Court of Los Angeles

County, Joseph W. Vickers, J., entered judgment adverse to city, and city appealed. The District Court of Appeal, Vallée, J., held that city zoning ordinance requiring discontinuance of nonconforming uses of land in city within five year period and discontinuance of nonconforming commercial and industrial uses of residential buildings in residential zones within the same five year period, was a constitutional exercise of the police power in so far as it required discontinuance of wholesale and retail plumbing business, which had been established prior to enactment of ordinance, in residence district, and was not clearly arbitrary, or unreasonable, and did not constitutionally impair property rights of owners.

Judgment reversed and Superior Court directed to render judgment for city.

Roger Arnebergh, City Atty., Bourke Jones, Alan G. Campbell, Asst. City Attys., Alfred E. Rogers, Deputy City Atty., for appellant.

Clyde P. Harrell, Jr., Tarzana, for respondents.

VALLÉE, Justice.

This appeal involves the constitutionality of the provisions of a zoning ordinance which require that certain nonconforming existing uses shall be discontinued within five years after its passage, as they apply to defendants' property.

Plaintiff brought this suit for an injunction to command defendants to discontinue their use of certain property for the conduct of a plumbing business and to remove various materials therefrom, and to restrain them from using the property for any purpose not permitted by the comprehensive zoning plan provisions of the Los Angeles Municipal Code. The cause was submitted to the trial court on admissions in the pleadings and a stipulation of facts. Defendants will be referred to as "Gage."

In 1930 Gage acquired adjoining lots 220 and 221 located on Cochran Avenue in Los Angeles. He constructed a two-family residential building on lot 221 and rented the upper half solely for residential purposes. He established a wholesale and retail plumbing supply business on the property. He used a room in the lower half of the residential building on lot 221 as the office for the conduct of the business, and the rest of the lower half for residential purposes for himself and his family; he used a garage on lot 221 for the storage of plumbing supplies and materials; and he constructed and used racks, bins, and stalls for the storage of such supplies and materials on lot 220. Later Gage incorporated defendant company. The realty and the assets of the plumbing business were transferred to the company. The case is presented as though the property had been owned continuously from 1930 to date by the same defendant. The use of lots 220 and 221 begun in 1930 has been substantially the same at all times since.

In 1930 the two lots and other property facing on Cochran Avenue in their vicinity were classified in "C" zone by the zoning ordinance then in effect. Under this classification the use to which Gage put the property was permitted. Shortly after Gage acquired lots 220 and 221, they were classified in "C-3" zone and the use to which he put the property was expressly permitted. In 1936 the city council of the city passed Ordinance 77,000 which contained a comprehensive zoning plan for the city. Ordinance 77,000 re-enacted the prior ordinances with respects to the use of lots 220 and 221. In 1941 the city council passed Ordinance 85,015 by the terms of which the use of a residential building for the conduct of an office in connection with the plumbing supply business was permitted. Ordinance 85,015 prohibited the open storage of materials in zone "C-3" but permitted such uses as had been established to continue as nonconforming uses. The use to which lots 220 and 221 was put by defendants was a nonconforming use that might be continued. In 1946 the city council passed Ordinance 90,500. This ordinance reclassified lots 220 and 221 and other property fronting on Cochran Avenue in their vicinity from zone "C-3" to zone "R-4" (Multiple dwelling zone). Use of lots 220 and 221 for the conduct of a plumbing business was not permitted in zone "R-4." At the time Ordinance 90,500 was passed, and at all times since, the Los Angeles Municipal Code (§ 12.23 B & C) provided: "(a) The nonconforming use of a conforming building or structure may be continued, except that in the 'R' Zones any nonconforming commercial or industrial use of a residential building or residential accessory building shall be discontinued within five (5) years from June 1, 1946, or five (5) years from the date the use becomes nonconforming, whichever date is later. * * *

"(a) The nonconforming use of land shall be discontinued within five (5) years from June 1, 1946, or within five (5) years from the date the use became nonconforming, in each of the following cases: (1) where no buildings are employed in connection with such use; (2) where the only buildings employed are accessory or incidental to such use; (3) where such use is maintained in connection with a conforming building."

Prior to the passage of Ordinance 90,500, about 50% of the city had been zoned. It was the first ordinance which "attempted to zone the entire corporate limits of the city." Prior to its passage, several thousand exceptions and variances, were granted from restrictive provisions of prior ordinances, some of which permitted commercial use of property zoned for residential use, "and in some cases permitted the use of land for particular purposes like or similar to use of subject property which otherwise would have been prohibited." Under Ordinance 90,500, the uses permitted by these exceptions and variances that did not carry a time limit may be continued indefinitely.

The business conducted by Gage on the property has produced a gross revenue varying between $125,000 and $350,000 a year. If he is required to abandon the use of the property for his business, he will be put to the following expenses: "(1) The value of a suitable site for the conduct of its business would be about $10,000; which would be offset by the value of $7,500 of the lot now used. (2) The cost incident to removing of supplies to another location and construction of the necessary racks, sheds, bins and stalls which would be about $2,500. (3) The cost necessary to expend to advertise a new location. (4) The risk of a gain or a loss of business while moving, and the cost necessary to reestablish the business at a new location, the amount of which is uncertain."

The noise and disturbance caused by the loading and unloading of supplies, trucking, and the going and coming of workmen in connection with the operation of a plumbing business with an open storage yard is greater than the noise and disturbance that is normal in a district used solely for residential purposes.

The court found: the business conducted by Gage has a substantial value; he could not, either prior to June 1, 1951, or at any time thereafter or in the future, remove the business without substantial loss or expense; the value of Gage's property has not been increased or stabilized by the passage of Ordinance 90,500, nor will observance or enforcement of the ordinance increase the value of the property; the use of the property for the purpose that it has been used continuously since 1930 will not adversely and detrimentally effect the use or value of other property in the neighborhood thereof; the use to which the property has been put by Gage has not been unsanitary, unsightly, noisy, or otherwise incompatible with the legal uses of adjoining property; Gage has not, nor will he in the future, operate to disturb the peace and quiet of the residents of the neighborhood as long as the property is operated substantially as it was operated at the date of the filing of the complaint; the use to which the property has been put does not interfere with the lawful and reasonable use of the streets and alleys in the vicinity by the residents in the neighborhood or others entitled thereto.

The court concluded: Gage became vested with the right to use the property for the purpose that it was used; insofar as the Los Angeles Municipal Code purports to require the abandonment of the use of the building on lot 221 as an office for the plumbing and plumbing supply business or the use of lot 220 for the open storage of plumbing supplies in the manner that it has been and is being used by Gage, it is void and of no legal effect; Ordinance 90,500 is void insofar as it affects Gage's use of the property in that it deprives him of a vested right to use the property for the purpose it has been used continuously since 1930 and deprives him of property without due process of law. Judgment was that plaintiff take nothing. Plaintiff appeals.

Plaintiff contends that the mandatory discontinuance of a nonconforming use after a fixed period is a reasonable exercise of the police power, and that on the agreed facts the Los Angeles ordinance is a valid exercise of such power as applied to Gage's property. Gage does not question the validity of the ordinance as a whole, but he contends it may not be constitutionally applied to require the removal of his existing business. He asserts that under Jones v. City of Los Angeles, 211 Cal. 304, 295 P. 14, the decision of the trial court was correct.

[1-5] When a cause is submitted to a trial court on an agreed statement of facts without any other evidence, findings of fact are unnecessary; the only question before the trial court is the law applicable to the agreed facts; and on review any findings of fact may be disregarded. Crawford v. Imperial Irrigation Dist., 200 Cal. 318, 335, 253 P. 726. However, where the stipulation sets forth evidentiary material only, it is proper for the trial court to make findings of the ultimate facts. Taylor v. George, 34 Cal.2d 552, 556, 212 P.2d 505. In the present case the agreed facts consist of admissions in the answer and the stipulation of facts comprising evidentiary material only, including a number of exhibits which are photographs of defendants' property and property in its vicinity and a map showing the uses made of all of the property within 500 feet in all directions from lots 220 and 221. If the findings are supported by any substantial evidence the judgment may not be disturbed. However, if only one conclusion can be reasonably drawn from the agreed facts and that conclusion is that Ordinance 90,500 is a valid exercise of the police power as applied to defendants' property—the findings must be disregarded and the judgment reversed.

[6-9] Zoning laws are enacted in the exercise of the police power. Miller v. Board of Public Works, 195 Cal. 477, 485-488, 234 P. 381, 38 A.L.R. 1479. A zoning law is presumptively valid, and the burden is on the one assailing it to overcome the presumption. Hart v. City of Beverly Hills, 11 Cal.2d 343, 348, 79 P.2d 1080; Sunny Slope Water Co. v. City of Pasadena, 1 Cal.2d 87, 92, 33 P.2d 672; City of Yuba City v. Cherniavsky, 117 Cal.App. 568, 572, 4 P.2d 299. The police power is not restricted to the suppression of nuisances. It includes the regulation of the use of property to the end that the public health, morals, safety, and general welfare may not be impaired or endangered. Zoning deals with many uses of property which are in no way harmful. Ex parte Hadacheck, 165 Cal. 416, 419, 132 P. 584, L.R.A.1916B, 1248; Miller v. Board of Public Works, 195 Cal. 477, 485, 234 P. 381, 38 A.L.R. 1479. A municipality has the power to establish and maintain residential and quasi-residential districts, and to exclude therefrom all nonconforming and conflicting uses. 12 Cal.Jur. 10 Yr. Supp. 147, § 8, and cases there cited.

[10, 11] The power to declare a zoning ordinance unconstitutional should be exercised only where no reason exists to support the determination of the legislative body. In passing upon the validity of legislation "the rule is well settled that the legislative determination that the facts exist which make the law necessary must not be set aside or disregarded by the courts, unless the legislative decision is clearly and palpably wrong and the error appears beyond reasonable doubt from facts or evidence which cannot be controverted, and of which the courts may properly take

notice." Matter of the Application of Miller, 162 Cal. 687, 696, 124 P. 427, 429.

"In considering the scope or nature of appellate review in a case of this type we must keep in mind the fact that the courts are examining the act of a coordinate branch of the government—the legislative—in a field in which it has paramount authority, and not reviewing the decision of a lower tribunal or of a fact-finding body. Courts have nothing to do with the wisdom of laws or regulations, and the legislative power must be upheld unless manifestly abused so as to infringe on constitutional guaranties. The duty to uphold the legislative power is as much the duty of appellate courts as it is of trial courts, and under the doctrine of separation of powers neither the trial nor appellate courts are authorized to 'review' legislative determinations. The only function of the courts is to determine whether the exercise of legislative power has exceeded constitutional limitations. As applied to the case at hand, the function of this court is to determine whether the record shows a reasonable basis for the action of the zoning authorities, and, if the reasonableness of the ordinance is fairly debatable, the legislative determination will not be disturbed." Lockard v. City of Los Angeles, 33 Cal.2d 453, 461, 202 P.2d 38, 43, 7 A.L.R.2d 990.

[12, 13] The Fourteenth Amendment to the Constitution of the United States does not impair the police power of a municipality. Barbier v. Connolly, 113 U.S. 27, 5 S.Ct. 357, 28 L.Ed. 923, 925. Whether a zoning ordinance is unreasonable, arbitrary and discriminatory is related to its application to the particular property involved. Morris v. City of Los Angeles, 116 Cal.App.2d 856, 861, 254 P.2d 935. Each case must be determined on its own facts. Livingston Rock, etc., Co. v. County of Los Angeles, 43 Cal. 2d —, —, 272 P.2d 4.

[14-18] The fact that various exceptions and variances were granted under zoning ordinances prior to Ordinance 90,500, and that some of them permitted the use of land for particular purposes like or similar to the use of defendants' property which otherwise would have been prohibited, presents a question for the zoning authorities of the city. They are the persons charged with the duty of deciding whether the conditions in other parts of the city require like prohibition. Ex parte Hadacheck, 165 Cal. 416, 420, 132 P. 584, L.R.A. 1916B, 1248; Lockard v. City of Los Angeles, 33 Cal.2d 453, 465, 202 P.2d 38, 7 A.L.R.2d 990; County of San Diego v. McClurken, 37 Cal.2d 683, 691, 234 P.2d 972; Beverly Oil Co. v. City of Los Angeles, 40 Cal.2d 552, 560, 254 P.2d 865. The mere fact that a prior ordinance excepts a parcel of land in a residential district does not give the owner thereof a vested right to have the exception continued so as to entitle him, on that ground, to attack the validity of a later ordinance repealing the former. Marblehead Land Co. v. City of Los Angeles, 9 Cir., 47 F.2d 528, certiorari denied 284 U.S. 634, 52 S.Ct. 18, 76 L.Ed. 540.

A zoning ordinance may be amended from time to time as new and changing conditions warrant revision. Jardine v. City of Pasadena, 199 Cal. 64, 76, 248 P. 225, 48 A.L.R. 509. The fact that nearby business property has the same characteristics as the parcels involved in the proceeding does not justify the court in substituting its judgment for the judgment of the city council. Reynolds v. Barrett, 12 Cal.2d 244, 249, 83 P.2d 29. Permitting some persons to violate a zoning regulation does not preclude its enforcement against others. Donovan v. City of Santa Monica, 88 Cal.App.2d 386, 396, 199 P.2d 51; Annotation 119 A.L.R. 1509, 1517. The adaptability and suitability of defendants' property for business purposes is not controlling. The best interests of the entire district is the controlling factor. Reynolds v. Barrett, 12 Cal.2d 244, 250, 83 P.2d 29.

[19-22] The right of a city council, in the exercise of the police power, to regulate or, in proper cases, to prohibit the conduct of a given business, is not limited by the fact that the value of investments made in the business prior to any legislative actions will be greatly diminished. A business which, when established, was entirely unobjectionable, may, by the growth or change in the character of the neighborhood, become a source of danger to the public health, morals, safety, or general welfare of those who have come to be occupants of the surrounding territory. Ex parte Hadacheck, 165 Cal. 416, 420, 421, 132 P. 584, L.R.A.1916B, 1248; Curtis v. City of Los Angeles, 172 Cal. 230, 234, 156 P. 462; Brown v. City of Los Angeles, 183 Cal. 783, 785-786, 192 P. 716; Miller v. Board of Public Works, 195 Cal. 477, 486-489, 234 P. 381, 38 A.L.R. 1479; In re Ellis, 11 Cal.2d 571, 574, 81 P.2d 911. The effect of zoning restrictions may be to depreciate sharply the value of a particular parcel.[1] The mere fact that some hardship is experienced is not material since "Every exercise of the police power is apt to affect adversely the property interest of somebody." Zahn v. Board of Public Works, 195 Cal. 497, 512, 234 P. 388, 394. An individual cannot complain of incidental injury if the police power is exercised for proper purposes of health, safety, morals, or general welfare, and if there is no arbitrary and unreasonable application in the particular case. Wilkins v. City of San Bernardino, 29 Cal.2d 332, 338, 175 P.2d 542. Damage caused by the proper exercise of the police power is merely one of the prices an individual must pay as a member of society.

[23, 24] A nonconforming use is a lawful use existing on the effective date of the zoning restriction and continuing since that time in noncon-

---

1. In Village of Euclid v. Ambler Realty Co., 272 U.S. 365, 47 S.Ct. 114, 71 L.Ed. 303, 54 A.L.R. 1016, the Supreme Court of the United States sustained zoning restrictions on vacant land with the effect that value was reduced from $10,000 to $2,500 an acre.

formance to the ordinance. A provision permitting the continuance of a nonconforming use is ordinarily included in zoning ordinances because of the hardship and doubtful constitutionality of compelling the immediate discontinuance of nonconforming uses. County of San Diego v. McClurken, 37 Cal.2d 683, 686, 234 P.2d 972; Wilkins v. City of San Bernardino, 29 Cal.2d 332, 175 P.2d 542; Rehfeld v. City and County of San Francisco, 218 Cal. 83, 84, 21 P.2d 419. It is generally held that a zoning ordinance may not operate to immediately suppress or remove from a particular district an otherwise lawful business or use already established therein. 58 Am.Jur. 1022, § 148.

No case seems to have been decided in this state squarely involving the precise question presented in the case at bar. Until recently zoning ordinances have made no provision for any systematic and comprehensive elimination of the nonconforming use. The expectation seems to have been that existing nonconforming uses would be of little consequence and that they would eventually disappear. See 9 Minn.L.Rev. 593, 598. The contrary appears to be the case. 35 Va.L.Rev. 348, 352; Wis.L.Rev. (1951) 685; 99 Univ.Pa.L.Rev. 1019, 1021. It is said that the fundamental problem facing zoning is the inability to eliminate the nonconforming use. 17 Ill.Munic.Rev. 221, 232.[2] The general purpose of present-day zoning ordinances is to eventually end all nonconforming uses. Ricciardi v. County of Los Angeles, 115 Cal.App.2d 569, 576, 252 P.2d 773. There is a growing tendency to guard against the indefinite continuance of nonconforming uses by providing for their liquidation within a prescribed period. County of San Diego v. McClurken, 37 Cal. 2d 683, 686, 234 P.2d 972. It is said, "The only positive method of getting rid of nonconforming uses yet devised is to amortize a non-conforming building. That is, to determine the normal useful remaining life of the building and prohibit the owner from maintaining it after the expiration of that time." Crolly and Norton, Termination of Nonconforming Uses, 62 Zoning Bulletin 1, Regional Plan Assn., June 1952.

Amortization of nonconforming uses has been expressly authorized by recent amendments to zoning enabling laws in a number of states. Ordinances providing for amortization of nonconforming uses have been passed

---

2. "It has always been assumed that nonconforming uses would gradually eliminate themselves from the district in which they exist if they were not permitted to expand. Such has not proven to be the case. They not merely continue to exist, but to send down deeper roots. They become clear monopolies and special privileges. Their existence is a continual threat to the conservation of property values in the districts where they exist. The time has come when cognizance should be taken of this situation and provision made, probably in the state law, whereby non-conforming uses may be gradually eliminated under some equitable method of procedure." Bartholomew, The Zoning of Illinois Municipalities, 17 Ill.Munic.Rev. 221, 232.

in a number of large cities.[3] The length of time given the owner to eliminate his nonconforming use or building varies with the city and with the type of structure. In Austin v. Older, 283 Mich. 667, 278 N.W. 727, 730, it is said: "Certainly the maximum benefit of zoning ordinances cannot be obtained as long as nonconforming businesses remain within residential districts, and their gradual elimination is within the police power. DeVito v. Pearsall, 115 N.J.L. 323, 180 A. 202; Thayer v. Board of Appeals of City of Hartford, 114 Conn. 15, 157 A. 273, 276; Rehfeld v. City [and County] of San Francisco, 218 Cal. 83, 21 P.2d 419 420."

In State ex rel. Dema Realty Co. v. McDonald, 168 La. 172, 121 So. 613, the defendants had used their property as a retail grocery store for a great many years prior to 1927. In 1927 the city passed a zoning ordinance which established the area in which the property was located as a residential district and provided that all businesses then in operation within that area should be liquidated within one year from the passage of the ordinance. It was contended that this provision was unconstitutional as being arbitrary and unreasonable, and that it amounted to a taking of the defendants' property without due process of law. After referring to, and quoting at some length from, Village of Euclid v. Ambler Realty Co., 272 U.S. 365, 47 S.Ct. 114, 71 L.Ed. 303, 54 A.L.R. 1016, the first case in which the Supreme Court of the United States considered and upheld the validity of a zoning ordinance, the court stated, 121 So. 617: "It is be to observed, too, that the ordinance there under consideration provided for the establishment and maintenance of residential districts from which every kind of business was excluded. The ordinance did not deal specially with any already established business in the zoned district. But, if the village had the authority to create and to maintain a purely residential district, which the court held it did have, and if such an ordinance was not arbitrary and unreasonable, it follows necessarily that the village was vested with the authority to remove any business or trade from the district and to fix a limit of time in which the same shall be done." The Supreme Court of the United States denied certiorari. 280 U.S. 556, 50 S.Ct. 16, 74 L.Ed. 612. In State ex rel. Dema Realty Co. v. Jacoby, 168 La. 752, 123 So. 314, the validity of a zoning ordinance of New Orleans was attacked. The ordinance prohibited any business establishment from operating within a prescribed area, and gave all businesses in operation at the time one year in which to liquidate. The defendant had operated a small retail drugstore on her property for some

---

3. Chicago, Ill. Zoning Ord. § 20 (1944); Mass.Acts 1948, c. 214, § 9; Cleveland, Ohio, Ord. § 1281-9(c) (1930); New Orleans, La., Zoning Ord.; Richmond, Va. Zoning Ord. Art. XIII, § 1 (1948); Seattle, Wash. See State ex rel. Miller v. Cain, 40 Wash.2d 216, 243 P.2d 505, 507; Tallahassee, Fla. See Standard Oil Co. v. City of Tallahassee, 5 Cir., 183 F.2d 410; Wichita, Kan. Zoning Ord. § 24 (1948).

time prior to the passage of the ordinance. She disregarded the ordinance. The court said, 123 So. 316: "It is also suggested that the ordinance is unconstitutional, because it grants only one year to liquidate and close an established business in the district. Defendant's drug store is a small one, and it is obvious that one year affords ample time within which to liquidate the business and close it. The validity of that provision of the ordinance was decided unfavorably to defendant's contention in State ex rel. Dema Realty Co. v. McDonald, supra. [168 La. 172, 121 So. 613.]"

In Standard Oil Co. v. City of Tallahassee, 5 Cir., 183 F.2d 410, the plaintiff was operating a motor vehicle service station at the time the area in which it was located was, by a zoning ordinance, made a residence district. The ordinance, adopted in April 1948, provided that all locations then used for motor vehicle service stations should be discontinued as such on and after January 1, 1949. In upholding the validity of the ordinance the court stated, 183 F.2d at page 413: "The power of a municipality to require by ordinance the discontinuance of an existing property use also appears to be well established law in Florida. [Citations.] Here, plaintiff's service station is near the State Capitol and the State Supreme Court Building, as well as several other state office buildings and a public school. It therefore becomes manifest that its discontinuance under the ordinance cannot be viewed as arbitrary and unreasonable, or as having no relation to the safety and general welfare of the community affected. [Citations.] We find no merit in appellant's contention that enforcement of this ordinance would entail any unjust discrimination, or would be tantamount to depriving it of its property without due process merely because the site was acquired and improved at considerable expense before the zoning ordinance was enacted. The general rule here applicable is that considerations of financial loss or of so-called 'vested rights' in private property are insufficient to outweigh the necessity for legitimate exercise of the police power of a municipality." The Supreme Court of the United States denied certiorari. 340 U.S. 892, 71 S.Ct. 208, 95 L.Ed. 647. See, also, People v. Miller, 304 N.Y. 105, 106 N.E.2d 34; Bazinsky v. Kesbec, Inc., 259 App.Div. 467, 19 N.Y.S.2d 716. There is one case to the contrary. City of Akron v. Chapman, 160 Ohio St. 382, 116 N.E.2d 697. See comment on this case, 67 Harv.L.Rev. 1283.

In Livingston Rock, etc., Co. v. County of Los Angeles, 43 Cal.2d—, —, 272 P.2d 4, 8, the court stated: "However, zoning legislation looks to the future in regulating district development and the eventual liquidation of nonconforming uses within a prescribed period commensurate with the investment involved. * * * Here the rezoning permits plaintiffs to continue their nonconforming use of the property for twenty years as an 'automatic exception' to the rezoning restrictions, § 531, supra; Edmonds v. County of Los Angeles, supra, 40 Cal.2d 642, 651, 255 P.2d 772, but

authorizes revocation of such exception where it can be done without the
impairment of 'constitutional rights' (§ 533, supra). Manifestly, care has
been taken in such rezoning regulations to refrain from the interference
with constitutional guarantees, and in the light of such express language
it would be a contradiction in terms to hold that the regulations are nevertheless unconstitutional."

Jones v. City of Los Angeles, 211 Cal. 304, 295 P. 14, relied on by Gage,
held unconstitutional, as applied to existing establishments, an ordinance
making it unlawful to erect, operate, or maintain, in certain residential
areas, a sanitarium for the treatment of persons suffering from mental or
nervous diseases. The Jones case was distinguished in the recent case of
Livingston Rock, etc., Co. v. County of Los Angeles, supra, 43 Cal.2d—,
272 P.2d 4. In the Livingston case an ordinance of the County of Los
Angeles allowed certain existing nonconforming uses to continue for 20
years unless such exception should be revoked as provided in the ordinance. One ground of revocation specified was if the use was so exercised "as to be detrimental to the public health or safety, or so as to be
a nuisance." Distinguishing the Jones case the court said, 43 Cal.2d—,
272 P.2d 8: "Moreover, the ordinance under consideration in the Jones
case differed materially from the one here involved. There the ordinance,
cast in the form of a penal statute rather than in the form of a comprehensive zoning law, prohibited the maintenance of sanitariums of a certain
type in designated districts. By its terms the ordinance, unlike the ordinary zoning laws, purported to have both a retroactive as well as a prospective effect, thereby automatically prohibiting the continued maintenance
of several established sanitariums representing large investments. In other
words, no provisions was made for any automatic exception for existing
nonconforming uses. In the present case, the zoning ordinance does
provide for automatic exceptions of reasonable duration for existing nonconforming uses, subject, however, to earlier revocation of the automatic
exception if the use for which approval was granted is so exercised 'as
to be detrimental to the public health or safety, or so as to be a nuisance'
(§ 649, supra); and the power to determine, upon notice, the question of
whether the property was being so used was vested in the Regional Planning Commission." Assuming, as suggested by Gage, that the foregoing
was dictum, we think it a correct statement of the distinction between the
Jones case and the case at bar. There are other differences between Jones
and the present case. There the regulation was of one type of commercial use. Here the regulation is of all commercial uses. There the ordinance affected a substantial investment in land and special buildings
designed and built for the use to which they were being put. Here the
ordinance affects only the use of land and the nonconforming use of a
conforming building. The building has been, and may continue to be,
used for the purpose for which it was designed and built. There the

property could not have been used immediately for other purposes. Here the property can be used immediately for the uses for which it is zoned. In the Jones case the court said 211 Cal. at pages 319, 321, 295 P. at page 21: "We do not mean to hold that those engaged in the zoning of cities must always be faced with the impossibility of eradicating the nonconforming uses. ° ° ° Our conclusion is that where, as here, a retroactive ordinance causes *substantial* injury and the prohibited business is not a nuisance, the ordinance is to that extent an unreasonable and unjustifiable exercise of police power." (Italics added.)

[25-27] The theory in zoning is that each district is an appropriate area for the location of the uses which the zone plan permits in that area, and that the existence or entrance of other uses will tend to impair the development and stability of the area for the appropriate uses. The public welfare must be considered from the standpoint of the objective of zoning and of all the property within any particular use district. Rehfeld v. City and County of San Francisco, 218 Cal. 83, 85, 21 P.2d 419. It was not and is not contemplated that pre-existing nonconforming uses are to be perpetual. State ex rel. Miller v. Cain, 40 Wash.2d 216, 242 P.2d 505. The presence of any nonconforming use endangers the benefits to be derived from a comprehensive zoning plan. Having the undoubted power to establish residential districts, the legislative body has the power to make such classification really effective by adopting such reasonable regulations as would be conducive to the welfare, health, and safety of those desiring to live in such district and enjoy the benefits thereof. There would be no object in creating a residential district unless there were to be secured to those dwelling therein the advantages which are ordinarily considered the benefits of such residence. It would seem to be the logical and reasonable method of approach to place a time limit upon the continuance of existing nonconforming uses, commensurate with the investment involved and based on the nature of the use; and in cases of nonconforming structures, on their character, age, and other relevant factors.

Exercise of the police power frequently impairs rights in property because the exercise of those rights is detrimental to the public interest. Every zoning ordinance effects some impairment of vested rights either by restricting prospective uses or by prohibiting the continuation of existing uses, because it affects property already owned by individuals at the time of its enactment. People v. Miller, 304 N.Y. 105, 106 N.E.2d 34, 35. In essence there is no distinction between requiring the discontinuance of a nonconforming use within a reasonable period and provisions which deny the right to add to or extend buildings devoted to an existing nonconforming use, which deny the right to resume a nonconforming use after a period of nonuse, which deny the right to extend or enlarge an existing nonconforming use, which deny the right to substitute new buildings for those devoted to an existing nonconforming use—all of which have been held to be valid exercises of the police power. See County of Orange v. Goldring, 121 Cal.App.2d 442, 263 P.2d 321; 58 Am.Jur. 1026, 1029, §§ 156, 158, 162; annotation 147 A.L.R. 167; 1 Yokley, Zoning Law and Practice, 2d ed., §§ 151-157.

The distinction between an ordinance restricting future uses and one requiring the termination of present uses within a reasonable period of time is merely one of degree, and constitutionality depends on the relative importance to be given to the public gain and to the private loss. Zoning as it affects every piece of property is to some extent retroactive in that it applies to property already owned at the time of the effective date of the ordinance. The elimination of existing uses within a reasonable time does not amount to a taking of property nor does it necessarily restrict the use of property so that it cannot be used for any reasonable purpose. Use of a reasonable amortization scheme provides an equitable means of reconciliation of the conflicting interests in satisfaction of due process requirements. As a method of eliminating existing nonconforming uses it allows the owner of the nonconforming use, by affording an opportunity to make new plans, at least partially to offset any loss he might suffer. The loss he suffers, if any, is spread out over a period of years, and he enjoys a monopolistic position by virtue of the zoning ordinance as long as he remains. If the amortization period is reasonable the loss to the owner may be small when compared with the benefit to the public. Nonconforming uses will eventually be eliminated. A legislative body may well conclude that the beneficial effect on the community of the eventual elimination of all nonconforming uses by a reasonable amortization plan more than offsets individual losses.

The ordinance in question provides, according to a graduated periodic schedule, for the gradual and ultimate elimination of all commercial and industrial uses in residential zones. These provisions require the discontinuance of nonconforming commercial and industrial uses of residential buildings in the "R" zones within the same five-year period. These provisions are the only ones pertinent to the decision in this case. However, it may be noted that other provisions of the ordinance require the discontinuance of nonconforming billboards and, in residential zones, the discontinuance of nonconforming buildings and of nonconforming uses of nonconforming buildings, within specified periods running from 20 to 40 years according to the type of building construction.

We have no doubt that Ordinance 90,500, in compelling the discontinuance of the use of defendants' property for a wholesale and retail plumbing and plumbing supply business, and for the open storage of plumbing supplies within five years after its passage, is a valid exercise of the police power. Lots 220 and 221 are several blocks from a business center and it appears that they are not within any reasonable or logical extension of such a center. The ordinance does not prevent the operation of defendants' business; it merely restricts its location. Discontinuance of the non-conforming use requires only that Gage move his plumbing business to property that is zoned for it. Such property can be found within a half mile of Gage's property. The cost of moving is $5,000, or less than 1% of Gage's minimum gross business for five years, or less than half of 1% of the mean of his gross business for five years. He has had eight years within which to move. The property is usable for residential purpose. Since 1930 lot 221 has been used for residential purposes. All of the land within 500 feet of Gage's property is now improved and used for such purposes. Lot 220, now unimproved, can be improved for the same purposes.

[28] We think it apparent that none of the agreed facts and none of the ultimate facts found by the court justify the conclusion that Ordinance 90,500, as applied to Gage's property, is clearly arbitrary or unreasonable, or has no substantial relation to the public's health, safety, morals, or general welfare, or that it is an unconstitutional impairment of his property rights.

It is enough for us to determine and we determine only that Ordinance 90,500 of the city of Los Angeles, insofar as it required the discontinuance of Gage's wholesale and retail plumbing business on lots 220 and 221 within five years from the date of its passage, is a constitutional exercise of the police power.

The judgment is reversed, and the superior court is directed to render judgment for plaintiff as prayed for in the complaint.

SHINN, P. J., and PARKER WOOD, J., concur.

LIVINGSTON ROCK & GRAVEL CO.

v.

LOS ANGELES COUNTY

260 P.2d 811 (1953), rev'd, District Court of Appeal, Second District,

43 Cal. 2d 121, 272 P.2d 4(1954).

Division 2, California.

Sept. 8, 1953.

Rehearing Denied Sept. 25, 1953.

Hearing Granted Nov. 5, 1953.

Action to enjoin a county from enforcing an ordinance rezoning an unlimited industrial district as a light manufacturing district so as to prohibit operation of plaintiffs' cement mixing plant therein. From a judgment of the Superior Court of Los Angeles County, J. T. B. Warne, J., for plaintiffs, defendant appealed. The District Court of Appeal, McComb, J., held that provisions of the ordinance, authorizing revocation of exceptions automatically granted thereby to permit continuation of particular existing uses of buildings or premises in the respective zones immediately before the ordinance became effective and revocation or modification of permits, exceptions or other approvals granted for uses so exercised as to be detrimental to public health or safety, were unconstitutional with respect to plaintiffs' plant as depriving them of vested property rights without due process of law and fair and reasonable compensation.

Judgment affirmed.

Harold W. Kennedy, County Counsel, and Edward H. Gaylord, Deputy County Counsel, Los Angeles, for appellant.

Denio, Hart, Taubman & Simpson, Long Beach, for respondents.

McCOMB, Justice,

From a judgment in favor of plaintiffs Livingston, in an action for an injunction to restrain the County of Los Angeles, hereinafter referred to as deendant, from enforcing certain provisions of the Los Angeles County zoning ordinance which would prohibit plaintiffs from conducting their cement mixing plant in an area of Los Angeles County known as the "Artesia Industrial District", defendant appeals.

Facts: On January 31, 1950, the Pacific Electric Corporation owned a parcel of land in Los Angeles County in a district designated as the Artesia Industrial District. Over it passed a main double track railway line with two separate spur tracks to serve the commercial and industrial plants on the adjoining land. The latter was held and used for industrial and manufacturing purposes exclusively, and was surrounded by lands being devoted to commercial, industrial and manufacturing uses. The Pacific Electric leased 20,000 square feet of their land to plaintiffs.

At such time and at all times prior to March 21, 1950, all of this land was by ordinance No. 1494 (new series), of the County of Los Angeles, zoned as being in zone M-3 (unlimited) with the provision that (except as otherwise provided in Article 4 of said ordinance, which is not here involved) any building, structure, improvement or premises might be erected, constructed, established, altered, enlarged, used, occupied or maintained thereon without restriction under the provisions of the ordinance as to use and occupancy.

Plaintiffs leased such property and erected thereon a batching plant for the loading of readymix concrete mixer trucks with concrete aggregates which use was then permissible in any M-3 zone in the County of Los Angeles. This plant was erected pursuant to building permit issued by the duly authorized building department of defendant and was completed prior to March 21, 1950. The plant cost $18,000 to erect and plaintiffs purchased $80,000 worth of mixer trucks to use with their plant. Since such date the plant and mixer trucks have been in continuous operations.

In the construction and operation of their plant, plaintiffs conformed to, complied with, and at all times now are complying with all requirements of the smog control and air pollution ordinances of Los Angeles County. In addition plaintiffs secured from the proper authority having control of smog and air pollution a permit authorizing the operation of their plant and certifying that after inspection it was found to be complying with all smog control and air pollution ordinances and requirements.

Defendant, by Urgency Ordinance adopted March 21, 1950, purported to rezone the Artesia Industrial District, theretofore in zone M-3 (unlimited), putting it in zone M-1 (light manufacturing).

On November 25, 1950, plaintiffs received a notice through the mail that a hearing would be held December 1, 1950, before the regional planning commission with reference to revocation of exception (Case No. 61).

The owner of the property, Pacific Electric Company, was never given any notice of this hearing.

On December 6, 1950, the regional planning commission sent plaintiffs a notice that it had revoked plaintiffs' right to operate their plant. Plaintiffs exhausted their administrative remedies before instituting the present action.

In addition to the foregoing facts the trial court found that plaintiffs by erecting and operating their plant had "acquired property rights which are entitled to protection against unconstitutional encroachments which will have the effect of depriving them of property without due process of law," and that defendant claims that by reason of the purported action of its regional planning comission, plaintiffs will lose all right to operate their plant and will be guilty of a criminal act if they continue operation.

[1-4] This appeal is upon the judgment roll alone.* Therefore our review is confined to a determination of whether (a) the complaint states a cause

---

* The fact that in the notice to the clerk to prepare a record, defendant requested in addition to the judgment roll, that there be included "that certain document entitled 'Return and Supplemental Return to Writ of Review and Affidavit' filed on August 4, 1952," does not change the character of the appeal. It still remains an appeal upon the judgment roll alone.

Mr. Presiding Justice White in Hunt v. Plavsa (hearing denied by the Supreme Court), 103 Cal.App.2d 222, 224 (1), 229 P.2d 482, 483, thus accurately states the rule:

"The present appeal is here upon the judgment roll. And as is said in Kompf v. Morrison, 73 Cal.App.2d 284, 286, 166 P.2d 350, 352. 'It is elementary and fundamental that on a clerk's transcript appeal the appellate court must conclusively presume that the evidence is ample to sustain the findings and that the only questions presented are as to the sufficiency of the pleadings and whether the findings support the judgment.' In this type of appeal, since 'the evidence is not before this court, we are confined to a determination of the questions as to whether the complaint states a cause of action; whether the findings are within the issues; whether the judgment is supported by the findings and whether reversible error appears upon the face of the record.' (Montaldo v. Hires Bottling Co., 59 Cal.App.2d 642, 646, 139

of action; (b) the findings are within the issue; (c) the judgment is supported by the findings and (d) whether reversible error appears upon the face of the record. (Hunt v. Plavsa, (hearing denied by the Supreme Court), 103 Cal. App.2d 222, 224 [2], 229 P.2d 482.)

In view of this rule, we are further limited under the circumstances of this case to be a determination of whether reversible error appears upon the face of the record.

The determination of the problem depends upon this question:

Were sections 533 and 649 of the county zoning ordinance, so far as applicable to plaintiffs, unconstitutional and was the order of the reg'onal planning commission thus void?

This question must be answered in the affirmative. The following are provisions of the urgency ordinance adopted March 21, 1950 by defendant purporting to change the Artesia Industrial District from zone M-3 to zone M-1:

"Section 531. Existing Uses.

"An exception is granted automatically, hereby, so as to permit the continuation of the particular existing uses of any building, structure, improvement or premises existing in the respective zones immediately prior to the time this ordinance or any amendment thereof becomes effective if such existing use was not in violation of this or any other ordinance or law.
❋ ❋ ❋

"Such exception shall remain in force and eff〜ct for the following length of time, except that it may be extended or revoked as provided in this article;

"(a) Where the property is unimproved, one year.

"(b) Where the property is unimproved except for structures to replace which said Ordinance No. 2225 does not require a building permit, three years.

"(c) In other cases twenty years, and for such longer time so that the total life of the improvement from date of construction will be:

❋   ❋   ❋

"Section 533. Revocation of Automatic Exception.

"In addition to other grounds stated in Article 2 of Chapter 6, an exception which has been automatically granted may be revoked if the Commission finds:

"(a) That the condition of the improvements, if any, on the property are such that to require the property to be used only for those uses permitted in the zone where it is located would not impair the constitutional rights of any person.

P.2d 666, 668). Appellants cannot, by designating for inclusion in the clerk's transcript documents not properly a part of the judgment roll, or by requesting that the exhibits received in evidence be transmitted to the appellate court, enlarge the scope of the appellate court's review. (In re Estate of Larson, 92 Cal.App.2d 267, 268, 269, 206 P.2d 852.)"

"(b) That the nature of the improvements are such that they can be altered so as to be used in conformity with the uses permitted in the zone in which such property is located without impairing the constitutional rights of any person.

"Section 649. Revocation.

"After a public hearing as provided for in this Article, the Commission may revoke or modify any permit, exception or other approval which has been granted either automatically or by special action of either the Board of Supervisors or the Commission, pursuant to either the provisions of this ordinance or of any ordinance superseded by this ordinance on any one or more of the following grounds:

               ❂   ❂   ❂

"(c) Except in the case of a dedicated cemetery, that the use for which the approval was granted is so exercised as to be detrimental to the public health or safety, or so as to be a nuisance."

[5] The 5th amendment to the Constitution of the United States reads in part: "No person shall be ❂ ❂ ❂ deprived of ❂ ❂ ❂ property, without due process of law."

The 14th amendment to the Constitution of the United States is to the same effect, and a similar provision apears in the Constitution of the State of California as Article 1, § 13.

The foregoing constitutional provisions protect plaintiffs in their vested property rights to conduct their lawful business in which they had engaged prior to the time the property on which their plant is located was placed in an M-1 zone. This rule has been established by our Supreme Court under similar circumstances in various cases. In County of San Diego v. Mc-Clurken, 37 Cal.2d 683, 691 [9], 234 P.2d 972, our Supreme Court held that an owner of real property who had legally undertaken construction of a building thereon before the effective date of a zoning ordinance might complete the building and use it for the purposes designated, which were legal at the date of the commencement of the building, after the effective date of the zoning ordinance restricting its uses to purposes other than that for which it had been originally intended.

[6, 7] A similar rule was stated in Jones v. City of Los Angeles, 211 Cal. 304, 309 [7], 295 P. 14, 17, in the following language: "In other words, does the broad view of the police power which justifies the taking away of the *right to engage* in *such businesses* in certain territory, also justify the *destruction of existing businesses?* We do not think that it does." And again 211 Cal. at page 321, 295 P. at page 22, " 'It has also been held that any regulation which deprives any person of the profitable use of his property constitutes a taking of property and entitles him under the Constitution to compensation, unless the invasion of rights is to slight as to permit the regulation to be justified under the police power. ❂ ❂ ❂ ' "

[8] In Édmonds v. County of Los Angeles, 40 Cal.2d 642, 255 P.2d 772, 777, our Supreme Court said: "The rights of users of property as those rights existed at the time of the adoption of a zoning ordinance are well recognized and have always been protected. (Yokley, Zoning Law and Practice § 132, p. 255.) Accordingly, a provision which exempts existing nonconforming uses is ordinarily included in zoning ordinances because of the hardship and doubtful constitutionality of compelling the immediate discontinuance of non-conforming uses. (County of San Diego v. McClurken, 37 Cal.2d 683, 686, 234 P.2d 972.)"

[9] Similarly, in Wilkins v. City of San Bernardino, 29 Cal.2d 332, 340, 175 P.2d 542, 548, Chief Justice Gibson, speaking for the court, says "An examination of the California decisions discloses that the cases in which zoning ordinances have been held invalid and unreasonable as applied to particular property fall roughly into four categories: 1. Where the zoning ordinance attempts to exclude and prohibit existing and established uses or businesses that are not nuisances (citing cases). 2. Where the restrictions create a monopoly (citing cases). 3. Where the use of adjacent property renders the land entirely unsuited to or unusable for the only purpose permitted by the ordinance (citing cases). 4. Where a small parcel is restricted and given less rights than the surrounding property, as where a lot in the center of a business or commercial district is limited to use for residential purposes, thereby creating an 'island' in the middle of a larger area devoted to other uses (citing cases)."

In the present case it was expressly admitted by defendant in its answer that it did not claim it had instituted any proceedings to abate a public nuisance as provided by section 3491 of the Civil Code.

[10] There is, of course, no merit in defendant's contention that plaintiffs were not being deprived of their property without just compensation, but that an automatic exception to the ordinance was merely being revoked. Such argument overlooks the basic facts in this case and says in effect that a rose by another name is not in fact a rose. In other words defendant may not do indirectly that which it could not do directly. Constitutional guaranties and rights may not be thus frittered away through specious reasoning.

[11] Mr. Justice Holmes, of the Supreme Court of the United States, in Pennsylvania Coal Co. v. Mahon, 260 U.S. 393, at page 416, 43 S.Ct. 158, at page 160 (67 L.Ed. 322) very aptly states, "We are in danger of forgetting that a strong public desire to improve the public condition is not enough to warrant achieving the desire by a shorter cut than the constitutional way of paying for the change."

[12] Applying the foregoing constitutional provisions in the light of the rules announced by the Supreme Court of California in the cases set forth above, it is evidence that the provisions of the ordinances as applied to the facts in this case were unconstitutional so far as plaintiffs' plant was concerned, and of course, that the order of the regional planning commission

was void. It is apparent that at the time plaintiffs erected their plant, made their investment in equipping it, and commenced to use it, its operation was perfectly legal, which fact was recognized in the urgency ordinance of defendant. It is likewise obvious that plaintiffs had a vested property right in the operation of their plant of which they could not be constitutionally deprived without due proces of law, which presupposes plaintiffs' being awarded a fair and reasonable compensation for the property rights of which defendant was attempting to deprive them.

In view of such conclusions it is unnecessary to discuss other points presented by counsel in their respective briefs for the reason that irrespective of the solutions the judgment, for the reasons set forth above, must be affirmed.

Affirmed.

MOORE, P. J., and FOX, J., concur.

LIVINGSTON ROCK & GRAVEL CO.

v.

COUNTY OF LOS ANGELES

43 Cal.2d 121, 272 P.2d 4 (1954).

Sept. 8, 1953.

Rehearing Denied Sept. 25, 1953.

Hearing Granted Nov. 5, 1953.

Supreme Court of California.

June 25, 1954.

Rehearing Denied July 21, 1954.

Action for an injunction against defendant county's interference with plaintiff's operation of a cement batching plant in an area rezoned by a county ordinance as a light manufacturing district after erection of the plant and for a declaration of the parties' rights and duties respecting the plant and determination of the construction and validity of the Regional Planning Commission's revocation of plaintiff's right to operate the plant. From a judgment of the Superior Court, Los Angeles County, J. T. B. Warne, J., granting an injunction, defendant appealed. The Supreme Court, Spence, J., held that provisions of the rezoning ordinance authorizing the Commission to revoke automatic exceptions of existing uses, are constitutional and within prescribed objectives of the police power and that plaintiff had an adequate remedy at law by certiorari or mandamus for review of the Commission's proceedings, so as to preclude injunctive or declaratory relief.

Judgment reversed.

Carter, Shenk and Schauer, JJ., dissented.

Prior opinion, 260 P.2d 811.

Harold W. Kennedy, County Counsel, Edward H. Gaylord, Deputy County Counsel, Los Angeles, for appellant.

Denio, Hart, Taubman & Simpson, Long Beach, for respondents.

SPENCE, Justice.

Plaintiffs sought to enjoin the county of Los Angeles from enforcing against them certain zoning ordinance provisions which would prohibit them from conducting a cement mixing plant in a rezoned district. They recovered judgment upon the premise that the ordinance provisions in question could not be constitutionally applied to require the removal of their existing business as a nonconforming use, and therefore "any action purportedly taken under * * * such provisions [was] invalid and [had] no effect as to * * * plaintiffs." Defendant challenges the propriety of this judgment on these grounds: (1) the ordinance provisions are not constitutionally objectionable in application to plaintiffs' business; and (2) plaintiffs' remedy is by writ of certiorari or mandamus, precluding injunctive or declaratory relief. Settled principles of law sustain defendant's position.

The Pacific Electric Railway Company owned a parcel of land in an area in Los Angeles County known as the Artesia Industrial District. The area was used exclusively for industrial and manufacturing purposes. Over Pacific Electric's land there passed a main double track railway line with two separate spur tracks to serve the neighboring commercial and industrial plants. On January 31, 1950, Pacific Electric leased 20,000 square feet of its land to plaintiffs. At that time all of this area was in an M-3 zone (unlimited), under ordinance No. 1494 (new series) of the county of Los Angeles, permitting any building structure or improvement to be erected, established or maintained thereon without restriction as to use or occupancy.

Plaintiffs erected on the leased property a batching plant for the loading of readymix concrete mixer trucks with concrete aggregates, a use then permissible in any M-3 zone in the county. The plant was erected pursuant to a building permit issued by the county building department and was completed prior to March 21, 1950. Plaintiffs complied with all the smog control and air pollution ordinances of the county, and they secured a permit authorizing the operation of their plant and certifying that after inspection, it had been found to be complying with these requirements. The plant cost $18,000 to build; $80,000 worth of mixer trucks were purchased; and both the plant and trucks have been in continuous operation.

On March 21, 1950, after the erection and operation of the plant and purchase of the trucks, the county adopted an urgency ordinance (No. 5508) rezoning the Artesia Industrial District into an M-1 zone (light manufacturing). Upon such rezoning, existing uses were protected as automatic exceptions (§ 531) with such structure as plaintiffs' plant allowed twenty years for continued use unless such time period should be extended or the automatic exception should be revoked as provided in the amending ordinance. Section 533 provided for the revocation of an automatic exception "if the [Regional Planning] Commission finds: (a) That the condition of the improvements, if any, on the property are such that to require the property to be used only for those uses permitted in the zone where it is located would not impair the constitutional rights of any person; (b) That the nature of the improvements are such that they can be altered so as to be used in conformity with the uses permitted in the zone in which such property is located without impairing the constitutional rights of any person." Section 649, as here material, authorized the planning commission, after a public hearing as therein provided, to "revoke or modify any permit, exception or other approval which has been granted either automatically or by special action of either the Board of Supervisors or the Commission, pursuant to * * * the provisions of [the] ordinance [where] (c) * * * the use for which the approval was granted is so exercised as to be detrimental to the public health or safety, or so as to be a nuisance."

On November 25, 1950, plaintiffs received a notice through the mail that a hearing would be held December 1, 1950, before the Regional Planning Commission with reference to the revocation of their exception. Pacific Electric, owner of the property, was never given notice of the hearing. Following the scheduled public hearing and on December 6, 1950, the planning commission notified plaintiffs that their "use of the property with a cement batching plant thereon" was "being exercised in such a manner as to be detrimental to public health, and so as to be a nuisance"; and that their right to operate their plant was therefore revoked "effective as of January 31st, 1952." On January 16, 1951, plaintiffs appealed to the county board of supervisors, which affirmed the planning commission's decision. In August, 1951, the board added to the basic zoning ordinance (No. 1494) section 404 of ordinance No. 5800, expressly confirming the expiration date on plaintiffs' exception as "January 31, 1952." Thereafter plaintiffs brought this action seeking (1) to enjoin defendant county from "interfering with" the operations of the cement batching plant "after January 31, 1952" and (2) to have the court "declare the rights and duties of plaintiffs and defendant with respect to the property and batching plant * * * and determine the construction and validity of the purported action taken by [the] Regional Planning Commission * * * "

Defendant admitted in its answer that its proceedings against plaintiffs were not taken under the provisions of section 3491 of the Civil Code relating to the abatement of a public nuisance but rather were instituted under authority of sections 533 and 649 of the zoning ordinance, supra, providing for the "revocation of automatic exceptions." The trial court determined that these sections, as well as section 404, supra, affirming the expiration date on plaintiffs' exception, were "invalid" in permitting "unconstitutional encroachments" upon plaintiffs' property rights and therefore "any action * * * taken" by the Regional Planning Commission "under * * * such provisions [was] invalid and [would] have no effect as to * * * plaintiffs." Upon such premise the court expressly refrained from making "any findings as to what occured at the hearing before the Regional Planning Commission on December 1, 1950, or whether or not there was any competent evidence at said hearing to prove any cause for revocation." Plaintiffs accordingly were granted the injunctive relief sought. Defendants attack the propriety of such judgment upon the merits as well as upon the procedural phases.

[1] It is well settled that zoning ordinances, when reasonable in object and not arbitrary in operation, constitute a justifiable exercise of the police power. Miller v. Board of Public Works, 195 Cal. 477, 487, 234 P. 381, 38 A.L.R. 1479; Acker v. Baldwin, 18 Cal.2d 341, 344, 115 P.2d 455; Wilkins v. City of San Bernardino, 29 Cal. 2d 332, 337, 175 P.2d 542. Plaintiffs concede the general validity of the zoning ordinance here as a whole but they contend that the rezoning amendment may not be constitutionally applied to require the removal of their existing business from the rezoned district. They maintain that their unlimited right to operate their cement batching plant in the district, a lawful use of the property as originaly zoned, could not be curtailed or limited by subsequent rezoning without violating the constitutional guarantee of due proces of law. They rely on Jones v. City of Los Angeles, 211 Cal. 304, 295 P. 14, wherein the court refused to apply retroactively, so as to destroy a valuable sanatorium business, an ordinance which prohibited such institutions in areas rezoned as residential. Under the particular circumstances of that case, showing "substantial injury" to be involved, 211 Cal. at page 321, 295 P. 14, it was deemed unreasonable and arbitrary to destroy the esablished enterprise. But each case must be determined on its own facts. Cf. Beverly Oil Co. v. City of Los Angeles, 40 Cal.2d 552, 560, 254 P.2d 865.

Moreover, the ordinance under consideration in the Jones case differed materially from the one here involved. There the ordinance, cast in the form of a penal statute rather than in the form of a comprehensive zoning law, prohibited the maintenance of sanitariums of a certain type in designated districts. By its terms the ordinance, unlike the ordinary zoning laws, purported to have both a retroactive as well as a prospective effect, thereby automatically prohibiting the continued maintenance of several established sanitariums representing large investments. In other words, no provision was made for any automatic exception for existing non-conforming uses. In the present case, the zoning ordinance does provide for automatic exceptions of reasonable duration for existing nonconforming uses, subject, however, to earlier revocation of the automatic exception if the use for which approval was granted is so exercised "as to be detrimental to the public health or safety, or so as to be a nuisance" (§ 649, supra); and the power to determine, upon notice, the question of whether the property was being so used was vested in the Regional Planning Commission. As a result of these distinctions, plaintiffs may not urge that the remedy of injunction which was sought in the Jones case is the appropriate remedy in the present case. It is apparent that the only remedy available to plaintiffs in the Jones case was preventive, by way of an action for injunctive relief; whereas, as will hereinafter appear, other remedies were available in the present case to review the action taken by the planning commission in revoking plaintiffs' automatic exception.

[2-5] The rights of the users of property as those rights existed under prevailing zoning conditions are well recognized and have always been protected. Edmonds v. County of Los Angeles, 40 Cal.2d 642, 651, 255 P.2d 772. Accordingly, a provision which exempts existing non-conforming uses is ordinarily included in rezoning ordinances because of the hardship and doubtful constitutionality of compelling the immediate discontinuance of nonconforming uses. (Ibid.) Protection of an undertaking involving the investment of capital is akin to the protection of a nonconforming use existing at the time that rezoning conditions become effective. County of San Diego v. McClurken, 37 Cal.2d 683, 691, 234 P.2d 972. However, zoning legislation looks to the future in regulating district development and the eventual liquidation of nonconforming uses within a prescribed period commensurate with the investment involved. Ibid., 37 Cal.2d at page 686, 234 P.2d 972. The mere fact that some hardship may thereby be experienced is not controlling, for "Every exercise of the police power is apt to affect adversely the property interest of somebody." Zahn v. Board of Public Works, 195 Cal. 497, 512, 234 P. 388, 394. Implicit in the theory of the police power, as differentiated from the power of eminent domain, is the principle that incidental injury to an individual will not prevent its operation, once it is shown to be exercised for proper purposes of public health, safety, morals, and general welfare, and there is no arbitrary and unreasonable application in the particular case. Wilkins v. City of San Bernardino, supra, 29 Cal.2d 332, 338, 175 P.2d 542, Beverly Oil Co. v. City of Los Angeles, supra, 40 Cal.2d 552, 557 254 P.2d 865.

[6, 7] Here the rezoning permits plaintiffs to continue their nonconforming use of the property for twenty years as an "automatic exception" to the rezoning restrictions, § 531, supra; Edmonds v. County of Los Angeles, supra, 40 Cal.2d 642, 651, 255 P.2d 772, but authorizes revocation of such exception where it can be done without the impairment of "constitutional rights" (§ 533, supra). Manifestly, care has been taken in such rezoning regulations to refrain from the interference with constitutional guarantees, and in the light of such express language it would be a contradiction in terms to hold that the regulations are nevertheless unconstitutional. Likewise, there can be no constitutional objection to the authorized revocation by the planning commission of an automatic exception where after a public

hearing, upon notice, it is found that the nonconforming use is "so exercised as to be detrimental to the public health or safety, or so as to be a nuisance." § 649, supra; Ricciardi v. County of Los Angeles, 115 Cal.App.2d 569, 577, 252 P.2d 773. Revocation of the right to continue a previously existing lawful business because of such finding would be a legitimate exercise of the police power. Ex parte Quong Wo, 161 Cal. 220, 230, 118 P. 714; Jones v. City of Los Angeles, supra, 211 Cal. 304, 316, 295 P. 14; In re Jones, 56 Cal.App.2d 658, 663-664, 133 P.2d 418; Cantrell v. Board of Supervisors, 87 Cal.App.2d 471, 477, 197 P.2d 218. It therefore follows that the rezoning regulations authorizing the revocation of "automatic exceptions" are constitutionally valid as a whole and come within the prescribed objectives of the police power. There now remains the question of whether in application to plaintiffs' existing cement plant there has been an unconstitutional impairment of property rights.

[8-10] The Regional Planning Commission was a local board exercising quasi-judicial powers under the ordinance in determining the facts in plaintiffs' case. Greif v. Dullea, 66 Cal.App.2d 986, 1009, 153 P.2d 581; North Side etc. Ass'n v. Hillside etc. Park, 70 Cal.App.2d 609, 616, 161 P.2d 618; Cantrell v. Board of Supervisors, supra, 87 Cal.App.2d 471, 475, 197 P.2d 218. Either certiorari or mandamus is an appropriate remedy to test the proper exercise of discretion vested in a local board. Walker v. City of San Gabriel, 20 Cal.2d 879, 881, 129 P.2d 349, 142 A.L.R. 1383; La Prade v. Department of Water & Power, 27 Cal.2d 47, 53, 162 P.2d 13. Under such review, the chief issues are whether the person affected has been accorded a hearing, and if so, whether there is any evidence to support the order of the local board. (Ibid.)

[11-13] In the present case, the transcript of the hearing before the planning commission is not a part of the record. Plaintiffs allege that there was "no competent evidence to prove any cause for revocation" in their case, and that Pacific Electric, owner of the property, was never given notice of the hearing as required by the ordinance regulations. In answer to this latter point, defendant asserts that "Pacific Electric * * * was represented at the hearing," a voluntary appearance which eliminates any cause for complaint in failing to give the required notice, see Hopkins v. MacCulloch, 35 Cal.App.2d 442, 451, 95 P.2d 950, and that in any event the presence of Pacific Electric was of no concern to plaintiffs in the determination of their case before the planning commission. Although plaintiffs admittedly did comply with smog and air pollution regulatory requirements, their plant might be still so operated "as to be detrimental to the public health or safety, or so as to be a nuisance." (§ 649, supra.) The propriety of the planning commission's finding on these issues cannot be determined without recourse to the proceedings taken before it "in the manner provided by law". Ricciardi v. County of Los Angeles, supra, 115 Cal.App.2d 569, 580, 252 P.2d 773, 780, and examination of the evidence there submitted. The valid-

ity of section 404 of the ordinance, supra, affirming the expiration date of plaintiffs' right to continue the operation of their cement plant in the rezoned district, would necessarily depend on whether the planning commission's action was unreasonable, arbitrary or oppressive in ordering revocation in plaintiffs' case. Under all the circumstances, plaintiffs have an adequate remedy at law for review of the planning commission's proceedings, and therefore they are not entitled to injunctive or declaratory relief. North Side etc. Ass'n etc. v. Hillside etc. Park, supra, 70 Cal.App.2d 609, 615, 161 P.2d 618; Hostetter v. Alderson, 38 Cal.2d 499, 500, 241 P.2d 230.

The judgment is reversed.

GIBSON, C. J., and EDMONDS and TRAYNOR, JJ., concur.

CARTER, Justice.

I dissent.

The ordinance in this case changed the zone in which plaintiffs' business (concrete aggregates loading plant) was then established to embrace only "light manufacturing" to which class plaintiffs' business did not belong. As is customary, the ordinance excepted from its operation for a period of 20 years, existing uses such as plaintiffs'. Yet in the next breath it provided that any exception could be revoked if the planning commission found that that could be done without violating the constitutional rights of the existing user or where the existing use was detrimental to the "public health or safety" or was a "nuisance." For all practical purposes, therefore, no exception was granted for existing uses because the exception could be taken away at any time, and in the case at bar, was taken away from plaintiffs with impunity.

It is settled in this state as elsewhere that a zoning ordinance which requires the discontinuance of nonconforming uses existing when the ordinance was adopted is a deprivation of property without due process of law contrary to the federal and state constitutions. Jones v. City of Los Angeles, 211 Cal. 304, 295 P. 14; Beverly Oil Co. v. City of Los Angeles, 40 Cal.2d 552, 254 P.2d 865; Wilkins v. City of San Bernardino, 29 Cal.2d 332, 175 P.2d 542; Clemons v. City of Los Angeles, 36 Cal.2d 95, 222 P.2d 439; Price v. Schwafel, 92 Cal.App.2d 77, 206 P.2d 683; Acker v. Baldwin, 18 Cal.2d 341, 115 P.2d 455; Yokley, Zoning Law & Practice, § 133; 58 Am.Jur.Zoning, § 148; McQuillin, Municipal Corporations (3rd ed.) § 25.181. In Village of Terrace Park v. Errett, 6 Cir., 12 F.2d 240, a zoning ordinance was held invalid which prohibited plaintiff from operating his gravel processing plant which was operating when the ordinance was passed. In In re Kelso, 147 Cal. 609, 82 P. 241, 2 L.R.A.,N.S., 796, it was held that an ordinance could not validly prohibit the maintenance of a rock quarry in the city. In Dobbins v. City of Los Angeles, 195 U.S. 223, 25 S.Ct. 18, 49 L.Ed. 169, reversing our court's decision in Dobbins v. City of Los Angeles, 139 Cal. 179, 72 P. 970, the court held an ordinance unconstitutional which prohibited a gas works as applied to an existing gas works.

As a zoning ordinance which does not exempt existing nonconforming uses is invalid it necessarily follows that an ordinance, like the one here, which excepts such uses but authorizes a planning commission to revoke those exceptions where the public safety or health is involved, is also invalid. If public health and safety (police power), the basis for the zoning, cannot justify the destruction of existing uses, an administrative agency cannot be given such power. Those uses cannot be eliminated unless they inherently, or as exercised, are nuisances. Jones v. City of Los Angeles, supra, 211 Cal. 304, 295 P. 14.

Assuming the commission could be given the authority to determine that an existing non-conforming use was a nuisance, and hence not under the exception for such uses, it is difficult to see how the plaintiffs' business could be a nuisance. It is in an area zoned for light manufacturing. Hence there is no question of disturbing the residents in a residential area. Plaintiffs obtained a permit to conduct its business and it complied with all "smog control and air pollution" ordinances.

In the disposition of the case the majority reverses the judgment granting an injunction in an action for preventive and declaratory relief and in so doing states that plaintiffs cannot review the action of the commission in a proceeding for declaratory relief or injunction. In effect the trial court is told to dismiss the action. Although it is said in Hostetter v. Alderson, 38 Cal.2d 499, 241 P.2d 230, that a determination by a local administrative agency cannot be reviewed in a declaratory relief action, it has been done. See Edmonds v. County of Los Angeles, 40 Cal.2d 642, 255 P.2d 772; Otis v. City of Los Angeles, 52 Cal.App.2d 605, 126 P.2d 954; Hoyt v. Board of Civil Service Com'rs, 21 Cal.2d 399, 132 P.2d 804; 15 Cal.Jur.2d Declaratory Relief, § 63; 2 Cal.Jur.2d Administrative Law, § 199. In any event, the declaratory relief action may be treated as mandamus, a proper remedy for review, Hostetter v. Alderson, supra, 38 Cal.2d 499, 241 P.2d 230; 2 Cal.Jur. 2d Administrative Law, § 200, and it was alleged by plaintiffs that the commission had no competent evidence to prove any cause for revocation of its exemption from the ordinance. This should be pointed out to avoid a dismissal of the action.

I am convinced that the trial court correctly applied the law to the facts of this case, and the judgment should be affirmed.

SHENK and SCHAUER, Justices.

We dissent.

In our view the opinion prepared for the District Court of Appeal by Justice McComb and concurred in by Presiding Justice Moore and Justice Fox (reported in 260 P.2d 811) adequately discusses and correctly resolves the questions presented on this appeal. For the reasons therein stated we would affirm the judgment of the trial court.

Rehearing denied; SHENK, CARTER and SCHAUER, JJ., dissenting.

Questions and Notes

On Gage

1. What was Mr. Gage doing on his house and lot? (For pictures, see Williams, v.5, plate 19.)
2. Was this a conforming use when established?
3. When did it become non-conforming?
4. What, according to the court, was the original policy on non-conforming uses in zoning? How did this work out, and why? Is this equally true for all types of non-conforming uses?
5. On what basis did the court uphold the requirement for termination here?
6. For what happened after this, see Williams, sec. 116.06.

On Los Angeles County

1. How were non-conforming uses treated in the County ordinance?
2. Does a rose by any other name smell just as sweet?

HARBISON

v.

BUFFALO

4 N.Y.2d 553, 176 N.Y.S.2d 598, 152 N.E.2d 42 (1958).

Court of Appeals of New York.

June 25, 1958.

Landowners brought proceeding in the nature of mandamus against city and its director of licenses directing issuance of a wholesale junk license to landowners. The Supreme Court, Special Term, Erie County, Carlton A. Fisher, J., entered an order directing issuance of a license, on ground that city ordinance requiring termination of nonconforming use of premises as a junk yard within three years from date of ordinance was not a valid exercise of the police power, and the city and its director of licenses appealed. The Supreme Court, Appellate Division, Fourth Department, 4 A.D.2d 999, 169 N.Y.S.2d 598, on November 8, 1957 modified the order of the Special Term by deleting provisions for injunctive relief, and affirmed the order as modified. The city and its director of licenses appealed to the Court of Appeals. The Court of Appeals, Froessel, J., reversed the order and remanded the matter to the Special Term for trial of issue whether resultant injury to landowners would be so substantial that ordinance would be unconstitutional as applied to the particular facts of case.

Order of Appellate Division reversed and matter remanded to Special Term for trial of material issues and further proceedings.

Van Voorhis, J., Conway, C. J., and Dye, J., dissented.

FROESSEL, Judge.

Petitioner Andrew Harbison, Sr. purchased certain real property located at 35 Cumberland Avenue in the city of Buffalo on January 5, 1924. Shortly thereafter he erected a 30- by 40-foot frame building thereon, and commenced operating a cooperage business, which, with his son, he has continued to date. The building has not been enlarged, and the volume of petitioners' business is stated to be the same now as then. The only difference is that, whereas petitioners formerly dealt mainly with wooden barrels, they now recondition, clean and paint "used" steel drums or barrels. No issue of that difference is made here. These drums, or barrels, are stacked to a height of about 10 feet in the yard, and on an average day about 600 or 700 barrels are stored there.

When petitioner Andrew Harbison, Sr., established his business in 1924, the street upon which it was located was an unpaved extension of an existing street, the city operated a dump in the area, and there was a glue factory in the vicinity. At the present time, the glue factory has gone, and there are residences adjoining both sides of petitioners' property and across the street. The change in the surrounding area is reflected by the fact that in 1924 the land was unzoned, but since 1926 (except for the period between 1949 and 1953, when it was zoned for business), the land has been zoned for residential use; and it is presently in an "R3" dwelling district.

Thus it is clear that at the time of the enactment of the first zoning ordinance affecting the premises, petitioners had an existing nonconforming use, that is, the conduct of a cooperage business in a residential zone. In 1936, under an ordinance which included the operations of petitioners in a definition of "junk dealers", petitioners applied for and received a license to carry on their business. Licenses were obtained by petitioners every year from 1936 through the fiscal year of 1956.

However, the ordinances of the City of Buffalo were amended, effective as of July 30, 1953, so as to state in chapter LXX (§ 18): "1. Continuing existing uses: Except as provided in this section, any nonconforming use of any building, structure, land or premises may be continued. Provided, however, that on premises situate in any 'R' district each use which is not a conforming use in the 'R5' district and which falls into one of the categories hereinafter enumerated shall cease or shall be changed to a conforming use within 3 years from the effective date of this amended chapter. The requirements of this subdivision for the termination of non-conforming uses shall apply in each of the following cases: * * * . (d) Any junk yard". (Defined in § 23, subd. 24.)

On November 27, 1956 the director of licenses of the City of Buffalo sent a letter to petitioners stating: "At a meeting of the Common Council under date of November 13, 1956 * * * [it] evinced its intention not to amend or modify the provisions of Chapter 18, Subdivision I of Chapter LXX of the Ordinances relating to non-conforming uses by junk yards ° ° °in 'R' districts. ° ° ° you are hereby notified to discontinue the operation of your junk yard ° ° ° at once". A subsequent application by petitioners for a wholesale junk license and one for a "drum reconditioning license" were refused on the ground that "said premises lie within an area zoned as 'R3' Dwelling District ° ° ° and the operation of a junk yard and the outside storage of used materials is prohibited therein." Petitioners then brought this article 78 proceeding in the nature of mandamus in which they sought an order directing the city to issue a wholesale junk license to them, and the lower courts sustained them.

On this appeal, the City of Buffalo argues (1) that petitioners did not have a *lawful* nonconforming use when the zoning ordinance was enacted in 1926, since at that time they had not complied with an ordinance enacted in 1892 requiring the licensing of wholesale junk dealers; (2) that petitioners are not entitled to the peremptory grant of a license since they have not enclosed their premises with a solid wood or sheet metal fence or masonry wall not less than 6 feet high, as required by section 194 of article XIII of chapter V of the ordinance, and (3) that the ordinance, held invalid by the courts below, is a valid exercise of the police power.

The first point need not detain us long. The ordinance of 1892, upon which the city relies, related to "the business of purchasing or selling old silver, iron, brass, copper scraps or other secondhand or partially ruined or damaged materials, [or] carry[ing] on ° ° ° a junk shop". It is argued that this ordinance does not clearly encompass petitioners' business of repairing and reconditioning barrels. In any event, I might note that petitioners operated a *licensed* wholesale junk business from 1936 to 1956, and the city never raised the foregoing objection on any of the applications for renewal of the license. Hence this argument has no merit.

Nor does the second point appear to be a sound ground for refusal to issue a license here. If, as appears, petitioners have not complied with the letter of the ordinance since their property is enclosed by a picket fence rather than one of solid wood or metal, an order directing the issuance of a license could readily be conditioned upon compliance with such provisions inasmuch as petitioners are quite willing to comply with this requirement. It may be noted that this defense was not interposed until the close of the hearings.

In the major point involved on this appeal, the city argues that the ordinance requiring the termination of petitioners' nonconforming use of the premises as a junk yard within three years of the date of said ordinance is a valid exercise of its police power. Its claim is not based on the theory of nuisance (see People v. Miller, 304 N.Y. 105, 107, 106 N.E.2d 34, and cases there cited; Noel, Retroactive Zoning and Nuisances, 41 Col.L.Rev. 457), and indeed this record contains little evidence as to the manner of operation of petitioners' business and the nature of the surrounding neighborhood. Rather, in this case, the city bases its claim largely on out-of-State decisions which have sustained ordinances requiring the termination of nonconforming uses or structures after a period of permitted continuance, where such "amortization" period was held reasonable.

When zoning ordinances are initially adopted to limit permissible uses of property, or when property is rezoned so as to prevent uses of property previously allowed, a degree of protection is constitutionally required to be given owners of property then using the premises in a manner forbidden by the ordinance. Thus we have held that, where substantial expenditures were made in the commencement of the erection of a building, a zoning ordinance may not deprive the owner of the "vested right" to complete the structure (People ex rel. Ortenberg v. Bales, 250 N.Y. 598, 166 N.E. 339; see City of Buffalo v. Chadeayne, 134 N.Y. 163, 165, 31 N.E. 443). So, where the owner already has structures on the premises, he cannot be directed to ease using them (see 440 East 102nd St. Realty Corp. v. Murdock, 285 N.Y. 298, 304-305, 34 N.E.2d 329, 331), just as he has the right to continue a prior business carried on there (Town of Somers v. Camarco, 308 N.Y. 537, 127 N.E.2d 327; Crossroads Recreation v. Broz, 4 N.Y.2d 39, 172 N.Y.S. 2d 129, 149 N.E.2d 65; People v. Miller, supra).

However, where the benefit to the public has been deemed of greater moment than the detriment to the property owner, we have sustained the prohibition of continuation of prior nonconforming uses. These cases involved the prior use of property for parking lots (People v. Wolfe, 272 N.Y. 608, 5 N.E.2d 355, motion for reargument denied 273 N.Y. 498, 6 N.E.2d 422; People v. Kesbec, Inc., 281 N.Y. 785, 24 N.E.2d 476, motion for reargument denied 282 N.Y. 676, 26 N.E.2d 808). We have also upheld the restriction of projected uses of the property where, at the time of passage of the ordinance, there had been no substantial investment in the noncomforming use (e. g., New York Trap Rock Corp. v. Town of Clarkstown, 3 N.Y.2d 844, 166 N.Y.S.2d 82, 144 N.E.2d 725; Rice v. Van Vranken, 255 N.Y. 541, 175 N.E. 304; Fox Lane Corp. v. Mann, 243 N.Y. 550, 154 N.E. 600). In these cases, there is no doubt that the property owners incurred a loss in the value of their property and otherwise as a result of the fact that they were unable to carry out their prospective uses; but we held that such a deprivation was not violative of the owners' constitutional rights. In People v. Miller, supra, 304 N.Y. at page 108, 106 N.E.2d at page 35, we explained these cases by stating that they involved situations in which the property owners would sustain only a "relatively slight and insubstantial" loss.

It should be noted that even where the zoning authorities may not prohibit a prior nonconforming use, they may adopt regulations which restrict the right of the property owner to enlarge or extend the use or to rebuild or make alterations to the structures on the property (Koeber v. Bedell, 280 N.Y. 692, 21 N.E.2d 200; Cordes v. Moore, 308 N.Y. 761, 125 N.E.2d 112; Marcus v. Village of Mamaroneck, 283 N.Y. 325, 28 N.E.2d 856; Town of Hempstead v. Goldblatt, 4 A.D.2d 970, 168 N.Y.S.2d 609, motion for leave to appeal denied 4 N.Y.2d 674, 171 N.Y.S.2d 1027; see Crossroads Recreation v. Broz, supra).

As these cases indicate, our approach to the problem of permissible restrictions on nonconforming uses has recognized that, while the benefit accruing to the public in terms of more complete and effective zoning does not justify the immediate destruction of substantial businesses or structures developed or built prior to the ordinance (People v. Miller, supra, 304 N.Y. at page 108, 106 N.E.2d at page 35), the policy of zoning embraces the concept of the ultimate elimination of nonconforming uses, and thus the courts favor reasonable restriction of them. But, where the zoning ordinance could have required the cessation of a sand and gravel business on one year's notice, we have held it unconstitutional (Town of Somers v. Camarco, 308 N.Y. 537, 127 N.E.2d 327, supra).

The development of the policy that nonconforming uses should be protected and their existence preserved at the stage of development existing at the time of passage of the ordinance seems to have been based upon the assumption that the ultimate ends of zoning would be accomplished as the nonconforming use terminated with time. But this has not proven to be the case, as commentators have noted that the tendency of many of these uses is to flourish, capitalizing on the fact that no new use of that nature could be begun in the area (see, e. g., 9 U.Chi.L.Rev. 477, 479, 481; 102 U.Pa.L. Rev. 91, 94; 35 Va.L.Rev. 348, 352-353; 1951 Wis.L.Rev. 685). Because of this situation, communities have sought new forms of ordinances restricting nonconforming uses, and in particular have turned to provisions which require termination after a given period of time.

With the exception of a decision of the Ohio Supreme Court (which may be explained on the basis of the particular language and application of the ordinance) in City of Akron v. Chapman, 160 Ohio St. 382, 116 N.E.2d 697, 42 A.L.R.2d 1140 [criticized in 67 Harv.L.Rev. 1283], the decisions have sustained ordinances where the time provided was held reasonable (Livingston Rock & Gravel Co. v. County of Los Angeles, 43 Cal.2d 121, 123-127, 272 P.2d 4; City of Los Angeles v. Gage, 127 Cal.App.2d 442, 453-458, 274 P.2d 34; Standard Oil Co. v. City of Tallahassee, 5 Cir., 183 F.2d 410, certiorari denied 340 U.S. 892, 71 S.Ct. 208, 95 L.Ed. 647; Spurgeon v. Board of Com'rs of Shawnee County, 181 Kan. 1008, 317 P.2d 798; Grant v. Mayor & City Council of Baltimore, 212 Md. 301, 129 A.2d 363; State ex rel. Dema Realty Co. v. Jacoby, 168 La. 752, 123 So. 314; State ex rel. Dema Realty Co. v. McDonald, 168 La. 172, 121 So. 613, certiorari denied 280 U.S. 556, 50 S.Ct. 16, 74 L.Ed. 612; see Robinson Brick Co. v. Luthi, 115 Colo. 106, 111-112, 169 P.2d 171, 166 A.L.R. 655; City of Corpus Christi v. Allen, 152 Tex. 137, 142, 254 S.W.2d 759; Stoner McCray System v. City of Des Moines, 247 Iowa 1313, 1320, 78 N.W.2d 843; United Adv. Corp. v. Borough of Raritan, 11 N.J. 144, 152, 93 A.2d 362).

A number of States and municipal bodies have adopted statutes authorizing this approach to the problem (as e. g., Ill.Ann.Stat., S.H.A., ch. 24,

§ 73-1; 3 Va.Code (1950), § 15-843; see, also, list in n. 1 in Grant v. Mayor & City Council of Baltimore, supra); and the textwriters generally express the opinion that they would be constitutional if reasonable (1 Antieau on Municipal Corporation Law, § 7.03 [3]; Bassett on Zoning, pp. 115-116; 8 McQuillin on Municipal Corporations [3d ed.], § 25.190; see, also, Law Reviews cited supra). Bassett, in his text on Zoning, states (p. 115) that "Several ordinances in Long Island provide [for] * * * the ousting of automobile junk yards with accessory buildings * * * the owner being given from three to six years to amortize."

Leaving aside eminent domain and nuisance, we have often stated in our decisions that the owner of land devoted to a prior nonconforming use, or on which a prior nonconforming structure exists (or has been substantially commenced), has the right to continue such use, but we have never held that this right may continue virtually in perpetuity. Now that we are for the first time squarely faced with the problem as to whether or not this right may be terminated after a reasonable period, during which the owner may have a fair opportunity to amortize his investment and to make future plans, we conclude that it may be, in accordance with the overwhelming weight of authority found in the courts of our sister States, as well as with the textwriters and commentators who have expressed themselves upon the subject.

With regard to prior nonconforming *structures,* reasonable termination periods based upon the amortized life of the structure are not, in our opinion, unconstitutional. They do not compel the immediate destruction of the improvements, but envision and allow for their normal life without extensive alterations or repairs. Such a regulation is akin to those we have sustained relating to restrictions upon the extension or substantial repair or replacement of prior nonconforming structures.

As to prior nonconforming *uses,* the closest case we have had is Town of Somers v. Camarco, 308 N.Y. 537, 127 N.E.2d 327, supra; see discussion thereof in this connection in 7 Syracuse L.Rev. 158-161. In that case we held that, in view of defendant's investment and the business which had been built up and carried on over the years, the provisions of the ordinance which required defendant to apply for a permit to continue its business every year, and provided further that on the termination of any approval period any structure or improvement on the premises could be ordered removed and the premises restored to their original condition as nearly as practicable, were unreasonable. There the land involved had unusual resources which made it especially suitable for the nonconforming use carried on; the improvements were necessary for the operation of the business, and the period of termination was unreasonably short. Under these circumstances the ordinance would have deprived the property owner of his "vested rights". As was pointed out in the opinion (307 N.Y. at pages 540-541, 127 N.E.2d at page 328), "The courts, in order to afford stability to property owners who do have existing nonconforming uses, have imposed the test of reasonableness upon such exercise of the police powers. Therefore broad general rules and tests, such as expressed in People v. Miller, 304 N.Y. 105, 106 N.E.2d 34, must always be considered in this context."

If, therefore, a zoning ordinance provides a sufficient period of permitted nonconformity, it may further provide that at the end of such period the use must cease. This rule is analogous to that with respect to nonconforming structures. In ascertaining the reasonable period during which an owner of property must be allowed to continue a nonconforming use, a balance must be found between social harm and private injury. We cannot say that a legislative body may not in any case, after consideration of the factors involved, conclude that the termination of a use after a period of time sufficient to allow a property owner an opportunity to amortize his investment and make other plans is a valid method of solving the problem.

To enunciate a contrary rule would mean that the use of land for such purposes as a tennis court, an open air skating rink, a junk yard or a parking lot—readily transferable to another site—at the date of the enactment of a zoning ordinance vests the owner thereof with the right to utilize the land in that manner in perpetuity, regardless of the changes in the neighborhood over the course of time. In the light of our ever expanding urban communities, such a rule appears to us to constitute an unwarranted restriction upon the Legislature in dealing with what has been described as "One of the major problems in effective administration of modern zoning ordinances" (1951 Wis.L.Rev. 685). When the termination provisions are reasonable in the light of the nature of the business of the property owner, the improvements erected on the land, the character of the neighborhood, and the detriment caused the property owner, we may not hold them constitutionally invalid.

In the present case, the two lower courts have expressed the view that, "Whatever the law may be in California or Florida or other jurisdictions, in this State" no regulation infringing at any time the perpetual right of an owner to continue a prior nonconforming use is valid. Accordingly, neither court considered the question of whether the particular period prescribed by the ordinance was reasonable under the facts of this case.

Their conclusion is not in accord with the general rule applicable to protection of nonconforming uses as stated in People v. Miller, 304 N.Y. 105, 106 N.E.2d 34, 35, supra. In that case we decided that where the enforcement of an ordinance requiring the termination of a prior nonconforming use caused "relatively slight and insubstantial" loss to the property owner, it would be constitutional. While it is true that the ordinance there involved did not have an "amortization" provision, nevertheless the general test enunciated is no less germane when such a provision is included in the ordinance. As previously pointed out, the period of "amortization" allowed by the ordinance is a crucial factor in determining whether the ordinance has been constitutionally applied in a given case.

Here, petitioners are engaged in the business of reconditioning barrels or used steel drums. We are told that the value of the property together with the improvements is $20,000; but there is no indication of the relative value of the land and improvements separately. It was further alleged that the improvement consists of a 30- by 40-foot frame building erected in 1924, and in addition thereto, petitioners claim that at the insistence of the City of Buffalo, three years before the ordinance went into effect, they were obliged to install a special sewage system at a cost of $2,000 and a boiler at a cost of $700.

Material triable issues of fact thus remain, and a further hearing should adduce evidence relating to the nature of the surrounding neighborhood, the value and condition of the improvements on the premises, the nearest area to which petitioners might relocate, the cost of such relocation, as well as any other reasonable costs which bear upon the kind and amount of damages which petitioners might sustain, and whether petitioners might be able to continue operation of their business if not allowed to continue storage of barrels or steel drums outside their frame building. It is only upon such evidence that it may be ascertained whether the resultant injury to petitioners would be so substantial that the ordinance would be unconstitutional as applied to the particular facts of this case.

The order of the Appellate Division should be reversed, without costs, and the matter remanded to Special Term for a trial of the material issues and further proceedings as outlined in this opinion.

VAN VOORHIS, Judge (dissenting).

The decision which is about to rendered marks, in my view, the beginning of the end of the constitutional protection of property rights in this State in pre-existing nonconforming uses under zoning ordinances. Special Term and the Appellate Division unanimously followed the existing law in holding this amendment to the zoning ordinance of the City of Buffalo to be unconstitutional. In my view the traditional rule is right, and should not be abrogated.

Petitioners-respondents in 1924 began what has been described as a wholesale junk yard business at 35 Cumberland Avenue, in that city. Their principal line has been cooperage, although the city recognizes no distinction between that and the junk business. The opposite side of the street, at that time, was a rubbish dump being filled in by the city. Later residences commenced to be built in the area, after the fill had settled across the street, and the residential newcomers did not like the continuance of petitioners' business in their new neighborhood. Although petitioners' business has been conducted legally in every respect, the City of Buffalo refused to renew their license for 1956, although licenses covering this business had been issued annually for the last 20 years. The basis on which their license was refused was that although after the enactment of a zoning ordinance their business had been licensed as a nonconforming pre-existing use, nevertheless in 1953 the zoning ordinance was amended to outlaw nonconforming uses of this nature at the expiration of three years from the effective date of the amendment. For this reason petitioners' license was not renewed for the year 1956.

The phraseology of this 1953 zoning amendment is important. It reads as follows:

> "§ 18. Non-conforming uses and buildings. 1. Continuing existing uses: Except as provided in this section, any non-conforming use of any building, structure, land or premises may be continued. Provided, however, that on premises situate in any 'R' district each use which is not a conforming use in the 'R5' district and which falls into one of the categories hereinafter enumerated shall cease or shall be changed to a conforming use within 3 years from the effective date of this amended chapter. The requirements of this subdivision for the termination of non-conforming uses shall apply in each of the following cases:
>
> "(a) Any such non-conforming use involving the use of land only and not accessory to an adjacent building or structure assessed as a real estate improvement.
>
> "(b) Any such non conforming use involving the use of or accessory to one or more buildings or structures on the same lot, the aggregate assessed value of which improvements for tax purposes is not more than five hundred dollars ($500.00).
>
> "(c) Any such non conforming use consisting of a sign.
>
> "(d) Any junk yard, auto wrecking or dismantling establishment."

No contention is made that petitioners' business has been enlarged, altered in character or abandoned. Neither is the city acting on the basis that the the assessed value of buildings or structures on the lot does not exceed $500, although that clause in the ordinance has been mentioned and will be discussed. The city is terminating the continuous use of this real property upon the ground that the real property is being used as a junk yard, and that the amount of capital investment which plaintiffs have made in land or build ngs makes no difference inasmuch as three years have elapsed since the zoning amendment of 1953.

It appears from the petition, without denial in the answer, that at the insistence of the City of Buffalo petitioners spent $2,000 for the installation of a special sewage system for use in their business as recently as 1950. The petit on further alleges that at the same time they spent $700 for the installation of a boiler also for use in their business. Although the answer denies that the city has knowledge or information sufficient to form a belief about the boiler, this denial is palpably frivolous in view of the admission that this boiler was inspected by city inspectors for the years 1951 to 1956 inclusive. It is thus established that petitioners had at least $2,700 invested in this construction upon this property, in addition to the other structures and the land.

The plaintiffs' business is being confiscated, as has been mentioned, not on the basis that the improvements are assessed within $500, but regardless of how much the improvements may be worth. It is being terminated under the language of this ordinance for the sole reason that it is classified as a junk yard. I agree with what was said by the Appellate Division [169 N.Y.S.2d 599] that "Whatever the law may be in California or Florida or other jurisdictions, in this state, the rule is as stated in People v. Miller, 304 N.Y. 105, 107, 109, 106 N.E.2d 34, 35, to wit: 'It is the law of this state that nonconforming uses or structures, in existence when a zoning ordinance is enacted, are, as a general rule, constitutionally protected and will be permitted to continue, notwithstanding the contrary provision of the ordinance'." Not less than nine cases are cited in our opinion in People v. Miller, 304 N.Y. 105, 106 N.E.2d 34, as authority for this statement (304 N.Y. at page 107, 106 N.E.2d at page 34). Plaintiffs' business is not a nuisance. It is not injurious to life or health or morals. The neighbors whose sensibilities are offended would have found difficulty in abating it (even if it were a nuisance) for the reason that they "came to the nuisance," in the time honored phrase, by purchasing and moving into the neighborhood while petitioners' business was in operation. Neither, in my mind, can the city abolish this business under this ordinance. Even if this case came under the clause abrogating nonconforming uses where the buildings or structures on the lot do not exceed $500 in assessed value, the ordinance would still be unconstitutional. Zoning relates to the future development of municipalities. Areas in cities that have already been developed cannot be zoned retroactively. That is the function of municipal redevelopment, which is constitutionally authorized by statutes directing payment of just compensation for property that is appropriated. It is arbitrary, in my view, to draw the line at buildings or structures valued at $500 or less. That sum is negligible in the case of large stores or factories, whereas it may represent the savings of years to small proprietors. If the line can be drawn at $500, it will soon be extended to $5,000 or perhaps to $50,000. If, in principle, the city is allowed to confiscate property without payment of just compensation, it is no answer to say that it is taking only $500. It would be a novel proposition that a municipality can take private property for a public use without compensation provided that it does not take too much. Retroactive zoning, as this clearly is, resembles slum clearance more than zoning, which is for the future. If $500 is so small an amount, then why should not the city be obliged to pay it before confiscating this use, by the same token whereby it would be required to pay just compensation in cases of slum clearance? That there is no existing statutory authority to make such a payment in this case is not justification for confiscating the prior use which is a vested right. It would be no answer to argue that the small businessman does not need to be compensated provided that he is small enough. No such rule as that can be applied in zoning administration. If any distinction of that kind were relevant, it would be more appropriate to be guided by what proportion of the businessman's assets have been invested in improvements to his property. Observing the vagaries of modern zoning, many a businessman (large or small) might properly hesitate to invest his life savings in a store or other commercial or industrial property knowing that this investment is liable to be expropriated after the enterprise has been successfully launched, if some pressure group succeeds in obtaining favorable action from a municipal legislature. That is not in the public interest. Constitutional security against such developments is infinitely more important to the public at large than the occasional presence of a noncomforming use, or the possibility that a nonconforming use may acquire some advantage by way of monopoly in the use district. The comment by Chief Judge Hutcheson, of the United States Court of Appeals in the Fifth Circuit, is relevant in his dissenting opinion in Standard Oil Co. v. City of Tallahassee, 183 F.2d 410, 413-414: "recognizing that even in this age of enlightenment the Constitution still protects the citizen against arbitrary and unreasonable action, I am in no doubt that in sustaining this admittedly confiscatory ordinance, a good general principle, the public interest in zoning, has been run into the ground, the tail of legislative confiscation by caprice has been permitted to wag the dog of judicial constitutional protection." This accords with the statement in Incorporated Village of North Hornell v. Rauber, 181 Misc. 546, 552, 40 N.Y.S.2d 938, 944: "Rather is it argued that what used to be called confiscation is justifiable in an enlightened age, if enough people desire it, and the amount to be taken away from the owner is not too great."

An incidental defect in the same subsection of this municipal ordinance is that if the amount of money involved were to be deemed to be controlling on the issue of confiscation, the ordinance could not constitutionally bind the owner to the assessed value of buildings or structures to be taken without compensation. Quoting again from Incorporated Village of North Hornell v. Rauber, supra, 181 Misc. at pages 552-553, 40 N.Y.S.2d at page 944: "The assessed valuation of real estate is some evidence of fair market value. Matter of Simmons [Ashokan Reservoir], 132 App. Div. 574, 576, 116 N.Y.S. 952; Adler v. Berkowitz, 229 App.Div. 245, 249, 240 N.Y.S. 597, modified on other grounds 254 N.Y. 433, 173 N.E. 574; Heiman v. Bishop, 272 N.Y. 83, 88, 4 N.E.2d 944; President & Directors of Manhattan Co. v. Williams, 152 Misc. 901, 902, 274 N.Y.S. 338. It is to be taken into consideration along with other factors, Heiman v. Bishop, supra, but is not conclusive, and is not made conclusive by the reference to assessed valuation in the zoning ordinance. * * * Certainly the reasonableness of the ordinance in a particular case must be decided on the basis of the real facts. The Court cannot be estopped by anything contained in it from deciding whether its operation is confiscatory. The reference to assessed valuation in § 7 does not render less oppressive a deprivation of property without due process of law where the assessed valuation is beneath the true value.

The remedy for an inadequate assessed valuation is to raise it, not to put the taxpayer out of business by an injunction."

In this instance, as has been said, the limitation to $500 assessed valuation in this zoning ordinance does not apply. Petitioners come under a different subdivision which outlaws after three years "Any junk yard, auto wrecking or dismantling establishment." This subdivision has no relation to the amount of money invested in physical improvements. In the case of petitioners' business, it stands admitted by the pleadings that petitioners have recently invested a substantial sum in the improvement of their property at the instance of the city, much more than $500. Junk yards or cooperage businesses are not operated without buildings and other improvements upon the land. Auto dismantling establishments, it is well known, are frequently conducted by unit auto parts companies which require sizable structures in which to dismantle the discarded automobiles and to store and merchandise the variety of used automobile parts and equipment. The reason on account of which these nonconforming uses are interdicted does not relate to the quantity of capital invested in buildings or improvements, but is that they are of a kind which is frequently disliked by the neighbors.

The circumstance that this is a cooperage establishment or junk yard ought not to obscure that the principle of the decision applies to any kind of business which, due to lapse of time, has been overtaken by changes in the neighborhood. The principle of the decision applies equally to stores, shops or service organizations which are retroactively legislated out of existence by the abolition of prior nonconforming uses. If petitioners' establishment is not secure against this kind of invasion, no one else's business is better protected. The neighbors or the officials of a municipality in one year may look askance at a junk or cooperage yard, and in another year may frown upon the conduct in a particular locality of any other type of commerce or industry. The people who moved into petitioners' vicinity and now find their business offensive may not be aware that the principle of this decision unsettles their own property rights, and that it may suddenly be used against them in unexpected ways if agitation arises to legislate them out of business by a similar procedure. It makes little difference what the nature of their businesses may be. The smaller they are the more vulnerable they become to this kind of attack, which is based on the misfortune of unpopularity. Democracy depends upon respect for the individual as well as upon majority rule. The relaxation of constitutional safeguards protecting commonly accepted personal and property rights, goes hand in hand with the multiplication of pressure groups. People should not be obliged to organize to preserve rights the safeguarding of which is the proper function of law. The small manufacturer or merchant feels this acutely, since he ordinarily finds it more difficult to succeed in wielding organized power for his own protection when property rights depend upon the discretion of legislative bodies. No question is raised here concerning the good faith of the enactment or administration of this ordinance. Nevertheless petitioners find themselves confronted by the organized civil power of the municipality, set in motion by the complaints of their neighbors who wish to eliminate them from the locality in which petitioners settled first. If this part of the city is to be redeveloped, it should be done through the enactment of a statute similar in principle to slum clearance acts, whereby just compensation can be paid for private property that is confiscated for a public use. Petitioners have well-recognized legal property rights which ought to be protected in court.

Zoning, as originally conceived, related to the future development of municipalities. It was not an attempt to reconstruct the past. Cases such as Village of Euclid v. Ambler Realty Co., 272 U.S. 365, 47 S.Ct. 114, 71 L.Ed. 303, and Lincoln Trust Co. v. Williams Bldg. Corp., 229 N.Y. 313, 128 N.E. 209, were decided in this frame of reference. Pre-existing nonconforming uses were uniformly excepted from the operating of zoning ordinances, and the proprietors thereof were held to have the constitutional right to continue such uses (People v. Miller, supra; City of Buffalo v. Chadeayne, 134 N.Y. 163, 31 N.E. 443; People ex rel. Ortenberg v. Bales, 250 N.Y. 598, 166 N.E. 339; Caponi v. Walsh, 228 App.Div. 86, 238 N.Y.S. 438; New York State Investing Corp. v. Brady, 214 App.Div. 592, 212 N.Y.S. 605; Pelham View Apts. v. Switzer, 130 Misc. 545, 224 N.Y.S. 56; People v. Stanton, 125 Misc. 215, 211 N.Y.S. 408). We are now told that the protection of nonconforming uses in the beginning was a strategem of city planners, "prompted by a fear that the courts would hold unconstitutional any zoning ordinance which attempted to eliminate existing nonconforming uses." (1951 Wis.L.Rev. 685; 35 Va.L.R. 352, citing Bassett on Zoning, p. 108, n. 1; also Noel, Retroactive Zoning and Nuisances, 41 Col.L. Rev. 457, 473.) The Virginia Law Review note, citing these authorities, states: "Those who led the zoning movement in its early stages adopted a lenient attitude towards nonconforming buildings. They did so because they did not wish to arouse the animosity of a large segment of property owners at a time when opposition might have jeopardized the whole success of zoning." The reasoning of these and other commentators, and of some decisions in other States, is that all zoning interferes with property rights to some degree, even in case of unused vacant land, and that now another step should be taken by eliminating pre-existing uses which were formerly held to constitute vested property rights. (State ex rel. Dema Realty Co. v. McDonald, 168 La. 172, 121 So. 613; State ex rel. Dema Realty Co. v. Jacoby, 168 La. 752, 123 So. 314; Livingston Rock & Gravel Co. v. County of Los Angeles, 43 Cal.2d 121, 272 P.2d 4; City of Los Angeles v. Gage, 127 Cal.App.2d 442, 274 P.2d 34; Spurgeon v. Board of Com'rs, of Shawnee County, 181 Kan. 1008, 317 P.2d 798; Standard Oil Co. v. City of Tallahassee, 5 Cir., 183 F.2d 410, certiorari denied 340 U.S. 892, 71 S.Ct. 208, 95 L.Ed. 647, supra; Grant v. Mayor & City Council of Baltimore, 212 Md. 301, 129 A.2d 363). In the Louisiana cases it was held that a grocery store and a drugstore could be eliminated in one year by passing a zoning ordinance; in the California cases, a plumbing establishment and a cement batching plant were required to be removed respectively in five years and one year after the enactment or amendment of such an ordinance; in the Federal case in Florida, an automobile service station was required to be eliminated on the amendment of such an ordinance in ten years; in the Kansas case an automobile wrecking business was required to be removed within two years; and in the Maryland case billboards, which may be in a different category, were required to be removed from residential areas after a tolerance period of five years. Most of these cases were decided over vigorous dissents. There are decisions to the opposite effect in other states (O'Connor v. City of Moscow, 69 Idaho 37, 202 P.2d 401, Annotation, 9 A.L.R.2d 1039; City of Akron v. Chapman, 160 Ohio St. 382, 116 N.E.2d 697, Annotation, 42 A.L.R.2d 1146; James v. City of Greenville, 227 S.C. 565, 88 S.E.2d 661; City of Corpus Christi v. Allen, 152 Tex. 137, 254 S.W.2d 729, affirming Tex.Civ.App., 247 S.W.2d 130). Our Town of Somers v. Camarco, 308 N.Y. 537, 127 N.E.2d 327, has been cited in the same context (see Grant v. Mayor & City Council of Baltimore, supra). The Texas case held unconstitutional an ordinance compelling the removal of an automobile salvage and wrecking yard, which is included in the same category as a junk yard under the ordinance of the City of Buffalo under adjudication herein. In American Jurisprudence (Vol. 58, Zoning, § 148 [1948]) the statement is made that "it is generally held that a zoning ordinance may not operate to suppress or remove from a particular district an otherwise lawful business or use already established therein. Even if the general welfare, for the promotion of which zoning legislation is justified, were interpreted to include the protection of economic values of adjacent property, so that the establishment of a new business may be prohibited to protect such value, that is considered a different matter from ousting a business already there, with reference to which the economic value of the adjacent property has long since been fixed." The 1957 annotation recognizes that "In several cases the validity of such a requirement has been upheld," but adds: "However, in a number of cases the view has been taken that an ordinance or other regulation intended to terminate a lawful nonconforming use in existence when such ordinance or regulation was adopted, and permitted to continue thereafter, was invalid, at least as to the particular application sought."

This citation of authority is enough to display the confusion into which this subject is becoming involved in some jurisdictions in consequence of departing from the established rule. The courts find themselves obliged, without any guiding principle, to pick and choose between instances where a prior nonconforming use will or will not be protected in the courts. It is generally implied in discussions of the subject that the sponsors of the zoning movement were merely temporizing with the courts by leading them in the beginning to hold that a prior use constituted a vested right. The facts in the cases cited, where there has been a departure from that rule, illustrate how impossible it would be to confine a ruling like the one in this case to a junk yard, or to determine judicially what would be a reasonable period of time for removal in a specific case within the meaning of the Constitution. In some of them stores were removed, in another a gasoline service station, in one a plumbing shop and in another a cement batching plant. The grace periods allowed bear no discoverable relation to the kinds of property or businesses involved. An auto wrecking establishment was given five years, and a gasoline service station ten years, whereas a grocery store, drugstore and cement batching establishment were allowed but one year. Different periods purport to be allowed by ordinances elsewhere. Thus it is stated (9 U.Chi.L.Rev. 481-482): "The proposals vary greatly. Some pertain only to particular uses such as billboards, garages, gasoline stations, and junk yards. Still others attempt to eliminate many more non-conforming uses. Nor are the lengths of the amortization periods uniform. Under some proposals a two-year period is allowed, others allow ten or twenty years. Although most of the provisions are silent as to the administrative techniques by which the amortization provisions are to be applied, the boards of zoning appeals will probably be given varying degrees of discretion by which individual hardships may be mitigated within the larger, less flexible framework of the definite elimination period."

In practice this spells confusion, instability, inability to diagnose what are legal rights, inconsistency, arbitrariness and discrimination in administrative and court decisions, and an avalanche of litigation. That Pandora's box is opened, regardless of the best possible intentions on the part of all concerned. Nor is the judgment appealed from an unwarranted interference by the courts in the province of the municipal legislature. It simply follows precedent from the beginning of zoning practice. The new rule has the additional infirmity that it opens wide new fields of discretion in administrative law without any workable standards by which it is to be guided.

The lack of any principle in applying the novel theory of "amortization" betrays a fundamental weakness in the theory. Zoning, like other public programs, is not always best administered at the hands of its enthusiasts. The existence of non-conforming uses has spoiled the symmetry in the minds of zoning experts. It has bulked so large in this context that, desirable as the elimination of nonconforming uses may be, it has sometimes been presented as though it were more important than ordinary property rights. "Many means of eliminating and controlling nonconforming uses have been proposed and tried. Among these means are retroactive zoning, amortization of nonconforming uses, abatement of nonconforming uses as nuisances, public purchase and eminent domain, prohibition of the resumption of a nonconforming use after a period of discontinuance, and refusal to provide governmental services to nonconforming users" (1951 Wis.L.Rev. 687). This Wisconsin Law Review article points out how most of these different proposals have been tried and found wanting, particularly the method by exercising the power of eminent domain which is said to have been discarded mainly for the reason that it is too expensive. The same is said at page 93 of Volume 102 of the Pennsylvania Law Review. The fault found with eminent domain is that it failed to achieve the object of destroying the owner's right in his property without paying for it. Consequently the most promising legal theory at the moment is known as "amortization". This theory is discussed in some of the cases and in most of the law review articles which have been cited as upholding constitutionality of these measures. "Amortization" is explained as follows:[1] " 'The only positive method of getting rid of non-conforming uses yet devised is to amortize a non-conforming building. That is, to determine the normal useful remaining life of the building and prohibit the owner from maintaining it after the expiration of that time.' " The opinion in City of Los Angeles v. Gage, 127 Cal.App.2d at page 455, 274 P.2d at page 41 adds: "The length of time given the owner to eliminate his nonconforming use or building varies with the city and with the type of structure."

This theory to justify extinguishing nonconforming uses means less the more one thinks about it. It offers little more promise of ultimate success than the other theories which have been tried and abandoned. In the first place, the periods of time vary so widely in the cases which have been cited from different States where it has been tried, and have so little relation to the useful lives of the structures, that this theory cannot be used to reconcile these discordant decisions. Moreover the term "amortization", as thus employed, has not the same meaning which it carries in law or accounting. It is not even used by analogy. It is just a catch phrase, and the reasoning is reduced to argument by metaphor. Not only has no effort been made in the reported cases where this theory has been applied to determine what is the useful life of the structure, but almost all were decided under ordinances or statutes which prescribe the same time limit for many different kinds of improvements. This demonstrates that it is not attempted to measure the life of the particular building or type of building, and that the word "amortization" is used as an empty shibboleth. This comment applies to the ordinance at issue on this appeal. There could be no presumption that all junk yards, all auto wrecking or dismantling establishments, and all improvements assessed for tax purposes at not more than $500 will or have any tendency to depreciate to zero in three years. This shows that the ordinance in suit could not possibly have been based on the amortization theory.

Moreover this theory, if it were seriously advanced, would imply that the owner should not keep up his property by making necessary replace-

---

1. Crolly and Norton, Termination of Non-conforming Uses, 62 Zoning Bulletin 1, Regional Plan Assn., June, 1952, quoted in City of Los Angeles v. Gage, supra, 127 Cal.App.2d at pages 454-455, 274 P.2d at page 41.

ments to restore against the ravages of time. Such replacements would be money thrown away. The amortization theory would thus encourage owners of nonconforming uses to allow them to decay and become slums.

Although the courts of other States are divided on this question, the better reason seems to me to be on the side of the rule heretofore established in this State, wherefore I vote to affirm.

BURKE, J., concurs with FROESSEL, J.

DESMOND and FULD, JJ., concur in result upon the principles stated in People v. Miller, 304 N.Y. 105, 108, 109, 106 N.E.2d 34, 35, 36.

VAN VOORHIS, J., dissents in an opinion in which CONWAY, C. J., and DYE, J., concur.

Order reversed, etc.

Questions and Notes

1. How many judges signed the first opinion?

2. Nonetheless, since the New York Court had been the great holdout on amortizing non-conforming uses, this was an important decision in turning the tide.

3. On what basis did this opinion uphold the requirements?

4. For what happened after this, see 44 Cornell Law Quarterly 450 (1959).

CROSS-REFERENCES

In Anderson, see Index, this topic.
In Hagman, see § 87-88.
In Rathkopf, see ch. 62-1.
In Williams, see ch. 109-117.

C. *Signs*

MID-STATE ADVERTISING CORPORATION

v.

BOND

274 N.Y. 82, 8 N.E.2d 286(1937).

Court of Appeals of New York.

April 27, 1937.

Appeal from Supreme Court, Appellate Division, Third Department.

Proceeding in the matter of the application of the Mid-State Advertising Corporation, for a mandamus order against John A. Bond, as Fire Marshal and Superintendent of Buildings of the City of Troy. From an order of the Appellate Division (249 App.Div. 681, 291 N.Y.S. 441), which reversed on the law an order of the Special Term granting a motion for a peremptory order of mandamus to compel the defendant to issue to petitioner a permit for the erection of certain billboards on vacant lots of land in the city of Troy, and denied the motion, the Mid-State Advertising Corporation appeals.

Order of Appellate Division reversed, and order of Special Term affirmed.

John H. Boderick, of Troy, for appellant.

Frank S. Parmenter, Corp. Counsel, of Troy (John P. Judge, of Troy, of counsel), for respondent.

LOUGHRAN, Judge.

Appellant applied to the respondent, as Superintendent of Buildings of the City of Troy, for permits to erect billboards for general advertising purposes on property of the appellant in that city. The application was denied under an ordinance of the city which provides: "It shall be unlawful to construct or erect any billboard and/or signboard within the corporate limits of the City of Troy, except upon real property owned or leased by the occupants thereof and for the sole purpose of advertising the sale of such real property or of merchandise kept for sale upon such premises. The provision of this Ordinance shall not apply to sky signs, as provided for in section 172 of the Building Code, erected or to be erected upon buildings three stores or more in height."

A peremptory order of mandamus directing issuance of the permits so applied for was granted by the Special Term. The Appellate Division reversed on the law. The single question presented to us is that of the constitutional validity of the foregoing ordinance.

We think the ordinance is void on its face. It is not an attempt by zoning to exclude billboards or other advertising signs from localities where such devices might mar the beauty of natural scenery or distract travelers on congested city streets. Even were we to assume that outdoor advertising on private property within public view may without compensation be restricted by law for cultural or aesthetic reasons alone, this prohibition, which includes all land in the city of Troy, without definition of the structures prescribed or other standard of regulation, cannot be sustained consistently with fundamental constitutional principles. N.Y. Const. art. 1, § 6; U.S.Const. Fourteenth Amendment, § 1; cf. People ex rel. Wineburgh Adv. Co. v. Murphy, 195 N.Y. 126, 88 N.E. 17, 21 L.R.A.(N.S.) 735; People ex rel. Publicity Leasing Co. v. Ludwig, 218 N.Y. 540, 113 N.E. 532; People v. Rubenfeld, 254 N.Y. 245, 248, 249, 172 N.E. 485; Perlmutter v. Greene, 259 N.Y. 327, 182 N.E. 5. See In re Opinion of Justices, 232 Mass. 605, 124 N.E. 319; General Outdoor Advertising Co. v. Department of Public Works, 289 Mass. 149, 193 N.E. 799; Freund, Police Power, § 182; Larremore, Public Aesthetics, 20 Harvard Law Review, 35.

The order of the Appellate Division should be reversed and that of the Special Term affirmed, with costs in this court and in the Appellate Division.

FINCH, Judge (dissenting).

The city of Troy, through its duly chosen representatives, has enacted an ordinance prohib.ting the erection of billboards or signboards within the city limits, except for the purpose of advertising the sale of the real property upon which they are placed or of merchandise kept for sale upon the premises. Excepted, also, are sky signs erected upon buildings three stories or more in height. This court is about to declare the ordinance void as being unconstitutional.

It is not unreasonable for a municipality or a state to desire to beautify its streets or highways. Legislation designed to eliminate advertising signs which tend to mar such beauty and annoy travelers upon the highway should not be deemed arbitrary.

Such a restriction upon the rights of a property owner is not a taking of private property for public use for which the city must compensate the owner. There has been no taking of private property. There has been merely a restriction on the use of the property retained by the property owner. "This is very different from the right of eminent domain, the right of a government to take and appropriate private property to public use, whenever the public exigency requires it; which can be done only on condition of providing a reasonable compensation therefor. ° ° ° [The owner] is restrained; not because the public have occasion to make the like use, or to make any use of the property, or to take any benefit or profit to themselves from it; but because it would be a noxious use, contrary to the maxim, sic utere tuo, ut alienum non lædas. It is not an appropriation of the property to a public use, but the restraint of an injurious private use by the owner, and is therefore not within the principle of property taken under the right of eminent domain." Ch. J. Shaw in Commonwealth v. Alger, 7 Cush. (Mass.) 53, 85.

Every restriction upon the use of property imposed under the police power deprives the owner of some right and is in that sense an abridgment of rights in property without making compensation. Nevertheless, such restrictions, where reasonable, have been held not to deprive the owner of property in violation of the Constitution. The property remains in the possession of the owner. The state does not appropriate it or make use of it. Thus it is not a taking of private property for public use for a state to authorize encroachment by party walls in cities (Jackman v. Rosenbaum Co., 260 U.S. 22, 43 S.Ct. 9, 67 L.Ed. 107), to fix the height of buildings (Welch v. Swasey, 214 U.S. 91, 29 S.Ct. 567, 53 L.Ed. 923), to exclude from residential areas offensive trades (Reinman v. City of Little Rock, 237 U.S. 171, 35 S.Ct. 511, 59 L.Ed. 900), or to establish zoning areas (Zahn v. Board of Public Works of City of Los Angeles, 274 U.S. 325, 47 S.Ct. 594, 71 L.Ed. 1074). Restrictions upon the use of property are limited by the due process clause of the Federal and State Constitutions. Legislation that is unreasonable, arbitrary, or capricious cannot be sustained, but laws which have a reasonable relation to a proper legislative purpose, and are neither arbitrary nor discriminatory, satisfy requirements of due process, and where the law applies equally to all property owners there is no denial of equal protection of the laws. We are inclined to overlook the fact that save for the three exceptions above mentioned, namely, a taking of property, a compliance with the clauses of due process, and an equal protection of the laws, the legislative power of a state of the United States is absolute and unlimited, and every act of the Legislature must be presumed to be in harmony with the Constitution until the contrary is made clearly to appear.

The appellant refers us to cases in this state and others which have held that statutes restricting the display of advertising signs are unconstitutional if they are based solely upon asthetic grounds. People ex rel. Wineburgh Adv. Co. v. Murphy, 195 N.Y. 126, 88 N.E. 17, 21 L.R.A.(N.S.) 735; In re Opinion of Justices, 232 Mass. 605, 124 N.E. 319; Varney & Green v. Williams, 155 Cal. 318, 100 P. 867, 21 L.R.A.(N.S.) 741, 132 Am.St.Rep. 88. Although such a law may have been unwarranted in New York in 1909, when the Wineburgh Case was decided, it does not follow that it is unconstitutional today. The Constitution, it is true, does not change with the times, nor does an emergency or unusual circumstances warrant a disregard of constitutional provisions. A determination of what is due process, aside from procedural matters, however, depends upon the reasonableness of the legislation. Circumstances, surrounding conditions, changed social attitudes, newly-acquired knowledge, do not alter the constitution, but they do alter our view of what is reasonable. Restrictions upon the use of property, which were deemed unreasonable in 1909, are regarded today as entirely reasonable and natural. "The field of regulation constantly widens into new regions." On innumerable occasions the courts have found that with the passage of years, legislation, at one time deemed unreasonable, has become entirely acceptable. Cf. Adkins v. Children's Hospital, of District of Columbia, 261 U.S. 525, 43 S.Ct. 394, 67 L.Ed. 785, 24 A.L.R. 1238; West Coast Hotel Co. v. Parrish, 57 S.Ct. 578, 81 L.Ed. —, decided March 29, 1937; Block v. Hirsh, 256 U.S. 135, 41 S.Ct. 458, 65 L.Ed. 865, 16 A.L.R. 165; Chastleton Corp. v. Sinclair, 264 U.S. 543, 44 S.Ct. 405, 68 L.Ed. 841; Home Bldg. & Loan Ass'n v. Blaisdell, 290 U.S. 398, 54 S.Ct. 231, 78 L.Ed. 413, 88 A.L.R. 1481. See Sharp, Movement in Supreme Court Adjudication, A Study of Modified and Overruled Decisions, 46 Harv.Law Rev. 361, 593, 795.

Moreover, People ex rel. Wineburgh Adv. Co. v. Murphy, 195 N.Y. 126, 88 N.E. 17, 21 L.R.A.(N.S.) 735, dealt only with sky signs, which have been specifically excepted from the effect of the ordinance in the case at bar, and this court has only recently stated: "One of the unsettled questions of the law is the extent to which the concept of nuisance may be enlarged by legislation so as to give protection to sensibilities that are merely cultural or æsthetic." People v. Rubenfeld, 254 N.Y. 245, 248, 172 N.E. 485, 487; Perlmutter v. Greene, 259 N.Y. 327, 332, 182 N.E. 5.

Can it be said that it is unreasonable to decide that a city without ugly and distracting billboards is a more attractive and a more desirable place to dwell in than a city so disfigured? In a number of cases the courts have held that statutes and ordinances limiting or prohibiting billboards are constitutional. Perlmutter v. Greene, 259 N.Y. 327, 182 N.E. 5; Thomas Cusack Co. v. City of Chicago, 242 U.S. 526, 37 S.Ct. 190, 61 L.Ed. 472, L.R.A.1918 A, 136, Ann.Cas.1917C, 594; St. Louis Poster Adv. Co. v. City of St. Louis, 249 U.S. 269, 39 S.Ct. 274, 63 L.Ed. 599; Gibbons v. Missouri, K. and T. Ry. Co., 142 Okl. 146, 285 P. 1040; Horton v. Old Colony Bill Posting Co., 36 R.I. 507, 90 A. 822, Ann.Cas.1916A, 911; Cream City Bill Posting Co. v. City of Milwaukee, 158 Wis. 86, 147 N.W. 25; Kansas City Gunning Adv. Co. v. Kansas City, 240 Mo. 659, 144 S.W. 1099; General Outdoor Adv. Co. v. City of Indianapolis, Dept. of Public Parks, 202 Ind. 85, 172 N.E. 309, 72 A.L.R. 453, 465. In many of these cases it has been admitted in the opinion that the primary motive of the statute seemed to be an æsthetic one, but the courts, still hesitant to uphold the legislation on that ground alone, have made reference to the fact that the statutes might be sustained also as health or safety measures. Often the health or safety element has been slight indeed.

"The [police] power is not limited to regulations designed to promote public health, public morals or public safety or to the suppression of what is offensive, disorderly or unsanitary but extends to so dealing with conditions which exist as to bring out of them the greatest welfare of the people by promoting public convenience or general prosperity." Wulfsohn v. Burden, 241 N.Y. 288, 298, 150 N.E. 120, 122, 43 A.L.R. 651.

Recently Massachusetts held, despite an earlier decision to the contrary, that prohibitions against, and restrictions upon, the display of billboards are constitutional, although they can be justified only upon æsthetic grounds. General Outdoor Adv. Co. v. Dept. of Public Works, 289 Mass. 149, 193 N.E. 799; Gardner, Mass., Billboard Decision, 49 Harv.Law Rev. 869. The United

States Supreme Court has upheld an ordinance zoning a village which entirely excluded billboards from most of the zones. Village of Euclid, Ohio, v. Ambler Realty Co., 272 U.S. 365, 47 S.Ct. 114, 71 L.Ed. 303, 54 A.L.R. 1016. It is submitted that it cannot be said today that an ordinance forbidding the display of billboards is unreasonable, arbitrary, or capricious, even though it is based solely upon the desire to improve the appearance of the city.

It is objected by some that, while the prohibition of advertising signboards would be lawful if applied to a residential district alone, such prohibition is not lawful if extended to business districts. Perhaps the prohibition is more desirable in a residential area than in a business district. Perhaps factories, stores, and the industrial sections of a city naturally tend to be ugly, but it does not follow that business may not be carried on amid more pleasant surroundings. Certainly any city enacting such an ordinance would present a more pleasing picture to the eye than one plastered with blatant signboards. Psychologists and business men themselves tell us that in pleasant surroundings work is done more efficiently. A city might well conclude that it is more likely to attract commercial enterprises and permanent residents if it improves its appearance; that its residents will gain financially by such an improvement; or that the elimination of distracting and annoying billboards will add to the physical and mental well-being of its inhabitants. Such a conclusion is not unreasonable. The billboard eyesore is in many ways akin to annoying sounds and undesirable odors which undoubtedly can be prohibited. Although such restrictions may be more desirable in residential areas, nevertheless, their extension to business districts cannot be termed unreasonable. It is said that in business districts such signs do not mar the beauty of natural scenery or distract travelers on the city streets. Beauty in such areas, may not be so obvious, but that does not prevent the city from restraining additional ugliness.

The order of the Appellate Division should be affirmed, with costs.

CRANE, C. J., and LEHMAN, O'BRIEN, and RIPPEY, JJ., concur with LOUGHRAN, J.

FINCH, J., dissents in opinion.

HUBBS, J., taking no part.

Ordered accordingly.

CROMWELL

v.

FERRIER

19 N.Y. 2d 263, 279 N.Y.S. 2nd 22, 225 N.E. 2d 749 (1967).

Court of Appeals of New York.

March 2, 1967.

Proceeding on application by operator of diner and service station to annul town zoning board of appeals determination suspending completion of billboards as zoning law violation, and to direct board to issue permit for completion. The Supreme Court, Special Term, Orange County, Joseph F. Hawkins, J., denied the application and applicant appealed. The Supreme Court, Appellate Division, Second Department, 24 A.D.2d 998, 266 N.Y.S.2d 188, affirmed and the applicant appealed. The Court of Appeals, Breitel, J., held that ordinance permitting erection of signs on lots devoted to particular use advertising, wherein "lot" is defined as parcel used by one principal building with its accessory buildings, and otherwise proscribing advertising signs is constitutional even though based primarily on esthetic considerations.

Affirmed.

Van Voorhis and Keating, JJ., dissented.

Samuel W. Eager, Jr., Middletown, for appellant.

Angelo J. Ingrassia and Victor O. Smith, Middletown, for respondents.

BREITEL, Judge.

Petitioner appeals from an order of the Appellate Division, Second Department. He brought this proceeding under article 78 of CPLR to review determinations of the respondents Building Inspector and Zoning Board of Appeals of the Town of Wallkill that two billboards on petitioners land violated a town zoning ordinance. Special Term denied the application and the Appellate Division affirmed in a short memorandum by a divided court.

An important constitutional issue is involved. Petitioner concedes that the signboards violate the provisions of the local law in question but argues that the ordinance is unconstitutional.

Since 1961, petitioner has been the co-owner of a 200-acre parcel of land in the Town of Wallkill. The tract is bisected by a highway, Route 17, which passes through the parcel in a general north-south direction. Shortly after acquiring the land, petitioner constructed a service station and a diner upon a portion of the premises west of the highway.

The zoning ordinance was adopted March 14, 1963. In July, 1964 petitioner contracted with a display advertiser for the construction and installation of two signs, advertising petitioners service station and restaurant. The signs were to be located on the portion of petitioners land east of Route 17. Before the signs had been completed respondent Building Inspector served a stop order on petitioner on the ground that the signs violated the town zoning ordinance. Petitioner appealed to the Zoning Board which affirmed the action of the Building Inspector.

The ordinance contains a number of sections which set forth a comprehensive and detailed plan for the regulation of signs in the township. The town is zoned into a number of use districts (e. g., "business, highway commercial, industrial") and there are detailed provisions regulating the size, location and number of signs allowed in each district. The regulations, however, cover only signs which are "related to an establishment located on the same lot" ("accessory" signs) and "non-accessory" signs are implicitly prohibited throughout the township.

As the signs advertising petitioner's service station and restaurant are not on the same lot as the establishments they advertise, they are "non-accessory" signs and, therefore, are excluded by the ordinance. Petitioner argues that the zoning ordinance, insofar as it prohibits the maintenance of nonaccessory signs anywhere within the township, is "arbitrary and unreasonable" and that its application results in "an unconstitutional deprivation of the property of Petitioner".

Special Term held that "The basic issue to be resolved is whether the Zoning Law regulates or prohibits billboards". The court dismissed the petition because the law "does not prohibit; it does regulate". On appeal, the majority in the Appellate Division came to the same conclusion as it regarded the ordinance "as reasonably regulating the erection of signs in the Town", and that the ordinance "promotes symmetry and protects the Town from becoming an eyesore". The two Justices who dissented concluded that the "flat prohibition of all advertising signs on all vacant land" was "unreasonable and confiscatory", citing Matter of Mid-State Adv. Corp. v. Bond (274 N.Y. 82, 8 N.E.2d, 286).

The Appellate Division distinguished the ordinance at issue from the one ruled unconstitutional in the *Bond* case (supra) "where erection of billboards or signboards, save for three isolated exceptions, was prohibited throughout the City of Troy". The dissenting Justices in that court, however, are correct in their conclusion that *Bond* is in point. The ordinance in that case read as follows: "It shall be unlawful to construct or erect any billboard and/or signboard within the corporate limits of the City of Troy, except upon real property owned or leased by the occupants thereof and for the sole purpose of advertising the sale of such real property or of merchandise kept for sale upon such premises. The provision of this Ordinance shall not apply to sky signs, as provided for in Section 172 of the Building Code, erected or to be erected upon buildings three stories or more in height." (274 N.Y., p. 84, 8 N.E.2d p. 286).

The petitioner in *Bond* (supra) applied for a permit to erect billboards on vacant lots in the City of Troy and the application was denied on the ground that they would violate this ordinance. Special Term then granted the petitioner a peremptory order of mandamus to compel the city to issue the permit, but the Appellate Division, one Justice dissenting, reversed on the law (Kahl v. Sinclair Refining Co., 249 App. Div. 681, 291 N.Y.S. 719).

On appeal, this court reversed the order of the Appellate Division and affirmed that of Special Term. The majority held: "We think the ordinance is void on its face. It is not an attempt by zoning to exclude billboards or other advertising signs from localities where such devices might mar the beauty of natural scenery or distract travelers on congested city streets. Even were we to assume that outdoor advertising on private property within public view may without compensation be restricted by law for cultural or aesthetic reasons alone, this prohibition, which includes *all* land in the city of Troy, without definition of the structures proscribed or other standards of regulation, cannot be sustained consistently with fundamental constitutional principles. N.Y.Const. art. 1, § 6; U.S. Const. Fourteenth Amendment, § 1. cf. People ex rel. Wineburgh Adv. Co. v. Murphy, 195 N.Y. 126, 88 N.E. 17, 21 L.R.A. (N.S.) 735; People ex rel. Publicity Leasing Co. v. Ludwig, 218 N.Y. 540, 113 N.E. 532; People v. Rubenfeld, 254 N.Y. 245, 248, 249, 172 N.E. 485; Perlmutter v. Greene, 259 N.Y. 327, 182 N.E. 5 [81 A.L.R. 1543]. See In re Opinion of Justices, 232 Mass. 605, 124 N.E. 319; General Outdoor Adv. Co. v. Dept. of Public Works, 289 Mass. 149, 193 N.E. 799; Freund, Police Power, § 182; Larremore, Public Aesthetics, 20 Harvard Law Review, 35." (274 N.Y., supra, pp. 84-85, 8 N.E.2d p. 286; emphasis in orginal.)

Judge FINCH, the sole dissenter, argued that "It is not unreasonable for a municipality or a state to desire to beautify its streets or highways", and that the ordinance should not be deemed unconstitutional simply because it sought to achieve that end (274 N.Y., supra, p. 85, 8 N.E.2d p. 287).

For present purposes, then, the ordinance involved in *Bond* (supra) and the one at issue here are indistinguishable. The provisions of the Wallkill zoning ordinance are "substantially different" from those considered in *Bond* only insofar as the prohibition of nonaccessory signs may be implied from the comprehensive provisions of the ordinance regulating accessory signs. But the effects of the two ordinances upon prospective owners of nonaccessory signs are the same: the signs are prohibited.

Both Special Term and the majority in the Appellate Division fell into an analytical trap when they distinguished *Bond* (supra) from this case on the ground that one ordinance "prohibited" nonaccessory signs while the other "regulates" signs.

It is possible to manipulate concepts by the selection of a different level of verbalization, that is, a different level of generalization. An entirely different result can be "logically" forced. In this case, by selecting a wider generalization, namely, that of regulation of signs, it can be said that there is no prohibition of nonaccessory signs because any kind of regulation must embrace incidental and subordinate prohibition. On the other hand, by declining to consider all signs in one class and, instead, by insisting that there are two classes of signs each independent of the other, namely, accessory signs and nonaccessory signs, one forces the conclusion that there is an absolute prohibition of nonaccessory signs and only regulation with respect to accessory signs. That kind of analysis is fruitless because the conclusion is dictated by the way one starts the train of reasoning. The real question is more often whether particular conduct is prohibited regardless of one's method of nomenclature or verbal classification.

On any realistic view, the ordinance involved in this case is indistinguishable in effect from the one ruled unconstitutional in *Bond* (supra). Consequently, reexamination of the *Bond* case is required if the ordinance at issue is to be sustained as constitutional.

[1-3] It is concluded that the decisional as well as the practical bases for the holding in *Bond* (supra) are either no longer valid or have changed so considerably that the case should be overruled. As Judge FINCH commented in his dissent in *Bond*: "The Constitution, it is true, does not change with the times, nor does an emergency or unusual circumstances warrant a disregard of constitutional provisions. A determination of what is due process, aside from procedural matters, however, depends upon the reasonableness of the legislation. Circumstances, surrounding conditions, changed social attitudes, newly-acquired knowledge, do not alter the Constitution, but they do alter our view of what is reasonable. Restrictions upon the use of property, which were deemed unreasonable in 1909, are regarded today as entirely reasonable and natural." (274 N.Y. 82, 87, supra, 8 N.E.2d 286, 288.)

The question, then, is whether the rule in the *Bond* case (supra) reflects present conditions and understanding of present-day community conditions.

One important factor in the courts' increasingly permissive treatment of similar zoning ordinances has been the gradual acceptance of the conclusion that a zoning law is not necessarily invalid because its primary, if not its exclusive objective, is the esthetic enhancement of the particular area involved, so long as it is related if only generally to the economic and cultural setting of the regulating community. On this point, People v. Stover, (12 N.Y.2d 462, 240 N.Y.S.2d 734, 191 N.E.2d 272) is now the leading case. In *Stover*, this court held that a city ordinance which prohibited the erection of clotheslines in certain areas of residential districts was not invalid even though the obvious purpose of the ordinance was almost exclusively esthetic. Writing for the majority, Judge FULD, now Chief Judge, traced the history of the courts' treatment of zoning ordinances designed partly or primarily to satisfy esthetic objectives, commencing with the early cases such as People ex rel. Wineburgh Adv. Co. v. Murphy (195 N.Y. 126, 88 N.E. 17) which had held that esthetic considerations alone would be insufficient to justify exercise of the police power. But "since 1930", Judge FULD noted that the question has been an open one in New York (12 N.Y.2d, p. 466, 240 N.Y.S.2d 734, 191 N.E.2d 272). He then concludes: "Once it be conceded that aesthetics is a valid subject of legislative concern, the conclusion seems inescapable that reasonable legislation designed to promote that end is a valid and permissible exercise of the police power." (12 N.Y.2d, p. 467, 240 N.Y.S.2d at p. 738, 191 N.E.2d p. 275.)

This holding is important for present purposes not only because, realistically, the primary objective of any anti-billboard ordinance is an esthetic one (Dukeminier, Zoning for Aesthetic Objectives: A Reappraisal, 20 Law & Contemp.Prob. 218,220) but also because it at least partially undermines the authority of *Bond*, (supra). While the majority opinion in that case held that the ordinance before it would be unconstitutional even if "aesthetic reasons alone" could support such a legislative enactment, it is significant that the first case cited by the court in support of its holding was People ex rel. Wineburgh Adv. Co. v. Murphy (195 N.Y. 126, 88 N.E. 17, supra) upon which Judge FULD commented in the *Stover* case (supra). Moreover, *Bond* also cited People v. Rubenfeld (254 N.Y. 245, 172 N.E. 485) and Perlmutter v. Greene (259 N.Y. 327), two decisions also cited by *Stover* for its observation that the esthetic issue had been an open one since 1930.

In the only other New York case cited by *Bond* (supra), People ex rel. Publicity Leasing Co. v. Ludwig (218 N.Y. 540, 113 N.E. 532), the court held that an ordinance passed by the Board of Aldermen of New York City limiting the height of signs on roofs was not arbitrary and unreasonable (218 N.Y., p. 543, 113 N.E. 532).

[4] Consequently, insofar as the *Bond* holding (supra) was predicated on the now discarded notion that esthetic objectives alone will not support a zoning ordinance, it may no longer be a valid precedent. But, as pointed out in *Stover* (supra), the question remains whether such an ordinance should still be voided because it constitutes an " 'unreasonable device of implementing community policy' " (12 N.Y.2d 462, 467, 240 N.Y.S.2d 734, 738, 191 N.E.2d 272, 275, quoting from Dukeminier, 20 Law & Contemp.Prob. 218, 231, supra). Moreover, *Bond* is cited in *Stover* as a case in which "the legislative body [went] too far in the name of aesthetics" (12 N.Y.2d, p. 468, 240 N.Y.S.2d p. 738, 191 N.E.2d p. 275).

In this respect, petitioner argues that the legislative distinction between identification signs and nonaccessory signs is unreasonable and discriminatory. Neither *Bond* (supra) nor any other decision of this court has dealt specifically with this point but numerous cases from other jurisdictions have had occasion to do so. In nearly all, zoning ordinances which have distinguished between accessory and nonaccessory signs have been upheld, providing that the distinctions were applied in a reasonable manner. The following excerpt from the opinion of Mr. Justice BRENNAN in United Adv. Corp. v. Borough of Raritan (11 N.J. 144, 93 A.2d 362) is typical: "The business sign is in actuality a part of the business itself, just as the structure housing the business is a part of it, and the authority to conduct the business in a district carries with it the right to maintain a business sign on the premises subject to reasonable regulations in that regard as in the case of this ordinance. Plaintiff's placements of its advertising signs, on the other hand, are made pursuant to the conduct of the business of outdoor advertising itself, and in effect what the ordinance provides is that this business shall not to that extent be allowed in the borough. It has long been settled that the unique nature of outdoor advertising and the nuisances fostered by billboards and similar outdoor structures located by persons in the business of outdoor advertising, justify the separate classification of such structures for the purposes of governmental regulation and restriction." (11 N.J. 150, 93 A.2d 365.)

To similar effect, see, also, Murphy, Inc. v. Town of Westport, (131 Conn. 292, 40 A.2d 177, 156 A.L.R. 568); Opinion of the Justices (103 N.H. 268, 169 A.2d 762); Ghaster Props. v. Preston (176 Ohio St. 425, 200 N.E.2d 328; Petition of Franklin Bldrs. (207 A.2d 12, 30 [Del.Super.]); Metromedia, Inc. v. City of Pasadena (216 Cal.App.2d 270, 276-277, 30 Cal.Rptr. 731); Schloss v. Jamison(262 N.C. 108, 136 S.E.2d 691); cf. Township of Superior v. Reimel Sign Co. (362 Mich. 481, 107 N.W.2d 808); but see Triborough Bridge & Tunnel Auth. v. Crystal & Son (2 A.D.2d 37, 40-41, 153 N.Y.S.2d 387, affd. 2 N.Y.2d 961, 162 N.Y.S.2d 362, 142 N.E.2d 426).

Nearly all of the decisions last cited, however, upheld ordinances which prohibited nonaccessory signs in certain areas of a town but not in others. In the relatively few cases which have passed upon ordinances similar to the one involved here, the results have not been uniform.

In Norate Corp. v. Zoning Bd. of Adjustment (417 Pa. 397, 207 A.2d 890) the ordinance at issue prohibited all nonaccessory signs throughout the township. The Supreme Court of Pennsylvania, while recognizing the validity of the distinction between accessory and nonaccessory billboards, held that the ordinance nevertheless "does not attempt to regulate, but to prohibit" and that it must be declared invalid as "too general, too broad and unreasonable" (417 Pa. 407, 207 A.2d 895). On the other hand, in United Adv. Corp. v. Borough of Raritan (11 N.J. 144, 93 A.2d 362, supra), the Supreme Court of New Jersey upheld the constitutionality of a nearly identical statute. The opinion noted "It is enough that outdoor advertising has characteristic features which have long been deemed sufficient to sustain regulations or prohibitions peculiarly applicable to it" (11 N.J., p. 151, 93 A.2d, p. 366). See, also, Murphy, Inc. v. Town of Westport (131 Conn. 292, 40 A.2d 177, 156 A.L.R. 568, supra) where the Supreme Court of Errors of Connecticut upheld in principle a similar statute but remanded the case to the trial court for further facts.

While the proliferation of nonaccessory signs or billboards was a burgeoning problem in 1937, when the *Bond* case (supra) was decided, since that time the amounts expended on outdoor advertising have increased nearly fourfold (Statistical Abstract of the United States [1966], p. 836). It is, of course, unnecessary to discuss at length the effect that this blight has had upon the national landscape; suffice it to say that it has probably exceeded the most pessimistic forecasts of the pre-World War II years.

During the same period, however, the proportional share of the advertising dollar expended on outdoor advertising has markedly declined (Statistical Abstract, p. 836, supra). This may be explained in part by the increasing number of restrictive State statutes and local ordinances which have been enacted to check the spread of billboards (see Dukeminier, 20 Law & Contemp.Prob., pp. 220, 221, 233, supra, for a partial compilation). (Perhaps the major reason for the decline has been the corresponding increases in the expenditures allocated to other media, particularly television and magazines.)

In other words, since 1937, outdoor advertising has become a less and less important facet of the advertising business while, at the same time, its deleterious effects have substantially increased. Moreover, the attitude of the courts both in the general field of economic regulation as well as in the specific area under discussion here has also changed with the passage of time.

[5-9] In concluding that the ordinance is constitutional and that the restrictive outlook of the *Bond* case (supra) should no longer be followed, it does not mean that any esthetic consideration suffices to justify prohibition. The exercise of the police power should not extend to every artistic conformity or nonconformity. Rather, what is involved are those esthetic considerations which bear substantially on the economic, social, and cultural patterns of a community or district. Advertising signs and billboards, if misplaced, often are egregious examples of ugliness, distraction, and deterioration. They are just as much subject to reasonable controls, including prohibition, as enterprises which emit offensive noises, odors, or debris. The eye is entitled to as much recognition as the other senses, but, of course, the offense to the eye must be substantial and be deemed to have material effect on the community or district pattern. Such limitations are suggested in the *Stover* case (12 N.Y.2d 462, 467-468, 240 N.Y.S.2d 734, 191 N.E.2d 272, supra). No doubt, difficult cases will arise in which there will be the necessity for discrimination on very fine bases, but that is not a new difficulty for Legislatures, administrative agencies, or courts. This case does not involve, however, such a difficulty.

Lastly, petitioner suggests that a town, as distinguished from a village, does not have the legislative power to adopt the ordinance in question. The recent decision of this court in Koffman v. Town of Vestal (23 A.D.2d 199, 259 N.Y.S.2d 958, affd. 18 N.Y.2d 855, 276 N.Y.S.2d 113, 222 N.E.2d 733) disposes of that issue.

Accordingly, the order of the Appellate Division should be affirmed, with costs to respondents.

VAN VOORHIS and KEATING, Judges (dissenting).

We dissent and vote to reverse. Although we have recognized esthetic considerations in certain instances as a ground for sustaining zoning regulations, there is no showing in this case that prohibition of nonaccessory signs, as opposed to regulation, is necessary. To proscribe all such signs here constitutes a serious interference with a man's right to use his own property to advertise his own business conducted on his own property across the street. We believe our holding in Matter of Mid-State Adv. Corp. v. Bond (274 N.Y. 82, 8 N.E.2d 286) should be followed on this record.

FULD, C. J., and BURKE, SCILEPPI and BERGAN, JJ., concur with BREITEL, J.

VAN VOORHIS and KEATING, JJ., dissent and vote to reverse in a memorandum.

Order affirmed.

Questions and Notes

On Troy

1. In which district did this case arise?
2. Was Troy a good choice for a test case on this point?

On Cromwell

1. Where was the sign located in reference to the principal use? Why was it an "advertising sign"?
2. Would it have been possible to distinguish the Troy case?
3. Why do you think the New York court did not do so? In this connection, compare the comic-opera case of People v. Stover, 12 N.Y. 2d 462, 240, N.Y.S. 2d 734, 191 N.E. 2d 272 (1963), appeal dismissed per curiam 375 U.S. 42 (1963).

UNITED ADVERTISING CORPORATION

v.

METUCHEN

76 N.J. Super. 301, 184 A.2d 441(1962), affd, 42 N.J. 1, 198 A.2d 447(1964).

Superior Court of New Jersey

Law Division.

Sept. 17, 1962.

Action attacking validity of borough's zoning ordinance prohibiting off-premises outdoor advertising in business and manufacturing district. On remand from the Supreme Court, 35 N.J. 193, 172 A.2d 429, the Superior Court, Convery, J. C. C., temporarily assigned, held that in view of small size of community, its predominantly residential character, and its plans for future, ordinance prohibiting off-premises outdoor advertising, even in business and manufacturing district, did not lack reasonable basis.

Order accordingly.

Martin J. Loftus, Newark, for plaintiff (Marilyn H. Loftus, Newark, attorney).

Robert F. Moss, Metuchen, for defendants.

CONVERY, J. C. C. (temporarily assigned).

This is an action in lieu of prerogative writs wherein plaintiff challenges the validity of the defendant borough's zoning ordinance which prohibits off-premise outdoor advertising signs throughout the entire community. The determination sought is that the absolute prohibition, as applied to the business and manufacturing districts, is unreasonable.

Plaintiff United Advertising Corporation is engaged in the business of erecting, maintaining and leasing standard outdoor advertising signs. On or about December 4, 1959 it applied to Metuchen's building inspector for a permit to erect two billboards. Both were to be located on land owned by the Pennsylvania Railroad and leased to plaintiff. Billboard #1 was proposed to be erected in the B-1 business district and billboard #2 in the M-1 manufacturing district. Metuchen's zoning ordinance prohibited the use of outdoor advertising signs throughout the entire borough which do not advertise business conducted on the premises, services rendered on the premises, and/or products offered for sale on the premises. Accordingly, the applications were denied, and plaintiff commenced this in lieu proceeding challenging the validity of those sections of the ordinance which so restrict the erection of billboards and seeking an order requiring the issuance of the permits to it. Defendant's answer admitted all of the allegations in the complaint except those appearing in paragraphs 7 and 8, which contend:

> "7. The refusal to issue the permit was arbitrary, unreasonable, and discriminatory.
>
> 8. Article VII, Section 1(g) and those phases of Article IX, Section 1, which prohibit billboards in those districts except to advertise the business conducted on the premises, services rendered on the premises, and/or products offered for sale on the premises are invalid and unconstitutional; violate the equal protection clause of the Federal Constitution; constitute an unreasonable, arbitrary and discriminatory exercise of the police power; bear no reasonable relation to the police power under the Municipal Home Rule Act; are not authorized by the police power or any valid law of the State of New Jersey."

Defendant's motion for summary judgment was granted, but on appeal the matter was reversed and remanded to this court to the end that evidence be taken to determine whether "under the particular facts and circumstances existing in the business and manufacturing districts of Metuchen, the manner and method in which its signs are to be erected and maintained and the resulting benefits redounding to the community at large, the specific prohibitory features of the ordinance here challenged constitute an improper exercise of police power and are arbitrary and unreasonable."

United Advertising Corp. v. Borough of Metuchen, 35 N.J. 193, 196, 172 A.2d 429, 430 (1961).

[1] On April 17, 1962 Metuchen's zoning ordinance was amended and the following are its pertinent provisions:

"ARTICLE I

*   *   *

Section 2.   Definitions

*   *   *

ADVERTISING SIGNS—A sign which directs attention to a business, commodity, service or entertainment conducted, sold or offered elsewhere than on the lot where the sign is located.

*   *   *

ARTICLE XII

Signs

Section 1: * * *

C. *Advertising Signs.* No advertising signs shall be permitted in any district in the Borough of Metuchen."

Both counsel agree that the amendment does not alter the issues here involved. However, the effect of this decision will bear upon the ordinance adopted on April 17, 1962, for it is fundamental that "[t]he zoning ordinance in effect at the time the case is ultimately decided is controlling." Hohl v. Readington Tp., 37 N.J. 271, 279, 181 A.2d 150, 155 (1962).

[2] The Legislature is empowered by our Constitution to enact general laws pursuant to which municipalities may adopt zoning ordinances "limiting and restricting to specified districts and regulating therein, buildings and structures, according to their construction, and the nature and extent of their use, and the nature and extent of the uses of land, and the exercise of such authority shall be deemed to be within the police power of the State." N.J.Const. Art. IV, Sec. VI, par. 2. Municipalities were granted extensive power to create districts and regulate structures and the use of land therein through zoning by R.S. 40:55-30, 31, N.J.S.A. But the power must be exercised to accomplish one of its legitimate aims, i. e., the statutorily stated purposes set forth in R.S. 40:55-32, N.J.S.A., which provides:

"Such regulations shall be in accordance with a comprehensive plan and designed for one or more of the following purposes: to lessen congestion in the streets; secure safety from fire, panic and other dangers; promote health, morals or the general welfare; provide adequate light and air; prevent the overcrowding of land or buildings; avoid undue concentration of population. Such regulations shall be made with reasonable consideration, among other things, to the character of the district and its peculiar suitability for particular uses, and with a view of conserving the value of property and encouraging the most appropriate use of land throughout such municipality."

Judicial review of a zoning ordinance is limited. The court may not interfere unless the presumption in favor of its validity is overcome by affirmative proofs that it was not adopted to accomplish one of the legitimate aims for which the power was granted. Vickers v. Tp. Com. of Gloucester Tp., 37 N.J. 232, 181 A.2d 129 (1962).

Plaintiff urges essentially two grounds to support its contention that the ordinance is unreasonable, arbitrary and unconstitutional: (1) there exists no reasonable basis upon which legitimate constitutional classifications may be formulated which would distinguish, and therefore permit, different treatment of on-premise outdoor advertising and off-premise outdoor advertising; and (2) the absolute prohibition of off-premise outdoor advertising in the business and manufacturing districts of Metuchen has no legal justification in fact and is accordingly unreasonable, arbitrary and unconstitutional.

I.

[3] As to plaintiff's first contention that the ordinance's classification is unconstitutional, the law in this State would appear to be to the contrary. In United Advertising Corp. v. Raritan, 11 N.J. 144, 93 A.2d 362 (1952), the same ground was urged as to the invalidity of the ordinance there in question. In answer to that contention, the Raritan court said "that [off-premise] outdoor advertising has characteristic features which have long been deemed sufficient to sustain regulations or prohibitions peculiarly applicable to it." United Advertising Corp. v. Raritan, supra, at p. 151, 93 A.2d at p. 366. See also Bd. of Com'rs, Ridgefield Park v. A. S. Pater Realty Co., 73 N.J.Super. 155, 179 A.2d 169 (Ch.Div. 1962). Metuchen's ordinance would therefore seem to possess no constitutional infirmity in this regard.

It is clear that the Raritan case sustained the power of a municipality through its zoning to regulate outdoor advertising. This, plaintiff does not dispute. What is put in issue, however, is the reasonableness of the regulations. The thrust of plaintiff's position is that the particular facts and circumstances existing in Metuchen's business and manufacturing districts, considered with the nature of plaintiff's business, its method of operation and its effect upon the community, make unreasonable and arbitrary the prohibition found in the ordinance. This necessitates an inquiry into the character of Metuchen and, in particular, the districts involved; the zoning end sought to be accomplished by the restriction; and the private rights affected.

II.

As to this issue of reasonableness, the problems framed by the testimony adduced before me are primarily these: (a) would off-premise outdoor advertising signs in the manufacturing and business districts, by their effect on vehicular traffic, produce safety hazards; and (b) would off-premise outdoor advertising signs in the manufacturing and business districts be detrimental to the general welfare of the community.

A.

As to the safety problem, the expert testimony was authoritative and well documented. Dr. Leonard Strulowitz, a licensed optometrist of the State of New Jersey and an active participant in a committee on traffic safety formed by the New Jersey Board of Trustees of Optometrists, testified that roadside outdoor advertising signs were actually a stimulus to the driving public. He said that long stretches of monotonous highway driving tended to "lull" the driver and cause a phenomenon known as "highway hypnosis." In that condition the automobile operator is actually not consciously aware of what he is doing and is thus a danger to the safety of others. Roadside signs act as a stimulus which keep his brain busy and his mind alert. Although the road in question probably would cause little, if any, "highway hypnosis," Dr. Strulowitz could not "conceive of any situation in which the stimuli ° ° ° such as road signs, would not be beneficial." With respect to the signs and locations involved here, based upon his own personal knowledge of the areas, Dr. Strulowitz concluded that the signs would in no way be detrimental to safe driving.

J. Carl McMonagle, a civil engineer, supervised a field study conducted by the Planning and Traffic Division of the Michigan State Highway Department. The project was carried out at the request of the Bureau of Public Works, Division of the U. S. Department of Commerce, and The National Safety Council, its purpose being according to McMonagle, "to determine in what way each roadside feature, whether it be a driveway, tavern, store, a sign, or other feature studied, contributed in any way to accidents." The survey was conducted on about 70 miles of U.S. Highway 24. This road was selected because it possessed nearly every type of land use and roadside feature, and the effect of each of these factors on traffic safety could be, and, ultimately was, analyzed and measured. The report concluded that roadside signs, whether on- or off-premise, had no effect on traffic safety. Based upon his personal investigation of Metuchen, McMonagle felt that these results were applicable to its business and manufacturing districts because of their similarity to a portion of U.S. Highway 24, and, further, that the erection of the two outdoor standard poster signs at the locations in question would not cause traffic hazards.

In addition to his supervision of the Michigan report, he also collaborated with Dr. Lauer on an article entitled "Do Road Signs Affect Accidents?" which appeared in the July 1955 Traffic Quarterly Dr. Lauer is a Professor of Psychology and Director of the Driving Laboratory at Iowa State College. He had conducted a laboratory investigation of the effect of advertising signs on traffic accidents to determine whether it would confirm the Michigan field study supervised by McMonagle. The article referred to above is a fusing of the two studies and concludes that "there is no significant relationship shown between outdoor advertising signs and highway accidents. The evidence, if any, is slightly in favor of having something along the highway to arouse the motorist and keep him alerted as far as efficient driving is concerned." Traffic Quarterly, July 1955, p. 329. See also by Dr. Lauer, The Psychology of Driving (1960).

Dr. Ernest C. Blanche, a statistician, offered expert testimony with respect to the Michigan survey. He contended that the statistical method used in that report to analyze the cause and effect relationship between roadside features and highway accidents is scientifically accurate. Utilizing that procedure one can measure precisely the effect of one feature or a group of features on traffic accidents. Based on his study of the report Dr. Blanche concluded that its results are definite mathematical proof that there is no positive relationship between advertising signs and accidents.

[4] The evidence on the safety issue was uncontroverted. It has persuaded me, and accordingly I find, that outdoor advertising signs would constitute no safety hazard in the business and manufacturing districts of Metuchen.

B.

Metuchen's contention as to the problem of the general welfare is grounded upon the character of the community. The borough's area is 2.9 square miles. It may roughly be divided into quadrants in the following manner: Main Street runs in a generally north-south direction and the Pennsylvania Railroad is a generally east-west direction. These two arteries, of course, cross and thus divide Metuchen into four sections. The business districts are situated largely in the center of the town and the manufacturing district is located generally in the northwest and southwest sections. The business districts have a diversity of uses; e.g., parking lots, gasoline stations, automobile sales, food markets, real estate offices, residences which have been converted into commercial and professional uses, and funeral homes. The manufacturing district is largely vacant land or utilized for agricultural purposes. Only a small portion of it is crossed by major streets.

Metuchen is serviced by two railways: the Pennsylvania which, as noted above, runs in a generally east-west direction, and the Lehigh Valley which crosses it from northwest to southwest. The community for the most part is a residential one and, in fact, this is the essence of defendant's position. Metuchen contends that it is reasonable for a municipality about 85% residential to exclude off-premise outdoor advertising signs, for in so doing the high quality of land use is maintained.

[5] The purposes and criteria of valid zoning as laid down by our Legislature in R.S. 40:55-32, N.J.S.A. are set forth above. However, it has been stipulated between the parties that the *proposed billboards* "would not prevent adequate light or air from getting to any surrounding build-

ings or dwellings * * * would not cause overcrowding * * * would not decrease the property value of land in the Borough of Metuchen * * * would not produce objectionable noise, vibration, odor, smoke, gas, glare, offensive or radioactive waste materials or effluent" and would not conceal immoral acts. It was further agreed that "the business and manufacturing character of the said districts in Metuchen would not be changed by the creation of the proposed billboards." These agreed upon points do much to allay fears Metuchen may have that its highly residential character would be jeopardized by the presence of plaintiff's signs at the *proposed locations.* Indeed, as applied to these sites, the prohibition may be without legitimate basis and unreasonable. But plaintiff is not here seeking relief in the nature of a variance or a special exception. The scope of its attack goes to the constitutionality of the ordinance *in toto* as applied to the business and manufacturing districts, and "[o]rdinarily the invalidity of an ordinance as to a small parcel will not vitiate the treatment of the entire district within which it is situated." Kozesnik v. Montgomery Twp., 24 N.J. 154, 183, 131 A.2d 1, 17 (1957); Fischer v. Bedminster Tp., 11 N.J. 194, 205, 93 A 2d 378 (1952); Fanale v. Hasbrouck Heights, 26 N.J. 320, 324, 139 A.2d 749 (1958). Thus the inquiry precipitated by plaintiff's challenge should not be confined merely to the two proposed locations, but must be at least as broad as the business and manufacturing districts in their entirety.

It is clear that outdoor advertising is a legitimate business, United Advertising Corp. v. Raritan, supra, and is so recognized by our Legislature, N.J.S.A. 54:40-50 et seq. It is generally conceded to be the medium that can expose an advertising message to more people, more often, for less money than any other. The testimony reveals that its primary function is to accelerate "the fulfillment of desires, and in doing so it provides mass distribution which is essential in our economy with mass production, and it is a means of speeding up the movement of the product to the consumer." When an individual responds to the message his purchase is, of course, made at a store in some community. For this reason all advertising is directed to local community purchasing. Plainly, this could contribute in some measure to the economic betterment of any community in terms of tax revenue and employment.

It was further testified that outdoor advertising is related to the social betterment of communities. Advertising "space" is contributed to the State of New Jersey to promote safety campaigns; to the New Jersey Education Association to promote public understanding of the schools and teacher recruitment problems; to the Red Cross, to 4–H Clubs, to the Girl Scouts, to Crippled Children appeals, to Cerebral Palsy, to Multiple Sclerosis and many other organizations dedicated to and working for the social good. The evidence in these areas of social and economic betterment persuasively shows that outdoor advertising could have some definite and useful role in the affairs of community life. However, each municipality need not provide for every use which, in the abstract, may be potentially beneficial and zoning regulations may be sustained on the broad concept of "general welfare" if it "is reasonably calculated to advance the community as a social, economic and political unit." Vickers v. Tp. Com. of Gloucester Tp., supra, 37 N.J. at p. 247, 181 A.2d at p. 137.

Sound zoning requires that local officials anticipate the long range needs of the future as well as those of the present and the immediately foreseeable future. Vickers v. Tp. Com. of Gloucester Tp., supra. However, plaintiff contends that the exclusion did not result from any rational process and was not designed to accomplish a legitimate end in accordance with a comprehensive plan, in that no attention was given to it in the master plan. But "a plan may readily be revealed in an end-product—here the zoning ordinance—and no more is required * * *." Kozesnik v. Montgomery Twp., supra, 24 N.J. at p. 166, 131 A.2d at p. 8. If a prohibition as an integral part of a zoning ordinance is reasonably calculated to meet or anticipate the needs of the total community its absence from the master plan is of little moment.

[6, 7] As noted above, Metuchen is largely residential, with only limited areas zoned for business and manufacturing It is urged that sound planning for this community requires that its highly residential character be maintained. Nearly every artery leading into Metuchen reflects the high quality of the land use, and the plans for the future include high quality industrial developments, upgrading the quality of stores, and development of quality shopping areas which would provide merchandise "appealing to the higher level income clientele." Considering Metuchen in its entirety, the prohibition of off-premise advertising signs does not appear to be arbitrary or unreasonable. Certainly a community of this character, to promote the general welfare, may plan to retain through zoning the high quality of its land use. To this end Metuchen has made a legislative judgment that the purposes of R.S. 40:55-32, N.J.S.A. would be served, *inter alia,* by the exclusion of off-premise advertising signs throughout the entire community. In my opinion, its size, the nature of its land uses and its plans for the future form a reasonable basis for that judgment and therefore this court may not interfere.

Thus, I conclude that the prohibition found in the ordinance is not unreasonable and must remain undisturbed. An appropriate order may be submitted.

UNITED ADVERTISING CORPORATION

v.

METUCHEN

42 N.J. 1, 198 A.2d 447 (1964).

Supreme Court of New Jersey.

Argued Jan. 20, 1964.

Decided March 16, 1964

Case involving validity of zoning ordinance provision. The defendant borough obtained summary judgment on motion but the case was reversed, 35 N.J. 193, 172 A.2d 429. On remand to the Superior Court, Law Division, the defendant again prevailed, 76 N.J.Super. 301, 184 A.2d 441. The plaintiff advertising company's appeal was certified by the Supreme Court before the Appellate Division heard it. The Supreme Court held that a zoning ordinance prohibiting outdoor advertising signs other than those related to business conducted on the premises made a supportable classification and did not violate the statute requiring uniformity for each class or kind of buildings or other structures or uses of land throughout each district.
Affirmed.

Hall, J., dissented.

Martin J. Loftus, Newark, for appellant (Marilyn H. Loftus, Newark, on the brief, Loftus & Loftus, Newark, attorneys).

Robert F. Moss, Metuchen, for respondents.

The opinion of the court was delivered

PER CURIAM.

This case involves the validity of a provision of a zoning ordinance prohibiting outdoor advertising signs other than those related to a business conducted on the premises. Off-premise signs are prohibited throughout the municipality. Plaintiff sought to erect one such sign in a business district and another in a manufacturing district. Defendant obtained summary judgment on motion. We reversed, holding that plaintiff was entitled to adduce facts in support of its constitutional challenges. United Advertising Corp. v. Borough of Metuchen, 35 N.J. 193, 172 A.2d 429 (1961). The case was thereafter tried and judgment again rendered in favor of defendant. We certified plaintiff's appeal before the Appellate Division heard it.

Plaintiff wishes to erect billboards 12 feet in height by 25 feet in width. These are standard dimensions for billboards throughout the country. Plaintiff concedes its billboards do not belong in residential or scenic areas, but its business being lawful, it claims it should be permitted to operate among other businesses and in industrial districts as well.

Plaintiff's position was rejected in United Advertising Corp. v Borough of Raritan, 11 N.J. 144, 93 A.2d 362 (1952), where the Court refused to strike down an ordinance barring off-premise signs throughout the municipality. Plaintiff contends that case was wrongly decided because the evils once thought to abound in this setting were unreal or had been eliminated by the time of that decision and in truth no zoning purpose remained to be furthered by the ban. Further, plaintiff urges the discrimination between off-premise and non-premise signs violates the mandate of N.J.S.A. 40:55-31 that "All such regulations shall be uniform for each class or kind of buildings or other structures or uses of land throughout each district * * *."

As to the first proposition, plaintiff starts with an analysis of Thomas Cusack Co. v. City of Chicago, 242 U.S. 526, 37 S.Ct. 190, 61 L.Ed. 472 (1917), one of the cases cited n the Raritan opinion. Cusack did not involve a zoning ordinance. Rather the ordinance was addressed to the special evils then charged to billboards. They included the accumulation of offensive materials and rubbish, and the shield afforded for immoral practices and for loiterers and criminals. As to such matters, plaintiff says that today billboards are so constructed, positioned and maintained that these ills no longer exist. In other words, plaintiff says that proper regulation will suffice and enforcement is not so burdensome that prohibition is warranted.

With respect to whether billboards create traffic hazards, a topic which came to the scene after Cusack, plaintiff says that, as to obstruction of view, appropriate setbacks are sufficient; and as to distraction of the motorist, plaintiff claims the billboard, although designed to attract, presents no hazard because a driver's peripheral vision will embrace the roadway while he looks left or right to read the advertisement, and in fact such momentary diversions prevent road hypnosis and thus mean safer driving. Expert testimony was offered to maintain the last proposition, and the trial court was persuaded by it. We have some reservations as to whether billboards would not be a hazard in heavy traffic where a driver has quite enough to do to watch for sudden movements of men and machines. At any rate, for present purposes we accept the trial court's agreement with that testimony.

That the evils which prompted earlier legislation may be gone or be well in hand does not end the inquiry, for new circumstances generate new problems. Since the time Cusack was decided, it has been universally recognized that the growth in population, in commerce, in industry, and in land utilization call for order in land uses, to preserve human values and to conserve property values. Hence our zoning statute authorizes ordinances to achieve aims made necessary by the new scene and expressed in R.S. 40:55-32, N.J.S.A.:

> "Such regulations shall be in accordance with a comprehensive plan and designed for one or more of the following purposes: to lessen congestion in the streets; secure safety from fire, panic and other dangers; *promote* health, morals or *the general welfare;* provide adequate light and air; prevent the

overcrowding of land or buildings; avoid undue concentration of population. Such regulations shall be made with reasonable consideration, among other things, to the character of the district and its peculiar suitability for particular uses, *and with a view of conserving the value of property and encouraging the most appropriate use of land throughout such municipality.*"

We have italicized the portion which we think here pertinent.

As we have said, plaintiff concedes a billboard does not belong in a residential area or in places of scenic beauty. The concession is put in terms that billboards are a business use and hence may be barred wherever business does not belong. We think the concession is correct, not merely because billboards are a business use, but because they would clash with those settings whether they solicited an interest in toothpaste or in some charitable cause.

[1] Much is said about zoning for aesthetics. If what is meant thereby is zoning for aesthetics as an end in itself, the issue may be said to be unexplored in our State, but if the question is whether aesthetics may play a part in a zoning judgment, the subject is hardly new. There are areas in which a discordant sight is as hard an economic fact as an annoying odor or sound. We refer not to some sensitive or exquisite preference but to concepts of congruity held so widely that they are inseparable from the enjoyment and hence the value of property. Even the basic separation of industrial from commercial from residential, although obviously related to so much of the quoted statute as speaks of health and hazard, rests also on the aesthetic impact of uses upon the value of properties. Surely no one would say today that an industrial structure must be permitted in a residential district upon a showing that the operation to be conducted therein involves no significant congestion in the streets, or danger of fire or panic, or impediment of light and air, or overcrowding of land, or undue concentration of population. So also the recognition of different residential districts, with varying lot sizes, setbacks, and the like, rests upon the proposition that aesthetics should not be ignored when one seeks to promote "the general welfare," as the statute says, "with a view of conserving the value of property and encouraging the most appropriate use of land throughout such municipality" Our cases deem aesthetics to be relevant when they bear in a substantial way upon land utilization. Vickers v. Township Committee of Gloucester Tp., 37 N.J. 232, 247-248, 181 A.2d 129 (1962); Napierkowski v. Gloucester Tp., 29 N.J. 481, 494, 150 A.2d 481 (1959); Pierro v. Baxendale, 20 N.J. 17, 27-30, 118 A.2d 401 (1955).

[2] Accordingly we are not persuaded that Raritan should be discarded on the thesis that it relied upon evils no longer pervasive. The aesthetic impact of billboards is an economic fact which may bear heavily upon the enjoyment and value of property It is a relevant zoning consideration. See Moore, "Regulation of Outdoor Advertising for Aesthetic Purposes," 8 St. Louis L.J. 191 (1963); "Zoning, Aesthetics, and the First Amendment," 64 Colum.L.Rev. 81 (1964).

This brings us to the charge that the ordinance, in barring off-premise signs while permitting on-premise signs, violates N.J.S.A. 40:55-31, which provides in part that "All such regulations shall be uniform for each class or kind of buildings or other structures or uses of land throughout each district * * *." This issue of classification is in substance the same issue projected by plaintiff in Raritan and there decided against it, notwithstanding that here the stress, is more upon the statute than upon constitutional provisions barring unequal treatment.

[3,4] The zoning statute relates to the uses of structures as well as to their nature, and the section upon which plaintiff relies must be read in that light. N.J.S.A. 40:55-30 provides that zoning ordinances may regulate "buildings and structures according to their construction, and the nature and extent of their use * * *." A structure or use may be permitted if it is merely ancillary or incidental to a permitted principal use and still be barred if it is a separate, independent use. Here, the on-premise sign is a mere adjunct to a permitted business or industrial use, whereas the off-premise sign would be a separate, independent business effort. Hence it proves nothing to say that a sign is a sign.

[5] There are obvious differences between an on-premise sign and an off-premise sign. Even if the baleful effect of both be in fact the same, still in one case the sign may be found tolerable because of its contribution to the business or enterprise on the premises. The hurt is thus supported by a need or gain not present in the case of the off-premise sign. This difference, it seems to us, suffices to support the classification.

And the classification is not impaired by the fact that the ordinance before us, if exploited relentlessly according to its literal terms, would permit on-premise signs with a total square footage in excess of that of the standard billboard. It would still be true that the permitted signs advance the business or industry on hand while an off-premise sign does not. Moreover, the sensibilities of neighbors and customers may offer a restraint which the off-premise advertiser would not feel. Still further, if experience should show that the maximum limitations upon size were ill-conceived, there is probably power to revise the ordinance and to compel compliance by existing on-premise signs whereas an off-premise sign, as part of separate business activity, might be claimed to be a nonconforming use, as Raritan suggested, and for that reason impervious to corrective measures. Finally, if the total impact of on-premise signs should prove to be too much, surely too much is enough. For all of these reasons we adhere to Raritan. Cf Metromedia, Inc. v. City of Pasadena, 30 Cal. Rptr. 731 (D.Ct.App.1963), appeal dismissed for want of substantial federal question, 84 S.Ct. 636 (1964).

[6, 7] We find Raritan is appropriate here. Metuchen is a small municipality, covering 2.9 square miles, with a population of 14,000. Its essential character is residential. Its business and industrial areas are relatively limited and the municipal aim is to achieve the maximum degree

of compatibility with the residential areas. The most that can be said with respect to the proof is that reasonable men can disagree as to whether the addition of off-premise signs would disserve the general welfare. Such policy questions are committed to the judgment of the local legislative bodies. As we have said so many times with respect to zoning and other legislative or *quasi*-legislative decisions, a judge may not interfere merely because he would have made a different policy decision if the power to decide had been his. A court can concern itself only with an abuse of delegated legislative power, and may set aside the legislative judgment only if arbitrariness clearly appears. Plaintiff has not sustained its burden.

We think it unnecessary to discuss the other points raised.

The judgment is affirmed.

For affirmance: Chief Justice WEINTRAUB and Justices JACOBS, FRANCIS, PROCTOR, SCHETTINO and HANEMAN—6.

For reversal: Justice HALL—1.

HALL, J. (dissenting).

The majority decides that a zoning ordinance prohibition of all "off-premises" advertising signs in a municipality with the characteristics and aspirations of Metuchen is valid even if "on-premises" signs should be allowed without restriction. While the controversy commenced over the right to erect two standard-size billboards against embankments on railroad property—one in a business district and the other in a manufacturing zone—for temporary leasing by the plaintiff to various advertisers, the challenge which the court ultimately was called upon to decide was much more abstract and broad. The two locations and their surroundings became merely illustrative. Though confined to Metuchen and similar type communities, the ruling upholds an outright prohibition of all signs, no matter what their kind, size or setting, which do not refer to a business or activity conducted on the premises where located. I am concerned with the rationale upon which result is reached, as well as with the intertwined problem of discrimination in relation to on-premises signs.

This is an unusual billboard case in certain fundamental respects not fully adverted to in the majority opinion which, when considered, seem to me to make the true rationale somewhat different from that expressed and in turn place the classification question in a different light. I refer to the fact that, by stipulation of the parties, all of the stereotyped reasons ordinarily utilized to support the use of the police power in billboard cases were removed from consideration. It was agreed that the erection of the proposed billboards would not prevent adequate light and air from reaching any surrounding buildings or dwellings, would not produce objectionable noise, vibration, odor, smoke or the like, would not conceal immoral acts and would not decrease the property value of land in the borough or change the character of the business and manufacturing districts. The only conventional factor not excluded was highway safety and trial court's finding in plaintiff's favor on this aspect (the municipality offered no affirmative evidence to attack the opinion of plaintiff experts) has not been challenged.[1] While these stipulations specifically referred to the two proposed signs, the argument of both sides indicates they were considered to have general application beyond the particular sites.

Accordingly, the municipality's defense of the ordinance provisions, presented primarily through the opinion of its planning expert, offered an approach entirely different from that customarily used in these cases. It was, in essence, grounded on an "image," if you will, in the minds of its own citizens and the world at large of a high class built-up residential community, with a quality local business district and a relatively small industrial district (with commercial business also permitted) on one border, which it desires and plans to maintain and even up-grade. The thesis is that off-premises advertising signs are a jarring visual note and do not belong anywhere in such a picture It is basically very different and much more frank than the old, stereotyped police power shibboleths which led this court in United Advertising Corp. v. Borough of Raritan, 11 N.J. 144, 93 A.2d 362 (1952) to justify billboard prohibition by simply saying abruptly: "It has long been settled that the unique nature of outdoor advertising and the nuisances fostered by billboards and similar outdoor structures located by persons in the business of outdoor advertising, justify the separate classification of such structures for the purposes of governmental regulation and restriction.' (11 N.J., at p. 150, 93 A.2d, at p. 365) and "It is enough that outdoor advertising has characteristic features which have long been deemed sufficient to sustain regulations or prohibitions peculiarly applicable to it." (11 N.J., at p. 151, 93 A.2d, at p 366).

In reality, as Metuchen's counsel conceded at oral argument, the thesis rests upon exercise of the police power, here through the medium of a zoning ordinance, for purely aesthetic reasons and purposes. The majority recognizes this to some extent, but seems unwilling to give it the exclusive effect which I think it can and should have in this particular situation. My colleagues dilute the concept by leaning upon the well accepted basis of economics, related to an alleged effect of off-premises signs upon the value of property throughout the municipality. Cf. People v. Stover, 12 N.Y.2d 462, 240 N.Y.S.2d 734, 191 N.E.2d 272 (Ct.App.1963), commented upon in "Zoning, Aesthetics, and the First Amendment," 64 Colum.L.Rev. 81 (1964). I strongly doubt that the reliance is factually sound or a meaningful crutch in the situation before us. Effect upon property values in any zoning district seems negatived by the parties' stipulation. But even if it is not,

---

1. There is at least one study which finds a correlation between billboards and traffic accidents. See Moore, "Regulation of Outdoor Advertising for Aesthetic Purposes", 8 St. Louis L.J. 191, 197 (1963). It does not take an expert to appreciate that street and highway signs of all kinds can be distracting—indeed, purposely so— to the motorist. But this evil is not confined to off-premises advertising. Every automobile driver knows that equal or worse offenders are highway on-premises signs and signs in central business districts which obscure or confuse traffic signals.

I find it impossible to think that a billboard in the manufacturing district can have any dollar effect on the value of a dwelling in a residential zone.

It seems to me that courts ought to face up to realities squarely and begin to give frank recognition to aesthetics as an appropriate basis in some areas for exercise of the police power to attain proper community objectives. See Dukeminier, "Zoning for Aesthetic Objectives: A Reappraisal," 20 Law and Contemporary Problems 218 (1955). While this has actually been done for a considerable time, judicial opinions generally expound some other reason. Many police power regulations are upheld where the true but unexpressed basis is that the activity or condition is considered by practically everyone to be an eyesore or offensive to some other sense. Many zoning regulations actually rest on aesthetic considerations, such as those prescribing suburban residential setback and yard distances.

The concept is admittedly a most difficult one to put into fair practice. Beauty and taste are almost impossible to legislate affirmatively on any very broad scale because they are generally such subjective and individual things, not easily susceptible of objective, non-arbitrary standards. See Vickers v. Township Committee of Gloucester Township, 37 N.J. 232, dissenting opinion, at p. 269, 181 A.2d 129, at p. 140 (1962). But that does not mean that they cannot be judicially recognized in some situations as proper community objectives. It would seem that the approach could validly be made and legislation sustained squarely on this basis at least with respect to the prohibition or strict regulation of those activities or conditions which a court can find that practically everyone agrees are non-beautiful in their particular environment, so long as more important values are not overridden. Junkyards and automobile graveyards, except in a special setting, come to mind as instances. (They are prohibited by the Metuchen zoning ordinance.) See e.g., Jasper v. Commonwealth, 375 S.W 2d 709 (Ky.Ct. App.1964); but cf. Delawanna Iron and Metal Co. v. Albrecht, 9 N.J. 424, 88 A.2d 616 (1952); Pfister v. Municipal Council of Clifton, 133 N.J.L. 148, 43 A.2d 275 (Sup.Ct.1945). And I think a court can properly say that we have reached that point with respect to outdoor advertising signs in many settings. The saturation of so much of the landscape with signs, both those with changing faces which plaintiff erects and those of all sizes and kinds conveying a permanent message, has caused a very widespread public revulsion because of their ugliness and marring effect. Blake, God's Own Junkyard 11-16 (1964). The situation has become one of the "concepts of congruity held so widely," as the majority puts it. Since zoning and other local police power exercise in this state is confined by municipal boundaries, the predominant character of Metuchen seems to me to justify the prohibition of off-premises advertising signs throughout the borough for aesthetic reasons, and we ought to frankly put the conclusion on that ground. Whether similar action would be justified in other types of communities, as for example, in a large city with many heavy industrial uses, must await another day.

This leads to my point of difference with the result reached by the majority. The true basis for prohibition being aesthetics, the concept must extend to all similar situations and should be reasonably applied to on-premises signs as well. If not, the municipality is guilty of unfair, unequal and unreasonable treatment which would invalidate the off-premises prohibition. And that is the difficulty I find with the Metuchen scheme.

Granted that an owner or operator of a business or a factory, whether it be on Main Street or in an outlying highway area, is entitled to identify his enterprise and seek to attract customers or generate good-will and that the aesthetically minded municipality must accordingly put up with some nonaesthetic conditions, it seems to me that the local businessman cannot have an unlimited right to put up signs without commensurate limitation. I cannot find any such right simply because the sign relates to the business and, whatever the privilege should be called, it should not be denominated an accessory use or given nonconforming use protection (and indeed even off-premises signs do not seem to me a sufficient land use to be entitled to that protection). It is common knowledge that on-premises signs are frequently just as ugly and offensive as conventional billboards, if not even more garish. Photographs in evidence in this case illustrate that such conditions do exist to some degree in the business districts of Metuchen.

I cannot read United Advertising Corp. v. Borough of Raritan. supra, 11 N.J. 144, 93 A.2d 362, to sanction unrestricted on-premises signs if those off-premises are prohibited, as the majority appears to. The court was careful to point out that the on-premises right was "subject to *reasonable* regulations" and went on to detail the restrictions in that ordinance which it characterized with the statement "that the municipality has *strictly regulated* all signs to confine their use to the *reasonable requirements* of signs incident to and part of businesses authorized on the premises." 11 N.J. at pp. 150, 151, 93 A.2d, at p. 366 (emphasis supplied).

Courts elsewhere have gone both ways on the question. Some, like Metromedia, Inc. v. City of Pasadena, 30 Cal.Rptr. 731 (D.Ct.App.1963), appeal dismissed for want of a substantial federal question, 84 S.Ct. 636 (1964), sanction practically unlimited distinct treatment simply because on-premises signs relate to the business conducted at the site. Others forbid, and I think soundly, unreasonable discrimination. An example is Sunad, Inc. v. City of Sarasota, 122 So.2d 611 (Fla.Sup.Ct.1960). There the court said:

> "Bearing in mind that aesthetics is the criterion by which the merits of the ordinance should be judged, we find insurmountable difficulty to a decision that a wall sign 300 square feet in size at non-point [*sic*] of sale would not offend while a sign of the same size on one of petitioner's billboards would, or that an unrestricted wall sign, at point of sale, would be inoffensive but one of petitioner's signs would shock refined senses, or for that matter, that a roof, ground, or other sign could be only 180 square feet while a wall sign could be at least 300 square feet and, if at point of sale, unlimited." (122 So.2d, at pp. 614-615).

While the Metuchen ordinance purports to restrict on-premises signs, in my opinion the regulation is so illusory in fact that it goes beyond the bounds of reasonable differentiation when off-premises signs are prohibited on the basis of aesthetics. While the square foot *size of single signs* in the business district is confined to 100 square feet, the *number* of such signs on one property is limited only by the front footage of the lot. For example, in the B-2 district, an enterprise on a 100-foot lot can have 1000 square feet of advertising sign space, with any number of signs in any place thereon, so long as no single sign is larger than 100 square feet. In the manufacturing district, if the property (and it may be a commercial as well as an industrial use) has a 300-foot frontage, it may maintain 4500 square feet of advertising space made up of any number of signs. Any sign may be as large as plaintiff's 300-square-foot billboards and erected anywhere on the premises so long as the top does not project higher than the maximum permissible height of principal structures in the district. It is obvious that there is substantially no recognition of aesthetics in these regulations and I feel strongly that such recognition must be given where aesthetics is the basis to exclude billboards. Compare the restrictions imposed by the Raritan ordinance. 11 N.J., at pp. 151-152, 93 A.2d 362. I cannot but conclude that there is consequently such unreasonable leniency as to on-premises signs in Metuchen that, as the ordinance provisions now stand, complete prohibition of off-premises signs cannot be justified. It is no answer that the municipality can change the ordinance if actual installations of on-premises devices get out of hand. That thought affords no legal warrant for present unreasonable discrimination. Moreover, it is well known that, as a practical matter, it is most difficult to tighten restrictions which affect enterprises operated by substantial taxpayers or local residents.

I therefore believe that the prohibitory provisions of the Metuchen ordinance are invalid and so would reverse the judgment of the trial court and decide in favor of plaintiff. I would, however, not give this determination effect for a reasonable period of time in order that the municipality might have an opportunity, if it so desired, to make the on-premises regulations appropriately stricter so that thereby off-premises prohibition would become valid. See Morris County Land Improvement Co. v. Township of Parsippany-Troy Hills, 40 N.J. 539, 559, 193 A.2d 232 (1963).

Questions and Notes

1. What arguments did the billboard company lawyers make in the lower court? How were they received? Did you find the ending of that opinion rather unexpected?

2. In the appellate (majority) opinion, note the two rationales which fall just short of a full acceptance of aesthetic regulations—the

economics-plus-aesthetics rationale, and the lowest-common denominator approach.

3. What did that court think about the safety argument?

4. Why did Justice Hall dissent? What was his approach to aesthetic regulations?

KELBRO, INC.

v.

MYRICK

113 Vt. 64, 30 A.2d 527 (1943).

Supreme Court of Vermont. Washington.

Jan. 5, 1943.

Exceptions from Washington County Court of Chancery; Charles B. Adams, Chancellor.

Suit in chancery by Kelbro, Inc., against Rawson C. Myrick, Secretary of State, and others for injunction against removing billboards. On defendants' exceptions to decree for plaintiff.

Decree reversed and judgment rendered in accordance with opinion.

Before MOULTON, C. J., and SHERBURNE, BUTTLES, STURTEVANT, and JEFFORDS, JJ.

Sylvester & Ready, of St. Albans, for plaintiff.

Clifton G. Parker, Deputy Atty. Gen., of Vermont, for defendant.

John J. Bennett Jr., Atty. Gen., of New York, William C. Chanler, Corp. Counsel of New York City, and Raymond P. McNulty, of Babylon, L. I., N. Y. (Henry Epstein, Sol. Gen. of New York, and Jeremiah H. Evarts, both of New York City, of counsel), for amici curiae.

BUTTLES, Justice.

The plaintiff corporation is engaged in the business of outdoor advertising for direct profit through rentals or compensation received for the erection, maintenance and display of painted bulletins, poster panels and other outdoor advertising devices, commonly called bill-boards, located upon real property at various places in the State of Vermont. In this suit in chancery the plaintiff prays for an injunction restraining the defendants, their agents, employees and representatives from removing certain bill-board structures erected and maintained by the plaintiff, because of alleged violations of certain provisions of the statutes regarding such structures, authority for such removal being claimed by the defendants under P.L. §§ 8352, 8353 and 8354, as amended Pub. Acts 1939, No. 221, § 7. The defendants demurred to the complaint and upon hearing the demurrer was overruled pro forma, the complaint adjudged sufficient and the defendants were enjoined until further order of the court, in accordance with the prayer of the complaint. The case comes to this Court upon the defendants' exceptions.

[1] By their demurrer the defendants have admitted the following allegations of the plaintiff's complaint. The plaintiff has paid the fee required by P.L. § 8340 and has obtained from the Secretary of State the license required in order to engage in such business. It has erected and for a number of years has maintained bill-board structures designated as Numbers 304 and 308 on private property of one Seymour in the town of St. Albans on the easterly side of the highway known as Route 7; also a bill-board structure designated as Number 307 on private property of one Wood located on the westerly side of said highway. Each of these structures has been erected and maintained pursuant to written agreements between the plaintiff and the respective land owners. These bill-boards are not located in a city or incorporated village or in the thickly settled part of a town or in the business part thereof as defined by P.L. § 8338, as amended, Pub.Acts 1941, No. 287, §1. They are each 24 feet long by ten feet high, having an area of 240 square feet each.

On April 18, 1942, the Secretary of State refused to issue a renewal of the permits previously issued to the plaintiff to maintain or display advertising matter on said bill-board structures, such refusal being based upon the ground that such structures were located within 300 feet of a highway intersection and within 240 feet from the center of the travelled part of the highway, in violation of provisions of P.L. § 8350, as amended, Pub.Acts 1939, No. 221, § 6. It is conceded that all three of the bill-boards are within the forbidden distance from the center of the highway and that Numbers 308 and 304 are less than 300 feet from a highway intersection. It is the plaintiff's contention, however, that the section of the statutes referred to together with other provisions of Chapter 332, hereinafter referred to by which greater privileges are accorded, under certain circumstances, to an advertiser who is not engaged in the business of outdoor advertising for direct profit than to one who is so engaged, deny to the plaintiff the rights guaranteed to it by the constitutions of the United States and of Vermont in that they deny equal protection of the laws to it, deny due process of law, and fail to provide compensation for the taking of its private property for public use.

[2] The established rule is that every presumption is to be made in favor of the constitutionality of an act of the legislature and it will not be declared unconstitutional without clear and irrefragable proof that it infringes the paramount law. State v. Auclair, 110 Vt. 147, 156, 4 A.2d 107; Village of Waterbury v. Melendy et al., 109 Vt. 441, 447, 199 A. 236; Nebbia v. New York, 291 U.S. 502, 54 S.Ct. 505, 516, 78 L.Ed. 940, 89 A.L.R. 1469.

It is necessary to consider the exact nature of the plaintiff's alleged property rights which it claims have been invaded. It is obvious that something more is claimed than the mere right to erect and maintain bill-board structures upon lands adjacent to the highway. In its essence the right that is claimed is to use the public highway for the purpose of displaying advertising matter. This has been well stated by the Philippine Supreme Court which has said that "the success of bill-board advertising depends not so much upon the use of private property as it does upon the use of the channels of travel used by the general public. Suppose that the owner of private property * * * should require the advertiser to paste his posters upon the bill-boards so that they would face the interior of the property instead of the exterior. Bill-board advertising would die a natural death if this were done, and its real dependency not upon the unrestricted use of private property but upon the unrestricted use of the public highways is at once apparent. Ostensibly located on private property, the real and sole value of the billboard is its proximity to the public thoroughfares. Hence, we conceive that the regulation of bill-boards and their restriction is not so much a regulation of private property as it is a regulation of the use of the streets and other public thoroughfares." Churchill and Tait v. Rafferty, 32 P.I. 580, 609, appeal dismissed 248 U.S. 591, 39 S.Ct. 20. In General Outdoor Adv. Co. v. Department of Pub. Works, 289 Mass. 149, 168, 169, 193 N.E. 799, 808, it is said: "The only real value of a sign or billboard lies in its proximity to the public thoroughfare within public view. * * * The object of outdoor advertising in the nature of things is to proclaim to those who travel on highways and who resort to public reservations that which is on the advertising device, and to constrain such persons to see and comprehend the advertisement. * * * In this respect the plaintiffs are not exercising a natural right, * * * they are seizing for private benefit an opportunity created for a quite different purpose by the expenditure of public money in the construction of public ways. * * * The right asserted is not to own and use land or property, to live, to work, or to trade. While it may comprehend some of these fundamental liberties, its main feature is the superadded claim to use private land as a vantage ground from which to obtrude upon all the public traveling upon highways, whether indifferent, reluctant, hostile or interested, an unescapable propaganda concerning private business with the ultimate design of promoting patronage of those advertising. Without this superadded claim, the other rights would have no utility in this connection." See, also, Perlmutter v. Greene, 259 N.Y. 327, 182 N.E. 5, 81 A.L.R. 1543; Fifth Ave. Coach Co. v. City of New York, 194 N.Y. 19, 86 N.E. 824, 21 A.L.R.,N.S., 744, 16 Ann. Cas. 695, and an exhaustive article by Ruth I. Wilson entitled "Billboards and the Right to be Seen from the Highway", 30 Georgetown Law Journal, 743 et seq.

The plaintiff avers that its property rights, for which it claims the protection of the national and state constitutions are derived by contract from the abutting land owners, Wood and Seymour. We will consider the rights that these abutters had which they could convey, omitting, for the present, consideration of any preferential treatment that the statute may give to Wood because of his being also the owner and operator of a business located less than 500 feet from two of the billboards upon which certain goods are advertised which happen to be offered for sale in connection with that business.

[3-5] The rights of an abutting owner in an adjacent street or highway are of two kinds, public rights which he enjoys in common with all other citizens, and certain private rights which arise from the ownership of property contiguous to the highway which are not common to the public in general, and this irrespective of whether the fee to the highway is in him or in the public. Certain of the latter rights constitute property, or property rights of which an abutter cannot be unlawfully deprived. While the cases involving such rights relate, mainly, to questions of ingress and egress, light and air, and lateral support, neither logic nor sound legal principle exclude the recognition of other rights equally valuable to an abutting owner. Skinner v. Buchanan, 101 Vt. 159, 165, 142 A. 72; Barnett v. Johnson, 15 N.J.Eq. 481, 487.

[6] These private property rights are usually termed easements. Even if it can be questioned whether they are true easements in the strictest sense they are at least rights in the nature of appurtenant easements, the abutting property being the dominant and the highway the servient tenement, and they are governed by the law of easements. An important right of this nature is the abutter's right of view to and from the property, from and to the highway; that is, his right to see and to be seen. This right of reasonable view has been generally recognized by the weight of authority and has been protected in numerous cases where encroachments on streets or sidewalks obscured the visibility of signs, window displays or show cases. Among such cases may be cited First Nat'l Bank v. Tyson, 133 Ala. 459, 32 So. 144, 59 L.R.A. 399, 91 Am.St.Rep. 46; Klaber v. Lakenan, 8 Cir., 64 F.2d 86, 90 A.L.R. 783; Perry v. Castner, 124 Iowa 386, 100 N.W. 84, 66 L.R.A. 160, 2 Ann.Cas. 363; Bischof v. Merchants Nat. Bank, 75 Neb. 838, 106 N.W. 996, 5 L.R.A.,N.S. 486; Williams v. Los Angeles R. Co., 150 Cal. 592, 89 P. 330; Yale Univ. v. City of New Haven, 104 Conn 610, 134 A. 268, 47 A.L.R. 667; Davis v. Spragg, 72 W.Va. 672, 79 S.E. 652, 48 L.R.A.,N.S., 173. See 25 Am.Jur. Highways, Secs. 155 and 319. While authority contra may be found we are in accord with the rule above stated which we believe to be the sounder and more logical one. It is to be noted that in each of the authorities above cited this right is designated an easement.

[7] It is said in Goddard on Easements, p. 383, 8th Ed., that "a right of way appurtenant to a dominant tenement can be used only for the

purpose of passing to or from that tenement. It cannot be used for any purpose unconnected with the enjoyment of the dominant tenement, neither can it be assigned by the dominant owner to another person and so be made a right in gross, nor can he license anyone to use the way when he is not coming to or from the dominant tenement." McCullough v. Broad Exch. Co., 101 App.Div. 566, 92 N.Y.S. 533, affirmed 184 N.Y. 592, 77 N.E. 1191; Bang v. Forman, 244 Mich. 571, 222 N.W. 96; Miller v. Weingart, 317 Ill. 179, 183, 147 N.E. 804, 805, 806. While this principle has been applied most frequently to rights of way it is applicable to other appurtenant easements and should, in our opinion, be applied in the present case where the servient tenement is the public highway, built with public funds, designed for public use, and under the exclusive regulation and control of the Legislature. Especially is this so since it is a principle which underlies the use of all easements that the owner of the easement cannot materially increase the burden of it upon the servient estate or impose thereon a new and additional burden. 17 Am. Jur., Easements, § 98; Hopkins the Florist Inc. v. Fleming, 112 Vt. 389, 391, 26 A.2d 96; Dernier v. Rutland Ry. L. & P. Co., 94 Vt. 187, 194, 110 A. 4.

The result, as to the claim here made, is that the right of view of the owner or occupant of the abutting property is limited to such right as is appurtenant to that property and includes the right to display only goods or advertising matter pertaining to business conducted thereon. His appurtenant easement does not include the right to display advertising matter foreign to a business conducted on the property, and he could not convey to this plaintiff a right that he did not himself possess.

The greater privileges accorded to advertisers who are not engaged in the advertising business for direct profit, to which we have referred, are to be found in P.L. c. 332, Sections 8340, 8341, 8342, 8343, as amended, Pub.Acts 1941, No. 187, § 2,8349 as amended Pub.Acts 1941, No. 187, § 4, and 8350, as amended Pub.Acts 1939, No. 221, § 6. They include preferential treatment as to payment of license fees and obtaining permits; as to the required distance from the abutting highway and from intersecting highways, of bill-boards upon which are displayed advertisements of goods manufactured or offered for sale or of a business carried on within 500 feet thereof; also as to advertisements by or on behalf of a municipality, by common carriers upon certain kinds of property and as to highway lighthouses and purely direction signs.

[8, 9] That the Legislature has seen fit to extend these privileges cannot avail this plaintiff. They are a matter of sufferance rather than of right. The plaintiff is admittedly not in the excepted class, but is, rather, seeking to use the highway for commercial purposes analogous to the use made of it by common carriers. Such use, this Court has held, the Legislature in the exercise of its police powers may wholly deny, or may permit to some and deny to others as will best promote the general good of the public. There is no inherent right to use the highways for commercial

purposes. State v. Gamelin, 111 Vt. 245, 250, 251, 13 A.2d 204; In re James, 99 Vt. 265, 270, 132 A. 40, 44; State v. Caplan, 100 Vt. 140, 155, 135 A. 705. This is in accord with the holdings of the United States Supreme Court which has recently said: "Whether, and to what extent, one may promote or pursue a gainful occupation in the streets, to what extent such activity shall be adjudged a derogation of the public right of user, are matters for legislative judgment. The question is not whether the legislative body may interfere with the harmless pursuit of a lawful business, but whether it must permit such pursuit by what it deems an undesirable invasion of, or interference with, the full and free use of the highways by the people in fulfillment of the public use to which streets are dedicated." Valentine v. Chrestensen, 316 U.S. 52, 54, 55, 62 S.Ct. 920, 921, 86 L.Ed. 1262.

[10] No invasion of the plaintiff's constitutional rights appears. Decree reversed. Defendant's demurrer sustained; injunction dissolved and plaintiff's bill of complaint dismissed.

On Motion for Reargument.

After the foregoing opinion was handed down the plaintiff, upon leave duly obtained, moved for a reargument, basing its motion upon several grounds.

The plaintiff is in error in saying that the opinion proceeds on the theory that an easement was created between the plaintiff and the abutting land owners. We merely assumed the correctness of the averment in the complaint that the bill-board structures in question were erected and maintained pursuant to written agreements between the plaintiff and the respective land owners. We made no finding or assumption, and did not consider it necessary to do so, as to the relationship created by such agreements between the parties. It appears, however, that the plaintiff did not become the agent or servant of the abutters. No doubt the plaintiff is correct in saying that an easement between them was not created.

The plaintiff urges that by the concluding clause in our quotation from the opinion in Churchill and Tait v. Rafferty, 32 P.I. 580, 609, we conceded that private rights are here secondarily involved. We do not think that inference is warranted but if it were it needs no argument to demonstrate that claimed private rights must yield so far as they are inconsistent with paramount public rights. We consider that in the present case there is such inconsistency. It should be noted that we did not follow in toto the reasoning either of the Churchill case or of General Outdoor. Adv. Co. v. Department of Public Works, 289 Mass. 149, 193 N.E. 799. We merely adopted the trenchant and accurate language used in those opinions to describe the nature of the claims which this plaintiff is making. Upon reading the Massachusetts constitutional amendment to which the plaintiff refers it becomes obvious that it had nothing to do with the use of the language quoted from the latter case.

Our holding that the right which the plaintiff here claims is in the nature of an easement appurtenant to the abutting land and servient upon the public's interest is challenged upon several grounds. It is said that this holding is inconsistent with the fact that the fee to highways in this State is in the abutting owners, subject to the use by the public for highway purposes. While it is true that this is the general rule it is not the universal rule in Vermont or elsewhere. In Skinner v. Buchanan, 101 Vt. 159, 142 A. 72, the premises involved abutted upon the street but did not include the fee to any part of that street, and in Ferre v. Doty, 2 Vt. 378, it appeared that the plaintiff, who had the fee to abutting land, had no fee to any part of the adjoining common, which was held to be in some respects similar to a highway. The record before us does not disclose whether in the present case the fee to the highway is in the public or in one or the other or both of the abutting owners.

Furthermore, it is stated in Skinner v. Buchanan, supra, as set forth in the foregoing opinion, that the abutting owner has certain special rights in the highway irrespective of whether the fee to the highway is in him or in the public. The right of view is of the same nature as those referred to in that statement and has often been included with them. There is abundant authority for the statement in the Skinner case. Sec. 29 C.J. 547; Donahue v. Keystone Gas Co., 181 N.Y. 313, 320, 321, 73 N.E. 1108, 70 L.R.A. 761, 106 Am. St.Rep. 549; Anzalone v. Metropolitan Dist. Comm., 257 Mass. 32, 36, 153 N.E. 325, 47 A.L.R. 897; City of Denver v. Bayer, 7 Colo. 113, 2 P. 6; Town of Norwalk v. Podmore, 86 Conn. 658, 86 A. 582; Brakken v. Minneapolis & St. L. Ry. Co., 29 Minn. 41, 42, 11 N.W. 124; 4 McQuillin, Munic. Corp., 2nd Ed., § 1426; 3 Dillon, Munic. Corp., 5th Ed., § 1136, where it is said: "The later and best considered judgments hold that it is comparatively unimportant, as respects the relative rights of an abutting owner and the public in and over streets, whether the bare fee is in the one or the other. If the fee is in the public, the lawful rights of the adjoining owners are in their nature equitable easements; if the fee is in the abutter, his rights in and over the street are in their nature legal; but in the absence of controlling legislative provisions, the extent of such right is, in either event, substantially, perhaps precisely, the same."

The rules stated in the opinion by which dominant easements are restricted apply here if the rights of the abutter are such easements. If they are not true easements because of the fee of the highway being in the owner of the rights, those restrictions are equally applicable, since "the extent of such rights is, in either event, substantially, perhaps precisely, the same." The plaintiff invokes the rule, often stated in the books, that an owner cannot have an easement in his own land. If the fee of the highway is in the public the abutter's easement would not be in his own land, but if the fee is in him the extent of his rights, as above stated is the same. In that event the situation is somewhat analogous to that which sometimes results in the creation of an implied easement. Strictly speaking, a man cannot subject one part of his property to another part by an easement, on the theory that he cannot have an easement in his own land, but if he makes one part of it servient to another by an alteration which is obvious and permanent or apparent and continuous, and then conveys one of the parcels, his grantee takes such part benefited or burdened by the easement which the alteration created. Provident Mut. Life Ins. Co. v. Doughty, 126 N.J.Eq. 262, 265, 8 A.2d 722, 724; 17 Am.Jur., Easements, § 32.

The plaintiff seems to have misunderstood the opinion in one respect. We discussed only the abutter's right of view to and from the highway and did not intend to assert any corresponding right of view on the part of the public. One sentence of the opinion has been amended to prevent any such misapprehension. The plaintiff's statement that an easement must be created for the benefit of corporeal property is, therefore, not at variance with the opinion.

The right of view was, as the plaintiff asserts, in existence before the billboard structures were erected. The manner in which the plaintiff has sought to increase the servitude of that right fully appears, we think, from the opinion.

We make no assumption as to the purpose for which the land may have been rented to the plaintiff. The demurrer admits the averment of the complaint that the use to which the land has been put by the plaintiff is pursuant to written agreements with the land owners, and it does not appear that that use by the plaintiffs is connected with the enjoyment or use of the land by its owners. It is alleged that Wood owns the land upon which billboard number 307 is erected, but the fact that he sells gas and oil at retail at a building more than 500 feet distant and across a road from that billboard, upon which gas and oil are advertised, does not establish such connection. It does not appear that the brands of gas and oil advertised are the same brands sold by Wood, nor that if they are the same brands attention is called by the advertisement to his station as a place where they may be bought. Apparently the billboard advertises Wood's business no more than it does thousands of others—even less if the brands of gas and oil are different.

The record does not indicate that the plaintiff in displaying this advertisement was acting as the agent or servant of Wood, but rather that it acted independently in furtherance of its own business which Wood had by contract attempted to give the plaintiff the right to conduct at that location. It is not necessary to assume aesthetic considerations for the enactment of restrictions which apply to this billboard. In the view we take the Legislature's undoubted right to restrict or forbid the use of highways for commercial purposes sufficiently justifies such enactment. The classification, for legislative purposes, of a person, firm or corporation engaged in the business of outdoor advertising for direct profit through rentals or compensation in a class apart from one engaged in advertising, not for such direct profit but for the purpose of fostering a local business, a community enterprise or public safety, is clearly not unconstitutional, the object sought by the Legislature being, it may be assumed, the limitation of the use of highways for commercial purposes. State v. Auclair, 110 Vt. 147, 160, 4 A.2d 107; State v. Haskell, 84 Vt. 429, 437, 79 A. 852, 34 L.R.A.,N.S., 286; State v. Hazelton, 78 Vt. 467, 471, 63 A. 305. Mr. Wood is therefore properly placed in a different class from this plaintiff, even if it be true that because he sells coca-cola and Chesterfield cigarettes at his store he could lawfully advertise those products which the plaintiff advertises—upon billboards "identical in size and location" with two of those maintained by this plaintiff.

The fundamental trouble with the plaintiff's position is that it claims certain property rights in the highway which we hold do not exist to the extent claimed.

The plaintiff's motion for reargument is denied. Let full entry go down.

PERLMUTTER

v.

GREENE

259 N.Y. 327, 182 N.E. 5(1932).

Court of Appeals of New York.

July 19, 1932.

Action by Joseph Perlmutter and others, copartners doing business under the firm name and style of the Perlmutter Furniture Company, against Frederick Stuart Greene, as State Superintendent of Public Works, and others. From a judgment of the Appellate Division (234 App. Div. 896, 254 N. Y. S. 542), affirming a judgment of the Trial Term in favor of plaintiff on agreed and stipulated facts (140 Misc. 42, 240 N. Y. S. 495), the defendants appeal.

Judgments reversed, and the complaint dismissed.

John J. Bennett, Jr., Atty. Gen. (Henry Epstein and Timothy F. Cohen, both of New York City, of counsel), for appellants.

John E. Mack and Edward A. Conger, both of Poughkeepsie, for respondents.

POUND, C. J.

Plaintiffs are lessees of a parcel of land immediately south of the east approach to the Mid-Hudson bridge at Poughkeepsie. They purposed to erect a large display sign or billboard thereon for advertising purposes in full view of travelers along the adjacent approach which is a part of the state highway. The state of New York is the owner of the fee of the highway. The defendant Greene, as state superintendent of public works, for the purpose of blocking a view of the sign from the highway, purposed to construct a screen or shield on the highway in front of the billboard. The billboard would be about fifty-three feet long, ten feet high, and thirty-five feet from the traveled part of the bridge approach, on a pronounced curve in a narrow road. It may be illuminated at night.

Plaintiffs have obtained a judgment restraining defendants from placing the screen in the highway where it would prevent motorists from seeing their sign. The courts below have held that the state may not lawfully erect the screen so as to obscure plaintiffs' sign, that it may not thus prevent plaintiffs from using their property for advertising purposes, and that the erection of the screen for the purpose of obscuring the billboard does not safeguard the traveler or serve any highway purpose.

[1-3] When the fee of the highway has been transferred to the state, the state may use the highway for any public purpose not inconsistent with or prejudicial to its use for highway purposes. Thompson v. Orange & Rockland Electric Co., 254 N. Y. 366, 369, 173 N. E. 224. The mere disturbance of the rights of light, air, and access of abutting owners on such a highway by the imposition of a new use, consistent with its use as an open public street, must be tolerated by them, and no right of action arises therefrom, although such use interferes with the enjoyment of their premises. Kane v. New York Elev. R. R. Co., 125 N. Y. 164, 176, 26 N. E. 278, 11 L. R. A. 640. The highway must, however, be kept open as a public highway, and not diverted to wholly inconsistent uses. This right to have the highway kept open for light, air, and access as well as for travel has been termed an "easement," but it is the right deduced by way of consequence from the purposes of a public street. Muhlker v. New York & H. R. R. Co., 197 U. S. 544, 25 S. Ct. 522, 49 L.Ed. 872.

Shall we, on this basis, imply as against the state an easement of visibility from the highway which arises from the necessity that the highway be "kept open"; hold that the screen would be an unlawful structure, and that plaintiffs are entitled, by virtue of proximity to the highway, to protection from the injuries "to the easements of light, air, view and access belonging to them" which would result therefrom? Bradley v. Degnon Contracting Co., 224 N. Y. 60, 72, 120 N. E. 89; Donahue v. Keystone Gas Co., 181 N. Y. 313, 319, 73 N. E. 1108, 70 L. R. A. 761, 106 Am. St. Rep. 549; Muhlker v. New York & H. R. R. Co., supra. Or shall we invoke the principle that considerations of an esthetic purpose may enter into the reasons for improving a state highway and thus sustain the superintendent of public works in his action if it has any direct relation to a highway purpose? Welch v. Swasey, 214 U. S. 91, 108, 29 S. Ct. 567, 53 L.Ed. 923; Matter of Wulfsohn v. Burden, 241 N. Y. 288, 300, 150 N. E. 120, 43 A. L. R. 651.

We are dealing not with a statute passed in the exercise of the police power of the state, prohibiting billboards on private property where the primary motive is esthetic (Public Esthetics and the Bill Board, 16 Cornell Law Quarterly, 151, 154), but with the act of the administrative officer in constructing and controlling a state highway placed in his charge. The question is as to the limits of his authority. The state superintendent of public works has control of the Mid-Hudson Bridge (Laws 1923, c. 900, § 3; Laws 1927, c. 88, § 4), and has general supervision over all state highways (Highway Law [Consol. Laws, c. 25], art. 2, § 15). In the exercise of such supervision and control, doubtless he may plant shade trees along the road to give comfort to motorists and incidentally to improve the appearance of the highway. By so doing he aims to make a better highway than a mere scar across the land would be. If trees interfere with the view of the adjacent property from the road, no right is interfered with. So, if the superintendent desires to shield the travelers on the highway from obnoxious sights of public nuisances or quasi nuisances by the erection of screens more pleasing to the eye, he still acts within his jurisdiction. He aims to make the highway free from sights which would offend the public. No adjacent owner has the vested right to be seen from the streets in his backyard privacy. Again, if the purpose is to shut out from view scenes which might distract the attention of the driver of a car, the superintendent may aim to make the highway safer for those who use it by erecting screens to keep the eye of the driver on the road as he may erect barriers to keep the car on the road on dangerous curves. All these things are as incidental to the construction and operation of the highway as are the matters of grade, materials, or drainage.

[4] Authorities are agreed that any considerations, other than purely esthetic ones, which are relevant to the operation of the highway, may influence the superintendent's action, and, if such considerations exist, the fact that considerations of an esthetic nature also exist does not take away his authority to act. Our lower courts have differed on the question whether artistic considerations alone are sufficient to warrant the general prohibition of billboards on private property (People v. Wolf, 127 Misc. 382, 216 N. Y. S. 741; Id., 220 App. Div. 71, 220 N. Y. S. 656, appeal dismissed, 247 N. Y. 189, 159 N. E. 906), and this court has said: "One of the unsettled questions of the law is the extent to which the concept of nuisance may be enlarged by legislation so as to give protection to sensibilities that are merely cultural or aesthetic." People v. Rubenfeld, 254 N. Y. 245, 248, 172 N. E. 485, 487.

The Supreme Court of the United States has held that billboards may be prohibited in the interest of the safety, morality, health, and decency of the community (Cusack Co. v. City of Chicago, 242 U. S. 526, 37 S. Ct. 190, 61 L. Ed. 472, L. R. A. 1918A, 136, Ann. Cas. 1917C, 594), and that they may be excluded from residence districts by zoning ordinances. (Village of Euclid, Ohio, v. Ambler Realty Co., 272 U. S. 365, 47 S. Ct. 114, 71 L. Ed. 303, 54 A. L. R. 1016).

[5] Beauty may not be queen, but she is not an outcast beyond the pale of protection or respect. She may at least shelter herself under the wing of safety, morality, or decency. It is, however, needless for the decision of the case to delimit her sphere of influence. The immediate question is not whether the state superintendent of public works may, as an incident to his power of highway control, shut off from the eyes of the traveling public all advertising signs erected on private property, nor is it whether the highway, created by public money, is controlled in part by those who desire to thrust upon the notice of the public the ostentatious display of private advertising from the adjoining premises for their own profit wherever they see fit; nor is it whether advertisers have a right, independent of environment, to have a highway "kept open" visually so that their signs may compel the eye of the passerby. The question is whether the superintendent was justified in erecting this screen to shut off the view of this sign in this location.

The elevated railway cases (Story v. New York Elev. R. R. Co., 90 N. Y. 122, 43 Am. Rep. 146; Lahr v. Metropolitan Elev. R. R. Co., 104 N. Y. 268, 10 N. E. 528), much relied on herein, went far to protect adjacent owners whose light, air, and access had been interfered with by the construction of the elevated railroads in front of their premises on the city-owned street. Some expressions in the opinions, read apart from the context, may suggest that any disturbance in such a street, not essential to highway purposes, suffered by the owner of an adjacent lot, creates a cause of action in his favor. They do not go to that extent. This court has never discussed easements of prospect or view, although it has mentioned them. Doubtless they may exist in certain cases. Great diminution of values may impel the courts to find a remedy when the street, although still a street, is partially closed to common street uses, but every diminution of value does not call for compensation. Muhlker v. New York & H. R. R. Co., supra. Aside from the Elevated Railway Cases, it is generally held that any change in the street for the benefit of public travel is a matter of public right as against the private right of the adjacent owner. The highway in suit is still "open to" the plaintiffs. It is not closed to them in any sense. It is the same highway that it would be without the screen.

From new conditions of travel new rights and obligations arise. The state creates new values for adjacent owners by building good roads. It does not then destroy old values, as happened in the case of the elevated structures, by blocking the roadway. No contract exists between the state and the owner that the latter may forever use his property to erect billboards anywhere along the highway; no right in rem exists, for the adjacent owner has no title to the highway. As one of the sovereign people for whom the title is held in trust, the adjacent owner may compel the state to limit the use of the highway to highway purposes when a proposed excess use would be to his disadvantage.

[6, 7] Some future case may call for new definitions of highway purposes. New highways and new uses arise. Enough for this decision to say that

the superintendent of public works may act reasonably in his discretion for the benefit of public travel in screening a billboard at a dangerous curve when by its enormity such a structure may divert the attention of the motorist from the road. He then interferes with no property right of the adjacent owner, and he should not be interfered with by the courts. If, incidentally, the outlook from the road is improved by shutting off the view of the billboard, so much the better. We deal with the act and not with the motive. An act, lawful in itself and not done with malice, will not be restrained, nor will the courts assume the management and control of state highways.

The judgments should be reversed and the complaint dismissed, with costs in all courts.

CRANE, LEHMAN, KELLOGG, O'BRIEN, HUBBS, and CROUCH, JJ., concur.

Judgments reversed, etc.

Questions and Notes

On Vermont

1. Explain the Vermont theory of billboards as a unique type of land use. What happens at the point where the billboard's supports enter the ground? What happens on the highway?

2. How does the court translate this theory into legal terms?

3. Under this theory, why does a billboard increase the burden on the servient estate (the highway)?

4. For the ultimate tribute to the Vermont billboard legislation, see Williams, v.5, plate 20.

On New York

1. If you have some doubt on the Vermont theory, consider this case.

2. What did plaintiff propose to do on his land? Where was his land?

3. What did the Superintendent propose to do on his land?

4. Did you get an impression from Judge Pound's attitude towards billboards, that he might have adopted a broader rationale if the narrower one were not available?

5. While written by Pound, the language sounds like Cardozo.

CROSS-REFERENCES

In Anderson, see §§ 11.76-11.82, and see Index, this topic.
In Hagman, see § 77.
In McQuillin, see § 24, and see Index, this topic.
In Rathkopf, see Index under "Billboards and Signs".
In Williams, see ch. 118-127.
In Yokley, see § 28.

Part C

Housing and Urban Redevelopment Renewal

Section 12

The Background In The West

CLARK

v.

NASH

ERROR TO THE SUPREME COURT OF THE STATE OF UTAH.

198 U.S. 361(1905).

Argued April 19, 20, 1905.—Decided May 15, 1905.

Whether the statute of a State permitting condemnation by an individual for the purpose of obtaining water for his land or for mining, is or is not a condemnation for public use and, therefore, a valid enactment under the Constitution, depends upon considerations relating to the situation of the State and its possibilities for agricultural and mining industries.

The rights of a riparian owner in and to the use of water flowing by his land, are not the same in the arid and mountainous western States as they are in the eastern States.

This court recognizes the difference of climate and soil, which render necessary different laws in different sections of the country, and what is a public use largely depends upon the facts surrounding the subject, and with which the people and the courts of the State must be more familiar than a stranger to the soil.

While private property may not in all cases be taken to promote public interest and tend to develop the natural resources of the State, in view of the peculiar conditions existing in the State of Utah, and as the facts appear in this record, the statute of that State permitting individuals to enlarge the ditch of another and thereby obtain water for his own land, is within the legislative power of the State, and does not in any way violate the Federal Constitution.

1555

Statement of the Case.

This action was brought by the defendant in error Nash, to condemn a right of way, so called, by enlarging a ditch for the conveying of water across the land of plaintiffs in error, for the purpose of bringing water from Fort Canyon Creek, in the county and State of Utah, which is a stream of water flowing from the mountains near to the land of the defendant in error, and thus to irrigate his land.

The plaintiffs in error demurred to the complaint upon the ground that the same did not state facts sufficient to constitute a cause of action against them. The demurrer was overruled, and the defendants then waived all time in which to answer the complaint and elected to stand on the demurrer. Thereafter there was a default entered against the defendants, and each of them, for failing to answer, and the case was under the practice in Utah then tried and evidence heard on the complaint of the plaintiff, showing the material facts as stated in the complaint. The trial court found the facts as follows:

"That the plaintiff during all the times mentioned in said complaint, to wit, from the first day of January, 1902, down to the present time inclusive, was, has been and now is the owner of, in possession of and entitled to the possession of the south half of the northwest quarter of section 24, in township 4 south of range 1, east of Salt Lake meridian, in Utah County, State of Utah.

"That Fort Canyon Creek is a natural stream of water flowing from the mountains on the north of plaintiff's said land, in a southerly direction to and near to plaintiff's said land.

"That said land of plaintiff above described is arid land and will not produce without artificial irrigation, but that with artificial irrigation the same will produce abundantly of grain, vegetables, fruits and hay.

"That the defendants own land lying north of and adjacent to plaintiff's said land, and said defendants have constructed and are maintaining and jointly own a water ditch which diverts a portion of the said waters of the said Fort Canyon Creek on the west side of said creek (being the side on which the plaintiff's said land is situated) at a point about one mile north of plaintiff's said land in section 13 of said township, down to a point within a hundred feet of plaintiff's said land, which said ditch is begun on the defendants' land and runs in a southerly direction over said defendants' land and on to and over the lands of the said defendants to said point about a hundred feet of plaintiff's said land.

"The plaintiff is the owner of and entitled to the use of sufficient of the remainder of the flow of the waters of the said Fort Canyon Creek to irrigate his said land, and that the irrigation of said land by the waters of said creek and the uses of the said waters in the irrigation of the said lands of the defendant is under the laws of this State declared to be, and the same is a public use.

"That the said waters of said Fort Canyon Creek cannot be brought upon the said plaintiff's said land by any other route except by and through the ditch of the defendants, owing to the canyon through which said ditch runs being such as to only be possible to build one ditch.

"That plaintiff has no other way of irrigating his said land except by the use of the waters of said Fort Canyon Creek and that unless plaintiff is allowed to enlarge the ditch of the defendants and have a right of way through said ditch for the flow of the waters of said Fort Canyon Creek, down to the plaintiff's said land, that said land of plaintiff will be valueless and the waters of said Fort Canyon Creek will not be available for any useful purpose.

"That said ditch of defendants is a small ditch about 18 inches wide and about 12 inches deep; that if the plaintiff is permitted to widen said ditch one foot more it will be sufficient in dimensions to carry plaintiff's said water to which he is entitled to his said land and the same can and will be put to a beneficial and public use, in the irrigation of the soil on plaintiff's said land hereinbefore described.

"That on the sixteenth day of January, 1902, and while the said defendants were not in the actual use of their said ditch, and while the widening of said ditch at said time would not in any manner interfere with said defendants, other than the act of widening of same, the plaintiff requested of the said defendants the right to so widen the said ditch of the said defendants so to make it one foot wider, for the purpose of using the same to carry the water of the plaintiff onto his said land from said creek, and at said time and place offered to pay to said defendants all damages which the said defendants might suffer by reason of said enlargement, and offered to pay his proportion of the maintenance of keeping the same in repair, and asked of said defendants a right to continue the use of said ditch in common with said defendants, and to use the same so as not to interfere with the use of said ditch by said defendants, and it further appearing to the court that the said plaintiff is now and has ever since been willing to pay said damage and all damage incident thereto—and to pay his just proportion of the cost of maintaining said ditch. That the said defendants then and there and ever since have refused to permit plaintiff to enlarge said ditch or to use the same, or in any manner to interfere with the same.

"And it further appearing to the court that the said defendants would suffer damages by reason of the enlarging of said ditch one foot in width, in the sum of $40.00, and no more. And that the said plaintiff has deposited with the clerk of this court to be paid to the order of the said defendants the sum of $40.00, in full payment of such damages. That the land of the defendants not sought to be condemned by plaintiff would suffer no injury or damage.

"And it further appearing from said evidence that said ditch of the defendants can be widened by the plaintiff one foot more without injury to defendants or to said ditch, and that said widening of said ditch and the use thereof by the plaintiff will not in any manner interfere with the free and full use thereof by the defendants or the carrying of all waters of the said defendants."

Upon these facts the court found the following—

Conclusions of Law.

"The court finds and decides that the plaintiff is entitled to a decree of this court condemning a right of way through defendants' said ditch, to the extent of widening said ditch one foot more than its present width and to a depth of said ditch as now constructed through the entire length thereof down to plaintiff's said land, for the purpose of carrying his said waters of said Fort Canyon Creek to the land of the plaintiff for the purpose of irrigation, and is entitled to an easement therein to the extent of the enlarging of said ditch and for the purposes aforesaid, and to have a perpetual right of way to flow waters therein to the extent of the said enlargment.

"That the defendants are entitled to have and recover from the said plaintiff the sum of $40.00 damages for injury sustained by reason of the enlargement and improvement above stated and such right of way and easement.

"That the plaintiff is required to contribute to the cost and expense of maintaining and keeping the said ditch in repair in an amount and proportion bearing the same relation to the whole amount of cost and expense as the waters he flows therein bears to the whole amount flowed therein both by the plaintiff and defendants.

"That the plaintiff recover no costs herein and judgment is hereby ordered to be entered accordingly."

Judgment having been entered upon these findings, the defendants appealed to the Supreme Court of the State, where, after argument, the judgment was affirmed. 27 Utah, 158.

*   *   *

MR. JUSTICE PECKHAM, after making the foregoing statement, delivered the opinion of the court.

The plaintiffs in error contend that the proposed use of the enlarged ditch across their land for the purpose of conveying water to the land of the defendant in error alone is not a public use, and that, therefore, the defendant in error has no constitutional or other right to condemn the land, or any portion of it, belonging to the plaintiffs in error, for that purpose. They argue that, although the use of water in the State of Utah for the purpose of mining or irrigation or manufacturing may be a public use where the right to use it is common to the public, yet that no individual has the right to condemn land for the purpose of conveying water in ditches across his neighbor's land, for the purpose of irrigating his own land alone, even where there is, as in this case, a state statute permitting it.

In some States, probably in most of them, the proposition contended for by the plaintiffs in error would be sound. But whether a statute of a State permitting condemnation by an individual for the purpose of obtaining water for his land or for mining should be held to be a condemnation for a public use, and, therefore, a valid enactment, may depend upon a number of considerations relating to the situation of the State and its possibilities for land cultivation, or the successful prosecution of its mining or other industries. Where the use is asserted to be public, and the right of the individual to condemn land for the purpose of exercising such use is founded upon or is the result of some peculiar condition of the soil or climate, or other peculiarity of the State, where the right of condemnation is asserted under a state statute, we are always, where it can fairly be done, strongly inclined to hold with the state courts, when they uphold a state statute providing for such condemnation. The validity of such statutes may sometimes depend upon many different facts, the existence of which would make a public use, even by an individual, where, in the absence of such facts, the use would clearly be private. Those facts must be general, notorious and acknowledged in the State, and the state courts may be assumed to be exceptionally familiar with them. They are not the subject of judicial investigation as to their existence, but the local courts know and appreciate them. They understand the situation which led to the demand for the enactment of the statute, and they also appreciate the results upon the growth and prosperity of the State, which in all probability would flow from a denial of its validity. These are matters which might properly be held to have a material bearing upon the question whether the individual use proposed might not in fact be a public one. It is not alone the fact that the land is arid and that it will bear crops if irrigated, or that the water is necessary for the purpose of working a mine, that is material; other facts might exist which are also material, such as the particular manner in which the irrigation is carried on or proposed, or how the mining is to be done in a particular place where water is needed for that purpose. The general situation and amount of the arid land, or of the mines themselves, might also be material, and what proportion of the water each owner should be entitled to; also the extent of the population living in the surrounding country, and whether each owner of land or mines could be, in fact, furnished with the necessary water in any other way than by the condemnation in his own behalf, and not by a company, for his use and that of others.

These, and many other facts not necessary to be set forth in detail, but which can easily be imagined, might reasonably be regarded as material upon the question of public use, and whether the use by an individual could be so regarded. With all of these the local courts must be presumed to be more or less familiar. This court has stated that what is a public use may frequently and largely depend upon the facts surrounding the subject, and we have said that the people of a State, as also its courts, must in the nature of things be more familiar with such facts and with the necessity and occasion for the irrigation of the lands, than can any one be who is a stranger to the soil of the State, and that such knowledge and familiarity must have their due weight with the state courts. *Fallbrook Irrigation District* v. *Bradley*, 164 U. S. 112, 159. It is true that in the *Fallbrook case* the question was whether the use of the water was a public use when a corporation sought to take land by condemnation under a state statute, for the purpose of making reservoirs and digging ditches to supply land owners with the water the company proposed to obtain and save for such purpose. This court held that such use was public. The case did not directly involve the right of a single individual to condemn land under a statute providing for that condemnation.

We are, however, as we have said, disposed to agree with the Utah court with regard to the validity of the state statute, which provides, under the circumstances stated in the act for the condemnation of the land of one individual for the purpose of allowing another individual to obtain water from a stream in which he has an interest, to irrigate his land, which otherwise would remain absolutely valueless.

But we do not desire to be understood by this decision as approving of the broad proposition that private property may be taken in all cases where the taking may promote the public interest and tend to develop the natural resources of the State. We simply say that in this particular case, and upon the facts stated in the findings of the court, and having reference to the conditions already stated, we are of opinion that the use is a public one, although the taking of the right of way is for the purpose simply of thereby obtaining the water for an individual, where it is absolutely necessary to enable him to make any use whatever of his land, and which will be valuable and fertile only if water can be obtained. Other land owners adjoining the defendant in error, if any there are, might share in the use of the water by themselves taking the same proceedings to obtain it, and we do not think it necessary, in order to hold the use to be a public one, that all should join in the same proceeding or that a company should be formed to obtain the water which the individual land owner might then obtain his portion of from the company by paying the agreed price, or the price fixed by law.

The rights of a riparian owner in and to the use of the water flowing by his land are not the same in the arid and mountainous States of the West that they are in the States of the East. These rights have been altered by many of the Western States, by their constitutions and laws, because of the totally different circumstances in which their inhabitants are placed, from those that exist in the States of the East, and such alterations have been made for the very purpose of thereby contributing to the growth and prosperity of those States arising from mining and the cultivation of an otherwise valueless soil, by means of irrigation. This court must recognize the difference of climate and soil, which render necessary these different laws in the States so situated.

We are of opinion, having reference to the above peculiarities which exist in the State of Utah, that the statute permitting the defendant in error, upon the facts appearing in this record, to enlarge the ditch and obtain water for his own land, was within the legislative power of the State, and the judgment of the state court affirming the validity of the statute is therefore

Affirmed.

Mr. Justice Harlan and Mr. Justice Brewer dissented.

MT. VERNON—WOODBERRY COTTON DUCK COMPANY

v.

ALABAMA INTERSTATE POWER COMPANY

ERROR TO THE SUPREME COURT OF THE STATE OF ALABAMA.

240 U.S. 30

Submitted January 10, 1916.—Decided January 24, 1916.

Prohibition is a distinct suit and the judgment finally disposing of it is a final judgment by common law as well as under the statutes of Alabama within the meaning of Judicial Code, § 237.

The fact that the denial of a petition for writ of prohibition does not decide the merits of the principal suit is immaterial so far as finality of the judgment is concerned.

Where the state court has denied a petition for writ of prohibition, all the points urged exclusively under the state constitution must be taken to have been decided adversely to plaintiff in error and this court in such respect follows the state court.

To manufacture, supply and sell to the public, power produced by water as motive force, *held* in this case, following the judgment of the state court, to be a public use justifying the exercise of eminent domain, and the statute of Alabama providing for condemnation of property for water power purposes is not unconstitutional as taking property without due process of law.

186 Alabama, 622, affirmed.

The facts, which involve the construction, application and constitutionality of statutes of Alabama providing for proceedings to condemn land and water powers, are stated in the opinion.

Mr. *Hollins N. Randolph* and Mr. *Edwin G. Baetjer*, for plaintiff in error.

Mr. *Thomas W. Martin* and Mr. *Ray Rushton* for defendant in error.

Mr. Justice Holmes delivered the opinion of the court.

This is a petition for a writ of prohibition to prevent the Probate Court of Tallapoosa County from taking jurisdiction of condemnation proceedings instituted by the Alabama Interstate Power Company to take land, water and water rights belonging to the petitioner. An alternative writ was issued but the Supreme Court of the State ordered it to be quashed and the writ to be dismissed. 186 Alabama, 622. The grounds of the petition are that the statutes of Alabama do not authorize the proceedings and that if they do they contravene the Fourteenth Amendment of the Constitution of the United States. * * *

The principal argument presented that is open here, is that the purpose of the condemnation is not a public one. The purpose of the Power Company's incorporation and that for which it seeks to condemn property of the plaintiff in error is to manufacture, supply, and sell to the public, power produced by water as a motive force. In the organic relations of modern society it may sometimes be hard to draw the line that is supposed to limit the authority of the legislature to exercise or delegate the power of eminent domain. But to gather the streams from waste and to draw from them energy, labor without brains, and so to save mankind from toil that it can be spared, is to supply what, next to intellect, is the very foundation of all our achievements and all our welfare. If that purpose is not public we should be at a loss to say what is. The inadequacy of use by the general public as a universal test is established. *Clark* v. *Nash,* 198 U. S. 361. *Strickley* v. *Highland Boy Mining Co.,* 200 U. S. 527, 531. The respect due to the judgment of the State would have great weight if there were a doubt. *Hairston* v. *Danville & Western Ry. Co.,* 208 U. S. 598, 607. *O'Neill* v. *Leamer,* 239 U. S. 244, 253. But there is none. See *Otis Co.* v. *Ludlow Manufacturing Co.,* 201 U. S. 140, 151. We perceive no ground for the distinction attempted between the taking of rights below the contemplated dam, such as these are, and those above. Compensation is provided for according to rules that the court below declares to be well settled and that appear to be adequate. The details as to what may be taken and what not under the statutes and petition are not open here. Before a corporation can condemn rights it is required to have obtained, by other means, at least an acre on each side of the stream for a dam site, and this is supposed to show that the use is not public. It is only a reasonable precaution to insure good faith. A hardly consistent argument is that the dam should be built before the necessity of taking waters below can be shown. But a plan may show the necessity beforehand. All that we decide is that no general objection based on these grounds affects the jurisdiction of the Probate Court or the constitutionality of the act.

Certain exceptions from the powers conferred, such as private residences, lands of other corporations having similar powers, and cotton factories, subject to the taking of the excess of water over that in actual use or capable of use at normal stages of the stream, are too plainly reasonable so far as they come in question here to need justification. Discrimination is alleged but not argued. We see nothing that runs against the Fourteenth Amendment. The right given to take possession before the compensation is finally determined also is not argued. *Williams* v. *Parker*, 188 U. S. 491, 502. Without further discussion of the minutiæ, we are of opinion that the decision of the Supreme Court of Alabama upon the questions arising under the Constitution of the United States was correct.

Judgment affirmed.

Questions and Notes

On Clark

1. Who was the judge in this case? For what is he famous?—or, more precisely, which one of his opinions provoked a famous dissent by Mr. Justice Holmes?
2. What did plaintiff seek in this case?
3. Why were the special climatic conditions in Utah relevant to this problem?
4. How would it have been possible to settle the land in the dry western states for agricultural use, if this case (and similar ones) had gone the other way? What type of pattern of land-ownership would you then expect?
5. *Clark* was preceded by *Fallbrook Irrigation District v. Bradley*, 164 U.S. 112 (1896), a much longer opinion, with essentially the same holding.

On Mount Vernon-Woodberry

1. Who was the judge here?
2. What did the court say about the adequacy of use by the general public as the universal test of public use?
3. On what background cases did the court rely?

Section 13

Excess Condemnation

PENNSYLVANIA MUTUAL INSURANCE CO.

v.

PHILADELPHIA

242 Pa. 47, 88 A. 904.

Supreme Court of Pennsylvania. June 27, 1913.

Appeal from Court of Common Pleas, Philadelphia County.

Action by the Pennsylvania Mutual Life Insurance Company against the City of Philadelphia and others. From a decree awarding an injunction, plaintiff and defendant appeal. Affirmed.

Bill in equity for an injunction to restrain the city of Philadelphia from appropriating certain land under the provisions of the Act of June 8, 1907, P. L. 466. From the record it appeared that by ordinance of July 3, 1912, the councils of the city of Philadelphia undertook to appropriate certain land within 200 feet of a proposed parkway. By ordinance of January 16, 1913, the mayor was authorized to enter into an agreement on behalf of the city, with the Bell Telephone Company, whereby the land so appropriated should be conveyed to the telephone company in fee, subject to certain building restrictions. The purpose of the transaction was admittedly to protect the parkway from the construction of an unsightly building in the vicinity. There were no allegations of fraud. The court held the act constitutional, but awarded the injunction on the ground that the ordinance of January 16, 1907, was defective, in that it was not preceded by an ordinance prescribing general restrictions for the protection of the parkway.

Argued before FELL, C. J., and BROWN, MESTREZAT, ELKIN, and MOSCHZISKER, JJ.

Joseph P. McCullen, Asst. City Sol., and Michael J. Ryan, City Sol., both of Philadelphia, for the City of Philadelphia. Joseph Gilfillan, J. Washington Logue, and John C. Grady, all of Philadelphia, for the Pennsylvania Mut. Life Ins. Co. John G. Johnson, of Philadelphia, for the Bell Telephone Co.

MESTREZAT, J. By section 1 of the Act of June 8, 1907, P. L. 466, cities of the commonwealth are authorized to purchase, acquire, use, and appropriate private property for the purpose of making, enlarging, extending, and maintaining public parks, parkways, and playgrounds whenever councils shall determine thereon. Section 2 confers like authority on cities for appropriating "neighboring private property, within two hundred feet of the boundary lines of such property so * * * appropriated for * * * parkways * * * in order to protect the same by the resale of such neighboring property with restrictions, whenever the councils thereof shall, * * * determine thereon: Provided, that in the said ordinance * * * the councils shall declare that the control of such neighboring property * * * is reasonably necessary, in order to protect such * * * parkways * * * their environs, the preservation of the view, appearance, light, air, health, or usefulness thereof." Section 3 confers upon cities the right "to resell such neighboring property, with such restrictions in the deeds of resale in regard to the use thereof as will fully insure the protection of such * * * parkways * * * their environs, the preservation of the view, appearance, light, air, health and usefulness thereof, whenever the councils thereof shall * * * determine thereon." Section 4 declares the appropriation of property for such purposes "to be taking * * * for public use."

Pursuant to the authority conferred by the act and for the purposes therein specified the council of Philadelphia passed an ordinance on July 3, 1912, section 1 of which appropriated certain described private property located outside and within 200 feet of the parkway, a projected street extending northwestward from city hall to Fairmount Park, which appropriation includes property owned by the plaintiff company declared to be necessary to protect the parkway. By an ordinance of January 16, 1913, the mayor was authorized on behalf of the city to enter into an agreement with the Bell Telephone Company of Pennsylvania by which the company should convey in fee to the city, for the consideration of $1, three certain lots of ground at the northeast corner of North Seventeenth and Arch streets, and abutting on the parkway, and the city should acquire by deed or condemnation proceedings the property outside of and adjacent to the parkway and adjoining the property of the telephone company, Arch street, Appletree street, and property then owned by the city, which includes plaintiff's property, and with certain restrictions convey the same and the lots agreed to be conveyed to the city by the company, except the small portion thereof included in the parkway, to the telephone company. The consideration to be paid by the company to the city was 90 per cent. of the cost of acquiring the property by condemnation.

The Pennsylvania Mutual Life Insurance Company filed this bill against the city, averring, inter alia, that it is the owner in fee of two certain lots, together with the brick houses erected thereon, located on the north side of Arch street, containing in front 66 feet and extending northwardly to the south side of Appletree street, a depth of 160 feet; that the city has authorized the proper officials to acquire title to the property within the lines of the parkway, and within 200 feet thereof; that the parkway passes diagonally across the rear of the plaintiff's lots; that the property taken under the ordinance of July 3, 1912, includes not only the portion of the plaintiff company's lots included within the lines of the parkway, but also the entire balance of its property which lies within 200 feet of the parkway; that the portion of its property lying outside of the parkway was taken by the city to resell to the Bell Telephone Company of Pennsylvania, a private corporation, or to other private parties; that it objects to the city taking so much of its property as lies outside the parkway, and avers its intention to improve such property by the erection of new structures thereon, with such uniform restrictions as the city may constitutionally impose; that it is advised that the proposed taking of its property beyond the lines of the parkway is without authority of law, as the same is not being taken for public use, and because plaintiff's property is being taken to an extent greater than the city is legally authorized to appropriate. The bill prays that the act of 1907, section 1 of the ordinance of July 3, 1912, and the ordinance of January 16, 1913, be declared unconstitutional, null, and void, and that the mayor and director of the department of public works be enjoined from condemning and taking and from selling or transferring to any person such parts of the plaintiff's property as are not within the lines of the parkway. The answer admits substantially such averments of the bill as are necessary to the disposition of the case here. It denies that the part of the plaintiff's property outside of the parkway was appropriated to sell to the telephone company, but admits that it was taken to secure the control of the property in order to protect the parkway, as authorized by the act of 1907. This denial must be read in connection with the ordinance of January 16, 1913, which became effective after the answer of the city was filed, authorizing the mayor to execute an agreement, selling the property appropriated outside the parkway, including plaintiff's property, to the telephone company.

[1] The view we take of this case requires us to determine the single question whether the purpose of use for which the city intends to take the plaintiff's land is a public use within the constitutional provision permitting its appropriation under the power of eminent domain. Under our former Constitutions it was declared that no man's property can be justly taken from him or applied to public use without his consent and just compensation being made. The present Constitution, however, provides that private property shall not be taken or applied to public use without authority of law, and without just compensation being first made or secured. The right, therefore, to appropriate private property in this state for a

public use must now be conceded, and it is equally true that private property cannot be taken for a private purpose.

[2] The difficulty is in determining in the particular case what is a public use for which such property may be taken. Primarily this is a question for the legislative department of the government, but ultimately for the courts. "Whether it be expedient or wise for the Legislature to exercise this authority, to take property for public use," says Mr. Justice Dean, in Philadelphia, Morton & Swarthmore Street Railway Company's Petition, 203 Pa. 354, 362, 53 Atl. 191, 193, "is purely a political question, and one solely for the Legislature. But whether the use to which it is sought to appropriate the property authorized to be taken is a public use is a judicial question for the determination of the courts." There is no constitutional or statutory definition of the words "public use," and none of the adjudicated cases has given a definition of the words which can have universal application. It has been held that the words are equivalent to public benefit or advantage, while numerous other cases hold that to constitute a public use the property must be taken into the direct control of the public or of public agencies, or the public must have the right to use in some way the property appropriated. See 1 Lewis, Em. Dom. (3d Ed.) par. 257. The learned author, after discussing both views of the subject and referring to the many cases which have aligned themselves on either side, says (paragraph 258): "The use of a thing is strictly and properly the employment or application of the thing in some manner. The public use of anything is the employment or application of the thing by the public. 'Public use' means the same as 'use by the public,' and this it seems to us is the construction the words should receive in the constitutional provisions in question." This interpretation, says the same author (paragraph 258), will cover every case of appropriation that has been deemed lawful by any court, except a few in relation to mills, mines, and drainage.

Judge Cooley (Const. Lim. [7th Ed.] 766) says: "The public use implies a possession, occupation, and enjoyment of the land by the public at large or by public agencies. * * * It may be for the public benefit that all the wild lands of the state be improved and cultivated, all the low lands drained, all the unslightly places beautified, all dilapidated buildings replaced by new; because all these things tend to give an aspect of beauty, * * * and gratify public taste; but the common law has never sanctioned an appropriation of property based on these considerations alone."

In delivering his opinion in Bloodgood v. Mohawk & Hudson Railroad Co., 18 Wend. (N. Y.) 9, 65 (31 Am. Dec. 313), Tracy, Senator, said: "Can the constitutional expression, 'public use,' be made synonymous with 'public improvement,' or 'general convenience and advantage,' without involving consequences inconsistent with the reasonable security of private property, much more with that security which the Constitution guarantees? If an incidental benefit, resulting to the public from the mode in which individuals in pursuit of their own interests use their property, will constitute a public use of it, within the intention of the Constitution, it will be found very difficult to set limits to the power of appropriating private property."

[3] Mr. Justice Pearce, delivering the opinion in Arnsperger v. Crawford, 101 Md. 247, 253, 61 Atl. 413, 415 (70 L. R. A. 497), says: "There will be found two different views of the meaning of these words which have been taken by the courts; one, there must be a use, or right of use, by the public, or some limited portion of the public; the other, that they are equivalent to public utility or advantage. If the former is the correct view, the Legislature and the courts have a definite, fixed guide for their action; if the latter is to prevail, the enactment of laws upon this subject will reflect the passing popular feeling, and their construction will reflect the various temperaments of the judges, who are thus left free to indulge their own views of public utility or advantage. We cannot hesitate to range this court with those which hold the former to be the true view." We think this interpretation of the words "public use" is in accord with their plain and natural signification and with the weight of the best considered authorities. It furnishes a certain guide to the Legislature as well as to the courts in appropriating private property for public use. It enables the state and the owner to determine directly their respective rights in the latter's property. If, however, public benefit, utility, or advantage is to be the test of a public use, then, as suggested by the authorities, the right to condemn the property will not depend on a fixed standard by which the legislative and judicial departments of the government are to be guided, but upon the views of those who at the time are to determine the question. There will be no limit to the power of either the Legislature or the courts to appropriate private property to public use, except their individual opinions as to what is and what is not for the public advantage and utility. If such considerations are to prevail, the constitutional guaranties as to private property will be of small moment.

[4] Let us now turn to the case under consideration. Applying the doctrine that to constitute a public use for which private property may be appropriated there must be a use or right of use by the public it is apparent, we think, that the sections of the act of 1907, authorizing the acquisition of private property outside a public park, parkway, or playground, are not a constitutional exercise of legislative authority. It will be observed that these sections confer authority to appropriate and resell with such restrictions as may be prescribed property outside the lines of the parkway, and it is justified by declaring that it is done in order to protect the parkway, and for "the preservation of the view, appearance, light, air health or usefulness thereof." The protection of the highway is the only "public use" to which the land is to be applied. The property is not to be taken and held by the city for any use for which a statute confers on the city the right to appropriate it. Saving the restriction contained in the conveyance, the city can exercise no control over it, and hence cannot use it for any purpose. The only possible "use," therefore, which the city can

make of the property is to impose restrictions on it or impress it with an easement in the hands of the city's vendee. As said by the learned court below, the act contains a feature entirely new in this state, and authorizes the taking by the city of property which is not to be used by the public as part of its park, parkway, or playground, but is to be sold in fee to private parties for private use after it has been charged with an easement for the protection of the public improvement. Prior to this legislation the state had not authorized the taking of private property by the exercise of the power of eminent domain for such purpose. It is a step far in advance of the policy of the state as heretofore declared in her organic law, and is a liberal construction of a power which we have uniformly held must be strictly construed. "The exercise of the right of eminent domain, whether directly by the state or its authorized grantee," says Thompson, J., in Lance's Appeal, 55 Pa. 16, 26 (93 Am. Dec. 722) "is necessarily in derogation of private right, and the rule in that case is that the authority is to be strictly construed."

A municipality has the unquestioned right to appropriate property for its highways, and it determines in the first instance the necessity for taking the property for the purpose. It may lay out its streets in the manner it deems proper. It may fix the width of and divide the highways as it thinks should be done. It is not compelled to use the ground appropriated for the highway solely for sidewalks and cartways, but may devote part of it to æsthetic purposes, and ornament and beautify it. This is a legitimate use of the land in connection with the primary purpose for which property may be appropriated for a public thoroughfare. It, however, contemplates occupancy or possession by the city of the land taken for the highway, and not that it shall be owned and in possession of a private party. This construction of the powers of the municipality to condemn property will permit the city in the present case to carry into effect the purpose the learned trial judge says it has "to build a noble highway from the city hall to Fairmount Park, which shall by its character beautify the city and increase its attractiveness and renown," without invading the constitutionally protected right of private property.

Holding, as we do, that the use to be made of property located outside a public highway is not a public use, for which private property may be taken by the city against the consent of the owner, the effect of the act of 1907, authorizing the appropriation of property for such purpose, is to permit by the exercise of eminent domain the taking of the property of one citizen without his consent and vesting the title thereto in another. No court in this country has yet sanctioned such action by the state or its representative exercising the power of eminent domain. Says Mr. Justice Story, speaking for the court in Wilkinson v. Leland, 2 Pet. (27 U. S.) 658, 7 L. Ed. 512: "We know of no case in which a legislative act to transfer the property of A. to B., without his consent has ever been held a constitutional exercise of legislative power in any state in the Union. On the contrary, it has been constantly resisted as inconsistent with just principles, by every judicial tribunal in which it has been attempted to be enforced." It is true that in the present case the declared purpose in taking the property is to protect the highway and preserve the light, air, etc., but, if that be conceded to be a legitimate public use, the city is not permitted to hold it for that or any other purpose. The statute compels the city to sell and divest itself of the control or use of the property. The restriction imposed by the act which is to be inserted in the deed does not remove the objection that the act authorizes the city to take the property from one citizen without his consent and transfer it to another. The act does not require the property to be resold to the party from whom it has been taken, which might justify the contention that the only purpose in making the appropriation was to impose an easement for the benefit of the highway, but it is to be held by the city as a fee-simple owner who can sell to whomsoever it pleases. It deprives the owner of his right to accept the restrictions and retain the property on the same terms as the city's vendee would hold it. It empowers the city, at the pleasure of its officials, to transfer property on which is a business plant owned by one individual or corporation to another who is engaged in the same or another business. One man may be deprived of his home for the benefit of another. In view of its provisions conferring almost unlimited discretion on cities or their officials in exercising the powers granted, it is idle to say that the statute furnishes no opportunity to produce such results or to promote a private purpose.

We are all of the opinion that so much of the act of 1907 as authorizes and provides for the appropriation by cities of neighboring private property within 200 feet of the boundary lines of property taken and appropriated for public parks, parkways, and playgrounds, and section 1 of the ordinance of July 3, 1912, and the ordinance of January 16, 1913, passed in pursuance thereof, are unconstitutional, null, and void. It follows that the city is without authority under the act to appropriate the plaintiffs' land and resell it to the Bell Telephone Company, or to any other party, in pursuance of the ordinances passed for that purpose, and that the prayer of the plaintiff's bill restraining such action by the city should have been granted. The plaintiff's appeal must therefore be sustained, and the defendant's appeal be dismissed. The court below is directed to enter a decree declaring unconstitutional and void so much of the Act of June 8, 1907, P. L. 466, as authorizes cities to take and appropriate neighboring private property within 200 feet of the boundary line of property appropriated for public parks, parkways, and playgrounds, and section 1 of the ordinance of July 3, 1912, and the ordinance of January 16, 1913, passed in pursuance and by authority of said act, and enjoining perpetually the city from appropriating plaintiff's property outside of and adjacent to the parkway.

The decree of the court below, as thus amended, is affirmed. Costs in both appeals to be paid by the city of Philadelphia.

Questions and Notes

1. What kind of a civic improvement was proposed here?
2. Why did the city propose to use excess condemnation?
3. Who was the chosen redevelopment sponsor?
4. Who was the plaintiff? (Note that the allegations are a fine example of the "widows and orphans" school of plaintiff-brief-writing.)
5. It would be interesting to know exactly what happened after this case. As of 1941, the Bell Telephone Company building on this parkway had, as its tenant on the upper floors, Pennsylvania Mutual Life.

CROSS-REFERENCES

In Hagman, see § 177.
In McQuillin, see § 32.23.

Section 14

Public Purpose

GREEN

v.

FRAZIER

ERROR TO THE SUPREME COURT OF THE STATE OF

NORTH DAKOTA.

253 U.S. 233.

Argued April 19, 20, 1920.—Decided June 1, 1920.

THE case is stated in the opinion.

Mr. Thomas C. Daggett for plaintiffs in error.

Mr. Frederic A. Pike for defendants in error.

MR. JUSTICE DAY delivered the opinion of the court.

This is an action by taxpayers of the State of North Dakota against Lynn J. Frazier, Governor, John N. Hagan, Commissioner of Agriculture and Labor, William Langer, Attorney General, and Obert Olson, State Treasurer, and the Industrial Commission of that State to enjoin the enforcement of certain state legislation. The defendants Lynn J. Frazier, as Governor, William Langer, as Attorney General, and John Hagan, as Commissioner of Agriculture and Labor, constitute the Industrial Commission, created by the Act of February 25, 1919, [Laws 1919, c. 151] of the Sixteenth Legislative Assembly of the State of North Dakota.

The laws involved were attacked on various grounds, state and federal. The Supreme Court of North Dakota sustained the constitutionality of the legislation. So far as the decision rests on state grounds it is conclusive, and we need not stop to inquire concerning it. *Davis* v. *Hildebrant*, 241 U. S. 565. The only ground of attack involving the validity of the legislation which requires our consideration concerns the alleged deprivation of

1573

rights secured to the plaintiffs by the Fourteenth Amendment to the Federal Constitution. It is contended that taxation under the laws in question has the effect of depriving plaintiffs of property without the due process of law.

The legislation involved consists of a series of acts passed under the authority of the state constitution, which are: (1) An act creating an Industrial Commission of North Dakota [Laws, 1919, c. 151] which is authorized to conduct and manage on behalf of that State certain utilities, industries, enterprises and business projects, to be established by law. The act gives authority to the Commission to manage, operate, control and govern all utilities, enterprises and business projects, owned, undertaken, administered or operated by the State of North Dakota, except those carried on in penal, charitable or educational institutions. To that end certain powers and authority are given to the Commission, among others: the right of eminent domain; to fix the buying price of things bought, and the selling price of things sold incidental to the utilities, industries, enterprises and business projects, and to fix rates and charges for services rendered, having in mind the accumulation of a fund with which to replace in the general funds of the State the amount received by the Commission under appropriations made by the act; to procure the necessary funds for such utilities, industries, enterprises and business projects by negotiating the bonds of the State in such amounts and in such manner as may be provided by law. $200,000 of the funds of the State are appropriated to carry out the provisions of the act. (2) The Bank of North Dakota Act, [Laws 1919, c. 147] which establishes a bank under the name of "The Bank of North Dakota," operated by the State. The Industrial Commission is placed in control of the operation and management of the bank, and is given the right of eminent domain to acquire necessary property. Public funds are to be deposited in the bank, and the deposits are guaranteed by the State of North Dakota. Authority is given to transfer funds to other departments, institutions, utilities, industries, enterprises or business projects, and to make loans to counties, cities or political sub-divisions of the State, or to state or national banks on such terms as the Commission may provide. Loans to individuals, associations, and private corporations are authorized, when secured by duly recorded first mortgages on lands in the State of North Dakota. An appropriation of $100,000 is made immediately available to carry out the provisions of the act. (3) An act providing for the issuing of bonds of the State in the sum of $2,000,000, the proceeds of which are to constitute the capital of the Bank of North Dakota. [Laws 1919, c. 148.] The earnings of the bank are to be paid to the State Treasurer. Tax levies are authorized sufficient to pay the interest on the bonds annually. The bonds shall mature in periods of five years, and the Board of Equalization is authorized to levy a tax in an amount equal to one-fifth of the amount of their principal. The State Treasurer is required to establish a bank bond payment fund into which shall be paid moneys received from taxation, from appropriations and from bank earnings. $10,000 is appropriated for the purpose of carrying the act into effect. (4) An act providing for the issuing of bonds in the sum of not exceeding $10,000,000, to be known as "Bonds of North Dakota, Real Estate Series." [Laws 1919, c. 154.] These bonds are to be issued for the purpose of raising money to procure funds for the Bank of North Dakota to replace such funds as may have been employed by it from time to time in making loans upon first mortgages upon real estate. The faith and credit of the State of North Dakota are pledged for the payment of the bonds. Moneys derived from the sale of the bonds are to be placed by the Industrial Commission in the funds of the bank, and nothing in the act is to be construed to prevent the purchase of the bonds with any funds in the Bank of North Dakota. It is further provided that the State Board of Equalization shall, if it appears that the funds in the hands of the State Treasurer are insufficient to pay either principal or interest, accruing within a period of one year thereafter, make a necessary tax levy to meet the indicated deficiency. Provision is made for the repeated exercise of the powers granted by the act, for the purposes stated. An appropriation of $10,000 is made for carrying into effect the provisions of this act. (5) An act declaring the purpose of the State of North Dakota to engage in the business of manufacturing and marketing farm products, and to establish a warehouse, elevator, and flour mill system under the name of "North Dakota Mill and Elevator Association" to be operated by the State. [Laws 1919, c. 152.] The purpose is declared that the State shall engage in the business of manufacturing farm products and for that purpose shall establish a system of warehouses, elevators, flour mills, factories, plants, machinery and equipment, owned, controlled and operated by it under the name of the "North Dakota Mill and Elevator Association." The Industrial Commission is placed in control of the Association with full power, and it is authorized to acquire by purchase, lease or right of eminent domain, all necessary property or properties, etc.; to buy, manufacture, store, mortgage, pledge, sell and exchange all kinds of raw and manufactured farm food products, and by-products, and to operate exchanges, bureaus, markets and agencies within and without the State, and in foreign countries. Provision is made for the bringing of a civil action against the State of North Dakota on account of causes of action arising out of the business. An appropriation is made out of state funds, together with the funds procured from the sale of state bonds, to be designated as the capital of the Association. (6) An act providing for the issuing of bonds of the State of North Dakota in a sum not exceeding $5,000,000, to be known as "Bonds of North Dakota, Mill and Elevator Series," providing for a tax and making other provisions for the payment of the bonds, and appropriations for the payment of interest and principal thereof. [Laws 1919, c. 153.] The bonds are to be issued and sold for the purpose of carrying on the business of the Mill & Elevator Association. The faith and credit of the State of North Dakota are pledged for the pay-

ment of the bonds, both principal and interest. These bonds may be purchased with funds in the Bank of North Dakota. Taxes are provided for
sufficient to pay the bonds, principal and interest, taking into account the
earnings of the Association. The sum of $10,000 is appropriated from the
general funds of the State to carry the provisions of the act into effect.
(7) The Home Building Act declares the purposes of the State to engage
in the enterprise of providing homes for its residents and to that end to
establish a business system operated by it under the name of "The Home
Building Association of North Dakota"; and defines its duties and the
extent of its powers. [Laws 1919, c. 150.] The Industrial Commission is
placed in control of "The Home Building Association," and is given the
power of eminent domain, and the right to purchase and lease the requisite
property. Provision is made for the formation of home building unions.
The price of town homes is placed at $5,000, and of farm homes at $10,000.
A bond issue of $2,000,000, known as "Bonds of North Dakota Home Build-
ing Series," is provided for.

There are certain principles which must be borne in mind in this connection, and which must control the decision of this court upon the federal
question herein involved. This legislation was adopted under the broad
power of the State to enact laws raising by taxation such sums as are deemed
necessary to promote purposes essential to the general welfare of its people.
Before the adoption of the Fourteenth Amendment this power of the State
was unrestrained by any federal authority. That Amendment introduced a
new limitation upon state power into the Federal Constitution. The States
were forbidden to deprive persons of life, liberty and property without due
process of law. What is meant by due process of law this court has had
frequent occasion to consider, and has always declined to give a precise
meaning, preferring to leave its scope to judicial decisions when cases from
time to time arise. *Twining* v. *New Jersey*, 211 U. S. 78, 100.

The due process of law clause contains no specific limitation upon the
right of taxation in the States, but it has come to be settled that the authority of the States to tax does not include the right to impose taxes for merely
private purposes. *Fallbrook Irrigation District* v. *Bradley*, 164 U. S. 112, 155.
In that case the province of this court in reviewing the power of state
taxation was thoroughly discussed by the late Mr. Justice Peckham speaking for the court. Concluding the discussion of that subject (p. 158) the
Justice said: "In the Fourteenth Amendment the provision regarding the
taking of private property is omitted, and the prohibition against the State
is confined to its depriving any person of life, liberty or property, without
due process of law. It is claimed, however, that the citizen is deprived of
his property without due process of law, if it be taken by or under state
authority for any other than a public use, either under the guise of taxation
or by the assumption of the right of eminent domain. In that way the question whether private property has been taken for any other than a public
use becomes material in this court, even where the taking is under the

authority of the State instead of the Federal government." Accepting this as settled by the former adjudications of this court, the enforcement of the principle is attended with the application of certain rules equally well settled.

The taxing power of the States is primarily vested in their legislatures, deriving their authority from the people. When a state legislature acts within the scope of its authority it is responsible to the people, and their right to change the agents to whom they have entrusted the power is ordinarily deemed a sufficient check upon its abuse. When the constituted authority of the State undertakes to exert the taxing power, and the question of the validity of its action is brought before this court, every presumption in its favor is indulged, and only clear and demonstrated usurpation of power will authorize judicial interference with legislative action.

In the present instance under the authority of the constitution and laws prevailing in North Dakota the people, the legislature, and the highest court of the State have declared the purpose for which these several acts were passed to be of a public nature, and within the taxing authority of the State. With this united action of people, legislature and court, we are not at liberty to interfere unless it is clear beyond reasonable controversy that rights secured by the Federal Constitution have been violated. What is a public purpose has given rise to no little judicial consideration. Courts, as a rule, have attempted no judicial definition of a "public" as distinguished from a "private" purpose, but have left each case to be determined by its own peculiar circumstances. Gray, Limitations of Taxing Power, § 176, "Necessity alone is not the test by which the limits of State authority in this direction are to be defined, but a wise statesmanship must look beyond the expenditures which are absolutely needful to the continued existence of organized government, and embrace others which may tend to make that government subserve the general well-being of society, and advance the present and prospective happiness and prosperity of the people." Cooley, Justice, in *People* v. *Salem*, 20 Michigan 452. Questions of policy are not submitted to judicial determination, and the courts have no general authority of supervision over the exercise of discretion which under our system is reposed in the people or other departments of government. *Chicago, Burlington & Quincy R. R. Co.* v. *McGuire*, 219 U. S. 549, 569; *German Alliance Insurance Co.* v. *Lewis*, 233 U. S. 389.

With the wisdom of such legislation, and the soundness of the economic policy involved we are not concerned. Whether it will result in ultimate good or harm it is not within our province to inquire.

We come now to examine the grounds upon which the Supreme Court of North Dakota held this legislation not to amount to a taking of property without due process of law. The questions involved were given elaborate consideration in that court, and it held, concerning what may in general terms be denominated the "banking legislation," that it was justified for the purpose of providing banking facilities, and to enable the State to carry out the purposes of the other acts, of which the Mill & Elevator Association Act is the principal one. It justified the Mill & Elevator Association Act by the peculiar situation in the State of North Dakota, and particularly by the great agricultural industry of the State. It estimated from facts of which it was authorized to take judicial notice, that 90% of the wealth produced by the State was from agriculture; and stated that upon the prosperity and welfare of that industry other business and pursuits carried on in the State were largely dependent; that the State produced 125,000,000 bushels of wheat each year. The manner in which the present system of transporting and marketing this great crop prevents the realization of what are deemed just prices was elaborately stated. It was affirmed that the annual loss from these sources (including the loss of fertility to the soil and the failure to feed the by-products of grain to stock within the State), amounted to fifty-five millions of dollars to the wheat raisers of North Dakota. It answered the contention that the industries involved were private in their nature, by stating that all of them belonged to the State of North Dakota, and therefore the activities authorized by the legislation were to be distinguished from business of a private nature having private gain for its objective.

As to the Home Building Act, that was sustained because of the promotion of the general welfare in providing homes for the people, a large proportion of whom were tenants moving from place to place. It was believed and affirmed by the Supreme Court of North Dakota that the opportunity to secure and maintain homes would promote the general welfare, and that the provisions of the statutes to enable this feature of the system to become effective would redound to the general benefit.

As we have said, the question for us to consider and determine is whether this system of legislation is violative of the Federal Constitution because it amounts to a taking of property without due process of law. The precise question herein involved so far as we have been able to discover has never been presented to this court. The nearest approach to it is found in *Jones* v. *City of Portland*, 245 U. S. 217, in which we held that an act of the State of Maine authorizing cities or towns to establish and maintain wood, coal and fuel yards for the purpose of selling these necessaries to the inhabitants of cities and towns, did not deprive taxpayers of due process of law within the meaning of the Fourteenth Amendment. In that case we reiterated the attitude of this court towards state legislation, and repeated what had been said before, that what was or was not a public use was a question concerning which local authority, legislative and judicial, had especial means of securing information to enable them to form a judgment; and particularly, that the judgment of the highest court of the State declaring a given use to be public in its nature, would be accepted by this court unless clearly unfounded. In that case the previous decisions of this court, sustaining this proposition, were cited with approval, and a quotation was made from the opinion of the Supreme Court of Maine justifying the legislation under the conditions prevailing in that State. We think the principle of that decision is applicable here.

This is not a case of undertaking to aid private institutions by public taxation as was the fact in *Citizens' Savings & Loan Association* v. *Topeka*, 20 Wall. 655, 665. In many instances States and municipalities have in late years seen fit to enter upon projects to promote the public welfare which in the past have been considered entirely within the domain of private enterprise.

Under the peculiar conditions existing in North Dakota, which are emphasized in the opinion of its highest court, if the State sees fit to enter upon such enterprises as are here involved, with the sanction of its constitution, its legislature and its people, we are not prepared to say that it is within the authority of this court, in enforcing the observance of the Fourteenth Amendment, to set aside such action by judicial decision.

Affirmed.

Questions and Notes

1. What was proposed in this program?
2. What is the historical background of this legislation?
3. What is the special significance of grain warehouses in North Dakota?
4. *Frazier* was preceded by *Jones v. Portland*, 245 U.S. 217 (1917), which upheld a municipal fuel yard on the ground that special local conditions in Maine were involved. However, the Supreme Court later affirmed by memorandum (275 U.S. 504, 1927) the lower court decision in Standard Oil Company v. Lincoln, 114 Neb. 243, 207 N.W. 172 and 208 N.W. 162 (1926), which involved a filling station in Lincoln—not something which was created in response to special and peculiar local conditions. Query whether these opinions may be summarized by the principle that socialism is constitutional?

Section 15

Housing as a Nuisance

HEALTH DEPARTMENT OF

CITY OF NEW YORK

v.

DASSORI

21 App. Div. 348, 47 N.Y.S. 641 (1897), appeal dismissed,
159 N.Y. 245, 54 N.E. 13(1899).

Supreme Court, Appellate Division. First Department. October 15, 1897.

Appeal from special term.

Procedings by the health department of the city of New York against
Frederick Dassori and others. From a final order in favor of plaintiff, defendant Dassori apeals. Reversed.

Argued before PATTERSON, RUMSEY, WILLIAMS, O'BRIEN, and
PARKER, JJ.

David Keane, for appellant.

Roger Foster, for respondent.

RUMSEY, J. This proceeding was begun under the authority of section
659 of the consolidation act, as amended by chapter 567 of the Laws of
1895, for the purpose of condemning certain buildings situated in the rear of
Nos. 308, 310, 312, and 314 Mott street, in the city of New York, by a petition
praying for the condemnation of the buildings, filed by the department of
health. In that petition it was alleged, substantially, that the buildings
sought to be condemned were in such condition as to be dangerous to public
health, and that they were not reasonably capable of being made fit for
human habitation and occupancy, and that the evils caused by said buildings could not be remedied in any other way than by their destruction. To

this petition an answer was filed, in which the appellant denied the existence of a nuisance upon said premises, or that the premises were not fit for human habitation, and practically put in issue the existence of all the facts which, by the statute in question, are necessary to authorize the condemnation of the buildings. Upon this issue a reference was ordered to hear and determine, and the referee found that the condition of affairs alleged in the petition existed, and that the plaintiffs were entitled to judgment for the appointment of commissioners. Judgment to that effect was accordingly entered, and thereupon three commissioners were appointed to appraise the value of the property, and a hearing was had before them in due form. As the result of that hearing, the compensation was fixed at the value of the materials of the building, and a final order confirming the report was entered, by virtue of which the amount awarded to the appellant was the sum found by the commissioners to be the value of the materials of the buildings, which was $110; and it was ordered that upon the payment of that sum to the appellant the health department should be entitled to enter upon the possession of the property condemned, and to hold it for public use, and to destroy the rear tenement house described in the petition. From that final order this appeal is taken, and in the notice of appeal it is stated that the defendant will bring up for review the judgment entered upon the report of the referee, and all proceedings antecedent thereto.

Before considering the reasons given by the appellant why this order should be reversed, it is advisable to examine the statute, to ascertain just what the object of the legislature was in passing it, and the means they have adopted to attain that object. The statute is in that part of the consolidation act which relates to the health department, and contains the provisions with regard to tenement houses. As is well known, the condition of many buildings used for that purpose has been for years a menace to the public health, and grave questions have arisen as to the best manner in which the evils arising from their condition could be remedied, and the dangers to the public health averted. The condition of these houses arose, not alone from the habits of the inmates, but principally and largely from the construction, plans, and location of the buildings themselves. It was well understood that these evils were such as to seriously threaten the health of the community, and to render likely severe epidemics, with all the consequences which follow such a condition of affairs in a crowded community; and to meet that condition, and to avert these perils, careful inspection was required, and it might often be necessary to take summary measures to abate nuisances which, if permitted to exist, would endanger the health of the people of the city. To meet and provide for this condition of affairs was the object of the statute. It provides, in the first place, that whenever it shall be certified to the board of health that any building is infected with contagious diseases, or by reason of want of repair has become dangerous to life, or is unfit for human habitation because of defects in drainage, plumbing, ventilation, or the construction of the same, or because of the existence of a nuisance on the premises, and which is likely to cause sickness among its occupants, the board of health might, in a manner prescribed in the statute, require all persons to vacate the building. The statute provided for notice of the order to be given to the occupants of the building and to its owner or his agent, and it contained a further provision that whenever the defects mentioned in the order shall be remedied, or the danger shall cease to exist, the board of health might revoke the order. The statute further provided that "whenever, in the opinion of the board of health, any building or any part thereof, an order to vacate which had already been made by the board, is, by reason of age, defects in draining, plumbing, infection with contagious diseases or ventilation, or because of the existence of a nuisance on the premises which is likely to cause sickness, or because it stops ventilation in other buildings or otherwise makes or conduces to make other buildings adjacent to the same unfit for human habitation or dangerous or injurious to health, or because it prevents proper measures from being carried into effect for remedying any nuisance injurious to health or other sanitary evils in respect of such other buildings, so unfit for human habitation that the evils in or caused by said building cannot be remedied by repairs or in any other way than by destruction of said building or a portion of the same," the board was authorized to condemn the building, and order it to be removed. It provided, however, that, upon such condemnation being made, the owner might demand a survey of the building in the manner provided for in case of unsafe buildings. The proceedings for condemnation were to be taken by the board of health, and were to be proceeded with in the manner prescribed by the general law. The statute provided that upon the institution of the proceedings the owner, or any person interested in the building, might dispute the necessity of the destruction of the building, or any part thereof; and in that case the court was not authorized to appoint commissioners, unless proof was made of the necessity of such destruction. The foregoing is all that need be recited of the statute at present. It is quite clear that the object of this statute was to provide a summary way in which any nuisance in a building, as the result of which the building was dangerous to the health of its occupants or any other persons, might be summarily abated, and to provide further a way in which the existence of the nuisance should be adjudged, and the necessity of the destruction of the property upon which the nuisance existed might be decreed. When that had been done, the object of the statute was, further, to provide for the fixing of the compensation to which the owner of the building would be entitled, if its destruction was found to be necessary. The appellant here insists that the judgment appointing the commissioners to appraise the damages is erroneous, because there was no sufficient evidence that his buildings were unfit for human habitation, or that they were not capable of being made fit. No evidence upon this subject was offered by the defendant, and the case stands solely upon the proof made by the plaintiff of the situation and condition of these buildings, and such proof is entirely undisputed. The evidence showed that the building or buildings in question were situated in the rear of four other buildings owned by the appellant, which fronted upon Mott street, and were also occupied as tenement houses. These rear houses were 91 feet long from north to south, and a little over 20 feet wide. The length of the buildings was parallel with Mott street, and they extended across the premises of the defendant, occupying in their north and south course the whole width of those premises. They were five stories high. From the front of these buildings to the rear of the buildings occupying the front of the lot was a court extending the whole width of the lot, and being 5 feet in width on the northern extremity, and 7 feet at its widest part. This court was entirely surrounded by buildings, the lowest of which were three stories high. The front buildings, facing on Mott street, the rear of which formed the front wall of this court, were four stories high. On each end of this narrow court were buildings over 40 feet high, and the rear of the court was formed by the wall of the buildings in question, which were five stories high. At the southeast corner of this court there was a space of 11 inches between the rear wall of the building on the next lot and the south wall of the building in question, but, except for that space of 11 inches, there was no way in which fresh air could reach that court except from the top. The north and south walls of these buildings were dead walls, without any windows or ventilation whatever, except a small window on the north side of each story. The east wall stood next to a dead wall, and about 8 inches from it, so that the space between the east wall of the tenements in question and a blank wall of the buildings several stories in height, just east of it, was 91 feet long and 8 inches wide. As might be expected, this space was full of all sorts of filth, and its condition was such as to be unmentionable. The apartments in these buildings consisted of three rooms,—a front room, lighted and ventilated by two windows, each 5 feet by 3, opening into the front court yard; and two bedrooms in the rear, each 8 feet high and 6 feet 10 inches square, and lighted by a single window 2 feet square, opening onto the court 8 inches wide, and having no other ventilation except that the bedrooms on the northeast corner on each floor had a window opening on the north into a yard. But, except for that, the bedrooms had no ventilation whatever, save such as they might get from the living room, or from the windows opening onto this ill-smelling and narrow court, 8 inches wide. The cellars of these buildings were occupied by school sinks for the use of all the tenants of both front and rear buildings. These cellars opened into the court yard, and had no other means of ventilation. They were damp, the floor being constantly wetted by the water from the hydrants in front of the buildings and by the sinks. The smell from the cellars going through the whole house was almost unendurable. The stairways in the buildings are narrow and steep, and always were dark and foul; and smoke and coal gas from the defective chimney flues have discolored the walls and ceilings so that it is impossible to make them white. The roofs leak, causing the rooms to be wet. The plaster on the walls and ceilings is cracked in many places, and portions of it have fallen. The places around the sinks in the hall are constantly damp from the waste splash. The houses swarm with vermin throughout. Every room is damp, and filled with air which is foul, and unfit to breathe. There is no possible way in which the sun could shine into these buildings. The only sunlight which could approach them is that which at certain hours of the day filters down into this court 7 feet wide, along their front; but the rays of the sun which fall into that court yard for a short time during the day cannot enter any of the rooms of the house, and are insufficient to properly light the lower floors, which are so dark that for a large portion of the time artificial light has to be used in them, as might be expected. What little sunlight filters into this court is obstructed by the fire escapes along the front of the buildings, which are used for the deposit of various articles by the tenants. This has been the condition of these buildings for a long time. The population in May, 1896, was 115 men, women, and children in the rear houses, and 150 in the front houses. Whereas the death certificates show that during the past six years the annual death rate in New York was 24 to 1,000, in these houses the death rate was 45.87 to 1,000. The death rate in these buildings was considerably higher than the death rate in the ward, and the infant death rate was abnormally high, so that in one year more than one-third of the children under five years of age in these buildings died. These deaths were largely caused by the diseases which are nourished by dampness and exposure to foul air. All these facts not only appeared by the testimony, but were entirely undisputed or unexplained; and, although it was made to appear that such had been the condition of affairs in these buildings for several years, there was no pretense that any effort had ever been made to remedy such of them as were remediable, or that the buildings themselves were capable of being repaired, or put into such condition as to be fit for human habitation.

From this testimony the learned referee was justified in his findings that these rear tenement houses were unfit for habitation. But the testimony was far from establishing that they were not capable of being made fit for habitation, or that the nuisance upon them could not be abated in any other way than by their destruction. It was quite clear from the testimony that the unsanitary condition of the buildings was caused, to a very considerable extent, if not entirely, by the filthy habits of the persons who inhabited them, and grew out of the fact that they were used for human habitation. It did not appear that, after the buildings had been vacated, they might not easily have been put into a sanitary condition by proper repairs, and the removal of those offensive appurtenances which were more particularly complained of as the cause of its unhealthy condition. Even if it be said, however, from this testimony, that the referee would have been justified in finding that the buildings could not have been made fit for human habitation, still the necessity for their destruction was not made to appear. A thing is a nuisance when, because of its inherent qualities, or the use to which it is put, it works an injury to people who live in its neighborhood. The right to abate it arises from the necessity of the case, exists only because of that necessity, and is to be exercised only so far as the necessity requires. A thing which is a nuisance because of the use to which it is put cannot be destroyed by way of abating the nuisance, unless such destruction is necessary. If the nuisance can be abated by discontinuing the use, it must be abated in that way. Wood, Nuis. § 33; Ely v. Supervisors, 36 N.Y. 297. The case of Meeker v. Van Rensselaer, 15 Wend. 397, which has sometimes been relied upon as establishing the proposition that a building which was in a filthy condition, and calculated to breed disease, and was thereby a public nuisance, might be torn down by way of abating the nuisance, was decided upon the facts of that case. It was there made to appear, and was not disputed, that the only way of abating the nuisance was by the destruction of the buildings; and for that reason alone it was held by the supreme court that the destruction was justifiable. But in this case no such fact has been made to appear. Although the buildings may not have been capable of being made fit for habitation, still, if they were so put in repair that the evil smells should be removed, and the sources of contagion taken away,—as it is plain from the evidence might be done,—the buildings would cease to be a nuisance; and the fact that they might not thereby be made fit for human habitation would not authorize their destruction. If they ceased to be in such a condition as to breed pestilence and spread disease, and were rendered innoxious, the owner of them had a right to have them remain upon the premises, even though he might not be permitted to use them as a tenement house. There are many other uses to which he might lawfully put them; and the undoubted power of the public to refuse him permission to rent them to be used for human habitation did not necessarily involve the right to destroy them if they were not fit for that purpose.

One of the allegations in the petition was that the buildings prevented proper measures from being carried into effect for remedying nuisances dangerous to health and other sanitary evils in respect of other buildings to which they were adjacent. As has been said, it was made to appear that these buildings were erected within a very short distance of other buildings, which were also used as tenement houses; and it is quite likely that the proximity of the two buildings deprived each of them of the ventilation necessary to make them fit for the uses to which the owners intended to put them. But, if these particular buildings were themselves in a proper condition, or were put in a proper condition, the fact that, located as they were, they stopped ventilation of other buildings, so that those other buildings were not fit to be used as tenement houses, was no warrant for the destruction of these buildings. It might furnish a good reason why the other buildings—not being supplied with sufficient air, so that they could be occupied by a great number of people—might be vacated, but was not a reason for the destruction of these buildings so that the other buildings might become more fitted for use as tenement houses, and thereby more valuable. In this country the right of one owner of property to have light and air for his buildings at the expense of land of another owner is not recognized, except it comes to exist by express contract. Myres v. Gemmel, 10 Barb. 537. All that the owner of any building can be called upon to do with regard to that building, if he desires to use it as a tenement house, is to keep it in such a condition as the statute requires. If he does that, he has complied with the law, and his building is not a nuisance. He cannot be compelled to submit to the destruction of his building, if it is on his own land, because some other building adjacent to it is thereby deprived of proper ventilation.

The case, then, so far as the plaintiff is concerned, must stand upon the condition of these buildings themselves, and upon the fact that they were not capable of being put in such a condition that they would not be of themselves dangerous to public health. Unless that was made to appear, the right to destroy them did not exist. In such cases the right to condemn grows out of the right to destroy the building because it is a public nuisance, and can be abated in no other way; and, unless that is made to appear, there can be no final order for condemnation. For the reason, therefore, that there was a complete failure of evidence to show that it was not practicable so to repair these buildings as that they might be put in a wholesome condition, and not remain a public nuisance, without their destruction, the judgment which is brought up on this appeal was erroneous, and must be reversed, and the final order must fall with the judgment.

PATTERSON, WILLIAMS, and O'BRIEN, JJ., concur. PARKER, J., not voting.

Questions and Notes

1. On what street was this building located? Where is that street? —and for what is it better known?
2. Where on the lot was this building located?
3. Was compensation proposed for its demolition?
4. Give a description of this charming building.
5. What was the court's idea of an appropriate remedy?

Section 16

Restrictive Housing Legislation

HEALTH DEPARTMENT OF
CITY OF NEW YORK

v.

RECTOR OF TRINITY CHURCH

145 N.Y. 32, 39 N.E. 833 (1895).

Court of Appeals of New York.   Feb. 26, 1895.

Appeal from common pleas of New York city and county, general term.
Action by the health department of the city of New York against the
rector, church-wardens, and vestrymen of Trinity Church, to recover a
penalty for failure to supply the floors of a tenement house with Croton or
other water.   From a judgment of the general term of the court of common
pleas of New York city and county (17 N. Y. Supp. 510) reversing a judgment for plaintiff, the latter appeals.   Reversed.

Th's is an appeal from an order of the general term of the court of common pleas for the city of New York, which reversed a judgment on a verdict
directed for the plaintiff, and granted a new trial.   The action was brought
by the plaintiff, by virtue of several acts of the legislature giving it power,
in certain cases, to commence an action in its own name, for the purpose
of recover'ng the amount of $200, being the penalty for 20 days' violation
by the defendant of the act hereinafter mentioned, relative to the supply of
water in several tenement houses owned by the defendant.   The defendant
denied some of the allegations of the complaint, and set up, also, as one of
the defenses to the action, that the statute upon which the complaint is
founded is unconstitutional.   Each party moved, after the evidence was in,
that a verdict be directed in its favor. The motion on the part of the plain-

tiff was granted, and that on the part of the defendant was denied. The defendant excepted to these decisions of the court, and, judgment having been entered, it appealed to the general term of the court of common pleas. There the judgment was reversed, and from the order of reversal the plaintiff appeals here.

The cause of action is founded upon section 663 of the consolidation act, relating to the city of New York, as such section was amended by chapter 84 of the Laws of 1887. After making various provisions in prior sections for the proper construction and ventilation of tenement houses in the city of New York, the legislature, by the amendment of 1887, enacted as follows: "Sec. 663. Every such house erected after May 14th, 1867, or converted, * * * shall have Croton or other water furnished in sufficient quantity at one or more places on each floor, occupied or intended to be occupied by one or more families, and all tenement houses shall be furnished with a like supply of water by the owners thereof whenever they shall be directed so to do by the board of health. But a failure in the general supply of water by the city authorities shall not be construed to be a failure on the part of the owner, provided that proper and suitable appliances to receive and distribute such water are placed in said house. Provided, that the board of health shall see to it that all tenement houses are so supplied before January first, eighteen hundred and eighty-nine." The rest of the section is not material. It appeared upon the trial that the defendant was the owner of certain houses in the city of New York, known as "Numbers 59, 77, 84, and 86 Charlton Street," and on the 20th of March, 1891, the plaintiff caused to be served on the agent of the defendant a notice requiring the defendant, in conformity with the provisions of the Sanitary Code, to alter, repair, cleanse and improve the premises above mentioned, and directing that suitable "appliances to receive and distribute a supply of water for domestic use be provided on the top floor of No. 59; the basement, first and second floors of No. 77; the basement, first, second, and third floors of No. 84; and the basement and attic of 86." And the defendant was required to comply with the requirements within five days from the receipt of the notice, and it was also stated in the notice that any application for a necessary extension of time, or for the suspension of any part of the requirements contained in the written notice, should be made to the health department, at the time and place designated in the notice. This action was brought against defendant as owner of houses Nos. 77 and 84 Charlton street. The defendant claims that the houses in question were not "tenement" houses, as that word is popularly used; that they were houses constructed many years ago as dwelling houses, and they have never been altered, with reference to their internal arrangement, so as to convert them into what would popularly be called "tenement houses." They were old-fashioned dwelling houses,—two-story, attic, and basement. There were hydrants in the back yards, accessible to all tenants of the houses. But the proof in the case shows that at No. 77 Charlton street there were three families, and in No. 84 there were six families; and the houses came clearly and distinctly under the definition of "tenement houses," as enacted by section 666 of the consolidation act, as amended by the Laws of 1887 (chapter 84, p. 100). It is claimed on the part of the defendant that the buildings are in a transition neighborhood, which will be shortly required for business structures; that they are not in a neighborhood where all or many of the large buildings, which are known as "tenement houses," in the popular meaning of the word, are situated; and that these houses are not really within the reason of the statute. The defendant offered on the trial to give testimony as to the necessary cost of complying with the order of the board of health, which was excluded, and the defendant excepted. Defendant also offered to prove that the introduction of appliances to furnish water on each floor, and the required sinks and waste pipes to connect with the sewer, would cause great danger of injury to the property, through the water in the pipes freezing and the pipes bursting in the winter season; also, that no complaints had been made to the defendant corporation by occupants of these houses, in reference to the want of water. All this evidence was excluded, under the objection of the plaintiff, and upon the exception of the defendant. The general term of the common pleas granted leave to plaintiff to appeal from its order of reversal and granting a new trial, on the ground that a question of law was involved, which ought to be reviewed by this court.

Roger Foster for appellant. Stephen P. Nash, for respondent.

PECKHAM, J. (after stating the facts). The recovery in this case is founded upon that portion of the consolidation act which requires that all houses of a certain description, upon the direction of the board of health, shall be provided with Croton or other water in sufficient quantity at one or more places on each floor, occupied, or intended to be occupied, by one or or more families. The defendant, among other things, alleges as a defense that the order of the board of health directing the defendant to furnish the water as provided by the statute was made without notice to it, and that, as it could not be complied with excepting by the expenditure of a considerable amount of money, the result would be to deprive the defendant of its property without a hearing and an opportunity to show what defense it might have, and that it in fact deprived the defendant of its property without due process of law. There was no arrangement in either of these houses in question for the supplying of the Croton or other water to the occupants of each floor at the time when the order of the board of health was made. Such order could not, therefore, be complied with on the part of the defendant without the expenditure of money for that purpose. That fact must be assumed, and, even upon that assumption, we do not think the act is invalid on the alleged ground that it deprives the defendant, if enforced, of its property without due process of law. The act must be sustained, if at all, as an exercise of the police power of the state. It has frequently been said that it is difficult to give any exact definition which shall properly limit and describe such power. It must be exercised subject to the provisions of both the federal and state constitutions, and the law passed in the exercise of such power must tend, in a degree that is perceptible and clear, towards the preservation of the lives, the health, the morals, or the welfare of the community, as those words have been used and construed in many cases heretofore decided. Such cases have arisen in this state, where the power of the legislature was questioned, and where the exercise of that power was affirmed or denied for the reasons given therein. See People v. Marx, 99 N. Y. 377, 2 N.E. 29; In re Jacobs, 98 N. Y. 98; People v. Gillson, 109 N. Y. 389, 17 N.E. 343; People v. Arcusberg, 105 N. Y. 123, 11 N.E. 277; and many cases cited in these cases. See, also, Slaughter-House Cases, 16 Wall. 36, 62; Barbier v. Connolly, 113 U. S. 27, 5 Sup. Ct. 357; New Orleans Gaslight Co. v. Louisiana Light & Heat Producing & Manuf'g Co., 115 U. S. 650, 6 Sup. Ct. 252; Beer Co. v. Massachusetts, 97 U. S. 25. The act must tend, in some appreciable and clear way, towards the accomplishment of some one of the purposes which the legislature has the right to accomplish under the exercise of the police power. It must not be exercised ostensibly in favor of the promotion of some such object, while really it is an evasion thereof, and for a distinct and totally different purpose; and the courts will not be prevented from looking at the true character of the act, as developed by its provisions, by any statement in the act itself, or in its title, showing that it was ostensibly passed for some object within the police power. The court must be enabled to see some clear and real connection between the assumed purpose of the law and the actual provisions thereof; and it must see that the latter do tend, in some plain and appreciable manner, towards the accomplishment of some of the objects for which the legislature may use this power.

Assuming that this act is a proper exercise of the power, in its general features, we do not think that it can be regarded as invalid because of the fact that it will cost money to comply with the order of the board, for which the owner is to receive no compensation, or because the board is entitled to make the order, under the provisions of the act, without notice to and a hearing of the defendant. As to the latter objection, it may be said that, in enacting what shall be done by the citizen for the purpose of promoting the public health and safety, it is not usually necessary to the validity of legislation upon that subject that he shall be heard before he is bound to comply with the direction of the legislature. People v. Board of Health, 140 N. Y. 1, 6, 35 N. E. 320. The legislature has power, and has exercised it in countless instances, to enact general laws upon the subject of the public health or safety without providing that the parties who are to be affected by those laws shall first be heard before they shall take effect in any particular case. So far as this objection of want of notice is concerned, the case is not materially altered in principle from what it would have been if the legislature had enacted a general law that all owners of tenement houses should, within a certain period named in the act, furnish the water as directed. Indeed, this act does contain such a provision, but the plaintiff has not proceeded under it. If, in such case, the enforcement of the direct command of the legislature were not to be preceded by any hearing on the part of any owner of a tenement house, no provision of the state or federal constitution would be violated. The fact that the legislature has chosen to delegate a certain portion of its power to the board of health, and to enact that the owners of certain tenement houses should be compelled to furnish this water after the board of health had so directed, would not alter the principle, nor would it be necessary to provide that the board should give notice and afford a hearing to the owner before it made such order. I have never understood that it was necessary that any notice should be given under such circumstances before a provision of this nature could be carried out.

As to the other objection, no one would contend that the amount of the expenditure which an act of this kind may cause, whether with or without a hearing, is within the absolute discretion of the legislature. It cannot be claimed that it would have the right, even under the exercise of the police power, to command the doing of some act by the owner of property, and for the purpose of carrying out some provision of law, which act could only be performed by the expenditure of a large and unreasonable amount of money on the part of the owner. If such excessive demand were made, the act would, without doubt, violate the constitutional rights of the individual. The exaction must not alone be reasonable, when compared with the amount of the work or the character of the improvement demanded. The improvement or work must, in itself, be a reasonable, proper, and fair exaction, when considered with reference to the object to be attained. If the expense to the individual under such circumstances would amount to a very large and unreasonable sum, that fact would be a most material one in deciding whether the method or means adopted for the attainment of the main object were or were not an unreasonable demand upon the individual for the benefit of the public. Of this the courts must, within proper limits, be the judges. We may own our property absolutely, and yet it is subject to the proper exercise of the police power. We have surrendered, to that extent, our right to its unrestricted use. It must be so used as not improperly to cause harm to our neighbor, including in that description the public generally. There are sometimes necessary expenses which inevitably grow out of the use to which we may put our property, and which we must incur, either voluntarily, or else under the direction of the legislature, in order that the general health, safety, or welfare may be conserved. The legislature, in the exercise of this power, may direct that certain improvements shall be made in existing houses at the owners' expense, so that the health and safety of the occupants, and of the public through them, may be guarded. These exactions must be regarded as legal so long as they bear equally upon all members of the same class, and their cost does not exceed what may be termed one of the conditions upon which individual property is held. It must not be an unreasonable exaction, either with reference to its nature or its cost. Within this reasonable restriction, the power of the state may, by police regulations, so direct the use and enjoyment of the property of the citizen that it shall not prove pernicious to his neighbors, or to the public generally. The difference between what is and what is not reasonable frequently constitutes the dividing line between a valid and void enactment by the legislature in the exercise of its police power. In commenting on the difference of degree in any given case which would render an act valid or otherwise, Mr. Justice Holmes, in Rideout v. Knox, speaking for the supreme court of Massachusetts, said: "It may be said that the difference is only one of degree. Most differences are, when nicely analyzed. At any rate, difference of degree is one of the distinctions by which the right of the legislature to exercise police power is determined. Some small limitations of previously existing rights incident to property may be imposed for the sake of preventing a manifest evil. Larger ones could not be, except by the exercise of the right of eminent domain." 148 Mass. 308, 372, 19 N. E. 390. See, also, Miller v. Horton, 152 Mass. 540, at page 547, 26 N. E. 100. The case of Stuart v. Palmer, 74 N. Y. 183, is an example of the exercise of the taxing power of the state, and other considerations obtain in such cases.

Laws and regulations of a police nature, though they may disturb the enjoyment of individual rights, are not unconstitutional, though no provision is made for compensation for such disturbances. They do not appropriate private property for public use, but simply regulate its use and enjoyment by the owner. If he suffers injury, it is either damnum absque injuria, or, in the theory of the law, he is compensated for it by sharing in the general benefits which the regulations are intended and calculated to secure. 1 Dill. Mun. Corp. (4th Ed.) § 141, and note 2; Com. v. Alger, 7 Cush. 83, 84, 86; Baker v. City of Boston, 12 Pick. 183, 193; Clark v. Mayor, etc., 13 Barb. 32, 36. The state, or its agent in enforcing its mandate, takes no property of the citizen when it simply directs the making of these improvements. As a result thereof, the individual is put to some expense in complying with the law, by paying mechanics or other laborers to do that which the law enjoins upon the owner; but, so long as the amount exacted is limited as stated, the property of the citizen has not been taken, in any constitutional sense, without due process of law. Instances are numerous of the passage of laws which entail expense on the part of those who must comply with them, and where such expense must be borne by them, without any hearing or compensation, because of the provisions of the law. Thorpe v. Railroad Co., 27 Vt. 140-152. One of the late instances of this kind of legislation is to be found in the law regulating manufacturing establishments. Laws 1887, c. 462. The provisions of that act could not be carried out without the expenditure of a considerable sum by the owners of a then existing factory. Hand rails to stairs, hoisting shafts to be inclosed, automatic doors to elevators, automatic shifters for throwing off belts or pulleys, and fire escapes on the outside of certain factories,—all these were required by the legislature from such owner, and without any direct compensation to him for such expenditure. Has the legislature no right to enact laws such as this statute regarding factories, unless limited to factories to be thereafter built? Because the factory was already built when the act was passed, was it beyond the legislative power to provide such safeguards to life and health, as against all owners of such property, unless upon the condition that these expenditures to be incurred should ultimately come out of the public purse? I think to so hold would be to run counter to the general course of decisions regarding the validity of laws of this character, and to mistake the foundation upon which they are placed. Coates v. Mayor, etc., 7 Cow. 583; Stuyvesant v. Mayor, etc., Id. 604; Cooley, Const. Lim. (5th Ed.) p. 706, c. 16, etc.

Any one in a crowded city who desires to erect a building is subject at every turn, almost, to the exactions of the law in regard to provisions for health, for safety from fire, and for other purposes. He is not permitted to build of certain materials, within certain districts, because, though the materials may be inexpensive, they are inflammable; and he must build in a certain manner. Theaters and hotels are to be built in accordance with plans to be inspected and approved by the agents of the city; other public buildings, also; and private dwellings within certain districts are subject to the same supervision. And in carrying out all these various acts the owner is subjected to an expense much greater than would have been necessary to have completed his building, if not compelled to complete it in the manner, of the materials, and under the circumstances prescribed by various acts of the legislature. And yet he has never had a hearing in any one of these cases, nor does he receive any compensation for the increased expense of his building, rendered necessary in order to comply with the police regulations. I do not see that the principle is substantially altered where the case is one of an existing building, and it is to be subjected to certain alterations for the purpose of rendering it either less exposed to the danger from fires, or its occupants more secure from disease. In both cases the object must be within some of the acknowledged purposes of the police power, and such purpose must be possible of accomplishment at some reasonable cost, regard being had to all the surrounding circumstances. There might at first seem to be some difference as to the principle which obtained in enacting conditions, upon complying with which the owner might be permitted to erect a structure within the limits of a city or village, or for certain purposes, and the enactment of provisions which would necessitate the alteration of structures already in existence. In the first case it might be urged that the discretion of the legislature in enacting conditions for building might be more extensive, because the owner would be under no necessity of building; it would be a matter of choice, and not of compulsion; and, in choosing to build, it might be said that he accepted the condition,—while in the second case he would have no choice, and would be compelled to alter or improve the existing building as directed by the law.

The difference, however, is, as it seems to me, really not one of principle, but only of circumstances. Although the owner, in the one case, is not compelled to build, yet he is limited in the use to which he may put his property by the provisions of the law. He cannot build as he wishes to, unless upon the condition of a compliance with the law; and he may very probably be so situated, as to location of property, and in other ways, that it is really a necessity for him to use his property in the way proposed, and which he cannot do without expending considerable sums above what he otherwise would be called upon to do, in order to comply with those provisions. They must therefore be reasonable, as already stated. When one's use of his property is thus circumscribed and limited, what might otherwise be called his rights are plainly interfered with, and the justification therefor can only be found in this police power. So, when the owner of an existing structure is called upon to make such alterations, while the necessity may seem to be more plainly present, still it may exist in both cases, and the only justification in either is the same. Under the police power, persons and property are subjected to all kinds of restraints and burdens in order to secure the general comfort and health of the public.

The citizen cannot, under this act, be punished in any way, nor can any penalty be recovered from him for an alleged noncompliance with any of its provisions, or with any order of the board of health, without a trial. The punishment or penalties provided for in section 665 cannot be enforced without a trial under due process of law, and upon such trial he has an opportunity to show whatever facts would constitute a defense to the charge; to show, in other words, that he did not violate the statute, or the order of the board, or that the statute itself or the order was unreasonable and illegal. He might show that the house in question was not a tenement house, within the provision of the act, or that there was a supply of water as provided for by the act, or any other fact which would show that he had not been guilty of an offense with regard to the act. City of Salem v. Eastern R. Co., 98 Mass. 431, 447. The mere fact, however, that the law cannot be enforced without causing expense to the citizen who comes within its provisions, furnishes no constitutional obstacle to such enforcement, even without previous notice to and a hearing of the citizen. What is the propriety of a hearing, and what would be its purpose? His property is not taken without due process of law, within any constitutional sense, when the enforced compliance with certain provisions of the statute may result in some reasonable expense to himself. Any defense which he may have is available upon any attempt to punish him, or to enforce the provisions of the law.

An act of the legislature of Massachusetts which provided that every building in Boston used as a dwelling house, situated on a street in which there was a public sewer, should have sufficient water closets connected therewith, was held valid as to existing houses, and applied, in its penalties, to their owners, if such houses continued without the closets after its passage. Com. v. Roberts, 155 Mass. 281, 29 N. E. 522. And see Train v. Disinfecting Co., 144 Mass. 529, 11 N. E. 929. No notice or hearing was provided for, in the above statute as to water closets, before the act could be enforced; and yet to enforce it would, of course, cost the owner of the building some money. The same may be said as to the disinfecting of the rags, in above case in 144 Mass. and 11 N. E. If the citizen be charged with any violation of such a statute, and any penalty or punishment is sought or attempted, then is the time for a hearing, and then is the time he can make defense, if any he may have. But to assert that he must be heard before the authorities assume or endeavor to act under and to enforce the law, as against him, is to say, in substance, that each citizen is to be heard upon the general question whether it is right to enforce the law in his particular case. This is not to be permitted. Com. v. Alger, 7 Cush. 53, 104; City of Salem v. Eastern R. Co., 98 Mass. 431, 443. Everything that the individual could urge upon the hearing, if given prior to the attempted enforcement of the act by the making of the order in question, can be said by him when he is sued, or when the attempt is made to punish him for the alleged violation of the law. Upon the prior hearing, if granted, it would be no defense to him if he showed that the law could not be complied with, unless at some reasonable expense to himself. That would have been matter to urge upon the legislature prior to the enactment of the statute, as a question of reasonable cost and of public policy. Boston & M. R. Co. v. County Com'rs. 79 Me. 386, 393; State v. Wabash, St. L. & P. Ry. Co., 83 Mo. 144-149; Thorpe v. Railroad Co., 27 Vt. 140, 149, 156, note. We do not think that the cost of making the improvements called for by this act exceeds the limits which have been defined, assuming the amount thereof which the defendant offered to prove.

This is not the case of a proceeding against an individual on the ground of the maintenance of a nuisance by him, nor is it the case of an assumed right to destroy an alleged nuisance without any other proof than the decision of the board itself (with or without a hearing) that the thing condemned was a nuisance. Nor is it the case of the destruction of property which is in fact a nuisance, without compensation. Where property of an individual is to be condemned and abated as a nuisance, it must be that somewhere between the institution of the proceedings and the final result the owner shall be heard in the courts upon that question, or else that he shall have an opportunity, when calling upon those persons who destroyed his property to account for the same, to show that the alleged nuisance was not in fact. No decision of a board of health, even if made on a hearing, can conclude the owner upon the question of nuisance. People v. Board of Health, 140 N. Y. 1, 35 N. E. 320; Board v. Copcutt, 140 N. Y. 12, 35 N. E. 443; Miller v. Horton, 152 Mass. 540, 26 N. E. 100; Hutton v. City of Camden, 39 N. J. Law, 122, We are therefore of the opinion that the act, if otherwise valid, is not open to the objection that it violates either the federal or state constitution, in the way of depriving the defendant of its property without due process of law.

We think the act is valid as an exercise of the police power with respect to the public health and also with respect to the public safety regarding fires and their extinguishment. We cannot say, as a legal proposition, that it tends only to the convenience of the tenants in regard to their use of water. We cannot say that it has no fair and plain and direct tendency towards the more speedy extinguishment of fires, in crowded tenement houses. That the free use of water, especially during the summer months, tends towards the healthful condition of the body, by reason of the increased cleanliness occasioned by such use, there can be no reasonable doubt. The supply of water to the general public in a city has become not only a luxury, but an absolute necessity for the maintenance of the public health and safety. The city of New York itself has spent millions upon millions of dollars for the purpose of securing this great boon for the inhabitants thereof. The right of eminent domain in the taking of land around the sources the water supply has been granted to and exercised by that city to a very large extent, so that all sources of supply of this vital necessity of life should be rendered as free from contamination and danger to health and life as it possibly could be. This use of the water is not confined, so far as the necessities of the case are concerned, to the public hydrants. The water is brought into the city so that it may be used in every house and building within its limits; and although we may, and indeed must, admit that no health law could practically be enforced which should provide that every individual inhabitant of the tenement houses should use the water, yet we think it is perfectly clear that facilities for the use of the water will almost necessarily be followed by its actual use in larger quantities and more frequently than would be the case without such facilities, and to the great benefit of the health of the occupants of such houses. Those occupants require it more even than their favored brethren, living in airy, larger, more spacious, and luxurious apartments. Their health is matter of grave public concern. The leg'slature cannot, in practice, enforce a law so as to make a man wash himself; but, when it provides facilities therefor, it has taken a long step towards the accomplishment of that object. That dirt, filth, nastiness in general, are great promoters of disease; that they breed pestilence and contagion, sickness and death,—cannot be successfully denied. There is scarcely a dissent from the general belief on the part of all who have studied the disease. The so-called "ship fever" or "jail fever" arises from filth. Most diseases are aggravated by it. That opportunities—conveniences—for the use of water in these tenement houses will unquestionably tend towards, and be followed by, more cleanly living on the part of the occupants of those houses, cannot, it seems to me, admit of any rational doubt; and, if so, then the law which provides, at a reasonable cost, for the furnishing of such facilities, is plainly and honestly a health law.

The learned counsel for the defendant asks where this kind of legislation is to stop. Would it be contended that the owners of such houses could be compelled to furnish each room with a bath tub, and all the appliances that are to be found in a modern and well-appointed hotel? Is there to be a bath room and water closet to each room, and every closet to be a model of the very latest improvement? To which I should answer, certainly not. That would be so clearly unreasonable that no court, in my belief, could be found which would uphold such legislation, and it seems to me equally clear that no legislature could be found that would enact it. The tenement house in New York is a subject of very great thought and anxiety to the residents of that city. The number of people that live in such houses; their size; their ventilation; their cleanliness; their liability to fires; the exposure of their occupants to contagious diseases, and the consequent spread of the contagion through the city and the country; the tendencies to immorality and crime where there is very close packing of human beings of the lower order in intelligence and morals,—all these are subjects which must arouse the attention of the legislator, and which it behooves him to see to, in order that such laws are enacted as shall directly tend to the improvement of the health, safety, and morals of those men and women that are to be found in such houses. Some legislation upon this subject can only be carried out at the public expense, while some may be properly enforced at the expense of the owner. We feel that we ought to inspect with very great care any law in regard to tenement houses in New York, and to hesitate before declaring any such law invalid, so long as it seems to tend plainly in the direction we have spoken of, and to be reasonable in its provisions. If we can see that the object of this law is without doubt the promotion or the protection of the health of the inmates of these houses, or the preservation of the houses themselves, and consequently much other property, from loss or destruction by fire, and if the act can be enforced at a reasonable cost to the owner, then, in our opinion, it ought to be sustained. We believe this statute fulfills these conditions. We think that in this case it is not a mere matter of convenience of the tenants as to where they shall obtain their supply of water. Simple convenience, we admit, would not authorize the passage of this kind of legislation. But where it is obvious that, without the convenience of an appliance for the supply of water on the various floors of these tenement houses, there will be scarcely any but the most limited and scanty use of the water itself, which must be carried from the yards below, and when we must admit that the free use of water tends directly and immediately towards the sustaining of the health of the individual, and the prevention of disease arising from filth either of the person or in the surrounding habitation, then we must conclude that it is more than a mere matter of convenience in the use of water which is involved in the decision of this case. The absence of the water tends directly towards the breeding of disease, and its presence is healthful and humanizing.

Looked at in the light of a fire law, the act is also valid. The section of the consolidation act in question belongs to title 7, which treats of tenement and lodging houses; and various provisions are made in the preceding sections looking towards the prevention and the prompt extinguishment of fires, as well as towards the protection and promotion of the health of the occupants of such house. And it seems to me that the facility for the extinguishment of fires, which would result from the presence of a supply of water on each floor of these houses, is plain, and the act must be looked upon as a means for securing such an important result. We are inclined therefore, to the belief that the act may be upheld under both branches alike, as a health law, and as one calculated to prevent destruction of property from fires which might otherwise take place.

The act is somewhat vague as to what shall be regarded as a sufficient quantity of water on each floor, but it must have in this respect, as in others, a reasonable construction: and when an appliance for its supply is placed on a floor where it might be open and common to all those on that floor, and easy of access, and the supply sufficient in amount for general domestic purposes, then and in such case there would be a full compliance with the provisions of the act.

Some criticism is made in regard to the wording of the order of the board of health. The order directed that suitable appliances to receive and distribute a supply of water for domestic use should be provided at these various houses; and it is claimed that there is no language in the act which requires appliances for the distribution of water, nor that the water shall be furnished for domestic use. The act provides that the water shall be furnished in sufficient quantity at one or more places on each floor occupied, or intended to be occupied, by one or more families. This necessarily requires some appliance for that purpose. The statute must also mean that the water is to be provided for the use of the one or more families that are to be occupants of the floor, and that must include a sufficient quantity of water for domestic purposes. The provision in the law that the water shall be furnished in sufficient quantities at one or more places on each floor cannot be so construed as to leave the number of places of supply entirely to the discretion of the board of health. As the water is to be supplied in sufficient quantity for domestic and not for manufacturing purposes, when that point is reached the law is satisfied. Looking at the purpose of the supply, it is, as I have said, reasonably apparent that one such place on each floor, fairly accessible to all the occupants of the floor, would be all that could usually and reasonably be required, and anything further would be unreasonable, and therefore beyond the power of the board to order. The facilities thus given would at the same time furnish the means necessary for obtaining water to extinguish such fires as might accidentally break out, and before they had obtained such headway as to render necessary the aid of the fire department. This is clearly a most important safeguard.

The question alluded to in the brief of the respondent's counsel, whether the penalties might not be said to have commenced running immediately after the passage of the amended act of 1887, because of the provision requiring all tenement houses to be supplied with suitable appliances before January 1, 1889, and so have amounted to a confiscation of property, is not before us, as the proceeding herein was to recover only those incurred since the order was made by the board. If such a case arises where penalties so enormous in amount are claimed, there will probably be not much difficulty in refusing enforcement, under the circumstances of that case. Upon the whole, we think the order of the general term of the court of common pleas should be reversed, and the judgment of the trial court affirmed, with costs.

BARTLETT, J. (dissenting). I am unable to discover the limit of legislative power, if this act is to stand. Upon the face of the proceeding, it is not an exercise of the police power to promote the safety of property by the prevention of fire. The order of the health department, served upon the defendant, directs that suitable appliances "to receive and distribute a supply of water for domestic use be provided" on certain floors in the houses named. The act provides that tenement houses "shall have Croton or other water furnished in sufficient quantities at one or more places on each floor," etc. The order undertakes to construe the act, and requires the landlord to distribute a supply of water for domestic use on each floor. The board of health is not confined to compelling one place on each floor at which water may be obtained, but the act reads, "one or more places on each floor." So that it is left with the board of health to determine how many water faucets upon each floor shall be provided by the landlord for the use and convenience of his tenants. In other words, the legislature seeks to vest in one of the departments of the city government the power to decide the extent of the plumbing in tenement houses for Croton water purposes. It must, of course, be admitted that water is essential to the public health, and more particularly in crowded tenement districts. It would undoubtedly be a legitimate exercise of the police power to compel the introduction of water into tenement houses at some convenient point where all the tenants could obtain an adequate supply; and it may be that the legislature could go so far as to require a faucet upon each floor of the large tenement houses, in the public hall, in order to encourage the free use of water, by enabling the tenants to procure it without too great exertion, but certainly it cannot be possible that the legislature may leave the number and location of faucets on each floor for the domestic use of water to be determined by the board of health. There is no limitation as to whether the faucets shall be in the public hall, or in the room of the tenant. To my mind, such an exercise of the police power is spoliation and confiscation under the forms of law. It deprives the landlord of the control of his property, and leaves it to a stranger to decide in what manner the house shall be plumbed. It is a direct interference with the right of the landlord to regulate the rental value of his property. It is a matter of common knowledge that in rented apartments in the city of New York the convenience and volume of the water supply is regulated by the rental value of the premises, and that in the cheap tenement districts the convenience of the tenants is not and cannot be consulted to the same extent as in first-class localities. The vice of the act we are considering lies in the fact, already pointed out, that it is too general in its terms, and clothes the health department with unlimited and undefined powers. If it be the legislative intent to compel the introduction of a more abundant supply of water into tenement houses, either to promote the public health, or to provide for the timely extinguishment of fires, I think this very proper exercise of the police power should be manifested in an act containing details and limitations, so that capitalists may understand the burdens imposed upon tenement property, and decide, with a full knowledge of the facts, whether they care to embark their money in that class of buildings. This court has held (In re Jacobs, 98 N. Y. 108) that the limit of police power "cannot be accurately defined, and the courts have not been able or willing definitely to circumscribe it." Each case must be decided very largely on its own facts. A sound public policy certainly dictates that at this time, when the rights of property and the liberty of the citizen are sought to be invaded by every form of subtle and dangerous legislation, the courts should see to it that those benign principles of the common law which are the shield of personal liberty and private property suffer no impairment. I think the judgment should be affirmed, with costs.

All concur with PECKHAM, J., for reversal, except BARTLETT, J., who reads for affirmance. Judgment reversed.

Questions and Notes

1. Who was the judge involved here?
2. Where was the building involved? (This is in the area now known as "Soho," just below Greenwich Village.)
3. What were the new requirements involved here? Did they apply both to new and existing buildings?
4. Had any of the tenants asked the Rector for the improvements now required?
5. What was the allegation on what might happen in winter, if these improvements were made? What does this tell you about the heating system in the building?
6. On what ground did the court uphold the restrictions?
7. Note the fine example of the parade-of-horrors technique—where will such regulations stop?

ADAMEC

v.

POST

273 N.Y. 250, 7 N.E. 2d 120.

Court of Appeals of New York.

March 9, 1937.

Appeal from Special Term.

Proceeding for injunction by John B. Adamec against Langdon W. Post, as Tenement House Commissioner of the City of New York. From a judgment of Special Term granting a motion to dismiss the complaint, plaintiff appeals.

Affirmed.

Theodore Ornstein, Edward Elman, and Henry H. Silverman, all of New York City, for appellant.

Paul Windels, Corp. Counsel, of New York City (William S. Gaud, Jr., Paxton Blair, and Francis J. Bloustein, all of New York City, of counsel), for respondent.

John J. Bennett, Jr., Atty. Gen. (Henry Epstein, of Albany, and John C. Crary, Jr., of counsel), for the State.

LEHMAN, Judge.

The plaintiff is the owner of a plot of land in the city of New York, twenty-five feet in width and one hundred feet in depth, with a four-story brick building erected upon it prior to 1901, and still used as an apartment or tenement house. It contains eight five-room apartments, two on each floor, and also two two-room apartments in the basement.

Under the provisions of the Multiple Dwelling Law (Consol.Laws, c. 61-a; Laws 1929, c. 713, as amended by Laws 1930, cc. 839, 840, 841, 842, 843, 844, 845, 846, 847, 861, 863, 864; Laws 1931, cc. 129, 213, 228, 229, 681, 765; Laws 1932, c. 626; Laws 1933, cc. 210 and 398; Laws 1934, cc. 526, 527, 528, 529, 530, 531, 532, 552, 719, 742; and Laws 1935, cc. 335, 336, 863, 864, 865, 866, 904 and 941), buildings used as multiple dwellings though erected prior to 1901 in accordance with the requirements of the laws of the State which were then in force, must now comply with new requirements and higher standards enacted by the Legislature, for the protection of the safety and health of those who may live in these houses and, indirectly, of the people of the State. The plaintiff, claiming that the statute as amended is arbitrary and unreasonable and deprives him and others similarly situated of their property without due process of law, has brought this action, praying that the court declare the statute null and void in so far as it applies to buildings erected before 1901 and that an injunction issue against the Tenement House Commissioner restraining him from taking any steps to enforce the statute.

[1] The plaintiff moved at Special Term for an injunction pendente lite. The defendant moved for judgment dismissing the complaint on the ground that it failed to state facts sufficient to constitute a cause of action. The defendant's motion was granted, and from the judgment of dismissal the plaintiff has appealed directly to this court pursuant to the provisions of the Civil Practice Act, § 588, subd. 3. The scope of the plaintiff's appeal is limited to the constitutional question of the validity of the statute. No procedural question survives. The appellant can succeed in the court only if from the allegations of the complaint the conclusion must be drawn that the legislative command arbitrarily deprives the plaintiff of his property.

[2] The complaint alleges that the plaintiff's building is "one of many thousands of similar buildings in the city of New York, commonly known as 'old law' tenements, having been constructed prior to January 1st, 1901." The State has prohibited the use of any building, erected since that time, as a "tenement house" or "multiple dwelling" unless such building complies with requirements exacted and standards prescribed from time to time for the protection of the health and lives of those living there. During the last thirty-five years there have been improvements in sanitation; new devices have been invented which provide added comfort or safety; noncombustible or slow burning materials have been perfected. During these years, too, there has come a general recognition that dwellings which are unsafe or unsanitary or which fail to provide the amenities essential to decent living may work injury not only to those who live there, but to the general welfare. Economic self interest—the incentive to obtain the higher rentals which might be exacted of those able and willing to pay adequately for increased comfort and safety—would, doubtless, be a force sufficient, even without legislative compulsion, to induce the erection of some buildings which would embody the latest improvements and the most advanced ideas in safety and construction. In steadily descending scale, less conveniences, less space, less light, less air, less safeguards of health and safety, will be provided for lower rentals. At the point where economic self-interest ceases to be a sufficiently potent force for the promotion of the general welfare, or, indeed, becomes a force which may actually injure the general welfare, the Legislature may intervene and require that buildings intended for use as tenement houses or multiple dwellings shall conform to minimum standards which may reasonably be regarded as essential for safe, decent, and sanitary dwelling places.

Conformity to such standards may cause additional expense to owners of land and result in increased rentals and thus cause incidental hardship to tenants who have small incomes. Nevertheless the Legislature has power to prohibit the use of land for the erection of buildings, to be used for housing, which provide accommodations below such standards. The power of the State to place reasonable restrictions upon the use of property for the promotion of the general welfare is no longer subject to challenge and regulations governing the erection or use of buildings as multiple dwellings which are reasonably calculated to safeguard the public health and safety constitute a proper exercise of that power. Cf. Adler v. Deegan, 251 N.Y. 467, 167 N.E. 705.

[3] This court has said that there is no difference of principle but "only of circumstance" between a legislative enactment of "conditions upon complying with which the owner might be permitted to erect a structure within the limits of a city or village or for certain purposes, and the enactment of provisions which would necessitate the alteration of structures already in existence." In both cases the enactment is an attempted exercise of the police power "in order to secure the general comfort and health of the public" and in both cases the use of his property by the owner is "circumscribed and limited, what might otherwise be called his rights are plainly interfered with, and the justification therefor can only be found in this police power." Health Department of City of New York v. Rector, etc., of Trinity Church, 145 N.Y. 32, 45, 39 N.E. 833, 837, 27 L.R.A. 710, 45 Am. St.Rep. 579.

[4] Difference "of circumstance" may, nevertheless, be an important factor in determining whether a particular regulation is reasonable. A small additional cost in erecting a new building in conformity with a regulation calculated to "secure the general comfort and health of the public" even in a matter, perhaps, not of vital importance, may be reasonably justified by the result to be attained, while the cost of alteration of an old building to conform to such a regulation may be too great to be reasonably required for a doubtful or slight public benefit. Then, too, costly alterations may be economically impractical for old buildings, perhaps deteriorated by years of use, perhaps obsolescent, perhaps in neighborhoods no longer suitable for dwellings. In such case a requirement of such alterations may result in discontinuance of the use of such buildings with consequent loss of revenue to the owner of the building, and perhaps hardship to the tenants who must move out and find other quarters, where, in return for better dwellings, they may be compelled to pay higher rents.

These are matters which are primarily the concern of the Legislature and must reasonably affect its judgment as to what differentiation should be made between regulations for the construction of buildings presently to be erected and provisions necessitating alterations in old buildings constructed in accordance with standards formerly approved but now discarded as inadequate. Even so, as the court pointed out in Health Department of City of New York v. Rector, etc., of Trinity Church, supra, 145 N.Y. 32, at page 41, 39 N.E. 833, 836, 27 L.R.A. 710, 45 Am.St.Rep. 579, the discretion of the Legislature is not absolute. "The improvement or work must in itself be a reasonable, proper and fair exaction when considered with reference to the object to be attained. If the expense to the individual under such circumstances would amount to a very large and unreasonable sum, that fact would be a most material one in deciding whether the method or means adopted for the attainment of the main object were or were not an unreasonable demand upon the individual for the benefit of the public." In the same case the court quoted with approval from the opinion of Mr. Justice Holmes, speaking for the Supreme Court of Massachusetts in Rideout v. Knox, 148 Mass. 368, 19 N.E. 390, 2 L.R.A. 81, 12 Am.St.Rep. 560: "It may be said that the difference is only one of degree; most differences are when nicely analyzed. At any rate, difference of degree is one of the distinctions by which the right of the legislature to exercise police power is determined. Some small limitations of previously existing rights incident to property may be imposed for the sake of preventing a manifest evil; larger ones could not be except by the exercise of the right of eminent domain."

[5] General statements in judicial opinions can be understood only when read in their context. In Health Department of City of New York v. Rector, etc., of Trinity Church, supra, this court sustained on broad grounds a statute requiring owners of tenement houses at their own cost to make alterations which would promote the comfort and health of their tenants. The court held, too, that, at the trial, evidence of the probable cost of such alterations was properly excluded when it appeared that the cost even as claimed by the owner of the tenement would not be an unreasonable exaction for the resulting benefit. Lest the decision might be construed as a holding that the Legislature had power to require landlords to make improvements at their own expense for purposes other than the *public* health and welfare or to require *unreasonable* expenditures even for such a purpose, the court in the sentences above quoted from its opinion gave warning that it was not discarding the well-recognized limitations imposed by the Constitution upon the power of the Legislature.

The attack of the plaintiff in this case upon the validity of the statute which requires the alteration of existing buildings, which do not conform to the minimum standards prescribed in the statute, is based upon the claim that the cost of alterations, required to make "old law tenements" conform to the new standards prescribed by the Multiple Dwelling Law and the amendments thereto, would be prohibitive and unreasonable. The plaintiff leans heavily upon these extracts from the opinion in Health Department of City of New York v. Rector, etc., of Trinity Church, supra. It is said in imposing such an expense the Legislature has transcended the constitutional limitations upon its power. The statute maintains the differentiation recognized in all earlier statutes between the standards which should be prescribed for buildings to be erected thereafter and the standards which should be required in existing buildings which had been erected in conformity with the standards prescribed in earlier statutes. Article 7 of the statute (sections 210 et seq.), which formulates the requirements for existing buildings, prescribes higher standards for buildings erected prior to 1901, than had been prescribed at the time the buildings were erected, but less than the Legislature prescribed for buildings to be erected thereafter.

The plaintiff in his complaint set forth sixteen "changes, additions, eliminations and alterations" in his building which will be required to meet the new standards prescribed in the statute as amended. These requirements are not challenged on the ground that they are not calculated to promote in some degree the public health, safety, and welfare. They are challenged solely on the ground that the cost of conforming to them would be unreasonable.

The complaint alleges that the expense of all these "changes, additions, eliminations and alterations" would be "upwards of $5,000," although the plaintiff's property is assessed only "in the total sum of $13,500.00; the land being assessed at the sum of $5,000 and the building being assessed at the sum of $8,500.00." Until now, the Tenement House Commissioner, charged with the duty of enforcing the statute, has served upon the plaintiff an order requiring the plaintiff to conform to the statute only in two particulars and the plaintiff does not attempt to show that the cost of complying with that order would be excessive or unreasonable. Even though we should assume for the purpose of this appeal that the plaintiff may complain of the cost of other alterations, required by the statute, before he has been ordered to make such alterations by the officer charged with the duty of enforcing the statute, yet we should be constrained to hold that the complaint fails to state facts from which the conclusion follows that the Legislature has sought to impose unreasonable restrictions upon the use of the plaintiff's property and that the statute is, therefore, invalid.

[6] The imposition of the cost of the required alterations as a condition of the continued use of antiquated buildings for multiple dwellings may cause hardship to the plaintiff and other owners of "old law tenements" but, in proper case, the Legislature has the power to enact provisions reasonably calculated to promote the common good even though the result be hardship to the individual. "It is not the hardship of the individual case that determines the question, but rather the general scope and effect of the legislation as an exercise of the police power in protecting health and promoting the welfare of the community at large. It is a well-recognized principle in the decisions of the state and federal courts that the citizen holds his property subject not only to the exercise of the right of eminent domain by the state, but also subject to the lawful exercise of the police power by the legislature; in the one case property is taken by condemnation and due compensation; in the other the necessary and reasonable expenses and loss of property in making reasonable changes in existing structures, or in erecting additions thereto, are damnum absque injuria." Tenement House Department of City of New York v. Moeschen, 179 N.Y. 325, 330, 72 N.E. 231, 232, 70 L.R.A. 704, 103 Am.St.Rep. 910, 1 Ann.Cas. 439.

Certainly the proportion of cost of the alteration to the assessed or even the market value of the old law tenement can be no criterion of whether the

Legislature has acted reasonably in requiring the alteration. The value of a tenement house decreases as year by year it becomes more antiquated, less suited to its purpose and departs further from the reasonable standards prescribed by the State for such buildings; yet the same reasons which cause such decline in value may present most cogent argument that the Legislature as a condition of the continued use of these old buildings as dwellings should require alterations which will make them reasonably fit for use as dwellings according to modern standards of health, safety and decency and thus prevent them from becoming a source of danger to the community.

"The improvement or work must in itself be a reasonable, proper and fair exaction when considered with reference to the object to be attained." Health Department of City of New York v. Rector, etc., of Trinity Church, supra, 145 N.Y. 32, 41, 39 N.E. 833, 836, 27 L.R.A. 710, 45 Am.St. Rep. 579. The object to be attained here is greater safety from fire and more sanitary conditions in tenement houses erected prior to 1901 and which do not even at this date conform to the standards set for all buildings erected since 1901. It does not appear and it is not claimed that the alterations are not reasonably calculated to attain their object and it can hardly be argued that the imposition of a cost of $5,000 to attain that result in a tenement house containing forty rooms is unreasonable even though it may cause hardship in an individual case. Because the State has tolerated slum dwellings in the past, it is not precluded from taking appropriate steps to end them in the future. When a building used as a dwelling house is unfit for that use and a source of danger to the community, the Legislature in order to promote the general welfare may require its alteration or require that its use for a purpose which injures the public be discontinued; and, subject to reasonable limitation, the Legislature may determine what alterations should be required and what conditions may constitute a menace to the public welfare and call for remedy. The result, as we have said, may be the closing of many tenement houses and the eviction of the tenants. Argument may be made that before the Legislature causes the closing of tenement houses because they are unfit for habitation, provision should be made for better housing elsewhere for the evicted tenants. Such arguments must be addressed to the Legislature. The plaintiff cannot complain to the court because the Legislature has decided otherwise.

The judgment should be affirmed, with costs.

CRANE, C. J., and O'BRIEN, HUBBS, LOUGHRAN, FINCH, and RIPPEY, JJ., concur.

Judgment affirmed.

QUEENSIDE HILLS REALTY CO.

v.

SAXL

328 U.S. 80 (1946).

Appeal from the Court of Appeals of New York.

Argued March 28, 1946.—Decided April 22, 1946.

Appellant sued in the New York courts for a declaratory judgment holding certain provisions of the New York Multiple Dwelling Law (L. 1929, c. 713) as amended in 1944 (L. 1944, c. 553) unconstitutional and restraining their enforcement. The Supreme Court dismissed the suit. The Appellate Division affirmed. 269 App. Div. 691, 54 N. Y. S. 2d 394. The Court of Appeals affirmed, 294 N. Y. 917, 63 N.E.2d 116, certifying by its remittitur that questions involving the Fourteenth Amendment were presented and necessarily passed upon. 295 N. Y. 567, 64 N.E.2d 278. *Affirmed,* p. 85.

George G. Lake argued the cause and filed a brief for appellant.

Edward G. Griffin argued the cause for appellee. With him on the brief were *John J. Bennett* and *Joseph F. Mulqueen, Jr.*

Mr. Justice Douglas delivered the opinion of the Court.

In 1940 appellant constructed a four-story building on the Bowery in New York City and since that time has operated it as a lodging house. It was constructed so as to comply with all the laws applicable to such lodging houses and in force at that time. New York amended its Multiple Dwelling Law [1] in 1944,[2] providing, *inter alia*, that lodging houses "of non-fireproof construction existing prior to the enactment of this subdivision" [3] should comply with certain new requirements.[4] Among these was the installation of an automatic wet pipe sprinkler system. Appellant received notice to comply with the new requirements and thereupon instituted this suit in the New York courts for a declaratory judgment holding these provisions of the 1944 law unconstitutional and restraining their enforcement.

The bill alleged that the building was safe for occupancy as a lodging house and did not constitute a fire hazard or a danger to the occupants; that it complied with all building laws and regulations at the time of its construction; that part of it was fireproof and that the rest was so constructed as not to be dangerous to occupants; that the regulations existing

---

1. L. 1929, ch. 713; Cons. L. ch. 61A.
2. L. 1944, ch. 553.
3. *Id.*, § 4.
4. This followed a disastrous fire in an old lodging house in New York City in which there was a considerable loss of life.

prior to 1944 were adequate and sufficient to prevent loss of life in lodging houses of this particular type. It was further alleged that this lodging house has a market value of about $25,000, that the cost of complying with the 1944 law would be about $7,500; and that the benefits to be obtained by the changes were negligible. By reason of those circumstances the 1944 law was alleged to violate the due process clause of the Fourteenth Amendment. It was also alleged to violate the equal protection clause of the Fourteenth Amendment since it was applicable to lodging houses "existing" prior to the 1944 law but not to identical structures erected thereafter. Appellee answered, denying the material allegations of the bill, and moved to dismiss. The Supreme Court granted the motion. The Appellate Division affirmed without opinion. 269 App. Div. 691, 54 N. Y. S. 2d 394. On appeal to the Court of Appeals the judgment was likewise affirmed without opinion. 294 N. Y. 917, 63 N. E. 2d 116. The case is here on appeal, the Court of Appeals having certified by its remittitur that questions involving the Fourteenth Amendment were presented and necessarily passed upon. 295 N. Y. 567, 64 N. E. 2d 278.

Little need be said on the due process question. We are not concerned with the wisdom of this legislation or the need for it. *Olsen v. Nebraska,* 313 U.S. 236, 246. Protection of the safety of persons is one of the traditional uses of the police power of the States. Experts may differ as to the most appropriate way of dealing with fire hazards in lodging houses. Appellant, indeed, says that its building, far from being a fire-trap, is largely fireproof; and to the extent that any fire hazards exist, they are adequately safeguarded by a fire alarm system, constant watchman service, and other safety arrangements. But the legislature may choose not to take the chance that human life will be lost in lodging house fires and adopt the most conservative course which science and engineering offer. It is for the legislature to decide what regulations are needed to reduce fire hazards to the minimum. Many types of social legislation diminish the value of the property which is regulated. The extreme cases are those where in the interest of the public safety or welfare the owner is prohibited from using his property. *Reinman v. Little Rock,* 237 U.S. 171; *Hadacheck v. Sebastian,* 239 U.S. 394; *Pierce Oil Corp. v. Hope,* 248 U.S. 498. We are dealing here with a less drastic measure. But in no case does the owner of property acquire immunity against exercise of the police power because he constructed it in full compliance with the existing laws. *Hadacheck v. Sebastian, supra,* p. 410. And see *Chicago, B. & Q. R. Co. v. Nebraska,* 170 U.S. 57; *Hutchinson v. Valdosta,* 227 U.S. 303. The police power is one of the least limitable of governmental powers, and in its operation often cuts down property rights. *Block v. Hirsh,* 256 U.S. 135, 135. And see *Plymouth Coal Co. v. Pennsylvania,* 232 U. S. 531. Appellant may have a lodging house far less hazardous than the other existing structures regulated by the 1944 law. Yet a statute may be sustained though some of the objects affected by it may be wholly innocent. *Purity Extract Co. v.*

Lynch, 226 U.S. 192, 204. The question of validity turns on the power of the legislature to deal with the prescribed class. That power plainly exists here.

Appellant's claim of lack of equal protection is based on the following argument: The 1944 law applies only to existing lodging houses; if a new lodging house were erected or if an existing building were converted into a lodging house, the 1944 law would be inapplicable. An exact duplicate of applicant's building, if constructed today, would not be under the 1944 law and hence could be lawfully operated without the installation of a wet pipe sprinkler system. That is said to be a denial of equal protection of the laws.

The difficulty is that appellant has not shown that there are in existence lodging houses of that category which will escape the law. The argument is based on an anticipation that there may come into existence a like or identical class of lodging houses which will be treated less harshly. But so long as that class is not in existence, no showing of lack of equal protection can possibly be made. For under those circumstances the burden which is on one who challenges the constitutionality of a law could not be satisfied. *Metropolitan Casualty Insurance Co.* v. *Brownell,* 294 U. S. 580, 584. The legislature is entitled to hit the evil that exists. *Patsone* v. *Pennsylvania,* 232 U. S. 138, 144; *Bryant* v. *Zimmerman,* 278 U. S. 63; *Bain Peanut Co.* v. *Pinson,* 282 U. S. 499. It need not take account of new and hypothetical inequalities that may come into existence as time passes or as conditions change. So far as we know, the 1944 law may have been designed as a stop-gap measure to take care of a pressing need until more comprehensive legislation could be prepared. It is common knowledge that due to war conditions there has been little construction in this field in recent years. By the time new lodging houses appear they, too, may be placed under the 1944 law; or different legislation may be adopted to take care of the old and the new on the basis of parity. Or stricter standards for new lodging houses may be adopted. In any such case the asserted discrimination would have turned out to be fanciful, not real. The point is that lack of equal protection is found in the actual existence of an invidious discrimination (*Truax* v. *Raich,* 239 U. S. 33; *Skinner* v. *Oklahoma,* 316 U. S. 535), not in the mere possibility that there will be like or similar cases which will be treated more leniently.

Affirmed.

MR. JUSTICE RUTLEDGE concurs in the result.

MR. JUSTICE JACKSON took no part in the consideration or decision of this case.

Questions and Notes

On Adamec

1. What was the test invoked here as to when public intervention is appropriate?

2. What did the courts think of the formula relating to the assessed valuation of buildings?

On Queenside

1. What type of building was involved here? When was it built?
2. What facilities were required to be installed?
3. Note that Mr. Justice Douglas is playing the conservative role here. Nonetheless, this is an important holding on the role of safety in policy-power regulations.

Section 17
Public Housing

UNITED STATES

v.

CERTAIN LANDS IN LOUISVILLE

78 Fed. 2d 684 (C.A. 6th, 1935), appeal withdrawn

294 U.S. 735 (1935) and 297 U.S. 726 (1963).

Circuit Court of Appeals, Sixth Circuit.

July 15, 1935.

As Amended Oct. 9, 1935.

* * * Appeal from the District Court of the United States for the Western District of Kentucky; Chares I. Dawson, Judge.

Condemnation proceeding by United States of America against Certain Lands in the City of Louisville, Jefferson County, Ky., Edward J. Gernert, and others, for the purpose of securing fee-simple title to certain lands in order to erect thereon a low-cost housing and slum-clearance project. From a judgment dismissing plaintiff's petition (9 F. Supp. 137) plaintiff appeals. Affirmed.

H. W. Blair and Lloyd H. Landau, both of Washington, D. C. (Aubrey Lawrence and H. A. Berman, both of Washington, D. C., George C. Bunge, of Chicago, Ill., and Shackelford Miller, Jr., of Louisville, Ky., on the brief), for appellant.

Charles Middleton, of Louisville, Ky. (Chesley H. Searcy, of Louisville, Ky., on the brief), for appellees.

Before MOORMAN, HICKS, and ALLEN, Circuit Judges.

MOORMAN, Circuit Judge.

1613

This is an appeal from a judgment of the District Court for the Western District of Kentucky dismissing the petition in a suit filed by the United States to condemn four city blocks within the city of Louisville for the construction of a low-cost housing and slum-clearance project under the provisions of title 2 of the National Industrial Recovery Act (48 Stat. 195). The petition alleged that the action was brought at the request of the Federal Emergency Administrator of Public Works, who, pursuant to and acting under authority vested in him by the National Industrial Recovery Act, had prepared a program of public works which included the construction of a low-cost housing and slum-clearance project in the city of Louisville, known as the Louisville housing project; that by virtue of the authority vested in him by the act the Administrator had found it necessary and advantageous to acquire an estate in fee simple in the lands described in the petition for the purpose of constructing a low-cost housing and slum-clearance project thereon; that acting through the Administrator pursuant to the provisions of the act the United States proposed to construct, erect, and build such a project on the lands; and that they were needed for a public use and purpose. Subsequent to the filing of the action, the government filed a written motion for the appointment of commissioners to assess the damage to owners of the property sought to be condemned, but before commissioners were appointed one of the owners, Gernert, filed a demurrer to the petition. The trial court sustained the demurrer, and, upon the failure of the government to plead further, dismissed the petition on the ground that it was not within the power of the government to condemn the property for the purposes for which it was designed. (D. C.) 9 F. Supp. 137.

Section 201 (a) of title 2 of the National Industrial Recovery Act (40 USCA § 401 (a) authorizes the President to create a Federal Emergency Administration of Public Works and to appoint a Federal Emergency Administrator. Section 202 (40 USCA § 402) authorizes the Administrator to prepare a comprehensive program of public works to include, among other things, "construction, reconstruction, alteration, or repair under public regulation or control of low-cost housing and slum-clearance projects." Section 203 (a), 40 USCA § 403 (a), quoted in the margin,[1] authorizes the

---

1. "With a view to increasing employment quickly (while reasonably securing any loans made by the United States) the President is authorized and empowered, through the Administrator or through such other agencies as he may designate or create, (1) to construct, finance, or aid in the construction or financing of any public-works project included in the program prepared pursuant to section 202 [section 402]; (2) upon such terms as the President shall prescribe, to make grants to States, municipalities, or other public bodies for the construction, repair, or improvement of any such project, but no such grant shall be in excess of 30 per centum of the cost of the labor and materials employed upon such project; (3) to acquire by purchase, or by exercise of the power of eminent domain, any real or personal property in connection with the construction of any such project, and to sell any security acquired or any property so constructed or acquired or to lease any such property with or without the privilege of purchase. * * *"

President, through the Administrator or through such other agencies as he may designate, to acquire, by the exercise of the power of eminent domain, any real or personal property in connection with the construction of any low-cost housing or slum clearance project, and to sell any property so acquired, or to lease such property, with or without the privilege of purchase. Section 220 (40 USCA § 411) authorizes an appropriation of $3,300,000,000 to carry out the purposes of the act. By the Fourth Deficiency Act passed the same day (48 Stat. 274), Congress made the appropriation to carry into effect the provisions of the act.

There is nothing in the act under which the appellant is proceeding to serve as a guide to the President in exercising the powers conferred upon him; no requirement that his actions be conditioned upon findings of fact made by himself or the administrator; no standards supplied with reference to low-cost houses and slum-clearance projects. Nothing is said as to what shall be deemed a slum or a low-cost house or housing project. There is no designation of the cities or counties or states in which such projects shall be established, nor any standards fixed by which the administrator is to determine where they are to be established. Neither is there any limitation or requirement imposed upon the administrator with reference to the spending of the money appropriated for these purposes. All of this is left to the unfettered discretion or choice of the President through his administrator without any standards by which he is to act. It is argued for the appellee, with much force and persuasiveness, that this unlimited power given to the President or his administrator to determine such matters without the aid of congressional standards is an illegal delegation of legislative authority under the rulings of the Supreme Court in Panama Refining Co. v. Ryan, 293 U. S. 388, 55 S. Ct. 241, 79 L. Ed. 446, and A. L. A. Schechter Poultry Corporation v. United States, 55 S. Ct. 837, 79 L. Ed. —, decided May 27, 1935. We place our decision upon the second objection to the proceeding, viz., the lack of right in the government to exercise the power of eminent domain for the purposes contemplated by the act.

[1-3] The government of the United States is one of delegated powers. There is no constitutional provision expressly authorizing it to exercise the power of eminent domain. It is nevertheless well settled that this power belongs to the government as an attribute of its sovereignty. Kohl v. United States, 91 U.S. 367, 23 L. Ed. 449; Shoemaker v. United States, 147 U. S. 282, 299, 13 S. Ct. 361, 37 L. Ed. 170; Chappell v. United States, 160 U. S. 499, 509, 510, 16 S. Ct. 397, 40 L. Ed. 510. Equally well settled is it that the right can only be exercised where the property is to be taken for a public use. The contention of the government is that the property here sought to be condemned is to be devoted to a public use because, first, the construction of the project will relieve unemployment during the period of construction, and, secondly, the leasing or selling of the new buildings at reasonable prices will give to persons of low incomes an opportunity to improve their living conditions. We do not think the first of these pur-

poses, if made effective, could be said to constitute the use to which the property is to be put. While the act purports to authorize the construction with the view of relieving unemployment, it provides that the property when taken and after the project is constructed is to be leased or sold. The assertion that the taking of property to relieve unemployment and to improve living conditions among low-salaried workers is a taking for a public use rests upon the view that any taking which will advance the interest or well-being of a selected group of citizens will result in a benefit or advantage to larger groups or the entire community and must be regarded as a taking for a public use. It is argued that the right to take the property is conferred by clause 1, § 8, art. 1 of the Constitution which gives Congress the power "to lay and collect Taxes, * * * to pay the Debts and provide for the common Defence and general Welfare of the United States." The contention is that under this clause of the Constitution the power of Congress to levy taxes and appropriate the receipts therefrom to such purposes as it may deem in the interest of the public welfare is practically unlimited, and that this power carries with it the right to acquire property by condemnation upon which Congress may expend tax funds. We need not inquire into the extent of the taxing powers of Congress under this clause of the Constitution—whether it may levy and collect taxes and make appropriations ad libitum, or cannot use its powers thereunder beyond those subjects over which it is elsewhere given express authority by the Constitution. It has been thought by many students of the Constitution that the authority of Congress, both as to levying taxes and spending the proceeds thereof, is limited to the purposes necessary to the exercise of the other enumerated powers delegated to it in the Constitution. Story on Constitution, vol. 1, p. 703; 4 Jefferson's Correspondence, 524; 17 Congressional Record, part 2, p. 1439. So far as we know, there is no Supreme Court case which undertakes to say how far this authority extends. An attempt to have it determined with respect to the Maternity Act (42 Stat. 224 [42 USCA §§ 161-174]) was unsuccessful. Commonwealth of Massachusetts v. Mellon, 262 U.S. 447, 43 S. Ct. 597, 67 L. Ed. 1078. It is true, as stated by the government in argument that Congress has established many bureaus and agencies and made appropriations of tax funds to support them for purposes which in its judgment would promote the general welfare. It is not to be inferred from these activities, however, that there is authority for the act here in question, for constitutional authority cannot be created by congressional act or purpose to aid beneficently established governmental bureaus and other agencies. It may be that the constitutional power of Congress goes far enough to justify donations of federal tax funds to a state, bureau, or other agency to use for the purposes which are said to be those of this proceeding. That question is not before us, and we, of course, do not undertake to decide it. Whatever its extent in that respect may be, in our opinion it does not carry with it the power here claimed, to condemn private property to the end that appropriations of tax funds may be made for purposes deemed by Congress to be for the public welfare.

[4] The term "public use," as applied to the federal government's power of eminent domain, is not susceptible of precise definition under the Supreme Court decisions. It includes, of course, property needed for use by the public through its officers and agents in performing their governmental duties. Chappell v. United States, supra. The trial court was of opinion that it means use by the government in carrying out its legitimate governmental functions, or a use in relation thereto open to all the public though practically available only to a part of it. The government contends that it means any use which will promote the general welfare through benefits or advantages conferred upon a considerable number of residents of the community. It points to statements in the authorities to the effect that use by the general public is not a universal test of the term. Strickley v. Highland Boy Mining Co., 200 U.S. 527, 531, 26 S. Ct. 301, 50 L. Ed. 581, 4 Ann. Cas. 1174. Reference is also made to decisions holding that it is not a fatal objection to the taking that the use is to be limited to a small group or to a single person. Fallbrook Irrigation District v. Bradley, 164 U.S. 112, 161, 17 S. Ct. 56, 41 L Ed. 369; Mt. Vernon-Woodberry Cotton Co. v. Alabama Power Co., 240 U.S. 30, 32, 36 S. Ct. 234, 60 L. Ed. 507; Rindge Co. v. Los Angeles County, 262 U.S. 700, 707, 43 S. Ct. 689, 67 L. Ed. 1186. The proceedings in these cases were instituted, however, under state statutes passed to effectuate the purposes of a declared public policy of the state. What the cases hold is that there is nothing in the Fourteenth Amendment to prevent a state from exercising the power of eminent domain to carry into effect a public policy which, in the light of the needs and exigencies of the state, may be regarded as promotive of the public interest. This was the ground of decision in Clark v. Nash, 198 U.S. 361, 25 S. Ct. 676, 49 L. Ed. 1085, 4 Ann Cas. 1171, and Green v. Frazier, 253 U.S. 233, 40 S. Ct. 499, 503, 64 L. Ed. 878. In the latter case, the court upheld state legislation authorizing the state to organize a bank and operate it, to establish elevators, warehouses, and flour mills, and to engage in the businesses of manufacturing and marketing, and the building of homes for residents of the state. The court said: "If the state sees fit to enter upon such enterprises as are here involved, with the sanction of its Constitution, its Legislature and its people, we are not prepared to say that it is within the authority of this court, in enforcing the observance of the Fourteenth Amendment, to set aside such action by judicial decision."

[5-8] Decisions dealing with condemnation proceedings are to be considered in the light of the powers possessed by the sovereign seeking to exercise the right. What is a public use under one sovereign may not be a public use under another. Clark v. Nash, supra. The state and federal governments are distinct sovereignties, each independent of the other and each restricted to its own sphere. Kohl v. United States, supra. Neither can invade or usurp the rightful powers or authority of the other. Hammer

v. Dagenhart, 247 U.S. 251, 275, 276, 38 S. Ct. 529, 62 L. Ed. 1101, 3 A.L.R. 649, Ann. Cas. 1918E, 724; Child Labor Tax Case, 259 U.S. 20, 37, 42 S. Ct. 449, 66 L. Ed. 817, 21 A.L.R. 1432. In the exercise of its police power a state may do those things which benefit the health, morals, and welfare of its people. The federal government has no such power within the states. Green v. Frazier, supra, and Jones v. City of Portland, 245 U.S. 217, 224, 38 S. Ct. 112, 114, 62 L. Ed. 252, L.R.A. 1918C, 765, Ann. Cas. 1918E, 660, dealt with State legislation enacted pursuant to this power. In the latter case the court pointed out that it was not its function, under authority of the Fourteenth Amendment, "to supervise the legislation of the states in the exercise of the police power beyond protecting against exertions of such authority in the enactment and enforcement of laws of an arbitrary character." Thus in these and other cases involving state action the court dealt with the subject of public use as it pertained to the powers of the sovereign claiming the right to take. It must be similarly dealt with in the case at bar. As so considered with reference to the federal government, it does not, in our opinion, include the relief of unemployment as an end in itself or the construction of sanitary houses to sell or lease to low-salaried workers or residents of slum districts. The tearing down of the old buildings and the construction of new ones on the land here sought to be taken would create, it is true, a new resource for the employment of labor and capital. It is likewise true that the erection of new sanitary dwellings upon the property and the leasing or the selling of them at low prices would enable many residents of the community to improve their living conditions. It may be, too, that these group benefits, so far as they might affect the general public, would be beneficial. If, however, such a result thus attained is to be considered a public use for which the government may condemn private property, there would seem to be no reason why it could not condemn any private property which it could employ to an advantage to the public. There are perhaps many properties that the government could use for the benefit of selected groups. It might be, indeed, that by acquiring large sections of the farming parts of the country and leasing the land or selling it at low prices it could advance the interest of many citizens of the country, or that it could take over factories and other businesses and operate them upon plans more beneficial to the employees or the public, or even operate or sell them at a profit to the government to the relief of the taxpayers. The public interest that would thus be served, however, cannot, we think, be held to be a public use for which the government, in the exercise of governmental functions, can take private property. The taking of one citizen's property for the purpose of improving it and selling or leasing it to another, or for the purpose of reducing unemployment, is not, in our opinion, within the scope of the powers of the federal government.

The judgment is affirmed.

ALLEN, Circuit Judge (dissenting).

I cannot agree that the condemnation prayed for is unauthorized under the United States Constitution. The case in my judgment does not fall within the doctrine of Panama Refining Co. v. Ryan, 293 U.S. 388, 55 S. Ct. 241, 79 L. Ed. 446, and A.L.A. Schechter Poultry Corp. v. United States, 55 S. Ct. 837, 79 L. Ed. —, decided May 27, 1935. In those decisions the delegation held invalid was a delegation of legislative power. The sections of the Act here involved provide for no code nor penalty, but relate to a purely executive function, namely, the preparation and carrying out of a comprehensive program of public works, including low-cost housing and slum-clearance projects.

If Panama Refining Co. v. Ryan, supra, and Schechter Poultry Corp. v. United States, supra, are controlling, the standards therein held to be necessary exist in these sections of the statute. The terms used are defined in the dictionary, and are understood in common speech. Slum clearance involves the wrecking of houses in a slum and the clearing of slum lands for new and sanitary dwellings. "Low-cost housing" is not ambiguous. Such projects have been carried out in civilized countries, including the United States, for many years. The self-liquidating feature of the project arising from the authority to lease and sell the properties is incidental to the main questions. We are not confronted with an arbitrary misuse of power, for the case is presented on demurrer, and the acts held by the trial court to be unauthorized come squarely within the purview of the statute.

The questions are whether under the Constitution (1) the Congress is authorized to levy a tax and make appropriations for a comprehensive program of low-cost housing and slum clearance, and (2) whether the United States Government can exercise the right of eminent domain in order to carry out such program.

The power of taxation to provide for the general welfare specifically granted to the Congress in article 1, § 8, cl. 1, authorizes the carrying on of low-cost housing and slum-clearance projects, national in scope. This project is comprehensive and national in scope.[1] Funds raised by taxation were actually appropriated for this particular purpose.

At the time the Constitution was adopted this general welfare clause was understood to confer upon the Congress an independent and substantive power, ceded to it by the states, totally distinct from those conferred in the succeeding clauses of Article 1, § 8. 4 Jefferson's Correspondence, 524; 4 Hamilton's Works (Lodge Ed.), 151; Monroe, Views of the Presidents of the United States on the Subject of Internal Improvements, 2 American State Papers, Misc., 443, 446. See, also, Story on the Constitution (5th Ed.),

---

1. Work on slum-clearance projects has been begun in Atlanta, Boston, Cleveland, Cincinnati, Chicago, Detroit, Indianapolis, Louisville, Milwaukee, Minneapolis, Montgomery, Nashville, New Orleans, New York City Richmond, and Pittsburgh. Similar projects are planned for other cities.

§ 913; Burdick on the Constitution, § 77, and Willoughby, United States Constitution, § 269.

It is only to the authority granted by this clause that much of the constructive legislation enacted by the Congress during the past one hundred years is referable. The Constitution made no provision for the Bureau of Education, the Department of Labor, the Department of Commerce, the Public Health Service, the Geological Survey, the Bureau of Mines, the Department of Agriculture, the Bureau of Fisheries, the Children's Bureau, the Smithsonian Institution, the Bureau of Standards. While certain of the activities of these departments or bureaus are authorized by the Constitution, as, for instance, the testing of weights and measures by the Bureau of Standards, there are many which relate to no other function specifically confided to the National Government by the Constitution, except that of providing for the general welfare through taxation. The Congress has continuously construed this clause as meaning that its power to tax and to make appropriations is not limited to the purposes set forth in the subsequent clauses of article 1, § 8, but includes the power to raise and appropriate money not "ad libitum" as pointed out by Jefferson (op. cit., supra) but to provide for the general welfare. This construction has prevailed too long and has been too uniform to be disregarded. McPherson v. Blacker, 146 U.S. 1, 36, 13 S. Ct. 3, 36 L. Ed. 869.

The individual states have power to enter into low-cost housing and slum-clearance projects within their borders. Green v. Frazier, Governor, 253 U.S. 233, 40 S. Ct. 499, 64 L. Ed. 878. However, the police power is reserved to the states under the Tenth Amendment. "But it is none the less true that when the United States exerts any of the powers conferred upon it by the Constitution, no valid objection can be based upon the fact that such exercise may be attended by the same incidents which attend the exercise by a State of its police power, or that it may tend to accomplish a similar purpose." Hamilton, Collector, v. Kentucky Distilleries & Warehouse Co., 251 U.S. 146, 156, 40 S. Ct. 106, 108, 64 L. Ed. 194. Cf. Lottery Case, 188 U.S. 321, 357, 23 S. Ct. 321, 47 L. Ed. 492.

In Hoke v. United States, 227 U.S. 308, 33 S. Ct. 281, 57 L. Ed. 523, 43 L.R.A. (N.S.) 906, Ann. Cas. 1913E, 905, it was urged that the Act under review was an attempt to interfere with the police power of the states to regulate the morals of their citizens. The court, in 227 U.S. 308, at page 322, 33 S. Ct. 281, 284, says: "Our dual form of government has its perplexities, State and Nation having different spheres of jurisdiction, as we have said, but it must be kept in mind that we are one people; and the powers reserved to the States and those conferred on the Nation are adapted to be exercised, whether independently or concurrently, to promote the general welfare, material and moral."

Also the court said "but there is a domain which the States cannot reach and over which Congress alone has power; and if such power be exerted to control what the states cannot, it is an argument for—not against—its legality."

The problem of slum elimination throughout the nation lies within a domain which the individual states cannot reach and over which the Congress alone has power. This is an argument for—not against—the legality of this enactment so far as it constitutes an exercise of the taxing power to provide for the general welfare. Here the Congress, in my judgment, is exercising a power expressly conferred and ceded to it by the states in taxing and making appropriations for these purposes.

But the further question arises whether the power of eminent domain can be exercised in order to carry out these projects. The National Government possesses the power of eminent domain within the field prescribed for it by the Constitution. Article 1, § 8, cl. 1, gives the taxing power and the power of appropriation to the Congress. The power of eminent domain may be exercised wherever necessary and proper for carrying into execution the power of taxation and appropriation for the general welfare. The Fifth Amendment, however, prohibits the taking of private property for public use without just compensation, and therefore by implication requires that the power of eminent domain be exercised only in the taking of private property "for public use." The specific question is narrow in scope. It does not involve nor hint at the condemnation of farm land nor the operation of factories by the government. The question is whether a national low-cost housing and slum-clearance project involves a public use. In my opinion taxation and appropriation by the Congress are authorized under article 1, § 8, cl. 1, for low cost housing projects to relieve unemployment so widespread as that which existed when this Act was passed, and this constitutes a public use. However, apart from the purpose declared in the statute, of creating nation-wide employment, this property is sought to be taken for a public use. Low-cost housing and slum-clearance subserve a public purpose, and when national in scope, they fall within the constitutional powers of the National Government.

The slum is the breeding place of disease and crime.[2] Also slum clearance cannot be completely effected without low-cost housing. If disease

---

2. Anti-social slum areas exist in New York, Chicago, Philadelphia, Richmond, Cleveland, Birmingham, Denver and Seattle, and other centers of population. "Despite the difference in character of these cities, their delinquency areas display similar characteristics—poor housing conditions; shifting and decreasing populations; great poverty and dependence; a marked absence of the home-owning class; a largely-foreign population of inferior social status; unwholesome types of recreation; inadequate open-air play facilities." 1 Report on the Causes of Crime—National Commission on Law Observance and Enforcement—page LV, Report of Henry W. Anderson.

"Where slum clearance has been effected and the population rehoused in sanitary homes, a sharp decline in morbidity and mortality, as well as delinquency, has resulted. An excellent example is that of Liverpool. Rotten slums in the heart of the city inhabited by casual dock workers were destroyed and the buildings replaced by new

and crime are to be rooted out of slum neighborhoods, the residents must be placed in homes which they can rent or buy. The wrecking of the rookeries must be followed by new and inexpensive housing.

The Congress has declared that this is a public use. A declaration so made will be respected by the courts unless the use be palpably without reasonable foundation. United States v. Gettysburg Electric Ry. Co., 160 U.S. 668, 680, 16 S. Ct. 427, 40 L. Ed. 576. That was a case involving not a declaration by a state legislature, but by the Congress, as in this case. The peculiar opportunity possessed by state legislatures for determining what is a public use within the state resides in the Congress with respect to determining what is a national public use when it acts, as here, within its constitutional powers.

The problem of housing is directly connected with the public morals. Its significance as bearing upon home environment is recognized by the United States Supreme Court in Village of Euclid v. Ambler Realty Co., 272 U.S. 365, 47 S. Ct. 114, 71 L. Ed. 303, 54 A.L.R. 1016. Since taxing to provide for the general welfare is one of the substantive powers of the Congress, the fact that national plans for low-cost housing may duplicate similar plans existing in the state does not affect the power. Hoke v. United States, supra.

No case precisely similar has been decided by the United States Supreme Court, which has wisely declined to lay down a rigid definition of public use. However, attention has repeatedly been called to the inadequacy of use by the general public as a universal test, and condemnation of private property, far less directly connected with the public good than these projects, has been held to involve a public use. In Clark v. Nash, 198 U.S. 361, 25 S. Ct. 676, 49 L. Ed. 1085, 4 Ann. Cas. 1171, condemnation of certain land was allowed for the use of irrigation of other land, belonging to one private individual. In Strickley v. Highland Boy Gold Mining Co., 200 U.S. 527, 26 S. Ct. 301, 50 L. Ed. 581, 4 Ann. Cas. 1174, condemnation of private land was allowed for the erection of an aerial tramway for one private corporation. Rindge Co. v. County of Los Angeles, 262 U.S. 700, 707, 43 S. Ct. 689, 693, 67 L. Ed. 1186, held that it is not essential that the entire community, nor even any considerable portion, should directly enjoy or participate in any improvement in order to constitute a public use, citing Fallbrook Irrigation District v. Bradley, 164 U.S. 112, 17 S. Ct. 56, 41 L. Ed. 369, which decided that a public use existed in the irrigation of arid land privately owned.

The uses declared to be public include purposes much wider than the mere erection of public buildings or the physical enjoyment of property

dwellings at low rentals. One clearance project restored 77 percent. of its old population, and another 99 per cent. Yet among this same population after a short period in the new structures crime had decreased to less than 20 percent of its former incidence, death rates had dropped from 50 to 27 per thousand, tuberculosis from 4 to 1.9 per thousand, and other sickness accordingly." 14 American Enc. of Social Science, 95.

owned by the United States Government. In Mount Vernon-Woodberry Cotton Duck Co. v. Alabama Interstate Power Co., 240 U.S. 30, 32, 36 S. Ct. 234, 236, 60 L. Ed. 507, which involved the condemnation of land under statutes authorizing the manufacture and sale of electric power, the court states that to draw energy from streams "and so to save mankind from toil that it can be spared, is to supply what, next to intellect, is the very foundation of all achievements and all our welfare. If that purpose is not public, we should be at a loss to say what is." In Rindge Co. v. County of Los Angeles, supra, the court said: "Public uses are not limited, in the modern view, to matters of mere business necessity and ordinary convenience, but may extend to matters of public health, recreation and enjoyment."

It is true that these cases, with the exception of United States v. Gettysburg Electric Ry. Co., supra, involved state statutes; but in every case the question was squarely raised that the use involved in the condemnation was private; and every case held that a public use existed.

The power of condemnation by the state is to be considered in the light of the police power. The power of condemnation by the National Government is to be considered in the light of the express and independent power of the Congress to levy and collect taxes and make appropriations to provide for the general welfare. In the exercise of this specific power, the National Government may undertake those projects which benefit the health, the morals, and the general welfare of the people. One such project is the elimination on a comprehensive scale of the slum.

The judgment should be reversed.

Questions and Notes

1. Can you make a guess as to the general political philosophy of the judges who signed the majority opinion?

2. What theory of public use was adopted in the majority opinion?

3. Note the distinction in this case between state and federal levels of government with respect to the power of eminent domain.

4. Note the problem here: that any given housing project can be used by only a relatively small number of people. Even under the old nineteenth century test of "public use," why was it not enough that public housing would be held by a public agency?

5. Judge Florence Allen was one of the first well-known woman judges, and her dissenting opinion in this case is the first expression anywhere of modern housing law. Earlier, as a member of the Ohio Supreme Court, she wrote one of the finest of the early opinions upholding zoning, Pritz v. Messer, 112 Ohio St. 628, 149 N.E. 30 (1925).

SPAHN

v.

STEWART

268 Ky. 97, 103 S.W.2d 651.

Court of Appeals of Kentucky.

Feb. 19, 1937.

As Extended March 26, 1937.

Appeal from Circuit Court, Jefferson County, Chancery Branch, First Division.

Suit by Charles R. Spahn and another, as taxpayers, to enjoin A. J. Stewart and others, as members of the Municipal Housing Commission, from proceeding further under ordinance for clearance of slums and erection and maintenance of low-cost houses. From a judgment sustaining a demurrer to their petition, the plaintiffs appeal.

Affirmed.

Wallace A. McKay, of Louisville, for appellants.

H. O. Williams and Mark Beauchamp, both of Louisville, for appellees.

MORRIS, Commissioner.

The 1934 General Assembly enacted chapter 113, authorizing cities of the first class to create a Municipal Housing Commission for the purpose of improving internal conditions by carrying out a plan for the clearance of slums and to erect and maintain low-cost houses in keeping with modern, sanitary, and safe methods.

The act and ordinance were so enacted and adopted that such cities might be entitled to the advantages of the provisions of Acts of Congress, extending to states and municipalities certain grants of money in furtherance of a purpose to better the standards of living.

Substantially the act provides that any city of the first class may establish an agency to investigate housing and living conditions; to plan and effectuate projects for the clearing of slum districts and to furnish instead reconstructed homes at reasonable rentals to persons of low incomes. The Commission is authorized to sell tax exempted bonds which are not to be obligations of the city, county, or state. Power of exercising the right of eminent domain is given the Commission. It was also empowered after reconstruction, to rent the new habitations, applying the proceeds of such rentals to payment of interest on and for retirement of the bonds and obligations of the Commission; to provide a sinking fund to be applied to upkeep, necessary improvements, and for deterioration. Any surplus is to go to the sinking fund of the city for the meeting of its bonded or other governmental indebtedness. Under the act the Commission may be paid limited compensation for services, either in form of a salary or per diem.

Conceiving both the act and ordinance to be invalid, appellants filed petition in the lower court seeking to perpetually enjoin the Commission from proceeding further under the ordinance mentioned. Appellant Spahn owns property within the subjected boundary; Silk, another appellant is the owner of rentable property outside the proposed boundary. Both are taxpayers and sue not only for themselves and others owning property within and without the boundary, but for all taxpayers of the city. The relief sought was denied by the lower court, demurrer to the petition being sustained, followed by dismissal upon a declination to plead further.

The pleadings fully state jurisdictional and other facts to the extent that a case is presented. The right of appellants to institute and prosecute such a suit is not challenged. The first contention of appellants is, that chapter 113 is void because it is in contravention of section 51 of the Constitution, which provides that no act shall relate to more than one subject, such subject to be expressed in the title, it being argued that there is nothing in the title of the act from which it might be inferred that there was to be extended the power of eminent domain, or that bonds were to be exempted from taxation. It is further asserted that the act undertakes to revise, amend, or extend existing laws without re-enacting such attempted revision or extension. We shall not quote the title; it may be observed by reference to Acts 1934, c. 113, p. 507. The substance of the act in terms has been set out above.

[1-3] The title to the act in question is not vulnerable to the aimed criticism. We have time and again in meeting such objections held that all required by section 51 of the Constitution is that the contents of the act be so related to the title as to be clearly embraced within its terms, or as it is sometimes expressed "germane." Kelley v. Hardwick, 228 Ky. 349, 14 S.W.(2d) 1098. The section of the Constitution supra, does not demand, nor is it intended thereby, that the title embrace a complete synopsis of the provisions of the act, nor that it act out details minutely. The title "need only indicate the general contents [purpose] and scope of the act, and if it gives reasonable notice thereof it is sufficient." Russell v. Logan County Board of Education, 247 Ky. 703, 57 S.W.(2d) 681, 683. The title of the act in question may be laid down by the side of the title of the act which was attacked on like grounds in Estes v. State Highway Commission, 235 Ky. 86, 29 S.W.(2d) 583, and the similarity (both of title and act) will be noted. In that case we held the title commensurate. The same may be said of Klein v. City of Louisville, 224 Ky. 624, 6 S.W.(2d) 1104. Reference is especially made to this court's opinion in the case of Talbott v. Laffoon, 257 Ky. 773, 79 S.W.(2d) 244, for a comprehensive exposition of the subject under discussion.

It is true that chapter 113, supra, comprises a diversity of details necessary to carry out its purpose and intent. These details do not differ materially from such as were contained in the acts involved in the cases mentioned above, the Estes and Klein cases being exemplary. The title here is amply broad in its scope to meet the requirements imposed by section 51 of the Constitution.

[4] The act does not extend revise, nor amend any existing law. At the time of its passage there was no law on our statutes in reference to slum clearance or cheaper housing. It is true we had laws, both constitutional and statutory, with relation to the power to condemn property for public use, and the exemption of property from taxation, but the act in question did not undertake to nor did it amend, revise, or repeal any of these laws. City of Bowling Green v. Kirby, 220 Ky. 839, 295 S.W. 1004; Williams v. Raceland, 245 Ky. 212, 53 S.W.(2d) 370; Wheeler v. Board of Com'rs of Hopkinsville, 245 Ky. 388, 53 S.W. (2d) 740.

[5, 6] Appellants contend that chapter 113, Acts of 1934, is void, since it delegates legislative powers, in that the Commission is vested with power to determine the type, nature, character, and extent of the projects to be undertaken under the ordinance, as well as to determine what properties may be acquired, the manner of acquirement and use, and to later control that use.

The two objections may be considered together and likewise answered. The act as we view it, does not delegate to the mayor of a city of the first class any legislative power. He is only given the power of appointment. This is not in any sense the exercise of more than the usual and ordinary executive power, such as filling any office created by appointment in a lawful manner. Neither do we find that the Commission is vested with legislative power. We need not again enumerate its functions.

The conclusion that there is no delegation of legislative power may well be based on the opinion in Estes v. State Highway Commission, supra, wherein the court held valid the Toll Bridge Act (Acts 1928, c. 172), vesting powers in the Highway Commission to fix rates of toll, issue bonds and fix their maturities and terms on which bids should be made and contracts accepted. The court held that no sections of the Constitution were violated by the act, the power vested being purely administrative. This case cited with approval Hunter v. Louisville, 204 Ky. 562, 265 S.W. 277, which held valid an act creating a commission to construct a memorial building in Louisville; to make and enforce rules and regulations in the management of its affairs, and to conduct its business. Klein v. Louisville et al., 224 Ky. 624, 6 S.W.(2d) 1104, upheld an act authorizing the building of the municipal bridge, giving a commission power to fix tolls, regulate rates and issue and retire bonds. In Craig v. O'Rear, 199 Ky. 553, 251 S.W. 828, powers to certain agencies to select locations for teachers' colleges and other powers were delegated, and in this and all cases cited, the court held that the acts were valid, since they did not delegate powers other than administrative, hence, they did not contravene the sections of the Constitution there and here invoked. Counsel for appellant has pointed to no authority from this or any other court which would militate against our conclusion that the point made is unmeritorious. Other cases in this jurisdiction may be noted as follows: Bell's Committee v. Board of Education of Harrodsburg, 192 Ky. 700, 234 S.W. 311; Douglas Park Jockey Club v. Talbott, 173 Ky. 685, 191 S.W. 474; Lawrence County v. Fiscal Court, 191 Ky. 45, 229 S.W. 139.

There are other objections urged as being sufficient to justify us in holding the act invalid. As we observe (and shall treat) them jointly and severally, it occurs that each and all inevitably turn upon the question as to whether or not the ultimate result sought constitutes a public use or purpose. A determination of this question will to all intents and purposes dispose of most, if not all of the objections forwarded, some of which are as follows:

"(a) The act and ordinance are both invalid because if carried into effect, the appellants and those for whom they speak will be deprived of their properties without due process of law, in contravention of the Fourteenth Amendment of the Constitution of the United States, and the bill of rights as set up in our Constitution [sections 1-26].

"(b) The condemnation of property as proposed under the empowering Acts cannot be legally effectuated because the purpose and intended use is not 'governmental.'

"(c) It is special or class legislation; for the benefit of one class of citizens to the exclusion of all others.

"(d) Neither the General Assembly nor the city possess the power to exempt from taxation the bonds issued by the Housing Commission to raise funds to carry out the project, because the purpose is not 'governmental'." Ky Const. §§ 171 and 174.

[7] "A public purpose * * * has for its objective the promotion of the public health, safety, morals, general welfare, security, prosperity, and contentment of all the inhabitants or residents within a given political division * * * the sovereign powers of which are exercised to promote such public purpose." Green v. Frazier, 44 N.D. 395, 176 N.W. 11, affirmed in the U.S. Supreme Court, 253 U.S. 233, 40 S. Ct. 499, 64 L. Ed. 878, see infra. See, also, Carman v. Hickman County, 185 Ky. 630, 215 S.W. 408; Barrow v. Bradley, 190 Ky. 480, 227 S.W. 1016; Barker v. Crum, 177 Ky. 637, 198 S.W. 211, L.R.A. 1918F, 673; Nourse v. City of Russellville, 257 Ky. 525, 78 S.W.(2d) 761.

The word "slum," harsh and objectionable to the aesthetic ear, has come to have a well-defined meaning, applicable to sections of almost every city or town of proportions. It is usually taken to mean, "A squalid, dirty street or quarter of a city, town or village, ordinarily inhabited by the very poor, destitute or criminal classes; overcrowding is usually a prevailing characteristic. The word is comparatively recent and is of uncertain origin. It has been doubtfully connected with a dialectal use of the word 'slump' in the sense of a swampy, marshy place." Ency. Br. 25, 246. Brewer, "Phrase and Fable" says, "Slums are purlieus of Westminster Abbey &c. * * * where the derelict may obtain a night's lodging for a few pence." Although the word may be of comparatively recent origin, the matter of properly housing persons living in unclean, unsanitary houses in congested portions of cities, has been a subject of public concern for many years. The importance of proper housing had received public recognition in England for more than 100 years; in 1909 it had reached considerable proportions. The motive was first purely philanthropic and the objective was to improve the condition of the working classes. As early as 1841 there existed at least two societies, one the "Metropolitan Association for Improving the Dwellings of the Industrial Classes." These societies, after successfully operating for a time, found that from better housing the moral improvement was almost "equal to the physical benefit." Legislation looking to the same end soon followed and has at intervals continued to the present time. Encyc. Br. vol. 13, p. 815. The requirements of public health are indeterminate and interminable; as knowledge increases standards of living, of health, and of safety constantly rise. It is the changing standard which gives most concern; housing at one period thought eminently satisfactory is presently condemned. In the present age, as in the past, material conditions of environment takes a leading position. These truths are recognized just as strongly in this, as in other countries which have outstripped ours in looking to the welfare of those whose conditions of life might be bettered by a more healthful surrounding. Encyc. Br. under title "Housing."

In 1933, under a survey of the city of Louisville, including the territory selected for the purposes here, conditions existed worthy of consideration and action. The number of tubercular patients in the selected area bore the average proportion of 1 to 187 inhabitants; whereas the ratio in the whole city was 1 to 463. The ratio of major crimes committed in the spotted area was 1 to 63, while in the total area it was 1 to every 171; in minor derelictions 1 to 82, and 1 to 129; in juvenile delinquencies 1 to 50 as against 1 to 182.

It takes little argument, if such conditions as are described exist, and no doubt they do, to convince one that there is presented a situation which has not been ameliorated in the past by those who own and control the properties, though aided by such safety and welfare measures as have been thus far adopted, and to some extent carried into effect by state and municipal governments. The solution of the problem calls for action in some way that may prove more efficacious.

[8] The General Assembly in empowering the city to undertake the clearance plan, declared the plan to involve "objects essential to public interest." Its conclusions are not at all binding, but they may be given considerable effect. They may be looked upon as being persuasive. New York City Housing Authority v. Muller, 270 N.Y. 333, 1 N.E.(2d) 153, 156, 105 A.L.R. 905. The opinions of legislative bodies are entitled to respect. Block v. Hirsh, 256 U.S. 135, 41 S.Ct. 458, 65 L.Ed. 865, 16 A.L.R. 165; People v. Charles Schweinler Press, 214 N.Y. 395, 108 N.E. 639, L.R.A. 1918A, 1124, Ann.Cas.1916D, 1059.

[9] The necessity, expediency, and propriety of enacting measures looking to the end here hoped for, are of general interest, the policy vested solely

in legislative bodies. "The motives that influenced it [the action] will not be inquired into, except in rare cases, where it is manifest that a flagrant wrong had been perpetrated upon the public." Henderson v. City of Lexington, 132 Ky. 390, 111 S.W. 318, 323, 33 Ky.Law Rep. 703, 22 L.R.A.(N.S.) 20; First National Bank of Paducah v. Paducah, 202 Ky. 48, 258 S.W. 938; Louisville & N. R. Co. v. Louisville, 131 Ky. 108, 114 S.W. 743, 24 L.R.A. (N.S.) 1213; Id., 190 Ky. 214, 227 S.W. 160.

[10] The question of the necessity for the exercise of eminent domain is one primarily and almost exclusively, addressed to the legislative branch, while the question of whether or not the use to which the proposed condemned property be put is a public use or purpose, is one to be determined by the judiciary. Tracy v. Elizabethtown, L. & B. S. R. Co., 80 Ky. 259; Henderson v. City of Lexington, supra; First Nat. Bank v. Paducah, supra. In carrying out that part of the administration of government, this court has not infrequently been called upon to determine the question of use, and has held that the power to condemn was rightfully conferred in many cases where the purpose was not as far reaching or as beneficial as it may prove to be here. A tramway, Chesapeake Stone Co. v. Moreland, 126 Ky. 656, 104 S.W. 762, 31 Ky. Law Rep. 1075, 16 L.R.A.(N.S.) 479; a pipe line, Paine's Guardian v. Calor Oil & Gas Co., 133 Ky. 614, 103 S.W. 309, 31 Ky.Law Rep. 754, 11 L.R.A.(N.S.) 727, 134 Am. St.Rep. 475; railroad rights of way, Riley v. Louisville, H. & St. L. R. Co., 142 Ky. 67, 133 S.W. 971, 35 L.R.A.(N.S.) 636, Ann.Cas. 1912D, 230; drainage ditches, Carter, v. Griffith, 179 Ky. 164, 200 S.W. 369.

In some of the earlier cases, e. g., Chesapeake Stone Co. v. Moreland, supra, a narrow view of the words "public use" was expressed. This view was somewhat extended in Carter v. Griffith, supra, which was an undertaking by condemnation to take private property for the use of constructing a drainage canal. The court therein indicated that a benefit to public health was not the sole purpose for which property might be acquired by condemnation for ditch purposes, but that the reclamation of low and swampy lands for agricultural and other economic purposes, brought the exercised power within the scope of governmental functions.

In this case quoting from Wilson & Co. v. Compton Bond & Mortgage Company, 103 Ark. 452, 146 S.W. 110, 112, we said: "Nor is it necessary that the entire state should directly enjoy or participate in an improvement of this nature in order to constitute it a 'public use' within the meaning of the words as used in our Constitution or the federal Constitution, providing that property shall not be taken without consent of the owner except for a public use. In the broad and comprehensive view that has been taken of the rights growing out of these constitutional provisions, everything which tends to enlarge the resources and promote the productive power of any considerable number of the inhabitants of a section of the state contributes, either directly or indirectly, to the general welfare and the prosperity of the whole community, and therefore to the public."

In Louisville & N. R. Co. v. Louisville, 131 Ky. 108, 114 S.W. 743, 748, 24 L.R.A.(N.S.) 1213, we said: "It is probable that in every case where the right of eminent domain is exercised private interests will be more or less benefited; but the existence of this fact will not be allowed to defeat the benefits that will accrue to the public."

In Rindge Co. v. Los Angeles County, 262 U.S. 700, 43 S.Ct. 689, 693, 67 L.Ed. 1186, condemnation of land for a road which appeared to serve no public purpose in so far as reaching one point from another was concerned, was upheld because, "A road need not be for a purpose of business to create a public exigency; air, exercise and recreation are important to the general health and welfare; pleasure travel may be accommodated as well as business travel; and highways may be condemned to places of pleasing natural scenery." See Cooley Const.Lim.(8th Ed.) vol. 2, p. 1131; Strickley v. Highland Boy Gold Mining Co., 200 U.S. 527, 26 S.Ct. 301, 50 L.Ed. 581, 4 Ann..Cas. 1174; Green v. Frazier, 253 U.S. 233, 40 S.Ct. 499, 64 L.Ed. 878; Block v. Hirsh, supra; Marcus Brown Holding Co. v. Feldman, 256 U.S. 170, 41 S.Ct. 465, 65 L.Ed. 877; Green v. Frazier, supra, is of fitting application here. It had to do with a Home Building Act (Laws N.D.1919, c. 150). The contention was that the act was contrary to both the State and Federal Constitutions. The Supreme Court upheld the favorable decision of the North Dakota Supreme Court. See also, Willmon v. Powell, 91 Cal.App. 1, 266 P. 1029; Village of Euclid v. Ambler Realty Co., 272 U.S. 365, 47 S.Ct. 114, 71 L.Ed. 303, 54 A.L.R. 1016; Tenement House Department v. Moeschen, 179 N.Y. 325, 72 N.E. 231, 70 L.R.A. 704, 103 Am.St.Rep. 910, 1 Ann.Cas. 439; New York Health Dept. v. Rector, etc., of Trinity Church, 145 N.Y. 32, 39 N.E. 833, 27 L.R.A. 710; Adler v. Deegan, 251 N.Y. 467, 167 N.E. 705, 711, in which Justice Cardozo concurring said: "The Multiple Dwelling Act is aimed at many evils, but most of all it is a measure to eradicate the slum. It seeks to bring about conditions whereby healthy children shall be born, and healthy men and women reared. * * * The end to be achieved is more than the avoidance of pestilence or contagion. * * * If the moral and physical fiber of its manhood and its womanhood is not a state concern, the question is, what is? Till now the voice of the courts has not faltered for an answer."

[11-13] The use here proposed, as argued by appellee and admitted by appellants, may be more beneficial in the way of direct aid to a particular class, but it also operates to the benefit of the general public and its welfare. The act limits the ultimate use of the improved property to such persons as may be selected to occupy. This does not brand the purpose as class or special legislation. Whether or not the persons chosen to occupy are to be ultimately benefited more than those who are not, is a sociological question because of differing circumstances. Who can say that in the long run those who live in sumptuous residences environed by the elite may not account themselves still more blessed, if by improved conditions of housing in another section they are relieved from the probabilities or possibilities

of an epidemic of smallpox, typhoid fever, or other diseases, or that they may sleep more serenely because of a lessened fear of the commission of crime against their persons or property. "The essential purpose of the legislation is not to benefit that class or any class; it is to protect and safeguard the entire public from the menace of the slums." New York City Housing Authority v. Muller, supra. The fact that all individuals may not be elected to occupy the reconditioned premises is not material. A power plant, because of limited equipment, may not be able at all times to serve all the public but it is none the less rendering public service. It is not essential to the validity of the proposal that all the public reap like direct benefits. Rindge Co. v. Los Angeles County, supra; Fallbrook Irrigation Dist. v. Bradley, 164 U.S. 112, 17 S.Ct. 56, 41 L.Ed. 369. The fact that those who may ultimately occupy the premises may have a preference is immaterial. Long Island Water-Supply Company v. Brooklyn, 166 U.S. 685, 687, 17 S.Ct. 718, 41 L.Ed. 1165. It is not material that some reap more benefit than others. Strickley v. Highland Boy Gold Mining Company, supra; Mt. Vernon-Woodberry Cotton Duck Company v. Alabama I. P. Co., 240 U.S. 30, 36 S.Ct. 234, 60 L.Ed. 507. Nor is the government competing with private enterprise. Green v. Frazier, supra; Madera Waterworks v. Madera, 228 U.S. 454, 33 S.Ct. 571, 57 L.Ed. 915; Knoxville Water Co. v. Knoxville, 200 U.S. 22, 26 S. Ct. 224, 50 L.Ed. 353; Springfield Gas & Electric Co. v. Springfield, 257 U.S. 66, 42 S.Ct. 24, 66 L.Ed. 131.

The bonds proposed are to be issued to retire 55 per cent of the total cost of the project. These bonds do not obligate the state, the county of Jefferson, nor the city of Louisville. They are payable, maturities and interest, from the revenues to be acquired from the rentals of the rehabilitated properties, secured by a first and prior lien on the properties. The plan of meeting the obligations in no material sense differs from plans which have heretofore been approved with regard to the building of interstate and intrastate toll bridges, financing certain educational institutions in the expanding and improvement of their properties, or in providing more adequate facilities for caring for tubercular patients, all under acts not dissimilar to the one in question. See Hughes v. State Board of Health, 260 Ky. 228, 84 S.W.(2d) 52; Williams v. Raceland, 245 Ky. 212, 53 S.W. (2d) 370; Wheeler v. Board of Com'rs of Hopkinsville, 245 Ky. 388, 53 S.W.(2d) 740; Estes v. State Highway Commission, supra; Bloxton v. State Highway Commission, 225 Ky. 324, 8 S.W.(2d) 392; Klein v. Louisville, supra; J. D. Van Hooser & Co. v. University of Kentucky, 262 Ky. 581, 90 S.W.(2d) 1029.

On both the dominant contentions here urged we are much persuaded by the able opinion of Justice Crouch of the New York Court of Appeals in New York City Housing Authority v. Andrew Muller et al., supra. The act there questioned was similar to the act here attacked. Only two contentions were urged, or at least considered by the court, and these two are common to the case here, i. e., power to condemn and exemption of the bonds from taxation. Both, there as here, turned on the question as to whether the intended use of the property was of such public nature as to permit the condemnation and exemption in the face of a similar state constitutional prohibition, and the Fourteenth Amendment to the Constitution of the United States. We quote: "Slum areas are the breeding places of disease which may take toll not only from denizens, but, by spread, from the inhabitants of the entire city and state. Juvenile delinquency, crime, and immorality are there born, find protection, and flourish. Enormous economic loss results directly from the necessary expenditure of public funds to maintain health and hospital services for afflicted slum dwellers and to war against crime and immorality. * * * Concededly, these are matters of state concern (Adler v. Deegan, 251 N.Y. 467, 477, 167 N.E. 705). * * * Time and again, in familiar cases needing no citation, the use by the Legislature of the power of taxation and of the police power in dealing with the evils of the slums, has been upheld by the courts. Now, in continuation of a battle, which if not entirely lost, is far from won, the Legislature has resorted to the last of the trinity of sovereign powers by giving to a city agency the power of eminent domain."

Quoting from In re Ryers, 72 N.Y. 1, 28 Am.Rep. 88, the New York Court said: " 'To take * * * for the * * * promotion of the public health, is a public purpose.' * * * Over many years and in a multitude of cases the courts have vainly attempted to define comprehensively the concept of a public use and to formulate a universal test. They have found here as elsewhere that to formulate anything ultimate, even though it were possible, would, in an inevitably changing world, be unwise if not futile. Lacking a controlling precedent, we deal with the question as it presents itself on the facts at the present point of time. * * * It is also said that since the taking is to provide apartments to be rented to a class designated as 'persons of low income,' or to be leased or sold to limited dividend corporations, the use is private and not public. This objection disregards the primary purpose of the legislation. Use of a proposed structure, facility, or service by everybody and anybody is one of the abandoned universal tests of a public use. Mt. Vernon-Woodberry Cotton Duck Co. v. Alabama I. P. Co. * * * ; Strickley v. Highland Boy Gold Mining Co. * * * ; Rindge Co. v. Los Angeles County * * * ; Fallbrook Irrigation District v. Bradley * * * [all supra]."

In commenting on the New York case (270 N.Y. 333, 1 N.E.(2d) 153, 105 A.L.R. 905) we do not overlook U. S. v. Certain Lands (C.C.A.) 78 F.(2d) 684, 687, or U. S. v. Certain Lands (D.C.) 12 F.Supp. 345, and Id. (D.C.) 9 F.Supp. 137, in which the Circuit Court of Appeals held that the federal government could not enter a state and condemn lands for housing purposes because, "The state and federal governments are distinct sovereignties," and "what is a public use under one sovereign may not be a public use under another." In short, the court apparently of the opinion that the use was for public purposes, held that the federal government could not condemn private property except for purely federal governmental purposes. The Attorney General of the United States recognized the propriety of these opinions, since certiorari in each was dismissed on his motion in the United States Supreme Court. The objectionable feature was abandoned by a more recent act of Congress. U.S.C.A. title 40, § 421.

[14] From what we have said above it is discernible that the property intended to be acquired here by condemnation, if such become necessary, is to be used for a public purpose. It follows that such condemnation, if undertaken, will not violate either the Fourteenth Amendment to the Federal Constitution or any section of our own, assuming that just compensation be made to owners. This conclusion we think should dispose of the contention that the bonds issued in furtherance of the project cannot be exempted from taxation. If the purpose is public, they are in express terms exempted by provisions of our Constitution. We have had this question in perhaps other forms before us not infrequently, and have consistently held that where the bonds are to be issued in furtherance of a public purpose the evidence of debt stands in the same light as other public property. Some of the cases where the contention of appellant has been adversely determined may be noted. Com. v. Covington, 128 Ky. 36, 107 S.W. 231, 32 Ky.Law Rep. 837, 14 L.R.A.(N.S.) 1214; Com. v. Newport, 107 S.W. 232, 32 Ky.Law Rep. 820; City of Covington v. District of Highlands, 110 S.W. 338, 33 Ky.Law Rep. 323; District of Highlands v. Covington, 164 Ky. 815, 176 S.W. 192; City of Harlan v. Blair, 251 Ky. 51, 64 S.W.(2d) 434; Estes v. State Highway Comm., Bloxton v. State Highway Comm., Klein v. City of Louisville, all supra. These cases and those added below, dispose of the contention that since the Housing Commission is merely an agency of the city, the bonds are obligations of the city, this notwithstanding the act and resolution distinctly provide otherwise. Board of Education v. City of Paducah, 108 Ky. 209, 56 S.W. 149, 21 Ky.Law Rep. 1650; Board of Education of Bowling Green v. Townsend, 140 Ky. 248, 130 S.W. 1105; Klein v. City of Louisville and Hunter v. City of Louisville, both supra.

[15] It is contended that the resolution and ordinance are invalid because in such contract as the Housing Commission may make, certain prescribed wages for labor are to be paid and the laborers to be limited to so many working hours. This provision in the resolution is there placed because it is a condition upon which the grant of financial aid is proffered by the government. It is said the resolution is contrary to public policy and violates such parts of the act of 1934 (section 4, c. 113) as require that all contracts be let upon competitive bidding to the best bidder. Two principal features of the act must be considered: One, that the act has as one of its outstanding purposes the procurement of financial aid from the government; second, that the work contemplated is of a public nature, as we think we have sufficiently pointed out. The work done in the consummation of the plan is essentially public work. A distinction as between liberty in contracting where private enterprise or public work is concerned, was recognized

by the Supreme Court in Morehead v. People of New York ex rel. Tipaldo, 298 U.S. 587, 56 S Ct. 918, 80 L.Ed. 1347, 103 A.L.R. 1445.

Our General Assembly, ready to accept the benefit of the national laws offering grants in aid of public enterprises, began in 1934 to take advantage of such offers. In that year the Assembly enacted chapters 68, 69, 72, and 113, and at an Extraordinary Session in the same year, chapters 14 and 15 were enacted, each and all adopted for the purpose of aiding municipalities in obtaining federal aid in the erection of public buildings; these may be, as some of them were termed, "Financial Distress Acts." The last two chapters, supra, extended to counties the authority to obtain relief in the erection of adequate public school quarters. By these acts the Assembly has determined and announced a definite policy in relation to conditions upon which aid may be accepted and applied in the erection of public buildings. The general plan provided in chapters 68 and 69 was approved in Davis v. Board of Education of Newport, 260 Ky. 294, 83 S.W.(2d) 34. Chapters 14 and 15 were approved in the case of Roberts v. Fiscal Court of Graves County (denying an injunction). Chapter 72 was approved in Van Hooser & Co. v. University of Kentucky, 262 Ky. 581, 90 S.W.(2d) 1029. Likewise, the general plan was approved in Hughes v. State Board of Health, 260 Ky. 228, 84 S.W.(2d) 52, 54, authorizing the improvement and expansion of Waverly Sanitorium on a plan similar to the one here.

[16] It is well settled that when the Legislature delegates a power to a municipal corporation that body has the implied right to select the means by which the purpose may be accomplished, provided always that the adopted means do not transcend any constitutional inhibition. Overall v. Madisonville, 125 Ky. 684, 102 S.W. 278, 31 Ky.Law Rep. 278, 12 L.R.A. (N.S.) 433; Marz v. Newport, 173 Ky. 147, 190 S.W. 670; City of Springfield v. Haydon, 216 Ky. 483, 288 S.W. 337; Simrall v. McKenna, 195 Ky. 580, 242 S.W. 587; Reconstruction Finance Corp. v. Richmond, 249 Ky. 787, 61 S.W.(2d) 631; 19 R.C.L. 768; 43 C.J. 190, p. 193.

There is no avoidance of competitive bidding here. We have defined "competitive bidding" to be such as "requires that all bidders be placed on a plane of equality, and that they bid upon the same terms and conditions." State Highway Commission v. King, 259 Ky. 414, 82 S.W.(2d) 443, 450. "Competitive bidding means that the council must by due advertisement give opportunity for every one to bid." Blanton v. Town of Wallins, 218 Ky. 295, 291 S.W. 372, 375. In City of Springfield v. Haydon, supra, we upheld a contract let on bid, in which the proposal called for a material possible of being furnished by only one concern in the entire country, saying that there is competitive bidding "unless the advantage, by its terms, excludes other bidders." Gathright v. Byllesby & Co., 154 Ky. 106, 133, 157 S.W. 45, 57. In the case of Denton v. Carey-Reed Co., 169 Ky. 54, 183 S.W. 262, 263, where only one bid was received for street reconstruction, we held that the contract was valid since there was a reasonable bid, "fairly made at a public letting, legally advertised and open to all." Appellants, or any party feeling aggrieved at any action taken by the commission in attempting to let proposed contracts, may in a proper proceeding raise any question of unfairness or illegal procedure.

[17] The question here presented has arisen in courts of other jurisdictions, to decisions of which we may point for authority for our conclusion that the resolution is in keeping with the act, and is not contrary to its terms, or contrary to public policy. We refer to City of Milwaukee v. Raulf, 164 Wis. 172, 159 N.W. 819; Wagner v. Milwaukee, 177 Wis. 410, 188 N.W. 487; Jahn v. Seattle, 120 Wash. 403, 207 P. 667; Malette v. Spokane, 77 Wash. 205, 137 P. 496, 51 L.R.A.(N.S.) 686, Ann. Cas.1915D, 225; Interstate Power Co. v. Cushing (D.C.) 12 F.Supp. 806; Iowa Southern Utilities Co. v. Lamoni (D.C.) 11 F.Supp. 581; Norris v. City of Lawton, 47 Okl. 213, 148 P. 123. These relate mainly to fixing of wage scale. The time schedule is upheld in Atkin v. Kansas, 191 U.S. 207, 24 S.Ct. 124, 48 L.Ed. 148; Jahn v. Seattle, supra; People v. Orange County Road Construction Co., 175 N.Y. 84, 67 N.E. 129, 65 L.R.A. 33; Norris v. Lawton, supra; Heim v. McCall, 239 U.S. 175, 36 S.Ct. 78, 60 L.Ed. 206, Ann.Cas.1917B, 287; Cornelius v. Seattle, 123 Wash. 550, 213 P. 17, and Ebbeson v. Board of Education of Wilmington, 18 Del.Ch. 37, 156 A. 286, it was held not to be a violation of the Constitution or any statutory law to give preference in employment to citizens of the state, where the employment was on public works. The provisions of chapter 113 directing competitive bidding in no wise prohibit the Commission from stipulating that bidders shall comply with a wage and labor scale set up by the Commission. To interpolate such an inhibition, as herein suggested by appellants, would require us to disregard the paramount purposes and intent of the act.

[18, 19] Nor is there any delegation of the powers of the state, the municipality, or the Commission to the Federal Government. The commissioners in all things required by the act are free to conduct the scheme of furnishing low-cost housing, without interference by the government. It may be presumed that the Commission has thus far exercised its free will and choice, and will continue to do so, even to the extent of accepting the government's proffer. It may so exercise its will in the acceptance or rejection of bids. The matter of contracting is one arising between the Commission and bidders. There is no attempt by the national government to control legislative functions, either of the state or municipality. When we say that the Legislature may not delegate its powers, we mean that it may not delegate the exercise of discretion as to what a law shall be, but not that it may not confer discretion in the administration of the law itself. Craig v. O'Rear, 199 Ky. 553, 251 S.W. 828; Douglas Park Jockey Club v. Talbott, 173 Ky. 685, 191 S.W. 474.

[20] Lastly, appellants contend that since section 4 of the act limits expenditures to the proceeds of the operation of the project, the Commission may not at the city's expense proceed with survey and mapping plans, and we assume, pay no salaries or expenses of the Commission except out of the

money arising frcm rentals. We do not so construe the act. It is provided that the Commission shall not proceed to exercise the power given it to bind the Commission beyond the extent to which money has been provided under "the authority of this act." The act gives the city the power to fix and pay salaries to the Commission and to defray preliminary expenses. The resolution passed by the council did these things. The purpose being a public one, as we have shown, we see nothing in the act which would prevent the city from providing for compensation and necessary expenses of the Commission. There is shown no attempt on the part of the Commission to contract for or expend any money "which has not been (or may not be) provided under the Act."

From a careful survey of the record, we are of the opinion that the act, the ordinance and the resolution are not out of harmony with any fundamental laws or statutory provisions, hence conclude that the court below properly sustained the demurrer and dismissed appellants' petition.

Affirmed.

The whole court sitting.

NEW YORK CITY HOUSING AUTHORITY

v.

MULLER

270 N.Y. 333, 1 N.E. 2d 153.

Court of Appeals of New York,

March 17, 1936.

O'BRIEN, J., dissenting.

Appeal from Supreme Court, Special Term, New York County.

Proceeding in the matter of the application of the New York City Housing Authority to acquire title to certain real property in the Borough of Manhattan, City and County of New York, for the purpose of altering, clearing, remodeling, constructing and/or reconstructing dwelling accommodations for persons of low income on the real property in Borough of Manhattan, City and County of New York, against Andrew Muller and another. From a final order of the Supreme Court confirming the report of the commissioners of appraisal and from a judgment and order of the Supreme Court granting the application for condemnation and appointing commissioners of appraisal, the defendants appeal on constitutional grounds.

Affirmed.

See, also, 155 Misc. 681, 279 N.Y.S. 299.

Charles Lamb and James A. McKaigney, both of New York City, for appellant.

Paul Windels, Corp. Counsel, of New York City (Paxton Blair, of New York City, of counsel), for respondent.

Ira S. Robbins, of New York City, for New York State Board of Housing, amicus curiæ.

Charles Abrams, of New York City, for New York City Housing Authority, amicus curiæ.

CROUCH, Judge.

The petitioner, a public corporation organized under the Municipal Housing Authorities Law (Laws 1934, c. 4, comprising sections 60 to 78, inclusive, of the State Housing Law, being Laws 1926, c. 823), seeks to condemn certain premises in the city of New York owned by the defendant Andrew Muller. The public use for which the premises are required is stated in the petition to be "the clearance, replanning and reconstruction of part of an area of the City of New York, State of New York wherein there exist, and the petitioner has found to exist, unsanitary and substandard housing conditions."

As part of its project the petitioner has acquired by purchase properties contiguous on both sides to the premises in question. Acquisition of the defendant's property is, therefore, necessary for the carrying out of the project. The premises consist of two old-law tenement houses. The owner resists condemnation upon the ground that the Municipal Housing Authorities Law violates article 1, section 6, of the State Constitution and the Fourteenth Amendment of the Federal Constitution, because it grants to petitioner the power of eminent domain for a use which is not a public use.

Briefly and broadly stated, the statute provides that a city may set up an authority with power to investigate and study living and housing conditions in the city, and to plan and carry out projects for the clearing, replanning, and reconstruction of slum areas and the providing of housing accommodations for persons of low income. It is empowered under certain limitations to issue and sell bonds which, however, shall not be a debt of the state nor of the city; and it may not in any manner pledge the credit of the state or city or impose upon either any obligation. It is granted the power of eminent domain, to be exercised as provided, and it is exempted from the payment of certain taxes and fees. In enacting the statute, the Legislature, after thorough investigation, made certain findings of fact, upon the basis of which it determined and declared the necessity in the public interest of the provisions enacted and that the objects thereof were "public uses and purposes for which public money may be spent and private property acquired." Section 61. The facts found were that "in certain areas of cities of the State there exist unsanitary or substandard housing conditions owing to overcrowding and concentration of population, improper planning, excessive land coverage, lack of proper light, air and space, unsanitary design and arrangement, or lack of proper sanitary facilities; that there is not an adequate supply of decent, safe, and sanitary dwelling accommodations for persons of low income; that these conditions cause an increase and spread of disease and crime and constitute a menace to the health, safety, morals, welfare, and comfort of the citizens of the state, and impair economic values; that these conditions cannot be remedied by the ordinary operation of private enterprise."

[1] It is true that the legislative findings and the determination of public use are not conclusive on the courts. Pocantico Water-Works Co. v. Bird, 130 N.Y. 249, 29 N.E. 246. But they are entitled at least to great respect, since they relate to public conditions concerning which the Legislature both by necessity and duty must have known. Block v. Hirsh, 256 U.S. 135, 41 S.Ct. 458, 65 L.Ed. 865, 16 A.L.R. 165; People v. Charles Schweinler Press, 214 N.Y. 395, 108 N.E. 639, L.R.A.1918A, 1124, Ann.Cas.1916D, 1059. The existence of all the conditions adverted to by the Legislature was alleged in the petition and proved with reference to the area included in the project, of which the premises in question are a part. The public evils, social and economic, of such conditions, are unquestioned and unquestionable. Slum areas are the breeding places of disease which take toll not only from denizens, but, by spread, from the inhabitants of the entire city and state. Juvenile delinquency, crime, and immorality are there born, find protection, and flourish. Enormous economic loss results directly from the necessary expenditure of public funds to maintain health and hospital services for afflicted slum dwellers and to war against crime and immorality. Indirectly there is an equally heavy capital loss and a diminishing return in taxes because of the areas blighted by the existence of the slum. Concededly, these are matters of state concern (Adler v. Deegan, 251 N.Y. 467, 477, 167 N.E. 705), since they vitally affect the health, safety, and welfare of the public. Time and again, in familiar cases needing no citation, the use by the Legislature of the power of taxation and of the police power in dealing with the evils of the slums, has been upheld by the courts. Now, in continuation of a battle, which if not entirely lost, is far from won, the Legislature has resorted to the last of the trinity of sovereign powers by giving to a city agency the power of eminent domain. We are called upon to say whether under the facts of this case, including the circumstances of time and place, the use of the power is a use for the public benefit—a public use—within the law.

There is no case in this jurisdiction or elsewhere directly in point. Governmental housing projects constitute a comparatively new means of remedying an ancient evil. Phases of the general subject were before the courts in Green v. Frazier, 44 N.D. 395, 176 N.W. 11, affirmed 253 U.S. 233, 40 S.Ct. 499, 64 L.Ed. 878, and in Willmon v. Powell, 91 Cal.App. 1, 266 P. 1029, where the power to spend public funds for such projects was upheld. See, also, Simon v. O'Toole, 108 N.J.Law, 32, 155 A. 449, affirmed 108 N.J.Law, 549, 158 A. 543. In United States v. Certain Lands in City of Louisville, Jefferson County, Ky. (C.C.A.) 78 F.(2d) 684, it was held that while such a project might be within the scope of a state's activities, it was not one which the federal government had power to undertake. The cases in this state, which, perhaps, afford the closest analogy are the drainage cases, where land was permitted to be taken by eminent domain in the interest of public health, even where there was incidental benefit to private interests. See e. g., Matter of Ryers, 72 N.Y. 1, 28 Am. Rep. 88; Board of Black River Regulating District v. Ogsbury, 203 App.Div. 43, 196 N.Y.S. 281, affirmed, 235 N.Y. 600, 139 N.E. 751. "To take," said the court, "for the maintenance and promotion of the public health, is a public purpose." Matter of Ryers, supra, 72 N.Y. 1, at page 7, 28 Am. Rep. 88. Over many years and in a multitude of cases the courts have vainly attempted to define use and to formulate a universal test. They have found here as alsewhere that to formulate anything ultimate, even though it were possible, would, in an inevitably changing world, be unwise if not futile. Lacking a controlling precedent, we deal with the question as it presents itself on the facts at the present point of time. "The law of each age is ultimately what age thinks should be the law." People ex rel. Durham Realty Corporation v. La Fetra, 230 N.Y. 429, 450, 130 N.E. 601, 608, 16 A.L.R. 152.

The fundamental purpose of government is to protect the health, safety, and general welfare of the public. All its complicated activities have that simple end in view. Its power plant for the purpose consists of the power of taxation, the police power, and the power of eminent domain. Whenever there arises, in the state, a condition of affairs holding a substantial menace to the public health, safety, or general welfare, it becomes the duty of the government to apply whatever power is necessary and appropriate to check it. There are differences in the nature and characteristics of the powers, though distinction between them is often fine. People ex rel. Durham Realty Corporation v. La Fetra, supra, 230 N.Y. 429, at page 444, 130 N.E. 601, 16 A.L.R. 152. But if the menace is serious enough to the public to warrant public action and the power applied is reasonably and fairly calculated to check it, and bears a reasonable relation to the evil, it seems to be constitutionally immaterial whether one or another of the sovereign powers is employed.

The menace of the slums in New York City has been long recognized as serious enough to warrant public action. The Session Laws for nearly seventy years past are sprinkled with acts applying the taxing power and the police power in attempts to cure or check it. The slums still stand. The menace still exists. What objections, then, can be urged to the application of the third power, least drastic, but, as here embodied, probably the most effective of all?

It is said that private enterprise, curbed by restrictive legislation under the police power, is adequate and alone appropriate. There is some authority to that effect in other states. A sufficient answer should be the page of legislative history in this state and its result referred to above. Legislation merely restrictive in its nature has failed because the evil inheres not so much in this or that individual structure as in the character of a whole neighborhood of dilapidated and unsanitary structures. To eliminate the inherent evil and to provide housing facilities at low cost—the two things necessarily go together—require large scale operations which can be carried out only where there is power to deal in invitum with the occasional greedy owner seeking excessive profit by holding out. The cure is to be wrought, not through the regulated ownership of the individual, but through the ownership and operation by or under the direct control of the public itself. Nor is there anything novel in that. The modern city functions in the public interest as proprietor and operator of many activities formerly and in some instances still carried on by private enterprise.

It is also said that since the taking is to provide apartments to be rented to a class designated as "persons of low income," or to be leased or sold to limited dividend corporations, the use is private and not public. This objection disregards the primary purpose of the legislation. Use of a proposed structure, facility, or service by everybody and anybody is one of the abandoned universal tests of a public use. Mount Vernon-Woodberry Cotton Duck Co. v. Alabama Interstate Power Co., 240 U.S. 30, 32, 36 S.Ct. 234, 60 L.Ed. 507; Strickley v. Highland Boy Gold Mining Co., 200 U.S. 527, 26 S.Ct. 301, 50 L.Ed. 581, 4 Ann.Cas. 1174; Rindge Co. v. County of Los Angeles, 262 U.S. 700, 43 S. Ct. 689; 67 L.Ed. 1186; Fallbrook Irrigation District v. Bradley, 164 U.S. 112, 161, 162, 17 S.Ct. 56, 41 L.Ed. 369. The designated class to whom incidental benefits will come are persons with an income under $2,500 a year, and it consists of two-thirds of the city's population. But the essential purpose of the legislation is not to benefit that class or any class; it is to protect and safeguard the entire public from the menace of the slums. The so-called limited dividend corporations referred to were provided for in the State Housing Law (Laws 1926, c. 823), and embody another and different attempt to solve the problem. The constitutionality of the scheme was unsuccessfully attacked in the courts. Mars Realty Corporation v. Sexton, 141 Misc. 622, 253 N.Y.S. 15; Roche v. Sexton, 268 N.Y. 594, 198 N.E. 420; cf. Mount Hope Development Corporation v. James, 258 N.Y. 510, 180 N.E. 252. After ten years of experiment, its use, for economic reasons, has proved inadequate as a solution.

[2, 3] Nothing is better settled than that the property of one individual cannot, without his consent, be devoted to the private use of another, even when there is an incidental or colorable benefit to the public. The facts here present no such case. In a matter of far-reaching public concern, the public is seeking to take the defendant's property and to administer it as part of a project conceived and to be carried out in its own interest and for its own protection. That is a public benefit, and, therefore, at least as far as this case is concerned, a public use.

The orders should be affirmed, with costs.

CRANE, C. J., and LEHMAN, HUBBS, and LOUGHRAN, JJ., concur.

FINCH, J., concurs in result.

O'BRIEN, J., dissents and votes to reverse.

Orders affirmed.

Questions and Notes

1. This is the other example of a first major opinion in modern housing law.

2. What was the point of the discussion about the three powers of government?

3. Note the holding that the primary purpose of public housing was slum clearance.

4. What test of public use was involved here?

5. Note the reliance on the Western irrigation cases—a dramatic example of how a principle, developed in one part of the country, in one particular type of situation, may play a major role in a totally different situation in another part of the country.

COLUMBUS METROPOLITAN
HOUSING AUTHORITY

v.

THATCHER

140 Ohio St. 38, 42 N.E. 2d 437.

Supreme Court of Ohio.

June 3, 1942.

Syllabus by the Court.

1. Public property may not be exempted from taxation unless it is used exclusively for a public purpose. The exclusive use for a public purpose must coincide with public ownership of property to entitle such property to exemption from taxation. City of Cincinnati v. Lewis, 66 Ohio St. 49, 63 N.E. 588, approved and followed.

2. No property may be exempted from taxation where such exemption would contravene the equal protection and benefit provision of the Constitution of Ohio. Section 2, Article I. State ex rel. Struble v. Davis, 132 Ohio St. 555, 9 N.E.2d 684, approved and followed.

ZIMMERMAN and WILLIAMS, JJ., dissenting.

Appeal from Board of Tax Appeals.

The Columbus Metropolitan Housing Authority made application for exemption from taxation of its realty. One Thatcher, county auditor, recommended that the realty should be exempted, and the Columbus Metropolitan Housing Authority sought the consent of the Board of Tax Appeals to such exemption. Ralph J. Bartlett, as prosecuting attorney of Franklin county, Ohio, and Francis M. Thompson, a taxpayer, each filed with the Board of Tax Appeals a complaint and protest against such exemption. Ralph J. Bartlett, Francis M. Thompson and Francis Baehr, a taxpayer, were made parties to the application by the Board of Tax Appeals. The Board of Tax Appeals denied the application for exemption, and the Columbus Metropolitan Housing Authority appeals.—[Editorial Statement.]

Decision affirmed.

Appellant, Columbus Metropolitan Housing Authority, is a body politic and corporate duly organized and existing under the Housing Authority Law (Section 1078-29 et seq., General Code).

Appellant is the owner of 22½ acres of land in the city of Columbus, popularly known as Poindexter Village, on which it has erected 426 dwelling units which are leased to families selected by appellant at rents ranging from $18.25 per month to $19.25 per month.

Appellant made application for exemption from taxation of its real property. In its application, appellant said, inter alia:

"Poindexter Village occupies what was a definite slum area, and there were 379 dwelling units therein. The authority demolished and removed all such dwelling units acquired by it from the area. The work of demolition began on April 3, 1939, and was completed on August 24, 1939. The authority has erected on the cleared area 426 new dwelling units of which 396 are now occupied. [All were occupied at the time of the hearing.] There are now more applicants than there are vacancies. The erection of said dwelling units was begun June 12, 1939, and was completed on July 25, 1940. The first dwelling unit was occupied May 1, 1940, and additional families have been moving in as fast as conditions permitted. ° ° °

"° ° ° In general, dwelling units are rented only to families of low income, and the authority has followed the definition of that term, found in Section 1078-49(d) as follows: 'The term "families of low income" shall mean persons or families who lack the amount of income which is necessary, as determined by the authority undertaking the housing project, to enable them, without financial assistance, to live in decent, safe and sanitary dwellings, without overcrowding.' Further, preference is given to families who lived in the area before demoliton, to families with children, to families living under housing conditions most injurious to health, safety and morals. Tenants will not be admitted whose monthly salary exceeds five times the monthly rents charged. Families to be admitted must have lived in and moved from a substandard home. ° ° °

"The above described premises, since date of acquisition, has been used exclusively for a public purpose, to wit: the preservation of the public health morals, safety and welfare by the elimination of slum conditions, and the renting of said dwelling units to families of low income, as hereinbefore set forth. ° ° °"

The county auditor recommended that the property should be exempted from taxation beginning with the duplicate year 1939–1940 and appellant sought the consent of the Board of Tax Appeals to such exemption (Section 5570-1, General Code).

Ralph J. Bartlett, as prosecuting attorney of Franklin county, Ohio, and Francis M. Thompson, a taxpayer, each filed with the Board of Tax Appeals a complaint and protest against such exemption from taxation, alleging that the real estate and improvements "in truth and in fact are now being used, and will at all times in the future, be used for rental purposes, for private living quarters for any persons and their families, who are able to qualify, and are selected by said authority according to standards of family, employment and income as fixed by statute and by said authority."

Messrs. Bartlett, Thompson and Francis Baehr, a taxpayer, were made parties to the application by the board.

Hearing was had before the Board of Tax Appeals on stipulation of facts, exhibits and oral evidence, to which reference will be made in the opinion.

The board denied appellant's application for exemption from taxation.

The case comes to this court by appeal under Section 5611-2, General Code, filed by Columbus Metropolitan Housing Authority, appellant.

Upon leave, the attorney general appeared in this court on behalf of the Tax Commissioner (Sections 1465-9 and 5624-8, General Code).

William Harvey Jones and George S. Marshall, both of Columbus, and Squire, Sanders & Dempsey, of Cleveland, for appellant.

Henry L. Holden and Robert P. Barnhart, both of Columbus, for appellee Newton A. Thatcher, auditor.

David B. Sharp and Francis M. Thompson, both of Columbus, for appellees Ralph J. Bartlett, pros. atty., and Francis M. Thompson.

Francis P. Howard and Edward J. Kirwin, both of Columbus, and W. Ray Skirvin, of Cincinnati, for appellee Francis Baehr.

Thomas J. Herbert, Atty. Gen., and Perry L. Graham, Asst. Atty. Gen., for Department of Taxation.

TURNER, Judge.

We cannot accept appellant's statement of the question of law involved, to wit: "The question of law involved is whether the property belonging to Columbus Metropolitan Housing Authority is exempt from taxation as public property used for a public purpose* * *."

[1] The question before the Board of Tax Appeals was whether the property belonging to appellant *is* used *exclusively* for any public purpose. Unless the property is exclusively so used, it may not be exempted from taxation.

[2, 3] As said by Judge Shauck in City of Cincinnati v. Lewis, Aud., 66 Ohio St. 49, 55, 63 N.E. 588, 589: "That the public ownership of property was not alone thought sufficient to exempt it from taxation is made obvious by the requirement that an exclusive use for a public purpose shall coincide with such ownership."

The question now before us is whether the decision of the Board of Tax Appeals is reasonable and lawful (Section 5611-2, General Code).

The Board of Tax Appeals being limited to determining whether the *present* use of the property is *exclusively* for any public purpose, we are not concerned with the former use of the property or the reasons for the change. Therefore, such subjects as slum clearance, the right of condemnation, housing conditions, and health and sanitary measures are not before us. Admittedly, the property is no longer slum property and the housing, health and sanitary conditions there obtaining are not now a ground of complaint.

The case of State ex rel. Ellis, City Solicitor, v. Sherrill, City Manager, 136 Ohio St. 328, 25 N.E.2d 844, is not in point here. In the case of State ex rel. Bartlett, Pros. Atty. v. Thatcher, County Aud., 138 Ohio St. 235, 34 N.E.2d 440, it was held in respect of the Sherrill case: "The majority opinion and decision did not take into consideration the question of tax exemption."

[4, 5] Appellant claims exemption under Section 5351, General Code. While this section reads, "Real or personal property belonging exclusively to the state or the United States, and public property used for a public purpose shall be exempt from taxation," yet this language is to be read in the light of the Constitution of Ohio and this court will not assume that the Legislature intended to violate any constitutional limitation.

Section 2 of Article XII of the Constitution of Ohio provides, in part: "Land and improvements thereon shall be taxed by uniform rule according to value. * * * and without limiting the general power, *subject to the provisions of article I of this constitution,* to determine the subjects and methods of taxation or exemptions therefrom, general laws may be passed to exempt * * * public property used *exclusively* for any public purpose * * *." (Italics ours.)

All land and improvements must be taxed except such as may be exempted by general law. Such general law must observe the constitutional mandate of equal protection. State ex rel. Struble v. Davis, 132 Ohio St. 555, 9 N.E.2d 684.

[6] The word "exclusively" may not be read out of this section and any statute which intentionally disregarded this feature would be unconstitutional.

[7] That it is the duty of the court to give a statute a constitutional construction, if possible, needs no citation of authority. If we were to hold Section 5351, General Code, invalid, appellant would fail. However, we hold that Section 5351 is not invalid and that it authorizes the exemption only of public property used exclusively for any public purpose.

Before the Board of Tax Appeals it was stipulated that appellant is a body politic and corporate, duly organized and existing under the housing laws of the state of Ohio.

Under the stipulations entered into before the Board of Tax Appeals, we assume that appellant comes within the term "housing authority" as used in Section 1078-36, General Code, which provides in part as follows: "All property, both real and personal, acquired, owned, leased, rented or operated by the housing authority shall be deemed public property for public use * * *." It will be noted that the Legislature has not attempted to declare that such property shall be deemed public property used *exclusively* for any public purpose. Here again, we assume that the Legislature was mindful of the constitutional limitation.

It would hardly be contended that the property of a limited dividend housing company created under the state housing law (Section 1078-1 et seq., General Code) would be exempt from taxation. Yet, in respect of such corporations it is provided in Section 1078-15, General Code, that the articles of incorporation shall contain a declaration that the corporation has been organized to serve a public purpose and "that all real estate acquired by it and all structures erected by it, shall be deemed to be acquired for the purpose of promoting the health and safety and subject to the provisions of the state housing law * * *."

[8] In Ohio, it is axiomatic that exemptions from taxation are to be strictly construed. As said by Judge Spear in Lee v. Sturges, 46 Ohio St. 153, 159, 19 N.E. 560, 2 L.R.A. 556: "Intent to confer immunity from taxation must be clear beyond a reasonable doubt, for as in case of a claim of grant, nothing can be taken against the state by presumption or inference."

We see no reason for a distinction being made in the case of publicly owned property. In the recent case of In re Estate of Taylor, 139 Ohio St. 417, 40 N.E.2d 936, it was held: "A right to exemption from taxation must appear with reasonable certainty in the language of the Constitution or valid statute and must not depend upon a doubtful construction of such language."

We pointed out in the Taylor case that this was not a declaration of any new or novel principle. From the earliest history of our state down to the present time, there has been no presumption favorable to the exemption of property from taxation. As stated by Judge Matthias in the case of Cullitan, Pros. Atty., v. Cunningham Sanitarium, 134 Ohio St. 99, 100, 16 N.E.2d 205, 206: "On the contrary, the right to such exemption must be shown 'indubitably to exist.'"

This brings us to an examination of the facts before the Board of Tax Appeals to determine whether the decision of the board was unlawful or unreasonable. It was stipulated before the board, inter alia.

"7. The authority has erected within the limits of the village 426 dwelling units together with a recreation center, central heating plan and playground. The erection of said dwelling units was begun June 12, 1939, and was completed June 25, 1940. Of the 426 new dwelling units 208 contained 3½ rooms each, 159 contained 4½ rooms each and 59 contained 5½ rooms each.

"8. The first dwelling unit was occupied May 1, 1940, and by September 26, 1940 97% of the dwelling units were rented and occupied. The last unit was rented and occupied October 5, 1940. * * *

"10. The lowest rent charged, including utilities is, per month $18.25. The highest rent charged, including utilities is, per month $19.25. The average shelter rent is per month $12.40. 'Shelter rent' as used herein shall mean the gross rent for a dwelling unit less the amount charged for utilities.

"Average charges for utilities for the 426 dwelling units is $6.18 per unit per month, which includes heat, light, gas, water asd sewer services.

"11. The present use of said dwelling units is for rental purposes, for private living quarters for such persons and their families as are admitted by the authority who are able to qualify according to standards as to family employment, income and living conditions, as are fixed by the statutes, and by the authority."

Under paragraph 15 of the stipulation it was shown that upon a valuation of $800,000 for the project costing approximately $2,000,000 the taxes would add $3.13 per month to the rent for each unit. The rents, exclusive of taxes and utilities, are fixed at approximately fifty per cent of the cost of the service.

In addition to the stipulation of facts, Mr. O. A. Corzelius, a director and secretary of appellant, testified orally before the Board of Tax Appeals.

The following selections from the testimony of Mr. Corzelius throw light upon the present use of the property:

"Q. Mr. Corzelius, the only people you take in the property are the ones that can afford to pay the rent; isn't that correct? A. That is right, either from their own income or any definite aid that they might be getting.

"Q. In other words, if they can't pay the rent, you don't take them? A. That is right.

"Q. And I understand you to say that 85 of the people that were in the original project were on direct relief, and, therefore, you couldn't take them; isn't that correct? A. That is right. However, on relief families, if some agency will definitely guarantee the rent, we will take the poor families in the project.

"Q. That is where you get a definite guarantee, but for instance I understood you to say there were 85 families getting direct relief that were in the project, and for that reason they were ineligible? A. We considered them ineligible until they could prove otherwise. * * *

"Q. Don't you have a rule like this, every tenant shall have an income which is sufficient to pay the rent and provide for necessary living expenses? A. We do."

"Q. And if a tenant can't pay his rent, you give him a notice to move just the same as a private land owner might, don't you? A. That is right.

"Q. He either has to move or you evict him? A. That is right. * * *

"Q. In the event any of the tenants fail to pay their rent, how soon after due date is notice served for vacation? A. We send them a notice within 10 days. We send a notice of delinquency usually within five days, and not to exceed ten, and if they run over 30 days they are given notice to vacate.

"Q. Upon failure to comply with that order, what do you do? A. We would have to evict them; but so far we have not had any of that to do. We have served notice on them and the families have moved. Since we have started occupancy, families have moved out owing less than $100 total. We have had 17 turnovers; 17 families have moved out, and the 17 families owe us less than $100."

"Q. Let me ask you this one question. Has any direct relief client ever been admitted as a tenant in this project? A. We have direct relief clients in this project, but the relief department will not guarantee a sufficient amount to cover the cost and unless the tenant can show that he can pay the difference, he would not be admitted. After admittance, if they go on relief, and a tenant can show he can continue to pay his rent with what he can get through relief, we don't give him a notice to vacate. * * *

"Q. * * * Did I understand you to say there were 30 former site tenants now in this project? A. The latest count was 27.

I think there were 30 out of the 60 that made application who could qualify, but some of them, for some reason or other, after they were notified, didn't want to—* * *

"Q. And when you talk about substandard dwellings, that is an altogether different thing than slum dwellings, isn't it? A. Not necessarily.

"Q. No. In other words a slum dwelling might be a substandard, but all substandard dwellings might not be slums; is that correct? A. That is right.

"Q. For example, if there is not hot and cold water in the house, that would be substandard under your rules, wouldn't it? A. That is right.

"Q. If there isn't an inside private tub and shower, that would be substandard under your rules, wouldn't it? A. That is right. * * *

"Q. And if the rooms were without electric outlets, that would constitute a substandard dwelling, wouldn't it? A. It would have to have electric lights, yes."

The Board of Tax Appeals had before it evidence which shows that the appellant selects, not from slums, but "regardless of where they formerly lived," tenants from what appellant considers substandard dwellings.

Appellant's resolution establishing rental schedules, policies and standards provides that for the purpose of determining housing conditions under which applicants for dwellings in the project are living, such dwellings should be scored by appellant's own scoring system.

Out of the residents of 379 dwellings replaced by appellant's project, but 30 families were found eligible to become tenants and only 27 became tenants.

The evidence shows that the premises in question are leased to private families for renewable terms and that the tenants must have sufficient income to assure that the rentals will be paid.

If it had been necessary to do so, the Board of Tax Appeals might have taken notice as a matter of common knowledge of the fact that under appellant's substandard housing score sheet and the explanation thereof a very large portion if indeed not a majority of the houses in this state could be declared substandard.

[9] It seems to us clear that where dwellings are leased to family units for the purposes of private homes, the use of such dwellings is private and not public. Under Anglo-Saxon law and tradition, there is nothing more private than one's home. Broom's Legal Maxims, 9th Ed., 283, Semayne's Case, 5 Coke, 91, 77 Eng.Rep.R., 194. That every man's house is his castle has not yet been erased from our laws.

[10] Furthermore, a tax advantage equal to $3.13 per month on home rental given to a selected few persons who are not paupers and who are not aged, infirm or without means of support is violative of the provisions of Section 2 of Article XII and Section 2 of Article I of the Constitution of Ohio. Such tax exemption would shift the tax burden to other home owners and taxpayers.

After hearing and upon consideration of the record and evidence before the Board of Tax Appeals, this court is of the opinion that the decision of the Board of Tax Appeals appealed from is reasonable and lawful and, therefore, affirms the same.

Decision affirmed.

WEYGANDT, C. J., and MATTHIAS, HART, and BETTMAN, JJ., concur.

WILLIAMS and ZIMMERMAN, JJ., dissent.

ZIMMERMAN, Judge (dissenting).

In the instant case the projected executed by the Columbus Metropolitan Housing Authority was the acquisition of a slum area, the demolition of the existing buildings and the erection thereon of safe and sanitary dwellings, rented exclusively to families which lived in unsafe and unsanitary homes and could not afford to pay the rent demanded by private owners for the same character of living accommodations.

The slum clearance and low rent housing program is essentially in the public interest, being a cooperative effort on the part of the federal and local authorities to solve a vital social problem. Its underlying objective is to protect and safeguard an entire community by lessening potent causes of disease, immorality and crime.

The conclusion therefore seems inescapable that the property of the Columbus Metropolitan Housing Authority here involved is "public property used exclusively for any public purpose" within the contemplation of Section 2, Article XII of the Constitution of Ohio, and Section 5351, General Code, that the property is consequently entitled to exemption from taxation on that basis and that the decision of the Board of Tax Appeals in refusing exemption is unreasonable and unlawful and should be reversed. Such action would be in harmony with the decision in the case of State ex rel. Ellis, City Solicitor, v. Sherrill, City Manager, 136 Ohio St. 328, 25 N.E.2d 844.

WILLIAMS, J., concurs in the foregoing dissenting opinion.

Questions and Notes

1. Is this a decision on statutory or on constitutional grounds?

2. Against what, precisely, was the complaint directed?

3. Why was this attack on public housing phrased in these terms?

4. What word, present in the state constitution, was not repeated in the statute?

5. The opinion near the end had some fine language on how every one's home is his castle. On the relevance of this point, see the superb article by McDougal and Mueller, *Public Purpose in Public Housing; An Anachronism Revisited*, 52 Yale L.J. 42 (1943).

6. Note that two judges dissented. This was the key to the whole tortured rationale of the case; see Ohio Constitution, Art. IV, Sec. 2, quoted in McDougal and Mueller, p. 53.

CROSS-REFERENCES

In Anderson, see §§ 7.06, 8.21.
In Hagman, see § 206.
In Rathkopf, see Ch. 6-6.
In Williams, see Index, this topic.

ADDITIONAL RECOMMENDED READING

McDougal and Mueller, *Public Purpose in Public Housing: An Anachronism Revisited*, 52 Yale L.J. 42 (1942).

Section 18

Urban Redevelopment/Renewal

BELOVSKY

v.

REDEVELOPMENT AUTHORITY
OF PHILADELPHIA

357 Pa. 329, 54 A.2d 277

Supreme Court of Pennsylvania.

July 29, 1947.

PATTERSON, J., dissenting.

Appeal No. 68, January term, 1947, from decree of Court of Common Pleas No. 1, Philadelphia County, June term, 1946, No. 1003; Kun, Judge.

Bill in equity by Martha Belovsky, as a taxpayer of City of Philadelphia, against the Redevelopment Authority of the City of Philadelphia, the City of Philadelphia, and others, for an injunction to prevent the Redevelopment Authority of the City of Philadelphia from entering upon any activities pursuant to the Urban Redevelopment Law, 35 P.S. § 1701, the Redevelopment Cooperation Law, 35 P.S. § 1741 et seq., or the Act of May 24, 1945, P.L. 977, 40 P.S. §§ 504-506, which amended the Act of May 17, 1921, P.L. 682, by authorizing life insurance companies to invest in city housing projects in redevelopment areas, wherein the Commonwealth of Pennsylvania, City of Pittsburgh, and others intervened. From decree dismissing the bill, the plaintiff appeals.

Affirmed.

Before MAXEY, C. J., and DREW, LINN, STERN, PATTERSON, STEARNE and JONES, JJ.

Irving W. Backman and Edmund Backman, both of Philadelphia, for appellant.

Abraham L. Freedman and Howard E. Stern, both of Philadelphia, for Redevelopment Authority of City of Philadelphia.

Frank F. Truscott, City Sol., G. Coe Farrier and Abraham Wernick, Asst. City Sol., both of Philadelphia, for City of Philadelphia.

Ralph B. Umsted, Deputy Atty. Gen., and T. McKeen Chidsey, Atty. Gen., for the Commonwealth.

Oscar G. Bender, of Philadelphia, for North Philadelphia Realty Board and West Philadelphia Realty Board.

William H. Eckert, Gen. Counsel, of Pittsburgh, for Pittsburgh Redevelopment Authority.

Henry C. Beerits, of Philadelphia, for Burholme Improvement Ass'n et al., amici curiae.

Anne X. Alpern, City Sol., of Pittsburgh, for City of Pittsburgh, intervening appellee.

HORACE STERN, Justice.

Plaintiff's bill in equity, filed by her as a taxpayer of the City of Philadelphia, challenges the constitutionality of the "Urban Redevelopment Law" of May 24, 1945, P.L. 991, 35 P.S. § 1701 et seq., the "Redevelopment Cooperation Law" of May 24, 1945, P.L. 982, 35 P.S. § 1741 et seq., and the Act of May 24, 1945, P.L. 977, 40 P.S. §§ 504-506, which amended the Act of May 17, 1921, P.L. 682, by authorizing life insurance companies to invest in city housing projects in redevelopment areas. The bill seeks an injunction to prevent the Redevelopment Authority of the City of Philadelphia from entering upon any activities pursuant to these statutes, and the City of Philadelphia and its officers from appropriating any public moneys to the Authority and from entering into any agreement with it. The Commonwealth of Pennsylvania intervened in the litigation, as have also the City of Pittsburgh and a great number of civic, philanthropic, social and business organizations of the City of Philadelphia. The learned court below dismissed the bill.

[1] The Urban Redevelopment Law determines and declares as a matter of legislative finding—(a) "That there exist in urban communities in this Commonwealth areas which have become blighted because of the unsafe, unsanitary, inadequate or over-crowded condition of the dwellings therein, or because of inadequate planning of the area, or excessive land coverage by the buildings thereon, or the lack of proper light and air and open space, or because of the defective design and arrangement of the buildings thereon, or faulty street or lot layout, or economically or socially undesirable land use. (b) That such conditions or a combination of some or all of them have and will continue to result in making such areas economic or social liabilities, harmful to the social and economic well-being of the entire communities in which they exist, depreciating values therein, reducing tax revenues, and thereby depreciating further the general community-wide

values. (c) That the foregoing conditions are beyond remedy or control by regulatory processes and cannot be effectively dealt with by private enterprise under existing law without the additional aids herein granted, and that such conditions exist chiefly in areas which are so subdivided into small parcels and in divided ownerships that their assembly for purposes of clearance, replanning and redevelopment is difficult and impossible without the effective public power of eminent domain. (d) That the acquisition and sound replanning and redevelopment of such areas in accordance with sound and approved plans for their redevelopment will promote the public health, safety, convenience and welfare." Therefore the act declares it to be "the policy of the Commonwealth of Pennsylvania to promote the health, safety and welfare of the inhabitants thereof by the creation of bodies corporate and politic to be known as Redevelopment Authorities, which shall exist and operate for the public purposes of acquiring and replanning such areas and of holding or disposing of them in such manner that they shall become available for economically and socially sound redevelopment. Such purposes are hereby declared to be public uses for which public money may be spent, and private property may be acquired by the exercise of the power of eminent domain."

Although such legislative declarations are subject to judicial review they are entitled to a prima facie acceptance of their correctness: Dornan v. Philadelphia Housing Authority, 331 Pa. 209, 222, 200 A. 834, 841.

The act creates for each city and county of the Commonwealth a so-called "Redevelopment Authority," which is not in any way to be deemed to be an instrumentality of the city or county or engaged in the performance of a municipal function. No Authority shall transact business or otherwise become operative until the governing body [1] of the city or county shall find and declare that there is need for it to function; upon such declaration being made the mayor or the board of county commissioners, as the case may be, shall appoint the members of the Authority. An Authority "shall constitute a public body, corporate and politic, exercising public powers of the Commonwealth as an agency thereof," and shall have all the powers necessary or appropriate to effectuate the purposes and provisions of the act—among them the power to acquire property whether by purchase, gift or eminent domain; to own, hold, improve and manage such property; to sell, lease or otherwise transfer, subject to approval by the local governing body, any development area, either as an entirety to a single redeveloper [2] or in parts to several redevelopers; and to borrow from private lenders or from the State or Federal Government funds necessary for its operation and work.

---

1. "Governing Body" is defined as being "In the case of a city, the city council or other legislative body thereof, and in the case of a county, the board of county commissioners or other legislative body thereof."

2. "Redeveloper" is defined as "Any individual, partnership or public or private corporation that shall enter or propose to enter into a contract with an Authority for the redevelopment of an area under the provisions of this act."

The scheme of redevelopment [3] proceeds under the act as follows: The local planning commission makes a "redevelopment area plan" designating an area which it finds to be blighted because of the existence of the conditions enumerated in the act and containing recommendations for the redevelopment of such area. The plan must set forth the boundaries of the area, information concerning its buildings and population, a statement of the existing uses of the real property therein, a statement of the proposed uses following redevelopment, a statement of the proposed changes in zoning ordinances and street layouts, an estimate of the cost of acquisition of the area and other costs necessary to prepare it for redevelopment, and a statement of such continuing controls as may be deemed necessary to accomplish the purposes of the act. Thereupon the Authority prepares a "redevelopment proposal" for the redevelopment of all or part of such area, including the proposed redevelopment contract and the selection of the redeveloper, and submits this proposal to the planning commission for review. The proposal, together with the planning commission's recommendations thereon, are then certified to the governing body, which, after a public hearing, approves or rejects the proposal and the redevelopment contract; in the event of the proposal being approved the Authority is empowered to execute the contract and to take such action as may be necessary to carry it out. The contract provides for the amount of the consideration to be paid by the redeveloper to the Authority and for the necessary continuing controls. Any deed or lease to a redeveloper in furtherance of the contract must contain such provisions as the Authority may deem desirable to run with the land in order to effectuate the purposes of the act. The Authority is granted the right of eminent domain and title to any property thus acquired shall be an absolute or fee simple title unless a lesser title shall be designated in the eminent domain proceedings. The Authority may issue bonds for any of its corporate purposes, the principal and interest of which are payable from its revenues generally; such bonds may be secured by a pledge of any of its revenues or by a mortgage of any of its property; the bonds and the income therefrom shall at all times be free from taxation for State or local purposes. Neither the bonds nor any other obligations of the Authority shall be a debt of any municipality [4] or of the Commonwealth, nor shall any municipality or the Commonwealth nor any revenues or any property of any municipality or of the Commonwealth be liable therefor.

The "Redevelopment Cooperation Law" provides that the city council or the county commissioners, as the case may be, may make such appropriations to an Authority as are deemed necessary to assist the Authority

---

3. "Redevelopment" is defined as "The acquisition, replanning, clearance, rehabilitation or rebuilding of an area for residential, recreational, commercial, industrial or other purposes, including the provision of streets, parks, recreational areas and other open spaces."

4. "Municipality" is defined as "Any county, city, borough or township."

in carrying out its public purposes. Any State public body [5] located in whole or in part within the field of operation of a Redevelopment Authority is granted the power from time to time to lend or donate money to the Authority.

Legislation similar to these Pennsylvania statutes has been adopted in 23 other States.

Pursuant to the authority given in the Urban Redevelopment Law the Council of the City of Philadelphia enacted an ordinance, on September 21, 1945, which stated that there existed in the city areas which had become blighted by reason of the conditions described in the Urban Redevelopment Law; the council therefore found and declared that there was need for a Redevelopment Authority to function within the city. Accordingly such an Authority was organized and subsequently the council made an appropriation to it for administrative expenses during the year 1946 and at the time of the hearing of this case in the court below had under consideration the making of another appropriation for the year 1947. A Redevelopment Authority has been similarly created and organized in and for the City of Pittsburgh.

[2] The present attack upon the constitutionality of the Urban Redevelopment Law centers largely upon the grant therein made to the Redevelopment Authorities of the power to exercise the right of eminent domain. It is contended that the taking of property under the act is not for a public purpose and therefore cannot constitutionally be effected by resort to the power of eminent domain.

Doran v. Philadelphia Housing Authority, 331 Pa. 209, 200 A. 834, may be regarded as the prototype of the present case since all the arguments now presented on this subject were there fully considered. The Urban Redevelopment Law closely parallels the provisions of the "Housing Authorities Law" of May 28, 1937, P.L. 955, 35 P.S. § 1541 et seq., with which the Dornan case was concerned. The fundamental purpose of both these acts was the same, namely, the clearance of slum areas, although the Housing Authorities Law aimed more particularly at the elimination of undesirable dwelling houses whereas the Urban Redevelopment Law is not so restricted. But the Housing Authorities Law had an important additional objective in that, as ancillary to the slum clearances, there were to be provided "decent, safe, and sanitary urban or rural dwellings, apartments or other living accommodations for persons of low income"; these were to be constructed and acquired by the Housing Authorities and leased out by them to the class of tenants for whose use such accommodations were designed. In the case of the Urban Redevelopment Law the operation of clearing and rehabilitating the "slums," now called "blighted areas", is not to be followed by a continuing ownership of properties by the Redevelopment Authorities

---

5. "State Public Body" is defined as "Any city, borough, town, township, county, municipal corporation, other subdivision, board, commission, housing authority or public body of this Commonwealth."

for any such further and ulterior social-welfare purpose as that of providing low rental homes for persons in moderate circumstances. In this additional feature of the Housing Authorities Law there was implicit the modern recognition of an enlarged social function of government which called for an advance over previous legal conceptions of what constitutes a public use justifying the exercise of the power of eminent domain, but this court sustained the constitutionality of that act, and the courts of numerous other States have, without exception, upheld similar legislation. In the case of the Urban Redevelopment Law, therefore, the justification of the grant of the power of eminent domain is even clearer than in the case of the Housing Authorities Law, there being in the present act only the one major purpose of the elimination and rehabilitation of the blighted sections of our municipalities, and that purpose certainly falls within *any* conception of "public use" for nothing can be more beneficial to the community as a whole than the clearance and reconstruction of those sub-standard areas which are characterized by the evils described in the Urban Redevelopment Law. It has long been clear that those evils cannot be eradicated merely by such measures, however admirable in themselves, as tenement-house laws, zoning laws and building codes and regulations; these deal only with future construction, not with presently existing conditions. Nor, as experience has shown, is private enterprise adequate for the purpose. The legislature has therefore concluded—and the wisdom of its conclusion is for it alone—that public aid must accompany private initiative if the desired results are to be obtained. The great cities of Europe have been improved and largely rebuilt through the expenditure of public moneys by the edicts of monarchs and dictators; if the governing bodies in our own democratic Commonwealth are to be held unable, under our constitution, to plan and support such reconstruction projects, our cities must continue to be marred by areas which are focal centers of disease, constitute pernicious environments for the young, and, while contributing little to the tax income of the municipality, consume an excessive proportion of its revenues because of the extra services required for police, fire and other forms of protection.

[3-6] One of the objections urged against the constitutionality of the Urban Redevelopment Act is the feature of the "redevelopment project" [6] which contemplates the sale by the Authority of the property involved in the redevelopment, it being claimed that thereby the final result of the operation is to take property from one or more individuals and give it to another or others. Nothing, of course, is better settled than that property cannot be taken by government without the owner's consent for the mere purpose of devoting it to the private use of another, even though there be involved in the transaction an incidental benefit to the public. But plaintiff misconceives the nature and extent of the public purpose which is the object of this legislation. That purpose, as before pointed out, is not one requiring

---

6. "Redevelopment Project" is defined as "A project undertaken by a redeveloper under a contract with an Authority in accordance with the provisions of this act."

a continuing ownership of the property as it is in the case of the Housing Authorities Law in order to carry out the full purpose of that act, but is directed solely to the clearance, reconstruction and rehabilitation of the blighted area, and after that is accomplished the public purpose is completely realized. When, therefore, the need for public ownership has terminated, it is proper that the land be re-transferred to private ownership, subject only to such restrictions and controls as are necessary to effectuate the purposes of the act. It is not the object of the statute to transfer property from one individual to another; such transfers, so far as they may actually occur, are purely incidental to the accomplishment of the real or fundamental purpose. However, it is of passing interest to note that there are some cases in which the constitutionality of statutes was sustained the very object of which was to effect such transfers of ownership. Thus in State ex rel. State Reclamation Board v. Clausen, 110 Wash. 525, 188 P. 538, 14 A.L.R. 1133, it was held to be a valid public purpose for the State to purchase and improve tracts of undeveloped agricultural lands and subdivide and dispose of them to individual farmers and settlers. And in People of Puerto Rico v. Eastern Sugar Associates, 1 Cir., 156 F.2d 316, certiorari denied 67 S.Ct. 190, it was held that the prohibition against taking property without due process of law was not violated by an act which, in order to establish a scheme of agrarian reform, authorized the condemnation of land by a Land Authority for the sole purpose of subdividing and disposing of it to individuals for homesteads and farms. True, it was held in Pennsylvania Mutual Life Insurance Co. v. City of Philadelphia, 242 Pa. 47, 88 A. 904, 49 L.R.A.,N.S., 1062, that an act was unconstitutional which authorized cities to acquire properties adjoining a parkway and then resell them subject to building restrictions, but this was because the only purpose was to beautify the parkway and aesthetic objectives are not sufficient to justify the exercise of the power of eminent domain. In the Housing Authorities Law the Authorities were given the power to sell, exchange, transfer or assign any property to any person, firm or corporation, public or private, when the Authority determined that such property was not needed for the purposes of the act, and we sustained the validity of that provision: Dornan v. Philadelphia Housing Authority, 331 Pa. 209, 227, 228, 200 A. 834, 843. Indeed, so far from it being legally objectionable that property acquired by eminent domain be resold or re-transferred to private individuals after the purpose of the taking is accomplished, the law actually requires that property be taken by eminent domain only to the extent reasonably required for the purpose for which the power is exercised (Bachner v. Pittsburgh, 339 Pa. 535, 539, 15 A.2d 363, 365) and upon cessation of the public use the public ownership is properly discontinued. Nor does the taking lose its public character merely because there may exist in the operation some feature of private gain, for if the public good is enhanced it is immaterial that a private interest also may be benefited.

[7, 8] As is not unusual when the constitutionality of an important statute is assailed, attacks are here made upon alleged violations of a considerable number of constitutional provisions, possibly in the hope that a stray shot may find its way to some vital target. One of these assaults is directed against an alleged delegation of legislative powers contrary to the provision of Article II, section 1 of the Constitution, P.S., it being claimed that insufficient standards are set up in the statute to guide the Authority in exercising the powers with which it is vested. The fact is, however, that the act contains as definite a description of what constitutes a blighted area as it is reasonably possible to express; in regard to such factors as the selection and the size of the areas to be redeveloped, the costs involved, and the exact form which the redevelopment in any particular case is to take, it was obviously impossible for the legislature to make detailed provisions or blueprints in advance for each operation. It is to be borne in mind that all the powers given to the Authority in regard to the making of the redevelopment proposal, including the redevelopment contract and the selection of the redeveloper, are subject to the approval of the city council or the county commissioners, and only after all the details of the particular project are formulated is the ultimate decision made by those governing bodies as to whether the proposed redevelopment is to be carried into effect. The planning necessary to accomplish the purposes of the act must necessarily vary from place to place within the same city or county and from city to city and county to county. All that the legislature could do, therefore, was to prescribe general rules and reasonably definite standards, leaving to the local authorities the preparation of the plans and specifications best adapted to accomplish in each instance the desired result, a function which obviously can be performed only by administrative bodies. While the legislature cannot delegate the power to make a law, it may, where necessary, confer authority and discretion in connection with the execution of the law; it may establish primary standards and impose upon others the duty to carry out the declared legislative policy in accordance with the general provisions of the act. So far as Article II, section 1 of the Constitution is concerned the validity of the Urban Rdevelopment Law finds support many authorities: Kelly v. Earle, 325 Pa. 337, 352, 353, 190 A. 140, 147; Dornan v. Philadelphia Housing Authority, 331 Pa. 209, 229, 230, 200 A. 834, 844; Williams v. Samuel, 332 Pa. 265, 273, 274, 2 A.2d 834, 838; Chester County Institution District v. Commonwealth, 341 Pa. 49, 61–64, 17 A.2d 212, 218, 219.

[9] The act does not violate Article III, section 3 of the Constitution because of any deficiency in its title. The title is virtually a complete index of the provisions of the statute. Although, as plaintiff points out, there is no mention of the fact that the properties acquired by the Authority may be resold to private individuals after the redevelopment has been accomplished, the title does state that the Authorities have the power of the leasing and selling of property, and also that they may contract with private redevelopers.

[10] The act does not offend the provision of Article III, section 20 of the Constitution that the legislature shall not delegate to any special commission or private corporation any power to make, supervise or interfere with any municipal improvement or perform any municipal function. The Redevelopment Authorities are purely administrative bodies enjoying no important power which is not subject to the approval of the city council or the county commissioners; the Authorities cannot independently exercise any municipal functions. Moreover they are public bodies and not special commissions or private corporations within the meaning of the constitutional prohibition: Tranter v. Allegheny County Authority, 316 Pa. 65, 77–79, 173 A. 289, 294, 295; Dornan v. Philadelphia Housing Authority, 331 Pa. 209, 230, 200 A. 834, 844; Williams v. Samuel, 332 Pa. 265, 274, 275 2 A.2d 834, 838, 839.

[11, 12] There is no violation of Article IX, sections 1 and 3 of the Constitution which provide that all taxes shall be uniform and that only certain prescribed property may be exempted from taxation. The provision of the Redevelopment Cooperation Law that any city, borough, town, township or county may contract with a Redevelopment Authority with respect to any sums which the Authority may agree to pay for special improvements, services and facilities to be provided by such city, borough, town, township or county for the benefit of the redevelopment, does not, either expressly or impliedly, have any bearing on, or relation to the subject of tax exemption of property within the redevelopment Law in the case of the bonds issued by an Authority, and it has been held that bonds issued by such a governmental instrumentality are not the kind of property contemplated by the constitutional prohibition against exemption of any property contemplated by the constitutional prohibition against exemption of any property from taxation other than that specified in the Constitution: Kelly v. Earle, 325 Pa. 337, 356, 190 A. 140, 149; Williams v. Samuel, 332 Pa. 265, 274, 275, 2 A.2d 834, 839.

[13, 14] The provisions of Article IX, section 8 and Article XV, section 2 of the Constitution concerning the debts of counties, cities and other municipalities and incorporated districts, and the incurring of liability by any municipal commission, are not violated by the Urban Redevelopment Law. A Redevelopment Authority is not a municipal commission. It is specifically provided by the act that neither the bonds nor any other obligations of an Authority shall be debts or liabilities of any municipality or of the Commonwealth. "In view of that declaration," as was said in Dornan v. Philadelphia Housing Authority, 331 Pa. 209, 231, 200 A. 834, 845, "it is difficult to understand how the act in any way impinges upon these constitutional provisions."

[15] In the provision of the Redevelopment Cooperation Law authorizing loans Court has never sustained a delegation of power to determine what shall constitute a *jurisdictional fact*. To the contrary, such delegation of power has been held unconstitutional: Wilson v. Philadelphia School District, supra.

The conclusion of the majority is contrary to established principles of constitutional law *and is a license to the legislature to place in the hands of persons, neither representatives of the people nor responsible to them in any manner, power to determine arbitrarily what shall constitute the law which is to be administered by them.*

The decree of the court below should be reversed and the relief prayed for granted.

Questions and Notes

1. In the 1940's the states began to move toward the use of the power of eminent domain to condemn slums and to provide for their reconstruction by private capital. Note that this Pennsylvania decision came down before the Federal Housing Act of 1949 (63 Stat. 413 *et seq.*), which provided federal financial and technical assistance for such a program, primarily by writing down the cost of land. During the 1950s the scope of federal aid was gradually expanded, to include different kinds of land use both before and after redevelopment, and to provide for action at different stages in the life cycle of a neighborhood (*i.e.* for conservation and rehabilitation as well as clearance); and the states gradually expanded their progress along the same lines (see, for example, the *Schenck* case below).

2. Note how the public housing rationale is applicable to redevelopment, as defined above, for this rationale consistently looks backwards to the preexisting conditions, rather than to the future. If slum clearance for public housing was Constitutionally valid, then slum clearance for redevelopment was likewise valid. The result of this was to divert attention from, and indeed to brush aside, the serious constitutional and practical questions involved in taking land from A and selling it to B, particularly at a bargain rate.

3. Which (according to the Pennsylvania court) presented the more serious constitutional question, public housing or redevelopment?

4. How would you state the opposite argument on this latter point?

OPINION TO THE GOVERNOR

76 R.I. 249, 69 A.2d 531

Supreme Court of Rhode Island.

Nov. 14, 1949.

Opinion to his Excellency John O. Pastore, Governor of the State of Rhode Island and Providence Plantations, in response to his inquiry as to constitutionality of Public Laws 1946, c. 1802, § 1 et seq.

The Supreme Court, advised that the act, in so far as it is limited to elimination of conditions inimical to public health, safety and welfare, relates to a "public purpose", and that the creation of redevelopment agencies with power of eminent domain pursuant to the act does not violate the constitution.

Flynn, C. J., and Condon, J., dissented.

November 14, 1949

To His Excellency John O. Pastore,
Governor of the State of Rhode Island
and Providence Plantations.

We have received from your excellency a request of our written opinion, in accordance with the provisions of section 2 of article XII of amendments to the constitution of this state, upon the following questions:

"1. Does the redevelopment of so-called blighted areas in accordance with Chapter 1802 of the Public Laws approved April 26, 1946, as amended by Chapter 2029 of the Public Laws of 1948 and by Chapter 2265 of the Public Laws of 1949, including the establishment of redevelopment revolving funds pursuant to Section 46 thereof as amended, constitute a public purpose for which public money may be spent, private property may be taken by condemnation, public debt may be incurred and taxes may be levied, within the fundamental principle of constitutional law that these things may be done only for a public purpose and not for a private purpose (See Opinion to the Governor [R. I.], 63 A.2d 724)?

"2. Does the creation of redevelopment agencies with the power of eminent domain pursuant to the legislation referred to in the preceding question violate Section 1 of Article IX of the Amendments of the Constitution of Rhode Island?"

Upon receipt of the above request the city of Providence, which apparently has a present interest in ascertaining the constitutionality of the act therein described, commonly known as the "Community Redevelopment Act" but which we will hereinafter call the act for convenience, asked and received permission to file a brief in support of the act. Pursuant to this permission the city filed a brief and later furnished us with an additional memorandum of authorities. The act is so lengthy as to preclude us from setting forth herein its many interlocking provisions with any pretence of completeness. We can only give here a summary in outline of its most important provisions.

Section 2 sets out in a most comprehensive manner the legislative finding, the policy of the state, and the purpose of the act. The legislature therein found and declared that there exists *"blighted areas,"* (italics ours) consisting of both improved and unimproved land, in many communities in this state; that such areas are "conducive to ill health, transmission of disease, infant mortality, juvenile delinquency and crime" because of the existence therein of buildings and structures, either used or intended to be used for living, commercial, industrial or other purposes, or any combination of such uses, which are "unfit or unsafe to occupy" by reason of overcrowding, inadequate provision for ventilation, light, sanitation, open spaces and recreation facilities, obsolescence, deterioration and dilapidation; that such areas present difficulties and handicaps which are beyond remedy and control solely by *regulatory process;* and that the menace to the public health, safety and welfare from blighted areas is becoming "increasingly direct and substantial in its significance and effect."

The legislature also found and declared that such conditions of blight tend to foster further obsolescence, deterioration and disuse because of lack of incentive on the part of individual landowners, who are unable of themselves to assemble the lands for rehabilitation because of "lack of the legal power" necessary for, and the excessive costs involved in, the private acquisition of the real property of the area; that the remedying of such conditions may require the "public acquisition" of adequate areas and the clearance thereof through demolition of inadequate, unsafe and insanitary buildings; and that the blighted areas should be redeveloped "under proper supervision, with appropriate planning, necessary financial assistance, and continuing land use and construction policies."

For the reasons more fully set forth in said section the legislature declared that it is the policy of the state to protect and promote the sound development and redevelopment of *blighted areas;* that when such end cannot be accomplished by private enterprise alone it is in the public interest to employ the power of eminent domain, to advance or expend public funds, and to provide a means whereby the blighted areas may be redeveloped for that purpose; and that the redevelopment of such areas with provision for appropriate continuing land use and construction policies therein "constitute public uses and purposes for which public money may be advanced or expended and private property acquired, and are governmental functions of state concern in the interest of the health, safety and welfare of the people of the state generally and particularly of the people of the communities of the state in which such areas exist * * *."

A "redevelopment area" is defined in sec. 5 as an area of a community which the legislative body thereof finds is a *blighted area* whose redevelopment is necessary to effectuate the public purposes declared in the act. Such an area is within the purview of the act if the buildings, improvements, or land therein that are inimical to the public health, safety or welfare, *"predominate and injuriously affect the entire area."* (Italics ours.)

Section 15 defines "redevelopment" as the planning, clearance, reconstruction or rehabilitation of a redevelopment area with provision for such residential, commercial, industrial and public structures or spaces, including recreational facilities, as may be appropriate or necessary to carry out the real purpose of the act. The term also includes the replanning or original development of undeveloped areas which by reason of certain specified causes have become stagnant and require reclamation. This section further provides that a blighted area may include therein buildings, improvements, or lands which of themselves are not detrimental to the public interests but whose inclusion is found necessary, with or without change in their condition or use, for the effective redevelopment of the area of which they are a part.

To accomplish its purpose the act creates in each community "a public body, corporate and politic, exercising public and essential governmental functions," sec. 45, to be known as the "redevelopment agency of the community," sec. 34, hereinafter called the agency, which shall not transact any business or exercise any of its powers unless and until the legislative body of the community shall by resolution declare that there is need for the agency to function in such community, sec. 35.

The powers of the agency are set forth in great detail in secs. 45, 71 and 73. The most important powers in sec. 45 are as follows: to acquire real or personal property by purchase, lease or otherwise; to acquire any real property by the exercise of the power of eminent domain; to clear the property so acquired of buildings and structures and to develop it as building sites; to sell, lease or otherwise dispose of such property at its value based on estimated income to be received from any legal use thereof; and to obligate buyers or lessees to use the property for the purpose designated in the redevelopment plans by covenants or conditions running with the land, whose breach shall cause the fee to revert to the agency. This section specifically denies to the agency the right "to construct any of the buildings for residential, commercial, industrial, or other use contemplated by the redevelopment plan * * *." In secs. 71 and 73 the agency is given power to issue tax exempt bonds for an essential governmental purpose, which bonds "shall not be a debt of the community, the state or any political subdivision thereof," and shall be payable exclusively from the income and revenues of the redevelopment projects for which they were issued together with any contributions or financial assistance from the state or federal governments.

In order for a municipality to come within the provisions of the act it *must* have a planning commission and a master or general community plan prepared in accordance with certain specified requirements, secs. 20, 21.

When by resolution the legislative body of a community shall declare that there is need for a redevelopment agency to function, sec. 35, the mayor or the president of the town council shall appoint five resident electors, possessing certain prescribed qualifications as members of the agency, sec. 37, who shall thereafter discharge the powers granted to the agency by the act.

Omitting reference to many provisions concerning the preparation and consideration of tentative plans, the act provides that before adopting a redevelopment plan the legislative body of the community shall consider (1) whether it conforms to the master or general community plan, sec. 50 and if carried out that it would redevelop the area therein described in the interests of the public peace, health, safety, and welfare, sec. 59; (2) whether the carrying out of the plan, which may provide for the issuance of bonds of the agency, sec. 65, is economically sound and feasible; and (3) whether partial tax abatement for the project area and its improvements is necessary to the carrying out of the plan, sec. 60. The official redevelopment plan must be adopted by ordinance, sec. 67, which will become effective unless stayed by legal proceedings within a specified time, sec. 69.

In section 46 the act further authorizes the legislative body of a community to establish a "redevelopment revolving fund" for the public purpose described in the act by the appropriation of tax money or the issuance of municipal revenue bonds, subject, however, to the express condition that if the amount of such bonds exceeds "any limitation, by general or special law," the excess bonded indebtedness must first be "approved by the voters of such community at any general or special election."

It is not to be denied that the program described in the act is broad. While the act, which is of state-wide application and directly creates for each community "a public body, corporate and politic, exercising public and essential governmental functions," may be novel with us as to the method therein prescribed for accomplishing its avowed public purpose, the answers to the constitutional questions now before us depend fundamentally upon whether property acquired by an agency for the purpose of eliminating *blighted areas* that are "conducive to ill health, transmission of disease, infant mortality, juvenile delinquency and crime," is a *public use* within the legal meaning of that term.

It is elementary in constitutional law that the public money may be expended for or devoted to a public use but not to a private purpose. The difficulty in this class of cases arises from the fact that the term "public use" is not capable of exact definition. In 2 Cooley's Const. Lim., 8th ed., 1131, it is said that a public use can be found to exist "where the government is supplying its own needs, or is furnishing facilities for its citizens in regard to those matters of public necessity, convenience, or welfare, which, on account of their peculiar character, and the difficulty—perhaps impossibility—of making provision for them otherwise, it is alike proper, useful, and needful for the government to provide."

There being no general test by which to determine whether the funda-mental purpose of a statute is for a public or private use, the decision in each case must therefore depend upon its own particular facts, especially if the statute presents a dual aspect: one looking definitely to the accom-plishment of a clearly public purpose, and the other indicating a possible advantage to private interests. In such a case, as in all instances of statutory construction, the legal problem presented is to determine the legislative intent from a consideration of the entire statute.

We concede that the act here in question might have been given a much broader construction and application than the one given to it in this opinion had it been enacted under an appropriate constitutional amendment, as was the case in Murray v. LaGuardia, 291 N.Y. 320, 52 N.E.2d 884, certiorari denied, 321 U.S. 771, 64 S.Ct. 530, 88 L.Ed. 1066. But it does not necessarily follow that in the absence of such explicit authority the statute is uncon-stitutional. Its constitutionality is unaffected if the primary purpose of the legislature, though limited in scope by construction, was to eliminate blighted areas in which the predominant conditions were a continuing menace to the public health and safety. The fact that following the elim-ination of such blighted areas some incidental advantage might enure to private interests does not make the statute unconstitutional, especially if that advantage is secured upon conditions for the public good.

We have no doubt that ordinarily a statute will be held void where it authorizes the taking of private property for a use partly public and partly private and the private use is so combined with the public use that the two cannot be separated. See Kessler v. City of Indianapolis, 199 Ind. 420, 157 N.E. 547, 53 A.L.R. 1; Smith v. Western Maine Power Co., 125 Me. 238, 132 A. 740. That is not the case here. Furthermore, in the situation now before us we need not concern ourselves with whether a mere advantage, benefit or convenience to the public is a public use, as the legislature's declared purpose is to eradicate sources of disease, juvenile delinquency and crime, which in our opinion clearly constitute a public use.

The wisdom or feasibility of a statute is not for the court to consider in determining the legislative intent. If in the present case, for instance, the legislature's primary purpose was to eliminate blighted areas in the interest of the public health, safety and welfare and to that end it adopted as a matter of policy the method specified in the act, we are not free to question its judgment as to such method. It is not for us to determine matters of policy or to express any opinion as to the adequacy of the method adopted by the legislature to accomplish its primary purpose. The responsibility for the successful operation of the act rests with the legislature. The sole question for our consideration is whether in adopting such an act the leg-islature acted within its constitutional power.

In the present circumstances the legislature has set out its findings, the purpose of the act and the policy of the state in great detail, far fuller in fact than in any statement that has come to our attention appearing in similar statutes in other jurisdictions.   As hereinbefore appears in our summary of the act the legislature found that "blighted areas," comprising both developed and undeveloped land, exist in this state, which areas are conducive to ill health, transmission of disease, infant mortality, juvenile delinquency and crime by reason of the existence in such areas of buildings and structures, either used or intended to be used for living, commercial, industrial or other purposes, that "are unfit or unsafe to occupy" because of insanitary conditions due to various causes, obsolescence, and deterioration.   The legislature further found that such buildings and structures should be demolished and the blighted areas redeveloped in the interest of the public health and safety of the people of the state generally and particularly of those in the communities in which such areas exist.   It therefore declared that the purpose of the act was to use public funds for a public purpose in order to remove deleterious conditions that are beyond ordinary "regulatory process" and that private interests are unable or unwilling to correct.

While the ultimate determination of the character of the use or purpose is a judicial and not a legislative question, yet where the legislature declares a particular use or purpose to be a "public use" such a declaration must be given weight and will control unless the use or purpose in question is obviously of a private character.   Narragansett Electric Lighting Co. v. Sabre, 50 R. I. 288, 298, 146 A. 777; City of Newport v. Newport Water Corp., 57 R.I. 269, 275, 189 A. 843.   In Block v. Hirsh, 256 U.S. 135, at page 154, 41 S.Ct. 458, at page 459, 65 L.Ed. 865, 16 A.L.R. 165, the supreme court said that "a declaration by a legislature concerning public conditions that by necessity and duty it must know, is entitled at least to great respect."

In considering the present act we are not left to speculate or conjecture as to what the legislature meant by the term "blighted areas."   It has defined such an area as one in which buildings, improvements, structures or land inimical to the public health, safety or welfare *predominate and injuriously affect the entire area.*" (Italics ours.)   To come within the act and thus be subject to redevelopment in accordance with its terms the area, irrespective of the private uses therein included, must be found to contain not only a predominance of buildings, improvements, structures or land which of themselves are "unfit or unsafe" for occupancy and use, but it must also be further found that collectively their present deleterious condition, due to overcrowding, insanitary conditions, obsolescence, deterioration or disuse, presently injuriously affects the entire area to the harm of its immediate inhabitants and of the people of the state generally.

When the language of the legislature in secs. 2, 5 and 15, hereinbefore outlined is read as a whole it is clear to us that such language requires a finding by the legislative body of the community that any blighted area, so called, is as a matter of fact predominantly affected by conditions which are the equivalent of or strongly similar to those existing in what is more plainly and commonly called a slum.   For instance, in Dornan v. Philadelphia Housing Authority, 331 Pa. 209, 200 A. 834, the constitutionality of a statute for slum clearance and the construction of adequate dwellings for persons of low income was in question. In that statute a "slum" was defined as "Any area in which there is a *predominance* of structures which, by reason of dilapidation, overcrowding, faulty arrangement or design, lack of ventilation, light or sanitary facilities, or any combination of these factors, are detrimental to safety, health, and morals." 35 P.S. § 1543. (Italics ours.) In a comprehensive majority opinion five justices of that court concurred in finding the statute constitutional inasmuch as its fundamental purpose was for a public use, while two justices dissented without stating their reasons therefor. All factors in the definition of a slum in the Pennsylvania statute, if not more, are expressed in greater detail in the act now before us.

[1] After serious consideration we are of the opinion that the primary purpose of the present act is the elimination of areas which, though perhaps not actually slums, predominantly show such a marked degree of degeneration as to constitute a menace to the life, health and safety of persons who are obliged to live or work within the limits of such areas and to the people of the state generally. Although the injurious effect from the continued existence of palpably deplorable conditions in such areas may appear to be local, nevertheless there is at least the threat, if not the probability, that the pernicious influences of disease, juvenile delinquency and crime engendered therein may spread to and manifest themselves in other localities to the detriment of the public generally. Construed in this manner we are of the opinion that the act was primarily intended to serve a public purpose and that the property taken in accordance with its terms is for a public use.

In reaching this conclusion we have followed the well-settled rule that a statute is presumed constitutional and should be sustained unless its unconstitutionality is clear beyond a reasonable doubt. In State v. District of Narragansett, 16 R.I. 424, 439, 16 A. 901, 906, 3 L.R.A. 295, this court said that in determining the constitutionality of an act "a becoming deference to the legislature inculcates caution." And in Fletcher v. Peck, 6 Cranch 87, 128, 3 L.Ed. 162, Chief Justice Marshall used the following language: "The question, whether a law be void for its repugnancy to the constitution, is, at all times, a question of much delicacy, which ought seldom, if ever, to be decided in the affirmative, in a doubtful case."

As already stated, it is not for us to consider whether the act in question is wise or unwise. On this point we have accepted and given weight to the findings of the legislature so fully expressed in the act, which findings, having been made by those charged with the duty of initiating and approving the act, we cannot say are obviously unreasonable or unwarranted in the absence of any evidence to the contrary. However, by our present opinion we are not to be understood as holding that under this act a community through an agency may engage in a redevelopment project based mainly upon esthetic views or upon considerations of economic advantage to the municipality, or a combination of both. Unless it is found that under the act, as herein construed and limited, a community redevelopment program is necessary to protect the public health, morals and safety through the elimination of blighted areas the act does not apply.

The eradication of the social evils existing in and emanating from a blighted area apparently being beyond the reach of private interests because of the difficulty and cost in assembling and clearing the land in such area, the legislature, acting under the police power of the state, granted the power of eminent domain to an agency which is defined as "a public body, corporate and politic, exercising public and essential government functions." The supreme court of the United States has been consistently liberal in sustaining the validity of acts as being for a public use whenever it happeared that the appropriation of private property under the right of eminent domain subserved a substantial public purpose. See Fallbrook Irrigation District v. Bradley, 164 U.S. 112, 17 S.Ct. 56, 41 L.Ed. 369; Mt. Vernon-Woodberry Cotton Duck Co. v. Alabama Interstate Power Co., 240 U.S. 30, 36 S.Ct. 234, 60 L.Ed. 507; Jones v. City of Portland, 245 U.S. 217, 38 S.Ct. 112, 62 L.Ed. 252, L.R.A.1918C, 765, Ann. Cas.1918E, 660. It is our judgment, therefore, that the assembly of property in a blighted area and the elimination therefrom of unsafe, insanitary and dilapidated structures in the manner and to the extent prescribed in the act as herein construed are legitimate objects for the exercise of the police power by the legislature and that the grant thereunder of the right of eminent domain to an agency as defined in this act violates no constitutional provision.

The present act, as limited in this opinion, does not authorize a municipality through an agency to engage in the real estate business generally; or to enter upon the utilization of so-called stagnant and unproductive vacant areas the development of which might be potentially more useful and remunerative to a community but which are not in themselves blighted areas, that is, undeveloped lands with conditions predominantly inimical to the public welfare; or to expend the public funds for the mere advantage of private interests. Its primary object is to assemble property, whether developed or undeveloped, in a blighted area and to remove therefrom all buildings, structures and other conditions that constitute a menace to the public health and safety. Upon the elimination of a blighted area, thus enhancing the public good, the primary purpose of the act has been accomplished. With the attainment of these fundamentally public purposes the property acquired and held by an agency has been thus clearly devoted to a public use. We see no valid objection to the constitutionality of the act on the ground that the agency may thereafter convey to private interests the property so reclaimed with conditions and restrictions intended to protect the public health and safety from the recurrence of blight in the future. In other words, it is of no consequence if in redeveloping the area private interests may derive some benefit as an incident to the accomplished public purpose.

We further believe that the act is not objectionable on the ground of improper delegation of legislative power. What shall constitute a blighted area within the meaning of the act is therein described in unmistakable language. The nature and extent of a blighted area must necessarily vary not only in the different cities and towns but also within the same community. All that the legislature can reasonably do in the circumstances is to prescribe a fixed standard and rules of general application adapted to accomplish the purpose of the act, leaving to the respective local authorities the responsibility of ascertaining as a matter of fact whether there exists in the community a blighted area within the meaning of the act as herein construed that requires redevelopment in the public interests. The determination of that factual question by the municipality is an administrative act and not the exercise of legislative power.

In our consideration of the first question the only other matters of fundamental importance that occur to us, as we are presently advised, are: first, whether the act authorizes a redevelopment agency to create a state debt in violation of article IV, sec. 13, of the Rhode Island constitution which provides that the general assembly shall have no power, without the express consent of the people, to incur state debts to an amount exceeding $50,000; and secondly, whether the act authorizes such an agency to incur obligations binding a municipality in excess of its debt limit.

We find no objection to the validity of the act on either of those grounds. While the agency is given the power to issue bonds in its discretion for any of its corporate purposes, the bonds are payable exclusively from the income and revenues of the redevelopment projects financed with the proceeds of those bonds, or with such proceeds together with financial assistance from the state or federal governments in aid of such projects. Further, the act specifically provides that "The bonds and other obligations of any agency (and such bonds and obligations shall so state on their face) shall not be a debt of the community, the state or any political subdivision thereof and neither the community, nor the state or any political subdivision thereof shall be liable thereon, nor in any event shall such bonds or obligations be payable out of any funds or properties other than those of said agency. The bonds shall not constitute an indebtedness within the meaning of any constitutional or statutory debt limitation or restriction." The foregoing pronouncement by the legislature is so explicit as to show clearly that a state debt could not be incurred in connection with a redevelopment project; and further, as hereinbefore indicated, that a municipality could not exceed its debt limit except by establishing a "redevelopment revolving fund" in aid of such a project *provided* that the amount of such fund was first "submitted to and approved by the voters of such community at any general or special election."

[2] The second question asks whether redevelopment agencies with the power of eminent domain violate article IX of the amendments of the Rhode Island constitution. In this instance we are clearly of the opinion that such agencies are not within the scope of that article, which, when adopted in 1892, took the place of sec. 17 of article IV of the constitution of this state. Taking into consideration its history, language and construction by this court in its original form it is clear to us that the intent and purpose of article IX of amendments was to impose more stringent limitations upon the legislature in the matter of granting the power of eminent domain to *private* corporations. See State v. District of Narragansett, supra; Wood v. Quimby, 20 R.I. 482, 485, 40 A. 161. This is not the case appearing in the present act. Here, as the act says, a redevelopment agency is a "public body, corporate and politic, exercising public and essential governmental functions," for the purpose of promoting and protecting the public good. As thus defined in the act, such an agency is in effect a public or quasi government body which is not affected by the provisions of the article under consideration.

In order that we might more clearly present our views on the questions submitted, we have purposely cited in the body of this opinion only a few authorities in support of our conclusions. But among such authorities that we have examined the following are most pertinent: Allydonn Realty Corp. v. Holyoke Housing Authority, 304 Mass. 288, 23 N.E.2d 665, where in the course of its opinion the court distinguishes the case of Salisbury Land & Improvement Co. v. Commonwealth, 215 Mass. 371, 102 N.E. 619, 46 L.R.A.,N.S., 1196; Murray v. LaGuardia, supra; Redfern v. Board of Com'rs of Jersey City, 137 N.J.L. 356, 59 A.2d 641; Belovsky v. Redevelopment Authority of City of Philadelphia, 357 Pa. 329, 54 A.2d 277, 172 A.L.R. 953; Dornan v. Philadelphia Housing Authority, supra; Zurn v. City of Chicago, 389 Ill. 114, 59 N.E.2d 18; Cremer v. Peoria Housing Authority, 399 Ill. 579, 78 N.E.2d 276; People ex rel. Tuohy v. City of Chicago, 399 Ill. 551, 78 N.E.2d 285; Housing Authority of Los Angeles County v. Dockweiler, 14 Cal.2d 437, 94 P.2d 794; Housing Authority of City of Dallas v. Higginbotham, 135 Tex. 158, 143 S.W.2d 79, 130 A.L.R. 1053. See also annotations 130 A.L.R. 1069; 172 A.L.R. 966; 29 B.U.L.R. 318

After serious consideration it is our opinion that the act as amended and as herein construed and limited is for a public use or purpose and therefore does not violate any fundamental principle of constitutional law. Under our view of the act we answer the first question in the affirmative. Our answer to the second question is in the negative.

ANTONIO A. CAPOTOSTO
HUGH B. BAKER

I entertain some doubts as to the constitutionality of the act under consideration. The primary purpose of the act appears to be to promote a redevelopment and use of land areas, to the end not only that such redevelopment and use may contribute to the elimination of conditions inimical to public health, safety and welfare, but also to promote a better utilization of such areas from an economic standpoint so that "economical liabilities" may be removed, higher tax values may be created and greater revenues thus assured to the several municipalities of this state. The exercise of the taxing power and of the power of eminent domain is undoubtedly constitutional as to the first purpose, but in my mind is questionable as to the second. Also running throughout the act there appears a concomitant though perhaps not a predominant purpose, to ensure greater symmetry and a more aesthetic assembly of the areas taken and redeveloped under the act. This purpose and the achievement of such results, in so far as they are *merely incidental* to the lawful purpose of eliminating conditions inimical to public health, safety and welfare, do not in my opinion militate against the constitutionality of the act.

The act expressly provides that blighted areas, which it is sought to eradicate, are characterized by *one* or *more* of certain conditions enumerated in art. 2, sec. 2, paragraphs (a), (b), (c) and (d). The latter paragraph refers to areas in which there is a lack of proper utilization, resulting in a stagnant and unproductive condition of land potentially useful and valuable for contributing to and serving the public health, safety and welfare. It is not necessary for the acquisition of land in some of the defined areas that such land actually constitutes a menace to public health, safety or welfare, which is a proper ground for the exercise of the power of eminent domain, since paragraph (b) of art. 2, sec. 2, expressly provides that such areas may include lands, buildings or improvements which of themselves are *not* detrimental to the public health, safety and welfare, but whose inclusion is found necessary, with or without change in their condition, for the effective redevelopment of the area of which they are a part.

Since the act provides that the existence of blighted areas characterized by *all* or *any* of the conditions enumerated in paragraphs (a) to (d) inclusive constitute grounds for the exercise of the power of eminent domain, it follows that whenever the utilization of land in a given area does not meet its full economic potential it may be acquired under the power of eminent domain on the ground that failure to utilize such land in a manner calculated to achieve its highest economic potential stamps such land as a blighted area or a segment thereof and permits its acquisition against the consent of the owner or owners thereof.

In so far as the act would permit the acquisition of an integrated area, which contains only unproductive or stagant land, or where there is merely an arrested development of such area, which constitutes no menace to public health, safety or welfare, I am of the opinion that such act is unconstitutional in that respect in that it would permit the acquisition of such area or any portion thereof, by the exercise of eminent domain and the expenditure of public money. But where such area is merely a part and not the whole of an area which the agency seeks to redevelop, and where such unproductive, stagnant or arrested area may constitute a menace to the public health, safety or welfare of the remainder of the area sought to be acquired, I am not prepared to state unequivocally that a taking under such circumstances is clearly unconstitutional.

Realizing that opinions of this nature are merely advisory, and not binding on this court, because they are not rendered in litigated cases, where the court has the benefit of the arguments and research of adversary parties, and being conscious of the well-settled rule of constitutional construction in this state and generally accepted in other jurisdictions, that courts should approach constitutional questions with great deliberation, exercising their power with extreme caution and even reluctance and that they should never declare a statute void unless its invalidity is, in their judgment, *beyond reasonable doubt,* I am constrained to concur, except as hereinbefore indicated, in the conclusion reached by Justices Capotosto and Baker, although I cannot concur fully with all of the reasons assigned for such conclusion.

While I entertain serious misgivings regarding various sections of the act I nevertheless find myself unable to say positively that it is unconstitutional beyond a reasonable doubt except as above stated. Such doubts as I may have are therefore, except in the particular above set forth, resolved, in accordance with the rule above referred to, in favor of the constitutionality of the act which is presented for the purpose of securing our advisory opinion.

JEREMIAH E. O'CONNELL

The first question should be answered in the negative and the second question in the affirmative since in my opinion the act is unconstitutional. Public Laws 1946, chapter 1802, as amended by P.L.1948, chap. 2029, and by P.L.1949, chap. 2265, known as the Community Redevelopment Act, hereinafter called the act, should not be confused with a so-called slum clearance act, or one based upon abnormal conditions of widespread distress created by an emergency or an acute shortage in housing, or one limited to a particular project and presently existing conditions or circumstances. It plainly provides, on a grand scale and under the most comprehensive plans and powers ever attempted in this jurisdiction, for future redevelopment of many areas coming within any one of the many conditions that may be found to constitute a so-called blighted or substandard area.

Only a careful study of the many interdependent provisions of the act can give an adequate understanding of the nature and extent of the legislative findings and the sweeping powers expressly granted. However, it is too long to be quoted in full and for our purposes some examples will be sufficient. Article 2, sec. 2, paragraphs (a), (b), (c) and (d) contain many elaborately stated findings by the legislature, any "one or more" of which conditions may constitute a blighted area requiring redevelopment. Accordingly in paragraph (a) "defective design and character of physical construction," or "faulty interior arrangement and exterior spacing," separately or in combination with other named characteristics may suffice to make the property "unfit or unsafe" for residential, commercial, industrial "or other purposes * * *." Such other purposes are not specified but evidently would include religious, educational and charitable uses.

Other such conditions in paragraph (b) include "An economic dislocation, deterioration or disuse" resulting from "faulty planning, the subdividing and the sale of lots of *irregular form and shape* and inadequate size for *proper usefulness and development*," or "the laying out of lots in *disregard of the contours* and other physical characteristics of the ground and surrounding conditions * * *." (Italics mine.) And an area may be declared blighted even though, as expressly provided, it includes "lands, buildings, or improvements which of themselves are *not* detrimental to the public health, safety and welfare, but whose inclusion is found necessary, with *or without change* in their condition, for the effective *redevelopment* of the area of which they are a part." (Italics mine.)

Further, in paragraph (c), "A prevalence of depreciated values," or "*impaired investments* and *social* and *economic maladjustment*" resulting in "reduced capacity to pay taxes and consequent *inadequacy of tax receipts* in relation to the cost of public services rendered" thereby may be declared to constitute a blighted area. (Italics mine.) Significantly, the act elsewhere authorizes a sale for less than cost and does not *require* the owner to pay taxes assessed on the increased valuation of the redeveloped area. It authorizes, however, taxes as low in amount as the average of those received from the old area during the three years preceding the acquisition thereof.

In paragraph (d), a growing "lack of proper utilization of areas" which is found to result "in a stagnant and *unproductive* condition of land *potentially useful*" either separately or with other factors may justify the conclusion that it is a blighted area subject to eminent domain and redevelopment. (Italics mine.)

"Redevelopment" as defined in art. 3, sec. 15, includes among other meanings the following: "The term *does not exclude* the continuance of existing buildings or uses whose demolition and rebuilding or change of use are not deemed essential to the redevelopment and rehabilitation of the area. The term *includes* provision for open space types of use, such as streets and other public grounds and space around buildings, as well as buildings, structures and improvements, public *or private,* and improvements of recreation areas, public *or private,* and other public grounds." (Italics mine.) The term also includes "the *replanning* or *redesign* or *original development* of *undeveloped* areas which by reason of * * * *faulty lot layout* in relation to size, shape, *accessibility,* or usefulness, *or for other causes*" may be determined to be "stagnant or *not properly util-*

ized" and for any one of these "or other reasons" it may be held to require *replanning* and *development*. (Italics mine.)

In art. 3, sec. 5, a "redevelopment area" is defined as one which has been found to be blighted, and in need of *redevelopment* to effectuate the public purposes of the act. According to express provisions, such an area may include lands, buildings, or improvements "which of themselves *are not detrimental* to the public health, safety or welfare, but whose inclusion is found necessary, with *or without* change in their condition, for the *effective redevelopment* of the area of which they are a part." (Italics mine.)

Generally speaking, therefore, the primary purpose of the act is to provide a plan for future wholesale *redevelopment* and the powers necessary to effectuate it. As an incident to the furthering of such purpose of redevelopment the act also authorizes the taking of private property by a legislative termed public body for *any one* of the reasons, grounds or conditions referred to in the act; and such body is not required to hold, rebuild and redevelop the area taken but is empowered to serve as a mere conduit through which property may be taken by eminent domain from one person and transferred to another without necessarily restricting the latter's title or subjecting him to the obligation of providing, in accordance with fixed standards and regulations, a use or service properly deemed to be essential for the public as such or a function of government.

The controlling question, therefore, is whether redevelopment in accordance with such extreme, comprehensive powers and plans as set forth in P.L.1946, chap. 1802, as amended, constitutes a public purpose, that is, a public use, within the fundamental principle of constitutional law. The "fundamental principle of constitutional law" thus stated in the propounded question relates of course to the provisions of the constitution of this state.

Article I, sec. 16, of the constitution of the state of Rhode Island, as a part of its bill of rights, provides that "Private property shall not be taken for public uses, without just compensation." While this is only a limitation upon the powers of the state and does not expressly prohibit the taking of private property, it is firmly established here, as elsewhere, that private property may be taken only for public purposes and by payment of just compensation. In re Rhode Island Suburban Ry. Co., 22 R.I. 457, 48 A. 591, 52 L.R.A. 879; City of Newport v. Newport Water Corp., 57 R.I. 269, 275, 189 A. 843.

Whether a public use is desirable or necessary is for the legislature to decide as a matter of policy. But what constitutes a public use and whether such a proposed use violates the constitutional provision against taking private property are judicial questions for the ultimate determination by the court. Narragansett Electric Lighting Co. v. Sabre, 50 R.I. 288, 298, 146 A. 777; In re Rhode Island Suburban Ry. Co., supra; Joslin Mfg. Co. v. City of Providence, 262 U.S. 668, 43 S.Ct. 684, 67 L.Ed. 1167. It is difficult perhaps to define public use precisely so that it may be applied universally and uniformly to all conditions and circumstances. Consequently in the application of the definition of public use to particular circumstances prevailing in several jurisdictions under varying constitutional provisions, or at different times in the same jurisdiction, some confusion and apparent conflict has arisen. However, notwithstanding these difficulties in the application of the doctrine to new conditions or particular facts, it seems to me that the underlying principle by which a public use should be distinguished from a private use in the fundamental constitutional sense was intended to remain substantially fixed.

Generally speaking, the various decisions of courts in relation to what constitutes a public use so as to justify the exercise of eminent domain have been classified into two main groups. The first appears to hold to the principle that the prospective use of property taken from private persons must provide the general public, or an appreciable portion thereof, with the *right* to use or employ such property or at least to have it used or employed by some agency, public or private, in the public interest under appropriate regulations and restrictions, in order to provide the public as such with some service deemed to be necessary to it or to a proper function of government.

Running through most of the decisions in this category seems to be the thought that the taking should be necessary to some well-recognized and proper governmental function in the interest of the public as such; that the public use or service must be of right and not dependent on permission of the new owner; and that private property taken by eminent domain for a public use is affected, at least to some extent, with a public interest. Such interest has been described as being in the nature of a quasi trust for the benefit of the public as a whole. In other words, the courts in this group adhere substantially to the primary and natural meaning of the term "public use" and to the fundamental principle relating to public use in the traditional constitutional sense.

The second group seems to hold that the term "public use" also has a *secondary* meaning which is substantially synonymous with public benefit, advantage, utility or convenience. Accordingly some courts have expressly held that whatever tends to benefit the public, even though only indirectly and in a general way, justifies a liberal extension of the meaning of public use to support the exercise of eminent domain; and that any use, for example, which tends to enlarge the resources, industrial energies, or productive powers of a number of inhabitants of the state, or to contribute to the welfare and prosperity of the community, is a public use in the constitutional sense.

It has been claimed that there is another or third group which seems to hold that the true interpretation of the term "public use" lies somewhere between the contrasting doctrines of the other two groups. However, some writers assert that such decisions really embrace the principle of the second group, differing only in a matter of the degree of public good or *public policy* which is found to be sufficient justification for its application.

Whatever may have been held elsewhere, Rhode Island appears to have adhered consistently to the primary meaning of the words "public use" and has applied substantially the traditional constitutional principle underlying public use as exemplified by the decisions generally included in the above-mentioned first group. In my opinion this classification has reasonable justification. According to Webster's New International Dictionary (2d ed.) 1946, p. 2005, the word "public" means: "Of or pertaining to the people; relating to, belonging to, or affecting, a nation, state, or community at large —opposed to *private* * * *." According to the same dictionary, page 2806, the verb "use" means: "To make use of * * * To convert to one's service; to avail oneself of"; and the noun "use" in its primary and usual sense means: "Act of employing anything, or state of being employed; application; employment * * * The fact of being used or employed habitually * * *." Moreover, according to that dictionary the noun "use" as particularly related to law conveys the idea of enjoyment through employment of property for the benefit of another, as something in the nature of a trust.

We find nothing in any of the several meanings found in the above-mentioned dictionary which entirely discards the concept of employment, and none which in my view satisfactorily supports the so-called secondary meaning as adopted and applied in many of the decisions classified in the second group. Therefore according to the dictionary it seems to me that the term "public use" in its primary and natural meaning contemplates some use or employment of property by the public, or a substantial portion thereof, or at least the right to have it thus employed. That concept is also supported by discussions of public use and eminent domain in various cases many of which are referred to in 14 Words and Phrases, Perm. Ed., page 324; 35 Words and Phrases, Perm. Ed., page 360; 18 Am.Jur. 660, § 36; 2 Cooley's Const. Lim., 8th Ed., 1108, and 1 Lewis on Eminent Domain, 3d Ed., 505, § 258.

Eminent domain is said to be an attribute of a sovereignty. It is a power, inherent or otherwise, in a sovereign state whereby private property may be taken for public use without the owner's consent. The philosophy behind its origin and exercise seems to be definitely affixed or reasonably and substantially related to some necessity in order to aid and protect the proper functioning of government, through a governmental or other agency, in discharging its essential obligations to the public as such, or a substantial segment thereof. The early cases, decided nearer to the dates of the various constitutions, seem to adhere to the primary and natural meaning of the term "public use" and to the above-mentioned fundamental philosophy as to the exercise of eminent domain. In more recent years, however, some courts appear to have adopted a so-called "liberal" view by expanding the meaning and extending the application of "public use" so as to support the exercise of eminent domain in cases which would not reasonably come within the primary meaning of public use. Many of such decisions seem to me to confuse that which may be merely beneficial or desirable as a matter of public policy with the constitutional meaning of public use and the requirements for the exercise of eminent domain. Others seem to stretch the meaning of public use in its application to a point where it becomes difficult in practice to distinguish any line of constitutional limitation.

But even in that connection it should be noted that there are still very few so-called acts for such wholesale *redevelopment,* as distinguished from special low rent housing or slum clearance, which have as yet been approved in a fully litigated case. In my opinion public use should not be confused with public policy or with mere general benefit or advantage to a community. Moreover, cases dealing with slum clearance or emergency conditions and those provided for by special constitutional provisions not present in our constitution are helpful but are not to be considered as binding authorities upon the instant question, namely, whether the *redevelopment* purpose in the instant act is a public use in the fundamental constitutional sense so as to justify the exercise of eminent domain.

In addition to the above considerations public use has been defined as "Anything which will satisfy a reasonable public demand for public facilities for travel, or for transmission of intelligence or commodities, and of which the general public under reasonable regulations will have a definite and fixed use independent of the will of the party in whom the title is vested is a public use." Narragansett Electric Lighting Co. v. Sabre, supra [50 R.I. 288, 146 A. 782]. By that definition the justices of this court plainly recognized and included the *right* of the public *to a definite and fixed use independent of the will of the party in whom the title is vested* as essential to the legal concept of public use. In substance and effect, therefore, that definition conforms to the primary and natural meaning of the words "public use" and to the principle underlying eminent domain as adhered to in the decisions within the above-mentioned first group.

Moreover, the settled practice in Rhode Island further exemplifies this conclusion. When the state desired to take more property than might be needed for actual construction in the "establishing, laying out, widening, extending or relocating of public highways, streets, places, parks or parkways * * *", it was evidently thought necessary to authorize eminent domain for such purposes by a special constitutional amendment. Article XVII of the articles of amendment to the constitution of this state was therefore adopted November 7, 1916. Moreover, in order to protect private ownership of property as guaranteed in the bill of rights that amendment significantly and expressly provided that the person or persons from whom the property was taken "shall have the first right to purchase or lease the same upon such terms as the state or city or town is willing to sell or lease the same", if it should be no longer strictly necessary for the public purpose supporting the original taking. In passing it may be noted that nothing of this kind has been done as to redevelopment nor are any such provisions found in the redevelopment act.

Finally a more recent case, Opinion to the Governor, R.I., 63 A.2d 724, concerned a particular housing project made necessary by the unusual widespread distress from conditions arising out of an emergency and acute shortage of housing. It was there pointed out in effect that in the absence of unusual and exigent circumstances the providing and rental of housing accommodations or of buying and selling houses by the exercise of the power of eminent domain and the expenditure of public funds therefor was a private and not a public use. We also noted that many things of a general and indirect benefit to the public through their substantial relation to health and safety of individuals, such as food, fuel, clothing and other things equally necessary to maintain life, generally speaking, were not the subject of a public use or purpose so as to support the power of eminent domain, unless its exercise conformed to the powers granted, reserved, or limited in the constitution.

Further, we concluded that a mere legislative declaration that an emergency existed did not of itself create an emergency warranting the enactment of such legislation, and that it was a judicial question for this court to determine whether the legislature could reasonably consider the use to which the property is to be devoted as amounting legally to a public use. If it were otherwise it is evident, as there stated, that "a legislative declaration that a use is public when it is obviously private would conclude the question of the constitutionality of the act." Opinion to the Governor, supra; Narragansett Electric Lighting Co. v. Sabre, supra.

If these and other statements of the law concerning a public use under our constitution are sound, I think it follows a fortiori that redevelopment for the reasons and under the extreme powers granted in numerous interdependent provisions of the instant act should not be considered as a public use. When the provisions of the act are read as a whole, having in mind the many extreme legislative findings and the blanket provisions based upon any "one or more" of named conditions or for "other purposes" or "other reasons," it seems clear to me that many of the conditions asserted by the legislature as justifying eminent domain and redevelopment as a public use are obviously not warranted in fact; that the purpose of redevelopment as set forth in the act does not conform reasonably and substantially to the natural and primary meaning of the words "public use," the philosophy and principle underlying the exercise of the power of eminent domain, and the traditional constitutional view and established practice in this state as to eminent domain and what constitutes a public use; and in any event that the extreme powers for *redevelopment*, which is the primary or at least the dominant purpose of the act, are not reasonably and substantially related to any continuing and independent right of the public as such to use the property thus taken or to have it employed, under appropriate regulations and restrictions, to provide services deemed necessary for the public or to effectively carry out some proper function of government.

In my opinion the dominant purpose of the act, the findings of fact and the grant of extreme powers by the legislature are manifestly clear, unequivocal and comprehensive. Obviously they were so intended and therefore the act requires no construction on our part. Nor is it our duty, as I view it, to attempt to separate the many interdependent provisions by interpretation and restriction. The act as passed, amended and approved is the basis for the proposed questions and my view is predicated thereon.

My conclusion has been reached reluctantly because an act of a coordinate department of the government is entitled to due consideration and should not be disturbed unless it violates constitutional principles beyond a reasonable doubt. However, after a review of many pertinent authorities in the light of definitions, opinions and practice relative to public use and eminent domain in Rhode Island, it seems to me beyond a reasonable doubt that the prospective purpose or use for redevelopment as set forth in the instant act does not constitute a public use in the fundamental constitutional sense so as to justify the exercise of the power of eminent domain.

This view also is amply supported by many cases from other jurisdictions. For example, in the Opinion of the Justices, 204 Mass. 607, 91 N.E. 405, 27 L.R.A.,N.S., 483, the question related to the taking of private property to insure the proper development of industrial facilities. It was there held that such purpose was primarily for the benefit of individuals and only incidentally for the promotion of the public weal. Accordingly it was not considered a public use in the constitutional sense.

In another case the justices of the same court held that the legislature had no power to authorize the use of public money to purchase and develop land for the purpose of providing homes for "mechanics, laborers, or other wage-earners," or for the purpose to improve "the public health by providing homes in the more thinly populated areas of the State for those who might otherwise live in the most congested areas of the State." In that opinion the court further stated: "If the power exists in the Legislature to take a tract of land away from one owner for the purpose of enabling another to get the same tract, the whole subject of such ownership becomes a matter of legislative determination and not of constitutional right." In re Opinion of the Justices, 211 Mass. 624, 625, 629, 98 N.E. 611, 612, 42 L.R.A.,N.S., 221. To a similar effect see also Salisbury Land & Improvement Co. v. Commonwealth, 215 Mass. 371, 102 N.E. 619, 46 L.R.A.,N.S., 1196, and cases there reviewed and cited.

In Healy Lumber Co. v. Morris, 33 Wash. 490, 509, 74 P. 681, 685, 63 L.R.A. 820, 99 Am.St.Rep. 964, the court was considering the general subject matter of eminent domain and used the following language: "the use under consideration must be either a use by the public, or by some agency which is quasi public, and not simply a use which may incidentally or indirectly promote the public interest or general prosperity of the state."

A similar thought has been stated as follows: "Different courts some-times arrive at different conclusions upon the same state of facts, but when-ever the remedy is applied, it should always be because there is a direct 'public use' of the property taken, and not a mere incidental or indirect public benefit." City of Richmond v. Carneal, 129 Va. 388, 398, 106 S.E. 403, 407, 14 A.L.R. 1341.

Likewise in Smith v. Cameron, 106 Or. 1, 210 P. 716, 720, 27 A.L.R. 510, the court points out by way of distinction different special provisions in the constitutions of certain other states and cites with approval the follow-ing expression from Cooley's Const. Lim., 7th Ed., 766: " 'The public use implies a possession, occupation, and enjoyment of the land' by the public or public agencies, and it is not enough 'that the public would receive incidental benefits, such as usually spring from the improvement of lands or the establishment of prosperous private enterprises.' "

For similar expressions and conclusions concerning the meaning of public use and eminent domain in the constitutional sense, see also Fountain Park Co. v. Hensler, 199 Ind. 95, 155 N.E. 465, 50 A.L.R. 1518; Connecticut College for Women v. Calvert, 87 Conn. 421, 88 A. 633, 48 L.R.A.,N.S., 485; and many others which are referred to in 14 Words and Phrases, Perm. Ed., page 324; 35 Words and Phrases, Perm Ed., page 360; 18 Amer.Jur. 660, § 36; 2 Cooley's Const.Lim., 8th Ed., 1108; 1 Lewis on Eminent Domain, 3d Ed., 505, § 258; 10 R.C.L. 24, § 22; Smith v. Cameron, 106 Or. 1, 210 P. 716, 27 A.L.R. 510; Fountain Park Co. v. Hensler, 199 Ind. 95, 155 N.E. 465, 50 A.L.R. 1518.

On the other hand, the courts in some states appear to have applied a different doctrine. They seem to me to treat "public use" as synonymous with either public policy or with a public benefit, advantage, utility or convenience. At least they stretch the meaning of "public use" to an extent that makes it difficult to have any reasonably fixed standard by which the question what constitutes a public use may be determined constitu-tionally. They are included in the second above-mentioned groups, and the cases of Dornan v. Philadelphia Housing Authority, 331 Pa. 209, 200 A. 834, Belovsky v. Redevelopment Authority of City of Philadelphia, 357 Pa. 329, 54 A.2d 277, 172 A.L.R. 953, and Zurn v. City of Chicago, 389 Ill. 114, 59 N.E.2d 18, represent that view.

However, I am not convinced that we should follow the reasoning or results enunciated therein. They are helpful but it should be noted that few, if any, of them are cases under a redevelopment act like ours and that all of them are litigated cases in equity where the particular project and issues are defined. Apart from that the thought seems to prevail, according to certain assertions and reasoning, that unless the words "public use" are given a so-called liberal meaning to conform with a declared public policy of the legislature, the community will be impotent or deprived of desirable advantages or benefits that might flow generally and indirectly from the exercise of eminent domain. Neither of these conclusions follows. In that connection the legally sound answer in my opinion is found in the practice and experience in the state of New York. Apparently the constitutional difficulties in trying to thus expand the meaning of the words "public use" beyond their primary meaning and the fundamental principle of constitutional law, in order to fit comparable proposed uses, were clearly and fully recognized in that state. Consequently in 1938, after an exhaustive study of the related problems, an appropriate amendment to the New York constitution was found to be the safe and sound procedure in order to insure the benefits of redevelopment, which at least in part are similar to the redevelopment here involved. See Murray v. LaGuardia, 291 N.Y. 320, 52 N.E.2d 884.

In the circumstances I prefer to follow what appears to be the weight of authority here and elsewhere and thus to recognize and approve the experience, procedure and decision in New York. See Murray v. LaGuardia, supra. That and other similar cases seem to me to conform substantially to the statement on eminent domain and public use to be found in 1 Lewis on Eminent Domain, 3d Ed., 506, § 258, which reads in part as follows: "The public use of anything is the employment or application of the thing by the public. * * * The reasons which incline us to this view are: First, That it accords with the primary and more commonly understood meaning of the words; second, it accords with the general practice in regard to taking private property for public use in vogue when the phrase was first brought into use in the earlier constitutions; third, it is the only view which gives the words any force as a limitation or renders them capable of any definite and practical application. If the constitution means that private property can be taken only for use *by* the public, it affords a definite guide to both the legislature and the courts. Though the property is vested in private individuals or corporations, the public retain certain definite rights to its use or enjoyment, and to that extent it remains under the control of the legislature. If no such rights are secured to the public, then the property is not taken for public use and the act of appropriation is void. * * * If exceptional circumstances require exceptional legislation in those respects in any State, it is very easy to provide for it specially in the constitution, as has been done in several States."

It is my opinion, therefore, that the redevelopment act, when considered as a whole in the light of all the reasons and authorities hereinbefore set forth, is unconstitutional. It follows that the first question propounded should be answered in the negative and the second question should be answered in the affirmative.

EDMUND W. FLYNN.

My study of this act has convinced me beyond a reasonable doubt that it authorizes the taking of private property for the express purpose of an ultimate private use and therefore violates article I, sec. 16, of the declaration of rights of the constitution of this state. Narragansett Electric Lighting Co. v. Sabre, 50 R.I. 288, 298, 146 A. 777. I am also of the opinion that it is constitutionally invalid because it expressly authorizes the use of public money raised by taxation for an ultimate private purpose.

In view of the analysis of the act in the majority opinion there is no need of a further exposition of its purposes and procedures here. The act is most comprehensive in vesting power in the redevelopment agency to take private property, clear the land of its improvements, relocate streets, assemble lots into larger tracts, replat and do other things necessary to prepare the cleared land for sale or lease to private persons or corporations who will agree to use it in accordance with such conditions and restrictions as the agency may prescribe pursuant to the express mandate of the act. It is, indeed, a far-reaching piece of legislation. That the draftsman of the act deliberately intended it to be so is apparent from its many sweeping and repetitive provisions. Certainly the legislature could not have failed to discern the ultimate design of the act and the comprehensiveness of the powers conferred upon the agency to effectuate such design. This being so, the only question for judicial determination is whether the legislature might reasonably find that such clear design of the act was a public use and therefore not within the inhibition of the declaration of rights that private property should not be taken except for a public use and upon just compensation. It is because I am firmly convinced that the legislature could not reasonably so find that I am constrained to differ with my brethren who subscribe to the contrary view.

I am fully aware of the rule of construction that courts should not declare legislative acts unconstitutional unless they are convinced beyond a reasonable doubt, and I realize that I am bound by that rule in giving my opinion here. I am also conscious of the fact, however, that to declare an act of the legislature unconstitutional is, to say the least, an extremely disagreeable duty. This is especially so where an act "because of some accident of immediate overwhelming interest," as was said in the dissent in Northern Securities Co. v. United States, 193 U.S. 197, 400, 24 S.Ct. 436, 468, 48 L.Ed. 679, "appeals to the feelings and distorts the judgment." Nevertheless the court must accept this grave responsibility and "when it is clear that the statute transgressses the authority vested in the Legislature by the Constitution, it is the duty of the court, a duty from which they cannot shrink without profaning their oaths of office, to see and to declare the invalidity of the statute." Salisbury Land & Improvement Co. v. Commonwealth, 215 Mass. 371, 373, 102 N.E. 619, 621, 46 L.R.A.,N.S., 1196. Such clearness in the statute in question is apparent to me notwithstanding the doubts of some of my brethren, and, therefore, I am constrained to differ with them. A decent respect for their opinions requires me to state as briefly as I may the reasons which impel me to this divergent view.

In the first place it is essential to keep in mind that this act is in no sense a *regulatory* statute based upon the exercise of the police power. It does not aim to regulate the use of private property but expressly authorizes the seizure of such property under the guise of necessity for a public use.

This is an exercise of the power of eminent domain. These are two separate and distinct powers and rest on entirely different principles. Horton v. Old Colony Bill Posting Co., 36 R.I. 507, 90 A.822, Ann.Cas.1916A, 911. The application of the police power to the activities of business is confined to regulating such activities and does not extend to authorizing the state to engage in them. State of Ohio v. Helvering, 292 U.S. 360, 54 S.Ct. 725, 78 L.Ed. 1307.

The acquisition of real estate and its renovation, improvement or redevelopment for the professed purpose of sale or lease to private persons is, therefore, not an exercise of the police power. But the proponents of the act nevertheless say it is valid because the land and the improvements thereon which are to be seized or otherwise acquired must be cleared and redeveloped to eradicate evils which inhere in or are necessarily incidental to such property in its present condition and which are detrimental to the public health, safety and morals. The short answer to their assertion is that even though such evils exist the police power furnishes no warrant for the *seizure* of the offending property.

The remedy is to hold the owner responsible for the illegal use which he makes or permits to be made of his property. In the event of his neglect or refusal to abate the alleged nuisance the authorities may abate it and charge the cost to him. Of course, in such a case they must be prepared to show that such evil or evils did in fact exist. This obligation, however, under the police power would also rest upon the redevelopment agency, even under this act, since their findings that any particular area was inimical in its existing condition to public health, safety or morals would be subject to judicial review premised upon the legislative policy as declared in article 2, sec. 2, of the act. Treigle v. Acme Homestead Ass'n, 297 U.S. 189, 56 S.Ct. 408, 80 L.Ed. 575, 101 A.L.R. 1284. The police power confers "no unrestricted authority to accomplish whatever the public may presently desire." Panhandle Eastern Pipe Line Co. v. State Highway Commission, 294 U.S. 613, 622, 55 S.Ct. 563, 567, 79 L.Ed. 1090.

Hence it is obvious that what the legislature has attempted under this act is to exercise two governmental powers in combination. Recognizing the inadequacy of the police power alone as a constitutional basis for the comprehensive provisions of the act, it has called upon its power of eminent domain by declaring that the taking of private property by the development agency under the act is for a public use. That declaration does not of itself determine the nature of such use. This is ultimately a judicial question. Here we must look behind the words to discover the actual use to which the property is to be put. In other words, it is not the immediate occasion of the taking that determines the nature of the use but the ultimate purpose to be served by such taking. That purpose is unquestionably for the same kind and character of private use as existed before the taking of the property, but without the evils attendant upon the prior private use. Some courts have held in passing upon similar legislative acts that such ultimate private use is only incidental to what they call the primary public use of eliminating certain evils which were found to be accompanying the prior private use and to be inimical to the public health, safety or morals. Prescinding from that view they state that the ultimate private use of the condemned property being only incidental to the taking of it for the elimination of public evils does not detract from what they term the primary public use.

I cannot accept such view. In my opinion it confuses the *taking* of the condemned property with the *use* to which it is designedly to be put. The taking is admittedly a public act and were the property intended to remain in the public for the purpose of providing parks, playgrounds, widened or straightened public highways for traffic relief, or for any other familiar type of public welfare projects definitely tending to promote the public health, safety or morals I would have no hesitancy in finding the intended use public. But here, aside from the elimination of the evils found to be attendant upon the prior private use of the property, the professed intention of the statute is to provide for the return of the property to private use unaccompanied by any use or right of use by the public generally.

This is quite unlike the act which was under consideration in Moore v. Sanford, 151 Mass. 285, 24 N.E. 323, 7 L.R.A. 151, where the primary object of the taking of the land was the development of Boston Harbor in order to promote cooperation between the various facilities engaged in foreign and domestic commerce. It is more like the situation that was passed upon in the Opinion of the Justices, 204 Mass. 607, 91 N.E. 405, 27 L.R.A.,N.S., 483, which concerned a proposed plan of taking by eminent domain private property adjoining the layout of a widened public thoroughfare and leasing it to private interests for the purpose of erecting improvements subject to certain prescribed conditions designed to promote the public interests and objects for which the thoroughfare was to be constructed. Whether such limited use of lands outside the highway was a public use which would justify the exercise of the power of eminent domain the opinion advised, 204 Mass. at page 610, 91 N.E. at page 407: "The city cannot be authorized to take the property of a private owner for such a purpose, nor can the city tax its inhabitants to obtain money for such a use."

But perhaps a closer case is Salisbury Land & Improvement Co. v. Commonwealth, supra, where a statute set up a park commission with power of eminent domain to take over a beach and adjoining property for the purpose of a park reservation. The act also contained broad powers authorizing the park commission to resell some of the property even though it continued within the territorial limits of the park. Holding the act invalid, the court said, 215 Mass. at page 377, 102 N.E. at page 622: "Legislation which is designed or which is so framed that it may be utilized to accomplish the ultimate result of placing property in the hands of one individual for private enjoyment after it has been taken from another individual avowedly for a public purpose is unconstitutional. It would enable that to be achieved by indirection which by plain statement would be impossible." This constitutional guaranty against the taking of private property except for a public use, it has been said by the supreme court of the United States, "grows out of the essential nature of all free governments" and "is fundamental in American jurisprudence". Madisonville Traction Co. v. Saint Bernard Mining Co., 196 U.S. 239, 251, 25 S.Ct. 251, 256, 49 L.Ed. 462.

We, ourselves, very recently advised that under our state constitution the state cannot engage in the buying and selling of land under the guise of exercising the power of eminent domain. Opinion to the Governor, R.I., 63 A.2d 724. And this view is consistent with the rule of law earlier announced by this court when it stated that the legislature had no power to take A's vested estate or any part of it and transfer it to B for private use, and *any circuity of proceeding in doing it will not defeat A's right*. Talbot v. Talbot, 14 R.I. 57. And it has been expressly held elsewhere that where the property to be taken for an admittedly public use is not to be retained for such purpose but is to be resold for private use it is not a valid taking for a public use. Pennsylvania Mutual Life Ins. Co. v. Philadelphia, 242 Pa. 47, 88 A. 904, 49 L.R.A.,N.S., 1062.

Perhaps the whole difficulty in this matter is the conception entertained by various courts of the term "public use" as employed in the federal constitution and practically all state constitutions. Formerly there was virtual uniformity in the judicial interpretation of that term along the line that it meant actual use or right of use by the public of the property taken. Latterly, however, there has been a definite departure from such interpretation tending to make it mean merely some public benefit or advantage flowing indirectly from the taking without actual use or right to use on the part of the public.

In Narragansett Electric Lighting Co. v. Sabre, supra [50 R.I. 288, 146 A. 782], this court, however, adopted the following statement in 20 C.J. 556, note (j): "Anything which will satisfy a reasonable public demand for public facilities for travel, or for transmission of intelligence or commodities, and of which the general public under reasonable regulations will have a definite and fixed use independent of the will of the party in whom the title is vested is a public use." See also 29 C.J.S., Eminent Domain, § 31, note 36. Earlier, however, some courts were already stretching this concept so that Potter, J., dissenting in Boston & Providence R. Corp. v. New York & New England R. Co., 13 R.I. 260, 285, was led to observe: "The logical outcome of many of the decisions and *dicta* on this subject of sacrificing private rights to a very slight public advantage is communism * * *." And earlier in his opinion he stated, 13 R.I. at page 278: "It is an enormous arbitrary power to seize the property of the citizen without or against his will, and apply it to public uses. But it *must be for the public use*, and for the *use of the people* of this State." (Italics mine.)

The question now is on which side shall this court be clearly ranged. I believe that it should continue to be on the side of the traditional interpretation of the term "public use" and not on the side of a loose construction. The reason for this conclusion, in my opinion, has been well stated by the court of appeals of Maryland in Arnsperger v. Crawford, 101 Md. 247, 61 A. 413, 70 L.R.A. 497. Referring in that case to the two divergent views of the term which had arisen among various courts they said, 101 Md. at page 253, 61 A. at page 415: "There will be found two different views of the meaning of these words which have been taken by the Courts; one, there must be a use, or right of use *by* the public, or some limited portion of the public; the other that they are equivalent to *public utility or advantage.* If the former is the correct view, the Legislature and the Courts have a definite, fixed guide for their action; if the latter is to prevail, the enactment of laws upon this subject will reflect the passing popular feeling, and their construction, will reflect the various temperaments of the Judges, who are thus left free to indulge their own views of public utility or advantage." For those reasons that court chose to adhere to the former view as the correct one.

Such is the choice which we are called upon to make in giving our opinions on the act here in question. It is a choice, in my opinion, fraught with grave consequences to the continuance of free government as we have known it and as the founding fathers sought, by explicit provisions in the bill of rights, to guarantee and preserve. The question involved is one of freedom. "The security of property, next to personal security against the exertions of government, is of the essence of liberty. They are joined in protection * * * and both the National Government * * * and the States * * * are forbidden to deprive any person 'of life, liberty, or property, without due process of law,' and the emphasis of the Fifth Amendment is that private property cannot be 'taken for public use, without just compensation.'" McKenna, J., dissenting in Block v. Hirsh, 256 U.S. 135, 165, 41 S.Ct. 458, 463, 65 L.Ed. 865, 16 A.L.R. 165.

At first blush it may seem extravagant to attribute such transcendent importance to the simple issue presented here, but I am confident that upon mature reflection its supreme importance will become more and more evident. We would do well to pause long and ponder earnestly before approving legislation which so clearly undertakes to authorize the seizure of private property of one person and its transfer to another. It was for the purpose of curbing governmental power that express protection to private property was written into the declaration of rights in our state constitution. The supreme court of the United States has well said in this connection: "Due protection of the rights of property has been regarded as a vital principle of republican institutions. 'Next in degree to the right of personal liberty,' Mr. Broom in his work on Constitutional Law says, 'is that of enjoying private property without undue interference or molestation.' [Page 228.] The requirement that the property shall not be taken for public use without just compensation is but 'an affirmance of a great doctrine established by the common law for the protection of private property. It is founded in natural equity, and is laid down by jurists as a principle of universal law. Indeed, in a free government almost all other rights would become worthless if the government possessed an uncontrollable power over the private fortune of every 'citizen.'" Chicago, Burlington & Quincy R. Co. v. Chicago, 166 U.S. 226, 235, 17 S.Ct. 581, 584, 41 L.Ed.979.

We are dealing here with the very cornerstone of our free society. If this guaranty of the right of private property against the arbitrary exactions of government is lost, then all is lost. No matter how beneficent legislation may at the moment appear to be it will be dear, indeed, if purchased at such a price. There are many things a benevolent despotism may do for the material well-being of its subjects that are denied to a constitutional democracy of free citizens, but the cost is loss of freedom and citizenship.

The people in their sovereign capacity of course may yield this right guaranteed to them under the constitution, if they so choose. But neither the legislature nor this court may directly or indirectly do so. If the objectives of the act under consideration are impossible of accomplishment under the constitution as it now stands, and if those objectives are so desirable and beneficial that the people are willing to surrender some portion of their guaranteed right of private ownership of property so that the government through the legislature may authorize the taking of such property for a use that is not truly public they may amend the constitution to permit the realization of those specific objectives. In this way it would be possible for them to restrict such surrender of their constitutional rights so as to extend it no farther than necessary to achieve those ends. Such was the method adopted in 1916 when the people were apparently convinced that the permissive authority specifically granted to the state under article of amendment XVII was desirable. That article reads as follows:

> "Section 1. The general assembly may authorize the acquiring or taking in fee by the state, or by any cities or towns, of more land and property than is needed for actual construction in the establishing, laying out, widening, extending or relocating of public highways, streets, places, parks or parkways: *Provided, however,* that the additional land and property so authorized to be acquired or taken shall be no more in extent than would be sufficient to form suitable building sites abutting on such public highway, street, place, park or parkway. After so much of the land and property has been appropriated for such public highway, street, place, park or parkway as is needed therefor, the remainder may be held and improved for any public purpose or purposes, or may be sold or leased for value with or without suitable restrictions, and in case of any such sale or lease, the person or person from whom such remainder was taken shall have the first right to purchase or lease the same upon such terms as the state or city or town is willing to sell or lease the same."

It will be noted that there the people even in the very act of constitutionally surrendering a portion of their rights jealously safeguarded some measure of them by expressly providing that the owner from whom the land or property was taken should have a preferred right to purchase ℒ lease such land or property in the event that all of it was not needed for the particular public use specifically described in the amendment.

The procedure there followed besides being the only constitutional way to effectuate the desired result, also avoids the danger of erosion of the right of private property by the process of loose judicial interpretation unconsciously affected as it may well be by momentary popular clamor. Reluctant as I am to delay the realization of the benefits which may flow from this seemingly worthwhile but clearly invalid legislation, I am in duty bound to do so out of respect to the constitution and my oath of office. If I did otherwise I would be recreant to both and be guilty of usurpation of the people's prerogative to amend their constitution. Furthermore I am profoundly of the opinion that unless this court resists what the late Mr. Justice Holmes called "the hydraulic pressure" of statutes so naturally appealing in their humane and civic aspects as the one here in question this great guaranty of the declaration of rights in our state constitution protecting the right of private property will soon live only in rhetoric.

My considered opinion is, therefore, that the act in question is unconstitutional on the grounds first hereinbefore mentioned.

FRANCIS B. CONDON.

Questions and Notes

1. What was the vote in this case? Incidentally this is the decision which gives the best insight into the attitudes in the Rhode Island Court, and so it is valuable in understanding its rather odd holdings on zoning.

2. What types of redevelopment were thought to be constitutionally objectionable, by one or more of the judges here?

BERMAN

v.

PARKER

348 U.S. 26

APPEAL FROM THE UNITED STATES DISTRICT COURT FOR THE DISTRICT OF COLUMBIA.

Argued October 19, 1954.—Decided November 22, 1954.

James C. Toomey and *Joseph H. Schneider* argued the cause for appellants. With them on the brief was *Albert Ginsberg.*

Solicitor General Sobeloff argued the cause for appellees. *Assistant Attorney General Morton, Oscar H. Davis, Roger P. Marquis, George F. Riseling* and *William S. Cheatham* were with him on a brief for the District of

Columbia Redevelopment Land Agency and the National Capital Planning Commission, appellees.

Vernon E. West, Chester H. Gray, Milton D. Korman, Harry L. Walker and *J. Hampton Baumgartner, Jr.* filed a brief for Renah F. Camalier and Louis W. Prentiss, Commissioners of the District of Columbia, appellees.

MR. JUSTICE DOUGLAS delivered the opinion of the Court.

This is an appeal (28 U. S. C. § 1253) from the judgment of a three-judge District Court which dismissed a complaint seeking to enjoin the condemnation of appellants' property under the District of Columbia Redevelopment Act of 1945, 60 Stat. 790, D. C. Code, 1951, §§ 5-701–5-719. The challenge was to the constitutionality of the Act, particularly as applied to the taking of appellants' property. The District Court sustained the constitutionality of the Act. 117 F. Supp. 705.

By § 2 of the Act, Congress made a "legislative determination" that "owing to technological and sociological changes, obsolete lay-out, and other factors, conditions existing in the District of Columbia with respect to substandard housing and blighted areas, including the use of buildings in alleys as dwellings for human habitation, are injurious to the public health, safety, morals, and welfare; and it is hereby declared to be the policy of the United States to protect and promote the welfare of the inhabitants of the seat of the Government by eliminating all such injurious conditions by employing all means necessary and appropriate for the purpose." *

Section 2 goes on to declare that acquisition of property is necessary to eliminate these housing conditions.

Congress further finds in § 2 that these ends cannot be attained "by the ordinary operations of private enterprise alone without public participation"; that "the sound replanning and redevelopment of an obsolescent or obsolescing portion" of the District "cannot be accomplished unless it be done in the light of comprehensive and coordinated planning of the whole of the territory of the District of Columbia and its environs"; and that "the acquisition and the assembly of real property and the leasing or sale thereof for redevelopment pursuant to a project area redevelopment plan . . . is hereby declared to be a public use."

Section 4 creates the District of Columbia Redevelopment Land Agency (hereinafter called the Agency), composed of five members, which is granted power by § 5(a) to acquire and assemble, by eminent domain and otherwise, real property for "the redevelopment of blighted territory in the

---

* The Act does not define either "slums" or "blighted areas." Section 3(r), however, states:

" 'Substandard housing conditions' means the conditions obtaining in connection with the existence of any dwelling, or dwellings, or housing accommodations for human beings, which because of lack of sanitary facilities, ventilation, or light, or because of dilapidation, overcrowding, faulty interior arrangement, or any combination of these factors, is in the opinion of the Commissioners detrimental to the safety, health, morals, or welfare of the inhabitants of the District of Columbia."

District of Columbia and the prevention, reduction, or elimination of blight-ing factors or causes of blight."

After the real estate has been assembled, the Agency is authorized to transfer to public agencies the land to be devoted to such public purposes § 6(b).

Section 6(a) of the Act directs the National Capital Planning Commission (hereinafter called the Planning Commission) to make and develop "a comprehensive or general plan" of the District, including "a land-use plan" which designates land for use for "housing, business, industry, recreation, education, public buildings, public reservations, and other general categories of public and private uses of the land." Section 6(b) authorizes the Planning Commission to adopt redevelopment plans for specific project areas. These plans are subject to the approval of the District Commissioners after a public hearing; and they prescribe the various public and private land uses for the respective areas, the "standards of population density and build-ing intensity," and "the amount or character or class of any low-rent housing."

Once the Planning Commission adopts a plan and that plan is approved by the Commissioners, the Planning Commission certifies it to the Agency. § 6(d). At that point, the Agency is authorized to acquire and assemble the real property in the area. *Id.* as streets, utilities, recreational facilities, and schools, § 7(a), and to lease or sell the remainder as an entirety or in parts to a redevelopment company, individual, or partnership. § (7)(b), (f). The leases or sales must provide that the lessees or purchasers will carry out the redevelopment plan and that "no use shall be made of any land or real property included in the lease or sale nor any building or structure erected thereon" which does not con-form to the plan, §§ 7(d), 11. Preference is to be given to private enter-prise over public agencies in executing the redevelopment plan. § 7(g).

The first project undertaken under the Act relates to Project Area B in Southwest Washington, D. C. In 1950 the Planning Commission prepared and published a comprehensive plan for the District. Surveys revealed that in Area B, 64.3% of the dwellings were beyond repair, 18.4% needed major repairs, only 17.3% were satisfactory; 57.8% of the dwellings had outside toilets, 60.3% had no baths, 29.3% lacked electricity, 82.2% had no wash basins or laundry tubs, 83.8% lacked central heating. In the judgment of the Dis-trict's Director of Health it was necessary to redevelop Area B in the interests of public health. The population of Area B amounted to 5,012 persons, of whom 97.5% were Negroes.

The plan for Area B specifies the boundaries and allocates the use of the land for various purposes. It makes detailed provisions for types of dwell-ing units and provides that at least one-third of them are to be low-rent housing with a maximum rental of $17 per room per month.

After a public hearing, the Commissioners approved the plan and the Planning Commission certified it to the Agency for execution. The Agency undertook the preliminary steps for redevelopment of the area when this suit was brought.

Appellants own property in Area B at 712 Fourth Street, S. W. It is not used as a dwelling or place of habitation. A department store is located on it. Appellants object to the appropriation of this property for the purposes of the project. They claim that their property may not be taken constitutionally for this project. It is commercial, not residential property; it is not slum housing; it will be put into the project under the management of a private, not a public, agency and redeveloped for private, not public, use. That is the argument; and the contention is that appellants' private property is being taken contrary to two mandates of the Fifth Amendment—(1) "No person shall . . . be deprived of . . . property, without due process of law"; (2) "nor shall private property be taken for public use, without just compensation." To take for the purpose of ridding the area of slums is one thing; it is quite another, the argument goes, to take a man's property merely to develop a better balanced, more attractive community. The District Court, while agreeing in general with that argument, saved the Act by construing it to mean that the Agency could condemn property only for the reasonable necessities of slum clearance and prevention, its concept of "slum" being the existence of conditions "injurious to the public health, safety, morals and welfare." 117 F. Supp. 705, 724-725.

The power of Congress over the District of Columbia includes all the legislative powers which a state may exercise over its affairs. See *District of Columbia* v. *Thompson Co.*, 346 U. S. 100, 108. We deal, in other words, with what traditionally has been known as the police power. An attempt to define its reach or trace its outer limits is fruitless, for each case must turn on its own facts. The definition is essentially the product of legislative determinations addressed to the purposes of government, purposes neither abstractly nor historically capable of complete definition. Subject to specific constitutional limitations, when the legislature has spoken, the public interest has been declared in terms well-nigh conclusive. In such cases the legislature, not the judiciary, is the main guardian of the public needs to be served by social legislation, whether it be Congress legislating concerning the District of Columbia (see *Block* v. *Hirsh*, 256 U. S. 135) or the States legislating concerning local affairs. See *Olsen* v. *Nebraska*, 313 U. S. 236; *Lincoln Union* v. *Northwestern Co.*, 335 U. S. 525; *California State Association* v. *Maloney*, 341 U. S. 105. This principle admits of no exception merely because the power of eminent domain is involved. The role of the judiciary in determining whether that power is being exercised for a public purpose is an extremely narrow one. See *Old Dominion Co.* v. *United States*, 269 U. S. 55, 66; *United States ex rel. T. V. A.* v. *Welch*, 327 U. S. 546, 552.

Public safety, public health, morality, peace and quiet, law and order—these are some of the more conspicuous examples of the traditional application of the police power to municipal affairs. Yet they merely illustrate the scope of the power and do not delimit it. See *Noble State Bank* v. *Haskell*, 219 U. S. 104, 111. Miserable and disreputable housing conditions may do more than spread disease and crime and immorality. They may also suffocate the spirit by reducing the people who live there to the status of cattle. They may indeed make living an almost insufferable burden. They may also be an ugly sore, a blight on the community which robs it of charm, which makes it a place from which men turn. The misery of housing may despoil a community as an open sewer may ruin a river.

We do not sit to determine whether a particular housing project is or is not desirable. The concept of the public welfare is broad and inclusive. See *Day-Brite Lighting, Inc.* v. *Missouri*, 342 U. S. 421, 424. The values it represents are spiritual as well as physical, aesthetic as well as monetary. It is within the power of the legislature to determine that the community should be beautiful as well as healthy, spacious as well as clean, well-balanced as well as carefully patrolled. In the present case, the Congress and its authorized agencies have made determinations that take into account a wide variety of values. It is not for us to reappraise them. If those who govern the District of Columbia decide that the Nation's Capital should be beautiful as well as sanitary, there is nothing in the Fifth Amendment that stands in the way.

Once the object is within the authority of Congress, the right to realize it through the exercise of eminent domain is clear. For the power of eminent domain is merely the means to the end. See *Luxton* v. *North River Bridge Co.*, 153 U. S. 525, 529-530; *United States* v. *Gettysburg Electric R. Co.*, 160 U. S. 668, 679. Once the object is within the authority of Congress, the means by which it will be attained is also for Congress to determine. Here one of the means chosen is the use of private enterprise for redevelopment of the area. Appellants argue that this makes the project a taking from one businessman for the benefit of another businessman. But the means of executing the project are for Congress and Congress alone to determine, once the public purpose has been established. See *Luxton* v. *North River Bridge Co., supra;* cf. *Highland* v. *Russell Car Co.*, 279 U. S. 253. The public end may be as well or better served through an agency of private enterprise than through a department of government— or so the Congress might conclude. We cannot say that public ownership is the sole method of promoting the public purposes of community redevelopment projects. What we have said also disposes of any contention concerning the fact that certain property owners in the area may be permitted to repurchase their properties for redevelopment in harmony with the over-all plan. That, too, is a legitimate means which Congress and its agencies may adopt, if they choose.

In the present case, Congress and its authorized agencies attack the problem of the blighted parts of the community on an area rather than on a structure-by-structure basis. That, too, is opposed by appellants. They maintain that since their building does not imperil health or safety nor contribute to the making of a slum or a blighted area, it cannot be swept into a redevelopment plan by the mere dictum of the Planning Commission or the Commissioners. The particular uses to be made of the land in the project were determined with regard to the needs of the particular community. The experts concluded that if the community were to be healthy, if it were not to revert again to a blighted or slum area, as though possessed of a congenital disease, the area must be planned as a whole. It was not enough, they believed, to remove existing buildings that were insanitary or unsightly. It was important to redesign the whole area so as to eliminate the conditions that cause slums—the over-crowding of dwellings, the lack of parks, the lack of adequate streets and alleys, the absence of recreational areas, the lack of light and air, the presence of outmoded street patterns. It was believed that the piecemeal approach, the removal of individual structures that were offensive, would be only a palliative. The entire area needed redesigning so that a balanced, inte-grated plan could be developed for the region, including not only new homes but also schools, churches, parks, streets, and shopping centers. In this way it was hoped that the cycle of decay of the area could be controlled and the birth of future slums prevented. Cf. *Gohld Realty Co.* v. *Hartford,* 141 Conn. 135, 141-144, 104 A. 2d 365, 368-370; *Hunter* v. *Redevelopment Authority,* 195 Va. 326, 338-339, 78 S. E. 2d 893, 900-901. Such diversification in future use is plainly relevant to the maintenance of the desired housing standards and therefore within congressional power.

The District Court below suggested that, if such a broad scope were intended for the statute, the standards contained in the Act would not be sufficiently definite to sustain the delegation of authority. 117 F. Supp. 705, 721. We do not agree. We think the standards prescribed were adequate for executing the plan to eliminate not only slums as narrowly defined by the District Court but also the blighted areas that tend to produce slums. Property may of course be taken for this redevelopment which, standing by itself, is innocuous and unoffending. But we have said enough to indicate that it is the need of the area as a whole which Congress and its agencies are evaluating. If owner after owner were permitted to resist these redevelopment programs on the ground that his particular property was not being used against the public interest, inte-grated plans for redevelopment would suffer greatly. The argument pressed on us is, indeed, a plea to substitute the landowner's standard of the public need for the standard prescribed by Congress. But as we have already stated, community redevelopment programs need not, by force of the Constitution, be on a piecemeal basis—lot by lot, building by building.

It is not for the courts to oversee the choice of the boundary line nor to sit in review on the size of a particular project area. Once the question of the public purpose has been decided, the amount and character of land to be taken for the project and the need for a particular tract to complete the integrated plan rests in the discretion of the legislative branch. See *Shoemaker* v. *United States*, 147 U. S. 282, 298; *United States ex rel. T. V. A.* v. *Welch, supra*, 554; *United States* v. *Carmack*, 329 U. S. 230, 247.

The District Court indicated grave doubts concerning the Agency's right to take full title to the land as distinguished from the objectionable buildings located on it. 117 F. Supp. 705, 715-719. We do not share those doubts. If the Agency considers it necessary in carrying out the redevelopment project to take full title to the real property involved, it may do so. It is not for the courts to determine whether it is necessary for successful consummation of the project that unsafe, unsightly, or insanitary buildings alone be taken or whether title to the land be included, any more than it is the function of the courts to sort and choose among the various parcels selected for condemnation.

The rights of these property owners are satisfied when they receive that just compensation which the Fifth Amendment exacts as the price of the taking.

The judgment of the District Court, as modified by this opinion, is

Affirmed.

Questions and Notes

1. Did Mr. Justice Douglas regard the power of eminent domain as one of the three separate powers of government (as in the *Muller* case above), or as merely the handmaiden of the police power?

2. Why do you suppose that Douglas handled it this way?

3. The famous passage on aesthetics is a fairly typical example of moralistic rhetoric, of the type that sometimes appears in Douglas' opinions.

4. Does the use of eminent domain for aesthetic purposes present the same legal question as the use of police power for aesthetic regulation?

5. Note how Douglas passes off the question of taking A's land and selling it to B—taking the conservative role, as the defender of private enterprise.

SCHENCK

v.

PITTSBURGH

364 Pa. 31, 70 A. 2d 612 (1950).

Supreme Court of Pennsylvania.

Jan. 11, 1950.

Rehearing Denied Jan. 30, 1950.

Albert W. Schenck filed bill in equity in the Supreme Court against City of Pittsburgh and others, for injunction against the carrying out, under the Urban Redevelopment Law of a project for redevelopment of a tract of land in defendant city, wherein others were permitted to intervene as plaintiffs.

The Supreme Court, Horace Stern, J., dismissed the bill on ground that no feature of the redevelopment project, the proceedings taken to effectuate it, or of contract by which it was to be accomplished, was violative of the Constitution or the Urban Redevelopment Law.

Robert Van der Voort, Pittsburgh, for plaintiff.

Anne X. Alpern, Pittsburgh, Theodore L. Hazlett, Jr., Pittsburgh, Robert J. Dodds, Pittsburgh, Charles E. Kenworthey, Pittsburgh, Ralph H. Demmler, Pittsburgh, Reed, Smith, Shaw & McClay, Pittsburgh, for defendants.

Before MAXEY, C. J., and DREW, LINN, STERN, PATTERSON, STEARNE and JONES, JJ.

HORACE STERN, Justice.

Because of the great importance to the City of Pittsburgh of the redevelopment project which is here under attack, and because of circumstances that require a prompt adjudication of the issue now raised as to its legality, we took original jurisdiction of these proceedings.

Plaintiff is the part owner of a property at 420-422 Penn Avenue, Pittsburgh; the intervening plaintiffs own, respectively, properties at 416-418 Penn Avenue, 427 Liberty Avenue, and 429 Liberty Avenue. Plaintiff filed the present bill of equity for an injunction against the carrying out, under the Urban Redevelopment Law of May 24, 1945, P.L. 991, 35 P.S. 1701 et seq., of a project for the redevelopment of a tract of land on which these properties are situated,—a tract which, constituting the original site of the City of Pittsburgh, is now covered almost exclusively by buildings devoted to commercial and industrial uses. The City Planning Commission certified approximately 59 acres which lie immediately to the east of the Point in Pittsburgh's "Golden Triangle" as a "blighted" area, and prepared a plan for its redevelopment. The Commonwealth of Pennsylvania had already acquired the westernmost 36 acres of this tract for the purpose of creating there a public park. The Urban Redevelopment Authority of Pittsburgh drafted a proposal for the redevelopment of the remaining 23 acres extending from Duquesne Way to Water Street and bounded on the east by Stanwix Street and Ferry Street; included therein was a proposed redevelopment contract with the Equitable Life Assurance Society of the United States as Redeveloper. The Authority's proposal, after being reviewed and approved by the City Planning Commission, was submitted to the City Council, which held a hearing thereon as prescribed by the Urban Redevelopment Law. Meanwhile plaintiff filed his bill to enjoin the City Council from approving the proposal and the contract, to enjoin the City from appropriating any money to carry out the proposal, to enjoin the Authority and the Redeveloper from executing the contract, and to enjoin the Authority from taking any steps to acquire land within the project area by the exercise of the power of eminent domain or to convey any such land to the Redeveloper.

The proposed contract provides that the Authority shall promptly acquire title to all the property (with a few exceptions) situated in the area; that the Redeveloper shall pay to the Authority all sums necessary for the acquisition of the title to such property, advancing to it from time to time and at its request the sums currently needed by the Authority for that purpose; that, after acquiring title to each of the parcels laid out on the plan, the Authority shall convey the same or any part thereof to the Redeveloper; that, upon the Redeveloper's acquiring such title, it shall clear the parcel of all existing structures thereon (other than the named exceptions), shall erect three modern office buildings not less than 18 stories in height, do appropriate landscaping, make provision for parking spaces, construct garage facilities, rehabilitate the buildings which are to remain standing, and plant certain designated portions of the area in grass; that the Authority shall secure the vacation of all streets in the project area, the relocation of a certain portion of Liberty Avenue, and the removal and reconstruction of sewer and water mains; that the redevelopment shall be completed within four years from the time of the acquisition of title by the Redeveloper; that the Redeveloper shall not have the power, without the consent of the Authority, to sell or lease any of the property until the Authority shall have certified that the redevelopment project has been completed; that any party acquiring or succeeding to the title and interest of the Redeveloper in any of the area shall be bound by the terms and covenants of the contract; that the Redeveloper shall not use or lease any of the property for other than the uses and buildings permitted by the plan during a period of 25 years from the date of the contract without the prior consent of the Authority; and that the Redeveloper shall secure housing for families residing in the project area who are displaced by the redevelopment operations. The contract is made terminable by the Redeveloper if a prescribed agreement with respect to sewers and streets is not made between the Authority and the City within 30 days after the execution of the redevelopment contract, or if the Authority shall have failed by June 1, 1950 to acquire title to all the property within the portion of the area on which the three office buildings are to be erected; in the event of such termination, however, the Redeveloper is to purchase all the property acquired by the Authority, paying to the latter the costs and expenses incurred in such acquisition. There are many other provisions contained in the contract, which, however, are not important in connection with the present discussion.

[1-3] Plaintiff asserts that the mere fact that the City Planning Commission has certified the tract as a blighted area does not conclusively establish that the redevelopment of this particular land is in fact for a public purpose. The answer to this contention is that, in the absence of any indication that the Commission did not act in good faith or was wholly arbitrary in certifying the area designated by it as blighted, its certification to that effect is not subject to judicial review. Among the conditions enumerated in the Urban Redevelopment Law as constituting a "blighted" area are "inadequate planning of the area," "excessive land coverage by the buildings thereon," "defective design and arrangement of the buildings thereon," "faulty street or lot layout," and "economically or socially undesirable land uses." Such conditions were found by the City Planning Commission to exist; it pointed out that the area certified by it had been laid out on a street pattern which dated from the year 1784 and which was wholly unsuited to the needs of a modern city because of poorly located street space and failure to provide for the ever increasing traffic; that the area was marred by too great a building density; and that the commercial and industrial uses of the buildings thereon were in large part economically undesirable, as shown by a continuous reduction in the appraised values of the properties for tax purposes. The existence of these conditions brings the situation clearly within the scope of the Urban Redevelopment Law, and, since the act gives the power of eminent domain to the Urban Redevelopment Authority, it is for that agency, and not for the courts, to determine whether or not the power should be exercised in this particular instance. It has been held in many cases that where the right of eminent domain is vested in a municipality, an administrative body, or even a private corporation, the question as to whether the circumstances justify the exercise of the power in a given instance is not a judicial one, at least in the absence of fraud or palpable bad faith.[1]

[4-6] Plaintiff contends that the commercial redevelopment of an existing commercial district, as in the present case, is not such a public purpose as the Urban Redevelopment Law envisages. He insists that redevelopment under the act must be aimed primarily to the relieving of undesirable

---

1. City of Philadelphia v. Ward, 174 Pa. 45, 34 A. 458; Price v. Pennsylvania R. Co., 209 Pa. 81, 58 A. 137; Wilson v. Pittsburgh & Lake Erie R. Co., 222 Pa. 541, 72 A. 235; Scranton Gas & Water Co. v. Delaware, Lackawanna & Western R. Co., 225 Pa. 152, 73 A. 1097; Sipe v. Tarentum Borough, 263 Pa. 838, 106 A. 637; Jury v. Wiest, 826 Pa. 554, 193 A. 6; King v. Union R. Co., 350 Pa. 623, 39 A.2d 831.

living conditions, and that any land which is not residential may be redeveloped only so far as the operation is ancillary and incidental to the redevelopment of a residential area; for support of this position he points to a cause in the title of the act which states as a purpose: to "supply sanitary housing in areas throughout the Commonwealth;" accordingly he argues that the erection of residential structures on the redevelopment area is a necessary concomitant of any project under the Urban Redevelopment Law. In Belovsky v. Redevelopment Authority of City of Philadelphia, 357 Pa. 329, 338, 54 A.2d 277, 281, 72 A.L.R. 953, it was said that "The Urban Redevelopment Law closely parallels the provisions of the 'Housing Authorities Law' of May 28, 1937, P.L. 955, 35 P.S. § 1541 et seq., * * *. The fundamental purpose of both these acts was the same, namely, the clearance of slum areas, although the Housing Authorities Law aimed more particularly at the elimination of undesirable dwelling houses *whereas the Urban Redevelopment Law is not so restricted.*" If the Urban Redevelopment Law were to be held to apply only to the clearing of blighted *residential* areas and the reconstruction of dwelling houses thereon there would have been no reason for its enactment since it would have added nothing to the Housing Authorities Law, 35 P.S. § 1541 et seq., already in force. On the contrary, the Urban Redevelopment Law was obviously intended to give wide scope to municipalities in designing and rebuilding such areas within their limits as, by reason of the passage of years and the enormous changes in traffic conditions and types of building construction, no longer meet the economic and zonal needs of modern city life and progress. Such needs exist, even if from a different angle, as well in the case of industrial and commercial as of residential areas. It is to be noted that the Urban Redevelopment Law defines the term "redevelopment," as used in the act, as "The acquisition, replanning, clearance, rehabilitation or rebuilding of an area for residential, recreational, *commercial, industrial* or other purposes, including the provision of streets, parks, recreational areas and other open spaces." 35 P.S. § 703(m).

[7, 8] Plaintiff urges that the proposed contract between the Authority and the Redeveloper is faulty in that its provisions do not absolutely insure the carrying out of the project, and he conjures up possible situations and contingencies of which the Redeveloper might take advantage and thereby relieve itself of the performance of its obligations. It is for the Authority and the Redeveloper, however, to decide upon the terms of their contract and for the City Council to approve or reject it, and if it contains the provisions stipulated in the Urban Redevelopment Law, as here it does, it is not for the courts to pass upon the merits of suggestions as to how the contract might be strengthened by amendments the desirability and effectiveness of which are for the consideration solely of the agencies and governing body to which the Urban Redevelopment Law has committed that responsibility. Plaintiff objects to the fact that by the terms of the proposed contract the title to property acquired by the Authority is to be con-

veyed to the Redeveloper instead of being retained until the redevelopment is actually completed. It would seem clear, however, that either the title must be transferred to the Redeveloper pending the process of redevelopment, with the Authority relying meanwhile upon the Redeveloper's covenants for the performance of its obligations under the contract, or the title must remain during that interim in the Authority, with the Redeveloper relying meanwhile upon the obligation of the Authority to convey the title after the redevelopment shall have been performed; whether the one or the other of these alternatives should be adopted is a practical, administrative matter for the contracting parties, and for them alone, to determine.

Our conclusion is that there is no feature of this redevelopment project, of the proceedings taken to effectuate it, or of the contract by which it is to be accomplished, that is violative of the Constitution or the Urban Redevelopment Law, and that therefore plaintiff and intervening plaintiffs are not entitled to the injunction which they seek.

The bill is dismissed at plaintiffs' costs.

Questions and Notes

1. Note the trend here toward nonresidential redevelopment at the state level.

2. The project involved here was the well known Golden Triangle project: an industrial slum located near the original site of Pittsburgh, where the Allegheny and Monongahela rivers join to form the Ohio, was cleared and turned into a park (much of which is now a highway interchange), together with new office buildings and hotels at the edge of the city's central business district.

DENIHAN ENTERPRISES

v.

O'DWYER

197 N.Y. Misc. 950, 97 N.Y.S. 2d 326 (1950), revd. 277 App. Div. 407, 100 N.Y.S. 2d 512 (appellate opinion) affd, 302 N.Y. 451, 99 N.E. 2d 235 (1951).
Supreme Court, Special Term, New York County, Part III.
April 27, 1950.

Denihan Enterprises, Inc., brought a taxpayer's action pursuant to section 51 of the General Municipal Law against William O'Dwyer, as Mayor of the City of New York; and others, to restrain the City of New York from performance of provisions of contract made with the New York Life Insurance Company for lease of lands acquired by the City of New York for purpose of erecting parking garages or areas. The Special Term, Hammer, J., held that the statute authorizing municipality to take private owned land for public parking and garage areas with resulting alleviation of traffic problems is valid as providing for a taking for a public use.

Complaint dismissed.

Raymond J. McGrover, Brooklyn, for plaintiff.

John P. McGrath, Corporation Counsel, New York City (Harry E. O'Donnell, Assistant Corporation Counsel, New York City, of counsel), for defendants.

HAMMER, Justice.

This is a taxpayer's action instituted pursuant to section 51 of the General Municipal Law.

Injunctive relief is sought restraining the City from performance of the provisions of a contract made with the New York Life Insurance Company dated February 16, 1950. In this agreement the insurance company, which is not a party to this action, is referred to as Nylic. For convenience, it will be at times similarly referred to herein.

The agreement in question provides that the City will acquire certain real property for street opening purposes and "to effectuate the purposes of Chapter 453 of the Laws of 1949" § 72-j of the General Municipal Law. The latter statute permits the acquisition of lands by a municipality for the purpose of erecting parking garages or areas to be operated by said municipalities or for sale or lease to private individuals or corporations for such purposes.

Under the agreement Nylic undertakes to bid on certain expressed terms, for a fifty-year lease if the condemned realty is offered at public auction by the City. The provisions of the lease are also agreed upon.

The real property in question is located in the easterly portion of the block bounded by East 64th and East 65th Streets and by Third and Second Avenues in the City and County of New York. Nylic has acquired the entire block immediately to the north and is erecting thereon a large apartment house.

The pertinent parts of the agreement and lease are these:

The lessee will erect a garage capable of storing 750 to 1,000 cars and may provide for stores and other commercial facilities on the Second Avenue front to a depth not in excess of 130 feet running west from Second Avenue.

The cost of condemnation and taxes on the condemned property from the date of condemnation to the closing date of the lease is payable as initial rent in two installments, one before the lease closing and the other, on demand, after the closing. In addition an annual rent of approximately $25,000 is to be paid.

All residential tenants are to be relocated at the lessee's expense.

There is a provision in respect of the zoning or rezoning of the area for garage purposes.

The entire roof of the structure, which will not be more than two stories high, will be landscaped as provided. The southern portion, or "approximately 50%" is to be improved as a public "sitting" park and is to be maintained by the City through its Park Department. The northerly portion of the landscaped area is to be maintained by the proposed lessee, Nylic. The use to which this latter portion will be put does not appear to be stated.

The lessee is obligated to repave East 65th Street between Second and Third Avenues and to install a mall.

The lessee does not have the privilege of assigning, mortgaging or pledging the lease.

The allocation of space between car owners who seek weekly or monthly storage as distinguished from transients is left to the lessee who shall, in determining this allocation, give consideration to the recommendation of the Traffic Commission contained in its report of May 23, 1949 which states "This garage will fill a need for storage space for the automobiles owned by the residents of the area and will afford a limited amount of space for transient parking during the day."

A provision is stated for fixing the rate to be charged those using the garage.

Plaintiff, a taxpayer, and an owner of some of the real property to be condemned seeks the injunctive relief urging (1) that Chapter 453 of the Laws of 1949 is unconstitutional; (2) that the property to be taken is not being taken for a public use; (3) that defendants have exceeded their authority in making the agreement.

The City moves to dismiss the complaint for legal insufficiency contending (a) that the acquisition of the land in question is in the public interest and (b) that it is not a valid objection that the project to be erected on the land acquired may result in an incidental private benefit if a public purpose is served.

Many of the legal questions which arise in considering the issues pointed upon these motions were discussed at length in Bronx Chamber of Commerce Inc. v. Fullen, 174 Misc. 524, 21 N.Y.S.2d 474, Hammer, J. There, the right of the City in the exercise of the power of eminent domain to acquire for demolition the elevated structures in Second and Ninth Avenues was challenged.

The recurring features of eminent domain referred to herein were fully considered there. Here we are concerned with a statute and a use which is therein "declared to be a public purpose." The statute in the Bronx Chamber of Commerce case did not contain such language but the implication of public use was drawn therefrom. At that time and prior thereto acquisition of land for garage purposes might not have been regarded as a public use. Whether or not it must be so regarded under the statute here requires further particularization.

The primary issue is the constitutionality of section 72-j of the General Municipal Law, Chap. 453 of the Laws of 1949. The test to be applied in determining the constitutionality of this law is whether or not acquisitions of land under said statute are taken for public purposes.

In adopting the enabling legislation previously referred to the Legislature provided: "It is hereby declared that there exists within municipalities in the state an acute shortage of parking and garage facilities as a result of which there is a serious condition of traffic congestion which constitutes a threat to the health, welfare and safety of the people of such municipalities; that such traffic congestion can be substantially relieved by providing adequate parking and garage facilities; that adequate parking and garage facilities and the relief of such traffic congestion will be facilitated by the provisions of this act and that the desirability in the public interest for the provisions hereinafter provided in this act is hereby declared as a matter of legislative determination. It is further declared that adequate provision of public parking and garage facilities is necessary and desirable to promote and aid in the clearance, replanning, reconstruction and rehabilitation of substandard and insanitary areas in such municipalities. The providing of public parking and garage facilities in the manner hereinafter set forth is hereby declared to be a public purpose." Section 1.

The pertinent parts of the statute itself, i. e., subdivisions 3 and 4 thereof are, as a matter of clarity in our consideration, set forth at length:

"3. Any municipal corporation, acting through its board of estimate or other governing body, may, in addition to exercising the powers granted to it by subdivision two hereof, sell, lease for a term not exceeding ninety-nine years, or otherwise dispose of any real property or any interest therein owned by it or acquired by it pursuant to this section, to any person, firm, or corporation at the highest marketable price or rental at public auction or by sealed bids pursuant to the provisions of any general, special or local law applicable to the sale, lease, or disposition of real property by such municipal corporation, for the purpose of the construction or establishment on such real property of public parking garages or public parking spaces for the relief of traffic congestion and for the maintenance and operation thereof. Any deed, lease, or instrument by which real property or any interest therein is conveyed or disposed of shall contain provisions requiring the purchaser, grantee, or lessee to construct or establish on such real property one or more public parking garages or public parking spaces and to maintain and operate the same for such period as may be prescribed by the board of estimate or other governing body, provisions fixing or providing for the approval by the board of estimate or other analogous body of rates to be charged for the use of such facilities by the operators thereof, and may also contain provisions authorizing the use of such portion of the property for other commercial purposes as may be necessary to provide revenue adequate to permit the operation of the principal portion of the property for public parking garages and public parking space. Such deed or instrument may contain such other provisions conditions and restrictions, including specifications relating to construction, and the rentals at which such property may be leased or subleased by the grantee or lessee as the board of estimate or other governing body may prescribe. The prior consent of the city planing commission or other analogous body of such municipal corporation shall be required for the acquisition by such municipal corporation of property for the purposes of this subdivision, which prior consent shall be based upon a finding by such city planning commission or other analogous body of the desirability thereof and after public hearings thereon.

"4. As used in this section, a public garage shall mean any building or facility where motor vehicles are parked, stored, serviced or repaired, and whose space and facilities are available to the public, with or without fee or charge, without regard to the residence, business or employment of the motor vehicle owner or operator seeking such space or facilities."

[1] The legislature has therefore held that an emergency exists in large cities with reference to parking and garage spaces. The legislative pronouncement conclusively establishes the necessity. While in respect of the question of public use such determinations are not binding on the courts, Pocantico Water-Works Co. v. Bird, 130 N.Y. 249, 29 N.E. 246, they are entitled "to great respect, since they relate to public conditions concerning which the Legislature both by necessity and duty must have known." New York City Housing Authority v. Muller, 270 N.Y. 333, 339, 1 N.E.2d 153, 154, 105 A.L.R. 905 and cases there cited.

[2] Passing to the question of whether or not the acquisition of land for parking and garaging of cars is a public use, consideration must, therefore, be given to the expression of legislative intent expressed in adopting section 72-j of General Municipal Law and, on the same reasoning although to a lesser degree, to the enactments of the local legislature and the reports of municipal commissions, offices and of public groups interested in the parking problem in this great city. These are before the court by stipulation. Even in the absence of such data, however, it is perfectly clear to anyone who traverses our streets whether he be pedestrian or operator of an automobile, regardless of its type, that there is a shortage of parking and garage space. This has come about for many reasons. The more obvious only will be indicated. City streets were not laid out in the contemplation that they would be intensively used by fast moving, easily manoeuvreable automotive vehicles which, in many instances are quite as large as railroad freight cars; zoning regulations, desirable as they are for orderly urban development, tend to keep parking areas and garages at considerable distance from desirable residential and business sections and the relocation of residential areas on the tremendous scale which has resulted from public and private housing projects such as Lillian Wald Houses, Parkchester and Stuyvesant Town, etc. has brought about parking and garaging problems beyond the existing capacity of these facilities in the areas in which these housing improvements have been located. The result has been the cluttering with parked cars of practically every available street in the business and residential areas of the city. Nor does the condition much improve at night, as previously it did when garage space was obtainable, although it may shift somewhat at home-going time, when residential areas are over-burdened. In such a situation does the taking

of privately owned land for public parking and garage areas with the resulting alleviation of the traffic problems constitute a taking for a public use? The answer lies in the definition of a public use. Crouch, J., in New York City Housing Authority v. Muller, supra, has said, "Over many years and in a multitude of cases the courts have vainly attempted to define comprehensively the concept of a public use and to formulate a universal test. They have found here as elsewhere that to formulate anything ultimate, even though it were possible, would, in an inevitably changing world, be unwise if not futile." Previously Cardozo, then Chief Judge of our Court of Appeals, in a similar vein observed: "A city acts for city purposes when it builds a dock or a bridge or a street or a subway ° ° °. Its purpose is not different when it builds an airport ° ° °." Hesse v. Rath, 249 N.Y. 436, 164 N.E. 342. The taking of private land for public housing has been approved as a public use, New York City Housing Authority v. Muller, supra, and such taking approved when the new housing was erected by private corporations. Murray v. La Guardia, 291 N.Y. 320, 52 N.E.2d 884. In this state the levy of a local improvement assessment in connection with land condemned for a public parking space has received judicial approval. Ambassador Management Corp. v. Incorporated Village of Hempstead, 186 Misc. 74, 58 N.Y.S.2d 880, affirmed 270 App.Div. 898, 62 N.Y.S.2d 165, appeal dismissed 296 N.Y. 666, 69 N.E.2d 819, certiorari denied 330 U.S. 835, 67 S.Ct. 971, 91 L.Ed. 1282. In Pennsylvania an act creating a Public Parking Authority, with a right of eminent domain, was held to be constitutional. McSorley v. Fitzgerald, 359 Pa. 264, 59 A.2d 142. Similar results have been reached in other states. Parr v. Ladd, 323 Mich. 592, 36 N.W.2d 157; Cleveland v. City of Detroit, 324 Mich. 527, 529, 37 N.W.2d 625; Miller v. City of Georgetown, 301 Ky. 241, 191 S.W.2d 403. Public highways, bridges, railroad rights of way, improvements of such rights of way, railway and other terminal facilities, elevated railroads, telegraph and telephone lines, water supply, drainage and irrigation projects, canals, piers, sewers, sewage disposal plants, levees, public markets, public buildings, slum clearance and apartment house developments and public cemeteries, have all, at various times and in various jurisdictions, been held public uses.

There is no means of transportation which serves the public more extensively than does the motor vehicle. The necessity for garaging is unquestionable. Obtaining garages through private enterprise in the present or approximately near future obviously may not be reasonably expected. The demand for parking and storage being so great, failure of garage building by private capital may be attributed only to the unprofitableness and consequent impracticability of such adventure. Public necessity requires that the multiplicity of parked cars be removed from the city streets where they are a menacing condition bringing about traffic congestion and a threat to the health, welfare and safety of the public. This can only be done by supplying parking and storage garages. Private enterprise is unwilling and unattracted and in any event has failed to supply the demand. It follows that there is only one available remedy to alleviate the condition which has caused the public necessity. That is for the public to undertake the obligation of supplying the necessary garages. This brings the fulfillment of such an obligation within the concept of a public use. What is to be done when completed, will enhance the public good.

The increasing "need for vision of the future in the governance of cities", Hesse v. Rath, supra, appears to require the holding that private land may be acquired for public storage and parking garages. That such a holding could not have been reasonably adjudicated in even the quite recent past is probably true, but that was also equally true when land was first taken by eminent domain for many of the public purposes previously adverted to, but such is the wisdom and benefit that has come to pass from unwillingness or inability of the courts to finally define a public use.

[3] It having been determined that the statute in consideration has in contemplation acquisition of land for public use, it follows that there can be no doubt of constitutionality.

[4, 5] The next question is the propriety of the taking considered in the light of the agreement between the City and Nylic to which there has been previous reference. Preliminarily it is noted that the statute permits the sale and leasing of the acquired land to private individuals or corporations for garage and parking purposes. The land to be acquired for the purpose provided for in the statute is to be acquired by the City in its trust and not its proprietary capacity. It may not, therefore, be used for any other use without specific legislation provision. American Dock Co. v. City of New York, 174 Misc. 813, 824, 21 N.Y.S.2d 943, 956, affirmed 261 App.Div. 1063, 26 N.Y.S.2d 704, Id., 286 N.Y. 658, 36 N.E.2d 696; People ex rel. Swan v. Doxsee, 136 App.Div. 400, 120 N.Y.S. 962, affirmed 198 N.Y. 605, 92 N.E. 1098; Merriwether v. Garrett, 102 U.S. 472, 26 L.Ed. 197. Such legislative provision is present in the statute under consideration and was similarly present in the legislative enactments under consideration in Murray v. La Guardia, supra, where it was held "Nor do we find merit in the related argument that unconstitutionality results from the fact that in the present case the statute permits the city to exercise the power of eminent domain to accomplish a project from which Metropolitan—a private corporation—may ultimately reap a profit. If, upon completion of the project the public good is enhanced it does not matter that private interests may be benefited. Board of Hudson River Regulating District v. Fonda, J. & G. R. Co., 249 N.Y. 445, 453, 164 N.E. 541". [291 N.Y. 320, 52 N.E.2d 888.] The authority of defendants to make an agreement such as that before the court is therefore absolute.

Some question has been raised as to the degree of alleviation which will result from the improvement. So long as it appears that the existing condition will be alleviated, it must be held that a public purpose is being served.

[6] Nor does the fact that the specifications contained in the agreement limit prospective bidders to corporations or individuals with large resources present grounds for enjoining the performance of the contract. From the very nature of the improvement it is desirable from the City's point of view that the lessee have ample means not only to erect but to maintain such an improvement.

With reference to the park on the roof of the structure it is noted that the southern half is to be a public "sitting" park maintained by the City and that the northern half is to be maintained by Nylic. No provision is made for the use of this portion of the property by Nylic exclusively and it must be assumed that none is in contemplation since a taking for such use would not be one for the public benefit. It may well be that any possible objection in this respect is to be remedied by further agreement.

The objections with reference to the commercial space provisions are of no avail. Such use is distinctly provided for in the statute for the purpose of establishing reasonable rates for the garage use. The right to fix these rates within the limitation of what appears to be a fair return to the lessee is retained by the City. In computing these rates the return from the commercial space must be considered as part of the fair return to the lessee.

[7] Lastly, reference is made to subdivision 4 of section 72-j of the General Municipal Law. The term there defined is "public garage". The term elsewhere used in the section is "public parking garage". The definition however is sufficiently broad to include not only the term "public garage" but also "public parking garage." It must therefore be held that both storage and parking garages were in the contemplation of the legislature and the agreement quite clearly has in contemplation both uses, quite naturally, from a business point of view, giving broad latitude to the lessee with reference to the allocation of each use.

The conclusion is that the statute is constitutional, that the use for which the land is being acquired is public and that the agreement is in no way at variance with the statute.

It follows that the complaint must be dismissed and the injunctive relief requested, denied. The motions are so determined.

DENIHAN ENTERPRISES

v.

O'DWYER

Supreme Court, Appellate Division, First Department.

Nov. 14, 1950.

Action by the Denihan Enterprises, Inc., against William O'Dwyer, as Mayor of the City of New York, and others, as constituti 1g the Board of Estimate of the City of New York, and the City of New York, to restrain city from performing provisions of a contract made with the New York Life Insurance Company for lease of land acquired by the city for purpose of erecting parking garages. The Special Term, Hammer, J., 197 Misc. 950, 97 N.Y.S.2d 326, entered an order granting defendants' motion to dismiss amended complaint and entered a judgment on said order and entered an order denying plaintiff's motion for an injunction and plaintiff appealed. The Supreme Court, Appellate Division, Per Curiam, held that the complaint stated a cause of action so as to test legality of contract between city and insurance company relating to condemnation of realty in question.

Order in accordance with opinion.

* * *

The fact that a private interest may be benefitted by a condemnation project does not render it illegal where the public good is enhanced.

Raymond J. McGrover, Brooklyn, for plaintiff-appellant.

Reuben Levy, New York City, of counsel (Harry E. O'Donnell, Bernard H. Friedman and Janet H. Lewin, all of New York City, on the brief; John P. McGrath, Corporation Counsel, New York City), for respondents.

Harry H. Chambers, New York City, of counsel (Chambers & Chambers, New York City, attorneys) for Abraham B. Cox et al. appearing as amici curiae.

Francis X Conlon, New York City (Sidney O. Raphael, New York City, on the brief; Raphael & Conlon, New York City, attorneys) for Shamrock Cleaners, Inc. appearing as amicus curiae.

Before PECK, P. J., and GLENNON, CALLAHAN, VAN VOORHIS, and SHIENTAG, JJ.

PER CURIAM.

This matter comes before us on the sufficiency of the complaint and the issue is the legality of a contract between the City of New York and the New York Life Insurance Company relating to the condemnation of real property between 64th and 65th Streets and Second and Third Avenues in the Borough of Manhattan. The proposed condemnation would be under General Municipal Law, § 72-j, which allows a municipal corporation to acquire by condemnation real property for the construction or operation of parking garages or parking spaces for the relief of traffic congestion, and permits the leasing of the property for the purpose to any person, firm or corporation at the highest marketable price or rental at public auction. Subdivision 3 of Section 72-j provides that any such lease shall contain provisions requiring the lessee to construct or establish on such real property public parking garages or public parking spaces as may be prescribed by the Board of Estimate or other governing body of the municipality, provisions for approval by the Board of Estimate or other analogous body of the rates to be charged for the use of such parking facilities, and may also contain provisions authorizing the use of such portion of the property for other commercial purposes as may be necessary to provide revenue adequate to permit the operation of the principal portion of the property for public parking garages and public parking space.

The City of New York has entered into a contract with the New York Life Insurance Company, which has under construction a large apartment house on the block between 65th and 66th Streets and Second and Third Avenues, providing that the City will condemn the property in question in this action and offer it for lease at public auction on terms specified in the contract and that the Insurance Company will bid for said lease for a term of 50 years an amount equal to the total condemnation costs plus annual rent of $25,000 a year and, if it is the successful bidder, will construct a garage in accordance with the specifications of the contract and proposed lease attached.

Plaintiff, a taxpayer and owner of a parcel of the land to be condemned, challenges the legality of the proposed condemnation and contract on various grounds, all adding up, as plaintiff contends, to a showing that the condemnation and contract are not for the public purpose envisioned by the statute or any permissible public purpose but are for the benefit of the Insurance Company in enabling it to get the control and use of the block opposite its apartment building to serve the tenants and its interest as landlord and to provide an attractive outlook for the apartment house. Plaintiff contends that the specifications for the garage building to be erected and other work to be done are such that no one but the New York Life Insurance Company would be interested in the undertaking and that the specifications are rigged to meet the requirements and desires of the Insurance Company and to foreclose other bids. We will not discuss the various claims in detail because the matter comes before us on the complaint alone, and the propriety of several of the clauses of the contract may depend upon the evidence and showing at the trial. It is sufficient for present purposes to indicate some of the respects in which we think the complaint states a cause of action and at least raises triable issues.

For one thing the contract provides that the garage building shall be only two stories in height above the surface and the entire roof shall be covered with at least four feet of earth and shall be improved with lawn, shrubs, trees, walks and landscaped areas, the southerly half of which shall be developed as a public park. The northerly half of the roof opposite the apartment building is thus reserved as a private park for the pleasant vista of the tenants of the apartment house. No purpose identifiable with a public park or a public garage appears to be served by requiring that half of the roof to be reserved and landscaped.

The plaintiff places considerable emphasis upon the fact that the contract permits the lessee to rent 30% of the ground floor and first basement space for commercial purposes not connected with garaging or parking. This gives the lessee the private allocation and disposition of a substantial portion of the building. Something of the kind is contemplated by the statute, with a view to allowing the more profitable use of some of the space for non-garage purposes to produce an income that will permit lower rates for the garage space than would otherwise be possible. We do not question the legality of this concept or its proper application, but think that there may be a question of proper proportion in this case in view of the limited size of the structure and the proportion of the space which is reserved for non-garage and non-public purposes.

[1, 2] In these respects and in other respects there is a triable issue as to whether the proposed lease is designed to attract bidders or provide the public parking facilities that would be expected from the use of the property for that purpose, or whether it reflects a compromise and pooling of the interests of the City and the Insurance Company to provide only a modicum of public parking facilities and otherwise give the Insurance Company use and control of the property for the benefit of its apartment development. We understand that the fact that a private interest may be benefited by a condemnation project does not render it illegal where the public good is enhanced, Matter of Murray v. La Guardia, 291 N.Y. 320, 52 N.E.2d 884, but that is a relative matter and one of proper proportions and purposes. It is possible that a trial of the action may dissipate any doubts as to the legality of the arrangement, but it is also possible that a trial may reveal that the project on the whole is not authorized by sound condemnation principles and is so imbued with a private purpose and private use of the land to be condemned as to render the proposed condemnation and contract arrangements invalid.

The order granting defendants' motion to dismiss the amended complaint and the judgment entered thereon dismissing the complaint should be reversed and the motion denied and the order denying the plaintiff's motion for an injunction should be reversed and the plaintiff's motion granted with costs to the plaintiff.

Order granting defendants' motion to dismiss the amended complaint and the judgment entered thereon dismissing the complaint unanimously reversed and the motion denied; order denying plaintiff's motion for an injunction unanimously reversed and the plaintiff's motion granted with costs to the plaintiff. Settle order on notice.

SHIENTAG, J., concurs in result.

DENIHAN ENTERPRISES

v.

O'DWYER

Court of Appeals of New York.

May 24, 1951.

Denihan Enterprises, Inc., brought a taxpayer's action against William O'Dwyer, as Mayor of the City of New York, and others, constituting the Board of Estimate of the City of New York, and others, to restrain the City from performance of provision of a contract made with an insurance company for lease of certain lands. The Supreme Court, Special Term, New York County, Hammer, J., 197 Misc. 950, 97 N.Y.S. 2d 326, rendered judgment for defendants, and the plaintiff appealed. The Supreme Court, Appellate Division, First Judicial Department, in 277 App.Div. 407, 100 N.Y.S.2d 512, entered an order on December 13, 1950, which reversed judgment for defendants, reversed an order of the lower court denying a motion by plaintiff for an order enjoining the carrying out of the contract and staying all proceedings pending determination of the action, denied motion by defendants for dismissal of the complaint, and granted plaintiff's motion for a temporary injunction enjoining the carrying out of contract in question and restraining defendants from taking any action during pendency of the action, and defendants appealed by permission of the appellate division. The Court of Appeals, Froessel, J., held that plaintiff's complaint stated a cause of action.

Order affirmed.

Desmond, Conway, and Dye, JJ., dissented.

John P. McGrath, Corporation Counsel, New York City (Harry E. O'Donnell, Reuben Levy and Benjamin Offner, all of New York City, of counsel), for appellants.

Raymond J. McGrover, Brooklyn, for respondent.

Francis X. Conlon and Sidney O. Raphael, New York City, for Shamrock Cleaners, Inc., amicus curiae, in support of respondent's position.

Harry H. Chambers, New York City, for Abraham B. Cox and others, amici curiae, in support of respondent's position.

FROESSEL, Judge.

In this taxpayer's action brought under section 51 of the General Municipal Law, Consol.Laws, c. 24, plaintiff-respondent seeks to enjoin the

City of New York and its board of estimate from carrying out a contract made with the New York Life Insurance Company, hereinafter called the Company. Special Term dismissed the complaint for legal insufficiency. The Appellate Division unanimously reversed, denied the motion to dismiss, granted a temporary injunction, and certified to us the following question: "Was the order of Special Term, dated May 2, 1950, granting defendants' motion to dismiss the complaint, on which judgment was entered May 12, 1950, properly made?"

Under the contract challenged, the city agrees (1) to acquire by condemnation, pursuant to subdivision 3 of section 72-j of the General Municipal Law, L.1949, ch. 453, about two thirds of the block (the easterly portion) bounded by East 64th and East 65th Streets, Second and Third Avenues, Manhattan; (2) to offer the same at public auction; (3) for a term of fifty years; (4) upon certain terms and conditions hereinafter referred to; (5) subject to conditions providing for the construction of a public parking garage, and (6) for commercial facilities.

The Company agrees to bid for the lease, as proposed, which shall be subject to the following conditions:

(a) The successful bidder shall construct on said real property a public parking garage (title to which shall vest in the city) accommodating at least 750 cars;

(b) the structure may include stores and other commercial facilities on the ground and basement floor along Second Avenue to a depth of 130 feet;

(c) the structure may not exceed 2 stories in height (with cellar and subcellar);

(d) the roof must contain 4 feet of sod, grass and planting;

(e) the initial rent shall consist of the total awards, interest and expense of this condemnation as well as for a condemnation for widening East 65th Street 14 feet, plus taxes accruing between condemnation and the execution of the lease, $836,450 of which must be paid five days prior to such execution, and the balance five days after the amount thereof is certified by the city comptroller; in addition, there shall be paid an annual rental of at least $25,200;

(f) the successful bidder (lessee) shall remove all tenants (of which there are more than 100);

(g) the city agrees to rezone "for the purposes of the said lease" the area condemned;

(h) the south half of the landscaped roof shall be improved "as a public sitting park;"

(i) the lessee may determine the amount of space allotted for "storage or transient use," but "shall consider" the following recommendations of the traffic commission:

"This garage will fill a need for storage space for the automobiles owned by the residents of the area and will afford a limited amount of space for transient parking during the day."

(j) The garage rates to be charged to be approved by the city, but lessee may charge "after operating expenses a return" of 6% annually "on the original investment [very broadly defined] to cover interest, yield, depreciation, obsolescence and amortization;" and

(k) the lessee shall pave, landscape, and construct a mall and improve East 65th Street and relocate the facilities therein, all of which shall be deemed part of the "investment."

Plaintiff contends that the contract is illegal because (1) the use contemplated is not public but private; (2) it is not authorized by the statute, General Municipal Law, § 72-j, subd. 3 since that statute relates to "*parking* garages or public *parking* spaces," (italics supplied) and the contract here contemplates primarily a *storage* garage; (3) even if authorized and found in some respects to be public in nature, it is so subordinated to the private benefit of the Company that the end result is a private use; (4) the contemplated use would violate the zoning resolution of the city, and its *contractual* obligation to rezone is illegal; (5) the contract specifications are such as to discourage competitive bidding and will insure that the only bidder at the sale will be the Company, particularly since it alone will receive many very valuable benefits therefrom, thereby depriving the city of the opportunity to obtain the highest marketable rental as required by the statute and the New York City Charter, and (6) the provision for a fifty-year lease is in violation of subdivision b of section 384 of the charter.

[1-4] It is well settled that whether or not a proposed condemnation is for a public purpose is a judicial question, Matter of Deansville Cemetery Ass'n, 66 N.Y. 569; Matter of Niagara Falls & Whirlpool Ry. Co., 108 N.Y. 375, 15 N.E. 429; Pocantico Water Works Co. v. Bird, 130 N.Y. 249, 29 N.E. 246; but legislative findings in this respect are entitled to great weight, Murray v. La Guardia, 291 N.Y. 320, 52 N.E.2d 884; New York City Housing Authority v. Muller, 270 N.Y. 333, 1 N.E.2d 153, 105 A.L.R. 905. Judicial examination is less critical, however, where the State itself is to be vested with the property, Long Sault Development Co. v. Kennedy, 158 App.Div. 398, 143 N.Y.S. 454, affirmed 212 N.Y. 1, 105 N.E. 849, writ of error dismissed, Long Sault Development Co. v. Call, 242 U.S. 272, 37 S.Ct. 79, 61 L.Ed. 294. It is equally well settled that proceedings in eminent domain to acquire property for *street* or *park* purposes are constitutionally permissible as serving a public purpose. Matter of City of New York [Clinton Ave.], 57 App.Div. 186, 171, 68 N.Y.S. 196, 199, affirmed 167 N.Y. 624, 60 N.E. 1108; Brooklyn Park Com'rs v. Amstrong, 45 N.Y. 234, 239, 240; People v. Adirondack Ry. Co., 160 N.Y. 225, 247-248, 54 N.E. 689, 696, affirmed sub nom. Adirondack Ry. Co. v. People of State of New York, 176 U.S. 335, 20 S.Ct. 460, 44 L.Ed. 492. Nor do we question the legality of the concept that private property may be condemned for parking motor vehicles when the public is primarily served in the taking of such vehicles from our streets to relieve traffic congestion. But whether or not the use here contemplated, and the method in which it is exercised, is authorized, is another question.

[5] We are here and now solely concerned with the legal sufficiency of plaintiffs complaint. Giving the pleader the benefit of every favorable inference, and assuming the truth of the allegations of its complaint, as we must, Blanshard v. City of New York, 262 N.Y. 5, 12, 186 N.E. 29, 31; Abrams v. Allen, 297 N.Y. 52, 74 N.E.2d 305, 173 A.L.R. 671, notwithstanding the fact that its proof may well fall far short of establishing them as facts, we cannot say as a matter of pleading that no cause of action whatsoever is set forth, and thus no triable issues are presented.

[6-8] Without setting out the detailed allegations of plaintiff's complaint, sufficient facts are alleged purporting to show that the public use here may be only incidental and in large measure subordinate to the private benefit to be conferred on the Company, and not for the purposes authorized by the statute. Of course an incidental private benefit, such as a reasonable proportion of commercial space, is not enough to invalidate a project which has for its primary object a public purpose, Murray v. La Guardia, supra; New York City Housing Authority v. Muller supra; Bush Terminal Co. v. City of New York, 282 N.Y. 306, 26 N.E.2d 269; Matter of Mayor, Aldermen & Commonalty of City of New York, 135 N.Y. 253, 31 N.E. 1043, but the use is not public where the public benefit is only incidental to the private. Matter of Eureka Basin Warehouse & Mfg. Co., 96 N.Y. 42. Moreover, the validity of a statute upon one set of facts is immaterial if in its application to an other situation it results in invalidity Nashville, C. & St. L. Ry. v. Walters, 25 U.S. 405, 414, 415, 55 S.Ct. 486, 79 L.Ed. 949; Municipal Gas Co. of City of Albany v. Public Service Comm., 225 N.Y. 89, 95, 96, 121 N.E. 772, 773, 774.

[9] Among other things, plaintiff alleges in effect that after the Company —the only probable lessee—has provided storage space for all of its tenants, and made provision for the 308 now existing car spaces in the area to be condemned, the net result will be that only 17 additional spaces will be available for the general public. Plaintiff also alleges with some particularity that many of the specifications are of such character as to benefit the Company privately and exclusively, and neither the public nor other bidders would or could derive any substantial benefit therefrom, such, e. g., as the low height limitation (notwithstanding expensive subcellar construction) which does not help materially to relieve parking congestion but grants a valuable easement of light and air for at least fifty years for the benefit of the Company's apartment house across the street, renting for $60 to $75 per room; the landscaping of the roof for an elevated public park on the southerly half, and a strictly private park on the northerly half, for its tenants to view, rather than employing same for parking purposes claimed by appellants to be necessary; the construction of the center mall, necessitating the widening of one block of East 65th Street, only to create a bottleneck at each end, and the location of entrances and exits across the street from the entrance to the Company's apartment house; the onerous financial arrangements, included in an ultimate probable outlay of $4,000,000, with-

out right to mortgage; all of which, taken together, with other allegations of the complaint, plaintiff asserts, amount not only to a taking primarily for a private rather than a public use, but also result in discouraging competitive bidding and in unduly discriminating in favor of the Company, thus assuring it of continued high rentals from its apartments.

In the face of the averments in the complaint before us, it cannot be summarily determined as a matter of law that no cause of action is stated, and that plaintiff, a taxpayer and owner of a substantial portion of the property sought to be condemned, must yield its property to the governmental power of eminent domain without at least a trial of the issues raised by it. As we said in Weiskopf v. City of Saratoga Springs, 269 N.Y. 634, 635, 200 N.E. 33, "This is not a case to be decided on the pleadings. The constitutionality of the regulations must be decided after the facts are determined on the trial."

Inasmuch as this is the only question now before us, we do not pass on any other question discussed in the briefs, such as the city's right to "contract" in advance for rezoning, and its powers to lease for more than ten years, New York City Charter 1938, § 384, subd. b. Accordingly, the question certified should be answered in the negative, and the order of the Appellate Division should be affirmed, with costs.

DESMOND, Judge (dissenting).

I dissent and vote to reverse the order, with costs, answer the certified question in the affirmative and dismiss the complaint. Nothing could be accomplished by a trial of any of plaintiff's allegations, since none of them exhibit any justiciable issue. We all agree that the Legislature has settled the question of whether condemnation of land for a public garage, to be built by the city but leased to a private operator, is for a public purpose. General Municipal Law, § 72-j. The public nature of such a use would not be destroyed by a demonstration, on a trial of this action, that this proposed garage will largely benefit, and is principally desired by, the owner of the apartment house across the street for its tenants, or that all concerned expect that this lease will be bought at auction by that particular owner, or that the terms of the lease are such as to make it probable that the owner across the street will be the successful bidder therefor, or that the project may accomplish only a little alleviation of traffic conditions, or that, in the end, the apartment house tenants across the street, rather than the general public, will have principal use of the garage. All those are, on their face, arguments not against the legality, but as to the feasibility, or wisdom, or fairness, of the expenditure. Such arguments, when rejected by the appropriate legislative body, cannot be re-examined by the courts. Rindge v. County of Los Angeles, 262 U.S. 700, 705, 706, 707, 43 S.Ct. 689, 67 L.Ed. 1186; New York City Housing Authority v. Muller, 270 N.Y. 333, 342, 1 N.E.2d 153, 155, 105 A.L.R. 905; Murray v. La Guardia, 291 N.Y. 320, 329, 330, 52 N.E.2d 884, 887, 888; Weitzner v. Stichman, 271 App. Div. 255, 64 N.Y.S.2d 50, affirmed 296 N.Y. 907, 72 N.E.2d 625.

LOUGHRAN, C. J., and LEWIS and FULD, JJ., concur with FROES-SEL, J.

DESMOND, J., dissents in opinion in which CONWAY and DYE, JJ., concur.

Order affirmed, etc.

Questions and Notes

1. What was regarded as the important issue in the lower court opinion?

2. What was the proposed net gain in parking spaces available to the general public?

3. How high was the proposed building?

4. What was to be on top of the proposed building, and who could use the various parts of it?

5. How much of the block would be occupied by the proposed development?

6. The apartment house owned by New York Life on the next block to the north (Manhattan House) is one of the largest luxury apartment houses in Manhattan. What is the significance of the fact that the apartment house is on the block to the north? This was the real point in the whole proceeding—but not mentioned in the opinions.

KASKEL

v.

IMPELLITTERI

306 N.Y. 73 and 609, 115 N.E. 2d 659 and 832 (1953).

Court of Appeals of New York

Oct. 23, 1953.

Taxpayer brought action against city officials for a determination that city officials acted improperly in acquiring realty for slum clearance. The Supreme Court, Special Term, New York County, Part III, Eder, J., 121 N.Y.S.2d 848, entered judgment for city officials on an order granting motion for dismissal of complaint, and entered an order denying motion of taxpayer for injunction pendente lite, and taxpayer appealed. The Supreme Court, Appellate Division, First Department, 281 App.Div. 962, 120 N.Y.S.2d 758, on April 21, 1953, unanimously affirmed judgment of Special Term, and taxpayer appealed on constitutional grounds and by permission of the Appellate Division. The following question was certified: "Was Special Term correct in denying plaintiff's motion for an injunction pendente lite?" The

Court of Appeals, Desmond J., held that city officials did not act unreasonably, arbitrarily, or capriciously in determining that area was substandard and subject to slum clearance.

Judgment affirmed, and appeal from order affirming denial of injunction pendente lite dismissed.

Van Voorhis and Fuld, JJ., dissented in part.

Harold L. Herzstein, Cecil A. Citron and Irving E. Kanner, New York City, for appellant.

Denis M. Hurley, Corp. Counsel, New York City (William S. Lebwohl, Seymour B. Quel, Harry E. O'Donnell, Reuben Levy, and Benjamin Offner, New York City, of counsel), for respondents.

Samuel I. Rosenman, Max Freund, Andrew J. Schoen, New York City, and Harvey L. Schein, Brooklyn, for intervener-respondent.

DESMOND, Judge.

[1] The nature of this suit and its procedural history, as well as the constitutional and statutory provisions which authorize slum clearance and redevelopment by cities, are so carefully described in the dissenting opinion as to make repetition unnecessary. The position is this: plaintiff, as a taxpayer, disputes the conclusion of various qualified public bodies and officers that the area, in Manhattan, bounded by Columbus Circle, Broadway, Eighth Avenue, Ninth Avenue, West 58th and West 59th Street, is "substandard and insanitary." Plaintiff says it is not, and demands that the courts hold a trial to settle this allegedly justiciable issue of fact. But there is no dispute as to the physical facts. In rounded figures, 20% of the land proposed to be taken is occupied by dwellings all but one of which are more than sixty years old, 7% of the site is covered by hotels and rooming houses, 34% is in parking lots where once there were outmoded buildings, and 39% is occupied by nonresidential structures. Of course, none of the buildings are as noisome or dilapidated as those described in Dickens' novels or Thomas Burke's "Limehouse" stories of the London slums of other days, but there is ample in this record to justify the determination of the city planning commission that a substantial part of the area is "substandard and insanitary" by modern tests, and that the whole 6.32 acres, taken together, may reasonably be considered a single "area" for clearance and redevelopment purposes. Power to make that determination has been lodged by the Constitution, N.Y.Const. XVIII, § 1, and the statute, General Municipal Law, McK.Consol.Laws, c. 24, § 72-k, in the city planning commission and the board of estimate, and when those bodies have made their finding, not corruptly or irrationally or baselessly, there is nothing for the courts to do about it, unless every act and decision of other departments of government is subject to revision by the courts, see Matter of Cruger, 84 N.Y. 619, 622; Ziegler v. Chapin, 126 N.Y. 342, 348, 27 N.E. 471, 472.

[2-4] The opinion of Judge Van Voorhis disposes of all plaintiff's contentions, except that stated in clause (D) of paragraph Twenty-Four of the complaint, "That the project area is not a substandard and insanitary

area, and that any finding, consent or report by the defendants to the effect that such area is a substandard and insanitary area is unreasonable, arbitrary, capricious and illegal." That part of the complaint apparently attempts to state a taxpayer's action under section 51 of the General Municipal Law. However, since no corruption or fraud is charged, plaintiff Kaskel, as a taxpayer, cannnot succeed in such a suit, unless there is a total lack of power in defendants, under the law, to do the acts complained of, Kittinger v. Buffalo Traction Co., 160 N.Y. 377, 54 N.E. 1081; Altschul v. Ludwig, 216 N.Y. 459, 111 N.E. 216. The decisions under section 51 make it entirely clear that redress may be had only when the acts complained of are fraudulent, or a waste of public property in the sense that they represent a use of public property or funds for entirely illegal purposes. Although the plaintiff here complains of the choice of this site for clearing and redevelopment as being "arbitrary and capricious," we must keep in mind that this is not an "article 78" proceeding dealing with a situation wherein it might be claimed that public officials, although acting within their powers, are doing so in a way that is arbitrary or capricious. The substance of plaintiff's contention in this respect is simply that this whole project is illegal because, according to him, the chosen site or area is not in fact substandard or insanitary.

[5, 6] There is no real question of fact here since the details as to age, condition and present use of the properties involved are undisputed and indisputable, as shown by the exhibits. Plaintiff does not dispute with defendants as to the condition of these properties or of the whole area. He is simply opposing his opinion and his judgment to that of public officials, on a matter which must necessarily be one of opinion or judgment, that is, as to whether a specified area is so substandard or insanitary, or both, as to justify clearance and redevelopment under the law. It is not seriously contended by anyone that, for an area to be subject to those laws, every single building therein must be below civilized standards. The statute (and the Constitution), like other similar laws, contemplates that clearing and redevelopment will be of an entire area, not of a separate parcel, and, surely, such statutes would not be very useful if limited to areas where every single building is substandard. A glance at the photographs, attached to the city's affidavit on these motions, shows that a considerable number of buildings in this area are, on a mere external inspection, below modern standards because of their age, obsolescence and decay. The other exhibits confirm this. Therefore, the question here is not whether certain public officials have acted arbitrarily or unwisely in coming to a certain conclusion. Here we have a naked question of legality, that is, of power, and the particular power to make a determination on this matter of judgment has been conferred by statute on these defendants. Four different public bodies have, after adequate investigation and consideration which appears in the record, determined that this area may properly be considered sub-

standard and insanitary (five such bodies if we include the Triborough Authority, and seven if we include the Special Term and the Appellate Division). One can conceive of a hypothetical case where the physical conditions of an area might be such that it would be irrational and baseless to call it substandard or insanitary, in which case, probably, the conditions for the exercise of the power would not be present. However, the situation here actually displayed is one of those as to which the Legislature has authorized the city officials, including elected officials, to make a determination, and so the making thereof is simply an act of government, that is, an exercise of governmental power, legislative in fundamental character, which, whether wise or unwise, cannot be overhauled by the courts. If there were to be a trial here and the courts below should decide in favor of plaintiff, there would be effected a transfer of power from the appropriate public officials to the courts. The question is simply not a justiciable one.

A persuasive authority quite closely in point is Stockus v. Boston Housing Authority, 304 Mass. 507, see beginning, page 509, 24 N.E.2d 333, 336. There a complaint was held insufficient in law which, much like our pleading here, said that the buildings in a certain area were in fact in such physical condition that the area could not be dubbed "substandard." The Supreme Judicial Court of Massachusetts said: "The extent that these various elements enter into and form the predominating and distinctive traits of a neighborhood is frequently and largely a matter of opinion" and a matter of "practical judgment, common sense and sound discretion." The Supreme Judicial Court of Massachusetts pointed out that men of training and experience might honestly differ as to whether a certain district was a slum area, but that in such cases the Legislature had undoubtedly given the local authorities power to make the determination; 304 Mass. at page 510, 24 N.E.2d at page 336, of the opinion, the court pointed out that "The allegation that the dwellings in this area are in good repair and condition is not an allegation that the defendants may not reasonably adjudge otherwise." The court stated, as is obviously correct, that the test is as to the area as a unit, and not as to any one or more particular structures, and that the allegations of the complaint stated no more than a mere opinion of the plaintiff on a perhaps debatable question which had been left by the Legislature to certain specified public officials, see, also, Schenck v. City of Pittsburg, 364 Pa. 31, 36, 70 A.2d 612; 11 McQuillin on Municipal Corporations [3d ed.], § 32.61, and decisions cited in notes to that section.

Another pertinent case is Davidson v. City of Elmira, 180 Misc. 1052, 44 N.Y.S.2d 302, affirmed 267 App.Div. 797, 46 N.Y.S.2d 655, motion for leave to appeal denied 292 N.Y. 723, 54 N.E.2d 831; the Special Term opinion, particularly at pages 1056 et seq. of 180 Misc. at page 306 of 44 N.Y.S.2d, is instructive and persuasive. Our decision in Denihan Enterprises v. O'Dwyer, 302 N.Y. 451, 99 N.E.2d 235, is not pertinent here; among the differences between that case and this, is that, in Denihan, we had before us the complaint only, and that pleading stated a triable issue of fact as to whether the dominant purpose of that proposed taking was public or private.

It is not necessary, nor would it be useful, for us to measure the full possible reach of section 1 of article VIII of the State Constitution, or section 72-k of the General Municipal Law. It is not to be assumed that responsible public officers will, in some future instance, label as "substandard or insanitary" an area in which there are no buildings at all, or fine, modern buildings only, or that they will attempt to condemn a number of such buildings by stretching the concept of "area." Such attempts can be dealt with if and when they are made.

[7] In addition to the appeals from the final judgment, plaintiff has appealed upon a certified question, pursuant to permission of the Appellate Division, from the order of the Appellate Division insofar as it affirms Special Term's denial of an injunction *pendente lite*. This appeal must be dismissed, Civil Practice Act, § 589, subd. 4, par. (b); § 603; Langan v. First Trust & Deposit Co., 296 N.Y. 60, 70 N.E.2d 15; Evadan Realty Corp. v. Patterson, 297 N.Y. 732, 77 N.E.2d 25.

The judgment should be affirmed, with costs.

VAN VOORHIS, Judge (dissenting).

[2] The basis for upholding the constitutionality of this statute, General Municipal Law, § 72-k, as outlined in this dissenting opinion, has been approved and adopted in the majority opinion written by Judge DESMOND. This court is unanimously of the opinion that municipal funds can legally be spent to acquire real estate by condemnation for slum clearance, but the money authorized to be spent by this statute has to be used for slum clearance and not mainly for some other public purpose, however commendable such other purpose may be. If the purpose of this project is not primarily slum clearance, if the comparatively small number of substandard and insanitary dwellings to be eliminated could not rationally require the redevelopment of the site area as a whole, plaintiff contends that this would be an indication that the object of the project is not slum clearance but the erection of a coliseum on Columbus Circle, which is not a slum area, and which the evidentiary facts in the papers before the court indicate does not need to be redeveloped in order to eliminate the substandard buildings on or near Ninth Avenue. The necessity for linking the Columbus Circle section to the other area is not so clear, in my view, in the face of the proofs to the contrary, as to justify dismissing the complaint on motion for summary judgment.

There is no rational basis, according to plaintiff, for linking the Columbus Circle portion of the site area to the Ninth Avenue section in order to eliminate tenements on or in the immediate vicinity of Ninth Avenue. The contention is that redevelopment of the Ninth Avenue section, where some substandard and insanitary tenements are located, is unrelated to the more valuable property to be acquired in the vicinity of Columbus Circle, where there are no tenements, that these are really two separate areas, and that the small amount of slum dwellings on and near Ninth Avenue could easily be eliminated separately, and would not have been undertaken jointly except for the coliseum. If that be true, plaintiff is entitled to enjoin the expenditure by the city of its share in the cost as a waste of public funds, regardless of however desirable a coliseum might be or however advantageous it might be to the city to have two thirds of its land cost paid from the Treasury of the United States. If the main purpose of combining these two areas is not slum clearance, but merely to lend color to the acquisition of land for a coliseum under the guise of a slum clearance project, then the combined project is not authorized by statute, and a taxpayer's action can be maintained to restrain it under section 51 of the General Municipal Law, Denihan Enterprises v. O 'Dwyer, 302 N.Y. 451, 99 N.E.2d 235. In that event, the courts would not be invading the administrative province, but performing their duty in limiting administrative officials, capable and public spirited as they may be, to spending public money for purposes authorized by law.

It is undisputed that not more than 27.1% of the entire site area is occupied for dwelling purposes of any kind. Thirty-three and eight-tenths per cent of the site area is vacant land devoted to parking lots; even if some of this vacant land was formerly occupied by substandard and insanitary dwellings, there is no need to spend public funds to eliminate them since they have already been eliminated by private capital. Thirty-nine and one-tenth per cent of the site area is occupied by business or commercial buildings which have not been classified as substandard or insanitary by the municipal authorities. It does very well to cite Dickens' novels, or Thomas Burke's "Limehouse" stories of the London slums of other days, but these have nothing to do with condemning the Manufacturers Trust Building in this "slum" area, assessed at $1,500,000, in order to make way for a coliseum—a laudable object, to be sure, but not one whose connection with slum clearance is so clear as to be taken for granted without a trial.

The report of the municipal slum clearance committee, on the basis of which the Columbus Circle project was approved by the city planning commission, states that there are 243 families consisting of 602 persons now living in tenement buildings in the entire 6.32-acre site area. The estimated cost of land alone for the redevelopment project is $9,500,000, or $15,780 per person living in existing tenements. The estimated amount to be recovered on resale is something less than one third of this sum. When it is considered that this per capita expense represents the cost of acquiring what will be merely vacant land, and that it does not include any of the expense of redevelopment by the construction of new buildings, this in itself presents a triable issue concerning whether the mainspring of the project is really slum clearance. Manifestly no such per capita land cost could be designed to extend to the 9,000 acres in New York City that the committee's report shows has been classified as slum, which is persuasive that this project would never have been undertaken for slum clearance alone. Even the above figure is computed on the hypothesis that all of the tenements in this site area are substandard and insanitary, whereas the land cost per individual slum dweller would be multiplied many times if the figures are adopted of the former chief of planning of the New York City housing authority, William C. Vladeck, who concludes, on the basis of his analysis of the area, that only 10% of the tenements therein are substandard or insanitary. Vladeck says that only 2% of the total site area is in reality slum.[1] Respondents contend that Vladeck is mistaken in failing to characterize all of the old law tenements (built before 1901) in the area as substandard and insanitary. He replies by asserting (what appears to be uncontradicted) that most of these tenements are equipped with sanitary toilet facilities, running water, central heating, fire retarding devices, suitable ventilation, and involve but slight violations of statutes, municipal ordinances or regulations. His report indicates that about one third in area of the city of New York consists of old law tenements. The far-reaching questions should not be decided, as it seems to me, on motion for summary judgment, whether a building can be condemned as being substandard and insanitary merely for the reason that it is an old law tenement even if it is well maintained, and under what circumstances, if at all, such an area may be labeled substandard and insanitary if but a small and apparently disconnected part of it consists of buildings so classified. Such determinations should as least be based upon evidence, taken at a trial. Many factors need to enter into such a decision which are not now before the court. A trial would present an opportunity for the reception of evidence concerning whether there is any rational basis for linking the Columbus Circle with the Ninth Avenue neighborhood, in order to redevelop the latter area. The evidence at present in the record is the other way. Whether this project as a whole bears any real relation to that objective is what plaintiff asks to try in court. By the judgment appealed from, his complaint has been dismissed without opportunity for a trial.

The complaint in this taxpayer's action charges that the expenditure of money for this project will constitute a waste of public funds. Waste, in this connotation, does not mean that it is claimed that the proposed coliseum will cost too much, or that the money will go for any private gain, but that funds earmarked by law for slum clearance will be "wasted" if they are spent contrary to what the statute authorizes.

---

1. Vladeck's basic facts are largely undisputed in the record on this appeal, but even if they were contested, it seems to me that it would not be in order to brush them aside as having no probative force on a motion for summary judgment.

It is said that plaintiff is not entitled to a trial for the reason that the city planning commission and the board of estimate have acted favorably upon the report of the slum clearance committee, and that the whole matter lies in the administrative domain into which the courts may not enter. The formulæ which the courts have adopted in defining the boundaries of administrative discretion such as "arbitrary or capricious," "bad faith," and so forth, sometimes sound as though they involved moral turpitude, which is not what they mean in this context, nor does plaintiff charge that it is present in this case. That is not a reason on account of which the courts should refrain from restraining the expenditure of municipal funds for nonstatutory purposes. Motive is not involved in the sense that it was in Kittinger v. Buffalo Traction Co., 160 N.Y. 377, 54 N.E. 1081, where the validity of legislative action was attacked by impugning the motives of the members of a legislative body. In this case the controversial question is simply whether public funds are to be spent for one public purpose which is authorized by statute or for another and different public purpose which is not authorized by statute.

It by no means follows, if these views are correct, that buildings or vacant land which are not slum in character cannot be condemned if that is incidentally necessary in order to redevelop a slum area. It cannot be done, however, if any slum clearance that may be involved is merely incidental to the redevelopment of other types of real property. If the existence of a few slum buildings within a particular site area is enough to divest the courts of jurisdiction to require that the dominant purpose of the project shall be the one which the statute requires, the door is opened to possible evasion of this law upon a large scale. The magnitude of the problem is disclosed by the statement in the slum clearance committees report, which has been referred to, that 9,000 acres in the city of New York have already been classified as slum, and that 1,328 acres are proposed to be eliminated by 1955. The power of taking private property for public use is a drastic one. It has long rested in the jurisdiction of the courts to decide whether, in particular cases, it is being invoked for a public purpose. By the same token, it is in the realm of the courts to decide whether the purpose, though public, is one sanctioned by the statute. This is far from saying that it is in the power of the courts to pass upon the advisability of every project of this kind. It is enough if the courts, in specific cases, define the boundaries of what is necessarily a wide administrative discretion. But that there are such boundaries can hardly be denied. If only 2%, or 8%, or 12% at most 20.3%—of this site area, under varying interpretations of the facts now before the court, is really substandard or insanitary, and if that be sufficient to authorize condemnation of the entire area, without any further showing that the major portion has to be included in order to redevelop the minor part, such a holding would mean that a large proportion of the City of New York could be taken under the power of eminent domain, acquiring title from one private owner and transferring it to another without substantial reason. In some measure this power undoubtedly exists, but its exercise is subject to restraints which the courts are competent to enforce.

Some guidance may be found in the definition of the term "area" in the Redevelopment Companies Law, L.1942, ch. 845, § 3, as amd. by L.1943, ch. 234, McK.Unconsol. Laws, § 3403. It is defined as "A section of a municipality wherein the planning commission finds that substandard conditions or insanitary housing conditions exist. An area may include land whether improved or unimproved, and buildings or improvements not in themselves insanitary or substandard, the inclusion of which is deemed necessary by such commission for the effective clearance, replanning, reconstruction or rehabilitation of the area of which such land or property is a part." In order to obtain urban redevelopment by private capital, which is the object of section 72-k and similar statutes, there are necessarily occasions when it is difficult to interest private developers in new projects considered to be desirable, unless some opportunity to build is allowed beyond the exact sites occupied by the substandard and insanitary structures to be removed, and, indeed, sensible planning demands just that. Nevertheless if the analogy with the Redevelopment Companies Law has force, the language just quoted from the definition of what constitutes an "area," establishes that land, buildings or improvements, not in themselves insanitary or substandard, are to be included only if necessary "for the effective clearance, replanning, reconstruction or rehabilitation of the area of which such land or property is a part"—viz., if it necessary as incidental to the redevelopment of the slums themselves. The statutory power fails if real property which is not slum is included in the site area for the sake of its own redevelopment, instead of being included as an adjunct to slum property that cannot be redeveloped satisfactorily without it. In this instance, the Columbus Circle section cannot be included unless it is necessary for the effective redevelopment of the Ninth Avenue neighborhood. The facts before the court tend strongly to show, on the contrary, that redevelopment of the Columbus Circle location, which is not substandard or insanitary in character, is the dominant purpose of the project.

In considering whether defendants were entitled to judgment dismissing the complaint, Table I annexed to the Vladeck report is significant, which shows that the existing site area is occupied in the following proportions:

Parking lot	33.8%
Nonresidential uses	39.1%
Hotels & rooming houses	6.8%
Elevator apartments	3.3%
Walk-up apartments	17.0%

Vladeck's report states that "a few buildings in the area can be construed as slum buildings" on the side toward Ninth Avenue, that the elevator apartments "would be considered standard housing under any definition," and it concedes that the age of the apartments would tend to classify them as slums "if they had not been rehabilitated and were not being decently maintained.' After stating the detailed facts of his survey of the site, Vladeck concludes that, based on these facts, and "predicated upon the accepted definition of slum dwelling, it is fair to state that at the most, less than 10% of the structures could be so considered. ° ° ° Less than 17% of the site area and less than 8% of the assessed value of the area is devoted to walk-up apartments. Using the previous assumption that not more than 10% of those walk-up structures can be considered as slum buildings, the percentage of slum condition for the site, as a whole, becomes ridiculously small, being 2% of the area and less than 1% of the value. Further interpretation of this Table shows that almost three-quarters of the site and more than four-fifths of the value is devoted exclusively to parking lots and non-residential structures, prominent among which is the Manufacturers Trust Company building, a 22-story structure, whose assessment, with its land, exceed[s] $1,500,000. ° ° ° Excluded from the analysis of slum conditions were the hotels, rooming houses and elevator apartments. These were excluded because of the fact that the hotels and rooming houses cater, in large, to transients and not to family groups and the two elevator buildings would be considered standard housing under any definition. ° ° ° The area is bounded on the east by Columbus Circle and the southerly end of Central Park, certainly not a slum area. The southern frontage of West 58th Street contains a number of substantial residential buildings and even those built prior to the turn of the century show a high standard of renovation and maintenance. The frontage on the west is almost completely occupied by the Roosevelt Hospital and its new extension, and a large church building; the north side abuts a highly developed commercial street, whose structures are well maintained and fully occupied. It is interesting to note that in a survey taken by the State of New York, Division of Housing, only two years ago, the area selected in west mid-town, between 42nd Street and 56th Street, lies entirely west of Ninth Avenue." The Vladeck report concludes that "It is obvious upon analysis of the data presented either in the report or in the survey that the Slum Clearance portion of the proposed Redevelopment Project is not the primary purpose of the proposed development."

The statements of fact in the Vladeck report are mainly undisputed in this record, although since plaintiff appeals from summary judgment dismissing the complaint, the judgment should be reversed if there is a showing of evidence creating a triable issue, even if some facts are disputed. There is no dispute that 33.8% of the site area is vacant land, which is not slum, neither is it disputed that at least 39.1% of the site area is devoted to commercial and business uses. The only adverse comment in the slum clearance committee's report against the latter property is 'Non-residential structures have not been classified, but most of them can be considered obsolete, occupying land the value of which is inconsistent with the age and type of buildings." A commercial or business building, which has no violation against it, and which is not a menace to health or safety, cannot become obsolete. The statute does not confer the power of eminent domain merely because the value of land may be inconsistent with the age and type of the building upon it. The power is given to eliminate slums. This is not to say that commercial or business structures may not be removed as part of redevelopment plans if to do so is required as an incident of rehabilitating slum area nearby; it does mean that the existence of merely obsolescent business or commercial structures is not enough, in itself, to characterize the area as slum. The commercial and other nonresidential buildings in this site area cannot, in any event, be counted for the purposes of this appeal as being in themselves substandard or insanitary, in view of the statement in the committee's report that they have not been so classified. This report contains the findings made by the committee, which were acted upon by the city planning commission and the board of estimate. Not only are no facts set forth on which a conclusion could be based that these buildings are slum, but the statement that they have not been classified as slum, is an affirmative showing that the particular features which render buildings substandard and insanitary have not been examined and analyzed by the committee, and that no administrative determination has been made that these nonresidential buildings fall within the category required by the statute. The court may not substitute such a determination of its own where the administrative body has omitted to make one.

It thus appears beyond serious dispute that at least 72.9% of the site area consists of vacant land or commercial structures which could not under any theory be regarded as slum in character on the basis of this record.

The maps supplied by both sides show commercial buildings or parking sites exclusively on the eastern half of the plot, the side toward Columbus Circle, except for one elevator apartment house fronting on the south side of West 60th Street. There are no residential structures of any sort in the easterly three quarters of the area between 58th and 59th Streets, nor in the easterly half of the area between 59th and 60th Streets, with the exception of the elevator apartment house above mentioned.

In order to sustain the administrative findings that this whole area is substandard and insanitary, respondents are really reduced to reliance upon the 17% of the area covered by the walk-up apartments, all in the Ninth Avenue section, to the west, away from Columbus Circle. The committee's report and the Vladeck report differ in minor respects concerning the condition of these walk-up apartments, but agree that a substantial number of them are provided with proper sanitation, heating, ventilation, fire retarding devices and are otherwise habitable. The reports also agree that they are old law tenements, and consequently occupy excessive portions of the lot areas as judged by present standards. Both agree that some of them are substandard and insanitary, Vladeck placing the number in that category at 2% of the site area. This is not an unsupported conclusion; it is based on Vladeck's examination of the premises, and on the particular facts which he states exist and which are enumerated in his report. He recognizes that all of these walk-up apartments would be classified as slum if they had not been rehabilitated and were not being decently maintained. The committee report contradicts this figure of 2% only by saying that 66.7% of the residence buildings are "badly run down" and 12.5% are "deteriorated." If these terms be construed to indicate that those percentages are all slum, it would mean that about 12% of the site area is of that character.

Approximately one third of the area of the city of New York has been stated to be occupied by "old law" tenements, constructed before 1901. It may well be that they comprise a substantial part of the 9,000 acres in the city which the committee's report states are "recognized slums" which it is ultimately proposed to remove. It is possible that lack of yards, size of rooms, lack of ventilation and other characteristics of old law tenements are enough so that any or all such buildings, regardless of how they are being maintained, can be classified as substandard and insanitary in the discretion of the administrative authorities. The present record, on appeal from a summary judgment, lacks the factual detail necessary in order to decide that important point. Assuming, however, the entire 17% in area occupied by these walk-up tenements, or even the 20.3% occupied by them and the elevator apartment houses, to be substandard and insanitary, it still remains true that there is no substantial evidence in this record that it is necessary to condemn the property between these apartment houses and Columbus Circle for slum clearance purposes. That property, as has been stated, is not substandard nor insanitary in itself, nor has a basis been shown for the exercise of administrative judgment that it must be redeveloped as incidental to the redevelopment of slum areas on or near Ninth Avenue.

By the Vladeck report and affidavits plaintiff has sustained whatever burden is upon him to come forward with evidentiary facts in opposing a motion for summary judgments, and also for the purpose of the motion, to rebut the presumption of regularity of official acts. Sufficient has been shown to draw in question that the determinations of the committee, the city planning commission and the board of estimate respecting this slum clearance site, had warrant in the record and a reasonable basis in law, Matter of Mounting & Finishing Co. v. McGoldrick, 294 N.Y. 104, 108, 60 N.E.2d 825, 827.

[3] As already indicated, I agree that section 72-k of the General Municipal Law is constitutional, in the respects in which it is attacked, and

the views that follow reflect those of the entire court. The ground of plaintiff's attack upon the validity of subdivision 2, under which respondents have proceeded, is that it fails to prescribe standards or safeguards governing the clearance, replanning, reconstruction and rehabilitation of substandard and insanitary areas. Section 1 of article XVIII of the State Constitution adopted in 1938, authorizes the Legislature to provide for slum clearance, cf. Matter of Murray v. LaGuardia, 291 N.Y. 320, 52 N.E.2d 884, 886, "by such means and upon such terms and conditions as it may prescribe." Plaintiff takes the position that this provision is not self-executing, and that the Legislature had to specify particular means, terms and conditions to carry it into effect. The contention on this point is not so much that the Legislature has failed to define or to describe what is meant by "substandard and insanitary areas," which is the phrase used in the Constitution to define what real property may be acquired, the meaning of which is elaborated in section 2 of the Urban Redevelopment Corporations Law, L.1941, ch. 892, McK.Unconsol.Laws, § 3302, and in section 2 of the Redevelopment Companies Law, L.1942, ch. 845, McK.Unconsol. Laws, § 3402, but it is argued that section 72-k is defective in not being more precise than the Constitution in prescribing how the municipality is to be regulated in disposing of the land to others so as to insure that the area will be effectively replanned, reconstructed and rehabilitated. The Redevelopment Companies Law, McK.Unconsol.Laws, § 3401 et seq., to be sure, is somewhat more specific and limited in this respect. Projects covered by it must be designed and used primarily for housing purposes, but portions may be planned and used for business, commercial, cultural or recreation purposes appurtenant thereto. L.1942, ch. 845, § 14, as amd. by L.1943, ch. 234. Instead of contemplating that the municipality shall take a loss on the projects, redevelopment law companies are required to pay to the municipality the entire cost of assembling the land, § 20. Nevertheless, except for limitation by statute to residential uses, maximum rentals and provision for partial tax exemption, the supervising agency, planning commission and local legislative body are allowed almost as much latitude in approving the design of the new projects under the Redevelopment Companies Law as in the case of section 72-k of the General Municipal Law (cf. Redevelopment Companies Law, §§ 4-5, 14-15, 17-21, 24). The constitutionality of the Redevelopment Companies Law was sustained, in these respects, in Matter of Murray v. La Guardia (supra).

Section 72-k of the General Municipal Law is drawn upon the basis, upheld in Matter of Murray v. La Guardia, that slum clearance is in itself a public purpose, which is separate and distinct from the objects to which the land may subsequently be devoted after being redeveloped by private capital. The State Constitution does not require that slums shall be rehabilitated exclusively by reconstruction for low cost housing, which is a different public purpose that may or may not be superimposed on slum clearance, Matter of Murray v. La Guardia, supra. Consequently, except where an applicable statute requires, the slum area may be cleared, reconstructed and rehabilitated according to any design and for any purpose which renders the area no longer substandard or insanitary. The Legislature is presumed to have interpreted those words in subdivision 1 of article XVIII of the Constitution, when it used them in section 72-k of the General Municipal Law, as having the same meaning which it ascribed to them in section 2 of the Redevelopment Companies Law, as amd. by L.1943, ch. 234, viz., "substandard conditions and insanitary housing conditions owing to obsolescence, deterioration and dilapidation of buildings, or excessive land coverage, lack of planning, of public facilities, of sufficient light, air and space, and improper design and arrangement of living quarters," and lack of "a sufficient supply of adequate, safe and sanitary dwelling accommodations properly planned and related to public facilities." Cf. Urban Redevelopment Corporation Law, § 2, L.1941, ch. 892. There appears to be agreement that, in general, as stated in the Vladeck report submitted by plaintiff: "It is generally accepted that a slum area is one, which because of lack of adequate open spaces and community facilities, and because of a preponderance of sub-standard buildings, does not provide an environment in accordance with the accepted standard of urban neighborhood life. A slum building, on the other hand, has been interpreted to mean a building which lacks private toilets, electric lighting, windows in each room, central heating, rooms of adequate size, adequate fire protection or a minimal standard of decent maintenance."

If the description "substandard and insanitary areas," commonly called slums, supplies a legal standard for the determination of what a slum is, so as to validate condemnation for public housing, urban redevelopment or under the Redevelopment Companies Law, it is equally adequate to furnish a standard by which to decide what is not a slum. All that is required by section 72-k is that the deed, lease, or other instrument by which real property is conveyed or demised by the municipality shall contain provisions requiring the purchaser or lessee to clear, replan, reconstruct or rehabilitate the property in such manner as to render certain that it shall not be substandard or insanitary in design or construction after the work shall have been completed. That is provided for by section 72-k, and is sufficient to establish its validity against plaintiff's attack.

Statutory or constitutional provisions authorizing local public agencies to undertake urban redevelopment projects for slum clearance have been adopted in at least thirty-seven States,[2] and their validity has been almost

2. Alabama, Arkansas, California, Colorado, Connecticut, Delaware, Florida, Georgia, Illinois, Indiana, Kansas, Kentucky, Louisiana, Maine, Maryland, Massachusetts, Michigan, Minnesota, Missouri, Nebraska, New Hampshire, New Jersey, New York, North Carolina, Ohio, Oregon, Pennsylvania, Rhode Island South Carolina, South Dakota, Tennessee, Virginia, West Virginia, Wisconsin, Alaska, Hawaii, Puerto Rico and the Virgin Islands.

uniformly upheld.[3]   Reference is made to the article by Philip H. Hill (1952) entitled: "Recent Slum Clearance and Urban Redevelopment Laws," in Washington and Lee Law Review (Vol. IX, p. 173) to indicate the extent of legislation of this character, and current trends in its construction and enforcement.   This is, of course, a different question from whether this particular (Columbus Circle) slum clearance project falls within the authorization of the statute.

The remaining questions raised by plaintiff are not substantial.   The contracts between the city and the redevelopers, described briefly as Apartments and Triborough, are adequate to insure that the area will be properly redeveloped if redevelopment is warranted.   Although Triborough is a public authority, it stands in the same position respecting the projects as any outside redeveloper, and subdivision b of section 384 of the City Charter requiring sale at public auction or by sealed bids does not appear to have been violated, in view of the contingent clauses in the contracts rendering them conditional on Apartments and Triborough being the highest bidders.   Although it is true that under the National Housing Act of 1949, U.S.C.A., tit. 42, § 1460, subd. (c), Federal funds are made available for slum clearance under State auspices only where the area to be acquired is "predominantly residential in character" or where it is to be redeveloped "for predominantly residential uses," and it is conceded by defendants that

---

3. In re Opinion of the Justices, 1938, 235 Ala. 485, 179 So. 535; Humphrey v. City of Phoenix, 1940, 55 Ariz. 374, 112 P.2d 82; Hogue v. Housing Authority of North Little Rock, 1940, 201 Ark. 263, 144 S.W.2d 49; Housing Authority v. Dockweiler, 1939, 14 Cal.2d 437, 94 P.2d 794; People ex rel. Stokes v. Newton, 1940, 106 Colo. 61, 101 P.2d 21; Marvin v. Housing Authority, 1938, 133 Fla. 590, 183 So. 145; Williamson v. Housing Authority, 1938, 180 Ga. 673, 199 S.E. 43; Lloyd v. Twin Falls Housing Authority, 1941, 62 Idaho 502, 113 P.2d 1102; Edwards v. Housing Authority, 1939, 215 Ind. 330, 19 N.E.2d 741; Spahn v. Stewart, 1937, 268 Ky. 97, 103 S.W.2d 651; State ex rel. Porterie v. Housing Authority, 1938, 190 La. 710, 182 So. 725; Matthaei v. Housing Authority, 1939, 177 Md. 506, 9 A.2d 835; Allydonn Realty Corp. v. Holyoke Housing Authority, 1939, 304 Mass. 288, 23 N.E.2d 665; Matter of Brewster St. Housing Site, 1939, 291 Mich. 313, 289 N.W. 493; Thomas v. Housing & Redevelopment Authority of Duluth, 1951, 234 Minn. 221, 48 N.W.2d 175; Laret Investment Co. v. Dickmann, 1939, 345 Mo. 449, 134 S.W.2d 65; Rutherford v. Grant Falls, 1939, 107 Mont. 512, 86 P.2d 656; Lennox v. Housing Authority, 1940, 187 Neb. 582, 200 N.W. 451, 291 N.W. 100; McLaughlin v. Housing Authority of City of Las Vegas, 1951, 68 Nev. 84, 227 P.2d 206; Opinion of Justices, 1947, 94 N.H. 515, 53 A.2d 194; Romano v. Housing Authority, 123 N.J.L. 428, 10 A.2d 181 affirmed 1940, 124 N.J.L. 452, 12 A.2d 384; Matter of New York City Housing Authority v. Muller, 1936, 270 N.Y. 333, 1 N.E.2d 153, 1050 A.L.R. 905; Wells v. Housing Authority, 1938, 213 N.C. 744, 107 S.E. 693; State ex rel. Ellis v. Sherill, 1940, 136 Ohio St. 328, 25 N.E.2d 844; Dornan v. Philadelphia Housing Authority, 1938, 331 Pa. 209, 200 A. 834; McNulty v. Owens, 1938, 188 S.C. 377, 199 S.E. 425; Knoxville Housing Authority v. Knoxville, 1930, 174 Tenn. 76, 123 S.W.2d 1085; Housing Authority v. Higginbotham, 1940, 135 Tex. 158, 148 S.W.2d 79, 180 A.L.R. 1053; Mumpower v. Housing Authority of City of Bristol, 1940, 170 Va. 420, 11 S.E.2d 732; Chapman v. Huntington Housing Authority, 1939, 121 W.Va. 819, 8 S.E. 2d 502.

53.54% of this size will be redeveloped for residential purposes only if 18,000 square feet of parking space in the coliseum is allocated to residential uses, and that otherwise less than 50% would be devoted to residential purposes, nevertheless the question whether the Federal appropriation was authorized by the Federal statute has been held to be subject to the sole cognizance of the Federal courts, Perkins v. Lukens Steel Co., 310 U.S. 113, 60 S.Ct. 869, 84 L.Ed. 1108.

On appeal from judgment: Judgment affirmed, with costs.

LEWIS, C.J., and CONWAY, DYE and FROESSEL, JJ., concur with DESMOND, J.

VAN VOORHIS, J., dissents in opinion in which FULD, J., concurs.

On appeal from order: Appeal dismissed, Civil Practice Act, § 589, subd. 4, par. (b); § 603; Langan v. First Trust & Deposit Co., 296 N.Y. 60, 70 N.E.2d 15; Evadan Realty Corp. v. Patterson, 297 N.Y. 732, 77 N.E.2d 25.

LEWIS, C. J., and CONWAY, DESMOND, DYE, FULD, FROESSEL and VAN VOORHIS, JJ., concur.

On appeal from judgment: Judgment affirmed.

On appeal from order: Appeal dismissed.

Questions and Notes

1. At the time of the proposed Coliseum, as originally presented, federal aid was available only if the project was predominantly residential *either* before or after redevelopment. What percentage of the land involved in this project was residential before redevelopment? Now you know why the apartment buildings were proposed on the 9th Avenue frontage to the rear. (Even then, the project was deemed "predominantly residential" only because a substantial part of the Coliseum garage was counted as residential space. (See Williams and Doughty, *Studies in Legal Realism*, 29 Rutgers L.R. 73, 90 (1975)).

2. What was the test adopted by the majority on the extent of judicial review over administrative determinations?

3. What were the five public bodies who made the findings that this land was "substandard and unsanitary"?

4. *Who* was the Triborough Bridge and Tunnel Authority?

5. *Who* was the Mayor's Committee on Slum Clearance?

6. *Who* was the dominant member of the New York City Planning Commission at that time?

7. For further background on the Moses mode of operation in urban renewal, see Caro, *The Power Broker: Robert Moses and the Fall of New York*, especially chapter 37 on relocation.

8. Is not the combination of Judges Fuld and Van Voorhis an unusual pair to dissent together, on an important case involving major issues of public policy? Why do you suppose this happened?

OPINION OF THE JUSTICES

152 Maine 440, 131 A.2d 904(1957).

Supreme Judicial Court of Maine.

April 26, 1957.

State of Maine

In Senate April 17, 1957

Whereas, it appears to the Senate of the 98th Legislature that the following is an important question of law and the occasion a solemn one and

Whereas, there is pending before the Senate of the 98th Legislature a bill (HP 983, LD 1407) entitled, "An Act Relating to Industrial Development in City of Bangor" and

Whereas, it is important that the Legislature be informed as to the constitutionality of the proposed bill, be it therefore

Ordered, that in accordance with the provisions of the constitution of the State, the Justices of the Supreme Judicial Court are hereby respectfully requested to give the Senate their opinion on the following question:

Would House Paper 983, Legislative Document 1407, "An Act Relating to Industrial Development in City of Bangor." if enacted by the Legislature, be constitutional?

> Transmitted by Director of Legislative
> Research pursuant to joint order.
> Ninety-Eighth Legislature

Legislative Document   No. 1407
H. P. 983   House of Representatives,
                                 March 26, 1957.

Referred to Committee on Legal Affairs. Sent up for concurrence and ordered printed.

                          Harvey R. Pease, Clerk.

Presented by Mr. Totman of Bangor.

State of Maine

In the Year of Our Lord Nineteen
Hundred Fifty-Seven
An Act Relating to Industrial Development in City of Bangor.

Emergency preamble. Whereas, industrial development is essential to the preservation and betterment of the economy of the city of Bangor and its inhabitants; and

Whereas, present opportunities for such development are limited under present conditions, and proposed imminent industrial development awaits the availability of an industrial area; and

Whereas, many citizens of said city of Bangor have urged the immediate enactment of a bill to provide for industrial expansion; and

Whereas, in the judgment of the Legislature, these facts create an emergency within the meaning of the Constitution of Maine and require the following legislation as immediately necessary for the preservation of the public peace, health and safety; now, therefore,

Be it enacted by the People of the State of Maine, as follows:

Sec. 1 P. & S. L., 1931, c. 54, Art. VIII, additional.   Chapter 54 of the private and special laws of 1931, as amended, is hereby further amended by adding thereto a new Article VIII, as follows:

"Article VIII.

"Industrial Development.

"Sec. 1.   Industrial development.   The city of Bangor is hereby empowered to acquire by purchase or lease or purchase and lease, or by the right of eminent domain, lots, sites, improvements and places within the city of Bangor to be used for industrial development.   The taking of real estate or any interest therein for the use of the city of Bangor for industrial park purposes by the right of eminent domain shall be effected as provided in sections 2, 3 and 4.

"Sec. 2.   Manner of taking.   Whenever the public exigencies require it, the city council may adopt an order of taking for any land within the following described area, which shall contain a description of the land to be taken sufficiently accurate for its identification and shall state the interest therein taken and the purposes for which such property is taken.

"Sec. 3.   Area defined.   The area in the city of Bangor within which the city of Bangor may take real estate or any interest therein for the use of the city of Bangor for industrial park purposes by right of eminent domain shall be as follows:

"Beginning at a point formed by the intersection of the center line of the Odlin road and the easterly right-of-way line of the Maine Central Railroad; thence southerly along said easterly right-of-way line of the main line of the railroad to the town line between the city of Bangor and the town of Hampden; thence easterly along said town line to an angle point in said town line; thence southeasterly along said town line to a point which is 825.5 feet northerly from the northerly side line of Crosby street; thence northeasterly parallel to and 825.5 feet northerly from said northerly line of Crosby street to Thatcher street; thence crossing Thatcher street and continuing on the same straight line to the center line of the Main

Street Industrial Spur; thence northwesterly by and along the center line of said Industrial Spur to the easterly side line of Thatcher street; thence northwesterly along the easterly side line of said Thatcher street to Webster avenue and continuing across said Webster avenue to the northwesterly side line of said Webster avenue; thence southwesterly by and along the northwesterly side line of said Webster avenue to the center line of the Main Street Industrial Spur; thence northwesterly along the center line of said Industrial Spur to the center line of Odlin road; thence southwesterly by and along the center line of said Odlin road to the point of beginning.

"Sec 4. Procedure. All proceedings under the provisions of sections 1, 2 and 3 shall be in accordance with the provisions of sections 12 to 22, inclusive, of chapter 52 of the Revised Statutes of 1954."

"Sec. 2. Referendum; effective date. In view of the emergency cited in the preamble, this act shall take effect when approved, only for the purpose of permitting its submission to the legal voters within the city of Bangor, voting at a regular or special election called and held for the purpose, by the municipal officers of the City of Bangor, to be held at the regular voting places in said city; the date of holding such election to be determined by said municipal officers. Such election shall be held not later than 8 months after the effective date of this act, and shall be called, advertised, and conducted according to the law relating to municipal elections; provided, however, that the board of registration shall not be required to prepare, nor the city clerk to post, a new list of voters. The city clerk shall reduce the subject matter of this act to the following question: "Shall the Act Relating to Industrial Development in City of Bangor, passed by the 98th Legislature, be accepted?" and the voters shall indicate by a cross or check mark placed against the words "Yes" or "No" their opinion of the same.

This act shall take effect for all the purposes hereof immediately upon its acceptance by a majority of the legal voters voting at said election; provided that the total number of votes cast for and against the acceptance of this act equals or exceeds 20% of the total votes cast for all candidates for Governor in said city of Bangor at the next previous gubernatorial election.

The result of the vote shall be declared by the city council of the city of Bangor and due certificate thereof filed by the city clerk with the Secretary of State. Failure of approval shall not prevent the municipal officers of said city of Bangor from against submitting said question to the voters of said city in the manner aforesaid.

Answer of the Justices

To the Honorable Senate of the State of Maine:

[1] In compliance with the provisions of Section 3 of Article VI of the Constitution of Maine, we the undersigned Justices of the Supreme Judicial

Court, have the honor to submit the following answer to the question propounded on April 17, 1957.

Question: Would House Paper 983, Legislative Document 1407, "An Act Relating to Industrial Development in City of Bangor." if enacted by the Legislature, be constitutional?

Answer: We answer in the negative.

The proposed Act is designed to provide for industrial expansion in Bangor by the acquisition by the city by purchase, lease or by the exercise of the right of eminent domain of "lots, sites, improvements and places within the city of Bangor to be used for industrial development."

The Act, it may be noted, does not set forth standards for action by the city either in the acquisition of property or in its use or disposition, for example, by sale or lease for industrial purposes. These are details, however, which we need not and do not consider. Deficiencies in these respects could be remedied, if the plan broadly speaking were constitutional.

[2] We prefer to place our answer upon consideration of the basic purpose of the Act. This, we are compelled to find, is a private purpose and not a public purpose under our constitution. It follows that the city may neither raise money by taxation nor acquire property by eminent domain for such purpose. There is neither the "public use" of taxation, nor the "public use" of eminent domain. The likelihood that public funds expended in acquisition of property might be repaid in whole or in part, or even with a profit, in its disposal does not alter the situation in its constitutional aspects. The taxpayer in the operation of the plan would be, or might be, called upon to pay therefor; and thus the constitutional bar remains firm.

We are not unmindful that the public exigencies or need for use of public monies for assistance in industrial development under the plan here proposed is determined by the Legislature (or under the Act by the city) and not by the Courts. See Mosley v. York Shore Water Co., 94 Me. 83, 46 A. 809 (water supply); Hayford v. Bangor, 102 Me. 340, 66 A. 731, 11 L.R.A.,N.S., 940 (library); Crommett v. City of Portland, 150 Me. 217, 233, 107 A.2d 841 (slum clearance). The value of the plan or its economic or social benefits, however, present no issues for judicial consideration. We mention these factors that it may plainly appear that our opinion does not touch the need or desirability of the plan, but solely the constitutionality thereof.

The pertinent provisions of the Maine Constitution are:

"He shall not ° ° ° be deprived of his life, liberty, property or privileges, but by judgment of his peers or the law of the land." Art. I, Section 6.

"Private property shall not be taken for public uses without just compensation; nor unless the public exigencies require it." Art. I, Section 21.

"The legislature ° ° ° with the exceptions hereinafter stated, shall have full power to make and establish all reasonable laws and regulations for the defense and benefit of the people of this state, not repugnant to this constitution, nor to that of the United States." Art. IV, Part Third, Section 1.

We are unable to escape the conclusion that action under the Act would be for the direct benefit of private industry. An existing shoe factory or paper mill, let us say, within the proposed industrial area or park could not, for reasons clear to all, be authorized under our Constitution to acquire additional facilities by eminent domain. That such a course could well be of great value to the particular enterprise and so to the city or community would not affect the application of the law.

[3] The test of public use is not the advantage or great benefit to the public. "A public use must be for the general public, or some portion of it, who may have occasion to use it, not a use by or for particular individuals. It is not necessary that all of the public shall have occasion to use. It is necessary that every one, if he has occasion, shall have the right to use." Paine v. Savage, 126 Me. 121, 126, 136 A. 664, 666, 51 A.L.R. 1194.

The Act in violation of these principles seeks to have the city do for private enterprise what private enterprise cannot be authorized to do for itself.

Our Court in 1954, in the Crommett case, supra, in upholding the constitutionality of slum clearance in Portland, said 150 Me. at page 236, 107 A.2d at page 852, in considering the redevelopment phase of the program:

> "Taken alone, the redevelopment of a city is not, in our view, a 'public use' for which either taxation or taking by eminent domain may properly be utilized.
> "However beneficial it might be in a broad sense, it would clearly be unconstitutional for the Legislature to provide for the taking of any area in a city for the purpose of redevelopment by sale or lease for private purposes. Such a proposal would amount to no more than the taking of A's property for sale or lease to B on the ground that B's use would be economically or socially more desirable."

The preamble of the Act before us reads in part:

> "Emergency preamble. Whereas, industrial development is essential to the preservation and betterment of the economy of the city of Bangor and its inhabitants; and
> "Whereas, present opportunities for such development are limited under present conditions, and proposed imminent industrial development awaits the availability of an industrial area; * * *."

The similarity of the purposes discussed in the extract from the Court's opinion and in the preamble to the Act is at once apparent.

Under the Act the city does not seek to regulate the use of land through zoning. The plan calls as we have seen for the acquisition of property against the will of the owner if need be, with its placement in industrial use by private enterprise.

In our opinion the Act attempts what is forbidden by our fundamental law, and is unconstitutional.

Among the cases illustrating the principles on which we base our conclusion are: Unconstitutional—private use: Allen v. Inhabitants of Jay, 60

Me. 124 (loan by town to manufacturing concern); Brewer Brick Co. v. Brewer, 62 Me. 62 (exemption of manufacturing plant from taxation); In re Opinion of Justices, 118 Me. 503, 508, 513, 515, 106 A. 865, 871, (water storage reservoir to increase value and capacity of water powers) "The dominant purpose here [water storage reservoir] is for private benefit and not for the 'benefit of the people,' and therefore the power of taxation to promote it does not exist."; Bowden v. York Shore Water Co., 114 Me. 150, 95 A. 779, where the real purpose of the taking was to serve a private use of protection of timberlands from fire, and not a public use of protection of a public water supply; Paine v. Savage, supra (a private logging road); Haley v. Davenport, 132 Me. 148, 168 A. 102 (a drain across a neighbor's land); Perkins v. Inhabitants of Milford, 59 Me. 315 (town cannot tax for gift to an individual). See also Opinion of Justices, 58 Me. 590.

Constitutional—public use: Laughlin v. City of Portland, 111 Me. 486, 90 A. 318, 51 L.R.A.,N.S., 1143 (Portland municipal fuel yard); State v. F. H. Vahlsing, Inc., 147 Me. 417, 88 A.2d 144 (potato tax).

Dated at Augusta, Maine, this 26th day of April, 1957.

Respectfully submitted:

ROBERT B. WILLIAMSON, Chief Justice
DONALD W. WEBBER
ALBERT BELIVEAU
WALTER M. TAPLEY, Jr.
FRANCIS W. SULLIVAN
Justices.

Memorandum:

Mr. Justice DUBORD was out of the State when the foregoing question was submitted. Despite his entire willingness to return for the purpose of answering it, it is the unanimous view of his Associates that such action on his part is entirely unnecessary. He has all the material before him, has considered the question and authorizes the statement that he concurs in the answer.

Questions and Notes

1. Why do you think the court regarded the proposed condemnation here as rather dubious?

2. What theory of public use did this opinion express?

CANNATA

v.

CITY OF NEW YORK

11 N.Y. 2d 210, 182, N.E. 2d 395 (1962).

Court of Appeals of New York.

April 26, 1962.

Action for judgment declaring statute authorizing cities to condemn for purpose of reclamation or redevelopment unconstitutional. The Supreme Court, Special Term, Kings County, Louis L. Friedman, J., 24 Misc.2d 694, 204 N.Y.S.2d 982, dismissed complaint and appeal was taken. The Supreme Court, Appellate Division, Second Judicial District, 14 A.D.2d 813, 221 N.Y.S.2d 457, modified judgment by striking out decretal paragraph dismissing complaint and appeal was taken. The Court of Appeals, Desmond, C. J., held that statute was not unconstitutional as applied to area which was 75 percent vacant and which had been subdivided into plots of such form and shape as to prevent effective economic development.

Affirmed.

Van Voorhis, J., dissented.

Raphael H. Weissman, Brooklyn, for appellants.

Leo A. Larkin, Corp. Counsel (Pauline K. Berger, New York City, of counsel), for respondent.

DESMOND, Chief Judge.

Sixty-eight home owners in the Canarsie section of Brooklyn bring this suit for a declaratory judgment that section 72-n of the General Municipal Law, Consol.Laws, c. 24 is unconstitutional on its face and as applied to the proposed redevelopment of the area in which these people live. Since April, 1961 this statute, or one like it, has become part of article 15 of the General Municipal Law but at the times here in question it was section 72-n of that law (L. 1958, ch. 924). The section authorizes cities to condemn for the purpose of reclamation or redevelopment predominantly vacant areas which are economically dead so that their existence and condition impairs the sound growth of the community and tends to develop slums and blighted areas. There are in the statute declarations by the Legislature that such reclamation and redevelopment of such areas are necessary to protect health, safety and general welfare, to promote the sound growth of the community, etc. Recited by the Legislature were a number of conditions "or combinations thereof" which "with or without tangible physical blight" impair or arrest the sound growth of the community or tend to create slums or blighted areas. There are seven of these listed conditions as follows: subdivision of the land into lots of such form, shape or size as to be incapable of effective development; obsolete and poorly designed street patterns with inadequate access; unsuitable topographic or other physical conditions impeding the development of appropriate uses; obsolete utilities; buildings unfit for use or occupancy as a result of age, obsolescence, etc.; dangerous, unsanitary or improper uses and conditions adversely affecting public health, safety or welfare; scattered improvements. The statute then goes on to declare that land assembly by individual or private enterprise for purpose of redevelopment in such areas is difficult of attainment, that the conditions above listed create tax delinquency and impair the sound growth of the community, that there is a shortage of vacant land in such communities for residential and industrial development, that it is necessary to clear, replan and redevelop such vacant land, and that for such purposes it is necessary that municipalities be given the condemnation and other powers provided by the act. It is particularly to be noted that the statute, while it becomes applicable on the existence of certain listed factors or combination of factors, expressly requires that the area is "predominantly vacant". Of the area here involved at least 75% is vacant. Section 72-n, beginning at paragraph a of subdivision 3 thereof, describes the procedure. The Planning Commission, after public hearing, may designate an area for these purposes providing there are findings that the area is vacant or predominantly vacant, and, in addition, findings as to the existence of some or all of the seven conditions above listed and findings that those conditions impair or arrest the sound growth of the community or tend to create slums or blighted areas. The Planning Commission must then make a detailed statement of the existing physical, economical and sociological conditions in the project area and a general statement of the new project and there must be hearings on a preliminary plan and approval of the preliminary and final plan by the local legislative body, whereupon the municipality may acquire the property by condemnation or otherwise and may sell it for the purpose of clearing, replanning, redevelopment, etc., in accordance with the final plan.

This action came into Special Term on the city's motion for a dismissal of the complaint and for summary judgment and the court held that plaintiffs are not entitled to relief. On appeal to the Appellate Division, Second Department, that court modified only to the extent of directing that judgment go for defendant city, the court holding that in an action for declaratory judgment the granting of a motion by the defendant for judgment on the pleadings properly results not in a dismissal of the complaint but in a declaration on the merits in favor of defendant. The Appellate Division, as stated, modified by directing a declaratory judgment for the city.

[1] This complaint does not allege any failure to carry out any of the statutory procedures. It points out that the Planning Board in this case made findings not only as to the vacancy of a large part of the area but also of these statutory factors: that the land is subdivided into plots of such form, shape and insufficient size as to prevent effective economic

development, that the streets are obsolete and of poorly designed patterns, and that the improvements are scattered and incompatible with appropriate development. The real basis of the complaint is its statement that there is in the area no such "tangible physical blight" as to constitute the area of slum. Plaintiffs' argument, most simply put, is that this taking is not for a "public use" because it is a taking of nonslum land for development into a so-called "Industrial Park" or area set aside for new industrial development. We agree with the courts below that an area does not have to be a "slum" to make its redevelopment a public use nor is public use negated by a plan to turn a predominantly vacant, poorly developed and organized area into a site for new industrial buildings.

[2–4] We see nothing unconstitutional on the face of this statute or in its proposed application to these undisputed facts. Taking of substandard real estate by a municipality for redevelopment by private corporations has long been recognized as a species of public use (Matter of Murray v. La Guardia, 291 N.Y. 320, 52 N.E.2d 884; see Kaskel v. Impellitteri, 306 N.Y. 73, 115 N.E.2d 659, cert. den. 347 U.S. 934, 74 S.Ct. 629, 98 L.Ed. 1085; Cuglar v. Power Authority of State of N.Y., 3 N.Y.2d 1006, 170 N.Y.S.2d 341, 147 N.E.2d 733). The condemnation by the city of an area such as this so that it may be turned into sites for needed industries is a public use (see Graham v. Houlihan, 147 Conn. 321, 160 A.2d 745; Opinion of the Justices, 334 Mass. 760, 135 N.E.2d 665; Wilson v. Long Branch, 27 N.J. 360, 142 A.2d 837; People ex rel. Adamowski v. Chicago Land Clearance Comm., 14 Ill.2d 74, 150 N.E.2d 792; Berman v. Parker, 348 U.S. 26, 75 S.Ct. 98, 99 L.Ed. 27).

The judgment should be affirmed, with costs.

VAN VOORHIS, Judge (dissenting).

The appeal is from a declaratory judgment upholding the constitutionality of former section 72-n of the General Municipal Law. Pursuant to this section, which is now repealed and has been re-enacted in modified form in article 15 of the General Municipal Law, the City of New York proposes to condemn about 95 acres in the Canarsie section of Brooklyn to be resold to private developers—who are as yet unidentified and uncommitted—for a project to be known as "Flatlands Urban Industrial Park", which, in the opinion of the Board of Estimate and the City Planning Commission, will be more advantageous to the future of the city than the lawful uses to which the properties are being devoted by their present owners. There is no finding that any of this area is substandard or insanitary—i. e., slum. Plaintiffs are owners of 68 private residences which are not claimed to be physically deteriorated. The statute under which condemnation is undertaken authorizes acquisition by the city without physical blight of "vacant or predominantly vacant areas". Vacant land comprises 75% of this area. The buildings are clustered together for the most part and not scattered through the vacant lands, nor is it necessary to condemn many of them in order to utilize the vacant land except as the city planners deem it wise to enlarge the vacant area by converting residential to industrial purposes. This is not a case of slum clearance as the condemnation site was held to be in Kaskel v. Impellitteri (306 N.Y. 73, 115 N.E.2d 659). The present exercise of the power of eminent domain transcends anything involved therein. This kind of municipal redevelopment is not based on what was thought to have been the full scope of such enterprises by the New York State Constitutional Convention of 1938, for it goes beyond what is authorized by the housing article (N.Y. Const. art. XVIII) then added to the State Constitution, which provides only for low-rent housing or the reconstruction and rehabilitation of areas that are actually substandard and insanitary. This proceeding is not instituted on the basis that this area is substandard or insanitary but that the city will be improved if real property in good condition is transferred to other private owners who, in the judgment of city planners, will use it for more progressive purposes deemed to be more in accord with development of the municipality. Such a practice may bear hard on the owner, who loses the good will connected with his location (Banner Milling Co. v. State of New York, 240 N.Y. 533, 148 N.E. 668, 41 A.L.R. 1019) and, in a world where politics is seldom absent from municipal administration, runs the risk of having his property taken from him to be transferred to more deserving owners.

Matter of Murray v. La Guardia, 291 N.Y. 320, 52 N.E.2d 884 and Kaskel v. Impellitteri (supra) marked a major step beyond what had theretofore been held to be public purposes in the exercise of the power of eminent domain. Property owners had been accustomed to parting with their real estate involuntarily where required for governmental uses such as highways, public buildings, parks, or for the use of transportation or public utility corporations deemed to be affected with a public interest. In 1936 it was held that substandard and insanitary real estate could be condemned to be replaced with public housing or limited dividend housing corporations (Matter of New York City Housing Authority v. Muller, 270 N.Y. 333, 1 N.E.2d 153, 105 A.L.R. 905). The Murray and Kaskel cases signified a departure in that there condemnation of real property was sanctioned for resale to other private owners, for ordinary private uses not affected with a public interest. The public purpose was conceived to be the elimination of slums to which resale of the subject property to other private owners was incidental. The difference of opinion on the court in Kaskel v. Impellitteri was confined to whether the site to be condemned in that case could be classified as being slum; the court was unanimous concerning the constitutionality of the statute there involved. Now we are faced with a further step in the socialization process. It does not necessarily follow that because the former statute was upheld this statute must be constitutional also. In ruling upon the validity of a statute like this, we are not to proceed upon the assumption that the Legislature has plenary power or none. "The state under the guise of paternal supervision may attempt covertly and gradually to mould its members to its will. The difference as so often is a difference of degree." (Cardozo: The Paradoxes of Legal Science, p. 111.) I see no escape from the duty and responsibility of courts in ruling upon the constitutionality of legislation of this kind to weigh the social values which are involved, including the social value of ownership of private property, in order to determine whether the Legislature has exceeded its power under the Federal and State Constitutions.

Conceding that the power of eminent domain has been extended to the elimination of areas that are actually slum, the question here is whether this power can be further extended to the condemnation of factories, stores, private dwellings or vacant land which are properly maintained and are neither substandard nor insanitary, so that their owners may be deprived of them against their will to be resold to a selected group of private developers whose projects are believed by the municipal administration to be more in harmony with the times. It begs the question, in my judgment, merely to assert that such properties are to be taken to prevent them from becoming actually blighted at some future date. It is possible that there are certain definable situations where conditions can constitutionally be eliminated which tend to produce slums, before the properties have deteriorated to that level. It is possible that some of what is contemplated by this statute, including portions of this project, could be accomplished under more limited legislation. What has been attempted under a statute in a particular instance does not determine its constitutionality which is adjudged in the light of what could be done according to its terms (Rosalsky v. State of New York, 254 N.Y. 117, 121, 172 N.E. 261, 262; McKinney's Cons. Laws of N.Y., Book 2, Part 1, Constitutional Interpretation, n. 39, p. 40). The 1958 statute *sub judice* is not satisfied by eliminating slums. It provides for the elimination of potential slums, which means anything that city planners think does not conform to their designs.

It might be thought, perhaps, that in the march of progress there is no limit to the power of the Legislature even short of authorizing municipal officials to determine, through zoning or eminent domain, who shall be permitted to own real estate in cities and to what purpose each separate parcel may be devoted. The sound view is still, however, that due process includes substantive as well as merely procedural limitations and that under the mores of the day there are substantive limits to what municipalities can do with private property, even by means of statutes enacted under the spur of single-minded city planners imbued with evangelistic fervor. At some stage the rights of private property owners become entitled to be respected, even if their use of their properties does not coincide with the ideas, however, enlightened, of the *avant garde*. The public theorists are not always correct; if they had full sway a century and a quarter ago the country would have invested its substance in the construction of canals,

which any intelligent theorist would have seen was the effective way to
promote the economic development of the United States. The railroads
were just around the corner, but their advent was obvious to nobody. Imposing some constitutional limit to the extremely wide scope of this statute
would be a far cry from returning to the days of *laissez faire*. There are
those among who the writer is one who believe that, although the Constitution does not enact Mr. Herbert Spencer's *Social Statics*, it nevertheless holds
substantive content in social matters and does mandate, at the minimum,
some sort of economic or social middle way. It is not for the courts to
question the wisdom of the Legislature in exercising the discretion which
it has within constitutional limits, but there are limits to legislative power
in dealing with private property and in my view they are exceeded by the
breadth of the statute on whose constitutionality we are now ruling. The
fundamental principle of government still applies which the mentor of the
young Cyrus tried to implant in him in ancient Persia. When asked
whether a ruler should compel a subject whose coat was too large for him
to trade it with another whose coat was too small, if one of them objected
to the exchange, the young future ruler replied in the affirmative, for the
reason that then each would have a coat that fitted him. The mentor told
him that he was wrong, since he had confused expediency with justice.
The question here, it seems to me, is where to draw the line between supposed expediency and justice. In Berman v. Parker, 348 U.S. 26, 75 S.Ct.
98, 99 L.Ed. 27, the actual decision of the court did not go beyond what
this court decided in Kaskel v. Impellitteri, 306 N.Y. 73, 115 N.E.2d 659,
supra, where it was recognized in both opinions that land, buildings or
improvements, not in themselves insanitary or substandard, may be included
in the condemnation site if necessary for the effective clearance, replanning,
reconstruction or rehabilitation of the essentially slum area of which such
land or property is a part. The question before the United States Supreme
Court in the Berman case was whether a department store could be condemned which was so connected with a blighted area that the latter could
not be rehabilitated without including the land occupied by the store.
That was not the case, like this, of so-called "intangible blight." The principal area there was substandard and insanitary without dispute: 64.3% of
the dwellings in it were beyond repair, 18.4% needed major repairs, only
17.3% were satisfactory; 57.8% of the dwellings had outside toilets, 60.3%
had no baths, 29.3% lacked electricity, 82.2% had no wash basins or laundry
tubs, 83.8% lacked central heating. All of those circumstances were noted
in the opinion of the court by Mr. Justice Douglas, who recognized that
there was a basis on which the municipal planning commission could determine that the subject property was so interrelated with the slum properties that the latter could not be effectively eliminated without the former.
Although the opinion uses broad language in certain paragraphs, which do
speak of unlimited power in the planning commission, these *obiter dicta*

should be limited and construed by what the same Supreme Court Justice said in his dissenting opinion in United States v. Wunderlich, 342 U.S. 98, 101, 72 S.Ct. 154, 96 L.Ed. 113: "Absolute discretion is a ruthless master. It is more destructive of freedom than any of man's other inventions." Nothing in the facts decided in Berman contravenes, it seems to me, the trenchant statements in the opinion in the same case of the three-Judge District Court (Schneider v. District of Columbia, D.C., 117 F.Supp. 705, 719–720), which are perhaps more applicable to this case than to that in which the words were spoken:

> "Even if the line between regulation and seizure, between the power to regulate and the power to seize, is not always etched deeply, it is there. And, even if we progress in our concepts of the 'general welfare,' we are not at liberty to obliterate the boundary of governmental power fixed by the Constitution.
>
> "The terms 'public use' and 'public purpose' have never been defined with precision, and cannot be. Localities, customs and times change, and with them the needs of the public may change. But even the most liberal courts have put boundaries upon the meanings. One eminent authority° sums up the matter by saying that the courts which go furthest in sustaining the power of eminent domain hold that 'anything which tends to enlarge the resources, increase the industrial energies, and promote the productive power of any considerable number of the inhabitants of a section of the state, or which leads to the growth of towns and the creation of new resources for the employment of capital and labor' constitutes a public use. We think so unqualified a definition cannot be sustained, because every factory or mercantile house of any size meets that definition to some degree, and most certainly the Government has not an unrestricted power to seize one man's property and sell it to another for the building of a factory or a store. The decisions of the courts which used such sweeping language and which are cited to us fall short of supporting the contention made to us in the present case. We shall discuss them in a moment.
>
> "It is said that the established meaning of eminent domain includes measures for the 'general welfare' and that new social doctrines have so enlarged the concept of public welfare as to include all measures designed for the public benefit. The difficulty lies somewhat in the unqualified philosophical declaration, but it lies more in the practicality that some person or persons must determine, if that be rule, what is the public benefit. Therein lies the insuperable obstacle, in the American view. There is no more subtle means of transforming the basic concepts of our government, of shifting from the preeminence of individual rights to the preeminence of government wishes, than is afforded by redefinition of 'general welfare,' as that term is used to define the Government's power of seizure. If it were to be determined that it includes whatever a commission, authorized by the Congress and appointed by the President, determines to be in the interest of 'sound development,' without definition of 'sound development,' the ascendancy of government over the individual right to property will be complete. Such ascendancy would logically follow over the rights of free speech and press, it seems to us."

"° 2 Nichols, Eminent Domain (3d ed., 1950), § 7.2 et seq."

Few more persuasive illustrations could be found than the statute (not necessarily the particular project) now before us for decision of situations where "Absolute discretion", in the language of Mr. Justice Douglas, can be "more destructive of freedom than any of man's other inventions." I do not imply that this power necessarily would be used to that end, but it potentially can be so employed. The constitutionality is to be tested by what can be done under this statute. If we uphold its validity, that means upholding everything which is an integral part of the act that can be done under its language.

Whether or not a proposed condemnation is for a public purpose is a judicial question (Denihan Enterprises v. O'Dwyer, 302 N.Y. 451, 457, 99 N.E.2d 235, 237). Perhaps the power of eminent domain might be invoked for the rehabilitation of vacant areas subdivided into lots of such irregular form and shape or insufficient size, depth, or width, as to render them incapable of effective or economic development; or rendered sterile by obsolete or poorly designed street patterns with inadequate access to such vacant areas rendering them unsuitable for appropriate development. It is possible that there are other conditions enumerated in former section 72-n of the General Municipal Law which could furnish a basis for condemnation. Nevertheless this act contains, in my judgment, fundamental defects which invalidate it. Thus it declares that in event of any of the factors existing which are enumerated in subparagraph a of subdivision 1, "with or without tangible physical blight," real property may be condemned if such areas impair or arrest "the sound growth of the community and tend to create slums and blighted areas." Among the factors enumerated are unsuitable topographical or other physical conditions *impeding the development of appropriate land uses;* an obsolete system of utilities serving the area, whatever that may mean; buildings and structures unfit for use and occupancy as a result of age, obsolescence, *improper uses and conditions which adversely affect the general welfare;* scattered improvements *which retard the development* of the land. When asked upon the argument of the appeal whether this means that the power of eminent domain may be invoked in any case of this nature where, in the judgment of municipal officers, the property should be acquired and sold to some other private owners who would agree to use it for purposes that would accord more nearly in their judgment with the progress of the municipality, the Corporation Counsel replied in the affirmative. He could hardly do otherwise, in view of the language of the statute.

Neither is it sufficiently clear or definite what constitutes a "predominantly" vacant area. In order that the power of eminent domain may be invoked for this purpose under this statute the area to be condemned must be "vacant" or "predominantly vacant." In the case of this project it appears that the area is 75% vacant. We were told upon the argument that it would be enough if it were 50% vacant. The land which is occupied by buildings (plaintiffs' own 68 private residences which have not been found to be in inferior condition or improperly maintained) appears to be linked to the project for the reason that a larger area than the vacant land is needed for the proposed industrial park, rather than that it is an integral part of an "intangibly" blighted area. However that may be in regard to this particular project, no such limitation is imposed by the statute itself whose constitutionality is being tested, which purports to render a finding by the governing body conclusive that an area to be condemned is "predominantly vacant" so as to enable almost any proportion of buildings to be condemned along with vacant land. On the basis of indefiniteness alone it seems to me that this statute fails to meet recognized constitutional requirements (People v. Grogan, 260 N.Y. 138, 145 et seq., 183 N.E. 273, 275, 86 A.L.R. 1266). Although the requirement of definiteness is most freqently presented in criminal cases, it has equal application to sumptuary statutes such as this depriving persons of property *in invitum.*

For the reasons stated, I dissent and vote to reverse the judgment appealed from and to grant to the plaintiffs the relief demanded in the complaint.

DYE, FULD, FROESSEL, BURKE and FOSTER, JJ., concur with DESMOND, C. J.; VAN VOORHIS, J., dissents in a separate opinion.

Judgment affirmed.

MUNICIPALITIES—SLUMS—PREVENTION
AND CLEARANCE
CHAPTER 924

An Act to amend the general municipal law, in relation to the prevention of the development or spread of slums and the promotion of the orderly growth of municipalities, through the clearance and redevelopment by municipalities of vacant or predominantly vacant areas which impair or arrest the sound growth of the municipality or tend to create slums and blighted areas.

Became a law April 22, 1958, with the approval of the Governor. Effective April 22, 1958.

The People of the State of New York, represented in Senate and Assembly, do enact as follows:

Section 1. The general municipal law is hereby amended by adding thereto a new section, to be section seventy-two-n, to read as follows:

§ 72-n. Prevention of the development of slums and blighted areas and the promotion of the orderly growth of municipalities through the clearance and redevelopment of vacant or predominantly vacant areas.

1. Legislative finding and declaration as to purpose of act. a. It is hereby found and declared that there exist in many municipalities within this state

vacant or predominantly vacant areas characterized by the following conditions, factors or characteristics or combinations thereof, with or without tangible physical blight: (1) subdivision of land into lots of such irregular form and shape or such insufficient size, depth or width as renders them incapable of effective or economic development; (2) obsolete and poorly designed street patterns with inadequate access to such vacant or predominantly vacant areas or street widths or block sizes which are unsuitable for appropriate development in such areas; (3) unsuitable topographical, subsoil and other physical conditions impeding the development of appropriate land uses; (4) an obsolete system of utilities serving the area; (5) buildings and structures unfit for use and occupancy as a result of age, obsolescence, dilapidation, inadequate maintenance, or other factors affecting their physical condition; (6) dangerous, unsanitary or otherwise improper uses and conditions which adversely affect the public health, safety and general welfare; and (7) scattered improvements which, because of their incompatibility with an appropriate pattern of land use and streets, retard the development of the land.

b. It is hereby further found and declared that, by reason of such conditions, factors or characteristics or combinations thereof, with or without tangible physical blight, such areas impair or arrest the sound growth of the community and tend to create slums and blighted areas.

c. It is hereby further found and declared that by reason of the subdivision of land in such areas into small parcels in subdivided ownerships, land assembly by individual owners or private enterprise for the purpose of development or redevelopment of such areas in a manner consistent with and in furtherance of the public health, safety, morals and general welfare, is difficult of attainment and uneconomic in nature; that by reason of the conditions, factors or characteristics set forth in paragraph a of this subdivision there is a high incidence of tax delinquency exceeding the fair value of the land in such areas; and that title is frequently defective or difficult to determine even through complex title searches, thereby rendering the land unmarketable and unusable without acquisition and assembly of such property by the municipality for the purpose of redevelopment thereof in a manner consistent with and in furtherance of the public health, safety and general welfare.

d. It is hereby further found and declared that while such vacant or predominantly vacant areas are appropriate for development at a greater intensity for residential, commercial, industrial, community, public or other uses or combinations thereof, the conditions, factors and characteristics described in paragraph a of this subdivision existing therein depress and destroy the economic value of such areas and also impair sources of public revenues normally capable of being derived therefrom.

e. It is hereby further found and declared that such vacant or predominantly vacant areas are presently impairing or arresting the sound growth of the community or municipality and should be made available for redevelopment in a manner consistent with and in furtherance of the public health, safety and general welfare; that there is an acute shortage of vacant or predominantly vacant land properly located for development in such manner within such municipalities; and that the clearance, replanning and development or redevelopment of such areas for residential, commercial, industrial, community, public or other uses or combinations of such uses is needed to foster the growth of said municipalities in a manner consistent with and in furtherance of the public health, safety and general welfare, by providing residential accommodations within reasonable proximity to existing employment centers, and by providing appropriately located commercial and industrial areas.

f. It is hereby further found and declared that the construction of needed public improvements throughout such municipalities, the clearance and redevelopment of substandard and unsanitary areas therein, and the rehabilitation and conservation of deteriorating areas therein are leading to a reduction in density and to the elimination of obsolete or incompatible land uses in such municipalities, and that therefore it is necessary to provide for the relocation and dispersion at proper densities of such displaced residential, commercial, industrial and other uses on properly located and suitable tracts within such vacant or predominantly vacant areas, in order effectively to prevent overcrowding and the resulting development or spread of slums and blight in other parts of the municipality.

g. It is hereby further found and declared that it is necessary to clear, replan and develop or redevelop such vacant or predominantly vacant areas for residential, commercial, industrial, community, public or other uses or combinations of such uses in order to promote and protect the public health, safety and general welfare; provide suitable areas for the relocation of persons and establishments displaced by clearance, redevelopment, rehabilitation or conservation activities or other needed public improvements elsewhere in such municipalities; that it is necessary for the accomplishment of such purposes to grant to the municipalities of this state the rights and powers herein provided and that the use of all the foregoing rights and powers for the accomplishment of such purpose or purposes is a public use and for a public purpose essential to the public interest.

2. Definitions. As used in this section, the following terms shall mean:

a. "Area." An area designated by the commission in the manner prescribed in subdivision three hereof as a vacant or predominantly vacant area which by reason of conditions, factors or characteristics described in paragraph a of subdivision one of this section or any combination thereof with or without tangible physical blight, impairs or arrests the sound growth of the community or tends to create slums and blighted areas therein.

b. "Agency." The officer, board, body, commission, committee or agency designated pursuant to paragraph f of subdivision nine hereof.

c. "Project area." All or part of an area selected by the agency for replanning and redevelopment.

d. "Commission." The planning commission or other analogous body of the municipal corporation.

e. "Municipal corporation" or "municipality." A city or town.

f. "Governing body." (1) In a city, the board of alderman, common council, council, commission or other body now or hereafter vested by its charter or other law with jurisdicition to enact ordinances or local laws, except that if there be a board of estimate, the term "governing body" shall mean only such board of estimate; (2) in a town, the town board.

3. Designation of area. An area shall be designated by the commission after a public hearing. Such designation shall be accompanied by:

a. a finding that the area is a vacant or predominantly vacant area which by reason of conditions, factors or characteristics described in paragraph a of subdivision one of this section or any combination thereof, with or without tangible physical blight, impairs or arrests the sound growth of the community or tends to create slums and blighted areas; and

b. a general statement of the proposed land uses, layout of streets, population and employment densities, building bulks and general standards for the development of the area, which form the basis for the replanning and redevelopment of the area.

4. Selection of project area; preparation of preliminary plan. The agency shall select one or more project areas. The agency shall prepare a preliminary plan of the project area, in accordance with the general standards established pursuant to subdivision three hereof. Such plan shall contain:

a. a detailed statement of existing physical, economic, and sociological conditions in the project area.

b. a general statement of (1) proposed land uses and their interrelationship with the existing and proposed pattern of traffic and transportation in the project area and the municipality. (2) proposed community facilities and open space in connection with any proposed development. (3) proposed demolition of designated structures, and new construction, with a preliminary estimate of the number of dwelling units or amount of floor space, density, and rent levels; and (4) proposed provision of offstreet parking and loading, and contemplated methods of financing.

5. Approval of preliminary plan. Such preliminary plan shall be submitted to the governing body for its approval. Before taking action on the preliminary plan, the governing body shall refer the plan to the commission, which, after a public hearing, shall certify whether the plan conforms to the master plan, if any, of the municipal corporation and to the general standards established pursuant to subdivision three hereof. The commission shall submit a report to the governing body, not later than six weeks from the date of referral, certifying its unqualified approval, its disapproval, or its qualified approval with recommendations for modifications therein. If the commission shall certify its unqualified approval, the governing body, by a majority vote after a public hearing, may approve the preliminary plan. If

the commission shall certify its disapproval or shall fail to make its report within six weeks from the date such plan was referred to it, the governing body after a public hearing, may nevertheless approve the preliminary plan, but only by a three-fourths vote. If the commission shall certify its qualified approval together with recommendations for modifications, the governing body, by a majority vote after a public hearing, may approve the preliminary plan and the modifications recommended by the commission or the governing body after a public hearing, may approve the preliminary plan without modifications, but only by a three-fourths vote.

6. Preparation and approval of final plan. If the preliminary plan is approved by the governing body, the agency shall prepare a final plan of the project area, which shall include, but shall not be limited to: a detailed statement of proposed land uses and their interrelationship with the existing and proposed pattern of traffic and transportation in the project area and the municipality; proposed improvement, alteration or vacation of streets; proposed provisions for off-street parking and loading; proposed locations and easements for public utilities; residential, commercial, industrial, community, public or other uses or combinations of such uses or for a purpose or purposes described in subdivision one of this section.

9. Additional powers. In proceeding under this section, in addition to all other powers which it may exercise, a municipal corporation, acting through its governing body, may:

a. Issue bonds or other obligations for the acquisition of property in the same manner as for other public purposes. The period of probable usefulness of such purpose is hereby determined to be fifteen years;

b. Provide, in the discretion of the governing body, for clearance of the property including the remedying of any unsuitable topographical, subsoil or other physical conditions impeding the development of the land for appropriate use by the person, firm or corporation to whom such property is sold. In the event that clearance is provided by the municipality, the cost of such clearance shall be financed in the same manner as acquisition costs.

c. It shall designate an appropriate board for each project area to carry out all activities connected with such project area.

§ 2. This act shall take effect immediately.

Note.—This bill will promote the establishment of new business and industry and greater improvement at little or no cost to the State or its municipalities. No tax exemption or other subsidy is involved. It is designed in fact to increase tax revenues through the utilization of land which would otherwise not be available for such uses. Many areas of substantial size exist in our municipalities which can be reclaimed and developed with highly useful and productive improvements. Through this bill the attack on deterioration of property will be intensified and a large gap will be closed in the efforts being put forth for that purpose.

REDEVELOPMENT AGENCY OF
SAN FRANCISCO

v.

HAYES

122 Cal. App. 2d 777, 266 P.2d 105 (1954), cert, den., 348 U.S. 897 (1954).

District Court of Appeal.　First District Division 1, California.

Jan. 26, 1954.

As Amended Jan. 29, 1954.

As Amended on Denial of Petitions for Rehearing Feb. 25, 1954.

Hearing Denied March 25, 1954.

Redevelopment agency and others bought mandamus proceeding against chairman of agency to compel him to execute certain loan and grant contracts with the United States, and taxpayers and residents and owners of realty in blighted area intervened. The District Court of Appeal, Bray, J., held that the Community Redevelopment Law was not unconstitutional on grounds raised.

Peremptory writ of mandate issued.

William A. O'Brien, Sp. Counsel, Redevelopment Agency of City and County of San Francisco, San Francisco, Dion R. Holm, City Atty. of City and County of San Francisco, John Elmer Barricklo, Morley Goldberg, Deputy City Attys., San Francisco, for petitioners.

Rose M. Fanucchi, San Francisco, for respondent.

Jack H. Werchick, San Francisco, for interveners.

Edmund G. Brown, Atty. Gen., Eugene B. Jacobs, Deputy Atty Gen., for the State, as amicus curiae in support of some of petitioners' contentions.

BRAY, Justice.

Petition for writ of mandate to compel respondent chairman petitioner Redevelopment Agency of the City and County of San Francisco [1] to execute certain loan and grant contracts with the United States of America.

Questions Presented.

1. Have intervenors the right to intervene?

2. Constitutionality of the Community Redevelopment Law, Part I, Division 24, sections 3300-33954, Health and Safety Code,[2] as applied to (1) slum clearance, (2) blighted area.

---

1. Hereafter referred to as "the Agency."
2. Hereafter referred to as "the act."

Record.

Respondent demurred and in answer to the petition denied none of the facts set forth in the petition, but based his refusal to execute the contracts on the alleged grounds of the unconstitutionality of the act. Two taxpayers in the Diamond Heights Area, Florence Van Hoff and Victor Berg, on behalf of themselves and all others similarly situated, filed a complaint in intervention in which they demurred to the sufficiency of the petition on the ground that the proposed proceedings of the Agency are prohibited by the Fourteenth Amendment to the United States Constitution, and article I, §§ 1, 11, 13, 14, 14½, 21; article III, § 1, and article IV, §§ 24, 31, of the California Constitution. They also answered, denying certain allegations of the petition. Thereupon petitioners demurred to the complaint in intervention both generally and specially and on the ground that intervenors have no right to intervene. Petitioners also moved to strike the whole and all parts of the complaint in intervention on the grounds of intervenors' lack of right and that the complaint is sham, irrelevant and argumentative. At the hearing, intervenors' demurrer to the petition and petitioners' demurrer to, and motion to strike, the complaint were submitted.

Petition.

The petition sets forth that the Agency is a public body corporate and politic created under the act, after a declaration of the board of supervisors of the need for such agency, and the fact that the city had satisfied the "Community Prerequisites" of the act in that the city's Planning Commission has a master plan which includes all the matters required by the act to be in such plan. The Agency has undertaken a program for the elimination and redevelopment of blighted areas, of which the first two are the ones to be considered here, one being known as Western Addition Project and the other as Diamond Heights Project. The petition then gives the steps taken antecedent to the formulation of the redevelopment plans for both projects. As no attack is made on the regularity of those proceedings, they need not be detailed.

Certain facts are then alleged as to each area. Western Addition is a blighted area which constitutes both a social and economic liability requiring redevelopment in the interest of the health, safety and general welfare of the people of the city and state. It includes approximately 28 blocks and is characterized by buildings used wholly or in part for residential purposes, which because of age, obsolescence, deterioration, dilapidation, mixed character and shifting uses, are unfit and unsafe for occupancy, and conducive to ill health, infant mortality, juvenile delinquency and crime. There are more than 2,000 substandard dwellings and hundreds of rooms in dilapidated rooming houses and row dwellings. More than 60 per cent of the dwelling units are dilapidated or lack private baths; more than 40 per cent have more than twice as many families than originally planned for; more than 50 per cent have inadequate toilet facilities; many lack installed heating; general use of portable coal oil heaters and storage of inflammable material constitute fire hazard; inadequate fire escape and exits add to the hazard of the inhabitants; extreme overcrowding is three and one-half times more prevalent in the area than in the city as a whole. The correction of these blighted conditions cannot be accomplished without redevelopment of the area as a whole, nor by private enterprise alone and without public participation. All of these conditions and this fact have been found by resolution and ordinance of the board of supervisors.

Diamond Heights is a blighted area constituting a social and economic liability requiring redevelopment in the interest of health, safety and general welfare. It includes approximately 325 acres. Much of the area was subdivided in 1863 and 1864; only 15 per cent of the area is occupied or used; 4 per cent is in improved boundary streets; 5 per cent playgrounds; less than 6 per cent interior streets and dwellings. Such unuse and lack of development is due to lots of irregular form and shape having been laid out without regard to the contours and other physical characteristics of the ground such as cliffs, steep gradings and outcroppings of rock; more than 500 parcels are in separate ownership which makes it impossible to effectively assemble the land by private means without public assistance and exercise of the power of eminent domain; there is wasteful street design, unsuited and unadapted to the topography of the area; mapped streets of usable grade are connected with mapped streets of unusable grade, so steep as to render impossible the construction of usable streets; one-third of said streets are too steep to be usable; 66 acres of such mapped streets remain unpaved and undeveloped, there being only 1.4 acres of paved streets. The major portion of the area is unserved by utilities of any kind; existing public open spaces would be inadequate to serve the area if built up. Approximately 85 per cent of the area is vacant and undeveloped; 115 acres are in private ownership, of which only 17.8 acres are improved with houses, the remainder of the private ownership improvements consisting of truck yards, deteriorated sheds and two quarries. As a result of said faulty planning there is an economic dislocation and disuse of the area; a subdivision of lots into irregular form and shape and inadequate size for proper use and development; a layout of lots in disregard of the contours and other physical characteristics of the ground and surrounding conditions; nonexistence of adequate streets and utilities in the area. The area is characterized by the growing or total lack of proper utilization resulting in stagnant and unproductive condition of land potentially useful and available for contributing to the public health, safety and general welfare. The blighted condition is aggravated by the shortage of useful land in the city for residential development to alleviate the acute housing shortage and tends to render the lands unmarketable and thereby to force an abnormal pattern of residential growth.

Redevelopment is necessary to facilitate the redevelopment of congested, deteriorated areas in other sections of the city, particularly in Western Addition. Correction cannot be accomplished without redevelopment of the areas as a whole. This cannot be done by private enterprise alone without public participation and assistance. All of the above has been found by the board of supervisors by resolution and ordinance. Intervenors admit the factual characteristics of the area but deny the conclusions and point out that for a long time past 210 acres have been and still are in public ownership.

The redevelopment of both projects requires (1) acquisition of lands by purchase or eminent domain, (2) demolition and clearance, (3) vacation and abandonment of certain street areas and dedication of other areas for street widenings and other improvements and the consolidation of certain blocks into continuous land areas, (4) rough grading and installation of necessary site improvements and utilities, (5) replatting and zoning in conformity with the city's master plan, (6) disposition of said lands as improved by sale under suitable safeguards, restrictions, covenants and conditions as set forth in certain ordinances. Such redevelopment will eliminate the blight conditions alleged by providing: clearance, elimination and prevention of slum and blighted areas; a proper, well-planned, economic utilization of said areas; adequate open spaces; utilities; streets designed to carry fast through traffic while closing off traffic on other streets, thereby contributing to the safety of the inhabitants of the areas; school, shopping and other community facilities; improved lands near the center of the city for the construction of needed dwelling units; a substantial increase in the number of safe and sanitary dwelling units to ease the acute housing shortage.

Title I of the Housing Act of 1949, P. L. 171, 81st Congress, 42 U.S.C.A. § 1451 et seq., authorizes certain financial assistance to petitioners to aid in this redevelopment. Pursuant to applications filed by the Agency with the Housing and Home Finance Administrator, the Administrator has advanced to the Agency $517,160.82, in addition to which the city has provided $78,962 to the Agency. On June 4, 1953, the Agency adopted a resolution directing respondent, as its chairman, to execute on behalf of the Agency a contract with the United States of America for a loan of $16,022,000 and a capital grant of $6,012,000 to aid in financing Western Addition Project and a contract for the loan of $5,049,000 and a capital grant of $334,000 to aid in financing Diamond Heights Project, both of which contracts have been approved by the board of supervisors. To satisfy the requirements of said contracts the city has undertaken to provide local grants-in-aid of $3,279,600 **for** Western Addition and $2,711,000 for Diamond Heights. The contracts have been executed by the administrator but respondent refuses to execute them.

Accompanying the petition are exhibits containing the various resolutions and ordinances of the board of supervisors, the tentative plans of the projects, reports on and photographs of the areas and other data.

*   *   *

(b) *Diamond Heights.*

[6] It is not contended that Diamond Heights constitutes a slum area. Its claimed necessity for redevelopment is its economic dislocation and disuse. It comes within the terms of section 33042 of the Health and Safety Code: "A blighted area is characterized by:

"(a) An economic dislocation, deterioration, or disuse, resulting from faulty planning.

"(b) The subdividing and sale of lots of irregular form and shape and inadequate size for proper usefulness and development.

"(c) The laying out of lots in disregard of the contours and other physical characteristics of the ground and surrounding conditions.

"(d) The existence of inadequate streets, open spaces, and utilities. * * *" 6

We have not included subdivision (e) dealing with submerged lots as there are none in the Diamond Heights area.

There are not as many cases dealing with redevelopment statutes concerning deteriorated areas, nor are they as uniform in their decisions as are those concerning slum areas. We have been cited to and found only five cases discussing the subject. The latest is Schneider v. District of Columbia, supra, 117 F.Supp. 705, which, as we have shown, upheld the validity of the District of Columbia Redevelopment Act as related to slum clearance. However, it held the act invalid as related to deteriorated areas, stating that Congress in legislating for the district has no power to authorize the seizure by eminent domain of property for the sole purpose of redeveloping the area according to its, or its agent's judgment of what a well-developed, well-balanced neighborhood would be.

The case then considers one further situation, *i.e.*, where a part of the deteriorated area contains slums. It holds that only that portion of the area geographically necessary to the elimination of slums may be taken.

The court distinguishes Foeller v. Housing Authority of Portland, supra, 256 P.2d 752, and Schenck v. City of Pittsburgh, infra, 364 Pa. 31, 70 A.2d 612, in both of which cases the properties seized were developed for nonresidential purposes, by pointing out that in each case the seizure and resale of the properties was a clear method of serving two purposes, (1) to prevent the

---

6. The statute includes both this type of area and slum areas under the term "blighted area." For brevity and in order to distinguish slum areas factually from areas of the type of Diamond Heights we will refer to the latter as "deteriorated" areas, not as a word of description but merely as a word of reference.

recreation of slums, and (2) to enlarge the potential activity upon which the city lived. The court seemed to consider that the first purpose could exist alone but that the second purpose must be concomitant with the first. It referred to Fallbrook Irrigation District v. Bradley, 1896, 164 U.S. 112, 17 S.Ct. 56, 41 L.Ed. 369, which involved an irrigation act of the State of California and the question was whether the construction of irrigation works is a public purpose, and also to Clark v. Nash, 1906, 198 U.S. 361, 25 S.Ct. 676, 49 L.Ed. 1085, where the doctrine of the Fallbrook case was applied to an irrigation project in the state of Utah, although the project, authorized by a state statute, was the condemnation of land by an individual for the purpose of irrigating his own land, and other cases. Concerning these and the Foeller and Schenck cases, supra, the court said that the basis of the decisions was "meeting a compelling community economic need is a public purpose." It then referred to People of Puerto Rico v. Eastern Sugar Associates, 1 Cir., 1946, 156 F.2d 316 certiorari denied 329 U.S. 772, 67 S.Ct. 190, 91 L.Ed. 664, which considered a statute of the insular legislature embodying a far-reaching program of agrarian reform designed to remedy desperate economic conditions existing in the islands. The act authorized the seizure of large holdings of land use for the raising of sugar, especially that owned by corporations, and the redistribution of the land to individuals in small parcels. The statute was upheld upon the public necessity for solution of the general and acute conditions and upon the conclusion that the statute was reasonably calculated to deal with these problems.

Thus, the Schneider decision recognizes that property may be taken for redevelopment for other than purely slum clearance purposes, namely, to meet a compelling community economic need. The case then considers whether as to the non-slum area in the District of Columbia the proposed taking was to meet such need. It states that the redevelopment plan is based on the opinion of its proponents that residential neighborhoods should be "well-balanced" and that the area should contain housing for all income groups. It points out that "No acute housing shortage is to be met," in fact the plan contemplates no more residents after redevelopment than now. "No pressing economic condition" is shown. No purpose of housing for the needy is shown. "No rearrangement of streets is contemplated," the streets in the Project Area being continuous lines of the streets in other parts of the District of Columbia. "In sum the purpose of the plan, in addition to the elimination of slum conditions, is to create a pleasant neighborhood, in which people in well-balanced proportions as to income may live." The court then states: "But as yet the courts have not come to call such pleasant accomplishments a public purpose which validates Government seizure of private property. The claim of Government power for such purposes runs squarely into the right of the individual to own property and to use it as he pleases. Absent impingement upon rights of others, and absent public use or compelling public necessity for the property, the individual's right is superior to all rights of the Government and is impregnable to the efforts of government to seize it. That the individual is in a low-income group or in a high-income group or falls in the middle of the groups is wholly immaterial. One man's land cannot be seized by the Government and sold to another man merely in order that the purchaser may build upon it a better house or a house which better meets the Government's idea of what is appropriate or well-designed." It should be noted that the act involved in the Schneider case, 60 Stat. 790, refers only to "substandard housing and blighted areas." It contains no definition of "blighted area" similar to that contained in section 330-42, Health and Safety Code.

[7] We are in accord with the Schneider decision that where no compelling community economic need is shown, the power of eminent domain may not be used. As hereafter shown, there appears to be such need in Diamond Heights.

The next most recent case is Kaskel v. Impellitteri, supra, 115 N.E.2d 659. There the appropriate New York municipal body proceeded under section 72-k of the General Municipal Law to find that a Columbus Circle area was "substandard and insanitary" and to plan a project for the removal of all buildings in it, redevelop it and then sell or lease portions of the area to private concerns. A taxpayer brought suit contesting the finding that the area was substandard and insanitary and asked that a court trial be had to determine that question. The majority opinion which held that as there was ample evidence to justify the City Planning Commission's findings and there was no charge that it acted corruptly or arbitrarily, the courts could go no further into this subject, adopts the minority opinion on all other questions in the case. It is held that the statute providing for slum clearance section 72-k of the General Municipal Law, is constitutional but can only be applied if the project is primarily for slum clearance. The minority opinion was to the effect that there was evidence supporting the plaintiff's claim that the area was not a slum area and slum clearance was not the primary object of the project but was secondary to turning the property over to private enterprise for the construction and operation of a sports coliseum, therefore, the case should be tried to determine the true factual situation.

People ex rel. Gutknecht v. City of Chicago, 1953, 414 Ill. 600, 111 N.E.2d 626, involved the validity of the 1949 amendments to the Illinois Blighted Areas Redevelopment Act of 1947, S.H.A. ch. 67½, §§ 63 et seq., 64, 65(1). As originally enacted that act was limited to "slum and blighted" areas—in substance, what we have considered here "slum areas" only—provided for their elimination and the construction of redevelopment projects financed by private capital. The amendment broadened the definition of "blighted areas" to include practically the same conditions set forth in section 33042 of the Health and Safety Code. Following the procedure provided in the act the Chicago Land Clearance Commission determined a certain 40 acre area to be blighted. Thereupon a private corporation submitted to the commission a redevelopment plan whereby it was to acquire the property, construct dwelling units thereon and sell them to private buyers. This plan required the use of public funds and the power of eminent domain. A quo warranto proceeding was brought to determine the validity of the amendment and the proposed procedure. No attack was made on the act as originally enacted as its validity had been sustained in People ex rel. Tuohy v. City of Chicago, supra, 78 N.E.2d 285, and Chicago Land Clearance Commission v. White, supra, 104 N.E.2d 236. While there is mention of slum eradication in the case, a study of it indicates that the question presented was clearly whether the acquisition of vacant land areas by a public agency for subsequent sale to private interests for development for residential use was an acquisition for a public use or public purpose permitting eminent domain to be employed. There was no slum condition in the area to be taken. The tie-in with slum eradication is based upon the statement that the development of areas for providing additional housing is necessary as an adjunct of clearing slum areas. "So far as we are aware, this is the first case in which governmental efforts to deal with unmarketable areas of vacant land have received judicial consideration. * * * What is involved here is, by the definition of the statute, and area which, because of characteristics of scattered ownership, undesirable platting, deteriorated site improvements, or excessive tax delinquencies, has in fact become unmarketable and because of its unmarketability has distorted the normal development of the community.

"The deleterious effect of such areas has been recognized by the Congress which has provided for Federal assistance in eliminating 'land which is predominately open and which because of obsolete platting, diversity of ownership, deterioration of structures or of site improvements, or otherwise substantially impairs or arrests the sound growth of the community * * *.' (42 U.S.C.A. par. 1460.) In the statute here involved, and in another statute known as the Blighted Vacant Areas Development Act of 1949, (Ill. Rev. Stat. 1949, chap. 67½, pars. 91.1-91.7), the General Assembly of Illinois has recognized that such vacant areas in their present condition are incapable of development for housing purposes by private enterprise. They are characterized as economic, social and physical waste lands, the elimination and development of which is declared to be a public use." 111 N.E.2d at page 634.

The court then held that the amendment was valid and constitutional. "The purpose and use to which the vacant blighted property is to be taken is both a public purpose and a public use, since the taking tends to alleviate a housing shortage, is an essential aid and adjunct to slum clearance, removes hazards to health, safety, welfare and morals of the community by developing the area, and eliminates factors impairing and arresting sound community growth." 111 N.E.2d at page 635.

The minority opinion points out that the majority opinion holds that the acquisition of vacant land and its development for residential uses even though unrestricted to low-rent accommodations is sufficiently related to the subject of slum clearance as to constitute the taking of land for a public use, a holding with which the minority opinion disagrees.

Foeller v. Housing Authority of Portland, supra, 1952, 256 P.2d 752 was brought to determine the validity of Oregon's Urban Redevelopment Law. While the project under consideration there was to take an area 53.8 per cent residential and redevelop it into an area completely commercial or industrial, the court held that the primary purpose was to prevent the development of slum conditions in that area. The case cannot be considered authority as to the situation where the area to be taken is a deteriorated one solely.

Thus we find that the only case which upheld the validity of a redevelopment statute as applied to a non-slum area is the City of Chicago case, and even in that case the court felt constrained to tie in the principle of the slum clearance cases by stating that providing additional housing was an adjunct of slum clearance. This constitutes a very elastic tie, for, based on that theory, any project of redevelopment could be supported as slum prevention if only it provided additional housing.

However, it appears from the cases on eminent domain dealing with a new subject to which the power is attempted to be applied that the right to its use depends upon what is referred to in the Schneider case as a "compelling community economic need." Our task, then, is to determine first whether the act is based on such a requirement, and secondly, whether in its application to the Diamond Heights Project such a need is shown. As to the basis of the act—in addition to sections 33041 and 33042, Health and Safety Code, heretofore quoted, there are a number of other significant sections. Section 33040 finds that in many communities there exist blighted areas which constitute social or economic liabilities, requiring redevelopment in the interest of the health, safety and general welfare of the people. These blighted areas are characterized by one or more of the conditions set forth in sections 33041-33044 inclusive. Section 33043 additionally characterizes a blighted area by a prevalence of depreciated values, impaired investments and social and economic maladjustments reducing the capacity to pay taxes so that tax receipts are inadequate for the cost of public services rendered. Section 33044 additionally characterizes a blighted area as one where in some parts a growing or total lack of proper utilization of areas results in a stagnant and unproductive condition of land potentially useful and valuable for contributing to the public health, safety and welfare. The section further refers to a loss of population and reduction of proper utilization of the area resulting in its further deterioration and added costs to the taxpayer for the creation of new public facilities and services elsewhere. Section 33045 declares the policy that the existence of blighted areas characterized by any or all of the conditions in the preceding sections constitutes a rising menace to public health, safety and welfare, cannot be remedied by use of the police power, necessitates excessive expenditures, and their removal is of benefit to the local population and property owners. Section 33046 continues the declaration of policy that such conditions cause continuing deterioration and disuse, that the blight cannot be corrected except by redeveloping the entire area, or substantial portions of it, that there is an impracticability of private assembly of small parcels in scattered ownership, and as a practical matter is so difficult and costly and lacking in legal power as to make it impossible to remedy by private owners. The only practical remedy is by public acquisition, clearance and planned redevelopment. Section 33047 declares that to protect and promote the sound development and redevelopment of blighted areas and the general welfare these conditions should be remedied by all appropriate means including the expenditure of public funds and the use of eminent domain and that the necessity of redevelopment in the interests of health, safety and welfare of the people is a matter of legislative determination.

[8] We do not deem it necessary to determine whether if only one of the designated conditions characterizing a blighted area under the statute exists, the statute could be enforced, as that question is not before us. However, it is clear that a combination of many of them establishes a menace to the health, safety and general welfare of the people of the community, and if such menace cannot be removed by private capital or police power, and requires redevelopment as outlined in the act, there would then exist a compelling community economic need.

Application to Diamond Heights Project.

This brings us to the question as to whether the petition shows a compelling community economic need for the project. Accompanying the petition are a series of exhibits setting forth the proceedings taken by the various city and county authorities, plans of the project, reports considered, maps of the present areas, and maps showing the projected uses to be made of the area. From these, it appears that the board of supervisors found, based upon substantial evidence, that the Diamond Heights area is a blighted one characterized, at least, by the conditions set forth in sections 33042(a) to (d) inclusive, 33044, 33045, 33046 and 33047.

The record shows that approximately 85 per cent of the area consists of vacant land which is in a state of economic disuse because private enterprise in the absence of governmental assistance cannot redevelop it in the community interest. This is due to the gridiron pattern of streets of approximately 66 acres of unimproved streets not adapted to the contour of the land, unsuited to the topography and too steep to be usable; to the fact that lots of irregular form and shape, many of them excessively long and narrow, have been laid out in disregard of the contours and other physical characteristics of the ground such as cliffs, out-croppings of rock, steep grades. There are 500 lots owned by separate individuals whose holdings vary in size from lots of 25 feet width to parcels of half an acre. Only

15 per cent of the area is used. There is a shortage of land in San Francisco and the welfare of the people requires that this unproductive area be used for dwelling and public places. In many instances the blighted condition of the area has resulted in sale of property to the state for delinquent taxes. The tentative plan shows that other than the public places the redevelopment is to be predominantly residential, consisting of single-family houses and multi-family houses. Open space, commercial, public (fire house, schools, park, playgrounds), institutional (churches, nursery schools, community buildings) and other uses are planned. It is not sufficient to say that the streets can be changed by ordinary eminent domain and street proceedings. Because of the peculiar layout of the streets as now shown on the map, the cost of abandonment proceedings and eminent domain proceedings would practically be prohibitive for, because of the many ownerships and the irregularity of the parcels, the cost of the taking and the resultant damage to the parts not taken would nearly equal the entire value of the private areas. While a large part of the area is in public ownership and could be developed by the authorities, it is so broken and interspersed with private ownerships as to require a consideration of the whole area. While probably no one element of the blight is sufficient to justify the taking by eminent domain, the combination of a great and pressing demand for more housing, the correlation of the area with other areas of the city, by streets and public places, the fact that without governmental help the area cannot be developed and will continue to deteriorate, together with all the circumstances shown by the record, demonstrate the compelling community economic need required to permit the application of the act.

[9] Intervenors contend that there is no necessity for the proposed Diamond Heights plan inasmuch as the private owners have had no opportunity to develop the area because 65 per cent of it has been held by public agencies, and the failure of the latter to act is a cause of the present condition. They claim that the area could have been developed many years ago when buildings costs were lower, the labor supply was more abundant, materials more available, and loans for construction were available at much lower rates. Regardless of the reason for the condition, and what might have been done, we are confronted with the present condition. Intervenors contend that there is no demand for dwellings of the class contemplated by the plan. This question is one for the city and the Agency to determine.

❋   ❋   ❋

Public Purpose.

[11] The contention that the proposed Diamond Heights plan does not constitute a public use, is answered in Oliver v. City of Clairton, 1953, 374 Pa. 333, 98 A.2d 47. While in that case there was some slum clearance in-

volved, it appears that the main attack on the redevelopment plan was that the area was not a blighted one because so much of it was vacant land. There the 5 acres which were to be redeveloped for heavy industrial purposes, consisted of 58 residential lots which, however, were not actually laid out with open streets; there were 7 small buildings in the area, and over 90 per cent of the land was vacant and unimproved. The assessed valuations over a decade had decreased, 15 of the lots were delinquent for many years in taxes, and the ownership of the lots was divided among approximately 22 individuals. Except for the fact that half of the few dwellings involved were substandard or slum grade, the situation was similar in many respects to that in Diamond Heights. Appellant there contended that as a large part of the area consisted of vacant land it could not be treated as blighted area. The court pointed out that, just as is the situation with regard to our act, there was nothing in the Pennsylvania act limiting the certification of blighted areas to improved property, but on the contrary vacant areas were expressly included. It then stated: "It may be well to point out once more what was said in the Schenck case, 364 Pa. [31] at page 37, 70 A.2d [612] at page 615, that the Urban Redevelopment Law is to be sharply distinguished from the Housing Authorities Law of May 28, 1937, P.L. 955 * * * in that the latter aimed principally at the elimination of undesirable dwelling houses, whereas the Urban Redevelopment Law 'was obviously intended to give wide scope to municipalities in redesigning and rebuilding such areas within their limits as * * no longer meet the economic and social needs of modern city life and progress.' Redevelopment authorities have the power, therefore, where the conditions prescribed in the act are found to exist, to exercise the right of eminent domain pursuant to a redevelopment proposal even though the redevelopment area may be predominantly open, vacant or unimproved." 98 A.2d at page 52.

The contention is further answered in People v. City of Chicago, supra, 111 N.E. 2d 626, 633: "Next to be considered is plantiff's contention that the acquisition of vacant land-areas of the type here involved by a public agency, for subsequent sale to private interests for development for residential use, is not acquisition for a public use or a public purpose, and that therefore eminent domain may not be employed and public funds may not be expended. This court has recognized the existence of an acute housing shortage, Cremer v. Peoria Housing Authority, 399 Ill. 579, 78 N.E. 2d 276, and the evidence in this case confirms the continued existence of that shortage. We have held that the expenditure of public funds for the acquisition of land by a public agency to be sold to a private developer for the construction of non-low-rent housing constitutes a public purpose. Cremer v. Peoria Housing Authority, 399 Ill. 579, 78 N.E.2d 276. In Zurn v. City of Chicago, 389 Ill. 114, 59 N.E.2d 18, we held that the elimination and redevelopment of slum and blighted areas is a public purpose and a public use regardless of the subsequent sale or lease of the property to private interests after redevelopment had been accomplished. And even more recently, in Chicago Land Clearance Commission v. White, 411 Ill. 310, 104 N.E.2d 236, we held that a condemnation proceeding under the Blighted Areas Redevelopment Act of 1947 was not a proceeding to acquire land for private purposes merely because a Land Clearance Commission had entered into a contract with a private corporation for the sale of the area after it was acquired. Chicago Land Clearance Commission v. White, 411 Ill. 310, 104 N.E.2d 236."

In Foeller v. Housing Authority of Portland, supra, 256 P.2d 752, it was pointed out that the transformation of an entire area which is struggling against obsolete planning and is otherwise blighted into one from which all hazards to the city's health, morals and safety have been eradicated and the placing in deeds conveying such portion of the area as may go into private ownership, of conditions and covenants to prevent the recurrence of blight constitutes a public use of such area. It must be pointed out that neither esthetic views nor considerations of economic advantage to the community or a combination of both are sufficient to justify the use of eminent domain for redevelopment purposes. The redevelopment program must be necessary to protect the public health, morals, safety or general welfare through the elimination of blighted areas. Opinion to the Governor, supra, 59 A.2d 531.

In Fallbrook Irrigation District v. Bradley, supra, 164 U.S. 112, 163, 17 S.Ct. 56, 65, a case arising in California, it was held that the state's power of eminent domain may be exercised if the taking "be essential or material for the prosperity of the community * * *."

[12] The act is premised upon the expressly declared policy that elimination of blighted areas of the Diamond Heights type and the redevelopment of such areas along the lines contemplated here are public uses and purposes and are governmental functions of state concern. As said in Housing Authority v. Dockweiler, supra, 14 Cal.2d 437 at page 449, 94 P.2d 794, at page 801 (dealing with slum clearance for public housing projects): "While such a declaration of policy by the legislative branch of the government is not necessarily binding or conclusive upon the courts, it is entitled to great weight and it is not the duty or prerogative of the courts to interfere with such legislative finding unless it clearly appears to be erroneous and without reasonable foundation."

Public Use.

While in Gravelly Ford Canal Co. v. Pope & Talbot Co. ,36 Cal.App. 556, 563, 178 P. 150, the court applied the strict definition of "public use," it is significant that in University of So. California v. Robbins, 1 Cal.App.2d 523, 37 P.2d 163, the court held that the taking of land by eminent domain by private institution, the University of Southern California, to be used as a library for its own students, was for a public purpose. In Tuolumne Water

Power Co. v. Frederick, 13 Cal.App. 498, at page 503, 110 P. 134, at page 136, the court said: "The courts would not be aiding the great enterprises of the West by adopting a narrow and restricted view of the meaning of the words 'public use,' as used by the Legislature and in our Constitution." Both cases advocate an expanded concept of what is use by the public.

Housing Authority v. Dockweiler, supra, 14 Cal.2d 437, 94 P.2d 794, adopted the broader interpretation as the rule to be followed in this state. It might be pointed out that as our community life becomes more complex, our cities grow and become overcrowded, and the need to use for the benefit of the public areas which are not adapted to the pressing needs of the public becomes more imperative, a broader concept of what is a public use is necessitated. Fifty years ago no court would have interpreted under the eminent domain statutes, slum clearance even for public housing as a public use, and yet, it is now so recognized. In addition, slum clearance for redevelopment purposes is likewise so recognized. To hold that clearance of blighted areas as characterized by the act and as shown in this case and the redevelopment of such areas as contemplated here are not public uses, is to view present day conditions under the myopic eyes of years now gone. As said in Miller v. Board of Public Works, 195 Cal. 477, 488, 234 P. 381, 385, 38 A.L.R. 1479: "'As the interest of society justifies restraints upon individual conduct, so also does it justify restraints upon the use to which property may be devoted. It was not intended by these constitutional provisions to so far protect the individual in the use of his property as to enable him to use it to the detriment of society. By thus protecting individual rights, society did not part with the power to protect itself or to promote its general well-being. Where the interest of the individual conflicts with the interest of society, such individual interest is subordinated to the general welfare.'"

[13] Pennsylvania Mut. Life Ins. Co. v. City of Philadelphia, 1913, 242 Pa. 47, 88 A. 904, 905, 49 L.R.A.,N.S., 1062 is not applicable. There the court held that taking private property adjoining a parkway merely to resell it to private persons subject to restrictions for "'the preservation of the view, appearance, light, air, health, or usefulness'" of the parkway was not a taking for public use. It pointed out that there have been two different interpretations of "public use" in this country, one the broader meaning of "public utility or advantage", the other narrower one of "use, or right of use, by the public," and that it preferred the narrower meaning. However, it indicated that there could be a taking for the purpose indicated if the city were to keep ownership of the property taken rather than resell it. Apparently the question of public use under this decision depended upon whether the use itself is a public one. In California our courts have followed the broader definition of "public use" and the cases hereinbefore cited have held that if property is taken for a public use, the fact that it is later to be returned to private ownership subject to restrictions protecting

the public use, does not make it any the less a public use. The later Pennsylvania cases have refused to follow the narrow interpretation in the Pennsylvania Mutual case, and in addition, have supported the last-mentioned statement. See Belovsky v. Redevelopment Authority, supra, 54 A.2d 277; Schenck v. City of Pittsburg, supra, 70 A.2d 612. While it has been held that private property may not be taken for purely esthetic reasons (that rule is discussed in the Pennsylvania Mutual case, 88 A. at page 906), it would seem proper in the light of the more modern cases, including the later Pennsylvania cases, to take private property if it were needed to protect a parkway and to provide light and air and usefulness for it. Section 14½, article I of the California Constitution (excess condemnation) provides this. Once it is determined that the taking is for a public purpose the fact that private persons may receive benefit is not sufficient to take away from the enterprise the characteristics of a public purpose. Housing Authority v. Dockweiler, supra, 14 Cal.2d 437, 94 P.2d 794; see also Chicago Land Clearance Commission v. White, supra, 104 N.E.2d 236; Herzinger v. Mayor & City Council of Baltimore, Md., 98 A.2d 87, 92; Zurn v. City of Chicago, supra, 59 N.E.2d 18; Waddell v. Chicago Land Clearance Commission, 7 Cir., 206 F.2d 748. "That purpose, as before pointed out, is not one requiring a continuing ownership of the property as it is in the case of the Housing Authorities Law in order to carry out the full purpose of that act, but is directed solely to the clearance, reconstruction and rehabilitation of the blighted area, and after that is accomplished the public purpose is completely realized. When, therefore, the need for public ownership has terminated, it is proper that the land be transferred to private ownership, subject only to such restrictions and controls as are necessary to effectuate the purposes of the act. It is not the object of the statute to transfer property from one individual to another; such transfers, so far as they may actually occur, are purely incidental to the accomplishment of the real or fundamental purpose." Belovsky v. Redevelopment Authority, supra, 54 A.2d 277, 282. See also Rowe v. Housing Authority, supra, 249 S. W.2d 551.

McCord v. Housing Authority of City of Dallas, Tex.Civ.App., 234 S.W.2d 108, is not in point here. It decided that the Housing Authority Law under which the Housing Authority purported to act contained no provision for selling or leasing the redeveloped land after slum clearance to private persons. For that reason it confined the definition of "public purposes" as used in the law to the continued ownership of the property after development by the authority. It contrasted the law with a federal law which expressly provided for making slum cleared land available for development by private enterprise.

Equal Protection.

[14] The claim that the Redevelopment Acts because they provide for acquisition of property by eminent domain and its later resale, violate the

Fourteenth Amendment to the Constitution in denying to the property owners the equal protection of the law, has been denied in several cases, among others, Ajootian v. Providence Redevelopment Agency, supra, 91 A.2d 21; Nashville Housing Authority v. City of Nashville, supra, 237 S.W.2d 946; Belovsky v. Redevelopment Authority, supra, 54 A.2d 277; Robinette v. Chicago Land Clearance Commission. D.C.Ill.1951, 115 F.Supp. 669; State ex rel. Bruestle v. Rich, supra, 110 N.E.2d 778. While the decision in the Robinette case is merely a "Memorandum and Order," the order dismissing the action for want of a substantial federal question, and is unpublished, it is of value for the reason that in Robinette v. Campbell, 342 U.S. 940, 72 S.Ct. 563, 96 L.Ed. 699, the Supreme Court denied motions for leave to file petitions for a writ of mandamus to compel the trial judge to expunge his order of dismissal. As said in Waddell v. Chicago Land Clearance Commission, supra, 206 F.2d 748, at page 750, where the same federal questions were raised: "Thus it is seen that the Supreme Court has refused to entertain an application to review the questions which appellants have attempted to present by this action."

As pointed out in those cases, the acquiring of the property is for a public use, its sale and the transfer of the property from one individual to another, so far as it may occur, are merely incidental to that use, and not the main object of the statute. The taking from the owner is not arbitrary. It is for a public purpose. The owner is guaranteed and will receive full compensation. In State ex rel. Bruestle v. Rich, supra, 110 N.E.2d 778, in discussing the contention made concerning the proposed redevelopment project, similar to the contention made here, that the plan contemplated taking the property of one person and reselling it to another and was therefore unconstitutional, the court stated that the primary purpose of the plan was to eliminate the blight conditions and provide against their recurrence. It then stated, 110 N.E.2d at page 785: "The exercise of the right of eminent domain under such a project, carried out pursuant to state law, has likewise been held by the Supreme Court of the United States as not to the contrary to the Fourteenth Amendment to the federal Constitution. Burt v. City of Pittsburgh, 340 U.S. 802, 71 S.Ct. 53, 95 L.Ed. 589." See also Waddell v. Chicago Land Clearance Commission, supra, 206 F.2d 748.

Due Process.

[15-19] The act does not violate the due process clause of the Fourteenth Amendment to the federal Constitution. See Robinette v. Chicago Land Clearance Commission, supra, D.C.Ill., 115 F.Supp. 669; People v. City of Chicago, supra, 111 N.E.2d 626, 636. To violate the due process clause a state statute permitting state action in economic affairs must be arbitrary and without reason. Olsen v. Nebraska, 313 U.S. 236, 61 S.Ct. 862, 85 L.Ed. 1305; U.S. v. Carolene Products Co., 304 U.S. 144, 58 S.Ct. 778, 82 L.Ed. 1234. The courts are restricted to an inquiry as to whether any state of facts

known or which reasonably could be assumed support the legislative judgment in enacting the statute. U.S. v. Carolene Products Co., supra, 304 U.S. 144, 154, 58 S.Ct. 778. While the legislative findings are not binding on the court, they are entitled to great respect. Block v. Hirsh, 256 U.S. 135, 41 S.Ct. 458, 65 L.Ed. 865; Weaver v. Palmer Bros. Co., 270 U.S. 402, 46 S.Ct. 320, 70 L.Ed. 654. Not only the California Legislature but the Congress of the United States and the legislatures of many states have made legislative findings of the necessity of redeveloping blighted areas by the use of private as well as public means. That modern conditions require such action is shown in the many books, articles and reports on community planning produced in the last few years. The courts, too, are entitled to take judicial notice of the need for and the change in attitude towards, such planning. See article by Hon. Emmet H. Wilson, Consideration of Facts in Constitutional Cases, vol. 17, So.Cal.Law Rev. 335. As article I, § 13 of the California Constitution is identical in scope and purpose with the Fourteenth Amendment of the federal Constitution, what has been said here concerning due process under the latter applies to it under the California Constitution.

Does the Act Unlawfully Delegate Legislative Power to the Agency?

[20] Intervenors contend that as the Agency is delegated the power to determine whether a given area is blighted, such delegation is contrary to article III, § 1 of the Constitution, which provides for the separation of powers into the three branches of government. It is contended that the characterization of blighted areas in the act is so broad as to provide no standards by which the agency may be guided, and hence it has the absolute power to determine what facts constitute any of the elements constituting blight. This same contention is almost identically the same language was made concerning the "Urban Redevelopment Law" of Pennsylvania in Belovsky v. Redevelopment Authority, supra, 54 A.2d 277. The answer given by the court there applies equally here, 54 A.2d at page 283: "One of these assaults is directed against an alleged delegation of legislative powers contrary to the provision of Article II, section 1 of the Constitution, P.S., it being claimed that insufficient standards are set up in the statute to guide the Authority in exercising the powers with which it is vested. The fact is, however, that the act contains as definite a description of what constitutes a blighted area as it is reasonably possible to express; in regard to such factors as the selection and the size of the areas to be redeveloped, the costs involved, and the exact form which the redevelopment in any particular case is to take, it was obviously impossible for the legislature to make detailed provisions or blueprints in advance for each operation. * * * All that the legislature could do, therefore, was to prescribe general rules and reasonably definite standards, leaving to the local authorities the preparation of the plans and specifications best adapted to accomplish in each instance the desired result, a function which obviously can be performed

only by administrative bodies. While the legislature cannot delegate the power to make a law, it may, where necessary, confer authority and discretion in connection with the execution of the law; it may establish primary standards and impose upon others the duty to carry out the declared legislative policy in accordance with the general provisions of the act." See also Housing Authority v. Dockweiler, supra, 14 Cal.2d 437, 462, 94 P.2d 794; People v. City of Chicago, supra, 111 N.E.2d 626. Blatz Brewing Co. v. Collins, 69 Cal.App.2d 639, 160 P.2d 37, is not opposed to our views here. That case held that "'the Legislature may not delegate authority to a board or commission to adopt rules which abridge, enlarge, extend or modify the statute creating the right.'" 69 Cal.App.2d at page 645, 160 P.2d at page 41. That principle is not involved here.

Special Privileges.

[21] Respondent contends that the act violates section 21, article I of the Constitution, which prohibits the granting of special privileges, in that the act provides that sale of the redeveloped property may be made on the basis of its "fair value" arrived at as provided in the act, and as there is no minimum price set, the "fair value" may be less than the actual cost to the Agency. Therefore, says respondent, the purchaser might profit on the transaction, giving him a special privilege over the rest of the public. The same contention was made in Housing Authority v. Dockweiler, supra, 14 Cal.2d 437, 460, 94 P.2d 794, concerning the fact that the houses to be erected were only to be rented to a certain class of citizens, and identically the same contention was made in Opinion to the Governor, supra, 69 A.2d 531, 534; In re Slum Clearance in City of Detroit, supra, 50 N.W.2d 340, 343; and in Belovsky v. Redevelopment Authority, supra, 54 A.2d 277. In all of them it was held that the fact that following the elimination of blighted conditions some incidental advantage might inure to private interests did not cause the taking to lose its public character nor make the statute unconstitutional.

Prohibition of Gifts of Public Moneys.

[22] Respondent contends that the furnishing of local grants-in-aid by the city provided for in the contracts sought to be executed here and the other public financial assistance to the agency proposed, constituted either the giving or lending of public moneys to private persons in violation of section 31, article IV of the Constitution. Actually there is no such gift or lending of money to private persons. The grants-in-aid are primarily for the providing of street improvements, fire protection, traffic control, schools, playgrounds, and other public services. The same objection was made to the Housing Cooperation Law in Housing Authority v. Dockweiler, supra, 14 Cal.2d 437, 458, 94 P.2d 794, and in Veterans' Welfare Board v. Jordan, 189 Cal. 124, 146, 208 P. 284, 22 A.L.R. 1515, to the statute authorizing a bond

issue to acquire lands, improve and sell them to veterans. In both cases it was held that the funds were being used by a public body for a public purpose, and were not given or loaned to private persons. In Patrick v. Riley, 209 Cal. 350, at page 357, 287 P. 455, at page 458, the court stated: "As indicated in the case of City of Oakland v. Garrison, supra, 194 Cal. [298] at page 302, 228 P. 433, the fundamental test of the constitutionality of a statute requiring the use of public funds is whether the statute is designed to promote the public interests, as opposed to the furtherance of the advantage of individuals; and such a statute should not be declared unconstitutional because of the fact that, incidental to the main purpose, there results an advantage to individuals." See also People v. City of Chicago, supra, 111 N.E.2d 626.

Effect of Section 19, Article XIII, Constitution

In 1952 this section was added to the Constitution by adoption by the people of an assembly constitutional amendment. In part it provides: "All of the provisions of the Community Redevelopment Law, as amended in 1951, which relate to the use or pledge of taxes or portions thereof as herein provided, or which, if effective, would carry out the provisions of this section or any part thereof, are hereby approved, legalized, ratified and validated and made fully and completely effective and operative upon the effective date of this amendment." In the analysis of this amendment by the Legislative Counsel sent to the voters appears the following: "In addition, the measure would validate all provisions of the Community Redevelopment Law consistent with the foregoing relating to the use or pledge of taxes." In the arguments in favor of the amendment appears the following: "This Constitutional Amendment provides a method of financing community redevelopment projects by relieving general taxpayers. Community redevelopment must be distinguished from public housing. The purpose is to eliminate blighted areas. Under the law, redevelopment, including the construction of streets, curbs, sidewalks and buildings, must be financed by private capital. However, a city or county must first acquire the property, if necessary by condemnation, because an individual, syndicate or corporation does not have the right of eminent domain and one property owner might refuse to sell and block the development.

"The difference between the expense of acquisition and clearing off the old, dilapidated buildings may be greater than the amount that may be received in the sale of the property for redevelopment in accordance with an officially approved plan. * *

"If adopted, this constitutional amendment will readily facilitate the redevelopment of blighted areas in cities and counties as now authorized by the Community Redevelopment Act of the State of California. Blighted areas are an economic and social drag upon the community and it is good public business to eliminate them."

"While an amendment to a state Constitution ratifying and confirming an act of its Legislature is ineffectual to validate that act, if it impair the obligations of a contract or divest vested rights, still such amendment may otherwise cure the infirmities of an act, and to that extent the act is thenceforth to be regarded as constitutional." Lee v. Superior Court, 191 Cal. 46, 53, 214 P. 972, 975.

[23] In view of the analysis sent to the voters, "If adopted, this constitutional amendment will readily facilitate the redevelopment of *blighted areas*" and the statement in the amendment that "*All* of the provisions of the Community Redevelopment Law, as amended in 1951 [the act with which we are dealing] ° ° ° are hereby approved, legalized, ratified" etc., it is obvious that the people were not restricting their ratification to such portions of the act as dealt with blight caused by slum conditions and refusing ratification to blight caused by the other conditions enumerated in the act. (Emphasis added.)

Excess Condemnation.

Section 14½, article I, California Constitution.

[24] This section, adopted in 1928, provides that in acquiring lands by gift, purchase or condemnation for memorial grounds, streets, squares or parkways, the state or any of its cities or counties may acquire additional lands within, in certain cases 150 feet, and in other cases within 200 feet, of the proposed improvement, and after the improvement is completed may sell the excess land not necessary for such improvement, with reservations concerning the use of such land so as to protect the improvement and to preserve its view, appearance, light, air and usefulness. The title to Senate Constitutional Amendment No. 16, Stats. 1927, p. 2371, the means whereby section 14½ was placed on the ballot, states that it is a resolution to propose to the people as addition to the Constitution a section "relating to the taking of parcels of land by eminent domain where such border upon public improvements." An examination of the argument to the voters concerning the proposed section, see Part I, page 17 of Arguments to Voters for the election of November 6, 1928, clearly shows that the section was intended primarily to apply to "little fractions of lots in the form of slivers or small triangles" left after making the particular improvements mentioned in the section, and in no manner was intended to apply either as an inhibition or otherwise to the projects contemplated in the act. Obviously there is no conflict between this section and the act. This section is limited to memorial grounds, streets, squares and parkways. Were there any such conflict the adoption in 1952 of section 19, article XIII, expressly recognizing the Community Redevelopment Law, would end the conflict. It is interesting to note that in State ex rel. Bruestle v. Rich, supra, 110 N.E.2d 778, at page 787, it was held "even if purchase or condemnation of the fee of the real estate in the slum area does involve acquisition of a greater interest

in such real estate than actually necessary to accomplish the purpose of eliminating slum conditions and providing against their recurrence," such acquisition was specifically authorized by section 10 of article XVIII of the Ohio Constitution, which provided for excess condemnation generally, rather than limiting it, as does our Constitution, to specified purposes.

*   *   *

Clean Hands.

[26, 27] Intervenors contend petitioners are not entitled to equitable relief as they do not come into court with clean hands. This is based upon the contention that the contract which petitioners seek to have executed contains inaccurate data which should be corrected and brought up to date before execution, and that petitioners have prevented development of the area. As we have heretofore shown, this is not the proper forum in which to raise such question, intervenors having no right to broaden the scope of the proceeding. Wright v. Jordan, supra, 192 Cal. 704, 714, 221 P. 915. Whether the agreement is an improvident and unwise one is for the Agency and the city to determine. As said in In re City and County of San Francisco, 191 Cal. 172, 185, 215 P. 549, 556, "In forming its judgment it must be presumed that the city considered the wisdom and policy of the whole plan in the light of the objects to be attained. The answer to adverse criticism is that the judgment of the city is conclusive in the absence of a showing of want of jurisdiction on the part of the city or a showing of bad faith on the part of its officers or gross extravagance or the existence of some fact sufficient to vitiate the contract." See also City and County of San Francisco v. Boyd, 22 Cal.2d 685, 690, 140 P.2d 666. " '* * * it is not for the courts to pass upon the merits of suggestions as to how the contract might be strengthened by amendments the desirability and effectiveness of which are for the consideration solely of the agencies and governing body to which the Urban Redevelopment Law has committed that responsibility.' " Oliver v. City of Clairton, 1953, 374 Pa. 333, 98 A.2d 47, 51.

[28] We fail to see how the failure of the city to develop its portion of the Diamond Heights Area in the past estops or prevents it from redeveloping the entire area.

[29-31] It should be emphasized that it is the combination in Diamond Heights of practically all the blight conditions mentioned in section 33042, subdivisions (a) to (d), showing a definitely compelling economic need, which permits the use of the act. Public agencies and courts both should be chary of the use of the act unless, as here, there is a situation where the blight is such that it constitutes a real hindrance to the development of the city and cannot be eliminated or improved without public assistance. It never can be used just because the public agency considers that it can make a better use or planning of an area than its present use or plan. As said in Schneider v. District of Columbia, supra, 117 F.Supp. 716 "* * * it

behooves the courts to be alert lest curently attractive projects impinge upon fundamental rights."

The demurrers of respondent and intervenors to the petition and of petitioners to the complaint in intervention are overruled. The motion of petitioners to strike all portions of the complaint in intervention other than those which constitute a demurrer to the petition is granted. It is ordered that a peremptory writ of mandate issue commanding respondent to execute the contracts referred to in the petition.

As we have herein stated, our decision is limited to questions of law, based upon the assumption that the findings of the administrative agencies involved in the redevelopment program are true. This decision in no wise bars a determination in a trial court of such issues of fact as may be properly raised in an attack upon an administrative proceeding.

PETERS, P. J., and FRED B. WOOD, J., concur.

Hearing denied; EDMONDS, CARTER and SCHAUER, JJ., dissenting.

Questions and Notes

1. Diamond Heights, on the shoulder of the Twin Peaks (straight southwest from downtown San Francisco, on Market Street) is one of the most spectacular residential sites in the United States.

2. What elements in a city planning program would be appropriate to demonstrate "compelling community economic need"?

3. Would it be fair to say that under this decision, the test of public use has shifted from slum clearance to housing to city planning?

DORSEY

v.

STUYVESANT TOWN CORPORATION

299 N.Y. 512, 87 N.E.2d 541 (1949), cert. den. 339 U.S. 981 (1950).

Appeal from Supreme Court, Appellate Division, First Department.

Separate actions by Joseph R. Dorsey and others, suing on behalf of themselves and others similarly situated, and by Shad Polier, as Taxpayer of the City of New York, against Stuyvesant Town Corporation, William O'Dwyer, as Mayor of the City of New York, an others, to enjoin defendants from refusing, withholding from or denying to any of the plaintiffs or others similarly situated any apartments in a certain housing project because of race or color of such persons. From two judgments of the Appellate Division of the Supreme Court in the first Judicial Department entered January 5, 1949, 274 App.Div. 992, 85 N.Y.S.2d 313, unanimously affirming (1) a judgment of the Supreme Court in the first action in favor of defendants, entered in New York County upon orders of the court (Benvenga, J.; 190 Misc. 187, 74 N.Y.S.2d 220) granting a motion by defendants dismissing the complaint for insufficiency under rule 112 of the Rules of Civil Practice and (2) a judgment of the Supreme Court in the second action, in favor of defendants, entered in New York County (Benvenga, J.) granting a motion by defendants for an order dismissing the complaint for insufficiency under rule 106 of the Rules of Civil Practice, plaintiffs appeal on constitutional grounds.

Judgment in first action affirmed, and appeal in second action dismissed.

Charles Abrams, New York City, Shad Polier, in person, Thurgood Marshall, Joseph B. Robison and Will Maslow, New York City, for Joseph R. Dorsey and others, appellants.

John P. Walsh, New York City, for Friendship House of Harlem, amicus curiæ, in support of appellants' position.

Carl Rachlin, New York City, and Lester C. Migdal, Brooklyn, for Citizens Housing & Planning Council, amicus curiæ, in support of appellants' position.

Paul L. Ross, New York City, for Town and Village Tenants Committee to End Discrimination in Stuyvesant Town, amicus curiæ, in support of appellants' position.

Andrew D. Weinberger, New York City, for the Board of Home Missions of the Congregational and Christian Churches and others, amici curiæ, in support of appellants' position.

Paul O'Dwyer and Lester M. Levin, New York City, for New York Chapter of National Lawyers Guild, amicus curiæ, in support of appellants' position.

Samuel Seabury, C. Frank Reavis, Jeremiah M. Evarts, George Trosk, Joseph C. Simpson and Churchill Rodgers, New York City, for Stuyvesant Town Corporation and another, respondents.

John P. McGrath, Corporation Counsel, New York City (William S. Lebwohl, Seymour B. Quel and Phillip V. Sherman, New York City, of counsel), for City of New York, respondent.

BROMLEY, Judge.

This appeal, involving two actions upon a consolidated record, raises the important question of whether a corporation organized under the Redevelopment Companies Law, McK. Unconsol. Laws, § 3401 et seq., has the privilege, admittedly possessed by an ordinary private landlord, to exclude Negroes from consideration as tenants. Appellants deny that respondents Stuyvesant Town Corporation and Metropolitan Life Insurance Company have such a privilege. They contend that these respondents are subject to the restraints of the equal protection clauses of the State and Federal Constitutions and that in their selection of tenants they cannot lawfully discriminate against Negroes, a policy which has been adhered to in renting apartments in the Stuyvesant Town development in New York City. Since the constitutional provisions referred to impose restraints on State action only, and not on private action, the precise question to be decided is whether Stuyvesant and Metropolitan in the circumstances of this appeal are subject to the constitutional limitations applicable to State action.

[1] The two actions involved in this appeal were brought simultaneously. In the Dorsey suit, plaintiffs are Negro veterans who have applied for apartments. In the Polier suit, plaintiff is a taxpayer. In both actions plaintiffs seek to enjoin Stuyvesant and Metropolitan from denying any of their accommodations and facilities in Stuyvesant Town to any person because of that person's race or color. In the Polier action, plaintiff seeks, in addition, to enjoin the City of New York from granting tax exemption to, and further performing a contract with, Stuyvesant and Metropolitan unless they cease discriminating against Negroes. Defendants' motions for judgment on the pleadings were granted below and judgments of dismissal unanimously affirmed by the Appellate Division, First Department. Since appellant Polier's status as a taxpayer does not support an action to challenge as unconstitutional the acts of respondent companies and officials, Bull v. Stichman, 273 App. Div. 311, 78 N.Y.S.2d 279, affirmed 298 N.Y. 516, 80 N.E.2d 661, his appeal does not present the constitutional question essential to our jurisdiction, Civil Practice Act, § 588, subd. 1, cl. (a), and must be dismissed. Subsequent references to appellants will indicate plaintiffs in the Dorsey suit, and to respondents will indicate Stuyvesant and Metropolitan.

Stuyvesant Town was built pursuant to a contract between the City of New York, Metropolitan and its wholly owned subsidiary Stuyvesant. The latter was organized by the former in 1943 as a redevelopment company under the Redevelopment Companies Law. Stuyvesant is a private corporation, all of its stock and debentures being owned and all of its working capital having been provided by Metropolitan. The entire cost of acquisition of the land in the project area and of the construction project has been advanced by Metropolitan. It represents an investment of not less than $90,000,000 of private funds held by Metropolitan for the benefit of its more than thirty-three million policyholders.

The project has been constructed in accordance with a plan approved by the city planning commission and the board of estimate of the City of New York, and the contract above referred to was approved by the State Superintendent of Insurance and the board of estimate, pursuant to the requirements of section 15 of the Redevelopment Companies Law, McK. Unconsol. Laws, § 3415.

The problems posed by this appeal require an understanding of the constitutional and statutory provisions applicable to housing in the State of New York. For that reason we proceed to set them forth in some detail. In 1938, the housing article of the State Constitution was adopted by the Constitutional Convention and approved by vote of the People. It is article XVIII, and in section 1 thereof it is provided that: "Subject to the provisions of this article, the legislature may provide in such manner, by such means and upon such terms and conditions, as it may prescribe for low rent housing for persons of low income as defined by law, or for the clearance, replanning, reconstruction and rehabilitation of substandard and insanitary areas, or for both such purposes, and for recreational and other facilities incidental or appurtenant thereto." The two purposes are distinct and different, and Stuyvesant Town involves the clearance and rehabilitation of a substandard and insanitary area and not low rent housing for persons of low income. Murray v. La Guardia, 291 N.Y. 320, 331-332, 52 N.E.2d 884, 888, 889. It may fairly be said that the whole housing article is instinct with the theory, consistent with its two purposes, that low rent housing for persons of low income is to be a function of government and the rehabilitation of substandard areas is to be the function of private enterprise aided by government. Section 2 provides that:

"For and in aid of such purposes * * * the legislature may: make or contract to make or authorize to be made or contracted capital or periodic subsidies by the state to any city, town, village, or public corporation, payable only with moneys appropriated therefor from the general fund of the state; authorize any city, town or village to make or contract to make such subsidies to any public corporation, payable only with moneys locally appropriated therefor from the general or other fund available for current expenses of such municipality; authorize the contracting of indebtedness for the purpose of providing moneys out of which it may make or contract to make or authorize to be made or contracted loans by the state to any city, town, village or public corporation; authorize any city, town or village to make or contract to make loans to any public corporation; authorize any city, town or village to guarantee the principal of and interest on, or only the interest on, indebtedness contracted by a public corporation; authorize and provide for loans by the state and authorize loans by any city, town or village to or in aid of corporations regulated by law as to rents, profits, dividends and disposition of their property or franchises and engaged in providing housing facilities; authorize any city, town or village to make loans to the owners of existing multiple dwellings for the rehabilitation and improvement thereof for occupancy by persons of low income as defined by law; grant or authorize tax exemptions in whole or in part, except that no such exemption may be granted or authorized for a period of more than sixty years; authorize cooperation with and the acceptance of aid from the United States; grant the power of eminent domain to any city, town or village, to any public corporation and to any corporation regulated by law as to rents, profits, dividends and disposition of its property or franchises and engaged in providing housing facilities.

"As used in this article, the term 'public corporation' shall mean any corporate governmental agency (except a county or municipal corporation) organized pursuant to law to accomplish any or all of the purposes specified in this article."

It will be noted that in specifying the powers of the Legislature, section 2 of article XVIII makes a distinction between a public corporation—which is defined to mean any corporate governmental agency organized for any of the specified purposes—and a corporation regulated by law as to rents, profits, dividends and disposition of its property or franchises and engaged in providing housing facilities. For instance, the Legislature is empowered to make State subsidies to public corporations, but only loans to corporations regulated as above described, and to authorize municipalities to guarantee principal and interest of obligations incurred by public corporations but not other corporations. Stuyvesant is not a public corporation but is a corporation regulated by law. Sections 3 to 7, inclusive, make provision for the creation of State debt for capital and periodic subsidies, impose certain limitations thereon, set up restrictions on the powers of cities, towns and villages to contract indebtedness in aid of the above-mentioned two purposes, impose liability on cities, towns and villages for State loans made to certain public corporations, empower the Legislature to make loans or subsidies on conditions consistent with the purposes of the article, such as restricting occupancy to persons of low income and according preference in occupancy to those who live or have lived in the area of the project, and prescribe the method of computing the liability for guaranties of the indebtedness of public corporations. Sections 8 and 9 provide for the taking and condemnation of property in excess of that actually and immediately required for the project if needed to effectuate the purposes of the article. There is nothing in the Constitution or, as will be demonstrated hereinafter, in the statute exercising the power granted by the Constitution indicating that the State is to have any part in the operation of dwellings resulting from the rehabilitation of substandard areas. Indeed section 10 provides that: "* * * nothing in this article contained shall be deemed to authorize or empower the state, or any city, town, village or public corporation, to engage in any private business or enterprise other than the building and operation of low rent dwelling houses for persons of low income as defined by law, or the loaning of money to owners of existing multiple dwellings as herein provided."

Thereafter the Legislature enacted the Redevelopment Companies Law, L. 1942, ch. 845, as amd. by L. 1943, ch. 234, and L. 1947, ch. 840, McKinney's Unconsol. Laws, §§ 3401-3426. In approving the amendment the Governor stated, in part: "The law permits and encourages the entrance into the housing field of life insurance companies. Since the enactment of the original law, there have been no projects. The amendments made by this bill are designed to attract private investment funds into the housing field."

Section 2 of the Redevelopment Companies Law, McK. Unconsol. Laws, § 3402, provides as follows: "* * * It is hereby declared that in certain areas of municipalities located within this state there exist substandard conditions and insanitary housing conditions owing to obsolescence, deterioration and dilapidation of buildings, or excessive land coverage, lack of planning, of public facilities, of sufficient light, air and space, and improper design and arrangement of living quarters; that there is not in such areas a sufficient supply of adequate, safe and sanitary dwelling accommodations properly planned and related to public facilities; that modern standards of urban life require that housing be related to adequate and convenient public facilities; that the aforesaid substandard and insanitary conditions depress and destroy the economic value of large areas and by impairing the value of private investments threaten the sources of public revenues; that the public interest requires the clearance, replanning, reconstruction and neighborhood rehabilitation of such substandard and insanitary areas, together with adequate provision for recreational and other facilities incidental and appurtenant thereto according to the requirements of modern urban life and that such clearance, replanning, reconstruction and neighborhood rehabilitation are essential to the protection of the financial stability of such municipalities; that in order to protect the sources of public revenue it is necessary to modernize the physical plan and conditions of urban life; that these conditions cannot be remedied by the ordinary operations of private enterprise; that provision must be made to encourage the investment of funds in corporations engaged in providing redevelopment facilities to be constructed according to the requirements of city planning and in effectuation of official city plans and regulated by laws as to profits, dividends and disposition of their property or franchises; that provision must be made to enable insurance companies to provide such facilities, subject to regulation by law as to the return from such facilities and the disposition of property acquired for such purpose; and that provision must also be made for the acquisition for such corporations and companies at fair prices of real property required for such purposes in substandard areas and for public assistance of such corporations and companies by the granting of partial tax exemption; that the cooperation of the state and its subdivisions is necessary to accomplish such purposes; that the clearance, replanning and reconstruction, rehabilitation and modernization of provision of adequate, safe, sanitary and properly planned housing accommodations in effectuation of official city plans by such corporations and companies in these areas are public uses and purposes for which private property may be acquired for such corporations and companies and partial tax exemption granted; that these conditions require the creation of the agencies, instrumentalities and corporations hereinafter prescribed for the purpose of attaining the ends herein recited; and the necessity in the public interest for the provisions hereinafter enacted is hereby declared as a matter of legislative determination."

Section 4, McK.Unconsol.Laws, § 3404, provides that a redevelopment company may be created by three or more persons filing a certificate which, among other specified information, shall contain:

"13. A declaration that the redevelopment company has been organized to serve a public purpose and that it shall be and remain subject to the supervision and control of the supervising agency except as provided in this act, so long as this act remains applicable to any project of the redevelopment company; that all real and personal property acquired by it and all structures erected by it, shall be deemed to be acquired or created for the promotion of the purposes of this act.

"14. A declaration that, after providing for all expenses, taxes and assessments, there shall be paid annually out of the earnings of the redevelopment company for interest, amortization, depreciation and dividends, a sum equal to but not exceeding six per centum if the total actual final cost of the project as defined by subdivision two of section thirteen of this act."

Sections 6 and 7, McK.Unconsol.Laws, §§ 3406, 3407, provide that the provisions of the Business Corporations Law, Consol.Laws, c. 4, General Corporation Law, Consol.Laws c. 23, and Stock Corporation Law, Consol. Laws c. 59, shall apply to redevelopment corporations, except where such provisions are in conflict with the provisions of the Redevelopment Companies Law, and that each such corporation shall have and may exercise such of the powers conferred by the General Corporation Law as shall be necessary in conducting its business and consistent with the provisions of the Redevelopment Companies Law. Limitations are imposed upon redevelopment companies in connection with various aspects of their businesses. Section 8, McK.Unconsol.Laws, § 3408, provides for a limited return on investment by stipulating that there shall be paid annually out of the earnings of the redevelopment company, after providing for all expenses, taxes and assessments a sum for interest, amortization, depreciation and dividends, equal to but not exceeding 6% of the total actual final cost of the project, which obligation shall be cumulative. Any cash surplus in excess of the amount so provided shall, upon dissolution of the company, be paid into the general fund of the municipality. Section 13, McK.Unconsol.Laws, § 3413, provides that a redevelopment company shall not have power to acquire any realty for a project unless the supervising agency and the local legislative body determine that such acquisition is necessary or convenient for the public purpose defined in the act. It also provides that no such company shall issue stock, debentures and bonds in an amount greater than the total actual final cost of the project and that no contract shall be made for the payment of salaries to officers or employees, or for the construction, substantial repair, improvement or operation of projects except subject to the approval of the supervising agency. The supervising agency referred to means only the Superintendent of Insurance where, as here, an insurance company owns the stock and debentures of a redevelopment company, and if, as here, a contract is entered into the parties to which are a municipality, a redevelopment company and an insurance company, the supervising agency shall have no continuing power of supervision once it shall have approved the contract. §§ 3, 15, McK.Unconsol. Laws, §§ 3403, 3415. This means that the general power of visitation, examination and control provided for by section 21, McK.Unconsol.Laws, § 3421, is inapplicable to Stuyvesant. There are other limitations upon methods of financing, mortgage, sale or disposition of property and alteration of structures. Section 9, 10, 11, 12, 14, 16, 23, McK.Unconsol.Laws, §§ 3409-3412, 3414, 3416, 3423.

Section 15 sets up a procedure for the submission and approval of a plan of a proposed project which requires the prior approval of the supervising agency and the local planning commission. Thereafter a contract shall be proposed which prior to its execution, must be approved by the local legislative body. It is provided that the contract shall regulate the rents to be charged and may contain other provisions for the financing, construction, operation and supervision of the project.

The statute provides that a municipality may take property by condemnation for a redevelopment company provided the latter shall pay all sums expended in connection with such acquisition, and it authorizes the municipality to convey such land to the company. § 20, McK.Unconsol.Laws, § 3420. It also authorizes any local legislative body to convey to such company land in any street which is duly closed or discontinued pursuant to the plan, upon payment therefor or upon exchange for other lands. § 20.

Section 24, McK.Unconsol.Laws, § 3424 provides that after the termination of tax exemption, in any manner, a redevelopment company may dissolve and convey its property to whomsoever it desires, and all limitations of the act shall cease.

Finally, section 26, McK.Unconsol.Laws, § 3426, provides as follows:

> "The local legislative body of any municipality in which a project of such company is or is to be located may by contract agree with any redevelopment company to exempt from local and municipal taxes, other than assessments for local improvements, all or part of the value of the property included in such project which represents an increase over the assessed valuation of the real property, both land and improvements, acquired for the project at the time of its acquisition by the redevelopment company which originally undertook the project and for such definite period of years as such contract may provide. The tax exemption shall not operate for a period of more than twenty-five years, commencing in each instance from the date of which the benefits of such exemption first become available and effective.
>
> "A redevelopment company which has been granted and has received tax exemption pursuant to this section may at any time elect to pay to the municipality the total of all accrued taxes for which exemption was granted and received, together with interest at the rate of five per centum per annum. Upon such payment the tax exemption of the project shall thereupon cease and terminate."

The Legislature deliberately and intentionally refrained from imposing any restriction upon a redevelopment company in its choice of tenants. The law contains none. Attempts, repeatedly made in the Legislature since the law was enacted, to alter the policy of the statute in this respect have failed. See e.g., 1948 Sess., Assem.Int. 127, Pr. No. 127; Assem.Int. 217, Pr. No. 217; Assem.Int. 1270, Pr. No. 1294; 1947 Sess., Assem.Int., 35,

Pr. No. 35; Assem.Int.,. 72, Pr. No. 72. On the other hand, the Public Housing Law, Consol.Laws, c. 44-A, § 223, which is applicable to State-constructed, low cost housing projects, expressly prohibits discrimination. There is no claim that the Legislature refused by amendment to make similar provision in the Redevelopment Companies Law because it thought the statute already barred discrimination, and it is undisputed, therefore, that the legislative intent is clear to leave private enterprise free to select tenants of its own choice.

The matter of the exclusion of Negroes from the development arose in connection with the approval by the Governor of the 1943 amendments to the Redevelopment Companies Law and in contract negotiations between Metropolitan and the city. Commissioner Robert Moses, active in the plan, stated publicly to the Governor and the board of estimate that if any requirement was imposed which deprived the landlord of the right to select its tenants, no private venture would go into the business. Certainly the general impression was created—which Metropolitan did nothing to dispel —that Stuyvesant Town would not rent to Negroes. For that reason and others, unsuccessful attacks were made upon the desirability of the project. In the board of estimate at least three votes were cast against approval of the contract on the ground that exclusion on racial grounds would be practiced. The contract was finally approved without any provision regarding discrimination in the selection of tenants. It may be noted in passing that thereafter the New York City Council passed legislation withholding tax exemption from any subsequent redevelopment company unless it gave assurance that no discrimination would be practiced in its rental policies. This provision, however, expressly excluded from its operation any project "hitherto agreed upon or contracted for." Administrative Code of City of New York, § J41—1.2.

In 1943, respondent Stuyvesant was formed by Metropolitan pursuant to the statute. A contract with the city was approved by the board of estimate of the City of New York in June, 1943. The contract embodied a plan for the rehabilitation of a substandard area comprising eighteen city blocks in the borough of Manhattan by the erection of thirty-five apartment houses capable of accommodating about twenty-five thousand people. Under the contract the City of New York agreed to condemn and bring under one good title the entire area. Stuyvesant agreed to acquire the area, demolish the old buildings and construct new ones, all without expense to the city. Metropolitan agreed to advance the necessary funds to Stuyvesant, guaranteed performance by the latter, and, with Stuyvesant, assumed all risks of the venture. The city granted tax exemption for twenty-five years only to the extent of the enhanced value to be created by the project. Stuyvesant agreed to convey to the city bordering strips around the periphery of the project in exchange for land in streets which the city agreed to close.

The contract regulates rents at rates intended to yield the statutory limited return, prohibits mortgaging and sale of the project, gives the city certain auditing privileges, and requires payment to the city upon the dissolution of Stuyvesant of any earned cash surplus after payment of all indebtedness. Upon the termination in any way of tax exemption, Stuyvesant may dissolve and convey its property to Metropolitan, and the statute and contract become inapplicable to the project.

In formulating an answer to the questions propounded at the beginning of this opinion we first consider whether there is anything in the Constitution of the State of New York which can be said to impose any broader or different restriction than is contained in the equal protection clauses of the Fourteenth Amendment of the Federal Constitution. Our conclusion is that the problem is precisely the same under the State Constitution as it is under the Federal Constitution.

Section 11 of article I of the State Constitution reads as follows: "No person shall be denied the equal protection of the laws of this state or any subdivision thereof. No person shall, because of race, color, creed or religion, be subjected to any discrimination in his civil rights by any other person or by any firm, corporation, or institution, or by the state or any agency or subdivision of the state."

The first sentence, which is obviously an equal protection clause, is no more broad in coverage than its Federal prototype, which reads: "No State shall * * * deny to any person within its jurisdiction the equal protection of the laws." U.S. Const., 14th Amendt., § 1. This conclusion follows from the plain meaning of plain words. It is strongly reinforced, however, by the fact that the chairman of the Bill of Rights Committee of the New York State Constitutional Convention of 1938, at which convention the section in question was approved, stated at the convention that the first sentence of section 11 "in effect embodies in our Constitution the provisions of the Federal Constitution which are already binding upon our State and its agencies." 2 Rev.Record of N.Y. State Constitutional Convention, 1938, p. 1065. It is significant that in previous New York cases arising under the equal protection clauses of the Federal and State Constitutions it has not been suggested that the reach of the latter differed from that of the former. Kemp v. Rubin, 298 N.Y. 590, 81 N.E.2d 325; Madden v. Queens County Jockey Club, 296 N.Y. 249, 72 N.E.2d 697, 1 A.L.R.2d 1160.

[2] The second sentence of section 11 is a civil rights clause and, although applicable to private persons and private corporations, protects only against "discrimination in * * * civil rights". Obviously such rights are those elsewhere declared. Again this conclusion is strongly supported by the statement of the chairman of the Bill of Rights Committee made at the convention to the effect that the provision in question was not self-executing and that it was implicit that it required legislative implementation to be effective. 2 Rev.Record of N.Y. State Constitutional Convention, 1938, p. 1144. Furthermore, it was stated at the convention that the civil

rights protected by the clause in question were those already denominated as such in the Constitution itself, in the Civil Rights Law or in other statutes. 4 Rev.Record of N. Y. State Constitutional Convention, 1938, pp. 2626-2627. At the 1938 Constitutional Convention attempts to provide explicitly against discrimination in housing in the housing and civil rights articles of the Constitution proved unsuccessful. See, e.g., N. Y. State Constitutional Convention, Pr. Nos. 10, 18, 49, 203, 380, 625, 691. No statute in New York recognizes the opportunity to acquire interests in real property as a civil right, although there are in existence today nearly twenty anti-bias laws covering many fields of activity. The conclusion that the opportunity to acquire such interests in New York is not a civil right is reinforced by the fact that bills introduced in the State Legislature in 1947 and 1948 to amend the Civil Rights Law in order to declare the "opportunity to purchase and lease real property without discrimination * * * to be a civil right", failed of passage. See e.g., 1947 Sess.Assem.Int. 34, Pr. No. 34; 1948 Sess.Assem. Int. 128, Pr. No. 128; Assem.Int. 715, Pr. No. 720; and Assem.Int. 1177, Pr. No. 1197; see, also, Pratt v. La Guardia, 182 Misc. 462, 47 N.Y.S.2d 359, affirmed 268 App. Div. 973, 52 N.Y.S.2d 569, appeal dismissed 294 N.Y. 842, 62 N.E.2d 394.

[3] Our decision then must rest on the co-ordinate commands expressed in the equal protection clauses of the Federal and State Constitutions. For many years it has been unquestioned that the great prohibitions of the Fourteenth Amendment are addressed to that action alone which "may fairly be said to be that of the States." Shelley v. Kraemer, 334 U.S. 1, 13, 68 S.Ct. 836, 842, 92 L.Ed. 1161, 3 A.L.R.2d 441; In re Civil Rights Cases, 109 U.S. 3, 3 S.Ct. 18, 27 L.Ed. 835. Upon that characteristic of the constitutional inhibition these parties have joined issue. Respondents contend that they are private companies, beyond the reach of the constitutional restraint and free to select arbitrarily the tenants who will occupy Stuyvesant Town. Appellants insist that the avowed discrimination falls under the constitutional ban because they say it has been aided and made possible by the action of the State. The issue is decisive, for the policy of respondents could not be followed by a governmental body. Cf. Buchanan v. Warley, 245 U.S. 60, 38 S.Ct. 16, 62 L.Ed. 149, L.R.A.1918C, 210, Ann. Cas.1918A, 1201.

In an early decision of the Supreme Court under the Fourteenth Amendment we find the statement that "a State acts by its legislative, its executive, or its judicial authorities. It can act in no other way." Ex parte Virginia, 100 U.S. 339, 347, 25 L.Ed. 676. In that case the court held the official conduct of a State judge subject to the mandate although he had acted on his own impulse and without authority from the law of the State. Subsequent cases have made it clear that the prohibited action of a State may be exerted through private individuals and corporations. Thus discrimination by private individuals offends the equal protection clause if they act under constraint of State law. Nixon v. Herndon, 273 U.S. 536, 47

S.Ct. 446, 71 L.Ed. 759; Buchanan v. Warley, 245 U.S. 60, 38 S.Ct. 16, 62 L.Ed. 149, L.R.A.1918C, 210, Ann.Cas.1918A, 1201, supra; Truax v. Raich, 239 U.S. 33, 36 S.Ct. 7, 60 L.Ed. 131, L.R.A.1916D, 545, Ann.Cas.1917B, 283.

In a more recent series of cases the Federal courts have held private groups subject to the constitutional restraints when they perform functions of a governmental character in matters of great public interest. Smith v. Allwright, 321 U.S. 649, 64 S.Ct. 757, 88 L.Ed. 987, 151 A.L.R. 1110; Nixon v. Condon, 286 U.S. 73, 52 S.Ct. 484, 76 L.Ed. 984, 88 A.L.R. 458; Rice v. Elmore, 4 Cir., 165 F.2d 387, certiorari denied 333 U.S. 875, 68 S.Ct. 905, 92 L.Ed. 1151; Kerr v. Enoch Pratt Free Library, 4 Cir., 149 F.2d 212. But compare Mason v. Hitchcock, 1 Cir., 108 F.2d 134. Speaking of the executive committee of the Democratic Party in the State of Texas, Mr. Justice Cardozo said: They are not acting in matters of merely private concern like the directors or agents of business corporations. They are acting in matters of high public interest, matters intimately connected with the capacity of government to exercise its functions". Nixon v. Condon, 286 U.S. at page 88, 52 S.Ct. at page 487, supra. The result is unchanged though the State cast off all fetters upon their discretion. Rice v. Elmore, supra. The Supreme Court of the United States has indicated that the inhibitions of the Fifth Amendment upon the action of the Federal Government would apply to a labor union whose power to act as sole collective bargaining agent for railroad employees was derived from Federal statute. See Steele v. Louisville & Nashville R. R. Co., 323 U.S. 192, 198-199, 65 S.Ct. 226, 89 L.Ed. 173.

In a final group of cases the State has lent its power in support of the actions of private individuals or corporations, and in so doing has clothed the private act with the character of State action. Shelley v. Kraemer, supra; Marsh v. Alabama, 326 U.S. 501, 66 S.Ct. 276, 90 L.Ed. 265. In the latter case an Alabama conviction for trespass in disseminating religious literature on the privately owned streets of a company town offended the due process clause of the Fourteenth Amendment. The language of the court indicates that if the right had been asserted in a different context the owner's action itself would have been condemned. Thus 326 U.S. at pages 505-506, 66 S.Ct. at page 278: "We do not agree that the corporation's property interests settle the question. The State urges in effect that the corporation's right to control the inhabitants of Chickasaw is coextensive with the right of a homeowner to regulate the conduct of his guests. We cannot accept that contention. Ownership does not always mean absolute dominion. The more an owner, for his advantage, opens up his property for use by the public in general, the more do his rights become circumscribed by the statutory and constitutional rights of those who use it."

Appellants here rely upon those cases in urging that we must characterize as governmental action the rental policy of Metropolitan and Stuyvesant. They point to the acknowledged contribution made by government to the project—principally the tax exemption amounting to many millions ɔf dollars, and aggregation of the land through use of the city's power of ɘminent domain and through exchange of bordering tracts for city streets which had been closed. Moreover, we are urged to consider the size of the project as in reality forming a large community within the city.

All of the previous decisions, and others cited, might be distinguished in that they disclose the exertion of governmental power directly to aid in discrimination or other deprivation of right, or the action of a private group in the exercise of a governmental function. Neither factor is present here, where the State has remained silent and has indicated that the public purpose has been fulfilled by the rehabilitation of a substandard area. Murray v. La Guardia, 291 N.Y. 320, 52 N.E.2d 884, supra. This conclusion is reinforced by the constitutional provision, hereinbefore referred to, which specifically negated any authorization to State or city to engage in any private business or enterprise in connection with the rehabilitation of substandard areas. Art. XVIII, § 10.

However, to rest our decision solely upon conceptual distinction would be to ignore the character of the Constitution which we construe and of the decisions through which the Supreme Court of the United States has preserved its nature as a living instrument of government. The language quoted above from Marsh v. Alabama, supra, has a different ring from the earlier words of Ex parte Virginia, supra. The evolution of our society has disclosed State action where doubtless it would not have been found in an earlier day. Institutions created to meet the social and industrial necessities of our times do not respond readily to the simple test enunciated in Ex parte Virginia, e.g., Marsh v. Alabama, supra. Those considerations might suggest the desirability of holding that the test can be satisfied, and State action discerned, in any case where the State has tolerated discrimination respecting a matter of high public importance. Invocation of the Constitution then might depend upon a balance of the two values asserted—here the privilege of Metropolitan and Stuyvesant as against the right of appellants to equality of treatment.

Such a development in constitutional law would clash with a fundamental policy inherent in the Fourteenth Amendment and the decision of the Civil Rights Cases, 109 U.S. 3, 3 S.Ct. 18, 27 L.Ed. 835, supra. Both are instinct with the idea that the rights defined in the amendment are to be protected by the States against the actions of private individuals. That high responsibility of the States, implicit in our Federal system, indicates that the political processes must furnish the appropriate means of extension of those rights in areas wherein they have not been heretofore asserted. The unquestioned value of that system suggests the limits to the expanding concept of State action, which has hitherto been found only in cases where the State has consciously exerted its power in aid of discrimination or where private individuals have acted in a governmental capacity so recognized by the State.

[4] The State of New York has consciously and deliberately refrained from imposing any requirement of nondiscrimination upon respondents as a condition to the granting of aid in the rehabilitation of substandard areas. Furthermore, it has deliberately refrained from declaring by legislation that the opportunity to purchase and lease real property without discrimination is a civil right. To say that the aid accorded respondents is nevertheless subject to these requirements, on the ground that helpful co-operations between the State and the respondents transforms the activities of the latter into State action, comes perilously close to asserting that any State assistance to an organization which discriminates necessarily violates the Fourteenth Amendment. Tax exemption and power of eminent domain are freely given to many organizations which necessarily limit their benefits to a restricted group. It has not yet been held that the recipients are subject to the restraints of the Fourteenth Amendment.

The increasing and fruitful participation of government, both State and Federal, in the industrial and economic life of the nation—by subsidy and control analogous to that found in this case—suggests the grave and delicate problem in defining the scope of the constitutional inhibitions which would be posed if we were to characterize the rental policy of respondents as governmental action. To cite only a few examples: the merchant marine, air carriers and farmers all receive substantial economic aid from our Federal Government and are subject to varying degrees of control in the public interest. Yet it has never been suggested that those and similar groups are subject to the restraints upon governmental action embodied in the Fifth Amendment similar to the restrictions of the Fourteenth upon the States. We do not read the language in Steele v. Louisville & Nashville R. R. Co., 329 U.S. 192, 65 S.Ct. 226, 89 L.Ed. 173, supra, as implying such a suggestion. Such restraints as have been imposed upon their freedom of action are derived from statute or common law, and we feel that those sources of control are the most appropriate.

We are agreed that the moral end advanced by appellants cannot justify the means through which it is sought to be attained. Respondents cannot be held to answer for their policy under the equal protection clauses of either Federal or State Constitution. The aid which the State has afforded to respondents and the control to which they are subject are not sufficient to transmute their conduct into State action under the constitutional provisions here in question.

The judgment in Dorsey v. Stuyvesant Town Corp. should be affirmed, with costs, and the appeal in Polier v. O'Dwyer should be dismissed, with costs.

FULD, Judge (dissenting).

Undenied and undeniable is the fundamental proposition that "Distinctions between citizens solely because of their ancestry are by their very nature odious to a free people whose institutions are founded upon the doctrine of equality." Hirabayashi v. United States, 320 U.S. 81, 100, 63

S.Ct. 1375, 1385, 87 L.Ed. 1774. The average citizen, aware of that truth but unschooled in legal niceties, will, I venture, find the decision which the court now makes extremely perplexing. While the Stuyvesant Town housing project was in blueprint and under construction, the public understood, and rightly, that it was an undertaking on which the State and the City of New York had bestowed the blessings and benefits of governmental powers. Now that the development is a reality, the public is told in effect that, because the Metropolitan Life Insurance Company (hereafter referred to as Metropolitan) and Stuyvesant Town Corporation (hereafter called Stuyvesant) are private companies, they are not subject to the equal protection clause, and may, if they choose, discriminate against Negroes in selecting tenants. That conclusion strikes me as totally at odds with common understanding and not less so with the facts and circumstances disclosed by the record.

In the City of New York as well as in other communities of this State, there are blighted areas whose rehabilitation has been the concern of public bodies for many years. Bent upon "the clearance, replanning, reconstruction and rehabilitation" of such areas, the People in 1938 adopted a new constitutional provision dealing with housing. N.Y.Const., art. XVIII. In aid of those purposes, the Legislature enacted the Redevelopment Companies Law, L.1942, ch. 845, as amd. by L.1943, ch. 234, and L.1947, ch. 840, McKinney's Unconsol. Laws, §§ 3401-3426. After announcing the State's concern over the existence of substandard and insanitary conditions which impaired real estate values, jeopardized public revenues, and depressed living standards, the Law declared that "these conditions cannot be remedied by the ordinary operations of private enterprise." § 2. Though providing that the actual work was to be done by privately-owned redevelopment companies (§ 4), the statute acknowledged and recognized that there was need for "the cooperation of the state and its subdivisions." § 2.

The co-operative activities set forth in the statute demonstrate that the state and city governments were to have a deep interest in, and a close connection with, these redevelopment enterprises. Not only did it fix their maximum rents and profits but it laid down careful limitations with respect to their financing and mortgaging, the selling or disposing of the property and the altering of the structures. §§ 15, 23. To the city governments, the statute gave authority to approve any plan for a proposed development, and power to include, by contract, provisions for the "operation and supervision of the project." § 15. In addition, the City was enabled to use certain of its governmental powers to aid the work. It was empowered to condemn property by eminent domain in order to assemble the area to be rehabilitated, and then to convey the property to the redevelopment companies at cost (§ 20); to close off and transfer public streets; and to grant tax exemption on the improvements for a twenty-five-year period. § 26. In sum, the companies and the enterprises were to be governmentally aided and effectuated, as well as supervised and regulated, in numerous ways.

In 1943, Metropolitan caused Stuyvesant to be formed pursuant to the statute. There followed negotiations, between the City on the one side and Stuyvesant and Metropolitan on the other, which culminated in a contract embodying a plan for the rehabilitation of a substandard area comprising eighteen city blocks in Manhattan, running north from East 14th Street to East 20th Street, and running east from First Avenue to the East River Drive or Avenue C. The plan and the proposed contract received the requisite approval from the State Superintendent of Insurance, from the Planning Commission and from the Board of Estimate of the City of New York. Following closely the contours of the Redevelopment Companies Law, the contract called for condemnation by the City of the site and its conveyance to Stuyvesant at cost; for grant by the City to Stuyvesant of all public streets within the project in return for an equivalent area on its periphery; and for tax exemption on improvements for twenty-five years. For its part, Stuyvesant agreed to acquire the area, demolish the old buildings and construct the Stuyvesant project. Metropolitan was to advance the necessary funds and to guarantee performance by Stuyvesant.

Condemnation of the land and its transfer to Stuyvesant, along with public streets, was accomplished in 1945, and construction of Stuyvesant Town began in that same year. The Town is now virtually completed, at a cost of over $90,000,000. It occupies eighteen city blocks and, with its thirty-five buildings, houses a population of about twenty-five thousand people. Streets in the area are "private" and signs at all entrances give the public notice of that fact.

Almost from the beginning, the question of exclusion of Negroes from the community was debated. While the project was under consideration by the Board of Estimate, Stuyvesant and Metropolitan insisted that they be given free choice in the selection of tenants and indicated that they planned to bar Negroes. Despite opposition to the contract on that ground, its execution was authorized. A local law was thereafter passed by the city forbidding racial discrimination in tax-exempt developments, but it expressly excepted from its coverage any project "hitherto agreed upon or contracted for", N.Y.C.Administrative Code, § J41—1.2—an exception which could relate only to Stuyvesant Town.

Though I digress for a moment, it is my opinion that there are present in the foregoing recital many factors which spell out governmental participation in illegal discrimination. Especially in the two items last mentioned, namely, the city contract sanctioning the very discrimination complained of and the city legislation actually ratifying that discriminatory conduct, do I find most clearly that "state action" which the Federal Constitution interdicts.

It is, of course, against the total background that we weigh appellants' claim that the admitted discrimination violates the equal protection clauses cf the Federal and State Constitutions. The court has rejected that claim cn the ground that such discrimination has neither been aided by the "consciously exerted" power of the State nor performed by private individuals acting in a recognized "governmental capacity." 299 N.Y. 534, 535, 87 N.E.2d 551. For that reason, it is held, the discrimination does not fall within the constitutional restraints. I cannot believe that the requirement of equal protection permits of such artificial qualifications or that the constitutional provisions designed to guarantee it are written in such gossamer phrases that formalities of that sort can obscure fundamentals. Doubly pertinent here is Chief Justice Marshall's century-old injunction that "we must never forget * * * it is a constitution we are expounding." McCul-loch v. Maryland, 4 Wheat. 316, 407, 4 L.Ed. 579.

The Fourteenth Amendment of the Federal Constitution, insofar as relevant, provides that "No State shall * * * deny to any person within its jurisdiction the equal protection of the laws." The Amendment, it is true, does not operate against purely private conduct, In re Civil Rights Cases, 109 U.S. 3, 3 S.Ct. 18, 27 L.Ed. 835, but it does prohibit discrimination even by private persons or agencies if such action can "fairly be said" to be that of the State. See Shelley v. Kraemer, 334 U.S. 1, 13, 68 S.Ct. 836, 842, 92 L.Ed. 1161, 3 A.L.R.2d 441. The concept of "state action" has enjoyed a career of aggressive expansion during the sixty-six years since the Civil Rights Cases were decided. 109 U.S. 3, 3 S.Ct. 18, 27 L.Ed. 835. It is no longer confined, if ever it was, merely to those affirmations of state authority which take the form of legislative enactments. It "refers to exertions of state power in all forms", Shelley v. Kraemer, 334 U.S. 1, 20, 68 S.Ct. 836, 845, supra, and has "the effect * * * of protecting the rights of individuals and minorities from many abuses of governmental power which were not contemplated at the time" of the Amendment's adoption. Rice v. Elmore, 4 Cir., 165 F.2d 387, 392, certiorari denied 333 U.S. 875, 68 S.Ct. 905, 92 L.Ed. 1151.

As long as there is present the basic element, an exertion of governmental power in some form, as long as there is present something "more" than purely private conduct, see Shelley v. Kraemer, 334 U.S. 1, 13, 68 S.Ct. 836, 92 L.Ed. 1161, 3 A.L.R.2d 441, supra, the momentum of the principle carries it into areas once thought to be untouched by its direction.

For example, a private individual who practices discrimination under the constraint of state power violates the equal protection clause. See, e.g., Buchanan v. Warley, 245 U.S. 60, 38 S.Ct. 16, 62 L.Ed. 149, L.R.A.1918C, 210, Ann.Cas.1918A, 1201; Truax v. Raich, 239 U.S. 33, 36 S.Ct. 7, 60 L.Ed. 131, L.R.A.1916D, 545, Ann. Cas.1917B, 283. In the latter case, Truax v. Raich, it was the action of a private employer, in discharging an alien pursuant to a statute limiting aliens to a stated percentage of the working force, that was deemed to deny equal protection. Similarly, a private association, a labor union, clothed with statutory power to bargain for a craft, has been implied to be under a constitutional duty to discharge its functions without discriminating against Negroes. See Steele v. Louisville & Nashville R. R. Co., 323 U.S. 192, 198, 65 S.Ct. 226, 89 L.Ed. 173. Indeed, even without a formal delegation of powers—formal in the agency sense—a private group is subject to the equal protection clause while it acts in a matter of high public interest with the aid of the State. See Smith v. Allwright, 321 U.S. 649, 64 S.Ct. 757, 88 L.Ed. 987, 151 A.L.R. 1110; Nixon v. Herndon, 273 U.S. 536, 47 S.Ct. 446, 71 L.Ed. 759, or with the sufferance and acquiescence of the State even without its aid. See Rice v. Elmore, 4 Cir., 165 F.2d 387, certiorari denied 333 U.S. 875, 68 S.Ct. 905, 92 L.Ed. 1151, supra. Thus, for instance in the Rice Case—which, stamps as unsupportable the court's rejection (299 N.Y. 534, 87 N.E.2d 550) of the proposition that "state action" is to be discerned "in any case where the State has tolerated discrimination respecting a matter of high public importance"—it was the unaided action of a private voluntary political association which denied equal protection to the Negro. Not even the formal disavowal on the part of the State of all interest in the process of selecting political candidates—by repealing all of its pertinent statutes—served to free "private" political parties from the duty to function without discrimination. Finally under recent decisions of the Supreme Court, private discriminatory conduct, freely and voluntarily initiated by private individuals, has been declared to violate the equal protection principle when facilitated or rendered effective by an assertion of state power. See, e.g., Shelley v. Kraemer, 334 U.S. 1, 68 S.Ct. 836, 92 L.Ed. 1161, 3 A.L.R.2d 441, supra; cf. Marsh v. Alabama, 326 U.S. 501, 66 S.Ct. 276, 90 L.Ed. 265.

As the majority opinion recognizes, 299 N.Y. 534, 87 N.E.2d 550, the Fourteenth Amendment is no longer satisfied by a mechanical finding that the discriminatory conduct was not perpetrated by legislative, judicial or executive officials of the State. The concept of "state" action has been vitalized and expanded; the definition of "private" conduct in this context has been tightened and restricted. When private individuals or groups move beyond "matters of merely private concern" and act in "matters of high public interest", the test is not, Mr. Justice Cardozo has written, whether they are "the representatives of the state in the strict sense in which an agent is the representative of his principal. The test is whether they are to be classified as representatives of the state to such an extent and in such a sense that the great restraints of the Constitution set limits to their action." Nixon v. Condon, 286 U.S. 73, 88-89, 52 S.Ct. 484, 487.

The fact that the constitutional right is invaded in the exercise of "private" property interests is no more decisive than that the owner himself is "private". In Marsh v. Alabama, 326 U.S. 501, 66 S.Ct. 276, 90 L.Ed. 265, supra, for instance, a Jehovah's Witness was convicted of trespass, in spite of her claim of constitutional right, for refusing to leave the streets of a company town completely owned by a private corporation. Relying upon its "private" proprietary rights, the owner urged that the Fourteenth Amendment was inapplicable to it, but the Supreme Court declared 326 U.S. at pages 505-506, 66 S.Ct. at page 278: "We do not agree that the corporation's property interests settle the question. The State urges in effect that the corporation's right to control the inhabitants of Chickasaw is coextensive with the right of a homeowner to regulate the conduct of his guests. We can not accept that contention. Ownership does not always mean absolute dominion. The more an owner, for his advantage, opens up his property for use by the public in general, the more do his rights become circumscribed by the statutory and constitutional rights of those who use it."

A kindred philosophy outlaws the enforcement of privately drawn restrictive covenants aimed at nonwhite ownership of property. See Shelley v. Kraemer, 334 U.S. 1, 68 S.Ct. 836, 92 L.Ed. 1161, 3 A.L.R. 2d 441, supra. It also runs through the numerous decisions which deny to the State and its subdivision, a city, the power to avoid their constitutional responsibilities by leasing or assigning to private persons important projects or functions in which discrimination is practiced. See, e.g., Lawrence v. Hancock, D.C., 76 F.Supp. 1004; Kern v. City Commissioners of City of Newton, 151 Kan. 565, 100 P.2d 709, 129 A.L.R. 1156; Culver v. City of Warren, 84 Ohio App. 373, 83 N.E.2d 82.

The teaching of this body of law is clear. On the one hand, the equal protection clause does not prohibit private persons from exercising rights of private ownership in matters merely private, however arbitrarily or capriciously they may discriminate. On the other hand, even the conduct of private individuals offends against the constitutional provision if it appears in an activity of public importance and if the State has accorded the transaction either the panoply of its authority or the weight of its power, interest and support.

Respondents' main defense to the charge of constitutional violation is that they, rather than the City, are behind the discrimination, and that they, as private corporations, are not answerable for it. Their premise is faulty. Stuyvesant is in no sense an ordinary private landlord. Its title bespeaks its character. With buildings covering many city blocks, housing a population of twenty-five thousand persons, Stuyvesant is a "Town" in more than name. Its very being depended upon constitutional amendment, statutory enactment and city contract. The exercise of a number of governmental functions was absolutely prerequisite to its existence. As a geographic entity, Stuyvesant Town was created by the City's exercise of its eminent domain and street-closing powers and by its act of transferring such condemned land and public property to respondents. As an economic enterprise, Stuyvesant Town was made possible by the acquisition of this land at its cost to the City—not augmented by reason of any increase in value through assembly of the entire tract under single ownership—and by the City's grant of tax exemption. As a going community, Stuyvesant Town functions subject to supervision by governmental agencies. Upon dissolution, its surplus assets revert to the public. All in all, the resemblance between Stuyvesant Town and the company town of Marsh v. Alabama, 326 U.S. 501, 66 S.Ct. 276, 90 L.Ed. 265, supra, is strong, the analogy between this case and that one, clear.

To intimate that this is just another instance of a government subsidy is to misconceive the case. To claim that the construction and operation of a project such as Stuyvesant is a matter of but private concern is to disregard the obvious. Unmistakable are the signs that this undertaking was a governmentally conceived, governmentally aided and governmentally regulated project in urban redevelopment. Everywhere in evidence are the voice and authority of the State and the City. Approval of the underlying constitutional housing article set in motion numerous governmental acts necessary to accomplish the "reconstruction and rehabilitation" of slum areas and to provide "incidental * * * facilities." § 1. Proceeding under that authority, the Legislature had in view more than merely the effacement or razing of blighted substandard buildings; their "modernization" and "reconstruction" to provide "adequate safe, sanitary and properly planned housing accommodations in effectuation of official city plans" were declared to be "public uses and purposes." § 2. And it was to achieve all these ends—not merely the clearance of a slum area—that the plans for Stuyvesant Town were conceived and executed, that the City condemned property for use by defendants, closed public streets and turned over their land area—comprising 19% of the total area of the project—granted tax exemption upon improvements and insisted upon regulation of the rents, profits and financing methods of the redevelopment corporation.

That there is "state action" here is supported and established, however, by more than the constitutional and statutory provisions which made the development possible, by more than the city and state participation and aid that brought Stuyvesant Town into being. In addition, there is the exceedingly significant fact that the City's Board of Estimate approved and authorized the contract for the construction and operation of Stuyvesant Town after having been apprised by city representatives and company officials that Negroes would be excluded from the development. Beyond that, the City Council deliberately excepted Stuyvesant from the coverage of the law, subsequently enacted, which barred discrimination in tax-exempt projects. In a most literal sense, in a most direct way, here was "action," and—if such a showing were necessary, but see, contra, Steele v. Louisville & Nashville R. R. Co., 323 U.S. 192, 65 S.Ct. 226, 89 L.Ed. 173, supra—"action, consciously exerted," by the State "in aid of" the discrimination being practiced. 299 N.Y. 535, 87 N.E.2d 551. To suggest that the Constitution's command does not apply because such action was not exerted "directly" in aid of the discrimination, 299 N.Y. 553, 87 N.E.2d 550, is to overlook the nature of the case. We cannot close our eyes to what led to the end result, nor properly hold that the final product of that action should be considered and appraised without regard to its roots or its background. Nothing to the contrary was decided in Murray v. LaGuardia, 291 N.Y. 320, 52 N.E.2d 884, wherein this court simply upheld the constitutionality of the exercise of eminent domain powers to assemble the area to be cleared.

If the City had zoned the site of Stuyvesant Town and closed it to Negroes, no one would doubt that the equal protection clause had been violated. See Buchanan v. Warley, 245 U.S. 60, 38 S.Ct. 16, 62 L.Ed. 149, L.R.A.1918C, 210, Ann.Cas.1918A, 1201, supra. If the City instead of doing that, had built a similar development and leased it to private operators for occupancy by white tenants only, the discrimination would have been condemned with equal vigor. Here, instead of a zoning ordinance or a city lease, there is a city-approved and city-executed contract, providing for a housing project from which it was realized Negroes would be barred, and a city law ratifying that discrimination. No one claims or even suggests that the City adopted an alternative stratagem to effect discrimination, but it may not be gains aid that the development plan, the contract and the local law brought about precisely the same situation as if the City had zoned or leased a "white" development. We draw distinctions too fine and too subtle when we say that the several cases are different or that they merit different consideration.

It is my conclusion, then, that the Fourteenth Amendment proscribes discrimination in Stuyvesant Town. And, since the equal protection clause of the Constitution of New York State (art. I, § 11) is at least as broad in coverage as its Federal counterpart, it is likewise my conclusion that the State Constitution also condemns it.

It is vehemently urged that to hold that Stuyvesant must discontinue its discriminatory practices would be to deprive respondents of an advantage implicit in their bargain with the City. The flaw in that argument is that the unseen protocol being relied upon was lawless from the start and may not be given effect. The argument overlooks that the constitutional rights of American citizens are involved and that such rights may not be used as pawns in driving bargains; respondents may not, by making a contract and bargain, succeed in avoiding the restraints imposed by Federal and State Constitutions upon their rights and powers. As Mr. Justice Holmes observed, "One whose rights, such as they are, are subject to state restriction, cannot remove them from the power of the state by making a contract about them." Hudson County Water Co. v. McCarter, 209 U.S. 349, 357, 28 S.Ct. 529, 531, 52 L.Ed. 828, 14 Ann.Cas. 560. In brief, the vice of the bargain asserted lies in its very effort to accomplish forbidden discrimination. In point of fact, the argument advanced proves too much. Insofar as respondents rely upon a bargain with the City for discrimination, we have confirmation indisputable that state action was present. If, on the other hand, respondents do not insist that there was such an agreement, they may not complain that they were led by the City to believe that they could practice discrimination.

As an enterprise in urban redevelopment, Stuyvesant Town is a far cry from a privately built and privately run apartment house. More, its peculiar features yield to those eligible as tenants tremendous advantages in modern housing and at rentals far below those charged in purely private developments. As citizens and residents of the City, Negroes as well as white people have contributed to the development. Those who have paid and will continue to pay should share in the benefits to be derived. Stuyvesant Town in its role as chosen instrument for this public purpose may not escape the obligations that accompany the privileges accorded to it.

It is impossible to balance the essence of democracy against fireproof buildings and well-kept lawns, and, fortunately, the Constitutions, Federal and State, forbid our putting the former into the judicial scales just as they forbade the city officials from putting it upon the bargaining table. The mandate that there be equal protection of the laws, designed as a basic safeguard for all, binds us and respondents as well to put an end to this discrimination.

I would reverse in the Dorsey action.

In Dorsey v. Stuyvesant Town Corp.:

LEWIS, CONWAY and DYE, JJ., concur with BROMLEY, J.

FULD, JJ., dissents in opinion in which LOUGHRAN, C. J., and DES-MOND, J., concur.

Judgment affirmed.

In Polier v. O'Dwyer:

LOUGHRAN, C. J., and LEWIS, CONWAY, DESMOND, DYE and FULD, JJ., concur.

Appeal dismissed.

Questions and Notes

1. In Pratt v. LaGuardia, 182 Misc. 482, 47 N.Y.S. 2d 359 (1944), affd. rev. 268 App. Div. 973, 52 N.Y.S. 2d 589 (1st Dept. 1944), appeal dismissed, 294 N.Y.S. 842, 62 N.E. 2d 394 (1945), a similar challenge was dismissed as premature. Here the majority held that the challenge was too late. When was the right time?

Appendix

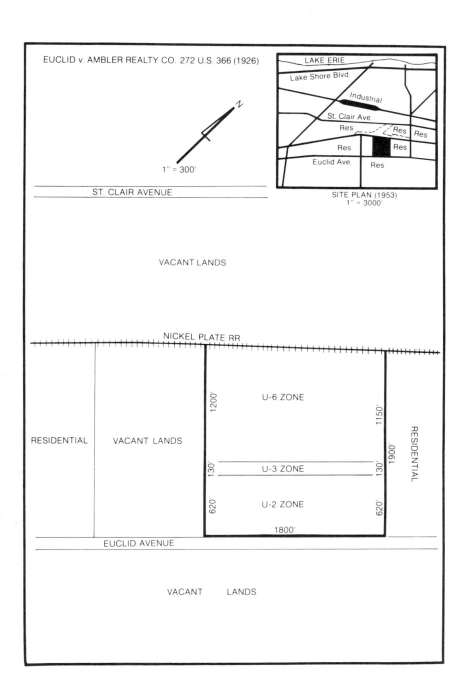

EUCLID v. AMBLER REALTY CO. 272 U.S. 366 (1926)

LAKE ERIE

Lake Shore Blvd.

Industrial

St. Clair Ave.

Res   Res   Res

Res   Res

Euclid Ave.   Res

SITE PLAN (1953)
1″ = 3000′

1″ = 300′

ST. CLAIR AVENUE

VACANT LANDS

NICKEL PLATE RR

RESIDENTIAL | VACANT LANDS

1200′

U-6 ZONE

1150′

RESIDENTIAL

1900′

130′   U-3 ZONE   130′

620′   U-2 ZONE   620′

1800′

EUCLID AVENUE

VACANT   LANDS